HUMAN COGNITIVE ABILITIES

Human cognitive abilities

A survey of factor-analytic studies

JOHN B. CARROLL
Professor of Psychology Emeritus
University of North Carolina at Chapel Hill

Published by the Press Syndicate of the University of Cambridge
The Pitt Building, Trumpington Street, Cambridge CB2 1RP
40 West 20th Street, New York, NY 10011-4211, USA
10 Stamford Road, Oakleigh, Victoria 3166, Australia

First published 1993

Printed in the United States of America

Library of Congress Cataloging-in-Publication Data
Carroll, John Bissell, 1916–
    Human cognitive abilities : a survey of factor-analytic studies /
John B. Carroll.
        p.   cm.
    Includes bibliographical references and indexes.
    ISBN 0-521-38275-0
    1. Cognition.   2. Psychology – Mathematical models.   3. Factor
analysis.   I. Title.
    BF311.C288   1993   92-12453
    153–dc20   CIP

A catalogue record for this book is available from the British Library.

ISBN 0-521-38275-0 hardback
ISBN-0-521-38712-4 paperback

Contents

v

Preface

This book is in a sense an outcome of work I started in 1939, when, as a graduate student at the University of Minnesota, I became aware of L.L. Thurstone's research on what he called "primary mental abilities" and undertook, in my doctoral dissertation, to apply his factor-analytic techniques to the study of abilities in the domain of language. Over the years of my career as a specialist in psychometrics, educational psychology, and the psychology of language I tried to keep abreast of both methodological and substantive developments in factor analysis, and from time to time I found it useful to conduct factor-analytic studies on topics of particular interest to me. Increasingly, however, I sensed the field's need for a thoroughgoing survey and critique of the voluminous results in the factor-analytic literature on cognitive abilities. It was not until 1974, when I came to the University of North Carolina at Chapel Hill as director of the L.L. Thurstone Psychometric Laboratory, that I felt that an appropriate use of my time would be to plan and execute such a survey.

A sabbatical year in 1979–80 supported by the Kenan Fund at the University of North Carolina and by the James McKeen Cattell Fund enabled me to start compiling materials systematically and make visits to prominent investigators in the U.S. and Europe. The major efforts starting in 1983, after I retired from the university, were supported chiefly by grant BNS-82-12486 from the National Science Foundation.

The book has three parts. Part I (Chapters 1–4) is introductory, historical, and methodological. Part II consists of chapters covering each of a number of domains of ability, ending with Chapter 15 on higher-order factors of ability, including g or general intelligence. In Part III, I consider more general issues about abilities. In Chapter 16 I propose a three-stratum theory of cognitive abilities. In Chapter 17 I outline the implications of such a theory for problems of nature and nurture, and more generally for cognitive psychology. In Chapter 18 I make recommendations for future research, for the application of

vii

currently available cognitive ability tests, and for problems of public policy on testing.

The book has been planned mainly as a monograph for use by researchers and students of cognitive abilities. As such, it should serve as a reference work and as a textbook in advanced courses in individual differences. But it also contains considerable material addressed to psychologists in general, particularly those parts dealing with the structure of cognitive abilities and what is known about the measurement and interpretation of such abilities. The general reader may be interested in some portions, especially those treating the history of cognitive ability studies and the implications for public policy on uses of cognitive ability tests.

A feature of the work is that it contains reanalyses of more than 460 data sets found in the factor-analytic literature. The reanalyses use techniques of what is called exploratory factor analysis as developed progressively over the last 60 years or more, rather than the currently more fashionable methods of confirmatory factor analysis. As I explain in Chapter 3, it is my view that properly controlled exploratory techniques are more suitable than confirmatory techniques for initially identifying cognitive abilities and their structure. Students may find it of interest, however, to attempt to verify or revise my findings by using confirmatory techniques. The final results of my exploratory reanalyses are contained in a set of files on computer disks that are available as a companion publication.

Because of its emphasis on the reanalysis of previous studies, the work may seem to look backward more than it looks forward. Currently the field of individual differences in cognitive abilities is very active. Since finishing the final draft of my manuscript I have become aware of many recent studies and discussions that I wish I could have considered. My hope is that future investigators will be able to profit from my analyses, and in this sense the work looks toward the future.

A word is in order about the name and subject indexes. To save space in the text, data sets are often cited without mentioning the names of the author or authors of the source publications. A reader wishing to find citations of the work of a particular investigator, therefore, should consult not only the name of that investigator in the name index but also, in the subject index, the one or more data sets of that investigator as listed in the list of references (pp. 715–89).

I wish to express gratitude to the many people who have helped me in this project. First of all I must mention appreciation to the investigators whose studies I have reviewed or reanalyzed here. I trust that none of them—at least those still living and active in the field—will take umbrage at the ways in which I have reinterpreted or even possibly distorted their findings and conclusions. My intention has been simply to present what was in my opinion the most accurate, reasonable, and consistent picture of the total domain of cognitive abilities.

During the period of greatest activity in collecting and reanalyzing materials from previous studies, I was ably assisted by two people who were then graduate students in the Quantitative Psychology program at my university, Christina M. Gullion and Ann C. Meade. They helped develop special main-frame computer programs and algorithms for this work, and executed a large number of analyses. Also assisting in the project at various periods were James Staszewski, Brynda Holton, and Melanie Miller, who helped assemble bibliographical materials or performed analyses on microcomputers.

I want also to mention my indebtedness to colleagues at the university, Lyle V. Jones, Edward S. Johnson, and Marcy Lansman, for insightful discussions of problems or for reviews of drafts of my manuscript. Richard E. Snow of Stanford University was a most capable outside reviewer of the manuscript, and made many suggestions that I was able to use in revising it. Ledyard R Tucker of the University of Illinois was most gracious in making certain computer programs available to me. Richard Helwig and Kenneth Pauwels gave unfailing help in connection with the use of computers. Ruth A. Childs and Valerie S. Williams gave useful comments as students in a course at UNC in which a preliminary version of the manuscript was a text. None of these people, of course, is to be held responsible for any errors or questionable points of view that may be found in this book.

As always, I am grateful to my wife, Mary S. Carroll, not only for her active assistance in a great variety of ways but also for her patience and encouragement over more years than I like to count.

Chapel Hill   J.B.C.
September 1992

PART I

Introduction to the Survey

1   *The Study of Cognitive Abilities*

SOME PROBLEMS OF DEFINITION

A predominant and recurring concern throughout this book is the identification and description of cognitive abilities. I had better be clear, at the outset, on what I mean by *ability*, *cognitive ability*, and related terms.

Ability

Although the term *ability* is in common usage both in everyday talk and in scientific discussions among psychologists, educators, and other specialists, its precise definition is seldom explicated or even considered. It is a word that seems to be accepted as a sort of conceptual primitive, and in fact it is intimately related to such commonly used words as *able* and the simple modal auxiliary *can*. It is sometimes used to characterize material objects, as in the sentence "This bullet has the ability to penetrate a wooden board three inches thick." More frequently, however, it is used to characterize attributes of human individuals, as in expressions like *athletic ability*, *musical ability*, and (in the context of this book) *cognitive ability*. It expresses a kind of *potential*, a term which has merited the attention of philosophers of education (Scheffler, 1985).

Oddly enough, dictionaries are of little help in developing an exact, analyzed meaning of the term. The *American Heritage Dictionary*, for example, defines ability as "the quality of being able to do something; physical, mental, financial, or legal power to perform." In the present context, of course, we can lay aside concern with financial and legal powers, but mental powers, and possibly physical powers, remain of interest. Dictionary definitions often have an air of circularity, as is the case here: *ability* is defined in terms of "being able to perform something" but *able* is defined as meaning "having sufficient ability." Dictionaries of psychology might be more useful, but it happens that the word *ability* does not appear either as an entry term or in the index of a recently issued *Encyclopedic Dictionary of Psychology* (Harré & Lamb, 1983), although it is used there in

3

numerous contexts, for example, in defining intelligence as "the all-round mental ability (or thinking skills) either of human or of lower animal species" (p. 313). In older dictionaries of psychology, considerable attention is devoted to defining ability and related terms. English and English (1958), for example, define ability as "actual power to perform an act, physical or mental, whether or not attained by training and education." They continue:

GENERAL ABILITY is concerned with all sorts of tasks, but especially those of a cognitive or intellectual sort. *Syn. intelligence.* SPECIAL ABILITY has to do with a defined kind of task. Each special ability should, when possible, be so defined as not to overlap with other special abilities.

Curiously, none of these definitions contains, in any explicit way, the notion that there can be variations in ability over individuals.

It seems, therefore, that we must pursue a bit of logical and semantic analysis to arrive at a more precise definition of the term *ability* as it is to be used in this book. Some issues to be addressed are: In what sense does ability imply "potential"? Is ability a matter of degree, and if so, to what extent can its degree be quantified? To what extent may ability vary within an individual and across different individuals? How general is ability, that is, does it apply only to single performances, to some class or classes of performances, or to all possible performances? To what extent is an ability to be construed as a "trait" of an individual? Let us first consider these questions in the case of the physical ability of strength, because this case affords a concrete, easily grasped context in which to do so – a context more easily handled than if we were to consider a mental ability of some kind.

Every ability is defined in terms of some kind of performance, or potential for performance. Physical strength would have to be defined in terms of a performance that would require physical strength. Lifting 100 pounds of weight on a barbell would be one such performance. Suppose that an individual is characterized as possessing the ability to lift a barbell with 100 pounds of weight on its ends. This implies that the individual has the *potential* of doing so *if conditions are favorable to it* – that is, if a 100-pound barbell is available, if the individual is fully conscious and attentive, is willing and motivated to do so if asked, and can assume an appropriate position and a good grip on the barbell to perform the task. Nevertheless, even the concept of potential has to be thought of in probabilistic terms. If the individual were tested for lifting a 100-pound barbell on 100 different occasions, he or she might succeed, say, on only 95 of these; various unforeseen or unknown conditions might prevent the person from performing on the other five trials. Still, we would be inclined to admit, on this basis, that the individual *does* have the ability to lift a 100-pound barbell. In fact, if the individual succeeded on only *one* occasion, we might still be inclined to ascribe that ability to the individual. Note that holders of world records in athletics often attain their records on only one or a very few out of many trials;

yet, we are willing to grant these people ability to attain the world record even if success is attained only occasionally. In such cases ability is defined in terms of maximal performance. As we shall see, however, this is not the way in which ability is best defined in psychometric terms.

Thus far we have considered physical strength only in terms of a single, narrowly defined task – lifting a 100-pound barbell. But this would hardly be a particularly difficult task for many individuals, although it might be difficult for many others (say, young children). Therefore, ability or lack of ability to lift a 100-pound barbell might tell us little about an individual's physical strength. If we want to ask "how strong is this individual?" a more informative procedure would be to give the individual trials with barbells of different weights, using both light ones and heavier ones. This means that physical strength ability would now be defined in terms of a *class* of highly similar tasks, less narrowly defined than before, but still restricted to the barbell-lifting task. The measure of physical strength would come out of finding at what weight, in this series or class of tasks, the individual would start to have difficulty, in the sense of having a less than 100% probability of being able to lift that weight. (We might have to control for fatigue effects, by randomizing the trials with respect to the weights used, but for now let us ignore this problem.) There are considerations, from the technical discipline known as psychophysics, whereby it turns out that the most accurate or reliable measure of individual differences in strength would be at that weight where the individual has just a 50% probability of being able to lift the weight, for example, 225 pounds for a certain individual. From a series of trials with different weights, it would be possible, at least in principle, to estimate the point on the weight scale where an individual's probability of success would be 50%, and this would be the most reliable *quantified* measure of barbell-lifting ability, even though it does not indicate the *maximal* weight the individual might be able to lift.

With this procedure, it would be possible to compare different individuals for barbell-lifting ability, and to form a statistical distribution of the measurements for different samples of individuals – individuals of different ages, genders, states of health, etc. The measurements, incidentally, would be given in absolute terms, that is, on what Stevens (1951) called a *ratio scale*; it would be reasonable, for example, to call an individual who has a 50% chance of being able to lift a 400-pound barbell twice as strong as one who has a 50% chance of being able to lift a 200-pound barbell.

It would be of interest, also, to plot curves of individuals' probabilities of successful weight-lifting performance as a function of the weights. A sample series of such curves for a few individuals might look something like those in Figure 1.1. I call such curves *person characteristic functions* (PCFs; see Carroll, 1990). The 50% points on these curves, referred to the baseline, are the measurements of weight-lifting ability; these may be called *liminal* or threshold levels. Thus, Curve A is for a comparatively weak individual, who has a 50% chance of lifting a

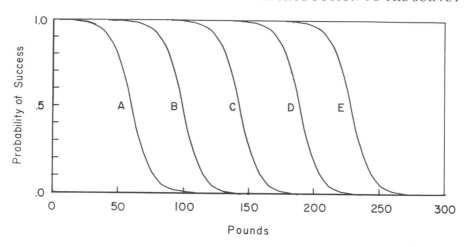

Figure 1.1. Illustrative Person Characteristic Function (PCF) curves for a barbell lifting task (hypothetical).

62-pound barbell and whose liminal level of weight-lifting ability is therefore 62 pounds. Curve E is for a comparatively strong individual – at least if we consider strength or weakness with respect to performance on the barbell-lifting task. This individual has a 50% chance of lifting a 228-pound barbell. The slopes of these curves are shown as fairly steep only because I assume they would have that degree of steepness; exactly how steep they could be is determined only by empirical investigation. In any case, the steepness of the curves would be associated with accuracy of measurement. If the curves were much flatter, this would imply that individuals' performances would be much more variable from trial to trial, even, possibly, that our barbell test of strength is for some reason not a good or appropriate one. Regardless of the steepness of the curves, they are in principle *monotonic descending*; that is, they always descend and never rise. It is unreasonable to expect that an individual who has a low probability of being able to lift a relatively light weight would nevertheless have a higher probability of being able to lift a heavier one.

The question now arises: How general is physical strength ability? It could be objected that barbell-lifting might be only a very specific skill. Common observation suggests, however, that a person who is very strong in the barbell-lifting task would also be strong in other physical strength performances, such as push-ups or pull-ups. This hypothesis could be examined by testing a group of people not only on the barbell task but also on a series of these other tasks. The group would have to exhibit some variability of performance on the barbell task; that is, it would have to include people whose abilities range from weak to strong on this task. The generality of physical strength ability would be judged from the correlations among the various tasks, that is, from the degree to which the individuals' measurements on the different tasks correspond to each other, or show similar rankings. If the correlations were all high – particularly if they were about as high as they could be in view of the reliabilities[1] of the measurements – we would conclude that physical strength ability is an ability that generalizes perfectly over the series of physical strength tasks that were employed. If the correlations were not significantly different from zero, despite high reliabilities of the measures, we would conclude that each task measures a different ability. If the correlations were significantly positive, but still somewhat lower than the maximal values they could attain in view of their reliabilities, we would probably conclude that there is a general physical strength ability measured to some extent by each task, but that each task measures, in addition, some rather restricted special ability. That is, we might infer that doing well in each task requires, in addition to a general physical strength ability, some special skill.

I am not aware that any thoroughgoing investigation of physical strength abilities like these is available (but see Fleishman, 1964). My guess is that the most likely outcome would be the last one mentioned in the preceding paragraph. Namely, there is a general physical strength ability measurable in a wide variety of physical tasks, but some tasks would require abilities more or less unique to themselves, possibly reflecting strengths or weaknesses in particular groups of muscles used in the tasks, or special strategies in performing particular tasks.

Still other questions would arise. How fixed is the ability? Does it vary over time? In the case of physical strength ability, common observation would suggest that over some short period of time – say a day or a week, or even longer – physical strength ability would not vary much at all, unless an individual takes special steps (like doing exercises) to improve his ability, or becomes subject to some debilitating conditions. Degree of physical strength ability can thus be regarded as a characteristic or trait of the individual, measurable at any particular point of time. It might vary somewhat more if measured at long intervals – in each of a number of years, say, in a mature adult. If considered developmentally – that is, if measured at each of a series of ages in a child – it would tend to increase, but the ranking of a number of children on this ability might tend to stay relatively the same, in which case we might infer that some developmental parameter of physical strength ability would be characteristic of each child. Such a developmental parameter could be calculated either on the basis of a series of measurements over a number of years, or possibly on the basis of noting a child's standing relative to those of a population of children of comparable age, physical size, or other attributes. In any case, such a developmental parameter would be a secondary, derived type of measurement, to be clearly labeled as such.

We have assumed here that an ability can be regarded as a *trait* to the extent that it exhibits some degree of stability or permanence even over relatively long periods of time. Many abilities do show this kind of stability. If an ability is found to be highly variable over time, a particular measurement of it would be best regarded as reflecting a *state* rather than a trait, just as a measure of a person's temperature might indicate presence of a fever.[2]

We are now in a position to define *ability* in a more precise way than before:

As used to describe an attribute of individuals, ability *refers to the possible variations over individuals in the liminal levels of task difficulty (or in derived measurements based on such liminal levels) at which, on any given occasion in which all conditions appear favorable, individuals perform successfully on a defined class of tasks.*

In this definition, levels are specified as *liminal* (threshold) values in order to take advantage of the fact that the most accurate measurements are obtained at those levels.

Something needs to be said about the concepts of "task" and "defined class of tasks." Dictionary definitions of the word *task* do not adequately convey the characteristics and structure of what is intended here, and some connotations of the word (its association with the notion of work, the assignment of tasks by superiors, and the difficulty, tediousness, and/or aversiveness of tasks) are irrelevant. We may define a *task* as *any activity in which a person engages, given an appropriate setting, in order to achieve a specifiable class of objectives, final results, or terminal states of affairs.* It is to be understood, however, that "finality" is only relative; the end result or terminal state may only lead to another task, either a repetition of the same task or a different one. The specifiability of the end result of a particular task is crucial, however, because the individual performing the task must have some notion of what type of end result is to be attained and possibly of the criterion or criteria by which attainment of the end result is to be assessed. Many tasks are imposed by others, as when an individual is asked a question, presented with an item on a psychological test, or requested to perform some action. Many other tasks, however, are self-imposed, as when an individual decides to write a letter, sing a song, memorize a poem, or seek some action on the part of another person or a group. It can be the case that some kind of ability, and its level, could be inferred from an individual's successful or unsuccessful performance on any of such tasks, whether self-imposed or imposed by another.

By a *class of tasks*, we mean a group or series of possible tasks that have at least some identical or similar attributes. These attributes may refer to the kinds of stimuli that must be dealt with, the kinds of actions that must be performed, or the means by which those actions can be performed. The greater the similarities, it may be assumed, the more likely it is that the same or similar abilities of performance are involved. In the illustration used above, a highly similar group of tasks was that represented in the series of tasks utilizing barbells of different weights; the only difference among the tasks, ideally, would be the weights used. A less similar group of tasks was that represented by the barbell task, the push-up task, and the pull-up task, taken together; their similarity consists mainly in the fact that they require some kind of muscular strength to achieve the desired end results.

It may be assumed that tasks vary in *difficulty*, that is, in the probabilities that individuals will be able to perform them. When the tasks vary in only one parameter, like the series of tasks involving weights on a barbell, it is possible to determine a liminal probability by giving trials with different values of the parameter. When the tasks differ in their parameters, but still can be found to tap the same ability, a measure of an individual's ability could be obtained only by somehow aggregating the measurements on a series of tasks. For example, if general physical strength were to be measured with three tasks – a barbell task, a push-up task, and a pull-up task, – the final measurement could be obtained from some function (for example, a weighted sum) of the scores on these three tasks.

It is on the basis of these concepts that we can begin to see how various human abilities may be defined and measured. In common parlance we may speak, for example, of musical ability, athletic ability, and learning ability. In each case, it is presupposed that a particular class of tasks is involved. Nevertheless, it would be recognized that some abilities could be more narrowly defined, with a corresponding restriction of the class of tasks to which they apply. For example, although there might be a rather general musical ability exhibited by relatively good performance in a wide variety of musical activities – singing, performing on one or more musical instruments, reading music at sight, composing music, etc. – one might recognize special abilities in each of these activities; that is, there is a special class of tasks called "singing," a special class of tasks called "playing classical music on the piano," and so forth, so that "singing ability" and "classical piano-playing ability" could be defined as somewhat separate abilities. Similarly, it is commonly recognized that there are different types of athletic abilities – in distance running, playing football, playing basketball, etc. – and that these abilities are only loosely related. People who are good distance runners are not necessarily good basketball players, and vice versa.

As we shall see, the investigations dealt with in this book can be regarded as attempts to identify abilities by systematically classifying different tasks with respect to the abilities they appear to require.

Cognitive Ability

Since this book is concerned with a class of tasks designated as *cognitive*, I must specify what I refer to by this word as used in the expression "cognitive ability."

Insofar as we have defined *task* as any activity that a person may engage in (or be made to engage in) in order to achieve a specifiable class of terminal states of affairs, and insofar as it may be assumed that the person must have a notion of what is to be performed, one might conclude that *any* task is automatically a *cognitive* task – even the task of lifting a barbell, or of digging a hole in the ground. By using the adjective *cognitive*, however, I mean to limit the range of cognitive tasks to those that centrally involve mental functions not only in the understanding of the intended end results but also in the performance of the task, most particularly in the *processing of mental information*. That is, a cognitive task is one in which suitable processing of mental information is the major determinant of whether the task is successfully performed. Although barbell lifting may involve certain kinds of processing of mental information (kinesthetic perceptions of the barbell's balance and one's grip on it, for example), successful performance of the task is determined mainly by the physical strength of the muscles involved, and thus we would not call it a cognitive task. In contrast, the task of repeating a series of digits (as in a memory-span test) is a cognitive task because it requires storing the digits and their order in short-term memory, and retrieving them, in addition to chunking or otherwise manipulating the materials to be repeated. I define a cognitive task, therefore, as *any task in which correct or appropriate processing of mental information is critical to successful performance*. A cognitive ability is *any ability that concerns some class of cognitive tasks, so defined*. At many points in this book we will be concerned with what kinds of mental information have to be processed or operated on in the classes of tasks associated with particular cognitive abilities. Here it is necessary to consider what *cognitive processes* are, and what kinds of processes are involved in mental information processing.

Cognitive Process

In general, a *process* refers to any action or series of actions by means of which something is operated on to produce some result. A *cognitive process* is therefore one in which mental contents are operated on to produce some response. These mental contents may be representations or encodings either of external stimuli or of images, knowledges, rules, and similar materials from short-term or long-term memory. The response may be either covert (generally unobservable) or overt (observable). In the context of mental testing, only observable responses are admissible as data, although it may be useful, to explain such data, to develop hypothetical constructs concerning covert responses.

Many cognitive tasks are complex, but can often be analyzed into distinct processes, stages, or components. Sternberg (1977), for example, has provided one possible way in which to analyze typical analogies tasks found on many intelligence and scholastic aptitude tests. He proposes (pp. 135–137) that such tasks (like evaluating the correctness of the verbal analogy *red:stop::green:go*, symbolized as $A:B::C:D$) can be analyzed into the following components:

> Encoding: The process of translating each stimulus into an internal representation upon which further mental operations can be performed.
> Inference: The process of discovering a rule, X, that relates the A term of the analogy to the B term, and storing the rule in working memory.

> Mapping: The process of discovering a higher-order rule, *Y*, that relates the *A* term to the *C* term, and storing the result in working memory.
>
> Application: The process of generating a rule, *Z*, that forms an image of the correct answer and tests it against the *D* term of the analogy.
>
> Justification: The (occasionally necessary) process of deciding whether the *D* term of the analogy is sufficiently close to the image formed by the application process to be regarded as correct.
>
> Preparation-response: The (control) processes of preparing to solve the analogy, monitoring the solution process, and translating the solution into a response.

Sternberg also developed experimental operations whereby the time taken by each of these processes, and the correctness or accuracy of the response, could be observed or estimated. In a series of experiments, he applied these operations to several types of analogy tasks. In one of his experiments, 16 subjects were given these analogy tasks along with several psychometric tests of reasoning and perceptual abilities. Although the data are limited to only 16 individuals and two tasks, I have pointed out (Carroll, 1980c, pp. 16–17) that the data suggested that these processes might generalize in certain ways over the tasks and psychometric ability measures. For example, measures of the encoding speed component and of the preparation-response component generalized over a verbal analogy task and a "People Piece" analogy task, as well as over three psychometric tests of reasoning. From evidence of this kind, it appears that cognitive abilities can sometimes be more sharply defined by associating them with classes of particular task components.

In pursuing the notion of cognitive task and attempting to analyze such tasks into processes that might be referred to particular abilities, it is convenient to define what I call an Elementary Cognitive Task (ECT), as follows:

> An elementary cognitive task (ECT) is any one of a possibly very large number of tasks in which a person undertakes, or is assigned, a performance for which there is a specifiable class of "successful" or "correct" outcomes or end states which are to be attained through a relatively small number of mental processes or operations, and whose successful outcomes depend on the instructions given to, or the sets or plans adopted by, the person.[3]

Any ECT, as studied in the laboratory, consists not only of the operations performed by the subject but also of a series of distinct operations performed by the experimenter: giving the subject instructions and any preparatory practice, the presentation of the stimuli in a specified procedure (including a specified time-schedule), and the observation, clocking, and evaluation of the responses. One aspect of a task's being cognitive is that the nature of the task can depend on the instructions given, even when stimulus presentations and other objective events remain the same. A simple example is the memory-span task: With the same stimuli (a series of spoken digits presented one per second, say), the outcome can differ depending on whether the subject is asked to repeat them in forward or in backward order, or with a numerical constant added to each digit. Strictly speaking, each such instruction makes for a different task.

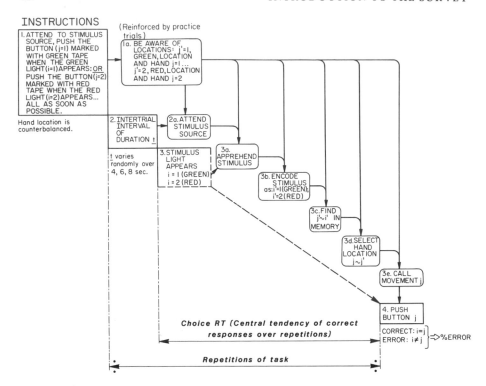

Figure 1.2. Dual time representation (DTR) for Keating and Bobbitt's (1978) choice RT procedure. Reproduced by permission from J. B. Carroll, 1980a, Figure 1, p. 15, *Individual difference relations in psychometric and experimental cognitive tasks.* Chapel Hill, N. C.: L. L. Thurstone Psychometric Laboratory Report No. 163.

In representing and analyzing ECT's (or, for that matter, any cognitive task), I have found it useful to develop a special kind of chart that I call Dual Time Representation (DTR). One such chart appears as Figure 1.2. It shows, along the diagonal, the objective events of the task, and in the space of the upper right triangle, the assumed cognitive processes performed by the subject, based on a logical and cognitive analysis of the requirements of the task. This particular task was one used by Keating and Bobbitt (1978) to measure choice reaction time. The subject was to press either a left-hand or a right-hand button depending on whether a red or a green light was the stimulus. I assumed, in this case, that the subject had to make a mental translation of the color code of the light to a code for the button position to be pushed, and that this mental translation process accounted for part of the reaction time. This mental translation process is shown in box 3c of the DTR chart. Note also that the measure of choice reaction time was taken from the onset of the stimulus to the onset of the button press.

INSTRUCTIONS:

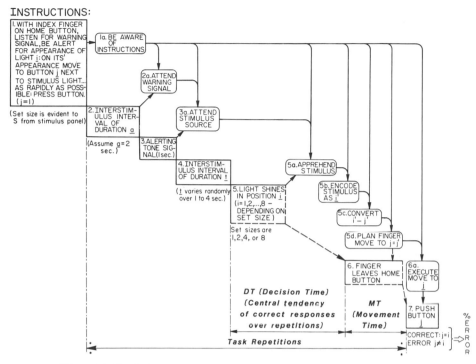

Figure 1.3. Dual time representation (DTR) for Jensen's (1980) RT-MT procedure. Reproduced by permission from J. B. Carroll, 1980a, Figure 2, p. 18, *Individual difference relations in psychometric and experimental cognitive tasks*. Chapel Hill, N. C.: L. L. Thurstone Psychometric Laboratory Report No. 163.

This chart is to be compared with a DTR chart (Figure 1.3) for a choice reaction-time task studied by Jensen (1980, pp. 688ff.) There are two important differences between the Jensen and the Keating and Bobbitt tasks, even though both were designed to measure choice reaction time. One difference has to do with what cognitive processes may be assumed to operate in the respective tasks. In Jensen's task, the subject has to move his/her finger to press a button just next to the *position* of a light, there being different numbers of light positions in the several experimental variations of the task. If there was any cognitive process in translating a light position to a hand movement code, it was very simple. Nevertheless, it is shown as box 5c of the DTR chart. In the Keating and Bobbitt task, however, choice of position depends on a translation of a color code into a position code, and it may be assumed that this translation would take more time than simply moving toward a light. The second difference between the tasks consists in the method of measuring times. In Jensen's task, reaction time was taken from the onset of the stimulus to the subject's finger leaving a "home" button, and was what may be called *decision time. Movement time* to move from the home button to a light was separately measured. In Keating and Bobbitt's task, reaction time, measured from the onset of the stimulus to the button-pushing, included both decision and movement time. Jensen was able to measure individual differences in both decision and movement time – largely unrelated, while Keating and Bobbitt were able only to measure individual differences in the sum of decision and movement times.

While it is debatable whether it is appropriate to distinguish decision and movement times (see, e.g., Smith and Stanley, 1983), or more precisely, whether "decision time" is really a valid measure of how long it takes an individual to make a decision, separate measurement of decision and movement times is never-theless often operationally useful in order to refine the definition of whatever cognitive ability is being measured. The construction of a DTR chart for any task being studied is also useful because it prompts the investigator to specify the cognitive processes that might be involved in ability measurements.

Most measurements of human ability are based on performances of individuals on psychological or educational tests.[4] Each such test, as I have pointed out (Carroll, 1976a), can be regarded as a collection of relatively similar cognitive tasks, many of which can also be considered elementary cognitive tasks because they involve a relatively small number of cognitive processes. The cognitive processes can, however, take many forms. Some of these processes are involved in understanding, or learning to understand, the requirements of a task – the types of stimuli to be presented, what is to be done to them, what kinds of responses are to be made, and (sometimes) the time allowed for performance and how the responses are to be scored or otherwise evaluated. These and still other processes are involved in the actual performance of each task; some of these can be very elementary processes such as attending to stimuli, encoding or recognition of stimuli, comparison of stimuli, transforming representations of stimuli, retrieving associations, executing responses, and monitoring one's performance. Some processes may depend on prior experience, learning, or knowledge of particular facts, procedures, algorithms, or rules. Particular abilities in the execution of different processes or in the knowledge of particular facts or procedures may be the source of individual differences in any one or more of these processes, but ordinarily the tasks are constructed in such a way as to emphasize only one or a few of such processes and abilities. That is, some of the required processes may be so simple as not to reflect possible individual differences, while other aspects of the task, such as variations in the familiarity of the stimuli, may cause striking individual differences to appear. Analysis of individual differences revealed by psychological or educational tests must appeal to detailed considerations of the types of processes and learnings called for by a test.

A psychological or educational test is meant to be administered in some uniform fashion to all individuals who are to take the test. That is, the procedure is meant to be applied according to some consistent set of rules for presenting tasks – even if different tasks are administered to different individuals depending on their responses, as can occur in what has been called "adaptive" or "tailored" testing (Lord, 1980; Weiss, 1983). Many tests are administered with time limits for the total test or for subtests; specified time limits constitute part of the standard procedure for administering the test, even if this means that there will be variations in what tasks or items different examinees attempt. A problem with this widely used procedure is that the scores may not adequately distinguish between rate of work (speed in task performance) and overall level of mastery (how accurate the examinee would be if allowed to attempt every item, without time constraints) (see further discussion in Chapter 11).

Some measurements of cognitive ability – appearing as variables in certain investigations – are not based on psychological or educational tests; instead, they can be based on judgments or ratings (either self-ratings or ratings by others), or on counts or evaluations of outputs (e.g., by noting the number of pages per year a writer publishes). In any case, the measurements can be viewed as resulting in some way from the performance of cognitive tasks, even if the tasks are self-imposed and far from "standardized" like a psychological test. Under many conditions, such measurements can have at least some validity in assessing given aspects of ability.

Most measurements are of ability assessed *at a particular point of time.* Nothing can be said about the fixity or over-time stability of an ability unless appropriate information is assembled on this matter. Even for a measurement taken at a particular point of time there must be concern with reliability, that is, the accuracy of a score. This is a matter that is dealt with in classical theory of measurements and will not be discussed here because it is well treated in many standard textbooks. It may be pointed out, however, that unless reliability is determined with "split-half" or internal consistency measures, as opposed to the use of equivalent measures or "alternate forms," coefficients of reliability inevitably have some implications for the possible over-time stability of ability scores, because the equivalent measurements must be taken at different points of time.

Analysis of the cognitive tasks presented in psychological ability measures shows that many of the processes involved in them also occur in various "real-life" situations. It is for this reason that measurements from psychological ability tests often show correspondences with individuals' performances – successful or unsuccessful – in various real-life situations, including schooling, occupation, and career. Some abilities appear to be more important or crucial in real life than others. This book deals with a very wide variety of abilities – that is, all that can be demonstrated from empirical studies, regardless of whether their importance in real life can be shown. This is because the book attempts to further the science of human abilities. That is, it seeks to contribute to the program of studies recommended by Carroll & Horn (1981), and not merely to investigate the more obviously important abilities. We cannot adequately appraise the importance of different human abilities until we have mapped the whole spectrum of those abilities.

Abilities, Aptitudes, and Achievements

I regard the term *ability* as entirely neutral and even uninformative as to whether any given ability is an "aptitude" or an "achievement." It is a term that refers only to variations in individuals' potentials for present performance on a defined class of tasks.[5] It is obvious that performance on any task, at any stage of life except possibly very early infancy, is affected to some extent by prior learning and experience. In this sense, any measurement can be regarded, trivially, as a measure of some kind of achievement, that is, as a measure of the extent that certain behaviors have been learned. On the other hand, level of performance, as reflected in a cognitive ability measurement, may be affected (in childhood and adolescence) by the individual's level of constitutional maturation or (at any age, but particularly in later adulthood) by the health of the individual's central nervous system. Further, it is possible that levels of performance can be associated to some extent with the genetic constitution of the individual. Behavioral geneticists (e.g., Plomin, DeFries, & McClearn, 1990) cite evidence that genes are implicated in "general intelligence" or general mental ability, and possibly in other abilities.

To the extent that cognitive abilities are at least relatively stable and relatively resistant to attempts to change them through education or training, and at the same time are possibly predictive of future success, they are often regarded as *aptitudes*. (Here, I use the term *aptitude* in a relatively narrow sense, i.e., to refer to a cognitive ability that is possibly predictive of certain kinds of future learning success; I exclude the notion of aptitude as interest in and motivation for a particular activity.) Conditions for regarding an ability as an aptitude are specified in Figure 1.4. That is, an ability is clearly a measurement of aptitude for some particular future learning success if, in a sample of individuals tested both in aptitude and in achievement in some specified learning or training activity at two points of times, once before training (time *A*) and once after training (time *B*):

1.   There is reliable variance in the measure of aptitude at time *A*.
2.   There is no reliable variance in achievement tested at time *A*, because no learning has occurred.
3.   As a consequence of condition 2, above, there is no significant correlation of aptitude and achievement at time *A*.
4.   No significant change in aptitude is observed from time *A* to time *B*.
5.   Significant change in achievement is observed from time *A* to time *B*, with reliable variance in achievement at time *B*.
6.   There is a significant correlation between aptitude measured at time *A* with achievement at time *B* (trivially, this will be the same as the correlation between aptitude and achievement both measured at time *B*).

Cases in which such conditions obtain, at least approximately, in the use of aptitude tests for predicting success in foreign language learning have been

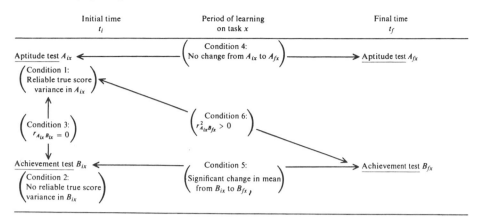

Figure 1.4. Ideal conditions for an aptitude test. Reproduced by permission from Carroll, 1974, Figure 9.1, p. 289, in D. R. Green (Ed.), *The aptitude–achievement distinction.* Copyright (C) 1974 by CTB-Macmillan/McGraw-Hill, Monterey, CA.

discussed by Carroll (1974). Cases are also to be found in studies of musical aptitudes (Stanton & Koerth, 1930), where it is shown that musical training does not significantly affect the aptitude measures even though they are significantly predictive of success in musical training.

Because it is seldom that *all* these conditions obtain, we can relax them somewhat, still retaining condition 5, by asserting that an ability measured at time *A* in a suitable sample of individuals is an aptitude if it contributes significantly to the prediction of achievement at time *B* over and above the prediction obtainable from a measurement of achievement at time *A*. That is, an ability is an aptitude if it helps in predicting degree of learning beyond a prediction from degree of prior learning. (It is sometimes said, in textbooks on psychological measurement, that a particular measure can be either a measure of aptitude or a measure of achievement, depending upon its use, but the account just given provides, in my view, a more accurate means of identifying an aptitude.)

Generally, I reserve the term *achievement* to refer to the degree of learning in some procedure intended to produce learning, such as a formal or informal course of instruction, or a period of self-study of a topic, or practice of a skill. Tests designed primarily to measure such degree of learning are measures of achievement, in addition to being measures of ability. (When *aptitude* is used to refer to any measure that is predictive of future performance, measures of achievement, in the narrow sense, could also be viewed as measures of aptitude to the extent that they might be found to be predictive of future learning progress.[6]

Given the definitions and discussion of the previous section, we can now ask what methods might be used to discover, identify, and differentiate human cognitive abilities.

Suppose we knew nothing about cognitive abilities or their measurement. A start toward identifying such abilities could presumably be made by inventing a wide variety of cognitive tasks. In view of the theory of ability offered above, it would probably be most effective to establish sets of tasks that would be highly similar within sets and in many ways different across sets. Within each set of tasks, tasks would differ only in attributes that might make them of differential difficulty – in the sense that different numbers of persons in typical samples would be expected to perform them successfully or with high levels of performance. The goal would be to establish that each given group of tasks would measure a single ability (or cluster of abilities). Administration of these tasks to typical samples of individuals would generate data analyzable in various ways. A preliminary sifting of the data would determine the difficulty levels of the tasks and permit elimination of any tasks that for some reason failed to show adequate discrimination among individuals with different degrees of average success on the tasks. An attempt would then be made to demonstrate that the data for a given set of tasks conform to a model whereby the tasks in that set could be regarded as measuring a single ability. One way of doing this might be to construct person-characteristic functions (PCF's) for groups of persons of different average levels of performance; if these curves showed characteristic shapes (like those illustrated in Figure 1.1) and at the same time differed markedly in their positions along the task difficulty baseline, the tentative conclusion might be reached that all the tasks in the set measure the same ability. Preliminary information on the nature of that ability would arise from an analysis of what task attributes are similar across all tasks in the set and what attributes of the tasks are associated with different levels of task difficulty.

Suppose, now, that we have established a series of task sets such that the tasks in each set conform to a model of a single ability. The question now arises: Do all these sets measure different abilities, or do they at least to some extent measure certain abilities in common? This question cannot be definitively answered solely from examination or logical analysis of the tasks in these sets. It can be answered only by analysis of empirical data obtained by administering all the task sets to a substantial representative sample of individuals and investigating the extent to which performances on different task sets correspond to each other. Ideally, the individuals ought to be comparable or homogeneous in any attribute, such as age, sex, or amount of education, that might be conceived to be associated with levels of performance in a similar way across task sets. (Otherwise, corresponding levels of performance across task sets might indicate only the common influences of such variables.) If performances on different task sets show no systematic correspondence, the conclusion would be that each task set measures a different ability from the abilities measured by the other task sets. If performances on different task sets show correspondences, the conclusion would be that there are one or more abilities that are common to two or more task sets. Just what abilities are measured by the several task sets would have to be determined by more detailed analysis.

Actually, the above paragraphs represent an attempt to give a simple, nontechnical description of the operations that investigators have been carrying out for some decades to discover and identify different abilities. It may be convenient to list here for the reader the correspondences between the nontechnical phrases we have used and the more technical terms that will generally be employed subsequently:

Nontechnical phrase	Technical term or phrase
Task sets	Psychological tests
Establishment of task sets measuring single abilities	Construction of psychological tests
Preliminary sifting of data	Item analysis
Correspondences between data from different task sets	Correlations among scores on different psychological tests

Procedures of test construction and of correlational analysis have become increasingly technical over the years. It is beyond the scope of this volume to elaborate on procedures of test construction, but certain suggestions arising from our analyses are made about these procedures in Chapter 18. Correlational analysis is treated in considerable detail in Chapter 3, but at this point it is useful to explain certain points about its logic.

Various measures of statistical association and dependence are available (Carroll, 1961). The Pearsonian correlation coefficient is the most frequently used measure, however, and this discussion assumes its use. It is often said that this coefficient is an indication of the degree to which two variables measure "the same thing," i.e., the same ability or the same combination of abilities. This statement would be completely correct only if the coefficient takes an absolute value of 1.00. If the coefficient is other than this value, a more accurate statement would be that it indicates the degree to which there is similarity or overlap in the abilities called upon for different members of the sample on which the correlation is computed.

An illustration of this can be offered in the following context. Suppose we have six measures:

1. A measure of visual acuity (such that an individual with 20/20 vision would get a high score, while blind individuals would receive a very low score, say zero).
2. An alternate measure of visual acuity that would be very highly correlated with variable 1.
3. A measure of hearing ability (such that an individual with no hearing loss of any

kind would receive a high score, while deaf individuals would receive a very
low score.

4   An alternate measure of hearing ability that would be very highly correlated
        with variable 3.

5.   A measure of performance success in a situation in which it is required to detect
        and locate stimuli with both visual and auditory components – for example,
        detecting and locating a bird singing and flying around high up in the trees
        in a forest. Thus, it would be possible to get a high score *either* by having
        excellent vision *or* by having excellent hearing, but not necessarily both. A
        low score would be obtained by individuals who have *both* poor vision and
        poor hearing. Let us call this measure "Bird task *A*."

6.   An alternate measure similar to variable 5, such that its correlation with variable
        5 is very high. Call this measure "Bird task *B*."

Suppose, now, that we obtain measures on all six variables on a sample of people
25% of whom have both vision and hearing (though with varying degrees of these
abilities), 25% have vision but are deaf, 25% have hearing but are blind, and 25%
are both deaf and blind. Further, we find the following correlations among these
measures:

Variable		1	2	3	4	5	6
Vision *A*	1	1.00	.95	.00	.00	.50	.50
Vision *B*	2	.95	1.00	.00	.00	.50	.50
Hearing *A*	3	.00	.00	1.00	.93	.48	.48
Hearing *B*	4	.00	.00	.93	1.00	.48	.48
Bird task *A*	5	.50	.50	.48	.48	1.00	.80
Bird task *B*	6	.50	.50	.48	.48	.80	1.00

The .95 correlation between variables 1 and 2 could be regarded as an indication
of the accuracy with which vision is measured by either variable.[7] Similarly, the
correlation between variables 3 and 4 could be taken as an indication of the
accuracy with which hearing ability is measured by either of these variables.
These high correlation coefficients establish that vision and hearing are well
measured by the respective variables. Cross-correlations between variables 1 and
2, on the one hand, and variables 3 and 4, on the other, are all zero, indicating
that in this sample there is no correlation between vision and hearing abilities,
or more precisely, that there is no overlap between the abilities measured by the
two sets of variables. The correlations of .50 between variables 1 and 2, on the
one hand, and variables 5 and 6, on the other, indicate some degree of overlap
between the abilities measured by the two sets of variables. One might conclude
that at least some of the sample perform the bird-detection task by virtue of their
vision, whatever their degree of visual acuity, and regardless of their hearing
ability. Similarly, the correlations with values of .48 between variables 3 and 4,
on the one hand, and variables 5 and 6, on the other, show that at least some of

the sample perform the bird-detection task by virtue of their hearing. Now consider the correlation, .80, between variables 5 and 6. From one point of view, it could be taken to be the reliability of either of these measures. Possibly the tasks on which they are based are constructed in such a way that whether the singing bird is detected is to some extent a matter of chance, regardless of the abilities required or used, thus contributing to a lack of perfect reliability. From another point of view, the correlation might be considered as indicating the extent to which the tasks measure the same ability or complex of abilities for every individual in the sample. Obviously they do not, however. What ability or abilities the tasks measure depends upon what combination of abilities a given individual possesses. If the individual has visual acuity ability, it may measure that ability if the individual detects the stimulus by seeing it. Similarly, if the individual has hearing ability, it may measure that ability if the individual uses it in performing the task. For individuals who are reasonably good in both vision and hearing, performance on the task provides no information on whether the task is performed by vision or by hearing. The correlation provides only an indication of the extent to which the task provides equal opportunities for the individual to use whatever abilities he/she possesses. This characterization of the meaning of a correlation may be generalized to all correlations between individual measures, *a fortiori* to all correlations in the above correlation table. Thus, the correlation of zero between variables 1 and 3 says that tasks 1 and 3 do not provide equal opportunities for a subject to use the same ability in performing them; in fact, it says that they possibly require different abilities. The correlation of .50 between variables 1 and 5 indicates that there is only partial equivalence between tasks 1 and 5 in providing for use of the same ability, and then possibly only for some individuals in the sample.

For this reason, identifying abilities from correlational data is often a complex problem, particularly when the tasks investigated permit use of different abilities in different combinations for different individuals. However, when relatively "pure" measures like tasks 1–4 in the above example are included in the analysis, tasks that might be demonstrated to measure single abilities by various operations of test construction and analysis, such as analysis of person-characteristic functions, the abilities become more apparent. (Thus, for task 1 the PCF's would have high slopes, and their positions on the ability difficulty scale for different individuals would be demonstrated to be dependent only on certain relevant visual attributes of the stimuli.)

In general, sophisticated correlational analysis can make use of the technique of factor analysis. Discussions of this technique and its development are to be found in Chapters 2 and 3. It may be noted at this point, however, that even factor analysis is not invulnerable to difficulties of the type found in the illustrative example shown above. What the example shows is that correlational analysis, including factor analysis that is based on correlations, should be regarded as a classificatory procedure, in that it classifies tasks with respect to the abilities that are called on *for at least some members of the sample.* If a factor analysis were performed on the correlations in the example, it would show two factors – a vision factor and an audition factor. Variables 5 and 6 would have substantial loadings on both of these factors, but such a result should not be interpreted to mean that these variables measure both vision and audition equally for all members of the sample. On the other hand, it would be possible from the data to determine separate scores on audition and vision for each individual, and to make a more precise determination of the meaning, for any given individual, of performance on the bird-detection tasks.

Abilities, Factors, and Latent Traits

Implicit in the above discussion is the assumption that an ability can be measured by any of a number of substantially correlated measures. Thus, in the example presented above it was assumed that visual acuity could be measured by either of two measures, and that this ability could underlie, at least to some extent, performance on the bird-detection task. If there are individual differences in performance on a task, or better, a set of tasks that conforms to a model whereby a single ability is measured, the individual differences can be said to be the immediate manifestation of individual differences in an underlying ability or *latent trait.* Further evidence for the existence of a latent trait derives from a demonstration that a number of similar task sets are highly correlated, or in factor-analytic terms, have weights on the same *factor.* A factor, if it is well established in a number of empirical investigations, is in essence a latent trait reflecting differences over individuals in ability characteristics or potentials.

It has been argued by some writers (e.g., Gould, 1981) that to speak of an ability, or a factor of ability, is to reify it. It is not clear what is meant by reification in this case, or what is supposed to be objectionable about it, although it appears that Gould is uncomfortable with the notion of ranking that accompanies it. Apparently the transgression imputed to psychometricians is that of assuming that ability is a thing or entity that somehow resides in the individual. No such assumption need be made. It would in fact be highly naive to make such an assumption, because to do so would entail an overly simplistic view of how the organism functions.

Consider, for example, the notion of physical strength ability, which we have mentioned as a possible latent trait or factor of ability. From what we know about the functioning of the human body and its parts, individual differences in physical strength ability have their source in the fact that individuals differ in conditions of their body build and musculature. It would not be necessary to specify the exact nature of these conditions, although physiologists and sports medicine specialists probably find it useful to do so. Physical strength ability, considered as a latent trait, functions at least as an *intervening variable*

(MacCorquodale & Meehl, 1948) that is useful as a parameter for describing and predicting individual differences in performances of various physical tasks.

A similar logic would apply in the case of cognitive abilities of various kinds. The definition of an ability arises from systematic observations of individual differences in performances on defined classes of tasks. These observations constitute the empirical basis of ability measurement. They require no assumptions or exact knowledge about neurophysiological functions that might be responsible for performance levels, although specialists outside the strict field of psychometrics may find it possible and useful to seek such knowledge. In any case, reification is not an essential or characteristic feature of the process of defining a cognitive ability. For our purposes, a cognitive ability can be viewed as an intervening variable, i.e., a calculational convenience, as it were, in linking together a particular series of observations.

Relations between Tasks and Abilities

The performance of any task, it can be assumed, calls on whatever ability or abilities it requires. Most, or perhaps all tasks, require more than one ability. For example, in a printed English vocabulary test, a subject might be asked to check "Yes" or "No" in response to being asked whether two words are opposites. Successful performance might be analyzed as depending on at least four abilities: (1) being able to read and recognize the words; (2) knowing the meaning of the words; (3) being able to evaluate their oppositeness, and (4) being able to make a check mark with a pencil. One could conceive of individuals with any of the $2^4 = 16$ combinations of these abilities, each ability being considered to have values of 0 or 1. A speaker of Chinese learning English, for example, might have no ability to read the words, yet know the words (in spoken form), be able to evaluate their oppositeness, and be able to make a checkmark. An English-speaking fourth-grader, in contrast, might be able to read and recognize the words, and be able to make checkmarks, yet not know their meanings well enough to evaluate whether they are opposites. Both individuals, one would assume, would fail to perform the task correctly, except possibly by guessing. Aside from the possibility of guessing, the only individuals performing the task correctly would be those having scores of 1 in all four abilities. In practice, however, only certain abilities are crucial to correct task performance, in the sense that individual differences in those abilities would be likely to be present in typical samples of individuals for whom the test is applicable. It is unlikely that a printed English vocabulary test would be presented to speakers of Chinese who had not learned to read English words; ordinarily it would be presented only to speakers of English who had learned to read and recognize words. It could be assumed that the ability to evaluate the oppositeness of the words would be closely associated with knowledge of the meanings of the words. Thus, in practice the only ability crucially required by the task would be that of knowing the word meanings (in this case, knowing both word meanings). All the operations of item (task) construction, item analysis, and determining ability dimensionality would be based on the assumption that knowledge of word meanings is the only ability in which individuals tested or likely to be tested differ significantly. Of course, if this assumption does not hold, the test might still require abilities other than knowledge of word meanings. This type of possibility – that a test may measure abilities others than those intended – is always worthy of consideration in interpreting test data.

At the same time, confusion can arise if one focuses more on the actual tasks assembled in a test than on the underlying ability. This is an issue that bears on matters of test use in predicting educational or occupational success. Suppose, for example, that it has been determined that vocabulary knowledge or general verbal ability is significantly predictive of success as a business executive. Such a determination would have been made, let us say, by establishing substantial correlations between a well-constructed vocabulary test and ratings of success in business administration. The vocabulary test would have been found to conform to criteria for measuring a single ability, being composed of a series of items varying in difficulty and producing satisfactory person characteristic functions.

Suppose, however, that a critic were to charge that this test was invalid or inappropriate because it contained items that required knowledge of words that are never needed or encountered in business administration. Such a critic would be confusing knowledge of particular items with the underlying ability being measured by the test. It is the underlying *ability* that is relevant to success in business administration, not the knowledge of particular items. When it is necessary, as it often is, to measure the upper reaches of vocabulary knowledge with words rarely encountered in business administration, this is a consequence of the way in which people acquire and organize their knowledge of words and their meanings; it has little if anything to do with the use of those words in business administration.

Similar logic applies to the use, in scholastic aptitude examinations, for example, of tasks that may seem to have little direct relevance or use in the college/university learning situations for which such examinations are claimed to be predictive. Assuming the appropriate evidence has been assembled (as it has for the College Board Scholastic Aptitude Examination, by Donlon, 1984), the underlying ability or abilities measured by these tasks are what is relevant to the predictiveness of the examinations, not the particular tasks contained in them.

Perhaps this point can be clarified and reinforced by noting that nobody would challenge the use of opticians' Snellen letter charts in appraising visual acuity, even though performance in reading such letter charts is unlikely to be directly involved in occupations in which high visual acuity is required.

THE IMPORTANCE OF COGNITIVE ABILITY STUDIES

The history of the study of cognitive abilities is presented in Chapter 2, but it is useful to consider here why cognitive ability studies are important in larger contexts of society.

For several thousand years – even in classical Greek and Roman times, and among the ancient Chinese (DuBois, 1970) – it has been recognized that there are individual differences in cognitive abilities, and that these differences have something to do with the roles and behaviors of individuals in society.

In the sixteenth century, the Spanish scholar Juan Huarte de San Juan (Huarte, 1575) examined the concept of intelligence. According to Linden and Linden (1968, p. 2), Huarte "invested the term with what today might be called *productive imagination*" and distinguished three characteristics of intelligence: "(1) docility in learning from a master, (2) understanding and independence of judgment; and (3) inspiration without extravagance." Huarte also recognized that some special aptitudes exist. According to Franzbach (1965), Huarte's ideas on the nature of genius influenced the thinking of various German writers and philosophers in the eighteenth and nineteenth centuries, including Goethe, Herder, and Schopenhauer, and his speculations about physical chararactistics of persons with different abilities and character traits found some echoes in the work of the early twentieth-century psychologist Kretschmer.

In England of the late nineteenth century, Galton (1869) revived interest in individual differences in intelligence that he thought were reflected in the different achievements of geniuses and of persons of lesser talent. Galton inspired a long tradition in British psychology to which such figures as Spearman (1904b, 1927) and Burt (1940) made contributions. Burt devoted many of his writings to correlations of intelligence with educational progress and success, occupational status, juvenile delinquency, and other phenomena of importance in society. To varying degrees, Galton, Spearman, and Burt were all convinced that intelligence was largely a matter of innate hereditary differences; that is, they believed that "nature" was more important than "nurture." This conviction crossed the Atlantic to become a dominant belief among many early American psychologists, like Terman (1916) and E. L. Thorndike (Thorndike et al., 1926). Purely as a scientific question, the nature–nurture issue has had its ups and downs throughout the history of psychology and the social sciences generally (Cravens, 1978). Already toward the close of the nineteenth century, the sociologist Cooley (1897) questioned Galton's conclusion that genius alone is sufficient to cause a person to rise to fame, but he appeared not to reject Galton's notion that genius is hereditary. The issue first became prominent in the 1920s, with Walter Lippmann's (1922) critique of intelligence testing, and again in the late 1930s with the claim of a group of University of Iowa psychologists (Skeels & Dye, 1939; see also Woodworth, 1941) that intelligence could be increased by special training and environmental adjustments. Most recently, the issue was again brought to the fore by Arthur Jensen's (1969) emphasis on the probable large role of nature in individual differences, particularly its possible role in white–black IQ differences. During the 1970s the so-called IQ controversy raged between adherents of either side (Block & Dworkin, 1974, 1976; Kamin, 1974; Eysenck & Kamin, 1981). At the present writing, the controversy seems to have come to a draw, neither side being willing to make concessions. Persons like myself, who are not directly engaged in active research on the nature–nurture issue, continue to believe that both genetic and environmental factors are important, but that it may be difficult to assess their relative importance with any exactness. In any event, the issue is of obvious social significance, because whatever the truth may be, it impinges on our concepts of equality of opportunity and social justice. The matter is so sensitive, Herrnstein (1982) claims, that the press and the media tend to suppress scientific findings that appear to favor hereditary factors in intelligence and cognitive abilities, and to feature any evidence favoring the role of training. Nevertheless, the press and the media have in the last several years shown keen interest in Bouchard's (1984) studies of twins reared apart – studies that now appear to support a strong genetic component in cognitive abilities (Bouchard, Lykken, McGue, Segal, & Tellegen, 1990). (For further discussions of the IQ controversy, see Aby, 1990; Cronbach, 1975; Kaplan, 1985; Snyderman & Rothman, 1988).

The role of mental abilities in education seems always to have been recognized, in the sense that learners have been classified as "apt" and "fast" or "inept" and "slow," and dealt with accordingly. Until modern times, those who appeared unable to keep up with instruction were often simply dropped from school. The work of the French psychologist Alfred Binet in introducing a series of intelligence scales (Binet & Simon, 1905) for assessing children's chances of school success is well known; this work was echoed in Germany, Spain, and many other countries, including the U.S. (Goddard, 1910; Terman, 1916). Volumes have been written about the role of mental abilities in education. The recent interest in issues such as the declines of mean scholastic aptitude test scores over the past several decades (Lipsitz, 1977; Advisory Panel on the Scholastic Aptitude Test Score Decline, 1977) and the levels of the nation's literacy (NAEP/ETS, 1985; Kirsch & Jungeblut, 1986) indicate public awareness of the importance of cognitive abilities in education and in the functioning of society and the economy.

The fairly strong correlation of intelligence with occupational status has been documented many times: on the basis of World War I mental testing data, by Yerkes (1921) and Fryer (1922); and on the basis of World War II data, by Stewart (1947). Gottfredson (1984) has made detailed analyses of the roles of intelligence and education in the division of labor. She presents evidence to show that (1) occupations differ in the general intellectual difficulty of the tasks they require workers to perform on the job, (2) the occupational prestige hierarchy reflects an ordering of occupations according to that intellectual difficulty level, (3) jobs that are higher in intellectual difficulty are more critical to the employing organization, and (4) large differences in intelligence in the population are evident by early school years and this distribution is not substantially changed by school or work environments. Recently (Gottfredson, 1986b), she has argued that it is virtually hopeless to expect that such differences can be circumvented in employee selection, even by extensive training programs, because while it may be possible to teach lower-ability persons certain job skills and knowledges (if enough time is taken to do so), it is practically impossible to teach the skills of good judgment and decision making that depend on level of intellect.

According to a reviewer in *Science,*

The relation of innate intelligence and crime is a central concern in *Crime and Human Nature* [Wilson & Herrnstein, 1985]. That IQ scores are correlated with delinquency and with school performance has long been known, though often ignored or interpreted by criminologists as reflecting social factors of class and culture and responses to school contexts. After describing studies of the relations between IQ test scores and other indices of behavior, such as school performance, the authors conclude that intelligence plays a prior and independent role in association with crime.

This is later explained:

Intelligence affects crime in that the individual of low intelligence is less aware of long-run consequences, less willing to defer present gratifications, and less able to restrict impulsivity (Gusfield, 1986, p. 413).

Undoubtedly there are many other areas of societal importance in which individual differences in cognitive abilities may be implicated to some extent, for example, consumer behaviors and extent and kind of television viewing, but any review of investigations of these topics is beyond the scope of this volume.

Nearly all studies of the societal correlates of cognitive abilities have focused on a very general mental ability, called *g* by Spearman (1927), and measured – though with some variations in exactly what is measured – by a wide variety of intelligence or IQ (intelligence quotient) tests. Likewise, most studies of the heredity–environment issue have utilized measures of general intelligence. It is the thesis of this book that there exist a substantial number of distinguishable and important mental abilities – as many as thirty or more. While it may well be the case that general intelligence – a recognized higher-order factor of cognitive abilities – is the most weighty element in all these relationships (Hunter, 1986), the possible importance of more specialized abilities cannot and should not be ignored. The predictive validity of several specialized abilities in military and occupational selection settings has often been demonstrated (Guilford & Lacey, 1947; United States Employment Service, 1970; Ghiselli, 1966.) My own work in foreign language aptitude strongly suggests that specialized abilities beyond general intelligence play an important role in learning a foreign language (Carroll, 1981b). It is commonly recognized that various specialized abilities in music and the arts are largely independent of general intelligence. Some evidence exists that there are genetic determinants for some special abilities, independent of any for general intelligence (Vandenberg, 1962; DeFries, Vandenberg, & McClearn, 1976).

Some special abilities are of such social importance that they have attracted the attention of historians. For example, in a book entitled *The Intelligence of a People*, Calhoun (1973) traces the development and importance of several special abilities – verbal and spatial-mechanical – in American social history since colonial times. Cohen (1982) has undertaken a similar task with respect to what she calls "numeracy," and Soltow and Stevens (1981) have chronicled the rise of literacy in America.

From all these considerations, it should be clear that the study of cognitive abilities is important from several social and practical standpoints. This volume attempts to present what is now known about cognitive abilities and its scientific basis. Social and educational policies need to take account of what cognitive abilities exist, how they are best measured, how they are formed, how they normally develop and change over the life span, how amenable they are to improvement, and by what means they can be improved, if that is possible.

NOTES

1. The reliability of a measurement is an index of its "accuracy," that is, the degree of agreement between successive applications of a measurement procedure. It is often expressed as the correlation, in a typical sample of cases showing dispersion of measurements, between scores or values obtained on two successive occasions, or from presumably equivalent measurement procedures. The correlation between any two variables A and B is reduced (in absolute magnitude) to the degree that the measurements of the variables lack perfect reliability. In theory, the maximum correlation that could be expected between variables A and B is the square root of the product of their respective reliability coefficients. See standard textbooks on psychological measurements for further details, particularly with respect to corrections for "attenuation."

2. According to the entry in Harré and Lamb (1983, p. 641), "a trait is a characteristic of a person...which varies from one individual to another.... Traits are conceived as reasonably stable and enduring attributes, distinguishing them from *states*, which are temporary behavioral predispositions." In personality theory, the concept of trait has been debated; some authorities reject the concept altogether, on the ground that behavior is so much situationally determined that there can be no stable traits. There is much evidence, however, that cognitive abilities exhibit a great degree of stability, even in diverse situations, and can therefore be regarded as traits. See Anastasi (1983) for further discussion. Note that the concept of trait as applied to cognitive abilities has no necessary connection with the concept of trait employed in genetics in discussing, e.g., dominant and recessive traits.

3. Some authorities dislike the expression "elementary cognitive task" because in their opinion it wrongly suggests that cognitive tasks can be "elementary" and simple when they are actually probably very complex, or that tasks can be decomposed into simple components when they are actually not amenable to such decomposition. In my usage of this expression, I only mean to suggest that some tasks are simpler than others; being "elementary" is a matter of degree. For example, a reaction time task studied in the laboratory is undoubtedly simpler than the task of writing a letter or essay. Whether

tasks can actually be decomposed into component processes is a matter for empirical determination.

4. Note that I imply a very broad definition of "test." The class of things that can be called *tests* includes not only the typical paper-and-pencil multiple-choice test that can be administered to groups of individuals at the same time, but also many types of individually administered examination schedules such as the Stanford–Binet intelligence scale or the Wechsler Intelligence Scale for Children (WISC). In his textbook on psychological testing, Cronbach (1990, p. 32) suggests that a test be defined as any "systematic procedure for observing behavior and describing it with the aid of numerical scales or fixed categories."

5. A reviewer has pointed out that the term *potential* implies future performance, and questions whether it is appropriate in this context. I use it only to refer to the idea that an individual's degree of ability on a particular dimension of ability implies a certain probability of success – that is, potential for success, in attempting *any* particular task involving that ability, depending, of course, on the level of difficulty of the task.

6. I strongly favor a distinction between aptitude and achievement, in opposition to a considerable body of opinion in the psychometric community to the effect that there is no useful distinction to be drawn. The issue was discussed extensively in a symposium whose proceedings were edited by Green (1974). In that symposium, I – along with several others – promoted the idea that aptitudes are basic characteristics of individuals that control rates of learning, while achievements are merely products of learning. Thus, in this context the distinction between *aptitude* and *achievement* bears on the nature of these constructs. This is in contrast to contexts in which variables – whether they be measures of aptitude or measures of achievement in the senses just mentioned – are considered to measure aptitudes to the extent that they are useful in predicting future performance.

7. If variables 1 and 2 were scores obtained by successive application of the same measurement procedure, their intercorrelation could be considered as a measure of the reliability of that measurement procedure. In this example, however, I envision two different measurement procedures, which could still have a high intercorrelation indicating that they tend to measure the same thing, namely, visual acuity.

2 *Historical Foundations of the Study of Cognitive Abilities**

> *I found that every science required
> a speciall and particular wit, which
> reaved from that, was little worth
> in other sorts of learning.*
>
> Juan Huarte (1575)

In Chapter 1, the kinds of questions deemed most important to ask about cognitive abilities were listed and discussed. The present chapter gives an account of how these questions have been dealt with in the past. It begins with a brief history of mental testing, followed by a history of the development of factor analysis as applied to the identification of cognitive abilities and the determination of their structure and organization. A third part consists of a treatment of the several models of intelligence that have been derived from factor-analytic investigations. Finally, there is a presentation of recent developments in cognitive psychology that suggest new ways of viewing problems of individual differences in cognitive abilities.

A BRIEF HISTORY OF MENTAL TESTING

Several histories of mental testing are available. Works by Peterson (1925) and Sokal (1987) are good sources for the early period; books or articles by Tuddenham (1962), Linden and Linden (1968), DuBois (1970), and R. M. Thorndike and Lohman (1990) bring the history up to a more recent date. In a chapter (Carroll, 1982) in Sternberg's (1982) *Handbook of Human Intelligence*, I have traced the history of the mental testing movement – with special attention to its methodological aspects and with a focus on group intelligence testing – through two somewhat arbitrarily defined periods: (a) an early or developmental period beginning in the late nineteenth century, during which the foundations of theory and practice in psychometrics were laid down; and (b) a modern period starting around 1935 with the founding of the Psychometric Society and its journal *Psychometrika* and continuing to the present, during which many refinements have been made in the technology of testing and during which testing became a major enterprise. I have also contributed (Carroll, 1987a) a chapter on the history of educational measurement, in a volume on the history of educational

*In this chapter, life dates are given in square brackets.

psychology. Jensen (1987) contributed to that same volume a chapter on the history of mental testing. To avoid too much repetition with materials in these other chapters, I give here only a summary that calls attention to developments that are particularly pertinent to the issues addressed in this volume, and that updates and amplifies the material where necessary.

The concept of individual differences in mental ability was slow to develop and become the subject of scientific investigation. Early in the nineteenth century, the astronomer Bessel [1784–1846] became aware that there were individual differences in reaction time, but it was not until the last third of the century that a number of investigations of individual differences in reaction time were carried out in the laboratory of the German psychologist Wundt [1832–1920], mainly by his American student James McKeen Cattell [1860–1944], who is credited with coining the term *mental test* (Cattell, 1885, 1890). Wundt himself is said to have had little interest in studies of individual differences.

The Englishman Francis Galton [1822–1911; see the biography by Forrest, 1974], a half-cousin of Charles Darwin, became much interested in individual differences, but only in the second half of his life, when he published one of his major works, *Hereditary Genius*, in 1869. In that work (Galton, 1869), he suggested that intellectual genius tends to run in families. In another work, *Inquiries into the Human Faculty and its Development* (Galton, 1883), he laid the foundations of a theory of cognitive abilities, proposing that a series of mental tests should be given to people in order to determine their mental strengths and weaknesses. From 1884 to 1890, Galton collected data from the general public on a variety of simple tasks, mainly physical and sensory. Although Galton was one of the first to conceive the idea of correlation, a correlational analysis of these data was conducted only recently by Johnson, McClearn, Yuen, Nagoshi, Ahern, and Cole (1985). These authors concluded, from a principal components factor analysis, that Galton's tests measured four components, identified as body length, reaction time, visual acuity, and body breadth. Only the second of these components could be regarded as a measure of anything like a cognitive ability, and there is little suggestion in their analyses that reaction time was consistently related to any correlate of intelligence such as socioeconomic class. Overall, Galton's efforts to measure intelligence by psychometric tests were a failure. The difficulty centered in the kinds of variables he chose to use. Nevertheless, Galton's influence on the field was immense; besides the notion of correlation, he also conceived the idea of the percentile, and drew attention to the kinds of statistical distributions (principally the Gaussian normal distribution) which measurements of individual differences typically form. He inspired the work of a number of British statisticians (Karl Pearson [1857–1936], G. U. Yule [1871–1951]) and psychologists (Spearman [1863–1945], Burt [1883–1971]) who helped develop the study of individual differences in the early years of the twentieth century.

In the 1890s and early 1900s, there were other efforts to associate results of simple mental tests with estimates of intelligence or scholastic success. From his studies with Wundt, Cattell returned to America and set about applying tests of reaction time, sensory discrimination, word association, picture-naming speed, and other such tests to college students (Cattell & Farrand, 1896). However, in what is purportedly the first extensive application of the correlational method, Clark Wissler [1870–1947] (1901), later to become a well-known anthropologist, found that the scores of the tests that Cattell had given several years earlier to Columbia University undergraduates showed no practically useful correlations with their college grades. The results of this study, as well as those of a somewhat similar one by Sharp (1898–99), were taken as persuasive evidence that tests of simple mental reactions had no promise as predictors of scholastic achievement or, for that matter, as measures of anything like intelligence.

From the debates in the literature of the times, one might have supposed that the mental testing movement was dying amidst its birth cries. Indeed, psychologists in the United States did not return to investigations in this field until they became aware of further work going on Europe. Historical priority must be given to the extensive work of Binet [1857–1911] in France. After a long period in which he investigated the simple tasks studied by Galton, Cattell, and others, Binet (1903) came to the conclusion that tests comprising more "complex" tasks, resembling mental activities required in school, were more promising as measures of intelligence. He and a colleague developed a scale of intelligence that adequately distinguished mentally retarded children from children of normal intelligence. The scale (Binet & Simon, 1905) consisted of a series of tasks of increasing difficulty, difficulty being assessed in terms of percentages of children passing at different chronological ages. The tasks were assigned mental age levels in terms of the typical performance of children at a particular chronological age. The tasks were highly varied, but most of them relied in some way on the understanding of language and the ability to reason with either verbal or nonverbal (spatial, numerical) materials. This scale, and the more refined one published shortly afterward (Binet & Simon, 1908), formed the basis for intelligence scales developed in a number of countries and languages. In fact, the contents of the present "Stanford–Binet" test developed in the U.S. by Terman (1916) and his colleague Maud Merrill (Terman & Merrill, 1937, 1960) can in most cases be traced back to those of the original scale. From the standpoint of my discussion of the definition of ability in Chapter 1, one important feature of the Binet test is its use of the mental-age scale as a difficulty scale. A child's mental age is determined by procedures that estimate the point on this scale where the child has about a 67% to 75% chance of performing a task correctly; thus the measurement structure of the Stanford–Binet test conforms well to the definition of ability that I offered in Chapter 1. From another standpoint, however, it does not conform well, since the scale is not homogeneous; that is, it can be shown that it measures a variety or melange of somewhat independent abilities (Wright, 1939; Jones, 1949, 1954; Stormer, 1966).

Tests of the Binet type are generally called *individual* tests of intelligence, because they are designed to be given to one person at a time by a trained examiner. The origin of the *group* test of intelligence, so called because it can be given to groups of examinees, usually as a "paper-and-pencil" printed test, is obscure, because the practice of giving written examinations to groups like school classes is very old. The German psychologist Ebbinghaus [1850–1909] – famed for his studies of memory – is said to have been one of the first to devise a group test of intelligence (Ebbinghaus, 1897). It was a "completion" test intended to measure the effects of fatigue on children's school performances. It resembled what today would be called a *cloze* test (Taylor, 1953), requiring the child to guess how to fill in blanks representing deleted syllables or words in a prose passage. Dividing classes into thirds on the basis of class standing or teachers' estimates of brightness, Ebbinghaus noted the substantial relation of scores on this test with these divisions, but techniques of computing correlation coefficients to quantify these relationships were not then available to him.

After Binet's success with individual tests of intelligence, group tests containing tasks or items modeled loosely on Binet's were developed, both in Great Britain (Burt, 1911) and the U.S. (Otis, 1918). Although most of these tests continued to require direct answers to questions or solutions to problems, some of them used the multiple-choice procedure whereby examinees were required to select the correct answer from a series of alternatives – two or more. Scores on the tests generally equaled the number of correct answers, it being assumed (correctly) that a ranking of examinees by the number of correct answers would correspond approximately to a ranking of the examinees by true ability.

The group tests of intelligence devised by Arthur Otis [1886–1963] as a student of Terman became the chief basis for the Army Alpha Examination developed and used for testing millions of recruits in World War I (Yerkes, 1921). The Army Beta examination was a nonverbal group test, designed for recruits who could not read or had little understanding of English. Shortly after World War I, numerous adaptations of such tests were made and widely used in American public schools. The publication of mental ability tests became a major commercial enterprise and has continued to the present day, as can be seen by inspecting a recent edition of a listing of tests in print (Mitchell, 1983).

The development and refinement of both individual and group tests was accompanied by a slow evolution of statistical procedures for deciding what was to be included in the tests and for evaluating the reliability and validity of the scores. Fundamental contributions to these problems were made by a group of mathematical statisticians in Great Britain led by Karl Pearson [1857–1936; see a biography by E. S. Pearson, 1938]. Pearson's group developed the statistics of linear correlation and multiple regression, estimations of statistical parameters, and other details relevant to mental test construction and evaluation (see Walker, 1929). The concept of test reliability and the theory and procedures for estimating the true correlation between two measurements corrected for unreliability or "attenuation" were developed by the British psychologist Charles Spearman

[1863–1945; see his autobiography, 1930] in a paper published in 1904 (Spearman, 1904a); the term now used for this concept, *reliability*, seems to have been first used by Burt (1909, p. 112). A further derivation of reliability theory, the so-called Spearman–Brown prophecy formula for predicting the effect of the length of a test (or the number of replicate measurements) on its reliability, was made by Spearman (1910) and also, independently, by William Brown (1910). Concepts of test scaling, standardization, and test norms were developed around 1917; simple item-analysis techniques were used in constructing the Army intelligence tests. Working with Terman [1877–1956] in the development of the Stanford–Binet intelligence test, Truman Kelley [1884–1961] was a major American contributor to test theory statistics (Kelley, 1927). Many contributions to this field, quite apart from his work in factor analysis (to be discussed below), were made by Thurstone [1887–1955; see Wood, 1962, for biography and listing of publications], for example, the development of an absolute scale for mental age (Thurstone, 1928) and a discussion of the speed–power problem in mental testing (Thurstone, 1937).

The major formulations of what is now called "classical test theory" were summarized by Gulliksen (1950) in a widely used textbook. Classical test theory proceeds from the assumption, first made by Spearman (1904a), that any test score is composed of two components, a "true score" and an "error" score representing the operation of random fluctuations. From these assumptions, along with the statistics of weighted sums, many formulations relating to test reliability and validity can be derived. These formulations continue to be useful in many contexts involving total test scores. What these formulations do not provide, however, is a clear specification of the relation between item response and the ability or latent trait underlying that response, at least in the case of tests that involve a series of item responses. Early formulations of this relation were made by David Walker (1931, 1936, 1940) and Louis Guttman (1941), and the contributions of Thurstone (1931) in postulating a normal ogive form of this relation should also be mentioned. A major contributor to what has come to be known as *item response theory* has been Frederic Lord [b. 1912] (1952; 1980; Lord & Novick, 1968). The theory incorporates a major simplification, due to Birnbaum (1968), of the relation between ability and item response by assuming that the relation is described by a logistic function rather than by the normal ogive function. It has many applications in practical testing problems, such as selection of items for best estimation of true ability and its distribution, the determination of the dimensionality of a test, equating different forms of a test either horizontally (for samples of the same average ability) or vertically (for samples of different levels of ability), and presenting items of appropriate difficulties in what has been called "adaptive" testing (Weiss, 1983).

Item-response theory is currently a very active area of psychometric research, since it presents many problems of parameter estimation that have not yet been solved satisfactorily, especially for the most popular and reasonably complete model for the ability-response relation, the three-parameter model that assumes parameters for the position and the slope of the function and a "guessing" parameter specifying the probability that an examinee of infinitely low ability will nevertheless choose a correct response by guessing or other means. This third parameter applies in the case of the multiple-choice items which appear in many mental ability and achievement tests. For free-response items in which alternative responses are not furnished, the one-parameter model proposed by Rasch (1960, 1980) is often considered more satisfactory (Wright & Stone, 1979), although many workers favor a two-parameter model (Carroll, 1990). In any event, successful use of item-response theory often requires large numbers of cases in tryouts of tests. Thus far, it has been applied mostly to scholastic aptitude and achievement tests designed to be administered to large numbers of examinees. Possibilities of using it for constructing and evaluating tests of specific mental abilities have not yet been widely explored.

Notions of Mental Ability

What does one seek to measure in developing a test of mental ability? We can interpret the efforts of Galton, J. M. Cattell, Binet, Terman, and many others in the developmental period of mental testing as being oriented toward the measurement of an ordinary language concept of intelligence that assumes that human beings exhibit, somewhat independently of the amount of education to which they have been exposed, grades of intelligence ranging from idiocy or feeblemindedness to genius. Galton was most concerned with the characteristics of superior mental ability or even genius; Binet was concerned with distinguishing grades of mental deficiency and contrasting them with the abilities of the average child. The psychologists who developed the Army intelligence examinations during World War I were evidently attempting to take seriously the advice offered by Galton, namely, that one should "obtain a general knowledge of the capacities of a man by sinking shafts, as it were, at a few critical points" (Galton, in a letter appended to Cattell, 1890). For these Army psychologists, the critical points were abilities to understand language, to follow directions, to perform reasoning with semantic and quantitative relationships, to make "practical judgments," to infer rules and regularities from data, and to recall general information.

A satisfactory definition of intelligence or mental ability was always elusive. In the early days, the definitions offered by leaders in testing seldom corresponded well with the actual measurement procedures embodied in their tests. For example, a definition of intelligence proposed by Binet would hardly yield suggestions about how to operationalize the concept: "What we call intelligence, in the narrow sense of the term, consists of two chief processes: First to perceive the external world, and then to reinstate the perceptions in memory, to rework them, and to think about them" (Binet, 1890, p. 582, my translation). A symposium on the meaning of intelligence published in 1921 (Thorndike et al., 1921) offered a great profusion of definitions and opinions. Intelligence was variously described as "ability to learn" (Buckingham, p. 273), as "the power of good responses from the point of view of truth or fact" (Thorndike, p. 124), as "the ability to carry on abstract thinking" (Terman, p. 128), as "the ability of the individual to adapt himself adequately to relatively new situations in life" (Pintner, p. 139), as "involving two factors – the capacity for knowledge and the knowledge possessed" (Henmon, p. 195), and as "the capacity to acquire capacity" (Woodrow, p. 207). Henmon insisted that "the so-called general intelligence tests are not general intelligence tests at all but tests of the special intelligence upon which the school puts a premium" (p. 197).

It is interesting, incidentally, to compare these views with a series of statements of twenty-five contemporary authorities on the concept of intelligence recently assembled by Sternberg and Detterman (1986), in a deliberate undertaking to update the 1921 symposium writings. Only a small sample of these statements can be given here. Anne Anastasi conceives of intelligence as a quality of adaptive behavior. J. W. Berry regards intelligence as the end-product of individual development in the cognitive–psychological domain. Carroll (the present writer) emphasizes that intelligence is a societal concept that operates in several domains – academic, technical, social, and practical. Hans Eysenck concentrates on intelligence from a biological point of view, arguing that it derives from the error-free transmission of information through the cortex. Howard Gardner describes the theory of multiple intelligences that he has expounded elsewhere (Gardner, 1983). Robert Glaser views intelligence as acquired proficiency. Arthur Jensen defines intelligence in terms of the general factor obtained in many studies of psychological tests. John Horn, however, thinks that intelligence is the reification of a functional unity that does not in fact exist; he prefers to think of intelligence in terms of a number of somewhat independent broad abilities. Lloyd Humphreys defines intelligence as the repertoire of intellectual knowledges and skills available to a person at a particular point of time. Robert Sternberg defines intelligence as "mental self-government."

Commenting on this collection, Sternberg and Berg (1986) conclude that although there was much agreement across the two symposia regarding the nature of intelligence, there are some differences. The 1986 symposiasts were more interested in understanding behavior than in measuring and predicting it. In attempting to understand intelligent behavior, they were motivated to appeal to concepts of information processing and cultural context, and their inter-relationships. The 1986 symposium did not produce any definitive definition of intelligence, nor was it expected to.

Throughout the history of mental testing, although much attention was devoted to the measurement of general mental ability, it was always recognized that there are many special abilities, aptitudes, achievements, and skills worthy of measurement, whatever their relation to general intelligence might be. For example, the first version of a battery for measuring musical aptitude was published as early as 1919 (Seashore, 1919). British psychologists were early interested in the measurement of spatial, "practical," and mechanical abilities (McFarlane, 1925; Cox, 1928; El Koussy, 1935), and mechanical and clerical abilities were investigated by several research groups in the U.S. (Andrew & Paterson, 1934; Paterson, Elliott, Anderson, Toops, and Heidbreder, 1930; Stenquist, 1923). Some of these early efforts to measure aptitudes were summarized in books by Hull (1928) and Bingham (1937). The question of exactly what types of abilities and aptitudes exist and are measurable was the concern of the developing field of factor analysis, to which we now turn our attention.

FACTOR ANALYSIS: ORIGINS AND DEVELOPMENT

At the age of thirty-four, Charles Spearman [1863–1945], a product of an English upper-class upbringing, decided to resign his officer's commission in the British Army in order to pursue long-held interests in psychology. He went to Leipzig to study experimental psychology with Wundt, taking seven years to obtain his Ph.D. with a dissertation on space perception. During those seven years, however, he spent some time in England, in military service connected with the Boer War of 1900–1902, and became acquainted with Galton's *Inquiries into the Human Faculty* (1883) and Galton's proposals about mental ability tests. As Spearman recalled in his autobiography,

One day, inspired by Galton's *Human Faculty*, I started experimenting with a little village school nearby. The aim was to find out whether, as Galton has indicated, the abilities commonly taken to be "intellectual" had any correlation with each other or with sensory discrimination (Spearman, 1930, p. 322).

The results of Spearman's "experimentation" were published by him in a classic paper (Spearman, 1904b) in the *American Journal of Psychology* (significantly, an American journal rather than a British one because Spearman considered no British journal appropriate; the *British Journal of Psychology* was then only in the process of being founded). This paper is worth study even today, because it contains not only a report of the tests given in the village school (and one other school, an upper-level preparatory school) but also a thorough review and critique of previous work by Binet and others, including many Americans such as Cattell and Wissler. Its importance for us consists in the fact that it was the first paper in which a set of correlations prompted an attempt to explain them in terms of a theory of individual differences in intelligence. The data are weak: there are five sets of data, none having more than 36 cases. The measurements themselves had weaknesses, and Spearman's own calculations of the correlations were not completely accurate (Fancher, 1985). Nevertheless, the seminal influence of this paper cannot be questioned, because it inspired decades of work on the problems it addressed. That work, in fact, is the focus of the present volume.

Actually, Spearman's chief concern in this paper, as noted above, was whether tests of sensory acuities were related to measures or ratings of abilities "commonly taken to be 'intellectual.'" This question, he believed, was answered in the affirmative, for after correcting the correlations for unreliability or attenuation, he computed the theoretical relationship between what he called General Intelligence and General Discrimination (based on measures of sensory acuity) to be equal to 1.01 for one sample, and 1.04 for another. The slight excesses over 1.0, the maximum meaningful value of a correlation, he attributed to random statistical error. The validity of these results is somewhat questionable, however, because of Spearman's choice of variables in assessing reliabilities. But these are not the results of most interest in the present context.

More important was Spearman's observation that the correlations, uncorrected for attenuation, formed a nearly perfect "hierarchy" if the variables are listed in order of their average correlation with the other variables. One of his tables of correlations, with the variables arranged in this way, is as follows:

	Classics	French	English	Math	Pitch	Music
Classics	—	.83	.78	.70	.66	.63
French	.83	—	.67	.67	.65	.57
English	.78	.67	—	.64	.54	.51
Math	.70	.67	.64	—	.45	.51
Pitch	.66	.65	.54	.45	—	.40
Music	.63	.57	,51	.51	.40	—

(Note, incidentally, that Spearman's use of the term *hierarchy* does not correspond to its contemporary use in speaking of the hierarchical arrangement of factors.)

Spearman observed that this hierarchy of correlations might signify that each variable could be accounted for, to some quantifiable extent, by a single factor common to all the variables. This factor, he suggested, is General Intelligence. From the observation that the variables had different levels of average correlation, he concluded that they had different levels of *saturation* with the general factor. In fact, it was possible to compute this level of saturation and form a table of the levels of saturation for the variables. The table of correlations with general intelligence that Spearman provided included the following values:

	Saturation (Spearman)	Recomputed
Classics	.99	.958
French	.92	.882
English	.90	.803
Math	.86	.750
Pitch	.72	.673
Music	.70	.646

Spearman's values were for "disattenuated" variables, however. I have computed the values for the original variables and shown them in the above table. Each of these saturations can be regarded as the correlation between the variable and a general factor. The expected correlation between any two variables would be the product of their respective saturations with the general factor. Thus, the expected correlation between Classics and French would be $.958 \times .882 = .845$; the difference between this value and the actual correlation (.83) could be attributed to random error in the data.

These results are perfectly analogous to results obtained in modern investigations conducted by factor analysis, except that today school marks would not generally be included as measures of a general factor. The above table of saturations would now be called a table of *factor loadings*, or a *factor matrix*, and a table of expected correlations would be called a table of *reproduced* correlations. One could form a table of *residuals* by forming a table of the differences between expected and observed correlations. The operation of computing expected correlations can be represented in matrix algebra by specifying that the matrix of reproduced correlations, R_r, is equal to the matrix of saturations, or factor loadings, F, multiplied by its transpose; that is,

$$R_r = FF'.$$

Spearman computed his table of saturations by certain simple formulas; it was only later that more formal computational methods for computing the loadings on a single factor were developed (Hart & Spearman, 1912). The important point here, however, is that as early as 1904 simple techniques of factor analysis were developed, parallel to procedures available today.

It was clear to Spearman that not all the variance in a given variable was accounted for by a single factor. He assumed that the remainder of the variance could be accounted for by random statistical error, by variance that was unique to the variable, or by some combination of these. For this reason he postulated what he called – somewhat misleadingly – a "two-factor" theory of intelligence. That is, each variable was to be accounted for by two factors – a *general factor* and a *specific factor* unique to that variable. (The term *two-factor* seems misleading in that Spearman's theory actually implies many factors – a general factor plus a specific factor for each variable that one might conceive of.) Spearman devoted the major part of his professional life as a psychologist to an attempt to establish the validity of the two-factor theory and, in addition, to explicate the psychological nature of the general factor, which he came to symbolize with the letter g. The major writing that bears on this subject is his book *The Abilities of Man* (1927), in which he described many investigations purporting to show the all-pervasive existence of g and in which he offered speculations as to its nature. A discussion of Spearman's theories of general intelligence will be deferred until a later point. Here the focus is on the development of factor analysis as a method for investigating dimensions of cognitive abilities.

In Spearman's time, the major problem raised by critics was whether it was indeed the case that a given table of correlations could be described by a single (general) factor, apart from a specific factor associated with each variable. Spearman provided several methods for investigating this problem. (See a discussion of these methods by Thurstone, 1947, pp. 259ff.) The method that was most used by him and his followers stemmed from his observation that the mathematics of his theory implied that if only a single factor were present, a certain function of the set of off-diagonal correlations for any four variables would have to equal zero. This function was called, consequently, the *tetrad difference*. (The first use of this term appears to be in a paper by Spearman and Holzinger, 1925). That is, for any four variables labeled 1, 2, 3, 4, the tetrad difference is

$$r_{13}r_{24} - r_{23}r_{14}.$$

For a real data matrix of correlations for which only a single factor is present, it could be expected that these tetrad differences, computed for all possible sets of four variables, would form a sampling distribution around zero, the variance in the sampling distribution being attributable to chance fluctuations. A provisional formula for the probable error of the tetrad difference was published by Spearman and Holzinger (1924). A more satisfactory formula was derived by Wishart (1928). Despite the large amount of effort required to compute the $n(n-1)(n-2)(n-3)/8$ tetrad differences for a matrix of n variables, Spearman and his followers used this method to judge the adequacy of a single-factor interpretation of a matrix. In some cases, Spearman eliminated variables that failed to yield vanishing (near zero) tetrads – a practice that made him the target of criticism. Undoubtedly, the amount of computation involved in these investigations and the inadequate computational facilities then available delayed the development of factor analysis. Another influence, however, was Spearman's persistent fascination with the idea that a single general factor could explain a large part of individual differences in cognitive ability.

Factorial investigations of many kinds proceeded, nevertheless, but in the period 1904–1928 they were conducted chiefly in Great Britain. Investigations such as one by Burt (1917) indicated that cognitive ability tests might measure factors beyond a general factor; the further factors were dubbed "group factors" because they appeared in particular groups of variables. Garnett (1919) pointed out that Spearman's formulations were a limited special case of a more general theory of multiple factors. On this basis Spearman and others began to work out methods whereby the existence of factors beyond a general factor might be demonstrated. At first, there was no great sophistication in these methods. A general factor was extracted, and then the further clustering of the variables was observed in the residuals. Over a number of years, fairly exact and reasonable methods were developed. Such methods were used in reporting some of the investigations included in Spearman's posthumous work *Human Ability*

(Spearman & Jones, 1950). Perhaps the best summary of these methods as they finally developed is that given by Burt (1940) in his book *Factors of the Mind*. Burt later published numerous papers concerning the development of factor analysis and his own role in it. Hearnshaw (1979, Chapter 9) has claimed that Burt indulged in some exaggeration and falsification in these papers, giving himself much more credit than was really due him, but Joynson (1989) has presented acceptable evidence for the view that Burt actually presented an honest and impartial account.

Responsibility for a further stage of development was taken mainly by American psychologists, at first largely following the lead of Spearman. Karl Holzinger [1892–1954], who took his Ph.D. in mathematics and education at the University of Chicago in 1922, studied for several years at the University of London with Karl Pearson and Spearman. On returning to the University of Chicago, he developed what he called a bi-factor method of factor analysis essentially an extension of Spearman's methods. Presented first informally around 1935 (see Holzinger & Harman, 1937), this and other closely related methods were summarized in a series of textbooks authored either by Holzinger and his student Harman [1913–1976] (Holzinger & Harman, 1941) or by Harman (1960, 1976) alone.

Much of Holzinger's work was carried out under the auspices of a so-called Unitary Traits Committee that was established in 1931 by the well-known educational psychologist Edward L. Thorndike [1874–1949]. Thorndike had become interested in the possibility of multiple factors of individual differences, even though he had earlier (Thorndike, Bregman, Cobb, & Woodyard, 1926) believed in the dominance of a single factor (or actually, in numerous small factors that in effect added up to one factor). The membership of the committee, under Thorndike as chairman, consisted of H. E. Garrett, Karl J. Holzinger, Clark L. Hull, Truman L. Kelley, K. S. Lashley, T. V. Moore, and C. Spearman. As described by Holzinger (1936), the work of the committee was divided among six subcommittees to study various aspects of the problems to be investigated, including the mathematical theory and practice of factor analysis, physiological correlates of intelligence, a survey of factorial tests, and a major effort to collect appropriate data for factor analysis. It appears that most of the work on this last problem was performed by Holzinger, who issued a series of preliminary reports on data collected in Illinois schools and on methods for analyzing these data (Holzinger, 1934a, b, 1935a, b, c, d; Holzinger & Swineford, 1936a, b, c). However, the committee supported a study by Garrett, Bryan, and Perl (1935) of the age differentiation of traits. A final summary report to be prepared by Spearman was never completed, due to Spearman's preoccupation with applications of psychology in World War II and his death in 1945.

Another American psychologist who took up the challenge to develop methods for investigating human ability traits was Truman Lee Kelley [1884–1961], well known for his statistical work in the development of Terman's

Stanford–Binet test. His book *Crossroads in the Mind of Man* (1928) reported new methods by which he was able to demonstrate the existence of a number of group factors (up to 5 or 6), in addition to a general factor, in several sets of data. This was apparently the first report of multiple factors of ability to be published in the U.S. Later, Kelley (1935) presented a method of analysis which would now be regarded as a principal components analysis similar to one originally proposed by Pearson (1901) and further developed by Hotelling (1933). It was by this method that Davis [1909–1975] (1944), one of Kelley's students, claimed that a set of reading tests measured 6 or 7 different factors, whereas Thurstone (1946), using his own methods, claimed that this same set measured only one factor. (The apparent conflict can be easily resolved by pointing out that Davis was analyzing total variance whereas Thurstone was seeking only common factor variance. Many of Davis's factors were largely specific factors.)

By all odds, the American psychologist who was most influential in the development of factor methods was Louis Leon Thurstone [1887–1955]. His biographer, Dorothy Adkins Wood (1962), wrote:

> Impatient with the long-standing debate on Spearman's single-factor method, Thurstone hit upon the expedient of posing the basic question in a new form. Instead of asking whether a table of correlation coefficients supported a general factor, he wondered how many factors must be postulated in order to account for the observed correlations. The power of this approach was that whether or not one factor should be regarded as general could be answered factually for each study (Wood, 1962, p. 22).

Thurstone published his first paper on what he called multiple factor analysis in 1931 (Thurstone, 1931). (Apparently, Thurstone was the first to use the term *factor analysis* extensively, although Spearman, as early as 1904, had used the term *factor*.) In a series of publications culminating in the book *Multiple Factor Analysis* (1947), he introduced many of the methods now regarded as essential or fundamental in factor analysis, at least in what is generally called "exploratory factor analysis." The principal elements of Thurstone's methods were:

1.   *The centroid method*: A computationally simple method of condensing a correlation matrix into an orthogonal factor matrix on arbitrary axes, each successive factor contributing less variance than the preceding. The number of factors extracted by this method was that number reached after which residuals were judged to be due mainly to chance fluctuations. The centroid method gives results somewhat similar to various other methods of condensation – for example, the principal factor method and Burt's simple summation method; it is now seldom used, however, because other methods are regarded as superior in several respects. Thurstone also contributed a "multiple-group" method of factor-analysis which is still occasionally used. It is similar in many respects to Holzinger's *B*-coefficient method.

2.   *The estimation of communalities*: The idea of communality was not original with Thurstone; it is to be found in earlier writings of Spearman and Burt, usually by that name (and spelling).[1] Thurstone provided several new methods for estimating the communalities of variables in a correlation matrix. In this connection, it should be noted that Thurstone was a strong supporter of what

is generally known as the *common factor model*, that is, a model in which it is assumed that meaningful and interpretable factors account not for the total variance but only the "common factor variance" embodied in the communalities. The common factor model was not original with Thurstone; essentially, it was Spearman's model, except that Spearman assumed in his early work that the common factor variance was accounted for by only one factor – *g* in the case of cognitive ability tests.

3. *Rotation of axes to "simple structure"*: Thurstone was among the first to recognize that multiple factors derived by the centroid and similar methods were not necessarily meaningful and appropriate for psychological interpretation, since they represented only successive extractions of decreasing amounts of variance. To make factors more meaningful, he developed judgmental criteria and methods – chiefly graphical – for rotating their reference frame axes either orthogonally or, if necessary, obliquely, to what he called "simple structure." This was a concept that met resistance among many factor analysts; British psychologists, for example, persisted in attempting to interpret unrotated factors in terms of their sign patterns. The idea of simple structure is now generally accepted, however.

4. *Computation of correlations among first-order or "primary" factors and factor-analysis at the second and (if necessary) higher order*: The idea of this procedure came relatively late (Thurstone, 1944b; Thurstone & Thurstone, 1941) but it is now regarded as an essential feature of Thurstonian methods.

Thurstone was also among the first to formulate factor analysis in terms of matrix algebra. He and his students and co-workers, principally Ledyard R Tucker [b. 1910], were instrumental in developing many procedures to facilitate factor-analytic computations, including, for example, a method of multiplying matrices using a specially adapted IBM test-scoring machine (Tucker, 1940). These methods enabled Thurstone to analyze larger matrices than had been studied previously, and to conduct an extensive program to study cognitive abilities in various domains.

In 1933, the mathematical statistician Harold Hotelling [1895–1973], having become aware of the work of Spearman and Kelley, pointed out that the condensation of a correlation matrix, as required in factor analysis, is analogous to the traditional mathematical problem of finding the latent roots and vectors of a matrix. He provided a new method of performing the required computations (Hotelling, 1933) and later a further simplified method (1936). Hotelling called this the *principal components* solution. Thurstone had developed a similar solution in 1932 (Thurstone, 1947), which he called the *principal-axes* solution. Kelley (1928, 1935) also developed solutions essentially equivalent to Hotelling's. In his later years, Burt pointed out that the theory of principal components had been developed by Pearson (1901), and complained that factor analysts had entirely overlooked Pearson's work; actually, Burt may have been as guilty of having neglected Pearson's work as anyone else (see Hearnshaw, 1979, pp. 171ff.). Thurstone recognized the theoretical utility of the principal-axes or principal components solution, but until at least the early 1950s, when electronic computers became available, the computational problems involved in its solution for large matrices discouraged its wide use. It was only after efficient and accurate algorithms and programs for the latent roots and vectors problem were devised (see Householder, 1964) that this type of solution replaced the somewhat less elegant centroid method.

There still exists, however, some confusion in terminology. As offered by Hotelling, the principal component solution calls for analyzing a matrix with unities in the diagonal; thus, it implies analysis of the total variance in each variable. Thurstone's centroid method assumed the common-factor model; that is, it assumed that only the common factor variance should be analyzed. It required, therefore, continual estimation and reestimation of the communalities to be inserted in the diagonal of the matrix of correlations or of residuals at any stage of the analysis. Thurstone (1947, p. 509) recognized that Hotelling's solution, insofar as it involved computing latent roots and vectors of a matrix, could equally well be applied to a matrix with estimated communalities inserted in the diagonal. By custom, this is now called the *principal factor* solution, whereas a solution based on unities in the diagonal is properly called a *principal components* solution. Both of these solutions are employed widely today. The characteristics and comparative advantages of these two types of solution are discussed in Chapter 3. (The term *principal axes solution* is still used, but often ambiguously, since it may refer to either a principal components or a principal factor solution.)

By 1940, much of the basic theory and methodology of factor analysis had become available (Wolfle, 1940). It had become possible to apply factor analysis to the determination of the common factors underlying large matrices of correlations among mental tests and other variables. Thurstone's (1938b) classic study, *Primary Mental Abilities*, analyzed 57 variables into 11 or 12 uncorrelated primary factors – and claimed that 7, or possibly 8, of these were clearly interpretable. (Interestingly, a preliminary presentation of these data (Thurstone, 1936b) reported some oblique rotations, but according to Thurstone's (1952) autobiography, the formal presentation had only uncorrelated factors due to a suggestion by E. L. Thorndike that it might be unwise to introduce too many innovations in one report.) Thurstone found no general factor like Spearman's *g*. This provoked a storm of controversy and criticism, principally from the British school of factor analysts led by Spearman, but also from Holzinger and Harman (1938). In a rather sardonic essay, Spearman (1939) complained that his *g* factor seemed to have entirely disappeared in Thurstone's study; he reworked Thurstone's data to show that there was indeed a general factor in these data. Burt (1939, p. 93) stated that he was "largely in agreement" with Spearman's criticisms. Thomson (1939), however, regarded Spearman's criticisms as superficial and easily answered, although he expressed his preference for the Spearman–Holzinger method because to him the results seemed more psychologically reasonable.

From today's standpoint, it is unfortunate that this debate ever took place. It caused, and has continued to cause, much distrust of factorial methods, particularly among those who have not bothered to understand the nub of the controversy. As Wolfle (1940, p. 24) pointed out, "When Thurstone's primary factors are correlated, as they may be, the method possesses the equivalent of a general factor." It had already been shown by Moore (1933) and Cox (1939) that a battery of tests involving a general factor and *n* uncorrelated group factors can be equally well analyzed into *n* correlated group factors without a general factor. Wolfle's conclusion seems quite appropriate today (except that better methods than the centroid method are now available):

> The methods of Spearman and Holzinger assume a general factor to exist – and find one. Thurstone's rotated centroid solution does not require a general factor but sometimes finds one explicitly or finds correlated group factors. The latter method seems preferable because of its greater flexibility (Wolfle, 1940, p. 25).

Thurstone himself acknowledged that data could reveal a general factor. Thurstone and Thurstone (1941) actually computed loadings on a second-order general factor in their study of primary mental abilities at the eighth grade. Chapter XVIII of Thurstone's (1947) text gives formulations for second-order factor analysis, and includes the following final statement:

> An interesting application of second-order factors is an attempt to reconcile three theories of intelligence, namely, Spearman's theory of a general intellective factor; Godfrey Thomson's sampling theory, with what he calls "sub-pools"; and our own theory of correlated multiple factors, which are interpreted as distinguishable cognitive functions. The tetrad differences vanish when there are no primary factors common to the four tests of each tetrad, the correlations being determined only by the general second-order factor (Thurstone, 1947, p. 439).

In the second edition of his textbook on factor analysis, Thomson (1946) showed how a correlated factor solution could be converted into a solution with "a *g* plus an orthogonal simple structure." An even more elegant resolution of the apparent disagreement between methods was presented by Schmid and Leiman (1957), who demonstrated how a correlated factor solution with factors at one or more higher-order levels or strata could be converted into a structure with solely orthogonal factors – some derived from higher-order factors and thus more general than others. The Schmid and Leiman technique of orthogonalizing a hierarchical solution is a generalization of Thomson's demonstration; it is superficially similar to a method that Cattell calls the Cattell–White formula (Cattell, 1978, pp. 209–211). None of these techniques has been widely used; until recently, none has been included, to my knowledge, in any commonly available computer package for factor analysis. More is said about the procedure in Chapter 3, because it has been used extensively in the present work.

If we restrict attention to what has come to be called *exploratory factor analysis* (a term that was introduced by Tucker, 1955), that is, to the methods developed chiefly by Holzinger and by Thurstone, the history of factor analysis since 1947 has consisted of the introduction of various refinements and special techniques, like that of Schmid and Leiman just mentioned, in addition, of course, to the enormous advances in computational methods permitted by modern electronic computers.

During the 1950s and 1960s, there was much concern with the problem of arriving at objective, analytic procedures of orthogonal or oblique rotation of axes of the initial factor matrix, to replace the rather subjective, graphical procedures developed by Thurstone and by others (e.g., Zimmerman, 1946). Tucker (1944) proposed what he called a "semi-analytical" method of rotation, consisting essentially of finding an oblique transformation that would optimally fit, in a least-squares sense, any hypothesized set of factor weights in a reference-vector matrix. Rotations were to be tried, iteratively, until the transformation appeared to yield an optimal simple structure. This method was still partly subjective, but the mathematics of Tucker's method were precisely the same as those of a so-called Procrustes solution proposed by Hurley and Cattell (1962), who seem to have been unaware of Tucker's procedure. Tucker's formulations were also the basis for a rather widely used Promax method proposed by Hendrickson and White (1964) whereby an oblique structure is to be found from the transformation that best fits a matrix containing powers (e.g., 2, 3, or 4, retaining signs) of loadings in an orthogonal simple structure matrix such as that produced by Kaiser's (1958) Varimax method.

Kaiser's method, yielding an orthogonal matrix that approximately meets simple structure criteria, was the latest development in a series of proposals by Saunders (1953), Carroll (1953), and others based on maximizing or minimizing certain functions of factor loadings. Saunders's proposal aimed at producing an optimal *orthogonal* solution, whereas Carroll's proposal was intended to produce an *oblique* reference structure, and his further proposals (Carroll, 1957, 1962a) concerned a so-called *oblimin* class of rotational procedures (see Harman, 1976, pp. 310–320). Jennrich and Sampson (1966) introduced a modification, which Harman called "direct oblimin," to produce an oblique *pattern* matrix (as opposed to a reference-vector matrix) that met simple structure criteria. Many other rotational procedures have been proposed, but it seems that no one of these has been generally accepted, except Kaiser's Varimax rotation for the orthogonal case. The choice of a rotational method still depends partly on the data and partly on the personal preferences of the investigator. Research on oblique rotational procedures has continued even in recent years (e.g., Tucker & Finkbeiner, 1981).

One problem with Thurstone's centroid method, and also with the principal factor method, was that it was difficult or impossible to assess the statistical significance of the results. The maximum likelihood solution for condensation of the factor matrix, due to Lawley (1940; Lawley & Maxwell, 1963), has come into fairly wide use because it offers statistical tests for significance of factors. Nevertheless, given the number of factors to be extracted, it produces a factor matrix which is approximately the same, after any necessary orthogonal transformation, as a converged iterated principal factor matrix for that number of factors. Furthermore, the maximum likelihood matrix solution usually requires further rotation to simple structure, just as a principal factor matrix does, and such rotation partly destroys the usefulness of the solution for assessing statistical significance since the statistical significance of factor loadings is indeterminate. These technical problems are the object of continued methodological research. Nevertheless, experience indicates that for well-designed sets of data, results given by different methods of condensation and axis rotation are seldom very different in their overall *patterns*; that is, the same factors are identified and the loadings for variables on those factors can generally be differentiated into those that clearly depart from zero and those that are close to zero.

Maximum likelihood methods are the basis for an approach, due chiefly to the Swedish statistician Karl Jöreskog, that has come to be called *confirmatory factor analysis*. Essentially, this approach, described most conveniently in a collection of papers by Jöreskog and Sörbom (1979), is closely related to Thurstone's simple structure concept. Using maximum likelihood procedures, it permits testing whether a set of data can be satisfactorily fitted to a model with the constraints imposed by a given set of hypotheses about the simple structure of the data. These hypotheses can be derived either from an exploratory factor analysis of the data or from psychological analysis and previous experience with the variables. Because of the fact that the results yield statistical significance assessments, even of factor loadings, it has been claimed (e.g., Long, 1983) that this approach is far superior to exploratory factor analysis techniques. In general this may be true, but the approach can be said to have certain problems, stemming from the fact that data sometimes appear to be equally well fitted by two or more sets of simple structure hypotheses. The procedure might better be called *disconfirmatory* factor analysis because it is more valuable for disconfirming hypotheses than for confirming them. But even this statement is not completely correct since significance tests tend to become unmanageable for datasets with large numbers of observations. Also, computations with sets of data for a large number of variables, as ordinarily performed with the so-called LISREL computer program (Jöreskog & Sörbom, 1984), are expensive and rather laborious. Although confirmatory factor analysis is valuable for lending more confidence to factorial findings and for dealing with certain special cases such as the multimethod–multitrait problem (Cole & Maxwell, 1985; Marsh & Hocevar, 1983; Schmitt & Stults, 1986), exploratory techniques continue to have an important place in the toolkit of the factor analyst (Carroll, 1985).

One of the more important recent developments in factor analysis is a technique, due principally to Bock and Aitken (1981), called full-information factor analysis. This technique (Muraki & Engelhard, 1985), based on maximum likelihood statistics and item-response theory, appears to circumvent the various technical problems that have arisen in factor-analyzing correlations among single dichotomously scored test items, particularly when the items differ widely in difficulty and can be passed by chance guessing (Carroll, 1945, 1961). Because of its recency, the technique has not as yet been applied widely, but it would appear to be highly promising for determining the homogeneity of items that are intended to measure a single factor of ability.

Partly to avoid confusion and undue complexity, this account of the history of factor analysis has deliberately omitted mention of numerous elaborations and special techniques of factor analysis (see Mulaik, 1986). The discussion has, for example, assumed that factor analysis is restricted to what Cattell (1952) has called R-technique, based on the correlations of variables over persons. No mention has been made of the obverse of this technique, Q-technique, the correlation of persons over variables, or several other possible types of analysis of the person × variable × occasion data box as described by Cattell (1978, Chapter 12). (Cattell's Q-technique should not be confused with the Q-sort technique developed by Stephenson, 1953.) This is because in fact these other techniques have seldom been used in discovering ability dimensions, and it is moot whether they would actually be useful in that search over and above what can be gained from use of R-technique. All the studies to be reviewed in this volume have used R-technique. Similarly, no mention has been made of several techniques of analysis due to Guttman (1954, 1966; see also Canter, 1985) because they assume models of factor analysis fundamentally different, in many respects, from those employed in most studies. It would take us too far afield to discuss them in the present context.

Factor analysis has been the subject of numerous textbooks and advanced treatises. Several of the earlier textbooks, up to 1947, have already been mentioned. A chronological listing of the more important texts that have appeared since then is as follows:

> Thomson (1951) (5th edition)
> Cattell (1952)
> Fruchter (1954)
> Harman (1960)
> Reuchlin (1964) (in French)
> Horst (1965)
> Harman (1967) (2nd edition)
> Pawlik (1967) (in German)
> Guertin & Bailey (1970)
> Mulaik (1972)
> Comrey (1973)
> Gorsuch (1974)
> Harman (1976) (3rd edition)
> Cattell (1978)
> Kim & Mueller (1978a, b)
> Revenstorf (1980) (in German)
> Cureton & D'Agostino (1983)

Gorsuch (1983) (2nd edition)
McDonald (1985)
Yates (1987)
Comrey & Lee (1992) (2nd edition)

Programs for computing exploratory factor analysis have appeared in all the standard statistical packages for large-frame electronic computers, such as BMD, SAS, and SPSS (MacCallum, 1983), but they vary considerably in what features they contain. Programs designed for use with personal computers are available from the author.

FACTOR-ANALYTIC MODELS OF COGNITIVE ABILITIES
AND THEIR ORGANIZATION

When applied to correlation matrices of a number of variables in the search for the underlying factors or latent traits that account for those correlations, factor analysis makes certain assumptions about abilities and the relation of factors to abilities and to variables. Many of these assumptions were brought together by Wolfle (1940, pp. 2–5) and it is worth quoting some of his statements (with certain clarifying materials added in square brackets):

1.   It is assumed that performance in any field, such as the cognitive, depends neither upon one undifferentiated ability nor upon a completely chaotic conglomeration of separate abilities. Rather, it is assumed that cognitive ability consists of a number of different factors, traits, faculties, or powers, each of which is elicited by a variety of different tests or problems... It is not necessary to make any assumptions regarding the total number of factors, except that, if the factorial methods are to effect any economy of thought, the number must be much smaller than the total number of different tests or tasks which could be constructed.

It is not necessary to make any assumptions regarding the fundamental nature of the factors or what produced them. Each factor may be unitary, or it may consist of a large number of separate causes which act together in a coherent and unitary manner. The factors may be produced by genetic differences or may be due to training. All that is assumed is that a cause or group of causes, however produced, acts as a functional or operational unit.

2.   Tests [read *variables*] may differ factorially in one or both of two ways – in their complexity and in their factor loadings. The complexity [read *factorial complexity*] of a test refers to the number of factors involved in it. For example, performance on test A may involve factors 1 and 2, while performance on test B involves factors 3, 4, 5, and 6. Test A, which depends on only two factors, is of low complexity; test B, which involves four factors, is of greater complexity.

It is usually hoped that any given test will involve only a few [say, one or two] of the factors or abilities present in an entire group of tests....

Tests may also differ in their factor loadings. Tests A and B may both involve factors 1, 2, and 3; but in the performance of A, factor 1 has a high loading or weight and plays a large and important role, while factors 2 and 3 are relatively unimportant....

3.   When the factors are not correlated with each other, the correlation between any two tests equals the sum of the products of the weights of those factors which are common to the two tests. For example, if factor 1 has weights of .6 and .4 in two tests and if this is the only factor common to both tests, the [expected] correlation between the tests will be .24. If factor 2 is also involved in the two tests, with weights of .5 and .8, then the correlation will be $(.6 \times .4) + (.5 \times .8)$, or .64.

4.   It is assumed that the abilities involved in performing any task combine by simple addition to determine the degree of excellence shown in the performance of that task. It would be possible to make any one of several other assumptions, but the additive one is the simplest to handle mathematically... These assumptions may be brought together and expressed in simple algebra. The result is the fundamental equation of factor analysis:

$$s_a = w_{1a}x_1 + w_{2a}x_2 + \cdots w_{na}x_n + w_a x_a;$$
$$s_b = w_{1b}x_1 + w_{2b}x_2 + \cdots w_{nb}x_n + w_b x_b,$$

where $s_a, s_b \cdots$ = standard scores [of any given individual] on tests A and B; $x_1, x_2, \cdots, x_n$ = standard scores [of any given individual] on the common factors $[1, 2, \ldots, n]$; $x_a, x_b, \cdots$ = standard scores [of any given individual] on the specific factors [i.e., factors that are not common but are specific to each test]; and $w_{1a}, w_{1b}, \cdots$ = the weights of these factors in determining s_a and s_b. (The weights in each of these equations are so chosen that the sum of their squares equals unity.)

5.   These score equations imply the existence of two other assumptions which are not usually stated very explicitly but which are, nevertheless, involved. Since parallel equations could be written for each subject on each test, it is obvious that every subject is assumed to possess every factor. The fact that this assumption may not be justified is not a serious handicap to the factorial methods....

6.   More serious misrepresentation of individual differences is likely to be involved in assuming that the weights, w_{1a}, w_{1b}, etc., are constant [over individuals]. Here it is assumed either that weights are the same for all individuals or that one is using an average weight. The retrospective reports of subjects sometimes indicate that they used quite different methods of attack on a test. When this is so, the weights should vary. Factor methods have not included this possibility. Until they do, the weights should be considered as averages of individual weights which vary among the subjects to an unknown extent....

     All the factor methods seek to transform the original table of correlations into a set of factor loadings [i.e., weights w_{1a}, w_{1b}, etc.] which will satisfactorily reproduce those correlations. This transformation may always be made in a number of different ways. The task is therefore one of finding a set of factor loadings which in some way is better than any of the others. Because of disagreement as to what constitutes the "best" set of loadings, the factor methods differ from each other (Wolfle, 1940, pp. 2–5).

We see, incidentally, that as early as 1940 Wolfle pointed out the limitation of the factor methods in assuming constant factor loadings over individuals, that is, parallel factor equations for all individuals. This limitation has been pointed out a number of times in the history of the factor methods, for example by Jeffress

(1948) and Sternberg (1977, p. 33). No way of getting around it has yet been proposed, even for the single factor case, except by performing different analyses for groups of individuals found to use different strategies (French, 1965), establishing experimental conditions whereby different factor weights might be determined, or testing different models of individuals' test performances (MacLeod, Hunt, & Mathews, 1978). For exploratory factor analysis studies, we may assume that this is not a serious limitation, because the chief goal is to determine what factors of ability exist, not to determine how these abilities are used by a given individual in performing a given task. (This problem was discussed, in an elementary way, in Chapter 1, in the context of a hypothetical bird-detection task.)

Several further assumptions not explicitly stated by Wolfle should be mentioned. One is the assumption that any variable entered into the computation of a Pearsonian correlation matrix is a linear function of whatever abilities (one or more) are involved in that variable, the abilities being assumed to be measured on at least an interval scale (with equal units). Ordinarily the variable is a score, such as number correct, on a psychological test, but it could be a variable derived in some other way, such as a judgmental rating of some ability, a count of number of products produced by an individual, a measurement of performance per unit of time, etc. Sometimes the raw variable (test score, or whatever) is subjected to some kind of nonlinear transformation before being entered into correlations, usually on the basis of the investigator's knowledge or judgment that the variable so derived better represents a linear function of interval-scaled true abilities. In most cases, however, there is no information concerning the most appropriate scaling of true abilities. Some investigators (e.g., Thurstone, in his classic *Primary Mental Abilities* study, 1938b) have attempted to circumvent the assumption of variables as linear functions of abilities by using tetrachoric correlations; such correlations, of course, assume that each variable is based on a normal distribution, with the implication that an ability is best scaled when it forms a normal distribution in a representative sample of a population. (For further discussion, see Carroll, 1961.)

More generally, it should be noted that factor analysis can be based only on variables that can be expressed quantitatively, and that result in some way – directly or indirectly – from people's performances.[2] If it is complained that factorial results are limited because they are based mainly on results of psychological testing (Lenk, 1983; Gould, 1981), the defense can be (1) that well-designed, well-administered psychological tests are scientifically appropriate means of assessing people's performances and potentials therefor and (2) that factor analysis permits, equally well, the study of individual difference variables that do not derive from psychological test performances.

Another assumption central to factor analysis is that a given ability or latent trait can indeed be involved, manifest itself, or be called for in a number of somewhat different performances. For example, the size and range of an individual's vocabulary could influence performance on (1) a conventional multiple-choice test of vocabulary, (2) a test in which the individual is required to give words specified by their definitions, (3) a spelling test, and (4) a reading comprehension test, if the reading passages contain considerable numbers of uncommon words likely to be unfamiliar to many examinees. The mathematics of factor analysis requires that in any factor study *several* possible measures of each factor or hypothesized factor must be included, in order that the factor may appear in the common factor space. (It is often recommended that there be at least three such variables for each factor.) Yet, the several possible measures of a factor should not be too similar, for if they are, a spurious common factor may emerge that would otherwise be treated as a specific factor. For example, including three parallel forms of a multiple-choice vocabulary test in a factorial battery might yield a factor (a "triplet") specific to that method of testing vocabulary.

The results of a factor analysis obviously depend upon what variables are entered (it is hard to see how the case could be otherwise). This fact has sometimes been appealed to in criticizing factor analysis on some such basis as "a factor analysis gives no more information than what you put into it" or even "garbage in – garbage out." Such criticisms are not reasonable; a well-designed factorial study *can* yield information that is by no means immediately apparent from the input. Nevertheless, the interpretation of the results of any particular study must take account of what variables were used as input. For example, it is quite possible for a "general" factor in one study to be rather different from the "general" factor in another, depending upon the variables employed.

All these assumptions and caveats having been stated, we can examine the various factorially derived models of intelligence or cognitive ability that have been proposed. As I have pointed out previously (Carroll, 1980c), factor analysis as such does not assume any particular model of intelligence or cognitive ability, except to the extent that the basic assumptions of factor analysis must apply to whatever variables are entered into it. Factorially derived models of intelligence attempt to specify the "structure" of mental abilities, in the sense of specifying what factors exist, and how these factors may be related to one another.

The Spearman–Holzinger Model

As sketched earlier, Spearman's earliest findings (1904b) caused him to adopt a view that a very general mental ability exists, involved to various degrees in many types of intellectual activity. What struck him most forcefully was the fact that many correlation matrices exhibited, or could be made to exhibit (by dropping some variables) what he called a "hierarchal" order such that all tetrad differences were close to zero. When this occurred, the matrix could most parsimoniously be explained as due to a single factor plus a specific factor for each variable. This was the basis for Spearman's so-called two-factor theory (which might better be called a "one-general-factor theory"). Spearman and his followers recognized that other analyses were possible. For example, it would be possible to explain a hierarchal matrix with two or more group factors, but the factors would have to be similarly ranked or have proportional weights; to assume more than one common factor would violate logic and the principle of parsimony.

Spearman (1927, Chapter XII) observed that when cognitive tests were involved, matrices exhibiting the hierarchal property contained a series of variables that all appeared to measure or reflect some kind of intellectual ability – reasoning, language understanding, ability to deal with quantitative relationships, and the like. "The leading part in intelligence," he said, "is played by the ability to handle, not merely abstract ideas, but above all symbols" (p. 211). The variables used in his studies tended to be psychological tasks, school marks, or ratings of intelligence or brightness. (Spearman pioneered in the development of group tests of intelligence and encouraged his students and followers to develop such tests.) Although measures of sensory discrimination were included in some of his early data sets, he gradually came to see that they had very little relationship to intellect, if any, and such measures were seldom included in his later data sets. Variables with the highest weights on the general factor were those that offered the greatest degree of evidence concerning the nature of this factor. Examples of such variables were tests of giving opposites, making inferences, and performing analogies. Spearman devoted considerable thought to the logical analysis of such cognitive tasks; indeed, he published a book specifically addressed to this matter, *The Nature of "Intelligence" and the Principles of Cognition* (Spearman, 1923). From this work, and from empirical data, he evolved the notion that the general factor of intelligence intrinsically involves three mental processes. The first of these is "the apprehension of experience." The other two, on which Spearman laid much stress, are the "eduction of relations" and the "eduction of correlates," where the word *eduction* means the drawing out of some logical abstraction or consequence from two or more stimuli. *Relations* are abstractions like "similarity" and "comparison"; *correlates* are the particular attributes of stimuli that are seen as identical, similar, compared, or related in some way. Spearman concluded that a task (or a test) calls upon the general factor to the extent that it requires the eduction of relations and/or correlates. Spearman also speculated that the ability to educe relations and correlates represented some sort of mental energy or power that might have a physiological substrate. In the intellectual ambience of the times, he was inclined to believe that this mental power had a genetic origin, i.e., that differences across individuals in degree of mental power could be traced at least in part to heredity.

Still, Spearman recognized that the general factor might not account for all the variance in tests of mental ability. His practice of pruning correlation matrices of variables that produced nonvanishing tetrad differences had the inadvertent effect of identifying tests that measured abilities beyond the general factor. Among these were tests of verbal ability, of spatial ability, or of other abilities.

Gradually there developed in his laboratory a broader, multifactor concept of mental ability. Garnett (1919) was actually the originator of multiple factor analysis – not Thurstone. When Holzinger went to study with Spearman shortly after 1922, the idea of multiple factor analysis burgeoned in a series of studies. Several of Spearman's students conducted studies that explored dimensions of ability beyond the general factor. For example, McFarlane (1925) studied "practical" ability; Hargreaves (1927) studied the "'faculty' of imagination"; and Cox (1928) studied "mechanical aptitude." El Koussy (1935) was one of the first of Spearman's students to publish a factor matrix with more than one common factor. This work implied a model of intellect that called for a general factor plus a number of group factors.

It was Spearman and Holzinger's purpose to explore such a model further that led to their work with the Unitary Traits Committee mentioned in a previous section. One outcome of this work was a set of data on 24 psychological tests, first analyzed by Holzinger and Swineford (1939) by their bi-factor method, that has been repeatedly analyzed by various other methods. By the bi-factor method (Harman, 1976, p. 127), these data yield a general factor and five group factors (spatial relations, verbal, perceptual speed, recognition, and associative memory), all factors being orthogonal. By Thurstonian methods (e.g., see Harman, 1976, p. 315), the data yield four or five correlated group factors, but the results can easily be transformed into a bi-factor pattern.

The Spearman–Holzinger model was also embodied in Spearman's (1939) abbreviated reworking of Thurstone's (1938b) data, and in Eysenck's (1939) more extensive reanalysis of those data. The model also is not unlike that presented by Kelley (1928), in that it contained a general factor plus several group factors.

Thurstone's Model of Cognitive Abilities

Thurstone's (1938b) first large study of cognitive abilities was planned to investigate "a number of tentative psychological categories or factors which served merely to insure that a wide variety of tests of the paper–pencil sort were included" (p. v). Using his multiple-factor methods (centroid condensation of a matrix of tetrachoric correlations and graphical orthogonal rotation to simple structure), he reported clear identification of seven "primary" factors, noting that "some of the primary factors ... correspond closely to group factors that have been previously identified" (p. 79). Nevertheless, "The primary factors that appeared have a general relation to the tentative categories with which we started, but they are not identical with the tentative categories" (p. v). The seven primary factors identified were labeled S (Space), P (only later explicitly named Perceptual Speed), N (Number Facility), V (Verbal Relations), W (later named Word Fluency), M (Memory), and I (Induction). In addition, two other factors were tentatively labeled R (perhaps for "Restriction") and D (Deduction), and there were four other factors that Thurstone did not attempt to rotate to simple structure or to identify.

In Thurstone's preface to this work, we find the following statement:

> So far in our work we have not found the general factor of Spearman, but our methods do not preclude it. The presence of a general factor could be indicated by a large part of the communality of each test that remains unaccounted for by the common factors that can be identified in a simple structure. So far we have not found any conclusive evidence for a general common factor in Spearman's sense, but some situations may be found in which such an interpretation is justifiable. As far as we can determine at present, the tests that have been supposed to be saturated with the general common factor divide their variance among primary factors that are not present in all the tests. We cannot report any general common factor in the battery of fifty-six tests that have been analyzed in the present study (p. vii).

Despite Thurstone's statement, it must be commented that his methods (as developed up to just before 1938) *did* tend to preclude the identification of a general factor. Of critical importance here is the fact that the 1938 study employed only orthogonal (graphical) rotations of axes. Thurstone's first publication on oblique rotation (Thurstone, 1938c) appeared only in 1938, apparently after work on the primary mental abilities study had been completed. If one makes pairwise plots of loadings of Thurstone's orthogonal rotated factors, it is clear in some instances (e.g., factors S and N) that simple structure criteria would have been better satisfied if rotations to oblique axes had been made. Oblique rotations would have shown many of the factors to be correlated, and it is conceivable that such correlations of primary factors could have been explained by a general factor at the second order. To my knowledge, no investigator has yet published a reanalysis of Thurstone's data by *oblique* simple structure procedures. There is, however, one unpublished reanalysis of this kind (Inman, personal communication), and I report my own reanalysis later in this volume. Snow, Kyllonen, and Marshalek (1984) present a multidimensional scaling of Thurstone's data.

We may also consider the possibility that the sample Thurstone used in this study was too highly selected to permit a general factor readily to emerge from the analysis. The sample consisted of 240 volunteers; some came from a YMCA college but the remainder apparently were from the University of Chicago student body. Although the sample was admittedly "a highly selected group" (Thurstone, 1938b, p. 16), it showed enough variance on all the tests, as well as on the psychological examination of the American Council on Education (that 113 of the volunteers had previously taken), to permit a general factor to appear if one existed. (One did appear, in fact, in both Spearman's (1939) and Eysenck's (1939) reanalyses by British methods.) On the other hand, the sample was perhaps too highly selected to force Thurstone to consider oblique rotations.

It was only later that Thurstone and his co-workers (principally L. R Tucker) developed techniques of higher-order factor analysis, and in a series of further studies, intercorrelations of primary (first-order) factors were regularly reported. In his later years, Thurstone (1947, Chapter XVIII) was willing to grant that his primary factors were or could be correlated, and to admit the possible existence of Spearman's general factor at the second order of analysis.

From this standpoint, the Thurstone model of cognitive abilities is not fundamentally different from the Spearman–Holzinger model. It permits a general factor to appear, along with group factors, if there is in fact such a general factor that can explain correlations among group or "primary" factors. In the meantime, however, acrimonious controversy between Spearman and his "British" school, on the one hand, and Thurstone and his "American" school, on the other, had arisen – taken up in many textbook discussions as if it represented a fundamental difference in viewpoint. I feel fairly certain that if Spearman had lived beyond 1945, it would have been possible for him and Thurstone to reach a rapprochement. The remaining differences between their viewpoints might have centered in the relative importance they attributed to primary and second-order factors. Spearman and his followers attached greatest importance to the general factor, and only subsidiary importance to various group or primary factors. Thurstone attached less importance to Spearman's general factor and in fact pointed out that there might be several factors at the second or higher orders; primary factors, he believed, were of considerable importance and utility in vocational guidance and other contexts. He and his wife and collaborator Thelma G. Thurstone [b. 1897] developed batteries for testing primary mental abilities – batteries that were in fairly wide use, at least in research and probably also in practice, for a number of years (Thurstone & Thurstone, 1938–65; see the hundred or more references in Buros, 1953, test 716 and in Mitchell, 1983, test 2269). In effect, a general factor was measured by the total scores for these batteries.

Thurstone's model recognized the possibility of a substantial number of primary or "group" factors, and the research of Thurstone and his students continued to find such factors and refine their interpretations; see, for example, studies by Thurstone (1944a, 1949), Schaefer (1940), Coombs (1941), Bechtoldt (1947), Taylor (1947), Jay (1950), Pemberton (1952), and Jeffrey (1957). Although I was not formally a student of Thurstone, I worked for a time in his laboratory, and my own study of verbal abilities (Carroll, 1941) can be added to this list. During the 1950s and 1960s many more studies of cognitive abilities were conducted in the Thurstonian tradition. In Ekstrom's (1979) summary of this work, several dozen primary or first-order factors were recognized as clearly confirmed.

The debate between British and American schools of thought over the relative importance of general vs. primary factors may have arisen by virtue of different interpretations of certain factorial statistics. Consider, for example, Eysenck's (1939; reprinted in Eysenck, 1973) reanalysis of Thurstone's (1938b) data. The reanalysis may be considered approximately analogous to a Schmid–Leiman orthogonalization of eight of Thurstone's primary factors if they had been rotated to an oblique structure. Eysenck's Table I shows factor saturations, by the group-factor method, for nine orthogonal factors, one of which is a general factor; the rest are group factors. The percentage of total variance contributed by each of the factors is shown in the last row of the table; these percentages sum to 54.3% (after correction for a slight typographical error). The percent variance for the general factor is much the largest of these, being 30.8%, or 56.7% of the common factor variance, while the percentages for group factors range from 6.61% down to 0.97%. From this standpoint the general factor might be regarded as the most important factor. But this type of computation (which occurs repeatedly in the factorial literature) allows the general factor variance to be counted as many times as there are tests, while the group factor variances are summed over only small to moderate numbers of tests. Obviously, the general factor variance is given undue weight. If we consider the respective percentages of common factor variance contributed by the general factor and some group factor for *each individual variable*, it is found that the average is 55.1% for the general factor and the remainder, 44.9%, for whatever group factor the variable contains. (For individual variables, the percentages contributed by a group factor range from 0% to 87.4%.) From this standpoint, group factors can be said to be, in this typical set of data, on the average nearly as important as the general factor in determining the common factor variance on any particular test. Thus, Thurstone's assessment of the importance of group factors seems to be justified.

Guilford's Structure-of-Intellect Model

Thurstonian methods of analysis were employed in a lengthy series of investigations conducted in the U.S. Army Air Force during and after World War II under the direction of J. P. Guilford [1897–1987]. The main results of these studies were published by Guilford and Lacey (1947), and appeared so promising that Guilford was encouraged to follow them up in a so-called Aptitudes Research Project conducted at the University of Southern California over the period 1949 to 1969. The results of these latter studies were published by Guilford and Hoepfner (1971), but as early as 1956 (Guilford, 1956; see Guilford & Hoepfner, 1971, pp. 25–27) Guilford concluded that it should be possible to arrange the many primary factors that he and others had claimed to have identified in a distinctive model that came to be known as the Structure-of-Intellect (SI, or SOI) model.

Because the SOI model has received much attention and is based on factorial methods that are in important respects unique to Guilford and his collaborators, these methods must be described and commented on. Until about 1960 Guilford employed the centroid method to condense a correlation matrix, carrying factorization to a rather larger number of factors than other investigators might have done. He did this on the basis of the opinion, often expressed by factor analysts, that overfactorization could do no harm, because residual, insignificant factors would presumably make themselves evident in factor rotation procedures, while underfactorization could seriously distort the findings, because the obtained factors might be in fact composites of other factors that should be separable. In his 1971 report (Guilford & Hoepfner, 1971), a principal factor method was used for condensation of correlation matrices, but it appears that this method was not applied with sufficient rigor to extract only the meaningful factors; generally, too many factors were extracted and subjected to a rotation process.

More importantly, Guilford argued for, and consistently employed, only orthogonal rotation of factors, because he believed that a set of data could be described most simply and directly by means of uncorrelated factors. In the earlier years of his researches, rotations were generally done graphically (Zimmerman, 1946), but in later years, he adopted a method designed by Cliff (1966) whereby it was possible to rotate axes – still orthogonally – to congruence or best fit with any specified matrix of hypothesized factor loadings. These hypothesized factor loadings were arrived at partly by logical analysis of tasks and their presumed factorial requirements, and partly on the basis of whatever evidence about the factorial compositions of the tests appeared to have accumulated from previous researches. Often, the hypotheses established to determine the target loadings for this method were derived from the SOI model that was evolving during the course of his investigations. Guilford must be given much credit for conducting a series of major factorial studies in which hypotheses were to be confirmed or disconfirmed by successive studies in which new tests were continually designed to permit such testing of hypotheses. Any evaluation of Guilford's findings raises the question, however, of how much these findings might be attributed to capitalization on chance or to the circularity that arose through the use of targeted rotation procedures. The wisdom of Guilford's adherence to orthogonal rotations and rejection of oblique rotations can also be questioned. Be that as it may, Guilford claimed to find a very large number of different, orthogonal factors of cognitive ability. At least up to the 1971 report, he never found a factor that resembled Spearman's g, and I can find little comment about this in his writings (but see Guilford, 1985). Guilford took it for granted that Spearman's factorial methodology and experimental program were deficient. (See discussion in Guilford, 1967, pp. 56–57.)

The SOI model was essentially an attempt to classify the many factors claimed to have been identified. Guilford called his model *taxonomic* or *morphological* rather than hierarchical. He took the point of view that any factor (or test variable, for that matter) would involve not one but three aspects or facets (at one time he called them "parameters"): *content*, *operation*, and *product*. That is, any factor, or the tests or tasks measuring it, would require the respondents to deal with some kind of content, perform some operation on this content, and have some kind of product as an outcome. By about 1958, the system was essentially complete. Four types of content, five types of operations, and six types of products were claimed to have been identified, and it was further postulated that the total number of possible factors would be 120, that is, the number of possible combinations of contents, operations, and products. The SOI model is most commonly depicted as a cube with "slabs" in the three dimensions corresponding to specified contents, operations, and products, and at least in many textbooks of general psychology and psychological testing, the model seems to have had wide acceptance and unreserved approval. Further, Guilford (1982) has claimed to have identified empirically most or all of the postulated factors; indeed, a number of cells in the SI cube appear to have contained two or more factors, and with the addition of an auditory content facet there may be as many as 150 different factors. Guilford (1981) has also claimed that some of the slabs of his SI cube may represent second-order factors, thus appearing to disavow his earlier rejection of hierarchical models.

Guilford's SOI model has been challenged on various grounds. In reviews (Carroll, 1968b, 1972) I questioned its logical validity, that is, the reasonableness of setting up a taxonomic system in which the parameters are universal and are assumed to interact in all possible ways to generate factors. I also expressed misgivings about the definitions and identifications of the claimed contents, operations, and products, and cited several empirical studies in which Guilford's classifications did not seem to hold. Cronbach and Snow (1977, pp. 155–160) called the SOI model "unprofitably complex." In an exchange of views with Guilford, Horn and Knapp (1973, 1974; Guilford, 1974) presented and defended their claim that Guilford's targeted rotation methodology was such as to permit him to accept almost any set of hypotheses about factor structure. It might have been expected that the modern British school, led by Eysenck (1967, p. 82) would reject Guilford's model in the strongest terms. Vernon (1961, p. 144) gave a number of reasons for having "grave doubts" regarding its ultimate validity. Harris (1967; Harris & Liba, 1965) reanalyzed a sample of Guilford's datasets and was unable to confirm the structures Guilford had claimed. Some psychometric researchers (e.g., Kelderman, Mellenbergh, & Elshout, 1981) have found partial support for certain aspects of Guilford's model, but on the whole the psychometric community has regarded the model as at least highly questionable, if not entirely rejected. On the other hand, some of Guilford's ideas, such as that of "divergent thinking," probably have at least some validity, and have been highly influential in studies of creativity.

In this historical survey it is not convenient or appropriate to pursue a detailed critique of the SOI model. At this point I will only state my conviction that the model is fundamentally defective. In Chapter 3, I consider the model further from the standpoint of Guilford's methodology, arguing against that methodology and defending the contrasting methodology that I favor. In later chapters I report numerous reanalyses of Guilford's data sets, showing that it is unlikely that his model can be confirmed, either in terms of its taxonomic structure or in terms of the large number of cognitive ability factors claimed by him.

Guilford's SOI model must, therefore, be marked down as a somewhat eccentric aberration in the history of intelligence models; that so much attention has been paid to it is disturbing, to the extent that textbooks and other treatments of it have given the impression that the model is valid and widely accepted, when clearly it is not.

Vernon's Hierarchical Model of Intelligence

The first truly hierarchical model of intelligence is usually associated with the name of Philip E. Vernon [1905–1987], a colleague of Spearman, Burt and Thomson in Great Britain during the 1930s and 1940s. Vernon himself, however, states that it was "first put forward by Burt, under the influence of McDougall" (Vernon, 1950, p. 24), and that its origin was described by Burt (1949). The most complete overview of this hierarchical theory has been given by Vernon in a survey published first in 1950 and issued in a slightly updated edition in 1961. There (Vernon, 1961, p.25), he states that the "strict hierarchical picture of mental structure is an over-simplification," if it is depicted, as it often is in textbooks, by a tree-diagram with g at the top, two major group factors $v:ed$ and $k:m$ just below it, a series of minor group factors at the next lower stage of the hierarchy, and numerous specific factors at the lowest level. Based on his review of many factorial studies conducted up to 1950 and later, Vernon presents (pp. 47, 85, 94, 127) much more complex diagrams of relations among factors in various domains (educational, psychological, sensory and perceptual, and occupational). The $v:ed$ (verbal:educational) and $k:m$ (spatial:mechanical) higher-order factors are dominated by g, and in turn dominate or subsume various minor group factors, which in turn dominate very narrow and specific factors.[3] Thus, $v:ed$ is depicted as dominating verbal, numerical facility, logical reasoning, attention, and fluency factors, while $k:m$ dominates educational grade factors in drawing, handwork, and technical subjects, as well as factors of spatial ability, mechanical information, psychomotor coordination, reaction times, and even athletic ability. Still, Vernon states his belief that "most of the variance of human abilities in daily life is attributable to g" – perhaps 40 per cent; the major and minor group factors contribute 10 per cent, and "the remaining 40 per cent would consist of very narrow group factors and unreliability" (p. 27).

It is difficult to appraise Vernon's model, partly because of its complexity, and partly because Vernon gives only his rather subjective impressions of the findings of widely diverse studies as the basis for his conclusions. Vernon gives a scholarly and useful review of the numerous studies available in the literature up to about 1960, but he made little if any attempt to rework or reanalyze them. Nevertheless, it is my judgment that many aspects of his model are correct. There is good evidence, for example, for clustering of variables around higher-order verbal–educational and spatial–mechanical factors, and for domination of all these factors by some sort of general factor. Vernon's admonition that factors' "pattern or structure changes according to the type of education or training" (p. 25) is to be taken seriously.

The Cattell and Horn Hierarchical Model of Cognitive Abilities

Raymond B. Cattell [b. 1905; for biographical information see *Multivariate Behavioral Research*, 1984, *19* (2 & 3)] was a student and research associate of Spearman in the 1930s. He moved to the U.S. in 1937 and for many years held a research professorship at the University of Illinois, where he devoted practically full time to factor-analytic methodology and research, chiefly in the personality field. As I have recounted elsewhere (Carroll, 1984), however, he took many excursions into the field of intelligence testing. In a paper on adult intelligence published in 1943 (Cattell, 1943), he proposed the possible existence of two kinds of intelligences: a "fluid" intelligence reflecting basic abilities in reasoning and related higher mental processes, and a "crystallized" intelligence reflecting the extent to which the individual has been able, partly on the basis of level of "fluid intelligence," to learn and profit from exposure to his or her culture through education and other experiences. (Throughout his career, Cattell has been much given to introducing new terminology, even coining new words from Greek roots and the like.) Fluid intelligence was given this term because it was conceived of as being able to flow into many kinds of mental activities; crystallized intelligence was so called because it was thought of as a kind of end product of experiences up to any given point in the life of an individual. Cattell noted the parallelism of this distinction with Hebb's (1942) distinction between "Intelligence A" and "Intelligence B," the former being, roughly, biologically determined capacity, the latter being intelligence as generated through experience and education. Although Cattell discussed it at various times in the intervening period, it was to be more than twenty years before the theory of fluid and crystallized intelligences, now often called Gf–Gc theory, was further developed and checked experimentally (Cattell, 1963, 1967a, b). A student of Cattell's, John Horn [b. 1928], provided the first clear test of the theory in his doctoral dissertation, using Thurstonian higher-order factoring techniques (Horn, 1965a; Horn & Cattell, 1967, 1982). This disclosed not only second-order Gf and Gc factors but also general visualization and speed factors. Further studies by Horn, Cattell, and others have refined the Gf–Gc theory; for example, an impressive study of twenty primary factors by Hakstian and Cattell (1978) disclosed six second-order factors, including not only Gf and Gc but also Gv (Visualization Capacity), Gps (General Perceptual Speed), Gm (General Memory Capacity), and Gr (General Retrieval Capacity). Further, correlations among these second-order factors were analyzed to suggest the existence of three third-order factors, "original fluid intelligence," "capacity to concentrate," and "school culture." These findings, however, must be regarded as in need of further confirmation from studies of different populations and samples.

Studies by Gustafsson (1984, 1988, 1989; see also Gustafsson, Lindström, & Björck–Akesson, 1981) suggest a further refinement of the Gf–Gc model in the form of what Gustafsson calls a HILI (hierarchical LISREL) model. According to the HILI model, a third-order "g" factor subsumes or dominates Gf, Gc, and Gv while at the same time being essentially identical to Gf.

An interesting feature of the Gf–Gc theory, as developed by Horn (1985; Horn, Donaldson, & Engstrom, 1981) is that fluid intelligence abilities tend to decline in old age, at least in some individuals, while crystallized abilities, like vocabulary, do not.

In his major book on abilities, Cattell (1971) incorporated Gf–Gc theory into a new and more general theory – the "triadic theory," which proposed that cognitive abilities fall into three types. "Capacities" are abilities reflecting "limits to brain action as a whole"; "provincial powers" are types of "local organization" for different sensory and motor modalities; and "agencies" are abilities to perform in different areas of cultural content, acquired through the "investment" of fluid intelligence in learning. Further, Cattell postulated a number of dimensions by which factors of ability could be characterized. Two of these dimensions had to do with "action phases" – input, processing, and output, and two of them referred to content – involvement of experiential-cultural dimensions, and involvement of neural-organization dimensions. The remainder were seven "process parameters" such as level of complexity, amount of committing to memory, and speed demand. This analysis of abilities comes very close to being a cognitive analysis.

The Cattell–Horn model, as summarized by Horn (1985, 1988), is a true hierarchical model covering all major domains of intellectual functioning. Numerous details remain to be filled in through further research, but among available models it appears to offer the most well-founded and reasonable approach to an acceptable theory of the structure of cognitive abilities. The major reservation I would make about it is that it appears not to provide for a third-order g factor to account for correlations among the broad second-order factors.

Miscellaneous Other Models

The major models presented thus far are seen not to be as different as might be supposed. All of them assume an organization of abilities whereby some abilities are more general than others. Any differences in the number of factors recognized by the models depend to a large extent on the extent of empirical evidence that each model had available at the time of its formulation. These differences also stem to some extent from the factorial methods available to, or favored by, the authors of these models and used by them to present their findings.

The Spearman–Holzinger model and the model deriving from the work of Thurstone and his followers are essentially similar in their final forms and are interconvertible through transformation operations. The Horn–Cattell model, insofar as it postulates more than one higher-order factor, can be regarded as an extension of both the Spearman–Holzinger model and the Thurstone model, and Gustafsson's HILI model may be considered a further refinement of some aspects of the Horn–Cattell model. Only the Guilford Structure-of-Intellect model represents a considerable departure from these models in that it postulates a large number of factors and gives much less credence to the notion of higher-order or general factors.

Other models that can be cited represent special forms of the general model attributable to Spearman, Holzinger, and Thurstone, emphasizing particular distinctions among classes of factors or special ways of interpreting those factors. Here we consider such models coming from the work of Godfrey Thomson, Richard Meili, Adolf Jäger, Arthur Jensen, Joseph Royce, Louis Guttman, Richard Snow, and a group headed by J. P. Das.

Godfrey Thomson [1881–1955] was a psychologist who worked in Scotland most of his life, mainly in educational research. He was the author of a popular textbook on factor analysis (1939) that went through five editions, to 1951. As early as 1916 (Thomson, 1916), he pointed out that Spearman's hierarchal correlation matrices could be interpreted not only by Spearman's two-factor theory but also by a theory in which the mind could be supposed to possess numerous "bonds" reflexes, habits, learned associations, and the like. Performance on any one task would call on a large number of these bonds, and individual differences would represent differences in the numbers of bonds possessed by different people. The correlation between performances on any two tasks, such as two mental tests, would indicate the extent of overlap between the pools of bonds they called on. A factor analysis of correlations among a series of tests might therefore yield the appearance of a general factor, when in fact what is common to the tests is a collection of bonds. Group factors would indicate special subgroups or "sub-pools" of bonds that tended to have developed together, or to have been acquired together. Thomson's theory, which is reminiscent of Thorndike's (Thorndike et al., 1927) theory of intelligence, is a model of cognitive abilities only to the extent that it provides an alternative explanation of what factors represent, or what an ability is. It is in no way incompatible with the models of the organization of abilities presented by Spearman, Holzinger, Thurstone, Cattell, and others.

A number of European psychologists have concerned themselves with discovering and interpreting intelligence factors, and in some cases their results have led them to posit models of intelligence somewhat similar to those offered by British and American psychologists. The Swiss psychologist Richard Meili [b. 1900] conducted a number of research studies (1946, 1979) that led him to assume the existence of four important group factors:

> Plasticity: This factor appears whenever a structure given by the data of a problem, or formed in the course of the solution, has to be broken or destroyed to make possible the formation of a new organization.

Complexity: This factor represents the capacity to apprehend complex structures clearly and with precision.

Fluency: This factor represents facility in abandoning, or "unhooking oneself" from, a certain idea.

Globalization: This factor represents facility in unifying relatively separate data or stimuli into a whole.

While it is possible to find correspondences between Meili's factors and those identified in American and British researches, Meili's interpretations betoken his attempt to give them a kind of dynamic generality for explaining the whole range of mental processes. He remarks, "It seems to me, therefore, that one must consider factors as the dynamic constant qualities of mental organization" (1946, p. 51, my translation). A final statement of Meili's model appears in a volume entitled *Struktur der Intelligenz* (Meili, 1981).

Another prominent European researcher on factors of intelligence is Adolf O. Jäger [b. 1920]. In a major work (1967) he was able to factor a wide range of mental tasks into six categories. Most of these appear to correspond to second-order factors identified by other investigators. I give his interpretations in German, with free English translations and comments:

1. *Anschauungsgebundenes Denken*: visuo-spatial thinking. This may correspond to the Gv second-order factor, visualization capacity, in the Cattell–Horn model.
2. *Einfallsreichtum und Produktivität*: Richness and productivity of ideas, possibly corresponding to Gr, general retrieval capacity, in the Cattell–Horn model.
3. *Konzentrationskraft und Tempo-Motivation*: power of concentration and motivation for pacing of performance. From the tests measuring it, this factor seems to correspond most closely to Cattell and Horn's Gps, general perceptual speed, but the interpretation given it suggests a more general process of attention and concentration.
4. *Verarbeitungskraftkapazität/formallogisches Denken und Urteilsfähigkeit*: Capacity for processing power/formal logical thinking and judgment ability. This may correspond quite closely to the Cattell–Horn Gf, fluid intelligence factor.
5. *Zahlengebundenes Denken*: Thinking that involves quantification. This apparently corresponds both to the numerical facility factor, N, of Thurstone's primary mental ability structure and to a more general quantitative reasoning (RQ) factor often found in American factor studies.
6. *Sprachgebundenes Denken*: Thinking that involves or depends on language. This probably corresponds to the often found V (verbal) factor of both British and American studies, or more generally to Cattell's (1971) Gc (crystallized intelligence) factor.

Recently, Jäger (1984) has proposed a "Berlin model of intelligence structure" that is reminiscent of Guilford's Structure-of-Intellect model in that it argues for a strict logical classification of factors or sources of variance. It provides for two modalities: operations (including speed, memory, creativity, and complex information processing), and contents (including verbal, number, and figural). The twelve combinations of these operations and contents, taken as a whole, represent general intelligence. The classifications of operations and contents are supported by factoring groups of variables that are each homogeneous either in terms of presumed operations or in terms of contents. For example, factoring groups of variables that are each homogeneous in operations but heterogeneous in content yields a factor for each operation. These results imply that any given variable is a linear function of both an operation factor and a content factor. Jäger claims to have confirmed these findings over a number of studies involving different types of samples. It would be of interest to attempt to align or compare Jäger's factors with those yielded by other studies.

Arthur Jensen's [b. 1923] hypothesis of two levels of intelligence, Level I and Level II, may be regarded as an elementary model of intelligence. As presented by Jensen (1968, 1970), it postulates two broad classes of abilities. Level I abilities involve the simple registration, storage, and recall of sensory inputs; these abilities are most prominent in short-term memory (memory span) and rote learning tasks. Level II is much like Spearman's *g* factor, measured by standard tests of intelligence, especially fluid intelligence. It is supposed to involve higher mental processes such as reasoning, manipulation of stored inputs, abstraction, problem solving, and the like. Differences between these hypothesized levels of intelligence become prominent, Jensen believes, when different socioeconomic, racial, or ethnic groups are compared. For example, he has observed (Jensen, 1973) major differences between American white and black samples on tests of Level II intelligence, but small or insignificant differences on Level I abilities.

It is not clear whether the Level I/II distinction is to be taken as a classification of abilities, factors, or processes. As P. A. Vernon (1981c) points out in a review of the distinction and its correlates, "Level I and Level II can be considered the poles of a continuum along which tasks can be arranged in terms of the degree of stimulus transformation they require for good performance" (p. 45). For example, in performing a memory-span task, which might *require* no more than Level I ability, an individual who uses chunking or other elaborative processes might be said to be using Level II ability. This consideration persuades me to think that the Level I/II distinction is not really a distinction but a continuum having to do with processes. It pertains, therefore, to interpretations of factors in terms of the degree to which stimulus transformations are involved, by being either required or optional. It is not necessarily a classification of factors because the various tasks that might be loaded on a factor vary in their requirements for stimulus transformation processes, depending in large part on their difficulty levels. The Level I/II distinction can be said to be misnamed if it in fact represents a continuum pertinent to a continous distribution of possible abilities.

Joseph R. Royce [1921–1989], who studied with Thurstone at the University of Chicago, was from 1967 associated with the Centre for Advanced Study of Theoretical Psychology at the University of Alberta, and conducted numerous factor-analytic studies, particularly in the domain of personality and emotionality. His last work, with Arnold Powell (Royce & Powell, 1983) presents an integrated theory of personality and individual differences that incorporates sensory, motor, cognitive, affective, style, and value systems into a broad conceptual framework. The cognitive system presented by these authors is essentially a hierarchical model of the Spearman–Holzinger–Thurstone type that includes 23 first-order cognitive factors subsumed by six second-order factors: *verbal, reasoning, spatiovisual, memorization, fluency*, and *imaginativeness*, which in turn are subsumed by three third-order factors: *perceiving, conceptualizing*, and *symbolizing*. These three third-order factors, they state, "also identify the three subsystems of the cognitive domain" (p. 108) but they do not admit a general factor, believing that "positive manifold can be attributed to cooperative functioning among all the cognitive abilities rather than general intelligence." Their further discussion of this hierarchical structure attempts to show how the several factors are related to information processing.

Louis Guttman [1916–1987], a consistent contributor to the theory of factor analysis methodology, interpreted mental abilities in terms of what he called *facets* (Guttman, 1965). Each facet is in effect a quantitative or qualitative classification dimension. According to Guttman's theory, a domain of inquiry, like intelligence, is to be described in terms of "mapping sentences" by which the relations among its facets are described (Canter, 1985). Thus, "an item belongs to the universe of intelligence items if and only if its domain asks about a [logical/scientific (factual)/semantic] objective rule, and its range is ordered from [very right to very wrong] with respect to that rule" (Guttman, quoted by Koop, 1985, p. 239). Koop gives an illustration of a facet analysis of intelligence by Guttman's methods. Data presented by Rimoldi (1951a) are reanalyzed by a nonmetric multidimensional scaling procedure called smallest space analysis, resulting in a two-dimensional plot of Rimoldi's variables whereby the mutual distances among the points represent their correlations. The smaller the distance, the higher the correlation. Closest to the center of the configuration are variables regarded as measuring inference of rules; farther out are variables measuring application of rules, and still farther out are variables measuring learning of rules, the distinction between inference, application, and learning of rules being one of the facets introduced to explain the findings. Another facet, having to do with the "language of communication" (verbal, numerical, or geometrical) is represented by partition of the space into pie-shaped portions. Presumably, other sets of data on cognitive ability tests could be analyzed in similar ways according to whatever facets are represented in the data. This analysis illustrates what Guttman has called a "radex" interpretation of intelligence (Guttman, 1957), apparently referring to the "radial" representation of points in factorial space. Other features of Guttman's proposals concern the "simplex" and the "circumplex" models for representing the fact that variables can often be ranged along a line or a circle such that the distances between them correspond to their correlations.

Over the past decade or more, Richard Snow [b. 1936] has led a group at Stanford University studying relations between aptitudes and learning processes. In the course of this work, he has come to believe that the radex, simplex, and circumplex models proposed by Guttman provide a more generally useful perspective on cognitive abilities and their relations than factor analysis (Snow, Kyllonen, & Marshalek, 1984). Using nonmetric multidimensional scaling methodology, he and his coworkers have reanalyzed data from the classic studies by Thurstone (1938b) and Thurstone and Thurstone (1941) to show that tests of the several Thurstonian primary mental abilities can be represented on a two-dimensional map in positions such that their mutual distances represent their degree of similarity in terms of content and processing complexity. The radex map is essentially a circular grid in which test variables appear closer to the center of the circle the more they measure a general factor, and cluster as factors in different sectors of the grid depending on content and complexity attributes. Snow et al. claim to show that although there are parallelisms between hierarchical factor analysis and the nonmetric multidimensional scaling model, the latter permits a theoretically more useful analysis. They state, "The radex thus emerges as the most general theoretical model to date on both substantive and methodological grounds" (p. 88). What is not clear, up to this time, is whether the radex model, if it is a more accurate representation of cognitive ability structure, requires the abandonment or radical modification of the mathematical apparatus associated with conventional factor analysis, such as the assumptions embodied in the fundamental factor equation.

Das, Kirby, and Jarman (1975, 1979) have developed a model of intelligence that attempts to relate mental abilities to a theory of neurological functions proposed by the Russian psychologist A. R. Luria [1902–1977] (1966). Mental functions are regarded as relying on two kinds of processing modes or "styles": simultaneous and successive. Simultaneous processing occurs in cognitive tasks when a large number of neural events occur simultaneously and cooperatively, as in visual pattern perception; successive processing occurs when neural events have to follow each other in succession, as in memory phenomena and in the production and understanding of speech. Das and his colleagues have used factor analysis extensively to find support for the theory by building and administering tests hypothesized to tap these two kinds of processes. They claim that separate factors corresponding to simultaneous and successive processing can be found over a wide range of samples with respect to age, socioeconomic status, and culture. Tests of spatial perception tend to be associated with simultaneous processing, while memory tests are found to be associated with successive processing. Thus far, the batteries of tests used in these studies are limited in variety, and it is not clear to what degree the theory of Das et al. can be extended to the total range of mental abilities.

All models of the structure of cognitive abilities appear to be attempts to classify the various manifestations of mental ability according to aspects of content, type of processing required, and type of response or outcome. Some authors prefer to classify factors; others are more comfortable with the notion of "facet." Which of these concepts, or some combination of them, will be most fruitful can be determined only by further testing them against different sets of empirical data.

It is clear that all the leading figures in psychometrics – Binet, Spearman, Thurstone, and Guilford (to name but a few) – have had an abiding concern for the nature of intelligence; all of them have realized, too, that to construct a theory of intelligence is to construct a theory of cognition. It is not without significance that one of Spearman's (1923) major works bore the title *The Nature of Intelligence and the Principles of Cognition*. Indeed, reading Spearman's (1930) autobiography one finds that Spearman was centrally much more interested in finding and establishing "laws" of cognition than in measuring individual differences, and it was apparently this interest that kept him focused on the factor of General Intelligence because he believed that *g* embodied general laws of cognition better than any group factor might do. Remembering this, and noting also works by Galton (1883), Binet and Henri (1896), Thurstone (1924), and Guilford (1967) whose titles signalled concern with the nature of intelligence and intellectual behavior, we may say that from the earliest years of the field up to the present, leaders in studying the nature and measurement of intelligence have been "cognitive psychologists" in the best sense of that term. "Cognitive ability" is not a new term: Wolfle (1940) used it more than fifty years ago, as did Spearman (1923).

Nevertheless, cognitive psychology did not become a recognized subfield of psychology until the 1960s (Kessel & Bevan, 1985). During long periods in the history of psychology when behaviorism, Gestalt psychology, and psychoanalysis were in the forefront, there were only islands of interest in cognitive processes. One may cite the work of Judd (1936) in education, of Huey (1908) in the study of reading, and of Bartlett (1932) in the study of conscious processes of memory. None of these developments seems to have had any influence on psychometrics or the study of intelligence, however.

With the publication of such works as *Plans and the Structure of Behavior* (Miller, Galanter, & Pribram, 1960) and *Cognitive Psychology* (Neisser, 1967), experimental psychologists made bold to write about such "mental events" as plans, sets, covert thoughts, imagery, covert rehearsal for memory performances, stimulus codings, short- and long-term memory stores, executive processes, etc. A "human information processing" viewpoint (Newell & Simon, 1972) was formulated in which the performance of cognitive tasks, such as problem solving, was described as taking place through the operation of integrated "programs" or "production systems" for the processing of information available from sensory channels and from memory stores assumed to exist in the central nervous system.

A natural application of this approach was to tasks represented in intelligence tests. Partly inspired by developments in the field of artificial intelligence, there were attempts to program computers to simulate human solutions of analogies problems, for example. Williams's (1972) Aptitude Test Taker program was one that developed its own rules for solving inductive tasks when presented with worked examples.

Experimenters in cognitive psychology concentrated on developing paradigms or special tasks for studying mental processes. Among the most prominent of these were:

> S. Sternberg's (1966) short-term memory paradigm: the subject is presented for a short period (a few seconds) with an array of visual or auditory stimuli, such as letters, digits, or words, then with a "probe" stimulus, being asked to indicate whether the probe was in the original array.
>
> Posner's letter-comparison task (Posner & Mitchell, 1967): Pairs of letters are presented visually (either simultaneously or sequentially); e.g., A A, or A a. Depending on instructions, the subject must indicate whether the letters are the same physically (A, A) or have the same name (A, a).
>
> The Clark & Chase (1972) sentence verification task: the subject must check whether a sentence correctly describes a visual presentation. For example, given the visual presentation the
>
>
>
> truth or falsity of a sentence such as "Star is not below cross" must be evaluated.
>
> The Shepard & Metzler (1971) mental rotation task: Presented with two pictures of complex forms, the subject must indicate whether they represent the same form in different rotations in space.

Some of these tasks resemble tasks found in various tests of aptitudes and abilities. For example, the Sternberg task has some similarity to a memory-span task; the Shepard and Metzler task is similar to tasks appearing in tests of spatial ability. It was almost inevitable that individual differences would appear in the speed and accuracy parameters of the tasks when studied experimentally in the laboratory. This gave rise to the notion that the operation of mental abilities, and thus intelligence, might be better understood by experimental analysis of typical tasks on mental ability tests.

Pellegrino and Glaser (1979) pointed out that this work could take either of two directions: the "cognitive correlates" approach in which correlations between specific task parameters and cognitive ability test results would be examined, and the "cognitive components" approach that would focus on identifying components of cognitive tasks such as those found in intelligence tests. The work of Earl Hunt (1978) exemplifies the former approach: He consistently found a correlation of about −.3 between scholastic aptitude scores and certain reaction-time parameters in the Posner letter-comparison task. The cognitive components approach is exemplified in the work of (Robert) Sternberg (1977) in analyzing analogies task performances into components (mentioned in Chapter 1). Sternberg has also employed the cognitive correlates approach in that he determines correlations between componential parameters and external reference tests. It is evident that the cognitive correlates and cognitive components approaches complement each other, rather than being contradictory or mutually exclusive.

In much of this work, there has been an emphasis on chronometric analysis, that is, the detailed analysis of the times, often measured in milliseconds, taken by people to perform the successive stages of some mental task like solving an analogies problem. Many of the tasks studied are so simple that subjects make few errors, but incorrect responses are usually excluded from analyses of response times. Where tasks are more difficult, or vary substantially in difficulty, analysis of task parameters associated with difficulty is appropriate.

In attempting to link the work in cognitive psychology with that in psychometrics and factor analysis, I (Carroll, 1976a) offered subjective analyses of a series of 24 well-recognized factors of cognitive ability in terms of a distributive memory model proposed by Hunt (1971). I also made reference to Newell's (1973) ideas about mental production systems.

In the early 1970s many investigators conducted studies of various cognitive tasks given in conjunction with more conventional paper-and-pencil cognitive ability tests. Illustrative work may be cited: Hunt, Frost, & Lunneborg's (1973) correlational studies of several cognitive tasks as related to performance on verbal and quantitative sections of the SAT (Scholastic Aptitude Test), and later a major factor-analytic study by Hunt, Lunneborg, and Lewis (1975); Chiang and Atkinson's (1976) study of two short-term memory tasks as related to SAT scores; Hundal & Horn's (1977) factor-analytic study of mental abilities and short-term memory performances; and Jensen's (1979, 1980) study of simple and choice reaction times as related to intelligence test scores. In a monograph (Carroll, 1980a), I reviewed many of these studies in an effort to determine, mainly by factor-analytic procedures, what basic abilities were measured by these varied cognitive tasks. (Many of these reanalyses are introduced in later sections of this volume.)

Since 1980, several groups have continued to conduct studies of this sort. Vernon and Jensen (1984) have conducted studies tending to show that intelligence measures have low but significant correlations with performance on simple and choice reaction-time tasks, but even more with speed of performance on tasks involving retrieval of semantic information from long-term memory. A group in the U.S. Air Force under the direction of Christal (1986) has been attempting to identify valid measures of learning abilities in cognitive tasks. Studies by Pellegrino and his associates (Pellegrino & Kail, 1982; Goldman & Pellegrino, 1984) have explored the parameters of inductive and spatial reasoning tasks often found in intelligence tests. They find that under certain conditions of training and practice, performance on such tasks can be improved.

There have been further detailed studies of cognitive components and "metacomponents" by R. J. Sternberg and his associates (e.g., Sternberg & McNamara, 1985; Sternberg & Turner, 1981), and Sternberg has published a cognitively oriented theory of intelligence (1985).

Following up on his collaboration with Cronbach (Cronbach & Snow, 1977) in reviewing the literature to identify possible aptitude-treatment interactions (ATIs), Snow (1976, 1978a, 1980, 1981) has been particularly concerned with the study of what he calls "aptitude processes." In this work, he has hoped to provide a theory for ATIs, that is, a theory for how aptitudes may interact with learning processes such that learners with different aptitude profiles may adopt different learning strategies, or require different types of instruction for optimal success in learning. He and his colleagues (Snow, 1978b; Kyllonen, Lohman, & Snow, 1984; Kyllonen, Lohman, & Woltz, 1984; Bethell–Fox, Lohman, & Snow, 1984) have reported a number of important empirical studies of detailed processes that students exhibit in the performance of cognitive tasks. Often, they find, students shift strategies from task to task, partly as a function of task difficulties and other attributes, and partly as a function of their levels of aptitude in dealing with the tasks. A recent summary of this and related work has been published by Snow and Lohman (1989).

The concept of test design as "specifying the aspects of individual differences that a test measures by constructing and/or selecting items according to their substantive properties" (Embretson, 1985, p. 3) seems to be much in the spirit of recent developments in cognitive psychology. The substantive properties of test items would presumably be influential in determining what abilities, and what levels of those abilities, successful performance of those items requires. Cognitive psychology would be pertinent to test design to the extent that the substantive properties of items could be described in terms of cognitive knowledges and processes.

Despite considerable work in the 1970s and 1980s in applying cognitive psychology to individual differences and psychometric studies, this line of investigation is still in its early stages (Leino, 1981). Only a few of the more important types of abilities have been studied in detail, and at this writing many questions remain to be resolved.

There are at least two ways in which this work is related to what will be reported on and discussed in the main body of this volume. First, the reanalyses of factorial and other studies presented there yield an enumeration of known cognitive abilities and the kinds of tasks and tests that can be used to measure them. This enumeration should offer cognitive psychologists a picture, clearer than any previously available, of the range of cognitive abilities that are to be explained in terms of concepts of cognitive psychology. Second, the chapters of this volume reporting information on cognitive abilities attempt, whenever possible, to interpret the findings in terms of cognitive psychology concepts.

NOTES

1. I have been unable to find any standard English dictionary, except the unabridged *Oxford English Dictionary*, that recognizes this technical term and its spelling. However,

it is recognized in Wolman's (1973) *Dictionary of Behavioral Science*, which also has an entry for *factor analysis*.

2. Factor analysis is sometimes used to determine the basic dimensions underlying any set of data – not necessarily the performances of individuals. For example, I (Carroll, 1960) used factor analysis to investigate dimensions of prose style, based on samples of prose taken from a variety of sources without reference to the writers of those samples. In physical anthropology, factor analysis has been used to determine basic dimensions of variation in the body and its parts, and in economics, it has been used to study variations in stock market quotations over periods of time. In the present context, however, it is assumed that the data come from individuals.

3. When factor A "dominates" factors B and C, it is implied that there exists a set of variables that all measure factor A, while different subsets of those variables measure factors B and C, respectively. Generally, factor A is at a higher order of analysis than factors B and C.

3 *Survey and Analysis of Correlational and Factor-Analytic Research on Cognitive Abilities: Methodology*

> *The factorial methods are still imperfect but can be developed to become more powerful analytical tools.*
>
> L. L. Thurstone (1938b)

THE NEED FOR THIS SURVEY

The chief goal of this volume is to present an up-to-date review and critique of the extant literature on the identification, characteristics, and interpretation of cognitive abilities. Much of the literature covered consists of studies using factor analysis, but some attention is also given to studies that did not use factor analysis but presented correlations among pertinent variables, in some cases with further analysis by various techniques such as multiple regression and multidimensional scaling.

Surveys of the correlational and factor-analytic literature on cognitive abilities have appeared periodically over the course of the last 60 years. Spearman's *Abilities of Man* (1927) considered a limited number of investigations of cognitive abilities; most were appraised in terms of whether they supported Spearman's two-factor theory of intelligence. Next in chronological sequence was Wolfle's (1940) survey of factor analysis to 1940, covering both methodological and substantive progress to that year. In the domain of cognitive factors, Wolfle reported that the factors most generally agreed upon were the verbal, number, space, memory, speed, and reasoning factors, besides, of course, the general factor recognized by Spearman.

Of major importance and influence was a monograph by French (1951) containing a compilation and comparison of the findings from 69 factorial datasets, available at the time, that met certain criteria. The datasets (1) had to deal primarily with aptitude and achievement tests, (2) had to be based on adolescents and adult subjects (datasets dealing with children below grade 8 were excluded), and (3) had to have been analyzed by multiple-factor methods including rotation of axes (either orthogonal or oblique). French did not attempt to reanalyze any of these datasets, but he offered new interpretations of many of the factors when factors from different studies appeared to be congruent. He found that these datasets, as analyzed by their authors, yielded altogether some 50 or more factors that had been "identified with sufficient certainty to receive a name" (p. 200). Some of these factors, however, were in the domains of personality and motor ability. About 35 of the factors that French accepted may be characterized as cognitive. French's monograph has continued to be a useful compendium of factor-analytic studies conducted up to about 1950.

French was also involved, over the years 1952 to about 1976, in a series of conferences and other activities sponsored by Educational Testing Service that were designed to develop "kits" of reference tests for factorial studies. Each of the kits, issued in the years 1954, 1963, and 1976, was based on a survey of the literature that had accumulated up to the time of issue. The survey was made to assist in deciding what cognitive factors were considered sufficiently well confirmed to justify issuing reference or "marker" tests for them. The kits included manuals that reported sources of factors and tests. For convenience, a concordance of cognitive and cognitive-related factors identified by French (1951) and in the 1963 and 1976 ETS kits (Ekstrom, French, & Harman, 1976; French, Ekstrom, & Price, 1963) is included here as Table 3.1. The table shows, for example, that 22 cognitive factors were recognized in the 1976 kit. Ekstrom (1979) published the review of cognitive factors that she performed in preparation for publication of the 1976 kit. It is to be noted that all 22 factors recognized in the 1976 kit were primary, first-order factors; no second-order factors were specified, much less a general factor, presumably because of the emphasis of the Thurstonian school on primary factors, as commented on in Chapter 2.

Useful monograph-length reviews of factorial literature are available in French (Oléron, 1957) and in German (Pawlik, 1967), but these reviews cover mostly American and British studies, there being at the time of their publication few studies indigenous to French- or German-speaking countries.

Two publications from Guilford's laboratory (Guilford, 1967; Guilford & Hoepfner, 1971) constitute book-length reviews of factor-analytic work, but they are now considerably out of date, and even though they consider work from other sources, the focus is on results from Guilford's studies, interpreted in terms of his Structure-of-Intellect (SOI) model.

Aside from relatively brief summaries by John Horn of recent factor-analytic work (Horn, 1976, 1978a, 1985, 1988), there appears to be no current extended summary of this field. What distinguishes the present summary is its attempt to survey a much broader range of studies and to base its conclusions upon reanalyses of the original studies, in order to provide factor analyses that were performed on a comparable basis. Also, except for Guilford's publications, this is the first broad survey of factor-analytic work to make a studied attempt to relate factorial findings to theories and findings of cognitive psychology, and to examine findings from a developmental point of view.

Thus, the purposes of the present survey can be listed as follows:

1.   To provide a current assessment of knowledge about cognitive abilities;
2.   To provide reanalyses of datasets, wherever necessary, by a consistent and currently acceptable methodology;

Table 3.1. *Concordance of selected cognitive and cognitive-related factors. Reproduced by permission from Carroll, 1983b, Table 2, in R. F. Dillon & R. R. Schmeck (Eds.), Individual differences in cognition, Vol. 1. Copyright © 1983 by Academic Press, Orlando, FL*

Factor code	Factor name	French (1951) code, name (no. of studies)	1963 ETS kit code, name	1976 ETS kit code, name	Guilford factors[b]	Cattell univ'l index[c]
Gf ("fluid intelligence") factors[d,e]						
I	Induction	I:Induction (9)	I:Induction	I:Induction	(Several)	T5
RL	Logical reasoning	D:Deduction (37)	Rs:Syllogistic reasoning	RL:Logical reasoning	EMR?	T4
RG	General reasoning	R:General reasoning	R:General reasoning	RG:General reasoning	CMS	T34
IP	Integrative process	In:Integration (1)	—	IP:Integrative process	—	—
J	Judgment	J:Judgment (5)	—	—	—	—
PL	Planning	Pl:Planning (4)	—	—	—	—
Gc (crystallized intelligence) factors:						
V	Verbal knowledge	V:Verbal comprehension (46)	V:Verbal comprehension	V:Verbal comprehension	CMU	T13
N	Numerical facility	N:Number (35)	N:Number facility	N:Number facility	NSI,MSI?	T10
Gv (general visual perception) factors:						
		S:Space (44)	{	{		
SO	Spatial orientation	SO:Spatial orientation (4)	S:Spatial orientation	S:Spatial orientation	CFS	T11
VZ	Spatial visualization	Vi:Visualization (16)	Vs:Visualization	VZ:Visualization	CFT	T14
CS	Speed of closure	GP:Gestalt perception (2)	Cs:Speed of closure	CS:Speed of closure	CFU	T3
CF	Flexibility of closure	GF:Gestalt flexibility (1)	Cf:Flexibility of closure	CF:Flexibility of closure	NFT	T2
SS	Spatial scanning	—	Sa:Spatial scanning	SS:Spatial scanning	CFI	—
LE	Length estimation	LE:Length estimation (4)	Le:Length estimation	—	—	—
CV	Verbal closure	—	—	CV:Verbal closure	—	—
P	Perceptual speed	P:Perceptual speed (34)	P:Perceptual speed[a]	P:Perceptual speed	(ESU,EFU)	T12
PA	Perceptual alternations	PA:Perceptual alternations (1)	—	—	—	—
IL	Figure illusions	FI:Figure illusions (1)	—	—	—	—

Table 3.1 (*cont.*)

Factor code	Factor name	French (1951) code, name (no. of studies)	1963 ETS kit code, name	1976 ETS kit code, name	Guilford factors[b]	Cattell univ'l index[c]
Ga ("general auditory perception") factors:						
AUI	Auditory integration	AI:Auditory integration (1)	—	—	—	—
AUR	Auditory resistance	AR:Auditory resistance (1)	—	—	—	—
LO	Loudness	Lo:Loudness (1)	—	—	—	—
PQ	Pitch quality	PQ:Pitch quality (1)	—	—	—	—
Gm ("general memory") factors:						
MA	Associative memory	M:Associative memory (16)	Ma:Associative memory	MA:Associative memory	MSR	T7
MS	Memory span	Sm:Span memory (2)	Ms:Memory span	MS:Memory span	MSU,MSS?	—
MV	Visual memory	VM:Visual memory (4)	—	MV:Visual memory	—	—
MMU	Musical memory	MM:Musical memory (2)	—	—	—	—
Fluency and production factors:						
FA	Associational fluency	—	Fa:Associational fluency	FA:Associational fluency	DMR	—
FE	Expressional fluency	FE:Fluency of expression (3)	Fe:Expressional fluency	FE:Expressional fluency	DMS	—
FI	Ideational fluency	IF:Ideational fluency (4)	Fi:Ideational fluency	FI:Ideational fluency	DMU	T6
FW	Word fluency	W:Word fluency (8)	Fw:Word fluency	FW:Word fluency	DSU	T15
XU	Flexibility of use	—	Xs:Semantic spontaneous flexibility	XU:Flexibility of use	DMC	—
XF	Figural flexibility	—	Xa:Figural adaptive flexibility	XF:Figural flexibility	DFT	—
NA	Naming speed	Na:Naming (1)	—	—	—	—
FS	Speech fluency	PS:Public speaking (1)	—	—	—	—
SA	Speed of association	SA:Speed of association (2)	—	—	—	—
O	Originality	—	O:Originality	—	DMT	—
RE	Semantic redefinition	—	Re:Semantic redefinition	—	NMT	—
SEP	Sensitivity to problems	—	Sep:Sensitivity to problems	—	EMI	—

Speed factors (not otherwise classified):

SD	Speed	Sp:Speed (3)
SDJ	Speed of judgment	SJ:Speed of judgment (1)

Selected psychomotor factors:

AIMG	Aiming	Ai:Aiming (7)
AMB	Ambidexterity	Am:Ambidexterity (2)
SDAR	Speed of articulation	Ar:Articulation (1)
FD	Finger dexterity	FD:Finger dexterity (11)
MD	Manual dexterity	MD:Manual dexterity (4)
PC	Psychomotor coordination	PC:Psychomotor coordination (10)
RT	Reaction time	RT:Reaction time (2)
TA	Tapping	Ta:Tapping (3)

Miscellaneous affective-cognitive factors:

AT	Attention	At:Attention (4)
CA	Carefulness	C:Carefulness (6)
PE	Persistence	Pe:Persistence (2)
PN	Perseveration	Pn:Perseveration (1)

[a] Identified by French (1951) and in the 1963 and 1976 ETS kits of factor reference tests (Ekstrom, French, & Harman, 1976; French, Ekstrom, & Price, 1963).

[b] Designations of Guilford factors are those shown in the 1963 ETS kit manual. A key to these designations is as follows:
First character: C, Cognition; D, Divergent production; E, Evaluation; M, Memory; N, Convergent production (Process)
Second character: F, Figural; M, Semantic; S, Symbolic (Content)
Third character: C, Classes; I, Implications; R, Relations; S, Systems; T, Transformations; U, Units (Products)

[c] Designations of Cattell (1957) Universal Index codes are those shown in the 1963 ETS kit manual.

[d] The classification of factors into higher-order groups is tentative; it generally follows the Cattell and Horn model (see Horn, 1978a, pp. 211–256).

[e] The two ETS kits distinguish two factors (Rs, RL; R, RG) derived from French's (1951) Deduction.

[f] French's (1951) Space appears as as two factors SO (Spatial orientation) and VZ (Visualization) in the ETS Kits.

[g] The 1963 ETS kit notes that Perceptual speed may consist of several subfactors.

3.   To compare, coordinate, and assemble the findings in convenient forms;
4.   To relate the findings, wherever possible, to theories and findings in cognitive
            psychology; and
5.   When possible, to relate the findings to problems of developmental psychology,
            particularly the development and change of abilities over the life span and
            the relative influences of genetic and environmental factors.

ASSEMBLY OF STUDIES AND THEIR DATASETS

The amount of available literature relevant to the subject matter of this volume is truly enormous. The bibliographical materials assembled for the survey presented here are much more extensive than what can be shown in the reference list for the volume. (The bibliography eventually compiled for the project contains more than ten thousand items.) The intent was to include as much as possible of the factor-analytic research of the past fifty years or more on cognitive abilities, in addition to related literature on individual differences and factorial methodology, problems of testing, experimental analysis of cognitive tasks, group differences, and effects of experimental treatments and educational interventions on abilities. Compilation of the bibliography was based initially on the writer's personal files maintained over more than forty years, but these materials were supplemented by the tracking of current journal and book literature, *Psychological Abstracts*, and similar sources. The bibliographical materials compiled by Bolton, Hinman, and Tuft (1973; Hinman & Bolton, 1979) on the factor-analytic literature were especially useful, as was the survey conducted by Ekstrom (1979). Efforts were made to make the bibliography international in scope, through personal visits to investigators in several European countries, correspondence, and tracking of relevant source materials.

From the bibliographical materials thus developed, a file of studies reporting correlational or factor-analytic investigations of cognitive abilities was established. On its completion, this file was found to contain approximately 1500 references. Although it cannot be claimed that the file is truly exhaustive, it represents all or nearly all of the more important and classic factor-analytic investigations of the past fifty years or more, as well as numerous others of potential interest. Any significant omissions would consist mainly of unpublished materials such as doctoral dissertations and internal reports of research organizations. A feature of this compilation is that all *reanalyses* that have been located are listed under the references to the original investigations.

The next step was to establish a file of photocopies of as many as possible of the 1500 publications identified as pertaining to the correlational or factor analysis of cognitive abilities, at least where the materials were not readily accessible in the author's collections of books and journals. In some cases requests were made to original authors or document repositories for correlation matrices, test descriptions, and similar materials that did not appear in the original publications; unfortunately, not all these attempts to retrieve materials were successful.

A further step was the establishment of a computerized file of information on factor-analytic (or correlational) datasets. (For convenience, the compound word *dataset* will be used here henceforth instead of the more conventional term *data set*.) A dataset was defined as a single set of data for a factor analysis, i.e., the data (usually, a correlation matrix) on the values for a distinct number of variables (n) for a distinct sample of individuals (usually, but not necessarily, with a distinct and constant number of cases, N). A given publication might report on one or more datasets. Each dataset was given a distinctive *dataset designation* consisting of (up to) the first four letters of the first author's name plus a two-digit number. For example, four datasets reported in a book by Clausen (1966) were given the designations CLAU01, CLAU02, CLAU03, and CLAU04. The two-digit numbers were assigned in such a way that the corresponding references would be in the correct bibliographical order, given that the four alphabetic characters of the designation could refer to several different authors, each with one or more publications of different dates, and given that references might have either single or multiple authors. For each dataset (at least for a major portion of them, and for all datasets actually considered and reanalyzed in this survey), the computer file (on microcomputer floppy disks) contained information on the following:

> Source of data set (bibliographical reference)
> Total N, and N's for males and females (if given)
> Age, grade, and/or other relevant attributes of sample
> Information on completeness of data
> Availability of correlation matrix and type of coefficient
> Number (n) and types of variables
> Type of factor analysis, if any, in original investigation
> Number of factors extracted in original investigation
> Type of factor-analytic rotations (if any)
> Higher-order analyses (if any)
> Citations of the original study (if any)
> Previous reanalyses (if any)
> Priority assignment for treatment in present project
> Remarks (special instructions, e.g., *re*: dropping variables)

It was impracticable to consider or reanalyze all of the approximately 1500 or more datasets found in the literature. Priorities were assigned by judging the probable relevance of the dataset for the purposes of the project, the adequacy of the original design, and other matters. The criteria for selection of datasets for consideration (and in general, for reanalysis) included the following:

1. Other things being equal, higher priorities were given to datasets with broader samplings of variables and individuals, and lower priorities to datasets whose variables represented, for example, only tests from small, self-contained batteries like one of the series of Wechsler tests.

2.   Higher priorities were assigned to datasets that were considered to be well-designed with respect to the representation of known or postulated factors, for example, by having at least three or more somewhat different variables representing each known or postulated factor. (In most instances, variables were omitted from the reanalysis when there was obvious experimental dependence among them, part-whole relationships, and the like.)

3.   As long as a dataset was considered to be reasonably well-designed and to be concerned at least in part with cognitive ability variables, there was usually no reason to drop it for any consideration of the types of variables selected, the types of samples employed, or the purpose of the analysis. For example, studies were not necessarily dropped from consideration if they involved very young or very old subjects, or subjects with highly special characteristics (e.g., brain-damaged individuals), although higher priorities were generally assigned to studies using adolescents and young adults from normal populations.

4.   A number of datasets were retained for consideration and reanalysis, even if they appeared to be poorly designed from a factorial viewpoint, when they contained variables rarely used in other studies and thus were of potential interest in defining new dimensions of cognitive ability.

In all, more than 450 datasets were selected for detailed attention in this project. A listing of them is included in the References for the volume.

Considerable effort was devoted to the accumulation of relevant material on tests, experimental procedures, and other instrumentation involved in the datasets selected for attention. This was necessary in order to have good information on the exact stimulus materials, test administration procedures, time limits, etc., associated with each variable. It was frequently found that variables named in the same way (e.g., "Designs") in different studies were actually quite different in their format and characteristics.

PROCEDURES IN REANALYSIS OF DATASETS
BY FACTOR ANALYSIS

The reader may wonder why it was considered necessary to reanalyze datasets for purposes of this survey project. As noted previously, it appears that no other general survey of factor-analytic results has employed procedures of reanalysis. Yet, there is ample precedent for reanalysis of factorial investigations, mainly because factorial methods have been under continuous development and refinement for the past fifty years or more. Successive investigators have been motivated to apply new methods to the reanalysis of older, previously analyzed datasets. For example, Harris and Liba (1965) applied four types of newer factor methods to datasets that had previously been studied by Guilford and his associates; the newer methods gave somewhat differing results among themselves, and all differed rather noticeably from Guilford's results.

Reanalysis can be regarded as a form of *replication* – a procedure recognized as critical in all scientific investigation. As a resource for further study, the reference list for this volume contains a compilation of numerous reanalyses of the datasets considered here.

Some of the datasets selected for this survey consisted solely of correlation matrices; that is, no factorial methods had been applied, and therefore in these cases the next step was analysis, not reanalysis.

For practically all datasets, procedures of reanalysis were applied at one or more stages of factor analysis (usually *all* stages beyond the correlation matrix itself). There are at least two reasons justifying this:

1. Even if many factor analyses extant in the literature have been performed by methods that can be regarded as acceptable by current standards, it is desirable to ensure that all of them are analyzed by methods that are as uniform as possible over the datasets. In this way results can be regarded as more comparable than they would be if the survey were based on the published analyses, whose methods were highly variable in a number of respects.

2. A large proportion of the factor analyses extant in the literature did not carry the analysis up to a second- or third-order when this might have been deemed desirable. The fact that such analysis was not carried out was due either to unavailability of advanced procedures at the time of the research or to the investigators' disapproval or lack of knowledge of the appropriate procedures. Even if analyses were carried out to higher orders, it is very rare that the analysis included use of an orthogonalization procedure such as the Schmid and Leiman (1957) technique, which is employed, when appropriate, in all analyses reported in the present survey.

The conduct of reanalyses of all or nearly all datasets selected for consideration here requires careful description, explanation, and defense of the methods actually employed.

Screening of Variables

As already indicated, in most instances certain variables were dropped from correlation matrices when it was evident that their inclusion would make for unwanted covariance due to experimental dependence or similar conditions. For example, if a correlation matrix contained a total score that was a sum of other variables, the total score would be dropped. In most instances, also, variables denoting age, sex, educational status, or similar background characteristics were dropped from matrices, because it was believed that including such variables would complicate the interpretation of results. Because the major interest was in the dimensions and structures of cognitive *abilities*, as opposed to cognitive achievements, it was generally the case that variables reflecting school or work performance were omitted from the matrices analyzed.

Use of Exploratory Factor Analysis (EFA)

As mentioned earlier, there is a considerable body of opinion (e.g., Long, 1983) that the techniques of confirmatory factor analysis (hereafter, CFA) are superior to those of exploratory factor analysis (EFA). This belief can be justified from some standpoints, but one must view it in the perspective of the purposes for which CFA is employed. CFA is best employed for testing particular hypotheses about the factor composition of a set of variables, and about the structure of the factors that are hypothesized. It is highly desirable, or perhaps mandatory, that the hypotheses to be tested have excellent logical or psychological support in some theory of individual differences and their measurements, or in prior analyses of datasets other than the one on which the hypotheses are to be tested. Application of CFA methods yields information on the probability that the dataset conforms to a hypothesized model, or more precisely, the probability that the data could be generated under the hypothesized model. It can happen that data can be generated about equally well under several alternative models, in which case it is difficult to choose among models. CFA methods, therefore, have certain limitations.

EFA methods, on the other hand, are designed to "let the data speak for themselves," that is, to let the structure of the data suggest the most probable factor-analytic model. They do not require testing hypotheses concerning models; thus, no hypotheses need be set up in advance (except to guide the design of studies and the selection of variables). From this standpoint, EFA methods appear to be more flexible. It might be argued that I should have used CFA methods to test hypotheses based on the results of the studies as published. But in view of wide variability in the quality of the analyses applied in published studies, I could not be certain about what kinds of hypotheses ought to be tested on this basis. It was considered necessary first to perform the reanalyses by EFA methods. Also, in the case of datasets with a large number of variables, EFA methods are much easier and less expensive to apply. For these and other reasons, it was decided to apply EFA methods uniformly to all datasets that were to be reanalyzed. CFA methods were to be used, sparingly, to assess certain problem cases.

The procedures of EFA actually employed were generally those I have recommended in another publication (Carroll, 1985) and are described below. They are described first in the abstract, and then in the context of several illustrative examples. Typically, analysis started with a correlation matrix, never from raw scores. It would have been desirable to start reanalysis from raw score data in order to check computations and to consider possible improvements that could result from nonlinear transformations of variables, but raw score data are rarely available from published analyses.

Many published correlation matrices are given to only two decimals. Experiments with making analyses, with a reduced number of decimals, of matrices given with more than two decimals suggested that little precision is lost by using two-decimal values. The values used in my reanalyses, however, were always those given in the published data, with numbers of decimals ranging from two to five.

For a few datasets, correlation matrices were not available even after attempts were made to obtain them from authors or from document archives. In such cases, analysis proceeded from the best set of values available: a principal component matrix, a principal factor matrix, a Varimax factor matrix, or an oblique, rotated factor solution. (For oblique matrices, it was necessary to devise a procedure for recovering an orthogonal solution on the basis of correlations among primary factors.) In such cases the value accepted for the number of factors was usually that represented in the data available.

All reanalyses were performed blindly, that is, without reference to the identifications of the variables or the nature of the factors. In the process of reanalysis, all variables and factors were designated only by numbers. The reanalyses were thus performed solely in terms of the numerical relationships found in the data and without the bias that might come from knowledge of the substantive characteristics of the data. This was true even for datasets that were in some sense parallel (e.g., different datasets for males and for females that employed the same variables). The number of factors was assessed independently for each dataset.

The basic steps in processing a dataset were as follows:

(1) *Reflection of correlations for variables in the correlation matrix, if necessary, such that all or nearly all columnar algebraic sums of off-diagonal entries were positive.* This was done to facilitate the assessment of positive manifold in later stages of the analysis. Moreover, the rotational methods to be employed are in some cases sensitive to the orientation of the variables. It is frequently the case in the published literature that variables are correlated in reverse orientation, e.g., variables based on time measurements such that the larger values represent slower speeds. Note, however, that variables (i.e., factors) in higher-order correlation matrices were never reflected, since it was desired to preserve the orientation of the space defined by the initial correlation matrix after any necessary reflections of variables.

(2) *Condensation of the correlation matrix and determination of the number of common factors.* (2a) This process was routinely started with computation of a principal component (PC) solution, with unities on the diagonal, to determine all latent roots of the correlation matrix. If the matrix was composed of Pearsonian correlations, this was done incidentally to test it for positive-semidefiniteness, i.e., for having only positive roots, partly as a means of checking the accuracy of the published correlation entries. When negative roots were encountered, as occasionally happened, efforts were made to identify and correct any errors in the matrix. Some errors were obvious, e.g., unequal values in upper and lower triangles in supposedly symmetric matrices. When the matrix was composed of tetrachoric correlations, negative roots were, as expected, fairly often encountered, but the condition was disregarded in this case since it was not

critical to further processing. (This implies that any errors in published tetra-choric matrices could usually not be detected, except in the case of obvious nonsymmetry across the diagonal.)

The chief purpose of the PC solution, however, was to apply Cattell's (1966) scree test to provide a tentative subjective estimate of the number of common factors. No attempt was made to apply a formal algorithm for determining the number of factors from the scree test, such as suggested by Gorsuch (1983, p. 167), because the scree test was used as only *one* guide to the number of factors. Plots were made of the values of the roots against successive root-numbers, and a preliminary indication of the number of factors was obtained by noting the number of roots just prior to an intersection of the curve with the scree (i.e., the later portion of the curve that typically shows an approximately linear descent of the smaller roots).

The PC solution also provided data for using the well-known Kaiser–Guttman rule (Kaiser, 1960a) of taking the number of factors as the number of roots greater than unity. I made little use of this rule because it is known to be inaccurate in many cases. It is likely to underestimate the number of factors when factors are substantially correlated, and to overestimate when the average correlation among variables is low and there are a large number of variables. Indeed, even completely random data can have multiple roots greater than unity.

PC solutions were not used in further analyses except as a last resort when a correlation matrix was unavailable. In PC solutions, factor loadings are generally inflated somewhat by the fact that they include specific as well as common factor variance, and these solutions may give an incorrect impression of the number of factors and of the magnitude of factor loadings.

I am aware that my non-use of PC solutions goes contrary to a considerable body of opinion (assembled by Velicer and Jackson, 1990, in a special issue of *Multivariate Behavioral Research*) to the effect that such solutions are in many respects more desirable than common factor solutions. I find, however, numerous theoretical and practical advantages for the common factor (or principal factor, PF) solutions that I used throughout the present study, and I believe that my use of PF methods would be supported by numerous experts in the field of factor analysis.

(2b) Processing continued with principal factoring of the matrix, iterating for communalities, normally starting with squared multiple correlations (SMC's) on the diagonal and proceeding with iterations until the maximum absolute difference between corresponding communalities in two successive iterations was less than .0005. This is a stricter criterion than the default values in standard computer packages, and sometimes requires a large number of iterations. It was chosen mainly in order to ensure that the solution accepted would not eventuate in a Heywood case, that is, a solution with at least one variable having a communality greater than unity. A solution with a less strict convergence criterion would sometimes have appeared acceptable when in fact it was not acceptable with the stricter criterion. Heywood case solutions were regarded as unacceptable because such solutions were believed to indicate poor definition of one or more factors, in the sense of a factor's not having a sufficient number of variables with salient loadings on it. Typically, such a factor has a very high salient loading on a particular factor, but very low or vanishing loadings on all other variables. In the process of iteration, communalities that exceeded unity were not replaced by unities for further iterations (as occurs in some computer package algorithms); instead, iteration was terminated.

In connection with principal factoring, Kaiser's (1981) Measure of Sampling Adequacy (MSA) was computed for each variable and for the set of variables as a whole. Since these statistics utilize the inverse of the correlation matrix, they could not be computed for singular matrices. Datasets with extremely low or "unacceptable" values of MSA for the set of variables as a whole were generally abandoned as unanalyzable. When the overall MSA was satisfactory but values for a few individual variables were low or unacceptable, these results were useful at a later stage in assessing the number of factors to be accepted. For example, a factor defined largely by variables with low or unacceptable MSA's was generally not accepted. In some cases variables with unacceptable MSA variables were dropped from the correlation matrix before further analysis.

Some matrices were found to be singular or otherwise such as not to permit computation of SMC estimates of communalities. In such cases initial communality estimates were the highest absolute off-diagonal values in the arrays of the matrix, and the initial estimate of number of factors was made from the scree plot of PC roots.

In the process of principal factoring, the first iteration from SMC values on the diagonal yielded information for using the so-called parallel analysis criterion proposed by Montanelli and Humphreys (1976). That is, it yielded the SMC roots – the latent roots of the matrix with SMC values on the diagonal; the sizes of these latent roots could be compared with the roots expected for a correlation matrix with given n and N based solely on random data. Tucker (personal communication) formulated a generalized algorithm for estimating these random data roots. Montanelli and Humphreys recommend that the number of factors be taken to be the largest number (m) for which it is the case that the first m latent roots of the data matrix are all larger than the expected random data roots. In practice, it was found inexpedient to follow this rule strictly, partly because of possible bias and random error in the estimation of the random data roots, and partly because it could happen that the curve of actual data roots never crossed the curve of random data roots. (This can often be the case for datasets with very large N's, or for matrices of tetrachoric correlations.) Instead, an initial estimate of the proper number of factors was arrived at by graphical inspection of plots of obtained and random data roots, selecting an initial estimate by noting where the curve of actual roots began to parallel closely the curve of random data roots, whether or not these curves actually crossed. It was also usually helpful to compare these curves with the scree plot of latent vectors for the principal component solution. In general, the initial estimate of the number of factors was selected to be very conservative.

Principal factoring was virtually always performed for a *range* of numbers of factors, starting with the initial estimate of the number of factors as described above, and then successively incrementing (by one) the number of factors in the solution until there were indications that the solution contained too many factors. Each principal-factor solution, for a given number of factors, was subjected to Kaiser's (1958) orthogonal Varimax rotation. When one or more factors in a Varimax solution failed to have at least two salient loadings, the solution was considered to have too many factors. The final number of factors was that largest number of factors that produced an acceptable Varimax solution in the sense just defined, where a salient factor loading is the highest, in absolute value, for the corresponding variable. However, this final number of factors was often increased by one, unless the solution with that larger number of factors failed to converge, to provide an additional dimension for rotational procedures.

The above is the description of the criterion for the number of factors for an ideal case, that is, for cases in which it was possible to follow this criterion without any reservations. In practice, it was fairly often necessary to make exceptions, namely for cases in which a factor appeared acceptable even if it did not have at least two salient loadings, in the strict sense, but still had one or more loadings (beyond a strict salient) that appeared to be high enough – say, greater than .30 in the Varimax solution – to be indicative of useful common factor variance. Occasionally, still other criteria were considered; for example, sometimes a factor was accepted if it was necessary to include it in order to bring the communality of a variable up to approximately the value indicated by the initial SMC value.

On the whole, the estimation of the number of factors by these criteria tended to be conservative. Factors with generally small loadings in the Varimax solution, or with only two loadings that were strikingly different in magnitude, were often rejected as being poorly defined and possibly the result of chance fluctuations. On the other hand, the criteria were such as occasionally to admit doublet or triplet factors, i.e., factors having high or substantial – and salient – loadings on two or three obviously very similar highly correlated variables.

The procedures and criteria used for selecting the number of common factors were generally those supported by a Monte Carlo simulation study conducted by Gullion (1985).

A possible criticism of the matrix condensation procedures described here is that iteration to a strict criterion can be argued to be unnecessary. Humphreys and Taber (1973) found, in a Monte Carlo analysis of samples drawn from populations with known factor loadings, that it made no essential difference, in predicting known factor loadings, whether SMC values or iterated communalities were used as the basis for the solution. Furthermore, they found that loadings based on SMC values had less sampling variance than those based on iteration. The major defense for using a strict criterion for iteration of communalities is that the iterations were thought to be useful in finding the correct number of factors, either by rejecting Heywood cases or by rejecting solutions that did not converge even after a large number of iterations, say 100. If SMC values are used as the basis for a solution without iteration, it is often possible to obtain a solution for a much larger number of factors than were obtained by our criteria, many of the factors having only trivial loadings and no salient loadings.

Many methods of matrix condensation other than principal factoring exist: maximum likelihood, image analysis, alpha factor analysis, etc. (Harman, 1976); investigators other than myself might have preferred one of these other methods. In my experience, however, all the methods yield substantially similar patterns of results. For a number of reasons (practicality, inexpensiveness, ease of operation) the iterated principal factor method appeared to be the method of choice for the present survey.

When it was possible to use special programs written for microcomputer, iterations were usually accelerated by a technique (which I developed) whereby estimated communalities for a given iteration (beyond the second) were projected or extrapolated from the communalities from the previous two iterations. Typically, the technique reduces the number of required iterations by approximately half, still yielding, to a high degree of approximation, the same final results as would be yielded by the standard procedures of replacing the communalities achieved in iteration $(X - 1)$ by those achieved in iteration X.

There were instances where convergence could not be obtained with *any* number of factors, or in which Heywood cases were encountered for a number-of-factors value that appeared clearly insufficient on the basis of the patterning of the correlations, magnitudes of SMC values, and other indicators. In such instances, a "Cureton procedure" was followed; that is, the solution was that obtained after *one* iteration (given some reasonable number of factors) beyond a solution from SMC values proportionally adjusted so that their sum was equal to the sum of the highest correlations in arrays. This procedure is recommended by Cureton and D'Agostino (1983, Chapter 5). In my reanalyses, it was particularly useful in factoring matrices at the second or a higher order, i.e., matrices of correlations among first-order or second-order factors, especially when it was hypothesized that there was only one second-order factor. It is believed that this procedure is justified in view of the larger amount of error undoubtedly latent in correlations among first-order factors due to uncertainties in methods of rotation.

On occasion, it became necessary to abandon the attempt to reanalyze a dataset because of unsatisfactory characteristics such as unresolvable nonpositive definiteness, presence of an unresolvable Heywood case, indeterminacy of the number of factors, insufficient number of cases, etc. Datasets whose correlation matrices could not be analyzed, as listed in the References, were as follows:

BANN11, DAVI41, GARD01, GARD02, HALL11, HAYN01, JENS01, LEIB01, PAIV11, PICK01, PORT01, RANK11, SEAS01, and STAN41.

(3) *Rotation of factors to simple structure.* Generally, at least at the first order, simple structure was expected to be oblique. Orthogonal Varimax solutions were inspected, often graphically (by a microcomputer plotting and rotation program), to see whether oblique rotation appeared to be demanded. If not, the final solution was usually the Varimax solution, except that sometimes slight orthogonal adjustments were made (by graphical inspection and judgmental procedures) to produce better simple structure. In the majority of cases at the first order, it was apparent that oblique simple structure rotation was required.

In the early phases of the project, much effort was devoted to deciding what method or criterion for rotation would be most satisfactory for uniform application to all datasets requiring oblique rotation. Some investigation of the possible stability and replicability of graphical rotations was made. Using certain guidelines and starting from Promax-rotated solutions, three persons independently made graphical rotations for ten selected datasets that had large numbers of variables and factors. Although the patterns of results were similar, there were enough differences among the solutions, particularly in the correlations among the factors, to make this procedure suspect. Extensive comparisons were made, for these selected datasets, of graphical, Promax (Hendrickson & White, 1964), optres (Hakstian, 1972), and Tucker and Finkbeiner (1981) DAPPFR (Direct Artificial Personal Probability Function Rotation) rotations. The appropriateness of a rotational solution was generally judged in terms of the apparent or tested viability of an analysis of the correlations among first-order factors. Eventually, it was decided to apply the Tucker/Finkbeiner DAPPFR procedure to all datasets requiring oblique rotation. This was done as uniformly as possible; appropriate programs were developed for both large-frame computers and microcomputers. About two-thirds of the way through processing all datasets, it was learned that Tucker (personal communication, 1984) had developed what he believed was an improved DAPPFR procedure. Programs were revised to take advantage of the improvements, and were used in processing datasets then remaining to be processed. The improved procedure was in general *not* applied to datasets already processed, because of diminishing time and funds available to do so. It is believed that the differences between the two procedures are not critical with respect to the patterns of final results. Tucker and Finkbeiner (1991, in preparation) have provided information about the currently favored DAPPFR procedure.

Like many other analytical procedures for oblique rotation, the Tucker/ Finkbeiner procedures are not completely objective because they permit a number of options in their parameters. One of the most critical options is whether the procedure is to be applied with the "one-sided" or the "two-sided" case. Essentially, with the one-sided case it is assumed that the structure is uniformly positive manifold; i.e., all salient loadings are to be positive. The two-sided case makes no assumption concerning signs of salient loadings; it allows them to be either positive or negative, except that positive loadings are favored by virtue of the fact that the starting position is usually a Promax solution (with its parameter $k = 2$). For the datasets of this project, the two-sided option was generally selected, on the ground that it readily permits negative manifold if such exists, and yet usually yields good positive manifold if such is characteristic of the dataset. In many cases, both the one-sided and the two-sided options were computed, and the final result was selected as that which yielded the more satisfactory higher-order correlation matrix – satisfactory, that is, in terms of the viability of the matrix for analysis at a higher order. Generally this was the two-sided option, but one-sided DAPPFR or even Promax rotations were used if they appeared to yield more satisfactory higher-order matrices. I can offer no apology for the apparent arbitrariness and lack of uniformity in selecting rotational solutions, except to remark that it appears that no analytic rotational solution exists that is completely satisfactory for all cases. The chief difference among rotational solutions appears in the correlations among the factors; the differences do not appear as much in the factor loadings or the identification of factors. I was forced to make some appeal to judgmental procedures in selecting rotational solutions, and I hope that my solutions can be examined and checked by other investigators. It remains true, in any case, that all rotational solutions reported here were achieved by *some* objective, analytic procedure; judgment was used only in deciding which procedure appeared to be most appropriate for a given dataset at a given stage of analysis.

(4) *Analysis of higher-order factor matrices.* When simple structure first-order factors were found to be significantly correlated, as was usually the case, they were subjected to higher-order factor analysis at the second order and sometimes, if necessary, at the third order. (It was never found necessary to carry out analysis at the fourth order.) This involved employing steps (2) and (3), as described above, to the correlation matrix of first-order factors, and then (if simple structure second-order factors were significantly correlated), to the correlation matrix of second-order factors. No reflection of factors (change of sign) was performed at these higher-order stages of analysis.

It is recognized that such analysis could involve considerable indeterminacy when the number of higher-order factors was small, say as small as two. It is well known that factor analysis requires at least three variables to be determinate for one factor (Thurstone, 1947, pp. 293f.), and even then, the single factor may be biased by sampling fluctuations, and if the variables are factors, by indeterminacy in factor rotations. When three factors were available, the best-fitting single factor was computed; with only two factors, the loadings of factors on the single higher-order factor were taken to be equal to the square root of the factor intercorrelation, even though they could have been taken to be any pair of values whose product equaled the factor intercorrelation. This type of indeterminacy is an inevitable consequence of the inadequate sampling of higher-order factors that is found in most empirical datasets. It is conceivable that it might be avoided if greater efforts were made to sample more higher-order factors. One dataset that exemplifies such broader sampling is that of Hakstian and Cattell (1978), here labeled HAKS21, except that the variables entered into this analysis were the second-order abilities themselves.

With second-order and sometimes third-order analyses available, the solutions were then subjected to the Schmid and Leiman (1957) orthogonalization procedure to produce a set of orthogonal factors, their number being the sum of the numbers of first-, second-, and third-order factors. The effect of this transformation is to produce an orthogonal factor pattern very similar to the Spearman–Holzinger bi-factor pattern, with factors varying in degree of generality. Each factor can be regarded as a source of variance that is independent of the others. The major difficulty with this procedure is that it is often strongly affected by the indeterminacy in the higher-order domains that has been commented on above. It is believed, however, that this difficulty can be partially overcome by noting whether results from different datasets are congruent with each other.

It may be noted, in any case, that a Schmid–Leiman orthogonalized factor matrix, when multiplied by its transpose, reproduces the original correlation matrix almost precisely as well as does the principal factor matrix from which it was derived. It has more factors, of course, but its rank is the same as that of the principal factor matrix because the loadings on the higher-order factors can be predicted from loadings on lower-order factors. The Schmid–Leiman transformation can be thought of as one that redistributes variances from correlated factors to orthogonal factors.

For convenience in inspecting results, the Schmid–Leiman orthogonalized factor matrix for each dataset was cast into a special format. The organization reflects the hierarchy of the factors and lists variables in the order of their salient loadings on each first-order factor. First-order factors are listed in order of their salient loadings on each second-order factor, and similarly for the ordering of second-order factors.

In the production of these specially organized orthogonalized matrices, tentative factor interpretations were included. At a later stage, the factors that appeared to be similar, from different datasets, were considered together and in many cases reinterpreted in the light of detailed examination of the variables (or factors) having high loadings on them. On this basis, factors were classified into broad domains to be considered in appropriate chapters of this volume.

Computer Procedures

Computations for this project were carried out with both large-frame computers and microcomputers, using programs that were essentially comparable in algorithms used, levels of accuracy, and final results. Because of memory limitations in the microcomputers used in the early stages of the project, initial factorization of matrices with more than about 30 variables was usually done with a large-frame computer, but the results could be downloaded to micro-computer files for further processing (rotation, Schmid–Leiman orthogonalization, etc.). A large proportion of the analyses were accomplished with a set of programs specially written in BASIC for the APPLE II + microcomputer (and compatibles) and compiled as object programs. The greater time required by microcomputer computations (as opposed to main-frame computations) was much offset by the inexpensiveness, convenience, immediate turnaround, ready accessibility of results, and flexibility in operation they offered. At a late stage of the project, the microcomputer programs were converted for use with the IBM Personal Computer (and compatibles), making it possible to do rapid initial factorization of correlation matrices with up to 70 variables, in addition to the usual further computations.

A WORKED EXAMPLE

A worked example is presented here in order to give the reader a concrete illustration of the processes of reanalysis that were followed, as described above. The example was selected because it represents a dataset with a relatively small number of variables and factors, so that it can be presented in relatively little space; yet, it is one that appears to require analysis up to the third order. It also presented a number of typical problems in analysis. The dataset was that designated SCHU11; the reanalysis was of the matrix published by Schutz (1958) of correlations among nine subtests of the Holzinger–Crowder Unifactor Tests (see Buros, 1959, test 610). Schutz published a four-factor centroid factor matrix, a four-factor obliquely rotated factor matrix, the transformation matrix pur-portedly yielding that rotated matrix, and a table of "cosine angles among factors." The latter is the same as the matrix $\Lambda'\Lambda$ used in computing correlations among first-order factors, the matrix Λ being the transformation matrix carrying the principal factor matrix to the oblique rotated reference-vector matrix. For convenience, in Table 3.2 I present Schutz's initial correlation matrix (from which my reanalysis started), and all of his results in parallel with those of my reanalysis. However, it turns out that there were errors in some of the tables presented by Schutz. In particular, some columns of his transformation matrix do not yield corresponding columns in his rotated oblique matrix, and the values in his table of cosines are not correct. It was possible, however (using a program for Procrustes rotation), to find a transformation of Schutz's centroid matrix that yields his rotated matrix to a close approximation. I have shown values for the correct rotated matrix, transformation matrix, and cosine matrix alongside Schutz's published values. All this, incidentally, illustrates a regrettable fact: that detectable errors in published results are not at all infrequent, even in publications

Table 3.2. *Original analysis of dataset SCHU11 and a reanalysis (see text for explanation)*

Section A: Correlation data and preliminary analysis
Below Diagonal: Correlation Matrix as given by Schutz (1958). Diagonal and Above Diagonal: Communalities and Correlations as Reproduced by the Centroid Matrix (decimals omitted)
N = 2562

Variable		1	2	3	4	5	6	7	8	9
Word Meaning	1	777	798	276	287	412	377	443	411	419
Odd Words	2	80	826	310	321	477	442	488	447	453
Boots	3	28	31	701	704	314	347	407	406	313
Hatchets	4	29	33	71	707	324	356	412	410	318
Mixed Arithmetic	5	41	49	32	32	769	760	489	376	379
Remainders	6	38	44	34	36	77	756	475	364	362
Mixed Series	7	44	50	41	42	50	48	599	567	500
Figure Changes	8	40	44	41	41	39	35	56	559	481
Teams	9	41	46	30	31	37	37	48	46	428
SMC Values		645	690	528	536	632	617	481	411	337
Kaiser MSA Values		832	848	836	839	851	848	956	948	966
Overall MSA										881

Section B: Correlation matrix condensations (decimals omitted)

Centroid matrix (Schutz)

	I	II	III	IV	h²
1	69	−26	37	−31	78
2	75	−22	37	−28	83
3	62	−30	−37	30	70
4	63	−30	−36	30	72
5	71	36	26	26	78
6	70	34	22	32	75
7	72	17	−16	−16	59
8	66	09	−25	−23	55
9	60	10	−10	−22	43
S^2	4128	588	754	651	6122

Principal factor matrix

	I	II	III	IV	h²
1	702	−388	335	−172	785
2	771	−384	284	−142	842
3	603	542	117	−154	695
4	617	535	118	−162	706
5	726	−141	−484	−065	785
6	707	−074	−502	−106	769
7	720	039	−005	283	601
8	644	099	109	314	535
9	587	−044	072	236	408
S^2	4137	917	724	350	6127

Section C: Schutz's analysis (decimals omitted)
Transformation Matrices to Oblique Rotated Matrices (Schutz)

− As given by Schutz:

	A	B	C	D
I	237	223	257	230
II	−682	−666	314	489
III	686	−372	461	−599
IV	−088	−608	790	−591

− Corrected:

	A	B	C	D
I	236	235	225	229
II	−680	−657	537	494
III	689	−404	461	−595
IV	−083	592	670	−591

Table 3.2 (*cont.*)

Corresponding cosine matrices

– As given by Schutz:					– Corrected:[a]				
	A	B	C	D		A	B	C	D
A	100	30	09	−62	A	1000	175	−051	−643
B	30	100	16	31	B	175	1000	−091	−380
C	09	16	100	−53	C	−051	−091	1000	−353
D	−62	31	−53	100	D	−643	−380	−353	1000

Section D: Reanalysis

Varimax matrix (from principal factor matrix)						Promax matrix ($k = 2$)				
	A	B	C	D	KIS	A	B	C	D	KIS
1	821s	129	185	247	811	709s	025	025	079	980
2	815s	143	256	302*	723	683s	020	082	123	940
3	115	780s	152	224	835	011	688s	024	073	983
4	130	783s	161	224	826	025	690s	031	069	982
5	223	141	807s	254	774	060	001	696s	098	965
6	181	197	808s	210	799	027	067	706s	053	979
7	240	254	317*	615s	510	043	071	138	489s	871
8	215	279	169	619s	625	034	107	−005	510s	939
9	277	159	208	513s	536	119	010	056	410s	877

	A	B	C	D	KIS
Overall KIS					753
S^2	1631	1485	1626	1386	6127
No. salients					
	2	2	2	3	9

					KIS
Overall KIS					964
Hyperplane Counts (.05)					
	5	4	3	0	12
No. Salients					
	2	2	2	3	9

Correlations among Promax factors				
	A	B	C	D
A	1000	232	346	468
B	232	1000	294	446
C	346	294	1000	443
D	468	446	443	1000

Section E

Oblique First-Order Rotated Reference-Vector Matrices

– Corrected from Schutz data:						– Tucker–Finkbeiner Rotation (2–sided case)				
	A	B	C	D	KIS	A	B	C	D	KIS
1	621s	000	−022	−008	998	662s	011	−023	−019	997
2	605s	005	033	008	996	630s	000	028	019	996
3	071	670s	008	037	981	−001	643s	002	007	1000
4	080	668s	015	033	977	013	645s	008	001	999
5	080	−021	647s	032	975	018	−028	649s	024	995
6	059	041	656s	008	984	−008	039	664s	−018	994
7	−042	027	072	439s	949	−021	003	073	418s	958
8	−058	061	−073	480s	932	−027	038	−067	447s	957
9	023	−015	−005	376s	993	063	−043	000	350s	939

Table 3.2 (*cont.*)

Overall KIS:				981	Overall KIS:				993
Hyperplane counts (.05):									
2	6	5	6	19	6	7	5	6	24
Number of salients:									
2	2	2	3	9	2	2	2	3	9

Correlations for above rotated factors:

	A	B	C	D		A	B	C	D	MSA
A	1000	223	430	715	A	1000	378	528	681	822
B	223	1000	324	461	B	378	1000	432	622	818
C	430	324	1000	573	C	528	432	1000	643	899
D	715	461	573	1000	D	681	622	643	1000	718

Overall MSA: 807

SMC Values 481 393 432 670

Section F: Higher-order analysis:
Second-order principal factor matrix:

	I′	II′	h^2
A	749	−323	666
B	641	317	512
C	690	035	477
D	937	067	882
S^2	2326	210	2536

Rotated reference-vector matrix:
 (1-sided Tucker–Finkbeiner solution)

	A′	B′	KIS
A	622s	−001	1000
B	001	544s	1000
C	338s	240	328
D	356*	431s	187

Overall KIS: 818

Correlations of 2nd-order factors:

	A′	B′
A′	1000	648
B′	648	1000

Third-order principal factor matrix:

	A″	h^2
A′	805	648
B′	805	648

Section G: Hierarchical analysis (decimals omitted)
Orthogonalized hierarchical factor matrix:

		A″	A′	B′	A	B	C	D	h^2
Word Meaning	1	565	428	−011	531	010	−022	−011	785
Odd Words	2	624	443	018	505	−000	027	012	842
Boots	3	487	004	355	−1000	577	002	004	695
Hatchets	4	497	012	354	010	578	008	001	706
Mixed Arith	5	556	250	160	015	−025	623	014	785
Remainders	6	533	217	175	−006	035	637	−011	769
Mixed Series	7	647	213	264	−017	002	070	250	601
Fig. Changes	8	597	175	266	−022	034	−064	268	535
Teams	9	532	211	181	051	−039	000	209	408
Sum of Squares		2843	609	480	541	671	803	179	6127

Table 3.2 (*cont.*)

Rearranged hierarchical factor matrix:

	A″	A′	A	C	B′	B	D	h²
Factor A″ (O3:F1) General Factor for this Battery, Order 3								
Factor A′ (O2:F1) Gc (Crystallized Intelligence), Order 2								
Factor A (O1:F1) Verbal Ability, Order 1								
+1 Word Meaning	**565**	**428**	**531**	−022	−011	010	−011	785
+2 Odd Words	**624**	**443**	**505**	027	018	−000	012	842
Factor C (O1:F3) Numerical Ability, Order 1								
+6 Remainders	**533**	217	−006	**637**	175	035	−011	769
+5 Mixed Arith	**556**	250	015	**623**	160	−025	014	785
Factor B′ (O2:F2) Gf (Fluid Intelligence), Order 2								
Factor B (O1:F2) Space, Order 1								
+4 Hatchets	**497**	012	010	008	**354**	**578**	001	706
+3 Boots	**487**	004	−000	002	**355**	**577**	004	695
Factor D (O1:F4) Reasoning, Order 1								
+8 Figure Changes	**597**	175	−022	−064	**266**	034	**268**	535
+7 Mixed Series	**647**	213	−017	070	**264**	002	**250**	601
+9 Teams	**532**	211	051	000	**181**	−039	**210**	408
Sums of Squares	2843	609	541	803	480	671	179	6127

Source: Material from Schutz (1958) reproduced by permission of Educational and Psychological Measurement, Inc. Copyright © 1958, G. Frederic Kuder.

[a]The rotated reference-vector matrix from this is shown in Section E; it is approximately the same as that given by Schutz.

of well-respected investigators. Such errors may, of course, occur for various reasons – investigators' computational errors, printers' errors, etc. I cannot emphasize too much that researchers and editors should be very careful in checking computations submitted for publication, and printed tables in galley and page proofs. (Despite my best efforts, I cannot guarantee that no errors are contained in the statistical tables presented in the present volume. All tables in Appendix B were produced from computer files and for that reason should not contain numerical errors. The tables may, however, present a number of minor disagreements from the text in the coding of factors.)

Section A of Table 3.2 contains, in the lower triangle (the entries below the diagonal), the correlation matrix published by Schutz to two decimal places. One gathers that it was extracted from the manual of the Holzinger–Crowder Uni-Factor Tests, for it is based on an unusually large sample, 2562 tenth-grade students in a standardization program. The diagonal of the correlation table contains the communalities actually produced from Schutz's centroid matrix (in Section B); the differences from the communalities reported by Schutz are presumably due to rounding error. Above the diagonal are correlations reproduced from the centroid matrix; it will be noted that they differ little from the actual correlations, a fact indicating that the information in the correlations is well summarized in the four factors of the centroid matrix. The rows of values just below the correlation matrix come from the preliminary phases of our reanalysis. The SMC values (squared multiple correlations) are initial lower-bound estimates of communalities inserted in the diagonal of the correlation matrix for the first iteration of principal factoring. They measure the extent to which each variable can be predicted from all the others. The MSA (Measure of Sampling Adequacy) values are computed by procedures due to Kaiser (1981). MSA values are square roots of a certain function of the correlation matrix. Acceptable values can range from 0 to 1; imaginary values indicate unacceptability. In the present case, they are all reasonably near unity, indicating that every variable is acceptable in a factor analysis. The overall MSA, .881, indicates that the battery as a whole is highly acceptable for factor analysis.

Section B contains, at the left, the centroid matrix published by Schutz to two decimal places, with a column of communality values. Various checks give confidence that the centroid factor matrix is correct: the sums of squares of loadings in each row are approximately equal to the communality value (h^2) for that row, and the matrix multiplied by its transpose reproduces the correlations in section A to a close approximation. (Schutz reports the residuals, but I prefer to report, in the diagonal and upper triangle of Section A, the communalities and reproduced correlations.) I have added a row of column sums of squares to indicate the amount of variance associated with each centroid factor. It is characteristic of the centroid method that the successive factors are not necessarily associated with decreasing amounts of variance (although usually they are).

Schutz extracted four factors by the centroid method, saying nothing about the criterion for stopping factoring. We may assume, however, that the criterion was the reduction of residuals to near zero, as shown in his Table 1 (not shown here).

In my analyses, it was a continual problem to determine the appropriate number of common factors for a dataset. Initial computations on the correlation matrix in Section A of Table 3.2 were by the principal component method, yielding the following sequence of 9 latent roots:

1	2	3	4	5	6	7	8	9	Sum
4.443	1.187	.949	.748	.545	.419	.291	.228	.190	9.000

A plot of these roots against root number is shown in Figure 3.1. All roots are positive, indicating positive-semidefiniteness of the matrix. Only two are greater than unity. By the Kaiser–Guttman rule, this would indicate that only two factors should be extracted. Noting that the "eibow" of the plot occurs at root 4, however, it appears that by the Cattell scree test, four factors should be considered. Experience has shown that both the Kaiser–Guttman rule and the Cattell scree test frequently underestimate the number of factors when first-order

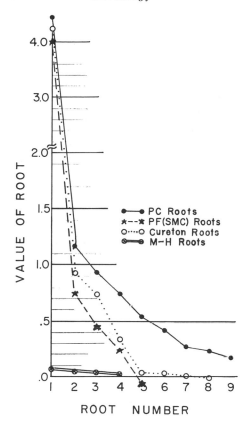

Figure 3.1. Scree plot of values of roots for the correlation matrix of dataset SCHU11 (Schutz, 1958).

factors are substantially correlated. In any case, my criteria for number of factors required consideration of results of principal factor computations, starting from SMC values as shown in Section A and as plotted in Figure 3.1. The principal factor matrix for the correlation matrix with the SMC values on the diagonal produced the following sequence of roots:

1	2	3	4	5	6	7	8	9
3.995	.759	.569	.225	−.075	−.121	−.132	−.161	−.183

The first four of these, all positive, are to be compared with Montanelli–Humphreys random data roots for $n = 9$, $N = 2562$:

1	2	3	4
.088	.058	.040	.022

The random data roots are quite small because of the large N. Clearly, the first four actual roots are larger than the corresponding random data roots, a fact suggesting that four factors should be extracted, that is, $m = 4$. Nevertheless, computations started conservatively with an assumed $m = 2$, then increasing to $m = 3$ and then to $m = 4$.

With $m = 2$, principal factoring converged in 11 iterations (a number of iterations within the normal range); a satisfactory Varimax solution ensued, but the value of m was to be increased to obtain the largest value giving a satisfactory Varimax solution. With $m = 3$, principal factoring converged in 19 iterations (a number of iterations still well within the normal range); a satisfactory Varimax solution was obtained, in that three factors each had at least two salient loadings. With $m = 4$, principal factoring converged extremely slowly and was arbitrarily stopped after 34 iterations. (Whether convergence would eventually occur after some large number of iterations was not ascertained.) The resulting Varimax matrix was satisfactory, in that each factor had at least two salient loadings. Nevertheless this solution was not accepted because it was not based on a converged principal factor solution. (After the 34 iterations, the maximum absolute difference between successive communalities was .001534, and this value was decreasing very slowly, for example by only .000036 from iteration 33 to iteration 34.) According to my rules, these circumstances required use of the Cureton procedure with $m = 4$. In this procedure, SMC's are multiplied by a factor (in this case 1.263) so that the sum of the adjusted values is equal to the sum (6.16) of the highest correlations in each array. Principal factoring is then performed, initially using the adjusted SMC's on the diagonal, and then carrying out exactly one further iteration. The resulting principal factor matrix is shown in Section B of Table 3.2, at the right, with a column of communalities and a row of roots (or variances, labeled S $\wedge$ 2 as the sums of squares of the loadings) at the foot. It is of interest to compare this matrix with the centroid matrix. The matrices agree closely in communalities and *total* variance extracted. They also agree closely in terms of the correlations they reproduce; the reproduced correlations in Section A of Table 3.2 are those from the centroid matrix. They do not agree in variances associated with factors; in the case of the principal factor matrix, the variances must decrease with successive factors. However, these differences with the centroid solution are actually immaterial; the principal factor matrix describes the variables about as well as the centroid, or perhaps a little better, but it does so in terms of a somewhat different set of coordinates. The major reason for preferring the principal factor solution over the centroid is that it is mathematically more elegant and in most cases can extract more variance than the centroid does, for a given number of factors.

No attempt was made to obtain a solution for five factors since it was already established that four factors were sufficient, and difficulty had been encountered even with the four-factor solution.

Section C of Table 3.2 gives information on Schutz's analysis, which as mentioned previously was incorrect in certain respects. His chief error, it seems, was in the sign of the fourth element of column B of his transformation matrix. The corrected matrices at the right of Section C were produced by a Procrustes rotation of the principal factor matrix to fit his oblique rotated matrix.

Section D of the table shows the Varimax rotation of the principal factor solution. It was regarded as satisfactory for supporting four first-order factors, because each Varimax factor had at least two salient loadings (salient loadings are marked with the letter *s*; loadings that are greater than |.3| but that are not salients are marked with an asterisk *). Also shown are the sums of squares of the loadings, labeled S^2, and a column of values labeled "KIS," the Kaiser Index of Simplicity (Kaiser, 1974). These values can range from 0 to 1. High values indicate that a variable has high loadings mainly on one factor; low values are for variables whose loadings are about equally high for a number of factors, and that are therefore factorially complex. The KIS values are not especially high for this Varimax matrix because it is evident that the factors are correlated.

Following this is a Promax rotation, obtained chiefly to provide a starting position for the Tucker–Finkbeiner DAPPFR procedure. The KIS values are distinctly higher, indicating a relatively clean simple structure, but the hyperplane counts (of loadings smaller than |.05|) are relatively small. The correlations among Promax factors are given chiefly as a matter of possible interest.

Section E of Table 3.2 shows, at the left, a corrected version of Schutz's oblique rotated reference-vector matrix. Its KIS values and hyperplane counts are somewhat better than those of the Promax matrix, but not as good as the rotated reference-vector matrix at the right, obtained by a revised version of the DAPPFR procedure (Tucker, personal communication). According to my usual procedure, the two-sided option was used. Convergence occurred very rapidly, after only 3 cycles. The two-sided option was successful in approximating a good simple-structure solution with positive manifold, even though it permitted negative manifold if such existed. This is probably due to the well-defined hyperplanes in the data.

Below, in Section E of the table, is a comparison of the correlations among first-order factors implied by the corrected Schutz transformation and those resulting from the DAPPFR procedure. The latter correlations tend to be somewhat higher. Their MSA values are given, indicating that each first-order factor is suitable for a further factor analysis, and this is confirmed by an overall MSA value of .807.

Section F of the table is devoted to the higher-order analysis of the factor correlation matrix produced by the DAPPFR procedure. A principal component (PC) analysis produced the roots 2.657, .640, .471, and .232, summing to 4.000. Only one of these roots is greater than unity, but it is assumed that this fact can be disregarded, particularly for higher-order correlation matrices. A principal factor (PF) analysis of the matrix with SMC's on the diagonal produced two positive roots, 2.173 and .063, both being larger than the corresponding random data roots, .042 and .008. It was concluded that the matrix supported two common factors. Continuation of the PF analysis converged in 18 iterations, producing a Varimax solution (not shown) in which each of the two factors had two salient loadings. It was clear, however, that the two factors required oblique rotation. This was accomplished first through a Promax rotation, and then through DAPPFR rotation, with the two-sided option. The two-sided option, however, produced an unsatisfactory reference-vector matrix, undoubtedly because the hyperplanes were inadequately defined. Therefore, the one-sided option was selected, producing what was regarded as a satisfactory solution (as shown next in Section F) because each factor had two salient loadings, and at the same time contained at least one vanishing loading and no large negative loadings. The correlation between the second-order factors was .648.

Next is shown the third-order analysis of the correlation matrix for the second-order factors. Since there are only two factors, their loadings on a single third-order factor are taken to be the square roots, .805, of their correlation. (This is in fact equivalent to a conventional iterated PF analysis of the second-order correlation matrix.)

Not shown in the table are computations that lead to the Schmid–Leiman orthogonalized matrix. Essentially, oblique reference-vector matrices at each order, along with the corresponding factor correlation matrices, are entered and converted successively into orthogonalized matrices. The final orthogonalized matrix at order 1, given at the top of Section G of Table 3.2, shows factor A'' as derived from the third-order factor, factors A' and B' as derived from the two second-order factors, and factors A, B, C, and D as derived from the four first-order factors. Communalities and column sums of squares of orthogonalized factor loadings are also shown. The communalities are identical to those computed for the first-order PF matrix. The column sums of squares, which sum to the total of the communalities, are measures of amounts of common factor variance associated with each factor, and when compared with column sums of squares for the PF or for the initial Varimax matrix, indicate how the orthogonalization process redistributes common factor variance.

In the second half of Section G of the table, the rows and columns of the orthogonalized hierarchical matrix are rearranged to facilitate interpretation of factors. Variables with salient loadings on first-order factors are listed in order of those loadings; the first-order factors are listed in order of their loadings on second-order factors, which in turn are listed in order of their loadings on the third-order factor. (In determining salient loadings and in ranking variables, the loadings in oblique reference-vector matrices are used rather than loadings in pattern matrices.) Columns of variables' loadings on factors are given first for the third-order factor, then for each second-order factor followed by the first-order factors which it dominates. Boldface printing of salient loadings makes this organization more apparent. In addition, the table includes identifications of variables and tentative interpretations of factors. All variables have substantial loadings on a third-order general factor. A second-order factor interpreted as crystallized intelligence (Gc) dominates first-order factors Verbal and Numerical; a second-order factor interpreted as fluid intelligence (Gf) dominates first-order factors Space and Reasoning.

COMPARISONS OF RESULTS WITH THOSE OF ORIGINAL INVESTIGATORS

In many instances, reanalyses performed by the methods and procedures described above produced results that did not differ markedly from those reported by the original investigators, especially if my procedures gave the same number of first-order factors as were used by those investigators. Even in these cases, however, my procedures often extended and refined the original findings by carrying them to higher orders.

There were other instances, nevertheless, in which my reanalyses gave results that differed in major respects from those of the original investigators. Sometimes this was due to computational errors or inadequate procedures used by the original investigators. There is a class of instances, however, where the differences between my results and those of the original investigators arise from major differences in the philosophy and procedures of factor analysis. This is particularly true of datasets from the series of investigations in the Aptitudes Research Project that Guilford directed over the period 1949–1969 (Guilford & Hoepfner, 1971). It is desirable, therefore, to set forth an illustrative comparison of an analysis made by Guilford and Hoepfner with my reanalysis, and to defend and justify my procedures of reanalysis in that instance. Any conclusions from such an illustrative comparison would presumably generalize to many other datasets where my results differ substantially from the findings originally reported.

Analysis of Dataset GUIL11

For this purpose I select the dataset, here designated GUIL11, first analyzed in Report No. 12 of the Aptitudes Research Project (Guilford, Berger, & Christensen, 1955). In that report, involving 52 test variables, 17 factors were extracted and rotated, of which 14 were interpreted psychologically. An archival publication by Berger, Guilford, and Christensen (1975) reports essentially the same analysis. A reanalysis is reported by Harris (1967; see also Harris & Liba, 1965) and there is further discussion by Harris and Harris (1971). In analyses by different methods, Harris found from 7 to 13 "effective common factors." The dataset was later reanalyzed by Guilford (with the number of variables reduced to 48) with 19 principal factors and a "targeted solution" rotation procedure; results were presented in skeletal form and discussed further by Guilford and Hoepfner (1971, pp. 148–150 and Tables 4.3 and 6.2). In that analysis, 11 factors were claimed to fit into the SOI (Structure-of-Intellect) model. Five of the remaining factors were singlets having only one variable loading significantly on each of them.

In my analysis, the 52-variable correlation matrix presented to three decimal places in Table 3 of Guilford's report No. 12 was solved first for principal components and then for principal factors. Pertinent results for arriving at an initial estimate of the number of factors are as follows:

Root No.	PC Roots	SMC Roots	Random Data Roots for $N = 364$, $n = 52$
1	9.771	9.197	1.025
2	3.993	3.407	.944
3	2.510	1.954	.870
4	1.966	1.358	.802
5	1.569	.956	.743
6	1.321	.676	.692
7	1.278	.644	.647
8	1.234	.562	.607
9	1.198	.533	.570
10	1.172	.491	.536
11	1.117	.459	.504
12	1.034	.366	.474
13	1.011	.354	.446
14	0.950	.308	.418
15	0.944	.296	.392
......	....	....	....

As is seen, 13 PC roots were greater than 1.0 but a scree plot suggested that only 5 factors were of any importance, unless one assumes that the remaining 8 roots formed a secondary scree. Cattell (1978, p. 91) states that the Kaiser–Guttman rule is likely to overestimate the number of factors when there are many variables, as in the present case. Using the Montanelli and Humphreys (1976) parallel analysis criterion, I found that only five of the SMC roots exceeded the corresponding random data roots, giving further support to the proposition that only five factors should be retained. The remaining SMC roots were smaller than the random data roots. Therefore, the starting point or initial estimate for iterated PF solutions was five factors. Iterations to my strict convergence criterion of .0005 were conducted for 5, 6, and 7 factors, and in each case the resulting factor matrix was rotated by the Varimax procedure. The numbers of salient loadings on each Varimax factor were counted, a salient loading being the highest in absolute value (generally positive) for the corresponding variable. The results are shown below:

Factor	$m = 5$	$m = 6$	$m = 7$
1	18	19	17
2	21	15	13
3	8	7	6
4	3	5	8
5	2	2	2
6	.....	4	5
7	.....	.....	1

Using a strict criterion that every factor must have at least two salients, one could conclude that only six factors should be retained. The rule was adopted, however, that one more factor should be retained than the strict criterion would allow. The rationale for this rule was that (1) rotations could reveal one or more factors as residuals, if in fact they were residuals, and (2) oblique rotations might produce conditions such that one more factor could show itself as valid. For the present data, therefore, seven factors were retained for all further analyses.

Rotations of first-order factors were performed by the early (1981) version of the Tucker and Finkbeiner DAPPFR procedure, since this dataset was dealt with early in the project, and subsequently, it was not considered worthwhile to redo the DAPPFR analysis in its later version. The parameters called for a two-sided solution; that is, salient loadings were allowed to be either positive or negative. On five of the factors, all salient loadings were positive; on a sixth factor, two salient loadings were positive and one negative; on the seventh factor, there was one positive and one negative salient, suggesting that this factor was a true residual factor.

All values were positive in the matrix of correlations among rotated first-order factors, although some were near zero. Analysis of this matrix suggested that only one second-order factor could be accepted, and this factor was extracted by principal factoring. The second-order factor loadings for the first-order factors were as follows (with tentative identifications of the latter):

First-Order Factor	Loading on Second-Order Factor
Reasoning	.904
Verbal Comprehension	.549
Conceptual Foresight	.430
Adaptive Flexibility	.390
(uninterpreted residual)	.348
Originality	.297
Numerical Facility	.282

On this basis, the final Schmid–Leiman orthogonalized factor-matrix at the first-order was computed; it is shown in Table 3.3 with variables and factors reordered to facilitate interpretation, and some factors renamed.

The table shows loadings on an orthogonalized second-order general factor and on seven first-order factors. The total variance represented here was 18.204, or 35.0%. This was somewhat less than what was extracted by Guilford with 17 factors, 22.42 (as can be estimated by summing the communalities in Table 5 of Report No. 12), but it can be noted that my seven PF factors represented 81.2% of the variance represented by Guilford's 17 factors. Considering the fact that remaining factors had roots close to random data roots, it would appear that the ten additional factors extracted by Guilford were probably due mainly to chance.

It is of interest to compare my seven factors with factors interpreted by

Table 3.3. Guilford JP/Berger RM/Christensen PR – A factor-analytic study of planning. Los Angeles: Reports from the Psychological Laboratory, Univ. of Southern California no. 12 (1955). Pearson r's table 3 pp. 8–9, Male aircrew trainees mean age 20.75 (SD 1.54)

N = 364
*** Hierarchical factor matrix, order 1 ***

V#		1	2	3	4	5	6	7	8	h^2
Factor 1: O2:F1 gen'l cognitive ability 2G; order 2										
Factor 2: O1:F2 sequential reasoning RG; order 1										
1	+40	Logical Reasoning	.53	.26	.02	.02	.01	-.08	-.06	-.01	.36
2	+29	Essential Operations	.55	.22	.08	.06	-.01	-.02	-.08	.11	.38
3	+48	Verbal Analogies I	.56	.22	.14	.04	.04	-.00	-.11	-.02	.39
4	+38	Ship Destination	.50	.22	-.07	-.03	.03	.13	.08	.03	.33
5	+35	Code Analysis	.42	.21	-.25	-.05	.08	.10	.00	.32	.40
6	+25	Word Matrices	.54	.16	.10	.02	.03	.19	.07	.03	.37
7	+#5	Awareness of Variables	.32	.15	.04	.05	-.07	.03	-.03	-.12	.15
8	+30	Ranking of Variables	.25	.15	-.00	-.05	-.08	-.01	.03	-.03	.10
9	+23	Outlining (Part I)	.33	.14	-.09	.06	-.07	.08	.11	.08	.17
10	+#3	Sensitivity to Order	.38	.12	.11	-.01	.16	-.01	.02	-.05	.20
11	+#1	Matrix Order	.44	.10	.12	.03	.12	.14	.12	-.02	.27
Factor 3: O1:F3 verbal ability V; order 1										
12	+37	Vocabulary	.47	-.02	.72	.01	-.05	.03	.11	.08	.76
13	+36	G–Z Verbal Comprehension	.52	.07	.63	-.00	-.06	-.02	-.00	-.00	.67
14	+49	Practical Judgement	.25	.00	.34	-.00	.18	.03	-.09	-.14	.24
15	+41	Inference	.48	.06	.30	.13	.08	.11	.05	.06	.37
16	+22	Sentence Order	.45	.05	.29	.06	.02	.25	.06	.03	.35
17	+31	Seeing Deficiencies	.51	.09	.25	.23	.10	.17	-.11	-.06	.43
18	+51	Symbol Manipulation	.25	.05	.16	-.08	.07	.05	-.05	.14	.13
Factor 4: O1:F1 sensitivity to problems SP; order 1										
19	+#7	Effects	.33	-.02	.08	.72	.02	-.08	-.02	-.01	.64
20	+#4	Pertinent Questions	.30	-.03	.08	.67	.10	-.04	-.08	-.07	.57

21	+13	Planning Skills II	.23	.06	−.05	**.60**	−.18	−.00	−.19	−.04	.49
22	+14	Planning Elaboration	.32	.04	−.01	**.59**	−.07	.04	−.10	.03	.47
23	+16	Alternate Methods	.34	.03	−.03	**.58**	.10	−.06	−.01	.03	.47
24	+26	Unusual Methods	.16	−.05	−.09	**.55**	.03	.03	.14	−.05	.36
25	+11	Contingencies	.36	−.00	.20	**.46**	−.04	−.01	.04	.06	.39
26	+43	Plot Titles (Low Quality)	−.05	−.10	−.12	**.45**	−.00	.02	−.06	.15	.26
27	+27	Verifications	.44	.16	.06	**.41**	−.02	−.22	.05	−.21	.49
28	+44	Consequences (Low Quality)	.02	−.06	−.04	**.41**	−.00	−.03	−.02	.02	.17
29	#8	Consequences (Remoteness)	.33	.06	−.02	**.40**	−.10	.02	.10	.08	.30
30	+15	Figure Production	.18	−.06	.05	**.39**	.07	.12	.11	−.08	.23
31	+32	Planning Skills	.22	−.04	.14	**.38**	−.09	.13	.06	−.03	.25
32	+28	Procedure Applications	.41	.04	.22	**.36**	−.04	.07	.02	−.03	.35
33	+45	Controlled Associations II	.34	−.00	**.32**	**.32**	.03	−.12	.01	.05	.34
34	+42	Plot Titles (Cleverness)	.27	.07	−.02	**.27**	−.11	−.03	.23	−.00	.22
35	+24	Outlining (Part II)	.33	.09	.02	**.22**	−.13	.03	.05	.13	.20
Factor 5: O1;F4 figural flexibility FX; order 1											
36	+17	Match Problems II	.30	.02	−.01	.03	**.58**	.01	−.09	.13	.44
37	+46	Match Problems	.33	.04	.01	−.02	**.54**	.01	.04	.03	.40
38	+12	Route Planning	.32	.04	.01	−.04	**.52**	−.02	.07	.03	.38
39	+34	Planning a Circuit	.19	−.03	.04	.09	**.44**	.07	.02	−.10	.26
40	+33	Planning Air Maneuvers	.30	.11	−.00	−.08	**.33**	−.11	.05	.01	.23
41	#9	Competitive Planning	.26	.07	−.13	.03	**.26**	.03	.08	.19	.20
42	+10	Symbol Grouping	.10	−.01	−.11	.06	**.18**	.11	−.02	.14	.09
Factor 6: O1;F7 uninterpreted I0; order 1											
43	+21	Picture Arrangement	.34	.02	.02	−.00	.24	**.51**	.02	−.04	.44
44	+50	Mechanical Principles	.28	.27	−.08	.01	.20	**−.52**	.05	*−.50*	71
Factor 7: O1;F6 originality FO; order 1											
45	+18	Symbol Production	.31	−.00	.05	.29	.07	−.05	**.47**	−.05	.41
46	#2	Seeing Trends	.44	.10	.08	.17	.01	−.07	**.30**	.03	.33
47	#6	Series	.39	.14	−.10	.07	.10	.05	**.26**	−.04	.27
48	+19	Line Drawing	.16	.02	.11	−.05	−.05	.07	**.23**	.02	.10
49	+20	Temporal Ordering	.45	.06	.20	.05	.15	.08	**.21**	.05	.32

Table. 3.3 (cont.)

N = 364
*** Hierarchical factor matrix, order 1 ***

V#		1	2	3	4	5	6	7	8	h²
Factor 8: O1;F5 numerical facility N; order 1										
50 +52	Numerical Operations	.23	-.02	.04	.05	.02	-.01	.03	**.72**	.58
51 +47	Sign Changes	.23	.01	-.01	.02	.01	-.02	.26	**.44**	.31
52 +39	Arithmetic Reasoning	**.51**	.18	.10	-.02	.07	-.14	-.01	**.32**	.43
	SMSQ:	6.72	.63	1.81	4.14	1.69	.92	.83	1.47	18.20

*** Hierarchical factor matrix, order 2 ***

HF #	.1st-order factor		1	h²
Factor 1: O2;F1 gen'l cognitive ability 2G; order 2				
HF 2 O1;F2	Sequential Reasoning	RG	**.90**	.82
HF 3 O1;F3	Verbal Ability	V	**.55**	.30
HF 4 O1;F1	Sensitivity to Problems	SP	**.43**	.19
HF 5 O1;F4	Figural Flexibility	FX	**.39**	.15
HF 6 O1;F7	Uninterpreted	IO	**.35**	.12
HF 7 O1;F6	Originality	FO	**.30**	.09
HF 8 O1;F5	Numerical Facility	N	**.28**	.08
		SMSQ:	1.75	1.75

Guilford, Berger, and Christensen (1955) in their Report No. 12. My Reasoning factor apparently represents a collapsing of Guilford's Factor D (General Reasoning) with his Factor E (Logical Evaluation). Actually, because of the high loading of this factor (before orthogonalization) on a general factor, much of the variance of this factor was absorbed into the general factor; thus, loadings of variables salient on this factor in Table 3.3 are relatively small. My Verbal Comprehension factor corresponds to Guilford's Factor A, Verbal Comprehension. The extensive factor that has been called here Conceptual Foresight corresponds not only to Guilford's Factor N (Conceptual Foresight) but also comprises variables he found as loading on several other factors, none of which was very clearly defined in his report. In a later analysis, Guilford and Hoepfner (1971) assigned many of these tests to several divergent thinking factors. A question could be raised about my results, therefore, to the effect that they missed important differences among these tests. Below, I look at this question further. But to proceed with the examination of factors, we can note that my Adaptive Flexibility factor corresponds quite well to Guilford's Factor K, Adaptive Flexibility. The next factor I regard as an uninterpretable residual, although it has some resemblance to Guilford's Factor L (Ordering). (The variables loading saliently on that factor have moderate loadings on my general factor.) My factor tentatively labeled Originality corresponds somewhat to Guilford's Factor I (Originality), and my factor Numerical Facility corresponds very well with Guilford's factor of that name.

I now examine the problem of why several of Guilford and Hoepfner's SOI factors seemed to collapse into one factor, here tentatively labeled Conceptual Foresight, as mentioned above. For this purpose, various special analyses of fourteen variables from this dataset were performed. I refer to Table 3.4 to explain these analyses and their results.

The fourteen variables selected for analysis were those that, according to Guilford and Hoepfner (1971, Table 6.2), had significant ($>.30$) loadings on five SOI factors. The variables (with their designation numbers and names) are listed in the first column of our table; they are grouped according to the SOI factors. (One variable, #26, Unusual Methods, had loadings on two of these factors; it is therefore grouped with both of them.) The SOI factors, and the reported significant loadings, are listed in the next column. In the third and fourth columns, the loadings on the second-order g factor and my Conceptual Foresight factor are listed. In the next portion of the table, a four-factor DAPPFR-rotated solution for these variables is reported, with the correlations among these factors at the foot of the table. (A five-factor solution was also obtained but appeared to show much less correspondence with the SOI factors.) We see here that this solution was able to separate some of the factors, namely DMI, DMU, and DMR; DFI and DMT, however, appear as a single factor. The factors are in general rather highly correlated. The DMR factor was not well defined, since the two variables supposed to define it had a correlation of only .202. In my complete

Table 3.4. *Reanalysis of selected variables from dataset GUIL11*
First-order rotated reference-vector matrix and correlations of factors
(decimals omitted)

Variable	Guilford's factor & loading	Our analyses					
		g	CF	A	B	C	D
15 Figure Production	DFI (36)	177	394	304s	000	−006	−012
7 Effects	DFI (36)	326	718	294#	106	043	150
26 Unusual Methods	DFI (34), DMT (39)	155	551	346s	010	042	−069
42 Plot Titles-Clever	DMT (43)	270	274	398s	−047	−212	−021
8 Consequences-Remote	DMT (35)	327	403	311s	035	−069	016
18 Symbol Production	DMT (54)	307	285	565s	−273	−175	−008
2 Naming Trends	DMT (37)	435	172	385s	−102	−248	108
14 Planning Elaborat'n	DMI (53)	317	592	209	236#	000	050
13 Planning Skills II	DMI (51)	226	600	010	564s	003	−018
32 Planning Skills	DMI (−)	220	382	261#	039	−020	068
43 Plot Titles (Low Q.)	DMU (45)	−052	452	−008	021	423s	−035
44 Consequences (Obv.)	DMU (43)	024	409	055	−032	326s	069
45 Controlled Assoc. II	DMR (45)	324	323	−008	005	004	736s
49 Practical Judgment	DMR (41)	247	−004	058	010	−148	209#

	Factor correlations			
A	1000	693	668	493
B	693	1000	565	362
C	668	565	1000	250
D	493	362	250	1000

s: Salient loading ⩾.3
#: Salient loading < .3

orthogonalized solution this variance falls under the Verbal Comprehension factor.

The conclusion from these analyses appears to be that my conservative rules for determining number of factors tend not to separate highly correlated factors when these factors are substantially loaded with higher-order variance. Detailed analysis of selected variables can under some conditions separate such highly correlated factors. It is questionable, however, whether it is worthwhile to separate these small and highly correlated factors, and whether they would stand up as distinct factors with more powerful tests. The factors identified by my conservative procedures are likely to represent major dimensions of ability that do not depend upon particular modes and conditions of testing, and that can be expected to be more generalizable and invariant than highly specialized, correlated factors corresponding to abilities claimed by Guilford in the SOI model.

Analysis of Dataset GUST11A

One other comparison can be presented, chiefly to illustrate differences between exploratory and "confirmatory" (structural modeling) procedures. This pertains to my reanalysis of the dataset, here designated GUST11A, used by Gustafsson (1984) to support his HILI model as mentioned in Chapter 2. Gustafsson used a special mode of Jöreskog and Sörbom's (1983) LISREL program to produce a third-order hierarchical analysis of 20 test variables administered to 981 sixth-grade Swedish pupils. Ten first-order factors, three second-order factors (Gv, Gf, and Gc), and one third-order factor were identified. The final model as presented in Gustafsson's (1984) Figure 1 was quite complex, with a number of correlated error links between factors or variables. At the second order, the Gv factor dominated first-order factors Vz (Visualization), S (Space), and Cf (Flexibility of Closure); the Gf factor dominated Cs (Speed of Closure), CFR (Cognition of Figural Relations), I (Induction), and MS (Memory Span); and Gc dominated V (Vocabulary), Ve Ach (Verbal Achievement), and Num Ach (Numerical Achievement). At the third order the factor G dominated the second-order factors Gv, Gf, and Gc, but because the coefficient for the link between G and Gf was 1.00 it appeared that G and Gf could be regarded as being identical. The final model was found to fit the data only with "borderline significance" (p. 191), chi-square = 185.35 with 144 degrees of freedom ($p < .011$). (A better fit would have produced p much larger than .011.)

My reanalysis started with the correlation matrix presented by Gustafsson to two decimal places. Kaiser's overall MSA was found to be highly satisfactory, .936. Only five PC roots were greater than unity, but Cattell's scree test suggested seven salient factors. This was the starting point for iterated PF solutions. The Montanelli–Humphreys parallel analysis criterion suggested nine significant first-order factors. Varimax-rotated, converged iterated PF solutions were obtained for 7, 8, 9, and 10 factors; it is of interest that the numbers of "accelerated" iterations required were unusually large, being 132, 111, 69, and 119 for 7, 8, 9, and 10 factors, respectively. (This may indicate that the factors were not well defined; indeed, the design generally allowed only two variables for each factor.) The table of the numbers of salient loadings for these solutions was as follows:

Factor	$m = 7$	$m = 8$	$m = 9$	$m = 10$
1	6	5	3	5
2	4	2	2	2
3	2	2	2	2
4	2	2	2	2
5	2	3	3	3
6	2	2	2	2
7	2	2	3	2
8	.....	2	2	2
9	.....	.....	1	0
10	.....	.....	.....	0

Table 3.5. *Gustafsson J.-E. A unifying model for the structure of intellectual abilities. Intelligence 1984 8 179–203, 6th grade students, exploratory factor analysis*

N = 981

*** Hierarchical factor matrix, order 1 ***

V#		1	2	3	4	5	6	7	8	9	10	11	12	13	h²
Factor 1: O3:F1 general intelligence 3G: order 3															
Factor 2: O2:F2 broad visual perception 2V: order 2															
Factor 3: O1:F5 closure flexibility CF: order 1															
1+7	Copying	.68	.20	.27	.03	-.02	-.04	.01	-.04	-.01	-.01	-.01	.00	-.00	.58
2+6	Hidden Patterns	.67	.19	.24	.03	.02	-.01	-.00	.04	.03	-.02	.01	-.01	.01	.55
3+5	Group Embedded Figures Test	.62	.14	.18	-.06	.03	.05	.13	-.00	.10	.05	-.01	.03	-.03	.47
Factor 4: O1:F4 spatial relations SR: order 1															
4+3	Card Rotation (Part I)	.56	.18	.01	.67	-.02	-.02	-.03	-.01	-.05	.01	.01	-.03	.02	.80
5+4	Card Rotation (Part II)	.60	.16	.00	.57	.03	.04	.04	.01	-.03	-.01	-.01	.04	-.02	.71
Factor 5: O1:F8 closure speed CS: order 1															
6+8	Disguised Words	.33	.07	.01	-.02	.64	.00	-.04	-.04	.10	-.01	-.00	-.00	.01	.54
7+9	Disguised Pictures	.28	.05	-.01	.03	.45	.08	.08	.06	.04	.02	.01	-.15	-.01	.32
Factor 6: O2:F3 fluid intelligence 2F: order 2															
Factor 7: O1:F3 visualization VZ: order 1															
8+1	Metal Folding (Odd Items)	.59	.07	.01	.01	-.01	.30	.58	.01	.04	.02	.01	-.04	.02	.79
9+2	Metal Folding (Even Items)	.61	.08	.00	.01	.01	.31	.57	.00	.02	-.02	-.00	.04	-.00	.80
Factor 8: O1:F2 CFR or induction I: order 1															
10+11	Raven (Even Items)	.53	.02	.02	-.01	-.01	.29	-.01	.70	.21	.00	-.01	.01	-.01	.89
11+10	Raven (Odd Items)	.48	.01	-.01	.01	.02	.27	.01	.62	.22	-.00	.01	.00	.01	.74
Factor 9: O2:F1 crystallized intelligence 2C: order 2															
Factor 10: O1:F9 verbal achievement A6 order 1															
12+20	English Achievement	.50	.02	.02	-.01	.00	-.06	.01	-.00	.63	.46	.01	.00	.01	.87
13+18	Swedish Achievement	.53	.01	-.01	.01	.03	-.01	-.02	.02	.63	.25	.21	.12	.04	.80
Factor 11: O1:F1 verbal (or lex knowl) VL: order 1															
14+16	Opposites (Odd Items)	.43	-.01	.02	-.04	-.02	.02	.01	-.01	.53	-.03	.60	-.02	-.00	.83
15+17	Opposites (Even Items)	.40	-.01	-.02	.05	.01	.01	-.01	-.00	.51	.06	.43	.03	-.01	.62

Factor 12: O1:F7 math achvt A3: order 1

16 + 12	Number Series II	**.59**	.07	.01	.03	.06	.00	.01	**.33**	.00	−.02	**.50**	.02	.71
17 + 19	Mathematics Achievement	**.59**	.05	.00	−.04	.05	.05	−.01	**.43**	.13	.02	**.39**	−.04	.71
18 + 13	Letter Grouping II	**.56**	.09	.07	.01	.04	−.02	.10	**.25**	.02	.05	**.17**	.05	.43

Factor 13: O1:F6 memory span MS: order 1

19 + 15	Auditory Letter Span	**.29**	.07	−.01	−.03	−.13	.00	.01	**.21**	.02	−.01	−.01	**.84**	.85
20 + 14	Auditory Number Span	.24	.06	.01	.05	−.06	.0:	−.02	**.12**	−.02	.02	.03	**.46**	.30
	SMSQ:	5.41	.20	.17	.62	.38	.70	.89	1.86	.30	.59	.47	.92	13.29

*** Hierarchical factor matrix, order 2 ***

HF # 1st-order factor

			1	2	6	9	h^2

Factor 1: O2:F1 general intelligence 3G: order 3
Factor 2: O2:F2 broad visual perception 2V: order 2

HF 3	O1:F5 Closure Flexibility	CF	**.81**	**.23**	−.03	.03	.71
HF 4	O1:F4 Spatial Relations	SR	**.57**	**.17**	.01	−.06	.36
HF 5	O1:F8 Closure Speed	CS	**.47**	**.08**	.04	.17	.26

Factor 6: O2:F3 fluid intelligence 2F: order 2

| HF 7 | O1:F3 Visualization | VZ | **.53** | .07 | **.25** | .02 | .35 |
| HF 8 | O1:F2 CFR or Induction | I | **.46** | .01 | **.23** | .23 | .31 |

Factor 9: O2:F1 crystallized intelligence 2C: order 2

HF 10	O1:F9 Verbal Achievement	A6	**.52**	.00	−.05	**.69**	.74
HF 11	O1:F1 Verbal (or Lex Knowl)	VL	**.48**	−.01	.02	**.62**	.61
HF 12	O1:F7 Math Achvt	A3	**.62**	.07	.05	**.40**	.55
HF 13	O1:F6 Memory Span	MS	**.34**	.07	−.10	**.22**	.18
		SMSQ:	2.70	.10	.13	1.15	4.08

*** Hierarchical factor matrix, order 3 ***

HF # 2nd-order factor

			1	h^2

Factor 1: O3:F1 general intelligence 3G: order 3

HF 2	O2:F2 Broad Visual Perception	2V	**.96**	.93
HF 6	O2:F3 Fluid Intelligence	2F	**.71**	.50
HF 9	O2:F1 Crystallized Intelligence	2C	**.62**	.39
		SMSQ:	1.82	1.82

Thus, only eight factors consistently had two or more salient loadings, and 8 was the highest number of factors for which every factor had two or more salient loadings. My rule required that one more factor than 8 be retained, given that convergence occurred at $m = 9$. After DAPPFR rotation of these nine factors, the matrix of correlations among factors appeared to demand at least three second-order factors, at least by the Montanelli–Humphreys parallel analysis criterion. Because convergence was not obtainable in the regular PF procedure, a Cureton procedure was used to obtain three factors. A two-sided DAPPFR procedure produced a good positive manifold with three correlated factors, for which it was of course possible to fit a single third-order factor. The final orthogonalized hierarchical matrix is shown in Table 3.5. This table also shows the hierarchical factor matrices at orders 2 and 3; in these tables one may find loadings of the first-order factors on second-order factors, and loadings of the second-order factors on the third-order factor.

My reanalysis identified nine of Gustafsson's ten first-order factors, except that my codings and interpretations were somewhat different from his, in some cases. Correspondences, such as they were, were as follows:

My factors		Gustafsson's factors
CF (Closure flexibility)	—	Cf (Flexibility of closure)
SR (Spatial relations)	—	S (Spatial orientation)
CS (Closure speed)	—	Cs (Speed of Closure)
VZ (Visualization)	—	Vz (Visualization)
I (Induction)	—	CFR (Cognition of Figural Relations) (Raven Progressive Matrices)
A6 (Verbal achievement)	—	Ve Ach (Verbal Achievement)
VL (Lexical Knowledge)	—	V (Vocabulary)
A3 (Math Achievement)	—	Num Ach (Numerical Achievement)
MS (Memory span)	—	Ms (Memory Span)

The major differences between our treatments were in the handling of so-called inductive tests. On the basis of my survey I have considered the Raven Progressive Matrices as primarily tests of I (Induction). Gustafsson's I (Induction) showed loadings primarily on the tests Number Series and Letter Grouping, separate from his CFR factor represented in the Raven tests. In my analysis, no such separate factor for Number Series and Letter Grouping appeared; instead, these tests were loaded (only weakly in the case of Letter Grouping) on the factor 12 that I interpreted as A3 (Math Achievement).

The alignment of first-order factors under second-order factors was somewhat different from Gustafsson's in my analysis. The Gv (broad visual perception) factor 2 dominated CF, SR, and (weakly) CS and VZ. The second-order factor 6, interpreted as Gf (Fluid Intelligence), dominated only VZ and I. The Gc factor (factor 9) dominated A6, VL, A3, and (weakly) MS.

At the third-order, the loadings of Gv, Gf, and Gc on the general factor were

.96, .71, and .62, respectively. There was no suggestion that the Gf factor was identical to, or most highly loaded on, the general factor. Indeed, according to my analysis the Gf factor was not well identified in this battery, being defined chiefly by the Raven matrices and Vz factors and their corresponding test variables. If anything, factor Gv was closer to the general factor for this battery, and the relatively low loadings of CF, SR, and CS variables on factor 2 (Gv) reflect absorption of their variances into the general factor. The exact nature of a general factor for a given battery of variables is, one must remember, a function of the composition of the battery. In the present case, it would seem that the general factor is biased toward variables involving visual perception. I would draw attention, however, to the loadings of variables on the third-order factor. It is notable, for example, that variables grouped under Verbal Achievement (factor 10) and Math Achievement (factor 12) had relatively high loadings on the general intelligence factor.

The results of my reanalysis of dataset GUST11A appear to serve as a reasonably satisfactory basis for interpreting the structure of abilities tested in this particular dataset, and in my view they make sense in the light of results from other datasets. They give a further basis for concluding that my procedures of analysis are generally satisfactory for the present survey, although I would welcome further tests by structural modeling techniques.[1]

COMMENT

My reanalyses of datasets in the factor-analytic literature were, I believe, the best that could be made under the circumstances. In the course of the project, over more than five years, various refinements in techniques were discovered or devised, but it was not deemed feasible to go back and apply these refinements uniformly to all datasets that had already been analyzed at a given stage of the work. (For example, at a late stage of the work it was discovered that the convergence criterion for DAPPFR rotations should have been made stricter than what was used in most cases.) Perhaps partly for this reason, but mostly because of characteristics inherent in the data, the reanalyses resulted in many indeterminacies and questions that the data left unresolved. Obviously, the reanalyses could not override difficulties arising from faults in the design of the studies examined and in the selection of variables in those studies. Beyond attempting to summarize and synthesize those conclusions that appeared to be well supported in the database, my purpose was also to disclose the problems and questions that could not readily be answered from available information but that presumably could be addressed in further research. It is to be hoped that my analyses will be found useful in designing and conducting new studies that can lead to more definitive answers and conclusions about the diversity and structure of cognitive abilities.

NOTE

1. In extensive discussions of hierarchical models and their analysis, Gustafsson (1988, 1989) has provided further data supporting his view that Gf (fluid intelligence) is equivalent to a third-order g (general intelligence). The exploratory factor analysis presented here of his 1984 study illustrates difficulties not only in analysis, but also in design, of studies to identify g and Gf and their possible equivalence. It should by no means be taken as a conclusive negative answer to the question of their equivalence.

4 *Survey and Analysis of Correlational and Factor-Analytic Research on Cognitive Abilities: Overview of Outcomes*

To what extent are the several traits of the body, of the senses and of mind interdependent: How far can we predict one thing from our knowledge of another? What can we learn from the tests of elementary traits regarding the higher intellectual and emotional life?

James McKeen Cattell and Livingston Farrand (1896)

This chapter is devoted, first, to the description of the 477 datasets that were initially selected for analysis in this survey. It presents statistics on various characteristics of these datasets, on the types of analysis that were employed, and on the general outcomes. Second, it tells how the results of the survey are to be presented in subsequent chapters.

Since the initial preparation of this chapter and its tables, a handful of datasets were dropped from the database for various reasons, chiefly because some were found not to be in the public domain. Also, a small number of datasets – fewer than a dozen – were added to the database, either because they had earlier been overlooked or because they were published subsequent to the initial selection of datasets that occurred in 1985. Nevertheless, the tables of information presented in this chapter, based on the datasets initially selected, can be taken to give trustworthy (albeit approximate) characterizations of the datasets actually employed in the survey.

THE DATASETS ANALYZED

A general characterization of the 477 datasets reported on here is that they include nearly all of those treated in a number of standard works: French's (1951) monograph summarizing factor-analytic work on aptitude and achievement tests to approximately 1950; Oléron's (1957) monograph, written for a French-speaking audience, on components of intelligence yielded by factor analysis; works of Guilford (1967; Guilford & Hoepfner, 1971) reporting results of his Aptitudes Research Project at the University of Southern California; Pawlik's (1967) monograph on factor analysis and factor-analytic results, written for a German-speaking audience; Horn's (1976) summary written for the *Annual Review of Psychology*; and Ekstrom's (1979) review of cognitive factors. Thus, they include nearly all the datasets studied by Thurstone, by Guilford, and by their students and followers. But they also include a large number of datasets from other sources, such as datasets studied by early British investigators (e.g.,

115

Table 4.1. *Frequency distribution by country of origin,[a] 461 factor-analyzed datasets*

Country of origin	f	%
United States	349	75.7
England	25	5.4
Canada	21	4.6
Germany	15	3.3
Australia	13	2.8
Sweden	8	1.7
South Africa	6	1.3
Japan	4	0.9
Netherlands	4	0.9
Norway	3	0.6
Switzerland	3	0.6
Italy	2	0.4
Scotland	2	0.4
Argentina	1	0.2
Ireland	1	0.2
Saudi Arabia	1	0.2
Spain	1	0.2
U.S.S.R.	1	0.2
Yugoslavia	1	0.2

[a]Country in which sample was collected.

Hargreaves, 1927; El Koussy, 1935), datasets from studies of particular test batteries like the Illinois Test of Psycholinguistic Abilities (Paraskevopoulos & Kirk, 1969), and datasets from Project Talent data collected by Flanagan, Davis, Dailey, Shaycoft, Orr, Goldberg, & Neyman (1964). They also include datasets treated in a monograph (Carroll, 1980a) which focused on relations between psychometric tests and experimental cognitive tasks. A complete list of the datasets (including those added since 1985) is contained in the list of references toward the end of the volume.

Because of various difficulties encountered in the process of analyzing the datasets, it became possible to obtain reasonable solutions for only 461 of them (96.6%). Further characterizations of these 461 datasets are presented here in a series of tables.

Table 4.1 shows their countries of origin, or more precisely, the countries in which the samples were collected. About 76% of the datasets had cases collected in the United States, but about 5% were collected in England, 5% in Canada, 3% in Germany, 3% in Australia, and the remainder (about 8%) in Argentina, Ireland, Italy, Japan, the Netherlands, Norway, Saudi Arabia, Scotland, South Africa, Spain, Sweden, Switzerland, the USSR, and Yugoslavia. Factor analysis has been

Table 4.2. *Frequency distribution, dates of publication, 461 factor-analyzed datasets, by countries of origin*

Yr. pub.	USA			Other countries			All countries		
	f	cf	c%	f	cf	c%	f	cf	c%
1925–29	1	1	0.3	2	2	1.8	3	3	0.7
1930–34	6	7	2.0	1	3	2.7	7	10	2.2
1935–39	19	26	7.4	1	4	3.6	20	30	6.5
1940–44	19	45	12.9	7	11	9.8	26	56	12.1
1945–49	30	75	21.5	2	13	11.6	32	88	19.1
1950–54	21	96	27.5	10	23	20.5	31	119	25.8
1955–59	24	120	34.4	8	31	27.7	32	151	32.7
1960–64	42	162	46.4	5	36	32.1	47	198	43.0
1965–69	66	228	65.3	13	49	43.7	79	277	60.1
1970–74	31	259	74.2	14	63	56.2	45	322	69.8
1975–79	41	300	86.0	34	97	86.6	75	397	86.1
1980–84	42	342	98.0	13	110	98.2	55	452	98.0
1985–87	7	349	100.0	2	112	100.0	9	461	100.0
Mean	1963.2			1967.2			1964.2		
S.D.	14.1			13.8			14.1		
Median	1965.5			1972.0			1966.5		

Note: f = frequency, cf = cumulative frequency, c% = cumulative percent.

a worldwide enterprise, even if initiated in England and much promoted in the USA.

Table 4.2 shows frequency distributions, separately for datasets originating in the USA and in other countries, of the dates of publication, which range from 1927 to 1987, with a mean at 1966 and a standard deviation of 14.1 years. It can hardly be said that the use of factor analysis for the study of cognitive abilities has declined in recent years, as sometimes claimed (Sternberg, 1979; see Royce, 1980); about 40% of the datasets were published in the years 1970–1987.

Table 4.3 shows distributions of the number of cases represented by the datasets, separately for exclusively male, exclusively female, and mixed-sex datasets. A substantial number of datasets, 141 (30.6%), are based on exclusively male samples, while 35 (7.6%) are based on exclusively female samples. The remainder (285, or 61.8%) are based on samples that generally contain approximately equal numbers of males and females.

As the table shows, about 24% of all datasets have fewer than 100 cases, 62% have fewer than 200 cases, and 91% have fewer than 500 cases. Only 16 (less than 4%) have 1000 cases or more. It is generally considered that for confidence in the results, a factor-analytic dataset should be based on at least 100 cases, preferably more. About 76% of the datasets studied here satisfy this criterion.

Table 4.3. *Number of cases in 461 factor-analyzed datasets, for male, female, and mixed-sex datasets*

No. cases	Datasets with males only			Datasets with females only			Datasets with M. & F.			All datasets		
	f	cf	c%	f	cf	c%	f	cf	c%	f	cf	c%
20–39	0	0	0.0	0	0	0.0	22	22	7.7	22	22	4.8
40–59	5	5	3.5	2	2	5.7	21	43	15.1	28	50	10.8
60–79	2	7	5.0	1	3	8.5	16	59	20.7	19	69	15.0
80–99	14	21	14.9	3	6	17.1	27	86	30.2	44	113	24.5
100–119	14	35	24.8	5	11	31.4	36	122	42.8	55	168	36.4
120–139	2	37	26.2	4	15	42.9	18	140	49.1	24	192	41.6
140–159	9	46	32.6	4	19	54.3	24	164	57.5	37	229	49.6
160–179	17	63	44.7	4	23	65.7	12	176	61.7	33	262	56.8
180–199	8	71	50.4	1	24	68.6	14	190	66.7	23	285	61.8
200–219	16	87	61.7	4	28	80.0	25	215	75.4	45	330	71.6
220–239	9	96	68.1	1	29	82.8	6	221	77.5	16	346	75.1
240–259	4	100	70.9	0	29	82.8	6	227	79.6	10	356	77.2
260–279	2	102	72.3	0	29	82.8	6	233	81.8	8	364	79.0
280–299	2	104	73.7	1	30	85.7	8	241	84.5	11	375	81.3
300–319	3	107	75.9	0	30	85.7	2	243	85.3	5	380	82.4
320–339	0	107	75.9	0	30	85.7	4	247	86.7	4	384	83.3
340–359	2	109	77.3	0	30	85.7	3	250	87.7	5	389	84.4
360–379	2	111	78.7	0	30	85.7	0	250	87.7	2	391	84.8
380–399	6	117	83.0	0	30	85.7	2	252	88.4	8	399	86.6
400–419	2	119	84.4	0	30	85.7	5	257	90.2	7	406	88.1
420–439	2	121	85.8	1	31	88.6	6	263	92.3	9	415	90.0
440–459	2	123	87.2	0	31	88.6	1	264	92.6	3	418	90.7
460–479	1	124	87.9	0	31	88.6	1	265	93.0	2	420	91.1
480–499	1	125	88.7	0	31	88.6	0	265	93.0	1	421	91.3
500–999	7	132	93.6	2	33	94.3	15	280	98.2	24	445	96.5
1000–1999	4	136	96.4	1	34	97.1	2	282	98.9	7	452	98.0
2000–2999	0	136	96.4	0	34	97.1	2	284	99.6	2	454	98.5
3000–3999	4	140	99.3	1	35	100.0	0	284	99.6	5	459	99.6
4000–4999	0	140	99.3	0	35	100.0	0	284	99.6	0	459	99.6
5000–5999	0	140	99.3	0	35	100.0	0	284	99.6	0	459	99.6
6000–6999	0	140	99.3	0	35	100.0	1	285	100.0	1	460	99.8
7000–7999	0	140	99.3	0	35	100.0	0	285	100.0	0	460	99.8
8000–8999	1	141	100.0	0	35	100.0	0	285	100.0	1	461	100.0
Total cases	55746			10357			65468			131571		
Mean	395.4			295.9			229.7			285.4		
S.D.	843.9			527.2			479.2			621.7		
Median	198			152			142			162		

Table 4.4. *Mean grade or age of samples, 454 factor-analyzed datasets*[a]

Samples characterized by mean grade				Samples characterized by mean age			
Grade	f	cf	c%	Age	f	cf	c%
0	4	4	1.6	6–11 mos.	1	1	0.5
1	8	12	4.8	12–23 mos.	5	6	2.9
2	5	17	6.8	2–3 yrs.	1	7	3.4
3	5	22	8.8	4–5 yrs.	6	13	6.3
4	11	33	13.3	6–7 yrs.	4	17	8.3
5	13	46	18.4	8–9 yrs.	13	30	14.6
6	15	61	24.5	10–11 yrs.	23	53	25.8
7	8	69	27.7	12–13 yrs.	13	66	32.2
8	8	77	30.9	14–15 yrs.	18	84	41.0
9	19	96	38.6	16–17 yrs.	3	87	42.4
10	10	106	42.6	18–19 yrs.	22	109	53.2
11	34	140	56.2	20–21 yrs.	53	162	79.0
12	15	155	62.2	22–23 yrs.	8	170	82.9
13	22	177	71.1	24–25 yrs.	1	171	83.4
14	63	240	86.1	26–27 yrs.	1	172	83.9
15	2	242	97.2	28–29 yrs.	3	175	85.3
16	5	247	99.2	30–31 yrs.	22	197	96.1
17	2	249	100.0	—	—	—	—
		Median: Grade	11.1	40–41 yrs.	1	198	96.6
				42–43 yrs.	3	201	98.0
				—	—	—	—
				50–51 yrs.	1	202	98.5
				—	—	—	—
				64–65 yrs.	1	203	99.0
				66–67 yrs.	1	204	99.5
				68–69 yrs.	0	204	99.5
				70–71 yrs.	1	205	100.0
						Median: Age	19.0

[a]Data must be considered approximate. Samples of "college" students were arbitrarily assigned Grade 14. Samples of "adults" (not otherwise specified) were assigned Age 30. Seven datasets are not included in this tabulation because of inadequate information or for other reasons.

In the original reports, samples underlying the datasets were characterized in terms of age, grade, or both. For purposes of tabulations here, the datasets were characterized in terms of school grade, where this was given, otherwise in terms of age. Sometimes means and ranges of ages were not stated explicitly; for our purposes, the age for an "adult" sample was arbitrarily coded as 30. Similarly, the grade of a "college" sample was arbitrarily coded as 14 when more explicit information was not given, and a "graduate student" sample was coded as grade 17. Where mean age was not given for samples from military sources, age was coded 21. Table 4.4 shows frequency distributions of mean grades and ages as could best be estimated from the published reports. For the 249 datasets for which grade information was given (about 54% of them), mean grades ranged from 0 (kindergarten or preschool) to 17 (graduate student), with a wide distribution over grades. Mean ages (for 205 datasets for which this could be estimated) ranged all the way from 6 months to 67 years, but the majority of the dataset samples were between ages 10 and 20; these ages would correspond approximately to grades 5 to 15, the range in which the bulk of the datasets classified by grade fall. Thus, it can be said that most of our data on the factor analysis of cognitive abilities come from samples with mean ages falling between 10 and 20.

Table 4.5 reports a classification of the types of samples underlying the 461 datasets, insofar as that information could be determined from the original published reports of studies. A majority (approximately 59%) are classified simply as "normal" samples, or students, from a given age or grade, but there is a wide range of special types of groups, or groups from "normal" populations selected with special constraints.

Table 4.6 reports the types of data available for reanalysis. In the majority of datasets (83.5%), the data consisted of Pearsonian correlation matrices, usually reported to two or three decimal places. (One would prefer at least three decimal places for accurately determining positive semidefiniteness, for example, but two-place accuracy was usually found to be adequate for purposes of analysis.) A small number of datasets consisted of matrices of tetrachoric, Spearman rho, partial, and other types of correlations, and for a further group of datasets, only factor matrices of several types were available.

For nearly all datasets (at least 95%) it appeared from the original reports that the data were complete, i.e., that the correlations or other types of data were not computed from incomplete data (with missing cases).

Table 4.7 reports the number of variables available in the original data, and also the number of variables actually used in our reanalyses. For 368 (80%) of the datasets, the number of variables used in reanalysis was equal to the number originally available. For other datasets, one or more variables were dropped for various reasons, principally: apparent experimental dependence or part-whole relationships, inappropriate variables such as age and sex, and lack of pertinence to the purposes of the study (e.g., measurements of vocational interest, specific knowledge, personality, or motivation). In general, dropping of variables was done conservatively. The number of variables employed in reanalysis ranged from 5 to 91, with a median of 18.6. The distribution was positively skewed.

Table 4.8 reports a somewhat subjective judgmental classification of the datasets in terms of the types of variables employed. The majority of the datasets, roughly 50%, employed what was classified as a relatively narrow sample of cognitive variables, i.e., variables in only one or a few cognitive domains, sometimes with variables also from achievement, personality, and/or interest domains. Relatively few, approximately 20%, included what was regarded as a

Table 4.5. *Types of samples underlying 461
factor-analyzed datasets*

Type of sample	f	%
Students at given age or grade	155	33.6
Normal sample at given age or grade	117	25.4
Military–officers, officer candidates, NCO's	44	9.5
Military–enlisted persons	18	3.9
Students in introductory psychology classes	16	3.5
Above normal in IQ or achievement	12	2.6
Students of a second/foreign language	9	2.0
Adult volunteers	8	1.7
Infants	6	1.3
Persons/students in lower-class areas	6	1.3
Prison inmates	6	1.3
Retarded persons	6	1.3
Deaf persons	4	0.9
Engineering students or apprentices	4	0.9
Students or professionals in education	4	0.9
Students in math. or science courses	4	0.9
Blacks (vs. other ethnic/racial groups)	3	0.7
Low-achieving, low IQ, or "referred" students	3	0.7
Restricted IQ range around 100	3	0.7
Technical high school or vocational college	3	0.7
Brain-damaged individuals; aphasics	2	0.4
Combined normal, remedial/retarded students	2	0.4
Mixture of normal and gifted persons	2	0.4
Mothers or parents of another sample	2	0.4
Remedial reading students	2	0.4
Whites (vs. other ethnic/racial groups)	2	0.4
Architecture students	1	0.2
Children of another sample (parents)	1	0.2
Clerical workers	1	0.2
Commercial students	1	0.2
Disadvantaged children in day care centers	1	0.2
Down's syndrome children	1	0.2
Emotionally disturbed persons	1	0.2
Employed, not otherwise specified	1	0.2
Healthy, recently recovered from head injury	1	0.2
Hispanics	1	0.2
Lobotomized schizophrenics	1	0.2
Music & non-music students	1	0.2
ROTC students	1	0.2
Schizophrenics (non-lobotomized)	1	0.2
Summer make-up students	1	0.2
Not stated, information unavailable	3	0.7
	461	100.0

Table 4.6. *Types of available data for 461
factor-analyzed datasets*

Types of available data	f	%
Pearsonian correlations, to 2 decimals	245	53.1
" " to 3 "	121	26.2
" " to 4 "	9	2.0
" " to 5 "	10	2.2
Total	385	83.5
Tetrachoric correlations, to 2 decimals	10	2.2
" " to 3 decimals	3	0.6
Total	13	2.8
Phi coefficients, to 2 decimals	1	0.2
Spearman rho coefficients, to 2 decimals	3	0.6
Enneachoric coefficients, to 2 decimals	2	0.4
Partial correlations, to 2 decimals	2	0.4
" " to 3 "	1	0.2
First factor residuals, to 3 decimals	1	0.2
Correlation coefficients, all kinds, total	408	88.5
Factor matrices:		
Principal component matrix	1	0.2
Principal factor matrix	7	1.5
Centroid factor matrix	1	0.2
Varimax-rotated factor matrix	15	3.3
Oblique factor matrix and phi	5	1.1
LISREL pattern matrix and phi	3	0.6
Orthogonal factor matrix, not otherwise specified	18	3.9
'Simple summation analysis'	1	0.2
Factor matrix from age-partialled correlations	2	0.4
Factor matrices, all kinds, total	53	11.5

broad sample of cognitive variables, for example, variables in all the domains included in Thurstone's (1938b) early study of "primary abilities." This fact limits the findings with respect to the structure of higher-order domains. On the other hand, the availability of a fairly large number of datasets concerned with narrow domains has the advantage that it makes these datasets more likely to disclose fairly narrow first-order factors, with results useful in distinguishing among such factors.

Similar interpretations can be made from the data of Table 4.9, which reports a judgmental classification of the datasets in terms of the apparent purpose of the factor analysis (or correlational analysis). Only 28 datasets (6.1%) were

Table 4.7. *Number of variables used in original analyses and in reanalyses for 461 factor-analyzed datasets*

Number of variables	Original analyses			Reanalyses		
	f	cf	c%	f	cf	c%
5	1	1	0.2	1	1	0.2
6–7	15	16	3.5	15	16	3.5
8–9	40	56	12.1	42	58	12.6
10–11	31	87	18.9	36	94	20.4
12–13	52	139	30.2	58	152	33.0
14–15	34	173	37.5	37	189	41.0
16–17	28	201	43.6	27	216	46.8
18–19	27	228	49.5	27	243	52.7
20–21	26	254	55.1	26	269	58.4
22–23	17	271	58.8	19	288	62.5
24–25	19	290	62.9	19	307	66.6
26–27	14	304	65.9	19	326	70.7
28–29	13	317	68.7	12	338	73.3
30–31	27	344	74.6	26	364	79.0
32–33	12	356	77.2	14	378	82.0
34–35	17	373	80.9	16	394	85.5
36–37	7	380	82.4	4	398	86.3
38–39	5	385	83.5	7	405	87.9
40–41	10	395	85.7	9	414	89.8
42–43	10	405	87.9	7	421	91.3
44–45	5	410	88.9	2	423	91.8
46–47	3	413	89.6	7	430	93.3
48–49	4	417	90.4	3	433	93.9
50–51	11	428	92.8	6	439	95.2
52–53	4	432	93.7	5	444	96.3
54–55	3	435	94.3	3	447	97.0
56–57	6	441	95.7	4	451	97.8
58–59	6	447	97.0	1	452	98.0
60–61	1	448	97.2	1	453	98.3
62–63	2	450	97.6	2	455	98.7
64–65	1	451	97.8	0	455	98.7
66–67	1	452	98.0	1	456	98.9
68–69	1	453	98.3	1	457	99.1
70–71	2	455	98.7	2	459	99.6
72–73	0	455	98.7	0	459	99.6
74–75	1	456	98.9	0	459	99.6
—	—	—	—	—	—	—
86–87	1	457	99.1	0	459	99.6
—	—	—	—	—	—	—
90–91	2	459	99.6	2	461	100.0
—	—	—	—	—	—	—
98–99	2	461	100.0			
Median		19.6			18.6	

Table 4.8. *Types of variables in 461 factor-analyzed datasets*

Type of variables	f	%
Broad sample of cognitive variables	59	12.8
Ditto, & information, interest, & achvt. vars.	3	0.7
Ditto, & achievement variables	9	2.0
Ditto, & behavior ratios	2	0.4
Ditto, & spelling tests	1	0.2
Ditto, & personality measures	9	2.0
Classification battery (military)	5	1.1
Cognitive variables in two languages	1	0.2
Broad sample of reading tests	7	1.5
Narrow sample of cognitive variables	204	44.3
Ditto, & achievement variables	6	1.3
Ditto, & markers for other cognitive vars	16	3.5
Ditto, & teacher ratings	1	0.2
Ditto, & Bloom taxonomy variables	1	0.2
Ditto, & personality measures	4	0.9
Ditto, & information processing variables	2	0.4
Restricted to standard battery (e.g. WISC, ITPA)	39	8.5
Several IQ & similar standard batteries	7	1.5
Items of 1 or more tests in standard battery	8	1.7
Learning measures	4	0.9
Information-processing variables	19	4.1
Ditto, & various IQ and other variables	17	3.7
Cognitive vars. scored for speed/level/power	1	0.2
Clinical diagnosis battery (personality, aphasia)	2	0.4
Measures of persistence	1	0.2
Language learning & proficiency measures	6	1.3
Infant behaviors	6	1.3
Infant language variables	1	0.2
Mothers' language variables	1	0.2
Broad sample of interest measures	1	0.2
Color wavelengths	1	0.2
Sensitivities to olfactory substances	1	0.2
Cognitive vars. & measures of deafness	1	0.2
Cog. vars. & information-processing vars	2	0.4
Cog. vars. & learning measures	2	0.4
Learning measures & cog. markers	1	0.2
Infor. processing & learning measures	1	0.2
Infor. processing & cognitive markers	1	0.2
Infor. processing & personality vars	1	0.2
Infor. processing & reading vars	1	0.2
Administrative behaviors	1	0.2
Cloze test scores	1	0.2
Speech communication variables	1	0.2
Speech perception variables	1	0.2
Speech characteristics (syntax)	1	0.2
Total	461	100.0

Table 4.9 *461 datasets classified by purpose of analysis[a]*

Purpose of analysis (in original study)	f	%
No factor analysis done	19	4.1
Study of a broad cognitive domain	28	6.1
Study of a restricted cognitive domain	150	32.5
Study tests in a narrow domain, no markers	49	10.6
Study of a particular battery or test	47	10.2
Test factor theory or construct validity	29	6.3
Study speed/level/power problem	5	1.1
Study the ability differentiation hypothesis	14	3.0
Study development of cognitive skills	5	1.1
Study development of 2nd-language abilities	4	0.9
Study correlates of a particular variable	36	7.8
Study correlates of learning measures	11	2.4
Study information-processing variables	32	6.9
Study factor structure of achievement gains	1	0.2
Study factor structure in special groups	26	5.6
Study relations of cog. vars. with personality	3	0.7
Study trait/method interactions	2	0.4
Total	461	100.0

[a]These are my classifications, not those of the authors of the datasets.

classified as coming from studies of the broad domain of cognitive abilities. One hundred fifty (32.5%) were classified as focused on the study of a restricted domain. A study of a particular battery, test, or variable was the concern in 47 datasets; 36 datasets had been collected for studies of correlates of particular variables. Factor structures in particular groups (e.g., retardates, lobotomized patients) were the concern in 26 datasets (5.6%), and the remaining datasets had been collected for various highly special purposes, e.g., the study of the differentiation hypothesis (the hypothesis that factor structure becomes more differentiated as age increases).

Of particular interest to methodologists in factor analysis are various data concerned with the number of first-order factors extracted and accepted for interpretation in source factor analyses vs. the number of first-order factors accepted in the reanalyses made here. Table 4.10 shows a cross-classification, according to these two variables, of the 359 datasets for which such a comparison was possible. (For the remaining datasets, either no original factor analysis had been done, the original factor analysis was not a multiple factor analysis – having been done by Spearmanian tetrad difference techniques – or the factor analysis in the original study was regarded as having been done so incorrectly that the number of factors was meaningless.) In general, the number of factors extracted

Table 4.10. *Number of factors in original analyses versus number accepted in reanalyses of 359 datasets[a] (frequencies)*

No. of factors accepted in reanalysis

No. of factors (orig.)	1	2	3	4	5	6	7	8	9	10	11	12	13	...	19	f	cf	c%
1	1	1	3	—	—	—	1	—	—	—	—	—	—	...	—	6	6	1.6
2	—	10	9	3	—	—	—	—	—	—	—	—	—	...	—	22	28	7.8
3	—	10	32	7	2	—	—	—	—	—	—	—	—	...	—	51	79	22.0
4	1	5	15	23	1	1	2	—	—	—	—	—	—	...	—	48	127	35.4
5	—	2	4	7	22	2	—	1	—	—	—	—	—	...	—	38	165	46.0
6	—	—	8	6	2	15	1	—	—	—	—	—	—	...	—	32	197	54.9
7	—	—	1	3	4	5	8	2	1	1	—	—	—	...	—	25	222	61.8
8	—	2	1	1	4	3	4	8	1	1	—	—	—	...	—	25	247	68.8
9	—	—	1	4	7	1	—	—	3	1	—	—	—	...	—	17	264	73.5
10	—	—	1	3	2	1	4	1	4	5	—	—	—	...	—	21	285	79.4
11	—	—	—	—	2	—	1	1	1	1	—	—	—	...	—	6	291	81.1
12	—	—	1	—	3	7	1	2	1	2	—	—	—	...	—	17	308	85.8
13	—	—	—	2	—	—	—	2	1	—	—	—	1	...	—	6	314	87.5
14	—	—	—	—	2	—	1	—	1	1	1	—	—	...	—	6	320	89.1
15	—	—	—	—	1	1	1	2	1	2	—	—	—	...	—	8	328	91.4
16	—	—	—	—	—	—	3	2	—	—	1	—	—	...	—	6	334	93.0
17	—	—	—	—	—	3	—	3	—	1	—	—	—	...	—	7	341	95.0
18	—	—	—	—	—	1	2	1	1	—	—	—	—	...	—	5	346	96.4
19	—	—	—	—	1	1	1	1	1	—	—	—	—	...	1	6	352	98.1
20	—	—	—	—	1	—	1	—	—	1	—	—	—	...	—	3	355	98.9
21	—	—	—	—	—	—	—	—	—	—	—	—	—	...	—	0	355	98.9
22	—	—	—	—	1	—	—	—	—	—	—	—	—	...	—	1	356	99.2
23	—	—	—	—	—	—	—	—	—	—	—	—	—	...	—	0	356	99.2
24	—	—	—	—	—	—	—	—	1	—	—	—	—	...	—	1	357	99.4
25	—	—	—	—	—	—	1	—	—	—	1	—	—	...	—	2	359	100.
Total	2	30	76	59	55	41	32	26	17	16	3	0	1	...	1	359		
cf	2	32	108	167	222	263	295	321	338	354	357	357	358	...	359	359		
c%	0.6	8.9	30.1	46.5	61.8	73.3	82.2	89.4	94.2	98.6	99.4	99.4	99.7	...	100.	100.		

Mean = 5.17; S.D. = 2.41; Median = 4.7; r = .674

Median = 6.0
Mean = 7.36
S.D. = 4.81

[a] For 102 datasets not tabulated here, a distinct number of factors had not been assigned in the original analysis, for various reasons.

and accepted in the reanalyses was smaller than the number of factors extracted in the original analyses, due mainly to the much more conservative criteria for number of factors employed in the reanalyses. For the 359 datasets compared in Table 4.10, the mean number of first-order factors extracted in the original analyses was 7.36, whereas the mean number accepted in the present reanalyses was 5.17. (For all 461 datasets, the latter figure was 4.93.) For only 128 datasets (35.6%) was the number of factors accepted in reanalysis the same as the number extracted in the original analysis.

A popular but often misleading indicator of the proper number of factors to extract and interpret, usually credited to Guttman and Kaiser (Kaiser, 1960a), is the number of eigenroots of the correlation matrix, with unities on the diagonal, that are greater than unity. Table 4.11 shows a comparison of this variable, for 406 datasets for which this variable was available, with the number of factors finally accepted in our reanalyses. In general, the latter number tends to be smaller than the Kaiser–Guttman number. Nevertheless, for 150 datasets (36.9%), the number of factors accepted was the same as the Kaiser–Guttman number.

One of the number-of-factor indicators that was used as a guide in the present set of reanalyses was the parallel analysis (M–H) criterion proposed by Montanelli and Humphreys (1976). Table 4.12 shows a comparison of the number of factors indicated by this criterion with the number of factors finally accepted in our reanalyses, for the 371 datasets for which such a comparison was possible. (For the remaining datasets, it was impossible to compute the M–H criterion because of various conditions such as singularity of the correlation matrix.) It should be pointed out that for this table, the number of factors by the M–H criterion was taken to be the number of factors (up to the largest factor number for which the difference continued to be positive) for which the eigenroots for correlation matrices with SMC's on the diagonal was greater than corresponding random-data roots, even if the difference was very small. In using the M–H criterion (actually, the version provided by Tucker, personal communication), I was generally inclined to ignore small differences, and there were many datasets for which other criteria indicated a greater number of acceptable factors than was indicated by the M–H criterion. (If it had been available, information on the confidence limits of the M–H random data roots might have been helpful.) Also, it should be mentioned that the M–H criterion, although computed and included in the table, was essentially useless or inapplicable in the case of tetrachoric correlation matrices; its logic makes it applicable only to Pearsonian correlation matrices. As the table shows, the number of factors accepted was the same as that indicated by the M–H criterion in only 127 datasets (34.2%), but was often smaller or larger than this number. The twelve cases where the M–H criterion is shown as indicating 15 or more factors are cases in which the SMC roots continued to be slightly larger than random data roots up to half the number of variables. For such cases, the M–H criterion cannot be a guide; use of a scree plot is advisable.

Table 4.11. *Number of greater-than-unity PC roots versus number of factors accepted in reanalysis[a]* (*frequencies*)

No. of PC roots >1	No. of factors accepted in reanalysis											f	cf	c%
	1	2	3	4	5	6	7	8	9	10	11			
1	4	7	3	—	—	—	—	—	—	—	—	14	14	3.4
2	1	25	22	7	1	—	—	—	—	—	—	56	70	17.2
3	1	12	37	14	8	2	—	—	—	—	—	74	144	35.5
4	—	4	15	29	9	2	2	—	—	—	—	61	205	50.5
5	—	2	10	8	21	4	5	1	1	—	—	52	257	63.3
6	—	—	6	3	9	15	4	1	2	—	—	40	297	73.2
7	—	—	2	1	3	7	6	1	1	—	—	21	318	78.3
8	—	—	1	—	4	7	4	9	3	—	—	28	346	85.2
9	—	—	—	—	4	1	3	4	2	4	—	18	364	89.7
10	—	—	—	—	—	4	7	—	—	2	1	14	378	93.1
11	—	—	—	—	—	—	2	2	—	—	—	4	382	94.1
12	—	—	—	—	—	1	—	2	2	1	—	6	388	95.6
13	—	—	—	—	—	—	1	5	—	1	—	7	395	97.3
14	—	—	—	—	—	1	—	1	—	2	1	5	400	98.5
15	—	—	—	—	—	—	1	—	2	1	—	4	404	99.5
16	—	—	—	—	—	—	—	—	—	—	—	0	404	99.5
17	—	—	—	—	—	—	—	—	1	—	1	2	406	100.0
Total	6	50	96	62	59	44	35	26	14	11	3			Median = 4.4
cf	6	56	152	214	273	317	352	378	392	403	406			Mean = 5.26
c%	1.5	13.8	37.4	52.7	67.2	78.1	86.7	93.1	96.6	99.3	100.			S.D. = 3.16

Mean = 4.74; S.D. = 2.21; Median = 4.3; $r = .813$

[a] For 55 datasets, the number of eigenvalues greater than unity could not be determined, usually because a correlation matrix was not available.

Table 4.12. *Number of factors by the Montanelli–Humphreys (1976) criterion versus number of factors accepted in reanalysis for 371 datasets for which the criterion was obtainable (frequencies)*

No. of factors (M–H)	Number of factors accepted in reanalysis											f	cf	c%
	1	2	3	4	5	6	7	8	9	10	11			
1	6	6	5	1	3	—	—	—	—	—	—	21	21	5.7
2	—	29	19	2	2	2	—	—	—	—	—	54	75	20.2
3	—	6	32	8	5	2	—	2	—	1	—	56	131	35.3
4	—	6	13	19	9	6	3	1	—	1	—	57	180	50.7
5	—	—	5	8	13	6	5	5	1	1	—	44	232	62.5
6	—	—	9	9	10	12	6	2	—	1	—	49	281	75.7
7	—	1	3	4	4	6	5	4	2	1	1	31	312	84.1
8	—	1	—	1	4	3	5	4	4	1	—	23	335	90.3
9	—	—	1	1	2	2	1	—	5	1	—	13	348	93.8
10	—	—	1	—	1	2	1	1	—	1	1	8	356	96.0
11	—	—	—	—	—	—	—	1	—	1	—	2	358	96.5
12	—	—	—	—	—	—	—	—	—	—	—	0	358	96.5
13	—	—	—	—	—	—	—	1	—	—	—	1	359	96.8
14	—	—	—	—	—	—	—	—	—	—	—	0	359	96.8
15	—	—	—	—	1	1	1	1	—	—	—	4	363	97.8
16	—	—	—	—	—	1	—	—	—	—	—	1	364	98.1
⋮														
19	—	—	—	—	—	—	—	1	—	—	—	1	365	98.4
20	—	—	—	—	—	—	—	—	—	1	—	1	366	98.7
⋮														
23	—	—	—	—	—	—	1	—	—	—	—	1	367	98.9
⋮														
26	—	—	—	—	—	—	—	1	—	—	—	1	368	99.2
27	—	—	—	—	—	—	—	—	1	—	—	1	369	99.5
⋮														
30	—	—	—	—	—	—	—	1	1	—	—	2	371	100.0
Total	6	49	87	53	54	43	28	25	14	10	2	371		Median = 4.4
cf	6	55	142	195	249	292	320	345	359	369	371			Mean = 5.18
c%	1.4	14.8	38.3	52.6	67.1	78.7	86.3	93.0	96.8	99.5	100.			S.D. = 3.83

Mean = 4.71; S.D. = 2.22; Median = 4.2; r = .585

Tables 4.10, 4.11, and 4.12 are included here not to justify the number-of-factors criteria employed in our reanalyses, but to show the extent to which our criteria gave number-of-factors values different from those indicated by certain commonly used criteria. I and my assistants also used, mainly through graphical inspection procedures, the scree test proposed by Cattell (1978), but this criterion is difficult to quantify in an unambiguous way, and therefore I have not tried to report how it compared with our criteria. Ultimately, our criteria must be judged mainly in terms of the interpretability of the results. However, in a doctoral dissertation completed by Gullion (1985) with the partial support of this project, a Monte Carlo investigation of number-of-factors criteria showed that the criteria used in this project (i.e., criteria based mainly on the pattern of loadings in a Varimax matrix) tended to predict known values in plasmodes better than other criteria such as the M–H criterion.

It may be of interest to compare the numbers of factors accepted in our reanalyses with the numbers of factors arrived at by Harris (1967) for several datasets from Guilford's studies. Harris used four different factor methods, which he describes in detail, to decide on numbers of factors; none of these methods was identical to the iterated principal factor method used here. Table 4.13 shows the comparison. In most instances the numbers of factors accepted in our reanalyses were identical to, or within the range of, the numbers of factors arrived at by Harris for one or more of his methods. It should be pointed out, however, that Harris defined an "effective common factor" as one that had loadings of .30 or greater on at least two variables in an orthogonal (Varimax) factor matrix. This criterion is less conservative than ours in that it takes no account of whether these loadings were largest for their variables, that is, "salient" by our definition of this term.

Of possible interest in characterizing a dataset is the algebraic mean of correlations, after any reflections of variables have been performed to make all arrays have a positive sum (as was almost always done in our reanalyses). Table 4.14 gives a frequency distribution for this statistic for 322 datasets – most with a number of variables less than 32. (This restriction occurred because the SAS computer package used for analyzing most of the larger datasets did not provide for computing this statistic, whereas it was provided for in the micro-computer program generally used for analyzing the smaller datasets.) In these 322 datasets, the mean correlation was .291, with a standard deviation of .129; the range was from .068 to .71.

Kaiser (1970, 1981; Kaiser & Rice, 1974) has proposed several versions of a Measure of Sampling Adequacy (MSA), intended to measure the degree to which a correlation matrix is appropriate for factor analysis in the sense that the variables adequately sample the one or more factor-analytic domains represented in the matrix. The latest version of this measure was presented in his 1981 paper, and this statistic (the overall MSA for a matrix) was computed, whenever possible, for the datasets analyzed here. (We also computed the statistic for each

Table 4.13. *Comparison of the number of common factors accepted in the present reanalyses with the number of "effective common factors" in Harris's (1967, Table III) reanalyses of data from Guilford's studies*[a]

Reanalyses			No. of effective common factors				No. of factors accepted by Guilford
Dataset designation	No. of factors accepted	Harris's code for matrix	Method (Harris)*				
			A	B	C	D	
GUIL66	11	08	14	11	15	10	15
GUIL18	7	09	14	13	†	13	14
GUIL11	7	12	13	10	7	8	14
GUIL19	4	14	6	6	4	7	9
GUIL21	5	16A	5	5	4	7	11
GUIL22	5	16B	6	6	4	7	9
GUIL23	3	16C	6	6	5	8	10
MERR41	9	22	12	†	7	8	13
GUIL51	7	23	5	5	5	7	13

*Method A: Principal components.
Method B: Alpha factor analysis.
Method C: Jöreskog's (1963) "early procedure."
Method D: "Related to Guttman's (1953) image theory."
In each case, the number of factors was "defined arbitrarily as the number of factors in the derived [Varimax] orthogonal solution for which at least *two* variables have a coefficient of .30 or greater (absolute)."
†According to Harris, "solution did not compute."
[a]Material taken from Harris (1967) reproduced by permission of the Psychometric Society and Chester W. Harris.

variable in each matrix, but results are too voluminous to be shown here.) The statistic has a functional range from 0 to 1; below zero the statistic – a square-root function – becomes an imaginary number indicating, according to Kaiser, unacceptability of the matrix. Table 4.15 shows a distribution of this statistic for 377 datasets for which it could be computed. (It cannot be computed for singular matrices; for various reasons it was also not computed for a number of nonsingular matrices.) Only 123 (32.6%) of these datasets had values of the MSA less than .8; on the average, the value was .768 with a standard deviation of .268. Because of the negative skewness of the distribution, however, the median, .862, is a more informative central tendency value. On the whole, the datasets had clearly acceptable MSA values. Nevertheless, some datasets, even with high overall MSA values, contained one or more *variables* with "unacceptable" MSA values; in general, such variables were not dropped from the matrix for reanalysis unless this was otherwise indicated, e.g., by encountering Heywood cases.

Table 4.14. *Algebraic means of correlations (after any necessary reflections), 322 datasets for which such means were computed*

Algebraic mean r	f	cf	c%
.06–.07	2	2	0.6
.08–.09	14	16	5.0
.10–.11	6	22	6.8
.12–.13	12	34	10.6
.14–.15	19	53	16.5
.16–.17	16	69	21.4
.18–.19	23	92	28.6
.20–.21	11	103	32.0
.22–.23	15	118	36.6
.24–.25	29	147	45.7
.26–.27	21	168	52.2
.28–.29	8	176	54.7
.30–.31	25	201	62.4
.32–.33	22	223	69.3
.34–.35	15	238	73.9
.36–.37	13	251	77.9
.38–.39	10	261	81.1
.40–.41	10	271	84.2
.42–.43	13	284	88.2
.44–.45	6	290	90.1
.46–.47	6	296	91.9
.48–.49	5	301	93.5
.50–.51	2	303	94.1
.52–.53	6	309	96.0
.54–.55	3	312	96.9
.56–.57	2	314	97.5
.58–.59	3	317	98.4
.60–.61	1	318	98.8
.62–.63	1	319	99.1
.64–.65	1	320	99.4
.66–.67	0	320	99.4
.68–.69	1	321	99.7
.70–.71	1	322	100.0

Mdn = .270; Mean = .291; S.D. = .129

Also of possible interest is the distribution of average SMC's (squared multiple correlations) for the 377 datasets for which this statistic could be computed. The frequency distribution of this statistic is shown in Table 4.16. The mean is .489 with a standard deviation of .137; the range is from .16 to .93. Datasets for which this statistic is very low have generally low correlations and tend to present

Table 4.15. *Frequency distribution of Kaiser's (1981) measure of sampling adequacy (MSA), for 377 datasets for which MSA was computable*

MSA	f	cf	c%
.00 or Unacceptable	29	29	7.7
.04–.07	1	30	8.0
.08–.11	1	31	8.2
.12–.15	1	32	8.5
.16–.19	1	33	8.8
.20–.23	1	34	9.0
.24–.27	2	36	9.5
.28–.31	0	36	9.5
.32–.35	2	38	10.1
.36–.39	1	39	10.3
.40–.43	4	43	11.4
.44–.47	4	47	12.5
.48–.51	2	49	13.0
.52–.55	3	52	13.8
.56–.59	5	57	15.1
.60–.63	3	60	15.9
.64–.67	10	70	18.6
.68–.71	18	88	23.3
.72–.75	14	102	27.1
.76–.79	21	123	32.6
.80–.81*	14	137	36.3
.82–.83	16	153	40.6
.84–.85	22	175	46.4
.86–.87	27	202	53.6
.88–.89	33	235	62.3
.90–.91	38	273	72.4
.92–.93	52	325	86.2
.94–.95	13	338	89.7
.96–.97	38	376	99.7
.98–.99	1	377	100.0

Mdn = .862; Mean = .768; S.D. = .268
*Note change of class interval here.

greater difficulties in factorization, because the factors are poorly defined, than datasets for which it is at least of moderate value.

The general plan for rotating primary factor axes called for use of the Tucker–Finkbeiner DAPPFR (Direct Artificial Personal Probability Function Rotation) procedure whenever the primary factors were significantly correlated. Table 4.17 reports the frequency with various rotational procedures were actually used. For a substantial number of datasets, the early version (1981) of the Tucker–Finkbeiner procedure was used; the later version did not become

Table 4.16. *Frequency distribution of average squared multiple correlations (SMC's) for 377 datasets for which SMC was computable*

Average SMC	f	cf	c%
.16–.19	3	3	0.8
.20–.23	2	5	1.3
.24–.27	20	25	6.6
.28–.31	12	37	9.8
.32–.35	38	75	19.9
.36–.39	34	109	28.9
.40–.43	38	147	39.0
.44–.47	24	171	45.4
.48–.51	58	229	60.7
.52–.55	50	279	74.0
.56–.59	30	309	82.0
.60–.63	12	321	85.1
.64–.67	20	341	90.5
.68–.71	17	358	95.0
.72–.75	8	366	97.1
.76–.79	3	369	97.9
.80–.83	5	374	99.2
.84–.87	0	374	99.2
.88–.91	2	376	99.7
.92–.95	1	377	100.0

Mdn = .442; Mean = .489; S.D. = .137

available until the project had been underway for some time, and it was not deemed expedient or necessary to re-rotate these datasets by the later procedure. For most of the DAPPFR rotations, the two-sided case was employed, permitting both positive and negative salients if the simple structure so demanded. Occasionally, however, the one-sided case was selected if this produced what appeared to be a more viable correlation matrix among first-order factors. As the table shows, a few datasets did not require rotation, either because they yielded only one factor or because the primary factors appeared not to be significantly correlated. Also, there were a few instances in which oblique rotations other than the Tucker–Finkbeiner DAPPFR procedure were employed because they appeared to produce more viable second-order factors.

Table 4.18 shows a frequency distribution of Kaiser's (1974) overall Index of Simplicity for the 455 rotated factor matrices with more than one factor. The index indicates the degree to which each variable in the rotated factor matrix tends, on the average, to measure one and only one factor. (These indices of

Table 4.17. *Type of rotational procedure employed at the first order, 461 factor-analyzed datasets*

Type of rotational procedure	f	%
DAPPFR*, 1981 version, 2-sided case	142	30.8
" , 1984 " , 2-sided case	207	44.9
" , " " , 1-sided case	50	10.8
Total	399	86.6
Promax, $k = 2$	9	2.0
Procrustes	1	0.2
Graphical starting from Varimax	2	0.4
Graphical starting from 2-sided DAPPFR*	3	0.7
Graphical starting from 1-sided DAPPFR*	2	0.4
Orthogonal graphical based on Varimax	2	0.4
(Orthogonal) Varimax not further rotated	36	7.8
Principal factor not rotated ($m = 1$)	6	1.3
Author's oblique rotation accepted	1	0.2

*Direct artificial personal probability function rotation (Tucker & Finkbeiner, 1981; Tucker, personal communication)

simplicity were also computed for individual variables, available for consideration in the interpretation of their factorial compositions.)

The most important results of this phase of the project are represented in the factors that were produced by the reanalyses. Table 4.19 presents a summary of the numbers of factors accepted at the first, second, and third orders, for all 461 datasets that were reanalyzed. There were 45 datasets which produced no second-order factors; i.e., the first-order factor matrix, if it had more than one factor, was left orthogonal. Only 36 datasets were analyzed to produce a third-order factor. In all, 2272 first-order factors, 542 second-order factors, and 36 third-order factors were produced, a total of 2850 factors. It should be remembered that the order at which a factor appears is not an intrinsic characteristic of the factor; rather, it is a function of the way in which the set of variables underlying the analysis is composed. For example, if a set of variables contained only one marker for each of a number of factors that might otherwise be analyzed as first-order factors, it is possible that the only factor determined from the matrix would emerge at the first order, whereas if the set of variables contained several markers for each of a number of factors, these factors would emerge at the first order and the factor reflecting their correlations would emerge at the second order.

The 2850 "token" factors counted in Table 4.19, of course, are not all different; the next problem to be addressed was that of determining how many distinctly different factors are represented among them, preparatory to interpreting them as basic dimensions of individual differences in cognitive abilities.

Table 4.18. *Frequency distribution of Kaiser's (1974) index of simplicity for the 455 rotated factor matrices with more than one factor*

Index of simplicity	f	cf	c%
.46–.47	1	1	0.2
.48–.49	1	2	0.4
...	...	...	...
.58–.59	1	3	0.7
.60–.61	4	7	1.5
.62–.63	1	8	1.8
.64–.65	14	22	4.8
.66–.67	8	30	6.6
.68–.69	23	53	11.6
.70–.71	28	81	17.8
.72–.73	30	111	24.4
.74–.75	37	148	32.5
.76–.77	15	163	35.8
.78–.79	28	191	42.0
.80–.81	59	250	54.9
.82–.83	33	283	62.2
.84–.85	6	289	63.5
.86–.87	28	317	69.7
.88–.89	41	358	78.7
.90–.91	28	386	84.8
.92–:93	20	406	89.2
.94–.95	10	416	91.4
.96–.97	29	445	97.8
.98–.99	10	455	100.0

Mdn = .805; Mean = .817; S.D. = .095

On completing the reanalysis of each dataset, each factor was given a tentative name reflecting the possible interpretation of that factor. These names were assigned by inspecting the names and also, in many cases, the descriptions of the variables having high loadings on the factor, in contrast to variables having low or vanishing loadings on the factor. Sometimes, factor names assigned by authors were used, but in many cases, names were assigned in the light of names and interpretations generally accepted in the factor-analytic literature. These tentative names were assigned in order to make the task of assessing the mass of results more manageable than it might otherwise have been. They were also assigned with an eye to giving apparently similar factors the same name throughout the numerous datasets. These names and interpretations were not regarded as fixed and unchangeable; in later phases of the work many of these names were changed as closer looks were taken at the variables grouped under

Table 4.19. *Number of factors at first, second, and third orders, 461 factor-analyzed datasets*

First order					Second order				
No. of factors	No. of datasets f	cf	c%	Total factors	No. of factors	No. of datasets f	cf	c%	Total factors
1	6	6	1.3	6	0	45	45	9.8	0
2	51	57	12.4	102	1	311	356	77.2	311
3	101	158	34.3	303	2	87	443	96.1	174
4	72	230	49.9	288	3	16	459	99.6	48
5	68	298	64.6	340	4	1	460	99.8	4
6	53	351	76.1	318	5	1	461	100.0	5
7	42	393	85.2	294					—
8	29	422	91.5	232					542
9	17	439	95.2	153				Mdn = 1.1	
10	16	454	98.7	160					
11	4	458	99.6	44	Third order				
12	0	458	99.6	0					
13	1	459	99.8	13	0	425	425	92.2	0
...	...	...	...	...	1	36	461	100.0	36
19	1	461	100.0	19					—
				——					36
				2272					
			Mdn = 4.5						

Summary
No. of first-order factors   2272
No. of second-order factors   542
No. of third-order factors   36
                              ——
Total   2850

a given factor. These "closer looks" involved detailed examination of the test instructions, test items, scoring procedures, administration times, and other things associated with each variable.

A further step was to group the factors into broad domains or classes. The results of this step are shown in Table 4.20, which lists 19 such domains, roughly in order of their relevance to the study of cognitive abilities. That is, the first nine of these groups are regarded as representing true cognitive abilities in the sense of being relatively fixed, long-term attributes of individuals respecting the kinds of cognitive tasks they can and cannot perform, or can perform with varying degrees of success, at a particular stage of development. Group 10 represents a set of abilities having to do with sensory processes; they are hardly "cognitive"

Table 4.20. *Number of factors by domain[a]*

Domain	No. of factors	cf
1) General abilities	459	459
(includes factors interpreted as *g*, *Gf*, *Gc* at 1st, 2nd, and 3rd orders, as well as miscellaneous factors of cognitive development, style, and learning ability)		
2) Reasoning abilities	241	700
(includes 91 factors interpreted as General Reasoning, 30 ” ” ” Verbal Reasoning, 25 ” ” ” Induction, 27 ” ” ” Quantitative Reasoning, 7 ” ” ” Syllogistic Reasoning, 5 ” ” ” Classification Ability)		
3) Abilities in the domain of language behavior	367	1067
(includes 190 factors interpreted as Verbal Comprehension, 20 ” ” ” Language Development, 14 ” ” ” Spelling Ability, 10 ” ” ” Phonetic Coding, 15 ” ” ” Vocabulary, distinct from Verbal Comprehension)		
4) Memory abilities	251	1318
(includes 43 factors interpreted as Associative Memory, 72 ” ” ” Memory Span, 17 ” ” ” General Memory)		
5) Visual perception abilities	405	1723
(includes 128 factors interpreted as Space, 106 ” ” ” Perceptual Speed, 35 ” ” ” Closure Speed, 25 ” ” ” Cognition of Figural Relations, 18 ” ” ” Visualization, 12 ” ” ” Closure Flexibility)		
6) Auditory perception abilities	42	1765
(includes 19 factors interpreted as Pitch Discrimination, 5 ” ” ” Auditory Closure)		
7) Number facility	81	1846
(This comprises only a single factor type)		
8) Mental speed abilities	95	1941
(includes 36 factors interpreted as General Mental Speed, 16 ” ” ” Simple Reaction Time, 10 ” ” ” Semantic Comparison Speed)		
9) Abilities in producing and retrieving words, ideas, and figural creations	252	2193
(includes 66 factors interpreted as Ideational Fluency, 37 ” ” ” General Fluency, 25 ” ” ” Word Fluency, 22 ” ” ” Originality,		

Table 4.20 (*cont.*)

Domain	No. of Factors	cf
15 " " " Associational Fluency,		
15 " " " Figural Fluency,		
9 " " " Adaptive Flexibility,		
14 " " " Expressional Fluency,		
11 " " " Naming Facility)		
10) Sensory abilities (thresholds, acuity)	34	2227
(includes 4 factors interpreted as Auditory Hearing Threshold		
10 " " " pertaining to visual acuity and color sensitivity,		
6 " " " pertaining to olfactory thresholds)		
11) Attention and concentration abilities	24	2251
(includes 9 factors interpreted as Attention & Concentration,		
7 " " " Carefulness, Attention to Detail)		
12) Abilities pertaining to interpersonal behavior	7	2258
(7 factors derived from tests of interpretation of facial expressions, gestures, etc.)		
13) Factors pertaining to knowledge of different subject-matters	72	2330
(includes 22 factors interpreted as Mechanical Knowledge,		
10 " " " Knowledge of English Usage, Spelling, etc.,		
12 " " " Knowledge of Mathematics		
11 " " " Technical Information)		
14) Factors pertaining to school achievement	32	2362
(includes 18 different factors, of which the most frequently occurring was a General School Achievement factor)		
15) Factors whose interpretation was doubtful or postponed	354	2716
(Includes such factors at 1st, 2nd & 3rd orders, plus 75 factors that were highly specific doublets or triplets)		
16) Psychomotor and physical ability factors	87	2803
(includes 15 factors interpreted as Finger Dexterity,		
10 " " " Psychomotor Coordination,		
11 " " " Writing Speed)		
17) Interest and motivation factors	12	2815
(Includes factors for different domains such as art and music, biology and health, science, business)		
18) Personality and affective factors	17	2832
19) Administrative behavior factors	9	2841
20) Educational & social status background factors	9	2850

[a]In this table, a "factor" is a dimension identified in a particular study, and is thus analogous to a *token*, not a *type*.

abilities in any true sense of the term. That they appear at all in our analyses is a result of the fact that some of the datasets included measurements of these sensory processes (usually in terms of absolute and difference thresholds). Group 11, attention and concentration abilities, includes a small set of abilities whose status as "cognitive" is at least debatable. Group 12 comprises a small number of abilities pertaining to interpersonal behavior, and again, their status as cognitive abilities is questionable. They need to be considered, however, as possible aspects of "social intelligence."

Groups 13 and 14 might have been classed together as a single group; the first reflects tested or otherwise observed *learned knowledge* of a subject matter – not necessarily acquired in school; the second reflects *school achievement* either in general or in a given subject matter area. They seem not to represent true cognitive skills, even though high knowledge and achievement in a given area might come about through, and accompany, the development of cognitive skills.

Group 15 represents a fairly large number of factors whose preliminary naming and interpretation could not readily be done, with reasonable confidence, from inspection of results at a superficial level. Their naming and interpretation was to be postponed until such time as more detailed examination of results could be carried out. This group also includes a number of factors that were obviously doublets or triplets resulting from highly specific variance entering the common factor space. It was thought probable that few if any of these specific factors would prove to be of importance as reflecting basic cognitive skills, but the possible importance of some of them could not be ruled out.

Group 16 comprises psychomotor and physical ability factors that were found in the datasets because of the inclusion of various psychomotor and physical ability variables in test batteries. Some of them may reflect cognitive abilities. Others, such as Writing Speed, may be regarded as traits with a possibly neurophysiological basis that nevertheless interact with various cognitive tasks, like those in Group 9 where subjects are often tested by asking them to produce responses as rapidly as possible in writing.

Groups 17, 18, and 19 are small groups of factors that are not regarded as cognitive skills, but that nevertheless appear in the reanalyses because measures of interest, motivation, or personality were sometimes included in datasets along with measures of cognitive abilities. They were not of interest in the present project and thus very few of the many studies of these types of variables – particularly personality variables – were included our datasets.

Group 20 consists of educational and social status background factors that appeared in a few datasets. There has been a long-standing interest in why they are correlated with cognitive ability factors.

The 2850 token factors identified in these reanalyses constitute a rich database for the further examination of cognitive abilities and their factorial structure that is the concern of subsequent chapters in this volume.

PLAN FOR PRESENTATION OF DETAILED RESULTS

Upon the compilation and analysis of the data from this project, I had to face the problem of how best to present the voluminous findings in a coherent, usable, and intelligible way. Obviously it was not possible to present all results in complete form in this volume. The main detailed results of the study are presented in the form of hierarchical factor matrices, one for each dataset, recorded on three high-density disks that are available with the volume (see Appendix B).

There remained, however, the problem of how selected results could be organized for presentation in this volume. The solution to this problem that I have selected involves the preparation of a number of separate chapters (Chapters 5 through 15), each devoted to a particular domain of abilities. In each of these chapters, a series of factorially distinct abilities are described. For each such ability, there is discussion of (1) the identification of the ability in factorial and other studies, (2) typical tests and variables that tend to be saliently loaded on the ability, and (3) interpretation of the ability in cognitive information-processing terms and knowledge bases, to the extent that that may be possible. On occasion, chapters also comment on: (4) information on life-span development and changes in the ability; and (5) information on genetic and environmental determinants of the ability, insofar as they are known. Space and time limitations, however, have precluded giving as much of this type of information as might be available.

In view of the fact that abilities vary in their generality (as reflected in the factorial order level at which they typically appear), two options present themselves: (1) the abilities could be presented in order from general to more specific, or (2) the abilities could be presented in order from specific to general, that is, considering primary or first-order factors first, followed by presentation of higher-order broad abilities. I have selected the second of these options, for several reasons. First, this order corresponds to the manner in which abilities at first- and higher-orders are actually identified in the procedures of exploratory factor analysis that have been used here. Second, the higher-order factors cannot be well understood unless one takes account of the nature of lower-order abilities whose intercorrelations lead to the identification of such factors. Third, there are many problems in the identification of higher-order abilities, not the least of which is the fact that the nature of a higher-order ability identified in a particular study is critically dependent on the composition of the battery of variables in that study. As will be seen, presently available data do not yet permit precise differentiation of higher-order abilities. It seems best, therefore, to defer discussion of higher-order factors until lower-order factors have been thoroughly set forth. That discussion is found in Chapter 15. Chapters 5–14 treat primary or first-order abilities in a number of domains.

It should be recognized that the "order" of a factor is somewhat arbitrary and dependent on the manner in which it is identified in a particular study. For example, it is sometimes possible to isolate extremely narrow factors by designing the battery to contain only a number of highly similar variables; Saunders' (1960a,b) studies of items in subtests of the WAIS are illustrations of this. At the same time, certain factors have come to be regarded as typically "primary" in nature, while others are recognized as being of higher-order or broader character. These conventions are observed in the chapters to follow. (See Chapter 15 for discussion of *order* and *stratum* as bases for classifying factors.)

It should also be recognized that the assignment of factors to domains is to a considerable extent arbitrary; the assignments made here are often simply for convenience.

PART II

The Identification and Description of Cognitive Abilities

5   *Abilities in the Domain of Language*

... language acquisition and reading ability may indeed be regarded as basic; they enhance potential in the sense of capability to learn.

Israel Scheffler (1985)

This survey of "primary" or first-order factors of cognitive ability found in the factor-analytic literature begins by considering factors interpreted as lying in the broad domain of language.The line between this domain and many others, such as that of reasoning, is difficult to draw. Many factors appear to depend on both language abilities and other abilities, such as reasoning and memory. I consider here the factors that appear to draw more on language abilities than other abilities. Furthermore, the tests loaded on any of a great many factors presuppose the subject's knowledge of his or her native language, either in its spoken form or – much more frequently – in its written, printed form, either in understanding instructions for these tests or in actually responding to the tasks presented in the tests. This very fact complicates the interpretation of any intercorrelations among factors and of any higher-order factors that are isolated in the analysis of test batteries (see Chapter 15). But it also justifies the consideration of factors in the language domain before all others, because it leads to establishing a kind of baseline for the consideration of those other factors.

Even the language domain itself is complex, for as this chapter shows, there are many different aspects of knowing and using a language. There is, however, a sense in which all language abilities tend to cohere, separately from other abilities. Many tests, measurements, and observational techniques are designed to tap directly the individual's competence and performance in that individual's native language, with only minimal reliance on other kinds of ability. If we take a developmental perspective, we note that a good portion of an individual's very early life is spent in learning to speak and understand the spoken form of the native language, that is, in acquiring an implicit knowledge of the structure and vocabulary of that language. Individuals differ in their rates of language acquisition, but their common experience is to develop by the age of about five years what can roughly be characterized as the competence of a "native speaker." In the normal child, this kind of language development takes precedence over the acquisition of skills in reading, writing, and certain more specialized skills. Individuals tend to become differentiated in levels of those other skills only at ages beyond the age of five or so. By the time of adulthood, however, the individual differences in various specialized language skills can become quite pronounced, and substantially independent of each other. At least in the language domain, it can be expected that abilities tend to become differentiated with age, as was first suggested by Garrett (1938).

Conceptually, these trends can be depicted graphically. Figure 5.1 presents a kind of raised umbrella structure. From the base of this structure, there is a single pole, rising vertically, that at its base represents the idea that language abilities are minimal, and minimally differentiated, in the earliest years of development, but that with advancing age, more and more abilities become differentiated, represented by the various "spokes" that depart from the central pole.

The spokes point in an upward direction, though at various angles to each other. Towards the top of the structure, we can imagine a surface on which the spokes are projected, and on which each spoke is labeled as a particular kind of skill or ability (the labels being two-character designations for factors, in the format used throughout this volume).

As depicted in the figure, spokes that lean towards the left represent abilities particularly concerned with oral language – listening and speaking. Spokes that point toward the right represent abilities concerned with written and printed language – reading and writing. The front-back dimension of the figure has meaning too: spokes leaning towards the front concern receptive skills – listening and reading, while spokes that point toward the back represent productive skills – speaking and writing.

But how does this relate to factor-analytic results? A factor isolated in a particular study can be thought of as representing a latent trait in which individuals differ, in this case principally with respect to the levels they attain along a particular spoke of the diagram. The spokes represent latent traits; their angular separations represent the degrees to which they are different. Spokes that are close together would represent highly correlated latent traits; widely separated spokes would represent latent traits that tend to be less correlated. The fact that all the spokes tend to be clustered in a fairly circumscribed way is intended to suggest that all language abilities tend to be rather highly correlated; their general degree of correlation can be attributed to the influence of a general higher-order factor of language ability or general language development. In concrete terms, individuals tend to differ – certainly over different ages, and also within groups of the same age – in general level of language development. But there is also some specialization of abilities: some individuals are specialized in speaking skills, others are specialized in reading and writing skills, and so on. Depiction of these skills as "spokes" in the language domain structure is intended to suggest this specialization of skills.

In actuality, of course, matters are not at all as simple as Figure 5.1 might suggest. Even though a series of factors might be cross-identified from different factorial studies as representing the same skill or latent trait, e.g., vocabulary

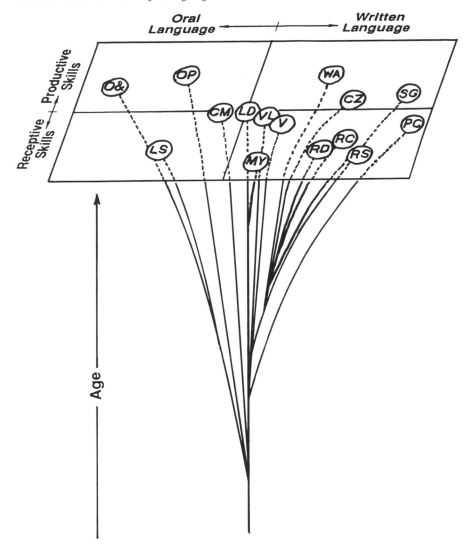

Figure 5.1. Conceptual representation of factors in the language ability domain (see text for explanation).

knowledge (lexical knowledge, VL), the actual composition of the factors might vary due to differential characteristics of the tests or measurements used to define those factors. Two vocabulary tests, for example, might be different in that one might have a higher proportion of literary words and another might have a higher proportion of scientific and technical words. The spokes of Figure 5.1 are to be thought of as centroids of closely related factors; the grouping of factors into such centroids has a certain arbitrary character. Also, no firm conclusions are to be drawn from the angular separations of the spokes in the figure as to the expected correlations of the factors. The correlations between factors in actual data will depend upon many characteristics of the data: the compositions of the test batteries, the nature of the samples, and so on. Figure 5.1 is intended to represent the domain of language abilities only in a conceptual, topological, non-metric way. At the same time the various labeled spokes of the figure represent factors, or actually clusters of factors, that appear to be identifiable in this domain. This chapter presents the evidence found for the identifiability and separability of these factors.

Each factor is dealt with in a separate section of the chapter, with discussion of the nature of the factor and the kinds of tests or other measurements that contribute to its definition. Special attention is devoted to the question of what evidence there is for the separability of each factor from others, or what may be called the *divergent validity* of each factor, at different stages of language development. However, the chapter deals only incidentally with problems of correlations among factors, since this matter will be taken up in a later chapter (Chapter 15).

In arriving at the clusters of factors presented here, there was an iterative process of classification and reclassification. Initially (as shown in Table 4.2) some 367 factors had been classified in the domain of language behavior. Reconsideration of these factors in terms of the types of measures that defined them and the kinds of skills, knowledges, and processes that they seemed to tap resulted in a refined classification that assigned 371 factors to 18 clusters. Some of the original 367 factors were assigned to other domains, and a few factors initially classified in other domains were brought into the language ability domain. In this chapter, the reasoning underlying this classification is discussed as each cluster is taken up.

Note that the language ability domain was defined to exclude fluency of idea and language production, a domain considered in Chapter 10.

LANGUAGE DEVELOPMENT (LD) FACTORS

Table 5.1 is the first of a large number of similar tables that appear in this and subsequent chapters. Some introductory remarks about the organization and intended use of such tables are in order.

Each table lists a series of factors that for one reason or another are thought most conveniently discussed together. The factors are *tokens*, not types, in the sense that each factor comes from a particular dataset and is thus only a particular instance of the factor type being discussed. The dataset from which each token factor comes is indicated by the standard 5-, 6-, or 7-character code used throughout this survey, and for convenience, further information about the dataset is given – date of the publication from which it comes, the code for the country in which the sample was collected, the approximate mean age of the sample, a code for the type of sample, and a code for whether the sample included only males (1), only females (2), or both males and females (3). (A list of codes for tables such as Table 5.1 is found in Appendix A. A complete list of datasets is to be found included in the References.) The particular factor being referred to is indicated by its number in the master hierarchical factor matrix for that dataset. The organization of each such hierarchical matrix is described in Chapter 3, and these hierarchical matrices are contained in Appendix B in the form of files on high-density floppy disks included with the volume. A final column in each table gives information on what higher-order factors (if any) dominate the factor, and on what other factors (if any) in the same domain occur in the dataset. This information is intended to be useful in assessing how distinct each factor is from other factors in the domain. The reader is encouraged, however, to consult the pertinent hierarchical matrix for detailed information as to the size of factor loadings and the identification of variables that have salient loadings on the given factor and other factors. I attempt to highlight pertinent details of this sort in my discussion of each factor, but due to limitations of space, many details will remain unmentioned. Space limitations also preclude giving detailed information on all of the more than 10,000 variables used in datasets studied here. Interested readers are advised to consult original sources and relevant reference materials, but alas, original sources are not always as helpful as might be desired.

As suggested, the token factors listed in a given table are regarded as belonging to one or more factor "types" – in any case a very small number of them – that represent a distinct cluster of abilities that are the same or closely similar throughout the table. For convenience in assessing the age range over which a given factor type occurs, the token factors are listed in order of the approximate mean age of the sample. (It should be borne in mind that many samples cover a considerable range of ages.) There is no assurance, of course, that factors derived from young samples are necessarily the same as factors derived from older samples, or still less that such factors would be found to be developmentally constant in longitudinal data. (There is in fact very little evidence about the longitudinal constancy of cognitive factors in general, apart from some materials about the constancy of gross measures such as IQ.) Nevertheless, the token factors grouped in a given table are regarded as being to a large extent similar in content and/or process aspects throughout the age range considered.

These introductory remarks having been made, we can now consider Table 5.1 in particular.

In the process of sorting and classifying the factors in the language ability domain, it became immediately evident that a broad distinction should be made between factors tapping general language development as such and factors that involved printed tests requiring reading skills in addition to language development. Developers of tests and measurements used in factor-analytic batteries have unfortunately paid very little attention to distinguishing language skills

Table 5.1. *49 Language Development (LD) factors in 47 datasets arranged in order of approximate mean age of sample*

Dataset	Date	C'y code	Age	Sample code	M/F code	Factor no.	Remarks (higher-order factors; others related)
RICH32	'39	U	12 mo.	N	3	3	1:2G
RICH33	'39	U	18 mo.	N	3	4	1:2G
PARA01	'69	U	3	1	3	2	1:2G
PARA02	'69	U	4	1	3	2	1:2G
WIEB11	'80	U	4	O	1	3	1:2G
WIEB12	'80	U	4	O	2	6	1:2G
WISL01	'69	U	4	8	3	2	1:2G
LUNZ11	'76	E	5	1	3	2	1:2G
PARA03	'69	U	5	1	3	4	Poorly defined;1:2G
TAYL31	'75	C	5	1	3	2	1:2C;7:PC
TAYL32	'75	C	5	1	3	2	1:2G
HUEF01	'67	U	6	6	3	2	1:GD;2:ITPA subtests
"	"	"	"	"	"	5	WISC subtests
MCCA21	'66	U	6	1	3	2	1:2G;3:IPD
PARA04	'69	U	6	1	3	4	1:2G
PARA05	'69	U	6	1	3	2	1:2C;4:PC
REYN01	'79	U	6	1	3	3	2:Symb.Manip.
STAN61	'84	U	6	6	3	4	—
JONE31	'49	U	7	1	3	2	1:2G
PARA06	'69	U	8	1	3	2	1:2G
CUMM01	'79	C	9	8	3	3	1:2D;2:O&
JONE32	'49	U	9	1	3	2	1:2G;4:V
NAGL01	'87	U	9	Z	3	2	1:2G
NAGL02	'87	U	9	W	3	3	1:2G
NAGL03	'87	U	9	6	3	3	1:2G
PARA07	'69	U	9	1	3	3	Poorly defined; 1:2G
UNDH01	'76	O	9	1	3	8	1:2G
KEIT21	'87	U	10	7	3	3	1:3G;2:2C;4:RC
PARA08	'69	U	10	1	3	2	Poorly defined;1:2G
PROG01	'73	U	10	J	1	3	1:2G
WILL11	'75	C	10	*	1	2	1:2G
WOOD15	'77	U	10	1	3	2	1:2G;3:RC
WRIG01	'39	U	10	1	3	3	1:2G
JONE33	'49	U	11	1	3	3	1:2G
VANH01	'75	U	11	R	3	3	1:2G
JONE34	'49	U	13	1	3	2	1:2G
STOR11	'66	U	14	8	3	4	1:2G;9:VL
STOR13	'66	U	14	7	3	8	1:2G
WOOD17	'77	U	17	1	3	2	1:2G;4:SG
SAUN03	'59	U	18	6	1	4	1:2G
"	"	"	"	"	"	5	5 = Similarities (specific)
SNOW12	'77	U	19	6	3	4	1:2G
SCHU01	'80	U	20	1	3	2	—
SPRA11	'66	U	27	R	3	2	1:2G
STAN21	'83	A	30	U	3	4	Poorly defined;1:2U

Table 5.1 (*cont.*)

Dataset	Date	C'y code	Age	Sample code	M/F code	Factor no.	Remarks (higher-order factors; others related)
WILL12	'75	C	30	Y	3	2	1:2G
ROYC11	'76	C	40	4	3	10	1:2G
SCHU00	'62	U	40	4	3	3	2:RC;6:Stim.Equiv.
SCHU02	'80	U	64	1	3	1	—

[a]See Appendix A for codes. In a few cases, the classifications of factors shown here were preliminary and may not agree with the final classifications shown in the tables of Appendix B.

according to the fourfold classification (listening, speaking, reading, writing) that has been traditional in measuring proficiencies in a second or foreign language. Test developers seem to have reasoned that because subjects beyond a certain age can be assumed to possess reading ability, their language skills could be effectively assessed with tests using the written (printed) form of the native language. It has often been noted that the most frequently found factor in factor-analytic studies is a "verbal" (V) factor. On close examination, however, these many "verbal" factors are in truth "reading ability" factors – at least in part. In the typical vocabulary test, for example, the words are presented as printed stimuli; a subject has to be able to recognize words in printed form in order to respond correctly. In actuality, the subject not responding correctly may indeed know the word in its oral form, and be able to respond correctly if the word is presented in a listening vocabulary test. For this and other reasons, it was decided to classify factors in the language ability domain with respect to whether they required reading ability. Factors measuring general language development but not requiring reading ability, or at least best represented by measurements not requiring reading ability, were classified as language development (LD) factors and listed in Table 5.1.

A few general observations about Table 5.1 may be made. Language development, it appears, is measurable from the earliest to the most advanced age – from 12 months, in dataset RICH32, to at least age 64, in SCHU02. In RICH32, it is measured most prominently by the variables "says 'bye-bye' and 'hello'" and "says three words"; in SCHU02, it is measured most strongly by the WAIS subtests Similarities and Vocabulary, but also by scores on the Raven Matrices test. (SCHU02 was a small dataset, with only eight variables selected in such a way as not to permit a second-order factor to appear. Thus this LD factor is confounded with a general intelligence factor.)

In nearly every case, the LD factor is dominated by a second-order or even a third-order factor, usually interpreted as a general intelligence factor (designated as 2G or 3G). By "dominated," we mean that the factor has a salient loading on a factor in the higher-order domain, and that on the average, its variables have substantial loadings on the higher-order domain factor. Language development, that is, tends to be accompanied by development in other cognitive abilities. In the few instances where a factor is not dominated by a higher-order factor, this is probably a result of the composition of the battery and/or of the sample such that a higher-order factor did not appear.

In most instances, the LD factor was clearly differentiated from cognitive abilities outside the language ability domain, such as factors from reasoning, space, memory, and perceptual speed domains. (This conclusion comes from consideration of the underlying hierarchical matrices; the evidence for it could not be included in the table, because of space limitations.)

Largely because of inadequacies in the test batteries, the LD factor could not be well differentiated from other factors in the language ability domain. There were, however, several datasets that differentiated LD from a reading comprehension (RC) factor; this was true of datasets KEIT21, WOOD15, and (for an aphasic sample) SCHU00. In STOR11, the factor was differentiated from a factor that contrasted lexical knowledge with expressional fluency, and in WOOD17 it was differentiated from a language usage and orthography (SG) factor.

Often the LD factor was measured most prominently by native-language vocabulary tests that were given in oral or pictorial form not requiring reading skills. Such tests were found in several standard individual intelligence tests such as the Stanford–Binet (in datasets JONE31, JONE33, JONE34, STOR11, WRIG01), the McCarthy scales (WIEB11), the Wechsler series – the WPPSI (TAYL31), the WISC or WISC–R (HUEF01, KEIT21, MCCA21, NAGL01–03, PROG01, UNDH01, VANH01, WILL11) and the WAIS (ROYC11, SAUN03, SCHU01, SNOW12, SPRA11), the Peabody Picture Vocabulary Test (MCCA21, STAN61, TAYL31, TAYL32), the K–ABC test (NAGL01–03), the Metropolitan Reading Readiness Test (REYN01), and the Woodcock–Johnson Psychoeducational Battery (WOOD15, WOOD17). Certain subtests from the ITPA appeared on factors assigned here (PARA01–08, PROG01, TAYL31, WISL01); even though these are not strictly vocabulary tests, they involve the child's lexical knowledge as well as ability to understand language of increasing complexity.

Tests of pure language development were often associated with tests of general or specialized information (SAUN03, SNOW12, SPRA11, UNDH01, WOOD15, WOOD17). Partly this may be due to the fact that information tests in standard batteries like the WISC–R frequently require knowledge of vocabulary items, along with knowledge of proper names that are of historical or geographical importance, and partly it may be due to the tendency of individuals to acquire generalized and specialized information along with vocabulary knowledge, and to do so in the same way as vocabulary is acquired (through reading, questioning, etc.).

There was one instance in which two factors were assigned to the LD category. The dataset was SAUN03, which was associated with Saunders's (1959) study of specific factors in the WAIS battery, using odd and even items. The WAIS

Vocabulary test was not included in the battery analyzed. Factor 4 was, however, loaded with information, arithmetic, and verbal comprehension items, and seemed most appropriately classified with the LD factor, if anywhere. The odd and even items of the Similarities test constituted a small specific factor, also classified here since this test loaded on LD in a number of other datasets.

The Language Development (LD) factor can best be characterized as reflecting general development in spoken native language skills. Nearly all the datasets covered here involved English as a native language; dataset UNDH01 involved an adaptation of the WISC for speakers of Norwegian. The factor is best measured by oral or listening vocabulary tests, but can also be measured by tests in which listening comprehension of language materials of increasing difficulty is involved. It is associated with tests of general information, but logically, general information is not critical to the factor since it is conceivable that a person could acquire good language comprehension without necessarily acquiring general information of the sort tested by the WISC Information subtest or similar measures.

Although Language Development is depicted as a single latent trait in the datasets considered above, one should not conclude that it is in reality a unitary trait. Other factors that are addressed in this chapter can be regarded as components of language development. Furthermore, it seems very probable that there are actually different trajectories of language development that begin at very early ages. Besides providing an illuminating review of previously accumulated evidence for this, Bates, Bretherton, and Snyder (1987) have used factor-analytic techniques to examine patterns of language development in 27 children studied at four age levels: 10, 13, 20, and 28 months. They report:

The factor structure from 10 to 28 months of age suggests the existence of three partially dissociable language acquisition mechanisms, which are emphasized to different degrees at different points in development. These are comprehension, rote production, and analyzed production. There is no evidence for a split between grammatical and lexical development within or across ages (p. 267).

VERBAL OR PRINTED LANGUAGE COMPREHENSION (V) FACTORS

Table 5.2, organized like Table 5.1, lists 150 token factors, in 148 datasets, that were classified as tapping general native language development measured by printed tests requiring ability to read. It is thus highly similar to the LD factor, and in fact in our sample there is no dataset in which the V and LD factors are clearly distinguished, even though in theory, it is believed, such separation could be accomplished by an appropriate factorial design. Undoubtedly there would be a high correlation between the two factors in any typical population. The axes for these factors are represented in Figure 5.1 as being very close together.

Because the factor involves printed language, the earliest age at which the

Table 5.2. *150 Verbal Ability (V) factors in 148 datasets arranged in order of approximate mean age of sample*[a]

Dataset	Date	C'y code	Age	Sample code	M/F code	Factor no.	Remarks (higher-order factors; others related)
STAN51	'81	U	6	1	3	2	1:2G;2:NA
ANDE01	'64	U	7	1	3	4	1:2G
PROG11	'71	U	7	1	3	2	1:2G;4:A2
SCHI11	'34	U	8	1	1	3	1:2G
SCHI12	'34	U	8	1	2	2	1:2G
SUMI04	'58	N	8	1	1	2	1:2G
VALT11	'81	G	8	1	3	3	1:2G;4:US
VALT12	'81	G	8	1	3	2	1:2G;3:SG;4:SG;6:US
GARR12	'35	U	9	6	2	4	1:2G
JAY01	'50	U	9	6	3	2	1:2C;3:SG;4:RS;7:20;8:V$
PROG12	'71	U	9	1	3	2	1:2G
ANDE02	'64	U	10	1	3	2	1:2G
BROW21	'33	E	10	6	1	5	1:2G
HARR51	'73	U	10	1	1	2	1:2G
HARR52	'73	U	10	1	2	2	1:2G
HARR54	'73	U	10	1	2	7	1:2G
SCHR11	'69	U	10	6	3	2	1:2&;3:VL;4:RS
SUMI03	'58	N	10	1	1	4	1:2G
WALL01	'65	U	10	6	3	1	—
DUNC11	'64	U	11	6	3	3	1:2G
MERR51	'63	U	11	1	3	3	1:2N
SATT01	'76	E	11	6	1	3	1:2G
SMIT11	'77	U	11	6	3	3	1:2G;2:SG
SPEA31	'77	A	11	6	1	2	1:2H; 3,6:R&
SPEA32	'77	A	11	6	2	4	1:2H
"	"	"	"	"	"	7	Sentence comprehension?
SPEA33	'77	A	11	O	1	3	1:2H
SPEA34	'77	A	11	O	2	2	1:2H
SULL01	'73	U	11	1	3	2	1:2G
TRAU01	'70	U	11	1	3	2	1:2G
UNDH11	'78	O	11	6	3	3	1:2G
CATT01A	'63	U	12	6	3	5	1:3G;2:2C
GARR13	'35	U	12	6	1	3	1:2G
HOLZ01	'39	U	12	6	3	2	1:2G
STAK01	'61	U	12	1	3	2	1:2G;10:A0
SUMI02	'58	N	12	1	1	2	1:2H
ANDE03	'64	U	13	1	3	2	1:2G
HARG12	'27	E	13	1	3	3	1:2G
SWIN11	'48	U	13	6	3	3	1:2G
THUR81	'41	U	13	6	3	3	1:3G;2:2H
THUR82	'41	U	13	6	3	3	1:3G;2:2C
DUPO01	'75	W	14	6	3	4	1:2G
GERS01	'63	U	14	1	3	4	Poorly defined;1:20
GUIL51	'61	U	14	1	3	4	1:2G
GUIL56	'61	U	14	1	1	9	1:3G;7:2H

Table 5.2 (*cont.*)

Dataset	Date	C'y code	Age	Sample code	M/F code	Factor no.	Remarks (higher-order factors; others related)
GUIL57	'61	U	14	I	2	9	6:2H
GUIL58	'61	U	14	8	3	9	1:2N
MURP01	'36	U	14	6	1	4	1:2G
PETE11	'63	U	14	M	3	3	1:2G
PETE12	'63	U	14	M	3	3	1:2G
SHAY01	'67	U	14	1	1	2	1:2H:4:SP;6:N
STOR12	'66	U	14	I	3	7	1:3G;2:2H
SUMI01	'58	N	14	1	1	5	1:2G
WEDE01	'47	E	14	1	2	4	1:2G
WERD01	'58	S	14	6	1	5	1:2G
WERD02	'58	S	14	6	1	3	1:2G
BAIR01	'51	U	15	D	3	5	1:2G
GARR15	'35	U	15	6	1	2	1:2G
REMO02	'62	Y	15	6	1	4	1:2G
REYB01	'41	K	15	6	3	3	1:2G
SCHU11	'58	U	15	1	3	3	1:3G;2:GC
SEGE01	'57	U	15	1	1	5	1:3G;2:2H
SEGE02	'57	U	15	1	2	5	1:3G;2:2H
WRIG21	'58	E	15	8	1	4	1:2G
BRAD01	'69	U	16	1	3	9	6:2V
BROW11	'66	U	16	6	3	3	1:2G
BURN11	'80	U	16	6	3	5	1:2G
COOM01	'41	U	16	6	3	5	1:2G
CURE11	'68	U	16	6	1	3	1:2G
CURE12	'68	U	16	6	2	2	1:2C;3:SP
DUNH11	'66	U	16	1	3	3	1:2G
HEND01	'69	U	16	6	3	7	1:2O
HEND11A	'82	E	16	6	3	6	1:3G;5:2C
HOEP21	'68	U	16	8	3	8	1:2O
HOLM11	'67	U	16	K	3	2	1:2G;4:PC
NIHI01	'64	U	16	8	3	4	1:3G;2:2H
NIHI02	'64	U	16	8	3	9	1:2G;6:A1
OSUL01	'65	U	16	6	3	3	1:2G
SUNG05	'81	U	16	1	2	7	1:3G;5:2C
WEIN11	'59	U	16	1	3	4	1:2C;5:CW
FLAN01	'64	U	17	1	3	2	1:2G;4:SP
GUIL32	'47	U	17	1	1	4	1:2G
HOEP31	'64	U	17	6	3	4	1:2H
MICH61	'51	U	17	6	1	4	1:2G
MICH62	'51	U	17	6	2	3	1:2G
PENF01	'67	E	17	8	3	10	1:3G;7:2N
TAYL01	'47	U	17	1	3	3	1:2H
THUR11	'38	U	17	1	3	11	9:2H
THUR31	'40	U	17	1	3	5	1:2G
VAND61	'78	U	17	1	3	2	1:2G
WOLI01	'65	U	17	1	1	6	1:2G;2:RC

Table 5.2 (*cont.*)

Dataset	Date	C'y code	Age	Sample code	M/F code	Factor no.	Remarks (higher-order factors; others related)
CARR11	'43	U	18	6	2	3	1:2G;5:VL
FREN11	'57	U	18	3	1	11	8:2H
GOOD01	'43	U	18	A	1	5	1:2G
GRIM01	'71	U	18	6	3	8	1:2I
GUIL20	'55	U	18	3	1	2	1:2G
HECK01	'67	U	18	6	3	11	10:2H
MORR11	'41	U	18	P	1	4	1:2G
SLAT01	'40	E	18	A	1	6	1:2V
STUM11	'74	G	18	6	1	5	1:2G
THOR21	'36	U	18	6	3	2	2 = Compreh/sense of humor
,,	,,	,,	,,	,,	,,	3	3 = Verbalsocial intell.
BLAC21	'80	U	19	P	2	4	—
BOTZ01	'51	U	19	6	1	6	—
FAIR01A	'84	U	19	2	3	7	5:2H
FAIR02	'84	U	19	2	3	2	1:2H
FLEI51	'71	U	19	2	1	2	1:2G
KARL01	'41	K	19	6	3	1	—
PIMS01	'62	U	19	F	3	7	3:LA;5:KL;6:2C
PIMS02	'62	U	19	F	3	5	1:KL;2:RS;7:IPD;8:GS
SCHN01	'29	U	19	6	1	2	1:2G
TAYL13A	'67	U	19	6	1	2	1:2!;3:FS;5:I5
THOR51	'39	U	19	6	3	5	1:2R
THUR21A	'38	U	19	6	3	8	7:2C
VERN21	'84	U	19	$	1	3	1:2G
VERY01	'67	U	19	6	1	5	1:2G
VERY02	'67	U	19	6	2	5	1:2G
VERY03	'67	U	19	6	3	7	5:2C
WALS21	'78	C	19	6	3	4	1:2G
WIND01	'67	U	19	P	3	1	—
CARR01	'41	U	20	6	3	3	1:2C;6:NA;9:FS
SMIT01	'33	U	20	P	1	3	1:2G
WEAV01	'63	U	20	6	3	2	1:2C;3:LA;4:CZ
ALLI02	'60	U	21	2	1	2	1:2H
ALLI03	'60	U	21	2	1	7	1:3G;6:2H
FEDE02	'80	U	21	2	3	6	5:2C
FRUC21	'52	U	21	2	3	2	5:2C
GUIL11	'55	U	21	3	1	3	1:2G
GUIL12	'56	U	21	3	1	10	8:2H;7:CW
GUIL14	'57	U	21	3	1	4	1:2H
GUIL17	'52	U	21	3	1	2	1:2G
GUIL19	'55	U	21	3	1	4	1:2G
GUIL31	'47	U	21	3	1	3	1:2G
GUIL32A	'47	U	21	3	1	4	1:2G
GUIL35	'47	U	21	3	1	5	1:2G
GUIL38	'47	U	21	3	1	4	1:2G

Table 5.2 (*cont.*)

Dataset	Date	C'y code	Age	Sample code	M/F code	Factor no.	Remarks (higher-order factors; others related)
GUIL42	'47	U	21	3	1	3	1:2G
GUIL46	'47	U	21	3	1	6	1:2G
HOFF01	'68	U	21	B	3	7	5:2H
LUCA01	'53	U	21	3	1	6	1:2H
MERR41	'60	U	21	3	1	5	1:2G
MESS01	'75	U	21	3	1	2	1:2G
ROFF11	'52	U	21	3	1	10	1:2G
TAYL11	'67	U	21	3	1	2	1:2G
TAYL12A	'67	U	21	2	1	4	1:2!;2:F8
KELL01	'64	U	22	3	1	5	1:2Y
MICH51	'50	U	22	6	1	4	1:2G
HAKS01	'74	C	24	1	3	16	1:3G;13:2C
DEMI01A	'62	U	30	L	3	3	1:2G
DEMI02A	'62	U	30	S	3	4	1:2H
HARR01	'40	U	30	5	1	7	6:2H
CORN01	'83	U	71	1	3	3	1:2G

*See Appendix A for codes. In a few cases, the classifications of factors shown here were preliminary and may not agree with the final classifications shown in the tables of Appendix B.

factor appears is 6 years, in dataset STAN51. The latest age at which it appears is age 71, in dataset CORN01. Most of the datasets in which it appears involve the English language, in one or another English-speaking country, but the factor also appears where other languages are involved: Afrikaans (REYB01), French (DUPO01), German (STUM11, VALT11–12), Italian (REMO02), Japanese (SUMI01 02, SUMI04), Norwegian (UNDH01, UNDH11), and Swedish (GUST11A, WERD01–02). In nearly every case the factor is dominated by a general factor (3G or 2G), or a factor (2C) interpreted as "crystallized intelligence." (As noted previously, the nature of any higher-order factor is at least partly a function of battery composition.) This fact can be interpreted as signifying that while the V factor is generally substantially or even highly correlated with general intelligence or crystallized intelligence, it is factorially distinct from these higher-order factors, in that there is variance in it even after higher-order variance is controlled or partialled out.

In general, factors were classified as V when (a) all or a majority of their variables involved printed tests requiring reading, and (b) the variables covered a wide range of test types measuring general language development including (typically) various types of vocabulary tests and reading comprehension tests. Factors were classified under several other categories in the language domain when the variables were more limited in their characteristics, or there was evidence that they could be distinguished from LD or V factors. For example, a special class of Lexical Knowledge (VL) factors, to be discussed below, was recognized and thus excluded from Table 5.2.

Nevertheless, variables that in various ways measure vocabulary knowledge were the most frequently occurring variables measuring factor V. Nearly all of these variables are of the multiple-choice variety, for example, tests requiring the subject to select the best *synonym* for a lead word, and tests requiring the subject to select the best *opposite* for a lead word. Most often, the words involved are presented in isolation, but sometimes they are presented in sentence contexts. Sometimes, but not always, the contexts dictate a choice of a synonym or opposite for a particular meaning of a word. Some vocabulary tests require the subject to give a definition of a word, or to supply a word, given its definition and/or an appropriate context. The precise format by which vocabulary knowledge is measured generally makes little difference in the factorial composition of the variables, to the extent that the underlying trait being measured is range of native-language vocabulary knowledge. Range of vocabulary can presumably be indexed in terms of the typical word-frequency, in word-frequency counts such as those of Thorndike and Lorge (1944) or Carroll, Davies, and Richman (1971), of words that are known by a subject at some liminal value such as 50%. Individuals with high range of vocabulary are more likely to know rarer, low frequency words than individuals with low ranges of vocabulary. Over individuals of different ages, range of vocabulary is correlated with age, of course, but there is wide variance in vocabulary ranges for individuals at any given age. (See an analysis, from this point of view, of the vocabulary test from the Woodcock–Johnson Psycho-Educational Battery, Carroll, 1992.)

Most vocabulary tests appearing as measurements of the V factor are general vocabulary tests in which words are sampled more or less randomly from the stock of vocabulary available in a language. A few, however, are specialized vocabulary tests. For example, technical vocabulary tests for navigator, bombardier, and pilot help to define the V factor in GUIL42, along with a reading comprehension test. Unfortunately, no dataset included a vocabulary test with subtests for different areas of vocabulary, such as Greene's (1937–1949) *Michigan Vocabulary Profile Test*, which might have permitted isolation of factors for groups of such areas.

As was the case for the LD factors, tests of general and specialized information often appeared, along with vocabulary and other types of tests, as helping to define a V factor (in datasets CURE11–12, FAIR01–02, HOLM11, SHAY01, SWIN11). This is due not only to the fact that such information tests frequently involve terminology, but also, probably, to the fact that individuals with much vocabulary knowledge also tend to have a wide range of information knowledge.

Besides vocabulary and information tests, a frequent test type that occurred as defining factor V was that of reading comprehension. Such tests, under various names (Reading Comprehension, English Comprehension, Paragraph Comprehension, Paragraph Meaning, etc.), are generally of a multiple-choice format requiring the subject to select answers to questions relating to the content of text that is presented to them in printed form. The physical format of such tests seems to make no consistent difference in factor compositions. Obviously, what is measured is a function of basic reading ability (i.e., ability to "decode" printed text), ability to understand text content (frequently involving vocabulary knowledge as well as ability to interpret the grammatical structure of prose), and ability to select answers correctly reflecting text content. In general, whether the test involves merely literal comprehension or also requires deductive and inferential processes seems to make little difference in the factorial composition of a variable, although it will be seen in Chapter 6 that some reading comprehension tests that make high demands on inferential processes can appear in the domain of reasoning tests.

Numerous other types of tests occasionally appear among those defining factor V. In most cases, their appearance can easily be interpreted as due to the involvement of vocabulary knowledge or general language comprehension in these tests. For example, "verbal analogies" tests that presumably measure analogical reasoning ability very often include relatively infrequent words in the test items. Low-scoring individuals tend to have more difficulty with vocabulary than with the analogical relations. (See Carroll, 1980b, for discussion of this point with respect to analogies items in the College Board Scholastic Aptitude Test.)

LEXICAL KNOWLEDGE (VL) FACTORS

Although vocabulary knowledge is a predominant element in the Language Development (LD) and Verbal (V) factors just discussed, there is some evidence that vocabulary knowledge can be regarded as a separable component of language development. In allocating token factors to factor types, a number of instances were found of factors that are defined *only* by tests of vocabulary knowledge, and in some cases these factors are defined separately from factors defined by measures of more general language comprehension or of other special skills in the language ability domain. These instances are listed in Table 5.3, arranged (as previously) in order of the approximate mean age of the samples. Most of the samples range in age from 18 to adulthood, that is, across ages at which it might be expected that vocabulary knowledge would be differentiated from more general language ability, because some individuals are able to attain, through reading and other experiences that occur in adolescence and adulthood, very high and wide ranges of vocabulary. This does not exclude the possibility, however, that lexical knowledge could be differentiated from more general language development at younger ages.

Of the datasets listed in Table 5.3, HANL01, HORN21, SEIB02, UNDE12, and WEIS11 have factors defined exclusively by tests of vocabulary, and have no other factors in the language domain. From inspection of the variables in

Table 5.3. *23 Lexical Knowledge (VL) factors in 23 datasets arranged in order of approximate mean age of sample*[a]

Dataset	Date	C'y code	Age	Sample code	M/F code	Factor no.	Remarks (higher-order factors; others related)
SCHR11	'69	U	10	6	3	3	1:2&;2:V;4:RS
GUST11A	'84	S	11	1	3	11	1:3G;9:2C
STOR11	'66	U	14	8	3	9	1:2G;9 = Vocab. vs Fluency (bi-polar factor)
ARNO01	'67	A	15	1	3	3	1:2G;6:Sentence Compreh.
WEIS11	'55	U	15	M	3	6	1:3G;4:2C
CARR11	'43	U	18	6	2	5	1:2G;3:V
LANG31	'41	U	18	6	2	5	1:2G;3:RS
LORD01	'56	U	18	3	1	8	4:VS;5:2H
CARR42	'76	U	19	P	3	2	1:MY;4:MY(Self-rated)
CARR43	'77	U	19	6	3	3	1:3G;2:2C;10:26;11:PC
GARD05A	'60	U	19	6	2	2	1:2G
HANL01	'52	U	19	6	3	6	1:2U
LUMS01	'65	A	19	P	3	12	8:2C;9:V
SCHA11	'40	U	19	6	1	3	1:3G;2:2H
SEIB02	'67	U	19	6	3	7	1:2V
UNDE12	'78	U	19	6	3	5	1:2Y (memory battery)
VERN01	'81	U	19	6	3	4	1:2G;2:G1
VERN61	'62	U	19	6	1	3	1:2C;2:RC
CARR21	'58	U	21	2	1	4	1:2G;2:MY;3:PC
VERN62	'62	E	21	1	1	2	1:2C;3:RC
WOTH01	'90	U	21	1	3	7	1:3G;2:2F
CURE01	'44	U	30	1	3	3	1:2C;2:RC
HORN21	'78	U	30	Q	1	4	1:2C

[a]See Appendix A for codes. In a few cases, the classifications of factors shown here were preliminary and may not agree with the final classifications shown in the tables of Appendix B.

these datasets, however, it appears that there are no variables (other than the vocabulary tests) that would be expected to fall in the language ability domain.

Several datasets present at least suggestive evidence for a separation between V (or RC) and VL. In LUMS01 factors 9 and 12 are dominated by a second-order Gc factor (factor 8). Factor 9 is interpreted as V or possibly RC (reading comprehension), being loaded with reading comprehension, reading speed, and reading vocabulary tests, whereas factor 12 is loaded only with vocabulary tests. VERN61 and VERN62 are two small datasets, one from an American sample and the other from a British sample, showing two factors dominated by a second-order Gc factor (factor 1). Factor 2 is a reading comprehension factor while factor 3 is loaded only with vocabulary tests. A similar separation between a V or RC factor and a VL factor is shown in CURE01.

Evidence from several other datasets (SCHR11 and CARR11), though promising, turned out on close examination to be inconclusive. The contrast between factors 2 and 3 of SCHR11, for example, is possibly attributable to the fact that factor 2 (tests of reading comprehension) is based on experimental tests whereas factor 3 is based on several tests (including a vocabulary test) from the Iowa Test of Basic Skills whose scores had been obtained from school records.

Further evidence is needed as to the possible separation between vocabulary knowledge, general reading comprehension skills that do not depend on vocabulary (in the sense of not involving knowledge of the meanings of relatively infrequent words), and general language development as represented by the LD factor. Obtaining such evidence would require careful control of measurements of these factors, limiting range of vocabulary in measuring LD or V and stressing it in measuring VL.

READING COMPREHENSION (RC) FACTORS

Table 5.4 lists datasets that provide evidence, though limited, for the identification of a reading comprehension (RC) factor linearly independent of other factors in the language ability domain. One of these, DAVI11, is from a famous article in which the author (Davis, 1944) had claimed to identify perhaps seven or eight separate reading skills, but which was reanalyzed by Thurstone (1946) to show a single common factor. At least two of the nine measures are tests of vocabulary, and thus in this dataset there is no evidence for the separation of reading comprehension ability from vocabulary knowledge. The single factor from this dataset could be classified under factor V equally as well as here.

Somewhat better evidence for an independent RC factor comes from other datasets. In WOOD13, for a Grade 1 sample, factor 3 is defined by Letter–Word Identification, Passage Comprehension, and Word Attack subtests, separate from factor 2, defined by several information-achievement subtests (Science, Social Studies, Humanities) and vocabulary (Picture Vocabulary, Antonyms–Synonyms) subtests. In KEIT21 we find a reading ability factor defined by the Reading–Decoding and Reading–Understanding subtests of the K–ABC battery, separate from an LD factor defined by Vocabulary, Comprehension, Similarities, and Information subtests of the WISC–R and the "Faces and Places" and "Riddles" subtests of the K–ABC. In WOLI01, factor 2 is defined by various reading comprehension variables, separate from factor 6, which is a verbal ability (V) factor defined by verbal subtests of the AGCT. The separation of a reading comprehension from a lexical knowledge factor in datasets LUMS01, VERN61, and VERN62 has already been mentioned above in the discussion of the VL factor. Dataset SCHU00 shows that in an aphasic population, factor 2, defined by tests and tasks involving visual discrimination and reading, is separate from a general language ability factor (factor 3).

Factor 2 of JACK11 is loaded with a measure of "raw comprehension" on a

Table 5.4. *10 Reading Comprehension (RC) factors in 10 datasets arranged in order of approximate mean age of sample[a]*

Dataset	Date	C'y code	Age	Sample code	M/F code	Factor no.	Remarks (higher-order factors; others related)
WOOD13	'77	U	6	1	3	3	1:2C;2:V
KEIT21	'87	U	10	7	3	4	1:3G;2:2C;3:V
STOL01	'72	U	10	V	3	1	2:PC
WOLI01	'65	U	17	1	1	2	1:2C;6:V
DAVI11	'44	U	18	G	3	1	—
JACK11	'79	U	18	6	3	2	1:2C;3:LS;4:RS
LUMS01	'65	A	19	P	3	9	8:2C;12:VL
VERN61	'62	U	19	6	1	2	1:2C;3:VL
VERN62	'62	E	21	1	1	3	1:2C;2:VL
SCHU00	'62	U	40?	4	3	2	1:2C;3:V; Aphasic sample

[a]See Appendix A for codes. In a few cases, the classifications of factors shown here were preliminary and may not agree with the final classifications shown in the tables of Appendix B.

short reading passage, as well as with the verbal and quantitative aptitude scores on the SCAT (School and College Aptitude Test), and is distinct from factor 3, interpreted as a listening comprehension (LS) factor, and factor 4, interpreted as a reading speed (RS) factor. Factors 2 and 3 are, however, not well defined.

It should be pointed out that factors loaded with reading comprehension tests often have further loadings with various sorts of reasoning tests, possibly indicating that the common element in the factor is not reading comprehension *per se*, but reasoning. Such factors (e.g., factor 2 in dataset ALLI02, and factor 2 in dataset CURE01) are generally assigned to factor RG (Reasoning) as discussed in Chapter 6.

Special Reading Comprehension (R&) Factors

Several investigators have attempted to refine the description of the reading comprehension subdomain. Table 5.5 lists special factors (designated R&) resulting from reanalyses of their studies. In several samples of Grade 6 children (datasets SPEA31–34), Spearritt, Spalding, and Johnston (1977) isolated "pure sentence comprehension" and "semantic context" factors, independent of more general V or VL factors, all dominated by a general verbal intelligence factor. Pure sentence comprehension was measured by several tests whose items asked the child to show understanding of very simple printed sentences by selecting correct paraphrases, or by answering simple questions. Presumably, only children with very poor reading ability had difficulty responding. Tests of the "semantic context" factor generally present short paragraphs, each describing a

Table 5.5. *9 Special Reading Comprehension (R&) factors in 5 datasets arranged in order of approximate mean age of sample[a]*

Dataset	Date	C'y code	Age	Sample code	M/F code	Factor no.	Remarks (higher-order factors; others related)
SPEA31	'77	A	11	6	1	3	1:2H;2:VL;4:EU;6:R&; 3 = "pure sentence comprehension"
"	"	"	"	"	"	6	1:2H;2:VL;4:EU;3:R& 6 = "semantic context"
SPEA32	'77	A	11	6	2	6	1:2H;2:EU;4:VL;5:S0 6 = "pure sentence comprehension"
SPEA33	'77	A	11	O	1	5	1:2H;3:V 5 = "pure sentence comprehension"
SPEA34	'77	A	11	V	2	6	1:2H;2:V;4:EU;5:2F 6 = "semantic context"
FRED12	'82	U	16	6	3	2	1:2C;2 = "extrapolating context"
"	"	"	"	"	"	3	3 = "semantic integration"
"	"	"	"	"	"	5	5 = "speed set for context utilization"
"	"	"	"	"	"	7	7 = "topicality set; location of referents"

[a]See Appendix A for codes. In a few cases, the classifications of factors shown here were preliminary and may not agree with the final classifications shown in the tables of Appendix B.

situation that the child has to understand in order to infer the correct answer to a multiple-choice question. Again, vocabulary load is restricted. For example:

Passage. A woman I met in London has an unusual job. Each day she disguises herself and visits a certain department store pretending to be a customer. Sometimes she has the manner of a duchess, other days she appears to be a poor housewife. Then she reports to the management on how she is treated by the sales clerks.

The woman in London is really:

A. an employee of the store
B. a customer of the store
C. an old lady

Frederiksen (1982) developed procedures – too complex to be described here – for isolating and confirming components in the process of understanding text discourse. Four of these components have to do with word recognition and are presented in Table 5.6. The remaining four are described, in brief, as follows:

> (Factor 2 in our reanalysis) Extrapolating a discourse representation
> (Factor 3) Semantic integration of antecedents with a discourse representation

Table 5.6. *15 Reading Decoding (RD) factors in 9 datasets arranged in order of approximate mean age of sample*[a]

Dataset	Date	C'y code	Age	Sample code	M/F code	Factor no.	Remarks (higher-order factors; others related)
JAY01	'50	U	9	6	3	8	7:20;8 = Decoding Accuracy
SING21	'65	U	9	1	3	2	1:2G;4:LS
VALT01	'70	G	9	V	3	3	1:2G;3 = Word Perception
VALT02	'70	G	9	1	3	3	1:2G;3 = Word Perception
VALT03	'70	G	9	%	3	4	1:2G;4 = Word Perception
STOL01	'72	U	11	V	3	2	1:RC;2 = Word Sense/ Phonics
FRED11	'78	U	16	6	3	2	1:2%;Others: see below; 2 = Grapheme Encoding
"	"	"	"	"	"	3	3 = Multiletter Array Facilitation
"	"	"	"	"	"	4	4 = Phonemic Contrast
"	"	"	"	"	"	5	5 = Depth of Processing in Word Recognition
FRED12	'82	U	16	6	3	4	1:2C;Others: see below; 4 = Letter Recognition
"	"	"	"	"	"	8	8 = Word Recognition
"	"	"	"	"	"	9	9 = Perception of Multiletter Units
"	"	"	"	"	"	10	10 = Decoding
HOEP21	'68	U	16	8	3	5	1:20

[a]See Appendix A for codes. In a few cases, the classifications of factors shown here were preliminary and may not agree with the final classifications shown in the tables of Appendix B.

(Factor 5) Speed in applying context
(Factor 7) Assignment of topicalized antecedent as referent

Frederiksen discusses the extent to which these "higher-level components" correlate with conventional measures of reading speed and comprehension; generally they correlate lower than do word-analysis components – even negatively, as in the case of the topicality set component. This latter finding, with respect to the topicality set component, is interpreted by Frederiksen as suggesting that "good readers are less influenced [than poor readers] by the topical status of a referent in analyzing anaphoric relations in a text" (p. 173).

READING DECODING (RD) FACTORS

There is evidence, indicated in Table 5.6, that a general skill of word recognition and decoding can be defined factorially independent of some other skills in the language ability domain, and further, that this word recognition skill can be broken down into detailed processes. My reanalysis of an early study (Jay, 1950) conducted under Thurstone's supervision identifies a second-order reading decoding factor that dominates two primary factors: factor 8, a reading decoding accuracy factor, and factor 9, a reading decoding speed factor, all independent of more general verbal comprehension, spelling, and reading speed factors. The word perception factors isolated in three datasets from Germany (VALT01–03) seem also to fall into this category, as well as a factor identified in several subtests of the Stanford Diagnostic Reading test (dataset STOL01).

In a series of studies, Frederiksen (1978, 1982) has shown that word recognition or decoding can be broken down into quite specific skills (the names or descriptions of these skills changed somewhat over the time period of the research):

> Grapheme Encoding, Letter Recognition
> Multiletter Array Facilitation, Perception of Multiletter Units (e.g. *sh*, *tion*)
> Depth of Processing in Word Recognition
> Phonemic Contrast, Decoding

READING SPEED (RS) FACTORS

Many standard measures of reading ability include measures of reading speed. There is good factorial evidence for distinguishing reading speed from reading comprehension. That is, it seems to be confirmed that individuals can attain equal degrees of comprehension at different speeds. Table 5.7 lists datasets disclosing reading speed factors, identified over ages 6 to 19.

Various ways of measuring reading speed are illustrated in these datasets. In PIMS01–02 reading speed would seem to involve comprehension only minimally; the measure is simply the time to read a passage aloud as fast as possible, i.e., to recognize the words (in sentences) and utter them. But such a measure may involve a motor component, Speed of Articulation (see Chapter 13). In most cases, reading speed is measured while the subject is comprehending the material as well as he/she may. For example, the Minnesota Speed of Reading Test, used in dataset LANG31, requires the subject to read short passages and mark words that are obviously nonsensical in relation to the passage. A similar test was used in dataset SPEA01. Many of the measures loading on the RS factor in these datasets are simple multiple-choice comprehension tests given in a time-limit. However, in a sample of deaf adolescents, Olson (1966; dataset OLSO51) used tachistoscopic techniques to measure the speed with which letter sequences or familiar words were perceived. Reading speed measured in this way was related to more conventional measures (e.g., scores on the Gates Reading Test) only through a second-order factor of general language development.

In a study that focused on the processing determinants of reading speed in college students, Jackson and McClelland (1979) measured both "raw speed" and "effective reading speed." The former was the speed with which subjects read

Table 5.7. *11 Reading Speed (RS) factors in 11 datasets arranged in order of approximate mean age of sample*[a]

Dataset	Date	C'y code	Age	Sample code	M/F code	Factor no.	Remarks (higher-order factors; others related)
STAN61	'84	U	6	6	3	3	1:20;2:PC;4:LD;
WALL51	'67	S	8	1	1	4	1:2C;3:SG;4 = Reading Speed
JAY01	'50	U	9	6	3	4	1:2C;2:V;3:SG
SCHR11	'69	U	10	6	3	4	1:2&;2:V;3:VL
SPEA01	'62	A	11	6	1	5	1:2H;3:LS
OLSO51	'66	U	14	E	3	3	1:2C;4:FE;6:Speech-reading
FRED11	'78	U	16	6	3	6	1:2&;See R& factors
JACK11	'79	U	18	6	3	4	1:2C;2:V;3:LS
LANG31	'41	U	18	6	2	3	1:2G;5:VL
PIMS01	'62	U	19	F	3	4	1:2F;3:LA;6:2C;7:V 4 = reading aloud tasks
PIMS02	'62	U	19	F	3	2	5:V;4 = reading aloud tasks

[a] See Appendix A for codes. In a few cases, the classifications of factors shown here were preliminary and may not agree with the final classifications shown in the tables of Appendix B.

passages "as fast as possible" but with the understanding they would be given a comprehension test. "Effective reading speed" was the raw speed multiplied by the percent correct for the comprehension questions. In dataset JACK11 it appears that raw speed defined a factor over two speed of reading tests. Raw speed was unfortunately not used as a variable in dataset JACK12, and there is only a "speed of mental comparison" factor in that dataset (discussed in Chapter 11), but these authors show that effective reading speed (a function of both raw speed and comprehension) was well predicted by reaction times in a several stimulus-matching tasks.

The weight of evidence from these studies indicates that reading speed is a cardinal variable in reading performance, and that it is associated with speed of accessing the memory codes involved in word recognition. Perfetti (1985) has assembled further evidence on this point, developing what he calls a "verbal efficiency theory" which proposes that "individual differences in reading comprehension are produced by individual differences in the efficient operation of local processes" (p. 100), important among which are processes of word recognition.

Reading speed will be factorially distinguished from reading comprehension only when both of these dimensions are adequately defined. For example, speed and comprehension were not separated in Holmes and Singer's (1966) study of "speed and power in reading" (dataset HOLM11) because there were not sufficient measures of either aspect; thus, both power of reading and speed of reading had loadings (.515 and .276, respectively) on a verbal ability factor V.

CLOZE ABILITY (CZ) FACTORS

A popular method of testing reading comprehension, either in a first or a second language, has been the "cloze" technique, originated by Taylor (1953) for measuring the readability of prose but subsequently widely applied for measuring language or reading proficiency. The standard cloze procedure is to ask subjects to supply words, represented by blanks, that have been deleted (say, every seventh word) in a prose passage. The question arises whether this technique measures reading or language comprehension in the same way as more conventional reading tests. Unfortunately there appears to be little evidence on this point from the factorial literature, at least from the datasets surveyed here. Table 5.8 lists several datasets that reveal factors associated with cloze tests.

It should be noted, incidentally, that cloze tests (unless they are in some kind of multiple-choice format) involve not only receptive skills but also productive skills, in that the subject has to supply words suggested by their contexts. For this reason, one might expect cloze ability tests to load on factors in the Idea Production domain (Chapter 10), but no dataset has been found in which this possibility was explored. McKenna (1986) has examined the cloze procedure as being a form of memory search.

The datasets listed in Table 5.8 disclose factors loaded almost exclusively with cloze tests, suggesting that such tests measure a special ability, even though it is dominated by a higher-order factor. Of these, only WEAV01 yields evidence to suggest that the cloze factor is linearly independent of a reading or more general language ability factor. Factor 4 is loaded with seven different cloze tests, in contrast to factor 2 loaded with reading, listening, and vocabulary tests. All tests, including those measuring factor 3 (a "foreign language aptitude factor"; see below) have substantial loadings on a second-order factor. There is thus little critical information on the nature of a cloze ability factor.

The seemingly arbitrary deletion scheme customarily used with cloze tests produces a condition in which the required fill-in responses are widely divergent with respect to form–class, vocabulary frequency, and other aspects of linguistic structure. Especially in connection with measuring English language proficiency among learners of English as a second language, there has been debate concerning whether there might be a more rational basis for selecting words for deletion, e.g., deleting only "function words" or deleting only heads of noun phrases. The studies of Ohnmacht, Weaver, and Kohler (1970; dataset OHNM11) and Weaver and Kingston (1963; dataset WEAV01), conducted on native English speakers, did not find radically different factorial compositions of variables corresponding to different deletion procedures. Using learners of English as a second language, Bachman (1982; dataset BACH01 listed in Table 5.18) claimed

Table 5.8. *6 Cloze Ability (CZ) factors in 6 datasets arranged in order of approximate mean age of sample*[a]

Dataset	Date	C'y code	Age	Sample code	M/F code	Factor no.	Remarks (higher-order factors; others related)
RAND01	'79	C	10	6	1	3	1:2G
RAND02	'79	C	10	6	2	2	1:2G
SPEA34	'77	A	11	O	2	7	1:2C;2:V
STOR13	'66	U	14	7	3	9	1:2G
OHNM11	'70	U	16	6	3	2	1:2G
WEAV01	'63	U	20	6	3	4	1:2C;2:V;3:LA

[a]See Appendix A for codes. In a few cases, the classifications of factors shown here were preliminary and may not agree with the final classifications shown in the tables of Appendix B.

to find three specific traits of cloze test ability depending on deletion procedures: "1) syntactic, which depended only on clause-level context, 2) cohesive, which depended upon the interclausal or intersentential cohesive context, and 3) strategic, which depended on parallel patterns of coherence" (p. 63). My exploratory factor analysis of his correlation matrix failed to show these traits as clearly as Bachman's confirmatory analysis, even though it isolated three factors and a general factor, as in Bachman's analysis. The problem obviously requires further research, but it is somewhat difficult to believe that different deletion procedures would yield replicably different factors, given that supplying a word to fill a deletion probably depends mainly on general language knowledge and comprehension ability.

SPELLING ABILITY (SG) FACTORS

There has long been speculation that spelling ability constitutes an ability rather independent of other language abilities, and there have been attempts to isolate the source of such an ability by studying its correlations with tests of hypothesized component abilities. Factor analysis has often been used for studying this problem. Table 5.9 lists factors identified in our survey that appear to measure an ability to spell that is linearly independent of other factors in the language ability domain. The studies cover the age range 8 to adulthood. Differences in spelling ability appear early in schooling and persist into adulthood and old age.

Unfortunately, it appears that factor-analytic work thus far provides little new insight into the nature of spelling ability, probably because it has been difficult to design studies to gain such insight. To be sure, many of the studies associated with the factors displayed in Table 5.9 have demonstrated that spelling ability is separate from general language ability as represented in tests of the V factor, and

Table 5.9. *18 Spelling Ability (SG) factors in 17 datasets arranged in order of approximate mean age of sample[a]*

Dataset	Date	C'y code	Age	Sample code	M/F code	Factor no.	Remarks (higher-order factors; others related)
VALT12	'81	G	8	1	3	3	1:2G;2:V;4:See below 3 = Phonetic Spelling Errors
"	"	"	"	"	"	4	4 = Orthographic Spelling Errors
WALL52	'67	S	8	6	2	2	1:2C
JAY01	'50	U	9	6	3	3	1:2C;2:V;4:RS;7:20
HARR53	'73	U	10	1	1	6	1:2G
REIN01	'65	G	10	1	3	4	1:2G
REIN03	'65	G	10	6	3	4	1:2G
WOOD15	'77	U	10	1	3	3	1:2C;2:V;5:2F
SMIT11	'77	U	11	6	3	2	1:2G;3:V
REIN02	'65	G	12	1	3	2	1:2G
REIN04	'65	G	13	6	3	4	1:2G
TENO01	'69	U	15	1	3	6	1:2G
CURE12	'68	U	16	6	2	3	1:2C;2:V
WOOD17	'77	U	17	1	3	4	1:2C;2:V
FOGA00	'86	A	19	P	3	9	7:2#
VERN51	'47	E	21	2	1	2	1:2H
HAKS01	'74	C	24	1	3	14	1:3G;13:2C;16:V
WOOD18	'77	U	30	1	3	3	1:2C;2:V;5:2F

[a] See Appendix A for codes. In a few cases, the classifications of factors shown here were preliminary and may not agree with the final classifications shown in the tables of Appendix B.

a few studies show, rather trivially, that spelling ability is different from reading speed.

Hakstian and Cattell (1974; dataset HAKS01) obtained a Spelling factor in a rather artificial manner by using three highly similar alternate forms of tests requiring subjects to recognize misspelled words. They state that they assume "this ability is the same as (but more easily measured than) that of correctly spelling dictated words." "Whether Spelling should be regarded as a relatively narrow primary ability," they continue, "or as a specific behaviour dependent upon both the V and W [word fluency] primaries and perhaps others, is not yet clear" (p. 149). A further dataset defining spelling ability in a somewhat similar way, i.e., by using highly similar forms of recognition spelling tests, is FOGA00, although in this dataset, both visual and auditory presentations of spellings were used, with and without secondary tasks. Spelling was equally well defined, according to my reanalysis, regardless of whether a secondary task was presented, and regardless of whether presentation of words was visual or auditory.

Several datasets were designed with the intention of exploring the effect of method of presentation. The most interesting of these is dataset SMIT11 (Smith, 1977), where the spelling factor was defined best by a spelling performance test using the "word-used-in-sentence dictation method" (factor loading .40), but also by a recognition-of-misspelling test (factor loading .35). (Both tests had high loadings on a second-order factor.) Also on this factor, but with lower loadings, were two tests (Root–Suffix Rules, and Phoneme–Grapheme Correspondence) in which subjects had to spell pseudowords from their pronunciations, or, for example, the plural or *ing* form of a pseudoword, according to conventional spelling rules. All the tests that were salient on the Spelling factor were linearly independent of another factor (factor 4) which is apparently a memory domain factor. One of the tests on the Spelling factor, named "Visual, Alternate Spellings," required the subject to remember which spelling of a word spoken by the examiner (like "fleem") occurred in a particular position in a grid. Conclusions that I would draw from this study are (1) that spelling ability can be equally well measured by dictation tests or misspelling-recognition tests, other things being equal, (2) that spelling ability includes at least implicit knowledge of conventional spelling rules and phoneme-grapheme correspondences, but (3) that spelling ability does *not* involve immediate memory for visual forms of words. (This last conclusion, incidentally, is contrary to Smith's (1977); Smith relied on the fact that the visual memory tests were highly correlated with spelling test scores, but actually it can be seen that this correlation is due to a higher-order intelligence factor.)

Nevertheless, evidence from dataset TENO01 possibly qualifies this last conclusion. In this dataset, two tests of memory for misspellings or for nonsense word spellings loaded on a Spelling factor that was also measured by a misspelling-recognition test and a test called Disemvowelled Words in which subjects had to fill in the vowels of a word presented as "m _ t _ l _ t _" [mutilate]. The latter two tests, presumably, measured spelling ability more or less directly, while the memory tests required memory for *deviations*, as it were, from normal spellings.

Evidence from two studies conducted in Germany throws some further light on the nature of spelling ability. In datasets REIN01–04, a spelling test tended to correlate with tests of "closure" ability, particularly a test ("Closure 1") that apparently required recognition of incomplete visual pictures (like the Street Gestalt test). (Nevertheless, spelling was separate from the Speed of Closure factor in dataset HAKS01, or was related to it only at the second order.) In dataset VALT12, it was found that measures of phonetic and of orthographic spelling errors defined two linearly independent factors, a finding that suggests different sources for these kinds of spelling errors.

Two datasets come from a study of spelling ability by Wallin (1967) in Grade 3 boys and girls in Sweden. The reanalyzed factor-analytic structures are somewhat different across the boys' and girls' samples. For boys (WALL51), a dictation spelling test comes out on a factor called Word Detail Perception, while a multiple-choice misspelling-recognition test comes out on another factor that is also loaded with a reading speed measure. It is possible that the time-limit for the multiple-choice test pushed it over into the reading speed factor. Word Detail Perception has a variety of measures having to do with manipulations of sounds and corresponding printed representations, for example a Dissected Words test that requires subjects to pick out printed "fragments" (like *so*) of a spoken word (e.g., *hälsosam*), in Swedish. This factor has been classified as measuring Phonetic Coding ability (see below) and is listed in Table 5.10.

In contrast, the spelling factor for the girls' sample includes both recall and recognition tests of spelling, the measure of reading speed, a synonyms test, and one of the sound manipulation tests that appeared on the spelling factor in the boys' sample. Dissected Words appears on a factor (factor 4) that is most probably to be interpreted as Perceptual Speed (see Chapter 8).

Somewhat related to this is the fact that a separate spelling factor appears only in the girls' sample (CURE12) of a study of PROJECT TALENT tests by Cureton (1968). In the boys' sample (CURE11), the variance of the spelling test is absorbed into the V factor. There are a number of other datasets (e.g., DUNC11) in which a spelling test appears on a V factor, with no separate spelling factor. It is not clear whether there is any consistent difference in factorial structures for boys as compared to girls; the results for datasets WALL51 and CURE12 appear conflicting.

The evidence from our survey on the nature of spelling ability is thus somewhat disappointing and inconclusive. The problem deserves further study.

PHONETIC CODING (PC) FACTORS

Table 5.10 lists twelve factors that are interpreted, at least tentatively, as belonging to a cluster of what may be called Phonetic Coding abilities. This cluster is very close to the Spelling cluster, and may in fact be identical to it. In the absence of convincing evidence on this point, however, the factors from these datasets have been categorized separately from the factors clearly measuring spelling ability.

The first intimation I had that a distinct "phonetic coding" factor might exist came from research (Carroll, 1958, 1962b; datasets CARR21–22) on foreign language aptitude. A number of tests that, incidentally, were highly predictive of foreign language learning rates seemed to cluster together because they tapped an ability to "code" phonetic data in memory. One of these was the Phonetic Script test, later incorporated in the *Modern Language Aptitude Test* (Carroll & Sapon, 1959), that required subjects to induce grapheme–phoneme relationships in an unfamiliar phonemic spelling system (or even in an unfamiliar writing system, such as Devanagari as used in Sanskrit and Hindi), given both auditory and graphemic information on these relationships. Yet scores on such tests tended to be correlated with several tests that had been used in batteries to predict

Table 5.10. *12 Phonetic Coding (PC) factors in 12 datasets arranged in order of approximate mean age of sample[a]*

Dataset	Date	C'y code	Age	Sample code	M/F code	Factor no.	Remarks (higher-order factors; others related)
PARA05	'69	U	6	1	3	4	1:2C;2:LD
STAN61	'84	U	6	6	3	2	1:20;3:V4;4:DL
TAYL31	'75	C	6	1	3	7	6:26
WALL51	'67	S	8	1	1	3	1:2G;4:RS
SPEA32	'77	A	11	6	2	9	1:2G;4:V
HOLM11	'66	U	16	K	3	4	1:2G;2:V
MULL01	'79	L	17	M	3	3	1:29;4:MY
CARR41	'76	U	19	6	3	3	1:2G
CARR43	'77	U	19	6	3	11	1:3G;2:2C;3:V;10:26
THUR21A	'38	U	19	6	3	10	7:2C;8:V
CARR21	'58	U	21	2	1	3	1:2G;4:V
CARR22	'58	U	21	2	1	2	1:2G;4:MY

[a]See Appendix A for codes. In a few cases, the classifications of factors shown here were preliminary and may not agree with the final classifications shown in the tables of Appendix B.

success in learning stenography. A phonetic script test was not included in dataset CARR21 but a possible phonetic coding factor appeared with highest loadings for the Turse Phonetic Association test (Turse, 1937–40) and a phonetic discrimination test. (The data discussed here are of course from a reanalysis of the battery correlations.) In the Turse test, the subject has to spell correctly a word suggested by a phonetic spelling such as *tox* (answer: *talks*). A correct-spelling recognition test also appeared on this factor, as well as several other tests whose appearance was not easy to explain. This factor appeared more clearly in dataset CARR22, although the loading for Phonetic Script (while salient for the first order) was low. Much of its variance was on a higher-order factor, possibly because of an induction component that seems to be involved in the task.

In a subsequent study (dataset CARR41) designed to examine the nature of the phonetic coding factor, the Phonetic Script test as well as an adaptation of the Turse Phonetic Association test appeared on a factor that was interpreted as Phonetic Coding. Associated with these tests were scores on two novel versions of the Atkinson–Shiffrin continuous paired-associate task (Atkinson & Shiffrin, 1968). In these tasks, one with stimuli given visually and the other with stimuli presented auditorily, the subject has to recall a CVC nonsense syllable that is currently associated with one of several digits; the associations change at various intervals during the task. In these tasks, even more than in the paper-and-pencil tasks, the subject has to encode and remember phonetic and graphemic material. Another experimental task that appeared on this factor was the Peterson and Peterson (1959) paradigm in which the subject is presented with a series of letters (the components of a CVC syllable) and then is asked to recall the letters after performing an interfering task (reading random numbers aloud). A similar factor appeared in a follow-up study (dataset CARR43), where the high loadings were for Spelling Clues (an adaptation of the Turse phonetic association test), Phonetic Script, a difficult spelling test, and a test of knowledge of pronunciation or grapheme–phoneme correspondence rules. Unfortunately, evidence from these studies for a separate Phonetic Coding factor is not as clear as might be desired, because the role of spelling knowledge is not adequately specified. Nevertheless, it appears that even if spelling ability is associated with phonetic coding, this association may come about because a phonetic coding ability is in some way basic to good spelling ability. Path-analytic studies might clarify this relation.

Several other datasets provide tentative evidence for a Phonetic Coding factor at relatively early ages (kindergarten and grade 1 samples). Dataset STAN61 shows a factor the authors (Stanovich, Cunningham, & Feeman, 1984) interpreted as "phonological awareness," which (according to my reanalysis) was measured principally by a Phonological Oddity task and a Strip Initial Consonant task. In the former, the child has to identify which of four words (presented auditorily) is different from the rest in not containing a common sound (e.g., in the set *bet*, *nut*, *get*, and *let*). In the latter, the child is asked to repeat a word spoken by the examiner, but without its initial consonant, to disclose another word, e.g., *pink → ink*. It would be interesting to determine whether such tests would correlate, in a longitudinal study, with measures of phonetic coding ability at later ages.

In a form of the Modern Language Aptitude Test designed for children in grades 3–6 (Carroll & Sapon, 1967), the subtest Hidden Words corresponds to the Phonetic Script subtest in the adult form; this test was loaded on what was interpreted as a Phonetic Coding factor in dataset SPEA32.

Reanalysis of dataset TAYL31, also involving young children, appears to show a phonetic coding factor (labeled 2U) at the second-order, with loadings on a variety of auditory tests in the Illinois Test of Psycholinguistic Abilities. At the first order, there are weak factors of Sound Blending and Auditory Closure.

A factor that is possibly related to Phonetic Coding appears in dataset HOLM11, but only some of its tests appear interpretable in these terms. A "word sense" test is essentially a cloze test, but the cues are abbreviated printed words somewhat like those in the Turse Phonetic Association test, and another test is very much like that test, requiring subjects to spell out words from printed cues such as *mlk*, *hpy*, and *rng*. Other tests require subjects to induce the meanings of Latin and Greek prefixes, suffixes, and roots, and these tests do not appear to involve phonetic coding.

Dataset MULL01 was collected on Arabic-speaking students (in Saudi Arabia) and appears to show a phonetic coding factor in several tests involving the learning of associations between sounds and printed symbols.

The variables loaded on factor 3 of dataset WALL51 (from Wallin's, 1967, study of factors in spelling ability in Swedish children) have some aspects that make this factor a possible candidate for a Phonetic Coding factor. A test Dissected Words has the highest salient loading; it requires the child to hear a spoken word and then find, in a printed list, which stimuli are "fragments" of the word. The test Exchange of Sounds presents a spoken word, e.g., FASLIG (a Swedish word), after which the child is to write this word with the S changed to R, the sounds being pronounced rather than the letter names. In a Sound Discrimination test, two words were presented; the child had to indicate whether the words were the same, or if not, at how many points they differed. These tests, as Wallin pointed out, required perception of word details. But other variables on this factor included a regular spelling/dictation test, a synonyms test, and a teachers' rating of attention and concentration.

Factor 10 in dataset THUR21A is loaded with two printed-test variables that may suggest a connection with a Phonetic Coding factor. In each item of Sound Grouping, S is presented with four printed words (e.g., *comb foam home come*) and is asked to indicate which one "sounds different." Performance obviously depends on reading decoding ability, but the factor is distinct from a verbal (V) factor; thus, it must also depend upon the subject's ability to detect differences in the rhyming sounds of words. Each item of the test Rhythm presents four lines of poetry; S is to indicate which line has a rhythm or meter that is different from the other three. Although this test does not depend on sensitivity to phonemic differences, its correlation with Sound Grouping suggests that both tests involve a sensitivity to the sound features of printed language. One hesitates to classify this factor with Phonetic Coding except in terms of a very broad grouping. These variables do not appear elsewhere in our database and deserve further investigation.

More research is needed on the nature of a phonetic coding or phonological awareness factor because of its possible importance in the learning of reading (Stanovich, 1988; Wagner & Torgeson, 1987) and foreign language skills (Carroll, 1974). The main question that needs to be answered is whether phonetic coding represents a basic characteristic of auditory–visual memory or is merely a reflection of individual differences in the learning of grapheme–phoneme correspondences.

GRAMMATICAL SENSITIVITY (MY) FACTORS

Another cluster of special skills in the language ability domain relates to the individual's awareness and knowledge of the grammatical features of the native language, quite apart from the skill with which the individual employs those features in using the native language in listening, speaking, reading, and writing. That is, although it may be assumed that the native speaker of a language implicitly learns or acquires a high degree of skill in *using* the grammatical structure of the language, it appears that there are wide differences in the degree

Table 5.11. *8 Grammatical Sensitivity (MY) factors in 7 datasets arranged in order of approximate mean age of sample*[a]

Dataset	Date	C'y code	Age	Sample code	M/F code	Factor no.	Remarks (higher-order factors; others related)
MULL01	'79	L	17	M	3	4	1:29;2:V;3:PC
CARR42	'76	U	19	P	3	1	2:V; 1 = Tested Grammatical Knowledge
"	"	"	"	"	"	4	4 = Self-rated Grammatical Knowledge
CARR43	'77	U	19	6	3	15	1:3G;10:26;11:PC
PIMS02	'62	U	19	F	3	8	1:KL;2:RS;5:V
CARR21	'58	U	21	2	1	2	1:2G;3:PC;4:V
CARR22	'58	U	21	2	1	4	1:2G;2:PC
SKEH01	'80	E	30	3	1	3	1:2G

[a]See Appendix A for codes. In a few cases, the classifications of factors shown here were preliminary and may not agree with the final classifications shown in the tables of Appendix B.

to which individuals are *aware* of the details of that structure. These individual differences may arise partly through school learning, but it is also possible that there are basic differences in aptitude for learning information about grammatical structure even with exposure to instruction in such information. Table 5.11 lists eight token factors from our survey that appear to measure or reflect such differences.

In early research on foreign language aptitude (Carroll, 1962b) I assumed that what I came to call "grammatical sensitivity" would be a useful predictor of foreign language learning. In an attempt to measure such a trait without at the same time measuring grammatical knowledge learned in formal instruction, I constructed a test called Words in Sentences. This is essentially a grammatical analogies test in which, given a sentence with one of its words or phrases specially marked (by printing it in capital letters), a subject had to identify which of five components in a second sentence (or set of sentences) had the same grammatical function as the component identified in the first sentence. This test was indeed found to be a strong contributor to the prediction of foreign language learning success in college students and adults, and it was included as Part IV of the *Modern Language Aptitude Test* (Carroll & Sapon, 1959). An adaptation of it was found useful in a form of the test designed for children in grades 3–6 (Carroll & Sapon, 1967). Further, two factor-analytic studies (datasets CARR21–22) appeared to support the conclusion that grammatical sensitivity constitutes a separate primary factor of language skill. In reanalyses of these datasets, Words in Sentences had the highest loadings on a possible grammatical sensitivity factor, but these factors were weak because of a lack of other variables that could be expected to measure this factor well. In a follow-up study (dataset CARR42), the factor was measured by a variety of grammatical tests, but both the verbal and mathematical scores of the Scholastic Aptitude test also appeared on this factor – suggesting that grammatical sensitivity may be correlated with a general intelligence or reasoning factor. (Possibly because of the test battery design or restriction of range in the sample, there was no higher-order factor in this dataset.) Orthogonal to this factor, but with loadings on it ranging from .11 to .25, appeared a factor (factor 2) interpreted as self-rated knowledge of grammar. Self-ratings of grammatical knowledge had low correlations with actual tests of grammatical knowledge or awareness, whether or not these tests employed grammatical terminology; people are poor judges of their own grammatical sensitivity. The study appeared to give good support for the existence of a grammatical sensitivity factor, but its separation from a more general factor of cognitive ability was not clear.

In a further follow-up study designed to study both Grammatical Sensitivity and Phonetic Coding (dataset CARR43), a Grammatical Sensitivity factor (factor 15) appeared more clearly, loaded most strongly with a test of grammatical knowledge and the Words in Sentences test, and somewhat less with self-ratings of grammar knowledge and a number learning test of the *Modern Language Aptitude Test* in which learning the "grammatical structure" of a number system in an artificial language is one aspect of the task. The SAT–V had an insignificant loading on this factor, while the SAT–M score had a loading of only .201. Several factors, including Grammatical Sensitivity, Phonetic Coding (factor 11), and a possible reasoning factor had loadings on a second-order factor (factor 10) intepreted as "linguistic element sensitivity." The results still did not conclusively settle the question of whether grammatical sensitivity is merely a learned ability.

Other datasets listed in Table 5.11 add little new information to the above. In dataset PIMS01, a possible grammatical sensitivity factor was poorly defined. In dataset SKEH01, such a factor was rather well defined by the Words in Sentences test as well as by several other tests in which subjects had to induce grammatical rules of unfamiliar or artificial languages, but age and education also loaded on this factor. A grammatical sensitivity factor also appeared in dataset MULL01, distinct from a Phonetic Coding factor and a factor defined only by an Aural Discrimination test and a vocabulary test (in Arabic).

Longitudinal research on the source and development of individual differences in grammatical sensitivity is needed.

FOREIGN LANGUAGE APTITUDE (LA) FACTORS

Because Grammatical Sensitivity and Phonetic Coding are important components of foreign language aptitude and are probably linked at a second-order, a distinct Foreign Language Aptitude (LA) factor occasionally occurs when a factor-analytic test battery does not contain enough first-order differentiation to permit these factors to appear separately. This is true of two datasets listed in

Table 5.12. *2 Foreign Language Aptitude (LA) factors in 2 datasets arranged in order of approximate mean age of sample*[a]

Dataset	Date	C'y code	Age	Sample code	M/F code	Factor no.	Remarks (higher-order factors; others related)
PIMS01	'62	U	19	F	3	3	1:2F;4:PT;5:AL;6:2C;7:V
WEAV01	'63	U	20	6	3	3	1:2C;2:V;4:CZ

[a]See Appendix A for codes. In a few cases, the classifications of factors shown here were preliminary and may not agree with the final classifications shown in the tables of Appendix B.

Table 5.12, and also of a dataset reported by Wesche, Edwards, and Wells (1982; see also Carroll, 1985). In WEAV01, for example, a foreign language aptitude factor appears, loaded with four subtests of the *Modern Language Aptitude Test*.

COMMUNICATION ABILITY (CM) FACTORS

At this point we turn attention to a series of factors that represent more general skills in communication, often involving listening and speech production, with or without involvement of reading and writing. Table 5.13 lists a few such factors in our datasets. The factor-analytic literature yields relatively little information on oral communication skills, presumably because it is difficult to measure such skills with anything like a paper-and-pencil test. The information reported in Table 5.13 is thus woefully inadequate for any thorough consideration of communication skills – their identification and their development. It cannot be claimed that the factors are all similar except to the extent that they concern various phenomena in oral communication.

Even at 22 months of age, it appears that there are individual differences in communication skills. In dataset WACH03 there is a factor saliently loaded with measures titled Schemas, Verbal Imitation, and Gestural Imitation from Uzgiris & Hunt's (1975) Infant Psychological Development Scale. (See also factor 3, dataset RICH32 and factor 4, dataset RICH33, classed as LD factors and listed in Table 5.1.)

In reanalysis of data from a study (Rondal, 1978; dataset ROND01) of characteristics of the speech of normal and Down's syndrome children, factor 2 is interpreted as indicating individual differences in degree of interactive communication with mothers. It is loaded with indices of the proportions of certain types of sentences and questions used in communicative interaction: "Wh-" questions, imperative sentences, and Yes–No questions.

Dataset BOLT11 reveals two linearly independent factors relating to the communication abilities of deaf adolescents. Factor 4 is a relatively broad factor that concerns reading and writing as well as communication by normal speech (by lipreading). Factor 5 has to do with ability in the use of manual signs and

Table 5.13. *3 Communication Ability (CM) factors in 3 datasets arranged in order of approximate mean age of sample[a]*

Dataset	Date	C'y code	Age	Sample code	M/F code	Factor no.	Remarks (higher-order factors; others related)
WACH03	'81	U	2	N	3	3	1:X2;2:X4
ROND01	'78	U	10	X	3	2	1:C1
BOLT11	'73	U	19	E	3	4	1:2G;5:KF;4 = Reading, Writing,Speech in Deaf

[a]See Appendix A for codes. In a few cases, the classifications of factors shown here were preliminary and may not agree with the final classifications shown in the tables of Appendix B.

fingerspelling. Both factors are dominated by a second-order factor that appears to represent general intelligence.

Aside from a study by Marge (1964) to be discussed later, the best available study of oral communication abilities is by Taylor, Ghiselin, and Yagi (1967) but it has received little attention because of the relative inaccessibility of the publication resulting from it. It yields three datasets, TAYL11, TAYL12A, and TAYL13A, the first of which is concerned mainly with abilities that can be measured by pencil-and-paper tests. The latter two involved elaborate observational and testing procedures that looked at language skills in various live communication situations, such as giving a lecture, participating in a group discussion, or instructing people on how to assemble and use a gun. The studies were conducted using either university students or officer candidates in the Air Force. Some of the factors were fairly specific and will be discussed subsequently. Factor 6 of dataset TAYL12A, however, is fairly general; it is loaded chiefly by two sociometric peer-rating measures of "listening ability" and performance in conducting a military drill. Factor 3 of TAYL13A appears to deal more directly with ability in speaking, being measured by performance in a conference situation, performance in a situation in which an emergency had to be dealt with by telephone, avoidance of unnecessary pauses in a public speaking situation, and overall rate of speech in public speaking. (It was also measured by a written test in which ideas had to be extracted from written material and placed correctly in an outline. Possibly such ability – to identify and structure important ideas – is involved in public speaking.) In each case, the factor is dominated by a second-order factor interpreted as "general communication ability" but which may in fact be more like a general intelligence factor since it covered a variety of cognitive abilities outside the language domain.

LISTENING ABILITY (LS) FACTORS

Educators generally recognize ability to listen to spoken prose as a skill somewhat distinct from reading ability, but it has always been difficult to measure

Table 5.14. *7 Listening Ability (LS) factors in 7 datasets arranged in order of approximate mean age of sample*[a]

Dataset	Date	C'y code	Age	Sample code	M/F code	Factor no.	Remarks (higher-order factors; others related)
SING21	'65	U	9	1	3	4	1:2G;2:V
SPEA01	'62	A	11	6	1	3	1:2H;5:V
SPEA02	'62	A	11	6	2	2	1:2H
JACK11	'79	U	18	6	3	3	1:2C;2:V;4:RS
JACK12	'79	U	18	6	3	2	1:2H
KAMM01	'53	U	19	F	3	7	1:2G;3:V
SCHO31	'80	U	21	F	3	3	1:29;2:RC (See KL factors)

[a] See Appendix A for codes. In a few cases, the classifications of factors shown here were preliminary and may not agree with the final classifications shown in the tables of Appendix B.

such an ability separate from reading skill factors. Partly this is due to the fact that many listening ability tests actually require reading ability at least to the extent of facility in reading printed answers to questions based on passages that are presented auditorily. Also, it can be said that, as compared to the voluminous research on reading skill, much less attention has been devoted to the measurement of listening ability. Nevertheless, there is some evidence from the factorial literature that supports the existence of listening ability as a separate skill. Table 5.14 lists some such evidence.

Dataset SING21 comes from a study of the Durrell–Sullivan Reading Capacity Test, which was designed on the principle that the *potential* reading achievement of a child should be equal to the child's auditory comprehension. The test has two parts in which listening comprehension is tested with spoken stimuli and pictorial alternatives, in the subtests Word Meaning and Paragraph Meaning; scores are to be compared with those on reading vocabulary and comprehension tests. In our reanalysis of Singer's varimax-rotated principal component matrix, these tests load on a listening comprehension factor along with Thurstone's PMA pictorial test of vocabulary and a test of range of information. These are linked to reading comprehension tests through a second-order verbal ability factor.

Probably the clearest indication of a listening comprehension factor comes from a study by Spearritt (1962) in which careful attention was paid to measuring this skill without the involvement of reading skill. For 6th-grade *boys* (SPEA01), a clear listening comprehension factor, measured by a variety of auditorily presented language tests, was obtained separate from a reading ability factor. This was not true for the comparable sample of girls, however (dataset SPEA02, factor 2), where both listening and reading tests loaded on the same factor. One may interpret this result as showing that for the samples involved, reading and listening skills develop in parallel for most (if not all) girls, but not for boys. It is well known that boys are more likely than girls to have difficulties in reading skills; thus, while their listening skills develop along with their general progress in language, reading skills for many boys are slower in development.

Jackson and McClelland (1979) were also concerned with differentiating listening skills from reading skills, but because they used only one measure of listening comprehension, a clear listening comprehension factor did not appear in either of the datasets analyzed from their study (JACK11–12), although in JACK11 a factor loaded with the listening comprehension measure was differentiated from reading speed and from a more general V factor. Also, listening comprehension had the highest loading in factor 2 of JACK12, along with several other measures that were obviously concerned with reading comprehension.

Although their numerous datasets were not included in our database, studies by Atkin, Bray, Davison, Herzberger, Humphreys, and Selzer (1977a, b) provide further evidence for a listening comprehension factor separate from other cognitive skills. These authors analyzed longitudinal data on students tested and retested in grades 5, 7, 9, and 11 and found that grade 5 scores on an aural comprehension test made a clearly independent contribution to the prediction of later cognitive development.

In the context of second-language acquisition studies, possible listening comprehension factors are found in datasets KAMM01 and SCHO31 (see Table 5.18).

Apparently there has been little attention to the way in which rates at which speech is presented may interact with individual differences in listening ability, controlling for the linguistic complexity of the material. A study by Friedman and Johnson (1968) offers some clues, however, that might well be followed up. These authors examined the predictability of scores on listening comprehension tests at four speech rates, 175, 250, 325, and 450 wpm. The 175 wpm rate was regarded as normal; the other three rates were achieved by compressed speech technology. Mean scores at these four rates were 14.55, 13.41, 10.41, and 4.93; performance thus fell off sharply for the 450 wpm rate. The best predictor of performance was a vocabulary test, with correlations of .67, .58, .50, and .54 for the four rates. Friedman and Johnson found that Guilford's Best Trend Name Test (a test that Guilford claimed measured Evaluation of Semantic Relations) had validity coefficients of .32, 22, .19, and .42 at the four rates. Friedman and Johnson's multiple regression analysis showed that Vocabulary and Best Trend Name had the highest beta-weights (.44 and .36, respectively) for the 450 wpm rate. Unfortunately, their analysis was incorrect. My computations from their published data show that only Vocabulary had significant beta-weights at all four rates; the correct beta-weights for Vocabulary and Best Trend Name at the 450 wpm rate are .54 and .18, respectively. Another problem with this study is that the authors did not demonstrate that scores on the listening comprehension test were significantly above chance and also above scores that would have been obtained if the relevant passage had not been presented. It is frequently the case that individuals can make above-chance scores on reading or listening comprehension tests even when they are not presented with the written or spoken texts on which the tests are based (Weaver & Bickley, 1967).

A study by Carver, Johnson, and Friedman (1971–72) addressing the factor analysis of the ability to comprehend time-compressed speech is not very informative, possibly because the battery was quite limited in the diversity of its variables. It disclosed a single factor for listening comprehension ability that had loadings that showed little variation dependent on rate of presented speech. This factor was largely independent of variables measuring 'cloze ability' (factor CZ) or speed of closure (factor CS).

Investigations of listening ability, whether for normal or compressed speech, need to take account of the possible effects of a factor of auditory ability, Resistance to Auditory Distortion (UR), discussed in Chapter 9. For example, a measure of ability to comprehend compressed speech in dataset STAN31 was loaded on that factor.

ORAL PRODUCTION (OP) FACTORS

Table 5.15 lists factors that appear to measure oral production (OP) abilities that are rather more specific than the general communication (CM) factors that were listed in Table 5.13. They come from a small number of studies that attempted to measure these skills quite directly, either by obtaining teachers' or peers' ratings of these abilities as observed in "real-life" situations (as opposed to artificial testing situations), or by assessing them in testing situations that were made to simulate "real-life" situations as closely as possible.

Marge's (1964; dataset MARG01) study utilized a battery of 40 measures of various oral production abilities, applied to a sample of Grade 6 children in a middle- to upper-middle-class suburb of Boston. Because this number of variables already approached unmanageability in a doctoral dissertation, it employed no printed tests of intelligence, vocabulary, reading, or writing, and thus relationships between oral production abilities and abilities in reading and writing were not investigated. However, it employed three types of measures: ratings by teachers, ratings by speech specialists who evaluated the children's spontaneous speech as recorded on tape, and a small set of special speech tests. Marge obtained seven factors; my reanalysis extended this to an eighth, second-order factor that can be interpreted as general oral communication ability. Of the seven primary factors, six are listed in Table 5.15. (The remaining factor, interpreted as Speech Motor Skill or Speed of Articulation, was assigned to the psychomotor domain; see Chapter 13.)

Factor 2 appeared with high loadings (> .50) on a variety of teachers' ratings of the children's speaking abilities – of "clarity of thought," "general communication of ideas," "vocabulary in speech," "correctness of pronunciation," "grammatical usage," "general behavior in oral reading," "skill in impromptu talks," "flow of words," "wealth of ideas," "articulation in conversation," and "ability in peer

Table 5.15. *15 Oral Production and Fluency (OP) factors in 9 datasets arranged in order of approximate mean age of sample*[a]

Dataset	Date	C'y code	Age	Sample code	M/F code	Factor no.	Remarks (higher-order factors; others related)
MCCA21	'66	U	6	1	3	3	1:2G;2:LD
HASS01	'74	U	8	1	3	1	Orthogonal factors; 2,3,4,5:O&
SNOW03	'79	H	10	F	3	4	1:2C;2,3:KL (Dutch)
MARG01	'64	U	11	6	3	2	1:2!;Others:See below; 2 = Speaking ability, Teacher-rated
"	"	"	"	"	"	3	3 = Language maturity, Specialist-rated
"	"	"	"	"	"	4	4 = Speech dominance
"	"	"	"	"	"	5	5 = Speaking ability, Specialist-rated
"	"	"	"	"	"	7	7 = Voice quality
"	"	"	"	"	"	8	8 = Non-distracting speech behavior
ROGE11	'53	E	14	6	3	4	1:2G;2:FI;3:WA
STOR11	'66	U	14	8	3	6	1:2G;4:V
TAYL13A	'67	U	19	6	1	3	1:2!;2:V
CARR01	'41	U	20	6	3	9	7:2N
TAYL12A	'67	U	21	2	1	3	1:2!;4:V;3 = Expressional ability (self-rated)
"	"	"	"	"	"	6	6 = Communication ability (peer-rated)

[a]See Appendix A for codes. In a few cases, the classifications of factors shown here were preliminary and may not agree with the final classifications shown in the tables of Appendix B.

group communication." It is possible, of course, that teachers' ratings were subject to a halo effect, and were influenced by teachers' impressions of the overall scholastic abilities of the children; note that one of the rating scales concerned oral *reading* behavior. If printed measures of intelligence, vocabulary, and reading ability had been employed, it is almost certain that they would have shown substantial correlations with the teachers' ratings of speaking abilities, but of course it is not clear from these data whether factor 2 would be distinct from one or more factors that might have been derived from such printed tests. At the same time, it should be observed that teachers did make distinctions among certain traits of speaking ability, since factors 4 and 8 were also derived primarily from teachers' ratings (as opposed to speech specialists' ratings). Factor 4 was interpreted as "Speech Dominance" and was derived from teachers' ratings of the children's typical behavior in group discussions, conversations, and situations in which a child might persuade a classmate of some point or idea. Factor 8 was interpreted as "Non-Distracting Speech Behavior," a general term for observations of "speech etiquette" and ability to speak with a minimum of hesitations, broken-off sentences, and the like. Teachers' ratings of "amount of talkativeness" had a high negative loading on this factor.

Factors 3, 5, and 7 were derived primarily from speech specialists' ratings of children's speech as tape-recorded in two contrived testing situations: (1) a picture description test in which the child was presented a picture, allowed to think what to say, and then asked to speak for 2 minutes about the picture; and (2) an impromptu speech test in which the subject was asked to describe a television program he or she had viewed recently. Factor 3 was loaded with ratings of grammatical usage, correctness of pronunciation, speech vocabulary, complexity of sentence structure, articulation, and formality of oral style. It was interpreted as "Language Maturity" because it appeared to represent the extent to which the child's speech approximated adult standards of educated standard speech. Factor 5 was measured by ratings of the continuity of speech, flow of words, amount of talkativeness, "non-distracting speech behavior," avoidance of hesitations, clarity of thought, and communication and wealth of ideas. Factor 7 centered in ratings of voice quality and appeal.

For the most part, all measures of factors 2, 3, 4, and 5 had high loadings (in the .40s, .50s, and .60s) on a general oral communication factor (factor 1); that is, these factors were substantially correlated though factorially distinct. The general trait of oral communication ability was perceived by both teachers and speech specialists. Variables for factors 7 (voice quality) and 8 (non-distracting speech behavior), however, had quite low loadings (ranging from .164 to .395) on the second-order factor.

Dataset CARR01 disclosed an Oral Language Production factor based on ratings and other measures from a picture description test somewhat similar to that used by Marge. Unfortunately, the measures were based on only one testing situation and were not as experimentally independent as might be desired. Of interest, however, is the fact that the second-order factor on which these measures loaded highest was a General Idea Production factor (factor 7), in what we are calling the Idea Production and Language Fluency domain (see Chapter 10). The measures had vanishing loadings on a second-order Crystallized Intelligence factor (factor 1); i.e., they did not correlate with measures of vocabulary and reading skills.

In measuring oral production ability, there arises the problem of controlling for variance from the first-order factor FI (Ideational Fluency) discussed in Chapter 10. That such control is possible is suggested from dataset ROGE11, where factor 4, interpreted as OP (Oral Production) was distinct from factor 2, interpreted as FI. Factor 4 was loaded with Pictures (total number of ideas given in oral responses to pictures of a tree and a street corner), Topic: Parcel (making up an oral story about a parcel), Inkblots (orally stating things that can be seen in three inkblots), and Picture Description (telling a story, orally, to describe a picture the subject has been shown). In contrast, factor 2 was loaded with a wide variety of *written* tests requiring giving a variety of responses.

Datasets TAYL12A and TAYL13A come from the large exploratory study by Taylor, Ghiselin, and Yagi (1967) already mentioned. According to my conservative reanalysis of these datasets, each yields only one factor that can possibly be interpreted as an oral production ability factor. Factor 3 is loaded primarily with self-rating and self-report measures of speaking ability, such as a Speech Attitude Scale (apparently that of Knower, 1938, also used in dataset CARR01), a self-rating of speaking ability, a biographical information inventory about experiences in speaking, a self-rating of "interest in speaking," etc. However, it also contains loadings (generally lower than for the speaking ability ratings) for some self-report scales on writing. Apparently the factor concerns subjects' feelings of confidence in expressing themselves *either* in speech or in writing. At the second order is a single general factor (factor 1) that has substantial loadings not only on this expressional ability factor but also on a V factor and a general idea production factor.

Factor 3 in TAYL13A has already been mentioned under Communication Ability (CM) factors, but it could also be regarded as an Oral Production factor since it is loaded with several measures derived from performances in contrived oral communication situations intended to simulate real-world oral communication tasks.

Dataset HASS01 (Hass & Wepman, 1974) is from a study of individual differences in the spoken syntax of groups of children at ages 5, 6, 7, 9, and 11. It is based on recorded spoken protocols of children responding to selected sex-appropriate cards of the TAT (Thematic Apperception Test; Murray, 1943). Our analysis is based on the unrotated principal component matrix presented by the authors; the correlation matrix for the 58 variables was not available. The factors were rotated to simple structure and appeared orthogonal. Factor 1 was loaded with a total word count and a large number of other variables reflecting the sheer number of various syntactic constructions occurring in the protocols. It is interpreted, therefore, as an oral production or speech fluency factor that applies at least for the kinds of stimulus situations represented by the TAT cards. Whether it would also apply for speech protocols obtained in other types of speech situations is of course unknown. (The other factors for this study were regarded as factors of oral style; they are considered in the next section.)

McCartin and Meyers (1966) sought to explore "six semantic factors," as specified by Guilford's (1967) Structure-of-Intellect model, in Grade 1 children. Using our criteria for the number of acceptable factors, we were not able to confirm the six factors they obtained in a factor analysis. Instead, we obtained two first-order factors and a second-order factor. Factor 2 was interpreted as a Language Development (LD) factor and is listed in Table 5.1. Factor 3 is loaded with various oral production variables (e.g., judged quality of response to "tell about your home" [Gewirtz, 1948], "make up a story about a house, a bucket of paint, and a boy or girl" [Loeffler, 1963]) and is thus interpreted as measuring factor OP. The correlation between the oblique forms of factors 2 and 3 was .532 and all variables had substantial loadings on the second-order factor, no doubt reflecting considerable variation in mental status in a sample of Grade 1 children.

Two other studies yield factors possibly to be interpreted as Oral Production (OP). In Snow and Hoefnagel–Höhle's (1979) study of English speakers learning Dutch, an English fluency variable was created by rating responses to a story-telling task. In early stages of learning Dutch, English fluency appeared on factors measuring acquisition of Dutch, but at a later stage, it appeared on a factor (factor 4 in dataset SNOW03) that reflects oral production ability. In dataset STOR11, factor 6 was loaded chiefly with a task from the Stanford-Binet test, Repeating Thought of a Passage. Since this factor was distinct from a verbal factor, it was assigned to factor OP.

Not included in our database was an analysis of data on school principals' public speaking performance by Hemphill, Griffiths, Frederiksen, Stice, Iannaccone, Coffield, and Carlton (1961, Chapter X) as part of a study of administrative performance. The principals in this study ($N = 232$) were asked to prepare and deliver, into a tape recorder, a 10-minute speech to a local P.T.A. on the topic, "The Value of Education in America." Few principals used the full ten minutes that they were given, and 15 recordings were blank or otherwise unusable. The recordings were scored by members of a speech faculty in terms of ratings on ten categories: Length, Introduction, Organization, Conclusion, Word Usage, Clarity, Voice Control, Voice Interest, Pronunciation, and Efficiency. These measures were factor-analyzed, yielding three oblique factors interpreted as follows: Factor A, Precision, Clarity, and Organization; Factor B: Effective Use of Time; and Factor C, Voice Control and Delivery. Some of the measures of Factor A, especially Word Usage, were positively and significantly correlated to scores on various tests of mental ability.

Somewhat in contrast to the findings of this study were those from a study by Ball (1952) of relationships between ratings of students' classroom speeches and scores on mental tests. The correlation of speech ratings with a combination of aptitude test scores was only .30.

ORAL STYLE (O&) FACTORS

Several datasets in our survey illustrate the use of factor analysis in isolating characteristics of language style. Factors from three such studies are listed in Table 5.16. Strictly speaking, it is questionable whether these factors should be regarded as cognitive abilities, even though they might be correlated with such abilities. Rather, they are dimensions by which particular samples of language productions may be characterized. Comparable dimensions were isolated factor-

Table 5.16. *11 Oral Style (O&) factors in 4 datasets arranged in order of approximate mean age of sample*[a]

Dataset	Date	C'y code	Age	Sample code	M/F code	Factor no.	Remarks (higher-order factors; others related)
HASS01	'74	U	5-11	1	3	2	1:OP; Others: see below 2 = Embeddedness
"	"	"	"	"	"	3	3 = Noun Phrase Structure
"	"	"	"	"	"	4	4 = Nominal Emphasis
"	"	"	"	"	"	5	5 = Finite Verb Structure
CUMM01	'79	C	9	8	3	2	Complexity Oral Language
ROND01	'78	U	10	X	3	1	2:CM;1 = Complexity
ROND02	'78	U	30	Y	2	2	Few Imperatives, Repetitions
"	"	"	"	"	"	3	Long Sentences, Frequent Modifiers
"	"	"	"	"	"	4	Few Repetitions, Expansions
"	"	"	"	"	"	6	Few Wh-Questions, Frequent Declarative Sentences
"	"	"	"	"	"	7	Wh-Questions more frequent than Yes–No Questions

[a] See Appendix A for codes. In a few cases, the classifications of factors shown here were preliminary and may not agree with the final classifications shown in the tables of Appendix B.

analytically by Carroll (1960) in written prose, and by Jones and Wepman (1967) in stories told by adult speakers.

Hass and Wepman's (1974; dataset HASS01) data have already been described, above. The five factors isolated were generally uncorrelated, and no higher-order factor was derived. Factor 1, Speech Fluency or amount of speaking, was considered as a measure of factor OP, listed in Table 5.15. The remaining factors are considered here as measures of oral style. Factor 2, Embeddedness, was loaded with various measures of surface structure elaboration, and was highly correlated with age (which has a loading of .638 on this factor). Age has a loading of .339 on Factor 3, Noun Phrase Structure, defined by such variables as the proportion of prepositions, the proportion of "indefinites", and the proportion of "common words." Age had insignificant loadings on Factors 4 and 5, respectively titled Nominal Emphasis and Finite Verb Structure. Space does not permit detailed descriptions of these factors; the interested reader is advised to consult the original source.

Factor 1 emerging from analysis of dataset ROND01 (based on several objective measures of children's speech) is titled Complexity and is possibly the same as the Embeddedness factor of dataset HASS01 just mentioned. Also, there was a second-order factor of speech complexity in dataset ROND02, based on analyses of the speech of the mothers in interaction with the children studied in dataset ROND01. Such a factor may also be related to the Language Maturity factor found in dataset MARG01 (Table 5.15). It is likely that this factor would be found to be related to language development (LD) or verbal ability (V) as measured by formal tests of these factors. The other factors from dataset ROND02 seem to reflect characteristic linguistic response tendencies in mothers' verbal behavior with their children: Factor 2, a tendency to utter few imperatives and not to repeat the mother's own utterances, vs. the tendency to utter many imperatives and make many speech repetitions; Factor 3, a tendency to utter long sentences, with frequent modifiers; Factor 4, a tendency to make few repetitions, give few approving utterances, and make few expensions of the mother's own utterances; and Factor 5, a tendency to ask few wh- questions, and to utter a high proportion of declarative sentences.

Factor 2 in dataset CUMM01 is loaded with two measures of the complexity of oral language elicited from nine year-old children in a story-telling task: words per T-unit and clauses per T-unit. (A T-unit is a grammatically defined utterance, or segment therof, as established by procedures due to K. W. Hunt, 1970, used in measuring degree of "syntactic maturity.") Factor 3 in this dataset was interpreted as Language Development and listed in Table 5.1, although it might equally well have been interpreted as Oral Production. Oblique factors 2 and 3 had a correlation of .498 and all variables on both of these factors had substantial loadings on a second-order factor interpreted as general cognitive development.

From these studies, one gets at least a glimpse of the possible dimensions of oral style. An important dimension is complexity of oral language, frequently found in children to be correlated with language development and amount of oral language, and thus an indicator of syntactic maturity. Other dimensions of oral style tend to be dependent on situational constraints.

WRITING ABILITY (WA) FACTORS

Factor-analytic studies have not generally been very successful in identifying a factor of writing ability distinct from other abilities in the language domain. Early studies such as those of Thurstone (1938b; dataset THUR21A) and Carroll (1941; dataset CARR01) had a Theme-Writing variable in their correlational matrices and found only that it loaded on a verbal factor V. If a Writing Ability factor is to be found distinct from other language abilities, there must be sufficient variables to define such a factor, and ideally, these variables should be experimentally independent. That is, the variables should not be merely different ways of scoring the same writing product.

Table 5.17. *8 Writing Ability (WA) factors in 8 datasets arranged in order of approximate mean age of sample*[a]

Dataset	Date	C'y code	Age	Sample code	M/F code	Factor no.	Remarks (higher-order factors; others related)
BENN01	'73	E	10	1	1	2	1:2C
BENN02	'73	E	10	1	2	2	1:2C
OLSO51	'66	U	14	E	3	4	1:2C;3:RS;6:LP
ROGE11	'53	E	14	6	3	3	1:2C;4:OP
WEIN11	'59	U	16	1	3	5	1:2G;4:V
GUIL12	'56	U	21	3	1	7	1:2S
TAYL11	'67	U	21	3	1	6	1:2!;2:V;3:FI;4:FE;5:WA?; 7:FO;8:FW
TAYL12A	'67	U	21	2	1	5	1:2!;2:WA?;3:OP;4:V

[a] See Appendix A for codes. In a few cases, the classifications of factors shown here were preliminary and may not agree with the final classifications shown in the tables of Appendix B.

At the same time, some doubts can be expressed that there *ought to be* a distinct writing ability factor, whether or not it would be linearly independent of general language ability as expressed in factor LD or V. Superior writing ability depends heavily on knowledge and ready recall of the facilities embodied in the language one is writing in, and thus on the abilities and knowledges expressed in factors LD, V, and VL. But writing has many varieties and purposes. If one is writing to inform, one needs knowledge of the material about which one is informing, and reasoning about the line of argumentation. If one is writing to persuade, one needs in addition to know one's audience and what kinds of ideas would appeal to and motivate that audience. There is also something called "creative writing," and this requires the production and organization of ideas, particularly novel or creative ideas. Writing ability, therefore, is not to be considered as a single dimension of ability – it could depend on many abilities. It is better thought of as a global, even nebulous variable that cannot be tied to any particular view of writing behavior and its antecedents and consequences. This probably explains the difficulty that educational authorities and organizations, such as the National Assessment of Educational Progress, have had in defining writing ability for the purpose of assessing the progress that schools are making in teaching students to write (Applebee, Langer, & Mullis, 1986).

Table 5.17 lists eight factors interpreted as writing ability (WA) in our datasets. There is only one case (dataset WEIN11) in which the writing ability factor is clearly distinct from a verbal factor V, and this is mainly because the writing factor is based on four experimentally dependent ratings of a theme that the subjects were given 30 to 35 minutes to write on a topic of their choice. Ratings were made by English teachers on Choice of Words, Organization, Sentence

Structure, and Originality. The other dataset – even one with a large number of variables (GUIL12) – did not contain variables sufficient to define a verbal factor.

In most cases, the writing ability factor is defined by multiple measures of a single writing product. In a report by Bennett (1973; datasets BENN01 for boys and BENN02 for girls) there is no information as to the instructions for, or the timing of, an imaginative story that subjects were asked to write. The writing factor (factor 2 in both datasets) is loaded with a variable derived from the "impression marks by teachers for the use of imagination, good ideas, and so on" (poor spelling and grammar not being penalized), and a word count of the story. Thus, longer stories tended to receive higher marks. It is debatable whether there should be control for the amount written. That is, should writing ability be assessed partly in terms of how much the subject can write in a given amount of time?

In dataset GUIL12, the writing factor is loaded with ratings on the "coherence of the story" and the total number of words written. The writing task in this case was to write a story containing ten specified words. In dataset OLSO51, the variables were *exclusively* a function of amount written, that is, the total number of sentences and the total number of words, obviously automatically correlated to such an extent that the factor could be said to be largely an artifact of experimental dependence.

In the case of dataset ROGE11 (Rogers, 1953) it is even questionable whether the writing ability factor (factor 3) should be regarded as truly writing ability or simply speed of handwriting, because although the highest salient loading was for the amount written in "writing more to an unfinished story," other loadings were for Handwriting – amount written in copying a familiar passage in 4 1/2 minutes, number of words written in a Letter–Star test, and number of responses produced in a Similes test (see Chapter 10 for descriptions of these tests). There was no consideration of the quality of the responses to any of these tasks. The factor was distinct from an oral production factor (factor 4), but this does not speak to the construct validity of the writing ability factor.

A thorough study of writing ability from a factorial point of view would have to involve consideration of different kinds of writing tasks, scored in a variety of ways, as criterion variables (or extension variables) for a matrix of a variety of relevant cognitive variables, including language, knowledge, reasoning, and idea production abilities. Using multiple scorings of writing products – both with and without control for amount written in a given amount of time – as extension variables would avoid the problems of experimental dependence that have beset the work reviewed here. To my knowledge, no such study has been conducted.

Studies done by Taylor (1947; dataset TAYL01) and Taylor, Ghiselin, and Yagi (1967; datasets TAYL11, TAYL12A, and TAYL13A) come close to meeting these desiderata, particularly as concerns dataset TAYL13A, in which various writing tasks were used along with a number of cognitive ability tests and measures of other communication skill. No general writing ability factor *as such* was disclosed, however. Scores from writing tasks tended to appear on a verbal ability (V) factor, a fact that confirms our suggestion that writing ability depends on basic language abilities. The factors from these datasets that are listed in Table 5.17 reflected what appears to be a rather specialized skill, namely, the ability to write telegrams with an economy of words, as opposed to being unnecessarily wordy.

FOREIGN LANGUAGE PROFICIENCY (KL) FACTORS

Up to this point discussion has concerned skills in individuals' native languages. We have emphasized that it is profitable to analyze such skills in the traditional categories of listening, speaking, reading, and writing generally considered by teachers of foreign languages. If it is useful to consider native language skills in terms of these traditional categories, this should also apply to the acquisition and learning of skills in a foreign or second language. A number of datasets in our survey pertained to this kind of language acquisition; factors of foreign or second language proficiency are listed in Table 5.18.

Some of the datasets come from studies in which little attempt was made to differentiate, factorially, aspects of foreign language proficiency. Second language proficiency was assessed in a variety of ways – by course grades, reading comprehension or cloze tests, and grades in language laboratory work, but no separate factors for different aspects of proficiency appeared. This was true of datasets MASN01, KAMM01, PIMS01, and PIMS02.

Datasets SNOW01–03 come from a study by Snow and Hoefnagel–Höhle (1979) of English speakers of various ages learning Dutch "naturalistically," i.e., in a Dutch environment but with little or no formal instruction. The three datasets pertain to data collected at 4–5 month intervals, the first being shortly after the individuals arrived in the Netherlands. Factorial structures differed somewhat over the three testing times, reflecting different stages in language acquisition, and possibly different stages of acquisition in persons of different ages (ages ranged from 3 to adult). The results are hard to interpret and summarize, but for present purposes it may suffice to point out that (1) phonological ability in Dutch tended to form a factor at each of the three testing times; (2) vocabulary and grammar tests, both in English and Dutch, formed a factor at each testing time, with the relations between English and Dutch strongest at the last testing time; and (3) fluency in English formed a separate factor only at the last testing time (see Table 5.15 and accompanying discussion). At all testing times, there was a second-order factor of general language ability in both English and Dutch.

Dataset SCHO31 comes from a study by Scholz, Hendricks, Spurling, Johnson, and Vandenberg (1980) done to answer a question raised by Oller (1976): Is language ability divisible or unitary? Oller had emphasized the claimed unitary nature of language ability. In my reanalysis of the Scholz et al. data and comment on the issue (Carroll, 1983a), I pointed out that language ability is *both* unitary *and* divisible, in that as illustrated by the Scholz et al. data, there was a general factor of proficiency in English as a second language (among foreign students at Southern Illinois University) and a classic division of primary factors into a reading and grammar factor, a listening factor, an oral interview factor, and a writing production factor. As I have argued elsewhere (Carroll, 1968a), it is reasonable to expect that proficiencies in a second language could be reflected in a series of linearly independent factors that would tend to parallel those obtained in measuring native-language skills.

Bachman's (1982; dataset BACH01) study of possible dimensions of cloze test performance among ESL students has already been mentioned. My analysis of Bachman and Palmer's (1982; dataset BACH11) study of ESL proficiency shows that while there is a strong general factor in such proficiency, there are separate trait and testing method factors, depending on how proficiency is measured – by interviews and written tests that are not multiple-choice, by multiple-choice tests, or by learners' self-ratings of proficiency. Bachman and Palmer's claim that there are separate aspects of proficiency associated with grammar, "sociolinguistics," and "pragmatics" seems not to be well supported in their data when exploratory factor analysis is used.

Presumably, if second language proficiency skills were studied as thoroughly as first language skills have been, much the same clusters of abilities would be found for those skills. The clusters could be represented in the same way as they are depicted in Figure 5.1 for first language skills.

SUMMARY AND COMMENT

This chapter has shown that language ability is a complex affair. It can be regarded, on the one hand, as a unitary factor that depends on the degree to which an individual has, on the whole, acquired the many thousands of competences and response capabilities associated with that individual's native language, or with a second language. All these competences tend to be learned together, *pari passu*, and in somewhat the same order by all individuals. For example, in vocabulary acquisition a certain set of vocabulary knowledges tends to be learned first (Brown, 1957), while low frequency, more specialized words tend to be learned much later. Similarly, Brown (1973) has shown that there is a fairly consistent order in which children learn certain grammatical phenomena in their native language. The general factors dominating the various primary factors of language skill can be regarded as measures of the extent to which an individual has learned the lexical and grammatical phenomena of a language (be it a native language or a second language), and roughly the point to which the individual has progressed along a scale of language development in that language. There are wide individual differences in rates of acquisition, and differences in acquisition rates are reflected in variance of test scores, ratings, or other relevant variables measured

Table 5.18. *21 Foreign Language Proficiency (KL) factors in 10 datasets arranged in order of approximate mean age of sample[a]*

Dataset	Date	C'y code	Age	Sample code	M/F code	Factor no.	Remarks (higher-order factors; others related)
SNOW01	'79	H	3–Adult	F	3	2	1:2G; 2 = Dutch productive ability
SNOW02	'79	H	3–Adult	F	3	2	1:2G;Others; See below 2 = Dutch phonological ability
"	"	"	"	"	"	3	3 = Dutch receptive ability
"	"	"	"	"	"	4	4 = Vocab. & grammar (English & Dutch)
SNOW03	'79	H	3–Adult	F	3	2	1:2G;Others: See below 2 = Dutch vocab. & grammar
"	"	"	"	"	"	3	3 = Dutch phonological ability
MASN01	'83	C	18	F	3	3	1:2G;2:V (in French) 3 = Proficiency in English
KAMM01	'53	U	19	F	3	5	1:2G;3:V;7:LS 5 = Proficiency in Spanish
PIMS01	'62	U	19	F	3	5	1:2F;3:LA; 5 = Proficiency in French
PIMS02	'62	U	19	F	3	1	1 = Proficiency in French
SCHO31	'80	U	21	F	3	2	1:29;Others: See below 2 = ESL Reading & grammar
"	"	"	"	"	"	3	3 = ESL Listening
"	"	"	"	"	"	4	4 = ESL in Oral interview
"	"	"	"	"	"	5	5 = ESL Writing production
"	"	"	"	"	"	6	6 = ESL Accent
BACH01	'82	U	22	F	3	2	1:29;Others: See below 2 = Cloze test (Strategic)
"	"	"	"	"	"	3	3 = Cloze test (Cohesion; syntactic)
"	"	"	"	"	"	4	4 = Cloze test (Cohesion; syntactic II)
BACH11	'82	U	23	F	3	2	1:29;Others: See below 2 = ESL proficiency by written test & interview

Table 5.18 (*cont.*)

Dataset	Date	C'y code	Age	Sample code	M/F code	Factor no.	Remarks (higher-order factors; others related)
BACH11	'82	U	23	F	3	3	3 = ESL proficiency as self-rated
"	"	"	"	"	"	4	4 = ESL proficiency in grammar & pragmatics by multiple-choice test

[a]See Appendix A for codes. In a few cases, the classifications of factors shown here were preliminary and may not agree with the final classifications shown in the tables of Appendix B.

at any given age. But rates of acquisition differ also with respect to specific aspects of language development, for example, vocabulary, grammar, reading comprehension, reading speed, oral production ability, etc. The various first-order or primary factors identified and reviewed in this chapter reflect a characteristic degree or rate of acquisition in some one cluster of language abilities.

It is beyond the scope of this work to detail more precise information about rates of acquisition of language abilities. I have reviewed some of this information previously (Carroll, 1971), but that review could undoubtedly be profitably updated. The purpose here has been to give more precise information, at least what information is now available from factor-analytic studies, about what particular aspects of language skill need to be attended to in any thoroughgoing consideration of the development of language skills.

It has been apparent that the development of language skills is substantially related to the development of more general cognitive skills, in that measures of language skills tend to be substantially correlated with measures of other cognitive skills, and various primary factors are dominated by more general factors. It has often been noted (e.g., Terman, 1916) that measures of vocabulary are among the best predictors of general intelligence. It is tempting to speculate that general intelligence is identical to rate and extent of language development, but such a speculation is only weakly supported in research. Language development as customarily measured (e.g., by vocabulary tests) is only one aspect of cognitive development, and its correlations with intelligence measures are not so high as to suggest that language development is the same as general cognitive development. There are many influences that govern individuals' rate and extent of language development – exposure to increasing levels of language complexity through exposure to model speakers, reading of increasingly difficult material, etc. Special traits associated with rates of learning to read may make estimates of general intelligence obtained from printed tests inaccurate. On the other hand, it is probable that the level of general cognitive development that is or can be attained by an individual at a given age tends to set limits on the level of language development that can be attained at that age. It is, again, beyond the scope of the present work to consider this matter, or the research on it, in any detail.

In confronting the problem of relating language abilities to cognitive processes and strategies, I find it extraordinarily difficult to set forth any summary statement or review. This is true for several reasons. First, language behavior is enormously complex and diverse, and we have seen that there appear to be a series of somewhat separate factors of language ability, reflecting that complexity and diversity. Second, the investigation of language acquisition and behavior has been very intense in recent years; it would be impossible to review here all of that activity and the present state of knowledge about language acquisition, competence, and performance. Third, any attempt to interpret cognitive processes as revealed by language abilities would entail discussion of an enormous range of detail and would quickly get out of hand. I must, therefore, limit myself to a few general remarks.

First, I would suggest that the factor-analytic results reviewed here are valuable in indicating what kinds of learnings and developments tend to cluster together, and what kinds of learnings and developments tend not to occur strictly in parallel. For cognitive psychology, there is the possible implication that for any given cluster of learnings, as represented by a given factor of ability, there is some similarity in whatever cognitive processes occur in the development of that ability, and some dissimilarity in the cognitive processes involved in different factors. If this speculation has any value, it would imply that studies of cognitive processes could be guided by factorial findings in the sense that they could be organized around the types of learnings indicated by those findings, with the understanding that generalizations would probably be more valid *within* a given domain of language ability than across domains. For example, it would make sense to assume that at least some of the processes involved in vocabulary acquisition are more or less uniform throughout the range of vocabulary, and somewhat different from processes involved in the acquisition of word recognition in reading. At the same time, it should be recognized that even within such a domain as vocabulary or word recognition, different processes may be involved depending on the nature of the items to be learned. For example, Marshalek (1981) has found interactions between reasoning abilities and the types of vocabulary items learned (e.g., concrete vs. abstract).

Second, a number of general remarks can be made about cognitive processes related to particular factors of language ability. For nearly all factors, processes of long-term semantic memory are involved. Language acquisition is, in fact, largely a matter of the development of long-term semantic memory – information, that is, about the meanings and uses of words and other aspects of language structure. Exactly how this information is acquired could be explicated, if at all, only by reviewing an enormous number of investigations and observations of the phenomenon. A critical point is that individuals differ widely in their rates of acquiring this information. To the extent that the various factors of language ability tend to be correlated, it is permissible to speculate that these rates are controlled more or less uniformly by a complex of both genetic and environmental influences that apply across the different factors.

Undoubtedly many aspects of language ability are acquired by processes of observation, inference, and memory on the part of the individual rather than by anything like formal training. Sternberg and Powell (1983) postulate that vocabulary acquisition occurs through such processes, operating on the contexts in which words occur; they find that persons with high vocabularies are better learners of new vocabulary than otherwise comparable persons with lower vocabularies. Tests of vocabulary are in the main tests of knowledge; the processes involved in immediately responding to such tests are of less interest than the processes by which that knowledge was acquired. I would speculate that acquisition processes are reflected more by the factorial loadings of vocabulary tests on higher-order cognitive factors than by their loadings on the vocabulary knowledge (VL) factor itself. The latter reflect, rather, an environmental influence on vocabulary learning, that is, the degree to which a particular individual happens to have had or sought opportunities to acquire vocabulary. (See McKeown & Curtis, 1987, for reviews of recent research on vocabulary acquisition.)

Some of the factorial studies surveyed here suggest components of skill, and thus differential processes, in particular areas. Results obtained by Frederiksen (1978, 1982) in the study of reading skills, for example, suggest the operation of such processes in reading behavior as grapheme recognition, response to multi-letter units, and perception of anaphoric relations. Similarly, results obtained in my studies of foreign language aptitudes (Carroll, 1981b) suggest the operation of distinct processes such as inferring phoneme-grapheme correspondences and perceiving grammatical relationships in foreign language learning.

6   *Abilities in the Domain of Reasoning*

Induction and deduction are not necessarily different intellectual processes. They are distinguished as problems rather than processes. A deductive problem calls for discovering the implications of certain given statements. What is given in an inductive problem consists of specimens, and the result to be attained is a definition, or at least a working knowledge, of the class represented by the given specimens. The process might be about the same in solving both sorts of problem; more probably, it will show much variation in both cases.

Robert S. Woodworth (1938)

Reasoning abilities are traditionally considered to be at or near the core of what is ordinarily meant by intelligence. Binet (1890, p. 582) offered the opinion that intelligence could be defined at least in part as the ability to "think about" materials drawn from the perception of the external world, and the Binet scale (Binet & Simon, 1905) included numerous tasks that relied in some way on the ability to reason with either verbal or nonverbal materials. In the famous symposium on intelligence organized by E. L. Thorndike (1921), Terman (p. 128) described intelligence as "the ability to carry on abstract thinking." The abilities – the eduction of relations and the eduction of correlates – that Spearman (1927) thought of as largely defining his g factor of intelligence may be regarded as elementary reasoning abilities, although Spearman recognized that the reasoning abilities involved in certain complex tests of thinking might define a special group factor separate from g (Spearman, 1927, p. 225). Successful thinking and problem solving were mentioned by numerous contributors as attributes of intelligent behavior in a recent symposium volume, edited by Sternberg and Detterman (1986), intended to provide a contemporary version of the 1921 symposium.

Nevertheless, in his classic study of 57 test variables that represented types of items typically included in standard intelligence tests, Thurstone (1938b) found only two factors, among some seven or eight, that could be said directly to reflect processes of reasoning. Five variables had significant saturations on a factor that he called I (Induction), and four variables had significant projections on a factor that he tentatively identified as D (Deduction). This study was among the first to indicate that special thinking and reasoning factors might exist apart from the general intelligence factor assumed by Spearman and presumably tapped by standard intelligence tests. Thurstone found no general intelligence factor, but as noted previously, Thurstone's methodology at the time was such as to emphasize group factors and to preclude the identification of higher-order factors.

Summarizing research in the Thurstonian tradition, French (1951) recognized only five first-order factors that could be said to lie in the domain of reasoning:

196

Thurstone's I (Induction) and D (Deduction), and from other sources, In (Integration), J (Judgment), and Pl (Planning). Based on the same tradition, the kits of factor tests assembled at Educational Testing Service (French, Ekstrom, & Price, 1963; Ekstrom, French, & Harman, 1976) have established the list of first-order reasoning factors as including mainly what are there called I (Induction), RL (Logical Reasoning), and RG (General Reasoning). (The 1976 kit also recognized, albeit with weak support, a factor called IP, Integrative Process; see Table 3.1, this volume.)

In a program of research that in many ways diverged from the Thurstonian tradition, Guilford and Hoepfner (1971, Chapter 5) devoted much attention to attempting to confirm a variety of hypothesized first-order reasoning and problem-solving factors. They claimed to identify a rather long list of factors in this domain – as many as 39 in their "cognition" and "convergent-production" operation categories. Reasoning and problem solving factors were claimed to be differentiated not only in terms of processes ("operations," namely cognition and convergent-production) but also in terms of types of stimulus material (figural, symbolic, and semantic) and types of "products" (units, classes, relations, systems, transformations, and implications). Guilford and Hoepfner gave short shrift to the notion that there might exist anything like general intelligence. But because of the many methodological problems involved in their analyses (commented on in Chapter 2 of this volume), the extreme factor differentiations implied by the Guilford Structure-of-Intellect model are to be viewed with much skepticism.

The present survey, based on a hierarchical model of cognitive abilities, is concerned with identifying both first- and higher-order factors, that is, factors of both narrow and broad extent, with the hope of establishing what factors can be confirmed in available factorial datasets. This chapter sets forth the findings on the narrower, lower-order factors in the domain of reasoning abilities. After a section describing tests that are frequently found to have loadings on reasoning factors, much of the chapter is devoted to establishing the evidence for its claim that there exist only three main first-order factors in this domain. Next, these three factors – RG (Sequential Reasoning), I (Induction), and RQ (Quantitative Reasoning – are each described in terms of the characteristic tasks that involve them and their appearance in the numerous datasets that have been studied in this survey. A brief section discusses evidence for special reasoning factors that are measured by Piagetian tasks. Some mention is made, in this chapter, of the loadings of reasoning factors on higher-order factors, but higher-order factors pertaining to reasoning are more extensively treated in Chapter 15. In a final summary and discussion section of the chapter, I draw attention to recent work in cognitive psychology that pertains to reasoning abilities.

ANALYSIS OF FIRST-ORDER REASONING FACTORS

As noted in Table 4.20, a preliminary sorting of the token factors that were identified in reanalysis of about 460 datasets yielded 241 factors tentatively interpreted as falling in the domain of reasoning abilities. Many of these were classified under categories proposed in previous factorial literature: General Reasoning, Verbal Reasoning, Induction, Quantitative Reasoning, Syllogistic Reasoning, and Classification Ability. General Reasoning factors were those, not otherwise classifiable, that had loadings on a variety of variables appearing to require reasoning. Verbal Reasoning factors were those in which the use of language in thinking was a prominent feature. Induction factors were those appearing to emphasize the need for subjects to discover rules or principles governing the test materials. Syllogistic Reasoning and Classification Ability factors were those in which syllogistic and classification problems, respectively, were explicitly presented.

Closer examination of this large array of factors involved detailed examination of the variables (tests and other procedures) that were found to have substantial loadings on them, in contrast to variables with vanishing loadings. Initially, an attempt was made to categorize factors into a large number of classes defined by distinct types of variables: e.g., classification tests, concept formation tests, figure analogies, number and letter series tests, matrix tasks, quantitative reasoning items, and verbal analogies tests. This closer examination of the data also involved consideration of instances in which a given dataset yielded two or more apparently distinguishable factors in the reasoning domain. It became clear, in this process, that it was going to be extremely difficult to clarify the domain in terms of an extended list of distinct factors. There were many grounds for arriving at this conclusion. Among them were the following:

1.　　Relatively few datasets yielded more than one factor classifiable in the domain of first-order reasoning factors. After rejecting a few factors for various reasons, it appeared that 236 token factors in the reasoning domain came from as many as 176 different datasets. Specifically, 134 datasets yielded only 1 reasoning-domain factor, while 2 such factors were yielded by 28 datasets, 3 factors by 10 datasets, and 4 by only 4 datasets. One of the datasets yielding 4 factors (CARL40) actually represented an item factor-analysis of a single test, the Raven Coloured Progressive Matrices test, and perhaps should not be counted in this tabulation. The reader must, of course, bear in mind the conservative principles guiding our reanalyses, designed to avoid overfactoring and tending to yield relatively small numbers of first-order factors (see Table 4.19).

2.　　First-order oblique factors in the reasoning domain were frequently quite highly correlated among themselves and/or with factors in other domains, with the result that in the process of Schmid–Leiman orthogonalization the orthogonalized loadings tended to become considerably attenuated from the corresponding values in oblique reference-vector or pattern matrices.

3.　　In the many datasets yielding only one reasoning-domain factor, it was frequently the case that there were numerous variables – say, 10 or more – having salient loadings on the factor, and these variables had much variety – sometimes apparently including tests traditionally associated with each one of the presumed factors in the reasoning domain. This was occasionally true even when the test battery had been designed to provide reasonably adequate marker variables for each of these presumed factors (see, for example, datasets GUIL17 and GUIL46 as presented in Appendix B).

In the search for possible reasons for the failure of clearly distinguishable factors to appear, it should be borne in mind that (a) many reasoning tasks are inevitably complex, involving (as the quotation from Woodworth at the head of this chapter reminds us) both inductive and deductive processes that may not be easily separated; (b) many of the tests used in factor studies are often very brief, and are given under a time-limit such that speed and level aspects are not clearly separated; (c) only rarely have the tests been subjected to careful test construction and item-analysis procedures to insure homogeneity in the test content; (d) even if it is possible to distinguish processes such as induction and deduction, these processes are likely to be developed or learned together, in the sense that those who can perform inductive processes are likely to be those who can also perform deductive processes, while those who cannot perform inductive processes are likely to be those who cannot perform deductive processes; and (e) many of the tasks designed to tap reasoning processes are likely to involve language, number, or spatial skills as well.

In view of these and other difficulties, guidance was sought from the relatively few datasets which yielded more than one factor apparently lying in the reasoning domain. Such datasets, it was thought, might indicate possibly generalizable distinctions among factors in the reasoning domain. Using the relatively fine classifications of factors previously mentioned, it was found, for example, that at least three datasets yielded a distinction between a Quantitative Reasoning factor and an Induction factor; at least four datasets yielded a distinction between a Quantitative Reasoning factor and what came to be called a Sequential Reasoning factor; and several datasets yielded a distinction between an Induction factor and the Sequential Reasoning factor. Furthermore, it was found that factors characterized mainly by loadings on matrix tasks (mainly, tests in the Raven progressive matrices series) could fit into the Induction factor classification without violating distinctions with the other two factors. It is not worthwhile to recount all the steps in making the final decision to postulate the existence of three chief factors in the reasoning domain, linearly independent of each other, and to attempt to assign all or nearly all the 236 token factors into these three classifications (13 token factors were assigned to a "Piagetian Reasoning" classification, for separate consideration). I will simply present the final outcomes of these decisions, with whatever comment is deemed useful.

Because of the large amount of detail that must be considered and the need to treat all these details together, the reader needs to be aware of the strategy of presentation that is employed. First, I give a list, with descriptions, of the variables that most frequently appear on one or more of the three main factors. In this connection, I give a table (Table 6.1) that shows the frequency with which these variables appear as salients on the factors, either when all salients are considered, or when only those salients are considered that appear as one of (up to) the three highest-ranking variables on a factor with Schmid–Leiman orthogonalized loadings greater than .25. Next, there is a discussion of evidence for distinguishing among the three main reasoning factors, based on data from 37 datasets that yield more than one factor in the reasoning domain. Associated with this discussion is a table (Table 6.2) showing the (up to five) highest-ranking variables on each token factor discussed, the token factors being classified tentatively into the three chief factors (RG, I, and RQ) in the reasoning domain. Finally, each main factor is discussed, with an accompanying table showing the dataset token factors assigned to that factor. In many cases the assignments were difficult or even in a sense arbitrary, and thus they must be viewed with caution.

VARIABLES IN THE REASONING DOMAIN

The 236 token factors initially identified as being in the reasoning domain were defined by a wide variety of variables – some 1250 of them. Many of these, however, appeared repeatedly in the datasets. No attempt was made to determine how many of these were actually different, for there were gradations of differences. Sometimes highly similar variables were found to have different names; for example, a certain type of inductive task was called "Locations" in some datasets and "Marks" in others. On the other hand, variables named simply "Reasoning" or "Puzzles" could involve quite different tasks in different datasets. Similarly-named variables could also differ in length, instructions, and time-limits, but for the most part these differences were not taken into account because it was not considered immediately necessary, and because of the volume of details involved. To aid in the interpretation of the factors, I present here a list and description of the variables that were found most frequently, as shown in Table 6.1 (to be introduced below). In most cases, the descriptions are adapted from those in the original studies, otherwise from information available in various compilations of test descriptions (e.g., French, 1951; Guilford & Hoepfner, 1971, Appendix B). The list also includes descriptions of most of the variables mentioned in Table 6.2 as defining factors found in datasets that yielded more than one factor. Wherever necessary, comments are given as to any differences among similarly named variables that may be critical to factor interpretation.

Over the numerous datasets studied here, there were many minor variations in names of variables. Also, many variables represent alternate forms of tests, progressively difficult subtests, or forms of tests that were progressively altered as research proceeded. For example, some studies utilized as separate variables up to five progressively difficult subtests of Raven's Progressive Matrices test. In such cases, the alternate variables are usually distinguished by suffixes such as I, II,... or A, B,....

Certain conventions are observed in the list of variables below. The keyed correct answers are usually italicized. The type of response is indicated by (M-C) [multiple-choice], (F-R) [free-response], (T-F) [true-false], or (Y/N) [yes/no]. A number of variables from the Stanford–Binet scale (Terman & Merrill, 1960) are indicated by [S–B] with the age-level indicated. There is an indication of one or more datasets in which each variable is to be found.

Abstract Words [S–B AA-8] (STOR12): Define (F-R) abstract words such as "generosity."

Abstraction (PENF01): A series completion task, from Vernon & Parry (1949).

Absurdities (ADKI03): Indicate (Y/N) whether given statements make sense; e.g., "Mrs. Smith has had no children, and I understand the same was true of her mother."

AFQT (Vocabulary & Reasoning) (CORY01): A subtest of the Armed Forces Qualification Test.

Algebra Test (VERY03): Solve (F-R) increasingly difficult algebra problems.

Alternating Operations (LUCA01): Presented with a series of six to twelve numbers, *S* is to perform a series of mathematical operations on successive numbers according to complex rules, the rules changing depending on certain outcomes.

Ambiguous Sentences (CARR42): Speed in detecting ambiguity of specially constructed sentences.

Analogies; Verbal Analogies (ANAS11; ANDE03; CARR42; GUIL16; GUIL21; GUIL22; MERR41; NIHI02): Choose words (M-C) to complete verbal analogies. Tests vary in vocabulary load and in the difficulty of the relationships involved.

Analysis-Synthesis (WOOD15): On the basis of a novel miniature mathematics system, analyze the components of an equivalency statement and reintegrate them to determine the components of a novel equivalency statement (F-R).

Applied Problems (WOOD15): Solve (F-R) practical problems in mathematics, ranging from very easy to very difficult. Some computational ability is involved.

Aptitude-Spatial (GUIL19): Identify how a folded and punched piece of paper would look when unfolded.

Arithmetic (COOM01; GOOD01; STOR11; STOR12; STOR13; VERY03; WERD01; WERD02): Perform (F-R) simple arithmetic operations.

Arithmetic Problems (HARR54): Perform (F-R) simple arithmetic problems involving addition, subtraction, multiplication, division, fractions, etc..; (WEIS11): Give (F-R) correct answer to verbally stated arithmetical reasoning problem. Problems have a wide range of difficulty and emphasize understanding rather than computational skill.

Arithmetic Reasoning (CORY01; DUNC11; GUIL32; STOR11; STOR12; VERY02; VERY03): Solve (F-R) short, verbally stated arithmetical problems.

Artificial Language (LUCA01): Translate (F-R) English verb forms into artificial language verb forms using a set of five rules governing tense, number, person, and selection of letters for verb endings.

Bead Chain [S–B 13–6] (STOR12; STOR13): Presumably by inducing a principle underlying the pattern of a series of beads (round, square, cylindrical), copy (F-R) the series from memory.

Best Number Class (HOEP31): Judge (M-C) into which of four classes each given number fits so as to receive most points, based on classes of numbers like primes, squares, even-multiples.

Best Number Pairs (HOEP31): Choose (M-C) one of three number pairs that makes the "best class"; e.g., *A*. 2–7; *B*. 5–2; *C*. 7–5 [both are odd].

Best Trend Name (NIHI02): Select (M-C) the word that best describes the order of four given terms, e.g., horse–pushcart–bicycle–car. *A*. speed *B*. *time C*. size.

Best Word Class (NIHI02): Select (M-C) one of four given classes to which a given object best belongs, e.g., PALM: *A*. plant; *B*. *tree*; *C*. flower; *D*. leaf.

Best Word Pairs (NIHI02): Select (M-C) the pair of words that makes the "best class," e.g., *A*. *handsome-dark B*. handsome-man *C*. man-dark.

Calculation (WOOD15): Perform (F-R) mathematical computations, from very easy to very difficult (including geometric, logarithmic, and calculus).

Circle Reasoning (BLAK01; GUIL19; GUIL21): Discover the principle by which one small circle is blackened in each of four rows of circles and dashes, then apply (M-C) the rule to the fifth row. (Similar to Locations; Marks; from Blakey, 1941)

Circle Square Triangle (GUIL19): Associate each of three verbally stated objects with a circle, square, or triangle; then place them according to instructions. E.g., given objects BLOTTER MARBLE GRAPE, make the most edible one the triangle, put the hardest one on the outside and the softest one on the inside. Six pictorial alternatives (M-C) show different enclosings of a circle, square, and triangle.

Classification (CATT01A): Find (M-C) the one pictorial figure that does not belong with four others having common characteristics.

Cofer Recall Task (CARR42): Free recall of 36 auditorily presented high-frequency words (12 nouns, 12 verbs, 12 adjectives). Scores intended to indicate sensitivity to parts of speech.

Commonsense Judgment (GUIL32; NIHI02): 1. Select (M-C) the two best of five given reasons why a briefly described plan is faulty. 2. Select (M-C) the two best of five given methods to demonstrate the truth of a given statement.

Concept Formation (DUNC11): In several tasks involving either verbal, numerical, or figural material, identify (Y/N) instances or non-instances of concepts; (WOOD15): When given instances and non-instances of a concept, identify and state the rule (orally, F-R).

Conditions (CANI01): Two versions of abstract logical reasoning tests involving linear syllogisms. 1. A conclusion is judged true or false (T-F) on the basis of a set of given conditions; 2. Task is to indicate (M-C) the relation ($>$, $=$, or $<$) which would express a true conclusion under a set of given conditions.

Correlate Completion (GUIL21; GUIL22; PETE11): Complete (F-R) analogies made up of words paired either for meaning or for letter composition. E.g., am – ma not – ton tool – ? Ans. *loot*

Critical Evaluation (GUIL18; GUIL21): Designate (M-C) given statements as being based on emotion or prejudice versus on reasoning and thought, e.g., "All people who drink liquor should have their driver's licenses taken away" [*emotion*]; "The police should revoke the licenses of people who drive while drunk" [*thought*]

Deduction; Deductive Reasoning (CORY01; GUIL32; VERY03): Identify (M-C) logical conclusion from a verbally stated problem situation.

Definitions (PENF01): A multiple-choice task concerning accuracy of definitions.

Dependence and Variation (WEIS11): Given an algebraic equation, indicate (M-C) how one variable will change as another is changed (increased or decreased).

Differences in Abstract Words [S–B AA-3] (STOR12): State (F-R) the difference in meaning between two spoken words, e.g., *laziness* and *idleness*.

Electronics: Electronic Technician Selection Test (CORY01): A test in the U. S. Navy enlisted classification battery, covering knowledge of mathematics, science, electricity, and electronics.

Episodes (MERR41): Write (F-R) two explanations for a specified action, e.g., "A man is sitting in his chair reading a magazine. Suddenly he closes the magazine and strides out of the room." Possible response: *He realizes he is late for an appointment.*

Enclosed Boxes [S–B SA-2] (STOR11): Orally presented arithmetical reasoning problems about numbers of boxes if different numbers of boxes are enclosed in others (F-R).

Essential Differences [S–B AA-7] (STOR11; STOR12): State (F-R) "principal difference" in meaning between two spoken words, e.g., "work" and "play."

Essential Operations: (GUIL16) Choose (M-C) one of five items of information that is irrelevant to the solution of a given arithmetical reasoning problem.

Essential Similarities [S–B SA I-6] (STOR11): State (F-R) the "principal" way in which two spoken words are alike in meaning; e.g., "farming" and "manufacturing."

Expressional Fluency (STOR11): Write (F-R) different four-word sentences using a given set of initial letters for the words.

False Premises; Nonsense Syllogisms (CORY01; GUIL16; THUR21A): Judge (T-F) correctness of conclusions to given nonsensical verbal syllogisms, e.g., "All haystacks are catfish. All catfish are typewriters. Therefore all haystacks are typewriters." [*T*]. Similar to Syllogisms.

Figure Analogies; Figure Analogies Completion (ADK103; GUIL16; GUIL21; GUIL22; GUIL32; GUIL32A; LUCA01; WEIS11): Select (M-C) one of five figures to complete a figural analogy of form *A:B::C:?*. In the completion form, *S* draws the figure.

Figure Changes (CANI01): A subtest of the Holzinger–Crowder Uni-Factor Tests: Figure Analogies items.

Figure Classification (ADK103; GUIL22): Given five classes of figures, discover principles underlying each class and assign (M-C) other figures to the classes.

Figure Grouping (CANI01): An adaptation of Thurstone's Figure Classification test, *q.v.*

Figure Matching (GUIL16; GUIL22): Select (M-C) one of five figures having most in common with another given pictorial figure.

Figure Matrix (GUIL22): Discover the trends in rows and columns of a 3 by 3 matrix of pictorial figures and choose one of five alternative figures to go in a specified cell. (Similar to Matrices; Progressive Matrices)

Find Reasons [S–B SA II-2] (STOR12): State orally (F-R) three reasons for a fact, e.g., why some people use typewriters rather than pen and ink.

Follow Directions (WEIS11): Given a mathematical statement, express (F-R) it in algebraic symbols and operations; e.g., "The sum of 8 and x is 5." Ans.: $8 + x = 5$.

Form Reasoning (BLAK01; GUIL19; PETE11; STOR11; STOR12; STOR13): Solve (F-R) equations stated in terms of figures, based on a table of equivalences of pairs of figures. Form Reasoning II is similar but more complex, using letters to specify different equivalences and the order of operations to be performed.

Form Series (WERD01): Similar to Number Series, but the stimuli are geometric forms. Cf. Series (CATT01A). In Form Series II, *S* is to cross out the form that does not fit into the series.

General Reasoning (VERY02; VERY03): From the Guilford–Zimmerman Aptitude Battery. Solve (M-C) problems requiring arithmetic reasoning in which numerical computation is minimized.

Geometry: T-F (WEIS11): Evaluate truth or falsity of verbal statement about geometric forms and relationships.

Gestalt Transformation (GUIL18; MERR41): Select (M-C) one of five objects, a part of which could be adapted for a new and unusual purpose. E.g., To start a fire: *A.* fountain pen; *B.* onion; *C. pocket watch; D.* bottle top; *E.* bowling ball.

Hidden Figures (GUIL16): Indicate (M-C) which one of five geometric figures is hidden in each complex figure.

Identical Words (PENF01): A multiple-choice task of finding best synonyms.

Induction; Inductive Reasoning (VERY01): Discover common relationships among numbers, letters, words, objects.

Inference; Inferences (ANDE01; ANDE03; CORY01; GUIL16; GUIL18; PENF01; WERD02): Select (M-C) one of five conclusions that follows from a verbally stated premise. (Employs syllogistic reasoning). In WERD02, Inferences I and II have categorical syllogisms.

Inventive Opposites (STOR11): Write (F-R) two antonyms for each given word, the first letters of the antonyms being given.

Judgment (VERY02): Make commonsense decisions regarding reasoning in everyday situations. E.g., why do clothes wear out? (4 M-C alternatives).

Judgment of Persons (LUCA01): Select (M-C, given traits and occupations) which traits best distinguish between people engaged in certain types of occupations.

Jumbled Words (HOEP31): Judge (Y/N) whether given words could be made just by rearranging the letters of a key word, e.g., from START, 1. stare (*N*), 2. starts (*N*), 3. tarts (*Y*).

Letter Classification (HARR54): Recognize classes of nonsense words, then assign (M-C) given nonsense words to the classes. E.g., classes: 1. ALF OSTE IMBR 2. CFCO AQOQ HCHY 3. GMB RGAD OFGE. Then *OMFA goes with class 1; WAWO with class 2; LSUG with class 3.*

Letter Grouping (GOOD01; GUIL22; GUST11A): Group (F-R) a list of twelve nonsense words into four classes, using each word only once. E.g. 1. LXD; 2. GOG; 3. LZQ; 4. BCD; 5. MAA; 6. SUS; 7. OPQ; 8. EEB; 9. RIR; 10. LWP; 11. KII; 12. RST. *Ans.:* Classes are 1, 3, 10; 2, 6, 9; 4, 7, 12; 5, 8, 11.

Letter–Number (PETE11; PETE12): Find the relations in two letter–number pairs and use them to specify (F-R) the number for a new letter–number pair. E.g., no = 56; po = 76; mo = ? (*46*)

Letter Reasoning (VERY03): Ability to discover a common rule from a series of examples involving series of alphabetical letters.

Letter Series (CANI01; CATT01A; GUIL21; PETE11; PETE12): Find the rule underlying a series of letters, then specify (F-R) the next two elements. E.g., A R B R C R D ? ? (*R E*)

Letter Sets (LUCA01): Find (M-C) the one letter group that does not belong in the class of four others; e.g., ABCD LMNO MNOP *DEFT* UVWX.

Letter Triangle (GUIL21; HOEP01; HOEP31; PETE11; PETE12): Choose (M-C) one of five letters to appear in a given place in a triangular pattern of rule-ordered letters.

Locations; Marks (CARR42; COOM01; LUCA01): Find rule for marking a space in rows of spaces and gaps; in principle similar to Circle Reasoning, *q.v.*

Logical Puzzles (ADKI03): Select (M-C) answers to verbally presented puzzles, the answers to which do not appear directly from the information given but must be deduced from it. (Items from Reasoning II and Reasoning III in BOTZ01).

Logical Reasoning (GUIL18; NIHI02; VERY02; VERY03): Choose (M-C) one of four conclusions that follows logically from two (syllogistic) meaningful premises. (Some alternatives are true but do not follow logically from the given premises.)

Logical Reasoning Judgment (GUIL32; GUIL32A): Select (M-C) best strategy for dealing with a military situation, using only logical reasoning.

Marks: See Locations.

Match Problems (STOR11): A variety of tasks involving removing a specified number of "matches" from a design, where "matches" form juxtaposed squares or triangles, to leave a specified number of complete squares or triangles. (Tests of this type frequently appear to measure a so-called Figural Flexibility (FX) factor; see Chapter 10.)

Matched Verbal Relations (NIHI02): Choose (M-C) one of four pairs of words with a relation most like that in another given pair. E.g., FISH–WORM: A. pole–hook; B. crumb–bird; C. water–swim; D. *mouse–cheese.*

Mathematical Reasoning (WERD02): Answer (F-R) verbally stated mathematical problems.

Mathematics; Mathematics Aptitude; Mathematics Achievement (GUST11A; DUNC11; VERY03). Various tests of mathematical aptitude or knowledge.

Matrices; Progressive Matrices; Matrix Test (CATT01A; GUST11A): On the basis of trends noticed in rows and columns of a figural matrix, find (M-C) figure that belongs in a specified cell.

Mechanical Movements (COOM01): Answer questions about mechanical movements in drawings.

Missing Sign (CANI01): Supply (F-R) the mathematical sign that will make an incomplete equation true.

Necessary Arithmetic Operations (DUNC11; GUIL19): Determine (M-C) what numerical operations (add, subtract, multiply, divide), in what order, are necessary in solving verbally stated arithmetic problems.

Necessary Facts (PENF01): Specify (F-R) what information necessary for a solution is missing from statements of arithmetic problems.

Necessary Operations (PENF01): Same as Necessary Arithmetic Operations, *q.v.*

Nonsense Syllogisms: See False Premises.

Number Analogies (WERD01): Indicate (M-C) which number (of five) is related to the third number in the same way as the second number is related to the first one.

Number and Operations Changes (GUIL16): Several tasks involving effects of changes in numbers, signs, or operations on correctness of mathematical equations.

Number Class Extension (HARR54): Given four numbers, infer its class, and select (M-C) another exemplar of the class from three given choices.

Number Classification (HOEP01; HOEP31): Recognize classes of three numbers each, and then assign (M-C) given numbers to them. E.g., classes: 1. 44 55 33 2. 10 45 15. Then 22 goes with (1); 25 with (2). The test in HARR54 is a further adaptation.

Number Exclusion (HARR54): Given four numbers, infer a class in three of them and indicate (M-C) the one that does not belong. E.g., 22 55 *26* 33.

Number Fluency (CANI01): Write (F-R) as many numbers as possible that satisfy certain given conditions.

Number Group Naming (HOEP01; HOEP31): State (F-R) what three numbers have in common. E.g., 1. 35 110 75 (*divisible by 5*); 2. 676 65 161 (*contain the digit 6*).

Number Oddities (CANI01): Essentially a series test. Supply equations continuing a pattern.

Number Patterns (COOM01): Fill in (F-R) missing number in matrices.

Number Relations (CANI01; HARR54): Identify (M-C) a pair of numbers that does not belong with other pairs for lack of common property. E.g., A. 1–5; B. 2–6; C. *5–8*; D. 3–7

Number Series; Number Series Completion (ANAS11; ANDE03; CANI01; GOOD01; GUIL21; GUST11A; WEIS11; WERD01): A variety of tasks in which rule-ordered series of _ umbers are to be continued with one or two elements. Items vary in the difficulty of the rule to be discovered. In Number Series II (WERD01, WERD02) the *S* is to cross out the number that does not fit in the series.

Numbers Reversed (WOOD15): Repeat (orally, F-R) a series of random numbers in an order opposite to that in which they are presented.

Numerical Operations (GUIL16; GUIL19; HOEP01): Highly speeded multiple-choice items of simple numerical computations; verbal arithmetic problems are not involved.

Object Naming (Shifts) (MERR41): Write (F-R, with time limit) a list of objects belonging to a very broad class, e.g., MINERAL. Score is number of shifts of category.

Object–Number (CORY01): A test of memory for pairs of objects and numbers.

Operations Sequence (HOEP31): Order (F-R) three specified numerical operations to get from one number to another. E.g., starting with 6, obtain 18. *A.* + 3; *B.* ÷ 2; *C.* × 3. *Ans.*: B, A, C.

Orientation [S–B AA-6] (STOR11; STOR12): Free response solutions to orally stated questions about proceeding with one or more changes of compass directions (North, South, East, West)

Paired Associates (DUNC11): Give (F-R) correct associate for stimulus, in learning task using the anticipation method over 16 trials.

Password (CORY01): Given five word clues, type the suggested word on a computer keyboard. E.g., given METAL, FINGER, CIRCLE, SHINY, WEDDING: Ans. *RING*.

Patterns; Pattern Reasoning (GUIL32; GUIL32A): A matrix test similar to Matrices.

Pedigrees (THUR81): A chart giving first names of persons and offspring covering three generations was the basis for 20 questions (F-R) concerning children, nieces, sisters-in-law, etc.

Perceptual Relations Naming (GUIL21): State (F-R) the relation that the first pictorial figure of a pair bears to the second figure. (E.g., *A is smaller than B*)

Phonetic Script (CARR42): Listening to auditorily presented pronunciations, discover and apply the system of relations between the pronunciations and phonemically spelled nonsense words.

Picture Arrangement (ADKI03; HARR54; PETE11): Reorder the panels of a cartoon strip so that it tells a meaningful sequence of events.

Picture Classification (GUIL21): Assign (M-C) pictures to classes defined by groups of three pictures each.

Plane Geometry (WERD02): A geometric reasoning problem (involving relations in two-dimensional space, often involving triangles, circles, etc.) is stated verbally. *S* is to give the correct answer (F-R).

Plotting (LUCA01): Given coordinates of a point, move it successively to different points according to indicated direction and distance; specify (M-C, eight compass points) direction of final point from starting point. A chart is used, but without actual plotting.

Practical Estimation (VERY02; VERY03): Using common experience as a basis, make quantitative estimates (M-C); e.g., Which coin will become the hottest after lying in the sun for an hour? dime; nickel; copper penny; steel penny.

Practical Judgment (LUCA01): Given a problem situation involving social relationships or minor emergencies, choose (M-C) which of four suggested modes of action would lead to the most satisfactory outcome.

Prescribed Relations (GUIL16): Choose (M-C) one of five pictorial figures that bears a described relation to another figure.

Problem Analysis (CANI01): I. Indicate the operations necessary to solve a simple (mathematical) word problem. II. Indicate (M-C) information irrelevant to the solution of a word problem.

Problem Solving (GUIL19): A five-choice arithmetic reasoning test; problems are stated verbally.

Product Choice (NIHI02): Select (M-C) best and worse of three objects that could be made by combining two stated objects, e.g., given LACE CURTAIN, WIRE HANGER: A. Christmas wrapping (*worst*); B. mop; C. butterfly net (*best*).

Progressive Matrices: See Matrices.

Proofing (WOOD15): Identify mistakes (punctuation, capitalization, word choice, spelling) in typewritten passages and indicate (F-R) how to correct each mistake.

Proverbs; Proverb Matching (CURE01; JAY01; STOR11 [S-B AA-5]): Orally state (F-R) meaning of a proverb like "large oaks from little acorns grow." Printed tests use M-C matching format.

Puzzles (HARR54): A syllogistic reasoning test. (WERD41): A test like Progressive Matrices, *q.v.*

Quantitative (ITED) (STOR11; STOR13): A score from the Iowa Tests of Educational Development; general mathematical reasoning ability and achievement.

Quantitative Aptitude (GUIL19): Part I: Word problems and series completions. Part II: Induce relationship among given columns of figures and identify a missing value.

Quantitative Concepts (WOOD15): Answer (orally, F-R) questions about quantitative concepts and vocabulary.

Reading (ADKI03): Consists of a number of paragraphs, on each of which two M-C questions are based. (From Chicago Reading Tests by M. Engelhart & T. G. Thurstone.)

Reasoning: The PMA Reasoning test used by CANI01 is essentially a letter-series test. Reasoning [S-B SA III-4] in STOR11 is an orally stated arithmetical reasoning problem. In WERD01 and WERD02 Reasoning is like Syllogisms I but involves comparisons of physical objects in length, weight, etc.

Recognition of Figures (DUNC11): Identify (M-C) figures as being those previously studied in a memory task.

Reconcile Opposites [S–B 14-6] (STOR12; STOR13): Orally state (F-R) in what way opposites are alike, e.g., "winter" and "summer."

Remote Verbal Similarities (GUIL22): Given a word, select (M-C) the one word of five that has the most in common with it, e.g., given FATHER: *A.* candidate; *B.* second baseman; *C.* agitator; *D. superintendent; E.* salesman.

Route Planning (GUIL34; GUIL46; MARK01): Identify (M-C) the points in a printed maze through which one *must* go from specified starting points to a specified goal. A test of this name in LUCA01 presents a map of a town and requires planning routes for most efficient deliveries to different points, considering distances and weights of objects.

Secret Writing (GUIL16,GUIL19): Identify (F-R) the letter that corresponds to each number in a decoding task. E.g., for TO ON NO = 36 68 86, $T = 3$; $O = 6$; $N = 8$.

Seeing Deficiencies (PENF01): Explain (F-R) how a plan or activity is faulty, e.g., "A city needs to improve both its streets and its sewer system. The council decides to work on the street-improvement program first." *The streets would have to be torn up later for the work on the sewer system.* (This test also appears to measure a Sensitivity to Problems (SP) factor; see Chapter 10.)

Seeing Trends (GUIL21; GUIL22; HARR54): A variety of tasks in which S must state (F-R) the trends in a series of words, based on letter compositions or meanings. E.g., mouse rat lion pig cow horse (*become larger*); rate crate morning dearth separate (*the "r" moves one position to the right in each successive item*). The test in HARR54 involves placing (M-C) an exemplar in the proper serial position, based on the trend inferred from the series.

Sentence Building [S–B SA I-5] (STOR11): Orally make up (F-R) a meaningful sentence containing three given words, e.g. *ceremonial, dignity, impression.*

Sentence Completion [SCAT] (STOR13): A subtest from the School and College Ability Test.

Sentence Order (ADKI03): Arrange (F-R) three statements of events in sensible order, e.g., A. She bought some food at the market; B. She cooked some of the food she had bought; C. She went to the market. (*C, A, B*)

Sentence Pairs (MERR41): Given a series of "lettered" sentences and a series of numbered sentences, match (*M-C*) sentences that express the same kind of idea, e.g., "*C. Exercise promotes good health*" goes with "*1. He walked home every night.*"

Sequential Association (MERR41): Arrange four words in a sequence so that each word is associated with words adjacent to it, e.g., given PEN PIG READ WRITE, correct sequence is *pig-pen-write-read.*

Series; Series Completion (CATT01A): Given a series of three pictured figures exhibiting systematic changes, select (M-C) the figure that correctly continues the series.

Ship Destination (GUIL16; GUIL19; PETE11; PETE12; STOR11; VERY02; VERY03): Given diagrammed information about the locations of ships and the ports to which they are to sail, as well as information about directions and strengths of winds and currents, compute (M-C) the miles they will have to travel. The numerical operations are simple; reasoning load increases.

Sign Changes (GUIL21; HOEP31; PENF01): A variety of tasks in which simple numerical equations are to be solved with specified or to-be-discovered changes of operation signs ($+$, $-$, $\times$, $\div$).

Similar Pairs (HOEP31): Judge (Y/N) whether the relation in the second pair of (meaningful or nonsense) words is the same as that in the first pair. E.g., 1. kire-lire fora-gora (*Y*); 2. moan-noam toes-seot (*N*).

Skywriting (LUCA01): Plan shortest, simplest, and most direct path a plane may take to write two adjacent letters, considering certain constraining rules.

Sound Grouping (GUIL16): Identify (M-C) a word that does not belong to a set of four because it sounds different. E.g., phrase *chase* maize phase.

Space; Spatial Reasoning (CANI01): The PMA Space test, level 11–17: identify all figures like the first figure in the row, when some are mirror images and all have been rotated into positions unlike the first.

Space Orientation; Space Positioning (GUIL16): Indicate (M-C) the direction from which a photograph of a pattern of balls was taken.

Spatial Relationships (VERY02): Ability to visualize objects in space, when rotated. E.g., "How many times between one and two o'clock will the hands of a clock be perpendicular to each other?"

Spatial Rotation (LUCA01): Given a two-dimensional figure having areas of black, white, and grey, select (M-C) figure it would be after mentally manipulating it through two moves (rotation or reversal).

Square Completion (LUCA01): Given groups of four squares in various stages of completion, plan alternating moves for two contestants so that each completes as many squares as possible for himself. The answer for each item is the number of squares "Black" can complete under the given conditions.

Story Titles (NIHI02): Select (M-C) the best and worst titles for a given short story.

Subtraction (CANI01): "of one-digit, two-digit, and three-digit numbers" (F-R).

Sunday–Tuesday Task (HUNT71): Perform computations based on non-decimal-base arithmetic, e.g., "add SUNDAY and TUESDAY" where SUNDAY = 0, TUESDAY = 2; Ans. *TUESDAY.* Or THURSDAY + FRIDAY = *TUESDAY.* Various scores based on speed, correctness.

Syllogisms (GUIL18; PENF01): A variety of tasks involving judging correctness of conclusions to pairs of verbally stated meaningful premises, or supplying correct conclusions. Categorical syllogisms. In WERD01 and WERD02, linear syllogisms.

Symbol Grouping (HOEP01): Rearrange scrambled symbols in a specified systematic order as efficiently as possible.

Symbol Manipulation (GUIL21; HOEP31; PENF01): Several tasks involving judging correctness of linear syllogisms, using symbols for Boolean operators.

Synonyms (NIHI02): Select (M-C) synonym closest in meaning to a given word, usually involving fine distinctions of meaning.

Teams (CANI01; a subtest of the Holzinger–Crowder Unifactor Tests): Categorical syllogisms based on overlapping memberships in sports teams.

Topology (CATT01A): Select (M-C) a pictorial figure that shows the same essential relational characteristics as a given figure.

Twelve Questions (CORY01) (Computerized): Like the well-known Twenty Questions game. Given a series of yes/no questions, select those providing the quickest identification of the object whose name is to be guessed.

Unlikely Things (NIHI02): Select (M-C) the two more unlikely or incongruous of four verbally stated features for a shown sketch of common objects.

Verbal Analogies: See Analogies.

Verbal Classification (GUIL18; MERR41; NIHI02): Given two classes of meaningful words, discover the principles of classification and assign further words to one of the classes, or to neither.

Verbal Concept Formation (ALLI01): In a rote learning paradigm over a number of trials, learn symbols associated with classes of words.

Verbal Meanings (CORY01): A Navy General Classification Test (GCT) testing word meanings and the ability to reason verbally.

Visual–Auditory Learning (WOOD15): Associate unfamiliar visual symbols (rebuses) with familiar oral words and translate (orally, F-R) sequences of rebuses into verbal sentences.

Vocabulary (ANAS11; GUIL16; STOR13 [ITED]): Find (M-C) a word that means about the same thing as a given word; context may or may not be supplied.

Water Jars [S–B AA-1, Ingenuity I] (STOR11): Mentally and orally, solve arithmetical reasoning problems about measuring given quantities of water using jars of given volumes.

Word Changes (HOEP01; HOEP31; PETE11): Arrange a list of words so that the first word is changed into the last one, one letter being changed each time. E.g., use 1. BAIL; 2. BALL; 3. MAIL as fillers to go from BELL to MAIN (*2, 1, 3*).

Word Classification (GUIL18; GUIL19; GUIL22): Select (M-C) the one word of four that does not belong with the others on the basis of meaning. E.g., horse cow man *flower*.

Word Grouping (CARR42) Judge how to group words in sentences. Several scores intended to indicate sensitivity to grammatical structure.

Word Groups (GUIL22): State (F-R) the feature of letter combination or other letter property common to four words, e.g., READ RETIRE REARMING RESTLESS all begin with "RE".

Word Relations (HOEP01; HOEP31): Recognize the same letter-combination relation between words in each of two pairs, then select (M-C) analogically the correct completion for a third pair. E.g., given ON – NO TOP – POT PART – ?, the correct completion is *TRAP*.

Word Systems (NIHI02): Select (M-C) one of three 2-by-3 word-matrices that shows the best trends and one that shows the worst trends, in both rows and columns.

CLASSIFICATION OF TASKS IN THE REASONING DOMAIN

Many of the variables in the foregoing list do not strictly belong in the reasoning domain; they are listed only because they occurred (usually, only once, and with relatively small loadings) among the salients for factors considered as belonging in the reasoning domain. Examination of the remaining variables, that is, those that appear more frequently as salients, and with relatively higher loadings, suggests that they fall into three main types, some with subtypes:

1. *Deductive Reasoning Tasks*: These require the subject to draw inferences from premises or combinations of premises. There are at least three subtypes:

1a. *Categorical Syllogism Tasks*: These are syllogisms that involve class memberships as stated in premises. Operators are terms such as "all," "some," and "no." The subject must either give the correct conclusion, evaluate the correctness of a stated conclusion, or select which of several conclusions is correct. Examples of tests (from the list given above) are: False Premises, Logical Reasoning, Puzzles (HARR54), and Teams.

1b.   *Linear Syllogism Tasks*: These are syllogisms in which the premises state comparisons of entities in terms of attributes that can vary continuously. Operators are words such as "greater than," "equal to," and "less than," or symbols for such terms ($>$, $=$, $<$). Response formats are similar to those for categorical syllogisms. Examples of tests are: Conditions, Reasoning (WERD01, WERD02), Syllogisms (WERD01, WERD02), and Symbol Manipulation.

1c.   *General Verbal Reasoning Tasks*: These involve problems stated verbally, sometimes accompanied by diagrams or pictures. (Some tasks involve only pictures or diagrams.) Sometimes the problems could indeed be formulated syllogistically, but this is not explicit. The subject must take one or more steps of inference or reasoning starting from the presented conditions, taking into account any further conditions or rules that are stated, finally giving a conclusion or evaluating stated possible conclusions (in either T-F, Y/N, or M-C formats). Some of the clearer examples in the list of variables are: Alternating Operations, Circle Square Triangle, Commonsense Judgment, Deductive Reasoning, Logical Puzzles, Logical Reasoning Judgment, Picture Arrangement, Plotting, Practical Judgment, Route Planning, Sentence Order, Seeing Deficiencies, and Square Completion. The variable Ship Destinations seems to fall into this category, particularly when it involves (as in the more difficult items) consideration of a number of factors determining the solution.

    Because these deductive reasoning tasks frequently utilize verbal statements, attention must be paid to the lexical and syntactic load in such statements. Not all investigators have been as careful in this matter as Adkins and Lyerly (1951), who deliberately designed their deductive reasoning tasks so as to minimize variance from verbal factors. Sometimes tasks in this category also involve variance from numerical, spatial, or other abilities, depending on test content.

2.   *Inductive Tasks*: These are tasks in which the subject is required to inspect a set of materials and from this inspection induce a rule governing the materials, or a particular or common characteristic of one or more stimulus materials, such as a relation or a trend. Subjects' abilities to induce the rule or common characteristic may be tested by asking them to state the rule or characteristic, to apply it by selecting a further exemplar to which the rule applies, or to classify one or more further stimuli according to this rule or characteristic. It should be noted that inductive tasks always involve at least one deductive step in arriving at a conclusion, classification, or other required response. Among the more commonly found subtypes of inductive tasks are the following:

2a.   *Simple Concept/Rule Discovery Tasks*: These require the subject to discover a common characteristic (e.g., a meaning, a concept, a simple rule or systematic correspondence) in two or more stimulus elements. Examples are: Perceptual Relations Naming, Reconcile Opposites, Remote Verbal Similarities, Secret Writing, Sentence Pairs. In addition we may list various tasks under the headings Concept Formation, Number Classification, Judgment of Persons, and Verbal Concept Formation.

2b.   *Series Tasks*: A series of literal (alphabetic letter), semantic, numerical, or figural stimuli is presented. The subject must notice what rule or trend is exemplified in the progression of the series, and show induction by supplying one or more elements that continue the series, by selecting from one or more further stimuli the one that correctly completes the series, or by evaluating whether a given further stimulus correctly completes it. Examples are: Abstraction, Best Trend Name, Form Series, Letter Series, Number Series, Seeing Trends, and Series (CATT01A).

2c.   *Multiple Exemplars Tasks*: These are in principle similar to simple series tasks, but require the presentation of a series of exemplars in order to illustrate the common characteristics or rules governing the series. Examples are: Correlate Completion, Circle Reasoning, Figure Classification, Figure Grouping, Letter Classification, Letter Grouping, Locations, Marks, and Verbal Classification.

2d.   *Matrix Tasks*: In these, the stimulus material is presented in the form of square or triangular matrices, and in this sense these tasks are extensions of multiple exemplars tasks. The material may be literal, numerical, semantic, or figural. The subject must notice the order in which materials are arranged in the matrix, or the trends or systematic changes in stimulus characteristics that take place over the rows and columns of the matrix. The rules governing these trends or changes can vary in ease or difficulty, from very obvious to more subtle changes, or with complex rules (e.g., with an alternation feature). Successful induction of the rule is tested by requiring the subject to specify or select a stimulus that would properly belong in a specified position in the matrix that has been left blank, or to identify a cell that is incorrectly filled in. Examples: Figure Matrix, Letter Reasoning, Letter Triangle, Matrices, Progressive Matrices (from the work of Raven, 1938), Pattern Reasoning, and Word Systems.

2e.   *Odd Element Tasks*: A set of stimulus materials (usually, four or five) is presented, all of which except one exemplify a rule or common characteristic. The subject's task is to identify the odd element. Examples: Classification, Induction (VERY01), Letter–Number, Letter Sets, Number Exclusion, Sound Grouping, and Word Classification.

2f.   *Analogies Tasks*: These tasks occur in considerable variety; they can vary in a number of aspects. The content may be literal, verbal, numerical, or figural. They may vary in the difficulty of the content and in the difficulty of the relationships on which an analogy is based. Many verbal analogies tests, for example, contain a heavy vocabulary load such as to bring them close to testing the VL factor (see Chapter 5). It is often difficult to discern this aspect from test descriptions. Even with a low vocabulary load, however, they may vary in the degree of difficulty of the inductive and deductive steps that are required to solve them. Induction is involved in the steps that Sternberg (1977) calls *inference* and *mapping*; deduction is involved in the steps he calls *application* and *justification*. The difficulty of the content affects the process he calls *encoding* (see Chapter 1). Because analogies tests vary in so many respects, and because they are likely to measure both inductive and deductive processes, it is difficult to predict, without detailed examination of item characteristics, what factor or factors they are likely to measure. It is also for these reasons that analogies tests tend to correlate highly with tests of general intelligence. Although analogies tests are here classified as inductive tasks, they are about equally likely to appear on deductive factors, that is, to correlate highly with deductive tests. Examples of analogies tasks appear in our list (above) under various names: Analogies, Verbal Analogies, Figure Analogies, Figure Changes, and Matched Verbal Relations. For a recent cognitive and psychometric analysis of analogical problem solving tasks, see Bejar, Chaffin, & Embretson (1991).

3.   *Quantitative Reasoning Tasks*: These are tasks requiring reasoning with quanti-
      ties or quantitative relationships, in particular, relations that can be described
      mathematically. They can emphasize either deductive or inductive processes,
      but their common characteristic is that they require an appreciation of
      quantitative concepts and relationships, particularly as treated in math-
      ematics in its various branches, from simple arithmetic to algebra, geometry,
      and calculus. No attempt is made here to classify such tasks further. It should
      be noted, however, that many of the tasks previously described under (1) and
      (2) can be given a quantitative emphasis by making the premises and
      necessary operations (in deductive tasks) or the rules or common character-
      istics (in inductive tasks) more elaborate in terms of mathematical attributes.
      For example, a Number Series task can be made more difficult, and thus
      classifiable as a quantitative task, by complicating the rules governing the
      series in terms of mathematical relations.

EVIDENCE FOR THREE MAIN FACTORS
IN THE REASONING DOMAIN

The 236 token reasoning factors yielded by 176 datasets were classified as well
as possible into three categories:

1.   *Sequential Reasoning (RG) factors*: Those whose salient variables, particularly
      the variables whose loadings were ranked highly, were predominantly in the
      first class of variables, i.e., various kinds of deductive tasks.
2.   *Inductive (I) factors*: Those whose salient variables were predominantly in the
      second class of variables.
3.   *Quantitative Reasoning (RQ) factors*: Those whose salient variables were
      predominantly in the third class of variables.

Lists of all variables appearing on the RG, I, and RQ factors so classified were
then made in order to see to what extent the factors appeared to be differentiated
by the variables on which they had salient loadings. To an extent, of course, they
would be expected to be differentiated as an artifact of the classification process
I used, but because a given factor might have salient loadings on many variables
in different classes, the differentiations could not be wholly artifactual. Table 6.1
shows a summarization of these results. In preparing it, I limited the variables
listed to those that appeared with a frequency of at least 2 on at least one of the
factors, under the restrictions that (a) the loading on the factor had to be at least
.26 and (b) the loading was one of the (up to) three highest salient loadings. (It
will be recalled that "salient" means that the loading was the highest, for a given
variable, among loadings for first-order factors in a reference-vector matrix.) The
frequencies shown in Table 6.1 are shown both for *all* salient loadings and for
loadings counted under the above restrictions (in the column headed "Restr.").

In interpreting information in Table 6.1, one should note the extent to which
frequencies are reduced when the restrictions are applied. For example, consider
the first variable listed, Absurdities. This variable was classed as a deductive task.
In classifying a factor on which it appeared as a salient, therefore, the inclination

Table 6.1. *Frequencies with which selected variables appear on three main factors in the reasoning domain*[a]

Variable	Factor					
	RG		I		RQ	
	All	Restr.	All	Restr.	All	Restr.
Absurdities	3	2	7	2	—	—
Analogies; Verbal Analogies	4	3	5	2	2	—
Arithmetic	8	4	3	3	12	12
Arithmetic Problems	—	—	1	1	3	3
Arithmetic Reasoning	6	4	2	1	22	14
Calculation	—	—	—	—	3	3
Classification	—	—	5	3	—	—
Concept Formation	—	—	8	7	—	—
Correlate Completion	1	—	4	2	2	1
Critical Evaluation	—	—	—	—	1	1
Deduction; Deductive Reasoning	3	1	—	—	3	2
False Premises	3	2	1	—	—	—
Figure Analogies	3	1	9	7	—	—
Figure Matching	—	—	3	3	—	—
Figure Matrix	—	—	5	2	1	—
Form Reasoning	—	—	—	—	1	1
Induction; Inductive Reasoning	3	—	8	7	—	—
Inference; Inferences	6	5	4	3	2	—
Letter Classification	—	—	3	2	—	—
Letter Grouping	3	—	10	6	2	1
Letter Series	7	5	15	10	—	—
Letter Sets	1	—	4	4	—	—
Letter Triangle	4	2	3	3	—	—
Locations; Marks	—	—	6	4	—	—
Logical Reasoning	10	4	1	—	2	1
Marks (See Locations)						
Match Problems	5	3	—	—	—	—
Mathematics; Math Aptitude	1	—	—	—	13	10
Matrices; Progressive Matrices	2	1	43	29	1	1
Number Classification	1	1	3	2	2	1
Number Series	13	12	11	7	13	12
Numerical Operations	1	—	—	—	4	3
Patterns; Pattern Reasoning	—	—	3	2	—	—
Pedigrees	—	—	3	3	—	—
Progressive Matrices (see Matrices)						
Proverbs; Proverb Matching	4	3	—	—	—	—
Reasoning	11	5	10	4	2	2
Route Planning	4	2	—	—	—	—
Sentence Completion	3	2	—	—	—	—
Series; Series Completion	—	—	5	2	1	1
Ship Destination	28	14	—	—	1	—
Sign Changes	5	2	—	—	3	1

Table 6.1 (*cont.*)

	Factor					
	RG		I		RQ	
Variable	All	Restr.	All	Restr.	All	Restr.
Similarities (and similarly named)	1	0	8	5	—	—
Space; Spatial Reasoning	2	1	12	4	1	1
Sunday–Tuesday Task	6	2	—	—	—	—
Syllogisms	12	7	—	—	1	1
Symbol Manipulation	4	2	—	—	1	—
Verbal Analogies (see Analogies)						
Verbal Classification	4	—	5	3	1	—
Verbal Concept Formation	—	—	3	2	—	—
Verbal Reasoning	8	6	—	—	—	—
Vocabulary	10	4	3	1	—	—
Word Changes	3	1	2	2	—	—

[a]Codes for factors: RG, Sequential Reasoning; I, Inductive Reasoning; RQ, Quantitative Reasoning. For each factor, frequencies are given in two columns: All, frequency with which the variable occurs for all salients on a token factor, regardless of size of loading; Restr., frequency with which the variable occurs as a salient with an orthogonalized loading > .25 and among the up to three highest ranked salient variables on a token factor.

would be to class it as a deductive (RG) factor, except that the classification would also be affected by other variables appearing on it as salients, which might, for example, be predominantly inductive tasks – in which case the factor would be classified as I (Induction). As the table shows, factors with Absurdities as a salient variable (with any size and rank of loading) were classified as Deductive (RG) 3 times, and Inductive (I) 7 times. They were never classified as Quantitative (RQ), and Absurdities therefore never appeared as a salient on factors classified as RQ. Nevertheless, under the restrictions stated, for RG factors the frequency of 3 was reduced only to 2, but the frequency of 7 for I factors was much reduced, to 2, indicating that Absurdities was less associated with inductive tasks. This result tends to support the proposition that Absurdities is indeed a deductive task. The reader is encouraged to make similar observations concerning other variables listed in the table; it is not worthwhile explicating all of them here. In general, it appears that the results in the table support the classifications of variables and factors proposed here.

The next step was to consider cases in which datasets yielded more than one factor in the reasoning domain – especially, cases in which more than one factor had been classified in one of the three categories of this domain. Of the 176 datasets yielding factors in the reasoning domain, only 37 yielded more than one such factor (excluding several datasets yielding factors classified as Piagetian

Reasoning factors). There are several reasons for the low percentage (21.0%). Many of the studies had relatively small numbers of variables, and few of them were intended or designed to study the dimensionality of the reasoning domain. Often, for example, the reasoning domain was represented by only two or three marker tests, mainly to provide what Cattell (1978, p. 112) calls "hyperplane stuff" for defining other factors of interest. Even when datasets were designed at least in part to study the dimensionality of the reasoning domain, they did not include a sufficient variety of variables, and/or the variables themselves were probably not adequately designed or controlled, to yield distinct factors. Finally, the methodology employed in my reanalyses can possibly have resulted in too few factors in some cases.

In any event, Table 6.2 lists 36 datasets yielding more than one factor classified as being in the reasoning domain, along with listings of the variables with the (up to) five highest salient loadings (regardless of absolute magnitude). (In some cases, all orthogonalized salient loadings were relatively small, even with all less than .30, either because of high correlations among factors or because of weakness in the definitions of factors, i.e., factors defined by relatively low intercorrelations among a small number of variables.) We study Table 6.2 in order to evaluate the evidence for factor differentiations, and in particular, to evaluate evidence for the proposed three main factors in the reasoning domain. Also useful in evaluating this evidence is Table 6.3, parallel to Table 6.2, which shows intercorrelations among reasoning domain factors and loadings on higher-order factors when these are present. The interested student may also find it useful to refer to the complete hierarchical matrix tables in Appendix B, but my discussion will mention pertinent information from these tables. Below, I discuss each dataset individually, finally stating a conclusion concerning factor differentiations.

Dataset ADKI03 was one of the few datasets that were specifically designed to study the reasoning domain. It shows a clear differentiation between factors RG and I even though they are highly correlated ($r = .66$); each factor is represented by numerous variables. There was no RQ factor, apparently because RQ variables were not strongly represented in the battery, but RG and I were differentiated from an N (Numerical Facility) factor. They were also differentiated from VZ (Visualization), CS (Closure Speed), FI (Ideational Fluency), and a possible P (Perceptual Speed) factor. Unfortunately, although several verbal ability and vocabulary variables were included, no separate V factor appeared and thus RG was not differentiated from the verbal domain. Factor I had a high loading (.96) on a second-order Gf factor. Factor RG had a loading of .69 on this factor, but also .46 on a second-order Gc factor.

Dataset ANAS11 came from a small, early study, with a total of only eight variables, designed to study memory abilities. The reasoning factors were interpreted as RG and RQ ($r = .27$), but neither was well defined. RG could have been a combination of RG and V, and RQ could have been a combination of

Table 6.2. *Variables having salient loadings on factors classified in the reasoning domain in 36 datasets yielding more than one such factor[a]*

Dataset	RG factor(s)	I factor(s)	RQ factor(s)
ADKI03	4(O1:F3) Absurdities Sentence Order Reading Reading II Logical Puzzles	2(O1:F1) Prog.Matrices D Prog.Matrices C Fig.Class'n IIB Prog.Matrices B Figure Analogies	—
ANAS11	4(O1:F2) Analogies Vocabulary	—	2(O1:F3) Arith.Reasoning No.Series Compl.
ANDE01	4(O1:F2) Delayed Recall Verbal Compreh	3(O1:F3) Similarities Manip'n Areas	2(O1:F1) Number Problems Numer'l Values Opposites Inferences Immed Recall
ANDE03	—	4(O1:F3) Similarities Rights & Lefts Immed.Recall Analogies	3(O1:F2) Number Series Number Problems Manip'n Areas Inferences Numer'l Values
CANI01	2(O1:F2) Conditions I Teams Figure Grouping Number Series (1) Problem Anal. II	4(O1:F1) Letter Series (PMA) Number Oddities Figure Changes Space (PMA) Missing Sign	3(O1:F4) Reasoning (CMT) Problem Analysis Subtraction Number Relations Number Fluency
CARR42	5(O1:F5) Ambiguous Sents. Cofer Recall Task Phonetic Script Verbal Analogies Entropy:Cofer Task	3(O1:F3) Locations Wd.Grouping I Figures (ETS Marker) Gramm'l Fluency Wd.Grouping II	—
CATT01A	3(O1:F5) Ltr.Series Form B Ltr.Series Form A	8(O1:F3) Matrices (IPAT) Series (IPAT) Classification (IPAT) Topology	—
COOM01	—	4(O1:F8) Marks Number Patterns	10(O1:F7) Number Series Arithmetic Mech'l Movements

Table 6.2 (*cont.*)

Dataset	RG factor(s)	I factor(s)	RQ factor(s)
CORY01	7 (O1:F6) Inference Password Twelve Questions Object-Number	—	3 (O1:F1) Arith.Reas'g AFQT (Vocab.& Reasoning) Verbal Meanings Electronics Nons.Syllogisms
DUNC11	—	7 (O1:F5) Conc.Form'n (Num) 1 Conc.Form'n (Fig) 1 Conc.Form'n (Num) 2 Conc.Form'n (Num) 3 10 (O1:F8) Conc.Form'n (Vrbl) 2 Conc.Form'n (Vrbl) 1 −Paired Assoc. 1	8 (O1:F6) Recog.Figures Math.Aptitude Arith.Reasoning Nec.Arith.Op'ns
GOOD01	—	2 (O1:F6) Number Series 8 (O1:F5) Letter Grouping Arithmetic	—
GUIL16	3 (O1:F1) Inference Verbal Anal. I Vocabulary Sound Grouping Verbal Anal. II 6 (O1:F6) Ship Destination False Premises Essen.Op'ns (Arith)	—	4 (O1:F3) No. & Op'ns. III No. & Op'ns. I No. & Op'ns. II Numer.Operations Secret Writing
GUIL18	3 (O1:F2) Syllogisms III Syllogisms II Logical Reasoning Inference Test	2 (O1:F1) Verbal Class'n Critical Eval'n Gestalt Transf'n Word Classification 7 (O1:F6) Figure Matching Object Synthesis II Figure Classification Titles Fig. Estimates (II)	—

Table 6.2 (*cont.*)

Dataset	RG factor(s)	I factor(s)	RQ factor(s)
GUIL19	2(O1:F1) Form Reasoning Secret Writing Ship Destination Aptitude–Spatial Circle Square Triangle	—	3(O1:F3) Nec.Arith.Op'ns Quant. Apt. Pt.I Circle Reasoning Quant. Apt. Pt.II Numer. Op'ns 5(O1:F4) Problem Solving
GUIL21	2(O1:F5) Verbal Anal. I Figure Analogics Fig.Anal.Compl'n Word Class'n Picture Class'n 3(O1:F2) Sign Changes II Symbol Manip. II Number Series Correlate Compl.II Seeing Trends	5(O1:F3) Circle Reasoning Perc.Rels.Naming Letter Series Letter Triangle	6(O1:F4) Sign Changes Form Reasoning Critical Evaluation
GUIL22	6(O1:F5) Word Class'n Verbal Anal. I Remote Verbal Similarities	3(O1:F2) Correlate Compl. II Word Groups Letter Grouping Seeing Trends II 4(O1:F3) Figure Analogies Figure Matrix Figure Matching Figure Class'n	—
GUIL32	2(O1:F2) Arith.Reasoning Logical Reas. Judgment Commonsense Judgment Deductive Reas'g	5(O1:F3) Figure Analogies Pattern Reasoning	—
GUIL32A	3(O1:F3) Arith.Reasoning Logical Reas. Judgment Deductive Reas'g	5(01:F4) Figure Analogies Pattern Reasoning	

Table 6.2 (*cont.*)

Dataset	RG factor(s)	I factor(s)	RQ factor(s)
HARR54	—	4(O1:F3) Ltr.Classification Number Class'n Puzzles Pict.Arrangement Number Exclusion	2(O1:F2) Arith.Problems Number Relations Number Series Seeing Trends Number Class Extension
HOEP01	—	2(O1:F1) Word Changes Letter Triangle Op'ns Sequence Word Relations Symbol Grouping	4(O1:F3) No.-Group Naming No. Class'n Numer Op'ns
HOEP31	3(O1:F4) Jumbled Words Similar Pairs Word Relations Word Changes Letter Triangle	—	2(O1:F1) Best No. Class No.Group Naming Best No. Pairs Symbol Manip'n Sign Changes II
LUCA01	2(O1:F7) Plotting Route Planning Skywriting 4(O1:F4) Alternating Operations Spatial Rotation Figure Analogies Artif. Language Operations	5(O1:F9) Locations Practical Judgment Judgment/Persons 9(O1:F8) Letter Sets Square Completion	—
MERR41	10(O1:F1) Verb.Anal. I-1 Logical Reasoning Verb.Anal. I-2 Sequential Assn. Gestalt Trans'n	8(O1:F6) Sentence Pairs Obj.Naming (Shifts) Verbl.Class'n 2 Verbl.Class'n 1 Episodes	—
NIHI02	3(O1:F4) Matched Verbal Relations Verbl.Anal. I-2 Verbl.Anal. I-1 Product Choice Best Trend Name	2(O1:F3) Verbl.Class'n 2 Verbl.Class'n 1 Synonyms Logical Reas'g Best Word Class	—

Table 6.2 (*cont.*)

Dataset	RG factor(s)	I factor(s)	RQ factor(s)
	5(O1:F2) Commonsense Judgment I Best Word Pairs Story Titles Unlikely Things Word Systems		
PENF01	4(O1:F4) Abstraction Symbol Manip'n Sign Changes Identical Words Seeing Deficiencies	—	3(O1:F6) Necessary Facts Necessary Op'ns Syllogisms
	6(O1:F7) Definitions Inferences		
PETE11	6(O1:F4) Ship Destination Letter Triangle Pict.Arrangement	?(O1:F2) Letter Series Letter–Number Word Changes Correlate Compl.II Form Reasoning	4(O1:F5) Symbol Grouping Necessary Facts Right Order Test
PETE12	4(O1:F4) Ship Destination Symbol Grouping Word Changes	2(O1:F2) Word Relations Correlate Compl.II Letter Triangle	—
	5(O1:F5) Sentence Order Pict. Arrangement Form Reasoning Camouflaged Wds. Word Patterns	Letter–Number Letter Series	
STOR11	3(O1:F2) Match Probs.V:A Match Probs.V:B Match Probs.II:A Ship Destinations Match Probs.II:B	5(O1:F5) Essen'l Sims. (S–B) Enclosed Boxes (S–B) Sent.Building (S–B) Essen'l Diffs. (S–B) Arith.Reas. (S–B)	8(O1:F6) Reasoning (S–B) Orientation (S–B) Quantit've (ITED) Orientation (S–B) Water Jars (S–B)
	10(O1:F7) Proverbs (S–B) Verbal Reas. B Verbal Reas. A		
STOR12	3(O1:F1) Abstract Words Orientation (S–B)	13(O1:F5) Orientation (S–B) Induction (S–B)	4(O1:F3) Arithmetic: B Arithmetic: A

Table 6.2 (*cont.*)

Dataset	RG factor(s)	I factor(s)	RQ factor(s)
	Diffs.Abst.Wds. Essen'l.Diffs (S–B) Arith.Reas. (S–B)	Proverbs (S–B)	Form Reasoning: B Bead Chain (S–B) Memory Symbols
	6(O1:F9) Reconcile Opp. (S–B) Finding Reasons (S–B)		
	11(O1:F8) Abstract Words (S–B) Enclosed Boxes (S–B) Essen'l Similarities (S–B)		
	12(O1:F9) Problems of Fact (S–B) Plan of Search (S–B) Verbal Reasoning:A		
STOR13	2(O1:F1) Verbl.Reasoning:B Sent.Compl. (SCAT) Quantitative (ITED) Vocabulary (ITED) Reconcile Opp. (S–B)	—	3(O1:F2) Arithmetic: B Arithmetic: A Bead Chain (S–B) Form Reasoning: B Memory: Symbols
	10(O1:F7) Plan of Search (S–B) Problems of Fact (S–B)		
	11(O1:F5) Verbal Absurdities (S–B) Abstract Words (S–B)		
VERY02	2(O1:F1) General Reasoning Ship Destination Arith.Reasoning Logical Reasoning Spatial Relations	—	6(O1:F5) Judgment Practical Estimation
VERY03	3(O1:F3) Logical Reasoning Ship Destination Deductive Reasoning Letter Reasoning Practical Estimation	—	6(O1:F1) General Reasoning Arith.Reasoning Math.Aptitude Arithmetic Test Algebra Test
WEIS11	—	9(O1:F10) Figure Analogies 10(O1:F9) Number Series II	11(O1:F6) Arith.Problems Follow Directions Number Series I Dependence & Variation Geometry:T–F

Table 6.2 (*cont.*)

Dataset	RG factor(s)	I factor(s)	RQ factor(s)
WERD01	2(O1:F4) Syllogisms II Syllogisms I Reasoning Number Analogies	8(O1:F7) Form Series II Number Series II	3(O1:F5) Arithmetic I Number Series I Arithmetic II Arithmetic III
WERD02	4(O1:F3) Syllogisms I Syllogisms IV Reasoning Math.Reasoning 7(O1:F5) Inferences I Inferences II	—	2(O1:F6) Arithmetic III Plane Geometry Arithmetic II
WOOD15	—	7(O1:F3) Concept Formation Numbers Reversed Analysis–Synthesis Vis–Aud Learning	4(O1:F4) Calculation Proofing Quan.Concepts Applied Problems

*a*Only up to five variables with the highest salient loadings are shown for each factor. Factors are identified by the numbers assigned in the hierarchical matrices shown in Appendix B, with an indication of the order in the hierarchy and the factor number in the first-order pattern matrix. Codes for classes of factors: RG, Sequential Reasoning; I, Inductive Reasoning; RQ, Quantitative Reasoning. S-B indicates a variable from the Stanford–Binet. Datasets yielding Piagetian Reasoning (RP) factors are excluded from this table.

RQ, I, and N. This dataset provides very limited support for differentiation of reasoning factors.

Datasets ANDE01 and ANDE03 were studies of the 11 subtests of the California Test of Mental Maturity, yielding only three factors. They provide limited support for differentiation of factors I and RQ, but neither was well defined in either of these datasets. The factor classified as I could almost equally well have been classified as RG, and it was poorly differentiated from a weakly defined verbal factor. The assignment of factor 4 to RG in ANDE01 is questionable.

Dataset CANI01, from a study of mathematical abilities, is one of the best instances of support for a differentiation of RG, I, and RQ, each represented by at least six variables. These factors were highly correlated and RG and RQ had particularly high loadings (each .93) on a general factor. A verbal factor V was not well represented, however, and RG was not differentiated from it.

Dataset CARR42 was from a study of grammatical sensitivity as a component of foreign language aptitude; it was not designed to study the reasoning domain

Table 6.3. *Intercorrelations and higher-order loadings of factors in the reasoning domain for 36 datasets yielding more than one factor in the domain*[a]

Dataset		Correlations			Loadings on higher-order factors			Remarks
ADKI03					2F	2C		No V. Dist. from
	RG	1.00			.69	.46		N, SR, CS, FI, P
	I	.66	1.00		.96	.00		
ANAS11					2G			Dist. from MA;
	RG	1.00			.34			No V, N
	RQ	.27	1.00		.79			
ANDE01					2G			
	I	1.00			.77			No N
	RQ	.73	1.00		.94			
	RG	.39	.58	1.00	.58			
ANDE03					2G			Dist. from V
	I	1.00			.61			No N
	RQ	.47	1.00		.77			
CANI01					2F			No V
	RG	1.00			.93			
	I	.61	1.00		.62			
	RQ	.83	.60	1.00	.93			Dist. from N
CARR42								
	RG	1.00			(Factors orthogonal)			
	I	.00	1.00					
CATT01A					3G	2F	2C	
	RG	1.00			.56	.08	.55	Dist. from
	I	.49	1.00		.57	.42	.23	V, N, SR
COOM01					2G			
	I	1.00			.65			Dist. from N, V
	RQ	.00	1.00		.09			

Study		(1)	(2)	(3)	(4)				
CORY01	RG	1.00				2Y .10	2H .85		No V
	RQ	−.18	1.00			2Y .59	2H −.26		No N
DUNC11	I1	1.00				2G .09			Dist. from V
	I2	.14	1.00			2G −.11			Dist. from N
	RQ	.08	−.04	1.00		2G .05			
GOOD01	I1	1.00				2G .64			Dist. from N, V, VZ
	I2	−.15	1.00			2G −.30			
GUIL16	RG1	1.00				3G .43	2H .69	2S −.09	No V
	RG2	.31	1.00			3G .26	2H .29	2S .07	" "
	RQ	.69	.48	1.00		3G .63	2H .69	2S .19	No N
GUIL18	RG	1.00				2G .76			No V
	I1	.66	1.00			2G .94			Dist. from VZ
	I2	.36	.16	1.00		2G .24			
GUIL19	RG	1.00				2G .83			Dist. from V
	RQ	.51	1.00			2G .56			No VZ, No N
GUIL21	RG1	1.00				2G .99			No V, no N
	RG2	.69	1.00			2G .70			
	I	.57	.43	1.00		2G .58			
	RQ	.13	.18	.28	1.00	2G .23			
GUIL22	RG	1.00				2G .43			
	I1	.20	1.00			2G .74			
	I2	.16	.62	1.00		2G .60			
GUIL32	RG	1.00				2G .89			No SR, No VZ
	I	.50	1.00			2G .57			Dist. from V

Table 6.3 (cont.)

Dataset	Correlations					Loadings on higher-order factors						Remarks
GUIL32A	RG	1.00				2G	.69					Dist. from V
	I	.34	1.00				.54					
HARR54	I	1.00				2G	.56					Dist. from V
	RQ	.41	1.00				.60					No N
HOEP01	I	1.00				2G	.63					No V
	RQ	.33	1.00				.52					No N
HOEP31	RG	1.00				2H	.63	2S	.02			Dist. from V
	RQ	.15	1.00				.70		.51			Dist. from N
LUCA01	RG1	1.00				2F	.79	2S	-.01			Dist. from V
	RG2	.53	1.00				.61		.25			
	I1	.46	.39	1.00			.57		.42			
	I2	.37	.49	.49	1.00		.48		.58			
MERR41	RG	1.00				2R	.26					Dist. from V
	I	.13	1.00				.37					
NIHI02	RG1	1.00				2G	.85					Dist. from V
	RG2	.44	1.00				.53					
	I	.74	.56	1.00			.87					
PENF01	RG1	1.00				3G	.15	2F	.40	2R	-.12	Dist. from V?
	RG2	.13	1.00				.19		.28		.05	No N
	RQ	.38	.27	1.00			.45		.76		.04	

PETE11 — Dist. from V

	RG	I	RQ	2G
RG	1.00			.24
I	.27	1.00		.83
RQ	.15	.60	1.00	.67

PETE12 — Dist. from V

	RG1	I	RG2	2G
RG1	1.00			.66
I	.68	1.00		.92
RG2	.33	.57	1.00	.65

STOR11

	RG	I	RQ	2G
RG	1.00			.00
I	.14	1.00		.57
RQ	−.01	.12	1.00	.25

STOR12

	RG1	RQ	RG2	RG3	RG4	3G	2H	2R	
RG1	1.00					.50	.79	.04	No V
RQ	.58	1.00				.26	.62	−.18	No N
RG2	.52	.35	1.00			.34	.42	.14	
RG3	.21	.05	.22	1.00		.22	.09	.27	
RG4	.01	.06	−.13	−.01	1.00	−.08	.04	−.17	

STOR13

	RG1	RQ	RG2	RG3	2G	
RG1	1.00				.93	Dist. from LD
RQ	.60	1.00			.67	No N
RG2	.08	.06	1.00		.08	
RG3	−.08	.11	.08	1.00	.01	

VERY02 — Dist. from V, N, VZ

	RG	RQ	2G
RG	1.00		.62
RQ	.24	1.00	.07

VERY03 — Dist. from V, N, VZ

	RG	RQ	2F	2C
RG	1.00		.36	.10
RQ	.22	1.00	.54	.68

WEIS11

	I1	I2	RQ	3G	2F	2C	2S
I1	1.00			.21	.75	.01	−.24
I2	.49	1.00		.06	.65	−.50	−.01
RQ	.40	.46	1.00	.41	.55	−.26	.25

Table 6.3 (cont.)

Dataset	Correlations			Loadings on higher-order factors		Remarks
WERD01				2G		
RG	1.00			.76		Dist. from V, N, VZ
I	.12	1.00		-.01		(Cross-out feature)
RQ	.56	-.32	1.00	.72		
WERD02				2G		
RG1	1.00			.58		Dist. from V, N, VZ
RG2	.18	1.00		.32		
RQ	.38	.31	1.00	.81		
WOOD15				2F	2C	
I	1.00			.60	.06	
RQ	.25	1.00		.34	.59	

[a] When two or more first-order factors in the same class appear, they are numbered (1,2,...) in the order in which they appear in Table 6.2. Codes for higher-order factors: 3G, 3rd-order General; 2G, 2nd-order General; 2F, Fluid Intelligence; 2C, Crystallized Intelligence; 2H, Fluid/crystallized Intelligence; 2R, General Fluency/Retrieval; 2S, Broad Speediness.

and reasoning variables were represented in it only rather adventitiously. The factors tentatively interpreted as RG and I were orthogonal, and neither was well defined by variables normally associated with these factors. This dataset is useful only because it suggests possible new features of the RG and I factors, with an ambiguous sentence task loading on RG and a grammatical word-grouping task loading on I.

Dataset CATT01A, based on only thirteen variables selected to represent second-order fluid and crystallized intelligence factors, provides some support for differentiation among factors RG, I, V, N, and SR (Spatial Relations), but the differentiation between RG and I is obtained only at the cost of regarding Letter Series tasks, normally and otherwise classified as measures of I, as measures of RG. The RG factor obtained here may in fact be a specific factor due to the format, content, and speededness of the letter-series tasks used in two forms of the Primary Mental Abilities (PMA) test. Nevertheless it is of interest that the I factor has its strongest loading on a second-order Gf (fluid intelligence) factor, while the RG factor has its strongest loading on a Gc (crystallized intelligence) factor.

Dataset COOM01, from a study of numerical facility, provides some support for differentiation of I and RQ, but neither factor is well defined. The factors are virtually orthogonal, though factor I has a substantial loading (.65) on a general factor. The factors are well differentiated from V, N, and SR (Spatial Relations).

In dataset CORY01, the classification of the RQ factor is questionable because of the loadings of several verbal tests on it; it may in fact be a verbal factor. The status of the RQ factor is thus unclear, though it loads highly (.59) on a second-order factor classified as Broad Memory (2Y). The factor classified as RG loads highly (.95) on what seems to be a combination of Gf and Gc (coded as 2H).

Results from dataset DUNC11, from a study of intelligence and learning ability, suggest that measures from several concept-formation learning tasks define two factors and that these are distinct from factor RQ. The two concept-formation factors are correlated only to the extent of .14 and have insignificant loadings on a general factor that is defined mainly by V, MA (Associative Memory) and N. It is not clear whether these factors should be classified as types of Induction factors, since the battery contained no conventional measures of Induction and thus did not provide information adequate to resolve this problem.

The two factors classified as Induction in dataset GOOD01, from a study of Thurstone's sixteen primary mental abilities tests, are not well defined, though differentiated from V, N, MA, and VZ.

Dataset GUIL16 comes from a study intended to study the reasoning domain. In our analysis, two factors were classified as RG, but one of them (factor 3) is close to being a verbal (V) factor, and there is no separate V factor. Factor 6, nevertheless, appears to be a conventional RG (sequential reasoning) factor. There was no clear I factor, although several inductive tests had loadings on a separate, poorly defined Visualization factor. The classification of factor 4 as RQ is dubious because there is no separate N factor; it appears that there were insufficient variables to define N. Factors 3 and 4 have appreciable loadings on a second-order factor that could possibly be interpreted as a broad reasoning factor, but the low loading of Factor 6 on this factor makes this interpretation doubtful. On the whole, this dataset fails to provide good evidence for the structure of the reasoning domain.

Dataset GUIL18, from a study of "evaluative" abilities, yielded three factors that were classified in the reasoning domain, including a poorly defined factor 7 for Induction. Factor 3, classified as RG, is defined mainly by categorical syllogism variables (the highest loading being for a completion, free response form). Factor 2 was classified as I because of the presence of several typical measures of I. There were insufficient variables to define factor RQ, and there is no separate V factor, so that factor 2 could well have verbal components. Both factors 2 and 3 have high loadings on a second-order general factor (.94 and .76, respectively).

Dataset GUIL19 comes from another study designed to investigate the reasoning domain. Factor 2 was classified as RG, but in view of its variables, it might almost equally well have been classified as I. It was differentiated from a V factor, however. Two factors (3 and 5) appeared to be classifiable as RQ, but only factor 3 was well defined.

Dataset GUIL21 (from a study of the domains of reasoning, creativity, and evaluation) yielded four factors classified in the reasoning domain, three of them substantially intercorrelated and with high loadings on a second-order factor. Factors 2 and 3 were classified as RG, but since there was no separate V factor, and in view of its variables, factor 2 may be a combination of V and RG. Factor 3 is a more credible RG factor. Factor 5, classified as I, contained typical variables measuring I. Factor 6 was tentatively classified as RQ, but the battery contained too few variables that might be expected to define RQ. The dataset provides limited support for a differentiation between RG and I; the status of the two RG factors is unclear. One possibility is that factor 2 contains the variables most highly correlated with a general factor, and thus was artifactually separated from factor 3.

Dataset GUIL22 came from the same investigation as GUIL21 but with a different sample and a somewhat different collection of variables. Factor 6 was somewhat hesitantly classified as RG. Factors 3 and 4 were classified as I; they are distinguished by the fact that factor 4 contains variables that might have a spatial component. A spatial factor was not otherwise represented in the battery and thus the status of factor 4 is unclear.

Dataset GUIL32 comes from a small USAAF study of judgment and reasoning tests. Of interest here is only that it provides limited support for a distinction between RG and I factors. The factors were highly correlated (.50) and had substantial loadings on a second-order factor (.89 and .57, respectively, for factors 2 and 3). Dataset GUIL32A was for the same variables as GUIL32 but for a different sample. Results were highly similar to those for GUIL32.

Dataset HARR54 shows a distinction between factor I and RQ, but RQ is not distinguished from a numerical facility factor. Dataset HOEP01 shows a distinction between an I and a RQ factor, but neither is distinguished from V or N. Dataset HOEP31 presents an RQ factor that is distinguished from factor N, but the classification and status of factor 3, assigned to RG, is unclear, though separate from a V factor, and an induction factor failed to appear. Dataset LUCA01 yielded two factors each for RG and I. Clearest is factor 4, assigned to RG. Factor 2, also assigned to RG, is not well defined and may represent specific variance due to facility with and knowledge of spatial coordinate systems. Neither I factor is well defined, the loadings being low in magnitude and the nature of the variables unclear.

Dataset MERR41, from a study of problem solving abilities, provides some support for a distinction between RG and I, separate from V. Dataset NIHI02 shows two RG factors, but only factor 3 is reasonably well defined by analogical reasoning variables. The assignment of factor 2 to I is plausible but not totally convincing. In dataset PENF01, a weak RQ factor is distinguished from two RG factors, neither of which is easily interpretable, partly because of the virtual impossibility of retrieving adequate information about some of the variables. Fairly clear distinctions between RG and I factors are apparent in both datasets PETE11 and PETE12.

Datasets STOR11, STOR12, and STOR13 represent studies of Stanford–Binet items, along with a number of paper-and-pencil marker variables, from three different levels of ability on the IQ scale. It is of interest to notice the degree to which the factor structures and loadings change over these samples, possibly due to the consequent restrictions of range and to sampling fluctuations. Nevertheless, all three datasets yield distinctions between RG factors and RQ factors, and an I factor appears in two of them.

Datasets VERY01, VERY02, and VERY03 are respectively for males, females, and males/females combined in a sample of college students. Results from VERY01 (for males) are not listed in Tables 6.2 and 6.3 because a factor that might be regarded as RQ was considered to be more a mathematical knowledge factor (to be considered in Chapter 12) than a reasoning factor. For the females in dataset VERY02 there was a strong RG factor that was separate from a weak factor (factor 6) classified hesitantly as RQ. For the combined sample (dataset VERY03) the distinction between RG and RQ was clear and strong, probably because of the decreased restriction of range in the combined sample. Although a couple of inductive tasks were included in the battery, an Induction factor failed to show up in any of these datasets.

Dataset WEIS11, from a study of mathematical abilities, showed no RG factor.

It had two weak factors classified as I. The only strong factor in the reasoning domain was an RQ factor that was separate from several other factors in the mathematical domain (to be discussed in Chapter 12).

On first inspection, datasets WERD01 and WERD02 (also from studies of mathematical abilities) promised to provide the strongest evidence for separations among all three proposed factors RG, I, and RQ. Closer inspection revealed several difficulties. An induction factor appeared only in WERD01, and then only weakly, in factor 8, whose highest-loading variables were series tasks which had a unique "cross-out" feature, in contrast to similar tasks elsewhere in the battery that required series completion. The RG and RQ factors in WERD01 were quite strong, though highly correlated ($r = .56$), but the RG factor was defined almost exclusively by *linear* syllogism tasks. Two *categorical* syllogism tasks (Inferences I and II) were introduced into dataset WERD02, and defined an RG factor (factor 7) separate from (and relatively uncorrelated with, $r = .18$) a factor that was defined by the linear syllogism tasks (factor 4). This study suggests, then, that reasoning in categorical syllogisms may be quite different from that employed in linear syllogisms. It also suggests that the RG factor proposed here may not be unitary.

Finally, consider dataset WOOD15, which was the only dataset, from a series based on analysis of the Woodcock-Johnson Psychoeducational Battery (1977 edition) at different age levels, to show two factors in the reasoning domain. These factors were classified as I and RQ, respectively, but neither was well defined, partly because the battery was designed for practical diagnostic use rather than as one for factor analysis. It yields only suggestive evidence for a distinction between I and RQ, and no evidence for an RG factor.

Reviewing the above mass of evidence from available datasets, we can conclude only that the evidence *suggests* the existence and separation of three factors in the reasoning domain, but this evidence is hardly compelling. Each of the three proposed factors can be found to be strong and well defined in *some* datasets, and all three possible pairs of factors are well separated in *some* datasets. No dataset can be found to give strong evidence for all three factors, except possibly dataset CANI01.

On the other hand, in view of the weak designs of available datasets, if three reasoning factors do in fact exist one could not expect these datasets to reveal strong evidence for such factors and their separation. This is not to fault the wisdom and perspicacity of previous investigators; it is only on the basis of the present survey and reanalysis that weaknesses have been disclosed, making it possible to ask new questions and propose new designs for further investigation.

Specifically, it would first be necessary to construct more adequate tests of the proposed factors – with techniques of item analysis (preferably utilizing latent trait item response theory and related techniques) to insure homogeneity of test content. In test construction, careful attention would have to be paid to hypotheses about the nature of the respective factors, and to hypotheses about what instructions and item stimulus characteristics make for variations in task difficulty. Careful attention would have to be paid, also, to controlling level of mastery as opposed to speed or rate of test taking effects. Few studies have been designed to take account of such effects.

Davidson and Carroll (1945; dataset DAVI01) showed that a level-of-mastery reasoning factor could be differentiated from a speed of reasoning factor. The study was not sufficiently well designed to differentiate factors RG, I, and RQ; the level-of-mastery reasoning factor contained variables that now appear to range over these three factors. Lord (1956; dataset LORD01) identified a level-of-mastery Quantitative Reasoning (RQ) factor best measured by variables based on number correct in unlimited time, less well measured by variables taken under time-limits. Although there are a few other studies, considered in Chapter 11, that demonstrate speed/level distinctions in the reasoning and other domains, it is strange and unfortunate that subsequent investigators have paid little if any attention to these findings in designing their studies. It is difficult to find evidence in our database concerning differential speed/level effects in the RG, I, and RQ factors proposed here.

Intercorrelations of Factors RG, I, and RQ and Loadings on Higher-Order Factors

In nearly all datasets listed in Table 6.3, factors had been rotated obliquely, with the result that their intercorrelations were generally non-zero. Considering all instances of RG, I, and RQ factors, the median intercorrelation between RG and I factors was .49; between RG and RQ factors, .36; and between I and RQ factors, .47. While these medians are all significantly different from zero ($p < .01$), it is unlikely that they are significantly different among themselves. The only conclusion that can be drawn is that these three proposed reasoning factors tend to be positively correlated, but that their correlations can vary widely, from near zero to very high, depending on such conditions as sample size, range of talent represented in the sample, and simplicity of factor structure. It may be assumed that these correlations are largely due to the effects of higher-order factors.

Along with the intercorrelations of factors, Table 6.3 also shows orthogonalized loadings of the first-order reasoning factors on higher-order factors. Any conclusions based on these loadings must be qualified by the observation that the nature of the higher-order factors is strongly conditioned by battery design, i.e., the selection of the variables of a dataset to represent factors. Most datasets listed in the table yielded only one second-order factor, generally interpreted as a general intelligence factor. In twelve cases, however, two or more higher-order factors appeared, with general factors either at the second or the third order. If all loadings of first-order reasoning factors on such general factors are considered, the median loading for RG factors was .60; for I factors, .58; and for RQ factors, .62. In view of these results, it is unlikely that these three types of factors differ in their typical loadings on higher-order general factors. There were several instances (ADKI03, CATT01A, GUST11A, VERY03, WEIS11, and WOOD15) in which datasets yielded second-order factors interpreted as Gf (fluid intelligence) and Gc (crystallized intelligence), respectively (in the table, these are coded as 2F and 2C). In these datasets, there was some tendency for RG and I factors to load more highly on Gf, and RQ factors to load more highly on Gc, but the sample of datasets was too small to permit drawing any conclusions about the status of these factors in the higher-order structure of cognitive abilities.

On the assumption that three types of factors can indeed be identified in the reasoning domain, each of these factors is discussed somewhat more fully in the following sections. Critical questions for further research are mentioned.

SEQUENTIAL REASONING (RG) FACTORS

All 91 token factors that were classified as Sequential Reasoning (RG) factors from 76 datasets are listed in Table 6.4, with date of publication, source country, median age of sample, male/female classification, factor number, and remarks. The structure of this table is similar to that of Tables 5.1 to 5.17 in Chapter 5.

It can be observed from Table 6.4 that RG factors can be measured at least from age nine to later adulthood. It is probable that they can be measured at ages earlier than nine; our sample of datasets happened not to include relevant data from earlier ages. One research question to be answered in the future is, in fact, at how early an age the RG factor can be distinguished from other reasoning factors.

The dominant feature of these RG factors is that they emphasize the ability to reason and draw conclusions from given conditions or premises, often in a series of two or more sequential steps. The stimulus or test material can be of almost any type – literal, verbal (semantic), numerical, pictorial, or figural. The operations in the reasoning process can be of many types, involving comparisons of stimuli in terms of continuous attributes or class memberships, or perception of relations of causality, implication, etc. Above all, the processes are deductive, in the sense that there is very little load of induction or rule-finding. The best tests of this factor impose little requirement on the subject to induce (educe) relationships or class memberships, since these relationships and class memberships are stated or otherwise immediately apparent to most subjects.

Some of the most characteristic tests of the RG factor are: Deductive Reasoning, False Premises (Nonsense Syllogisms), Inferences, Logical Reasoning, Proverbs, Reasoning (when based on syllogisms), Ship Destination, Syllogisms, Symbol Manipulation, and Verbal Reasoning. Preferably, these tests should be administered without a time limit, or at least scored in such a way that the subject's level of mastery of deductive skills, rather than speed in processing information, is emphasized. Administration of tests in a computerized format, as was done for dataset CORY01, should make for optimizing a distinction between level of mastery and speed. Load of vocabulary and sentence comprehension should be minimized.

The several instances in which datasets yielded more than one RG factor raise questions to be explored in future research:

1.   Are processes involved in the solution of categorical syllogisms different from those involved in the solution of linear syllogisms? This is suggested by results from datasets WERD01 and WERD02. It is also suggested by experimental data reviewed by Sternberg (1982, pp. 254ff.).

2.   A related question has to do with the factorial composition of tests involving conditional syllogisms – syllogisms in which the operators are words such as "if," "then," and "not." Our datasets provide few if any instances of such tests.

3.   Tests of analogies and series completion (letter series, number series, figure series) – ordinarily classified as inductive tasks – are frequently associated with tests of deductive reasoning. Under what conditions does this occur? Is it possible to vary the characteristics of such tasks to control their appearance on RG factors as opposed to I factors?

4.   Several datasets (e.g., GUIL34, GUIL35, LUCA01) yield a factor that has previously been interpreted as a "planning" factor. I regard it as a type of deductive reasoning factor because it requires drawing conclusions from stated conditions and planning actions accordingly. To what extent can such a factor be differentiated from other deductive reasoning factors? Are there fluency or idea production components in tests of planning ability?

5.   Several datasets (e.g., GUIL35, PARK01) yield a factor that has sometimes been interpreted as an "integration" or "integrative process" factor. Such a factor was recognized by French (1951) and in the 1976 version of the ETS kit of factor-referenced tests as "the ability to keep in mind simultaneously or to combine several conditions, premises, or rules in order to produce a correct response" (Ekstrom, French, & Harman, 1976, p. 87). My reanalyses of the relevant datasets and interpretations of resulting factors suggest that an integrative process factor is actually a type of sequential reasoning factor. For example, factor 3 of dataset GUIL35 and factor 2 of dataset PARK01 are classified as RG and listed in Table 6.4. The variables loaded on them are printed tests requiring reasoning about complex problems, and possibly also requiring a considerable load on working memory. Is this interpretation correct? Would it nevertheless be possible to differentiate an integrative process factor from factor RG?

It seems that at least some of the variance in performance on deductive reasoning tasks reflects biases in reasoning that depend upon whether the subjects perceive the conclusions as valid or invalid on the basis of common sense or general knowledge, rather than on the actual structure of the argumentation. Horn (1978b, pp. 23 ff.) studied responses to syllogisms cross-classified in terms of (a) the validity of the reasoning and (b) the apparent reasonableness of the conclusion, independent of the validity of the reasoning, and concluded that much of the reliable variance could be interpreted as response bias. "Some subjects," he reported, "systematically responded with the 'good reasoning' whenever there was doubt about the correct answer, while others in the same circumstances systematically responded with 'bad reasoning.'" Horn was unable,

Table 6.4. *91 Reasoning (RG) factors in 76 datasets arranged in order of approximate mean age of sample[a]*

Dataset	Date	C'y code	Age	Sample code	M/F code	Factor no.	Remarks (higher-order factors; others related)
JAY01	'50	U	9	6	3	6	1:2C
VALT01	'70	G	9	V	3	5	1:2G
BENN01	'73	E	10	1	3	3	1:2G
BENN02	'73	E	10	1	2	3	1:2G
MOUR01	'52	E	10	6	1	4	1:3G;2:2C
WRIG01	'39	U	10	1	3	5	1:2G
HIGG01	'78	A	11	1	3	2	1:2G
SPEA01	'62	A	11	6	1	2	1:2H
SPEA34	'77	A	11	O	2	8	5:2F
WERD51	'71	S	11	6	1	4	1:2G
CATT01A	'63	U	12	6	3	3	1:3G;2:2C;8:I
HARG11A	'27	E	13	6	3	2	1:2G
RIMO21	'51	T	13	6	3	2	1:2G;5:RQ?
WERD41	'69	S	13	6	3	4	1:2S
PETE11	'63	U	14	M	3	6	1:2G;2:I;4:RQ
PETE12	'63	U	14	M	3	4	1:2G;2:I
"	"	"	"	"	"	5	Also RG?
STOR11	'66	U	14	8	3	10	1:2G;2:RQ;5:I;8:RQ
STOR12	'66	U	14	I	3	3	1:3G;2:2H;4:RQ;13:I
"	"	"	"	"	"	6	Also RG?
"	"	"	"	"	"	11	Also RG?
"	"	"	"	"	"	12	Also RG?
STOR13	'66	U	14	7	3	2	1:2G;3:RQ;8:I
"	"	"	"	"	"	10	Also RG?
"	"	"	"	"	"	11	Also RG?
WERD01	'58	S	14	6	1	2	1:2G;3:RQ;8:I
WERD02	'58	S	14	6	1	4	1:2G;2:RQ
"	"	"	"	"	"	7	Also RG?
GARR16	'35	U	15	6	2	2	1:2G
REYB01	'41	K	15	6	3	2	1:2G
SCHU11	'58	U	15	1	3	7	1:3G;5:2F
BROW11	'66	U	16	6	3	7	1:2G
CANI01	'62	U	16	6	2	2	1:2G;3:RQ;4:I
DUNH11	'66	U	16	1	3	2	1:2F;4:I?;6:I?
JACO01	'75	U	16	1	3	4	1:2G
NIHI01	'64	U	16	8	3	3	1:3G;2:2H
NIHI02	'64	U	16	8	3	3	1:2G;2:I?
"	"	"	"	"	"	5	Also RG?
SNOW11	'77	U	16	8	3	5	1:2G
GUIL32	'47	U	17	1	1	2	1:2G;5:I
HOEP31	'64	U	17	6	3	3	1:2H;2:RQ
PENF01	'67	E	17	8	3	4	1:3G;2:2F;3:RQ
"	"	"	"	"	"	6	Also RG?
THUR31	'40	U	17	1	3	9	1:2G;2:I
CARR11	'43	U	18	6	2	2	1:2G
DAVI01	'45	U	18	P	3	3	1:2G

Table 6.4 (*cont.*)

Dataset	Date	C'y code	Age	Sample code	M/F code	Factor no.	Remarks (higher-order factors; others related)
HECK01	'67	U	18	6	3	12	1:3G;10:2H
SISK01	'39	U	18	A	1	3	1:2H
ADKI03	'52	U	19	2	1	4	1:2H;2:I
ANAS11	'32	U	19	1	2	4	1:2G;2:RQ
BUND11	'67	U	19	6	1	3	1:2G
CARR42	'76	U	19	P	3	5	3:I (All orthog.)
CARR43	'76	U	19	6	3	12	10:26
GARD05A	'60	U	19	6	2	5	1:2G
HUNT71	'75	U	19	6	3	1	(All orthog.)
KAMM01	'53	U	19	F	3	3	1:2G
PARK01	'60	U	19	T	1	2	1:2G;Integrative Process?
THUR21A	'38	U	19	6	3	3	1:2F
VERY01	'67	U	19	6	1	4	1:2G
VERY02	'67	U	19	6	2	2	1:2G
VERY03	'67	U	19	6	3	3	1:2F;6:RQ
CORY01	'77	U	21	2	1	7	1:2G;3:RQ;6:20
GUIL11	'55	U	21	3	1	2	1:2G
GUIL14	'57	U	21	3	1	3	1:2H
GUIL16	'51	U	21	3	1	3	1:3G;2:2F;4:RQ;5:I?
"	"	"	"	"	"	6	Also RG?
"	"	"	"	"	"	9	Also RG? (speeded)
GUIL19	'55	U	21	3	1	2	1:2G;3:RQ;5:RQ
GUIL21	'56	U	21	3	1	2	1:2G;3:RG?
"	"	"	"	"	"	3	Also RG?
GUIL22	'56	U	21	3	1	6	1:2G;3:I;4:I?
GUIL32A	'47	U	21	3	1	3	1:2G;5:I
GUIL34	'47	U	21	3	1	2	1:2G
GUIL35	'47	U	21	3	1	2	1:2G;Planning?
"	"	"	"	"	"	3	Integrative Process?
GUIL37	'47	U	21	3	1	4	1:2G
GUIL46	'47	U	21	3	1	2	1:2G
GUIL51	'60	U	21	3	1	2	1:2G
GUIL66	'52	U	21	3	1	2	1:2G
LUCA01	'53	U	21	3	1	2	1:2H;5:I?;9:I?;Integrative Process?
"	"	"	"	"	"	4	Also RG?
MERR41	'60	U	21	3	1	10	1:2R;8:I
MOON01	'54	C	21	3	1	3	1:2G
TAYL12A	'67	U	21	2	1	8	1:2!
GUIL18	'53	U	23	3	1	3	1:2G;2:I
CURE01	'44	U	30	0	3	2	1:2C
MARK01	'59	U	30	3	1	5	1:2R
DEMI01A	'62	U	42	L	3	2	1:2G
DEMI02A	'62	U	42	S	3	5	1:2G

*See Appendix A for codes. In a few cases, the classifications of factors shown here were preliminary and may disagree with the final classifications shown in the tables of Appendix B.

however, to find moderator variables that would predict bias behavior. Colberg and Nester (1987) have further studied illogical biases and recommend developing reasoning tests by making systematic use of all possible basic logical forms, including general-to-particular inductive tasks involving probabilistic reasoning (see also Colberg, 1985; Colberg, Nester, & Cormier, 1982; Colberg, Nester, and Trattner, 1985).

INDUCTION (I) FACTORS

Table 6.5 lists 107 factors classified as Induction (I), in 91 datasets. There are relatively few instances in which datasets yielded more than one induction factor, and our previous discussion indicated that most of these instances can be regarded as questionable, or based on the intrusion of variance from other factors such as Space or Spatial Visualization. One dataset, CARL40, had to do with an attempt to factorize the items of Raven's Progressive Matrix test, but the results are difficult to interpret and have not been replicated in other studies.

As mentioned previously, inductive tasks are those that require subjects to inspect a class of stimulus materials (nearly always with more than one instance) and infer (induce, educe) a common characteristic underlying these materials – a concept, a class membership, a rule, a process, a trend, or a causal relation, for example. Among the best and most characteristic tests of the Inductive Reasoning (I) factor are: Classification, Concept Formation, Correlate Completion, Induction, Letter Grouping, Letter Series, Letter Sets, Letter Triangle, Locations, Marks, Matrices, Patterns, Series, Similarities, and Verbal Classification. The factor is also frequently found to be measured by analogies tests and number series tests, but only if the tasks involve relations that are relatively difficult for subjects to discover. If there is a heavy vocabulary load, verbal analogies tests are often highly loaded on V or RG factors. If the mathematical relationships in a number series test are complex, requiring mathematical knowledge and insight, the loading on the RQ factor is likely to be high.

As the table shows, the inductive factor appears in datasets for samples taken even as early as age 4 (in dataset WIEB12, measured by two subtests, Conceptual Grouping and Opposite Analogies, of the McCarthy Scales of Children's Abilities), but it frequently occurs in datasets concerned with samples of later ages, even up to late adulthood.

QUANTITATIVE REASONING (RQ) FACTORS

Table 6.6 lists 59 factors from 59 datasets yielding factors classified as Quantitative Reasoning (RQ). These are factors requiring reasoning based on mathematical properties and relations. The reasoning processes may be either inductive or deductive, or some combination of them. This factor appears in datasets for

Table 6.5. *107 Induction (I) factors in 91 datasets arranged in order of approximate mean age of sample*

Dataset	Date	C'y code	Age	Sample code	M/F code	Factor no.	Remarks (higher-order factors; others related)
WIEB12	'80	U	4	O	2	5	1:2G
SCHI11	'34	U	5	1	1	2	1:2G
WOOD13	'77	U	6	1	3	5	1:2C
ANDE01	'64	U	7	1	3	3	1:2G;2:RQ
CARL40	'80	U	7	6	3	2	1:2Q;3, 4, & 5 are other
''	''	''	''	''	''	3	factors from analysis
''	''	''	''	''	''	4	of items of Raven Prog.
''	''	''	''	''	''	5	Matrix test
JONE31	'49	U	7	1	3	3	1:2D
CUMM01	'79	C	9	8	3	6	1:2D
JONE32	'49	U	9	1	3	4	1:2D
UNDH01	'76	O	9	1	3	5	1:2H
ANDE02	'64	U	10	1	3	3	1:2G
BROW21	'33	E	10	6	1	2	1:2G
HARR51	'73	U	10	1	1	5	1:2G
HARR52	'73	U	10	1	2	3	1:2G
HARR53	'73	U	10	1	1	4	1:2G
HARR54	'73	U	10	1	2	4	1:2G;2:RQ
REIN01	'65	G	10	1	3	2	1:2G
REIN03	'65	G	10	6	3	3	1:2G
WOOD15	'77	U	10	1	3	7	5:2F;4:RQ
DUNC11	'64	U	11	6	3	7	1:2G;8:RQ:Figural Concept Formation
''	''	''	''	''	''	10	Verbal Concept Formation
GUST11A	'84	S	11	1	3	8	1:3G;6:2F
JONE33	'49	U	11	1	3	4	1:2D
RIMO11	'48	U	11	1	3	3	1:3G;2:2F
SPEA02	'62	A	11	6	2	4	1:2H
SPEA31	'77	A	11	6	1	7	1:2H
SPEA32	'77	A	11	6	2	3	1:2H
SPEA33	'77	A	11	O	1	2	1:2H
SPEA34	'77	A	11	O	2	3	1:2H
UNDH11	'78	O	11	6	3	4	1:2G
CATT01A	'63	U	12	6	3	8	1:3G;6:21;3:RG?
ELKO01	'35	E	12	6	1	2	1:2G
''	''	''	''	''	''	3	Also I?
''	''	''	''	''	''	4	Also I?
REIN02	'65	G	12	1	3	4	1:2G
STAK01	'61	U	12	1	3	16	12:20
ANDE03	'64	U	13	1	3	4	1:2G;3:RQ
JONE34	'49	U	13	1	3	5	1:2D
REIN04	'65	G	13	6	3	3	1:2G
RIMO21	'51	T	13	6	1	3	1:2G;5:RG?
''	''	''	''	''	''	4	Also I?

Table 6.5 (*cont.*)

Dataset	Date	C'y code	Age	Sample code	M/F code	Factor no.	Remarks (higher-order factors; others related)
THUR81	'41	U	13	6	3	5	1:3G;2:2H
THUR82	'41	U	13	6	3	6	1:3G;2:2H
CRAW01	'76	C	14	1	3	5	1:2G
GERS02	'63	U	14	1	3	5	1:20
GUIL51	'61	U	14	1	3	6	1:2G;2:RG
MANG01A	'57	E	14	6	2	8	6:2S
PETE11	'63	U	14	M	3	2	1:2G;6:RG
PETE12	'63	U	14	M	3	2	1:2G;4:RG
STOR11	'66	U	14	8	3	5	1:2G;2:RQ;3:RG;8:RQ; 10:RG
STOR12	'66	U	14	I	3	13	1:3G;2:2H;3,6,11,12:RG?
WEDE01	'47	E	14	1	2	3	1:2G
WERD01	'58	S	14	6	1	8	1:2G;2:RG;3:RQ
TENO01	'69	U	15	1	3	2	1:2G
WEIS11	'55	U	15	M	3	9	1:3G;8:2F;10:I;11:RQ
”	”	”	”	”	”	10	Also I?
ARNO01	'67	A	16	1	3	2	1:2G
BLAK01	'41	U	16	6	3	2	1:2G
BURN11	'80	U	16	6	3	2	1:2G;3:RQ
CANI01	'62	U	16	6	2	4	1:2G;2:RG;3:RQ
DUNH11	'66	U	16	1	3	4	1:2F;2:RG
”	”	”	”	”	”	6	Also I?
”	”	”	”	”	”	8	Also I?
JEFF11	'57	U	16	$	3	4	1:21
NIHI02	'64	U	16	8	3	2	1:2G;5:RG?;Classes
SUNG01	'81	U	16	Z	3	10	8:28
SUNG02	'81	U	16	#	3	3	1:3G;2:2H
THUR71	'49	U	16	$	1	4	1:2G
WEIN11	'59	U	16	1	3	2	1:2C
COOM01	'41	U	17	1	3	4	1:2G;10:RQ
GUIL32	'47	U	17	1	1	5	1:2G;2:RG?
TAYL01	'47	U	17	1	3	2	1:2H
THUR31	'40	U	17	1	3	2	1:2G
WOLI01	'65	U	17	1	1	4	1:2G;3:RQ
GOOD01	'43	U	18	A	1	2	1:2G;8:I?
”	”	”	”	”	”	8	Also I?
MORR11	'41	U	18	P	1	5	1:2G
STUM11	'74	G	18	6	1	2	1:2G
ADKI03	'52	U	19	2	1	2	1:2H;4:RG
ALLI01	'60	U	19	2	1	3	1:2L
BARR00	'53	A	19	6	3	2	1:21
BOTZ01	'51	U	19	6	1	2	1:2G
”	”	”	”	”	”	5	Also I (speed)?
CARR42	'76	U	19	P	3	3	5:RG (All orthog.)
PIMS01	'62	U	19	F	3	2	1:2F
SCHE11	'52	C	19	6	3	6	1:2G

Table 6.5 (*cont.*)

Dataset	Date	C'y code	Age	Sample code	M/F code	Factor no.	Remarks (higher-order factors; others related)
SNOW20	'76	U	19	6	3	2	1:GV (All orthog.)
WHEA01	'73	U	19	1	1	2	1:2G
GUIL17	'52	U	21	3	1	7	1:2G
GUIL21	'56	U	21	3	1	5	1:2C;3:RG
GUIL22	'56	U	21	3	1	3	1:2G;4:I?;6:RG;semantic
"	"	"	"	"	"	4	Also I, figural
GUIL32A	'47	U	21	3	1	5	1:2G;3:RQ
HOEP01	'67	U	21	3	1	2	1:2G;4:RQ?
LUCA01	'53	U	21	3	1	5	1:2H;2:RG;4:RG;7:2S
"	"	"	"	"	"	9	Also I?
MERR41	'60	U	21	3	1	8	1:2G;10:RG
VERN51	'47	E	21	2	1	4	1:2H
GUIL18	'53	U	23	3	1	2	1:2G;3:RG
"	"	"	"	"	"	7	Also I?
HAKS01	'74	C	24	1	3	7	1:3G;5:21
ROYC11	'76	C	40	4	3	3	1:2G
"	"	"	"	"	"	4	Halstead Category Test
AFTA01	'69	C	43	1	3	10	9:20
CORN01	'83	U	71	1	3	2	1:2G

[a]See Appendix A for codes. In a few cases, the classifications of factors shown here were preliminary and may disagree with the final classifications shown in the tables of Appendix B.

ages ranging from age five to adulthood. There are no instances in which a dataset yielded more than one RQ factor.

Tests characteristically having high loadings on this factor are usually titled Arithmetic, Arithmetical Reasoning, Mathematical Aptitude, and the like. Typically these tests present a variety of mathematical reasoning problems such as word problems (solving verbally stated mathematical problems), number series, and problems requiring selection of appropriate arithmetical operations. Generally, the amount of actual numerical computation required is small. While tests are often given with a time-limit, the scores are expected to depend mainly on the level of difficulty in the problems that can be performed. It is probable that factorial validity could be maximized by minimizing speed components, vocabulary and syntax load, spatial vizualization components, and complexity of numerical computations, at the same time providing for an appropriate range of difficulty in the mathematical reasoning steps, algorithms, and operations required.

PIAGETIAN REASONING (RP) FACTORS

Eleven datasets yielded 15 factors that for convenience are termed Piagetian Reasoning factors because at least some of them involve reasoning tasks that

Table 6.6. *59 Quantitative Reasoning (RQ) factors in 59 datasets arranged in order of approximate mean age of sample*[a]

Dataset	Date	C'y code	Age	Sample code	M/F code	Factor no.	Remarks (higher-order factors; others related)
SCHI12	'34	U	5	1	2	3	1:2G
ANDE01	'64	U	7	1	3	2	1:2G;3:I
HARR54	'73	U	10	1	2	2	1:2G;4:I
WOOD15	'77	U	10	1	3	4	1:2C;7:I
DUNC11	'64	U	11	6	3	8	1:2G;7:I?;9:I?
TRAU01	'70	U	11	1	3	6	1:2G
ANDE03	'64	U	13	1	3	3	1:2G;4:RG
RIMO21	'51	T	13	6	1	5	1:2G;2:RG
SWIN11	'48	U	13	6	3	2	1:2G
PETE11	'63	U	14	M	3	4	1:2G;2:I;6:RG
STOR11	'66	U	14	8	3	8	1:2G;2:GH;5:I
STOR12	'66	U	14	I	3	4	1:3G;2:2H;3:RG;6:RG?
STOR13	'66	U	14	7	3	3	1:2G;2:RG
WERD01	'58	S	14	6	1	3	1:2G;2:RG;8:I
WERD02	'58	S	14	6	1	2	1:2G;4,7:RG
SEGE01	'57	U	15	1	1	3	1:3G;2:2H
SEGE02	'57	U	15	1	2	4	1:3G;2:2H
WEBE01	'53	G	15	6	1	3	1:2G
WEBE02	'53	G	15	6	2	2	1:2G
WEIS11	'55	U	15	M	3	11	1:3G;8:2F;9:I;10:I
BURN11	'80	U	16	6	3	3	1:2G
CANI01	'62	U	16	6	2	3	1:2G;2:RG;4:I
HOEP21	'68	U	16	8	3	9	6:20
OSUL01	'65	U	16	6	3	2	1:2G
COOM01	'41	U	17	1	3	10	1:2G;4:I
HOEP31	'64	U	17	6	3	2	1:2H;3:RG
PENF01	'67	E	17	8	3	3	1:3G;2:2F;4:RG;6:RG?
VAND61	'78	U	17	1	3	3	1:2G
WOLI01	'65	U	17	1	1	3	1:2C
WOOD17	'77	U	17	1	3	3	1:2C
GRIM01	'71	U	18	6	3	7	6:2H
GUIL20	'55	U	18	3	1	4	1:2G
LANG31	'41	U	18	6	2	4	1:2G
LORD01	'56	U	18	3	1	7	5:2H
THOR21	'36	U	18	6	3	4	1:2G
ANAS11	'32	U	19	1	2	2	1:2G;4:RG
FAIR01A	'84	U	19	2	3	6	5:2H
FAIR02	'84	U	19	2	3	3	.1:2H
FLEI51	'71	U	19	2	1	3	1:2G
SCHN01	'29	U	19	6	1	3	1:2G
SNOW12	'77	U	19	6	3	3	1:2G
VERN21	'84	U	19	$	1	2	1:2G
VERY02	'67	U	19	6	3	6	1:2G;2:RG
VERY03	'67	U	19	6	3	6	1:2F;3:RG
SMIT01	'33	U	20	P	1	2	1:2G

Table 6.6 (*cont.*)

Dataset	Date	C'y code	Age	Sample code	M/F code	Factor no.	Remarks (higher-order factors; others related)
CORY01	'77	U	21	2	1	3	1:2G;6:20;7:RG
GUIL16	'51	U	21	3	1	4	1:3G;2:2F;3:RG;5:I?; 6:RG?
GUIL17	'52	U	21	3	1	4	1:2G;7:I?
GUIL19	'55	U	21	3	1	3	1:2G;2:RG
GUIL21	'56	U	21	3	1	6	1:2C;3:RG;5:I
GUIL33	'47	U	21	3	1	2	1:2G
GUIL40	'47	U	21	3	1	2	1:2G
GUIL41	'47	U	21	3	1	2	1:2G
HOEP01	'67	U	21	3	1	4	1:2G;2:I
HOFF01	'68	U	21	B	3	4	1:2V
MESS01	'75	U	21	3	1	9	1:2G
WOTH01	'90	U	21	1	3	4	1:3G;2:2F
KELL01	'64	U	22	3	1	9	6:2H
WOOD18	'77	U	30	1	3	6	5:2F

[a]See Appendix A for codes. In a few cases, the classifications of factors shown here were preliminary and may disagree with the final classifications shown in the tables of Appendix B.

were devised and studied largely by Piaget and his collaborators over many years, as reviewed for example by Flavell (1977). These factors are listed in Table 6.7.

The datasets are for samples of individuals from very young ages (12 months) to late middle age. The youngest samples are for datasets WACH01, WACH02, and WACH03, for independent samples at ages 14, 18, and 24 months, respectively. The variables were from the Infant Psychological Developmental Scale (IPDS) of Uzgiris and Hunt (1975), based on these authors' developmental model of infant sensorimotor intelligence that postulates four levels of systematic changes: Level I (undifferentiated actions), Level II (differentiated actions), Level III (regulation by differentiated actions), and Level IV (anticipatory regulation). These variables represent simple tests of infant behavior that seem to require early forms of reasoning, such as noticing or anticipating the consequences of actions. Our principal-factor analysis yielded fewer factors than did the authors' principal component analysis, but the patterns of results were generally similar, and can be said to lend support to the developmental model, chiefly because the factor structures tended to differ over the age range considered. (The small sizes of the samples, $N = 25$ each, are troublesome.) Much more research is needed on the measurement and analysis of infant abilities with such scales.

Dataset DEVR02 (Carroll, Kohlberg, & DeVries, 1984) used a series of Piagetian tasks, mainly conservation tasks, along with measures from the Stanford–Binet scale, the California Test of Mental Maturity, and the Metropolitan Achievement Test, for a sample of bright and average kindergarten

Table 6.7. *15 Piagetian Reasoning (RP) factors in 11 datasets arranged in order of approximate mean age of sample*[a]

Dataset	Date	C'y code	Age	Sample code	M/F code	Factor no.	Remarks (higher-order factors; others related)
WACH01	'81	U	14 mo.	N	3	1	(Orthogonal Factors)
"	"	"	"	"	"	2	Also RP?
WACH02	'81	U	18 mo.	N	3	1	(Orthogonal Factors)
WACH03	'81	U	24 mo.	N	3	1	(Orthogonal Factors)
DEVR02	'74	U	5	9	3	4	1:2G;Conservation
LUNZ11	'76	E	5	1	3	3	1:2G;Operativity
"	"	"	"	"	"	7	Conservation
TOUS01	'74	C	6	O	3	1	(One factor only)
TOUS02	'74	C	7	O	3	1	(One factor only)
CUMM01	'79	C	9	8	3	5	1:2D;6:I
STEP01B	'72	U	12	%	3	2	1:2G; Spatial Operations
"	"	"	"	"	"	4	Conserv'n/Operativity
"	"	"	"	"	"	5	Classificatory Thought
DUPO01	'75	W	14	6	3	2	1:2G
STOR01A	'72	U	67	1	3	2	1:20

[a]See Appendix A for codes. In a few cases, the classifications of factors shown here were preliminary and may disagree with the final classifications shown in the tables of Appendix B.

children. The Piagetian measures defined a factor distinct from mental age and language and mathematics achievement factors, but all factors had substantial loadings on a general factor. Unfortunately the variety of measures was not such as to permit the isolation of separate reasoning factors such as RG, I, and RQ previously described. Further research is needed to investigate whether one or more Piagetian reasoning factors are distinct from these other reasoning factors.

Dataset LUNZ11, for a five-year-old sample, yielded at least two factors that can be regarded as lying in the reasoning domain: Operativity, measured by various tests of Piagetian seriation ability, and Conservation, measured by tests of conservation of number and of length. Raven's Coloured Progressive Matrices test had a small but possibly significant loading on the latter factor. These Piagetian reasoning factors were distinct from each other, and from verbal ability and memory factors, but all had appreciable loadings on a second-order factor of general mental ability. The data from this study provide little evidence for the status of the Piagetian reasoning factors with respect to the factors RG, I, and RQ previously described, except that the association between the Raven's progressive matrices test and the Conservation factor is suggestive of a relation with the Inductive Reasoning (I) factor.

Datasets TOUS01 and TOUS02 yielded only one factor each for a variety of Piagetian concrete operations tasks. Because the battery contained no other types of variables, it provides no evidence regarding the status of the one Piagetian factor vis-à-vis other reasoning factors.

Dataset STEP01B, for a sample averaging 12 years of age, yielded three Piagetian reasoning factors, interpreted as Spatial Operations, Conservation/Operativity, and Classificatory Thought. Note that Conservation was not distinguished from Operativity as it was in dataset LUNZ11 (for a younger age sample), but this may possibly be explained by the paucity of operational tasks in this dataset as opposed to conservation tasks. These factors were distinct from the mental abilities measured by the Wechsler intelligence test, at least the verbal components of that scale, except that several Wechsler performance scales appeared on the Piagetian Spatial Operations factor. All factors had high loadings on a general factor.

Dataset DUPO01, for a sample of Swiss children averaging 14 years of age, yielded a Piagetian reasoning factor that was distinct from numerical facility, verbal, and spatial factors. All factors had substantial loadings on a general factor. It would be difficult to align the Piagetian reasoning variables with the RG, I, and RQ factors described previously, and thus this dataset does not provide adequate information as to the nature of Piagetian reasoning in relation to more conventional measures of reasoning ability.

From these datasets, we can draw only the general conclusion that there are several dimensions of individual differences in Piagetian reasoning ability, perhaps as many as three, but that all measures of Piagetian reasoning tend to have high loadings on a general factor. The relation of possibly different kinds of Piagetian reasoning to the kinds of reasoning measured by more conventional tests is not yet clear from available research. Preliminary reports by Tuddenham (1970, 1971) from a major study of Piagetian measures suggested that his measures had generally low reliabilities and intercorrelations; these results might imply that Piagetian reasoning tasks involve highly specific kinds of reasoning.

SUMMARY AND DISCUSSION

The evidence presented in this chapter suggests that there are three main linearly independent dimensions of ability in the reasoning domain:

1. Factor RG, Sequential Reasoning. This factor operates in tasks or tests that require subjects to start from stated premises, rules, or conditions and engage in one or more steps of reasoning to reach a conclusion that properly and logically follows from the given premises.
2. Factor I, Induction. This factor operates in tasks or tests that present subjects with materials that are governed by one or more implicit rules, or that exhibit or illustrate certain similarities or contrasts. The subject's task is to discover the rules that govern the materials or the similarities and contrasts on which rules can be based, and then to demonstrate that discovery in some way, either by stating rules or relevant stimulus attributes, or by making appropriate choices among alternatives that are presented.

3.   Factor RQ, Quantitative Reasoning. This factor operates in tasks or tests that
         require subjects to reason with concepts involving quantitative or math-
         ematical relations in order to arrive at correct conclusions. The reasoning
         processes can be either inductive or deductive, or both.

In typical samples, these three factors can be expected to be substantially
correlated, and thus can be found to have high loadings on a general factor of
intelligence. In batteries of tests which are sufficiently diverse to support
second-order factors Gf and Gc, reasoning factors are often found to load on
either one or both of these. Generally, it is found that factors I and RG tend to
load more highly on Gf while factor RQ tends to load more highly on Gc, but
the particular patterns of loadings depend on types of samples and types of
variables included in test batteries.

In addition, one or more reasoning factors appear to reside in Piagetian
reasoning tasks. The relation of these factors to factors RG, I, and RQ is unclear
because research has not been adequate to reveal or clarify such relations, but
evidence suggests that Piagetian reasoning factors tend to load substantially on
one or more higher-order factors g, Gf, or Gc.

It is possible that subtypes of the three main reasoning factors exist, but it has
been difficult to differentiate these factors because of problems in constructing
tasks that feature a particular kind of reasoning process – deductive processes,
inductive processes, or reasoning with quantitative concepts, to the exclusion of
other processes.

The last several decades have seen an upsurge in interest among cognitive
psychologists in examining and explaining individual differences in reasoning
processes, as exhibited not only on psychological tests but also in performances
on various types of reasoning tasks exemplified in school curricula or studied in
the psychological laboratory. General reviews of this work may be found, for
example, in articles or chapters by Greeno and Simon (1988), Nickerson (1988),
and Polson and Jeffries (1982). Reading these materials, one gets the impression
that reasoning processes must be considered to be very diverse, defying easy
classification. The results reviewed in the present chapter, however, suggest that
individual differences in performance center around three kinds of processes that
correspond to the major factors found in the reasoning domain: deduction,
induction, and use of quantitative concepts. This suggests that future research in
reasoning might profit from focusing attention on these processes.

This would mean exploring the relation of reasoning task characteristics to
the ability scales implicit in each of these individual difference dimensions. For
example, one would like to know what kinds of deductive tasks are characteristically found at various levels of difficulty on the scale of factor RG.

Already some researchers have done research that is consistent with these
suggestions. For example, Rips (1984, Tables 3.1 and 3.3) has enumerated a
variety of inference rules involved in deductive arguments and has estimated
parameters for their "availability" (probability of correct employment). He has

offered some evidence (his Figure 3.2) for concluding there are actually two factors that need to be taken account of in the domain of deductive performance. (See Greeno and Simon, 1988, for references to other work on deductive processes.)

The domain of inductive processes has received much attention in recent research, but much of this work has focused on analogical reasoning. Pellegrino and Glaser (1982), for example, have carried out at least the early stages of an ambitious plan for the study of inductive reasoning as it occurs in the solution of figural, numerical, and verbal analogies. But the factor-analytic results reviewed here, as well as logical analysis, suggest that analogical reasoning involves both inductive and deductive steps (in addition to whatever is needed from the knowledge base). I would suggest, therefore, that these steps need to be investigated separately. A major question is what kinds of stimulus and task characteristics are associated with different levels of difficulty on the scale of inductive ability. Further, the level vs. speed aspects of performances must be given separate attention, particularly from the standpoint of developmental trends. Goldman and Pellegrino (1984) speculate that in adults, differences are chiefly in the efficiency with which materials are operated on, that is, in the speed with which correct performance takes place (as it usually does). In children, on the other hand, they believe that differences depend on the difficulties of task components, i.e., the probabilities that they can be handled correctly.

Studies of factor RQ (Quantitative Reasoning) would presumably be entailed, or implicit, in studies of mathematical ability as reviewed, for example, by Mayer (1986) and Mayer, Larkin, and Kadane (1984). I would assume that mathematical ability is actually a highly complex ability. If one had a good measure of it that could be included in an appropriate factor analysis, it would carry loadings on several factors, at different orders of analysis, including g, Gf, Gc, and the reasoning factors reviewed in this chapter. Nevertheless, one may conceive of studies that would focus on the role of factor RQ by investigating the nature of the quantitative and mathematical attributes of tasks found at different levels of a difficulty scale for factor RQ.

It is true that reasoning tasks usually involve many elements; factorially, they tend to be complex. This is perhaps one reason that they tend to have high loadings on second- and third-order factors; the higher-order factors would partly explain such complexity. Nevertheless, it would be analytically and theoretically satisfying to see such tasks broken down into the separate processes implied by the factorial results reviewed here. Also to be further investigated is the possibility, proposed by Kyllonen and Christal (1990), that capacity of working memory is centrally involved in many reasoning tasks.

7   *Abilities in the Domain of Memory and Learning*

> *Strength of memory is usually limited in every man to particular kinds of objects. ... He who easily remembers the technical expressions of a science that interests him has often a bad memory for the novelties of town.*
>
> J. F. Herbart (1816)

Learning and memory are broad, interrelated categories of behavior and performance that have received enormous attention in experimental psychology. Wide individual differences in learning and memory abilities have long been noted, and have been addressed in psychometric research. Unfortunately, there has been little interplay between experimental and psychometric approaches to these areas, with the result that little can be said about relations between processes studied in experimental investigations and the dimensions of individual differences isolated in psychometric research. In a recent review of memory measures (Richardson–Klavehn & Bjork, 1988) there was no reference to psychometric research, and only a little to individual differences as they occur in the contrast between normal and amnesic subjects.

Learning and memory are related because memory has to do with how the outcomes of learning are retained or forgotten. Nevertheless these categories tend to be treated, both in experimental and psychometric investigations, as if they were separate. Operationally, studies of learning focus on the rate at which information or skill is acquired under given conditions, while studies of memory focus on the amount of information or skill that is retained after a given amount of exposure to the learning situation and the materials to be learned, and after a given amount of time after that exposure is discontinued. These distinctions apply, in a general way, both in experimental and in psychometric research, and are almost of necessity observed in the treatment of learning and memory abilities in this chapter. Some observations are made, however, on relations between learning and memory abilities.

Of particular interest are the possible relations between intelligence, as ordinarily conceived, and learning and memory abilities. It has often been proposed that an important aspect of intelligence is the ability to learn, but for various reasons it has been difficult to demonstrate this relation convincingly. Results reviewed in this chapter have some pertinence to this issue, which is considered more at length in Chapter 17.

From very early on, tasks requiring learning and memory abilities were

248

included in procedures for measuring intelligence. The Binet scale (Binet & Simon, 1905), for example, included tests of memory span and sentence repetition, and many of its other tasks were tests of long-term memory for acquired information in such domains as language, number, and general culture. As early as 1921, Burt (1921, pp. 184, 195) identified a memory factor in the Stanford–Binet scale.

Spearman (1927, pp. 278ff.) recognized the possible existence of small group factors of memory separate from g, citing studies by Abelson (1911) and Carey (1915), both of whom employed simple tests of ability to memorize verbal, symbolic, and figural material. On the whole, however, he stressed that such factors had little relation to general intelligence. He suggested that g does not enter memory tests "where the influence of original understanding and subsequent reconstruction is comparatively slight" (p. 186).

A group factor of *delayed* memory was possibly indicated in an investigation by Hargreaves (1927), who tested the ability of children to reproduce the content of simple stories one week after presentation. (Our reanalysis of these data, dataset HARG11A, suggests that these measures actually tapped general intelligence as well as, to a small extent, verbal reasoning and creativity.)

Kelley (1928) found a group factor of rote memory in analyzing tests administered to seventh- and tenth-grade samples. The tests contributing to this factor measured the subject's ability to recognize, immediately after presentation, such materials as words, numbers, "meaningful" symbols, and "meaningless" symbols. Kelley found another memory factor at the kindergarten level, represented by several tests: the Knox Cube test, a test called Memory for Verbal Material, and two tests in which the child indicates what is missing from a row of forms which had previously been presented in toto. The first two of these tests, at least, are actually in memory span format, and in the light of subsequent results it appears that this factor is a memory span factor. In any case, Kelley's study was one of the first to identify clear group factors of memory.

Wolfle (1940) noted that a memory factor was the "fourth most frequently reported factor" (p. 31), referring to studies by Kelley and others such as Anastasi (1932), Carlson (1937), and Thurstone (1938b). The datasets from some of these studies are reanalyzed in the present survey and are discussed further below. Wolfle pointed out that the memory factor in most of these early studies was tested by paired associate or recognition tests of recently learned material, and that tests of memory over long intervals were not included in the test batteries. He suggested that "it might have been better to name the factor *rote learning* or *immediate memory*" (p. 32). Despite Wolfle's suggestion, however, in subsequent work this factor has most often been called simply Memory (*M*) or Associative Memory, and tests of paired associate learning have frequently been employed as markers for this factor. The associative memory factor was the only factor in this domain recognized in Cattell's proposed system of Universal Index Numbers for factors (Cattell, 1971, p. 30).

Based on results obtained up to the time of his review, French (1951) recognized four separate primary factors in the memory domain (using his designations): M (Associative Memory), MM (Musical Memory), Sm (Span Memory), and VM (Visual Memory). Of these, Associative Memory and Span Memory were recognized as well-established primary factors in the 1963 and 1976 kits of factor reference tests (French, Ekstrom, & Price, 1963; Ekstrom, French, & Harman, 1976). Based on Ekstrom's (1979) further review of factor-analytic work, Visual Memory was also included in the 1976 kit. (See Table 3.1, this volume). A possible Musical Memory or Memory for Sound Patterns factor is considered in Chapter 9.

In Guilford's Structure-of-Intellect system (Guilford & Hoepfner, 1971, Chapter 8), memory represents one of the five "operation" categories. In view of the hypothesized interaction of that category with four content and six product categories, however, 24 distinguishable abilities were called for. As of 1971, Guilford and Hoepfner claimed to have demonstrated 18 of these. My reanalyses of their datasets (mainly, datasets BRAD01, BROW11, DUNH11, HOEP21, HOFF01, and TENO11), based on more conservative procedures in factoring, confirm far fewer than 18 factors in the memory domain.

Many of the datasets reanalyzed here show Associative Memory and/or Memory Span along with various other well-established factors such as V, N, S, RG, and P, but were not concerned with studying the memory domain. Reanalyzed datasets specifically directed toward exploration of the memory domain, however, are as follows, in chronological order: ANAS11 (1932), CARL31 (1937), GUIL36 and GUIL37 (1947), INGH01 (1952), CHRI01 (1958), KELL01 (1964), LUMS01 (1965), BROW11 (1966), TENO01 (1966), BRAD01 (1969), PETR01 (1970), LANS21 and LANS22 (1978), UNDE12 (1978), MALM01 (1979), SKEH01 (1980), HUNT51 (1981), and GEIS01 and GEIS02 (1982). Datasets concerned specifically with memory span performances are BREN01 (1940) and BERG21 (1977).

One of the first studies to consider relations between intelligence and learning ability – that is, improvement with practice – was that of Woodrow (1938). This study has often been cited as revealing very little, if any, relation between intelligence and improvement with practice. Actually, the tasks that were practiced were in every case very simple motor or perceptual tasks involving very little cognitive activity. This study cannot be accepted as one that investigated relations between intelligence and ability to learn more difficult cognitive tasks. It was not reanalyzed in the present survey because correlational data were not available, and also because in any case there would be problems of overspecificity connected with the fact that correlations were obtained among initial, final, and gain scores. Examples of datasets more directly involving scores from relatively difficult learning tasks are as follows, again in chronological order: SIMR01 (1947), ALLI01 and ALLI02 (1960), STAK01 (1961), GAME01 (1962), JENS01 (1964), DUNC11 (1966), DUNH11 (1966), BUND11 (1967), HECK01 (1967),

Table 7.1. *Memory and learning factors identified in selected datasets (specified by number in hierarchical matrix)*

Dataset	Factor 2Y	MS	MA	M6	MM	MV	L1	Other
ALLE11	—	3	—	—	—	—	—	
ALLE12	—	2	—	—	—	—	—	
ALLI01	—	—	—	—	—	—	2, 3, 5, 6, 7	
ALLI02	—	—	7	—	—	—	—	
ANAS11	—	—	3	—	—	—	—	
ARNO01	—	5	—	—	—	—	—	
BACH21	—	5	—	—	—	—	—	
BERG21	1(2X)	2, 3, 4	—	—	—	—	—	10:Object Class?
BRAD01	1	—	2	8	—	3	—	
BREN01A	1(2X)	2, 3, 4	—	—	—	—	—	
BROW11	—	—	—	5	2	—	—	6:Order?
BUND11	—	6, 7	—	—	—	—	—	
CARL31	—	—	2, 3, 4, 5	—	—	—	—	
CARR01	—	—	2, 5	—	—	—	—	
CARR11	—	—	4	—	—	—	—	
CARR21	—	—	—	—	—	—	6	
CARR22	—	—	—	2, 6	—	—	3	
CARR41	—	5	—	—	—	—	—	6:Sachs tasks
CARR42	—	—	—	—	—	—	—	4:Sachs & Craik tasks
CARR43	—	—	—	—	—	—	—	7:Sachs tasks
"								8:Cont. memory tasks
"								9:Crowder tasks
"								14:Peterson/Peterson task
CHIA01	—	3	—	—	—	—	—	
CHRI01	2?	—	4, 6	—	—	—	—	3:Position
COOM01	—	—	9	—	—	—	—	

Table 7.1 (cont.)

Dataset	Factor							
	2Y	MS	MA	M6	MM	MV	L1	Other
CORN01	—	4	—	—	—	—	—	
CORY01	—	—	2?	4	—	—	—	—
CUMM01	—	4	—	—	—	—	—	
CURE11	—	—	7	—	—	—	—	
CURE12	—	—	5	—	—	—	7	
DETT00	—	—	—	—	—	—	6	
DUNC11	—	—	4,5	—	—	—	—	
FERN01	—	1	—	2	—	—	—	
FERN02	—	1	—	2	—	—	—	
GAME01	1,4	6	7	3	—	—	2,5	—
GARR12	—	—	3	—	—	—	—	
GARR13	—	—	4	—	—	—	—	
GARR14	—	4	3	—	—	—	—	
GARR15	—	—	3	—	—	—	—	
GARR16	—	—	4	—	—	—	—	
GEIS01	—	—	—	—	—	—	—	1:LTS vs. STS Storage
"								2:LTS processing
GEIS02	—	—	—	—	—	—	—	1:LTS vs. STS Storage
"								2:Processing Intensity
GOOD01	—	—	6	—	—	—	—	
GUIL37	—	—	3	—	—	—	—	
GUIL46	—	—	4	—	—	—	—	
GUST11A	2	13	—	—	—	—	—	
HAKS01	—	12	4	—	3	—	—	—
HANL01	—	—	11	—	—	—	—	Memory for Voices
HARR51	—	—	—	—	3	—	—	
HARR52	—	—	—	—	4	—	—	
HARR53	—	—	—	—	2	—	—	

Code	1	2	3	4	5	6	7	Notes
HARR54	—	—	—	—	6	—	—	—
HECK01	2,5	8	7	13?	4,6	—	—	3:Order? Events??
HISK03	—	3	—	—	—	—	—	3:Mem. for Misspelling
HOEP21	—	—	—	—	—	—	—	—
HOLZ01	—	—	4	—	—	—	—	2:Clustering/Free Recall
HORN21	—	—	—	—	—	—	—	5:Primary Memory
"	—	—	—	—	—	—	—	7:(Artifactual)
"	—	—	—	—	—	—	—	8:(Artifactual)
HUEF01	—	4	—	—	5	—	—	—
HUGH01	—	3	—	—	3	—	—	—
HUNT61	—	3,6	5	2	—	—	—	—
HUNT71	1	4	—	—	—	—	—	—
INGH01	1	—	—	—	—	—	2,3,4,5,6,7,8	7:Primary Memory
JAY01	—	—	—	—	5	—	—	—
JONE31	—	6	—	—	—	—	—	—
JONE32	—	5	—	—	3	—	—	—
JONE33	—	2	—	—	—	—	—	—
JONE34	—	6	—	—	—	—	—	—
KARL11	—	6	—	—	—	—	—	—
KEIT21	—	5	—	—	—	—	—	—
KELL01	1	4	3	—	2	7	—	—
LANS21	1	2	3	—	—	—	—	—
LANS22	—	2	—	—	—	—	—	—
LUMS01	—	4	5	—	—	—	—	—
LUNN21	—	2	—	—	—	6	—	—
LUNZ11	—	4,8	3	2	5	—	—	—
MALM01	1	—	—	2	4	—	—	—
MEEK01	2(2X)	3,4,5	—	—	.	—	—	—
NAGL01	—	4	—	—	—	—	—	—
NAGL02	—	4	—	—	—	—	—	—
NAGL03	—	4	—	—	—	—	—	—
PARA04	—	3	—	—	—	—	—	—

Table 7.1 (*cont.*)

Dataset	Factor							Other
	2Y	MS	MA	M6	MM	MV	L1	
PARA07	—	4	—	—	—	—	—	
PETR01	1?	2, 5	4	—	—	—	—	
PROG01	—	5	—	—	—	—	—	
RAND01	—	5	—	—	—	—	—	2 Reconstruction?
RAND02	—	5	—	—	—	—	—	3 "
REYB01	—	4	—	—	—	—	—	
RIMO11	—	6, 7	—	—	—	—	—	
ROBE11	—	—	—	3, 4	—	—	—	
SAUN03	—	6	13	—	—	—	—	
SCHA11	—	—	6	—	—	—	—	3:Short-Term Memory 1
SEIB02	—	8	—	—	4	—	—	5:Order?
"								9:Short-Term Memory 2
SIMR01	—	—	2	—	—	—	—	
SKEH01	—	—	2	—	—	—	—	
SMIT11	—	—	—	—	—	—	—	4:STM Visual Memory
SNOW11	—	4	—	—	—	—	—	
SNOW12	—	2	—	—	8	—	—	
SNOW20	—	4	—	—	3	—	—	
SNOW21	—	3	—	—	—	—	—	
SPEA01	—	4	6	—	—	—	—	
SPEA02	—	3	6	—	—	—	—	
SPRA11	—	3	—	—	—	—	—	
STAK01	—	—	7	—	—	—	4, 9, 11, 15	

Case						
STAN31		6				
STOR12		10				
STOR13		6				
SUMI01			4			
TAYL01			9	3		
TAYL31		5,8				
TENO01			3			
THUR11			7			
THUR21A			6			
THUR31			7			
THUR71				5,6		
THUR81			6			
THUR82			5			
TRAU01		7	3			4,8
UNDE12	1,6	4	2	3	8	
"						
UNDH01		2				
VERN01		6				
WHEA01			5			
WIEB11		5				
WIEB12		3				
WILL12		4				
WITT11			4			
WOOD17		6				
WOOD18		4				

7:Verbal Disc.'n
9:Clustering/Recall

SEIB02 (1967), TRAU01 (1970), HORN21 (1978b), HUGH01 (1983), and DETT01 (1986).

To give the reader an impression of the total scope of the learning and memory domain as it appears from the present series of reanalyses, Table 7.1 lists datasets that furnish the principal evidence concerning the differentiation of factors in this domain. The columns of the table report factors (specified by the numbers given them in the hierarchical factor matrices of Appendix B) that have been classified under the following factor-types:

> 2Y: One or more higher-order memory factors[1]
> MS: Memory span
> MA: Associative memory
> M6: Free recall memory
> MM: Meaningful memory, or "memory for ideas"
> MV: Visual memory
> L1: One or more learning ability factors

In addition, a number of miscellaneous memory factors tentatively identified in these studies are listed.

With some exceptions, each first-order factor (except for the miscellaneous ones) is differentiated from each of the others in at least two datasets, and usually more. The exceptions occur for factors MV (visual memory) and L1 (learning abilities). The Visual Memory factor is less well attested than the first five, and studies of learning abilities have generally not included clear marker variables for memory factors. Learning ability factors occur in too much variety to permit classification into a small number of categories.

The remainder of this chapter is devoted to detailed discussion of the first-order factors that have been identified in the learning and memory domain, with some attention to the status of higher-order factors.

MEMORY SPAN (MS) FACTORS

The standard memory span task included in numerous intelligence scales such as the Stanford–Binet (Terman & Merrill, 1960) and the Wechsler Intelligence Scale for Children – Revised (Wechsler, 1974) is an individually administered test in which the examiner reads aloud, at the rate of one per second and with "perfectly uniform emphasis," a series of digits. The subject is asked to repeat them in the same order, or in some tasks, backwards, immediately after the end of the series. The subject is not told how many digits will be in the series, but in the Stanford–Binet, there are always three series of identical length, and in the WISC-R, the series become progressively longer (2–7). It can be assumed that subjects acquire some information, therefore, about the probable length of a series and can adjust strategy of responding accordingly. In the Stanford–Binet, the Repeating Digits task employs from 2 to 6 digits, from a two-digit task at MA 2 to a six-digits reversed task at Superior Adult I.

The Stanford–Binet also employs Memory for Sentences tasks that apparently involve somewhat the same processes as the digit-span task, i.e., attention to a temporally ordered stimulus, registration of the stimulus in immediate memory, and output of its repetition. In the Memory for Sentences task, however, comprehension of meaning can play a role that it does not play in the Repeating Digits task. Lado (1965) found that a memory span task involving sentence repetition was a good measure of comprehension of a second language, when the sentences are in that second language. Therefore, verbal comprehension ability is likely to be involved in the sentence memory span task if the comprehension difficulty of the sentence taxes the subject's level of comprehension.

The ETS *Kit of Factor-Referenced Cognitive Tests* (Ekstrom, French, & Harman, 1976) offers, for research purposes, three memory span tests: Auditory Number Span Test (MS-1), Visual Number Span Test (MS-2), and Auditory Letter Span Test (MS-3). The stimuli in the first two of these are series of digits (ranging in length from four to twelve or thirteen, spoken or visually presented at one digit per second), while the stimuli in the third are series of spoken alphabetic letters (ranging in length from three to thirteen). In contrast to the memory span tests in the Stanford–Binet or Wechsler series, the length of the series varies randomly over items; scores are the numbers of series recalled correctly.

Because of its substantial correlations with other types of cognitive tasks, memory span tasks have often been regarded as measures of intelligence (Bachelder & Denny, 1977a, b). Early factor analyses of the Stanford–Binet scale (McNemar, 1938) were interpreted as indicating that the scale measures mainly a single general factor, memory span tasks having at least substantial loadings on such a factor. In an orthogonal multiple-factor analysis of ten-year-olds' performance on the Stanford–Binet, Wright (1939) identified a Number factor that had loadings on various numerical tasks, including digit-span tasks. Apparently variance in the digit-span tasks was associated with variance in other numerical tasks such as counting backward and making change; thus, it was not possible to identify a separate memory span factor. (Our reanalysis of this dataset, WRIG01, shows a similar pattern, but the Number factor has a high loading on a general factor.) These results support the idea that at the ten-year-old level, at least, digit-span performance depends in part on the child's ability to identify and manipulate digits and numbers. Reanalyzing correlation matrices for ages 7, 9, 11, and 13 originally analyzed by McNemar, however, Jones (1949) found clear evidence for group memory span factors; in my reanalyses of these datasets (JONE31, JONE32, JONE33, JONE34) these memory factors have substantial loadings on a second-order general factor. Tests loading on these factors include not only digit-span tasks but also memory for sentences tasks and Copying a Bead Chain from Memory, which involves memory for the order of a series of differently shaped beads.

In factor analyses of the WISC-R at different ages (Kaufman, 1975, 1978), the

Digit Span subtest consistently appears on what Kaufman has called a Freedom from Distractibility factor, along with the Arithmetic and Coding subtests. This appears to parallel the result from Wright's factor analysis of the Stanford–Binet mentioned above. But the WISC-R battery contains only one memory-span test and could not be expected to yield a separate common factor of memory span. Kaufman's "freedom from distractibility" factor is a complex factor, an artifact of the factor analysis of a severely limited battery of tests, and is not to be considered as a basic primary factor in mental organization. (I chose not to include Kaufman's matrices in my datasets for reanalysis because of the limited character of the WISC battery, by itself, for factor analysis purposes.)

Actually, the factorial literature offers much evidence for the existence of a memory-span (MS) factor separate from other memory factors and linearly independent of general intelligence. In fact, there is some evidence for the breakdown of the memory-span subdomain into several separate first-order factors. Table 7.2 lists 82 memory-span factors from 70 datasets reanalyzed in this survey, appearing at mean ages ranging from 4 to 71.

Because of the manner in which they were designed, or the characteristics of the variables included, many of the datasets listed yield only a single memory-span factor, and no other factors in the memory domain. This is true of the following datasets: ARNO01, BACH21, CORN01, CUMM01, GUST11A, HISK03, HUEF01, JONE31, JONE33, JONE34, KARL11, KEIT21, LUNN21, NAGL01, NAGL02, NAGL03, PARA04, PARA07, PROG01, RAND01, RAND02, REYB01, SAUN03, SNOW11, SNOW21, SPEA01, SPEA02, SPRA11, STAN31, STOR12, STOR13, UNDH01, VERN01, WILL12, WOOD17, and WOOD18. Typically, the tasks included in these datasets were auditory or visual, digit or letter span tasks with forward (or occasionally backward) reproduction of the series required. Occasionally (e.g., in dataset CORN01), the response was to be delayed for a short period of time. In dataset KARL11, nonsense syllables were presented auditorily or visually one letter at a time. In RAND01 and RAND02, digits or letters were presented either .5 or 1 second at a time; this variation made no difference in factor pattern. Rapid spelling tasks made their appearance on a memory span factor in datasets KARL11, SPEA01, and SPEA02; apparently such a task, in which the subject has to write a word presented a letter at a time, taps a memory span ability. In dataset STAN31, the highest salient loading on factor 6 is for a tonal figures test in which the subject is to select the correct reversal of a series of tones; digit span and letter span tests are also loaded on this factor.

A number of datasets, however, particularly those for ages 18 and above, show memory-span factors separate from other memory abilities that are discussed subsequently: JONE32 shows a separate factor (MM) for "memory for ideas"; datasets HAKS01, HUGH01, KELL01, LANS21, LUMS01, PETR01, SEIB02, TRAU01, and UNDE12 show memory span distinct from an Associative Memory factor (MA); and a number of datasets show memory span distinct from various other factors in the learning and memory domain.

Several datasets show two or more memory span factors because there were enough variables, with different attributes, to define separate factors.

Dataset LUNZ11, for five-year-old children, appears to yield separate verbal and visual memory span factors, but the visual memory span factor is not well defined, having small loadings only on memory span tests involving animals and shapes, and a discrimination learning task. These two factors are slightly negatively correlated ($r = -.12$).

In Brener's (1940; dataset BREN01A) study of the memory-span subdomain, seventeen memory-span variables were available for analysis. Ten tasks were visual presentations: digits, three-letter nonsense syllables, consonant letters, geometrical figures, color patches, concrete words, paired associates, abstract words, "commissions" (i.e., commands such as "Put a circle around A"), and simple sentences. Series of consonants, concrete words, and abstract words were also presented auditorily. Four variables (14–17) represented scoring of responses with credit being given for partially correct responses; these variables were dropped in my reanalysis to avoid the experimental dependence that would otherwise be entailed. All variables involved presentations of units in series of increasing length; subjects were required to reproduce each series in its original (forward) order. My analysis yielded three highly correlated memory span factors: one was for units with verbal or generally meaningful content; one was for units consisting of digits or consonant letters; and a third was for units with uniquely visual characteristics – colors, geometrical designs, and paired associate units such as "boy-31". (Presumably, at least some subjects encoded such units in visual terms.) In the case of the first two of these factors, some variables were presented visually, and others were presented auditorily; modality of presentation appeared to make no consistent difference in factor loadings. All factors and variables had high loadings on a general memory span factor (coded 2X). Since the battery was devoted exclusively to memory span tasks, it yielded no evidence concerning relations of memory span factors to other cognitive factors. Also, since all tasks required reproduction in the same order as was presented, it yielded no evidence concerning the factorial status of tasks requiring backward reproduction.

One dataset, MEEK01, yielded evidence concerning possible differences related to visual vs. auditory presentation and forward vs. backward reproduction. With tasks limited to units consisting of digits or words, it disclosed a second-order memory span factor (factor 2) subsuming three first-order factors: one (factor 3) dominated by auditory backward reproduction, a second (factor 4) dominated by visual backward reproduction, and a third (factor 5) dominated by auditory forward reproduction. However, these distinctions did not hold in every case; for example, a visual digits-forward task had a salient loading on factor 3 (along with two auditory digits-backward tasks). The distinction between digit and word units found in dataset BREN01A did not hold up in dataset MEEK01. A number of datasets (BACH21, KARL11, REYB01, SAUN03, SNOW11, SNOW12, VERN01) had both forward and backward reproduction

Table 7.2. *82 Memory Span (MS) factors in 70 datasets arranged in order of approximate mean age of sample*[a]

Dataset	Date	C'y code	Age	Sample code	M/F code	Factor no.	Remarks (higher-order factors; others related)
WIEB11	'80	U	4	O	1	5	1:2G
WIEB12	'80	U	4	O	2	3	1:2G
LUNZ11	'76	E	5	1	3	4	1:2G;5:M6;6:MV. Verbal
"	"	"	"	"	"	8	Visual Memory Span
HUEF01	'67	U	6	6	3	4	(Orthog.)
PARA04	'69	U	6	1	3	3	1:2G
TAYL31	'75	C	6	1	3	5	1:2C;6:2U. 5 = Vis. Mem. Span
"	"	"	"	"	"	8	Auditory Memory Span
JONE31	'49	U	7	1	3	6	1:2D
CUMM01	'79	C	9	8	3	4	1:2D
JONE32	'49	U	9	1	3	5	1:2D;3:MM
KEIT21	'87	U	9	7	3	5	1:3G;2:2C
NAGL01	'87	U	9	Z	3	4	1:2G
NAGL02	'87	U	9	6	3	4	1:2G
NAGL03	'87	U	9	6	3	4	1:2G
PARA07	'69	U	9	1	3	4	1:2G
UNDH01	'76	O	9	1	3	2	1:2G
PROG01	'73	U	10	J	1	5	1:2D
RAND01	'79	C	10	6	1	5	1:2G;Digits, .5 & 1 sec.
RAND02	'79	C	10	6	2	5	1:2G; " " " "
GUST11A	'84	S	11	1	3	13	1:3G;9:2C
JONE33	'49	U	11	1	3	2	1:2D
RIMO11	'48	U	11	1	3	6	1:3G;5:20
"	"	"	"	"	"	7	Cube Imitation task
SPEA01	'62	A	11	6	1	4	1:2H
SPEA02	'62	A	11	6	2	3	1:2H
TRAU01	'70	U	11	1	3	7	1:2G;3:MA;4:L7
BACH21	'77	C	12	7	3	5	1:2G
GARR14	'35	U	12	6	2	4	1:2G
JONE34	'49	U	13	1	3	6	1:2D
HISK03	'66	U	14	E	3	3	1:2G
MEEK01	'71	U	14	1	1	3	1:3G;2:2X;Auditory Backward
"	"	"	"	"	"	4	Visual Backward
"	"	"	"	"	"	5	Auditory Forward
STOR12	'66	U	14	I	3	10	1:3G
STOR13	'66	U	14	7	3	6	1:2G
REYB01	'41	K	15	6	3	4	1:2G
ARN001	'67	A	16	1	3	5	1:2G
KARL11	'42	U	16	6	3	6	Vis./Aud. Fusion
LUNN21	'77	U	16	6	3	2	(Orthog. Factors)
SNOW11	'77	U	16	1	3	4	1:2G;Forward & Backward
WOOD17	'77	U	17	1	3	6	5:2F
HECK01	'67	U	18	6	3	8	1:3G;5:2Y;6:MM;7:MA;13:M6
HUNT61	'73	U	18	6	3	3	1:20;2:M6;5:M6;7:PM, Registration
"	"	"	"	"	"	6	Interference

Table 7.2 (*cont.*)

Dataset	Date	C'y code	Age	Sample code	M/F code	Factor no.	Remarks (higher-order factors; others related)
SAUN03	'59	U	18	6	1	6	1:2G;Backward & Forward
BERG21	'77	U	19	1	3	2	1:2Y. Registration
,,	,,	,,	,,	,,	,,	3	Resistance to Interference
,,	,,	,,	,,	,,	,,	4	Proactive Inhibition
BREN01A	'40	U	19	6	3	2	1:2X;Verbal Units
,,	,,	,,	,,	,,	,,	3	Digits & Consonants
,,	,,	,,	,,	,,	,,	4	Visual Units
BUND11	'67	U	19	6	1	6	1:2G;Non-Auditory Stimuli
,,	,,	,,	,,	,,	,,	7	Auditory Stimuli
CARR41	'76	U	19	6	3	5	1:2G;2:M6;6:S0;7:I0
CHIA01	'67	U	19	6	3	3	(Orthog. Factors) 1:R7;2:R5
GAME01	'62	U	19	P	3	6	1:2Y;2:L*;3:M6;4:2Y;5:L1
HUGH01	'83	A	19	6	3	3	1:2G;5:MA
HUNT71	'75	U	19	6	3	4	(Orthog. Factors) 3:R5
LANS21	'78	U	19	6	3	2	1:2Y;3:MA
LANS22	'78	U	19	6	3	2	1:20;3:R8;4:R4
LUMS01	'65	A	19	P	3	4	1:2Γ;5:MA
PETR01	'70	R	19	1	3	2	1:2Y;4:MA. Vis./Aud.
,,	,,	,,	,,	,,	,,	5	Visual;Geometric Forms
SEIB02	'67	U	19	6	3	8	1:2V;3:M1;4:S0;5:M0;6:MA;9:MV
SNOW12	'77	U	19	6	3	2	1:2G;Forw.& Backw.;Vis./Aud.
SNOW20	'76	U	19	6	3	4	(Orthog. Factors);3:M0
SNOW21	'76	U	19	6	3	3	1:20
UNDE12	'78	U	19	6	3	4	1:2Y;2:MA;3:M6;6:2Y; 7:VN;8:M9;9:S0
VERN01	'81	U	19	6	3	6	1:2G;Forw. & Backw.
WOTH01	'90	U	21	1	3	5	1:3G;2:2F;11:MA
KELL01	'64	U	22	3	1	4	1:2Y;2:MM;3:MA;7:MV
HAKS01	'74	C	24	1	3	12	1:3G;5:21;3:MM;4:MA
SPRA11	'66	U	27	R	2	3	1:2G
STAN31	'80	U	27	Q	1	6	1:2G
ALLE11	'78	U	30	U	3	3	1:2H;4:M6;6:R5
ALLE12	'78	U	30	U	3	2	1:2H;4:M6;6:R5
FERN01	'78	U	30	U	3	1	(Orthog. factors) 2:M6
FERN02	'78	U	30	U	3	1	(Orthog. factors) 2:M6
WILL12	'75	C	30	Y	3	4	1:2G
WOOD18	'77	U	30	1	3	4	1:2C
CORN01	'83	U	71	1	3	4	1:2G

[a]See Appendix A for codes. In a few cases, the classifications of factors shown here were preliminary and may not agree with the final classifications shown in Appendix B.

tasks but not in sufficient numbers to reveal a distinction if such existed. The supposition that backward reproduction is more highly related to general intelligence, as claimed by Jensen and Figueroa (1975), is only weakly supported in datasets analyzed here, for example in datasets BACH21 and REYB01 where backward reproduction tasks had substantially higher loadings on second-order factors; in other datasets, no substantial difference in factor loadings for forward and backward reproduction tasks on higher-order factors can be observed.

Likewise, the data yield little evidence concerning a difference between auditory and visual presentation, except possibly in cases where the units presented are essentially visual (e.g., colors and geometrical designs, as in dataset BREN01A). But even colors and geometrical designs can be encoded verbally, i.e., by thinking of their names; it would be interesting to explore a possible difference between tasks where color or designs are presented visually and tasks where colors or geometrical figures are presented by their names. Such an experiment might disclose differences depending on subjects' strategies in encoding these visual units. In dataset BUND11, a possible difference between visual and auditory presentation is obscured by the fact that both its memory span factors (factors 6 and 7) have some salient loadings for variables other than memory span tasks.

In dataset UNDE12, which comes from one of the more searching studies of the domain of "episodic memory" (as the authors termed it), the highest loading on the memory span factor (factor 4) was obtained for a letter-span task in which the letters had *low* phonetic similarity; the loading for a task with letters of high phonetic similarity (e.g., B, C, D, G, E) was lower. This appears to indicate that phonetic similarity contributes only unwanted error variance in a memory-span task and does not contribute to the measurement of individual differences in memory span.

In summary, the datasets discussed above yield little solid evidence about the effect of several variations in memory-span tasks, and they give little information about the nature of the memory-span task or the processes involved in its performance. All that can be said, thus far, is that there are distinctive individual differences in a variety of memory-span performances, and that the nature of the stimuli, the method of presentation, and the type of reproduction required make little consistent difference in the factorial composition of such tasks (although, of course, these variations may make substantial differences in mean performance levels; it would take us too far afield to examine such differences).

At this point it is useful to draw attention to an important distinction pointed out by Martin (1978). As Martin notes, the standard digit-span task has traditionally been regarded as a measure of short-term memory capacity, i.e., the number of items or units that can be held in immediate working memory. Her study found that digit-span memory, when assessed in the manner recommended by Woodworth and Schlosberg (1954, p. 697), failed to correlate significantly with any of various measures of primary or of secondary memory applied to free recall tests. In two experiments, however, she showed that immediate digit span correlated with tests of ability to recall the *order* of items as distinguished from the *identities* of the items. From her results, it appears that a memory-span test measures two abilities: (1) the ability to recall the identities of the units presented and (2) the ability to recall the order of the units. A memory-span test is inherently a factorially complex measure. The degree to which it measures memory for order is a function of the stimulus set. If the stimulus set is very limited, as is the case when digits 0 to 9 (or a subset of them) are used, it probably measures order memory more than when letters or words are used, because in the latter case the subject has a greater problem remembering the identities of the items. It is fairly difficult to control, much less eliminate, the effect of stimulus-identity memory; Martin attempted to do this by constructing sequences of two-letter pairs (e.g., *BG, FM, RK*) with the letters selected from a fixed twelve-letter set that had been previously learned by subjects. Memory-span tasks have also been constructed with even more limited sets, e.g., by using sequences of consonant or vowel sounds drawn from a set of three (Crowder, 1971); variables of this sort appear in dataset CARR43. It may be hypothesized that in an appropriately designed factor analysis, it would be possible to differentiate memory for order from memory for stimulus identities. As matters stand, it appears that memory-span factors arise and are differentiated from free-recall factors mainly because they are more concerned with memory for order than with capacity for memory of stimulus identities – measured to a greater extent by free recall tests and thus embodied in free-recall factors (to be discussed below).

Some of the datasets surveyed here arose from experimental studies of memory span tasks. I analyzed data assembled from Berger's (1977) study of a variety of memory span tasks and their correlations with measures of field dependence/ independence. Berger's study was a follow-up to one by Jensen (1964), who had identified two factors in memory-span tasks: a "Registration" factor measured principally by immediate memory-span tests and an "Interference" factor measured principally by delayed digit-span tests. All of Berger's digit-span tests were of a standard type, with digits being presented auditorily at the rate of one per second, but some of them involved series of "superspan" length. They were administered in such a way that various types of delayed recall could be observed. The Retroactive Inhibition score was for cued recall of a given list *after* the subject was presented with a second list. The Proactive Inhibition score was for cued recall of the *second* list after the subject was presented with two lists. The delayed recall was recall after being required to echo a random series of the words "plus" and "minus" for 10 seconds after list presentation. Subjects were informed of the recall condition only after presentation of a list. Three first-order factors emerged from my analysis: Factor 2 was measured by two immediate digit-span measures, with high loadings on a general memory span factor (factor 1). It may be interpreted as a memory-span registration factor similar to Jensen's. Factor 3, Resistance to Interference, was measured by delayed digit-span tests, a "long" digit span test, and the Retroactive Inhibition variable. It also had loadings on two measures of field independence, namely, the Embedded Figures test and the Rod and Frame test. It was also highly related to scores on an "attention test" – actually a questionnaire having to do with feelings of boredom and inability to maintain attention during difficult tasks such as listening to lectures (Singer & Antrobus, 1963), with high scores indicating ability to maintain attention despite distractions. A third first-order factor (factor 4) was loaded with the Proactive Inhibition measure, i.e., a test of the ability to resist the effects of proactive inhibition, but also with one of the delayed digit-span measures. Factors 3 and 4 had only moderate loadings on the general memory-span factor. One may speculate that factor 3, Resistance to Interference, might be more relevant to appraising learning ability than the usual type of immediate memory-span test.

Factors 3 and 6 in dataset HUNT61 may be analogous, respectively, to the Registration and Interference factors just mentioned. Factor 3 had loadings on variables from two digit-span tasks; factor 6 had loadings on a number of variables in which materials stored in immediate memory could have been interfered with by extraneous material.

Possibly factor 4 in dataset HUNT71 may be interpreted as a type of delayed (interference) memory-span factor; it had loadings on several variables derived from a Peterson and Peterson (1959) task which concerned the subject's ability to retain order information in letter sequences, presentation of which was followed by an interfering task.

Datasets ALLE11 and ALLE12 employed a variant memory-span task in which series of 5 to 10 letters were presented auditorily, with instructions to recall the last 5 letters on hearing the word *recall*. The subject was not told how many letters would be in a given list. It was thought that this task would measure memory capacity more directly because the longer lists would require the subjects constantly to update the storage of items. Slopes and intercepts of percent correct as a function of list length were correlated -.81, and thus formed a factor – possibly artifactual – in my reanalysis. This factor was only moderately related to other factors in the analysis.

In datasets FERN01 and FERN02, a low-similarity letter span task was factorially associated with a running memory recognition task and an "interference susceptibility" task (a paired-associate task in which the pairings change over trials). The status of these factors in relation to other memory span factors is unclear.

Although the results reviewed here are suggestive, it is obvious that much further work is required to identify and characterize the basic dimensions of individual differences in memory span and related performances. Thus far, factorial investigation has not generally utilized a sufficient variety of memory-span tasks, and it has failed to differentiate possible processes such as memory for the identities of stimuli and memory for order.

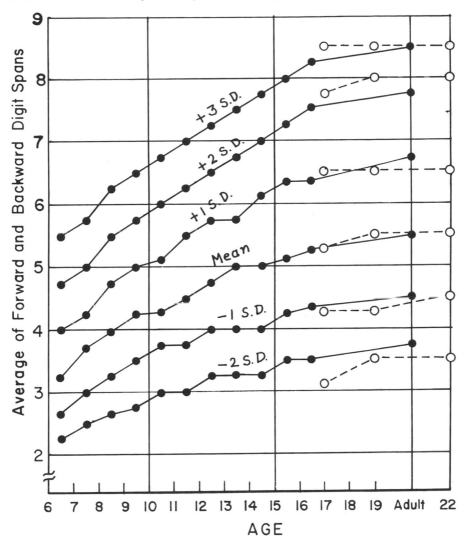

Figure 7.1. Norms, by chronological age, for average of Forward and Backward Digit Spans, from WISC-R (.————.) and WAIS (O————O) standardization samples (Wechsler, 1974, 1981). Separate curves are shown for standard deviation score points.

Granted that the factorial composition of memory-span scores on standard tests is still unclear, it may nevertheless be of use and interest to examine such scores from a developmental perspective. Figure 7.1 depicts norms of the average of forward and backward digit spans as a function of chronological age, using data from the manuals of the WISC-R (Wechsler, 1974) and the WAIS-R

(Wechsler, 1981). Such a depiction is especially meaningful because the average memory span computed in this way is on a ratio scale with a constant meaning over the scale. Of interest is the fact, as can be seen from the figure, that in the U.S. population, the average memory span develops from about 3.25 at age 7 to about 5.5 at age 22. Nevertheless, there are very wide individual differences at every age; at age 7, 2 S.D.s below and above the mean go from 2.25 to 4.75 (nearly as high as the age 22 mean), and at age 22, from 3.5 to 7.75. Although it is often stated that the average adult memory span is 7 digits, such a value is actually well above the average (about 1.3 S.D.s above the mean) for age 22. (Our figures, of course, are for the average of forward and backward digit span. Possibly the average adult *forward* digit span is as high as 7.)

It is now known that digit span can be enormously improved by special training techniques involving mnemonics (Ericsson, 1985), and that there are individuals who, using certain mnemonic systems, exhibit very high memory spans apparently without any special training (Luria, 1968). As far as I am aware, however, we have no information as to the improvability of digit-span performances for individuals with different levels of initial performance, i.e., individuals who do not use the mnemonic systems that can enhance performance. The standard digit-span test assumes that the examinee does not use a mnemonic system.

ASSOCIATIVE MEMORY (MA) FACTORS

As noted earlier, one of the clearest and most prominent factors in the memory domain is Associative Memory, here designated MA. In Thurstone's (1938b) primary mental abilities study (dataset THUR21A), it was designated *M* and represented mainly by three paired-associate learning tests, Number–Number, Word–Number, and Initials. These tests utilized a study-test paradigm frequently employed in studies of verbal learning; that is, the subject was asked first to study a series of paired stimuli (pairs of two-digit numbers, words paired with numbers, or personal names showing initials paired with surnames). After the study period, the subject was asked to lay aside the study page and recall (in writing) one member of the pair, given the other; the stimuli were given in rearranged order. Thurstone's *M* factor had significant loadings on two other tests: Word Recognition and Figure Recognition, which also use the study–test paradigm, but the memory task is one of recognition rather than recall. Subjects are given a set of words or figures to examine carefully so that they will be able to recognize which ones occur in a longer series that is subsequently presented. The factor loadings of the recognition tests were somewhat smaller than those of the paired-associates recall tests. Thurstone's results are typical of those that have been obtained in many later studies.

In the latest available version of the *Kit of Factor-Referenced Cognitive Tests* (Ekstrom, French, & Harman, 1976), the Associative Memory factor is designated

MA and is represented by three paired–associate tests: Picture–Number, Object–Number, and First and Last Names. Each has two presumably equivalent parts. In each part of the Picture-Number test, the subject is first presented with a page of 21 pictures of objects, each paired arbitrarily with a two-digit number, to study for four minutes. In the test phase, the subject is asked, given each of the object pictures, to write down the two-digit number that was paired with the picture on the study page. In Object–Number, the stimuli are *words* designating objects (e.g. *window*), paired arbitrarily with two-digit numbers; the response in the test phase is writing down the appropriate two-digit number, given the object word. In First and Last Names, names like Janet Gregory, Thomas Adams, and Roland Donaldson are presented in the study phase; in the test phase, the subject is asked to write the *first names* that go with each last name. There are fixed time limits for study and test phases, presumably set in such a way that individual differences in learning rate can be observed. These tests are designated as suitable for grade 6–16. The *Kit* includes no tests of MA using the recognition format.

The factor is described quite operationally by the *Kit*'s authors: "The ability to recall one part of a previously learned but otherwise unrelated pair of items when the other part of the pair is presented." They cite my remark (Carroll, 1976a) that the factor involves the storage and retrieval of information from intermediate term memory, and state that "the degree to which strategies, such as rehearsal in short-term memory and the discovery of mnemonic mediators in lexicosemantic and/or experiential long-term memory, are employed and the success of such strategies may be largely responsible for the individual differences observed."

Table 7.3 lists 58 token factors that are assignable to Associative Memory (MA), in most instances quite clearly. They appear in 51 datasets, with median ages of subjects ranging from 9 to 30 years. An examination of the tests having salient loadings on these factors shows that all tests employ a study–test format, in the sense that a first phase of the test involves presenting material to be studied or otherwise committed to memory, while a subsequent test phase requires the subject to give evidence of learning, either by recall or recognition. Usually there is only one study–test cycle, but some variables supporting these factors contain two or more study–test cycles, or multiple study phases, in order to increase the amount of learning in the study phases (see, for example, variables in datasets MALM01, TENO01, UNDE12).

It is true, of course, that memory span tests also involve the study–test paradigm. What distinguishes variables appearing on factor MA is the fact that as compared to memory span variables, relatively more time is given in the study phase – time enough to allow subjects to engage in rehearsal and long-term memory searches for associations that will help fix the material to be remembered. For this reason, factor MA can be said to depend on *intermediate*-term memory rather than short-term memory.

On the other hand, the test phase almost invariably occurs shortly after the study phase terminates. Probably this is due, usually, to the exigencies of

Table 7.3. *58 Associative Memory (MA) factors in 51 datasets arranged in order of approximate mean age of sample*[a]

Dataset	Date	C'y code	Age	Sample code	M/F code	Factor no.	Remarks (higher-order factors; other related)
GARR11	'35	U	9	6	2	3	1:2G
DUNC11	'64	U	11	6	3	4	1:2G;5:MA;6:L2
"	"	"	"	"	"	5	Figures & Digits
SPEA01	'62	A	11	6	1	6	1:2G;4:MS
SPEA02	'62	A	11	6	2	6	1:2G;3:MS
TRAU01	'70	U	11	1	3	3	1:2G;7:MS;4:L7;8:I0
GARR13	'35	U	12	6	1	4	1:2G
GARR14	'35	U	12	6	2	3	1:2G
HOLZ01	'39	U	12	6	3	4	1:2D
STAK01	'61	U	12	1	3	7	1:2G;3,9,11,15:Learning
THUR81	'41	U	13	6	3	6	1:3G; 2:2H
THUR82	'41	U	13	6	3	5	1:3G; 2:2H
SUMI01	'58	N	14	1	1	4	1:2G
CARL31	'37	U	15	1	3	2	1:2Y;See text
"	"	"	"	"	"	3	See text
"	"	"	"	"	"	4	See text
"	"	"	"	"	"	5	See text
GARR15	'35	U	15	6	1	3	1:2G
GARR16	'35	U	15	6	2	4	1:2G
TENO01	'69	U	15	1	3	3	1:2G
BRAD01	'69	U	16	1	3	2	1:2Y;3:MV
CURE11	'68	U	16	6	1	7	1:2G
CURE12	'68	U	16	6	2	5	1:2G
SIMR01	'47	U	16	6	3	2	1:2G
COOM01	'41	U	17	1	3	9	1:2G
TAYL01	'47	U	17	1	3	9	6:2N
THUR11	'38	U	17	1	3	7	4:20
THUR31	'40	U	17	1	3	7	1:2G
CARR11	'43	U	18	6	2	4	1:2G
GOOD01	'43	U	18	A	1	6	1:2G
HECK01	'67	U	18	6	3	7	1:3G;5:2Y;3:M9;4:M0;6:M9; 8:MS;13:M0
ALLI02	'60	U	19	2	1	7	6:2Y
ANAS11	'32	U	19	1	2	3	1:2G
CHRI01	'58	U	19	2	1	4	1:3G;2:2Y;3:I0
"	"	"	"	"	"	6	Memory for Color
GAME01	'62	U	19	P	3	7	1:2X;2:L*3:M6;5:L1;6:MS
GARD05A	'60	U	19	6	2	3	1:2G
HUGH01	'83	A	19	6	3	5	1:2G;3:MS
LANS21	'78	U	19	6	3	3	1:2Y;2:MS
LUMS01	'65	A	19	P	3	5	1:2F;4:MS
MALM01	'79	U	19	6	3	3	1:2Y;2:M6;4:S0
PETR01	'70	R	19	1	3	3	1:2Y;2:MS;5:MV
"	"	"	"	"	"	4	Also MA?
SCHA11	'40	U	19	6	1	13	1:3G;8:2S

Table 7.3 (*cont.*)

Dataset	Date	C'y code	Age	Sample code	M/F code	Factor no.	Remarks (higher-order factors; other related)
SEIB02	'67	U	19	6	3	6	1:2V;3:M1;4:S0;5:M0; 8:MS;9:MV
THUR21A	'38	U	19	6	3	6	1:2F
UNDE12	'78	U	19	6	3	2	1:2Y;3:M6;4:MS;7:VN;8:M9
WHEA01	'73	U	19	1	1	5	1:2G
CARR01	'41	U	20	6	3	2	1:2C
″	″	″	″	″	″	5	Also MA?
CORY01	'77	U	21	2	1	2	1:2G;4:M6;See text
GUIL37	'47	U	21	3	1	3	1:2G
GUIL46	'47	U	21	3	1	4	1:2G
WITT11	'43	U	21	2	1	4	1:2G
WOTH01	'90	U	21	1	3	11	1:3G;5:MS
KELL01	'64	U	22	3	1	3	1:2Y;2:MI;4:MS;7:MV
HAKS01	'74	C	24	1	3	4	1:3G;2:2Y;3:MM;12:MS
SKEH01	'80	E	30	3	1	2	1:2G

[a]See Appendix A for codes. In a few cases, the classifications of factors shown here were preliminary and may not agree with the final classifications shown in Appendix B.

paper-and-pencil testing. Only in dataset KELL01 do we find a case (for the test Sentence Completion) where the test phase was delayed for a short time (10 minutes) while subjects took another test. The individual differences found for factor MA variables will not necessarily correlate highly with individual differences in memory after much longer intervals (e.g., an hour, a day, or a week). Factor batteries rarely contain variables involving memory for learned material tested after such relatively long intervals.

Another characteristic of most MA factor tests is that the materials to be studied consist of stimuli that are distinctly paired, usually in an arbitrary way; the subject's task is to remember what stimulus is paired with another. Usually the subject is told which stimulus of a pair is to be presented in the test phase, and which stimulus is to be recognized or recalled as being paired with the presented stimulus. Normally the stimulus to be recognized or recalled is the second member of the pair, but not always. (For example, in the test First and Last Names mentioned above, the first member was to be recalled, given the second.) Factorial results give no indication that it makes any difference in the factor loadings which member of the pair is to be recognized or recalled; no studies of which I am aware have attempted to isolate separate dimensions for first-member and second-member recall even though this contrast was of much interest in the verbal learning studies of the 1960s (Cofer, 1961; Goss & Nodine, 1965).

The above observation may seem to have less force in connection with certain variables that involve a recognition paradigm whereby the subject's task, in the test phase, is to indicate which stimuli were presented in the study phase (e.g., variables Word Recognition and Figure Recognition in dataset THUR21A). Generally, MA factor loadings for variables involving this kind of recognition paradigm tend to be somewhat lower than those for variables in which there are distinct pairings. Nevertheless, numerous variables involving the recognition paradigm appear consistently on factor MA, with salient loadings. Even the recognition paradigm involves a kind of pairing, i.e., the pairing of the stimulus with the study phase event itself.

Although the evidence is relatively weak, it appears that serial learning tasks tend to load on factor MA. In dataset UNDE12, two such variables appeared on factor MA, though with lower loadings than paired-associate variables. In the serial learning task, the subject is presented with a series of stimuli; in the test phase, the subject must remember not only the stimuli (as in free recall learning) but also their order – for example, by writing them down in the order in which they occurred. It can be argued that the appearance of serial learning variables on factor MA is due to a tendency on the part of the better subjects to adopt a strategy of noting and remembering the pairings or associations of successive pairs of stimuli.

The importance of stimulus–response pairing for factor MA is supported by the fact that variables in which the subject is not given information about pairing, or about what specifically is to be remembered and recalled in the test phase, generally have low or insignificant loadings on the factor. This is illustrated in several findings. In dataset THUR21A, the variable Picture Recall has an insignificant loading (.128) on factor MA; its most salient loading, for some reason, is on a Perceptual Speed factor. In this test, the subject is asked to inspect a picture of a fairly elaborate scene, with many details, in order to answer questions about it later. Subjects probably differ substantially in what and how many aspects of the picture they pay attention to. Similarly, in dataset KELL01, the variable Meaningful Memory: Number has only a very low loading (.273) on factor MA. In the study phase of this test, the subject is presented with a number of facts about store inventories, about which various questions are asked in the test phase. In dataset LUMS01, the study phase for the Paragraph Memory test presents a paragraph describing a country; in the test phase, the subject must answer true–false questions based on the paragraph. This variable has a low (but salient) loading (.261) on factor MA. (It should be noted, however, that the variable has a low communality and probably low reliability.)

The nature and content of the stimuli presented in MA factor tests seem to make little difference in factor loadings, as long as the stimuli are distinct and more or less unitary and recognizable on presentation. The stimuli can be meaningful or non-meaningful; they can be verbal, numerical, or figural. What is important is that the subject "register" (or in the current terminology of cognitive psychology, "encode") and remember the obvious aspects of the stimuli, or those aspects of the stimuli to which his or her attention is directed; if the stimulus is paired with another stimulus, the subject must find some way to be able to reproduce one of the stimuli, given the other. Just how the stimulus is "registered," or just how the reproduction of one member of a pair occurs, is fundamentally unknown in the present state of psychological knowledge, despite numerous theories concerning this. Some subjects can probably rely mainly on some kind of iconic or imagic memory, but it has been shown (Underwood & Schulz, 1960, pp. 296–300; Adams & Montague, 1967) that many subjects come to rely on self-generated associative linkages ("natural language mediators") or various mnemonic devices. I have not found any studies on the possible correlation of performance on tests of factor MA with the degree to which subjects use natural language mediators or mnemonic strategies.

The best markers of the factor are tests in which pairings of stimuli are arbitrary but clearly presented, as in the case of the Picture–Number, Object–Number, and First and Last Names tests in the ETS *Kit of Factor-Referenced Cognitive Tests*. Nevertheless, tests in which pairings of stimuli are not clearly evident can still appear saliently on the factor. For example, in the Sentence Completion tests used in datasets KELL01 and LUMS01, a subject is required in the study phase to examine a series of unrelated sentences for which he will be asked to supply missing words in the test phase. He is not told which words will be omitted. Likewise, in several tests used in dataset TENO01, subjects have to induce information about classes of stimuli. In the test phase they must show memory for this information. In the Books and Authors test of dataset BRAD01, subjects study titles of books and the names of their alleged authors; in the study phase they must remember this material in guessing the probable occupations of the named authors.

In view of the wide variety of stimulus material used in tests appearing on factor MA, it seems unlikely that separate factors for different kinds of content can be established, provided that the basic element of associative pairing of stimuli is preserved in the tasks. Some evidence possibly contradictory to this proposition is reviewed below, for example, the evidence that a separate Visual Memory factor can be differentiated from factor MA.

Also, several datasets listed in Table 7.3 yielded separate factors for different kinds of content. One such dataset is CARL31, where reanalysis indicated at least four separate factors. This was a study using a recognition paradigm in which lists of words were presented visually (by film, two seconds for each word). Subjects were told to examine these words in order to recognize them in a later phase, immediately afterward, in which these words would be exposed along with an equal number of distractors. In all, 34 lists were presented and tested in this way. There were seven types of lists, differing in the relation between the words in the presentation list and the distractors. In type A, there was no obvious relation between presentation words and distractor words (e.g., *cruel, diagonal*).

In type B, each presentation word (e.g. *no*) was paired with a distractor word (e.g., *know*) that was alike in respect to what Carlson called "vocality" but different in visual appearance and meaning. The other types of list exhibited different combinations of these relations. In our factor analysis, scores on all lists were loaded very substantially on a general memory factor, but there were four first-order factors. Factor 2 mainly embraced list types A, B, and C, in which presentation and distractor words differed conspicuously in visual appearance (spelling) and variously in vocality and meaning. For factor 3, the pairs tended to be alike in vocality and meaning, but different in spelling, e.g., *through* vs. *thru*. For factor 4, the pairs differed in vocality (or in this case, accentuation; e.g., *con'tem-plate* vs. *con-tem'plate*). For factor 5, the pairs were homonyms alike in spelling and pronunciation but differing in meaning [e.g., *bark* (of dog) and *bark* (of tree)]. A possible interpretation of these findings is that (apart from differences in general memory ability) subjects differed not in memory ability *per se* but in what aspects of the stimuli they were able to note and attend to. For example, factor 3 might be related to spelling ability (the factor SG noted in Chapter 5). Unfortunately, this early study by Carlson (1937) was limited to scores on the 34 lists and used no marker variables.

A similar interpretation can be given to the finding in dataset CHRI01 of a first-order factor of memory for color that was linearly independent of a less specific associative memory factor. Aside from the distinct possibility that the subjects differed in color discrimination ability (due to incidence of various types of color blindness), some subjects might have been more prone to notice and remember the colors of stimuli.

A factor of "memory for voices" from dataset HANL01 is listed as an MA factor in Table 7.3, but only because it used the study-test paradigm typical of MA tests. The dataset contained no marker variables for different kinds of memory and consequently there is no way of telling whether a special "memory for voices" factor is represented here. This could be determined only with an appropriate factorial design.

In dataset DUNC11, two associative factors are present. Factor 4 is marked by the usual paired-associate tasks, including the three MA tests of the ETS factor kit. Factor 5 corresponds to what Duncanson (1964) regarded as a "nonverbal learning" factor, being loaded with numerical and figural rote-memory tasks. The distinction between these factors needs to be explored in further research. If confirmed, it is possibly explicable in terms of different kinds of associations that subjects can make between the stimulus elements in verbal as opposed to numerical and figural tasks.

The assignments of some factors listed in Table 7.3 to the MA factor were dubious or questionable. Possibly some of them could be better characterized as general memory factors. For example, factor 4 in dataset GUIL46 was loaded with a variety of tests, many involving visual elements and some seeming not to involve memory at all. Nevertheless, the majority of the tests employed the study-test paradigm and paired stimuli typical of the MA factor. Of various memory factors identified in dataset HECK01, factor 7 seemed best assigned to factor MA because it was loaded saliently with the ETS marker test First & Last Names, along with two variables requiring subjects to remember, about particular materials, what page number of the test they appeared on, or what position on the page they occupied.

Another questionable assignment is that of factor 2 in dataset CORY01. Although it was classified as MA, the one marker for MA (the ETS Object–Number Test) did not appear saliently on it. The variables appear not to measure associative memory very directly. For example, the highest salient loading is for a test called Memory for Patterns, in which subjects were asked to compare or reproduce consecutive patterns of sequentially blinking dots on a computer screen. Other tests on the factor were a Radio Code Aptitude Test, involving learning, remembering, and using sound patterns as symbols, and a Sonar Pitch Memory Test. It is not clear how this factor should be classified.

Reanalyses of several datasets assembled under the sponsorship of Guilford (e.g., BRAD01, TENO01) failed to confirm the differentiations among memory factors that their authors claimed to find. Factor 3 in dataset TENO01 is a combination of what Tenopyr (1966) identified as "semantic memory" factors for units, classes, relations, systems, and transformations. I believe that Tenopyr's conclusions resulted from the kind of overfactoring that I have described in Chapter 2.

The relatively unitary nature of factor MA, when properly measured, is illustrated in factor 2 of dataset UNDE12, comprising a series of variables the authors (Underwood, Boruch, & Malmi, 1978) had developed in a serious attempt to study correlations of memory tasks in terms of "attributes" of memory that they identified as imagery, associative, acoustic, temporal, affective, and frequency. As these authors remark,

The failure of attributes to form factors seems to have been due to two contrary forces. First, among tasks in which associative learning is required, the individual differences in associative learning are so strong that any additional variation that might be produced by attributes has little influence. The fundamental problem is to understand associative learning, and the attribute conception has little to contribute to this issue. Second, there was some evidence that experienced subjects can set aside attributes when use of attributes as a basis for responding produces interference. The presence of attributes in memory and the utilization of attributes for responding are two independent matters (Underwood et al., 1978, p. 393).

Despite the frequent appearance of the Associative Memory factor in factorial studies, the question can be raised as to whether it is an important dimension of individual differences, in the sense of contributing to prediction of performance on various real-life learning tasks. There is little evidence that the factor makes any significant *independent* contribution to the prediction of school learning performance in general, although Carroll (1962b) has shown that a paired associate learning task is likely to be a significant independent predictor of second-language acquisition rate in formal settings. Possibly the general failure of factor MA to predict learning performances can be explained as due to the fact that in most school learning performances, students are able to compensate for possible deficiencies in paired-associate memory by spending more time in learning than would otherwise be necessary. Factor MA is after all a measure of learning rate under severely controlled time conditions.

FREE RECALL MEMORY (M6) FACTORS

Table 7.4 lists 12 factors, from 12 datasets, whose variables are predominantly measures of free recall memory. In the free recall paradigm, a set of materials is presented to subjects in a study phase, after which, in a test phase, subjects are asked to recall the materials in any order. The set of materials presented in the study phase is generally larger than what subjects can register and reproduce in a memory span paradigm. The principal measure of free recall memory is the number of stimulus elements recalled. Other measures have to do with whether some parts of the materials are better recalled than others, and whether subjects tend to cluster the stimulus materials, when categorizations are introduced into the stimulus materials. Measures of clustering tend to constitute a factor separate from free recall memory (as in dataset UNDE12), or to be negatively correlated with free recall memory (as in factor 2, dataset HUNT61).

Table 7.1 indicates that the free recall memory factor, here coded as M6, is differentiated from factor MS in datasets GAME01 and UNDE12, and possibly in dataset HECK01. It also indicates that factor M6 is differentiated from factor MA, in datasets GAME01, MALM01, and UNDE12, and possibly dataset HECK01. In several datasets, the first-order memory factors are dominated by one or more higher-order memory factors, and in most of the datasets listed in Table 7.4, a higher-order general factor is also present. It should be remembered that the higher-order structure of a set of variables is a function of the variety of those variables.

In view of the nature of the free recall paradigm, this paradigm emphasizes the degree to which subjects are able to register or encode the stimulus materials for later recall. The paradigm contrasts with the memory-span paradigm in that the stimulus materials are generally beyond the subject's memory span, and memories for the order of the stimuli are not required. It contrasts with the paired-associate paradigm in that associations between particular pairs of stimuli do not need to be formed, nor is it necessary to form an association between stimulus presentation and the learning event itself in order to perform successfully in a recognition test. Thus, the fact that a free recall memory factor can be distinguished from the associative memory factor appears to demonstrate, so far as the available evidence can be trusted, that factor M6 focuses on a particular process involved in memory, namely, the encoding of stimuli for later recall of

Table 7.4. *12 Free Recall Memory (M6) factors in 12 datasets arranged in order of approximate mean age of sample*[a]

Dataset	Date	C'y code	Age	Sample code	M/F code	Factor no.	Remarks (higher-order factors; others related)
BRAD01	'69	U	16	1	3	8	1:2Y;2:MA;3:MV
BROW11	'66	U	16	6	3	5	1:2G;2:MM
HECK01	'67	U	18	6	3	13	1:3G;2:2Y;3:M9;5:2Y;6:MM; 7:MA;8:MS
HUNT61	'73	U	18	6	3	2	1:20;3:MS
CARR41	'76	U	19	6	3	2	1:2G
GAME01	'62	U	19	P	3	3	1:2Y;2,5:L1;6:MS;7:MA
MALM01	'79	U	19	6	3	2	1:2Y;3:MA;4:MM
UNDE12	'78	U	19	6	3	3	1:2Y;2:MA;4:MS;6:20;7:VN; 8:MM;9:S0
CORY01	'77	U	21	2	1	4	1:2G;2:MA
FERN01	'78	U	30	U	3	2	1:MS (Day 1)
FERN02	'78	U	30	U	3	2	1:MS (Day 2)
ROBE11	'76	U	50	U	1	4	1:2*

[a]See Appendix A for codes. In a few cases, the classifications of factors shown here were preliminary and may not agree with the final classifications shown in Appendix B.

those stimuli, under the condition that the stimuli are drawn from a relatively arbitrary, nonmeaningful set. This condition is introduced in order to explain the differentiation of factor M6 from the meaningful memory factor MM to be described shortly. At the same time, it shows that factor MA is relatively complex in terms of the memory processes involved, in that it involves *both* stimulus encoding and the formation of associations either between paired stimulus materials or between stimuli and the study phase of the learning event. (This would explain the occasional presence of free recall measures among variables loading on factor MA.)

Among the datasets listed in Table 7.4, the "cleanest" factors representing factor M6 are in datasets CORY01 and UNDE12. In dataset UNDE12, 5 of the 6 variables that are salient on factor M6 conform to the classical free recall paradigm, differing only in the types of stimulus materials presented or the detailed format of the learning trials. Furthermore, all free recall tests in the battery had substantial loadings on this factor, nearly all of them salients on this factor. Only variable 20, List Discrimination, has on this factor a salient loading that does not readily conform to the interpretation of the factor as free recall. In this test, developed to emphasize the temporal attribute of memory, subjects had to indicate memory of which of three successively presented lists a word had appeared on. No other pilot tests of the temporal attribute proved to be sufficiently reliable for inclusion in the battery.

Evidence for a free recall factor is somewhat weaker in dataset CORY01, in that only two tests had salient loadings on this factor. Both of them conformed to the classical free recall paradigm, except that they were administered by computer, and subjects typed in responses.

Factor 5 in dataset BROW11 was interpreted by the authors (Brown, Guilford, & Hoepfner, 1966, 1968) as "memory for semantic implications" (MSI in Guilford's Structure-of-Intellect system). Several of the variables, however, were clearly in the free recall format, and others (for example, Books and Authors, with the highest salient loading) required memory of previously seen material in order to perform the test phase. Despite some lack of clarity in the constructs measured by the variables, it seemed best to classify it as factor M6.

Two of the variables with salient loadings on factor 3 in dataset GAME01 were essentially memory-span tests, but with a superspan list of 10 consonant letters to be recalled after exposure. Two other variables were paired-associate tasks involving pairs of letters, but had a recall series which was "an interval in which S attempted to write down as many pairs as he could" (Games, 1962, p. 5). This factor was differentiated from a classical memory-span factor (factor 6) and from an associative memory factor (factor 7); therefore, in view of the nature of the tasks it seemed proper to assign it to factor M6, free recall.

Factor 13 in dataset HECK01 was not too clear as a free recall factor. It was classified here chiefly because its highest salient loading was for a Film Memory test in which Ss viewed a short motion picture filmed at a supermarket check-out counter; they were then asked to record the names of as many as possible of the objects appearing in the film. Its only other salient loading was for a Paired Words test in which a list of 15 pairs of common words was read by the examiner twice, with the order of the pairs changed for the second reading. In the test phase examinees had to write the second member of each pair, given the first member. The free recall aspect of this test seems to inhere in the fact that the superspan test list was read twice and recall was thus delayed more than in a more conventional paired-associate task. Also, this factor was differentiated from an associative memory factor (factor 7).

Factors classified as M6 in datasets FERN01, FERN02, and HUNT61 all had variables that were clearly in the free recall paradigm, but they also had variables less clearly requiring free recall. In the first two of these datasets (constituting replications on Day 1 and Day 2), a List Differentiation variable appeared, similar to the List Differentiation variable that appeared in dataset UNDE12 mentioned above. In dataset HUNT61, the second salient variable was a measure of clustering with a *negative* loading; it is not clear how this should be interpreted.

Factors 3 and 4 in dataset ROBE11 were from a study by Robertson–Tchabo and Arenberg (1976) in which an immediate free recall performance was scored in terms of (a) recall of words in the last five positions of a twelve-word list, as a measure of "primary" memory, and (b) recall for the words in the first seven positions, as a measure of "secondary" memory, that is, memory not in immediate attention. These scores had loadings on different, practically uncorrelated factors in our reanalysis: factors 3 and 4, respectively. It is noteworthy that a delayed free recall test, in which subjects were asked (after an interpolated task) to recall the words they had been given in the immediate recall test, had its salient loading on factor 4; this supports the interpretation of factor 4 as a measure of secondary memory, i.e., memory traces that are not in immediate working memory. Factor 3, on the other hand, represents primary memory, i.e., the presence of memory traces in an immediate working memory.

Factor 8 in dataset BRAD01 was saliently loaded with two variables, Matrix Trend Recall and Figural Class Recall, in which subjects were required to demonstrate recall of materials that had been previously studied – properties of figural matrices, in the first case, and common elements of sets of designs, in the second case.

Factor 2 in dataset CARR41 was saliently loaded with several memory task variables. Two of them were the total correct scores from specially adapted oral and written versions of a task developed by Crowder (1971) – essentially a superspan memory task in which subjects had to recall series of two-phoneme syllables. A third variable was a parameter, derived from the Peterson and Peterson (1959) task, indicating how well subjects were able to recall phonemic nonsense syllables after an intervening, interfering task (reading random numbers in time with a series of clicks).

Factor M6 thus seems to be describable as an ability to register in memory a superspan collection of materials and then to retrieve all or most of the materials, in any order, in a recall phase.

MEANINGFUL MEMORY (MM) FACTORS

Table 7.5 lists 18 factors, in 17 datasets, that have been interpreted at least tentatively as measures of a further memory factor, "meaningful memory" (MM) or "memory for ideas." It was shown in Table 7.1 that such a factor could be differentiated from other factors in the memory domain in a number of datasets, granted the proper assignment of factors to this classification. In all cases, factor MM is dominated by a second-order factor which in some cases is interpreted as a general memory factor 2Y.

The factor is not well defined in any dataset, and the variables that define it in any particular dataset are generally not common over different datasets. Assignment of factors to this classification is therefore somewhat speculative.

In nearly all cases, the test format involves a study phase and a test phase that usually follows immediately after the study phase. The special characteristic of this factor inheres in the fact that materials presented in the study phase are "meaningful" in the sense that there is a meaningful relation between paired stimuli (as opposed to the kind of arbitrary relation found in most tests of factor MA), or the materials constitute a meaningful story or connected discourse. Thus,

Table 7.5. *18 Meaningful Memory (MM) factors in 17 datasets arranged in order of approximate mean age of sample*[a]

Dataset	Date	C'y code	Age	Sample code	M/F code	Factor no.	Remarks (higher-order others related)
WIEB11	'80	U	4	O	1	6	1:2G
LUNZ11	'76	E	5	1	3	5	1:2G;4:MS;6:MV;8:MS
JAY01	'50	U	9	6	3	5	1:2C
JONE32	'49	U	9	1	3	3	1:2D;5:MS
HARR51	'73	U	10	1	1	3	1:2G
HARR52	'73	U	10	1	2	4	1:2G
HARR53	'73	U	10	1	1	2	1:2G
HARR54	'73	U	10	1	2	6	1:2G
BROW11	'66	U	16	6	3	2	1:2G;5:M6
HECK01	'67	U	18	6	3	6	1:3G;2:2Y;3:M9;5:2Y;7:MA; 8:MS;13:M6
"						4	Film Memory III
MALM01	'79	U	19	6	3	4	1:2Y;2:M6;3:MA
SEIB02	'67	U	19	6	3	4	1:2V;3:M1;5:MO;6:MA;8:MS; 9:M1
SNOW12	'77	U	19	6	3	8	1:2G;2:MS
SNOW20	'76	U	19	6	3	3	1:GV;4:MS
UNDE12	'78	U	19	6	3	8	1:2Y;2:MA;3:M6;4:MS;6:2%; 7:VN
KELL01	'64	U	22	3	1	2	1:2Y;3:MA;4:MS;7:MV
HAKS01	'74	C	24	1	3	3	1:3G;2:2Y;4:MA;12:MS

[a]See Appendix A for codes. In a few cases, the classifications of factors shown here were preliminary and may not agree with the final classifications shown in Appendix B.

subjects who are able to note and remember meaningful ideas or relations have an advantage. The factor is likely to be related to the verbal comprehension (V) factor and other linguistic ability factors discussed in Chapter 5, to the extent that language ability may be required to understand the stimulus materials, but most tests of language abilities minimize a memory component because they do not involve separate study and test phases. Factor MM is differentiated from factor V or other language and reasoning factors in nearly all the datasets listed in Table 7.5.

One of the clearest representatives of factor MM is factor 2 in dataset KELL01, with salient loadings of four variables. In variable 13, Memory for Limericks, examinees are given five minutes to study a group of 30 limericks; in the test phase, given the first four lines of a limerick the subject must "correctly reproduce the idea and key words of the fifth line" (Kelley, 1964, p. 8). In the Memory for Ideas test, subjects hear a brief, one-paragraph story (read once in about 50 seconds); in the test phase they must reproduce it in their own words. Memory is measured in terms of the number of idea units reproduced. With somewhat lower salient loadings, two Consequences tests appear on the factor. In Consequences I (non-verbal) subjects study 18 pairs of cartoon-type sketches, each pair being the first two panels of a meaningful three-panel sequence depicting a story. In the test phase, examinees are given only the first picture of a sequence and must select from three choices the third picture that correctly completes that sequence. In Consequences II (verbal), subjects hear 20 pairs of sentences read aloud; the first sentence in each pair states a condition and the second sentence states a consequence of that condition. In the test phase, when the first sentence of each pair is again orally presented to the subject, the examinee must correctly reproduce in his or her own words the consequence to that condition.

Three highly similar tasks define a Meaningful Memory factor in dataset HAKS01, differentiated from an associative memory (MA) factor and dominated by a general memory factor. The tasks, each called Object–Attribute Memorization, present in the study phase a series of paired-associate items consisting of the names of objects and meaningful attributes of these objects. In the test phase subjects reproduce the attribute, given the name of each object. There is obviously some question about the status of this factor in view of the high degree of similarity among the tasks and (due to the design of the battery) the absence of any other variables that might test meaningful memory.

Factor 6 in dataset HECK01 appears to belong to this MM factor. Its two highest salient loadings are on two forms of a test called Social Abstracts. This test, used also in dataset SEIB02, involves a study phase in which a film depicting the silent actions of five "actors" in a simple social encounter is shown. The actors, represented on the screen by different geometric figures, and the plot are adapted from a similar film constructed and used in studies of social perception by Heider and Simmel (1944). In the test phase subjects answer true-false questions about the actions and interactions that took place in the film. Other variables on the factor are a somewhat mixed lot, but include at least one other memory test, Film Memory II – similar to Social Abstracts but using live actors. Also in dataset HECK01 there is another possible memory factor, factor 4, for which the only positive salient loading is for the variable Film Memory III; the negative loadings are for several mathematical aptitude variables. Possibly this latter factor is a statistical artifact.

In dataset SNOW20, which is based on data from only 25 subjects, the variable Film Memory III is associated with a short-term visual memory variable and with two variables that generally load on spatial ability factors. Its assignment to the MM factor is dubious; alternatively, the finding suggests that performance in certain spatial tests depends on ability in handling meaningful memories.

Factor 4 in dataset SEIB02 is defined by three scores from the Social Abstracts test, already described.

Factor 2 in dataset BROW11 is a collapsing of two factors that the authors (Brown, Guilford, & Hoepfner, 1966, 1968) interpreted as semantic memory for classes (MMC) and semantic memory for transformations (MMT). The variables with salient loadings on it all involve study and test phases; the materials studied and the responses required in the test phases generally involve meaningful relations such as class membership or similarity of meaning. It therefore seemed appropriate to postulate assignment to the Meaningful Memory factor.

Memory factors appearing in datasets HARR51–HARR54 contain variables taken mainly from Guilford's studies of semantic memory, particularly memory for classes (because this study was chiefly concerned with learning of concepts). In line with our interpretation of factor 2 in dataset BROW11, these factors are interpreted as belonging to factor MM.

The highest salient loadings for Factor 5 in dataset LUNZ11 are for variables involving memory for meaningful stories read to children. Similarly, factor 5 in dataset JAY01 is loaded with variables requiring reproduction, in the child's own words, of meaningful material that has been read either silently or aloud. Factor 3 in dataset JONE32 is approximately of a similar nature, involving the reproduction or manipulation of meaningful material.

The assignment of factor 8 in dataset UNDE12 to the meaningful memory factor MM is somewhat questionable, and in this light its inclusion in Table 7.1 under factor MM is also questionable. Two of its salient variables are concerned with judgments of the frequency with which certain events (words and traffic signs seen in slide films of a drive through an urban area) occur in a presentation in the study phase. The other two variables are a Running Recognition test adapted from work of Shepard and Teghtsoonian (1961) and a free recall test involving lists of abstract (as opposed to concrete) words. Nevertheless, the factor may be thought of as one measuring memory for events, and to the extent that these events are seen as meaningful by the subjects, the factor can possibly be regarded as belonging to the MM factor class.

In dataset MALM01 appears a factor (4) that is differentiated from factors MA and M6; it concerns paired associate and free recall tasks involving complete sentences. On the hypothesis that these tasks involve a special capacity to memorize meaningful materials – in the form of complete sentences – the factor is tentatively assigned to factor MM.

VISUAL MEMORY (MV) FACTORS

The 1976 version of the ETS *Kit of Factor-Referenced Cognitive Tests* (Ekstrom, French, & Harman, 1976) claims the existence of a separate Visual Memory (MV) factor. It presents three marker tests for the factor, as follows:

> Shape Memory (MV-1): In each of two parts, the examinee has four minutes to study a 5″ × 6″ display containing numerous irregular meaningless shapes, after which the examinee has another four minutes to look at each of 16 smaller (1″ square) displays and judge whether (Y or N) the shapes in the display occurred in the study display in the same position and orientation.

Table 7.6. *6 Visual Memory (MV) factors in 5 datasets arranged in order of approximate mean age of sample[a]*

Dataset	Date	C'y code	Age	Sample code	M/F code	Factor no.	Remarks (higher-order factors; others related)
LUNZ11	'76	E	5	1	3	6	1:2G;4:MS;5:MM;8:MS
TAYL31	'75	C	6	1	3	3	1:2D
BRAD01	'69	U	16	1	3	3	1:2Y;2:MA;8,9,10:See text
THUR71	'49	U	16	$	1	5	1:2G
"						6	See text
KELL01	'64	U	22	3	1	7	1:2Y;2:MM;3:MA;4:MS

[a]See Appendix A for codes. In a few cases, the classifications of factors shown here were preliminary and may not agree with the final classifications shown in Appendix B.

Building Memory (MV-2): In each of two parts, the examinee has four minutes to study a large ($5\frac{3}{4}'' \times 7\frac{1}{2}''$) display containing a fairly elaborate street map showing the locations of 12 buildings. In the test phase, subjects are to indicate the locations of the buildings by responding to multiple-choice questions.

Map Memory (MV-3): In each of two parts, subjects are given three minutes to study a page containing 12 displays (each approximately 2 inches square) of different street maps. In the test phase, subjects have three minutes to indicate (Y or N) whether each of 12 further displays also occurred on the study page.

In claiming the existence of this factor, the authors of the *Kit* referred to a number of sources, including those covered by our datasets BRAD01, CHRI01, GUIL46, HOFF01, ROFF11, and TENO01. They also mentioned, without citations, work in cognitive psychology supporting the existence of "iconic memory" that would presumably be involved in visual memory.

Table 7.6 lists six possible Visual Memory (MV) factors identified in five datasets. Of the datasets referenced by the authors of the ETS *Kit*, only BRAD01 appears in the list. Even though dataset CHRI01 was designed as a study of visual memory, we regard its "visual memory" factors as special variants of other memory factors, principally factor MA (see Table 7.3). Nor can visual memory factors be clearly identified in datasets GUIL46, HOFF01, ROFF11, or TENO01. Further, Table 7.1 indicates that MV factors can be differentiated from other memory factors only in datasets BRAD01, KELL01, and LUNZ11, and possibly in dataset HECK01 if one considers factor 4 of that study a visual memory factor. (It has already been listed in Table 7.5 and discussed as a variant of a meaningful memory factor.) It should be pointed out, however, that two of the reference tests for factor MV in the ETS *Kit* do not appear as variables in any of the more than 450 datasets I have analyzed; although it is possible that I have missed finding relevant evidence because of the selection of the datasets, this is not likely because the reference tests in question are of relatively recent origin.

A visual memory factor, if it exists, would appear in tests that emphasize the person's ability to form and *remember* over at least a few seconds a mental image or representation of a visual shape or configuration that does not represent some easily recognized object. (Visual configurations that represent easily recognized objects or symbols could be encoded in a nonvisual manner – e.g., verbally – and their memorization would not rely on purely visual imagery.) This has been the criterion employed in assigning factors to Visual Memory (MV) in Table 7.6. A visual memory factor, by this criterion, is found most clearly in dataset KELL01. Variables having substantial and salient loadings on factor 7 in that dataset are the following, listed in descending order of their salient loadings on the factor (which range from .445 down to .153):

> Reproduction of Visual Designs: Immediately after a five-second flash-card exposure to a geometric design, the examinee must reproduce (draw) that design. (Note that the time over which memory is required is minimal.)
>
> Map Memory III (Recognition): After three-minute study of a map of an area of countryside, the examinee is given twelve five-choice items, for each of which he must indicate which of five representations of a section of the map is the correct match. (This test is apparently the model for the Map Memory test in the ETS *Kit*.)
>
> Memory for Relations: After six-minute study of a set of fourteen 3 × 3 progressive matrices of varied content (including letters, numbers, names of months, and geometric designs), the subject is presented with the upper left-hand cell of each matrix and asked to reproduce whichever of the other cells is called for. (This test does not employ purely nonmeaningful, not readily encodable materials, but perhaps its visual memory character arises from the necessity of remembering the positioning of cell contents.)
>
> Map Memory I (Reproduction): After two-minute study of a "product-type map of a fictional country" containing 31 features, the examinee must reproduce that map. Scoring gives credit for presence of features and correct location of the features. (Unfortunately, dataset KELL01 did not contain free recall tasks that might have generated a free recall factor; this test might have loaded on such a factor, as well as the visual memory factor. The test did, however, have a nonsalient loading of .244 on an associative memory factor.)
>
> Recognition Test III (Figures): After one-minute study of 40 geometric figures or symbols, the subject had to recognize these figures or symbols in a group of 80.
>
> Map Memory II (Verbal Recall): After thirty-second study of a map of a section of town and countryside, the examinees had to answer multiple-choice questions about the area portrayed by the map.
>
> Meaningful Memory (Picture): After five-minute study of a sketch representing a Venetian scene and a delay of approximately 20–24 minutes during which two other tests were administered, the subject was presented with a sketch of another Venetian scene and had to answer 30 true–false questions about the similarities and differences of the two pictures.

In my reanalysis of dataset BRAD01, all 18 variables having salient loadings on first-order factor 3 involve a study-test paradigm; they variously require recall or recognition in the test phase and therefore are clearly variables measuring memory. The test materials, furthermore, all involve figural material that is not readily verbally encodable: geometric designs, faces, different type-fonts, etc., in such a way as to support the notion of a visual memory factor by our criterion. The salient loadings, however, are relatively small, ranging from .135 down to .044, because a large portion of the variance of these variables is absorbed into a second-order general memory factor. (This is a consequence of the fact that the associative memory and visual memory first-order factors are highly correlated, $r = .623$.) In addition, nearly all of these variables also have substantial loadings on factor 6, a general visual perception factor 2V (to be discussed in Chapter 15). Thus, although there is evidence in this dataset for a visual memory factor, most of the variables measuring it are highly complex factorially. In the original analysis, the authors (Bradley, Hoepfner, & Guilford, 1969) claimed to find six factors for these figural memory tests memory for figural units, classes, relations, systems, transformations, and implications. My reanalysis failed to confirm such factors.

Dataset THUR71 (Thurstone's study of mechanical aptitude) gives evidence of a visual memory factor, my factor 5 being measured saliently by three variables:

> Memory for Pictures: The subject sees 84 pictures of persons or objects projected one at a time on a screen (five seconds per picture); in the test phase, there is a multiple-choice test in which the subject must select which of four pictures depicts the object or person in the same position or perspective.
>
> Memory for Geometric Designs: This has the same format as Memory for Pictures, but the stimuli are geometric designs, and the choices in the test phase are these same designs and variants of them in different positions.
>
> Visual Memory (a test with a salient loading of only .196 and communality of .140): A film test with 50 items; in each item a visual shape is exposed for five seconds, followed by a blank frame exposed five seconds and another visual shape that may be either the same as the first or slightly different. The examinee indicates S (same) or D (different) and the score is $R-W$. (This test is reminiscent of experiments on individual differences in shape recognition by Cooper, 1976; see Cooper & Regan, 1982, p. 154 for discussion.)

The status of this factor is unclear, however, because this dataset does not contain markers for other memory factors. It is distinct from one other possible memory factor, factor 6, which is loaded only with a Block Assembly test that was not described in the report because of its "classified" nature. In Thurstone's analysis, the tests for my factors 5 and 6 formed a single factor, about which he commented, "This factor seems to represent the ability to keep in mind some perceptual detail..." (Thurstone, 1949, p. 16).

Detailed descriptions of the tests loading on factor 6 in dataset LUNZ11 are not readily available, but the factor is tentatively assigned to factor MV because test performance appears to depend on visual memory. A special feature of this study is that there was a one-day interval between presentation and recall.

Suggestive evidence for a visual memory factor in young children comes from dataset TAYL31, where three visual memory tests from the Illinois Test of Psycholinguistic Abilities have loadings (only one being salient) on its factor 3.

In sum, there is good though not abundant evidence for a visual memory factor controlling performance on tasks in which the subject must form and retain a mental image or representation of a visual configuration that is not readily encodable in some other modality. But there is also evidence, as discussed by Cooper and Regan (1982, pp. 154–155) that there are individual differences in the manner in which visual configurations are encoded. Some subjects apparently encode stimuli analytically (noticing and encoding details); others do this more holistically (in terms of "templates"). If such differences in visual encoding strategies exist, they will affect factorial results. There is need for more research to show the effects of encoding strategies on the operation of individual differences in visual memory, and to explore the possibility of modifying individuals' strategies. I am not aware of any research attempting to enhance visual memory in general, nor of research on the usefulness of visual memory tasks in predicting educational or occupational success.

LEARNING ABILITIES (L1) FACTORS

As noted in the introduction to this chapter, learning and memory tend to be treated as separate categories in both psychometric and experimental research, even though the study of memory almost inevitably involves the study of learning. All the memory factors introduced up to this point are based on variables in which there is a *study phase* giving subjects an opportunity to learn certain stimulus material, and memory for this learning is measured in a *test phase* that usually follows immediately. Because exposure times in the study phase are normally strictly controlled, these factors could just as well – perhaps more correctly – be regarded as factors having to do with learning rates. In the factor-analytic literature, there are few studies that focus on the relation between learning rates and rates of forgetting that can occur after the learning phases, or on individual differences in those relations. There are, nevertheless, a number of psychometric studies that explore the parameters of learning and forgetting rates and their relations to other aspects of cognitive ability; 25 token factors identified in these studies are listed in Table 7.7. It is to be understood that these factors are not necessarily all the same; they are classified here partly as a matter of convenience and partly because available evidence does not permit more detailed classifications. It is useful to discuss these studies roughly in their chronological order.

Ingham's Study

Ingham's (1952) study was designed to study the retention phase of the learning/memory process. Ingham noted that previous studies of retention had

Table 7.7. *25 Learning Ability (L1) factors in 10 datasets arranged in order of approximate mean age of sample*[a]

Dataset	Date	C'y code	Age	Sample code	M/F code	Factor no.	Remarks (higher-order factors; others related)
DUNC11	'64	U	11	6	3	6	1:2G;4:MA;5:M6;9:M0
TRAU01	'70	U	11	1	3	4	1:2G;3:MA;7:MS
,,	,,	,,	,,	,,	,,	8	Errors/Programmed Learning
STAK01	'61	U	12	1	3	4	1:2G;7:MA;See text
,,	,,	,,	,,	,,	,,	9	See text
,,	,,	,,	,,	,,	,,	11	See text
,,	,,	,,	,,	,,	,,	15	See text
ALLI01	'60	U	19	2	1	2	1:2L;See text
,,	,,	,,	,,	,,	,,	5	See text
,,	,,	,,	,,	,,	,,	6	See text
,,	,,	,,	,,	,,	,,	7	See text
ALLI03	'60	U	19	2	1	3	1:2G;2:2Y;3:MA & c(2) params.
,,	,,	,,	,,	,,	,,	4	c(1) params. of learning tasks
GAMF01	'62	U	19	P	3	2	1:2Y;3:M6;6:MS;7:MA
,,						5	See text
CARR21	'58	U	21	2	1	6	1:2G
CARR22	'58	U	21	2	1	3	1:2G
DETT00	'85	U	21	2	3	7	1:22;6:2∗;See text
INGH01	'52	E	28	3	3	2	1:2Y;See text
,,	,,	,,	,,	,,	,,	3	See text
,,	,,	,,	,,	,,	,,	4	See text
,,	,,	,,	,,	,,	,,	5	See text
,,	,,	,,	,,	,,	,,	6	See text
,,	,,	,,	,,	,,	,,	7	See text
,,	,,	,,	,,	,,	,,	8	See text

[a]See Appendix A for codes. In a few cases, the classifications of factors shown here were preliminary and may not agree with the final classifications shown in Appendix B.

failed to provide evidence either for or against the existence of a retention factor (i.e., individual differences in ability to retain knowledge or skill) because the retention intervals were usually very short and "no attempt had been made to ensure that all individuals learned the material to the same level of proficiency" (p. 20). In his study, therefore, each testing session was divided into three phases: (1) learning the material to a fixed criterion; (2) a retention interval, fixed at 30 minutes, during which intelligence tests were administered; and (3) testing the amount retained in a "relearning" phase. All tests were administered individually, and consisted of paired-associates material administered by the anticipation and prompting method. Materials were either meaningful or meaningless, and either verbal or pictorial. Four types of score were used: (1) a *learning score*, the number of repetitions required to learn each item, summed over items; (2) a *retained items* score, the number of items recognized or recalled correctly on the first trial of the relearning phase; (3) a *savings* score, an alternate measure of retention, and (4) an *immediate memory* score, being the number of items recalled or recognized correctly on the first attempt in the learning phase. All the practicable combinations of types of score and conditions yielded 27 scores that were submitted to a factor analysis, after partialling out (by a special method) the effect of a g (general intelligence) factor defined as the first general factor from the correlations of all Wechsler intelligence subtests that were used. My reanalysis was of this correlation matrix of residuals from g (approximately the same as a conventional partial correlation matrix). Ingham employed a special method to analyze this matrix in such a way as to minimize the effects of spurious correlations between different scores from the same test; my reanalysis (perhaps mistakenly) did not do this, relying on hierarchical factor analysis to sort out effects of spurious factors. Ingham obtained a general m (memory) factor that he interpreted as a general "retentivity" factor because he showed that "it is the retention phase of the memory process which is influenced by 'm'" (p. 30). My reanalysis also obtained a general "retentivity" factor, but it also obtained a number of first-order factors, possibly due in part to spurious overlap of scores from the same learning tests. At the same time, these first order factors suggested that learning and memory for different types of content (words, nonsense syllables, objects, and nonsense figures) and method of testing (recall vs. recognition) might be different factors. Specifically, the first-order factors from my reanalysis of Ingham's study are interpreted as follows:

2: Learning and recalling *words*
3: Uninterpreted
4: Learning and recalling *objects*
5: Learning and recognizing *nonsense syllables*
6: Learning and recognizing *nonsense figures*
7: Learning and recognizing *objects*
8: Uninterpreted

It is possibly worthy of note that Ingham's Table 5 reports that g contributed more variance (32.6%) to Learning and Immediate Memory scores than to Retention and Savings scores (20.1%). In contrast, m contributed 22.5% variance to Learning and Immediate Memory scores, and 24.7% variance to Retention and Savings scores. Ingham's study illustrates the technical problems that can be encountered in the attempt to separate learning rates from retentivities.

Learning Rate Studies from ETS/Princeton

Important studies of learning rates were conducted by Stake (1961), Allison (1960), and Duncanson (1964, 1966) at Educational Testing Service and Princeton University under the general direction of Harold Gulliksen. Data from Stake's and Allison's studies have been reanalyzed by Snow, Kyllonen, and Marshalek (1984) with multidimensional scaling methods.

Stake's Study

Stake sought to investigate the possibility that "there is a general learning ability, independent of what intelligence tests measure, that is influential by itself or jointly with other factors in every learning situation" (Stake, 1961). "It seems that a reasonable hypothesis," he stated, "might be that the prediction of future course marks [in school] could be improved by sampling the pupil's 'achievement' in a controlled learning situation." Following up on proposals by Gulliksen (1934), Woodrow (1946), and others, he constructed a number of short-term learning tasks and determined, for each subject and task, parameters of the learning curve. These parameters constituted variables in a factor analysis battery that also included scores on a variety of factor reference tests, measures of intelligence, and school grades, for 240 seventh-grade children in Atlanta, Georgia, public schools. Stake obtained 14 oblique first-order factors, which he interpreted as follows:

  I. Race (approximately equal numbers of black and whites were in the sample)
 II. Number
III. Nonverbal Reasoning
IV. Vocabulary
 V. Perceptual Speed
VI. Rote Memory
VII. Course Marks
VIII. Uninterpreted
 IX. Achievement Scores
 X. Verbal Reasoning
 XI. Concentration
XII. Memory-Task Learning (I)
XIII. Numerical-Task Learning
XIV. Memory-Task Learning (II)

Stake summarized his conclusions as follows: "It was found that the curvature and asymptote parameters [of learning tasks] were substantially correlated, +.1 to +.6, with scholastic aptitude and achievement as measured by conventional standardized tests. Thus, unlike the majority of previous studies, there is support here for defining intelligence as the ability to learn. ... The findings of this study revealed no general learning ability other than the general aptitude that is measured by such tests as an intelligence test given just once. ... The association of one of the learning factors with a group of numerical tasks supports the hypothesis that learning ability can be specific to a type of task. No factors were found to support the hypothesis that a rote learning performance is fundamentally different from a relational learning performance" (Stake, 1961, pp. 44–45).

My reanalysis of Stake's data attempted to eliminate the effect of race (factor

I in Stake's analysis); also, a hierarchical factor analysis was performed. This was done by reconstituting an orthogonal factor matrix from factors II–XIV of Stake's oblique matrix (using his reported correlations among factors, and eliminating the variable of race) and proceeding with a standard hierarchical analysis according to procedures established for all datasets in the study.

The resulting hierarchical factor matrix (shown in Appendix B) bore only moderate similarity to Stake's analysis. Standard factors such as verbal knowledge (V), perceptual speed (P), number facility (N), space (S), associative memory (MA), and verbal reasoning (I) appeared mostly from marker tests included in the battery for those factors, but also occasionally from certain parameters that Stake computed for his experimental learning tasks. Such factors are listed and discussed at appropriate places in the present volume.

Factors 4, 9, 11, and 15 in the reanalysis appeared to be learning ability factors, saliently loaded exclusively with parameters from the experimental learning tasks. They showed only little correspondence to learning ability factors identified and interpreted by Stake. Factor 4 seemed closest to Stake's factor VIII, which he left uninterpreted; however, its loadings were primarily for error (asymptote) and curvature parameters for experimental tasks 11, 8, and 12, which were extremely simple paired-associate learning tasks in which subjects had to learn numbers associated with pictures or cells of a matrix, over six successive trials. Of interest is the fact that many of these variables had loadings on a second-order intelligence and school achievement factor.

Factor 9 was most similar to Stake's factor XI, which he interpreted as a measure of "sustained concentration"; its positive salient loadings were for "fit" parameters of experimental tasks 4 (a paired-associate task), 6 (learning the answers to a listening comprehension task), and 9 (essentially a verbal free recall task). According to Stake, the "fit" parameters indicated regularity of the learning curves over the 6 trials. Loadings of these variables on any second-order factors were negligible.

Factor 11 was most similar to Stake's factor XIII, which he interpreted as a memory-task learning ability, and factor 15 was slightly similar to Stake's factor XII, which he interpreted as regularity of learning performance in tasks involving memory of paired stimuli.

The general impression is that some of these learning ability factors may have been largely artifactual, and probably would not be replicable, being based on relatively low intercorrelations. The communalities of most learning curve parameter variables were low; Stake gives no data on reliabilities, but these were probably low also. There were many problems in administering the tests, and it could be argued that the experimental learning tasks were too easy and trivial. Nevertheless, the study as a whole tends to support Stake's conclusion that intelligence (i.e., cognitive ability) is related to ability to learn, and that there is no important learning ability factor that is independent of intelligence.

Allison's Study

The design of Allison's (1960) study was similar to that of Stake, in that it employed a series of learning tasks to define learning ability parameters, and included a series of factor reference tests, but it was performed on a sample of enlisted men in the U.S. Navy. Conventional factor analysis was used to study the intercorrelations of 28 learning parameters, resulting in seven interpretable learning parameter factors (five factors being discarded because of specificity or idiosyncratic factor loadings). Three of these were interpreted as rote learning parameters. The remaining four factors were interpreted as Verbal Conceptual Learning, Spatial Conceptual Learning, Mechanical-Motor Learning, and "Early versus Late" Learning. Allison then used Tucker's (1958) interbattery factor method to determine the factors in common between the learning parameters and the reference measures. Four of the seven resulting interbattery factors were relatively clearly defined and were interpreted as follows:

1. *Conceptual Process*: A factor in which the process of thinking or conceptualization was dominant.
2. *Rote Process*: A factor in which a rote memory process was required.
3. *Mechanical*: A factor primarily found in activities requiring use of mechanical principles, but also subtly dependent on conceptual processes.
4. *Psychomotor Coordination*: A factor for tasks that involved precision and speed of arm, wrist, and finger movements.

Allison concluded that (1) learning ability is multidimensional, containing several factors that are dependent upon the psychological processes involved in the learning task and the content of the material to be learned, and (2) measures of learning and measures of aptitude and achievement have factors in common with each other.

My reanalysis of Allison's data was conducted in three stages: (1) (dataset ALLI01) hierarchical factor analysis of 25 learning ability measures (variables 12, 25, and 27 being omitted because of the specificity reported by Allison); (2) (dataset ALLI02) hierarchical factor analysis of 37 reference measure variables (variables Age and Education being omitted); and (3) (dataset ALLI03) hierarchical factor analysis of 58 variables from both datasets, several further variables being dropped because of low correlations. Reanalysis of the matrix of reference measures was done because it constituted a further example of a battery of reference measures to be compared to other such batteries.

Hierarchical analysis of dataset ALLI01 yielded two second-order factors, interpreted as General Cognitive Learning (factor 1) and General Rote Learning (factor 4). The Cognitive Learning factor subsumed two factors: Factor 2 reflecting the curvature of the learning curves for a series of paired-associate learning tasks, and factor 3 reflecting mainly the average rate of learning of another series of cognitive tasks, most of them involving concept formation (this factor was classified as I and listed in Table 6.5). The second-order Rote Learning factor subsumed: factor 5, reflecting the average rate of learning of paired-associate tasks; factor 6, reflecting learning of tasks involving mechanical and motor performance; factor 7, an uninterpreted factor with positive and negative loadings on motor performance tests, and factor 8, a factor specific to rotary pursuit performance.

Analysis of dataset ALLI02, for the reference test variables, disclosed two general factors, one interpreted as Gf/Gc, and the other tentatively interpreted as general memory. First-order factors were (factor 2) a combination of verbal and reasoning abilities; (factor 3) uninterpreted; (factor 4) a combination of mechanical knowledge and space abilities; (factor 5) manual speed; (factor 7) associative memory MA; (factor 8) numerical ability. Despite the presence of reference tests for a large assortment of factors, this dataset failed to reveal a corresponding number of factors, perhaps because the sample consisted of Navy enlisted men whose intellectual ability was described by Allison as corresponding to an average IQ in the low 90's.

In the third stage of the analysis, dataset ALLI03 was factored, combining the learning measures and the reference test variables. It was a little surprising that the factor analysis yielded no more factors than did dataset ALLI02, but the overall structure was different. A weak third-order factor of general ability was obtained, on which there were moderate loadings for two second-order factors, (factor 2) general memory, and (factor 6) a combination of Gf and Gc abilities. Under general memory (factor 2) appeared a factor (factor 3) loaded with reference tests for associative memory (MA) and the $c(2)$ parameters for a series of associative learning tasks. The loadings for the $c(2)$ parameters were for *reflected* variables; the interpretation is that good performance on associative learning tests is associated with learning that is faster in the early phases of learning than in the later trials. But also subsumed under the general memory factor, and with moderate loadings on it, were the $c(1)$ parameters of the associate learning tasks; according to Allison, the $c(1)$ parameter is a measure of the average rate of learning.

The overall results of the Allison study, as reanalyzed here, suggest that there are moderate relations between cognitive abilities and learning rates, but there are special factors of learning rate that are independent of general cognitive ability. This study was well designed and well conducted; it is unfortunate that the sample was, on the average, of relatively low cognitive ability.

Duncanson's Study

Duncanson (1964, 1966) administered nine learning tasks and a battery of ability tests to 102 sixth-grade children. The tasks were of three types: concept formation, paired associates, and rote memory (free recall), and for each type there were tasks involving verbal, numerical, and figural content. Duncanson subjected each learning task to a separate factor analysis in order to determine the number of factors necessary to describe subjects' performances on that task. Factor scores on the tasks were then entered into a factor analysis together with scores on ability measures. Duncanson found seven factors. One factor was specific to the ability measures and interpreted as a speed factor. Three factors common to the ability and learning measures were interpreted as verbal ability, rote-memory ability, and reasoning ability. Three factors specific to the learning measures were interpreted as verbal learning, nonverbal learning, and concept formation.

In my hierarchical reanalysis of Duncanson's data (dataset DUNC11), I obtained one general factor and nine first-order factors. Many of the first-order factors were interpreted as standard reference factors and are listed and discussed elsewhere in this volume. Factor scores from Duncanson's learning tasks often loaded on one or more of these factors. Only factors 5, 6, 7, and 10 had loadings exclusively for factor scores from learning tasks, but the results were difficult to interpret. Factor 5 appeared to reflect skill in memorizing figures and digits, and it is listed under factor MA in Table 7.3. Factor 6 was loaded with components of learning curves for several learning tasks, but the meaning of these components may have differed over the tasks; no clear interpretation of this factor can be offered. Factors 7 and 10 were loaded exclusively with learning curve components from concept formation tasks; they are regarded as measuring factor I or special characteristics of inductive learning (see Table 6.5).

Games's Study

A factorial analysis of a series of verbal learning tasks, together with several reference tests for memory span (factor MS) and associative memory (factor MA, or what he called "rote memory") was made by Games (1962). All his experimental verbal learning tasks used as stimuli and responses only the 21 consonant letters of the English alphabet, and there was a variety of tasks given by either individual or group administrations. He confirmed his major hypothesis that "there are positive correlations between the reference and experimental tests and these correlations are accounted for by the two reference factors, Rote Memory and Span Memory" (p. 3). Various other hypotheses about verbal learning were either confirmed or rejected by detailed analysis of the data; the reader is referred to the study itself for further information.

My reanalysis of Games's data, based on an orthogonal factor matrix that Games developed to exclude the effects of experimental dependencies, generally confirms his conclusions. Two second-order factors were obtained, corresponding to (factor 1) general rote memory and (factor 4) general span memory. Most of the verbal learning tasks, grouped in a first-order factor (factor 5), loaded on both of these second-order factors, a finding that I would interpret as indicating that verbal learning depends on both associative and span memory abilities. In addition, I found specific first-order factors for serial anticipation tasks (factor 2), free recall tasks (factor 3, regarded as belonging under factor M6), memory span tasks (factor 6), and the reference tests for associative memory (factor 7, MA).

On the whole, this study makes little contribution to our present understanding of learning and memory tasks beyond its demonstration of the distinction between rote (associative) memory and memory span and their influences on traditional verbal learning tasks.

Other Learning Ability Factors

In studies of foreign language aptitude, Carroll (1958) used an inductive artificial language learning test devised by Sapon (1955). The test was administered by tape recorder and film strip and required the examinee to induce and remember details of spoken language grammar and vocabulary. Scores for three successive stages of learning on this test constituted a separate factor in datasets CARR21 (factor 6) and CARR22 (factor 3), linearly independent of an associative memory test and another artificial language test given in written form. Because of the absence of appropriate marker tests in these batteries, the status of this "inductive language learning" factor is unclear, but the finding is of possible interest for further research.

In a study of the influence of ability on programmed learning, Traub (1970) collected data on 23 ability tests and six measures of rate of work and errors made in learning from a linear program for teaching graphical addition of integers. My reanalysis of his correlation matrix – an analysis that was somewhat different from Traub's – yielded standard factors (V, MA, N, RQ, MS) for the cognitive ability tests, but in addition two factors unique to programmed learning performance. Factor 4 was interpreted as speed or rate of work during the performance, and factor 8 as level of mastery attained, being loaded with a count of errors and a post-test on the content of the program. Both of these programmed learning factors, and their measures, had loadings on a general second-order factor for the battery. At the same time my analysis supports Traub's conclusion that "programmed learning measures can...define factors which would not be identified using only those reference tests that were included in the present study" (p. 54).

In a study of scores on numerous information-processing tasks, Detterman (unpublished; personal communication, 1985) assembled a correlation matrix that I analyzed. One of the factors (factor 7, dataset DETT00) had salient loadings on three measures of study time in a self-paced probe recall task. This factor is possibly related to the study time or rate of work factor just mentioned in Traub's (1970) study. In any case it draws attention to the importance of investigating study times in self-paced learning situations.

MISCELLANEOUS FACTORS IN THE LEARNING AND MEMORY DOMAIN

This section describes and discusses a miscellany of factors, classified in the memory domain, that do not appear to fit readily into any of the categories previously presented and that therefore require special treatment. Some of them may have important implications for understanding the memory domain as a whole; they need to be investigated in future research. Others appear to introduce special memory abilities that may be of interest in certain domains of behavior. They are listed in Table 7.8 in the manner that has been adopted elsewhere.

Factors Pertaining to Memory Models

Datasets GEIS01 and GEIS02 come from a study by Geiselman, Woodward, and Beatty (1982) that used individual differences in verbal memory performance in a test of alternative information-processing models. These authors conducted two experiments in which several psychophysiological and verbal-report measures were recorded during learning. They used maximum-likelihood procedures to test alternative hypotheses concerning information processing. My use of exploratory factor-analysis procedures attempted to confirm at least the dimensional properties of their measurements. In the course of reanalyses it became evident that the correlation matrices *published* by the authors were incorrect (being nonpositive semidefinite). Fortunately, the authors were able to supply the correlation matrices on which their published (correct) structural equation results were based, and these were the matrices on which my analyses were performed. It is to be noted that both are based on small samples ($N = 20$ and 32 for the two datasets, respectively); however, pertinent correlation values were highly significant, and factor loadings were consequently high. The reader is referred to the original source for detailed explanations of the measurement procedures used and the alternative hypotheses that were tested. Briefly, in their first experiment the authors confirmed a dual-process conception of memory recall involving both short-term (STS) and long-term (LTS) stores, in contrast to a uniprocess model of the type proposed by Melton (1963). In addition, their second experiment suggested that the intensity with which a subject studies is associated with enhancement of LTS recall, but not STS recall.

The basic paradigm employed in the experiment was free recall of lists of nouns, and thus the results bear on the interpretation of the factor M6 that was discussed in connection with Table 7.4. In our reanalysis of dataset GEIS01, two orthogonal factors were obtained when signs of variables were reflected to produce positive manifold for purposes of Varimax rotation. However, the results are better interpreted when the original signs of variables are kept. Factor 1 is to be interpreted as indicating the extent to which recall was from LTS vs. STS. Positively loaded variables are those that according to the authors' theory indicate recall

Table 7.8. *28 Miscellaneous memory (M0) factors in 16 datasets*[a]

Dataset	Date	C'y code	Age	Sample code	M/F code	Factor no.	Remarks (higher-order factors; others related)
Factors pertaining to memory models							
GEIS01	'82	U	19	P	3	1	LTS vs. STS Storage
"	"	"	"	"	"	2	LTS Processing
GEIS02	'82	U	19	P	3	1	LTS vs. STS Storage
"	"	"	"	"	"	2	Processing Intensity
HORN21	'78	U	30	Q	1	5	Primary Memory?
"	"	"	"	"	"	7	Secondary Memory?
"	"	"	"	"	"	8	Artifactual?
HUNT61	'73	U	18	6	3	7	Primary Memory?
SEIB02	'67	U	19	6	3	3	Short-term Nonvisual?
"	"	"	"	"	"	9	Short-Term Visual?
Special factors in datasets CARR42 and CARR43							
CARR42	'76	U	19	P	3	6	Sachs Task
CARR43	'77	U	19	6	3	4	Sachs Task
"	"	"	"	"	"	7	Sachs Task, specific
"	"	"	"	"	"	8	Intermediate Term Memory?
"	"	"	"	"	"	9	Crowder Task
"	"	"	"	"	"	14	Peterson–Peterson Task
Factors in memory for events?							
CHRI01	'58	U	19	2	1	3	Memory for Position
HECK01	'67	U	18	6	3	3	Memory for Events
SEIB02	'67	U	19	6	3	5	Memory for Events
Memory for spellings							
HOEP21	'68	U	16	8	3	3	Misspellings, etc.
SMIT11	'77	U	11	6	3	4	Pseudoword Spelling
Special factors in datasets RAND01 and RAND02							
RAND01	'79	C	10	6	1	2	"Reconstruction" tasks
RAND02	'79	C	10	6	2	3	" "
A verbal discrimination memory factor							
UNDE12	'78	U	19	6	3	7	Verbal discrimination tasks
A factor in clustering in free recall							
HORN21	'78	U	30	Q	1	2	Clustering in free recall
UNDE12	'78	U	19	6	3	9	Clustering in free recall
General memory factors							
HAKS21	'78	C	16	6	3	4	MA and MM variables
HORN25	'67	U	30	Q	1	2	3 Memory tasks

[a]See Appendix A for codes. In a few cases, the classifications of factors shown here were preliminary and may not agree with the final classifications shown in Appendix B.

from LTS: Number of semantic confusions, number of immediate responses made only "slowly," i.e., after a two-second pause in the recalls had occurred, and number of responses made after delayed recall (following 24 seconds of distraction). The negatively loaded variables indicate recall from STS: number of immediate responses made "fast," (i.e., before a two-second pause occurred), an estimated STS recall measure, and number of acoustic confusions. On factor 2, the highest loadings were for measures of eye fixation during study of the lists, followed by loadings of approximately .4 for the LTS recall measures, a result tending to confirm that long and highly variable eye fixations were associated with recall from LTS. The implication is that subjects behave quite differently on a free recall task depending on whether they study in such a way as to place memories in a long-term store. It is not clear from this experiment whether these individual differences, though highly reliable for the experiment as such, are stable over time or over different kinds of learning tasks. It would be of interest to repeat this experiment with the addition of scores from several types of standard memory tests.

Factor 1 of dataset GEIS02 is similar to factor 1 of GEIS01 except that the eye fixation measures are directly included among positively loaded variables, indicating LTS processing during list study. Factor 2 is loaded with three measures of processing intensity during list study: heart rate variability, a self-report of processing intensity, and a measure of galvanic skin resistance. The results are consistent with the authors' interpretation that intensity of processing during list study enhances LTS processing but not STS processing, although admittedly the structural equation path model is more informative than the factor-analytic model. It should be noted that "long-term store" implies storage that is not very long, temporally; it is long-term only with respect to short-term storage. Elsewhere this is termed *intermediate-term* storage.

Dataset HORN21 comes from a study by Horn (1978b) that attempted to evaluate the contributions of various first-order factors to the interpretation of the second-order Gf (fluid intelligence) and Gc (crystallized intelligence) factors postulated by Horn and Cattell (1966). In particular, there was concern with the role of primary and secondary memory in these factors. A large number of tests were administered to 147 prison inmates and much work was done to derive theoretically interesting variables from the responses. Correlation matrices were not presented in Horn's report and my hierarchical reanalysis was based on a nine-factor Varimax solution for 47 variables in his Table 15. Factor 5 is interpreted as a factor of primary (recency) memory, loaded saliently with four variables (loadings are indicated):

> 30: (.558) Speed of answering Yes/No questions based on informational paragraphs presented by tape recorder, after a thirty-second interpolated task.
> 40: (.509) Total time to produce correct responses in an Esoteric Vocabulary test.
> 20: (.435) Recall of the last word in seven-word and nine-word free recall lists.

> 28: (.287) Score (number correct) for a "trivia" test for memory of various events inconspicuously introduced during the test series.

Horn himself labeled this factor "primary memory" but remarked that it did not seem to measure primary memory as usually discussed. Instead, he believed that it measured "a rather narrow facility in encoding and quickly retrieving words" (p. 96). Horn performed further analyses of his data by dropping variables that appeared to introduce too much experimental dependence. In fact, factors 7 and 8 of the reanalysis corresponded to factors in his analysis that he regarded as artifactual. Horn put more credence in a factor from his renalysis (his Table 16) that he labeled SAR, "Short-term acquisition and retrieval," that was saliently loaded on the following variables:

> 21: (.64) Murdock Intercept, Primary Memory
> 18: (.54) Murdock Slope, Secondary Memory
> 19: (.52) Primacy Score, Secondary Memory
> 16: (.42) Syllogisms not requiring flexibility
> 20: (.40) Recency, Primary Memory (see above)

In this list, variables 21, 18, 19, and 20 were all based on performance in a list-learning task due to Murdock (1960) in which Ss heard a word list and then immediately wrote down as many of the words as they remembered. Lists had 5, 7, 9, or 11 words. Variables 21 and 18 were, respectively, the intercept (I) and slope (S) of the linear equation $R = SL + I$, where R is the recall on a list of length L. Horn gave reasons why the intercept might be regarded as a measure of primary memory (or STS as Geiselman et al., 1982, would call it), and slope a measure of secondary memory (or LTS). Variable 19 was the number of recalls of the first two words in the seven- and eleven-word lists, and variable 20 the number of recalls of the last word in these lists. It is a little difficult to see why these variables were claimed not to exhibit experimental dependence. Variable 16 was the number correct score on syllogisms that did not make demands on the ability to resist certain kinds of response sets. Its presence on this factor may indicate a possible role of working memory capacity in solving such syllogisms.[2]

Factor 7 of dataset HUNT61 is positively loaded with two parameters, *tau* and *alpha*, of Atkinson and Shiffrin's (1968) model for a continuous paired-associate memory task, and negatively loaded with a measure of the degree of clustering manifested by subjects in free recall of unblocked word lists. The parameter *alpha* is supposed to indicate the probability of the entry of an item into short-term memory (STM) and the parameter *tau* the rate at which information becomes unavailable from "intermediate term memory" (ITM). While these results are intriguing, they are difficult to interpret, or even to accept, in view of the fact that in this experiment the N was only 40, and subjects were not extensively practiced.

Two factors from dataset SEIB02 are of considerable interest, being based on motion picture film presentations. Factor 3 is loaded with four variables in which subjects are presented with a 2 × 3 array that contains either colors, or photographs of objects. The array is shown in a brief presentation (from 1/3 to 1/2 second); after about a 60 milliseconds pause, subjects are required either to name the color or object cued in a particular position of the array, or to indicate its position in the array. Factor 9 is loaded only with two short-term visual memory tasks. Each item presents eight letters in a 4 × 2 array for about 31 milliseconds, with one element of the array marked by a circle or "doughnut" that can either precede or follow the presentation. The subject's task is to write the letter occupying the designated position. The tasks differ only in the way in which the position is designated. It is interesting that these tests, though superficially similar, yielded two linearly independent factors of visual short-term memory possibly differing in the type of memory coding required (color or object vs. letter recognition); the oblique factors actually correlated negatively, $r = -.150$.

Special Factors in Datasets CARR42 and CARR43

These datasets came from a study (Carroll, 1977) that attempted to determine correlates of subtests of the Modern Language Aptitude Test (Carroll & Sapon, 1959). Dataset CARR42 involved a number of measures designed to illuminate the nature of grammatical sensitivity (factor MY, discussed in Chapter 5). Factor 6 was loaded with several variables derived from a task devised by Sachs (1967) to test recognition of formal vs. semantic changes in sentences as passages are presented by tape recorder. Sachs had shown that recognition of semantic changes is much stronger than recognition of formal (grammatical or structural) changes. At odd intervals a bell was sounded and subjects were shown a test sentence to judge as being either "identical" or as "changed" from a sentence that was heard either zero or 80 syllables previously. Changes were either formal (changing positions of certain words), grammatical (changing between active and passive voice without essential change of meaning), or semantic (essential change of meaning, e.g., by reversing roles of persons, or by negation). The scores with positive loadings on factor 6 were measures of the degree to which the subject was able to notice and correctly recognize over an eighty-syllable interval whether formal (variable 26) or active–passive (variable 25) changes were made in the sentences. The negative loading was for a score reflecting recognition of identical sentences. That is, the factor represents ability to remember sentence *form* apart from total ability to remember changes of any type, including semantic changes. There was some evidence that this ability was related to variables defining a grammatical sensitivity factor (factor 1), in that variable 26 also had a loading of .32 on factor 1.

In dataset CARR43, for an enlarged set of variables and a different sample of subjects, variables from the Sachs task loaded on two factors. Factor 4 was loaded with a total score on the Sachs task and with number correct on the Craik (1971) recognition task – apparently a special factor of recognition memory. Factor 7 was loaded with variables indicating correct recognition of form and meaning changes in the Sachs task.

Three other factors in dataset CARR43 possibly index special aspects of memory. Factor 8 measured performance in a continuous paired-associate memory task in which visually presented nonsense syllables were successively paired with different digits, as well as performance in a task requiring recall of lists of auditorily presented phonemic nonsense syllables. Factor 9, independent of factor 8, was loaded principally with three variables from tasks in which memory span for lists of auditorily presented phonemic nonsense syllables was required. Some lists used vowels represented in names of alphabetic letters (e.g., /gey/, /giy/, /gow/, /gay/ – the vowels corresponding to the names of the letters *A, E, O, I*); other lists used English phonemic vowels that do not occur in alphabetic names; still others were mixed lists. Probably this was a memory-span factor (MS), but unfortunately there were no markers for this in the battery. Finally, factor 14 was loaded principally with two variables derived from the Peterson and Peterson (1959) task, in which a trial consisted of auditory presentation of one, two, or three nonsense syllables, followed by a tone, at which the subject read random numbers aloud (as an interfering task) for 0, 3, 6, 12, or 18 seconds and then attempted to recall the list originally presented. The two variables derived from this task and loaded on factor 14 were (1) a total score over all trials, and (2) a slope of number correct with respect to lag. A third variable from this task, a slope of number correct with respect to number of syllables in the list, was loaded highly on factor 9, lending support to the interpretation of that factor as short-term memory or memory span. Factor 14 could possibly be interpreted as long-term memory store, similar to factors found in datasets GEIS01 and GEIS02 as mentioned above.

Factors of Memory for Events

In dataset CHRI01 there occurs an interesting special factor that seems to represent long-term incidental memory for spatial position (which might be taken to be an "event"). Factor 9 is saliently loaded with two variables: variable 24, score on a number–word associative memory test, and variable 23, a score from a test administered unexpectedly four hours after the number–word association test, requiring subjects to recall the position on the page where each number–word association pair had occurred. The presence of variable 24 on this factor indicates that the better the word pairs were learned, the better subjects recalled the page position where they were presented.

Datasets HECK01 and SEIB02 contain factors interpretable as "memory for events." The stimuli for several variables loaded on these factors were motion picture films of either live actions of persons acting out a brief story or of geometric figures whose motions suggested stories (a film developed by Heider & Simmel, 1944). At the conclusion of film presentation, subjects were required to answer questions about the actions, in particular, the order in which they occurred. These factors are linearly independent of other memory factors in the datasets.

Factors of Memory for Spellings

Factor 3 in dataset HOEP21 and factor 4 in dataset SMIT11 appear to be highly similar, but in their respective batteries there are no other memory factors, nor markers for memory abilities. They are candidates for use in further investigation. In dataset HOEP21 salient loadings are on three variables:

> 20: (.624) Memory for misspelling: The subject studies a list of common words that are misspelled but presumably recognizable. In a test phase, each word is presented in its proper spelling and S is to reproduce how it was misspelled.

> 21: (.391) Memory for word transformations: In the study phase, S sees pairs of linked words such as EARN/ICE. In the test phase, S judges whether new pairs are the same or different (e.g. EAR/NICE) from before.

> 19: (.285) Memory for hidden transformations: S studies sentences in which certain underlined sequences of letters form embedded words, e.g., You must not bur*den t*he teacher. In the test phase, S is to indicate whether the embedding is in the same manner, e.g., in They loa*d ent*ire trucks, the embedding is different.

Three variables define factor 4 in dataset SMIT11:

> 5: (.489) Visual alternate spelling: In each item, S studies three phonemically similar pseudowords, e.g. *fleem, fleam, fliem*. In the test phase, these spellings must be written from memory, in the correct order.

> 3: (.450) Visual pictures: S studies misspellings associated with pictures; in the test phase S must reproduce the misspelling as cued by the picture.

> 4: (.281) Visual context: In a test phase, S is to remember the spelling of a pseudoword seen in reading a story.

All these variables appear to tap the ability to remember particular spellings and arrangements of letters. However, further investigation should attempt to control for the fact that some of them may also tap the factor identified as Phonetic Coding (PC) and discussed in Chapter 5, insofar as they require the subject to recognize the words cued by misspellings.

Special Factors in Datasets RAND01 and RAND02

Two rather ingenious tests of memory are loaded on factors (2 and 3, respectively) in datasets RAND01 and RAND02. The authors (Randhawa & Hunt, 1979) regarded the tests as perceptual, but it appears to me that there is a strong memory component in them. In the test Verbal Reconstruction there is a momentary presentation of a list of from 1 to 8 verbal cues that represent attributes of a stimulus, e.g, RED, SMALL. There is then a panel presenting various possibilities as to what the described stimulus is. S is to mark the position of the correct answer. In the test Visual Reconstruction, there is a momentary presentation of one or more attributes in figural form, after which a panel of figural stimuli is presented. S must answer a series of binary questions concerning what attributes are represented. The memory component consists in the requirement to remember what attributes are going to be represented in stimulus figures; it is interesting that items use as many as eight binary bits of information, well beyond the three or so bits implied by Miller's (1956) "magical number seven." These factors are shown to be distinct from memory span (MS) factors, but otherwise there is no information as to how they should be aligned with other memory factors.

A Verbal Discrimination Memory (VN) Factor

Distinct from several other memory factors in dataset UNDE12, from the study of episodic memory by Underwood, Boruch, and Malmi (1978), was factor 7, loaded principally with two variables from verbal discrimination tasks. The highest loading (.421) was for a control version of the task, which involved lists of 24 pairs of two-syllable words, the words being selected randomly from words with (relatively low) frequencies of 1–10 in the Thorndike and Lorge (1944) tables. These lists were given for a single study and test trial, each pair being presented for two seconds on the study trial and for four seconds on the test trial. On the study trial, one randomly chosen word in each pair was underlined to designate the "correct" member of the pair. On the test trial the underlining was omitted and the subject was to write the "correct" word for each pair. Score was number of correct responses over four such lists. The next highest loading (.372) was for an "affective cueing" version of the task, in which the underlined member of a pair had a high rating on a semantic differential scale (evaluation, for one list, and potency, for the other list). The hope was that subjects would learn which member of a pair was "correct" as a function of this affective cueing. Actually, the results gave little evidence that such learning occurred, so that this version could be regarded as simply an alternate form of the control version. (It is of interest that a "double function" version of the task had no significant loading on factor 7. The reader is referred to the source for a description of this version.)

It is debatable whether factor 7 is truly a distinct and replicable factor; possibly it is a specific factor associated with the particular format of this type of task. At the same time, it should be noticed that scores on these two tasks had high loadings (.600 and .539, respectively) on a second-order factor (factor 6) that was interpreted as a general factor for memory for events, since it had high loadings also for tests of factor 8 – interpreted as a meaningful memory factor (MM).

A Factor for Measures of Clustering

Also in dataset UNDE12 was evidence for a factor (factor 9) representing individual differences in the tendency to cluster responses in a free recall task, when the stimuli to be recalled presented obvious opportunities to do such clustering on the basis of categories of meaning. High loadings on this factor were observed for two variables: a clustering score (variable 8) based on responses to the conceptual associations free recall task (the number correct being variable 6), and a clustering score (variable 7) based on responses to the interitem associations free recall task (the number correct being variable 5). The conceptual associations task involved twenty-four–item lists of words made up of three instances of each of eight categories, the instances being more or less randomly distributed through the lists; the clustering score was calculated as the number of adjacent recalls of items from a category divided by total recall. The interitem associations task involved lists of 24 words made up of 12 pairs of associated words, e.g., *doctor–nurse* and *shallow–deep*, the members of these pairs being more or less randomly distributed through the list. Clustering scores were calculated as the number of two-item clusters divided by total recall. The authors reported that the distribution of scores showed bimodality. Some subjects recalled exclusively in a serial manner, others exclusively by associative clustering.

A similar factor was obtained by Horn (1978b) in factor 2 of dataset HORN21. The two highest loadings on this factor were for clustering scores calculated from the number of adjacencies in free recall responses. Horn's results tended to confirm his hypothesis that free recall clustering behavior would be indicative of high scores on factor Gc, crystallized intelligence.

Technically, deriving both clustering and total correct measures from free recall responses might be regarded as an instance of experimental dependence, but correlations between clustering scores and total correct scores are typically low enough to dispel any concern about experimental dependence.

General Memory (Gy) Factors

In many instances in our datasets, several memory factors were correlated in such a way that second-order memory factors appeared, distinct from other second-order factors. This is true, for example, of datasets CHRI01, GAME01, HECK01, KELL01, and UNDE12. Several investigators, however, designed datasets in such a way that what would usually be found as second-order factors appeared at the first order. This was the case for datasets HAKS21 and HORN25. In the first of these, factor 4 could be interpreted as a general memory factor, loaded with scores from first-order factors MA (Associative Memory) and MM (Meaningful Memory). In dataset HORN25, one test was used to measure each of a series of primary factors, including two memory factors: Memory for Designs (MD) and Memory Span (MS). Factor 2 contains loadings for these variables. It is not clear what factor was intended as Memory for Designs; apparently it would correspond to what has been called Visual Memory (MV) in the present chapter; it was measured by a test called Redraw the Figure but I have not been able to find an adequate description of this test.

A further discussion of the status of a general memory factor is contained in Chapter 15.

SUMMARY AND DISCUSSION

This chapter, devoted to ability factors in the domain of learning and memory, has reviewed evidence that appears to indicate the following:

1.   Individuals differ in a general memory ability that affects, to a considerable extent, performances in a wide variety of tasks and behaviors involving memory.

2.   In addition, there is evidence, strong in most cases, for additional, more specific factors of memory ability:

Memory Span (factor MS): An ability indicated by the amount of material (verbal, numerical, or figural) that the individual can immediately recall, in its correct order, after one exposure to that material. It is possibly a composite of two memory factors, one for the registration of the stimuli, and one for registration of their order, but as yet, clear evidence of this is not available.

Associative Memory (factor MA): The ability to form arbitrary associations in stimulus material such that on testing, the individual can recall what stimulus is paired with another, or recognize, in a series of test stimuli, which stimuli were experienced in a study phase.

Free Recall Memory (factor M6): Indicated by the fact that some individuals, after a study phase, are able in a test phase to recall more (arbitrarily unrelated) material from the study phase than others, when the amount of material to be remembered exceeds the individual's memory span.

Meaningful Memory (factor MM): Indicated by the fact that some individuals, after a study phase, are able to recall (reproduce) or recognize more material from a study phase than others, when the material in the study phase has meaningful interrelations.

Visual Memory (factor MV): The ability to form, in a study phase, a mental representation (or possibly an image) of visual material that is presented, when the visual material is not readily codable in some modality other than visual, and to use that representation in responding in a test phase by recognition or recall. (An analogous auditory memory factor UM is considered in Chapter 9.)

3.   There is a general learning ability that is positively and substantially correlated with performance on tests that are loaded with broad second-order factors of cognitive ability, particularly fluid and crystallized intelligence. It is possible that there is a component of general learning ability that is not predicted by cognitive ability tests, but no persuasive evidence for such a component exists in the available literature.

4.   There is evidence of factors of learning ability that are specific to particular kinds of learning situations.

The available literature on individual differences in learning and memory abilities leaves much to be desired, mainly because it has generally relied on observations of performances on one-shot cognitive ability tests and highly constrained learning situations such as those conducted in psychological laboratories. Work on abilities revealed in long-term training experiences has not been adequately subjected to factor-analytic methodology. Further, there is little work on individual differences in long-term "autobiographical" memory. Nor is there adequate study of individual differences in the types of memories that different persons are likely to retain over long periods of time. The assertion of Johann Friedrich Herbart, quoted at the head of this chapter, remains incompletely confirmed by the available scientific evidence.

NOTES

1. At the second order, General Memory is coded 2Y. Mnemonically, "Y" is the last letter of *memory*. A second-order memory-span factor is coded 2X.
2. No dataset examined in this survey yielded any factor that could be identified as a factor of "working memory capacity" as defined and studied, for example, by Baddeley (1986), Kyllonen and Christal (1990), and Woltz (1988). All the memory factors considered in the present chapter are defined by tasks that have clearly distinguished study and test phases, in contrast to tasks in which operations in "working memory" imply covert and unobservable interactions between memory storages and retrievals. See Chapter 16 for further discussion of the concept of working memory and its role in cognitive tasks.

8   *Abilities in the Domain of Visual Perception*

*Spatial ability has been defined in such
a variety of different ways that it is
often difficult to be precise about the
meanings which we ascribe to the term.*

John Eliot & Ian MacFarlane Smith (1983)

Abilities in visual perception have received much attention in psychometric studies. Over the years since Spearman first announced the identification of a general factor in intelligence, a number of separate abilities in the realm of visual perception, to some extent independent of general intelligence, have come to be recognized, but research studies have often led to contradictory and confusing conclusions about exactly what abilities exist and how they should be defined and measured. Often these abilities have been discussed under the heading of "spatial ability," because at least some of them have to do with how individuals deal with materials presented in space – whether in one, two or three dimensions, or with how individuals orient themselves in space. Dimensionality is, of course, an inherent attribute of space as commonly perceived, but it may not be the central attribute that is of concern in spatial ability or visual perception in general. What appears to be of more concern is the fact that objects, forms, or symbols are perceived as laid out in the space presented to the eyes (or in the "mind's eye," imaginal memory), whether in real-life interactions between the individual and his or her surroundings or in pictorial or printed representations of forms, objects, or text on paper. Spatial and other visual perceptual abilities have to do with individuals' abilities in searching the visual field, apprehending the forms, shapes, and positions of objects as visually perceived, forming mental representations of those forms, shapes, and positions, and manipulating such representations "mentally." I use the term "visual perception" to cover all these abilities, even though it may not be adequately descriptive.

Eliot and Smith (1983) describe, in three phases, the history of efforts to define what they regard as spatial abilities:

In the first phase (1904–1938), researchers investigated the evidence for and against the existence of a spatial factor over and above a general factor of intelligence. In the second phase (1938–1961), they attempted to ascertain the extent to which spatial factors differed from one another. And in the most recent phase (1961–1982), researchers have attempted to designate the status of spatial abilities within the complex interrelationship of other abilities, and to examine a number of sources of variance which affect performance on spatial tests (Eliot & Smith, 1983, p. 1).

304

The present survey and reanalysis of factor-analytic studies covers all three of these phases, considering not only some of the earliest studies, such as a study of mechanical ability by Paterson, Elliott, Anderson, Toops, and Heidbreder (1930), a study of space perception by El Koussy (1935), and a study of clerical abilities by Andrew (1937), but also the classic studies of Thurstone (1938b) and his colleagues and students (e.g., Bechtoldt, 1947; Pemberton, 1952; Jeffrey, 1957) that helped to establish a series of visual perception abilities variously designated Space, Visualization, Spatial Relations, Spatial Orientation, Perceptual Speed, Speed of Visual Closure, and Flexibility of Visual Closure. It also considers numerous studies of visual perception abilities conducted under the direction of Guilford in the U. S. Air Force (Guilford & Lacey, 1947), or later at the University of Southern California (e.g., Hoffman, Guilford, Hoepfner, & Doherty, 1968). There are important studies of visual perception abilities that have been conducted abroad (e.g., Werdelin, 1958; Werdelin & Stjernberg, 1969), particularly on the possible roles of these abilities in mathematical learning and achievement. Finally, important recent studies involving spatial abilities that are considered here include one by Lansman, Donaldson, Hunt, and Yantis (1982) showing relations between abilities measured by paper-and-pencil methods and those measured in the experimental laboratory.

In many respects, this survey of visual perception abilities is a replication of an intensive reanalysis of selected correlational literature that was conducted by Lohman (1979a). As in the present study, Lohman used hierarchical factor-analytic procedures, but he also used several other procedures – in particular, multidimensional scaling and cluster analysis. Lohman's reanalyses were of the following datasets (specified in terms of the designations used in this volume): THUR21A (1938), HOLZ01 (1939), THUR41 (1944), THUR71 (1949), GUIL40 (1947), GUIL46 (1947), MICH51 (1950), MICH61 and MICH62 (1951), HOFF01 (1968), and HORN01 (1966). In most cases he made reanalyses of subsets of variables selected as being of particular relevance to spatial or visual perception abilities.

Lohman concluded:

Spatial ability may be defined as the ability to generate, retain, and manipulate abstract visual images. At the most basic level, spatial thinking requires the ability to encode, remember, transform, and match spatial stimuli. Factors like Closure Speed (i.e., speed of matching incomplete visual stimuli with their long term memory representations), Perceptual Speed (speed of matching visual stimuli), Visual Memory (short term memory for visual stimuli) and Kinesthetic (speed of making left-right discriminations) may represent individual differences in the speed or efficiency of these basic cognitive processes. However, these factors surface only when extremely similar tests are included in a test battery. Such tests and their factors consistently fall near the periphery of scaling representations, or at the bottom of a hierarchical model (Lohman, 1979a, pp. 126–127).

In Lohman's view, then, Closure Speed, Perceptual Speed, and Visual Memory are minor factors that do not represent what is usually meant by "spatial ability."

Lohman urged recognition of three basic spatial ability factors, which he described as follows:

1.   Spatial Relations. This factor is defined by tests like Cards, Flags, and Figures (Thurstone, 1938b). The factor appeared only when these or highly similar tests were included in the same test battery. Although mental rotation is the common element, the factor probably does not represent speed of mental rotation. Rather, it represents the ability to solve such problems quickly, by whatever means.

2.   Spatial Orientation. This factor appears to involve the ability to imagine how a stimulus array will appear from another perspective. In the true spatial orientation test, the subject must imagine that he is reoriented in space, and then make some judgment about the situation. There is often a left–right discrimination component in these tasks, but this discrimination must be made from the imagined perspective. However, the factor is difficult to measure since tests designed to tap it are often solved by mentally rotating the stimulus rather than by reorienting an imagined self.

3.   Visualization. The factor is represented by a wide variety of tests such as Paper Folding, Form Board, WAIS Block Design, Hidden Figures, Copying, etc. In addition to their spatial–figural content, the tests that load on this factor share two important features: (a) all are administered under relatively unspeeded conditions, and (b) most are much more complex than corresponding tests that load on the more peripheral factors. Tests designed to measure this factor usually fall near the center of a two-dimensional scaling representation, and are often quite close to tests of Spearman's g (such as Raven Matrices or Figure Classification) or Cattell's (1963) Gf (Lohman, 1979a, pp. 127–128).

Lohman's conclusions about visual perception abilities were further developed in a subsequent article (Lohman, Pellegrino, Alderton, & Regian, 1987), from which I have extracted a table (Table 8.1) that lists what Lohman et al. regarded as the major and minor factors of the visual perception domain, with specifications of typical tests that load on these factors. This table provides the initial framework around which the present chapter is organized, with certain exceptions:

1.   Following conventions established here and elsewhere, factor designations are given as composed of one or two capital letters (one of the letters sometimes being replaced by a digit or other symbol). In some cases, I have used factor designations different from those used by Lohman et al.

2.   The order in which the factors are considered is somewhat different, in that the factor SR (Spatial Relations) is taken up immediately after factor VZ (Visualization), because there are questions about the differentiation of these two factors. Further, factors CS (Closure Speed), CF (Flexibility of Closure), PI (Serial Perceptual Integration), and SS (Spatial Scanning) are taken up in close succession, leaving P (Perceptual Speed) to be considered subsequently.

3.   Factor Vm (Visual Memory) has already been considered in Chapter 7 (there designated MV).

4.   There appears to be insufficient evidence for factors SO (Spatial Orientation) and K (Kinesthetic) to permit consideration of them separately from other visual perception factors.

Table 8.1. *Major spatial factors (after Lohman et al., 1987, p. 264)*[a]

Factor label	Factor name	Tests that often define the factor	Chapter in Eliot & Smith (1983)
Vz or Gv	Visualization or General Visualization	Paper Folding, Paper Form Board, Surface Development, Block Design, Shepard–Metzler Mental Rotations, Mechanical Principles	6, 8, 9, 11
SO	Spatial Orientation	Aerial Orientation, Chair–Window Test	12
Cf	Flexibility of Closure	Embedded Figures Test	4
SR	Spatial Relations	Cards, Flags, Figures	7
Ss	Spatial Scanning	Maze Tracing, Choosing a Path	3
Ps	Perceptual Speed	Identical Forms	
SI	Serial Integration	Successive Perception III, Picture Identification (Seibert & Snow, 1965)	
Cs	Closure Speed	Street Gestalt, Harshman Figures, Close Ups (Hoffman et al., 1968)	5
Vm	Visual Memory	Memory for Designs	
K	Kinesthetic	Hands (Thurstone, 1938b)	

[a]Copyright © 1987 by Martinus Nijhoff Publishers, Dordrecht, Holland. Reprinted by permission of Kluwer Academic Publishers.

5. A number of other minor factors in the visual perception domain have turned up in the database and appear to be worthy of consideration.

Also, account must be taken of the evolution of the structuring of the visual perception domain in the work of French (1951) and the several kits of factor-referenced tests developed at Educational Testing Service (ETS) by French and his colleagues (French, Ekstrom, & Price, 1963; Ekstrom, French, & Harman, 1976; Ekstrom, 1979).

French (1951) listed nine separate factors that can be regarded as belonging in the domain of visual perception. They are listed here, with brief descriptions. Further details are given later in the chapter when the factors are considered individually. The designations and names offered by French are used here, but with indications of the names and designations employed later. The reader must keep in mind that French accepted the analyses and rotations of factors that appeared in published studies; he made no reanalyses, and no study he surveyed used hierarchical analysis. Many of the studies he surveyed extracted more factors than would be accepted by the more conservative criteria adopted for my reanalyses.

> *S: Space*: "...the ability to perceive spatial patterns accurately and to compare them with each other" (corresponds approximately to the factor that I recognize as VZ, Visualization).
>
> *SO: Spatial Orientation*: "ability to remain unconfused by the varying orientations in which a spatial pattern may be presented" (not recognized as a separate factor in my analysis).
>
> *Vi: Visualization*: "...probably the ability to comprehend imaginary movements in a 3-dimensional space or the ability to manipulate objects in imagination" (corresponds approximately to the factor that I recognize as SR, Spatial Rotation).
>
> *GP: Gestalt Perception*: "...the ability to combine disconnected, vague, visual stimuli into a meaningful whole" (corresponds approximately to the factor that I recognize as CS, Closure Speed, or Speed of Closure).
>
> *GF: Gestalt Flexibility*: "...the manipulation of two configurations simultaneously or in succession" (corresponds approximately to the factor that I recognize as CF, Closure Flexibility, or Flexibility of Closure).
>
> *P: Perceptual Speed*: "...characterized by the task of finding in a mass of distracting material a given configuration which is borne in mind during the search" (corresponds approximately to the factor that I recognize as P, Perceptual Speed).
>
> *LE: Length Estimation*: "...the ability to compare the length of lines or distances on a sheet of paper" (corresponds to my factor LE, Length Estimation).
>
> *PA: Perceptual Alternations*: "Rate of Alternations" (corresponds to my factor PN, Perceptual Alternations).
>
> *FI: Figure Illusions*: "...limited to the resistance to illusions involving geometrical patterns" (corresponds to my factor or factors IL, Perception of Illusions).

PROBLEMS IN IDENTIFYING VISUAL PERCEPTION FACTORS

It becomes evident from the above account that considerable confusion exists about the identification of factors in the domain of visual perception. Names and interpretations of factors are in many cases ambiguous or indeterminate. Tests do not always load consistently on distinct factors, or they load rather indiscriminately on a number of factors. To some extent, this confusion may be only apparent, due to the fact that tests with the same or similar names in different datasets are often actually not very similar either in their stimulus content or the tasks required of subjects. In my reanalyses, it has been necessary to pay diligent attention to the nature of the test tasks, without regard to the names that have been assigned to these tasks by investigators.

Some sources of confusion are very real, and difficult to deal with. This is particularly true of confusion arising from the fact that test takers apparently can arrive at answers and solutions – either correct or incorrect ones – by a variety of different strategies. French (1965) demonstrated that different "cognitive styles" can cause wide fluctuations in factor loadings; some of his most dramatic cases had to do with spatial tests, as where a sample of subjects who reported "systematizing" their approach to the Cubes test yielded a large decrease of the loading of this test on a Visualization factor (that is, decreased correlations of Cubes with other spatial tests), as compared to a sample where subjects did not report systematizing. It has been shown (Kyllonen, Lohman, & Woltz, 1984), that subjects can employ different strategies even for different items within the same test. Lohman et al. (1987) have discussed this problem of solution strategies, even rendering the judgment that factor-analytic methodology is hardly up to the task of dealing with it because a basic assumption of factor analysis is that factorial equations are consistent over subjects.

Another source of serious confusion lies in the alleged "speeded" or "nonspeeded" conditions under which spatial tests are administered. Speededness is a relative term; its meaning varies for different individuals or different samples of individuals. Every test offered as a marker test in the ETS kits has an assigned time-limit; knowing such a time-limit does not enable one to judge how "speeded" a test is. Lohman (1979a) was particularly critical of psychometricians' general neglect of the speed-power problem. There are relatively few datasets in our present database that permit a critical examination of this problem as it applies to the domain of visual perception.

Finally, difficulty in factorial classification arises from the fact that most spatial test tasks, even the "simplest," are actually quite complex, requiring apprehension and encoding of spatial forms, consideration and possibly mental manipulation of these forms, decisions about comparisons or other aspects of the stimuli, and making a response – often under the pressure of being required to respond quickly. It can be expected that it would be difficult to prepare test variables that would emphasize individual differences in any one of these processes while minimizing the effects of individual differences in other processes.

About 230 datasets in the corpus yielded one or more factors that were classified as belonging in the domain of visual perception, broadly defined. These factors were tentatively classified according to the framework established by Lohman et al. (1987) (as reproduced in Table 8.1), despite much difficulty in doing so because of questions that arose. In attempting to sharpen the definition of these factors, Table 8.2 was constructed, listing 94 datasets that yielded two or more factors in this domain. In this way distinctions between factors could be examined. The major classifications were assumed to be as follows (using factor names previously established in the literature):

> *VZ: Visualization.* This classification contained factors that had loadings on a wide variety of test variables that appeared to reflect processes of apprehending, encoding, and mentally manipulating spatial forms, except those factors whose salient loadings were limited, in the main, to those on relatively simple, speeded tests such as *Cards*, *Figures*, and *Flags*; these latter factors were classified under factor SR, following the guidelines suggested by Lohman et al. (1987).
>
> *SR: Spatial Relations.* Factors which had loadings, in general, only on relatively simple speeded tests such as *Cards*, *Figures*, and *Flags*.

CS: *Closure Speed.* Factors having their higher loadings on such tests as *Gestalt Completion, Concealed Words,* and *Mutilated Words* in which the tasks were mainly those of apprehending a spatial form (not specified to the examinee in advance) that was in some way disguised or obscured by a "noisy" or distracting context.

CF: *Closure Flexibility.* Factors having their higher salient loadings on such tests as *Hidden Figures, Hidden Patterns,* and *Copying,* in which the tasks were mainly those of searching a visual field to find a spatial form (specified to the examinee in advance) despite a distracting context.

P: *Perceptual Speed.* This classification contained factors having their higher salient loadings on such tests as *Finding A's, Number Comparison,* and *Identical Pictures,* in which the characteristic task could be either (1) searching a visual field for one or more specified spatial forms, without there being highly distracting or obscuring material, or (2) comparing two or more visual presentations for identity.

The table also provided for an "Other" classification to which a variety of factors regarded as belonging in the visual perception domain could be assigned.

It can be seen that there are relatively few datasets that yield examples of more than two of the major assumed factors VZ, SR, CS, CF, and P. Indeed, there is only one dataset (EKST11) that yields examples of all five of these factors, but the results in this dataset are somewhat problematic, as will be discussed.

Considering all factors pairwise, we first examine the seven datasets that show a contrast between factors VZ and SR. CARR85 is a very limited battery in which the wisdom of separating a factor VZ could be questioned. Factor 3 is a specific containing the covariance associated with two subscores of a Block Counting test in which subjects have to count blocks in pictured piles. The factor was assigned to VZ because it is thought that the major problem of the subject is to visualize and include in the count the blocks in the piles that are not immediately visible. In contrast, factor 2 has salient loadings on four simple spatial tests, Spatial Rotations, Flags, Hands, and Cubes, all administered without time limit. Its assignment to factor SR is at least problematical. Both factors have loadings on a second-order factor Gv (often coded 2V in the tables).

Factor 5 in dataset EKST11 was classified as VZ because it has loadings on a variety of relatively complex spatial tasks, including Form Board, Paper Folding, and Punched Holes (all markers of VZ from ETS kits), but also, with lower loadings, Hidden Figures and Concealed Figures, markers for factor CF. The latter two tests had moderate loadings on factor 9, classified as CF, but their presence on factor 5, VZ, is reasonable in view of their requirement that subjects apprehend spatial forms. Factors 3 and 4 in dataset EKST11 were both classified as SR, factor 3 having salient loadings on Cube Comparisons (from the 1963 ETS kit) and Cubes (from the 1954 ETS kit), and factor 4 having salient loadings on Card Rotations (from the 1963 ETS kit) and Cards (from the 1954 ETS kit). All these tests had been regarded as markers for factor SR, but in my reanalysis they showed up on two factors, each of which could be regarded as a specific attributable to unique features of the respective pairs of highly similar tests. All

Table 8.2. *Visual perception factors identified in selected datasets (specified by number in hierarchical matrix of Appendix B)*

Dataset	Factor					
	VZ	SR	CS	CF	P	Other
ADKI03	3	—	6	—	10	—
ANDR01	4	—	—	—	2	—
ANGL11	—	—	3	2	—	—
BECH01	—	7	10	11	4,9	—
BLAC21	3	—	—	—	—	1:Imagery Vividness
BLAK01	3	—	—	—	4	—
BOLT11	2	—	—	—	3	—
BOTZ01	3	—	8	9	—	—
BRAD01	7	—	4	—	—	—
BROW21	3	—	—	—	4	—
CARR85	3	2	—	—	—	—
COOM01	—	6	—	—	8	—
CORY01	—	—	8,9	—	5	—
CURE11	2	—	—	—	9	—
CURE12	7	—	—	—	4	—
EGAN01	3	—	—	—	2	—
EKST11	5	3,4	6	9	8	—
ELKO01	6	—	—	—	7	—
FEDE02	4	—	—	10	—	—
FLAN01	5	—	—	—	6	—
FLEI51	4	—	—	—	5	—
FRED01	1	—	—	2	—	—
FRED13	—	—	3	5	4	—
FREN11	9	—	—	—	6	—
FRUC21	4	—	—	—	6	—
FULG21	—	—	1	—	—	2:S3?
GOOD01	7	—	—	—	4	—
GUIL16	5	—	—	—	8	—
GUIL17	5	—	—	—	3	—
GUIL31	2	4	—	—	5	—
GUIL35	8	—	—	—	4	—
GUIL38	3	—	—	—	—	6:LE (length estimation)
GUIL39	3	2	—	—	5	—
GUIL40	—	5	—	—	3	7 & 8:LE?
GUIL46	3	—	—	—	7	8:IL (Illusions)
GUIL66	7	—	6	—	—	9:I0
GUST11A	13	4	10	3	—	12:CFR?
HAKS01	—	6	19	8	9	—
HARR51	—	4	—	—	8	—
HARR52	7	—	—	—	6	—
HARR53	—	—	5	—	3	—
HARR54	—	—	3	—	5	—
HOFF01	3	—	8	—	—	2:I0
JEFF11	2	5	7	—	—	—

Table 8.2 (*cont.*)

Dataset	Factor					
	VZ	SR	CS	CF	P	Other
LANS31	5	—	—	—	2, 3	—
LORD01	6	—	—	—	3	—
LUCA01	3	—	—	—	10	4:I0
LUMS01	3	—	7, 11	—	—	—
MESS01	—	—	3, 8	4	5	—
MICH51	2	—	—	—	3	—
MICH61	2	3	—	—	5	—
MICH62	2	—	—	—	5	—
MOON01	—	—	4, 5	—	—	—
MORR11	6	—	—	—	2	—
MURP01	2	—	—	—	3	—
OLSO51	5	—	8	—	—	7:PI (Perceptual Integration)
PATE01	8	—	—	—	6	—
PEMB01	—	2	4	6	—	—
PRIC01	2, 3	—	—	—	—	—
RIMO11	4	—	—	—	—	7:SS (Spatial Scanning)
ROFF11	5	—	3	—	—	2:PQ (Plotting); 4:MD (Movement Detection) 7:Directional Thinking 9:LE (Length Estimation)
SCHA11	—	4, 11	—	—	9, 12	6:I0
SEGE01	4	—	—	—	7	—
SEGE02	3	—	—	—	7	—
SHAY01	7	—	—	—	8	—
SHAY02	3	—	—	—	4	—
SIMR01	—	6, 7	—	—	3, 4	—
SING21	3	—	—	—	6	—
SLAT01	3	—	—	—	—	2:I0,5:I0.
SNOW11	3	—	2	—	6	—
SNOW12	6	—	—	—	5	—
SNOW20	1	—	—	—	—	5:PI
SNOW21	—	—	—	—	—	2:PI;4:I0
SPEA32	—	—	9	—	8	—
STAK01	—	13	—	—	3	—
STOR31	4	—	—	—	—	5:I0
STUM11	3	—	—	—	4	—
SUMI01	—	—	—	—	2	6:LE?
TAYL32	3	—	—	—	—	4:I0
TAYL51	—	—	7	—	5	2, 4, 6:IL
THUR11	—	—	—	—	3, 5	—
THUR21A	2	—	—	—	4	—
THUR31	—	3	—	—	4, 6	—

Table 8.2 (*cont.*)

Dataset	Factor					
	VZ	SR	CS	CF	P	Other
THUR41	2	—	7	—	5	4:IL;8:S3
THUR71	9	3	7	2	—	10:S0?
THUR81	—	13	—	—	9	14:SS?
THUR82	—	10	—	—	9	—
UNDH01	3, 4	11	7	—	—	—
WALS21	3	—	2	—	—	—
WERD51	5	—	—	—	3	—
WHEA01	—	—	4	3	—	—
WITT11	—	5	—	—	3	—
WOTH01	—	13	10	—	6	—
YELA21	3	—	—	—	2	—

tests having loadings on factors 3, 4, and 5 had substantial loadings on a second order factor regarded as Gv.

In dataset GUIL31, there was a large factor 2 interpreted as VZ, having its highest salient loadings on two parts of Spatial Visualization [see Eliot & Smith, 1983, test 265, p. 288] which requires subjects to figure out how an alarm clock shown in its original position will look after being rotated one or more times in indicated directions in three dimensions. Much of the variance in these variables was absorbed into a second-order factor. The contrasting factor was factor 4, tentatively interpreted as factor SR because it had salient loadings on two tests (Instrument Comprehension and Planning Air Maneuvers) requiring subjects to visualize and indicate aircraft positions in three-dimensional space. A further loading on this factor was for a psychomotor test called Complex Coordination, described as follows:

...a serial, choice-reaction-time test in which each stimulus is one of 13 spatial patterns of 3 lights each. In systematic correspondence with each stimulus pattern, the correct response is a unique adjustment of imitation stick-and-rudder controls. Each correct reaction automatically brings a new stimulus. The score is the number of reactions completed in 8 minutes (Guilford & Lacey, 1947, p. 122).

We have here some evidence for a differentiation between factors VZ and SR, except that the SR factor in this dataset does not have tests characteristic of those for SR in other datasets (such tests not being present in the battery). It is possible that factor SR in this dataset emphasizes speed in arriving at decisions about simple spatial orientation problems. In contrast, factor 2, VZ, involves much more complicated spatial problems, and in fact some of its loadings are for variables that tend to tap reasoning ability (Spatial Reasoning, Figure Analogies).

In dataset GUST11A, there is a distinct contrast between factors interpreted as VZ and SR. Factor 13, VZ, has loadings on scores on odd and even items of a Metal Folding test that is probably similar to the Surface Development test that is a marker for VZ in ETS kits. Factor 4, SR, has loadings on Parts I and II of a Card Rotation test that is probably similar to the Card Rotation test in the 1963 ETS kit. Unfortunately, these factors could be regarded as specifics arising because of the high similarity of the respective pairs of variables. In my reanalysis, factor 13 (VZ) has only very weak loadings on a second-order GV factor; it has higher loadings on a second-order factor regarded as Gf (fluid intelligence). Factor 4 has somewhat higher loadings on the second-order factor GV.

Perhaps the best evidence for a differentiation between VZ and SR comes from dataset JEFF11, in which each of these factors has salient loadings on a fair variety of tests. For factor 2, VZ, salient loadings are for several form board and designs tests that probably involve complex problems in fitting and manipulating shapes, whereas for factor 5, SR, the salient loadings are for a variety of tests involving simple decisions about form rotations, forms turned over, and directions in which bolts must be turned.

Possible evidence for a differentiation between VZ and SR comes also from dataset MICH61, a study involving Grade 12 boys. Factor 2, interpreted as VZ, had loadings on a variety of tests (General Reasoning, Punched Holes, Form Board, and Spatial Visualization) that were, according to the author's plan, given under "power" conditions. In contrast, the highest loadings on factor 3, interpreted as SR, were for tests given under "speed" conditions (Spatial Orientation and a summation of scores on Flags, Cards, and Figures). This differentiation occurs despite the fact that some tests elsewhere considered as SR tests had their highest loadings on factor VZ. It should be noted, however, that much of the variance in tests of factor VZ was absorbed into a second-order general factor, so that the orthogonal loadings are relatively low. Also, the highest loading on factor 2 was for a General Reasoning test. Further, in contrast to its author's analysis, my reanalysis of dataset MICH62, involving Grade 12 girls given the same tests as the boys, failed to disclose separate VZ and SR factors; it yielded only a single factor, interpreted as VZ, that had salient loadings on nearly all the tests that yielded two factors for the male sample.

In dataset THUR71, VZ is represented only by two tests, Cubes and Surface Development, both requiring fairly complex spatial manipulation, while SR is represented by several simple speeded tests – Figures, Cards, and Reversals and Rotations.

Evidence from dataset UNDH01 for a differentiation between VZ and SR is complicated by the fact that it yielded *two* factors that were interpreted as VZ: one (Factor 3) with salient loadings on Paper Form Board ("indicate what pieces can be put together to make a certain figure") and Figure Classification ("assign each given figure to one of five classes, each defined by three examples"), and the other (Factor 4) with salient loadings on Punched Holes (imagining the folding and unfolding of pieces of paper), Block Design (from the WISC), and Block

Counting ("counting the number of blocks in a pile pictured"). The factor interpreted as SR (factor 11) had salient loadings only on Card Rotations ("indicate whether the same face of a figure is showing; each figure appears in eight different positions which are to be compared with a standard figure to the left") and Flag Rotations ("indicating whether the same face of the flag is showing. Two flags are to be compared"). We have insufficient information to judge the reasons for the presence of two factors interpreted as VZ in my analysis. Possibly the factors differed in the speededness of their tests; it is also to be noted that factor 3 involves two-dimensional representations whereas factor 4 has to do with three-dimensional representations.

On balance, the evidence from these datasets for a differentiation between factor VZ and factor SR is only suggestive. One gets the feeling that, as Lohman et al. (1987) have noted, the difference consists in the fact that tests of factor VZ emphasize power in solving increasingly difficult problems involving spatial forms, whereas tests of factor SR emphasize speed in solving relatively simple spatial analysis problems. This differentiation is not always clear, however. The matter needs to be investigated further using specially designed tests in which task difficulty and speed aspects are carefully controlled (but see Egan, 1978; Lohman, 1979b; Pellegrino, Alderton, & Shute, 1984).

Pairwise distinctions between VZ and CS, CF, and P, respectively, are well supported, there being at least six or seven datasets in which clear differentiation occurs.

The same can be said for pairwise distinctions between SR and CS, CF, and P. Given that SR, CS, CF, and P are all concerned with speed of performance, it appears that these factors have to do with speeds of different processes. SR concerns speed in simple decisions concerning turning over and rotating spatial forms; CS concerns speed in arriving at the apprehension of a single spatial form that is disguised or obscured in a visual presentation; CF concerns speed in disembedding a known form that is disguised by "geometrical camouflaging"; and P concerns searching visual presentations for comparisons with a given form. (Further discussion of these factor interpretations is to be found below where the evidence for each factor is presented in detail.)

Factor CS is distinguished from factor CF in 11 datasets, and from factor P in a different series of 11 datasets. Factor CF, found in only 13 datasets, is distinguished from factor P in only five of these, but the distinctions are clear in each case; in the remainder, there was little opportunity for P to appear because of the design of the respective test batteries.

We now turn to a detailed discussion of the first-order factors that can be identified in the domain of visual perception.

VISUALIZATION (VZ) FACTORS

French (1951) regarded the existence of a visualization factor as "certain, although its exact nature is not clear." He described it as "probably the ability to comprehend imaginary movements in a 3-dimensional space or the ability to manipulate objects in imagination." Continuing, he remarked that a proof of the separate existence of the factor is afforded by "Analysis AFN" – which is our dataset GUIL40, in reanalysis of which we find only a single spatial ability factor, here identified as SR. Among the tests he mentioned as having high loadings on this factor in some 16 datasets are Spatial Visualization (select drawing of alarm clock moved as described; see Eliot & Smith, 1983, test 265, p. 288), Punched Holes (indicate position of holes in paper folded and punched, see Eliot & Smith, test 312, p. 337), and Form Board (draw lines showing how pieces fit into an outline; see Eliot & Smith, test 127, p. 149).

The factor is represented in the 1963 ETS factor kit as factor Vz (Visualization), defined as "the ability to manipulate or transform the image of spatial patterns into other visual arrangements." The kit manual notes that "Visualization tests are given under relatively unspeeded conditions, whereas Spatial Orientation tests are speeded." It offers as marker tests:

> Vz-1, Form Board Test: "Each item presents 5 shaded drawings of pieces some or all of which can be put together to form a figure presented in outline form. The task is to indicate which of the pieces when fitted together would form the outline." (See Eliot & Smith, 1983, test 127, p. 149).
>
> Vz-2, Paper Folding Test (suggested by Thurstone's Punched Holes): "For each item successive drawings illustrate two or three folds made in a square sheet of paper. A drawing of the folded paper shows where a hole is punched in it. The subject selects one of 5 drawings to show how the sheet would appear when fully opened." (Essentially the same as test 312, Eliot & Smith, 1983, p. 337.)
>
> Vz-3, Surface Development Test (adapted from Thurstone's Surface Development): "In this test, drawings are presented of solid forms that could be made with paper or sheet metal. With each drawing there is a diagram showing how a piece of paper might be cut and folded so as to make the solid form. Dotted lines show where the paper is folded. One part of the diagram is marked to correspond to a marked surface in the drawing. The subject is to indicate which lettered edges in the drawing correspond to numbered edges or dotted lines in the diagram." (See Eliot & Smith, 1983, test 315, p. 341.)

These same tests are indicated as markers for factor VZ (Visualization) in the 1976 ETS kit.

Table 8.3 lists 147 token factors, in 144 datasets, that have been interpreted as very likely measuring the factor here designated VZ, Visualization. As noted previously, the Visualization factor is one of the factors most frequently found in factorial investigations.

The table arranges the datasets in order of approximate mean age of sample. A visualization factor can be measured at a wide range of ages. One dataset, RICH33, is for a sample of infants aged 18 months. Factor 2 in that dataset would seem to indicate a kind of spatial ability measurable at that age, to judge from the names of the variables with high loadings: Formboard/Shown; Formboard/Circle. (For descriptions of these variables, see Gesell, 1925, pp. 120–122.) Several

Table 8.3. *147 Visualization (VZ) factors in 144 datasets arranged in order of approximate mean age of sample*[a]

Dataset	Date	C'y code	Age	Sample code	M/F code	Factor no.	Remarks (higher-order factors; others related)
RICH33	'39	U	1	N	3	3	1:2G
PARA01	'69	U	3	1	3	4	1:2C
PARA02	'69	U	4	1	3	4	1:2C;3:CS?
WIEB11	'80	U	4	O	1	2	1:2G
PARA03	'69	U	5	1	3	2	1:2C
REYN11	'79	U	5	1	3	3	1:2G
HUEF01	'67	U	6	6	3	3	Orthogonal Factors
PARA04	'69	U	6	1	3	2	1:2C
TAYL32	'75	C	6	1	3	3	1:2G;4:I0
WOOD13	'77	U	6	1	3	6	4:2F
KEIT21	'87	U	8	7	3	7	1:3G;6:21
PARA06	'69	U	8	1	3	3	1:2C
SCHI11	'34	U	8	1	1	4	1:2G
SCHI12	'34	U	8	1	2	4	1:2G
VALT11	'81	G	8	1	3	2	1:2G
VALT12	'81	G	8	1	3	5	1:2G
GARR11	'35	U	9	6	1	4	1:2G;2:I0
GARR12	'35	U	9	6	2	2	1:2G
JARM31	'77	C	9	6	1	2	1:2G
JONE32	'49	U	9	1	3	7	1:2D
NAGL01	'87	U	9	Z	3	3	1:2G
NAGL02	'87	U	9	W	3	2	1:2G
NAGL03	'87	U	9	6	3	2	1:2G
SING21	'65	U	9	1	3	3	1:2G;6:P?
UNDH01	'76	O	9	1	3	3	1:2H;4:VZ?;6:CS;10:20;11:SR
"	"	"	"	"	"	4	An alternate VZ factor?
BROW21	'33	E	10	6	1	3	1:2G;4:P?
HARR52	'73	U	10	1	2	7	1:2G;6:P
MOUR01	'52	E	10	6	1	7	1:3G;5:2S?
PROG01	'73	U	10	J	1	4	1:2G
RAND01	'79	C	10	6	1	4	1:2G
RAND02	'79	C	10	6	2	4	1:2G
THOM11	'41	D	10	1	1	2	1:2V;3:S4
THOM12	'41	D	10	1	2	2	1:2V;3:S4
WALL01	'65	U	10	6	3	4	Orthogonal Factors
WILL11	'75	C	10	*	1	4	1:2G
WOOD15	'77	U	10	1	3	6	5:2F
WRIG01	'39	U	10	1	3	4	1:2G
GUST11A	'84	S	11	1	3	13	1:3G;2:2V;3:CF;4:SR;10:CS; 11:2F;12:CFR
HIGG01	'78	A	11	1	3	3	1:2G?
JONE33	'49	U	11	1	3	5	1:2D;4:S + I?
RIMO11	'48	U	11	1	3	4	1:3G;2:2F;5:20;7:SO?
SATT01	'79	E	11	6	3	2	1:2G;4:CF?
UNDH11	'78	O	11	6	3	6	1:2G

Table 8.3 (*cont.*)

Dataset	Date	C'y code	Age	Sample code	M/F code	Factor no.	Remarks (higher-order factors; others related)
WERD51	'71	S	11	6	3	5	1:2G;3:P
ELKO01	'35	E	12	6	1	6	1:2G;7:P?
GARR13	'35	U	12	6	1	2	1:2G
HOLZ01	'39	U	12	6	3	3	1:2G
VANH01	'75	U	12	R	3	4	1:2G
JONE34	'49	U	13	1	3	4	1:2G;3:I0
PATE01	'30	U	13	6	1	8	1:2G;6:P?
SWIN11	'48	U	13	6	3	4	1:2G
DUPO01	'75	W	14	6	3	5	1:2G
HISK03	'66	U	14	E	3	2	1:2G
MURP01	'36	U	14	6	1	2	1:2G;3:P?
OLSO51	'66	U	14	E	3	5	8:CS?
SHAY01	'67	U	14	1	1	7	1:2G;8:P
SHAY02	'67	U	14	1	2	3	1:3G;2:2V;4:P
STOR11	'66	U	14	8	3	11	1:2G;3:CF?(XF?)
STOR12	'66	U	14	I	3	5	1:3G;2:2H
STOR13	'66	U	14	7	3	4	1:2G;5:I0?
WERD01	'58	S	14	6	1	4	1:2G
WERD02	'58	S	14	6	1	5	1:2G
CARR85	'87	U	15	6	3	3	1:2V;2:SR
GARR15	'35	U	15	6	1	4	1:2G
REMO01	'62	Y	15	6	1	3	1:2G
SEGE01	'57	U	15	1	1	4	1:3G;2:2H;6:2S;7:P
SEGE02	'57	U	15	1	2	3	1:3G;2:2H;6:2S;7:P
WEIS11	'55	U	15	M	3	13	1:3G;8:2F
WRIG21	'58	E	15	8	1	3	1:2G
BLAK01	'41	U	16	6	3	3	—
BRAD01	'69	U	16	1	3	7	3:MV;6:GV
BURN11	'80	U	16	6	3	4	1:2G
CURE11	'68	U	16	6	1	2	1:2G;9:P
CURE12	'68	U	16	6	2	7	1:2C;4:P;6:21
HEND11A	'82	E	16	6	2	3	1:3G;2:2V
JEFF11	'57	U	16	$	3	2	1:21;5:SR;7:CS
SNOW11	'77	U	16	1	3	3	1:2G;2:CS;6:P
SUNG01	'81	U	16	Z	3	6	1:2G;5:2V
SUNG02	'81	U	16	#	3	4	1:3G;2:2H
SUNG03	'81	U	16	W	3	9	1:3G;8:2V
SUNG04	'81	U	16	1	1	4	1:3G;2:2H
SUNG05	'81	U	16	1	2	4	1:3G;2:2N
THUR71	'49	U	16	$	1	9	1:2G;2:CF;3:SR;7:CS
FLAN01	'64	U	17	1	1	5	1:2G;6:P
MICH61	'51	U	17	6	1	2	1:2G;3:SR;5:P
MICH62	'51	U	17	6	2	2	1:2G;5:P
WOLI01	'65	U	17	1	1	7	1:2G
WOOD17	'77	U	17	1	3	7	5:2F
FREN11	'57	U	18	3	1	9	1:2S;6:P;8:2H

Table 8.3 (*cont.*)

Dataset	Date	C'y code	Age	Sample code	M/F code	Factor no.	Remarks (higher-order factors; others related)
GOOD01	'43	U	18	A	1	7	1:2G;4:P
LANS31	'82	U	18	6	3	5	1:2S;2:P;3:P
LORD01	'56	U	18	3	1	6	3:P;5:2G
MORR11	'41	U	18	P	1	6	1:2G;2:P
SAUN03	'59	U	18	6	1	2	1:2G;3:I0
SLAT01	'40	E	18	A	1	3	1:2V;2:S?;4:2C;5:LE?
STUM11	'74	G	18	6	1	3	1:2G;4:P?
ADKI03	'52	U	19	2	1	3	1:2H;6:CS;10:P?
BARR00	'53	A	19	6	3	3	1:21;2:S?
BLAC21	'80	U	19	P	2	3	1:Image Vividness (Orthog.)
BOLT11	'73	U	19	E	3	2	3:P?;8:S?
BOTZ01	'51	U	19	6	1	3	1:2G;8:CS;9:CF?
EKST11	'67	U	19	6	2	5	1:3G;2:2V;3:SR?;4:SR?;6:CS; 7:2S;8:P;9:CF
FLEI51	'71	U	19	2	1	4	1:2G;5:P
FRED01	'65	U	19	6	3	1	2:CF? All orthogonal
LUMS01	'65	A	19	P	3	3	1:2F;7:CS?;8:2C;11:CS?
PARK01	'60	U	19	T	1	3	1:2G;6:P?
SNOW12	'77	U	19	6	3	6	1:2G;5:P
THUR21A	'38	U	19	6	3	2	1:2F;4:P
THUR41	'44	U	19	6	3	2	1:2G;4:IL;5:CS;7:I0
VERY01	'67	U	19	6	1	3	1:2H
VERY02	'67	U	19	6	2	4	1:2G
VERY03	'67	U	19	6	3	2	1:2F
WALS21	'78	C	19	6	3	3	1:2G
YELA21	'68	P	19	3	1	3	1:2G
SMIT01	'33	U	20	P	1	4	1:2G
EGAN01	'78	U	21	3	1	3	1:2G;2:Lat.Spd;4:P?
FEDE02	'80	U	21	2	3	4	1:2F;10:CF?
FRUC21	'52	U	21	2	1	4	1:2G;6:P
GUIL16	'51	U	21	3	1	5	1:3G;2:2H;7:2V;8:P
GUIL17	'52	U	21	3	1	5	1:2G;3:P
GUIL31	'47	U	21	3	1	2	1:2G;4:SR
GUIL35	'47	U	21	3	1	8	1:2G;4:P
GUIL36	'47	U	21	3	1	3	1:2G
GUIL38	'47	U	21	3	1	3	1:2G
GUIL39	'47	U	21	3	1	3	1:2G;2:SR;5:P
GUIL46	'47	U	21	3	1	3	1:2G;4:SO?;7:P;8:IL
GUIL66	'52	U	21	3	1	7	1:2G;6:CS?;9:I0
HOFF01	'68	U	21	B	3	2	1:2V;8:CFU
"	"	"	"	"	"	3	Alternate VZ?
LUCA01	'53	U	21	3	1	3	1:2H;7:2S;10:P
PRIC01	'40	E	21	6	1	2	1:2V;3:VZ?
"	"	"	"	"	"	3	VZ?
ROFF11	'52	U	21	3	1	5	1:2G;2:I0;3:CS;4:MD;9:LE
VERN51	'47	E	21	2	1	6	5:2F

Table 8.3 (*cont.*)

Dataset	Date	C'y code	Age	Sample code	M/F code	Factor no.	Remarks (higher-order factors; others related)
MICH51	'50	U	22	6	1	2	1:2G;3:P
GUIL18	'53	U	23	3	1	6	1:2G
SPRA11	'66	U	27	R	3	4	1:2G
HORN01	'66	U	28	Q	3	2	1:2G. 11:actually GV.
ANDR01	'37	U	30	C	2	4	1:2V;2:P;3:P?
HARR01	'40	U	30	5	1	8	6:2H
HORN21	'78	U	30	Q	1	11	9:2G. 11:actually GV.
VERS02	'81	K	30	U	2	2	1:2S
VERS03	'81	K	30	Z	1	3	1:2S
WILL12	'75	C	30	Y	3	3	1:2G
WOOD18	'77	U	30	1	3	7	5:2F
SCHU00	'62	U	40	4	3	4	1:2G

[a]See Appendix A for codes. In a few cases, classifications of factors shown here were preliminary and may not agree with the final classifications shown in the tables of Appendix B.

datasets involving the Illinois Test of Psycholinguistic Abilities (PARA01, PARA02, PARA03, PARA04, PARA06) disclose what would appear to be a visual perception factor measurable at ages 3 to 8. Dataset SCHU00 is for a sample of aphasics with estimated average age 40, and discloses a Visualization factor with loadings on individual performance tests such as Copy Greek Letters, Match Geometric Forms, Draw Man, and Assemble Manikin Head.

There were three datasets (UNDH01, HOFF01, and PRIC01) in which two alternate VZ factors appeared to emerge. I have already commented on the difficulty of interpreting any difference between factors 3 and 4 in dataset UNDH01, because of lack of complete information about the complexity and speededness of the tests. Factor 3 in dataset HOFF01 is a clear example of a VZ factor, with a variety of spatial ability tests loaded on it. The assignment of factor 2 to VZ is somewhat questionable, however, since only one variable (Block Rotation) is normally a test of VZ, and here it has no loading on factor 3. Because of the low salient loadings of all three variables, it is possibly a statistical artifact. In dataset PRIC01, factor 2 has its two highest loadings on tests called Cylinder Construction (a performance test requiring assembly of pieces to make a solid wooden cylinder in a rack ready for the purpose) and Shape Completion (a paper-and-pencil test requiring the subject to select a shape that completes one shape to make another). Factor 3 has its two highest loadings on tests called Fitting Shapes (essentially a paper form board test: "draw lines to show how the right-hand figure should be cut to give the shapes on the left") and Pool Image ("imagine the blank squares to represent pools of still water, and draw in each what you think would be the reflection of the figure above it"). Factor 2 seems to emphasize the construction of figures or solid objects, while factor 3 seems to emphasize ability to manipulate representations of shapes by drawing lines. The battery was too limited, and the information supplied about time limits, etc., was not sufficient to permit any further interpretations. It is possible that my criteria for extracting factors permitted too many factors. Since these factors do not seem to be replicated elsewhere, I conclude that their separation is probably an artifact.

At least two of the datasets (HORN01 and HORN21) were deliberately designed to yield, at the first-order of analysis, a factor that would otherwise be regarded as a second-order general visual perception factor GV, or what the author interpreted as Broad Visualization. Factor 2 in dataset HORN01 thus had loadings on measures of five possible first-order factors: Visualization (VZ), Spatial Orientation (here designated SR), Flexibility of Closure (CF), Adaptive Flexibility (here designated FX; see Chapter 10), and Speed of Closure (CS). Scores on each factor were determined by summing scores from one or more tests.

It is possible that some of the factors designated VZ in other datasets actually had more the character of a second-order GV factor, because the design of the datasets did not permit more first-order factors to emerge. This may be true, for example, of factor 2 in dataset JARM31, loaded with Memory for Designs, Figure Copying, Raven Matrices, and an Auditory-Visual Matching task, all designed to measure what Jarman and Das (1977) regarded as "simultaneous synthesis," a concept derived from Luria's (1973) theories of brain function (see Das, Kirby, & Jarman, 1975). The second-order visual perception factor GV could be interpreted as embodied in the concept of simultaneous synthesis.

Tests of the VZ factor

It would be possible to construct a list of the some 800 variables that have salient loadings on the VZ factor in our datasets. Exercising some selectivity, I have attempted to categorize those variables that tend to have the highest salient loadings, making some use of the categories identified in Eliot and Smith's (1983) compilation of spatial tests.

The most characteristic tests of VZ fall into six of Eliot and Smith's categories, namely 4: Paper Formboard Tasks, 6: Block Tasks, 7: Block Rotation Tasks, 8: Paper Folding Tasks, 9: Surface Development Tasks; and 10: Perspective Tasks. It is necessary to expand some of these categories to include tasks from performance tests (which Eliot & Smith did not consider), and to add a category for tasks involving mechanical movements and mechanical principles. All these categories, with the possible exception of 4: Paper Formboard Tasks, can and generally do involve spatial thinking in three dimensions, but there is no firm evidence for a factorial distinction between two- and three-dimensional tasks. People who are good in doing tasks in two-dimensional space tend to be equally good with tasks in three-dimensional space.

Paper Formboard and Assembly Tasks: "Subjects combine imaginatively the various parts of a figure to complete a whole figure" (Eliot & Smith, 1983, p. 147). Variables designated Form Board or Paper Formboard occur in numerous datasets, for example, GARR11, MICH62, EKST11, RIMO11, WERD01, PATE01, and UNDH01. Similar tasks, however, occur under other names: Fitting Shapes, in BARR00, BROW21, and PRIC01; Block Assembly, in LUCA01; Rosenstein Disc, in JEFF11; and Shape Assembly, in SUNG01. Various performance tasks belong in this category, since they all require putting together pieces (either in two or in three dimensions) to form a designated shape: from the Wechsler performance scales, Block Design and Object Assembly (in datasets HEND11A, PROG01, KEIT21, NAGL01); the Stenquist assembly task (dataset PATE01); and a Cylinder Construction task (dataset PRIC01).

Block Tasks. Most of these are named Block Counting, and take either of two basic forms: (1) the subject has to count the blocks in a pictured pile, assuming all blocks have the same shape, and (2) the subject is asked to count how many blocks *touch* indicated blocks in a pile. Either a free response or a multiple-choice format is used, most often the former. Good performance on such tasks requires the subject to comprehend, presumably by visualization, the interior structure of the block pile, i.e., recognizing how the blocks are laid out in the interior of the pile, recognizing what blocks support others, and realizing what blocks must be present but are not seen in the depiction of the pile. Examples are seen in datasets CARR85, UNDH01, FREN11, JONE33, and YELA21. Included in this category are also tasks that involve recognizing the shape of a section that could be cut through a solid figure; examples are Intersections, in LORD01, and possibly Solid Blocks, in BOTZ01 (a detailed description of the task is not readily available).

Block Rotation Tasks: "Subjects indicate which block, when turned or rotated imaginatively, is the same as a given block or object" (Eliot & Smith, 1983, p. 288). Strictly speaking, not all the stimulus objects are blocks; they can be analogs of blocks. For example, the pictured stimulus objects in a test called Spatial Visualization are spherical alarm clocks that are to be turned in different directions; this test is found in a number of datasets, e.g., GUIL31, GUIL46, HOFF01, and MICH51. But the category is well exemplified by the Cubes or Cube Comparison tests offered in the ETS factor kits. The three visible faces of two cubes with distinctive markings are shown, and the subject has to determine whether the cubes could be the same ones after rotation; see datasets FRED01, MICH62, and VERY03. Other tests represented here are Briques and Figures Complementaires (DUPO01) which probably are French adaptations of Bricks (Eliot & Smith, 1983, test 282) and Complementary Pieces (test 279). A task originally devised by Shepard and Metzler (1971) has received some attention in factorial studies; it is listed by Eliot & Smith (1983) as tests 298–300, and it appears in dataset LANS31 under the name Mental Rotations (in the form of several scores, both from a paper-and-pencil version of the test and from a computerized laboratory-presented form). Note that block rotation tasks are likely to appear on factor SR when they are simple and highly speeded.

Paper Folding Tasks. "Subjects are given drawings which illustrate successive foldings of a piece of paper. The final drawing has a mark or hole in a specified place. Subjects predict mark or hole pattern of unfolded paper" (Eliot & Smith, 1983, p. 326). This test occurs in numerous datasets either under the name Paper Folding (e.g., in datasets BRAD01, EKST11, HORN21, SNOW11) or the name Punched Holes (EKST11, GUIL16, GUIL17, HARR01, MICH51, SWIN11, WEIS11). Interestingly but confusingly, it also occurs under the name Spatial Visualization CP535 in several USAF datasets (e.g., ROFF11, variable 40) in a form in which the directions for paper folding in each item are given orally, presumably to force the examinee to visualize the process (see Eliot & Smith, 1983, test 305, misidentified as CP108A because of a printing error in the source).

Surface Development Tasks. "Subjects imagine how a pattern can be rolled or abstracted from a given [three-dimensional] figure" (Eliot & Smith, 1983, p. 341). Highly similar tasks occur under several names in a variety of datasets: Surface Development (datasets ADKI03, BLAC21, FRED01, LUCA01, SNOW11, UNDH21, YELA21); Pattern Comprehension (PARK01, ROFF11); Visualization in Three Dimensions (CURE11, FLAN01, SHAY01); Spatial Relations (SEGE02); and Metal Folding (GUST11A; "find the three-dimensional object which corresponds to a two-dimensional drawing").

Perspective Tasks: "Subjects align imaginatively two or more objects or reference points in drawing or picture in order to make judgments about viewpoints which differ from their own" (Eliot & Smith, 1983, p. 370). The most frequently found variable under this category is a test called Spatial Orientation, devised by Guilford and Zimmerman (1948) for their multifactor aptitude survey battery. (A number of quite different tests are found under the name Spatial Orientation.) The G–Z Spatial Orientation subtest (see Eliot & Smith, 1983, test 343) is one in which land and water scenery is shown as seen over the prow of a boat which moves slightly between two pictures; the examinee has to determine, by comparing the scenes and boat positions, how the boat has moved from the first picture to the second. This test has a high loading on factor VZ in several datasets (EGAN01, MICH51, VERY03). Another test named Spatial Orientation, CP503B (Eliot & Smith, 1983, test 346) has a high loading in VZ in dataset GUIL18; here, the subject is to locate on a map the area that is shown in an enlarged aerial photograph. It is not clear, in any of these tests, that subjects must necessarily consider a scene from a perspective different from their own.

Mechanical Movement Tasks. This category was not recognized by Eliot and Smith (1983), but such tasks frequently appear to involve factor VZ to an important extent. Typically these tasks depict mechanical objects such as geartrains and simple machines; the subject has to comprehend, and make decisions about, the movements, operations, and processes of these machines. Names of tests and datasets in which they occur are as follows:

> Mechanical Comprehension (FEDE02, VERN51)
> Mechanical Movements (ROFF11)
> Mechanical Principles (GUIL18, GUIL46, GUIL66)
> Mechanical Reasoning (FLAN01, SHAY01)

The tests frequently have secondary loadings on factor MK (Mechanical Knowledge), a fact that can indicate either or both of two possibilities: that individuals with experience with mechanical objects tend to have an advantage on these tests, or that individuals with high VZ ability are more likely to acquire and profit from experience with mechanical objects. The fact that they have high loadings on VZ, however, suggests that regardless of an individual's experience with mechanical objects, they tap a basic ability in spatial visualization.

Other Tasks Involving Spatial Visualization. High salient loadings on VZ are occasionally found for various other tests, mainly those placed in Eliot and Smith's Category 5: Figural Rotation Tasks, such as Flags, Cards, and Figures. Generally this is true only in datasets that did not yield a separate SR (Spatial Rotations) factor, because of the design of those datasets and/or our criteria for the number of factors to be extracted. Because I continue to entertain the possibility that there is a distinct SR factor, these tests will be described in the discussion of that factor. It is obvious, however, that performance on these tests depends at least to some extent on the process of spatial apprehension entailed in factor VZ.

Summary. In all these tests having salient loadings on factor VZ, it seems that the subject's task is to apprehend a spatial form, shape, or scene in order to match it with another spatial form, shape, or scene, often with the necessity of rotating it in two or three dimensions one or more times. The tasks can vary in difficulty; high scorers are those who can accurately handle the more difficult problems. Generally the tests are given under a fairly liberal time limit so that the individual's level of mastery, in terms of difficulty level that can be accurately handled, can be ascertained. Nevertheless, throughout the history of investigation of spatial ability, the speed/power aspects of spatial ability have rarely been properly controlled. Only in the case of a study like that of Egan (1978) has this problem been adequately addressed. Egan demonstrated the possibility of recasting spatial ability tests into better formats for measuring separate speed and accuracy aspects. Lohman (1979b) has proposed and illustrated a method of handling the additional complications introduced by variations in task complexity, together with speed and level.

It is difficult to make any simple statement about which kinds of tests (in the above categories) are likely to be the best and purest measures of factor VZ. Tests from any one of the categories (except possibly that concerned with mechanical processes) have been found to have high salient loadings in at least some datasets. In future research, however, it would be critical to insure that the scores depend as much as possible on level of difficulty that can be mastered and as little as possible on speed of performance.

SPATIAL RELATIONS (SR) FACTORS

The factor I call Spatial Relations was called Spatial Orientation by French (1951). It is not clear why he regarded it as distinct from what he called a Space factor. Tests he listed as having high loadings on it included Hands, Flags, Figures, Cards, Block Counting, and Punched Holes, but he mentioned these tests also in connection with his Space factor. The 1963 ETS kit of factor-referenced tests used the name Spatial Orientation and described it as "the ability to perceive spatial patterns or to maintain orientation with respect to objects in space." Three tests were suggested as markers for it (in all cases, quotations are from French, Ekstrom, & Price, 1963):

> S-1, Card Rotations Test (suggested by Thurstone's Cards test): "Each item gives a drawing of a card cut into an irregular shape. To its right are six other drawings of the same card sometimes merely rotated by different amounts and sometimes turned over onto its other side. The subject indicates which ones show the card not turned over." (See Eliot & Smith, 1983, test 176, p. 198.)
>
> S-2, Cube Comparisons Test (adapted from Thurstone's Cubes): "Each item presents two drawings of a cube. Assuming no cube can have two faces alike, the subject is to indicate which items present drawings that can be of the same cube and which ones present drawings that cannot be of the same cube." (See Eliot & Smith, 1983, test 266, p. 290.)
>
> S-3, Spatial Orientation: "This is Part V of the *Guilford–Zimmerman Aptitude Survey*. Each item presents two pictures of water and land scenery as seen looking out over the prow of a motor boat which has moved slightly between pictures. The task is to select the one of five dot and dash pairings in which the dot represents the old position of the prow and the dash the new position. Changes include any combination of tilt and of vertical and horizontal movement. Speed conditions are used." (See Eliot & Smith, 1983, test 343, p. 370.)

The 1976 ETS kit offers only the Card Rotations Test and the Cube Comparisons Test as markers of this factor. The Spatial Orientation Test was apparently eliminated because it is too likely to contain variance from factor VZ.

Table 8.4 lists 31 token factors that have been at least tentatively assigned to factor SR (Spatial Relations), in 28 datasets. Because all factors in the domain of

Table. 8.4. *31 Spatial Relations (SR) factors in 28 datasets arranged in order of approximate mean age of sample*[a]

Dataset	Date	C'y code	Age	Sample code	M/F code	Factor no.	Remarks (higher-order factors; others related)
UNDH01	'76	O	9	1	3	11	1:2H;3&4:VZ?;7:CS;10:20
HARR51	'73	U	10	1	1	4	1:2G;8:P
GUST11A	'84	S	11	1	3	4	1:3G;2:2V;3:CF;10:CS;13:VZ
CATT01A	'63	U	12	6	3	7	6:21
STAK01	'61	U	12	1	3	13	3:P;12:20
THUR81	'41	U	13	6	3	13	1:3G;8:2S;9:P;12:2V;14:SO?
THUR82	'41	U	13	6	3	10	1:3G;8:2S;9:P
CARR85	'87	U	15	6	3	2	1:2V;3:VZ
SCHU11	'53	U	15	1	3	6	1:3G;5:21
ARNO01	'67	A	16	1	3	4	1:2G
JEFF11	'57	U	16	$	3	5	1:21;2:VZ;7:CS
SIMR01	'47	U	16	6	3	6	1:2G;3:P;4:P?
"	"	"	"	"	"	7	Alternate SR?
THUR71	'49	U	16	$	1	3	1:2G;2:CF;7:CS;9:VZ?
COOM01	'41	U	17	1	3	6	1:2G;8:P
MICH61	'51	U	17	6	1	3	1:2G;2:VZ;5:P
THUR31	'40	U	17	1	3	3	1:2G;4:P
BECH01	'47	U	19	6	3	7	1:2S;4:P?;9:P?
CHRI01	'58	U	19	2	1	9	1:3G;7:2V
EKST11	'67	U	19	6	2	3	1:3G;2:2V;4:SR?;5:VZ;6:CS; 7:2S;8:P;9:CF
"	"	"	"	"	"	4	Alternate SR factor?
SCHA11	'40	U	19	6	1	4	1:3G;2:2H;6:I0;8:2S;9:P?; 11:SR?;12:P?
"	'	"	"	"	"	11	Alternate SR?
EGAN01	'78	U	21	3	1	2	1:2V;3:VZ
GUIL31	'47	U	21	3	1	4	1:2G;2:VZ;5:P
GUIL39	'47	U	21	3	1	2	1:2G;3:VZ;5:P
GUIL40	'47	U	21	3	1	5	1:2G;3:P;6&7:LE?
WITT11	'43	U	21	2	1	5	1:2G;3:P
WOTH01	'90	U	21	1	3	13	1:3G;10:CS;12:2V
PEMB01	'52	U	22	6	3	2	1:2G;4:CS;6:CF
HAKS01	'74	C	24	1	3	6	1:3G;5:21;8:CF;9:P;19:CS

[a]See Appendix A for codes. In a few cases, classifications of factors shown here were preliminary and may not agree with the final classifications shown in the tables of Appendix B.

visual perception deal with spatial relations in one way or another, the term Spatial Relations fails to indicate what may be uniquely characteristic of factors so designated. Lohman et al. (1987, p. 267) suggest that a better name for the factor might be "speeded rotation or reflection."

My assignment of factors to this category was strongly influenced by the suggestion of Lohman et al. (1987) that the factor is usually defined by simple, speeded tests such as Cards, Flags, and Figures that require the subject to compare two stimuli to determine whether one is only a rotated version of the other, or is a reflected (turned over) version of the other, rotated or not. As they point out,

Many subjects solve such problems by mentally rotating and reflecting the stimuli although some subjects use other strategies. Thus, the factor appears to represent the ability to solve simple rotation problems quickly, by whatever means. More difficult rotation tests usually show stronger loadings on the Gv factor than on the SR factor. Here, we may take Gv to be equivalent to VZ (p. 267).

Thus, I have assigned token factors to this category when their highest salient loadings are in general *only* on simple speeded tests involving rotations and reflections, particularly when no VZ factor that contained such variables appeared in the dataset. When a dataset also appeared to contain a VZ factor, I took advantage of this to delineate the distinctions between the factors.

A historical note on spatial factors is of interest and pertinence. A single Space factor was isolated by Thurstone (1938b) in his large study of primary mental abilities (dataset THUR21A), likewise by Thurstone and Thurstone (1941) in a subsequent study. In his orthogonal graphical reanalysis of the centroid analysis made by Thurstone (1938b), Zimmerman (1953) found two factors in the visual perception domain, one that he called Spatial Relations, with major loadings on tests such as Flags, Lozenges B, Cubes, and Hands, and the other that he called Visualization, with major loadings on Form Board, Punched Holes, and Lozenges A. In my hierarchical principal factor reanalysis of Thurstone's data (dataset THUR21A), I could not find two factors in the visual perception domain; rather, I identified only a single factor that I assigned to VZ (as noted previously), containing variables that appeared on both of Zimmerman's factors. According to my criteria for factor extraction, it would appear that any covariance that might be assigned to a separate spatial-visualization factor would be regarded as a statistical artifact (possibly due to the fact that tetrachoric correlations, less reliable than Pearsonian correlations, formed the basis for the analysis).

The battery of variables that Thurstone and Thurstone (1941) used for their study of cognitive abilities omitted many of the tests that Zimmerman (1953) regarded as measures of visualization, and their analysis disclosed only a single spatial factor, loaded mainly on tests Cards, Figures, and Flags – all simple speeded tests that Lohman et al. (1987) regard as measures of Spatial Relations. These tests – or at least Cards and Figures – formed the basis of the "space" factor in the commercially published SRA Primary Mental Abilities tests (Thurstone & Thurstone, 1938–65) that were subsequently used in a number of factorial studies by various investigators. It is partly for this reason that a spatial factor has come to be thought of as primarily measured by these tests; more complex tests measuring visualization have tended to drop out of the range of tests used by some investigators. It is also the reason that most of the variables found to measure the SR factor in my reanalyses are limited to tests such as those classified as Figural Rotation Tasks by Eliot and Smith (1983).

Indeed, some of these variables are simply scores on the Space factor of appropriate levels of the Thurstone and Thurstone Primary Mental Abilities (PMA) tests – for example in datasets CATT01A, HARR51, SIMR01, and STAK01. One of the variables in dataset GUIL40 is a sum of scores on Flags, Figures, and Cards. Most studies, however, use separate scores on the Cards and Figures subtests of the PMA, or separate scores on tests offered in the 1963 or 1976 ETS factor kits.

Some version of a Cards or Card Rotation test (see Eliot & Smith, 1983, tests 176, 210, 214) is found with a salient loading on factor SR in datasets ARNO01, BECH01, COOM01, EKST11, GUST11A, JEFF11, PEMB01, SCHA11, THUR31, THUR81, THUR82, and UNDH01. In several cases (EKST11, GUST11A), however, the loadings are on two highly similar forms of the test.

Some version of a Figures test (see Eliot & Smith, 1983, tests 215, 218, 219) is found with a salient loading on factor SR in datasets ARNO01, BECH01, COOM01, HAKS01, JEFF11, THUR31, THUR71, WITT11. The tests Hatchets, and Boots, in dataset SCHU11, Reversals and Rotations, in JEFF11, and Flags (Eliot & Smith, 1983, tests 175 and 213) in datasets BECH01, CARR85, and UNDH01 are constructed on the same principle.

The test Hands (see Eliot & Smith, 1983, test 211) occasionally appears on this factor. It requires the examinee to decide whether two pictured hands are from the same or different hands (left or right). Following Thurstone (1949), Lohman et al. (1987) suggest that it measures a separate Kinesthetic factor, but no evidence for such a factor appeared in my reanalyses. The test Hands seems to be an example of a test that can be performed by either of two strategies: (1) one can examine the first stimulus and then decide whether it can be turned over and rotated to match the second stimulus, as in other tests of SR like Cards or Figures, or (2) one can attempt to "feel" whether each hand is a left or a right, and respond accordingly.

Various other spatial tests occasionally appear as salients on this factor, but with lower loadings and frequently also with loadings on other spatial factors; an example is Designs, in dataset BECH01, with an additional loading on CS. The SR component appears to consist in speed in apprehending the stimuli and making decisions about them.

Three datasets have two factors classified as SR. In SIMR01, factor 6 is loaded with two "spatial" tests that are not fully described; they are apparently tests modeled on Thurstone's Cards and Figures tests. Factor 7 is loaded with scores on an initial practice trial and a final practice trial for a further (unspecified) spatial test; it probably contains specific variance associated with this particular test. In any event, the oblique forms of factors 6 and 7 are substantially correlated ($r = .440$), yielding a second-order factor 5. In EKST11, factors 3 and 4 capture specific variance associated with alternate forms of a Cards test (factor 3) and a Cubes test (factor 4); the corresponding oblique factors are substantially correlated ($r = .58$) and together with a VZ and a CS factor yield a second-order factor 2, interpreted as GV (or 2V).

Factors 4 and 11 of dataset SCHA11, from an unpublished dissertation by Schaefer (1940), are of considerable interest because they seem to exhibit different aspects of a Spatial Relations factor. Factor 4 is loaded with Thurstone's paper-and-pencil tests Cards, Figures, and Flags, and the scores reflect accuracy as well as speed. In contrast, factor 11 is loaded with several variables resulting from experimental laboratory tests in which latencies of correct responses to spatial relations items were determined. The tasks were such that two-choice responses were made by keys for the left and right hands. The highest loading (.773) was for Figures II, presenting capital letters in different rotations and reflections; the task was to determine whether the stimulus was simply rotated from its normal form, or was a rotated mirror image. The next highest loading (.542) was for a similar task with "strange" figures, i.e., not letters. The lowest salient loading (.314) was for a task using capital letters presented either normally or in mirror image form, but without rotations. These results seem to indicate that rotation of the stimulus is a critical aspect of the factor. Also loaded here (.376) was Pursuit, a task in which the stimulus was two wavy lines like those in a pursuit maze; the subject had to determine whether the marked line ended at the left or the right of the bottom part of the figure. This purely perceptual task seems to suggest that accuracy in visual scanning is a component of the factor. The oblique forms of factors 4 and 11 were correlated .253, a finding that suggests that speed and accuracy of spatial performance are largely independent.

For most purposes, probably the best tests of factor SR are Cards, Flags, and Figures as used by Thurstone. Card Rotations – S-1 in the 1976 ETS kit can be used, but Cube Comparisons – S-2 in the kit is probably somewhat too complex, often with loadings on VZ. For research purposes it is recommended that latency measurements as used in datasets EGAN01 and SCHA11 be employed.

CLOSURE SPEED (CS) FACTORS

Relying on only two datasets (which are designated BECH01 and THUR41 in my reanalyses), French (1951) identified a factor GP, Gestalt Perception, hypothesizing that it represented "the ability to combine disconnected, vague, visual stimuli into a meaningful whole." Tests mentioned as measuring the factor included Street Gestalt Completion ("interpreting incomplete pictures") and Mutilated Words ("interpret words with incomplete letters"), although there was some inconsistency in the factor loadings in the two datasets. By the time the 1963 ETS factor kit was published, the factor had received considerably more support, and was labeled Cs: Speed of Closure. It was defined as "the ability to unify an apparently disparate perceptual field into a single percept." Tests offered as markers were as follows:

> Cs-1, Gestalt Completion Test (adapted from the Street Gestalt Completion Test, Street, 1931): "Drawings are presented which are composed of black blotches representing parts of the objects being portrayed. The subject writes down the name [*sic*] of the objects, being as specific about them as he can." (Essentially the same as test 99, Eliot & Smith, 1983, p. 118.)
>
> Cs-2, Concealed Words Test (suggested by Thurstone's Mutilated Words): "Words are presented with parts of each letter missing. The subject is to write out the full word in an adjacent space."

As markers of the factor, the 1976 ETS kit offers these same two tests, but in addition, a test called Snowy Pictures: "The subject is asked to identify objects which are partly obliterated by snow-like spatters." (See Eliot & Smith, 1983, test 100, p. 119.)

Table 8.5 lists 43 factors, in 38 datasets, that are assigned to factor CS, Closure Speed. The factor appears in datasets for a wide range of age levels.

The characteristic process in variables measuring factor CS is one of apprehending a visuospatial form in a visual presentation when that form is presented incompletely or with a context such that the form is disguised or obscured. Generally the subject is not informed what the form is (i.e., what its name is, or what its category is), but experience with such presentations suggests that knowledge of what the form is does not necessarily lead to speedy apprehension. For example, in items of the Street Gestalt test (Street, 1931; Eliot & Smith, 1983, tests 099, 110) a subject will often not be able to apprehend the form immediately even if told what to look for (e.g., a flag, or a head of a hammer). Apparently the factor concerns individual differences in people's ability to access spatial representations in long-term memory when presented incomplete or disguised cues to those representations. Of course, performance in these tests also depends on whether the spatial representations actually exist in long-term memory. A person who has never seen a flag, or whatever the test designer intended to represent, could not be expected to apprehend it. For this reason, items in CS tests usually involve only objects in common experience, but the range of a person's experiences would have to be considered in assessing performance.

It should be noted that Eliot and Smith (1983) categorize certain typical CS tests, for example Gestalt Completion, as tests of visual memory (perhaps because they have in mind the long-term memory access aspect of such tests), but their tests of visual memory also include many tests that are better regarded as tests of factor MV (see Chapter 7), in which a standard memory paradigm (presentation followed by attempted recall) is involved. Eliot and Smith do not list certain other CS tests, such as Mutilated Words, probably because they do not regard such tests as spatial tests. Nevertheless, it should be recognized that printed materials such as letters, digits, and words can be regarded as spatial forms to be apprehended.

It has been pointed out (Ekstrom, French, & Harman, 1976, p. 25) that factor CS differs from factor CF (Flexibility of Closure) in the fact that in the former,

Table 8.5. *43 Closure Speed (CS) factors in 38 datasets arranged in order of approximate mean age of sample*[a]

Dataset	Date	C'y code	Age	Sample code	M/F code	Factor no.	Remarks (higher-order factors; others related)
PARA02	'69	U	4	1	3	3	1:2C;4:VZ?
UNDH01	'76	O	9	1	3	7	1:2H;3&4:VZ;10:20;11:SR
HARR53	'73	U	10	1	1	5	1:2G;3:P
HARR54	'73	U	10	1	2	3	1:2G;5:P
GUST11A	'84	S	11	1	3	10	1:3G;2:2V;3:CF;4:SR;5:2C; 11:2F;13:VZ
BACH21	'77	C	12	7	3	2	1:2G;4:CF
MCGU01	'61	U	12	1	1	5	1:2G;6:P
HOEP21	'65	U	14	6	3	4	1:20;5:CF?
OLSO51	'66	U	14	E	3	8	1:2C;5:VZ;7:PI
HOLM11	'67	U	15	E	3	3	1:2C
BRAD01	'69	U	16	1	3	4	1:2Y;5:DFU;6:2V;7:S?
FRED13	'82	U	16	6	3	3	1:20;4:P;5:CF
JEFF11	'57	U	16	$	3	7	1:21;2:VZ;5:SR
OHNM11	'70	U	16	6	3	3	1:2C
OSUL01	'65	U	16	6	3	8	1:2G
SNOW11	'77	U	16	1	3	2	1:2G;3:VZ;6:P
THUR71	'49	U	16	$	1	7	1:2G;2:CF;3:SR;9:VZ
HOEP31	'64	U	17	6	3	9	1:2H;6:P;7:2S
ADKI03	'52	U	19	2	1	6	1:2H;3:VZ;10:P?
BECH01	'47	U	19	6	3	10	1:2S;4:P?;7:SR;9:P?;11:CF?
BOTZ01	'51	U	19	6	1	8	1:2G;3:VZ;9:CF?
EKST11	'67	U	19	6	2	6	1:3G;2:2V;3:SR?;4:SR?;5:VZ; 7:2S;8:P;9:CF
FULG21	'66	U	19	P	3	1	2:S3
LUMS01	'65	A	19	P	3	7	1:2F;3:VZ;8:2C;11:CS?
"	"	"	"	"	"	11	Alternate CS factor?
TAYL51	'76	K	19	1	1	7	1:20;2,3,4,6:IL;5:P
THUR41	'44	U	19	6	3	5	1:2G;2:VZ;4:IL;?
"	"	"	"	"	"	7	Alternate CS?
WHEA01	'73	U	19	1	1	4	1:2G;3:CF
CORY01	'77	U	21	2	1	8	1:2F;5:P;6:2C;9:CS?
"	"	"	"	"	"	9	Alternate CS factor?
GUIL66	'52	U	21	3	1	6	1:2G;7:VZ;9:I0
HOEP01	'67	U	21	3	1	3	1:2G
HOFF01	'68	U	21	B	3	8	1:2V;2:I0;3:VZ;5:2H
MESS01	'75	U	21	3	1	3	1:2H;4:CF;5:P
"	"	"	"	"	"	8	Alternate CS factor?
MOON01	'54	C	21	3	1	4	1:2G;5:CS?
"	"	"	"	"	"	5	Alternate CS factor?
ROFF11	'52	U	21	3	1	3	1:2G;2:S0;4:MD;5,7:VZ;9:LE
WOTH01	'90	U	21	1	3	10	1:3G;8:20;12:2V;13:VZ
ANGL11	'75	G	22	6	3	3	1:2G;2:CF?
PEMB01	'52	U	22	6	3	4	1:2G;2:SR;6:CF
HAKS01	'74	C	24	1	3	19	1:3G;5:21;6:SR;8:CF;9:P;11:2C

[a]See Appendix A for codes. In a few cases, classifications of factors shown here were preliminary and may not agree with the final classifications shown in the tables of Appendix B.

"the subject sees no obvious closure to start with and does not know what to look for, whereas in flexibility of closure the subject knows what the required configuration is, but must disembed it from a more complex figure" (Ekstrom, French, & Harman, 1976, p. 25). Nevertheless, factors here assigned to CS occasionally have loadings on tests in which the subject is given a form to look for. This can occur for at least two possible reasons: (1) even if the subject knows what to look for, a test of factor CF can require a process of apprehending a spatial form that is very similar to the process required in tests of factor CS, and (2) the test battery does not contain sufficient variables to define a separate factor CF, with the result that any variance from a general visual perception factor (GV) appears aligned with that from factor CS. Among the datasets with token factors assigned to factor CS in Table 8.5 that sporadically contain tests more characteristic of factor CF, because of a missing CF factor, are: CORY01, FULG21, OHNM11, OSUL01, SNOW20, and WHIT01. Supportive of the notion that CF tests can involve CS processes are findings from datasets FRED13 and PEMB01. In FRED13, the test Hidden Figures (characteristically a test of CF) has a loading of .480 on CS and .312 on CF; in PEMB01, characteristic CF tests Copying and Concealed Figures have substantial loadings on both CS and CF, although the characteristic CF test Designs loads only on CS. In any event, one may speculate that the apprehension process characteristic of CS is more basic and general than the processes characteristically involved in factor CF (discussed below).

Tests of the Closure Speed (CS) Factor

Tests of CS, Speed of Closure, have four critical characteristics:

1. In any given item or task, a visual stimulus is presented, constructed in such a way that a pattern contained in or represented by the stimulus is obscured in some way. Obscuration can be of any of several types (or combination of types), e.g., partial effacement, addition of irrelevant material (by speckling with dots), camouflaging, or putting part of the stimulus in peripheral vision.

2. The pattern that is obscured can be either a design, a pictured object, a symbol such as an alphabetic letter or digit, or a printed word. Target patterns are usually selected to be familiar so that it can be assumed that subjects have their representations in long-term memory.

3. The subject is asked to recognize and identify the pattern by naming it. Usually the testing format employs free response; multiple-choice format is generally not used because the alternative choices that might be given would provide excessive cueing. The subject is not told what to look for, but usually is made aware of the *class* of the pattern, that is, whether it is a familiar design, a pictured object, a letter or digit symbol, or a word. Sometimes further information on the class of the pattern is given, e.g., that a word names a type of fruit. (There have come to my attention no instances in which the subject is told nothing about the class of the target pattern; in future research

it might be interesting to construct a test in which the class of the pattern (pictured object, word, etc.) is selected randomly over items.)

4. The response is evaluated mainly for its speed. Paper-and-pencil tests are constructed so that the number of successful responses within a given time limit can be counted. Apparatus or computerized tests are designed so that the latency of a successful response can be measured.

The two most frequently used types of tests of factor CS illustrate these characteristics. Both use partial effacement as the method of obscuration or degradation.

The first of these goes under a variety of names: Gestalt Completion, Street Gestalt Completion, Street Pictures, Closure Test, Disguised Pictures, Incomplete Pictures, Figure Completion, and Harshman Figures; for examples see Eliot & Smith, 1983, tests 099 and 124. Subjects are required to identify familiar objects whose pictorial representations have been degraded by partial effacement; scores are the number of correct responses attained within a time-limit that is short enough to yield individual differences in speed of response. Some of the datasets in which this type of test appears with high salient loadings on factor CS are ADKI03, CORY01, EKST11, GUST11A, HAKS01, JEFF11, LUMS01, PEMB01, SNOW11, and THUR71.

The second type of test goes under such names as Concealed Words, Disguised Words, and Mutilated Words. Subjects are told to read familiar words (usually 5-7 letters long) whose letters have been partially effaced in a seemingly random way. Datasets with this type of test appearing on factor CS are ADKI03, BECH01, BOTZ01, and CORY01.

Both of these types of tests are offered in the 1976 ETS kit as measures of factor CS. They are nearly always correlated highly enough to produce high salient loadings, despite the difference in the classes of patterns that are effaced (pictures, words). In general, the evidence suggests that it makes no difference, in tests of CS, what kind of thing is presented in an obscured form, as long as it is familiar as a pictured object or a graphemic symbol or configuration.

Nevertheless, there are several datasets that yielded alternate CS factors in our reanalyses. In LUMS01, factor 11 is possibly to be interpreted as involving closure for pictured objects, while factor 7 concerns closure for degraded letters or digits. The separation of the factors, however, is somewhat questionable because factor 11 may be mainly a specific produced by the presence of two forms of Gestalt Completion. Furthermore, several tests loaded on factor 7 also have substantial loadings on factor 11, and Mutilated Words (not concerned with pictured objects) has a substantial loading on factor 11. It is possible that the separation of factors 7 and 11 in dataset LUMS01 is artifactual.

Dataset MESS01, however, presents clearer evidence for the separation of two versions of factor CS, one (factor 8) concerning closure for pictured objects and the other (factor 3) concerning closure for printed words. It is possible that when two versions of a closure factor appear, a greater variance in the reading (word perception) ability of the subjects is reflected in tests involving printed words.

Factors 4 and 5 in dataset MOON01 present a different kind of problem. Factor 5 appears to be a conventional CS factor, with loadings on (a) a Closure Test that is similar to Gestalt Completion, and (b) a Mutilated Words test. The salient loadings on Factor 4 are for tests called Mutilated Sentences, Hidden Words, and Disjointed Sentences. All seem to depend more on semantic comprehension than closure. In Hidden Words there is first a series of items in which subjects are asked, for example, to find a name of a fruit spelled out in the letters of the sequence PGETAXCNH [peach], and then to perform tasks in which the set presumably established by this task needs to be overcome. Degrading a word stimulus by supplying extra letters does not seem to be characteristic of other tests of Closure Speed. It is probably best to dismiss factor 4 in dataset MOON01 as a test of CS.

Another problematic factor is factor 4 in dataset HOEP21. Its only salient loading (.380) is on a test called Camouflaged Words, in which subjects have to find within a sentence a group of consecutive letters that spells the name of a sport or game, e.g., in "I did not know that he was ailing" subjects are supposed to find the word *sailing*. The next highest loading (nonsalient, .313) is for a test called Correct Spelling. Probably, therefore, the factor should not be classified as CS.

A number of successful tests of CS require subjects to recognize single alphabetic symbols: Concealed Letters (HARR53, using partial effacement); Dotted Outlines (THUR41, using a minimal number of dots to represent letters); and Hidden Digits (THUR41), Hidden Print (HOFF01), and Hidden Letters (LUMS01), using a speckled background for dotted-line symbols.

Besides partial effacement and the use of speckled or snowy backgrounds, there is a wide variety of methods of obscuration. A few of these are:

> Use of irrelevant surrounding or interpolated material, such as random letters, as in Hidden Words (MOON01), or use of irregular spacing of letters that spell words, as in Disjointed Sentences (MOON01) (but see discussion above).
>
> Use of close-up or out-of-focus, blurred photography, as in the test Close-Ups (HOFF01).
>
> Having stimuli viewed tachistoscopically in peripheral vision, as in the test Peripheral Span (THUR41), or under dark-adaptation conditions, as in the test Dark Adaptation (THUR41).

In most cases, there is only one presentation of the stimulus material. The exact degree of obscuration that is selected by test constructors is a matter of their judgment as to what will be effective in producing individual differences. There has apparently been little investigation of the effect of the degree of obscuration on item difficulty or individual differences. There are two instances in the datasets, however, in which different degrees of obscuration are produced.

In dataset CORY01, a variable called Recognizing Objects is essentially a computerized Gestalt Completion test. As the authors describe it,

The first presentation showed 10 percent of the area, and more area was added in random increments of 10 per unit until 90 percent of the picture was exposed. Subjects entered the names of the stimuli on the keyboard. The score was the total number of frames shown before the objects were identified. Thus, the lower the score, the better the performance (Cory, Rimland & Bryson, 1977, p. 102).

In my analysis, as in the authors', Recognizing Objects came out on a different factor (factor 8) from one (factor 9) that was loaded with more conventional CS tests. Also on factor 8 was a loading (though nonsalient) for a test called Memory for Patterns. The authors concluded that Recognizing Objects appeared to be measuring a substantially different attribute from that measured by the paper-and-pencil tests which have been previously used to define perceptual closure. They remarked that "the computerized measure appears to place greater reliance on short-term memory factors than do paper-and-pencil tests of closure, but the extent and character of the other differentiations between the modes are not clear at the present time" (p. 109). One is reminded of the interference effect found by Bruner and Potter (1964) whereby performance on series of increasingly less degraded stimuli is less accurate than performance for a single presentation of a stimulus at the highest level in the series. In any event, individual differences in performance of closure tests are possibly dependent on whether the tests involve single presentations or involve presentations of ascending series. This matter deserves further investigation.

In dataset OLSO51, a test called Perception of Pseudosymbolic Forms was conducted with tachistoscopic presentation of symbols (in alphabets other than English) at two levels of exposure, 15 ms and 55 ms. A symbol was presented on the screen, after which the examinee was allowed to look at four alternatives to choose which symbol had been seen (this test was one of the few that utilized multiple-choice format). On factor 8, regarded as CS, the 15 ms score had a considerably higher loading (.59) than the 55 ms score (.45).

What was particularly interesting about this study, involving deaf adolescents with some training in lipreading, was that factor CS was also highly loaded with two measures of lipreading performance. Subjects saw a film in which a person was shown pronouncing either single words or brief sentences; they were to write down what was said. It is striking that apparently a similar process of perceptual closure was involved both for apprehending unfamiliar alphabetic symbols and for interpreting visually perceived speech movements, which of course can be regarded as stimuli that are degraded in a special way. Whether such a lipreading test would function as a test of CS for hearing subjects needs to be determined.

Messick and French (1975) sought to determine whether the concept of closure speed would apply to cognitive tasks not directly involving visual perception. They constructed a task called What Are You Doing? in which subjects read series of words that were intended to suggest some particular activity, such as the following:

aroma clean table cloth
fork   red   teeth lean
cut   pass   tough good

The task was (apparently) to write down the suggested activity – in this case, sitting at a dinner table eating meat. The notion was that in this task, a kind of cognitive closure would occur for the array of semantic suggestions afforded by the word list. This task, however, did not load on a closure speed factor (factor 8 in dataset MESS01); instead, it loaded on a weakly defined verbal comprehension factor. Possibly the task did not adequately measure the *speed* aspect of any cognitive closure that might have occurred.

From the evidence available, it appears that factor CS is restricted to *visual* closure. Auditory analogs of visual closure tests have apparently not been investigated in the factor-analytic literature. (But see a discussion of dataset WHIT01 in connection with factor CF below.)

For most purposes, the best tests of factor CS are the Gestalt Completion and Concealed Words tests offered in the 1976 ETS kit. However, for research purposes it would probably be well to use several tests in addition to these in order to investigate the possible separation of closure for *pictured objects* from closure for *printed words* as was suggested in the results for datasets LUMS01 and MESS01 discussed above. There is as yet inadequate research to support the use of the test Snowy Pictures in the ETS kit as a marker for CS. In all cases, it would be desirable to obtain latency scores for correct responses for computerized versions of closure speed tests.

CLOSURE FLEXIBILITY (CF) FACTORS

French (1951) recognized a factor that he called GF, Gestalt Flexibility. Such a factor had been found by Thurstone in what French listed as Analysis ThD (identified here as dataset THUR41) and had been described as concerned with "the manipulation of two configurations simultaneously or in succession" (Thurstone, 1944a, p. 110). Among tests mentioned as having high loadings on it were Two-Hand Coordination (an experimental performance task in which the subject had to simultaneously tap specified sectors of two disks with a stylus in each hand; the task was scored for lack of interference in using two hands as opposed to tapping the disks separately), Hidden Pictures (speed in finding hidden pictures in a snow scene), and Gottschaldt Figures (finding simple figures embedded in complex ones). In the Two-Hand Coordination Test it was theorized that "the subject improves his performance if he can suppress the separate configurations for the two hands and combine them into a single configuration involving the two plates" (French, 1951, p. 212). French claimed that "the *Gottschaldt* and *Hidden Picture* tests obviously involve flexibility of gestalts."

This factor was represented in the 1963 ETS kit as Factor CF: Flexibility of Closure. Marker tests were offered as follows:

> Cf-1, Hidden Figures Test: (An adaptation of the Gottschaldt Figures Test; see Eliot & Smith, 1983, test 080, p. 98): "The task is to decide which of 5 geometrical figures is embedded in a complex pattern. The difficulty level of the test is high." (See Eliot & Smith, 1983, test 053, p. 71.)
>
> Cf-2, Hidden Patterns Test (suggested by Thurstone's Designs; see Eliot & Smith, 1983, test 083, p. 100): In the instructions, the subject is shown a single geometrical configuration. Each item presents a geometrical pattern. Some of the items contain the given configuration, embedded. The task is to mark each pattern in which the configuration occurs. These are easy items given under speeded conditions. (See Eliot & Smith, 1983, test 054, p. 72.)
>
> Cf-3, Copying Test (adapted from a subtest in MacQuarrie's Test for Mechanical Ability; see Eliot & Smith, 1983, test 026, p. 43): "Each item consists of a four-line geometrical figure and a square matrix of dots. The task is to copy the figure onto the dots. It is believed that the copying test requires Closure Flexibility in the act of superimposing the particular configuration on a strong visual field consisting of the matrix of dots." (See Eliot & Smith, 1983, test 002, p. 18.)

Despite the claimed high loadings of the Two-Hand Coordination Test on a possible flexibility of closure factor in both Thurstone's 1944 study and a study by Bechtoldt (1947), this test was not suggested as a marker for the factor, probably because the inclusion of an experimental performance task in the kit would have been impractical.

As markers for factor CF, Closure Flexibility, the 1976 ETS kit offered the same three tests mentioned above, in some cases with minor modifications in items and/or time limits.

Table 8.6 lists 19 factors, in 19 datasets, that are assigned to factor CF, Closure Flexibility. As in other such tables, the datasets are arranged in order of approximate mean age of the sample. In this case, most of the datasets are for adolescents and young adults.

For continuity with previous literature, I employ Closure Flexibility, or Flexibility of Closure, as the name of the factor. The name seems to have arisen partly from Thurstone's remark, about his factor E, that "freedom from *Gestaltbindung* might be an appropriate description in that it implies flexibility in manipulating several more or less irrelevant or conflicting gestalts" (Thurstone, 1944a, p. 111). French (1951) called the factor Gestalt Flexibility, citing only Thurstone's study as evidence for it, but the term Flexibility of Closure was adopted in the 1963 ETS kit, and the factor was defined as "the ability to keep one or more definite configurations in mind so as to make identification in spite of perceptual distraction" (French, Ekstrom, & Price, 1963, p. 9). The definition offered in the 1976 kit was "the ability to hold a given visual percept or

Table 8.6. *19 Closure Flexibility (CF) factors in 19 datasets arranged in order of approximate mean age of sample*[a]

Dataset	Date	C'y code	Age	Sample code	M/F code	Factor no.	Remarks (higher-order factors; others related)
GUST11A	'84	S	11	1	3	3	1:3G;4:SR;10:CS;12:VZ
BACH21	'77	C	12	7	3	4	1:2G;2:CS
WHIT01	'54	U	15	6	3	1	Orthogonal factors
FRED13	'82	U	16	6	3	5	1:20;3:CS;4:P
THUR71	'49	U	16	$	1	2	1:2G;3:SR;7:CS;9:VZ;10:K
BECH01	'47	U	19	6	3	11	1:2S;4:P?;7:SR;9:P?;10:CS
BOTZ01	'51	U	19	6	1	9	1:2G;3:VZ;8:CS
EKST11	'67	U	19	6	2	9	1:3G;3:SR?;4:SR?;5:VZ;6:CS; 7:22;8:P
FOGA00	'87	A	19	P	3	4	1:2G
FRED01	'65	U	19	6	3	2	1:VZ. Orthogonal factors
GARD05A	'60	U	19	6	2	4	1:2G
WALS21	'78	C	19	6	3	2	1:2G;3:VZ
WHEA01	'73	U	19	1	1	3	1:2G;4:CS
WIDI01	'80	U	19	P	3	6	4:2F
FEDE02	'80	U	21	2	3	10	1:2F;4:VZ;5:2C
MESS01	'75	U	21	3	1	4	3,8:CS;5:P
ANGL11	'75	G	22	6	3	2	1:2G;3:CS
PEMB01	'52	U	22	6	3	6	1:2G;2:SR;4:CS
HAKS01	'74	C	24	1	3	8	1:3G;6:SR;9:P;19:CS

[a]See Appendix A for codes. In a few cases, classifications of factors shown here were preliminary and may not agree with the final classifications shown in the tables of Appendix B.

configuration in mind so as to disembed it from other well-defined perceptual material" (Ekstrom, French, & Harman, 1976, p. 19). These definitions derive from subjective judgments about processes in performing tests that are loaded on factor CF, not (as far as I am aware) from experimental investigations of such processes. There is no objective evidence, for example, that the critical element is the "ability to hold a given visual percept in mind."

The psychometric evidence for the factor is somewhat ambiguous. My reanalysis of Thurstone's study (dataset THUR41), in which the factor was first identified, did not yield a distinct CF factor similar to Thurstone's factor E. Instead, the tests that loaded on Thurstone's factor E had loadings on several factors, principally a factor (factor 2) assigned to factor VZ. Studies cited in the 1963 ETS factor kit manual as evidence for the factor included those forming datasets BOTZ01, MOON01, PEMB01, ROFF01, and THUR71, but I could not confirm the factor in MOON01 and ROFF01, and the factor was not particularly clear in some others. In BOTZ01 the factor was almost indistinguishable from factor VZ, having no salient loadings. In PEMB01 the factor had its highest loadings on the tests False Premises and Figure Classification – tests that are hard to interpret as tests of CF. Only in THUR71 was the factor reasonably clear, with salient loadings only on tests interpretable as measuring CF.

Factors in other datasets listed in Table 8.6 are not always clear. Factor 2 in ANGL11 was assigned to CF chiefly following its author's suggested interpretation, but it could equally well be a broader visualization factor. Factor 11 in BECH01 is poorly defined; it is defined only by the variables Shape Constancy and Hidden Pictures. Factor 9 in EKST11 has two tests (Designs and Hidden Patterns) that are acceptable as measures of CF, but its highest salient loading is for Mutilated Words, ordinarily regarded as a test of CS (on which it has a supplementary loading). Factor 10 in FEDE02 was assigned to CF only because its highest loading was for Hidden Figures; the other three tests with salient, albeit low, loadings would be interpreted as measuring factors other than CF. Factor 2 in FRED01 has three acceptable CF tests (Copying, Hidden Patterns, and Hidden Figures), but also Form Board and Card Rotation (interpreted as tests of VZ and SR, respectively). Factor 8 in HAKS01 is defined only by three alternate forms of Hidden Figures and thus may overemphasize specific variance in this test.

Although the evidence for factor CF is far from clear, there is enough of it to suggest that this factorial dimension exists and can be well measured if further research is devoted to it. Specifically, it appears that further research must be devoted to the formats, item construction methods, and administration procedures of CF tests. This dimension appears to be important in assessing cognitive structure, intellectual development, and personality, in that it is substantially related to the "cognitive style" factor that Witkin and Goodenough (1981) call *field dependence and independence* (see Chapter 14).

Tests of the Closure Flexibility (CF) Factor

A large class of measures of factor CF derives from the work of Gottschaldt (1926) in the experimental investigation of the influence of experience on visual perception. Thurstone (1944a) used Gottschaldt's figures in his factorial study of perception, but divided the test into two parts because preliminary investigation suggested that the more difficult items measured different functions from the easier ones. In the easier part (see Eliot & Smith, 1983, tests 039 and 085), the subject is shown two geometrical designs, the one at the left being simpler than the one at the right, which contains the design at the left; the subject is asked to trace the simpler design in the more complex design. In the supposedly more difficult part (see Eliot & Smith, 1983, test 080), the subject is shown two simple designs and then is asked to show, by tracing, which of these simple designs is contained in each of a series of more complex designs. Nevertheless, in my reanalysis of dataset THUR41 there was no significant difference in the factorial composition of these variables; both were found to be loaded on a factor that I classified as VZ.

The Gottschaldt test was further developed by Witkin, Oltman, Raskin, and Karp (1971) in the form of an Embedded Figures Test that is to be administered to one individual at a time. In each item, a card with a complex figure is shown to the subject for 15 seconds, and the subject is asked to describe it. Then a card containing a simple figure is shown for 10 seconds. Following this, the complex figure is again presented and the subject's task is to find the simple figure and trace it with a blunt stylus. The score is a function of the amount of time that subjects take to find the figures. The items range in difficulty, with average times for college males ranging from 10 seconds to 2 minutes. A score on the Embedded Figures Test appears with a relatively low loading on a CF factor in dataset WALS21. There is also a group test adaptation of this, the Group Embedded Figures Test (Eliot & Smith, 1983, test 375), and scores on this appear with substantial loadings on factor CF in datasets BACH21, WIDI01, and GUST11A.

In contrast to those given for factor CS the four critical characteristics of tests of the Gottschaldt figure variety are as follows:

1. The target visual stimulus (that in which a simple form is contained) is constructed in such a way that the simple form is obscured by what may be called *geometrical camouflaging*, i.e., adding lines in the region contained in and surrounding the simple form.
2. The pattern that is obscured is a geometric design.
3. The subject is shown the simple form and presumably apprehends and "knows what it is" before being asked to find it in the more complex form.
4. As in the case of factor CS, the response is evaluated mainly for its speed or latency.

These critical characteristics are embodied, with minor variations, in various other tests that have been constructed to measure factor CF:

Concealed Figures (Eliot & Smith, 1983, test 052, p. 70): In each row of the test, a simple figure is shown; the subject must indicate which figure in a series of more complex figures contains the simple figure. The target forms vary from row to row. This test appears on factor CF in datasets PEMB01, WALS21, WHEA01, and WHIT01.

Designs (Eliot & Smith, 1983, test 083, p. 100): The subject is shown a "model" which is in the shape of the capital Greek letter *sigma*; he is given four minutes to indicate which of a series of 300 more complex designs contain the model. The model is the same throughout the test. This test appears on factor CF in datasets BOTZ01, EKST11, THUR71, and WHEA01.

Hidden Figures (Eliot & Smith, 1983, test 053, p. 71): The subject is presented with *five* simple designs, labeled *A* through *E* (available for inspection at all times throughout the test), and then must indicate which of these designs is contained in each of 32 more complex forms. This test appears on factor CF in datasets BACH21, FEDE02, FOGA00, FRED01, FRED13, HAKS01, and WALS21.

Hidden Patterns (Eliot & Smith, 1983, test 054, p. 72): This test is essentially the same as *Designs* except that a different model (simple form) is used for each item throughout the test. The test appears on factor CF in datasets EKST11, FRED01, GUST11A, and WALS21.

A further test frequently found on factor CF is Copying, mentioned above as a marker in ETS kits. In effect, the grid on which a form is to be copied constitutes the geometrical camouflaging that is characteristic of CF tests, and in fact, the format is very similar to that in the easier part of the Gottschaldt figure test, where the subject is to trace the form at the left onto the more complex form at the right (see above). This test appears on factor CF in datasets FRED01, GUST11A, PEMB01, THUR71, and WHIT01.

One other test that is a possible measure of factor CF is Hidden Pictures, described by Pemberton (1952) as having "items like those in children's books, in which one can see objects hidden in the lines of a larger picture." The subject is told at least the class of objects to be seen (faces), and the camouflaging is somewhat similar to that in the Gottschaldt figures. The test appeared on factor CF in dataset BECH01, but not in PEMB01, where it (somewhat more reasonably) appeared on factor CS.

A Shape Constancy test appeared on the rather weak factor 11 interpreted as CF in dataset BECH01, mainly by being strongly contrasted to two tests (Size Comparison and Word Checking) that had negative loadings. This elaborate experimental test requires subjects to judge the shape of a retinal image that is presented by tipping a square card, rotated to the diagonal, through a certain number of degrees. (See Thurstone, 1944a, pp. 80–81.) One could possibly rationalize its appearance on CF by noting that it requires subjects to maintain memory of a retinal image despite the geometric camouflaging incident to the exposure conditions and the natural tendency to see the stimulus as a square because of depth perception phenomena.

White (1954) was interested in seeing whether the closure process involved in factor CF would extend to the auditory modality. A test that he developed, Hidden Tunes, appears on a factor that I interpret as CF in the dataset WHIT01 generated in his study, along with several visual tests of CF. The test consists of a series of items in which simple 3-, 4-, or 5-note melodies are presented, followed after a pause by a longer melody. The subject's task was to indicate whether the short melody was contained in the longer melody. In this way, the test was an analogue of Gottschaldt Figure tasks. This suggested finding, that "flexibility of closure" extends to the auditory modality, deserves further investigation.

From my analysis, it appears that there is no true element of flexibility of closure in tasks that measure factor CF. A better name, and interpretation, might be simply "speed of detecting and disembedding a known stimulus array from a more complex array." CF tasks bear some similarity to the S. Sternberg (1966, 1969, 1975) memory search task in which a stimulus element, for example a letter or digit, is to be detected (or not) in a more complex array. As far as I am aware, there are no studies that investigate correlations between scores on the Sternberg memory search paradigm and scores on CF tasks. In any case, it is possible that speeds (or latencies) of search and detection in CF tasks are a function of whether the instances are positive or negative, as they are in the case of the Sternberg task.

The best available tests of the CF factor are probably those offered for it in the 1976 ETS kit, but they present several problems that are difficult to overcome: (1) variance from other spatial factors, especially VZ and SR, is frequently present in these tests, and (2) implicitly or explicitly, both Hidden Figures and Hidden Patterns contain both positive and negative instances. Use of the Group Embedded Figures Test and Copying can be recommended because in effect they involve only positive instances.

SERIAL PERCEPTUAL INTEGRATION (PI) FACTORS

Table 8.7 lists five factors, in five datasets, that are tentatively assigned to factor PI (Serial Perceptual Integration). In my reanalyses I have been able to confirm this factor, noted by Lohman et al. (1987). Not recognized in ETS factor-reference kits, it was apparently first isolated by Seibert and Snow (1965; see also Seibert, Reid, & Snow, 1967) using motion picture film tests. Factor 2 in dataset SEIB02 is loaded with three film tests in which pictorial material is presented successively, in parts. The technique has some similarities to the partial presentation involved in the Street Gestalt Completion test, and in fact a paper-and-pencil form of the Street Gestalt Completion test has a salient loading on the factor along with the three film tests. It is altogether possible that this factor is to be classified as factor CS, on which the Gestalt Completion test normally loads, since there is no independent CS factor in this dataset. The same is true of factor 9 in dataset HECK01 (also developed under the direction of Seibert and Snow), which is loaded with two of the tests (Successive Perception III, Successive Perception IV) found on factor 2 in dataset SEIB02. Successive Perception III is also found on factor 5 in dataset SNOW20, but the battery was not extensive enough to provide differentiations from other factors in the domain of visual perception.

A possible example of a Serial Perceptual Integration factor is factor 7 in dataset OLSO51, loaded with three variables deriving from film presentations of successive letters in four-letter words at various tachistoscopic speeds. The factor is differentiated from what may be a speed of closure factor (factor 8) that is loaded with lipreading and tachistoscopic symbol perception tasks.

The status of a Serial Perceptual Integration factor is thus moot at the present time. Computer technology should make it possible to explore this factor with renewed interest. It would be important to try to show clear differentiation from factor CS, Speed of Closure. If it is not differentiated from factor CS, the film presentation tests claimed to measure factor PI may be simply alternate measures of factor CS.

Seibert and Snow (1965) found that measures of PI were related to performance in a visual masking task especially when the masking stimulus occurred at a delay of only 10 ms, that is, when the stimulus was still registered in an iconic memory store. This finding would suggest that factor PI may refer to some aspect of iconic memory – its capacity or its resistance to decay. Snow and Lohman (1989, p. 273)

Table 8.7. *5 Serial Perceptual Integration (PI) factors in 5 datasets arranged in order of approximate mean age of sample*[a]

Dataset	Date	C'y code	Age	Sample code	M/F code	Factor no.	Remarks (higher-order factors; others related)
OLSO51	'66	U	14	E	3	7	1:2C;5:VZ;8:CS
HECK01	'67	U	18	6	3	9	1:3G;2:2Y
SEIB02	'67	U	19	6	3	2	1:2V
SNOW20	'76	U	19	6	3	5	1:GV
SNOW21	'76	U	19	6	3	2	1:20;4:CS?

[a]See Appendix A for codes. In a few cases, the classifications of factors shown here were preliminary and may not agree with the final classifications shown in the tables of Appendix B.

suggest that use of the visual masking technique "would provide a new method of studying [PI and other abilities] in more detail."

A SPATIAL SCANNING (SS) FACTOR?

The authors of the 1963 ETS factor-reference kit (French, Ekstrom, & Price, 1963) defined a Spatial Scanning (Ss) factor as "speed in visually exploring a wide or complicated spatial field," citing several factorial studies (e.g., those on which datasets THUR81 and GUIL46 were based) that seemed to support the existence of such a factor. They offered three marker tests for it: Maze Tracing Speed, Choosing a Path, and Map Planning. This factor continued to be supported in the 1976 Kit, and the same three tests were offered as markers for it, described as follows:

> SS-1. Maze Tracing Speed Test. "The task is to find and mark an open path through a moderately complex series of printed mazes."
>
> SS-2. Choosing a Path. "Each item consists of a network of lines (as in an electrical circuit diagram) having many intersecting and intermeshed wires with several sets of terminals. The task is to trace the lines and to determine for which one of 5 pairs of terminals, marked S (start) and F (finish), there is a complete circuit through a circle at the top. There is some orderliness in the layout to encourage comprehension of the pattern by scanning rather than simple visual pursuit of lines."
>
> SS-3. Map Planning Test. "The examinee sees diagrammatic sections representing city maps. The streets are blocked at various points by barriers represented by circles. The examinee must plan routes between given points in such a way that no roadblocks need to be crossed. The task is to find the shortest available route as quickly as possible."

Little evidence for such a factor appears in the datasets I have reanalyzed, either because my database did not include all the datasets referenced by the authors of the ETS kits, or because my analyses yielded results somewhat different

Table 8.8. *5 Spatial Scanning (SS) factors in 4 datasets arranged in order of approximate mean age of sample*[a]

Dataset	Date	C'y code	Age	Sample code	M/F code	Factor no.	Remarks (higher-order factors; others related)
THUR81	'41	U	13	6	3	14	1:3G;8:2S;9:P;12:2V;13:SR
BARR01	'82	U	21	6	3	3	(Orthogonal factors)
BARR02	'82	U	21	6	3	2	(Orthogonal factors)
SU"L01	'54	G	21	6	3	2	1:2S
"	"	"	"	"	"	3	Alternate SS?

[a]See Appendix A for codes. In a few cases, the classifications of factors shown here were preliminary and may not agree with the final classifications shown in the tables of Appendix B.

from those yielded by the original analyses. Table 8.8 lists five token factors, in four datasets, that were assignable to this classification. I confirmed that in dataset THUR81 there occurs a factor, labeled X2 by Thurstone and Thurstone (1941) and factor 14 in the reanalysis, with loadings on two maze tracing tests and a "pursuit" task which is essentially another maze-tracing task. The factor may be a "specific" due to the high similarity of the three tests. But I find no factor in any of the datasets that has loadings on tests identical to or corresponding to all three, or even only two, of the tests offered in the ETS factor kits. Furthermore, maze tracing or pursuit tasks often appear on factors VZ or P. The status of a Spatial Scanning factor must be considered at least questionable if not highly dubious.

Nevertheless, several factors can be cited as of possible interest in this connection. In datasets BARR01 and BARR02 there occurs a factor whose two highest salient loadings are for tests labeled Linear Scanning and Matrix Scanning, respectively. In Linear Scanning, the subject is shown (on a computer screen, for 1.5 seconds) a row of 20 equilateral triangles. All the triangles have lines drawn through them except for one, two, three, or four of them (randomly over 20 trials). The subject's task is to indicate, by pressing a computer key, how many triangles do not have a line drawn through them. The score is the number correct. Matrix Scanning is almost the same task except that the triangles are arrayed in a 4 x 5 matrix. In dataset BARR02 several other visual search tasks also have loadings on the factor. These search tasks seem somewhat different from those required in tests of factor P (Perceptual Speed), in that the presentation time is probably too short to permit a true scanning operation; rather, the presentation must be apprehended as a whole, more or less as is required for efficient performance of the maze tracing task. This is a possibility that could be investigated by placing the BARR01 and BARR02 scanning tasks in a battery with maze tracing and other visual search tasks.

Reanalysis of a German study of attention abilities by Süllwold (1954) disclosed several factors that pertain to searching a visual field. One (factor 4) was assigned to factor P because it involved cancelling particular digits to be found in columns of numbers. Two others, however, seemed of interest in connection with a possible spatial scanning factor. Factor 2 had loadings for tests in which visual fields were presented with two-digit numbers randomly placed throughout the field. In one of the tests, the subject's task was to find and point to the numbers in ascending order. In another test, the visual field contained both numbers and letters and the task was to find the numbers and letters, alternately, in ascending order. For Factor 3, the tasks involved (1) finding the one repeated number in a display, and (2) finding which figure (circle, square, triangle, etc.) occurred most frequently in the display and stating how frequently it occurred.

PERCEPTUAL SPEED (P) FACTORS

French (1951) recognized a factor P, Perceptual Speed, found in numerous studies and

characterized by the task of finding in a mass of distracting material a given configuration which is borne in mind during the search. This includes the ability to compare pairs of items or to locate a unique item in a group of identical items. In all of these cases a perceived configuration is compared with a remembered one. The tests of this ability are all speeded; in no case is the configuration sought after so hidden as to cause difficulty if plenty of time were available. The high loadings of this factor on tests like *Name Comparison* (check sameness of names in pairs) and *Number Comparison* (check sameness of numbers in pairs) indicate that clerical ability as usually tested is mainly *Perceptual Speed* (French, 1951, p. 227).

A large number of tests, with various names, were mentioned as typically having high loadings on this factor.

The factor was extensively discussed in the 1963 ETS factor kit. It was defined as "speed in finding figures, making comparisons, and carrying out other very simple tasks involving visual perception." Further,

The concept of Perceptual Speed being defined here can be considered to be the centroid of several sub-factors which have been separated (Bechtoldt, 1953), but which, for most purposes, are likely to be useful when considered as a unitary concept. The sub-factors have been named or defined as (a) speed of symbol discrimination, Cattell's U. I. T12, Guilford's ESU,... (b) speed of making comparisons as in many tests of "clerical aptitude"..., (c) speed of form discrimination as in recognizing predetermined but novel configurations, Guilford's EFU,..., (d) speed of classification of readily discriminable configurations into categories, and possibly others (French, Ekstrom, & Price, 1963, p. 31).

As markers for the factor, the 1963 kit offered the following:

> P-1, Finding *A*'s Test (adapted from Thurstone's Letter *A*): "In each column of 41 words, the task is to check the 5 words having the letter 'a.'" The score is the number of words correctly checked in the time limit.

P-2, Number Comparison Test (adapted from the Minnesota Vocational Test for Clerical Workers): "The subject inspects pairs of multi-digit numbers and indicates whether the two numbers in each pair are the same or different."

P-3, Identical Pictures Test (adapted from tests originally by Thurstone): "For each item the subject is to check which of 5 numbered geometrical figures or pictures in a row is identical to the given figure at the left end of the row." Each of two parts has 48 rows for which a time-limit of 1.5 minutes is allowed, and the score is the number of items correctly answered in the time-limit.

These same tests, with minor changes, are suggested as markers by the 1976 kit, whose manual again notes the possibility that the factor is the centroid of several subfactors.

None of the marker tests suggested for factor P is displayed in Eliot and Smith's (1983) compilation of spatial tests, such tests apparently being regarded as outside the scope of spatial tests.

Table 8.9 lists 100 token factors, in 92 datasets, classified as belonging in the category Perceptual Speed. Assignment of factors to this category was in general fairly easy, being based on the presence of high salient loadings for tests such as Finding A's, Number Comparisons, and Identical Pictures, the markers offered in the 1976 ETS Kit. Among datasets where such a factor was particularly well defined are BAIR01, COOM01, CORN01, FLAN01, GUIL17, HOEP31, SHAY01, and SHAY02. In dataset CORN01, the *only* salient loadings on the factor were for the three tests for P in the 1976 ETS factor-reference kit. Aside from these cases, it is seldom that other datasets contain representatives of all three of these types of variables, and a perceptual speed factor is not always well defined. It is frequently the case that variables from other factors in the visual perception domain, or even other domains such as reasoning, appear on the factor.

Several datasets appear to present variants of P factors, but evidence for multiple kinds of P factors is meager. In dataset ANDR01 there are two factors classified as P, factor 2 being loaded with a variety of clerical tasks (Clerical Name Checking, Clerical Number Checking, Spelling II, and Verifying Arithmetic) and factor 3 being loaded mainly with two "cancellation" tests. Nevertheless, the oblique factors underlying these orthogonalized factors are substantially correlated ($r = .534$).

In dataset BECH01, factor 4 is the clearest example of a P factor, with loadings on several speeded symbol-finding and cancellation tests, but factors 2, 6, and 9 are possible variants. The highest loadings on factor 2 are for variables (Verbal Enumeration and Finding Boys' First Names) emphasizing speed in using verbal knowledge to perform search tasks, but other variables include several (apparently speeded) vocabulary tests. The highest salient loading on factor 6 is for a variable (Two-Hand Coordination/Ratio) that was thought to characterize the "resistance to conflict" aspect of factor CF, but the remainder of the saliently loaded variables all involve search of visual fields. The two highest loadings for factor 9 are

Table 8.9. *100 Perceptual Speed (P) factors in 92 datasets arranged in order of approximate mean age of sample[a]*

Dataset	Date	C'y code	Age	Sample code	M/F code	Factor no.	Remarks (higher-order factors; others related)
WALL51	'67	S	8	1	1	2	1:2G
WALL52	'67	S	8	6	2	3	1:2G
UNDH01	'76	O	9	1	3	6	1:2G;3,4:VZ?;7:CS;11:SR
BROW21	'33	E	10	6	1	4	1:2G;3:VZ
HARR51	'73	U	10	1	1	8	1:2G;4:SR
HARR52	'73	U	10	1	2	6	1:2G;7:VZ?
HARR53	'73	U	10	1	1	3	1:2G;5:CS
HARR54	'73	U	10	1	2	5	1:2G;3:CS
REIN01	'65	G	10	1	3	3	1:2G
SPEA31	'77	A	11	6	1	5	1:2G
SPEA32	'77	A	11	6	2	8	1:2G;9:CS?
SPEA33	'77	A	11	O	1	4	1:2G
WERD51	'71	S	11	6	3	3	1:2G;5:VZ
ELKO01	'35	E	12	6	1	7	1:2G;6:VZ
STAK01	'61	U	12	1	3	3	1:2G;13:SR
SUMI02	'58	N	12	1	1	6	1:2H;5:2S
PATE01	'30	U	13	6	1	6	1:2G;8:VZ
THUR81	'41	U	13	6	3	9	1:3G;8:2S;12:2V;13:SR;14:SS?
THUR82	'41	U	13	6	3	9	1:3G;8:2S;10:SR
WERD41	'69	S	13	6	3	3	1:2S
GERS02	'63	U	14	1	3	7	6:20
MURP01	'36	U	14	6	1	3	1:2G;2:VZ
SHAY01	'67	U	14	1	1	8	1:2G;7:VZ
SHAY02	'67	U	14	1	2	4	1:3G;2:2V;3:VZ
SUMI01	'58	N	14	1	1	2	1:2G;6:LE?
SEGE01	'57	U	15	1	1	7	1:3G;2:2H;4:VZ;6:2S
SEGE02	'57	U	15	1	2	7	1:3G;2:2H;3:VZ;6:2S
TENO01	'69	U	15	1	3	4	1:2G
BAIR01	'51	U	16	D	3	3	1:2G
BLAK01	'41	U	16	6	3	4	1:2G;3:VZ?
CURE11	'68	U	16	6	1	9	1:2G;2:VZ
CURE12	'68	U	16	6	2	4	1:2C;7:VZ
FRED13	'82	U	16	6	3	4	1:20;3:CS;5:CF
SIMR01	'47	U	16	6	3	3	1:2G;4:P?;5:2V;6:SR;7:IO
"	"	"	"	"	"	4	Alternate P
SNOW11	'77	U	16	1	3	6	1:2G;2:CS;3:VZ
COOM01	'41	U	17	1	3	8	1:2G;6:SR
FLAN01	'64	U	17	1	1	6	1:2G;5:VZ
HOEP31	'64	U	17	6	3	6	1:2H
MICH61	'51	U	17	6	1	5	1:2G;2:VZ;3:SR?
MICH62	'51	U	17	6	2	5	1:2G;2:VZ
TAYL01	'47	U	17	1	3	8	6:2N
THUR11	'38	U	17	1	3	3	1:20;4:20
"	"	"	"	"	"	5	Alternate P?
THUR31	'40	U	17	1	3	4	1:2G;3:SR
"	"	"	"	"	"	6	Alternate P?

Table 8.9 (*cont.*)

Dataset	Date	C'y code	Age	Sample code	M/F code	Factor no.	Remarks (higher-order factors; others related)
FREN11	'57	U	18	3	1	6	1:2S;8:2H;9:VZ
GOOD01	'43	U	18	A	1	4	1:2G;7:VZ
LANG31	'41	U	18	6	2	2	1:2G
LANS31	'82	U	18	6	3	2	1:2S;3:P;5:VZ.
							P:Paper & Pencil Tests.
"	"	"	"	"	"	3	P:Experimental Settings.
LORD01	'56	U	18	3	1	3	1:2S;5:2G;6:VZ;9:Spatial Speed.
MORR11	'41	U	18	P	1	2	1:2G;6:VZ
STUM11	'74	G	18	6	1	4	1:2G;3:VZ
ADKI03	'52	U	19	2	1	10	1:2H;6:CS;7:20
ALLI02	'60	U	19	2	1	3	1:2H
BECH01	'47	U	19	6	3	2	1:2S;7:SR;9:P;10:CS;11:CF?
"	"	"	"	"	"	4	Alternate P
"	"	"	"	"	"	6	Alternate P
"	"	"	"	"	"	9	Alternate P
BOLT11	'73	U	19	E	3	3	1:2G;2:VZ
BUND11	'67	U	19	6	1	5	1:2G
EKST11	'67	U	19	6	2	8	1:3G;2:2V;3:SR?;4:SR?;5:VZ;
							6:CS;7:2S;9:CF
FLEI12	'54	U	19	2	1	2	1:2G
FLEI51	'71	U	19	2	1	5	1:2G;4:VZ
HUNT71	'75	U	19	6	3	2	Orthogonal factors
SCHA11	'40	U	19	6	1	9	1:3G;2:2H;4,11:SR P(verbal)
"	"	"	"	"	"	12	Alternate P (letters)
SNOW12	'77	U	19	6	3	5	1:2G;6:VZ
TAYL51	'76	K	19	1	1	5	1:20;2,3,4,6:IL;7:CS?
THUR21A	'38	U	19	6	3	4	1:2F;2:VZ
YELA21	'68	P	19	3	1	2	1:2G;3:VZ
CORY01	'77	U	21	2	1	5	1:2F;6:2C;8,9:CS?
FRUC21	'52	U	21	2	1	6	1:2G;4:VZ
GUIL16	'51	U	21	3	1	8	1:3G;2:2H;5:VZ;7:2V
GUIL17	'52	U	21	3	1	3	1:2G;5:VZ
GUIL31	'47	U	21	3	1	5	1:2G;2:VZ;4:SR
GUIL33	'47	U	21	3	1	4	1:2G
GUIL34	'47	U	21	3	1	5	1:2G
GUIL35	'47	U	21	3	1	4	1:2G;8:VZ
GUIL37	'47	U	21	3	1	2	1:2G
GUIL39	'47	U	21	3	1	5	1:2G;2:SR;3:VZ
GUIL40	'47	U	21	3	1	3	1:2G;5:SR;6,7:LE?
GUIL42	'47	U	21	3	1	2	1:2G
GUIL43	'47	U	21	3	1	2	1:2G
GUIL44	'47	U	21	3	1	2	1:2G
GUIL45	'47	U	21	3	1	3	1:2G
GUIL46	'47	U	21	3	1	7	1:2G;3:VZ;4:MV;8:IL
KELL01	'64	U	21	3	1	8	6:2H;7:MV
LUCA01	'53	U	21	3	1	10	1:2H;3:VZ;7:2S
MESS01	'75	U	21	3	1	5	1:2H;3,8:CS;4:CF

Table 8.9 (*cont.*)

Dataset	Date	C'y code	Age	Sample code	M/F code	Factor no.	Remarks (higher-order factors; others related)
WITT11	'43	U	21	2	1	3	1:2G;5:SR
WOTH01	'90	U	21	1	3	6	1:3G;2:2F;10:CS;12:2V;13:SR
MICH51	'50	U	22	6	1	3	1:2G;2:VZ
HAKS01	'74	C	24	1	3	9	1:3G;5:21;6:SR;8:CF;13:2C;19:CS
ANDR01	'37	U	30	C	2	2	1:2V;3:P?;4:VZ
HORN21	'78	U	30	Q	1	3	1:2C;9:2G;12:GV
VERS01	'83	K	30	U	1	3	1:2S
ROYC11	'76	C	40	4	3	2	1:2G
CORN01	'83	U	71	1	3	6	1:2G

[a]See Appendix A for codes. In a few cases, the classifications of factors shown here were preliminary and may not agree with the final classifications shown in the tables of Appendix B.

for tests (Concrete Association and Gottschaldt Figures) that appear to tap processes not characteristic of the P factor, but loadings ranked 3 and 4 are for variables (Letters IV and Letters I) that require subjects to search a visual field rapidly for a given symbol and in their response indicate whether it is on the left or the right of the field. These results suggest that variants of factor P involve differences in types of stimulus content.

Dataset LANS31 reveals two factors that may be considered as belonging to the Perceptual Speed classification: factor 2 is the more conventional one, measured by paper and pencil tests (including a paper-and-pencil version of the Posner letter matching task), while factor 3 (in its oblique form highly correlated with factor 2) is loaded on four variables which are reaction times from a computerized version of the Posner task. This finding suggests that measures of P may be affected by format or "method" variance.

Dataset SCHA11 yielded two factors assigned to P. Factor 12, with loadings on two laboratory-administered visual search tasks (finding the letter X in arrays of 4 or 18 letters and indicating whether it is on the left or the right of the field) bears greater similarity to P factors found elsewhere, but it should be noted that the scores are latencies of response. Factor 9 has some aspects of a P factor in that visual search is required, and scores are latencies of response, but the two highest loadings are for variables Enumeration I and Enumeration II. In the former, the task is to indicate in which of two columns of words (left or right) is found a member of the class named at the top of the display (e.g., *green* as a *color*). In the latter, the task is similar; it is to find a word *with an association to* the concept named at the top of the display (e.g., *fever* as related to HEAT). Other variables on this factor are two choice reaction time tasks, responding L (left) or R (right) depending on where a letter is in the display, and two variables measuring speeds in judging the same vs. opposite meanings of words. It is difficult to interpret this factor as pure perceptual speed in view of the several other elements embodied in it – semantic judgments, choice-reaction time, and left–right judgments. One is tempted to assign this factor to a reaction-time category, but the variables on this factor had both positive and negative loadings on factor 7 in this study, interpreted as a reaction time (RT) factor. One can only say that the variables explored in this early study by Schaefer (1940), using laboratory presentations, deserve further investigation.

The author of dataset BUND11 (Bunderson, 1967) postulated a Spatial Scanning factor separate from Perceptual Speed and was able to confirm its separation in a confirmatory factor analysis; in my reanalysis, however, the two variables postulated to measure Spatial Scanning (Maze Training and Map Planning, from the ETS factor kit) appeared on factor 5, interpreted as P, and did not define a factor separate from P.

Tests of the Perceptual Speed (P) Factor

There are two main types of tests of Perceptual Speed, closely related in terms of the processes they appear to tap:

1. Tests of speed in locating one or more given symbols or visual patterns in a extended visual field, with or without distracting stimuli. Tests of this kind are found under various names: Cancellation, Finding *A*'s, First Digit Cancellation, Identical Numbers, Identical Patterns, Inspection, Letter Cancellation, and Scattered *X*'s. For example, in Finding *A*'s the task is to look through columns of words and cross out all words that contain the letter *a*.

2. Tests of speed in comparing given symbols presented either side-by-side or more widely separated in a visual field. Names of typical tests of this kind are: Clerical Checking, Faces, Identical Forms, Name Comparisons, Number Checking, and Object Inspection. In some of these, a stimulus is presented at the left of a row of stimuli, and the task can be to find which other stimulus in the row is either identical to, or different from, the first stimulus. Sometimes the task is to find which stimulus, in a row, is different from the others.

From evidence in dataset LANS31, speed in performing the Posner Letter-Matching Task (Posner & Mitchell, 1967) can be a measure of factor P. In this task, subjects are visually presented with pairs of letters such as *AA*, *Aa*, *Ab*, and *ab*. The task can be administered under either of two conditions: (1) Physical Identity – the subject is instructed to respond S (Same) or D (Different) depending upon whether the letters in the pair are "physically identical." Thus, among the stimuli cited, only the letters *AA* are physically identical. (2) Name Identity – the subject is instructed to respond S or D depending upon whether the letters in a pair "have the same name"; thus, in the pairs *AA* and *Aa*, the letters have the same name, letter "*a*". Mean reaction times for name identity (NI) are significantly longer than those for physical identity (PI), and it has been found by Hunt (1978) that the difference (NI − PI) is correlated about −.3 with typical scholastic aptitude tests. In dataset HUNT71, this difference had a loading on factor P along with at least two variables measuring clerical checking speed. However, these findings for difference scores possibly reflect only the fact that physical and name match speeds are highly correlated. A study by Schwartz, Griffin, and Brown (1983) supported Carroll's (1980a) suggestions that (1) the variable (NI − PI) is related more to speed than to power or level of mastery in scholastic aptitude tests, and (2) the (NI − PI) statistic, as computed, is not the optimal formula for predicting standardized test scores.

The two types of tests mentioned above – those involving search and those involving comparison – are closely related in the sense that both are concerned with comparisons of stimuli. In tests of the first type, the comparisons are with a stimulus that is held in mind during the search task, and in tests of the second kind, the comparisons concern whether immediately given pairs of stimuli are identical or not.

A number of other types of tests occasionally appear with significant or salient loadings on P. One frequently occurring type requires some kind of table look-up, either explicitly, as in a test called Dial & Table Reading (studied in FLEI12, GUIL44, KELL01), or implicitly, as in various kinds of Digit–Symbol and Coding tests, where examinees are likely to make frequent reference to the list of codes. The connection with factor P apparently arises because the task can require the subject to make a visual search of information presented in a tabular arrangement of some form.

Factor P must to some extent involve peripheral motor behavior, such as eye movements in making visual searches, or finger movements in making check-marks or other indications of choices. As yet, there is inadequate evidence on how much variance in P measures is attributable to such peripheral effects. (But see datasets GUIL35 and FLEI12, which contain variables such as Marking Accuracy and Speed of Marking that were the result of efforts to measure these peripheral effects.) There is a role for central processes, however, consisting of decisions arising from comparisons of stimuli for identity or other attributes. Generally, higher loadings on P are for variables in which decisions are relatively simple rather than complex. For example, in dataset BAIR01, loadings for two variables involving number comparisons are higher than those for two variables involving comparisons of names.

The tests offered for P in the 1976 ETS factor kit are generally satisfactory as markers of the factor if paper-and-pencil tests are to be used. Finding *A*'s exemplifies an easy visual search task requiring successive inspection of words, arranged in columns, for the presence of the lower-case letter *a*; because of its content, it may tend to have supplementary loadings on a verbal or reading skill factor. The Number Comparison Test involves careful checking of paired multidigit stimuli for exact identity, and the Identical Pictures Test requires searching a row of figural stimuli for identity with a given stimulus at the left. It does not appear to be as difficult as a similar test, Identical Forms, that was used extensively by Thurstone and others (see datasets MICH51, MICH61, MICH62, THUR11, THUR21A).

The paper-and-pencil Letter Matching tests developed by Lansman et al. (1982), based on the Posner and Mitchell (1967) task, would constitute desirable supplementary tests of P, and if it is feasible to give computerized tests and record latencies of response, these computerized versions would be useful.

The P factor can be defined by means of a mapping sentence that would look approximately as follows:

$$\text{Speed in}
\begin{bmatrix}
\text{searching for} \\
\text{and finding} \\
\text{or correctly} \\
\text{comparing}
\end{bmatrix}
\begin{bmatrix}
\text{one or} \\
\text{more}
\end{bmatrix}
\begin{bmatrix}
\text{literal} \\
\text{digital} \\
\text{figural}
\end{bmatrix}
\text{stimuli}$$

$$\text{in a visual field arranged}
\begin{bmatrix}
\text{by pairs} \\
\text{by rows} \\
\text{in columns} \\
\text{at random}
\end{bmatrix}
\text{for}
\begin{bmatrix}
\text{identity.} \\
\text{difference.} \\
\text{size.} \\
\text{etc.}
\end{bmatrix}$$

The values taken by each of the mapping variables in a given case probably make for differences in mean performance, but as far as can be determined from the data, they do not make for systematic differences in factor loadings.

IMAGERY (IM) FACTORS

Table 8.10 lists two token factors that may be assigned to a possible factor of Imagery (IM).

Interpretations of several of the factors in the domain of visual perception, especially VZ and SR, sometimes make reference to the notion that good performers use "imagery" in arriving at solutions to certain kinds of spatial problems. It is supposed, for example, that they can mentally manipulate abstract spatial forms in the course of doing tests like Paper Folding or Card Rotation. If this supposition is correct, one might expect measures of imagery vividness to be correlated with scores on factors VZ or SR. Dataset BLAC21 suggests that measures of vividness of imagery are *not* correlated with scores on spatial tests. Factor 1 in this dataset is loaded with at least three subjective measures of imagery vividness, and it is totally independent of factor 4, labeled as VZ. Variable 9, for example, was the average of self-reports of vividness when the subject was requested to form mental images of various events. Of course, the fact that subjective reports of imagery vividness do not correlate with performance on tests of factor VZ does not exclude the possibility that some kind of mental manipulation of images occurs in such tests.

The datasets yield no further information on this point. Dataset PAIV11, concerned with eidetic imagery, proved to be unanalyzable, possibly due to errors in the published correlation matrix. However, Poltrock and Agnoli (1986) have

Table 8.11. *26 Length Estimation (LE) factors in 9 datasets arranged in order of approximate mean age of sample[a]*

Dataset	Date	C'y code	Age	Sample code	M/F code	Factor no.	Remarks (higher-order factors; others related)
THUR71	'49	U	16	$	1	10	1:2G;2:CF;3:SR;7:CS;9:VZ?
BLAC21	'80	U	19	P	2	1	3:VZ (orthogonal factors)

[a]See Appendix A for codes. In a few cases, the classifications of factors shown here were preliminary and may not agree with the final classifications shown in the tables of Appendix B.

contributed an important and useful discussion of possible relations between imagery and spatial abilities. They conclude that various imaging processes can play an important role in performing spatial tasks. Poltrock and Brown (1984) found evidence that there may be as many as five or more separate imagery abilities, of which vividness is only one.

Reanalysis confirmed a small factor isolated by Thurstone (1949) that he called "kinesthetic imagery." Factor 10 in dataset THUR71 has loadings on two tests: Hands and Bolts. The test Hands requires subjects to judge whether pairs of pictured hands in different positions are the same or different in terms of being right or left. Many subjects are apparently able to approach this task by matching the pictures to subjective, kinesthetic images of left or right hands, and making the judgment accordingly. The test Bolts has pictures of bolts in position to screw into a block. Subjects have to indicate which of two directions each bolt should be turned to screw it in, given that all bolts shown have right-hand threads. Some subjects apparently report giving answers on the basis of kinesthetic experiences in turning screws. It is not clear whether this is truly a case of imagery. In any event, the status of the factor is questionable because it has not been isolated in other datasets. Indeed, these variables (Hands; Bolts) are loaded on factor SR (Spatial Relations) in dataset JEFF11.

LENGTH ESTIMATION (LE) FACTORS

French (1951) reported a Length Estimation factor from several US Army Air Force datasets and described it as "the ability to compare the length of lines or distances on a sheet of paper." Marker tests for the factor were included in the 1963 ETS kit, as follows:

> Le-1, Estimation of Length Test (adapted from a USAF test of the same name, Guilford & Lacey, 1947, p. 463): "Each item consists of lines 1/2 to 1 1/2 inches in length oriented in different directions. This is to be compared with a set of 5 pairs of companion lines at the center of the page. The test lines may be as long as or twice as long as the companion lines. This is a speeded test."
>
> Le-2, Shortest Road Test (adapted from the USAF test Shortest Path, Guilford & Lacey, 1947, p. 452): "Each item consists of 2 points. Three curved or angular

Table 8.11. *26 Length Estimation (LE) factors in 9 datasets arranged in order of approximate mean age of sample*[a]

Dataset	Date	C'y code	Age	Sample code	M/F code	Factor no.	Remarks (higher-order factors; others related)
SMIT51	'66	U	8	1	3	1	Age; V; Curvature Judgments
"	"	"	"	"	"	2	Failure of Size Constancy
"	"	"	"	"	"	4	Fractionation Judgments
"	"	"	"	"	"	5	Arm Length Estimation
"	"	"	"	"	"	6	Overestimation Arm Length
"	"	"	"	"	"	7	Motion Parallax Judgments
"	"	"	"	"	"	8	Distance Judgments
"	"	"	"	"	"	9	Uninterpreted
"	"	"	"	"	"	10	Uninterpreted
SUMI03	'58	N	10	1	1	6	1:2G
SUMI01	'58	N	14	1	1	6	1:2G;2:P
SLAT01	'40	E	18	A	1	5	1:2V;3:SR;4:2C
SMIT52	'66	U	18	1	3	2	Fractionation Judgments
"	"	"	"	"	"	3	Failure of Size Constancy
"	"	"	"	"	"	4	Uninterpreted
"	"	"	"	"	"	5	Arm Length Estimation
"	"	"	"	"	"	6	V;S;Age;Curvature Judgments
"	"	"	"	"	"	7	Size Constancy?
"	"	"	"	"	"	8	Motion Parallax Judgments
"	"	"	"	"	"	9	Distance Judgments
"	"	"	"	"	"	11	Overestimation Arm Length
WICK01	'80	U	20	6	1	3	1:2G
GUIL38	'47	U	21	3	1	6	1:2G
GUIL40	'47	U	21	3	1	6	1:2G;3:P;5:SR
"	"	"	'	"	"	7	Alternate LE?
ROFF11	'52	U	21	3	1	9	1:2G;2:Plotting;3:CF?;5,7:VZ

[a]See Appendix A for codes. In a few cases, the classifications of factors shown here were preliminary and may not agree with the final classifications shown in the tables of Appendix B.

> lines are drawn between these 2 points. The task of the examinee is to select the shortest of these lines."
>
> Le-3, Nearer Point Test (adapted from the USAF test Nearest Point, Guilford & Lacey, 1947, p. 451): "Each item consists of 2 dots, a reference point, and some distracting lines and figures. The task is to select the dot that is nearer to the reference point."

This factor was one of those dropped from the 1976 ETS kit "because they seem to refer to achieved skills rather than to what are normally called aptitudes" (Ekstrom et al., 1976, p. 5).

Evidence for the existence of a Length Estimation factor remains meager, because there has been very little interest in it since the 1940s and 1950s, possibly because little practical utility was seen for measures of it. Table 8.11 lists 26 token factors, in 9 datasets, that were assigned to LE in our database; few if any are clear in their interpretation. Psychologists have not been successful in constructing good measures of the factor, if it in fact exists. This is surprising in view of the fact that length estimation ability should be readily measurable with the use of basic psychophysical principles.

Tests of the Length Estimation (LE) Factor

The simplest tests of a possible LE factor are to be found in dataset SLAT01: Parallel Lines – a test of judging whether two lines are really parallel, and Divided Lines – a test of judging whether a line has been divided into two equal parts. Slater remarked, in this connection, "There is a deep conviction among many people unfamiliar with the evidence, that such tests should be of use in selecting trainees for mechanical trades. Previous investigations have indicated that this [belief] is probably unwarranted" (Slater, 1940, pp. 46–47). Although it appears that such tests can reveal reliable individual differences in making elementary spatial distance judgments, their validity may not hold up in practice because length estimation judgments may not be critically necessary for workers in mechanical and construction trades, in view of the ready availability of instruments for measuring lengths.

Length Discrimination Tests used in several datasets of Sumita and Ichitani (1958) – SUMI01 and SUMI03 – require subjects to bisect lines by sight, or to adjust an apparatus to bisect a fixed length. In these datasets, it is of interest that a weight discrimination task also loaded on a length estimation factor.

Several tests of Length Estimation show up in factor 6 of GUIL38 and factors 6 and 7 of GUIL40. In Nearest Point, the task is to judge which of two points in a geometrical design is nearer to a reference point. The various features of the geometrical design can tend to create distracting and illusory effects. This is even more true in Shorter Line (in GUIL38) or Line Length (in GUIL40, apparently the same test but under a different name), where the subject has to judge which of two labeled lines radiating from a point is shorter; the lines are accompanied by other lines both straight and wavy that could cause judgments to be in error due to illusory effects. In GUIL40, Map Distance adapts Nearest Point to the context of a map, and in Path Length, subjects compare lengths of routes on a map – an "upgrade" of the Shorter Line test.

The element of illusion is even more pronounced in several tests loaded on factor 9 in dataset ROFF11. In Normality of Perception, judgments of length are to be made for various standard illusions; the instructions for the task make no attempt to produce an illusion-resisting set. In Objectivity of Perception, the task is the same but instructions emphasize the desirability of resisting the illusion. Nevertheless, the loadings of these tests on factor 9 are substantially the same (.50 and .41 respectively). Significantly lower is the loading (.338) of a further test, Estimation of Length, in which the subject matches the length of a number of lines with one of five standard lengths that are given.

Although marker tests for a Length Estimation factor were offered in the 1963 ETS factor-reference kit, there is as yet inadequate research to justify the use of these or other tests as markers for the factor. Development of adequate tests would probably require special, focused effort, but whether the effort would be worthwhile is moot. Length Estimation ability appears to be a dimension of individual differences that could be reliably measured, but that is practically valueless for assessing or predicting any behavior of importance. I am not aware of, and have not attempted to locate, research literature on the potential trainability of this ability.

Smith and Smith's (1966) Study of Spatial Judgments

Smith and Smith (1966) conducted an extensive study of children's and adults' judgments of various kinds of spatial distances, a study that may have some relevance to the Length Estimation factor. From 182 subjects ranging in age from 5 1/2 to 42 years, they obtained 40 variables, most of which were judgments of size, distance, motion, visual direction, and curvature of various objects. The reader is referred to the original report for details of the quite elaborate experimental settings for these judgments. Age, arm length, measures of visual acuity, and scores on a vocabulary test and a specially prepared analogue of Thurstone's Cards test were also obtained, although it should be noted that the battery contained an inadequate number of markers of spatial and other abilities.

For factor analysis, the group was divided into those less than 12 years of age (dataset SMIT11) and those at 12 years and over (dataset SMIT12). The authors employed principal component analysis and (apparently) oblique rotation by a procedure that cannot be easily grasped from their description, based on the extraction of 15 factors for the "adult" group and 16 for the "child" group. My more conservative factoring of their matrices produced only 10 factors in each case; the Varimax factors for dataset SMIT11 were left unrotated, and the oblique factors for dataset SMIT12 produced only a single weak second-order factor. My results show rough parallelism with those of the authors, but with much less clarity of factors, and less congruence between the two groups. Here follows a summary, showing what parallelism and consistency there appear to be:

	Factor number	
Factor description	"Child" group	"Adult" group
Age; Verbal ability; Curvature Judgments	1	6
Failure of Size Constancy	2	3,7
Visual Acuity	3	10
Fractionation Judgments	4	2
Distance Judgments by Arm length	5	5
Self-initiated movement (Overestimation of arm length in wagon tasks)	6	11
Motion Parallax Judgments	7	8
Unrestricted Distance Judgments	8	9

The remainder of the factors appear to be uninterpretable. Even the interpretations given here are dubious in some cases, being based on only two or three variables that were highly similar to one another. One can agree with the authors that spatial judgments of the sort they studied are multifactorial, suggesting that the Length Estimation (LE) factor discussed above should also be regarded as multifactorial.

FACTORS IN THE PERCEPTION OF ILLUSIONS (IL)

French (1951) reported a Figure Illusions factor that had appeared only in a study by Thurstone (1944a); he described it as being "limited to the resistance to illusions involving geometrical figures" (p. 210). The factor was not considered for inclusion in any of the ETS factor-reference kits.

Table 8.12 lists seven token factors, in four datasets, that predominantly have salient loadings on measures of what subjects perceive – or misperceive – in visual illusions. I do not attempt to summarize or synthesize these data for several reasons: (1) the data are relatively incomplete and not always well enough described to make synthesis possible; (2) the data are to a considerable extent outdated by the publication of a major factor-analytic study of visual illusions by Coren, Girgus, Ehrlichman, and Hakstian (1976; see also Coren & Girgus, 1978); and (3) any summary or synthesis that I could make in this space would be too brief to be of use. I show Table 8.12 only for its possible use by researchers who may wish to compare the results with those published by Coren et al. (1976).

I will, however, summarize the findings of Coren et al. On the basis of the responses of 221 observers to 45 illusion configurations, they performed an analysis that yielded five factors. In describing these factors, I quote from their report:

1.   *Shape and direction illusions.* "This grouping predominantly includes distortions in apparent shape, parallelism, and colinearity, which seem to arise in patterns with numerous intersecting line elements. ... The Poggendorff, Wundt, and Zöllner illusions are characteristic of this class."

2.   *Size contrast illusions.* "This classification ... represents those illusory distortions in which the apparent size of an element appears to be affected by the size of other elements that surround it, or form its context. ... The Delboeuf, Ebbinghaus, Jastrow, and Ponzo illusions are characteristic of the illusions on this factor."

3.   *Overestimation illusions.* "The illusions that show the highest loadings on this factor include all the apparently longer versions of the Müller–Lyer illusion, both parts of the Baldwin illusion, the apparently longer segment of the horizontal–vertical illusion, and the apparently longer segment of the Oppel–Kundt illusion."

4.   *Underestimation illusions.* "Since it includes most of the apparently shorter segments of the Müller–Lyer illusion, the apparently shorter segment of the Oppel–Kundt, and the horizontal–vertical illusions, it seems to be a factor that is the complement to Factor III [the overestimation illusions], representing predominantly underestimations of linear extent."

Table 8.12. *7 Visual Illusion (IL) factors in 4 datasets arranged in order of approximate mean age of sample*[a]

Dataset	Date	C'y code	Age	Sample code	M/F code	Factor no.	Remarks (higher-order factors; others related)
TAYL51	'76	K	19	1	1	2	1:20;5:P;7:CS? (Poggendorf)
"	"	"	"	"	"	3	(Hering, Zöllner, Wundt)
"	"	"	"	"	"	4	(Sanders, Müller-Lyer)
"	"	"	"	"	"	6	(Ehrenstein, Gatti)
THUR41	'44	U	19	6	3	4	1:2G;2:VZ;5:CS?
GUIL46	'47	U	21	3	1	8	1:2G;3:VZ;7:P
AFTA01	'69	C	43	1	3	5	1:20

[a]See Appendix A for codes. In a few cases, the classifications of factors shown here were preliminary and may not agree with the final classifications shown in the tables of Appendix B.

5.   *Frame of reference illusions.* "We have tentatively identified this as a frame-of-reference factor. If this interpretation is correct, illusions like the rod-and-frame ought to fall into this classification. Further experimental investigation is clearly necessary to specify this grouping more clearly." (Coren et al., 1976, pp. 134–135).

Coren et al. proceeded to compute a higher-order analysis, showing two correlated ($r = .49$) second-order factors: Factor A, they suggest, deals mainly with distortions of linear extent, while Factor B deals predominantly with distortions involving area, shape, and direction. They emphasize that while their classification is somewhat provisional, it has the virtue of being based on behavioral data rather than on theoretical suppositions.

One may ask whether these factors represent *abilities* in the usual sense, that is, as defined in Chapter 1. Probably they are better described as response tendencies, i.e., as extents to which individuals are affected by illusory aspects of stimuli. It may help to realize that the measurements taken, in the Coren et al. study, were the actual lengths of lines that subjects indicated when asked to mark "the apparent linear extent" of a given part of an illusory figure. The finding of five factors in these measurements suggests that subjects differ not only in the extent to which they are affected by illusory aspects of stimuli but also in what kinds of illusory phenomena they are affected by.

PERCEPTUAL ALTERNATIONS (PN) FACTORS

The factor Perceptual Alternations, listed by French (1951), had appeared in a study by Thurstone (1944a, dataset THUR41), where it had been called Rate of Alternations. It received loadings on several experimental tasks involving perceptual alternations, such as a Retinal Rivalry task, Windmill Alternations, and the Necker Cube. It was not represented in ETS factor-reference kits, either

Table 8.13. *3 Perceptual Alternations (PN) factors in 3 datasets arranged in order of approximate mean age of sample*[a]

Dataset	Date	C'y code	Age	Sample code	M/F code	Factor no.	Remarks (higher-order factors; others related)
FULG21	'66	U	19	P	3	2	1:CS (Orthogonal factors)
THUR41	'44	U	19	6	3	8	1:2G;2:VZ;4:IL;5:CS
AFTA01	'69	C	43	1	2	2	1:20;5:IL

[a]See Appendix A for codes. In a few cases, the classifications of factors shown here were preliminary and may not agree with the final classifications shown in the tables of Appendix B.

because it was not regarded as sufficiently well established or because it was thought impractical to include these experimental tasks in a paper-and-pencil factor reference kit.

Table 8.13 lists three token factors, in three datasets, classified as Perceptual Alternations (PN) factors.

One of the factors was that in dataset THUR41 already mentioned. According to my reanalysis it had loadings for three variables: Retinal Rivalry Reversals (number of reversals perceived for rival blue and yellow fields in two one-minute trials); the Necker Cube (number of alternations perceived in two one-minute exposures); and Windmill Illusion (number of alternations passively perceived in three minutes). This finding suggests that subjects tend to have substantial consistency, over several phenomena, in the rate at which they tend to alternate between the possible perceptions. Nevertheless, this rate did not correlate with any other factor in this study of perceptual abilities.

This was also essentially the finding of Fulgosi and Guilford (1966; dataset FULG21), whose data yielded a perceptual alternations factor that was orthogonal to a factor that could be interpreted as GV (general visual perception). The finding was a disconfirmation of Guilford's hypothesis that perceptual alternations measures would have loadings on his Divergent Production of Figural Classes (DFC) factor. Perceptual alternations were obtained in three experiments: (1) retinal rivalry, (2) the Necker cube, and (3) the Rubin vase figure, where perception alternates between profiles of human faces and of vases. The correlation between rates of alternation in the Necker cube and the Rubin vase figure was so high (.82) that these variables were combined for the factor analysis.

A Perceptual Alternations factor was also identified in dataset AFTA01, with loadings on Retinal Rivalry and Critical-Fusion Frequency. (There is also a small loading for a Modified Word Learning variable, which seems difficult to interpret.) The Critical-Fusion Frequency variable is produced by a task in which the subject adjusts the rate of flashing of an intermittent light source until fusion (appearance of steadiness of the light) occurs. The finding that critical-fusion

Table 8.14. *10 miscellaneous factors (V &) in the domain of visual perception*[a]

Dataset	Date	C'y code	Age	Sample code	M/F code	Factor no.	Remarks (higher-order factors; others related)
JOHA01	'65	S	7	1	3	4	1:2D. Nonverbal intelligence
JONE34	'49	U	13	1	3	3	1:2C;4:VZ. Orientation tasks.
ROFF11	'52	U	21	3	1	2	1:2G. Plotting ability (PQ)
,,	,,	,,	,,	,,	,,	4	Movement detection (MD)
,,	,,	,,	,,	,,	,,	7	Directional thinking?
SAUN03	'59	U	18	6	1	3	1:2G;2:VZ. Specific for WAIS Picture Completion
SAUN11	'60	U	18	6	1	2	1:2V. WAIS Picture Completion: Maintenance of Perspective
,,	,,	,,	,,	,,	,,	3	Effect of Uncertainty
,,	,,	,,	,,	,,	,,	4	Maintenance of Contact
VOSS01	'77	G	8	1	3	1	Visual Exploration

[a]See Appendix A for codes. In a few cases, the classifications of factors shown here were preliminary and may not agree with the final classifications shown in the tables of Appendix B.

frequency is related to rate of alternation in retinal rivalry suggests that these variables relate to a common neuropsychological function.

OTHER POSSIBLE VISUAL PERCEPTION FACTORS

Table 8.14 lists 10 token factors, in 6 datasets, that appeared not to be classifiable under any visual perception factors that have been presented above, but that deserve mention and description here for their possible interest in future research.

Factor 4 in dataset JOHA01 appears to represent nonverbal intelligence measured at age 7 by three variables: Levin's School Readiness test, the revised Goodenough Draw-a-Man test, and a nonverbal intelligence test, with nine subtests, called Picture Choice. It corresponds approximately to Johansson's (1965) factor IV: "ability to form concepts and perceive and organize spatial relationships." It is classified here because nonverbal intelligence tests usually emphasize perception of spatial relationships.

Factor 3 in dataset JONE34 is loaded chiefly with two items from Stanford–Binet scales called Orientation: Direction and thus may represent a rather specific dimension indexing children's ability to answer questions like "Suppose you are going south and then turn to your left; in what direction are you facing now?"

Factors from Roff's (1952) Study

In an extensive study of visual perception abilities, Roff (1952) isolated three factors that seem not to have been subsequently studied, but they are of sufficient clarity and interest to mention here, and they were confirmed in my reanalysis.

Factor 2 in dataset ROFF11 can be interpreted as a Plotting (PQ) factor, i.e., ability to plot points on orthogonal coordinates, or to solve problems requiring the plotting or use of such points. Although its highest salient loading was for the test Dial and Table Reading – a fact that might make it a candidate for assignment to the Perceptual Speed factor P – many of the variables loaded on it support its interpretation as a Plotting Ability factor, e.g., Directional Marking, Plotting, Directional Plotting, and Coordinate Reading (all tests developed by the U.S. Air Force; for details, see Roff's monograph). Performance on many of these tests could well be a reflection of specific experiences and training in plotting of points on coordinates.

Factor 4 can be interpreted as Movement Detection (MD), having loadings on a number of motion-picture tests that require subjects to detect movements of various kinds and judge their size, rate, or direction.

Factor 7 can tentatively be interpreted as Directional Thinking. It has loadings on a number of paper-and-pencil tests that involve verbalization of directional information, for example, information about compass directions, and horizontal vs. vertical directions. Again, performance may be a reflection of specific experiences with the verbalization of compass and other kinds of direction.

Factors from Saunders's (1959, 1960a) Studies

In two studies, Saunders (1959, 1960a) addressed the dimensionality of the Wechsler Adult Intelligence Scale in groups of high school and college males. Dataset SAUN03 divided most subtests of the scale into odd item and even item portions in such a way as to show that the Performance scales actually measured two somewhat separate dimensions. One had its highest loadings on Block Designs and Object Assembly scales; this was factor 2 in the dataset and I assigned this to factor VZ. The other dimension (factor 3) was largely specific to the Picture Completion scale, though Picture Arrangement shared its variance between this and a Verbal/Information factor. This would indicate that the Picture Completion scale has specific variance. It is not clear how this should be interpreted; possibly it is associated with the specific requirement of the items that subjects find missing parts of pictures of various more-or-less-familiar objects. All first-order factors in this dataset had at least moderate loadings on a second-order general factor.

In dataset SAUN11 Saunders attempted to make an even more fine-grained analysis of the items of the Picture Completion scale. My reanalysis confirmed the three correlated factors he found; space permits only an abbreviated report of his interpretations of these factors:

> Factor 2: Maintenance of Perspective
> Factor 3: Effect of Uncertainty
> Factor 4: Maintenance of Contact

Loadings of particular items on a second-order general factor ranged from .026 to .741, suggesting that items were far from equally effective in measuring whatever the Picture Completion scale as a whole measures. The reader is referred to Saunders's article for further details.

Dynamic Spatial Reasoning (Pellegrino & Hunt, 1989)

Pellegrino and Hunt (1989) report a study of computer-controlled assessments of what they call "static" and "dynamic" spatial reasoning. Static spatial reasoning encompasses some of the visual perception factors that are ordinarily measured by paper-and-pencil tests, such as VZ, SR, and P as discussed above, but Pellegrino and Hunt find that these factors are even more reliably measured by computerized tests. Dynamic spatial reasoning concerns the prediction of "where a moving object is going and when it will arrive at its predicted destination" (p. 181). They claim that this kind of spatial reasoning is measurable only in the context of computerized testing (but actually, it has been studied with motion picture tests; cf. Gibson, 1947; Seibert & Snow, 1965). Their preliminary results suggest that one or more factors over and above those associated with static spatial reasoning are necessary to account for performance of tasks involving prediction of directions and arrival times of moving points and objects.

Possible "Ecological" Spatial Abilities

Lorenz and Neisser (1986) reported a factor-analytic study of a series of variables thought to reflect "ecological" dimensions of spatial ability, i.e., dimensions concerning the individual's ability to orient the self in a real-world space and to maintain a sense of direction. Data on these variables were obtained on 76 undergraduate subjects, along with scores on more traditional spatial ability tests such as Flags, a visualization test involving cubes, and a surface development test. The authors reported three independent ecological dimensions: landmark memory, route knowledge, and awareness of geographic directions, all being "essentially independent of psychometrically measured spatial ability." The resulting factors need further study, however, because of possible relationships with verbal and visual memory dimensions. Moreover, many of the variables appeared to depend on degree of familiarity with a particular spatial locality (a college campus).

SUMMARY

The major discriminable first-order factors in the domain of visual perception are as follows:

> VZ: Visualization: Ability in manipulating visual patterns, as indicated by level of difficulty and complexity in visual stimulus material that can be handled successfully, without regard to the speed of task solution.

> *SR: Spatial Relations*: Speed in manipulating relatively simple visual patterns, by whatever means (mental rotation, transformation, or otherwise).
>
> *CS: Closure Speed*: Speed in apprehending and identifying a visual pattern, without knowing in advance what the pattern is, when the pattern is disguised or obscured in some way.
>
> *CF: Flexibility of Closure*: Speed in finding, apprehending, and identifying a visual pattern, knowing in advance what is to be apprehended, when the pattern is disguised or obscured in some way.
>
> *P: Perceptual Speed*: Speed in finding a known visual pattern, or in accurately comparing one or more patterns, in a visual field such that the patterns are not disguised or obscured.

Available evidence for the existence and linear independence of the above factors is persuasive, except possibly in the case of factor CF. It is believed, however, that with better and more rationally constructed measures of the above spatial factors, each factor could be measured with high reliability and clearly discriminated from the other factors.

There is some evidence for the independent existence of a number of other factors in the visual perception domain, but further research is necessary to establish and provide adequate interpretations of these factors. Among such factors are the following:

> *PI: Serial Perceptual Integration*: The ability to apprehend and identify a visual pattern when parts of the pattern are presented serially or successively at a high rate. (It would be desirable to determine whether this factor is distinct from factor CS.)
>
> *SS: Spatial Scanning*: Speed in accurately following an indicated route or path through a visual pattern.
>
> *IM: Imagery*: Ability in forming internal mental representations of visual patterns, and in using such representations in solving spatial problems. (It would be desirable to show that this factor is distinct from factor VZ.)
>
> *LE: Length Estimation*: Ability to make accurate estimates or comparisons of visual lengths or distances (without using measuring instruments).

There is some evidence for individual differences in response tendencies in the presence of visual illusions and conditions, such as retinal rivalry and flicker fusion, giving rise to perceptual alternations.

Recent research suggests the existence of one or more factors, beyond those mentioned above, in tasks involving predictions of the directions and arrival times of moving points and objects.

Although there exists a considerable amount of knowledge about individual differences in the visual perception domain, there are many gaps in this knowledge, and procedures of measurement are in need of much refinement.

9   Abilities in the Domain of Auditory Reception

> ...if there are marked individual differences in the
> predispositions of individuals to appreciate various
> aspects of rhythm, pitch, melody, harmony, and timbre,
> then a fuller understanding of these differences should
> be relevant to music education.
>
> Roger Shepard (1981, p. 154)

It is difficult to define the domain of auditory receptive abilities in such a way that it properly excludes many abilities that in some way involve auditory reception, but that are not strictly auditory abilities, for example, speech comprehension ability or musical appreciation. Roughly, for this category I have in mind any ability that depends mainly on the characteristics of the auditory stimulus itself and the individual's capacity to apprehend, recognize, discriminate, or even ignore those characteristics, independent of the individual's knowledge of structures in language or in music, for example, that determine the overall pattern of an extended auditory signal. Speech comprehension ability, for example, would be regarded as an auditory receptive ability only when the auditory signal is distorted or attenuated in special ways that interfere with normal speech comprehension; in most contexts speech comprehension ability depends mainly on knowledge of a language and only secondarily on auditory ability. Similarly, music appreciation ability (if it exists and can be measured) would be regarded as an auditory receptive ability only to the extent that it might depend on the individual's capacity to perceive and discriminate those features of a musical auditory signal that make its appreciation possible. Some of the abilities discussed in this chapter involve special capacities to perceive musical structures.

The domain of individual differences in auditory receptive abilities has received relatively little attention in the factor-analytic literature. This statement can be made despite the fact that over a period that reaches as far back as 1919 or even earlier (Seashore, 1919), there has been considerable research on musical talent or aptitude, as reviewed for example by Shuter–Dyson and Gabriel (1981). But there are few if any trustworthy and *extensive* factor-analytic studies of musical talent; those reviewed here prove to be relatively unsatisfactory, in that they fail to yield conclusive statements about the structure of musical abilities. In the area of speech perception, I have been able to find only a single study (Hanley, 1956) that provides a reasonably satisfactory factor-analytic account of speech perception abilities, and even this leaves various questions unanswered. The vast

364

majority of factor-analytic studies in our database have totally neglected the domain of auditory abilities, largely because of their being restricted to the analysis of data from tests that involve no auditory stimuli (other than, say, spoken verbal instructions).

Nevertheless, the database yielded 38 datasets, listed in Table 9.1, that provide some basis for structuring the domain of auditory reception abilities. In constructing this table, a preliminary analysis of the factors identified was made by sorting them into eight groups, listed in a footnote to the table. Some of the groups are fairly restricted, while others comprise a considerable variety of factors. This grouping is, however, the basis for the detailed discussion that follows. In general, it can be assumed that factors in any one group are linearly independent of abilities in other groups, but further research may force modification of this assumption. The question of the higher-order structuring of auditory reception abilities is addressed in Chapter 15.

For convenience, the table also specifies the factor codes assigned to each identified first-order factor. The first letter of these codes is *U*, mnemonically recalling the second letter of *auditory*. (The letter *A* was not used because it also suggests such words as *achievement, aptitude,* and others.)

HEARING AND SPEECH THRESHOLD FACTORS (FACTORS UA, UT, AND UU)

It is well known that there are individual differences in hearing sensitivity; persons with abnormal degrees of hearing loss are said to be deaf in some degree. The science of diagnosing and treating hearing loss has advanced to a highly sophisticated state. It is well accepted that hearing loss is a purely sensory function that is almost by definition unrelated to any cognitive deficit (Corso, 1973). The factors listed in Table 9.2 reflect various measurements of hearing loss, either by pure tone audiometry or by speech audiometry. In the present context, they are of possible interest only to the extent that measurements of other auditory functions, particularly those of a cognitive nature, might be affected by sensory deficits. This point is well illustrated in the factors identified in datasets CLAU01, CLAU02, CLAU03, and CLAU04, which used both pure tone audiometry and speech audiometry to determine degrees of hearing loss in four samples of children (three of retardates at ages 9, 13, and 22, and one of children of normal intelligence at age 9). Hearing and speech threshold factors emerged for all samples, except that in dataset CLAU04 the audiometry threshold variable failed to appear on the hearing threshold factor, coded as UA. These factors, however, tended also to be loaded with a word association measure. It is not clear from the author's report exactly how the word stimuli for this association test were administered – whether by the spoken word of the examiner or by a recording (and if the latter, whether through earphones). In any case, the dependent variable was the average time of the subject's response, whatever that

Table 9.1. *Auditory reception factors identified in selected datasets (specified by number in hierarchical matrix, also by assigned factor code)*[a]

Dataset	Factor group[b]							
	1	2	3	4	5	6	7	8
AFTA01	—	—	—	—	—	—	—	12(UL)
BOLT11	7(UU)	—	—	—	—	—	—	—
CLAU01	5(UA)	—	—	—	—	—	—	—
CLAU02	4(UA)	—	—	—	—	—	—	—
CLAU03	7(UA)	—	—	—	—	—	—	—
CLAU04	6(UT)	—	—	—	—	—	—	—
ELKO01	—	—	5(U3)	—	—	—	—	—
FAUL11	—	—	1(U5)	—	—	—	2(UM)	—
FOGA00	—	—	5(U5)	—	6(UK)	—	—	—
GORD01	—	—	2(UI), 3(U9), 4(U3)	—	—	—	—	—
HANL01	4(UU), 8(UA), 9(UT)	—	3(U3)	2, 5, 10 (All UR)	—	—	11(UM)	—
HOLM11	—	—	5(U3)	—	—	—	—	—
HORN31	—	—	8(U3)	7(UR)	—	—	—	—
KAMM01	—	4(US)	—	—	—	—	—	
KARL01	—	—	2(U3), 3(U6)	—	—	—	—	—
KARL11	—	—	3(U6), 4(U5)	2(UR)	—	—	5, 8 (both UM)	—
LANG01	—	—	2(U9), 3(U6)	—	—	—	—	—
MORR11	—	—	3(U3)	—	—	—	—	—
MULL01	—	2(US)	—	—	—	—	—	—
PARA01	—	—	—	3(UR)	—	—	—	
PARA07	—	—	—	2(UR)	—	—	—	—
PIMS02	—	—	4(U5)	—	—	—	—	—
SING21	—	—	5(U3)	—	—	—	—	—
SNOW01	—	3(US)	—	—	—	—	—	—
STAN21	—	—	2(U5)	—	3(UK)	5(U8)	—	—
STAN31	—	3(US)	4(U1), 8(U3)	9(UR)	2(UK)	5(U8)	—	—
SUMI02	—	—	4(U3)	—	—	—	—	—
SUNG01	—	—	2(U3)	—	—	—	—	—
SUNG02	—	—	9(U3)	—	—	—	—	—
SUNG03	—	—	7(U3)	—	—	—	—	—
SUNG04	—	—	3(U3)	—	—	—	—	—
SUNG05	—	—	6(U3)	—	—	—	—	—
TAYL31	—	—	—	8(UR)	—	—	—	—
VALT11	—	4(US)	—	—	—	—	—	—
VALT12	—	6(US)	—	—	—	—	—	—

Table 9.1 *(cont.)*

Dataset	Factor group[b]							
	1	2	3	4	5	6	7	8
WHEA01	—	—	6(U3), 7(U6)	—	—	—	—	—
WHIT01	—	—	—	2(UR)	—	—	—	—
WING01	—	—	1(U5), 2(U9)	—	—	—	—	—

[a] Factor Codes:
  U1: Auditory Cognitive Relations
  U3: General Sound Discrimination
  U5: Pitch/Timbre Discrimination
  U6: Sound Intensity/Duration/Rhythm Discrimination
  U8: Maintaining and Judging Rhythm
  U9: Musical Sensitivity
  UA: Hearing Threshold
  UI: Tonal Imagery
  UK: Temporal Tracking
  UL: Binaural Sound Localization
  UM: Memory for Sound Patterns
  UP: Absolute Pitch (not identified in factor studies)
  UR: Resistance to Auditory Stimulus Distortion
  US: Speech Sound Discrimination
  UT: Speech Sound Threshold
  UU: "Speech Synthesis" in Speech Audiometry
[b] Factor Groups:
  1: Hearing and Speech Thresholds
  2: Speech Sound Discrimination
  3: Musical Sound Discrimination and Judgment
  4: Resistance to Auditory Distortion
  5: Temporal Tracking
  6: Maintaining and Judging Rhythm
  7: Memory for Musical Sounds
  8: Binaural Sound Localization

response might be. The most likely explanation for the appearance of the word association measure on the hearing threshold factor would be that the slower-responding subjects tended to have difficulty in clearly hearing the stimuli.

In pure tone audiometry, it is well known that individual subjects have patterns of response depending on the pitch (frequency) of the stimulus tones used. Some people have greater losses for certain high-frequency tones; others have greater relative loss for low frequencies. Hanley (1956) investigated factors in speech perception ability for a sample of 105 university students who were screened for having normal hearing acuity, defined as "a threshold for pure tones not exceeding a 15 db loss at 500, 1000, 2000, or 4000 cps" (p. 78). Nevertheless, measurements at these four levels had enough variance and covariance to

Table 9.2. *Auditory reception factors in group 1 (hearing and speech thresholds; factors UA, UT, and UU) arranged in order of approximate mean age of sample[a]*

Dataset	Date	Cy code	Age	Sample code	M/F code	Factor no.	Remarks (higher-order factors; others related)
CLAU01	'66	U	9	R	3	5	1:2G Hearing/speech threshold (factor UA)
CLAU04	'66	U	9	1	3	6	1:3G;2:2H Speech threshold (factor UT)
CLAU02	'66	U	13	R	3	4	1:2G Hearing/speech threshold (factor UA)
BOLT11	'73	U	19	E	3	7	1:2G Hearing (aided, unaided) (factor UU)
HANL01	'56	U	19	6	3	4	1:2U;2,5,10:UR;11:UM;Speech threshold (factor UU)
"	"	"	"	"	"	8	Hearing acuity (factor UA)
"	"	"	"	"	"	9	Speech threshold (factor UT)
CLAU03	'66	U	22	R	3	7	1:2G Hearing/speech threshold (factor UA)

[a]See Appendix A for codes. In a few cases, the classifications of factors shown here were preliminary and may not agree with the classifications shown in the tables of Appendix B.

produce a factor of hearing acuity (factor 8 in my reanalysis of Hanley's matrix, corresponding approximately to Hanley's factor B, "Threshold of Detectability for Tones," and coded factor UA), indicating that even for individuals of presumed normal hearing, there is a general factor of degree of loss over frequencies from 500 to 2000 Hz. Loadings for the frequencies 500, 1000, 2000, and 4000 on this factor were .76, .86, .57, and .53, respectively; thus, the higher loadings were for the middle range. Loadings on a general factor of speech perception were .19, .28, .11, and −.08, respectively; though of questionable statistical significance, it is possibly of interest that the highest loading on a general factor of speech perception (as measured in general by all of Hanley's measures) was for the frequency 1000.

Hanley also studied a series of four speech threshold tests, each employing different kinds of speech materials presented with progressively reduced intensities. In her analysis, she found that all these had loadings on the tone threshold factor, though these loadings were smaller than those of the pure tone tests. In my hierarchical reanalysis of Hanley's data, only Spondee Threshold and Sentence Threshold had significant loadings on the tone threshold factor, .46 and .39 respectively. Hanley found in the four speech threshold variables and also in several other speech-input variables a factor H, "Synthesis," that had insignificant loadings on the tone threshold factor. From this she concluded that "a synthesizing process, present in speech materials, must be absent in a detectability threshold" (p. 84). Reanalysis suggests, however, that the structure of the speech-input variables is somewhat more complex. I found two speech threshold factors, one (factor 9) loaded with the more conventional measures, a nonsense syllable (CVCs) test and a PB (phonetically balanced) word-recognition test, and the other (factor 4) loaded with a spondee threshold test (spondaic words presented with intensity gradually reduced), a sentence threshold test (the "Harvard intelligibility sentences," being questions answerable by one or two words or a number – again with reduction of intensity), a test in which intelligibility sentences were presented with masking of another voice, and a test in which the intelligibility sentences were presented with distortion through 50% interruption at 7 cycles per second. Speech Threshold I (factor 9, coded as factor UT) may be interpreted as dependent on individuals' absolute capacity to recognize phonemic signals at reduced intensity (holding hearing sensitivity constant), whereas Speech Threshold II (factor 4, coded as factor UU) would be interpreted as dependent on subjects' familiarity with certain characteristics of the English language – its syntactic structure, or the structure of spondaic words. Although neither factor had significant loadings on a lexical knowledge factor VL (factor 6), both these factors and the vocabulary factor had significant loadings on a general factor that pervaded most of Hanley's measures (all, in fact, except the tone threshold measures). These results suggest that conventional speech audiometry tests measure something more than sheer auditory threshold – a conclusion with which clinical audiologists would probably be quite comfortable, in view of the fact that for most people the most important use of hearing is to understand speech.

It may be pointed out here, in anticipation of further comments on Hanley's analysis, that some of the speech perception measures that Hanley found to measure her Synthesis factor are measures of factors discussed under our group 4, "resistance to auditory distortion" (see Table 9.7 and discussion of its factors).

Possibly to be assigned to the speech threshold factor is factor 7 from dataset BOLT11, loaded with measures of degree of verbal comprehension, with or without hearing aids, in a group of deaf adolescents. However, this factor probably measures much more than speech hearing threshold, namely, the subjects' abilities to understand speech.

FACTORS OF SPEECH SOUND DISCRIMINATION (US)

If speech audiometry testing shows individual differences when stimuli are presented under reduced intensity, what happens when similar stimuli are presented at normal or supraliminal intensities? *Tests in Print III* (Mitchell, 1983) lists (p. 557) a number of standardized tests of auditory discrimination that require respondents to detect differences between speech sounds, usually by presenting phonemically contrasting words in English. Wepman's (1958, 1973) Auditory Discrimination Test is one of the more popular of these. Designed for children ages 5–8, it yields a wide range of scores in typical normal populations of such children. Table 9.3 lists a number of factors in the datasets that can be interpreted as measuring speech sound discrimination ability, coded as factor US. Some are found in samples of young children, others in samples of college students or adults.

Interestingly, factor 4 in dataset VALT11 and factor 6 in VALT12 show that for eight-year-old German-speaking children, both the Wepman Auditory Discrimination test (presenting distinctions between English words) and a similar test in German (the Bremer Lautdiskriminationstest) have high loadings on these factors, indicating that a speech sound discrimination test operates similarly in English and German for these children.

Factor 3 in dataset SNOW01 has a single salient loading (.67) for a test of sound discrimination given to English-speaking persons (age range: age 3 to adult) learning Dutch (in the Netherlands). In each item, subjects were presented with a single Dutch word and then had to indicate which of two pictures depicted that word; the two pictures represented Dutch words whose phonemic differences are generally difficult for English learners of Dutch. This test of sound discrimination appeared on a sound discrimination factor only in dataset SNOW01; in datasets SNOW02 and SNOW03, for measurements taken at two later stages of language learning (at 4–5 month intervals), the test appeared on more general factors of Dutch language receptive and productive proficiencies – a "Dutch receptive ability" factor at time 2 and a "Dutch phonological ability" factor at

Table 9.3. *Auditory reception factors in group 2 (speech sound discrimination, factor US) arranged in order of approximate mean age of sample*[a]

Dataset	Date	C'y code	Age	Sample code	M/F code	Factor no.	Remarks (higher-order factors; others related)
VALT11	'81	G	8	1	3	4	1:2G
VALT12	'81	G	8	1	3	6	1:2G
SNOW01	'79	H	10	F	3	3	1:2C
MULL01	'79	L	17	M	2	2	1:2G
KAMM01	'53	U	19	F	3	4	1:2C
STAN31	'80	U	27	Q	1	3	1:2C;2:UK;3:US;4:U1;5:U8;7:2F;8:U3;9:UR

[a]See Appendix A for codes. In a few cases, the classifications of factors shown here were preliminary and may not agree with the classifications shown in the tables of Appendix B.

time 3, a result that suggested that sound discrimination ability was specifically critical only in an early stage of language learning, though it tended to affect general language skills at later stages.

Somewhat similar results for speech sound discrimination tests were obtained in datasets MULL01 (for Arabic-speaking high school students learning English) and KAMM01 (for English-speaking college students learning Spanish), although these datasets did not contain the longitudinal feature present in datasets SNOW01–03.

Factor 3 in dataset STAN31, for a sample of American prison inmates whose average age was about 27, was assigned here mainly because its highest salient loading was for an "intelligibility" test in which for each item, three English words were spoken, after which subjects had to select these words from a printed list that presented phonetically similar words. For example, after the words *border*, *shot*, and *insist* were spoken, subjects were to select them from the list:

order	mortar	border	water
shook	shout	shut	shot
enlist	insist	assist	resist

Although other factors (reading ability, short-term memory) may have been involved in this test, it would seem that the critical element may have been ability to discriminate speech sounds. This ability may have been critical in other measures appearing on this factor:

> Low Pass Filter: In each item, a spoken word was presented with frequencies below 1600 Hz filtered out; the subject was to select this word from among four printed words.
>
> Rapid Spelling: Familiar words were spelled very rapidly; the subject had to write these words.
>
> White Noise Masking: Like the Low Pass Filter test, except that the words were presented with a loud white noise background.
>
> Disarranged Sentences: Words were spoken in haphazard order; subjects had to write them rearranged to make sense.
>
> Cloze: Eight-word sentences were presented auditorily with two of the words replaced by clicks; subjects were to write the missing words.

Although the evidence cited above indicates the presence of individual differences in speech sound discrimination ability (factor US), as yet there has been little attempt to integrate this information with research (e.g., Miller & Nicely, 1955) on psychological processes in perceiving distinctions among speech sounds. It is possible, for example, that speech sound discrimination ability can be broken down into further factors that depend on different kinds of speech sound contrasts.

FACTORS IN PERCEIVING MUSIC AND MUSICAL SOUNDS (FACTORS U3, U5, U6, AND U9)

As noted previously, considerable work has been done in attempting to measure musical aptitude, that is, to measure person characteristics that predispose individuals to achievement and success in music. The history of these attempts has been recounted by Shuter–Dyson and Gabriel (1981), but it cannot be said that research has yielded a clear picture of what musical aptitudes exist. Seashore (1919) issued a series of tests of musical talent that were based on the notion that this talent consists of several distinct abilities in recognizing and discriminating different aspects of musical tones and patterns – their pitch, intensity, consonance, duration, and rhythm, all measured by tests that presented tonal stimuli with very little musical context, if any. It was early discovered, however, that these abilities tended to be at least moderately correlated. Various critics, notably James Mursell (1937), doubted that musical abilities could be viewed in terms of specific capacities; Mursell and others espoused what Seashore dubbed an "omnibus" theory that held that musical ability is a highly general capacity that is sensitive more or less in the same way to all aspects of musical materials. Critics also held that musical ability depends very little, if at all, on innate characteristics, as claimed by Seashore, but is acquired through training and exposure to music. Factor-analytic research has thus far had little success in delineating the dimensions of musical ability, even though there have been a number of investigations of musical aptitude tests.

According to Shuter–Dyson and Gabriel (1981), Whellams (1971) analysed relevant literature and claimed to identify 15 factors of musical talent. It is evident (see Shute–Dyson and Gabriel's Table 5.1), however, that these factors are not really distinct, since they overlap considerably in content. Our concern here is what the factor-analytic literature suggests with regard to the structure of musical aptitudes. (Whellams' reanalyses of a number of factorial studies are far short of yielding evidence for 15 separate factors, and his own investigation, concerned chiefly with relations of musical abilities to other cognitive abilities, contained too few musical tests – only seven! – to support the existence of any such number of factors.

Table 9.4 lists 31 factors, identified in reanalyses of the datasets in our corpus, that were assigned to Group 3 of auditory reception factors. They are classified into four subgroups:

> Group 3A: Factors (coded U3) for which the measures embrace discriminations with respect to two or more tonal attributes, such as pitch, timbre, intensity, duration, and rhythm.
> Group 3B: Factors (coded U5) for which the measures focus on discriminations with respect to pitch or timbre, i.e., the frequency attribute of sounds.
> Group 3C: Factors (coded U6) for which the measures focus on discriminations with respect to intensity, duration, and rhythm, that is, the amplitude and temporal attributes of sounds or of sequential patterns of sound.
> Group 3D: Factors (coded U9) for which the measures focus on ability to make judgments of the "musicality" or "musical taste" of short musical passages.

The appearance of factors in Group 3A would suggest that musical aptitude is a general ability to make discriminations and judgments with respect to all attributes of musical sounds, while the appearance of factors in the remaining

Table 9.4. *Auditory reception factors in group 3 (musical sound discrimination and judgment) arranged in order of approximate mean age of sample*[a]

Dataset	Date	Cy code	Age	Sample code	M/F code	Factor no.	Remarks (higher-order factors; others related)
Group 3A: General sound discrimination (factor U3 except as noted)							
SING21	'65	U	9	1	3	5	1:2G
ELKO01	'35	E	12	6	1	5	1:2G
SUMI02	'58	N	12	1	1	4	1:2H
HOLM11	'66	U	16	K	3	5	1:2C
SUNG01	'81	U	16	Z	3	2	1:2G
SUNG02	'81	U	16	#	3	9	1:2G
SUNG03	'81	U	16	W	3	7	1:2G
SUNG04	'81	U	16	1	1	3	1:2G
SUNG05	'81	U	16	1	2	6	1:2G
MORR11	'41	U	18	P	1	3	1:2G
GORD01	'69	U	19	1	3	4	1:2U;2:UI;3:U9;4:U3
HANL01	'56	U	19	6	3	3	1:2U?;2,5,10:UR;4:UU;8:UA;9:UT;11:UM
KARL01	'41	K	19	6	3	2	Orthogonal factors; 3:U6
WHEA01	'73	U	19	1	1	6	1:2G;7:U6
STAN31	'80	U	27	Q	1	4	1:2C;2:UK;3:US;5:U8;9:UR;Aud. Cog. Relations (U1)
"	"	"	"	"	"	8	Disc. Sound Patterns (U3)
HORN31	'82	U	30	Q	1	8	Disc. Sound Patterns (U3)

Group 3B: Sound-frequency discrimination: factor U5

WING01	'41	E	15	0	1	1	2:U9; Orthogonal factors
KARL11	'42	U	16	6	3	4	1:2U?;2:UR;3:U6;5,8:UM
FAUL11	'59	U	18	!	5	1	2:UM; Orthogonal factors
FOGA00	'87	A	19	P	3	5	1:2G;6:UK
PIMS02	'62	U	19	F	3	4	Orthogonal factors
STAN21	'83	A	34	U	3	2	1:2U;3:UK;5:U8

Group 3C: Sound-intensity/duration discrimination: factor U6

KARL11	'42	U	16	6	3	3	4:U5; Orthogonal factors
KARL01	'41	K	19	6	3	3	2:U3; Orthogonal factors
WHEA01	'73	U	19	1	1	7	1:2G;6:U3
LANG01	'76	C	22	6	3	3	1:2U;2:U9

Group 3D: "Musical" discrimination/judgment: factor U9 except as noted

WING01	'41	E	15	0	1	2	1:U5; Orthogonal factors
GORD01	'69	U	19	1	3	2	Tonal Imagery (UI); 1:2U;4:U3
"	"	"	"	"	"	3	Musical Sensitivity
LANG01	'76	C	22	6	3	2	1:2U;3:U6

[a]See Appendix A for codes. In a few cases, the classifications of factors shown here were preliminary and may not agree with the classifications shown in the tables of Appendix B.

groups would suggest that there are different abilities in this domain, depending on particular attributes of musical sounds or the types of musical materials presented. The evidence on the distinctness of abilities in this domain is very meager, however. Of the datasets I have analyzed, only GORD01, KARL01, KARL11, LANG01, STAN31, WHEA01, and WING01 yield more than one factor assignable to Group 3. In the light of present knowledge (or lack thereof), there is great need for thorough and extensive studies of abilities in this domain.

Nearly all measures of musical aptitude depend to a great extent on tests of quite elementary discriminations among tonal materials, with only meager musical contexts, if such contexts are present at all. This may be partly due to the desire on the part of those who construct musical aptitude tests to minimize the effects of musical training, so that the tests can be used to predict success in such training. At the same time, it may be due to failure to recognize the possibilities of preparing tests that include an appropriate musical context. Shepard (1981) has provided evidence that individuals "differ enormously in the extent to which they interpret musical tones in terms of an underlying tonal system" (pp. 167–168), and some of the experiments he reports could well be the basis for new tests of musical ability.

General Sound Discrimination (U3) Factors

These factors involve various tests of discrimination of musical materials. Many arise from including in the dataset two or more subtests from musical aptitude batteries such as the Seashore Tests of Musical Talents (Seashore, 1919; Seashore, Lewis, & Saetveit, 1939–1960) and the Kwalwasser–Dykema Music Tests (Kwalwasser & Dykema, 1930; also a revision developed by Holmes, 1954). Because such batteries, in addition to sets of author-constructed tests, contain similar series of tests, it is possible to construct a table (Table 9.5) presenting factor loadings of similar tests. From this table it is seen that tests of pitch or tonal memory frequently align themselves factorially with tests of rhythm, intensity, or time. The actual magnitudes of factor loadings are of course dependent on total battery structure, range of talent, and other effects, but loadings can legitimately be compared across tests if comparable reliabilities are assumed. Generally, loadings for tests of pitch and tonal memory are somewhat higher than those for rhythm, intensity, or time, at least for Seashore subtests. Results for tests from the Kwalwasser–Dykema series are inconsistent, possibly because of reliability and test-construction effects.

These results do not preclude the possibility that separate factors for different auditory attributes could be identified if provision is made for adequate definition of latent traits by including in a factorial battery several (preferably, three or more) measures to tap each factor. In the results shown in Table 9.5, it is often the case that communalities are much lower than test reliabilities, indicating that specific variance exists in the tests.

Table 9.5. *Factor loadings on selected test types for selected factors (coded U3) in group 3A*

Dataset	Test battery[a]	Test type					
		Pitch	Tonal memory	Timbre	Rhythm	Loudness/ intensity	Time
SING21	K–D–H	.412	—	—	.657	.657	—
ELKO01	Seashore	.666	—	—	—	.380	—
SUMI02	Seashore	.736	—	—	.520	—	—
HOLM11	K–D–H	.503	.468	.597	.471	.549	.474
SUNG01	Seashore	.403	.347	—	.091*	—	—
SUNG02	Seashore	.614	.544	—	.198*	—	—
SUNG03	Seashore	.507	.507	—	.316*	—	—
SUNG04	Seashore	.427	.540	—	.243*	—	—
SUNG05	Seashore	.358	.539	—	.278	—	—
GORD01	Seashore	.489	.506	.384	.315	.075	.358
MORR11	Seashore	.555	.682	—	.479	.374	.366
HANL01	Seashore	.661	.601	—	.254*	.324	.312
KARL01	Drake/						
	Seashore	.443	.760	—	.398	—	.714
WHEA01	Seashore	.591	.702	.499	.614	—	—

*Not salient.

[a]The K–D–H battery is the Holmes version of the Kwalwasser-Dykema series. When the battery is indicated as "Seashore" it refers either to one of the original Seashore series or to authors' adaptations of these tests. For dataset KARL01 the loadings are given either for a test from Drake's series or for a test from the Seashore series.

Because of their complexity, Table 9.5 does not include results from dataset STAN31, where two factors in the musical sound perception domain appeared. Loadings for factors 4 and 8 from this dataset are displayed in Table 9.6, with brief descriptions of the tests. Loadings are also shown for factor 1 and 7, which are second-order factors that the authors identify as Gc and Gf, respectively. It appears that factor 8, as a first-order factor, is similar to the factors with which Table 9.5 is concerned, because for the most part it involves simple discriminations of tonal materials with respect to pitch, timbre, or rhythm. It even includes a measure of ability to understand time-compressed speech. The authors designate this factor as "DASP" – Discrimination of Auditory Sound Patterns. The loadings of its measures on Gf suggest that the ability measured by factor 8 is in some sense more fundamental, and less influenced by training and exposure, than the ability measured by factor 4, whose measures generally have substantial loadings on factor Gc ("crystallized intelligence"). The measures that are loaded on factor 4 tend to involve tasks in which the subject must make analytical judgments concerning tonal relations – judgments, for example, as to what tone

Table 9.6. *Loadings for four orthogonalized factors in dataset STAN31*

Variable no. and description	Factor[a]			
	1 (Gc)	4 (U1)	7 (Gf)	8 (U3)
Factor 4: Auditory cognitive relations:				
#22 Tonal Series: What tone continues a series (e.g., given C,D,E,F: select G)	.396	.532	.355	−.117
#25 Chord Decomposition: Which tone sequence contains the same notes as a presented chord?	.256	.504	.463	.072
#23 Chord Series: Select correct temporally reverse order of presented chords	.432	.494	.320	−.027
#26 Notes per chord (Wing): How many notes in a presented chord (1–4)?	.136	.373	.409	.108
#27 Chord Parts Decomposition: Select which 2-note chord has the same notes as in a 3-note chord	.359	.373	.368	.180
#24 Tonal Analogies: Note 1 is to note 2 as note 3 is to which note (in terms of tonal intervals)?	.395	.336	.344	.162
#29 Pitch Differences (Seashore): Is 2nd tone higher or lower than 1st tone?	.367	.336	.485	.153
Factor 8: Discrimination of sound patterns:				
#31 Tonal Memory (Seashore): Given two short tone sequences, which note is different in the 2nd sequence?	.402	.028	.451	.523
#32 Memory for Pitch (Wing) : similar to #31	.407	.037	.429	.469
#36 Rhythm (Seashore): Are pairs of sound sequences Same or Different in rhythm?	.334	−.140	.313	.397
#34 Tonal Classification: Which chord does not belong in a series?	.271	.065	.334	.388
#37 Compressed Speech: Write sentences presented in time-compressed speech.	−.107	−.187	.369	.352
#33 Timbre (Seashore): Are pairs of tones Same or Different in timbre?	.086	.121	.458	.325
#35 Chord Matching: Select the chord that is "most similar" to a presented chord	.135	.056	.222	.316
#28 Pitch Change in Chords (Wing): In two chords presented, does a note change in the second chord, and if so, up or down?	.427	.280	.429	.298

[a]Factors 1 and 7 are second-order factors identified as Gc and Gf, respectively, by Stankov and Horn (1980) and also by me.

properly continues a given series of tones, or what the reverse order of a series of tones or chords would be. For this reason I can agree with the authors' designation of this factor as Auditory Cognitive Relations (coded as factor U1).

Dataset STAN31 was based on an unselected sample of adult prison inmates, mean age 25.64 (S.D. 7.75). The authors give no information about any musical training these subjects may have had, but it can be assumed that few if any had any considerable degree of such training. Although the tests of factor 4 would probably be quite easy for groups with musical training, they were relatively difficult for the prison inmate sample.

It should be noted that Karlin (1941) analyzed the musical tests (tests 10–19) in his battery with three factors, but my criteria for number of factors indicate that only one factor, here identified as factor 2 of dataset KARL01, could legitimately be extracted.

Summarizing: Most of the factors in Group 3A can be regarded as measuring a basic latent trait of ability to discriminate tones or patterns of tones with respect to their fundamental attributes of pitch, intensity, duration, and temporal relations. Factor 8 in dataset STAN31 appears to fall into this group, coded as factor U3. The one exception is factor 4 in dataset STAN31, which tests the ability to note and use more complex relations exhibited in tonal materials (Auditory Cognitive Relations, coded as factor U1).

Sound-Frequency Discrimination (U5) Factors

Factors in this group, as listed in Table 9.4, are generally similar to those in group 3A, except that they are focused on discriminations of the frequency attributes of tones.

Factor 1 in dataset WING01 has high loadings on three tests: Detecting a Changed Note in a Melody (.79), Detecting the Number of Notes in a Chord (.73), and Detecting a Changed Note in a Chord (.67). Because of the paucity of measures, it is not clear whether this belongs to a simple auditory discrimination factor or the Auditory Cognitive Relations factor mentioned in discussing Group 3A. Possibly it is a combination of these. It is in any case orthogonal to a "musical judgment" factor classified in Group 3D.

Factor 4 in dataset KARL11 has its five highest (and salient) loadings for tests involving pitch: #3, discrimination of pitches presented with very short durations (.69); #4, discrimination of pitches produced vocally (.68); #1, the Seashore Pitch test (.63); #26, the Seashore Tonal Memory Test (in which the subject must identify which note in a short sequence is changed on a second presentation) (.35); and #13, the Seashore Timbre test (.32). (A further test, with a loading of only .26, is Musical Rhythm, in which the subject must decide whether a selection is played in 2-, 3-, 4-, or 6-time. Since pitch would not be expected to play any large role in such a judgment, the loading is probably not significant.)

Factor 1 (an orthogonal factor) in dataset FAUL11 appears to represent a latent trait whereby pitch differences, or at least the pitch relations of the normal tempered scale, play a major role in test performance, as opposed to tests that are classified as tests of musical memory (Group 7, discussed below). Its highest loading (.89) is for a test of interval discrimination developed by Lundin (1949), that is, a test in which the subject has to detect whether tonal intervals (presented as sequences of two tones) are same or different, though at different pitch levels.

(E.g., is the sequence C–E the same tonal interval as F–A?) Other variables on this factor are Wing's Chord Change test; a Flat or Sharp Tune test in which one must detect whether the pitch of a simple melody "goes sharp" or "goes flat" with respect to the normal diatonic scale; an Octaves test measuring ability to detect that an octave interval is out of tune; the Seashore Pitch test; a Chord Sequences test in which the examinee has to say whether the first and last chords of a short sequence are Same or Different; and a Bands of Noise test where the average pitches of white noises are to be compared as Same or Different. Only Interval Discrimination has a negligible loading on the Musical Memory Factor, despite the fact that some short-term memory must be involved in its performance.

In Faulds's (1959) own analysis of his data, he extracted three factors, corresponding to what he called "pitch," "music," and "memory." My criteria for number of factors, however, revealed only two factors, so that Factor 1 is a combination of Faulds's Pitch and Music factors. Faulds's study is interesting particularly because it contrasted a group of subjects highly trained in music with a group of university undergraduates. Most of his tests revealed wide mean differences between these groups.

Fogarty's (1987) study, from which my factor 5 of dataset FOGA00 is derived, was concerned with effects of dual (simultaneous) tasks on factorial composition. Two tasks (Tonal Memory, similar to the Seashore Tonal Memory test, and Chord Decomposition, as studied in dataset STAN31) were presented either singly, or simultaneously with various other cognitive tasks. Of interest here is the result that nine measures involving these tasks all had salient loadings on a single factor, identified by Fogarty as "General Auditory Perception (Ga)." Considering the results from dataset STAN31, it would appear that this factor is a combination of a Sound Discrimination factor (U5) and an Auditory Cognitive Relations factor (U1).

Factor 4 in dataset PIMS02 is of interest in that it suggests that sound discrimination ability applies not only in the context of tonal material but also in the context of speech sound discrimination, particularly in discriminating tone patterns in Chinese syllables. The factor had loadings not only on the Seashore Pitch and Timbre tests, but also on a test of general speech sound discrimination and a test of perceiving tone pattern differences in Chinese syllables. This result is somewhat in contrast to that of Hanley (1956), whose dataset HANL01 showed a connection between tonal sound discrimination and speech sound discrimination only in a second-order factor of general auditory perception. But Pimsleur, Stockwell, and Comrey's (1962) results may be due to a battery design that precluded the isolation of separate factors for tonal discrimination and speech sound discrimination.

Factor 2 in dataset STAN21 had loadings on Chord Decomposition, Seashore's Tonal Memory, and Wing's Pitch Change in Chords and Notes per Chord. Probably because of battery design, it failed to reveal a distinction between Tonal Sound Discrimination and Auditory Cognitive Relations shown in dataset STAN31 (see Table 9.6).

Sound-Intensity/Duration Discrimination (U6) Factors

Four token factors, as listed in Group 3C in Table 9.4, give evidence for a separate factor of ability, here coded U6, to discriminate sound intensities, possibly associated also with ability to discriminate time relationships exhibited in rhythmic patterns. The clearest of these factors is factor 3 in dataset KARL11, which is distinct from a pitch-discrimination factor (factor 4) and is loaded saliently on four measures dealing with sound intensities:

> #5 Seashore Loudness test (.57): Of two tones, each about a second in duration, is the second louder or softer?
>
> #7 Loudness, Short Impulse (.49): Same as #5, but the duration of the tones was very short, "from a duration beneath the duration threshold for loudness perception to one well above it" (Karlin, 1942, p. 261).
>
> #6 Loudness Discrimination, Complex Sounds (.48): Stimuli were various sounds produced by setting objects in vibration.
>
> #8 Pitch-Loudness Function (.44): "In each item two pure tones of constant intensity, complexity, and duration but differing in frequency were compared in loudness. The two frequencies for each item were so chosen that they would normally be heard as differing in loudness on account of the differential sensitivity to frequency. A correct response would be one following the normal reaction" (Karlin, 1942, p. 261).

A further measure loaded on this factor was Sense of Time for Intervals of Silence (.39), from an early form of the Time test in Seashore's Tests of Musical Talents. Three clicks were presented; the subject was to compare the two time intervals.

My analysis of this dataset is somewhat different from Karlin's, in that I obtained only a single Loudness factor, whereas Karlin obtained in addition a factor that he called Auditory Integral for Perceptual Mass. Some of the variables loaded on his Loudness factor loaded also on this latter factor, including Sense of Time for Intervals of Silence. Possibly Karlin's interpretation (Auditory Integral for Perceptual Mass) should apply also to the factor 3 identified in his dataset.

The other factors listed here are not as clear. Factor 3 in dataset KARL01 has a moderate loading (.33) for the Seashore Loudness test, but a high loading (.73) for a nonauditory test entitled Classification. Factor 7 in WHEA01 has loadings (.46 and .39 respectively) for the Loudness and Time subtests of the Seashore battery, but a somewhat higher loading (.49) for a nonauditory test of clerical ability, Number Comparison. Because it would stretch credulity to argue that there is anything specifically in common between the Number Comparison test and the Seashore tests, this factor may be spurious.

Factor 3 in dataset LANG01 has substantial loadings (.58 and .55 respectively) on two subtests of an experimental battery called the Mundinger Musical Perception Test – constructed by a musical composer. The subtests are described as follows:

> #9 Rhythmic Perception: "Ability to detect similarities between barely dissimilar pairs of musical rhythms presented at various frequencies and decibel levels."

#10 Auditory Memory: "This bimodal coding task requires the subject to recall rhythmical patterns embodied in conventional musical pieces, and to reproduce these as graphic linear symbols or morse code notation (e.g. – –. – – –)..." (Lang & Ryba, 1976, p. 270).

Both tests appear to depend on sensitivity to temporal/rhythm aspects of tonal passages, and the factor is linearly independent of a factor of musical discrimination to be discussed under Group 3D. Unfortunately the battery is not sufficiently extensive to allow interpretations as to whether the factor also extends to other aspects of tonal stimuli, or to whether the factor can be cross-identified with the other factors mentioned here and coded U6.

Musical Discrimination and Judgment Factors (UI and U9)

Expert musicians and music educators tend to discredit simple tests of auditory discrimination, such as those in the Seashore battery, as possible tests of musical aptitude because they contain little or no musical meaning. It has apparently been difficult, however, to develop tests with a desirable level of musical meaning that do not at the same time become tests greatly influenced by musical training and experience. The four factors listed in Group 3D in Table 9.4 appear to contain measures that have a considerable amount of musical content, and in at least some of the studies in which they appear, they are shown to be linearly independent of factors assessing simple auditory discriminations.

Reanalysis of a set of data published by Wing (1941), for example, shows two orthogonal factors. Factor 1 is a factor of sound-frequency discrimination (U5), and factor 2 is identified as a factor of "musical judgment" (U9). Each of four tests of factor 2 is composed of 14 items presenting two versions of a brief musical passage. Subjects are asked to indicate which version "sounds best"; in order of the factor loadings, judgments are based on phrasing (.77), loudness (.69), rhythm (.59), and harmony (.45). Some of these tests, however, have moderate loadings on the auditory discrimination factor (factor 1, coded U5).

Reanalysis of a set of correlational data published by Gordon (1969, dataset GORD01) shows three first-order factors in addition to a second-order general factor (factor 1) of auditory perception. Factor 4 is an auditory discrimination factor that has loadings almost exclusively on subtests of the Seashore battery, and is classified in Group 3A (factor U3). Factors 2 and 3 have salient loadings on different subtests of Gordon's Musical Aptitude Profile, composed of a series of tests in which musical passages are presented by expert performers either on the violin alone or with violin and cello. These instruments are used both to add musical meaning to the passages and also to make it possible to present finer nuances of tone, intensity, phrasing, and tempo than is possible with pure tone presentations. I label factor 2 a factor of "tonal imagery," for want of a better term (the term is used by Gordon to describe some of the subtests); the code UI is assigned to this factor. Its highest loading (.58) is for a Harmony subtest; other loadings are for Melody (.54) and Tempo (.40) subtests, and for a measure of musical background (.28). Factor 3 may be labeled Musical Sensitivity (factor U9). Its salient loadings are for four subtests of the Musical Aptitude Profile, three of which involve judgments by subjects of which of two performances of a musical passage "sounds better" in style or actually mostly in tempo (.68), phrasing and expression (.63), or "balance" in the phrase ending (.61). A somewhat lower loading (.45) is for the Meter subtest in which subjects judge whether two renditions of a passage are the same or different in musical accent.

Finally, factor 2 in dataset LANG01 appears to be similar to the factor of Musical Sensitivity (factor U9) just mentioned. It has salient loadings on certain subtests from a battery cited as the Mundinger Musical Perception Test. Mundinger, a composer, set out to develop a test that would be musically interesting; unfortunately, the article by Lang and Ryba (1976) does not give adequate details on the nature of the test tasks and the Mundinger test appears not to be generally available. Test #5, Melodic Discrimination (with a loading of .47), is described as attempting to measure "the ability to discern similarities and subtle incongruities between two or more melodies." Test #11, Rhythmic Integration (.32), is described as "an elaborate cross-modal coding task" in which subjects are to "perceive musical meter by identifying accentuations, or by discriminating subtle nuances in harmony, and to reproduce these in the form of ordinal, symbolic units (e.g., beat patterns of 12, 123, 1234, etc.)." Test #8, Perceptual Awareness (.24), is described as "capacity to cognise similarity of compositional style between excerpts extracted from popular musical works." Test #7, Aesthetic Judgment (.20), concerns the ability to "select the most aesthetically pleasing musical composition from closely paired items comprised of the original version of a passage written by a notable composer, and a distorted, less harmonious version" (Lang & Ryba, 1976, p. 270). The orthogonalized hierarchical factor loadings are rather small, due to the fact that much of the test variance is absorbed into a general factor of auditory perception.

These findings are suggestive but cannot be regarded as leading to definitive descriptions of a factor or factors of musical sensitivity. Analysis of dataset GORD01 suggests that musical sensitivity is differentiated into a tonal imagery factor (UI) emphasizing melodic and harmonic aspects of music and a factor (U9) that stresses aspects of musical expression arising from variations in phrasing, loudness, and tempo.

RESISTANCE TO AUDITORY STIMULUS DISTORTION
(UR) FACTORS

A number of token factors, listed in Table 9.7, appear to reflect individual differences in the ability to resist or overcome the effects of distortions of speech stimuli that occur through masking or other types of interposition of extraneous auditory stimuli. Stankov and Horn (1980) have dubbed the underlying trait

Table 9.7. *Auditory reception factors in group 4 (resistance to auditory distortion; factor U R) arranged in order of approximate mean age of sample[a]*

Dataset	Date	Cy code	Age	Sample code	M/F code	Factor no.	Remarks (higher-order factors; others related)
PARA01	'69	U	3	1	3	3	Auditory Closure?
PARA07	'69	U	9	1	3	2	Auditory Closure?
WHIT01	'54	U	15	6	3	2	Orthogonal factors
KARL11	'42	U	16	6	3	2	1:2U?;3:U6;4:U5;5,8:UM
HANL01	'56	U	19	6	3	2	1:2U?;3:U3;4:UU;8:UA;9:UT;11:UM Distortion by Peak Clipping
,,	,,	,,	,,	,,	,,	5	Distortion by Masking
,,	,,	,,	,,	,,	,,	10	Distortion by Reverberation
STAN31	'80	U	27	Q	1	9	1:2C;2:UK;3:US;4:U1;5;U8;7:2F;8:U3. Distortion by Masking, etc.
HORN31	'82	U	30	Q	1	7	Auditory Info. Processing

[a]See Appendix A for codes. In a few cases, the classifications of factors shown here were preliminary and may not agree with the classifications shown in the tables of Appendix B.

"SPUD" – Speech Perception Under Distraction. Actually, there may be several underlying traits, depending upon the type of distortion, to judge from data gathered by Hanley (1956). Stankov and Horn's SPUD factor appears to be confirmed in data from studies by White (1954) and Karlin (1942), but for consistency it is here coded factor UR.

White (1954) investigated whether the phenomenon of visual closure, as implicit in the closure factor CS and CF as discussed in Chapter 8, could be replicated in the auditory domain. Reanalysis of his data yielded a factor that had substantial loadings on three tests:

> #6 Words in Noise (.83): Write words spoken against a background of simulated airplane noise (a test developed at Harvard's Psychoacoustic Laboratory; Karlin & Abrams, 1944).
>
> #7 Incomplete Words – Auditory (.61): The subject has to write words, presented by tape-recording, from which various consonant sounds had been excised (e.g., "door ep" for *doorstep*).
>
> #8 Distorted Words (.59): Write tape-recorded words with frequencies below 2400 Hz filtered out.

Although it can be argued that perception of speech distorted in these ways requires a kind of "closure" from an incomplete Gestalt, analogous to closure from distorted visual presentations, the factorial evidence suggests that the processes are not the same from an individual differences point of view, because White's auditory closure factor is orthogonal to his visual closure factor (see its mention in Table 8.6).

One of the subtests in the Illinois Test of Psycholinguistic Abilities (ITPA) (Paraskevopoulos & Kirk, 1969) is named Auditory Closure, and is similar to the Incomplete Words – Auditory test in White's study. The stimuli are words presented orally, but with some sounds omitted, e.g. "bo / le" [*bottle*], "/ype /iter" [*typewriter*]. The task is to give the complete word, and thus requires a process of auditory closure in that the underlying word must be perceived from an incomplete cue. This subtest appeared on factors in several datasets involving the ITPA: PARA01, PARA07, and TAYL31, usually also with a Sound Blending test in which the sounds of a word are spoken singly at half-second intervals, the task being to say the complete word.

Karlin's (1942; dataset KARL11) "auditory resistance" factor arises from covariance of a number of tests:

> #20 Singing (.57): Write words of a song sung to piano accompaniment.
>
> #22 Illogical Grouping (.53): Write, with appropriate rearrangement, phrases spoken with grouping contrary to sense.
>
> #21 Haphazard Speech (.48): Write words of phrases spoken with unusual inflection and pitch changes.

The factor also had loadings, though low, for the Seashore Rhythm test (.31); an "Intellective Masking" test (.30) in which subjects write isolated words heard against increasingly loud masking from a second continuous speaker; and the

Wepman Auditory Discrimination Test (.14 – this loading being too low to justify assigning the factor to factor US).

Dataset HANL01 yielded three auditory resistance factors: factor 2, with several tests of perception of mechanically distorted speech (by peak clipping or interruption at 7 cycles per second), as well as the Seashore Rhythm test; factor 5, with tests of speech distorted by masking with white noise or other speakers; and factor 10, with tests of speech distorted by reverberation. The finding of these three factors suggests that resistance to auditory distortion (factor UR) can be somewhat specialized dependent on the type of distortion. At the same time, all three factors had loadings on a second-order factor of speech perception (factor 1 in the analysis).

In dataset STAN31, resistance to auditory distortion was represented by a single factor, with tests of speech masked either by a second speaker or by cafeteria noise, but also tests of perception of mechanically expanded speech (the opposite of compressed speech), and of the perception of words with pauses inserted between phonemes (sound blending).

A question can be raised about the relation of the auditory resistance factor (UR) to the speech sound discrimination factor (US) underlying the factors discussed in Group 2 of auditory perception factors. Actually, there is no clear evidence separating these groups of factors. Only in dataset STAN31 is there a possible differentiation between speech sound discrimination and auditory resistance, but the assignment of factor 3 of that dataset to Group 2 is at least questionable. The speech sound discrimination factor US would presumably refer to a general ability to discriminate particular phonemes or speech sounds presented *with minimum distortion or distraction* (as with the Wepman Auditory Discrimination Test), whereas the auditory resistance factor UR would refer to an ability to overcome the effects of generalized distortion or masking in understanding extended speech passages. It should be noted that the Wepman Auditory Discrimination Test, which loads on some of the factors of Group 2 (Table 9.3), has a very low loading on the auditory resistance factor of dataset KARL11. Possibly the difference between the factors is an artifact of age sampling: the sound discrimination factor (Table 9.3) appears mostly with younger children or with samples of adults learning a foreign language. As far as I am aware, our research database is not yet sufficient to resolve the status of the auditory resistance factor relative to speech sound discrimination ability.

TEMPORAL TRACKING (UK) FACTORS

As indicated in Table 9.8, a Temporal Tracking factor, here coded UK, is claimed by Stankov (1983) and Stankov and Horn (1980) as being found in various auditorily presented tests involving the mental counting or rearrangement of temporal events. In dataset STAN21, such a factor (factor 3) is loaded with the following tests:

Table 9.8. *Auditory reception factors in group 5 (temporal tracking, factor UK) arranged in order of approximate mean age of sample*[a]

Dataset	Date	C'y code	Age	Sample code	M/F code	Factor no.	Remarks (higher-order factors; others related)
FOGA00	'87	A	19	P	3	6	1:2G;3:U8
STAN31	'80	U	27	Q	1	2	1:2C;4:U1;5:U8;8:U3;9:UR
STAN21	'83	A	34	U	3	3	1:2U;2:US;5:U8

[a]See Appendix A for codes. In a few cases, the classifications of factors shown here were preliminary and may not agree with the classifications shown in the tables of Appendix B.

> #5 Letter Reordering (.57): In each item, three letters of the alphabet (one each of the set *R, S, T*) are spoken, to be mentally labeled with numbers (1, 2, 3) by the subject. These same three letters are then heard in a different order. The subject is to write down, with numbers, the order in which they occur on the second hearing.
>
> #7 RST Test (.52): A sequence of letters from the set *R, S, T* is heard, e.g., *RSSRTST*; the subject must write down how many times each letter appears.
>
> #8 Do-Mi-Sol Test (.44): A sequence of musical notes is heard (e.g. *C–E–E–C–G–C*); the subject must write down how many times each note is heard.
>
> #6 Tonal Reordering (.42): Like Test #5, except that the stimuli are piano notes.

In dataset STAN31, a temporal tracking factor is loaded with tests either identical or somewhat similar to the above; e.g., Tonal Reordering occurs with stimuli that are either spoken letters of the alphabet, musical notes, or nonsense syllables. In other tests, series of eight stimuli (voices or tones) are heard, with repetitions, and the subject is to write down, by ordinal number in the series, when each different one (voice or tone) is first heard.

Without disputing that these findings indicate some sort of "mental tracking" factor, one can question whether this is really a specifically auditory factor. Mental tracking, one would think, could equally well be tested with sequences of visual presentations. Also, this factor appears to involve a special kind of short-term or working memory. As yet, its possible relations with tests with visual presentations and tests of short-term memory have not been adequately investigated, although it is true that dataset STAN31 contains a factor 6, loaded with several digit-span tests, that is linearly independent of factor 2, the so-called temporal tracking factor. About all that can be said at the present time is that Stankov and Horn appear to have invented a novel type of task for investigating cognitive operations, and demonstrated its potential status as a separate factor of individual differences.

MAINTAINING AND JUDGING RHYTHM (U8) FACTORS

Stankov and Horn (1980) also claim the identification of a factor that they call "Maintaining and Judging Rhythm" (abbreviated MaJR); it also appears in a

Table 9.9. *Auditory reception factors in group 6 (maintaining and judging rhythm; factor U8) arranged in order of approximate mean age of sample*[a]

Dataset	Date	C'y code	Age	Sample code	M/F code	Factor no.	Remarks (higher-order factors; others related)
STAN31	'80	U	27	Q	1	5	1:2C;2:UK;3:US;4:U1;7:2F;8:U3;9:UR
STAN21	'83	A	34	U	3	5	1:2U;2:US;3:UK

[a]See Appendix A for codes. In a few cases, the classifications of factors shown here were preliminary and may not agree with the classifications shown in the tables of Appendix B.

study by Stankov (1983), as indicated in Table 9.9. This factor is here coded U8. In dataset STAN21 factor 5 has salient loadings only on two tests from Drake's (1954) Musical Aptitude Tests, Tempo A and Tempo B, with loadings of .82 and .69 respectively. (Tempo B also has a loading of .31 on the Temporal Tracking factor, and the tests have loadings of .28 and .22 respectively on a second-order factor of auditory perception.) In Tempo A the subject hears a metronome establish a tempo while a voice counts with the metronome, "one, two, three, four." Subsequently, the metronome and the voice are silent and the subject is to continue counting to himself at the same tempo until the voice says "Stop." The subject then gives the count he has made at that point and this answer is evaluated with respect to what it should be according to the actual time involved. There are fifty items of this sort, with different metronome rates. Tempo B is similar except that during the silent interval *another* metronome is heard at a different tempo, to provide interference with the mental counting. In dataset STAN31 these same tests appear on the factor, with loadings of .74 and .72 respectively, but inexplicably, the Incomplete Words test (described above under Group 4) has a loading of .49 and a Loudness Series test has a negative loading (−.49). Both tests have low loadings on second-order factors interpreted as Gc and Gf by the authors.

It would appear that the ability to maintain a beat, tested in this way, is a distinguishable and independent dimension of individual differences. Musicians apparently consider it to be important in certain kinds of musical performances, for example, by orchestra members during *tacet* intervals. The question can be raised, as before, as to whether this is truly an auditory ability. Although beats are most often observed in the auditory modality, they are strictly speaking merely temporal events; beats could be established also in visual presentations, e.g., by flashing lights. Further research should establish whether Maintaining and Judging Rhythm is specific to the auditory domain, or more properly considered in a temporal domain. Also, Stankov and Horn report no evidence to support their interpretation of the factor as applying also to *judgments* of rhythm.

In future research, consideration might be given to the possibility of testing discriminations between tempi (i.e., different musical metronome markings), or even the ability to recognize or establish a given metronome marking (a kind of absolute tempo ability analogous to absolute pitch as discussed below). Musicians who perform solo, or conduct musical ensembles, are required to have such an ability.

MEMORY FOR SOUND PATTERNS (UM) FACTORS

Table 9.10 lists four token factors that I classified separately from other auditory reception factors because they seemed to involve memory in a more critical way than the others. Obviously, some degree of memory comes into play in nearly all testing, but some of the variables loaded on these four token factors involve longer-than-usual time intervals between stimuli and response.

In factor 5 of dataset KARL11, the highest salient loading (.48) was for the test Memory for Emphasis, in which a two-minute passage was read to subjects, with certain words uttered with marked emphasis; at the conclusion of the reading, the subjects were given the script and told to mark the words that were read with emphasis. Some degree of memory was involved in this task, but the factor also had salient loadings on tests with little involvement of memory – the Seashore Time test (.40), a Pitch Discrimination Test (.38), and a Sound Breakdown test (.25) in which subjects were to report how many of a group of five speakers read a word simultaneously. This set of loadings thus raises the question as to whether scores on the Memory for Emphasis test depended more on ability to *notice* speech emphasis than on memory for it. Factor 8 in this same dataset had a single salient loading (.46) on a test of Memory for Male Voices, in which a number of speakers were heard reading verbal materials in random order of speaker reappearance. The subject had to decide, for each passage, whether that speaker had been heard before. This variable had a correlation of .37 with a similar test using female speakers, but Karlin chose to drop this variable from his factor analysis (I made a similar decision, perhaps unwisely). If it had been included, it would probably have produced a stronger recognition memory factor. The problem arises, however, whether performance on this test relied more on ability to recognize voices than on recognition memory. In any event, both factors are coded as UM.

In reanalysis of Hanley's (1956) data (dataset HANL01) a separate factor Memory for Voices (factor 11) was obtained for two tests, Recognition Memory for Male Voices and Recognition Memory for Female Voices, also with loadings for two speech recognition tests.

Data from reanalysis of dataset FAUL11 raise the question of memory involvement even more acutely. Faulds's (1959) study was concerned mainly with the perception of pitch, but he sought to investigate the role of memory by administering some of his tests with and without a time delay between stimuli to

Table 9.10. *Auditory reception factors in group 7 (memory for sound patterns, factor UM) arranged in order of approximate mean age of sample[a]*

Dataset	Date	C'y code	Age	Sample code	M/F code	Factor no.	Remarks (higher-order factors; others related)
KARL11	'42	U	16	6	3	5	1:2U;2:UR;3:U6;4:U5; Memory for Emphasis
"	"	"	"	"	"	8	Memory for Voices
FAUL11	'59	U	18	!	3	2	1:U5 Orthogonal factors
HANL01	'56	U	19	6	3	11	1:2U?;2,5,10:UR;3:U3;4:UU;8:UA;9:UT

[a]See Appendix A for codes. In a few cases, the classifications of factors shown here were preliminary and may not agree with the classifications shown in the tables of Appendix B.

be compared for auditory attributes. He recognized also that many musical aptitude tests inevitably involve time delays (in the range of a few seconds) between stimuli to be compared, for example, Seashore's Tonal Memory test. Faulds in fact postulated three factors for his data, "pitch," "music," and "memory," and his criteria for number of factors led him to extract three factors from his correlation matrix. My criteria for number of factors, in contrast, led to extraction of only two factors – resulting essentially in collapse of Faulds's pitch and music factors into a single factor, as mentioned in the discussion of Group 3 factors above. This left factor 2 as loaded primarily on several tests with inserted time delays. In order of the salient loadings, these are:

#14 Seashore's Timbre test (.81) with a time delay of about 6 seconds between stimuli to be compared, with a negligible loading (-.03) on factor 1, the pitch factor.

#13 Seashore's Tonal Memory test (.75, with .47 on factor 1), which has an inherent time delay between the stimuli that are to be compared.

#10 Seashore's Pitch Test (.67; .36 on factor 1) with a time delay of about 6 seconds between stimuli to be compared.

#5 Scales (.55; .46 on factor 1): In each item, a succession of scale notes is heard, and they either "stay in tune" (in the tempered scale) or go slightly sharp or flat; the subject has to indicate which. Inevitably, the rendition of the scale notes occupies a certain amount of time.

#12 Seashore's Timbre test (.41; .01 on factor 1), but with no time delay.

#7 Pitch (Masked) (.38; .29 on Factor 1): Like Seashore's Pitch test, with no time delay, but with stimuli masked with white noise.

#8 Franklin's (1956) Tonality Test (.16; .10 on factor 1): Beginnings of melodies are heard, followed by endings that are either "right," "wrong," or "left out." The subject has to indicate which.

The data are generally, but not entirely, consistent with the notion that factor 2 is primarily a factor for memory of pitch. In any event, Fauld's study is an interesting pilot study of the possibility of distinguishing a pitch memory factor (possibly analogous to the MV (Visual Memory) factor discussed in Chapter 7). The matter deserves to be studied further.

ABSOLUTE PITCH (UP) ABILITY

One is reminded here of the phenomenon of absolute or "perfect" pitch (see, for example, Carroll, 1975; Ward & Burns, 1982), whereby some small proportion of individuals are able to give the musical name of a heard note without having a reference tone previously presented, that is, without using relative pitch. Indeed, Faulds cited several classic experiments (Bachem, 1954; König, 1957) showing a connection between musical memory and absolute pitch. It is not very likely, though conceivable, that an absolute pitch factor could be isolated in a factor-analytic study, partly because the phenomenon is relatively rare. It appears (Siegel & Siegel, 1977) that persons with absolute pitch have in long term memory categorical mental representations of the chromas of the musical scale, and can use these in either recognizing or producing specified chromas, or in recognizing the tonality of a musical passage (naming the key in which it is performed). (*Chroma* is the technical term for the position of a frequency on the horizontal dimension of the pitch helix; that is, the chroma for note A is the same regardless of the octave in which it occurs, assuming a given pitch standard such as A = 440 Hz.) According to Oakes (1955), absolute pitch ability is relatively independent of the ability to make very fine discriminations of pitch (as measured, say, by the Seashore Pitch test), except to the extent that absolute pitch ability implies ability to categorize pitches at least within semitones of the musical scale. Even if absolute pitch involves long-term memories, there is no implication that it is correlated with other dimensions of memory. In particular, it would not necessarily be correlated with the latent trait underlying Factor 2 of dataset FAUL11.

Because the phenomenon of absolute pitch ability is well established, I include it in my system of factors of individual differences by coding it UP, even though a distinct factor of absolute pitch ability has as yet not appeared in a factor-analytic study.

A FACTOR OF SOUND LOCALIZATION (FACTOR UL)

Table 9.11 lists one factor, from a study by Aftanas and Royce (1969), that may refer to individual differences in the ability to localize heard sounds in space, by binaural perception. It is measured chiefly by two procedures developed by Shankweiler (1961). Because this factor (to my knowledge) is not replicated elsewhere in the literature, it is listed here solely as a matter of record, without further comment.

Table 9.11. *Auditory reception factor in group 8 (binaural sound localization; factor UL)*[a]

Datset	Date	C'y code	Age	Sample code	M/F code	Factor no.	Remarks (higher-order factors; others related)
AFTA01	'69	C	43	1	3	12	9:20

[a]See Appendix A for codes.

SUMMARY

The evidence reviewed here suggests that the following linearly independent factors of individual differences in auditory receptive ability can be identified:

1. Factor UA: Hearing acuity (general over the range of audible frequencies, though possibly modulated by the pitch/loudness function). Possible sub-factors are:
   (a) Factor UU: Hearing acuity for phonemic materials, as tested by speech audiometry, and
   (b) Factor UT: A "speech synthesis" factor (Hanley, 1956) by which hearing level determined by speech audiometry is in part determined by the subject's success in perceiving speech materials through familiarity with certain characteristics of the language involved.

2. Factor US: Speech sound discrimination (general over the range of phonemes in a language, or possibly broken down over groups or types of phonemes).

3. Factor U3: Discrimination of tones and sequences of tones with respect to basic attributes such as pitch, intensity, duration, and rhythm; possibly there are also subfactors:
   (a) Factor U5: Discrimination of tones with respect to pitch and timbre;
   (b) Factor U6: Discrimination of tones with respect to intensity, or (possibly) discrimination of tonal patterns with respect to temporal, rhythmical aspects.

4. Factor U1: ACOR, Auditory Cognitive Relations: judgments of complex relations among tonal patterns.

5. Factor UI: Tonal imagery: Discrimination and judgment of tonal patterns in musicality with respect to melodic and harmonic aspects.

6. Factor U9: Discrimination and judgment of tonal patterns in musicality with respect to expressive aspects, particularly phrasing, tempo, and intensity variations.

7. Factor UR: SPUD (Speech Perception Under Distortion): Ability to understand speech that is masked or otherwise distorted; possibly there are subfactors, depending on the type of distortion (masking by white noise, by other speakers, or by reverberation).

8. Factor UK: Temporal tracking: Ability to track temporal events on a short-term basis so as to count or rearrange them. (This may not be a purely auditory function, inasmuch as events in other modalities could be dealt with in similar ways.)

9. Factor U8: Ability to recognize and maintain mentally an equal-time "beat"

(this may not be a purely auditory function inasmuch as it could also be tested with in other modalities).

10.   Factor UM: Ability to retain, at least on a short-term basis, images of auditory events such as tones, tonal patterns, and voices.
11.   Factor UP: Absolute pitch ability.
12.   Factor UL: Ability to localize sound accurately in space.

The above list is offered only as what is *suggested* by currently available research evidence. Development of a more definitive list awaits further research, for which many promising opportunities exist.

10   *Abilities in the Domain of Idea Production*

---

*Whereas creativity involves traits that make
a person creative, creating calls upon many
resources not intrinsically creative.*

David N. Perkins (1981, p. 275)

The ability of the individual to produce ideas expressed in language or other media is an important human characteristic. In this chapter, we consider a variety of factors that measure different aspects of such an ability. Many of these factors may be roughly described as "fluency" and "creativity" factors. These correspond generally to abilities that Guilford (1967) described as concerned with "divergent production," that is, with tasks in which the requirements are relatively unstructured and in which the individual must produce a variety of responses that might meet such requirements. Divergent production is regarded as being opposed to "convergent production," where the task is highly structured and the problem is only to produce a single "correct" or "best" answer. Some of the factors discussed in the present chapter are of a divergent character, but others are of a convergent character.

In describing this domain as one of idea production, I mean the term *idea* to be taken in its broadest possible sense. An idea can be expressed in a word, a phrase, a sentence, or indeed any verbal proposition, but it may be something expressed in a gesture, a figure, a drawing, or a particular action. It might be a musical phrase or composition, although there are no instances in our datasets where individuals are asked to produce musical materials. (Webster's, 1977, dataset concerning musical improvisation and composition proved to be inadequate for factorial analysis.)

It is characteristic of all the factors considered here that they involve the active *production* of ideas as opposed to the recognition, identification, selection, or comparison of ideas as represented in stimuli presented to subjects.

In his survey of results achieved in the early years of factor-analytic research, French (1951) recognized the following factors that could belong in the category considered here (French's symbols for the factors are given):

> Fluency of Expression (FE): "Verbal versatility" (Taylor, 1947) in producing a variety of verbal responses.
> Ideational Fluency (IF): "Characterized by tests on which the task is to write down ideas about a given topic as fast as possible" (French, 1951, p. 215).

394

Naming (Na): "Facility in naming" (French, 1951, p. 227).

Public Speaking (PS): "Ability to convert ideas into oral speech seems to be a fair description of this factor" (French, 1951, p. 233).

Word Fluency (W): "...entirely limited to the speed of producing any words which fit certain mechanical restrictions regarding the letters or affixes used" (French, 1951, p. 249).

The 1963 *Kit of Reference Tests for Cognitive Factors* (French, Ekstrom, & Price, 1963) provided tests for some of these factors, but also for others in this domain, as follows (we give here the 1963 designations for the factors and their descriptions in the manual for the *Kit*):

Factor Fa: Associational Fluency. "The ability to produce words from a restricted area of meaning" (p. 12).

Factor Fe: Expressional Fluency. "The ability to think rapidly of appropriate wording for ideas" (p. 14).

Factor Fi: Ideational Fluency. "The facility to call up ideas wherein quantity and not quality of ideas is emphasized" (p. 15).

Factor Fw: Word Fluency. "Facility in producing isolated words that contain one or more structural, essentially phonetic, restrictions, without reference to the meaning of the words" (p. 17).

Factor O: Originality. "The ability to produce remotely associated, clever, or uncommon responses" (p. 30).

Factor Sep: Sensitivity to Problems. "The ability to recognize practical problems" (p. 41).

Factor Xa: Figural Adaptive Flexibility. "The ability to change set in order to meet new requirements imposed by figural problems" (p. 49).

Factor Xs: Semantic Spontaneous Flexibility. "The ability to produce a diversity of verbally expressed ideas in a situation that is relatively unrestricted" (p. 50).

Of the above factors, the 1976 revision of the *Kit* (Ekstrom, French, & Harman, 1976) offered marker tests for the following (the 1976 designations and descriptions are given):

Factor FA: Associational Fluency. "The ability to produce rapidly words which share a given area of meaning or some other common semantic property" (p. 41).

Factor FE: Expressional Fluency. "The ability to think rapidly of word groups or phrases" (p. 51).

Factor FI: Ideational Fluency. "The facility to write a number of ideas about a given topic or exemplars of a given class of objects" (p. 67).

Factor FW: Word Fluency. "The facility to produce words that fit one or more structural, phonetic or orthographic restrictions that are not relevant to the meaning of the words" (p. 73).

Factor XF: Figural Flexibility (formerly, Figural Adaptive Flexibility). "The ability to change set in order to generate new and different solutions to figural problems" (p. 181).

Thus, Factor O: Originality, Factor Sep: Sensitivity to Problems, and Factor Xs: Semantic Spontaneous Flexibility were dropped from the 1976 *Kit* as not being sufficiently well established in the research literature. However, two new factors were offered, as follows:

> Factor FF: Figural Fluency. "The ability to draw quickly a number of examples, elaborations, or restructurings based on a given visual or descriptive stimulus" (p. 61).
>
> Factor XU: Flexibility of Use. "The mental set necessary to think of different uses for objects" (p. 197).

The new factors were offered mainly on the basis of work in Guilford's laboratory (Guilford & Hoepfner, 1971). According to Guilford (1967), Divergent Production is a facet of a general Structure-of-Intellect Model that interacts with other facets (Product and Content) to produce numerous factors, possibly as many as 24 or more, of which the factors recognized by the 1976 ETS *Kit* would be only a subset.

The purpose here is to examine currently available evidence, particularly that afforded by the database assembled for this volume, to identify what factors in the domain of idea and language production are adequately confirmed, and to discuss measurements of them. The higher-order structuring of the domain is considered in Chapter 15.

PRELIMINARY ANALYSIS OF THE DATABASE

In all, 121 datasets (listed in Table 10.1) were tagged as containing token factors that could be assigned to the domain of idea and language production. Although some of these contained only single factors and thus have little use in differentiating factors, about half of them contained more than one factor of interest. On the basis of preliminary examination of the variables loaded on factors and of general knowledge of authors' and reviewers' characterizations, factors were identified as falling into nine groups. Each group was given a two-character symbol that is used for convenient designation, in most cases being a designation used in ETS factor kits. The groups are as follows:

> FI: Ideational Fluency. Factors were assigned to this group when their variables were mainly concerned with tasks in which the subject was required to produce, within a fairly liberal time limit, a series of different words or phrases concerned with a specified topic or concept. Many such factors also contained variables that could be classified in other groups (such as FA and FE), apparently because the dataset did not contain sufficient variables adequately to define distinct separate factors in those groups. Such factors are indicated with an asterisk (*) in Table 10.1. (Asterisks are occasionally used for other factors listed in the table, for similar reasons.)
>
> NA: Naming Facility. Factors in this group have variables requiring subjects quickly to produce common names for concepts, usually as cued by visual displays (pictures).
>
> FA: Associational Fluency. Factors in this group tend to have variables requiring subjects to produce, in a limited time, a series of words or phrases that are associated, in meaning, with specified words or concepts.

FE: Expressional Fluency. Factors in this group have variables requiring subjects to produce, in a limited time, meaningful language sentences or phrases as cued by various means, e.g., the first letters of some or all of the words to be used. They may also have variables that require subjects to paraphrase verbal expressions or otherwise to manipulate the grammatical structuring of verbal materials in different ways.

FW: Word Fluency. Factors in this group have variables that appear to require subjects to recall, from long-term memory, a series of native language words that have certain phonemic or orthographic characteristics (independent of word meanings).

SP: Sensitivity to Problems. Factors in this group have variables that require subjects to see problems in practical situations and in a limited time to list what those problems might be and/or to suggest solutions for such problems. They may also have variables requiring subjects to think of new uses for objects or combinations of objects.

FO: Originality/Creativity. Factors in this group have variables that allow opportunity for subjects to suggest clever or unusual responses to the tasks presented. Scoring of the responses is often based on judgments of, or data bearing on, the degree to which responses are clever or unusual. Scoring can also be based on the degree to which subjects give an unusual variety of responses, as indicated by shifts of responses from one to another of certain categories of responses. (In the process of classifying factors into groups, factors in this group were initially assigned to either of two categories: (a) a "flexibility of use" category, in which the major emphasis was on the degree to which subjects could come up with a variety of unusual uses for objects, like a common brick; and (b) a "cleverness" category in which the major emphasis was on the degree to which responses were evaluated as clever or original. However, it was observed that although there were numerous instances of factors in each of these categories, there were practically no instances of datasets showing two distinct factors corresponding to the categories. Furthermore, there were a number of token factors that had variables falling into both categories. Therefore, these categories were collapsed into one.)

FF: Figural Fluency. Factors in this group have variables that ask subjects to produce, within a limited time, a variety of original drawings or sketches. Responses are evaluated for quantity and/or quality.

FX: Figural Flexibility. Factors in this group have variables that ask subjects to produce a variety of ways to solve certain problems presented figurally, principally tasks of the Match Problems type.

For convenience, Table 10.1 also lists factors concerned with tasks requiring the production of continuous discourse in spoken or written form. These factors are treated more extensively in Chapter 5 as language skills.

It can be seen that the classification of factors in the language and idea production domain is generally difficult because the tasks in all of them have many common elements – the production of a series of responses within a limited time, vagueness and ambiguity in the cuing of these responses, and the necessity on the part of the subjects to recall words, ideas, and other representations from long-term memory, or to discover or invent new ideas by manipulating such words and ideas. The fact that many token factors are asterisked in Table 10.1

Table 10.1. *Factors of idea and language production identified in 121 datasets (Entries are factor numbers in the dataset's hierarchical matrix)*

Dataset	Factor group[a]									Other[b]
	FI	NA	FA	FE	FW	SP	FO	FF	FX	
ADKI03	8	—	—	—	—	—	—	—	—	
BECH01	8*	—	—	—	—	—	—	—	—	
BENN01	4*	—	—	—	—	—	—	—	—	2:WA (Writing)
BENN02	4*	—	—	—	—	—	—	—	—	2:WA (Writing)
BERE01	4	—	5	3	7	—	—	2,6	—	
BERE02	3,4*	—	—	2*	7	—	—	5,6	—	
BOTZ01	—	—	—	—	7	—	—	—	—	
BRAD01	—	—	—	—	—	—	—	5	—	
BROW11	4*	—	—	—	—	—	—	—	—	
BUND11	—	—	—	—	—	—	—	—	4	9:OP (Speech)
CARR01	—	6	—	8	—	—	—	—	—	
CARR21	—	7	—	—	5	—	—	—	—	
CARR31	2*	3	—	—	—	—	—	—	—	
CRAW01	2*	—	—	—	—	—	—	6	—	
DEMI01A	—	—	—	—	—	—	4	—	—	
DEMI02A	—	—	—	—	—	—	2	—	—	
DENT01	3*	—	—	—	—	—	—	—	—	
DUNH11	—	—	—	—	5	—	7	—	—	
FEDE02	2*	—	—	—	—	—	—	—	—	
FLEI51	—	—	—	—	6	—	—	—	—	
FRED13	2*	—	—	—	—	—	—	—	—	
FREN11	—	—	—	3	—	—	—	—	—	
FULG31	3*	—	6	—	—	—	7	—	—	
GERS01	3	4	—	—	—	—	—	8	6	
GERS02	3*	—	—	—	—	—	—	4	2	
GUIL11	—	—	—	—	—	4*	7	—	5	
GUIL12	2,12	—	4	3	9	—	5	—	—	

	1	2	3	4	5	6	7	8	9
GUIL14	7*	—	—	—	—	—	—	—	2
GUIL15	2,4	3	—	—	—	—	—	—	—
GUIL18	8	—	5	—	—	—	—	—	—
GUIL20	6	—	3	—	—	—	5	—	—
GUIL21	4	—	—	—	—	—	—	—	—
GUIL22	2*	2	5	—	—	—	—	—	—
GUIL23	4*	—	3	—	—	—	—	6	4,7
GUIL51	—	—	—	—	3	—	—	—	—
GUIL55	2*,5	—	—	—	3*	—	8	6,10	11
GUIL56	3,4	—	—	—	5	—	4	2,10	5
GUIL57	3	—	—	—	7	—	2*	5	10
GUIL58	3,4	—	8	—	7	—	—	—	—
GUIL61	1	—	—	2	—	—	—	—	—
GUIL66	10	—	—	—	3	8,12	4	—	9
HAKS01	17	—	—	—	15	—	20,23	—	—
HAKS21	7*	—	—	—	—	—	—	—	—
HARG01	—	—	—	—	—	—	3,4	—	—
HARG11A	3	—	—	—	—	—	—	—	—
HARG12	2*	—	—	—	—	—	—	—	—
HARR51	—	—	—	—	6	—	—	—	—
HARR52	—	9	—	—	5	—	—	—	—
HEND01	3	—	—	—	—	—	5	—	—
HIGG01	4*	—	6*	—	—	—	—	—	—
HOEP11	9	—	—	—	—	—	—	7,8	2,4
HOEP21	—	—	—	—	2	7	10*	—	—
HOFF01	—	—	—	—	—	—	—	6,9*	—
HOLT11	3*	—	—	—	—	—	2	—	—
HORN01	8*	—	—	—	—	—	—	—	—
HORN25	5*	—	—	—	—	—	—	—	—
HORN26	4*	—	—	—	—	—	—	—	—
INNE01A	3*	—	—	—	—	—	2	—	—
INNE02A	2*	—	—	—	—	—	1	—	—
JACO01	2*	—	—	—	—	—	3	—	—

Table 10.1 (cont.)

Dataset	Factor group[a]									Other[b]
	FI	NA	FA	FE	FW	SP	FO	FF	FX	
JONE32	6	—	—	—	—	—	—	—	—	
JONE34	—	—	—	—	—	—	7	—	—	
KNOE11	2*	—	3, 5	6, 7	4	—	—	—	—	
LANG01	—	—	—	—	—	—	4	—	—	
LUMS01	2*	—	—	—	—	—	—	—	—	
MANG01A	2	—	—	—	—	—	—	—	—	
MARK01	2, 3	—	—	—	—	—	4	—	—	
MAY01	2, 3	—	—	—	—	—	4, 5	—	—	
MCGU01	4*	—	—	—	—	—	—	—	—	
MCGU02	4*	—	—	—	—	—	—	—	—	
MERR41	2, 4	—	7	—	—	3	6	—	—	
MERR51	5	—	—	—	—	4	2	—	—	
MESS01	7	—	—	—	6	—	—	—	—	
NIHI01	6, 9	—	—	—	—	10	—	—	—	
NIHI02	8	—	—	—	—	4, 5, 7	—	—	—	
OLIV01	2, 3	—	—	—	—	—	—	—	—	
OSUL01	—	—	—	—	—	7	6	—	—	
PARA05	3	—	—	—	—	—	—	—	—	
PARA06	4	—	—	—	—	—	—	—	—	
PEMB01	—	—	—	—	3	—	—	—	—	
PENF01	—	—	—	—	—	8, 9	—	—	—	
PIMS01	—	—	—	8	—	—	—	—	—	
PIMS02	—	—	—	7	—	—	—	—	—	
RIEB01	—	—	—	—	—	—	2, 3	—	—	
RIEB02	—	—	—	—	—	—	2, 3	—	—	
ROGE11	2	—	—	—	—	—	—	—	—	

3:WA (Writing),
4:OP (Speech)

Code	C1	C2	C3	C4	C5	C6	C7
SCHA11				5			
SCHU01						1	
SCHU02						2	
SNOW12					7		
STAN51	3	3					
STOR11						7*	
STOR12						9*	3
STOR13						7*	5
SULL01	3						
SULL02	3						
SUNG01	7						
SUNG02	11						
SUNG03	3						
SUNG04	8						
SUNG05	3						
TAYL01	4						
TAYL11	3		4	7		7	
TAYL12A	2*		3	8			
TAYL13A	7		9			4	
TAYL31	3						
THUR11				2			
THUR21A				9			
THUR31				10			
THUR81		10		4			
THUR82				2			
UNDH11							
UNDH21	5*						
VIDL01	2*						
VOSS01							
WALL01	2					2	
WEBE01	2*					3	

5,6:WA(Writing)

3,5:OP (Speech)

Table 10.1 (cont.)

Dataset	Factor group[a]									
	FI	NA	FA	FE	FW	SP	FO	FF	FX	Other[b]
WEBE02	4*	—	—	—	—	—	—	—	—	—
WEIN11	6*	—	—	—	3	—	—	—	—	5:WA (Writing)
WIND01	2*	—	3*	—	—	—	—	—	—	—
WOTH01	3	—	—	—	9	—	—	16	—	—

[a]Factor Groups:
FI: Ideational Fluency
NA: Naming Facility
FA: Associational Fluency
FE: Expressional Fluency
FW: Word Fluency
SP: Sensitivity to Problems
FO: Originality/Creativity
FF: Figural Fluency
FX: Figural Flexibility
[b]Speech and writing fluency factors are treated in Chapter 5.
*Variables loaded on the factor are diverse, covering several other primary factors in the domain. A factor so indicated is essentially at a second order of analysis.

reflects the notion, proposed by Cattell (1971; see also Hakstian & Cattell, 1978), that the primary factors in this domain are subsumed by a broad second-order factor of General Retrieval (*Gr*), the word *retrieval* referring to the involvement of long-term memory. More recently, Horn (1988) has termed this second-order factor "long-term storage and retrieval, TSR," proposing that it embraces not only such first-order factors as FI, FA, FE, and FO but also factors of long-term memory recall after learning.

Also of concern is the fact many of the tasks in this domain require the handwriting of responses, a consequence of which may be that individual differences in speed of performing a purely motor act may contribute to the variance of tests loaded on the various fluency factors. Some investigators have attempted to control this possibility by including tests of marking speed and/or handwriting speed in their test batteries. Either or both of two results can occur, depending on study design: separate factors of handwriting or marking speed can appear, or the marking/handwriting speed variables can have appreciable loadings on the fluency factors. Nevertheless, the overall pattern of results suggests that fluency tests requiring handwriting contain sufficient variance over and above what is contributed by motor speed to lend credence that the most important source of variance is the subject's ability to think of ("retrieve") substantively appropriate responses in the testing time allowed. On the other hand, it can be recommended that in order to control variance from handwriting speed, fluency variables should have handwriting speed variables partialled out of them, or should be administered in such a way as to call for oral responses. (See Chapter 13 for more information on writing speed factors.)

IDEATIONAL FLUENCY (FI) FACTORS

Table 10.2 lists 90 token factors, in 79 datasets, that are classified in the Ideational Fluency group. Mean age of sample ranges from 6 to 30 years, and the datasets come from both English-speaking and non-English-speaking countries. Many of the factors, indicated with an asterisk, are essentially factors at a second-order of analysis. Good examples are those in datasets HORN25 and HAKS21. Both of these datasets were designed to include just one variable to represent each of a number of factors known to be correlated, and thus to identify factors at a second order. Horn and Bramble (1967) included the variable Similar Words to represent factor FA and the variable Things to represent factor FI; their factor 5 had loadings of .76 and .68 on these variables respectively, and the factor was interpreted as General Retrieval capacity. (Although Horn and Bramble did not describe the tests in detail, the test Similar Words was apparently the same as Thurstone's Controlled Associations test, requiring subjects to give series of synonyms to words, and the test Things required the listing of instances of categories such as "things round.") Similarly, Hakstian and Cattell (1978) selected for their battery a single measure of each of factors they called Spontaneous

Table 10.2. *90 Ideational Fluency (FI) factors in 79 datasets, arranged in order of approximate mean age of sample*[a]

Dataset	Date	C'y code	Age	Sample code	M/F code	Factor no.	Remarks (higher-order factors; others related)
PARA05	'69	U	6	1	3	3	1:2C
TAYL31	'75	C	6	1	3	3	1:2C
PARA06	'69	U	8	1	3	4	1:2C
JONE32	'49	U	9	1	3	6	1:2D
BENN01	'73	E	10	1	1	4*	1:2R;2:Writing
BENN02	'73	E	10	1	2	4*	1:2R;2:Writing
WALL01	'65	U	10	6	3	2	3:FO Orthogonal Factors
HIGG01	'78	A	11	1	3	4*	1:2G
MERR51	'63	U	11	1	3	5	1:2G;2:FO;4:SP
SULL01	'73	U	11	1	3	3	1:2G
MCGU01	'61	U	12	1	1	4*	1:2G
MCGU02	'61	U	12	1	2	4*	1:2G
HARG11A	'27	E	13	6	3	3	1:2C
HARG12	'27	E	13	1	3	2*	1:2G;4:Writing Speed
MAY01	'65	U	13	1	3	2	1:2R;2:FI with "Uses"
"	"	"	"	"	"	3	3:FI with "Improvements"
SULL02	'73	U	13	1	3	3	1:2G
CRAW01	'76	C	14	1	3	2*	1:2G;6:FF
GERS02	'63	U	14	1	3	3*	1:20;2:FF
GUIL55	'61	U	14	1	3	2*	1:2G;3:FW;6:FF;7:FX;
"	"	"	"	"	"	5	Ideational Fluency (Alt)
GUIL56	'61	U	14	I	1	3	1:3G;2:2R;5:FW;6,10:FF; 8:FO;11:FX;
"	"	"	"	"	"	4	Ideational Fluency (Alt)
GUIL57	'61	U	14	I	2	3	1:2R;2,10:FF;4:FO;5:FX;7:FW
GUIL58	'61	U	14	8	3	3	1:2G;2:FO;5:FF;7:FW;
"	"	"	"	"	"	4	Ideational Fluency (Alt)
HOEP11	'65	U	14	6	3	9	1:2R;2,4:FX;6:FA;7,8:FF
MANG01A	'59	E	14	6	2	2	1:2S
ROGE11	'53	E	14	6	3	2	1:2C;3:Writing;4:Speech
BERE01	'60	U	15	8	2	4	1:2R;2:FF;3:FE;5:FA;7:FW
BERE02	'60	U	15	8	1	3	1:2R;2:FE;4:FI;5,6:FF;7:FW
"	"	"	"	"	"	4	Ideational Fluency (Alt)
GUIL15	'70	U	15	8	3	2	1:2R;3:NA;
"	"	"	"	"	"	4	Ideational Fluency (Alt)
WEBE01	'53	G	15	6	1	2	1:2G
WEBE02	'53	G	15	6	2	4	1:2G
BROW11	'66	U	16	6	3	4*	1:2G
FRED13	'82	U	16	6	3	2*	1:2R
HAKS21	'78	C	16	6	3	7*	1:2G
HEND01	'69	U	16	6	3	3	1:2G
JACO01	'75	U	16	1	3	2	1:2G;3:FO
NIHI01	'64	U	16	8	3	6	1:3G;2:2H;5:FX?;10:SP
"	"	"	"	"	"	9	Ideational Fluency (Alt)
NIHI02	'64	U	16	8	3	8	1:2G;4:FO
OLIV01	'72	U	16	6	3	2	1:2G;
"	"	"	"	"	"	3	Ideational Fluency (Alt)
SUNG01	'81	U	16	Z	3	7	1:2G

Table 10.2 (*cont.*)

Dataset	Date	C'y code	Age	Sample code	M/F code	Factor no.	Remarks (higher-order factors; others related)
SUNG02	'81	U	16	#	3	11	1:2G
SUNG03	'81	U	16	W	3	3	1:2G
SUNG04	'81	U	16	1	1	8	1:2G
SUNG05	'81	U	16	1	2	3	1:2G
WEIN11	'59	U	16	1	3	6*	1:2G;5:Writing
DENT01	'55	U	17	1	3	3*	1:2G + Personality Factors
TAYL01	'47	U	17	1	3	4	1:2H;7:FW
FULG31	'72	J	18	6	3	3*	1:3R;2:2R;4:NA;6:FA;7:FO
GUIL20	'55	U	18	3	1	6	1:2G;3:FA;5:FO
ADKI03	'52	U	19	2	1	8	1:2H
BECH01	'47	U	19	6	3	8*	1:2S
GERS01	'63	U	19	3	1	3	1:20;6:FX;8:FF
GUIL61	'74	U	19	P	1	1	2:FE (Orthogonal Factors)
KNOE11	'52	U	19	G	3	2*	1:2R;3,5:FA;4:FW;6,7:FE
LUMS01	'65	A	19	P	3	2*	1:2F
TAYL13A	'67	U	19	6	1	7	1:2G;3,5:Speech;4:FO;9:FE
VIDL01	'74	U	19	G	3	2*	1:2G
WIND01	'67	U	19	P	3	2*	3:FA Orthogonal Factors
INNE01A	'72	E	20	6	1	3*	1:2R;2:FO
INNE02A	'72	E	20	6	2	2*	1:FO Orthogonal Factors
FEDE02	'80	U	21	2	3	2*	1:2F
GUIL12	'56	U	21	3	1	2	1:2R;3:FE;4:FA;5,12:FO;9:FW
"	"	"	"	"	"	12	Ideational Fluency (Alt)
GUIL14	'57	U	21	3	1	7*	6:2R
GUIL21	'56	U	21	3	1	4	1:2C
GUIL22	'56	U	21	3	1	2*	1:2G;5:FA
GUIL23	'56	U	21	3	1	4*	1:2G;2:NA;3:FA
GUIL66	'52	U	21	3	1	10	1:2G;4:FO;8:SP
HOLT11	'71	U	21	2	1	3*	1:2R;2:FO
MERR41	'60	U	21	3	1	2	1:2G;3:SP;6:FO;7:FA;
"	'60	U	21	3	1	4	Ideational Fluency (Alt)
MESS01	'75	U	21	3	1	7	1:2H;6:FW
TAYL11	'67	U	21	3	1	3	1:2C;4:FE;5,6:Writing;7:FO
TAYL12A	'67	U	21	2	1	2*	1:2R;3:FE
WOTH01	'90	U	21	1	3	3	1:3G;2:2F;9:FW;16:FF
CARR31	'76	U	22	6	3	2*	1:2C;3:NA
GUIL18	'53	U	23	3	1	8	1:2G;5:FA
HAKS01	'74	C	24	1	3	17	1:3G;13:2C;15:FW;20,23:FO
HORN01	'66	U	28	Q	3	8*	1:2G
HORN25	'67	U	30	Q	1	5*	1:2G
HORN26	'67	U	30	Q	1	4*	1:2G
MARK01	'59	U	30	3	1	2	1:2R;4:FO;
"	"	"	"	"	"	3	Ideational Fluency (Alt)

*Variables loaded on the factor are diverse, covering several other primary factors in the domain. A factor so indicated is essentially at a second order of analysis.

[a]See Appendix A for codes. In a few cases, the classsifications of factors shown here were preliminary and may not agree with the final classifications shown in the tables of Appendix B.

Flexibility (multiple grouping of objects), Ideational Fluency (listing attributes of nouns), and Originality (object synthesis – constructing syntheses of two objects). On factor 7 of the reanalysis of their data, these factors had loadings of .23, .58, and .39, respectively.

Nevertheless, measures of Ideational Fluency tend to dominate (have the highest salient loadings on) even those FI factors indicated with an asterisk, and they of course also dominate factors that are not indicated with an asterisk. Among these measures are those that were offered as marker tests in both the 1963 and the 1976 editions of the ETS kits of marker tests (French, Ekstrom, & Price, 1963; Ekstrom, French, & Harman, 1976):

> Topics: In four minutes, write as many ideas as possible about a given topic, e.g., "A train journey." The score is the number of "appropriate ideas" (phrases or sentences) that are written; in practice there is usually no evaluation of appropriateness or differentness, so that the score is actually the number of ideas written.
>
> Theme: In four minutes, write "a few paragraphs" about a given theme, e.g., "a tree." Subjects are told to "write all you can about each theme" and to "use any idea whether or not it seems very closely related to the theme." Further, "expand on any idea as much as you like, and be sure you write as much as you can." The score is supposed to be based on "the amount of appropriate material written," but in practice there is usually no evaluation of what is written, and the score can be the number of words written.
>
> Thing Categories: In three minutes, "list the names of things that are alike in a specified way," e.g., "things that are always red or that are red more often than any other color." The score is the number of things listed.

In Guilford's Structure-of-Intellect model, Ideational Fluency was regarded as having to do with the *Divergent Production of SeMantic Units* (DMU). In a summary report (Guilford & Hoepfner, 1966b) the following tests were listed as good measures of this factor:

> Ideational Fluency: List members of a broadly defined class, e.g., FLUIDS THAT BURN (like gasoline, kerosene, alcohol), the score being the number of items listed.
>
> Topics: (same as the ETS factor kit test mentioned above)
>
> Theme: (same as the ETS factor kit test mentioned above)
>
> Thing Categories: (same as the ETS factor kit test mentioned above)
>
> Plot Titles (non-clever): Write titles for given story plots, only the "nonclever" titles being counted toward the score.
>
> Consequences (obvious): List consequences of a proposed unusual event, e.g., no babies being born for a year, only the number of "obvious" consequences being counted toward the score.
>
> Utility test (fluency): List many different uses for given common object, e.g., a brick, the score being the number of uses written.

The common element in all of these tests is facility in thinking of "ideas" that conform to the requirements of whatever particular task may be presented. The tasks are always restricted to those that require only recall of ideas from typical common experiences. Most cultures expose their members, even at early ages, to a variety of "things that are round," "things that are red," "attributes of trees," and the like. The Ideational Fluency factor measures the rate and extent to which individuals are able to think of, or recall, instances of given concepts or categories of experience. The factor appears to be generally applicable over a wide range of such common experiences, in the sense that measures taken for different categories are highly correlated.

The thus far untested assumption in all this is that individual differences in Ideational Fluency would also apply to the ability to think of ideas in highly specialized areas. Would it be the case, for example, that people trained in nuclear physics show differences in the ability quickly to recall instances of concepts like "subatomic particle," and if so, would these differences be correlated with scores on the marker tests of Ideational Fluency? Would it be the case that people specialized in political science or in law show differences in the ability to recall instances of particular political or legal concepts, and would any such differences load on factor FI as conventionally measured? To what extent would any such differences be of relevance to performance in specialized professions? For that matter, to what extent are differences in factor FI as conventionally measured relevant to performance in everyday life? There is need for research into such questions, as well as into the problem of the relation of factor FI to memory factors. On this last point, presently available evidence suggests that factor FI is largely independent, at least linearly, of the memory abilities described in Chapter 7.

There is little need to review the (token) factors listed in Table 10.2 with regard to the details of the measures loaded on them. In most cases, the measures are predominantly sampled from those already described (above), or they are variants of them. Of possible interest are the few cases in which alternative FI factors appear in our analyses. For example, in dataset MAY01 two FI factors are shown. Factor 2 is loaded with two "fluency" scorings of responses to tasks in which subjects were asked to think of different uses of common objects (a tin can, a book, a pencil, and a broom), whereas Factor 3 concerns responses to tasks in which subjects were asked to suggest "improvements" that could be made to common objects (a table fork, a chalkboard). The two factors were substantially correlated (.542), but their separation suggests that thinking of "uses" calls on slightly different processes or knowledges from those involved in thinking of "improvements." Whether this result could be replicated in further research is unknown, and even if it could, its ultimate meaning would be problematic.

In dataset GUIL55, factor 2 is loaded saliently with a wide variety of variables, most of which require thinking of, and writing down, a variety of responses to certain tasks – e.g., thinking of alternate uses for common objects, thinking of possible ways of completing a simile, thinking of possible problems that might arise in using certain common objects, etc. The highest salient loading (.31), however, is for a Verbal Comprehension variable (essentially, a vocabulary or lexical knowledge test), a result that might suggest that ideational fluency *as measured by factor 2* is correlated with the wealth of common experiences (as indicated by a vocabulary test) that an individual can draw upon in responding to fluency tasks. The fact that the highest salient loading is only .31 reflects the fact that factor 2 has a high correlation (.93) with a second-order factor that can be interpreted as *g*. It is difficult to see much contrast between factor 2 and factor 5, which is loaded saliently with only four variables – Plot Titles (scored for "low quality" responses), Utility (number of different uses suggested for common objects), Consequences (number of "obvious" consequences suggested for certain hypothetical events), and (with a much lower loading) Alternate Signs (number of different "symbols" drawn to express the meanings of given words). One is tempted to conclude that the differentiation between factor 2 and 5 in this dataset is a statistical artifact of some sort.

Similar remarks can be made about the apparent differentiation of factors 2 and 12 in dataset GUIL12, factors 3 and 4 in dataset GUIL56, factors 3 and 4 in dataset GUIL58, factors 2 and 4 in dataset GUIL15, factors 2 and 4 in dataset MERR41, factors 2 and 3 in dataset MARK01, and factors 2 and 3 in dataset OLIV01, for in none of these cases is there any compelling contrast between the sets of variables loaded on the two factors in each dataset. The differentiations could possibly be attributable to contrasts in how the responses are scored (i.e., whether they are scored for sheer number of responses – fluency, or for shifts in categories used), but even in this respect the contrasts are not uniform in the sense that one factor has only fluency scorings and the other has only shifts scorings. In any event, there would inevitably be a substantial or even high correlation between a fluency scoring and a shifts scoring; the more responses, the more likelihood of shifts in categories.

There seems to be little substantive differentiation between the sets of variables loaded on factors 3 and 4 in dataset BERE02; both factors were assigned to FI. Factor 3 is loaded with a Form Completion test in which subjects are asked to name objects that could be drawn by adding lines to given figures, and the test Brick Uses, in which subjects have to list different possible uses for a brick, the score being simply the number of uses given. Factor 4 has a melange of variables all of which seem to require fluency in thinking of ideas: Design Synthesis (draw different designs using three given figures), Plot Titles (write a series of titles for story plots), and Structural Functions (verbally produce ideas based on the formal relationships between objects – e.g., places to hide a rope, tasks suitable for an eight-foot-tall person).

Several factors tentatively assigned to FI emphasize thinking of different ways for dealing with numerical or algebraic expressions, – for example, factor 3 in dataset GERS01. This is saliently loaded with Number Grouping (group and regroup numbers in several different ways to form classes), Symbol Elaboration (given two simple equations, deduce a variety of other equations), Number Rules (given a starting number, relate one or more numbers to it in various ways to achieve a given result), and Letter Group Relations (given a set of four letters that are related in several possible ways, select other sets of four that have the same relations). Factor 3 in dataset GERS02 has a similar set of variables. Possibly these should not be assigned to FI; the datasets have no good markers for FI. A similar problem arises in the case of factor 1 in dataset GUIL61, loaded with a series of variables requiring invention of different ways of stating arithmetic problems, writing sentences, or creating letter-number codes.

NAMING FACILITY (NA) FACTORS

Even in the earliest days of research on individual differences (Cattell, 1885), speed of naming objects or colors was a variable of interest. It has not, however, been given much attention in factor-analytic investigations, and a factor of naming facility has not been recognized in the kits of marker tests issued by Educational Testing Service. Nevertheless, evidence now available strongly suggests the existence of a factor of naming facility. That is, it suggests that there are substantial and reliable individual differences in speed of producing names for objects or certain attributes of objects such as their color. Table 10.3 lists 9 token factors that can be assigned to this trait.

Probably the earliest evidence for a naming facility factor is to be found in dataset THUR81 (factor X3 in Table 5 of Thurstone & Thurstone, 1941), but the Thurstones neglected to interpret this factor or to comment on it in any way, since they apparently regarded it as a residual of little interest. In the reanalysis of this dataset, the two salient loadings on factor 10 are for the tests Picture Naming and Figure Naming. In Picture Naming, subjects were shown a series of drawings of common objects (house, apple, foot, bugle, etc.) and were asked to write the first letter of the name of each object. The score was the number of drawings (out of 147) so labeled in four minutes. Figure Naming was similar except that the 144 drawings were exclusively of the figures *triangle*, *rectangle*, *circle*, and *star*, randomly ordered. At about the same time as the publication of the Thurstone's study, Carroll (1941) conducted a study which involved individual administration of several oral naming tests:

> Naming States of the Union: Subjects were asked to list, orally, as many as they could of the (at that time) 48 states of the U. S., in 60 seconds.
> Color-Naming: Subjects were shown a display (the Woodworth–Wells color naming card) that had 100 square blotches of the colors *red*, *yellow*, *blue*, *green*, and *black*, randomly ordered, and were asked to name them as fast as possible (without a time limit); the score was the rate at which the colors were named.
> Form-Naming: Subjects were asked to name, as fast as possible, 100 randomly ordered forms *star*, *triangle*, *circle*, *square*, and *cross* (the Woodworth-Wells form-naming card); the score was the rate at which the forms were named.
> Giving First Names: Subjects were asked to give, as fast as possible, all the first names, either boys' or girls', that they could think of in 40 seconds. (Repetitions, if any, were not scored.)

Table 10.3. *9 Naming Facility (NA) factors in 9 datasets, arranged in order of approximate mean age of sample[a]*

Dataset	Date	C'y code	Age	Sample code	M/F code	Factor no.	Remarks (higher-order factors; others related)
STAN51	'81	U	6	1	3	3	1:2G
HARR52	'73	U	10	1	2	9	1:2G;5:FW
THUR81	'41	U	13	6	3	10	1:3G;4:FW;8:2S
GUIL15	'70	U	15	8	3	3	1:2R;2,4:FI
FULG31	'72	J	18	6	3	4	1:3R;2:2R;3:FI;6:FA;7:FO
CARR01	'41	U	20	6	3	6	1:2C;8:FE
CARR21	'58	U	21	2	1	7	1:2G;5:FW
GUIL23	'56	U	21	3	1	2	1:2G;3:FA;4:FI*
CARR31	'76	U	22	6	3	3	1:2C;2:FI*

*Variables loaded on the factor are diverse, covering several other primary factors in the domain. A factor so indicated is essentially at a second order of analysis.
[a]See Appendix A for codes. In a few cases, the classsifications of factors shown here were preliminary and may not agree with the final classifications shown in the tables of Appendix B.

Carroll identified a Naming Facility factor in his study, and this was confirmed in reanalysis (dataset CARR01, factor 10), where Naming States of the Union and Form-Naming had salient loadings of .51 and .45 respectively, and Color-Naming and Giving First Names had (nonsalient) loadings of .33 and .29. In a further study by Carroll (dataset CARR21), speed of performing Thurstone's Verbal Enumeration test had the highest salient loading (.85) on factor 7, interpreted as Naming Facility. Verbal Enumeration is a paper-and-pencil test in which subjects have to mark all words in a column that are instances of the concept (such as "color" or "fruit") named at the top of the column. Although this is not strictly speaking a test of naming facility, the responses depend on the subject's speedy recognition of a name or instance of a concept. Furthermore, Thurstone's Picture Naming test had the next highest salient loading on this factor. In a still later study, Carroll (1976b, dataset CARR31) established that an oral Picture Naming test and Thurstone's paper-and-pencil Picture Naming test both had loadings (.64 and .62) on a Naming Facility factor that was linearly independent of an Ideational Fluency factor.

In Guilford's (1967; Guilford & Hoepfner, 1971) studies, simple picture-naming or form-naming variables were never used. More complex tests of concept naming appear in his studies, however. For example, Picture-Group Naming requires subjects to give class names for groups of pictures (e.g., five pictures of hats, of animals, of fruits, etc.); Word-Group Naming requires giving class names to groups of five words that are instances of a particular concept. These tests, along with other tests that can require giving names, appear on factors that I interpret as NA factors in several datasets generated by Guilford or others, e.g.,

GUIL23 and HARR52. From this evidence, it is still not clear whether the critical element in these tests is the ability to produce names quickly or the ability to induce the class concept from a display of a series of instances of it. However, dataset FULG31 suggests that it is the former, because tests such as Picture-Group Naming and Word-Group Naming appear on a factor (factor 4) on which also appear a number of variables in which induction of class concepts from instances is not involved, but production of names *is*. Among such variables are:

> Attribute-Object Relations: "In each item, the response was so well described that it could hardly be anything else." For example, given the attributes "two-footed animal with feathers," the keyed response was "bird."
>
> Action-Agent Relations: The subject was asked to give "the *most likely* or *most natural agent* that performs the action." E.g., given the action "hears" the keyed response was "ear."

The evidence from this dataset lends support to interpreting its factor 4 as Naming Facility, particularly if it is assumed that test scores reflected speed in giving responses. It also supports interpreting factor 3 in dataset GUIL15 and factor 2 in dataset GUIL23 as Naming Facility, because among the variables saliently loaded on those factors are such variables as Attribute-Object Relations and Action-Agent Relations. Indeed, Guilford himself (1967, p. 172) interpreted these factors as measuring what he called Convergent Production of Semantic Units (or NMU) in his system of interpreting factors.

There has been some experimental investigation of naming responses. Oldfield and Wingfield (1964, 1965) reported that response times in naming pictures of objects are inversely related to the logarithms of the frequencies of the names in large word-counts such as that of Thorndike and Lorge (1944), but Carroll and White (1973a, b) found that some or all of this relation might be better accounted for by assuming that word frequency is at best only a moderately good indicator of the age-of-acquisition of the name. In fact, Carroll and White obtained direct measurements of the age-of-acquisition of names for a series of picturable objects and showed that these measures predicted naming latencies better than word frequency data. Other variables affecting the speed of naming particular pictured concepts are clarity of the pictorial representation and the "codability" of the stimulus (the degree to which the stimulus has only one name, as opposed to many possible names; Lachman, Shaffer, & Hennrikus, 1974). Codability, word frequency, and age-of-acquisition are variables pertaining to the stimuli used in naming latency studies; just how they interact with individual differences has as yet not been adequately investigated. It should be obvious that naming speed is not appropriately measured when the naming responses are not in the long-term memory stores of individuals, that is, when individuals do not know the name of an object. Individual differences in Naming Facility are best measured when the objects to be named have names that are well known by individuals in a sample to be tested.

ASSOCIATIONAL FLUENCY (FA) FACTORS

In the series of ETS kits of factor marker tests, the existence of an Associational Fluency factor was first recognized in the second edition (French, Ekstrom, & Price, 1963), mainly on the basis of work then recently completed in Guilford's laboratory (e.g., Guilford & Christensen, 1956, the source of our dataset GUIL12). This 1963 kit recommended three tests as markers of the factor:

> Fa-1 Controlled Associations: A test adapted from Thurstone's test of the same name. In each of two parts, the task is to write as many synonyms as possible (up to twelve) for each of four adjectives (like *good* or *hard*), in six minutes. The score is the number of acceptable responses.
>
> Fa-2 Associational Fluency: A test by Christensen and Guilford. The task is highly similar to that in Fa-1, but there are only two stimulus words in each part, with spaces for up to 20 responses to each, with two minutes working time.
>
> Fa-3 Associations IV: A test by J. P. Guilford. The task is to produce a word that is associated with both of the two given words but which has a different meaning in its relationship to each of them, e.g., *ring* in response to *jewelry* and *bell* (15 items, 7 minutes for each of two parts.)

In the 1976 edition of the kit, Controlled Associations (FA-1) is retained, but partly for the sake of providing greater variety, the second and third tests offered are:

> Opposites (FA-2): In each of two parts, the subject is asked to write up to six antonyms for each of four words, in five minutes.
>
> Figures of Speech (FA-3): In each of two parts, the subject is asked to think of up to three words or phrases that could be used in making figures of speech which compare one object with another, e.g., "She was as pale as . . . ." (5 items, 5 minutes). (In Guilford's work, this test was most often called Simile Insertions.)

These tests are essentially the same as those listed by Guilford and Hoepfner (1966b, p. 10) as good tests of the associational fluency factor, which he labeled DMU, the *D*ivergent Production of Se*M*antic *U*nits. It is to be noted that the tasks in all tests mentioned above are highly similar. In many respects, they are similar to tests of Ideational Fluency (FI) in that they require producing a variety of ideas. As may be seen in Table 10.1, factor FA is reasonably well differentiated from other factors in the domain; its distinctness appears to be attributable to the special character of the tasks loaded on it, namely, the fact that the responses are to be drawn from fairly restricted classes that can be said to be closely associated in meaning, e.g., synonyms, antonyms, and the like.

Table 10.4 lists 13 token factors in the database that were assigned to Associational Fluency (factor FA). The actual composition of the factors, in terms of the nature of the variables loaded on them, does not provide compelling evidence for an important and distinct dimension of individual differences. Two of the factors (from datasets HOEP11 and WIND01) are indicated (by asterisks) as being diverse, with some of their variables being normally associated with

Table 10.4. *13 Associational Fluency (FA) factors in 12 datasets, arranged in order of approximate mean age of sample*[a]

Dataset	Date	C'y code	Age	Sample code	M/F code	Factor no.	Remarks (higher-order factors; others related)
GUIL58	'61	U	14	8	3	8	1:2R;2:FO;3,4:FI;5:FF; 6,10:FX;7:FW;8:FA
HOEP11	'65	U	14	6	3	6*	1:2R;2,4:FX;5:2N;7,8:FF;9:FI
BERE01	'60	U	15	8	2	5	1:2R;2:FF;3:FE;4:FI;7:FW
FULG31	'72	J	18	6	3	6	1:3R;3:FI;4:NA;5:2R;7:FO
GUIL20	'55	U	18	3	1	3	1:2G;5:FO;6:FI
KNOE11	'52	U	19	G	3	3	1:2R;2:FI*;4:FW;6,7:FE;
"	"	"	"	"	"	5	Associational Fluency (Alt)
WIND01	'67	U	19	P	3	3*	2:FI* Orthogonal Factors
GUIL12	'56	U	21	3	1	4	1:2S:2:FI;3:FE;5,12:FO,9.FW
GUIL22	'56	U	21	3	1	5	1:2G;2:FI*
GUIL23	'56	U	21	3	1	3	1:2G;2:NA;4:FI*
MERR41	'60	U	21	3	1	7	1:2G;2,4:FI;3:SP;6:FO
GUIL18	'53	U	23	3	1	5	1:2G

*Variables loaded on the factor are diverse, covering several other primary factors in the domain. A factor so indicated is essentially at a second order of analysis.
[a]See Appendix A for codes. In a few cases, the classsifications of factors shown here were preliminary and may not agree with the final classifications shown in the tables of Appendix B.

other factors in the idea production domain. They were placed in the FA category mainly because associational fluency variables appeared to predominate and have the higher salient loadings. The same might be said for many of the other factors listed in the table. Indeed, with three exceptions, there is no case of a token factor loaded exclusively with variables set out as associational fluency measures in the ETS kits or by Guilford. One exception (in dataset GUIL12) may actually be a highly specific factor; its loadings are for three scores obtained from a single task, that of writing synonyms to the same set of stimulus words. The three scores were the numbers of synonyms written during three successive short time periods. Of possible interest is the fact that the number of synonyms written during the first half minute had a nonsignificant loading on the factor. The other exceptions arise for *two* factors from dataset KNOE11. One (factor 3) shows high salient loadings on two variables, both being scores from a single test (writing adjectives that could describe a house); variable 14 was the total number of words produced and variable 15 was the number of these describing "objective characteristics" such as color, size, and style of architecture. Factor 5 also had high salient loadings for two scores from a single test (producing three synonyms for each of 18 words such as *dark, happy,* and *huge*). Variable 6 was the number of words written in a column for the second synonym of a word, while variable 7 was the number of words written in a column for the third synonym.

Interestingly, the number of words written in the column for the first synonym loaded only .20 on the factor. As in the case of dataset GUIL12, it appears that variance in the early phases of the synonym-writing tasks is relatively inconsequential. Associational Fluency has to do with the ability to write the rarer and less commonly given synonyms. In both cases, it is obvious that there was serious experimental dependence, and it was not unexpected that two factors emerged for the associational fluency measures.

The conclusion to which we are forced is that Associational Fluency is a highly specific factor that appears only when highly similar measures of association production are obtained. Apparently the measures must require that a *series* of associations are to be given, and the score is the number of associations produced (written) in a limited time.

It is somewhat surprising, incidentally, that factor-analytic research has given little attention to the production of associational responses to stimuli such as those in the well-known Kent-Rosanoff test (Rosanoff, 1927) which have been studied extensively by such scholars as Jenkins and Palermo (1964) and Deese (1965). The only datasets in our database in which Kent–Rosanoff variables appear are INNE01A and INNE02A; results are to be discussed in the later section on factor FO (Originality/Creativity).

EXPRESSIONAL FLUENCY (FE) FACTORS

What was later recognized as an Expressional Fluency factor was first identified by me (Carroll, 1941; dataset CARR01) in several variables that were interpreted as measuring "the rate of production for meaningful and syntactically coherent discourse where there is little restriction to definite responses" (Carroll, 1941, p. 297). Reanalysis of this dataset by hierarchical factor methods yielded a clearer presentation of this factor; its highest salient loadings were for:

> Theme – Word Count (number of words written in a theme in a 20-minute time-limit, loading .47).
> Letter-Star Test, Number of items completed: In each of 75 items, the subject was presented with a series (two to six) of capital letters and asterisks (e.g., *P*H) and asked to write a meaningful phrase or sentence such that each letter is the first letter of a word, while an asterisk could represent any word; loading .44).
> Similes: For each of four items (each with a two-minute time limit), the subject was asked to give up to ten ways of completing a simile taken from poetry; the score is the number of completions written. Subjects were told that responses could have more than one word (loading .43).

These and various other tests were used by Taylor (1947; dataset TAYL01), who obtained both an ideational fluency factor and a factor that he called "verbal versatility." Reanalysis of his data failed to reveal a separate verbal versatility or expressional fluency factor; I obtained only an Ideational Fluency factor that was saliently loaded with a Sentence Fluency test (write different sentences to persuade friends to vote for a certain candidate), a Similes Test (like Carroll's, but with simpler stimuli), a Topics Test (write different ideas about "going up a ladder"), Carroll's Letter–Star test, and several other tests requiring writing of ideas in continuous discourse.

In an early study conducted in Guilford's laboratory (Guilford & Christensen, 1956; dataset GUIL12) an expressional fluency factor was obtained, chiefly with several variants of Carroll's Letter–Star Test (listed in order of salient loadings on factor 3):

> Four-word combinations CEF03A (.54): Write four-word sentences, the first letter of each word being given.
>
> Two-Word Combinations CEF04A (.42): Write a number of two-word phrases (no first letters given)
>
> Four-Word Combinations CEF02A (.40): Write a number of four-word sentences (no first letters given).
>
> Word Arrangement CEF09A (.37): Write a number of sentences containing four specified words (e.g., SEND, ALMOST, SHORE, LARGE).
>
> Two-Word Combinations CEF05A (.34): Write a number of two-word phrases, the first letter of each word being given.

On the basis of this and several other studies, Guilford and Hoepfner (1966b) interpreted the expressional fluency factor as "the ability to organize words in various meaningful complex ideas," or as factor DMS, the *D*ivergent Production of Se*M*antic *S*ystems. As good marker tests of this factor he listed Expressional Fluency (construct a variety of 4-word sentences, given four initial letters), Simile Interpretations (complete in a number of ways a statement involving a simile), and Word Arrangements (write a number of sentences, each containing four specified words). These were also precisely the tests recommended as markers in the 1963 ETS kit (French, Ekstrom, & Price, 1963). In the 1976 ETS kit (Ekstrom, French, & Harman, 1976), the marker tests for factor FE are mostly the same as those in the 1963 kit but the names were changed:

> Making Sentences: Make sentences of a specified length when the initial letter of some of the words is provided.
>
> Arranging Words: Write up to twenty different sentences using the same four words.
>
> Rewriting: Rewrite each of three sentences in two different ways.

Table 10.5 lists 12 token factors in the database that were assigned to Expressional Fluency, in 11 datasets. In nearly every case, the variables with higher salient loadings on the factor consist exclusively of those that have been mentioned above, or minor variations of them. They appear to reflect ability readily and quickly to construct (at least in writing) syntactically acceptable language responses under various kinds of constraints such as:

> (a) requirements about the first letters of words to be used (as in the Letter–Star or similar tests);
>
> (b) requirements about some of the words to be used (as in Arranging Words);

Table 10.5. *12 Expressional Fluency (FE) factors in 11 datasets, arranged in order of approximate mean age of sample[a]*

Dataset	Date	C'y code	Age	Sample code	M/F code	Factor no.	Remarks (higher-order factors; others related)
BERE01	'60	U	15	8	2	3	1:2R;2:FF;4:FI;7:FW
BERE02	'60	U	15	8	1	2*	1:2R;5,6:FF;7:FW
FREN11	'57	U	18	3	1	3	1:2S
GUIL61	'74	U	19	P	1	2	Orthogonal Factors
KNOE11	'52	U	19	G	3	6	1:2R;2:FI*;3,5:FA;4:FW;
"	"	"	"	"	"	7	Expressional Fluency (Alt)
PIMS01	'62	U	19	F	3	8	1:2H
PIMS02	'62	U	19	F	3	7	(Orthogonal factors)
TAYL13A	'67	U	19	6	1	9	1:2G;3,5:Speech;4:FO;7:FI
CARR01	'41	U	20	6	3	8	1:2C;6:NA
GUIL12	'56	U	21	3	1	3	1:2S;2:FI;4:FA;5,12:FO;9:FW
TAYL11	'67	U	21	3	1	4	1:2C;3:FI;5,6:Writing;7:FO

*Variables loaded on the factor are diverse, covering several other primary factors in the domain. A factor so indicated is essentially at a second order of analysis.
[a]See Appendix A for codes. In a few cases, the classsifications of factors shown here were preliminary and may not agree with the final classifications shown in the tables of Appendix B.

   (c) requirements about the meanings to be communicated in different ways (as in Similes, Rewriting, or Theme);
   (d) requirements about the number of words in the response.

Factor 2 in dataset BERE02 is asterisked because the highest salient loading is for a variable (Word Fluency), normally regarded as a marker for the factor FW, Word Fluency, in which the task is to write a variety of words containing a specified letter – with no requirement for syntactical construction. But the Letter–Star test and its variations, also loaded on this factor, impose a somewhat similar requirement – thinking of words with a given first letter, as well as requiring syntactic construction. Factor 2 is distinct from factor 7 in this dataset, assigned to factor FW because of several salient and nonsalient loadings of word fluency variables on the factor.

Factor 3 in dataset TAYL12A does not truly belong in the set. It is loaded with a series of variables consisting of *self-ratings* of various aspects of expressional fluency – in speaking and in writing, or of interest in self-expression. Scores on Knower's (1938) *Speech Attitude Scale* have the highest salient loading. This factor is linearly independent of factor 2, which was assigned to factor FI (Table 10.2) and asterisked there, although it could equally well have been assigned to factor FE because of the presence of many FE variables on it.

The table shows two factors appearing in dataset KNOE11, both arising from multiple scorings of single test performances, specifically, the Letter–Star test developed and used by Taylor (1947). Factor 6 concerns three measures of quantity of responses – Number of Adjectives and Adverbs, Number of Words of Two or More Syllables, and Number of Items Completed. Factor 7 is loaded with three measures of quality or nature of responses: Number of Popular Responses, Number of Responses Showing Relationships between People, and Number of Commands. Apparently this factor says something about strategies that many individuals employ in constructing responses.

It is difficult to be impressed with the sophistication of the measures of Expressional Fluency that have been developed thus far, if the factor is of any importance in revealing differences in cognitive processes. Tests of expressional fluency tend to look like the kinds of games and puzzles with language that appear in newspapers and similar media. One suspects, however, that there exist important opportunities for developing new and more theory-based measurements of this factor, which appears to pertain to individuals' abilities to readily and quickly manipulate linguistic elements, constrained by syntactical and other requirements, to produce a variety of satisfactory responses. For example, tests of the ability to combine syntactic elements into a variety of acceptable sentences (Mellon, 1969) might be found to be good measures of factor FE. It is at least conceivable that this ability could be shown to be an important element in writing good prose.

WORD FLUENCY (FW) FACTORS

The so-called Word Fluency (FW) factor was first identified by Thurstone (1938b); it was the only factor in the idea production domain that was disclosed by Thurstone's classic study (other than, possibly, Naming Facility, that Thurstone did not recognize). This being the case, Thurstone took the Word Fluency factor to be an important primary ability and an indicator of general language fluency. It was frequently cited, in textbooks and similar summary presentations, as being one of the "seven primary abilities of intelligence." Tests of Word Fluency were included at least in early editions of the *Primary Mental Abilities* battery published by Thurstone and Thurstone (1938–1965), and the manual for the battery suggested that word fluency might be an important ability in writers and others concerned with language production. From our present perspective, such a suggestion was probably overly optimistic.

In reanalysis of dataset THUR21A, tests of factor 9 (interpreted as Word Fluency) were the following, listed in order of their salient loadings on the factor:

> Anagrams (.51): "Make as many different words as you can, using only the letters in the word *G-E-N-E-R-A-T-I-O-N-S*." (10 minutes; score is number of words accepted).
> First and Last Letter (.50): "Devised as a test of the facility with which words come to mind. The subject is given the first and last letter and asked to write as many words as possible that have the given initial and terminal letters" (3

minutes for each of two parts, with different first and last letters; score is number of words accepted).

Inventive Synonyms (.41): For each item, subjects are asked to write two synonyms of a given word, each to begin with the letters that are given, e.g. tiny .... s ____ l ____ [*small, little*] (6 minutes for 29 items; score is number right).

Disarranged Words (.40): In each item, rearrange given letters to spell the name of something indicated, e.g., an animal: ebar; a boy: lpau, etc. (8 minutes; 72 items, 12 for each of 6 class names).

Grammar (.35): An objective test of English grammatical correctness in which the subject is asked to correct each wrong sentence by changing a single word (15 minutes; 50 items; score is number correct).

Inventive Opposites (.31): Similar to Inventive Synonyms, except that antonyms are to be given (6 minutes for 30 items; score is the number of correct responses).

For the most part, these tests involve calling words to mind when cued by alphabetic and sometimes other stimuli. Only the test Grammar does not involve alphabetic cuing, but it is not surprising that knowing rules of grammatical correctness as taught in English classes is likely to be associated with being able to use alphabetic cues in recalling words.

Another pioneering study that disclosed a Word Fluency factor was that of Thurstone and Thurstone (1941; dataset THUR81). Reanalysis of that dataset yielded the following tests loaded highly and saliently on factor 4 (I list only the first seven variables, in order of loadings):

First Letters (.61): "Write as many words as you can that begin with *S*" (4 minutes).

Prefixes (.57): "Write as many words as you can that begin with *con*——" (4 minutes).

First and Last Letters (.54): "Write as many words as you can which begin with *T* and end with *E*. The length of the words does not matter" (5 minutes).

Suffixes (.53): "Write as many words as you can which end with *-tion*" (4 minutes)

Synonyms (.51): "In each row write three words which mean almost the same as the given word...." (18 words; 4 minutes; initial letters are not given).

Rhyming Words (.49): "In each row write four words which rhyme with the given word...." (20 words; 5 minutes).

Four-Letter Words (.48): "Write as many words as you can which have four letters and begin with *C*" (4 minutes).

Based on this work and that of a number of other investigators, the 1963 ETS factor-reference kit offered the following three tests as markers of factor FW:

Fa-1 Word Endings Test (similar to Thurstone's Suffixes)
Fa-2 Word Beginnings Test (similar to Thurstone's Prefixes)
Fa-3 Word Beginnings and Endings Test (similar to Thurstone's First and Last Letters)

These same tests were retained as markers in the 1976 Kit. It can be complained

Table 10.6. *31 Word Fluency (FW) factors in 31 datasets, arranged in order of approximate mean age of sample*[a]

Dataset	Date	C'y code	Age	Sample code	M/F code	Factor no.	Remarks (higher-order factors; others related)
HARR51	'73	U	10	1	1	6*	1:2G
HARR52	'73	U	10	1	2	5*	1:2G;9:NA
UNDH11	'78	O	11	6	3	2	1:2G
THUR81	'41	U	13	6	3	4	1:3G;2:2H;10:NA
THUR82	'41	U	13	6	3	4	1:3G;2:2H
GUIL55	'61	U	14	1	3	3*	1:2G;2,5:FI;6:FF;7:FX
GUIL56	'61	U	14	I	1	5	1:3G;2:2N;3,4:FI;6,10:FF; 8:FO;11:FX
GUIL57	'61	U	14	I	2	7	1:2R;2,10:FF;3:FI;4:FO;5:FX
GUIL58	'61	U	14	8	3	7	1:2G;2:FO;3,4:FI;5:FF;10:FX
BERE01	'60	U	15	8	2	7	1:2R;2:FF;3:FE;4:FI;5:FA
BERE02	'60	U	15	8	1	7	1:2R;2:FE;5,6:FF
DUNH11	'66	U	16	1	3	5	1:2G;7:FO
HOEP21	'68	U	16	8	3	2	1:20;6:20;7:SP;10:FO
WEIN11	'59	U	16	1	3	3	1:2G;5:Writing;6:FI*
TAYL01	'47	U	17	1	3	7	1:2H;4:FI
THUR11	'38	U	17	1	3	2	1:2S
THUR31	'40	U	17	1	3	10	1:2G
BOTZ01	'51	U	19	6	1	7	1:2G
FLEI51	'71	U	19	2	1	6	1:2G
KNOE11	'52	U	19	G	3	4	1:2R;2:FI*;3,5:FA;6,7:FE
SCHA11	'40	U	19	6	1	5	1:3G;2:2H
THUR21A	'38	U	19	6	3	9	1:2F;7:2C
CARR21	'58	U	21	2	1	5	1:2G;7:NA
GUIL12	'56	U	21	3	1	9	1:2S;2:FI;3:FE;4:FA:5,12:FO
GUIL51	'60	U	21	3	1	3	1:2G
GUIL66	'52	U	21	3	1	3	1:2G;4:FO;8,12:SP;9:FX;10:FI
MESS01	'75	U	21	3	1	6	1:2H;7:FI
TAYL11	'67	U	21	3	1	8	1:2C;3:FI;4:FE;5,6:WA;7:FO
WOTH01	'90	U	21	1	3	9	1:3G;3:FI;8:20;16:FF
PEMB01	'52	U	22	6	3	3	1:2G
HAKS01	'74	C	24	1	3	15	1:3G;13:2C;17:FI;20,24:FO;21:21

*Variables loaded on the factor are diverse, covering several other primary factors in the domain. A factor so indicated is essentially at a second order of analysis.
[a]See Appendix A for codes. In a few cases, the classsifications of factors shown here were preliminary and may not agree with the final classifications shown in the tables of Appendix B.

that these tests are more similar than they should be, and fail to represent the somewhat wider range of tests that have been found to load on the factor, tests such as Inventive Synonyms and Rhyming Words. Guilford and Hoepfner's (1966b) list of marker tests is similarly somewhat constricted, probably because of their insistence that the factor represented DSU, the *D*ivergent *P*roduction of

Symbolic Units, words or letter strings being considered as the "symbols" pertinently involved in the factor:

> Word Fluency–Write words containing a specified letter.
> Suffixes–Write words ending with a specified suffix.
> Word Beginnings Test (same as the ETS Kit test of this name)
> Word Beginnings and Endings Test (same as the ETS Kit test of this name).

Guilford regarded factor DSU as "the ability to produce many symbolic units, like words, that conform to simple specifications not involving meanings." But at least some tests of FW involve meanings, e.g., Inventive Synonyms, if the reliable appearance of this test on FW is accepted.

The available evidence on the FW factor does not permit firm conclusions on its scope. Table 10.6 lists 31 token factors, in 31 datasets, that were assigned to the Word Fluency (FA) factor. Mean age of sample ranged from 10 to 24. As can be seen from this table, as well as Table 10.1, the Word Fluency factor is reasonably well differentiated from other factors in the language and idea production domain. Nevertheless, close examination of the variables that have salient loadings on these factors suggests that the factor has possibly been conceived, too narrowly, as dependent only on use of alphabetic cues. Most studies have used only a restricted number of marker tests, sampled from those mentioned above, and all requiring written responses. Little imagination or creativity has been brought to the task of defining what the factor measures. It is not satisfactory to conclude that the factor is simply facility in thinking of native language words that have certain simple orthographic characteristics. The role of vocabulary and spelling ability has not been adequately investigated (occasionally, a vocabulary or spelling test has a moderate loading on the factor), and the factor called Phonetic Coding ability (see Chapter 5) may be relevant. Except in the case of dataset ROGE11, where a factor involving some word fluency tests has been assigned to factor OP (Oral Production), there are no investigations that employ oral responses, thus avoiding variance from writing speed. Finally, to my knowledge, there is little evidence that factor FW has any relevance to any important real-life performances. Nevertheless it might have relevance to the interpretation of certain cognitive processes in recalling words, such as the "tip-of-the-tongue" phenomenon studied by Brown and McNeill (1966).

SENSITIVITY TO PROBLEMS (SP) FACTORS

A factor called Sensitivity to Problems was recognized in the 1963 *Kit of Reference Tests for Cognitive Factors* (French, Ekstrom, & Price, 1963), where it was noted that the factor was "entirely confined to Guilford's laboratory." The tests offered as markers were taken from Guilford's work:

> Sep-1, Apparatus Test: In each of two parts, the subject is asked to think of and

write, in ten minutes, two suggested improvements for each of 10 common appliances, like the telephone. (Interestingly, one of the suggested sample answers for *telephone* is what is now available as "caller ID," a fact that illustrates how easily tests can go out of date!)

Sep-2, Seeing Problems: The subject is asked to list problems that might arise in connection with common objects, such as a *candle* (four parts, each specifying three objects; total time 12 minutes).

Sep-3, Seeing Deficiencies: The subject is asked to point out, in writing, the way in which a described plan or activity is faulty (10 items, 10 minutes for each of two parts).

In 1966, Guilford and Hoepfner (1966b, p. 7) listed four tests as markers for a factor whose designated "common name," they stated, was Conceptual Foresight, but whose designation in their then recently developed Structure-of-Intellect model was CMI, the *C*ognition of Se*M*antic *I*mplications:

Pertinent Questions: Write as many as four questions, the answer to which should help to reach a decision in a conflict situation.

Alternate Methods: List as many as six different ways of accomplishing a certain task.

Seeing Problems: (as above)

Apparatus Test: (as above)

Guilford described this factor as "the ability to anticipate or be sensitive to the needs of or the consequences of a given situation in meaningful terms." It is noteworthy that he classified this factor under his Cognition facet, rather than a production facet (Convergent or Divergent), in view of the fact that at least three of the tests he listed as markers required what might be described as "divergent production," i.e., the *production* (not merely the cognition or recognition) of a variety of solutions for stated problems; also, all his marker tests required free response writing rather than selection of alternatives in multiple-choice questions.

The 1976 edition of the ETS *Kit* (Ekstrom, French, & Harman, 1976) dropped the Sep or Conceptual Foresight factor from its list, on the ground that the factor did not seem to be well confirmed in the research literature, and efforts to develop new marker tests for it had not been successful. Despite this, I feel called upon to present what evidence has been found in support of this factor, which I designate as SP, Sensitivity to Problems.

Table 10.7 presents 13 token factors that were assigned to the SP factor. With a few exceptions, they come from studies conducted in Guilford's laboratory. Variables loaded on these factors nearly always include one or more of the marker tests mentioned above, and the factors appear to be reasonably well defined. Furthermore, the factor is differentiated from at least some other factors in the domain under consideration here – at least FI and FO, in some of the datasets. No dataset appears, however, to have been designed to differentiate the factor from factor FE, a possible "close relative." Factor 4 in dataset GUIL11 is a good example of a Sensitivity to Problems factor, with many examples of variables that can be interpreted as measurements of such a factor. The highest

Table 10.7. *13 Sensitivity to Problems (SP) factors in 10 datasets, arranged in order of approximate mean age of sample*[a]

Dataset	Date	C'y code	Age	Sample code	M/F code	Factor no.	Remarks (higher-order factors; others related)
MERR51	'63	U	11	1	3	4	1:2G;2:FO;5:FI
HOEP21	'68	U	16	8	3	7	1:20;2:FW;6:20;10:FO
NIHI01	'64	U	16	8	3	10	1:3G;2:2H;6:FI;8:2N;9:FI
NIHI02	'64	U	16	8	3	4	1:2C;8:FI
"	"	"	"	"	"	7	Sens. Problems (Alt.)
OSUL01	'65	U	16	6	3	7	1:2G;6:FO
PENF01	'67	E	17	8	3	8	1:3G;7:2R;
"	"	"	"	"	"	9	Sens. Problems (Alt)
SNOW12	'77	U	19	6	3	7	1:2G
GUIL11	'55	U	21	3	1	4*	1:2G;5:FX;7:FO
GUIL66	'52	U	21	3	1	8	1:2G;3:FW4:FO;9:FX;10:FI
"	"	"	"	"	"	12	Sens. Problems (Alt)
MERR41	'60	U	21	3	1	3	1:2G;2,4:FI;6:FO;7:FA

*Variables loaded on the factor are diverse, covering several other primary factors in the domain. A factor so indicated is essentially at a second order of analysis.
[a]See Appendix A for codes. In a few cases, the classsifications of factors shown here were preliminary and may not agree with the final classifications shown in the tables of Appendix B.

salient loading is for a variable called Effects, in which subjects are asked to predict future events from specified present trends. Predicting future events would arguably imply good sensitivity to the problems inherent in present trends. But there is a catch: factor 4 in dataset GUIL11 is asterisked, and could equally well have been assigned to factor FI; and there is no separate FI factor in that dataset, at least in our reanalysis.

Factors 8 and 9 in dataset PENF01 are from a study of "verbal critical thinking" performed in England (Penfold & Abou–Hatab, 1967), using many of Guilford's tests. Each of these factors was loaded with certain variables presumably marking factor SP; in the case of factor 8, Seeing Problems had the highest salient loading (.428) while factor 9 was loaded with the Apparatus test, the Alternate Methods test, and several other variables plausibly interpreted as measuring factor SP. It is possible that the separation of the factors was artifactual; both factors were dominated by a second-order General Retrieval factor, and it is also possible to interpret either one of them as factor FI.

From my present perspective, it is unfortunate that there has not been further research on a possible Sensitivity to Problems factor, with studies designed to confirm or disconfirm a differentiation of it from other fluency factors. At this point I can only suggest the *possible* existence of the factor. One hypothesis about it that deserves investigation is that it focuses on problems in real life, as opposed to the purely verbal or linguistic problems that are typically presented in tests of factor FI. That is, high scorers could be assumed to have more experience in solving practical problems, using objects in novel ways, assessing the feasibility of plans, etc. Several datasets (GUIL66, NIHI02) had two or three factors tentatively assigned to factor SP, exhibiting possible variations in this ability that could be investigated.

ORIGINALITY/CREATIVITY (FO) FACTORS

Much of the factor-analytic work on the study of language production and other types of production behavior has been motivated by a desire to develop methods of measuring or predicting the tendency or predisposition of an individual to be "creative" (Guilford, 1950), and in this light it is hardly surprising that most of our evidence on production factors has emanated from Guilford's laboratory at the University of Southern California. Guilford and his colleagues (Guilford & Hoepfner, 1971) addressed not only the factors of intelligence but also factors that might underlie creativity. This is not the place to discuss the very large literature that has arisen concerning the nature of creativity (see, for example, Koestler, 1964; Perkins, 1981) or its relations with intelligence and other cognitive factors (see, for example, Getzels & Jackson, 1962; McNemar, 1964; Crockenberg, 1972). It is not amiss to mention, however, two important lines of research on creativity, namely, those conducted by E. Paul Torrance (Torrance, 1963, 1966) and by Michael Wallach and Nathan Kogan (Wallach & Kogan, 1965) because the Torrance Tests of Creative Thinking and the Wallach and Kogan Creativity Battery figure in a number of the factor-analytic investigations reviewed here.

Based on recommendations of Guilford and Merrifield (1960), the 1963 edition of the *Kit of Reference Tests for Cognitive Factors* (French et al., 1963) offered three marker tests for a factor designated O, Originality, "the ability to produce remotely associated, clever, or uncommon responses":

> O-1, Plot Titles (clever): The task is to write titles for story plots. The subject is told that the titles can be clever or not. (In each of two parts, one story plot; 3 minutes to write up to 20 titles; the score is the number of "clever" titles written.)
>
> O-2, Symbol Production: The task is to produce (by drawing) figural symbols to represent given activities and objects. (In each of two parts, 31 or 30 items, 5 minutes; score is the number of symbols produced that are acceptable according to a scoring guide.)
>
> O-3, Consequences (remote): The task is to list, in writing, the consequences of certain hypothetical situations, e.g., "What would be the consequences if people no longer needed or wanted sleep?" (In each of two parts, 2 minutes for each of 10 hypothetical situations; the score is number of consequences written that are "indirect" or "remote," according to a scoring guide.)

These are also three of the four tests listed by Guilford and Hoepfner (1966b) as markers for a factor they designated as DMT, the *D*ivergent Production of Se*M*antic *T*ransformations. A Riddles test (giving clever solutions to riddles) was the fourth test in their list.

In the 1976 edition of the *Kit* (Ekstrom et al., 1976), factor O, Originality, was among those dropped because of its dubious status and the investigators' lack of success in creating new markers. However, Ekstrom et al. thought that possibly "parts of these factors ... are represented by the Expressional Fluency and Flexibility of Use factors" (p. 5); presumably they had in mind Flexibility of Use as a "relative" of the Originality factor. As noted previously, in making a preliminary analysis of all factors in the database assigned to the language and idea production domain, I initially formed two groups, one corresponding to the Originality or DMT factor, and another corresponding to the Flexibility of Use factor as set out in the 1976 edition of the *Kit*. But I observed that in virtually no case did a dataset contain both an Originality factor and a (separate) Flexibility of Use factor. Furthermore, many token factors had variables saliently loaded on them that fell into both classifications. (Examples are factor 8 in dataset GUIL56, factor 2 in dataset GUIL58, factor 4 in dataset GUIL66, and factor 10 in dataset HOEP21.) These factor groups were therefore collapsed into one. The only dataset that might be thought to contain both an Originality factor and a separate Flexibility of Use factor was GUIL12, whose data are discussed below.

The Flexibility of Use (XU) factor declared in the 1976 edition of the *Kit* was described as "the mental set necessary to think of different uses for objects" (p. 197), and was stated to be a combination of two factors considered separately in the 1963 edition: (a) semantic redefinition, and (b) semantic spontaneous flexibility. (In our preliminary analysis of factors in this domain, it was not found necessary to consider these two factors as useful classifications.) Four tests were suggested as markers for factor XU:

> Combining Objects: The subject is asked to name two objects which, when used together, would fulfill a particular request, e.g., to rub dirt off the inside of a small bottle, *rag* and *pencil* (In each of two parts, 10 items, 5 minutes).
>
> Substitute Uses: The subject is asked to think of a common object that could serve as a substitute for a specified object or purpose, given the circumstances or location; e.g., for one shipwrecked on an island, a *shirt* could serve to make a small sail (In each of two parts, 10 items, 5 minutes).
>
> Making Groups: Given a list of seven words for objects or things, the subject is asked to specify up to seven ways of grouping or classifying the items, and to provide a reason for each grouping (similar to Guilford's test Multiple Grouping) (In each of two parts, 2 items, 5 minutes).
>
> Different Uses: The subject is asked to think of up to six different uses for an object, e.g., a *magazine* (swat mosquitos, start a fire, etc.). (In each of two parts, four items, 5 minutes; the score is based on the number of "changes" or "shifts" of use, not on the total number of responses. The manual does not indicate how changes or shifts are to be determined.)

Table 10.8 lists 42 factors, in 37 datasets, that were assigned to the Originality/

Table 10.8. *42 Originality/Creativity (FO) factors in 37 datasets, arranged in order of approximate mean age of sample[a]*

Dataset	Date	C'y code	Age	Sample code	M/F code	Factor no.	Remarks (higher-order factors; others related)
RIEB01	'77	W	6	1	3	2	1:2R;2:Wallach–Kogan Tests
"	"	"	"	"	"	3	Torrance Tests
RIEB02	'77	W	8	1	3	2	1:2R; 2:Wallach–Kogan Tests
"	"	"	"	"	"	3	Torrance Tests
VOSS01	'77	G	8	1	3	2	Orthogonal Factors
HARG01	'72	E	10	6	3	3	1:2G;
"	"	"	"	"	"	4	Originality/Creat. (Alt)
WALL01	'65	U	10	6	3	3	2:FI Orthogonal Factors
MERR51	'63	U	11	1	3	2	1:2R;4:SP;5:FI
JONE34	'49	U	13	1	3	7	1:2G
MAY01	'65	U	13	1	3	4	1:2R;2,3:FI;
"	"	"	"	"	"	5	Originality/Creat. (Alt)
GUIL56	'61	U	14	I	1	8	1:3G;3,4:FI;5:FW;6,10:FF;11:FX
GUIL57	'61	U	14	I	2	4	1:2R;2,10:FF;3:FI;5:FX;7:FW
GUIL58	'61	U	14	8	3	2	1:2G;3,4:FI;5:FF;7:FW;10:FX
STOR11	'66	U	14	8	3	7	1:2G;3:FX
STOR12	'66	U	14	I	3	9	1:3G;8:2N
STOR13	'66	U	14	7	3	7	1:2G;5:FX
DUNH11	'66	U	16	1	3	7	1:2G;5:FW
HEND01	'69	U	16	6	3	5	1:2G;3:FI
HOEP21	'68	U	16	8	3	10	1:2O
JACO01	'75	U	16	1	3	3	1:2G;2:FI*
OSUL01	'65	U	16	6	3	6	1:2G;7:SP
FULG31	'72	J	18	6	3	7	1:3G;2,5:2R;3:FI*;4:NA;6:FA
GUIL20	'55	U	18	3	1	5	1:2G;3:FA;6:FI
TAYL13A	'67	U	19	6	1	4	1:2G;3,5:Speech;7:FI;9:FE
INNE01A	'72	E	20	6	1	2	1:2R;3:FI*
INNE02A	'72	E	20	6	2	1	2:FI Orthogonal Factors
SCHU01	'80	U	20	1	3	1	Orthogonal Factors
GUIL11	'55	U	21	3	1	7	1:2G;4:SP;5:FX
GUIL12	'56	U	21	3	1	5	1:2S;2:FI;3:FE;4:FA;9:FW
GUIL66	'52	U	21	3	1	4	1:2G;8:SP;10:FI
HOLT11	'71	U	21	2	1	2	1:2R;3:FI*
MERR41	'60	U	21	3	1	6	1:2G;2,4:FI;3:SP;7:FA
TAYL11	'67	U	21	3	1	7	1:2C;3:FI;4:FE;5,6,6:Writing
LANG01	'76	C	22	6	3	4	1:2G
HAKS01	'74	C	24	1	3	20	1:3G;13:2C;15:FW;
"	"	"	"	"	"	23	Originality/Creat. (Alt)
MARK01	'59	U	30	3	1	4	1:2R;2,3:FI
DEMI01A	'62	U	42	L	3	4	1:2G
DEMI02A	'62	U	42	S	3	2	1:2G
SCHU02	'80	U	64	1	3	2	Orthogonal Factors

*Variables loaded on the factor are diverse, covering several other primary factors in the domain. A factor so indicated is essentially at a second order of analysis.

[a]See Appendix A for codes. In a few cases, the classsifications of factors shown here were preliminary and may not agree with the final classifications shown in the tables of Appendix B.

Creativity group. The mean age of sample ranged from 6 to 64 years, an unusually wide range that probably reflects the great interest that has been shown in studying creativity. On the other hand, the latest study noted was published in 1980 (datasets SCHU01 and SCHU02); there seems to have been a decline, in factor-analytic investigations, in attention to dimensions of creativity.

A number of questions present themselves for discussion in reviewing the information contained in Table 10.8. (a) Do the data support the existence of a single factor of originality/creativity, or are there a number of subfactors in this category? (b) If there is a single factor of originality/creativity, how well is it differentiated from other factors in the domain of language and idea production? (c) How well is it differentiated from factors outside the domain; in particular, does it appear to be at least linearly independent of factors ordinarily thought of as components of intelligence? (d) Can anything be said, from this evidence, about what the factor measures? Does it represent an underlying trait of creativity as it might be exhibited in the creation of works of art, inventions, and the like? (e) What are the best and most consistently construct-valid measures of the factor (in the sense of having consistently high salient loadings on it)?

As may be seen from the table, there are only six instances of datasets having more than one factor in this group (assuming the soundness of our decisions about factor assignments).

Dataset MAY01 has two factors assigned to FO; though clearly distinct, they are dominated by a second-order factor that may be interpreted as General Retrieval ability. Factor 4 has chiefly "unusual uses" tests given under a set for fluency, and scored for fluency. Factor 5 also has "unusual uses" tests, but they are given under a set for "flexibility" and scored in special ways devised by the authors (May & Metcalf, 1965) to measure what they called "adaptive flexibility." The authors interpreted factor 4 as "spontaneous flexibility" and factor 5 as "adaptive flexibility." The result is clearcut but deserves further investigation.

For groups of six- and eight-year-old children, results from datasets RIEB01 and RIEB02 indicate a possible differentiation between the kinds of creativity measured by the Wallach–Kogan (Wallach & Kogan, 1965) tests and the Torrance Tests of Creative Thinking (Torrance, 1966), at least in French language versions of them. There is, however, a second-order factor linking the two first-order factors. Also, note that the variables employed in these datasets are sums of two different scorings of the Wallach–Kogan tests and the Torrance tests, each taken as a whole. Artifactually high correlations can be expected between different scorings (fluency as the total number of responses, and flexibility as the number of category shifts); therefore, the factors are probably specific and their differentiation is probably artifactual. In other datasets, e.g., HARG01, there is no differentiation between Wallach-Kogan and Torrance tests.

There is a suggestion of a true difference between factors 3 and 4 in dataset HARG01. Factor 3 has loadings on a variety of fluency tests, some inspired by Guilford's work, others taken or adapted from tests in the Torrance and

Wallach–Kogan series; only the fluency (total number of responses) scores were considered in the factor analysis because they had high and possibly artifactual correlations with flexibility and originality scores. This factor is thus aligned well with most of the other FO factors listed in Table 10.8. Factor 4 has only one positive salient loading, .37, for a test (Picture Preferences/Polygons) in which subjects got credits for "liking" complex abstract polygons as opposed to simple polygons. There were also nonsalient loadings on this factor, .42 for a test called Images – essentially a paired-associates test in which subjects were told to form associations by making images of the stimulus words in a common situation (e.g., shoes–tree; imagine a tree wearing a pair of shoes on its roots), and .31 for Mednick's (1962) Remote Associates Test (e.g., given the words *rat, blue, cottage,* think of a word related to all three, but in different ways: *cheese*). The authors of this study cited evidence that performance on these tests might indicate some aspect of creativity. The factor is in any case not well defined, and could not be accepted as a measure of originality without much further evidence.

In dataset HAKS01, two originality factors appeared, but both are based on three highly similar forms of a single test type – factor 20 for three tests of Multiple Grouping (where the subject has to suggest different ways of grouping a series of things – animals, foods, etc.), and factor 23 for three tests of Object Synthesis (a Guilford test in which the subject is to suggest how two or more objects could be used together for a new purpose). It is probable that the differentiation observed in dataset HAKS01 is artifactual, i.e., that factors 20 and 23 are specifics that arise because of undue similarities in test format. On the other hand, they are not dominated by the same second-order factors; their differentiation might be confirmed in further research.

There is at least one dataset, and in many cases more than one, differentiating factor FO from each of the other factors in the language and idea production domain, but this fact does not guarantee that the factor is adequately differentiated from all the other factors because it depends on judgments in classifying and interpreting factors in terms of the variables loaded on them. Nevertheless, the bulk of the evidence suggests that factor FO represents a distinct dimension of individual differences that is linearly independent of other such dimensions. It is reassuring that there are a number of datasets that yielded three or four of the fluency/production dimensions, for example GUIL12 in which factor FO is differentiated from factors FI, FA, FE, and FW, and datasets GUIL56, GUIL57, and GUIL58 (using the same set of variables on different samples) in which factor FO is differentiated from factors FI, FW, FF, and FX.

The evidence also indicates quite clearly that factor FO is linearly independent of many of the factors in other domains, or more generally, of what is regarded as intelligence as measured by standard tests. Numerous datasets listed in Table 10.8 contain factors such as V (verbal ability), VZ (visualization ability), and RG (reasoning) that are linearly independent of factor FO. These factors, however, are usually linked to factor FO with a second-order factor, and thus measures of FO commonly have substantial orthogonalized loadings on such a second-order factor. In dataset HARG01, for example, all variables having salient positive loadings on factor FO have loadings on a second-order general factor that range from .56 to .73, reflecting their substantial correlations with measures of verbal and performance IQ. Measures of factor FO in dataset GUIL56 have moderate loadings (ranging from .36 to .48) on a third-order general factor, and also loadings ranging from .17 to .38 on a second-order factor that is interpreted as a combination of Gf (fluid intelligence) and Gc (crystallized intelligence). That is to say, in the populations sampled in these studies, there are significant correlations between measures of originality and measures of various types of general intelligence. It appears to require a considerable degree of general cognitive ability for an individual to be able to make high-scored responses to tests of factor FO. Because of the linear assumptions underlying standard factor analysis, these data provide no evidence for or against the hypothesis that there is a threshold of intelligence above which there is little relationship between intelligence and creativity; see Crockenberg (1972) for a discussion of studies bearing on this hypothesis. (Even at the present writing, there appear to be no studies that have adequately addressed this hypothesis.)

The common element in variables that have high salient loadings on factor FO is that they require examinees fairly quickly to think of, and write down, a series of responses fitting the requirements of the task or situation that is presented; the task, furthermore, is one such that it is difficult and challenging for individuals to think of responses beyond the more obvious, commonsense ones. When an individual can give a large number of responses, therefore, at least a few of these responses are likely to be the more unusual, "creative" responses. Considerable attention has been given to problems of scoring; generally, scoring systems fall into four categories:

1. *fluency*: total number of responses;
2. *flexibility*: number of times the individual changes spontaneously from one category of response to another, the categories having been defined by a test's author or user, on the basis of logical classifications or studies of response protocols;
3. *originality*: assignments of points according to whether the response is "unusual," "clever," or "original," on the basis of scorers' judgments or on the basis of how rare the response is found to be in a series of response protocols; and
4. *elaboration*: assignment of points to the response according how "elaborate" it is, in terms of multiple details given.

Generally it has been found that all the above scoring systems are highly correlated. Hargreaves and Bolton (1972), for example, concluded that the use of anything other than fluency scores adds little useful information. Nevertheless, many investigators have chosen to use scoring systems other than fluency because of their belief, possibly justified, that such systems yield better measures of creativity. For example, the test Alternate Uses is often scored by "flexibility" –

the number of shifts in response categories. Also, the tests Consequences and Plot Titles often receive separate scores for (a) "common" or "low quality" responses, and (b) "unusual, remote, clever" or "high quality" responses. It remains true, however, that these scores tend to be substantially (positively) correlated because of tendencies on the part of individuals to give either a small number of responses or a large number of responses – possibly a reflection of their status on the FI factor.

It will be asked how factor FO differs from factor FI, given that both factors involve tasks requiring series of different responses. The hypothesis that presents itself on review of the evidence is the following: factor FI is a measure of the tendency of individuals to think of a large number of different responses – whether obvious or nonobvious – to *any* task lending itself to the giving of numerous responses, whereas factor FO is a measure of the tendency to give the more *unusual* or creative responses, when the task permits or requires such responses. Tasks measuring FI generally do not permit or require unusual responses, whereas the tasks measuring FO tend to do so. For example, it does not take much creativity to think of a long list of "things that are round" or of "things to eat," because there are in common experience many round things and many kinds of things to eat, whereas it apparently requires some originality to think of ways of using bricks or pencils beyond their few obvious uses.

Probably some of the ambiguity of results in the fluency domain arises because of variations in administration procedures or in instructions given to subjects. There is insufficient evidence conclusively to evaluate Wallach and Kogan's (1965) claim that creativeness is better tested when procedures of administration encourage a "playful, gamelike" mental set, as opposed to the competitive, anxiety-laden atmosphere that often accompanies mental testing. Authors of studies using tests of creativity usually give little or no information on what kind of ambience their procedures seek to generate, and even when they try to give such information, it may have no relation to actual attitudes and mental sets of the subjects who are tested. Authors also tend to give insufficient information as to whether subjects are made aware that they are being tested for originality or creativity, or as to whether subjects are instructed to try to give original or creative responses.

Laying aside the recommendations of Guilford and Hoepfner (1966b) or the ETS kits as to the best markers for factor FO, we can inspect the variables that most frequently have high salient loadings on the factor.

By all odds the most frequently occurring variables of this sort are those that require subjects to think of different uses for common objects. The variables go under names that differ considerably from one dataset to another, and there can be slightly different scoring procedures:

> Alternative/Alternate Uses: DEMI01A, DEMI02A, DUNH11, GUIL56, GUIL57, GUIL58, HOEP21, WALL01

Brick Uses (shifts/flexibility): DEMI01A, DEMI02A, GUIL12, GUIL66, MARK01, SCHU01, SCHU02
Different Uses: MERR51
Ideational Fluency: INNE02A, JACO01
Originality: Cans: STOR11, STOR12, STOR13
Unusual/Unconventional Uses: GUIL66, MARK01, MAY01
Uses for Things (fluency): HARG01
Utility Test (shifts/flexibility/uniqueness): DUNH11, GUIL56, GUIL57, GUIL58, HEND01, HOLT11
Ways to Use It: MERR51

The second most frequently occurring type of variable is one that requires subjects to think of titles for plots or stories, or punch lines for cartoons. Usually the subject is told to try to invent clever titles or punch lines, but not always. Scoring is either for fluency, cleverness, or uniqueness (originality). Examples of such variables are to be found loaded on factor FO in datasets FULG31, GUIL12, GUIL20, JACO01, MERR41, and MERR51, under such names as Plot Titles, Cartoons, Originality, and Names for Stories.

The third most frequent type of variable is a score from the test Consequences, in which the subject has to think of, and write down, a series of possible consequences of a hypothetical event. The score that is most likely to load on factor FO is one based on the number of "remote" or "original" consequences that are listed. Datasets in which this variable occurs with high salient loadings are FULG31, GUIL56, GUIL66, HOLT11, and MERR51.

A fourth type of variable goes under such names as Grouping, Multiple Grouping, Similarities, or What Kind Is It? – exemplified in datasets DUNH11, HAKS01, HARG01, HOLT11, and WALL01. The basic task is to suggest as many ways as possible of classifying a group of common objects, or to suggest as many ways as possible of indicating how two or more objects are alike. Closely related are variables such as Similes or Simile Interpretations requiring the subject to complete similes in as many ways as possible. One may say that the essential element here is flexibility or fluency in thinking of how attributes can define classes.

A fifth type of variable goes under such names as Picture Meanings, Stories, Nonsense Words, Blots, and Line Meanings – in datasets HARG01, HOLT11, SCHU01, and SCHU02. Essentially the variables involve what are often called projective tests; indeed, the test Stories as used in dataset HARG01 is adapted from the Children's [Thematic] Apperception Test (Bellak, 1950). That is, the stimuli and tasks are intentionally ambiguous, prompting the subject to invent an imaginative variety of responses – for example, possible meanings for nonsense words, stories that could explain what pictures or inkblots might represent, or drawings that are suggested by a small collection of lines. The scores can be fluency (number or quantity of responses) or originality (ratings).

Still other types of variables are occasionally found with high salient loadings on factor FO. As a general rule, the best variables are those that confront the subject with a serious problem in thinking of responses – beyond possibly a few obvious ones – that still reasonably meet the requirements of the task.

Factor 1 in dataset INNE01A and factor 2 in dataset INNE02A were listed in Table 10.8 as possible measures of originality. They reflect a tendency to give original responses to the Kent–Rosanoff free association test (Rosanoff, 1927). However, there is no evidence of significant correlation with other measures of factor FO, such as Guilford's Unusual Uses test (called Ideational Fluency in these datasets). Therefore, these free-association measures are not to be considered measures of FO as measured elsewhere, but they are distinct from measures of factor FI, and possibly deserve further investigation.

The assignment of factor 7 of dataset JONE34 was made with some hesitation. The two highest salient loadings are for the Ingenuity test at level 14 in the Stanford–Binet scale and the test Problems of Fact at level 13. The Ingenuity test calls for solutions to "water jar" problems; Problems of Fact calls for explanations of unusual events – even the scoring manual remarks that many responses can be ingenious and far-fetched (Terman & Merrill, 1960, p. 202).

Whether FO tasks truly measure creativity in some general sense is a question that cannot be answered with the data at hand. All one can say is that factor FO appears to be represent a distinct dimension of individual differences that can be measured with considerable reliability, particularly if a variety of measures are used. It is distinct, at least, from other dimensions in the domain of language and idea production; in particular, it is distinct from factor FI – interpreted as merely the ability to think of a large number of responses (whether original or not) to certain tasks calling for such responses. In practice, particularly in studies of the validity of creativity tests, it is possible that measures of factor FO should be controlled for variance in factor FI, by some type of partialling technique. They might also be controlled for variance in general intelligence, general information, and verbal ability, inasmuch as producing responses in many creativity tests would appear to require a considerable amount of real world knowledge. For example, producing original responses to the Consequences test requires an appreciation of possibilities and impossibilities presented by conditions in the real world.

In his book *The Mind's Best Work*, from which the quotation heading this chapter is taken, Perkins (1981) takes a skeptical view of the validity of creativity tests. Nevertheless, as the quotation suggests, creativity depends on a variety of resources. Factor FO as discussed here may represent one of those resources.

FIGURAL FLUENCY (FF) FACTORS

Table 10.9 lists 19 token factors, in 13 datasets, that were assigned to a Figural Fluency (FF) group for examination as measures of one or more latent trait factors in a special subdomain of language and idea production. Figural Fluency could belong in such a domain because it has to do with the production of ideas in a visual, figural form. Most of the samples for the factors listed are of adolescents aged 14–16 years; only the samples for datasets GERS01 and HOFF01 are for young adults. In the assignment of token factors to this group, some reliance was placed on evidence surveyed by Ekstrom, French, and Harman (1976) in offering marker tests of a Figural Fluency Factor in the 1976 edition of the *Kit of Factor-Referenced Cognitive Tests*, these marker tests being the following:

> FF-1, Ornamentation Test: The subject is asked to make, by drawing, as many different decorations as possible on common objects, such as a lampshade (In each of two parts, 24 objects, 2 minutes; score is the number of objects decorated, minus duplicates).
>
> FF-2, Elaboration Test: In each item, a partially decorated design is given. The subject is asked to add pictorial material to the existing decoration, by drawing or sketching. Because all the given designs in a section of the test are identical, the subject is told to make as many different decorations as possible (In each of two parts, 20 identical designs, 2 minutes; score is the number of designs decorated, minus duplicates).
>
> FF-3, Symbols Test: The subject is asked to draw up to five different symbols for each of several words or phrases, e.g., a drawing of a crossed fork and spoon to represent the word *food* (In each of two parts, 5 items, 5 minutes; score is the number of different symbols drawn for each item, summed over items).

The factor FF or Figural Fluency was characterized in the *Kit* as "the ability to draw quickly a number of examples, elaborations, or restructurings based on a given visual or descriptive stimulus" (Ekstrom et al., 1976, p. 61). Ekstrom et al. remark that the Figural Fluency factor "is probably a figural form of the ideational fluency factor," and that "the emphasis is on the number of responses produced, not on the quality or unusualness of the drawings produced."

The marker tests in the *Kit* were adapted from some recommended by Guilford and Hoepfner (1966b, p. 9) for measuring various figural production factors postulated in their Structure-of-Intellect model. One of these factors was DFU, the *D*ivergent *P*roduction of *F*igural *U*nits, characterized by Guilford and Hoepfner as "the ability to produce many figures that conform to simple specifications." Other figural production factors claimed by them had to do with production of figural "classes," "systems," "relations," "transformations," and "implications." (Except for a factor for figural transformations, which I designate as FX, I find no clear evidence for the existence of these other figural production factors.) As good measures of factor DFU, whose common name was given as Figural Fluency, Guilford and Hoepfner recommended the following:

> Make a Figure: Given three lines, e.g., two short straight lines and a curved line, make different combinations in limited time (scored for number of combinations produced).
>
> Make a Mark: Make simple figures of a specified kind, e.g., open figures composed of curved lines.
>
> Sketches: Add figural details to several replications of the same basic design to produce a variety of recognizable objects.

Table 10.9. *19 Figure Fluency (FF) factors in 13 datasets, arranged in order of approximate mean age of sample*[a]

Dataset	Date	C'y code	Age	Sample code	M/F code	Factor no.	Remarks (higher-order factors; others related)
CRAW01	'76	C	14	1	3	6	1:2G;2:FI*
GERS02	'63	U	14	1	3	4	1:20;2:FX;3:FI*
GUIL55	'61	U	14	1	3	6	1:2G;2,5:FI;3:FW*;7:FX
GUIL56	'61	U	14	I	1	6	1:3G;2:2R;3,4:FI;5:FW;8:FO; 11:FX;
"	"	"	"	"	"	10	Figural Fluency (Alt.)
GUIL57	'61	U	14	I	2	2	1:2R;3:FI;4:FO;5:FX;7:FW;
"	"	"	"	"	"	10	Figural Fluency (Alt.)
GUIL58	'61	U	14	8	3	5	1:2G;2:FO;3,4:FI;7:FW;10:FX
HOEP11	'65	U	14	6	3	7	1:2R;2;4:FX;5:2R;6:FA*;9:FI;
"	"	"	"	"	"	8	Figural Fluency (Alt.)
BERE01	'60	U	15	8	2	2	1:2R;3:FE;4:FI;5:FA;7:FW
"	"	"	"	"	"	6	Figural Fluency (Alt.)
BERE02	'60	U	15	8	1	5	1:2R;2:FE;7:FW;
"	"	"	"	"	"	6	Figural Fluency (Alt.)
BRAD01	'69	U	16	1	3	5	1:2Y?
GERS01	'63	U	19	3	1	8	1:20
HOFF01	'68	U	21	B	3	6	1:2V;
"	"	"	"	"	"	9*	Figural Fluency (Alt.)
WOTH01	'90	U	21	1	3	16	15:2R

*Variables loaded on the factor are diverse, covering several other primary factors in the domain. A factor so indicated is essentially at a second order of analysis.
[a]See Appendix A for codes. In a few cases, the classsifications of factors shown here were preliminary and may not agree with the final classifications shown in the tables of Appendix B.

> Dot Systems: Draw two copies of a given alphabetic letter in different, relative positions within a matrix of equally spaced dots.

Reanalyses of factorial datasets in the literature, including many generated by Guilford and his students, yield only fragmentary and puzzling evidence for more than one factor in the divergent figural domain as defined by Guilford, other than the factor FX discussed below.

Examining Table 10.1, one notes that the FF group is differentiated from most of the other eight groups in at least one dataset, and usually more than one. It is well separated from groups FI and FW, and distinct from factors FA, FE, and FO in two datasets. No datasets are found in which it is differentiated from groups NA or SP, but this is probably a result of there having been no studies designed (in terms of the selection of variables) to provide such differentiation. In terms of content and description, FF would seem to be clearly different from NA. Its separation from SP needs to be investigated.

Most of the factors listed in Table 10.9 are clearly measures of a "figural ideational factor," i.e., a factor measuring the ability of a subject to produce, within a very short time, a variety of simple drawings or pictorial materials. This assertion can be supported by information on the measures found to be saliently loaded on these factors (test descriptions are introduced the first time a test is mentioned; in many cáses they are taken from Appendix B of Guilford & Hoepfner, 1971):

CRAW01, factor 6: loaded with four scorings (for fluency, flexibility, elaboration, and originality) of performances on the three figural tests in Torrance's (1966) Tests of Creative Thinking: Picture Construction (draw something clever on an egg-shaped piece of paper), Incomplete Figures (given a variety of abstract lines or designs, use them to sketch unusual pictures or objects), and Parallel Lines (same as Incomplete Figures except that all the given materials are pairs of straight parallel lines). The fluency score had the highest loading (.88), the originality score the lowest (.48). Given that these four variables were all based on the same set of responses, the appearance of this factor is somewhat artifactual. It is, however, distinct from a factor (factor 2) based on scores from verbal production tests in the Torrance series.

GERS02, factor 2: loaded with Make a Figure, Monograms (invent monogram designs for triplets of alphabet letters), Sketches, Making Objects (combine figures in various ways to form named objects), Designs (given five figural elements, e.g., a line, a curve, a dot, an angle, and a circle, combine them in various ways to produce designs such as appear on wallpaper, linoleum, or fabrics), Make a Mark, and Dot Systems – all tests scored for number of responses in simple drawing tasks.

GUIL55, factor 6: loaded with Decorations (adding lines, decorate two identical outline drawings of objects differently), Figure Production (add lines to given lines to produce sketches of a variety of meaningful objects), Production of Figural Effects (add details to a simple figure without drawing real objects), and (note!) a test of Marking Speed. The former three are simple drawing tasks scored for fluency; the presence of Marking Speed (though with the lowest salient loading) suggests that factor FF is partly a measure of motor speed in drawing.

GUIL56, factor 10: loaded with the same simple drawing tasks as those used in GUIL55.

GUIL57, factor 2: loaded with Decorations (.630) and only weakly with Production of Figural Effects (.280).

GUIL58, factor 5: The same simple drawing tasks as in GUIL55.

HOEP11, factor 7: loaded with fluency scores from Make a Figure, Monograms, Sketches, and Designs.

BERE01, factor 2: loaded rather weakly with fluency scores for three tests that Bereiter (1960) designed to measure "figural ideational fluency" – Design Synthesis (draw different designs using three given figures), Form Completion (name objects that could be made by adding lines to given figures), and Product Design (draw designs for car grills and lampshades).

BERE02, factor 5: loaded chiefly with fluency scores for two tests designed by Bereiter for figural ideational fluency – Alphabet Design (design possible new letters for the alphabet), and Product Design.

BRAD01, factor 5: loaded only with fluency scores for Make a Figure and Sketches.

GERS01, factor 8: loaded with Monograms, Sketches, Making Objects, Make a Mark, Designs, and fluency and shifts scores for Make a Figure.

> HOFF01, factor 9: loaded with Monograms, Designs, and Sketches, but in addition Plot Titles (fluency) and Possible Jobs, measures of factor FI that were described in the section dealing with that factor.

This leaves six token factors to consider as possible measures of one or more factors distinct from what has been described as Figural Fluency. Four of them come from work in Guilford's laboratory and are possibly measures of a trait that may be called Figural Creativity, since their measures appear to require more originality than measures commonly loaded on Figural Fluency:

> GUIL56, factor 6: saliently loaded only with Alternate Signs (draw a variety of different signs to express the meaning of each given word), and nonsaliently also with Figure Production and Planning Air Maneuvers. In view of low loadings, this factor could be a statistical artifact, but if not, it may represent a measure of figural creativity distinct from FF.
>
> GUIL57, factor 10: saliently loaded with Alternate Signs and Figure Production, but also with Associational Fluency I and Consequences (remote), lending support to interpreting the factor as Figural Creativity.
>
> HOEP11, factor 8: saliently loaded with Figure Production, Making Objects, Decorations, and Production of Figural Effects.
>
> HOFF01, factor 6: saliently loaded with Figure Production (.42) and very weakly (.17) with Circle Continuations (select a point that would fall on a circle, given only an arc and five alternative points), a test quite outside the realm of figural fluency. The factor could be a statistical artifact, except that it may be noteworthy that Figure Production is also found for the other three token factors considered here.

Factor 6 in dataset BERE02 (for a sample of academically talented girls in grade 10) has salient loadings for two tests (out of four) that Bereiter (1960) hypothesized might measure a factor of "structural ideational fluency – the production of formal systems as opposed to concrete figures or substantive ideas": Partitions (draw different ways to separate objects into pairs by the use of a limited number of straight lines) and Linkages (draw devices for connecting objects A and B so that when A is moved in an indicated direction, B will move in an indicated direction). The other two tests hypothesized to measure this factor had insignificant loadings. In dataset BERE01 (for academically talented boys), the factor hypothesized to measure structural ideational fluency was loaded with different tests: Connections (draw lines connecting specified objects without one line crossing another) and Alphabet Design (cited above). The status of a "structural ideational fluency factor" is thus questionable, and the tests are not found in other datasets. If such a factor exists, it would have to be confirmed in further investigations.

It can be concluded that a factor of Figural Fluency – the ability to produce a variety of simple drawings or sketches in a limited time – is well confirmed. However, its importance as a factor of individual differences is debatable. For one thing, it may be largely a reflection of motor speed and manual control in drawing; nearly all its measures require responses in a limited time, and scores are in part measures of rate of performance. For another, it is hard to believe that subjects tested regard this kind of performance as anything but trivial or even silly. Figural Fluency, as commonly measured, may be nothing more than speed of doodling. I suggest research with tests that are given under no time-limit restrictions and that are scored more for artfulness, meticulous detail, and originality than for fluency.

FIGURAL FLEXIBILITY (FX) FACTORS

The 1963 edition of the *Kit of Reference Tests for Cognitive Factors* (French, Ekstrom, & Price, 1963) recognized a factor called "Figural Adaptive Flexibility, Xa" characterized as "the ability to change set in order to meet new requirements imposed by figural problems" (p.49). It pointed out that the factor had been found only in Guilford's laboratory, and that it appeared to be limited to the "figural content area." Three marker tests were offered:

> Xa-1, Match Problems II: "A test developed in Guilford's project. The task is to indicate up to four different sets of a specified number of lines, representing matches, which may be taken away from a pattern of such lines in order to leave a certain number of squares or triangles" (In each of two parts, there are five problems, each provided with four identical designs on which the examinee is to indicate ways of taking away matches; 7 minutes; score is the number of *different* solutions given).
>
> Xa-2, Match Problems V: "The task is to indicate several different patterns of matches that can be removed to leave a specified number of squares. Many set-breaking solutions are needed" (In each of two parts, three problems, each provided with six to eight identical designs for answers; 5 minutes; scoring as in Match Problems II).
>
> Xa-3, Planning Air Maneuvers: "Following certain rules, the examinee is required to select the most direct path in 'skywriting' pairs of capital letters" (In each part, 36 items, 8 minutes).

In the 1976 edition of the *Kit* (Ekstrom, French, and Harman, 1976), the name for this factor was changed to XF, Figural Flexibility, and the tests offered were somewhat different:

> XF-1, Toothpicks Test: "The subject is asked to present up to five different arrangements of toothpicks according to sets of specified rules." The task is actually very similar to that in Match Problems II, i.e., showing how a specified number of toothpicks can be taken away from the design to leave exactly a specified number of squares, and no more (In each of two parts, five problems, each with five identical designs for indicating answers; 6 minutes; score is the number of *different* solutions, not counting reflections or rotations).
>
> XF-2, Planning Patterns: "The subject is asked to arrange a certain number of specified capital letters in up to 12 different positions or orientations on matrices of dots" (In each part, three problems, each with twelve 5 x 5 dot matrices for indicating answers; 2 minutes; scoring is the number of solutions that are *different* by certain scoring rules).

XF-3, Storage Test: "The subject is asked to show the different ways small boxes can be arranged inside of a large container" (In each of two parts, 1 problem, with 16 identical designs for answers; 3 minutes; scoring is based on the number of solutions that are *different* according to certain scoring rules).

None of this last set of tests appears in any of our datasets; designers of recent factor-analytic investigations have not chosen to use them. In fact there are few investigations using FX variables other those conducted in Guilford's laboratory. The tests are difficult to score properly, and there is probably a lack of interest in the factor.

The tests listed in the 1963 edition of the *Kit* are essentially the same as those suggested by Guilford and Hoepfner (1966b) as good markers of the factor they called Figural Adaptive Flexibility, or DFT, the *D*ivergent Production of *F*igural *T*ransformations, "the ability to process figural information in revised ways." The Match Problems tests had been developed by Guilford and his colleagues to measure an aspect of "flexibility in thinking"; the Planning Air Maneuvers test had been developed in the course of investigations during World War II in the U.S. Air Force.

Largely on the basis of whether factors had high salient loadings on Match Problems tests, the Planning Air Maneuvers test, or both, I assigned 15 token factors, in 13 datasets, to the group here called FX, Figural Flexibility. These factors are listed in Table 10.10. Mean ages of samples ranged from 14 to 21 years.

Inspection of Table 10.1 shows that factor FX is well differentiated from factors FI, FW, FO, and FF. Differentiation from other factors in the language and idea production domain is less well established. Indeed, there are no datasets separating it from NA and FE, but on logical grounds it would appear that it is distinct from them. Because of the possible visual and reasoning components in tests of FX, some concern can be observed about differentiating FX from factors in the visual perception and reasoning domains, and in fact Match Problems variables and Planning Air Maneuvers are occasionally found to load on factors VZ (e.g., factor 5 of dataset STOR12) or RG (see Table 6.1). I can find only two datasets, STOR11 and STOR13, in which FX is differentiated from VZ, though not very conclusively.

Practically all the datasets listed in Table 10.10 have Match Problems tests – one or more – saliently loaded on the factor: this is true of datasets BUND11, GERS01, GERS02, GUIL11, GUIL14, GUIL55, GUIL56, GUIL57, GUIL58, GUIL66, HOEP11, STOR11, and STOR13. Some of these – BUND11, GUIL11, GUIL14, GUIL55, GUIL56, GUIL57, and HOEP11 – have the factor also saliently loaded with Planning Air Maneuvers. Factor 2 of dataset HOEP11 has loadings on three Match Problems tests, along with Dot Systems and Planning Air Maneuvers. Factor 4 of this same dataset has Match Problems II along with Make-a-Code and Multiple Grouping; it is difficult to see any basis for interpreting this factor as distinct from factor 2. There is reason for thinking that factor FX is actually a highly specific factor, absorbing the specific variance

Table 10.10. *15 Figural Flexibility (FX) factors in 13 datasets, arranged in order of approximate mean age of sample[a]*

Dataset	Date	C'y code	Age	Sample code	M/F code	Factor no.	Remarks (higher-order factors; others related)
GERS02	'63	U	14	1	3	2	1:20;3:FI*;4:FF
GUIL55	'61	U	14	1	3	4	1:2R;2,5:FI;3:FW*;6:FF
"	"	"	"	"	"	7	Figural Flexibility (Alt.)
GUIL56	'61	U	14	I	1	11	1:3G;3,4:FI;5:FW;6,10:FF;8:FO
GUIL57	'61	U	14	I	2	5	1:2R;2,10:FF;3:FI;4:FO;7:FW
GUIL58	'61	U	14	8	3	10	1:2G;2:FO;3,4:FI;5:FF;7:FW
HOEP11	'65	U	14.	6	3	2	1,5:2R;6:FA*;7,8:FF;
"	"	"	"	"	"	4*	Figural Flexibility (Alt.)
STOR11	'66	U	14	8	3	3	1:2G;7:FO
STOR13	'66	U	14	7	3	5	1:2G;7:FO
BUND11	'67	U	19	6	1	4	1:2G
GERS01	'63	U	19	3	1	6	1:20;3:FI;5:20;8:FF
GUIL11	'55	U	21	3	1	5	1:2R;4:SP;7:FO
GUIL14	'57	U	21	3	1	2	1:2G;6:2R;7:FI
GUIL66	'52	U	21	3	1	9	1:2G;3:FW;4:FO;8,12:SP;10:FI

*Variables loaded on the factor are diverse, covering several other primary factors in the domain. A factor so indicated is essentially at a second order of analysis.

[a]See Appendix A for codes. In a few cases, the classsifications of factors shown here were preliminary and may not agree with the final classifications shown in the tables of Appendix B.

of the Match Problem tests. But the occasional presence of other tests, such as Planning Air Maneuvers, lends some support to its interpretation as one reflecting an ability to be flexible in adopting and changing hypotheses and mental sets about figural and spatial problems. More evidence about the nature and scope of factor FX is needed; it would probably be illuminating to try using Planning Patterns and the Storage Test (marker tests suggested in the 1976 ETS *Kit*) as possible measures. But experimentation with inducing different mental sets – for fluency or flexibility, for example – would also possibly be productive. Finally, the speed/level dimension of test administration should be explored.

SUMMARY

The domain of idea production can be accounted for with nine first-order linearly independent factors, as follows:

> *FI: Ideational Fluency*: speed in thinking of, and reporting (usually in writing) a series of different verbal responses falling in a specified class.
> *NA: Naming Facility*: speed in evoking and reporting (orally or in writing) an accepted name for a given thing, as cued by the thing itself or a picture of it, or in some other appropriate way.

FA: Associational Fluency: speed in thinking of, and reporting (usually in writing) a series of different verbal responses that are semantically associated with a given stimulus.

FE: Expressional Fluency: speed in thinking of, and reporting (usually in writing) a series of syntactically coherent verbal responses under highly general or more specific cueing conditions.

FW: Word Fluency: speed in thinking of, and reporting (usually in writing) one or more language units (usually words) that have specified phonemic or (more usually) graphemic properties. The factor is also measured by tasks (e.g., anagrams) that indirectly involve this type of language unit evocation in their solution.

SP: Sensitivity to Problems: speed and success in thinking of, and reporting (usually in writing) solutions to "practical" problems, or new ways of using objects.

FO: Originality/Creativity: speed and success in thinking of, and reporting (usually in writing) unusual or original verbal/ideational responses to specified tasks.

FF: Figural Fluency: speed and success in producing (usually by drawing) a variety of figural responses to specified tasks.

FX: Figural Flexibility: speed and success in dealing with figural tasks that require a variety of approaches to a solution.

The above characterizations of the factors are those that seem to be suggested by available research. In most cases, further research is needed to refine these characterizations and to provide clarification of the extent to which the factors can be differentiated from one another, and on what basis they are differentiated. There is need for greater creativity on the part of researchers in devising appropriate and highly reliable measurement procedures. (See Maxwell, 1977, for empirical analysis of a variety of fluency tasks and discussion of parameters of rate of production in tasks studied by factor-analysts and experimental psychologists.)

11   *Abilities in the Domain of Cognitive Speed*

> *If speed deserves any weight in determining the measures of intellect it is by virtue of the principle that, "Other things being equal, the more quickly a person produces the correct response, the greater is his intelligence."*
>
> Edward L. Thorndike et al. (1926, p. 24)

This chapter is concerned with two major issues:

What dimensions of ability exist in the domain of cognitive speed?

and

How are these abilities related to, or indicative of, cognitive abilities in which speed of performance is involved only minimally, or not at all? Asking this question loosely, how is "speed" related to "intelligence"?

Answering these questions from presently available knowledge requires prior discussion of several terminological and methodological issues. Such terms as "speed," "power," and "level" have had varying interpretations and operationalizations that must be carefully observed and distinguished. After reviewing the ways in which these terms have been used and setting forth the definitions that are to be employed in subsequent discussion, I review a number of models that have been proposed for interpreting the rates at which cognitive tasks are performed.

Next, studies of relations among rates of task performance, levels of task mastery, and task difficulty are reviewed. In the course of this review, attention is directed to the relatively few factor-analytic studies that have been specifically addressed to identifying speed-of-performance abilities as distinct from level-of-mastery factors.

Because many or perhaps nearly all of the factors of cognitive ability discussed in previous chapters involve speed or rate-of-work components, an attempt is made to assess the relative contributions of speed and level-of-mastery in these factors, and to classify them as being characteristically either *speed* or *level*.

The traditional Number or Numerical Facility factor is one of the dimensions of individual differences that are essentially dimensions of rate of performance or speed of response. It has not been treated in previous chapters and is discussed here, along with various other speed-of-response factors that have been identified in the database.

Of continuing interest are issues concerning the relationships of speed-of-response abilities to other cognitive abilities – in particular, to those abilities that compose what is ordinarily thought of as intelligence. Because such issues were raised even in the earliest days of psychological investigation, a historical review is necessary to provide proper context for a discussion, occupying the final portion of the chapter, of more recent researches that appear to indicate that relations of speed-of-response abilities to intelligence may be somewhat closer than they were believed to be during the middle decades of this century.

SPEED, LEVEL, POWER, AND RELATED TERMS

It seems best to introduce a discussion of the terms *speed* and *level* in the context of considering what aspects of performance can be observed when persons are given a single cognitive task to perform in unlimited time, that is, when persons are allowed to take as much time as they wish. Logically, and in the most general terms – regardless of the nature of the task – two aspects of performance can be distinguished: (1) whether the task is performed "correctly" (or satisfactorily according to some given criterion), and (2) the time that is spent in performing the task – whether correctly, incorrectly, or to the point where a person gives up attempting to perform it. With respect to (2), it should be possible to measure (a) time spent before the person renders a correct (final) response, (b) time spent before the person renders an incorrect (but final) response, (c) time spent before the person decides not to work on the task or attempt a response, and (d) the time the person spends working on the task before abandoning the attempt to render a response. On the assumption that the person has been instructed regarding at least the general nature of the task and what kind of response is expected, time spent is to be measured from the initial presentation of the task to the actual rendering of a response or to the time when work is abandoned. It is also assumed that persons are motivated to "do the best they can."

In this framework, the correctness of the individual's response is to be taken as an indication of the individual's level of ability with respect to the task, or with respect to the range of tasks, of varying difficulty, defining an ability. (See discussion, Chapter 1.) According to well-known models of task response, such as the Rasch (1960) model, the probability that the response will be correct is a function of the person's level of ability and the difficulty of the task. Persons with high levels of ability are expected to make correct responses to the more difficult tasks (items), while persons with low levels of ability are expected to make correct responses, if at all, only to tasks of low difficulty, difficulty being defined in terms of (complements of) probabilities of correct response aggregated over groups (samples or populations).

The term *level* was proposed by E. L. Thorndike (Thorndike et al., 1926, p. 24; Chapters VI, XI); he also used the terms *altitude* and *height*. For present purposes, I adopt the term *level*, or *level-of-mastery*, to denote a concept that is to be distinguished from the concept of speed of performance. (Level-of-mastery is approximately the same as what Spearman, 1927, Chapter xiv, called "goodness" of response.)

Measurements of time spent in performing a task may be taken as indicants of some kind of cognitive *speed*. Thorndike et al. (1926) recognized speed as a possible component of intelligence logically independent of level or altitude (and also independent of *width*, the range or quantity of tasks at a given level of difficulty that could be performed). Historically, it was recognized by Thorndike et al., as well as by McFarland (1928, 1930), Slater (1938), and others that speed measurements should properly be taken only for *correct* responses if they were to be studied in relation to measurements of level. In current research in cognitive psychology, this rule continues to be generally followed, but for certain purposes it has also been of interest to study speed in rendering incorrect responses, or time spent in working on problems even when the person never finds the solution. More generally, measurements of rate of work in attempting series of tasks, as those found in typical psychometric tests, may help to define dimensions of cognitive speed abilities.

Nevertheless, dimensions of speed-of-performance abilities and relations of these dimensions to dimensions of altitude or level-of-performance abilities are ideally studied only when accuracy (level) and speed measures are taken separately for each item of tests containing multiple items. A few such studies are discussed below, some conducted before the advent of computers (when collection of data was highly labor-intensive), and others utilizing computer-administered tests.

Time taken to perform a task in unlimited time can be a function of at least several variables: the difficulty or complexity of the task in relation to the individual's ability and experience, the individual's attention, motivation, and set for speed versus accuracy, and whether the individual can recognize successful completion of the task. Just how these effects operate will depend on the nature of the task. Generally, the time taken to indicate an answer for a multiple-choice item is often composed mainly of the times the examinee needs to inspect the stem and the alternative choices, and then to consider the comparative correctness-likelihoods of the choices if the correct choice is not immediately recognized. Inspection times may depend on reading speeds if the material is verbal. Times to complete open- or free-response tasks are generally longer than those for completing multiple-choice items. Some types of problem-solving tasks – for example, solving an anagram – have the feature that the examinee has to search for a solution, but when the solution is found, it can easily be recognized as correct. For such "self-revelatory" items, examinees tend to work until a correct solution is found, or until the attempt to find a solution is abandoned. Many types of tasks or problems, however, are such that individuals cannot easily recognize whether a response is correct or otherwise satisfactory; in such cases, they may terminate work on an item after arriving at a response or solution that is incorrect.

From the earliest days of psychological testing, it became customary to construct tests as series of separate tasks or items, often arranged in order of difficulty as determined either judgmentally or on the basis of try-out data. For practical considerations, time-limits for test performance were set, usually such that at least a majority of examinees could attempt most or all of the items. No widely accepted standards were established concerning the setting of time-limits; constructors of tests followed their own guidelines, depending on the kinds of tests and subject samples with which they were working. Scores were typically number correct within a time-limit (sometimes formula-corrected for guessing), and these were often called *time-limit* or *speed* scores. The distinction between level-of-mastery and speed of performance (whether only for correct responses or for all responses, including item omissions) thus became blurred. "Speed" scores were not really measures of speed of performance; they were unknown functions of level-of-mastery and speed-of-performance, depending on the generosity of the time-limits and the difficulty of the items.

Early investigators recognized this problem of "speed versus power," as they called it. They defined *power* in terms of the number of correct scores that an examinee could attain in some time that was considerably greater than the time-limit initially set for a test. In attempting to resolve the "speed–power" problem, May (1921), for example, found a correlation of .97 between the usual time-limit scores for the Army Alpha examination and scores obtained (on the total test) when examinees were allowed to work for an additional time equal to the initial time-limit (i.e., double time). Similarly, for this same test Ruch and Koerth (1923) found correlations of .97 and .94 between the usual scores and scores obtained in double time and unlimited time, respectively. These investigators concluded that for practical purposes time-limit scores were virtually equivalent to power scores and could be substituted for them, at least in the case of tests in which items varied widely in difficulty. What these investigators failed to realize (as pointed out by Odoroff, 1935) was that the correlations between time-limit and power scores were part–whole correlations, automatically and artifactually high if time-limit scores constitute substantial parts of power scores. (The part–whole nature of the problem is seen if it is noted that a power score is equal to the time-limit score plus whatever additional number correct are attained in the additional time.) They also neglected the fact that the degree of speededness is a function of the time-limit. If the time-limit is liberal, the time-limit score can approach the power score; if the time-limit is much shorter, the time-limit score can be largely a measure of speed of work, particularly if the early items of the test are easy for most examinees. In any event, these investigators failed to recognize possible speed components in time-limit or speed scores, with consequent confusion about the respective roles of speed and level in test scores.

Tests in which items were of low or even zero difficulty for a given sample of examinees were called *speed tests* (as opposed to power tests), and it was recognized that time-limit scores (number correct within a time-limit) were, in effect, measures of speed of performance for these tests. The distinction between "speed tests" and "power tests" was, as it were, canonized by Kelley (1927, p. 31), who nevertheless expressed concern that "[o]ur knowledge as to the educational and social situations in which speed is of prime importance and those in which power is especially demanded is quite limited." "Such data as are available," he continued, "incline the writer to the view that power is generally the more important."

These definitions of *speed* and *power* have persisted even to the present day. For example, in the sixth edition of Anastasi's (1988) textbook on psychological testing, it is stated that

an important distinction is that between the measurement of speed and of power. A pure *speed test* is one in which individual differences depend entirely on speed of performance. Such a test is constructed from items of uniformly low difficulty, all of which are well within the ability level of the persons for whom the test is designed. The time limit is made so short that no one can finish all the items. Under these conditions, each person's score reflects only the speed with which he or she worked. A pure *power test*, on the other hand, has a time limit long enough to permit everyone to attempt all items. The difficulty of the items is steeply graded, and the test includes some items too difficult for anyone to solve, so that no one can get a perfect score (pp. 127–128).

It is to be noted that Anastasi's definitions were for "pure" speed and "pure" power tests. In practice, speed scores are often determined as number correct within a time-limit even when not all items are done correctly by all examinees, and power scores are number correct within a fairly generous time-limit even when not all individuals are able to attempt all items. The important point is that the degree to which timed tests are speeded is not usually evident, even when information is available on the time-limit and the number of items. This is true of most tests that have been used in factorial studies, and it is therefore difficult to assess the extent to which cognitive factors are determined by dimensions of speed of performance. In effect, speed is an influential and undesirable confound in many factor-analytic studies.

The terms *time-limit* and *work-limit* have also been employed to refer to speed and power scores, respectively. But even these terms have not had consistent definitions. Paterson & Tinker (1930), for example, found high correlations between work-limit and time-limit scores for a test of reading speed, especially when corrected for attenuation. But as pointed out by Davidson and Carroll (1945, p. 413),

the work-limit score was not the number of items correctly performed in unlimited time but, instead, the time taken to read all the paragraphs in the test. The time-limit score was the number of paragraphs read within a time-limit. What Paterson and Tinker showed, then, was that in the measurement of a *rate* of performance it makes little difference whether the scores are expressed in terms of performance-per-unit-of-time or time-per-unit-of-performance. A convenient paradigm is that of a runner's speed, which can be expressed either in terms of feet per second or in terms of seconds per foot. It is a mistake, however, to generalize the results of the Paterson and Tinker study by inferring that "work-limit" and "time-limit" scores in the usual sense will be highly correlated in situations where elements of test performance other than rate are measured.

Baxter (1941) defined *speed* scores in terms of the time taken by a subject to work from the beginning to the end of a test, attempting every item once, and *level* scores in terms of the number of items correctly answered when each subject is allowed all the time he desires to try every item and to check over his work. Baxter showed a marked independence of speed and level scores, defined in this way, in a single omnibus test of intelligence (the Otis Self-Administering Intelligence Examination); the correlation between speed and level was $-.06$. He also recommended that the more usual time-limit scores be regarded as measures of power, on the analogy of the interpretation of *power* in physical measurements such as horsepower. However, such a recommendation seems not to have been widely accepted in subsequent writings on speed and power, even though it was adopted in a study by Davidson and Carroll (1945). Also, the definition of speed adopted by Baxter, as well as by Davidson and Carroll, has been criticized (Lohman, 1979a, p. 156; see also Rindler, 1979) for its failure to be restricted to speed of correct responses, and for its neglect of a "perseverance" element in speed scores. This criticism does not, however, diminish Baxter's and Davidson and Carroll's demonstrations that time-limit scores are composites of speed and level; it only reflects the difficulty of determining true speed scores from group test administration.

Miller and Weiss (1976) recommend that the terms *speed* and *power* be restricted to characterizations of *tests*, while the terms *rate* and *accuracy of response* be restricted to characterizations of *individuals*. This recommendation is attractive, but to my knowledge it has not been widely accepted. One can only recommend that readers be properly attentive to what is meant when terms such as *speed*, *rate*, *level*, and *power* are used.

In order to avoid the inclusion of speed-of-performance variance in time-limit scores intended to measure level-of-mastery, some investigators (e.g., Kyllonen, 1985) have adopted the strategy of obtaining proportion-correct scores, i.e., the ratio of the number of correct responses to the number of items attempted (the number of items to which any response is made within a time-limit). A minor disadvantage of this procedure is that the reliability of a proportion-correct score can decrease dramatically with a decrease in the number of items attempted. If only one item is attempted, for example, the only proportion-correct scores possible are 0 and 1. In most cases, however, the number of items attempted is large enough to make proportion-correct scores have satisfactory reliability. The procedure is therefore to be favorably considered for future research, but a further caution to be observed is that proportion-correct scores may be biased upward for individuals who attempt only the easier items – often the earlier items in a test in which items are arranged in approximate order of difficulty.

A possibly better strategy for obtaining level-of-mastery scores that are un-affected by variance due to speed is to construct a test as a series of blocks, each containing a series of items arranged in order of difficulty from easy to hard. Given an appropriate amount of time to do so, examinees are instructed to attempt all items within each block, omitting or guessing at those that they cannot answer or solve. Scores are based on the proportion of correct answers in all blocks completed. An advantage of this procedure is that examinees can be given a uniform time-limit, and there is enough test material to keep all examinees – even the speedier – working throughout the time limit. Moreover, with this procedure it is possible to determine a rate-of-work score from the number of items or blocks attempted. A disadvantage is that scores are less reliable for slow test-takers.

There is a logical problem in defining a speed or rate-of-performance as an ability if the notion of *ability* presented in Chapter 1 is accepted. That is, if ability refers to possible variations over individuals in the liminal levels of task difficulty at which individuals perform successfully on a defined class of tasks, what are the "liminal levels of task difficulty" in the case of cognitive speed abilities? We can apply this notion of ability to cognitive speed by assuming that each (infinitely possible) speed at which a task can be performed constitutes a possible liminal level at which a task (reformulated as "performing the task at a given speed or within a given amount of time") can be performed with, say, 50% probability. Because performing a task in a short time is generally more difficult or unlikely than performing it in a longer time, the baseline for a person characteristic curve for a cognitive speed ability would be scaled in terms of amounts of time ranging from infinite time to zero time. Mathematically, a convenient scale might be a/x or perhaps $\ln(a/x)$, where x is the time of successful performance (in whatever unit is convenient) and a is a suitable constant. The person characteristic curves for three individuals, with low, average, and high (fast) speed abilities might appear as in Figure 11.1. It should be noted, however, that these curves are only conceptual; actually determining data to plot such curves would require repeated trials for a given task with varying time-limits (or "stopping times") per response, and of course this would possibly involve practice or fatigue effects. It would be as if one attempted to determine whether a given individual could perform a task in $x, x + 1, x + 2, \ldots, x + n$ seconds (for example, asking whether a runner could run 100 meters in 9.5, 10, 10.5, 11, ... seconds). The individual's limen would be the value of x where the probability of success would be equal to .5. Even though such a determination would generally be impractical, the point is that it is possible to conceive speed ability in terms of ability limens.

MODELS OF TIMED OR SPEEDED TASK PERFORMANCE

Specialists in mental measurement have long been concerned with the definition of ability independent of any considerations of the time taken to perform a

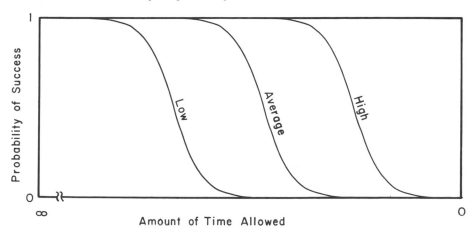

Figure 11.1. Hypothetical person characteristic curves for individuals with low-, medium-, and high-speed ability. Probability of success is plotted against amount of time allowed, scaled from infinite time to zero time.

cognitive task. In a classic article, "Ability, motivation, and speed," Thurstone (1937, p. 251) proposed a definition of "the ability of the individual subject with special reference to power or altitude which is independent of the speed of any performance." This was, "*The ability of an individual subject to perform a specified kind of task is the difficulty* E *at which the probability is 1/2 that he will do the task in infinite time.*" This definition was made with reference to a graph, reproduced here as Figure 11.2, showing the three-dimensional ability surface for a *single examinee,* that is, a surface showing the probability that the examinee would perform the task correctly as a function of the difficulty D of the task and the amount of time T allowed to perform the task. The plane AB shows the "psychometric curve" ACB when the value of T is infinite (or at least very large and generous). E is a value of difficulty D at which the probability of success is $C = .5$. At lesser values of T, the psychometric curves for this hypothetical examinee comprise a surface such that the individual would perform only progressively easier tasks with probability .5 as the time allowed decreases.

Thurstone also considered motivation to be an important variable. The graph in Figure 11.2 was drawn on the assumption that motivation to perform any of the tasks was at some constant value greater than zero. An increment of motivation, however, would move the surface parallel to the axis T "so as to augment the ordinates P for finite values of T" (p. 252). That is, higher motivation would enable the examinee to perform tasks at faster speeds (or in less time). Thurstone thus conceived of motivation as a "rate concept" (p. 253) that could be independent of ability. Thurstone does not tell us what kinds of tasks he had in mind – only that they could be "problem solving and ... discrimination of many kinds," but

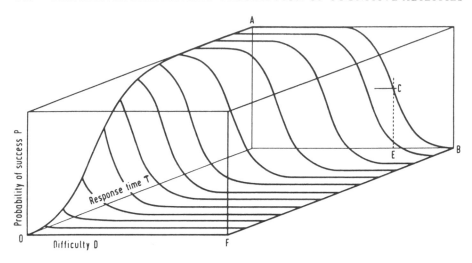

Figure 11.2. Hypothetical ability surface for a single individual, showing probability of success as a function of task difficulty D and response time T (from Thurstone, 1937, p. 250). Reproduced by permission of the Psychometric Society.

not a "task which is by definition a rate of work." It appears that it would be difficult to apply the model to multiple-choice tasks.

To my knowledge, the experimental procedures that Thurstone suggested could be carried out to determine rates of work and motivation have never been given a proper tryout. It is interesting that his psychometric curve ACB, where probability of success is plotted against task difficulty for unlimited time, is essentially the same as the person characteristic function that has been discussed at various points in this volume.

Probably the most complete description and discussion of models and procedures for measuring mental speed is provided by Berger (1982). He mentions various problems of Thurstone's model and criticisms of it, continuing with a historical review of investigations of mental speed. He describes an approach that was developed by Furneaux (1948, 1960) as conceptually important but difficult to realize in practice. An appraisal of Furneaux's contributions was made by White (1973, 1982), who also developed his own very elaborate "probabilistic latent trait model" designed to estimate speed, accuracy, and persistence scores from data on cognitive test performance. Further, White described a model that would in addition provide estimates of "propensity to guess," presumably similar to the pseudo-guessing parameter in Birnbaum's (1968) three-parameter item response model.

Taking off from White's (1973) and Birnbaum's (1968) formulations, Thissen (1980) developed a latent trait model for estimating speed and level (accuracy) parameters from item response and latency data for individual items of a test (as might be obtained from computerized test administration). In contrast to White's (1973) model, the latencies were assumed, "like the item responses themselves, to be fallible data reflecting underlying trait values" (p. 257). This model, requiring extensive computations, was applied to selected items from three tests: a verbal analogies test, the Progressive Matrices Test, and a test of spatial ability called Clocks (Guilford & Zimmerman, 1947–56). The tests were administered to 78 undergraduates by slide projector in such a way that item responses were individually timed. On the basis of a correlation matrix presented by Thissen for the individual scores for six parameters estimated for the tests (an ability parameter *theta* and a speed parameter *s* for each), Carroll (1980d) presented a Varimax-rotated principal factor-analysis matrix showing loadings on two factors (Table 11.1). As Carroll remarked,

Obviously, the two uncorrelated factors, together accounting for about 77% of the variance, may be interpreted as ability and speed, respectively. What is of particular note is that the factors generalize over different tasks. The best "pure" measure of ability is the parameter θ for the Analogies test, while the purest measure of speed is the *s* (slowness) parameter for the Clocks test. Nevertheless, the factors show up in interesting ways on other tasks (Carroll, 1980d, p. 280).

For example, it is interesting that the Progressive Matrices items are complex measures of both ability and speed. Carroll further suggested that if Thissen's model were applied to a much wider range of cognitive tests, the structure might be "much more multidimensional than Thissen's preliminary results show" (p. 282).

Miyajima (1972) presented a model and evidence that working time may be determined by two speed factors, one dependent completely on power (level) and the other independent of power.

Several investigators in the Netherlands (van der Ven, 1971, 1976; Pieters & van der Ven, 1982; Roskam, van Breukelen, & Jansen, 1989) have presented models for estimating parameters of concentration, speed, and accuracy in time-limit tasks. Speed is conceived of as having two components: processing time and distraction time. Other such models have been proposed by Birke (1981), Fairbank (1988), and Traub (1983).

In studying relations between IQ and choice reaction time, Matthews and Dorn (1989) postulate that there may be two mechanisms underlying these relations, one interpreted as "lower level encoding speed" and the other regarded as reflecting "upper level processing."

The concept of "personal tempo" studied by Rimoldi (1951b) and Mangan (1959; dataset MANG01) is possibly a further dimension of speed in timed performance of cognitive tasks. The notion is that individuals differ in their preferred rate of performing tasks, or indeed, in simple activities like walking and talking, and that this rate-preference affects performance in cognitive tests. The various evidence reviewed here fully supports the notion that there are reliable individual

Table 11.1. *Varimax-rotated principal factor analysis of Thissen's (1980, Table 2) correlations among estimated person parameters for three tests (from Carroll, 1980d, Table 1)[a]*

	Factor loadings	
Test	Factor I (ability level)	Factor II (speed)
Analogies		
θ (Ability)	.97	.01
s (Speed)	.62	.52
Matrices		
θ (Ability)	.59	.71
s (Speed)	.41	.91
Clocks		
θ (Ability)	.45	.09
s (Speed)	−.09	.67

[a]Reprinted by permission of David J. Weiss.

differences in rate of performing cognitive tests, but there is no clear evidence that these speeds are dependent on or even correlated with "personal tempos" established in such activities as walking, talking, or setting a metronome to beat at a preferred rate. (See also Harrison, 1941; Marr & Sternberg, 1987.)

As a general remark, it is fair to say that models are now available to study effects of one or more dimensions of mental speed in the performance of mental tests, but as yet these models have not been applied to a sufficient variety of mental test performances to permit making generalizations about how speed factors operate in different domains of cognitive ability.

THE DISTINCTNESS OF SPEED AND LEVEL: HISTORICAL OVERVIEW

We have seen how, largely through misunderstandings of methodology, cognitive speed and level were in the early days of psychological testing perceived as being two sides of the same coin. Spearman (1927, Chapter 14) did not recognize speed as a separate component of intelligence. Realization developed slowly that mental speed, properly measured, is or can be distinct from mental level. Bernstein (1924) claimed to find no clear evidence for a hypothetical speed ability, but his negative results are criticized by Vernon (1961, p. 83) as probably being attributable to the fact that his "leisure" tests (intended to be performed in a generous amount of time) were still done within a time limit. Hunsicker (1925) was one of the first to find that rate of performing easy sentence completion and arithmetic items had relatively low correlations with measurements of level. Peak and Boring (1926) reported high correlations between speed and intelligence level, but the number of subjects was only five! Thorndike et al. (1926), Lemmon (1927), and Longstaff and Porter (1928) compiled considerable evidence that speed in performing intelligence tests had low correlations with level. Yet McFarland (1928) concluded that speed and level (or power, as he termed it) are fairly closely correlated in mental performances. This idea was given indirect support by the apparent finding of Travis and Hunter (1928) that speed of the patellar reflex correlated .87 with scores on the Otis intelligence test. Later, however, it appeared that this correlation resulted from a computational error; in a large sample ranging in age from 4 to 35, Travis and Young (1930) found no correlation between intelligence scores and several measures of reflex times.

Probably the first investigator to find a general speed factor in a series of mental measurements was DuBois (1932), who gave 139 university students a "speed battery" consisting of a series of easy tests scored for time of performance. The time scores had intercorrelations ranging from .324 to .687 and had low correlations with number-correct scores on arithmetic reasoning, vocabulary, and paper form board tests. Reanalysis of DuBois's correlation matrix (dataset DUBO01) shows two orthogonal factors, one for the speed tests and the other for the level variables. At about the same time, Line and Kaplan (1932) reported insignificant correlations between speed scores and intelligence tests given to third-grade children. Similar findings were reported by Tryon (1933), Tryon and Jones (1933), and Lanier (1934). Sutherland (1934) concluded that for problems of low difficulty, a speed ability is apparent, but for more complicated problems, response rates show "almost complete dependence on the 'level' factor" (p. 289).

Raskin's (1937) Study

To my knowledge, the first careful study of the dependence of speed-level relations on task difficulty was conducted by Raskin (1937) in an unpublished doctoral dissertation that is rarely cited in the literature. Individually to each of 90 psychology students, Raskin administered ten items from each of levels F through Q of the sentence completion subtest of Thorndike's CAVD test, timing the performances and noting the correctness of the responses. After certain transformations, mean times for correct responses were intercorrelated, yielding a matrix that would now be called a quasisimplex. That is, average correlations between speeds ranged from .65 for speeds one level apart down to .35 for speeds eleven levels apart. This result might be interpreted as showing that a general rate-of-work factor was weakly present, but that the rate of work maintained by an individual could vary depending on the difficulty of the task. For some individuals, rate would decrease with item difficulty; for others, it would increase. Raskin also correlated rates of work with accuracy (altitude) scores on levels grouped by relative difficulty. For the "easy" levels F through K, correlations of speed scores ranged from $-.07$ to $.23$, in no distinct pattern. For levels L through N, of "medium" difficulty, the correlations ranged from $-.03$ to $.20$, again with no obvious pattern. For the hardest levels O through Q, the correlations ranged from $.11$ to $.39$, with some tendency for the higher correlations to be for levels of medium difficulty. One might interpret this finding as showing that there is a small but significant correlation between speed and accuracy for tasks of medium difficulty, but that this correlation is overridden by countervailing tendencies for tasks of low and high difficulty.

Significant studies of the speed-level problem appearing shortly after Raskin's are those of Saum (1938), Slater (1938), Baxter (1941, 1942), Thomson (1941), and Davidson and Carroll (1945). Saum noted that time taken to finish an intelligence test did not correlate significantly with certain measures of school achievement, and that correlations of number correct in unlimited time tended to have higher validity against school achievement than time-limit scores. Slater found that times for correctly completing levels of Thorndike's CAVD showed "no close association" with various verbal and nonverbal intelligence tests. Already mentioned is Baxter's work showing that time-to-finish had vanishing correlations with number correct scores on a group intelligence test.

Thomson (1941) studied performance times and number correct scores in a series of standardized performance tests given to children averaging 10.5 years of age; his correlation matrices (for boys and girls, respectively) were included in our datasets for reanalysis (datasets THOM11 and THOM12), each showing two distinct first-order factors (level and speed, respectively), and a second-order factor on which both level and speed scores were loaded. This result implies, at least for these tests and samples, moderate relations between speed and level, accounted for by the operation of a second-order factor.

Davidson and Carroll's (1945) Study

Probably the first fairly extensive battery of tests scored both for speed and level whose factor analysis was published in the literature is that employed by Davidson and Carroll (1945, dataset DAVI01). The sample consisted of 91 students who were given a battery consisting of subtests of the Army Alpha examination, plus several other tests. Speed, level, and time-limit scores were obtained by first having students work on each subtest within a given time-limit, then having them complete the tests in unlimited time; time-to-finish was recorded, and students recorded responses for the time-limit and extended portions of the test with differently colored pencils. Time scores were converted to their reciprocals (performance per unit of time) in order to make score distributions approximately normal. Initial factor analysis was conducted only on speed and level scores. Time-limit scores were added to the analysis by the procedure known as Dwyer's (1937) extension; that is, the time-limit scores were projected into the space defined by the speed and level scores. (This procedure is necessary to minimize or eliminate the effects of the experimental dependency of time-limit scores on speed and level scores.) In the reanalysis, factor 1 was a second-order factor on which all four first-order factors were loaded substantially. The four first-order factors were interpreted as follows (factor numbers are those given in the hierarchical orthogonalized factor matrix): factor 2, speed of performing mainly verbal items such as same–opposites and verbal analogies; factor 3, level of reasoning ability; factor 4, speed of performing reasoning tasks; and factor 5, number facility. Speed and level variables in general had clear salient loadings on respective speed and level factors; time-limit scores had projections on both speed and level factors. It was noteworthy that in the domain of reasoning, both speed and level factors were obtained. Unfortunately the battery was not extensive enough to permit the isolation of separate speed and level factors in the verbal domain; level scores for verbal tests had low but salient loadings on the Level of Reasoning factor. At the same time, first-order speed and level factors were strongly enough correlated to support the identification of a second-order factor.

As noted above, Lohman (1979a, p. 163) has criticized the Davidson and Carroll study for using rate-of-work measurements that were not controlled for correctness of response. However, rates of work for correct and incorrect responses tend to be substantially correlated. For example, data reported by Tate (1948, Table 2) permit computation of correlations between speed of performance for correct and for incorrect items in the case of a free-response Arithmetic Reasoning test. At a level of medium difficulty, the correlation is .528, and for items of higher difficulty, the correlation is .586. (Correlation of speeds for correct items at the two levels is .779, $N = 36$.) Thus it appears that speeds for correct and incorrect items are substantially positively correlated, at least for this test. This result tends to justify using rate-of-work measurements without controlling for correctness, but caution must be observed inasmuch as the correlations might be quite different for other types of tests.

Tate's (1947, 1948) Study

Tate's study (1947, 1948) is deserving of examination in its own right. In design and procedure, it is highly similar to Raskin's (1937) study, of which Tate was apparently unaware. The sample consisted of 36 high school sophomores and juniors in college preparatory mathematics classes. Students were individually tested with selected items, ranging widely in difficulty, from arithmetic reasoning, number series completion, sentence completion, and spatial relations tests. All items were free response rather than multiple-choice, and performance on each item was timed in seconds. Times were converted to logarithmic units. Altitude scores were also developed for each test. Thus, correlations between speed and level scores can be computed from Tate's results; these correlations, based on raw data presented in Tate's (1948) Table 9, are shown in Table 11.2.

Table 11.2. *Correlations among altitude and speed scores for four psychological tests (computed from data reported by Tate, 1948, Table 9) N = 36*

Score, test		1	2	3	4	5	6	7	8
Alt.: Arith Reasoning	1	1.00	.66	.63	.33	-.07	.03	.13	-.25
" : Number Series	2	.66	1.00	.71	.32	-.01	.05	.13	-.28
" : Sentence Completion	3	.63	.71	1.00	.26	-.08	-.06	-.01	-.20
" : Spatial Relations	4	.33	.32	.26	1.00	-.24	-.04	-.09	-.04
Speed: Arith Reasoning	5	-.07	-.01	-.08	-.24	1.00	.66	.31	.24
" : Number Series	6	.03	.05	-.06	-.04	.66	1.00	.22	.31
" : Sent. Completion	7	.13	.13	-.01	-.09	.31	.22	1.00	.07
" : Spatial Relations	8	-.25	-.28	-.20	-.04	.24	.31	.07	1.00

For each of the four tests, correlations between speed and altitude scores are negligible. At the same time, correlations among the altitude scores are in most cases substantial, probably reflecting the influence of a general intelligence level factor in reasoning, verbal, and spatial tests. Also, some of the correlations among speed scores are substantial, possibly indicating the influence of a speed factor affecting at least the reasoning and verbal tests – similar to the speed-of-reasoning factor identified in the Davidson and Carroll (1945) study. It should be noted, incidentally, that Tate adjusted the speed scores for correctness by a regression technique.

Results of studies such as Raskin's, Davidson and Carroll's, and Tate's tend to contradict Lohman's (1979a, pp. 186–187) opinions that "[s]peed factors for level constructs such as reasoning are impossible, since individual differences in speed can be measured only over error free items," that "studies in which total time and number correct were obtained for each test, and then used to define level and speed factors are flawed," and that "no evidence for a general speed factor was found." Speed factors for level constructs such as reasoning *can* be obtained, even if their reliability and possible validity are lowered by involvement of incorrect responses, guesses, and omissions. At least, there is no logical reason why latent traits of speed of performance cannot be obtained for concepts established by use of level or altitude scores. The separate existence of speed factors for verbal ability, reasoning ability, spatial ability, and so forth is thus conceivable. The existence of a higher-order speed factor is also conceivable. The fact that such factors have not been well established is very likely due to inadequacies in the design of the available research studies, most of which have paid no attention whatsoever to the speed–level problem.

I conclude this historical review, however, with discussion of several further factorial studies that *have* been concerned with speed–level relations; all of them tend to confirm the linear independence of speed and level factors.

Myers's (1952) Study

Myers (1952) studied the factorial composition and validity of differently speeded portions of a single nonverbal reasoning test (figure classification) given to cadets at the U.S. Naval Academy. Sections of the test were arranged into three different forms such that there could be either 10, 20, or 30 items given in a standard time-limit of twelve minutes. Rotation of sections over forms made it possible to observe whether practice on the test items would change the effect of speededness. For each form, factor analysis disclosed two orthogonal factors, one interpreted as "ability to answer the problems correctly," the other as "the tendency to answer the problems quickly." The effect of practice was found to be negligible. Because the correlation matrices included course grades, it was possible to observe validities of scores against these grades. The conclusion was that "the most valid figure-classification test for predicting grades ... is a moderately speeded test which can be finished by about 70% of the candidates" (p. 352). This would imply that both level and speed contribute to the prediction of grades, but the study did not disclose the optimal weighting of these two factors.

Porebski's (1954, 1960) and Howie's (1956) Studies

Wishing to question the widely accepted view (following Spearman, 1927) that "speed" and "power" are synonymous, Porebski (1954, 1960) conducted three pilot factor-analytic investigations using nine tests, six of which were highly speeded and three of which were power tests given to the subjects to take home and complete at their leisure. In each case, orthogonal independent speed and power factors were obtained, though the speeded tests tended to have loadings on both speed and power. I did not consider these datasets worthy of reanalysis because of the small number of variables and the questionable manner in which a speed dimension was represented in the speeded tests. It is likely, however, that hierarchical analysis would have shown a second-order general factor plus first-order speed and level factors.

Similarly, Howie (1956) attempted to show that speed and accuracy dimensions are independent contributors to intelligence test scores. Because of the unavailability of the correlation matrix and possible problems of experimental dependence in it, this dataset was not subjected to reanalysis, but the published results at least give further support to the notion that linearly independent dimensions of speed and level can be identified in typical subtests of intelligence.

Lord's (1956) Study

Lord's (1956) study of speed factors in a series of tests remains one of the few available studies that are truly informative on the speed–level issue, although from my point of view it is not completely satisfactory because the speed dimensions were represented partly by time-limit correctness scores and also by three variables (9, 17, 25) that identified the last item attempted in three tests as estimates of rate of work. In my reanalysis of this dataset (LORD01), these last three variables were not used (because of experimental dependence) in a seven-factor principal factor solution of the correlation matrix. Also, criterion variables (course grades at the U.S. Military Academy) were omitted because the interest was only in the space defined by test scores. This seven-factor principal factor solution was rotated (by a Procrustes technique) to reproduce the first seven factors of Lord's own rotated solution as closely as possible. Two orthogonal second-order factors were extracted from the correlations among oblique first-order factors. The three variables initially omitted (9, 17, and 25) were added to the analysis by Dwyer's (1937) extension, followed by hierarchical orthogonalization.

At the second order, the two orthogonal factors (labeled 1 and 5) could clearly be interpreted as speed and level, respectively. Subsumed under the second-order speed factor were three first-order factors of numerical, perceptual, and verbal speed, respectively. Subsumed under the second-order level factor were factors of visualization, quantitative reasoning, and lexical knowledge, but also (very weakly) a small speed or rate-of-work factor defined by the last-item-attempted measures for the spatial ability test (intersections) and the arithmetic reasoning test. Lord noted that "there is reason to believe that many or all of the examinees who answered the last item of the speeded tests skipped many items or responded at random" (p. 34), implying that these "last item attempted" variables were not necessarily good measures of rate of work.

Lord had attempted to differentiate speed and level dimensions by using tests with different time-limits, i.e., tests that were differentially speeded. All were, however, scored as number correct less a correction for guessing. Even the tests designed to measure level had time-limits, though these were very generous. These differentiations failed to be well manifested in the factor loadings on the respective first-order factors. For example, speeded test scores had somewhat higher loadings than did level tests of Intersections on factor 6, interpreted as the level visualization factor. Similar patterns were observed for loadings of speeded and level tests on factor 7 (Level of Quantitative Reasoning) and factor 8 (Level of Vocabulary Knowledge). The differentiations between speeded tests and level tests tended to show themselves, instead, in the loadings on the second-order factors. For example, speeded arithmetic reasoning and vocabulary tests had higher loadings (though still small) on factor 1 (a second-order speed factor) than did the level tests of arithmetic reasoning and vocabulary. Similarly, there was a weak tendency for level tests to have higher loadings than speeded tests on factor 5 (the second-order level factor).

A further disturbing result in these data was that variables 9, 17, 25, measures of "last item attempted" on the vocabulary, intersection, and arithmetic reasoning tests, respectively, did not consistently have high loadings on the second-order speed factor, as they might have been expected to have. Variables 9 and 25 behaved properly in that they had high or moderate loadings on factor 1 (speed) and low loadings on factor 5 (level), but variable 17 had a loading of only .113 on factor 1. The ambiguities in these results are possibly attributable to the fact that the rate-of-work dimension was poorly represented in Lord's study, as mentioned above.

Mangan's (1959) Study

Mangan (1959) published "a factorial study of speed, power, and related temperament variables," conducted with 38 test scores from 200 13- and 14-year-olds. He reported finding "five clearly identifiable and two less definite factors – content factors $g + v$ and N, speed factors P, verbal tempo and fluency, and temperament factors persistence and speed–accuracy" (p. 144). It appeared, however, that a number of Mangan's variables were experimentally dependent on others, leading to erroneous factorization. Furthermore, it was noted that level (or "power," in Mangan's terminology) was not well represented in the battery. In my reanalysis, I selected 30 variables that appeared not to be affected by experimental dependence and performed a standard hierarchical analysis on these, yielding two orthogonal second-order factors and seven first-order factors. The remaining eight variables were added to the analysis by Dwyer's (1937) extension. The second-order factors were interpreted as (factor 1) broad speediness (for relatively easy tasks) and (factor 6) level and rate-of-work in performing difficult tasks.

Subsumed under the "broad speediness" factor were first-order factors: factor 2, Ideational Fluency; factor 3, Motor Speed in Writing; factor 4, a composite factor of Numerical Facility and Perceptual Speed; and factor 5, an uninterpretable factor on which was loaded one of the fluency tests and Thurstone's Identical Pictures test. Subsumed under factor 6 ("level and rate of work in difficult tasks") were first-order factors: factor 7, "persistence" (adopting Mangan's interpretation); factor 8, "level of ability in reasoning"; and an uninterpretable factor 9.

In general, the factors disclosed by this study were poorly defined, but at least it was possible to distinguish speed factors from level factors.

SPEED VS. LEVEL CLASSIFICATION OF FACTORS

A basic question that can be asked about any factor of cognitive ability is that of whether it essentially refers to *level* or to *speed*. That is, does it conform to the paradigm of a *level* factor, for which probabilities of success (when subjects are given as much time as they desire for any specific task) decrease with the difficulties of relevant tasks (as described in Chapter 1), or does it conform to the paradigm of a *speed* ability, where probabilities of success approach unity when time permitted for any task is as much as a subject desires, and decrease as the time permitted decreases?

A convenient analog, in the domain of athletic events, would be the distinction between such tasks as the standing high jump, the pole vault, or weight lifting, where the *level* of an individual's ability is stated in terms of the maximum height or weight the individual can achieve in the task, as opposed to an event such as the 100-meter dash, where the achievement is measured in terms of the maximum *speed* (or rate) that can be attained.

Determining whether a cognitive ability factor is to be classified as *level* or *speed* is not the same as determining the extent to which a test is speeded (e.g., by techniques suggested by Cronbach & Warrington, 1951; Helmstadter & Ortmeyer, 1953). It is asking a question about a *factor* or latent trait, rather than about a specific test. A given test of a level factor might or might not be "speeded"; if speeded, it would be speeded to the extent that the time-limit does not permit all examinees to finish the test or some portion of it. A "pure" test of a speed factor would contain items that all or nearly all examinees could perform correctly, and the score would be simply a function of the rate at which examinees perform the items. Classifying a factor as "speed" or "level" involves a conceptual analysis of the range of tasks that measure the factor, that is, determining whether this range of tasks shows variation in difficulty such that when subjects are given unlimited time to perform them, subjects would vary in the difficulty of tasks they could perform correctly. If so, the factor would be classified as a level factor. Otherwise, the factor would be classified as a speed factor, in that the only essential variation in subject performance would be, not the variation in probability of correct performance, but in the rate at which tasks are performed.

Of course, if relevant data are available on variation in task difficulties and rates of performing them, it would be relatively easy to make the speed vs. level classification for a given factor, but such data are only occasionally, and certainly not systematically, available in the factorial literature because of the widespread use of time-limit tests.

The problem considered here is somewhat similar to that considered by Furneaux (1960):

Suppose there are two relatively independent attributes, say "speed" and "accuracy," each of which affects test performance separately in a way which varies with the difficulty of the test and with the time allowed for completion, but not with test content. In any heterogeneous set, tests will vary in difficulty and in the time allowed for completion, and the correlations between tests could therefore reflect these differences as well as, or *even rather than* [italics added], those associated with content. In view of this possibility each of the fifty-seven tests used in the original P.M.A. experiment [Thurstone, 1938b] was considered in turn, and a decision made as to whether it was likely to have served as a measure for speed or for accuracy in the experimental population used. In making this decision consideration was given to any experience the writer might have had in using the same, or a similar test within a British population of university students, to the method of scoring adopted, to the shape of the distribution of scores, to the time allowed, and to the apparent difficulty of the test items as gauged from a brief scrutiny. In respect of thirteen tests no decision could be made with even moderate confidence. Sixteen seemed to be concerned mainly with speed, ten with accuracy, and eighteen with both. In order to simplify the analysis the factors isolated from Thurstone's matrix by Eysenck (1939), using Burt's group-factor method, were used instead of the oblique solution favoured by Thurstone himself. In Eysenck's study only four factors were of any great importance, the remaining five each accounting for less than 2 per cent of the total variance. One of the four factors concerned was a general factor accounting for some 31 per cent of the total variance, the others being Verbal–Literary (5 per cent), Arithmetical (4.6 per cent) and Visuo-Spatial (6.6 per cent).

After the speed/accuracy dependence of all fifty-seven tests had been estimated the nine tests having loadings greater than 0.3 on the Arithmetical axis were examined. Six of them had been designated measures of speed, one of accuracy, one mixed, and one unclassified. Of the fifteen tests defining the Visuo-Spatial factor, five had been designated measures of accuracy, seven mixed, two speed, and one unclassified. Both speed and accuracy are represented to an approximately equal degree within the Verbal–Literary tests, four being measures of speed, three mixed, and two accuracy. Of the seventeen tests having loadings above 0.65 on the General-Factor only one represents speed, while no less than six had been designated accuracy. At g saturations below 0.4, on the other hand, four of the nine classifiable tests measured speed, and only one accuracy.

It would be absurd to make too much of so cursory an examination. The evidence could, however, be interpreted as supporting the hypothesis that at least part of the apparent differentiation between Visual–Spatial and Arithmetical tests is not due to differences of content at all, but to differences in the extent to which they measure speed as opposed to accuracy. The association of tests measuring accuracy with high loadings on the General-Factor is of interest in that it helps with the interpretation of the Factor. It is not however really relevant to the point under discussion, and in the present context the analysis will have served its purpose if it illustrates the difficulties which attend the use of the kind of complex test that still represents the psychologist's chief measuring instrument. It is rather as if the electrician had no means of measuring current and voltage independently, but could only use a wattmeter, to measure their product; or as if a tailor had to fit his customers from a knowledge of their weights (Furneaux, 1960, pp. 169–170).

Several comments may be made to help the reader appreciate the context and import of the above quotation. Furneaux focused on the interpretation of the traits measured by specific tests, but by considering these in terms of the factors on which these tests loaded in Eysenck's reanalysis of Thurstone's data (roughly comparable to our orthogonalized hierarchical analysis of these data), he was actually concerned with the classification of these factors as level (accuracy) vs. speed. It is unfortunate that Furneaux did not identify which tests he classified as speed, accuracy, or "mixed." I believe he properly interpreted the "Arithmetic axis" (our Number Facility factor) as a speed factor because of the large number of speed tests that loaded on it. With regard to the other factors, Furneaux was perhaps misled into using the perceived speededness of specific tests as a basis for classifying the factors on which they were loaded. According to my own analysis, the General factor, Spatial Visualization, and the Verbal factor are all essentially *level* factors, regardless of how speeded particular tests of these factors may be. A possible qualification of this statement, however, would be that the spatial domain is complex. As noted by Lohman (1979a), some spatial factors are essentially *level*, while others are essentially *speed*. It is probable that the general speededness of the Space tests used by Thurstone precluded separation, in his study, of one or more speed factors in this domain from one or more level factors.

There is an interesting but subtle suggestion in Furneaux's statement at a point where I added emphasis: "... the correlations between tests could therefore reflect these differences [in speed vs. accuracy] as well as, or *even rather than*, those associated with content." The implication is that it is conceivable that correlations among tests could be due *only* to common elements of speed. Of course, the almost overwhelming body of evidence goes counter to such an implication. Most first-order factors show clear differences in content. But what about correlations among *factors* – correlations that are often used to support the notion of a higher-order general factor? If tests of all first-order factors are characteristically speeded (given with a fairly severe time-limit), could not the second-order general factor reflect mainly differences in speed abilities rather than the operation of a factor reflecting differences in levels of cognitive functioning that individuals can attain? This is a possibility that must be entertained, because it is by no means completely ruled out by the evidence presently at our disposal.

The above remarks serve as background and partial justification for an attempt to classify, into separate and mutually exclusive level and speed categories, the factors that have been identified in Chapters 5 through 10, with, in addition, some reference to factors that were cited above in the course of discussing certain correlational and factor-analytic studies addressed to the speed/level problem. Factors are considered in each of the domains of cognitive ability established in Chapters 5 through 10.

Factors in the Domain of Language (See Chapter 5)

Nearly all the factors in the domain of language can be classified as level factors, because in each case individual differences are with respect to the liminal point on some scale of task difficulty that the individual can attain.

Level factors in the language domain are listed as follows, with remarks concerning the relevant difficulty scale. These remarks are in many cases somewhat speculative because there is inadequate knowledge of what aspects of pertinent tasks make them easy or difficult for relevant populations.

> LD: *Language Development.* Language tasks or products are scaled with respect to their complexity, the relative rarity or unfamiliarity of the language features (words, syntactic structures, etc.) involved in them, and the stage of language development at which language learners manifest the ability to perform or produce them.
>
> V: *Printed Language Comprehension.* Verbal tasks (vocabulary items, reading comprehension items) are scaled with respect to complexity and the relative rarity or unfamiliarity of printed language features.
>
> VL: *Lexical Knowledge.* The difficulty scale is an ordering of lexical items with respect to unfamiliarity, relative rarity, abstractness, or other aspects that make for vocabulary test item difficulty (Marshalek, 1981).
>
> RC: *Reading Comprehension.* This factor is similar to V except that the tasks are restricted to comprehension of connected discourse. An example of a difficulty scale for this factor is the Reading Proficiency Scale established in recent work sponsored by the National Assessment of Educational Progress (Beaton, 1987; Carroll, 1987b, 1988b).
>
> RD: *Reading Decoding.* Speculatively, reading decoding tasks are scaled with respect to the type and number of orthographic–phonemic features that make for difficulty in pronouncing printed words or pseudowords.
>
> CZ: *Cloze Ability.* Cloze items are scaled with respect to whatever features (e.g., amount and informativeness of context, rarity of words, etc.) may make for difficulty in supplying missing words in continuous text.
>
> SP: *Spelling.* Spelling items in languages like English, French, and German vary in difficulty as a function of the extent to which knowledge of correctness requires frequent exposure, knowledge of spelling rules, etc.

PC: *Phonetic Coding.* Speculatively, phonetic coding tasks vary in difficulty as a function of the amount of material to be coded, the familiarity of this material, etc.

MY: *Grammatical Sensitivity.* Speculatively, grammatical sensitivity tasks vary in difficuly as a function of type of grammatical context, familiarity of the material, etc.

CM: *Communication Ability.* Speculatively, communication ability tasks would vary in difficulty as a function of the pragmatic features of the communication situation, the complexity of the ideas to be communicated, etc.

LS: *Listening Ability.* Tasks vary in difficulty mainly as a function of the same factors of language complexity that make for difficulty in reading comprehension. In addition, difficulty may vary as a function of the rate at which stimulus material is presented, and to this extent speed may be a component.

OP: *Oral Production.* The relevant scale on which performances are evaluated is probably more one of quality than of difficulty. That is, the scale concerns the quality of oral production with reference to such aspects as "clarity of thought," "grammatical correctness," "articulatory clarity," etc.

WA: *Writing Ability.* Analogously to the case of OP (*Oral Production*), the relevant scale concerns the quality of written production with reference to such aspects as "clarity of thought," "organization," "good sentence structure," etc.

Speed factors in the language domain are probably limited to:

RS: *Reading Speed.* This factor would presumably refer to a parameter governing the individual's speed or rate of silently reading different kinds of materials for different purposes, over and above the parameters associated with types of materials, purposes, etc. (See Carver, 1990.)

Rate of Work in Performing Verbal Tasks: A factor of this type was hypothesized, above, in examining Raskin's (1937) unpublished data on speeds in performing sentence completion tasks. The matrix of correlations among these speeds, for different levels of difficulty, was of the quasisimplex type, suggesting that the operation of a rate-of-work parameter would vary with the difficulty of the task. Also, factor 4 in the analysis of dataset LORD01 could be interpreted as a factor governing rate of work in performing multiple-choice vocabulary tests.

(The reader is reminded that the "language domain" is here limited mainly to language competence abilities; it does not include the domain of "idea and language production," as discussed below.)

Factors in the Domain of Reasoning (See Chapter 6)

Chapter 6 identified three major factors in the domain of reasoning. All three can be characterized as *level* factors:

RG: *Sequential Deductive Reasoning.* Sequential reasoning tasks can be arranged on a difficulty scale that presumably reflects their complexity in terms of the types of relationships involved, the number of steps in the solution process, and other elements, as yet not adequately researched (but see, for example, Johnson–Laird, 1985; Colberg, Nester, & Trattner, 1985). Kyllonen and

Christal (1990) have suggested that reasoning ability is affected by working memory capacity.

I: *Induction*. Inductive tasks can be arranged on a difficulty scale that reflects the complexity of the rules, regularities, or concepts to be induced or otherwise derived from the stimulus materials (Pellegrino, 1985). An example of such a scale for a series of concept formation tasks is given by Carroll (1992).

RQ: *Quantitative Reasoning*. The difficulty scale would reflect increasing complexity and involvement of advanced quantitative concepts in problem solutions.

There is evidence, though limited, for a *Speed of Reasoning* factor in this domain. For example, factor 4 in dataset DAVI01 is such a factor, loaded on rate-of-work measures for an Arithmetic Reasoning test (whose level scores are normally measures of factor RQ), a Letter Grouping test (whose level scores are normally measures of factor I), and the test Disarranged Morphemes (whose level scores have high loadings on a Verbal Reasoning factor). The substantial correlation (.66) between speed measures for the tests Arithmetic Reasoning and Number Series in Tate's (1948) study (as shown in our Table 11.2) is further evidence for a speed of reasoning factor, as is also the speed factor identified by Myers (1952) in a figure classification test, in contrast to the level factor for this same test, interpreted as a measure of Induction.

What is problematical about a Speed of Reasoning factor is that there is no good evidence as to its possible distinctiveness from the Rate-of-Work factor mentioned in the domain of language abilities. Note, for example, the speed factor identified in dataset DUBO01, which is loaded with rates of work on vocabulary, directions, and reasoning tests.

Factors in the Domain of Learning and Memory (see Chapter 7)

The only true level factor identifiable in this domain is Memory Span (MS). The relevant difficulty scale is represented by the number of elements to be recalled, as is evident even in the manner in which a memory span test is typically administered – with stimulus sets of increasing length given until the subject fails to pass a criterion.

It is difficult to classify other factors in this domain as either level or speed. On the assumption that any subject (regardless of amount of memory ability) could learn to recall any amount of memorial material if given enough time (or trials) to do so, memory factors might be regarded as speed factors, in the sense that scores on memory tests measure simply what subjects are able to recall (in a test phase) on the basis of exposure to the material in some given time limit, that is, in a study phase. (Memory tests used in factor studies typically have set time-limits for the study phase, usually with a generous time-limit for the test phase.) Persons who are able to give perfect recall after exposure in the time-limit could be said to demonstrate fast learning; persons who have poor recall after exposure to the material in the set time-limit could be said to exhibit slow learning.

The memory factors identified in Chapter 7 of which this could be said include the following:

> MA: *Associative Memory*: Rate of learning arbitrary associations between paired stimuli.
>
> M6: *Free Recall Memory*: Rate of learning supra-span series of stimuli.
>
> MM: *Meaningful Memory*: Rate of learning meaningful material.
>
> MV: *Visual Memory*: Rate of learning material that is characteristically visual, figural, or pictorial.

Chapter 7 also discussed factors of "learning ability" identified in a number of factorial studies. Most or all of these can probably best be characterized as speed or rate-of-learning factors.

Mathematical psychologists (e.g., see Atkinson, Bower, & Crothers, 1965) have provided mathematical models of the learning/memory process, often in the form of mathematical equations showing relations between amount of learning, time to learn, various experimental conditions, and one or more individual difference parameters. For example, Thurstone (1930) proposed an equation showing total learning time as a function of list length (number of items to be learned, for example in a paired-associate memory task), a subject's learning ability, and two other parameters. Carroll and Burke (1965) found good fit of this equation for a set of data on paired-associate learning, especially when individual differences were taken account of. Stake (1961; dataset STAK01) used a version of Gulliksen's (1934) rational learning equation to derive learning ability parameters for individual subjects. It is beyond the scope of this volume to explore the literature of mathematical learning theory, but it may be suggested that the factors of individual differences in learning and memory could be represented as individual difference parameters in mathematical learning models. To the extent that learning and memory factors are distinct, each factor would presumably provide a distinct parameter for a model to account for a given type of learning or memory task.

Factors in the Domain of Visual Perception (See Chapter 8)

Considering only the major factors of visual perception discussed in Chapter 8, only one factor, VZ: *Visualization*, appears to be clearly classifiable as a level factor. The difficulty scale associated with this factor involves, in some general sense, the complexity of the spatial representations that are involved or required in performing spatial visualization tasks. Carroll, Meade, and Johnson (1991) have studied parameters predictive of the difficulty of items in several spatial tasks (Block Counting, Cubes, Flags, Hands, and Spatial Rotations) administered to tenth-grade children in unlimited time (in contrast to the time-limits often imposed in factorial studies), with the general conclusion that difficulty is associated with complexity of spatial perception. In the Block Counting test, for example, difficulty is associated with items that show piles of blocks in which blocks not directly seen must be visualized. Pellegrino and Kail (1982) have shown that the difficulty of items on a paper form board test is a function of the number and complexity of processes of encoding, search, rotation, and comparison of visual elements.

Most other factors in this domain can be characterized as speed factors, because people can perform the respective visual tasks with a low rate of error if they are given unlimited time. Tests of these factors are generally speeded, that is, given with a time-limit such that only a small proportion of subjects, if any, can complete all items. Scores are generally number correct, with or without correction for guessing, but because of the low error rates such scores are essentially measures of rate of performance.

Speed factors in the domain of visual perception include the following:

> SR: *Spatial Relations*: rate of performing simple tasks involving rotation and/or reflection of visual forms.
>
> CS: *Closure Speed*: rate of apprehending what is represented by a visual presentation that has been subjected to some degree of obscuration or degradation. It is with some hesitation that I classify this as a speed factor because some people are seemingly unable to perform very difficult items at all, even when given a very generous time-limit. Note that closure speed items are usually "self-revelatory"; that is, when apprehension is achieved, the response is recognized as being correct. In fact, incorrect apprehensions are relatively uncommon. The factor could perhaps just as well be classified as a level factor in the sense that it is in effect a measure of the degree of obscuration or degradation that an individual can tolerate. Carroll (1992) has analyzed a Visual Closure test in these terms, but this was a test in which items graded in difficulty are administered individually in such a way that if items are not perceived within a certain time, they are scored as incorrect. On the other hand, typical group-administered tests of this factor, such as the Street Gestalt Completion test, tend to be designed and administered in such a way that the scores reflect speed in attaining closure for relatively easy items. More research is needed to determine the speed and level parameters pertaining to this factor and items used in testing it.
>
> CF: *Closure Flexibility*: rate of apprehending or finding a given (known) visual form that is embedded in another form.
>
> P: *Perceptual Speed*: rate of search and comparison of visual forms.

Factors in the Domain of Auditory Reception (See Chapter 9)

Every factor identified in this domain appears to be a level factor, even though temporal aspects of stimuli are involved in some cases. Each of these factors is listed here, with a statement of the nature of the difficulty scale by which the factor is defined:

UA: *Hearing Threshold*: Stimulus presentations (usually, pure tones) are scaled in terms of decreasing loudness in decibels (db), generally controlling for pitch frequency (Hz).

UT: *Speech Threshold I*: Phonemic signals (words in a language) are scaled in terms of decreasing loudness.

UU: *Speech Threshold II*: Phonemic signals (words or short sentences in a language) are scaled in terms of decreasing loudness, but also in terms of intelligibility as determined by tryouts.

US: *Speech Sound Discrimination*: Pairs of spoken words or syllables are scaled in terms of difficulty in their being discriminated.

U3, U5, U6: *Musical Sound Discriminations*: Pairs of musical sounds are scaled in terms of difficulty in their being discriminated on the basis of pitch, intensity, or other attributes of sound.

U9: *Musicality Judgments*: Musical materials are scaled in terms of distance or closeness to accepted criteria of aesthetic pleasingness.

UR: *Resistance to Auditory Stimulus Distortion*: Stimuli are scaled in terms of the amount of distortion introduced into normal versions.

UK: *Temporal Tracking*: Speculatively, items are scaled in terms of the complexity of the subject's task in counting temporal stimuli or in manipulating temporal representations.

UP: *Absolute Pitch*: Performances are evaluated in terms of accuracy in identifying or naming pitches, or in producing specified pitches.

UL: *Sound Localization*: Performances are evaluated in terms of accuracy in localizing sounds.

Factors in the Domain of Idea and Language Production
(See Chapter 10)

Nearly all the factors in the domain of idea and language production are labeled as measures of fluency – a word that suggests that they are measures of speed or rate. The only factor in this domain that might be considered to be a level factor is FO: *Originality/Creativity*, for its performances are evaluated for the extent that they appear to be "original" or "creative." But even in this case the responses are typically obtained under time-limit constraints, as in the case of many other level factors that have been discussed. I am not aware of research that adequately explores the extent to which measures of this factor would have more construct validity if subjects were permitted extended time.

Speed or *rate-of-response* factors in this domain, with brief and somewhat speculative statements about what kinds of speeds or rates they concern, are the following:

FI: *Ideational Fluency*: rate of producing responses that fit given semantic criteria, e.g., instances of given categories, ideas about a topic.

NA: *Naming Facility*: speed or latency in naming pictured objects, colors, geometric figures, etc.

FA: *Associational Fluency*: rate of producing responses that are drawn from restricted classes that are associated in meaning with given stimuli.

FE: *Expressional Fluency*: rate of producing meaningful discourse, or manipulating stimulus materials to produce sentences that are semantically similar.

FW: *Word Fluency*: rate of producing different verbal responses that are cued by the orthographic or phonemic characteristics of the stimuli.

SP: *Sensitivity to Problems*: rate of producing different ideas that are pertinent to real or imagined problems of a practical nature. Conceivably, however, there could be a level component if ideas are evaluated for pertinence or quality.

FF: *Figural Fluency*: rate of producing (with a writing or drawing instrument) different figural designs.

FX: *Figural Flexibility*: rate of producing different hypotheses and mental sets about figural and spatial problems.

NUMBER OR NUMERICAL FACILITY (N) FACTORS

A group factor of Number ability or Numerical Facility was recognized in the early years of factor-analytic investigation, even by Spearman (1927, pp. 230f.). According to Wolfle (1940), it was reported almost as frequently as the Verbal and Space factors. French (1951) listed 35 datasets in which it had appeared. He stated that it "represents facility in manipulating numbers in any form," but claimed that it "is not limited to tests involving the arithmetical operations" (p. 225). As an example, he cited the test Highest Number, in which the examinee has to find the highest number in each column of numbers, a test which had at least a moderate loading on a Number factor (in dataset THUR11 its highest loading on a first-order factor, .35, is on factor 6, interpreted as Number Facility). In his opinion, "the best tests of the *Number* factor are those with the greatest amount of number handling, namely, tests of the four arithmetical operations," and he further pointed out that arithmetic reasoning tests are not pure tests of N, tending to have loadings also on a reasoning factor.

The Educational Testing Service Reference Tests for Cognitive Factors have consistently offered tests for a Number Facility factor N. The 1976 version (Ekstrom, French, & Harman, 1976, p. 115) defines the factor as follows:

The ability to perform basic arithmetic operations with speed and accuracy. This factor is *not* a major component in mathematical reasoning or higher mathematical skills.

Further:

It is possible that this factor may be broader than simple arithmetic manipulation. For example, several studies by Thurstone show non-numerical coding tasks to have a moderate loading on N. Other researchers have suggested that N may be part of an "automatic process" factor, incorporating both number facility and perceptual speed, which is operant when responding to overlearned material.

The 1976 Kit offers four tests of N:

Addition (N-1): A speeded test of the addition of sets of three one- or two-digit numbers. Each problem is presented as a vertical column of numbers, with a box supplied for the subject to write the answer. In each of two parts of the test, two minutes are allowed to answer up to 60 problems. The score is number correct, and thus the score has both speed and level components.

Division (N-2): Each item requires division of a two- or three-digit number by a single-digit number; all correct answers are integers. In each of two parts, two minutes are allowed to answer up to 60 problems of this type. Score is number correct.

Subtraction and Multiplication (N-3): In each of two parts, two minutes are allowed for answering up to 60 problems, alternating between rows containing 10 subtraction problems (subtracting a two-digit number from a larger two-digit number) and 10 multiplication problems (multiplying a two-digit number by a single-digit number). The score is number correct.

Addition and Subtraction Correction (N-4): In each of two parts, the subject is to mark C (correct) or I (incorrect), to indicate the correctness of answers given for simple addition or subtraction problems such as $11 + 23 = 34$ and $35 - 10 = 20$. The score is number correct minus number incorrect, as a correction for guessing.

According to the manual, the Kit tests "should be considered suitable for persons who have reached ninth grade or higher." It is obvious that these tests presuppose considerable training and practice in elementary arithmetic. As far as I am aware, there is no published information on the distribution of the number of items attempted or the proportion of items correct. It is not possible, therefore, to make any general statements about the speededness of the tests or the extent to which they measure speed or level. Nevertheless, the factor appears to conform more to the paradigm of a speed factor than to that of a level factor, in that there would probably be a relatively low error rate in typical samples of subjects if unlimited time were permitted. For this reason, the factor is considered in the present chapter; it did not appear to fall into any of the domains previously considered.

In Guilford's (1967; Guilford & Hoepfner, 1971, p. 242) Structure-of-Intellect model, the factor underlying tests of numerical facility has been regarded as primarily a factor with specific variance associated with numerical operations, but with some additional variance associated with a factor labeled MSI (Memory for Symbolic Implications) because of correlations with the Wechsler Digit–Symbol test, in which no numerical operations (as such) are involved. This interpretation of the factor neglects the possibility that the number factor involves not only number operations (addition, etc.) but also any kind of number perception or manipulation that requires recognition of digits and their significations, for example, their order on the number line.

In Table 11.3, 88 token Numerical Facility factors found in 88 datasets are listed, along with relevant information on source, age of sample, type of sample, sex composition of sample, hierarchical factor number in the pertinent matrix shown in Appendix B, and remarks on any higher-order factors that dominate the factor, and on the identities of any other first-order factors whose distinctions from the factor are of interest. The three first-order factors that are mentioned in any such remarks are: P (Perceptual Speed), RQ (Quantitative Reasoning), and KM (Mathematical Knowledge, considered in Chapter 12). In some datasets (e.g., REIN03, REIN02, UNDH21, MANG01A, and VERY02) there is a tendency for variables normally loaded on P to load on N in such a way that a separate P factor does not appear. However, numerous datasets show a distinction between N and P. Similarly, a number of datasets show a distinction between N and RQ, or between N and KM.

Instances of the Numerical Facility factor occur in samples as early as age 8, although the majority of instances occur for samples of older ages. The numerical tasks used for young samples tend to be simpler than those used for older samples, but even for the latter, the tasks are often quite simple.

Detailed examination of the variables that have high loadings on factor N suggests that the interpretation of the factor is very straightforward, differing little if at all from the interpretations offered by French (1951) and the ETS factor kits, as cited above. Factor N refers simply to the degree to which the individual has developed skills in dealing with numbers, from the most elementary skills of counting objects and recognizing written numbers and their order, to the more advanced skills of correctly adding, subtracting, multiplying, and dividing numbers with an increasing number of digits, or with fractions or decimals. These are skills that are learned through experiences in the home, school, or even in the workplace. In the early years, skills deal with simple numbers and operations, and the important object is to be able to deal with number problems correctly, at whatever speed. In later years, practice is aimed at handling computations with greater speed as well as accuracy. More complex problems can be dealt with effectively and efficiently only if skills with simple problems are increasingly automatized.

Typical tests of factor N emphasize speed as well as accuracy in handling simple problems. It appears that the most construct-valid tests of N are those that deal with simple problems, that is, addition, subtraction, multiplication, or division of numbers with a small number of digits. Apparently, problems with larger numbers of digits often pose too great a demand on the subject's attention or working memory, and are too likely to be solved incorrectly at some point in the process.

Tests of factor N would be more informative if they were designed to distinguish level (accuracy) and speed aspects of skill. Tests typically used in factor-analytic studies, at least, do not distinguish speed and level, and one gets the impression that they are more influenced by speed than level, in that time-limits are usually set fairly severely. There are no factor-analytic studies in our database that reveal separate dimensions of speed and level for skills in numerical operation, even though it is logically possible for such separate dimensions to exist, as they do, for example, for arithmetic reasoning tasks (see Table 11.2, where the correlation between altitude and speed scores on an arithmetic reasoning test is shown as $-.07$). However, a study by Kyllonen (1985) found separate numerical speed and level factors.

The status of an individual on factor N can be reflected in almost any task in which dealing with numbers, or performing numerical operations, is required.

Table 11.3. *88 Numerical Facility (N) factors in 88 datasets, arranged in order of approximate mean age of sample[a]*

Dataset	Date	C'y code	Age	Sample code	M/F code	Factor no.	Remarks (higher-order factors; others related)
KEIT21	'87	U	8	7	3	8	1:3G;6:2V;8:N & P
VALT11	'81	G	8	1	3	5	1:2G
VALT12	'81	G	8	1	3	7	1:2G
UNDH01	'76	O	9	1	3	9	1:2H
REIN03	'65	G	10	6	3	2	1:2G;2:N & P
WRIG01	'39	U	10	1	3	2	1:2G;2:N & MS
DUNC11	'64	U	11	6	3	2	1:2G;8:RQ
TRAU01	'70	U	11	1	3	5	1:2G;6:RQ
WERD51	'71	S	11	6	3	2	1:2G;3:P
CATT01A	'63	U	12	6	3	4	1:3G;2:2C
HOLZ01	'39	U	12	6	3	5	1:2G;5:N & P
REIN02	'65	G	12	1	3	3	1:2G;3:N & P
STAK01	'61	U	12	1	3	6	1:2G;3:P
REIN04	'65	G	13	6	3	2	1:2G
THUR81	'41	U	13	6	3	7	1:3G;2:2H;9:P
THUR82	'41	U	13	6	3	7	1:3G;2:2H;9:P
WERD41	'69	S	13	6	3	2	1:2S;3:P
DUPO01	'75	W	14	6	3	3	1:2G
GUIL55	'61	U	14	1	3	8	1:2G
HOEP11	'65	U	14	6	3	3	1:2R
MANG01A	'59	E	14	6	3	4	1:2S;4:N & P
PETE11	'63	U	14	M	3	5	1:2G
PETE12	'63	U	14	M	3	6	1:2G
SHAY01	'67	U	14	1	1	6	1:2G;3:KM
WERD01	'58	S	14	6	1	7	1:2G;3:RQ;6:KM
WERD02	'58	S	14	6	1	6	1:2G;2:RQ; 6:N & Alphabet Tasks
REMO02	'62	Y	15	6	1	2	1:2G
SCHU11	'58	U	15	1	3	4	1:3G;2:2C
WEBE01	'53	G	15	6	1	4	1:2G;3:RQ
WEBE02	'53	G	15	6	2	3	1:2G;2:RQ
WEIS11	'55	U	15	M	3	12	1:3G;8:2F; see text.
WRIG21	'58	E	15	8	1	6	1:2G;2:KM;5:27
CANI01	'62	U	16	6	2	5	1:2G;3:RQ
CURE11	'68	U	16	6	1	5	1:2G;9:P
CURE12	'68	U	16	6	2	8	4:P;6:21;9:KM
COOM01	'41	U	17	1	3	3	1:2G;2:Alphabet Tasks; 8:P;10:RQ
HOEP31	'64	U	17	6	3	8	6:P;7:2S
MICH61	'51	U	17	6	1	6	1:2G;5:P
MICH62	'51	U	17	6	2	4	1:2G;5:P
TAYL01	'47	U	17	1	3	5	1:2H;8:P
THUR11	'38	U	17	1	3	6	1:2S;3:P
THUR31	'40	U	17	1	3	8	1:2G;4:P
DAVI01	'45	U	18	P	3	5	1:2G

Table 11.3 (*cont.*)

Dataset	Date	C'y code	Age	Sample code	M/F code	Factor no.	Remarks (higher-order factors; others related)
FREN11	'57	U	18	3	1	13	12:20
GOOD01	'43	U	18	A	1	3	1:2G;4:P
LORD01	'56	U	18	3	1	2	1:2S;3:P;7:RQ
SAUN21	'60	U	18	6	1	4	1:2G;4:N & Information
ADKI03	'52	U	19	2	1	5	1:2H;10:P?
ALLI02	'60	U	19	2	1	8	6:2Y
ALLI03	'60	U	19	2	1	9	6:2H
BECH01	'47	U	19	6	3	5	1:2S;4 & 9:P
BOTZ01	'51	U	19	6	1	4	1:2G
CHRI01	'58	U	19	2	1	11	1:3G;10:2C
FAIR01A	'84	U	19	2	3	8	5:2H;6:RQ
FAIR02	'84	U	19	2	3	7	6:2S
GUIL61	'74	U	19	P	1	3	Orthogonal factors
KAMM01	'53	U	19	F	3	6	1:2C
LUMS01	'65	A	19	P	3	6	1:2F
SCHA11	'40	U	19	6	1	10	1;3G;8·2S;9,12:P
SCHE11	'52	C	19	6	3	3	1:2G
THUR21A	'38	U	19	6	3	5	1:2F;4:P?
VERN21	'84	U	19	$	1	4	1:2G;3:RQ
VERY01	'67	U	19	6	1	6	1:2H;2:KM
VERY02	'67	U	19	6	2	3	1:2G;3:N & P?
VERY03	'67	U	19	6	3	4	1:2F
EGAN01	'78	U	21	3	1	4	1:2S;4:N & P
FEDE02	'80	U	21	2	3	3	1:2F;3:N & KM?
FRUC21	'52	U	21	2	1	3	1:2G;6:P
GUIL11	'55	U	21	3	1	8	1:2G
GUIL17	'52	U	21	3	1	8	1:2G;3:P
GUIL31	'47	U	21	3	1	6	1:2G;5:P
GUIL34	'47	U	21	3	1	3	1:2G;3:N or RQ?;5:P
GUIL35	'47	U	21	3	1	6	1:2G;4:P
GUIL42	'47	U	21	3	1	6	1:2G;2:P
GUIL43	'47	U	21	3	1	6	1:2G;2:P;6:N & RQ
GUIL45	'47	U	21	3	1	6	1:2G;3:P?
GUIL51	'60	U	21	3	1	5	1:2G
GUIL66	'52	U	21	3	1	5	1:2G
LUCA01	'53	U	21	3	1	8	7:2S;10:P
VERN51	'47	E	21	2	1	3	1:2H
WITT11	'43	U	21	2	1	2	1:2G;3:P
WOTH01	'90	U	21	1	3	6	1:3G;6:N & P
MICH51	'50	U	22	6	1	5	1:2G;3:P
HAKS01	'74	C	24	1	3	18	9:P;13:2C
ALLE11	'78	U	30	U	3	2	1:2H;5,7:P?
ALLE12	'78	U	30	U	3	3	1:2H;7:P?
DEMI01A	'62	U	42	L	3	5	1:2G
DEMI02A	'62	U	42	S	3	3	1:2G

[a]See Appendix A for codes. In a few cases, the classifications of factors shown here were preliminary and may not agree with the final classifications shown in the tables of Appendix B.

Tests of factor RQ (Quantitative Reasoning) often have subsidiary loadings on factor N. When factor RQ is not well defined in a given dataset, tests of RQ such as Arithmetic Reasoning can even have their highest (salient) loadings on factor N.

Factor 3 in dataset HOEP11 corresponds to a factor that Hoepfner and Guilford (1965) classified as DSR (Divergent Production of Symbolic Relations). Although some of the variables required "divergent production" of a variety of responses to numerical tasks, other variables did not, and it seems evident that the common element in most of the saliently loaded variables was degree of success in handling numerical problems, regardless of the type of responses required. The factor was therefore classified as N.

Of interest is the fact that in dataset WRIG01, which contains data on responses of ten-year-olds tested with the Stanford–Binet, factor 2 is loaded not only with several items requiring manipulation of numbers (e.g., counting backward from 20 to 1, and making change), but also with items normally measuring memory span (e.g., repeating five digits backward). Indeed, it appeared to be impossible to separate a numerical facility factor from a memory span factor in this dataset, possibly because all memory span tasks in this dataset involved numbers. It is also noteworthy that most of the variance in the oblique version of factor 2 was absorbed into a general factor (factor 1 in the hierarchical factor matrix).

A number of datasets (e.g., REIN03, UNDH21, VERY02, WOTH01) show, for variables that are normally loaded on factor P (Perceptual Speed), substantial loadings on factor N, so that the resulting factor N appears to be a composite of N and P. Such a result is partly due to failure of factor P to be adequately defined in these datasets, but it may also be due to the fact that some perceptual speed variables involve number manipulation. Digit–Symbol coding, for example, usually involves looking up the required symbols in an array in which digits are placed in numerical order; individuals with better ability to recognize digits and to find a given digit in the ordered array are at an advantage in performing the digit–symbol coding task. This observation goes toward answering Guilford's (1967, p. 133) concern about the fact that some tests of N appear not to involve numerical operations. Table 11.3 exhibits numerous datasets in which factor N is clearly distinguished from factor P.

Factor N is also to be distinguished from factor RQ, Quantitative Reasoning, and from a factor KM, Mathematical Knowledge, although tests of N sometimes show loadings on these factors, presumably because numerical computation is often required in tests of RQ and KM. As discussed in Chapter 6, factor RQ involves reasoning with quantitative concepts. Factor KM (considered in more detail in Chapter 12) concerns knowledge of mathematical concepts that are more advanced than those of simple numerical operations, and it is a level factor rather than a speed factor.

Dataset WEIS11 was developed in a factor-analytic study of mathematical ability (Weiss, 1955). It yielded not only a factor (factor 12 in the hierarchical matrix) interpreted as N, but also a factor (factor 14) interpreted as Algebraic Computation Facility. The factor probably contains a considerable amount of variance due to speed, because its tests – Algebraic Computation, Equations, and Computational Speed – were given with fairly short time-limits. Algebraic Computation is a free-response test of 18 items requiring simplification and reduction of algebraic expressions. Equations is a free-response test of 12 algebraic equations that are to be solved. The Computational Speed test was intended to reveal ingenuity in using algebraic skills to short-cut computational work.

An early study that attempted to test hypotheses concerning factor N is that of Coombs (1941; dataset COOM01). Coombs reviewed evidence on arithmetical prodigies and cases of acalculia or arithmetic disability and concluded that numerical ability is a special dimension of ability that is largely independent of intelligence and education. "It is reasonable, therefore," he remarked, "that tests like addition and multiplication really measure some more fundamental process than mere number manipulations per se. Hence it should be possible to devise tests of a non-numerical character which would measure this fundamental process" (p. 163).

Coombs therefore developed tests to investigate the following hypotheses:

1. Tests involving new rules for manipulation of a symbolic system are better tests of number ability after practice than they are before.
2. Of several tests involving manipulation of a symbolic system, the one in which the symbolism is more familiar provides the better measure of number ability.

Non-numerical tests of a hypothesized rule-manipulation ability were the tests AB, ABC, Forms, and Alphabet I, II, and III. The AB test consisted of 210 problems each presenting pairs of letters A, B, and C. If the two letters were different (e.g., $A\,B$), the subject was to mark the remaining letter (C); if they were the same (e.g., $B\,B$), the answer was that same letter (B). The somewhat more complicated ABC test consisted of 60 problems using the same rules, but with groups of letters to be operated on. Thus, the problem $C\,B\,B = ?$ would be solved by first finding $C\,B = A$ and then combining it with the next letter, $A\,B = C$. The Forms test was exactly like the ABC test, but three non-meaningful geometrical designs replaced the letters A, B, and C. The Alphabet tasks (I, II, and III) were constructed to check the hypothesis that practice with a set of rules would improve a test as a measure of number ability; they utilized all the letters of the alphabet and several rules concerning how pairs such as $M\,P$ should be answered depending on whether there are letters of the alphabet between them, and whether the letters are in alphabetical order. Initial learning occurred with Alphabet I; further practice was given with the tests Alphabet II and Alphabet III.

The factor analysis, as such, was not particularly helpful in testing Coombs's hypotheses. Both in Coombs's analysis and in my reanalysis, the special tests (AB, ABC, Forms, and the Alphabet tasks) defined a factor that was linearly independent of factor N. Study of relevant correlations, however, persuaded Coombs that practice with a set of rules increases the correlation of a test with factor N. For example, Alphabet III (performed after practice with Alphabet I and Alphabet II) tended to have slightly higher correlations with number tests than Alphabet I. (The increases were very small, however, and found only for addition tests.) Somewhat more convincing was the finding that tests using a familiar symbol system (the AB and ABC tests) were more highly correlated with number tests than the Forms test – with a structure identical to that of the ABC test but with nonmeaningful figural stimuli as elements. These findings of Coombs are somewhat unconvincing because differential reliability was not controlled.

Coombs also found, as have a number of other investigators, that the simpler numerical tests were better measures of N than more elaborated tests. For example, Two-Digit Addition had a higher loading on N than Three- or Four-Digit Addition. Coombs argued that this evidence tended to contradict the hypothesis that "number ability is in the nature of a serial response process."

Werdelin (1958) further investigated Coombs's automatization hypothesis by using Coombs's ABC and Alphabet tests. In general his results confirmed Coombs's hypothesis, which Werdelin stated as supposing that "a test involving an automatizable process will show successively higher loadings on the numerical factor the more the process underlying the test is practised" (p. 207). As did Coombs, Werdelin found that the alphabet tasks defined a factor separate from factor N. However, reanalysis of his matrix (dataset WERD02) had the alphabet tasks loading on the same factor as the numerical facility tests, a result that tends to yield even greater support for the hypothesis that factor N is a measure of an automatized ability. This work of Coombs and Werdelin on processes involved in factor N is in need of extension using modern computerized administration techniques. The group-administered tests used by Coombs and Werdelin did not permit adequate control of speed and accuracy aspects of the tests.

Worthy of some note is the fact that in my reanalyses of Coombs's and Werdelin's studies, the alphabet tasks tended to have somewhat higher loadings on a second-order factor than did the numerical operations tests. If the second-order factors in these studies are interpreted as measures of g or general intelligence, the implication might be that the ability to automatize a new rule-following skill is more related to intelligence than the degree to which an "old" skill such as numerical facility has been automatized. This result is consistent with R. J. Sternberg's (1985) proposal that one component of intelligence is the ability to automatize a skill.

One other researcher who attempted to confirm Coombs's notion of an expanded number factor was Remondino (1962), working with samples of male students aged 14–16 years in Italy, but publishing his report in French. As an interesting measure of a highly automatized skill, he developed a Weekday test (*Test de la Semaine*) in which subjects had to answer questions like (I translate)

"If yesterday was Saturday will the day after tomorrow be Tuesday? (Possible? Impossible?)." Scores on this Weekday test tended to correlate highly with more conventional tests of the number factor; indeed, in our reanalysis of one of his datasets (REMO02) the Weekday test had the highest salient loading on a Number factor (factor 2). But possibly this result was due, not to skill automatization as such, but to subjects' operating with days of the week on the analog of a number line – a matter that needs to be further investigated.

As may be seen in Table 11.3, the age distribution of samples in which factor N has been studied is strongly biased toward samples of older adolescents and adults. More work is needed on the developmental aspects of numerical facility. According to Groen and Parkman (1972), most adults perform computations using automatic look-up of long-term memory stores (containing number facts such as those in addition and multiplication tables), while at least in early stages children use incremental counting processes (see also Birren & Botwinick, 1951). Questions to be investigated are (1) when and how rapidly automatic look-up processes appear in the development of numerical facility, and (2) whether the numerical facility factor reflects individual differences in rate of developing automatic processes.

RATE-OF-TEST-TAKING (R9) FACTORS

Table 11.4 lists 12 factors that can provisionally be interpreted as Speed of Test Performance or Rate-of-Test-Taking factors (symbol: R9). In most cases, they are contrasted with accuracy factors that are also found in the same datasets. They are classified here by virtue of the fact that in every case they represent measures of the rate at which individuals perform tests, but these rates do not appear to be associated with any particular type of test content, provided it is of a cognitive performance nature. Generally the tests are relatively easy. Some of the factors are labeled or interpreted as "broad speediness," implying that they cover rates of performance in a variety of cognitive tasks.

THOM11 and THOM12 are, respectively, datasets deriving from a study (Thomson, 1940, 1941) of young boys' and girls' responses on a variety of intelligence tests, including "performance tests" such as the Seguin test, the Manikin test, and a Cube Construction test. The tests were individually administered and scored both for accuracy and the time taken. In each case, hierarchical analysis of the correlations with age partialed out showed first-order accuracy and times factors, with a second-order general factor. In reporting time scores, Thomson reflected their orientation so that fast performance correlated positively with accuracy. Most of the time scores had substantial loadings on the second-order general factor.

Factor 5 of the hierarchical matrix for dataset UNDH11 might well have been classified under either P (Perceptual Speed) or N (Number Facility); it was classified here largely because the author (Undheim, 1978) labeled it "general

Table 11.4. *12 Speed-of-Test-Performance (R9) factors in 12 datasets, arranged in order of approximate mean age of sample*[a]

Dataset	Date	C'y code	Age	Sample code	M/F code	Factor no.	Remarks (Higher-Order factors; others related)
THOM11	'41	D	10	1	1	3	1:2G;2:Accuracy
THOM21	'41	D	10	1	2	3	1:2G;2:Accuracy
UNDH11	'78	O	11	6	3	5	1:2G
FREN11	'57	U	18	3	1	2	1:2S;6:P
CARR42	'76	U	19	P	3	7	Orthogonal Factors
CARR43	'77	U	19	6	3	6	1:3G;5:20
DUBO01	'32	U	19	6	3	1	2:Accuracy scores
HORN01	'66	U	28	Q	3	3	1:2G
HORN02	'82	U	28	Q	3	9	8:2S?
VERS01	'83	K	30	U	1	2	1:2S;3:P;4:2P
VERS02	'83	K	30	U	2	3	1:2S;2:P
VERS03	'83	K	30	Z	1	6	5:2S

[a]See Appendix A for codes. In a few cases, the classifications of factors shown here were preliminary and may not agree with the final classifications shown in the tables of Appendix B.

speed." Two of its variables, Symbol Identities and Letter Identification, are typical tests of Perceptual Speed; the remaining two, Addition and Multiplication, are typical tests of Number Facility.

The variables loaded on factor 7 for dataset FREN11 (French, 1957) included:

> Social Judgment: "Each item consisted of pairs of names of personal qualities. The subject checked the quality he would prefer to characterize someone with whom he had to associate closely. The score was the number checked [within a brief time-limit]."
>
> Visual Preferences: "Each item consisted of a pair of somewhat similar, simple line drawings or figures. The subject checked the one he liked best. The score was the total number checked [within a brief time-limit]."
>
> Size Judgment: "Each item consisted of pairs of descriptions of objects. The subject checked the larger (assuming standard or average sizes). The score was the number checked [within a brief time-limit]."

Thus, each variable measured rate of making very simple decisions, and accuracy or correctness was not a factor. It is not possible to tell, from the design of French's study, whether this factor would be similar to a performance-time factor derived from tests in which correctness would also be a factor.

In dataset CARR42, two of the variables with salient loadings on factor 7 ("Speed of test-taking") were scores representing rate of performance (number of items completed within a time-limit) of tests that were also scored for accuracy under unlimited time. This was true of the variables Verbal Analogies and Grammatical Fluency. The third variable was the Letter–Star test in which subjects have to give meaningful sentences to patterns like "S * R *" in which each symbol is to be replaced by a word, with the restriction that a letter is to be replaced by a word starting with that letter, and an asterisk may be replaced by any word. Correctness is essentially not a factor. The common element, then, is the speed with which these tasks are performed. A similar factor was found in dataset CARR43, in which the rate in performing a Verbal Analogies test was one of the variables.

Factor 1 in DUBO01 is loaded exclusively with rate-of-performance scores on a variety of verbal, reasoning, and arithmetic tests; the accuracy scores on these same tests appear on another factor orthogonal to factor 1.

Factor 3 in dataset HORN01 is a good example of a dataset designed so that what is normally a second-order factor becomes available for analysis at a first-order by including only one variable for each of a heterogeneous set of first-order factors. The variables included in this factor, with their loadings on a second-order general factor and their salient loadings on this factor 3 (R9), were as follows:

	2G	R9
Speed of Copying (SC)	.476	.620
Perceptual Speed (P)	.482	.442
Writing Flexibility (WF)	.299	.426
Number Facility (N)	.380	.394
Ideational Fluency (FI)	.381	.361

Although correctness may be involved in the scoring of some of these variables, the common element appears to be rate of performance. Dataset HORN02 has the same source as dataset HORN01, but its correlations were adjusted for age differences; results reported for this dataset are essentially similar to those reported for dataset HORN01, except that the Perceptual Speed (P) and Number Facility (N) variables are no longer *saliently* loaded on a Broad Speediness factor, but still retain substantial loadings on this factor.

Datasets VERS01, VERS02, and VERS03 come from a study (Verster, 1983) that focused on a hypothesized theoretical distinction between speed and accuracy at different cognitive levels (psychomotor, sensory, perceptual, and conceptual). In my reanalyses, each of these datasets shows first-order speed factors at each of these levels, with two second-order factors: (1) general cognitive speed, dominating a speed factor at the conceptual level and one at the perceptual level, and (2) general motor speed, dominating a speed factor at the psychomotor level and one at the sensory level. The speed factors at the conceptual level are listed in Table 11.4 because they appear to be generally comparable to the other factors listed there. The Verster study, incidentally, is useful for its data on processing rates and accuracies as a function of test complexity.

Not included in the database for reanalysis because of unavailability of the correlation matrix is a study by Kyllonen (1985, Study 1) that analyzed a series of more or less traditional psychometric tests that were administered to 508 Air

Force basic trainees by computer in such a way that speed (latency) and accuracy (percent correct) scores could be obtained, along with subtests of the ASVAB battery (Armed Services Vocational Aptitude Battery). An oblique factor matrix showed eight factors, as follows:

> Reasoning Level (percent correct scores)
> Reasoning Speed (latency scores)
> Verbal Level (percent correct scores)
> Verbal Speed (latency scores)
> Numerical Level (percent correct scores)
> Numerical Speed (latency scores)
> Technical Knowledge
> Clerical Speed [or Perceptual Speed]

Kyllonen reported that at the second-order, a general speed and a general level factor were obtained, virtually uncorrelated ($r = -.05$). The general speed factor can be interpreted as a general rate-of-test-taking factor. The first-order speed factors appear to correspond to similar factors we have obtained in reanalyses as mentioned above.

FACTORS IN REACTION TIME AND OTHER ELEMENTARY COGNITIVE TASKS (ECTs)

The phrase *elementary cognitive task* (ECT) has come into fairly general usage among cognitive psychologists. My "tentative and somewhat loose" definition (Carroll, 1980a) was cited in Chapter 1. Among ECT's that have been studied by cognitive psychologists are the following:

> *Simple reaction time*: The reaction time (RT) or latency to the onset of a single stimulus (visual or auditory), presented at a particular point of time. It can be argued that the response is a cognitive process because attentional resources are involved (Carlson, Jensen, & Widaman, 1983), and latency depends on various conditions that are prompted by instructions to the subject (e.g., the use of a warning signal and random delays from the warning signal). In some experimental arrangements (as used particularly by Jensen, 1979), the reaction time can be divided, at least operationally, into two phases, (1) decision time (DT) – time to decide to make a response and leave a home button, and (2) movement time (MT) – the time to move, say, a finger, from the home button to a button at which the response is physically made and recorded.

(In all paradigms from this point on, accuracy as well as speed of response is involved, but interest here is in *speed* of response. Stimuli are usually chosen so that error rates are very low, but speed measurements are usually taken only on correct responses.)

> *Choice reaction time*: Time to make a response to one of two or more alternative stimuli, depending on which alternative is signaled. A popular form of experimental arrangement is the so-called Hick paradigm, named after Hick

(1952) who formulated a law in which reaction time is a function of the number of bits ($\log_2 n$) implied in the number (n) of alternatives. (See Jensen, 1987, for a historical review and discussion, also Widaman & Carlson, 1989, on methodological problems.) When $n = 1$, the paradigm reduces to simple reaction time. As in the case of simple reaction time, the latency can be divided into decision time and movement time, and these times can be separately recorded with appropriate experimental arrangements. Various statistics for these measurements can be computed. Of frequent interest have been statistics (slope, intercept) concerned with the (normally linear) regression of response times on the number of bits. There has been some debate in the literature (e.g., Smith & Stanley, 1983) as to whether the use of a home key procedure adequately distinguishes decision time from movement time. Some subjects apparently leave the home key before they complete making a decision, tending to hover over alternative response keys before making the final response. Nevertheless, in my view it is useful to make separate measurements of decision and movement times even if there is systematic or random error in them. Factorial results suggest that decision and movement times have low intercorrelations and that decision times are more likely to have significant correlations with accuracy variables. One other problem with the Hick paradigm is that apparently some subjects do not conform to the Hick law (Barrett, Eysenck, & Lucking, 1986). In pointing this out, Eysenck (1987, pp. 48, 51) suggests investigating what individual difference variables may be responsible for variation in subjects' conforming to Hick's law.

The categorization paradigm: In a sense, this is a variant of the choice-reaction paradigm. It differs from it in that only a single stimulus is presented, and the signal for the choice is contained in the stimulus. In the simplest form, the stimulus might be, for example, a single letter *L* or *R*, indicating whether the response is to be made to the left or the right. In a more complicated form, the stimulus might be the name of an object, and the subject makes the response on the basis of whether the object is a living or a non-living thing.

The Odd-Man paradigm: This paradigm has been used by Kranzler (1990). It employs the same experimental arrangement as the Hick paradigm, but the stimuli are three lights presented at different positions on a display. Two lights are close together; the subject's task is to move to the third light, that is clearly farther from the first two.

The Posner paradigm: In this paradigm, popularized by Posner (1978; Posner & Mitchell, 1967), two stimuli are presented either simultaneously or sequentially (with a short but controlled delay between the stimuli); the subject is to decide, and respond accordingly, whether the two stimuli are "same" or "different" with respect to criteria stated in instructions that have been given to the subject prior to a trial or a series of trials. For example, the letters "A" and "a" can be regarded as "physically different" but "same in name." For a given set of trials, subjects can be instructed to respond according to the "physical" difference, and for other trials, they can be instructed to respond according to the "name" difference. With appropriate experimental arrangements, latencies can be divided into decision and movement times, and statistics such as means and standard deviations can be computed over trials. Hunt (1978) reports that the difference between name-identity and physical-identity RTs is related to certain intellectual measures, but see Schwartz, Griffin, and Brown (1983) for a critique of this result.

Visual search: In this paradigm, a visual stimulus is presented (for example, a particular letter or digit), followed shortly by a series of further stimuli; the subject's task is to decide whether the initial stimulus is present or absent in the series. Measurements include not only reaction times and accuracies but also the linear regression parameters (intercept, slope) of RTs on the number of stimuli in the series to be searched.

Scan and search: This is a variant of visual search. In Scan and Search, as studied for example by Neisser (1967), the stimulus to be searched for is presented initially; there is then a long series of items (each containing a series of stimuli) in which this stimulus is to be searched; the subject's task is to indicate whether the initial stimulus is present or absent in each set of target stimuli. The task is thus very similar to many that are used in measuring the Perceptual Speed factor, for example the Finding A's test (see Chapter 8).

Memory search: This paradigm, studied extensively by S. Sternberg (1969), is in a sense the obverse of visual search. In each item, one or more stimuli are presented (to be "put in memory"), after which a single "probe" stimulus is presented. The subject's task is to decide as rapidly as possible whether the probe stimulus was present or absent in the initial series of stimuli, held in memory. As with visual search, measurements include reaction times and the parameters of the (normally linear) regression of latencies on the number of stimuli presented for memorization.

Inspection time: In this paradigm, discussed by Nettelbeck (1987), the object is to determine the threshold amount of time that is required for a subject to detect a difference in two simple visual stimuli, for example, a difference in the length of two vertical lines. Auditory inspection time has been studied by Irwin (1984) and Deary, Head, and Egan (1989).

Sentence verification: In this paradigm, studied by Clark and Chase (1972) and used in dataset LANS31 (Lansman, Donaldson, Hunt, & Yantis, 1982), the subject must evaluate whether a sentence such as "Star is not above cross" correctly describes a pattern showing an asterisk ("star") and plus sign ("cross") in vertical relation to each other. Mean response time has been shown to depend on the presence of negation and the use of "above" vs. "below," as well as the correctness of the sentence in relation to the visual presentation.

The tasks described above are only a sample of the many types of cognitive tasks that have been studied. Our concern here is with what and how many dimensions of individual difference abilities underlie the various measurements that can be obtained from these and other ECTs. By including ECT measurements of various sorts in their batteries, many factorial studies have provided information intended to throw light on these questions. Table 11.5 shows 39 datasets in our database, with more than 76 token factors that have been classified as relevant to possible ECT abilities.

In format, this table is slightly different from similar tables elsewhere in this volume. Datasets are listed in alphabetical order; there is little point in arranging them by mean chronological age of the samples because most samples are age 18 or above. Each factor is listed with a symbol indicating a very preliminary and tentative classification. The list of symbols, with their intended interpretations, is as follows:

R∗: A factor that may be specific to a particular paradigm, not otherwise classified.

R1: Simple reaction time. Factors are classified here if the dominant or only loadings are for simple reaction time measures – either decision times or total RT, when separate decision and movement times are not reported. Often these factors are loaded with various other RT measurements, for example, those from choice reaction tasks.

R2: Choice reaction time. Factors are classified here if the dominant or only loadings are for choice reaction time measures – either decision times or, when separate decision and movement times are not reported, total RT.

R3: Movement time, from any paradigm for which separate movement times are reported.

R4: Semantic processing speed. Factors are classified here when the dominant loadings are reaction times for ECTs in which the decisions to be made by the subject require some encoding and mental manipulation of stimulus content, as in the more complex forms of the Posner task, or in categorization tasks.

R5: Visual and/or memory search, slope parameters.

R6: Visual and/or memory search, RT and/or intercept parameters.

R7: Speed of mental comparison. Factors are classified here when the dominant loadings are for reaction time parameters derived from tasks in which stimuli must be compared for particular attributes, as in the Posner task.

S1: Accuracy of mental comparison. Accuracy scores from tasks whose speed scores produce factors classified as R7.

2S: A second-order cognitive speed factor.

Some abbreviations used in the table must be explained:

RT: a general abbreviation for reaction time, especially where decision time and movement time are not distinguished.

RTSD: standard deviation (over trials) of RTs.

DT: decision time, and DTSD, standard deviation of decision time, when measured separately from movement time.

MT: movement time, and MTSD, standard deviation of movement time.

For each factor, a "Remark" is given, intended to indicate the types of variables loaded on the factor. Space does not permit giving complete details of variables and factor loadings; for such details, the reader is advised to consult the complete hierarchical factor matrices shown in Appendix B.

The datasets listed in the table vary enormously in quality, in terms of number of cases, adequacy of design, freedom from experimental dependence, and other matters. In several cases, parallel batteries were given on different occasions to the same sample, but for some reason the factors derived show less congruence than might be desired. For example, as between datasets ROSE11 and ROSE12, representing a battery being given to the same sample on different days, only factors 1 and 2 show satisfactory congruence. Factor congruence was so poor for datasets ROSE01, ROSE02, and ROSE03 (a battery given to the same small samples on three occasions, with some attrition) that it was decided to drop them from consideration.

Table 11.5. *39 datasets and 76 (or more) factors pertaining to reaction times and other temporal measures of elementary cognitive tasks (see text for explanations)*

Dataset	Date & C'y code	Age code	Sample code	M/F code	Factor no. & symbol	Remarks
AFTA01	'69C	43	1	3	7:R1	Simple & Choice RT
ALLE11	'78U	30	U	3	5:R*	Scan & Search: Slope & Intercept
"	"	"	"	"	6:R5	Memory Search: Slope
"	"	"	"	"	7:R4	Posner Physical; Memory Search Intercept
ALLE12	'78U	30	U	3	5:R4	Posner Physical; Memory Search Intercept
"	"	"	"	"	6:R5	Memory Search: Slope
"	"	"	"	"	7:R*	Scan & Search: Slope & Intercept
BARR01	'82U	21	6	3	1:R6	Memory Search Intercept
"	"	"	"	"	2:S1	Memory Search Accuracy
"	"	"	"	"	4:R5	Memory Search Slope
BARR02	'82U	21	6	3	1:R6	Memory Search Intercept
"	"	"	"	"	3:S1	Memory Search Accuracy
"	"	"	"	"	4:R5	Memory Search Slope
CARL41	'83U	12	6	3	2:R2	Hick: DTSD, DT Slope
"	"	"	"	"	5:R2	Hick: DT, Attention
"	"	"	"	"	6:R3	Hick: MTSD & MT
CHIA01	'76U	19	6	3	1:R6	Visual & Memory Search/Intercept
"	"	"	"	"	2:R5	Visual & Memory Search/Slope
CLAU01	'66U	9	R	3	2:R1	Simple & Choice RT
CLAU02	'66U	13	R	3	2:R1	Simple & Choice RT
CLAU03	'66U	22	R	3	3:R1	Simple & Choice RT
CLAU04	'66U	17	1	3	7:R1	Simple & Choice RT
DETT00	'85U	21	2	3	3:R2	DT to Hick, Recognition Memory, & Learning Tasks
"	"	"	"	"	4:R*	Recog.Memory:Low MTSD; Stimulus Disc.:Fast DT
"	"	"	"	"	5:R3	Tachistoscopic, Stimulus Disc. Tasks: Fast MT
"	"	"	"	"	9:R*	Tachistoscopic Tasks: Low DTSD, Fast DT
"	"	"	"	"	10:R*	Probed Recall Task: Low DTSD
FAIR01A	'84U	19	2	3	1:2S	General Speed; Dominates factors 2,3,4
"	"	"	"	"	2:R7	Posner Physical & Name Identity
"	"	"	"	"	3:R4	Word Categorization Tasks
"	"	"	"	"	4:R1	Simple & Choice RT
FAIR02	'84U	19	2	3	5:R5	Memory search slope
"	"	"	"	"	6:2S	General Speed; Dominates factors 7 (Number) & 8
"	"	"	"	"	8:R6	Memory search intercept
FLEI12	'54U	19	2	1	4:R1	RT and other speed measurements

Table 11.5 (*cont.*)

Dataset	Date & C'y code	Age code	Sample code	M/F code	Factor no. & symbol	Remarks
HUGH01	'83A	19	6	3	2:R7	Posner task measures
HUNT51	'81U	19	6	3	2:R4	Semantic verification/simul.
"	"	"	"	"	3:R7	Word matching, categorization
"	"	"	"	"	4:R4	Semantic verification/sequential
HUNT61	'73U	19	6	3	5:R6	Visual memory search
HUNT71	'75U	19	6	3	3:R5	Visual memory search/slope
"	"	"	"	"	5:R7	Speed of mental comparison tasks
JACK12	'79U	18	6	3	3:R7	Speed of mental comparison tasks
"	"	"	"	"	6:R5	Visual memory search/slope
JENS41	'79U	19	6	2	1:R2	Choice DT/slope re bits
"	"	"	"	"	3:R3	Movement time and MTSD
KRAN01A	'90U	22	U	3	2:R4	Odd-man: DTSD, DT
"	"	"	"	"	3:R7	Visual & Memory Search, Posner Physical & Name: DT
"	"	"	"	"	6:R1	Hick; Inspection Time: DT
"	"	"	"	"	8:R3	Posner Tasks: MT
"	"	"	"	"	9:R3	Search, Hick, Odd-man: MT
LANS21	'78U	19	6	3	4:R1	RT of a probed response
LANS22	'78U	19	6	3	4:R4	Sentence verification task
LANS31	'82U	18	6	3	4:R4	Sentence verification task
LUNN21	'77U	16	6	3	1:R1	Simple RT & other measures
PARK01	'60U	14	T	1	6:R1	Simple RT & other measures
ROBE11	'76U	50	1	1	2:R2	Mainly choice RT measures
[ROSE01,ROSE02,ROSE03: data omitted due to inadequacy of the batteries]						
ROSE11	'77U	19	6	3	2:R5	Visual & Memory Search: Slope
"	"	"	"	"	3:R4	Various semantic tasks
"	"	"	"	"	4,5,6,7,8:	Various specific factors
ROSE12	'77U	19	6	3	2:R7	Posner task measures
"	"	"	"	"	3:R6	Memory search intercepts
"	"	"	"	"	4:R5	Memory search slopes
"	"	"	"	"	5:R4	Various semantic tasks
"	"	"	"	"	6,7,8:	Various specific factors
SCHA11	'40U	19	6	1	7:R1	Simple reaction time
SNOW21	'76U	19	3	3	6:R7	Speed of Mental Comparison
THUR41	'44U	19	6	3	3:R1	RT (Auditory, visual)
VERN01	'81U	19	6	3	3:R7	Semantic tasks (see text)
"	"	"	"	"	5:R2	Hick: DT & MT
VERN11	'81U	21	R	3	2:R1	Simple DT
"	"	"	"	"	3:R2	Choice DT
VERN21	'84U	19	$	1	5:R4	Various semantic tasks
VERS01	'83K	30	U	1	6:R2	Sensory RT
VERS02	'83K	30	U	2	6:R2	Sensory RT
VERS03	'83K	30	Z	1	2:R2	Sensory RT

The tasks studied vary considerably in design over datasets. Each paradigm allows for many possible subtle variations that apparently can give rise to conflicting results. For example, it may make some difference whether the Posner task is given with simultaneous or with sequential presentation of the pair of stimuli to be compared (Hunt, Davidson, & Lansman, 1981; dataset HUNT51). Further, the tasks can vary sufficiently in content to make for differential factorial results. For example, a categorization task can be either very easy or more difficult depending on the selection of stimuli.

For these reasons, among others, it is not possible to derive from the datasets listed in Table 11.5 clear evidence for a definite set of speed factors in ECTs. Our only option at this writing is to rely mainly on several datasets whose designs were relatively more adequate and that appear to give the clearest and most consistent results. There are inconsistencies in the results of even these datasets, however. It is obvious that further research is needed.

Evidence from Kranzler's (1990) Study

One of the most interesting and apparently reliable datasets is KRAN01A (Kranzler, 1990), based on 101 volunteer subjects, aged 17 to 25, all students at the University of California at Berkeley. The original dataset had 37 ECT variables derived from eight paradigms:

> Inspection time: DT estimated by a special algorithm
> Hick paradigm: 0 bits: DT, DTSD, MT, MTSD
> "   "   : 3 bits: DT, DTSD, MT, (MTSD)
> Odd-man paradigm: DT, DTSD, MT, (MTSD)
> Posner paradigm, Physically Same–different for common words presented simultaneously (side-by-side):
>
> > DT, DTSD, MT, MTSD
>
> Posner paradigm, Semantically Same–different for synonym or antonym pairs of common words presented simultaneously (side-by-side):
>
> > DT, (DTSD), MT, (MTSD)
>
> Memory search: Target series, 1 to 7 digits:
>
> > DT, (DTSD), MT, MTSD, (DT Slope),
> > DT Intercept, (MT Slope), MT Intercept
>
> Visual search: Target series, 1 to 7 digits:
>
> > DT, (DTSD), MT, MTSD, (DT Slope),
> > DT Intercept, (MT Slope), MT Intercept

In addition, the dataset contained eleven psychometric variables: scores for Raven's Advanced Progressive Matrices (untimed) and scores for ten timed subtests of the Multidimensional Aptitude Battery (MAB) (Jackson, 1984). (Kranzler kindly supplied me with the complete correlation matrix for the 48 variables, not included in his dissertation.)

In my analysis of the matrix, most ECT variables (being response times or functions thereof) had to be reflected in order to yield a positive manifold. Ten of them (those placed in parentheses in the above list) failed to satisfy Kaiser's (1981) revised Measure of Sampling Adequacy and were dropped from the matrix before principal factoring of the remaining 38 variables. Many of these eliminated variables were reported by Kranzler as having low test–retest reliabilities. (Dunlap, Kennedy, Harbeson, & Fowlkes, 1989, found low reliabilities for derived variables such as slopes and intercepts from ECTs, but in the present case the unreliable variables were mainly slopes, not intercepts.) Seven acceptable principal factors were obtained and processed to produce an orthogonalized hierarchical matrix with two second-order factors (factors 1 and 7). Factor 1 subsumed the following first-order factors (with loadings as indicated):

2   .704 Odd-Man Task: DT variables
3   .574 Memory and Visual Search Tasks; Posner Task: DT variables
4   .519 MAB Performance tests (Spatial, Object Assembly, Picture Arrangement); Raven
5   .425 MAB Verbal tests (Vocabulary, Information, Comprehension)
6   .370 Hick tasks; Inspection Time: DT variables

Factor 7 subsumed the following first-order factors:

8   .876 Posner Tasks: MT variables
9   .473 Memory & Visual Search Tasks; Hick & Odd-man Tasks: MT variables

Thus, the results indicate quite clearly that decision time and movement time variables are generally orthogonal to each other, being loaded on different second-order factors. At the first order, decision and movement times appear on different factors, respectively, depending on the type of task. In the case of decision times, factor 2 involves speed in making the special kind of decision required by the Odd-man task – locating the light that is farthest from the other two of three. Factor 3 involves decisions about whether stimuli are same or different with respect to a given criterion; it can be interpreted as a Speed of Mental Comparison factor. Factor 6 involves simple or choice reaction time, as well as inspection time. In the case of movement times, factor 8 arises only in connection with Posner tasks, while factor 9 arises for all the other ECTs.

In most cases, standard deviation variables tend to have loadings on the same factors as the corresponding means, and in the same directions, but the loadings are lower. That is, greater variability over trials is associated with longer reaction times, but reaction times are more dependable measures of factors. Intercept parameters also loaded on the same factors as the corresponding means. All slope parameters were eliminated from the analysis because of unacceptable MSA values (and low reliabilities).

Evidence from Other Studies Listed in Table 11.5

Numerous studies (AFTA01, CARL41 – factor 5, CLAU01, CLAU02, CLAU03, CLAU04, DETT00 – factor 3, FAIR01 – factor 11, FLEI12, LANS21, LUNN21, PARK01, SCHA11, THUR41) show Simple Reaction Time factors similar to the simple decision time factor 6 of dataset KRAN01A described above. In most cases, however, decision time was not measured separately from movement time, so that these factors are possibly less construct-valid than factor 6 of KRAN01A. Further, some of these factors show loadings not only on simple reaction time but also choice reaction time, possibly because these studies' designs led to failure to distinguish simple and choice RT factorially. A few studies show distinctions between decision time and movement time factors, like KRAN01A: datasets CARL41 (factors 5 and 6), DETT00 (factors 3 and 5), and possibly JENS41 (factors 1 and 3, although factor 1 relies on slope and SD parameters). In any case, the evidence from these studies is consistent with the notion that separate movement time and simple decision time factors can be held to exist. (Movement time factors can be interpreted as special cases of the psychomotor factor Speed of Limb Movement, R3, mentioned in Chapter 13.)

Evidence bearing on the possibility that various factors of information processing speed (as represented by factors 2 and 3 of dataset KRAN01A) can be confirmed over studies is very confusing. Many of the datasets listed in Table 11.5 show one or more factors that might be cross-identified with some of those in dataset KRAN01A, but there is little basis for asserting adequate factor differentiation and interpretation, apparently because of wide variations in the types of cognitive tasks studied and in the types of variables used. About the only conclusion that seems clear is that tasks involving mental classification or comparison of stimuli tend to load on factors different from simple decision time and movement time factors. Among datasets that can be cited as evidence of this are:

> FAIR01: A general cognitive speed factor (8:2S) dominates not only a Simple and Choice RT factor, but also factor 9, with a physical and a name identity reaction time for a Posner task that uses letter pairs like AA, Aa, AB, etc.; and factor 10, with two meaures from word categorization tasks.
> FAIR02: Factor 5 is for two slope parameters from Sternberg memory search tasks; Factor 6 is a second-order speed factor dominating factor 7 (Number) and factor 8 with three other parameters from Sternberg memory search tasks.
> VERN01: Factor 5 is loaded mainly with DT and MT measures from the Hick tasks (because of the design, DT and MT could not be distinguished factorially); Factor 3 is loaded with RT (or DT?) measures from a variety of symbol and word comparison tasks.
> VERN21: Factor 5 is loaded with a variety of measures from Posner and Sternberg tasks. There is no separate factor for a reaction time measure from the Hick paradigm, but this measure has a quite low loading (.336) on factor 5.

It might be thought that variables from visual or memory search tasks, as opposed to Posner mental comparison tasks, would appear on different factors; some evidence for this comes from datasets ALLE11, ALLE12, JACK12, ROSE11, and ROSE12. But in KRAN01A we have seen that decision times from these tasks appear on the same factor. Further, results in dataset HUNT51 suggest that Posner tasks with sequential presentation of stimuli appear on a different factor from Posner tasks with simultaneous presentation of stimuli, but such separation does not occur in datasets BARR01 and BARR02.

It is possible that the difficulty of analyzing the individual difference dimensions underlying ECTs is due to the inappropriateness of ordinary factor analysis for the study of tasks that may have successive component stages. At least one dataset (Kyllonen, 1985, Study 2) in the literature can be cited as being an interesting effort to circumvent this difficulty. Because the underlying data and correlations were not available for reanalysis, it was not included in the database. Kyllonen administered a series of computerized ECT's to 178 Air Force basic trainees. The tasks were conceptualized as falling into five classes, as shown in Table 11.6, in the sense that they were thought to require successively more numerous stages of component processing. All tasks required a response component (possibly corresponding to the simple reaction time factor discussed above). Choice reaction time tasks also required a "decision" component; categorization tasks also required an "encoding" component; and matching tasks (like those in the Posner task) further required a "comparison" component in addition to the other components.

Based on this model (somewhat similar to a model proposed by Verster, 1983), Kyllonen used what he called a stage-analysis approach, computing estimates of separate times for processing stages. That is, parameters were estimated by taking the difference between response time on a given task and response time on the next simpler task. Reliabilities of the four parameters computed in this way were uniformly high, all exceeding .80 (in contrast to the findings of Dunlap et al., 1989, that difference parameters have low reliabilities), but interestingly, none of the between-parameter correlations were significantly different from zero. As Kyllonen states, "If additivity of processing stages can be assumed in this paradigm, then the lack of significant correlation among parameters can be taken to indicate that four independent dimensions of processing speed were present in this study" (Kyllonen, 1985, p. 11).

Because the additivity assumption might be questioned, Kyllonen proceeded to perform a conventional factor analysis of the 16 log latency variables, resulting in the oblique factor pattern matrix shown (in skeleton form) in Table 11.7. Six factors were identified:

> RT: Simple Reaction time (response component)
> CRT: Choice Reaction time (decision component)
> CAT: Categorization time (the encoding component)
> SQM: Sequential Matching time (the comparison component)
> SMM_w: a component associated with word matching
> SMM_l: a component associated with letter matching

Thus, four of the factors appeared to correspond to the hypothesized processing components, and two were associated with particular types of task content. It is noteworthy that the factor correlations approximate a simplex matrix, which is what one might expect if tasks are assumed to contain systematically increasing

Table 11.6. *Tests and processing components (from Kyllonen, 1985, Table 2)*[a]

Tests	Test label	Processing Component			
		Respond	Decide	Encode	Compare
Simple Reaction Time	(SRT)				
Left Hand	(SRT-LH)	X			
Right Hand	(SRT-RH)	X			
Choice Reaction Time	(CRT)				
"L" vs. "D"	(CRT-LD)	X	X		
"even" vs. "odd"	(CRT-EO)	X	X		
"positive" vs. "negative"	(CRT-PN)	X	X		
"vowel" vs. "consonant"	(CRT-VC)	X	X		
Categorization	(CAT)				
Words	(CAT-W)	X	X	X	
Letters	(CAT-L)	X	X	X	
Sequential Matching	(SQM)				
Words (Block 1)	(SQM-W1)	X	X	X	X
Words (Block 2)	(SQM-W2)	X	X	X	X
Letters (Block 1)	(SQM-L1)	X	X	X	X
Letters (Block 2)	(SQM-L2)	X	X	X	X
Simultaneous Matching	(SMM)				
Words (Block 1)	(SMM-W1)	X	X	2	X
Words (Block 2)	(SMM-W2)	X	X	2	X
Letters (Block 1)	(SMM-L1)	X	X	2	X
Letters (Block 2)	(SMM-L2)	X	X	2	X

[a] X means the column component was required for the particular row test; 2 means the component had to be executed twice.

numbers of stages. Indeed, it is possible that if the pattern matrix were orthogonalized by the Schmid–Leiman technique used extensively in this volume (or some variant of it), the orthogonalized matrix would approximate the pattern shown in Table 11.6, although of course with two more factors. (Such an analysis has not been attempted here.) Kyllonen himself performed a multidimensional scaling of the factor intercorrelations, showing two dimensions, one for the number of cascaded processes, and one for differential content.

A further study of this sort reported by Kyllonen (1985, Study 3) obtained, for a sample of 710 basic trainees, latencies on six tasks varying in the criteria by which decisions were to be made ("match decision rules"). Besides simple and choice reaction time, tasks required one of four bases of matching: physical identity, name identity, category identity, or meaning identity. Intercorrelations of the latencies formed a quasisimplex pattern which multidimensional analysis showed to be based on two dimensions: (1) amount of perceptual processing required, and (2) amount of memory search required.

Table 11.7. *Factor pattern matrix of log latency scores from reaction time tests, with factor intercorrelations (N = 178) (adapted from Kyllonen, 1985, Table 3)[a]*

	Factor					
Task	RT	CRT	CAT	SQM	SMM$_w$	SMM$_l$
SRT-LH	.76					
SRT-RH	.92					
CRT-LD		.75				
CRT-EO		.94				
CRT-PN		.93				
CRT-VC		.78				
CAT-W			.64			
CAT-L			.87			
SQM-W1				.72		
SQM-W2				.80		
SQM-L1				1.00		
SQM-L2				.81		
SMM-W1					.85	
SMM-W2					.87	
SMM-L1						.71
SMM-L2						.54
Factor						
RT	1.00					
CRT	.61	1.00				
CAT	.42	.62	1.00			
SQM	.31	.57	.65	1.00		
SMM$_w$	.34	.63	.57	.63	1.00	
SMM$_l$	.08	.42	.37	.42	.33	1.00

[a]Factor pattern loadings less than .25 are omitted.

Further research using procedures of task construction and analysis similar to those used by Kyllonen is recommended to clarify the dimensionality of the domain of cognitive speed.

As has been intimated at various points, processes in performing some ECT tasks bear much similarity to those involved in performing perceptual speed tasks; that is, both seem to require rapid mental comparisons. The study by Lansman, Donaldson, Hunt, and Yantis (1982; dataset LANS31) throws some light on these relations. Factor 3 in this dataset (according to my reanalysis of the published correlation matrix) was saliently loaded with four variables obtained from a computerized version of the Posner letter-matching tasks, i.e., subjects' mean reaction times for correct responses to each of the four possible types of stimuli – physical identity (e.g., AA), name identity (Aa), different–same case (AB), and different–different case (Ab), all given under instructions to respond according to whether the pairs of letters had the same name. Factor 2, however, was loaded with two variables from a paper-and-pencil version of the letter-matching tasks – estimated time for physical identity stimuli and estimated time for name identity stimuli. It was also loaded with a time score from a paper-and-pencil version of a sentence verification task and with three standard measures of Perceptual Speed – Finding A's, Identical Pictures, and Cancelling Numbers. Both factors were classified as Perceptual Speed and listed in Table 8.9. They might equally well be classified as Speed of Mental Comparison (R7) factors. In Chapter 8, it was commented that these results might suggest that measures of factor P are affected by "format" or "method" variance. However, another possible interpretation is suggested by the fact that in the reanalysis of this dataset, both factors 2 and 3, and their variables, had substantial or even high loadings on factor 1, a second-order "broad speediness" factor. The letter-matching and sentence verification tasks – whether from paper-and-pencil or computerized administrations – had much higher loadings on the broad speedi-ness factor than the standard Perceptual Speed tests. This suggests that the letter-matching and sentence verification tasks, as such, are much better measures of a cognitive speed factor than the standard Perceptual Speed tests. But this cognitive speed factor appears to be subject to some restrictions. Although letter-matching and sentence verification tasks appear on it, various spatial tasks (even computerized versions of a mental rotations task), as well as various psychometric tests (including verbal ability tests), had small or vanishing loadings on it. (Unfortunately, Lansman et al. did not control speed vs. level aspects of their psychometric tests; all were given with time-limits.)

The Stroop Color-Word Naming Task

The color-word naming task, introduced by Stroop (1935), has engaged the attention of cognitive psychologists because it appears to reveal some sort of psychological process involved when a subject is asked to read names of colors printed in colors other than the colors they name. It almost invariably takes subjects longer to read such color names than to name the colors themselves or to read the names of colors printed in black and white.

Although there seems to be no standard form of the Stroop test or its scoring, it can include three tasks (although it is frequently the case that only tasks A and C are employed):

A: (Color) Giving the names, as rapidly as possible, of a series of easily recognized colors, as represented by patches of color. Score A is time of this performance.

B: (Word) Reading, as rapidly as possible, the names of a similar series of colors printed in black and white. Score B is time of this performance.

C: (Color-word) Naming, as rapidly as possible, the colors in which a series of words is printed, when the words are printed in colors other than the colors they name. Score C is time of this performance. (In one variant of the task, the words are printed in white, say, against colored backgrounds.)

Noting wide variation in methods of scoring the task, Jensen (1965; dataset JENS02) factor-analyzed the three basic scores A, B, and C together with eleven other scores derived from them, as applied to data from two administrations of the three parts of the Stroop test to 436 college students. It was legitimate to tolerate the experimental dependence inherent in the matrix in order to determine the underlying dimensions. In my reanalysis of the matrix for the first administration, I dropped variables F, I, and J because their intercorrelations among themselves and with other variables approached unity. As did Jensen, I obtained three factors, interpreted as (1) color/print interference, measured best by the formula $(C - A)$, (2) color naming controlled for reading speed, measured best by the formula $(A - B)$, and (3) reading speed, measured best by the score B. Jensen himself recommended the score $A/(A + B)$ for the second factor, but the difference is probably inconsequential.

There has been some debate in the literature (e.g., Hintzman, Carre, Eskridge, Owens, Shaff, & Sparks, 1972) concerning whether the "Stroop effect" is actually a case of interference between the color and print aspects of the stimulus, or a matter of suppressing the highly practiced response to the printed word. Hintzman et al. favor the latter interpretation.

Other datasets give a confusing pattern of results on the correlates of the Stroop effect as measured by any one of several possible scores for it. In analyzing dataset THUR41, Thurstone (1944a) used the score A/C (giving high scores for least interference), but found that this score had such low correlations with his other variables that it was dropped from the analysis. (I did not include it in the reanalysis, for the same reason.)

The earliest use of the Stroop test in a cognitive test battery apparently occurred in a study by Rose (1974), from which I drew datasets ROSE01, ROSE02, and ROSE03 for factor analysis. (These datasets come from administrations on three successive days.) Rose used two scores from the Stroop task: $(C - A)$ and A. This was unfortunate for two reasons: (1) according to Jensen's analysis, score A has high and opposite-signed loadings on Jensen's factors 2 and 3 – that is, it does not control for speed as measured by score B, and (2) these two scores have too much experimental dependence. It might have been more satisfactory if Rose had limited himself to the score $(C - A)$, which is a good measure of the Stroop effect according to Jensen's analysis. Consequently, in each of Rose's datasets, there is a first-order factor loaded about equally on the two scores, with no interpretable loadings for other variables. On the other hand, in each dataset these two scores had the highest loadings on a second-order speed-of-information-processing factor, along with scores on a variety of information-processing tasks. There was no way to assess the specific nature of the Stroop test scores in this dataset.

A similar problem arises in dataset HUNT71, which used the experimentally dependent scores $(C - A)$ and A. The score $(C - A)$, the interference or response suppression score, or in effect a score $(A - C)$ after reflection, appeared on factor 2, interpreted as a Perceptual Speed factor, along with two clerical speed variables and the $(PI - NI)$ score (reflected name identity minus physical identity score) from a version of the Posner task. The score A (color naming speed) had very low communality but appeared, uninterpretably, with a salient loading of only .290 on a factor loaded with scores from the Peterson and Peterson (1959) memory storage task.

The only other dataset with a score – only the score $(C - A)$ in this case – from the Stroop task was LUNN21 (Lunneborg, 1977), where it had low communality and uninterpretable small loadings. At least from the datasets examined, therefore, it is impossible to make any confident report about the nature of the Stroop effect in terms of other factors of cognitive ability. In future research it would be profitable to derive scores on each of the three largely independent factors identified by Jensen (1965) and to use other tasks in which similar interference or response suppression effects appear (see an extensive review of Stroop effects by MacLeod, 1991).

It may be useful to point out that the score A from the Stroop test can be interpreted as a measure of the factor NA (Naming Speed; see Chapter 10). Score B possibly measures factor RS (Reading Speed; see Chapter 5). Note also that B and C scores are both a function of the individual's skill in reading the language in which color names are printed; for an English speaker with no knowledge of Arabic writing, for example, the Stroop effect would be unlikely to occur if color names were printed in Arabic. In fact, the Stroop task has occasionally been used as a measure of competence in reading a language. If the Stroop effect depends on strength of responses, from the standpoint of individual differences it is an epiphenomenon dependent on the practiced strength of responses in factors NA and RS as they function in a particular task (Cohen, Dunbar, & McClelland, 1990).

HOW IS "SPEED" RELATED TO "INTELLIGENCE"?

Having reviewed what evidence is available on the dimensions of ability that exist in the domain of "mental speed," we are now in a position to address the second of the two major issues raised at the beginning of this chapter, namely, how are cognitive speed abilities related to, or indicative of, cognitive abilities in which speed of performance is involved only minimally, or not at all?

We have seen that the dimensionality of cognitive speed is undoubtedly complex. Earlier chapters of this volume have reviewed much evidence that suggests that the dimensionality of what is ordinarily thought of as "intelligence" is likewise complex. It is therefore not possible to give any simple answer to the question of how speed is related to intelligence. I take the view that it is necessary to examine detailed relationships between particular dimensions of cognitive speed and particular dimensions of cognitive ability represented in mental tests purporting to measure "intelligence."

One problem besetting the present discussion is that we have not yet systematically addressed the higher-order structure of cognitive abilities, that is, the evidence as to what broader abilities can be identified, such as the second-order factors postulated by such investigators as Cattell (1971), Horn (1987), and Hakstian and Cattell (1978), or a "general intelligence" or *g* factor, as postulated by Spearman (1927), even though many of our tables report factors identified as *g*, Gf, Gc, etc. The higher-order structuring of cognitive abilities is addressed in Chapter 15. For the present, let us assume that there exists a higher-order structure of abilities roughly similar to what has been described, for example, by Horn (1987). It appears that relations between cognitive speed and level factors can be usefully considered by looking at them at higher-order levels of structure, or with reference to correlations among factors.

Evidence from Studies of Speed/Level Relations

At many points, our earlier discussions of the linear independence of speed and level touched on relations between cognitive speed and intellectual abilities. It is useful to consider again some of the factorial datasets that give evidence on these relations, in particular, datasets showing speed-of-test-performance factors along with factors representing dimensions of level or accuracy of cognitive ability. Some of these datasets were listed in Table 11.4, but Table 11.8 summarizes further information, from such datasets, that is pertinent to the present discussion.

It is evident from the table that correlations between speed and level factors vary considerably, from zero (in the many cases of orthogonal factors) to quite high. The correlations among speed and level factors in datasets THOM11 and THOM12 are the highest obtained; these are for a series of performance tests of intelligence given to ten-year-old children. Other datasets in which fairly high correlations among first-order speed and level factors are found are:

> DAVI01: Verbal Speed with
>   Verbal Reasoning (level):   .548
> HORN01: Broad Speediness with
>   Broad Visualization: .398
> LORD01: Visualization & Quantitative Reasoning Speed with
>   Visualization (level):   −.491
> UNDH11: General Speed with
>   Verbal Fluency: .498

These correlational values, of course, are dependent on the particular rotational methods employed in the reanalysis of the datasets, but they are also possibly dependent on the types of abilities involved and the degree to which the tests underlying level factors are actually speeded, as may be the case for some of the datasets (HORN01, LORD01, and UNDH11). The negative correlation found in dataset LORD01 suggests that high-level performance in visualization and quantitative reasoning is associated with low speed, a finding that has

Table 11.8. *Data on correlations between speed and accuracy factors in selected datasets (see text for explanations)*

Dataset	Intercorrelations of first-order factors and other relevant information
CARR42	All factors are orthogonal. For example, F7 (Speed of Test-Taking) is orthogonal to F5 (Reasoning Level); two scores from Verbal Analogies – No. Completed in a time-limit and No. Correct in unlimited time, are loaded .677 and .507 on these, respectively, and are correlated .188.

DAVI01 *Correlations of first-order factors:*

	O1:F1	O1:F2	O1:F3	O1:F4
O1:F1 Verbal (speed)	1.000	.548	−.111	.431
O1:F2 Verbal Reasoning (level)	.548	1.000	.063	.246
O1:F3 Number (speed)	−.111	.063	1.000	.230
O1:F4 Speed of Reasoning	.431	.246	.230	1.000

A test of Perceptual Speed (Scattered X's) showed no significant correlations with other tests and was not included in the battery analyzed.

DUBO01   Speed and level factors were orthogonal.

FREN11   At the second order, three orthogonal factors:

O2:F1 Speed: Number, Writing
O2:F2 General Speed of Judgment
O2:F3 Gf/Gc dominating Space/VZ, V, MK(Mechanical Knowledge)

HORN01 *Correlations of selected first-order factors:*

	O1:F1	O1:F2	O1:F3	O1:F4	O1:F5
O1:F1 Fluid Intelligence	1.000	.574	.332	.184	.131
O1:F2 Broad Visualization	.574	1.000	.398	.072	.202
O1:F3 Broad Speediness	.332	.398	1.000	−.163	.012
O1:F4 Crystallized Intelligence	.184	.072	−.163	1.000	.421
O1:F5 Broad Fluency	.131	.202	.012	.421	1.000

KYLL01   (Kyllonen, 1985, Study 1)
Speed and level factors at second-order correlated −.05

LORD01 *Correlations of first-order factors:*

	O1:F1	O1:F2	O1:F3	O1:F4	O1:F5	O1:F6	O1:F7
O1:F1 Verbal (level)	1.000	.071	.460	−.046	−.043	−.102	.143
O1:F2 Visualiz'n (level)	.071	1.000	.451	.131	−.193	.255	−.491
O1:F3 RQ (level)	.460	.451	1.000	.237	−.062	.104	−.104
O1:F4 Number (speed)	−.046	.131	.287	1.000	.546	.648	−.305
O1:F5 Perceptual Speed	−.043	−.193	−.066	.546	1.000	.419	.301
O1:F6 Verbal (speed)	−.102	.255	.104	.648	.419	1.000	−.413
O1:F7 VZ & RQ speed	.143	−.491	−.055	−.305	.301	−.413	1.000

At the second order, O2:F1 (General Speed) and O2:F2 (General level) are orthogonal.

Table 11.8 (*cont.*)

Dataset	Intercorrelations of first-order factors and other relevant information

MANG01A *Correlations of selected first-order factors:*

	O1:F1	O1:F2	O1:F3	O1:F4	O1:F5
O1:F1 N & P	1.000	.029	.061	.230	.220
O1:F2 Persistence	.029	1.000	.283	−.103	.057
O1:F3 Reasoning (level)	.061	.283	1.000	.285	.136
O1:F4 Ideational Fluency	.230	−.103	.285	1.000	.320
O1:F5 Writing Speed	.220	.057	.136	.320	1.000

At the second-order, O2:F1 (Broad Speediness) and O2:F2 (Difficult Tasks: Rate of Work and Level) are orthogonal.

THOM11

O1:F1 (Accuracy Scores) & O2:F2 (Rates): $r = .717$ (boys)

THOM12

O1:F1 (Accuracy Scores) & O2:F2 (Rates): $r = .708$ (girls)

UNDH11 *Correlations of first-order factors:*

	O1:F1	O1:F2	O1:F3	O1:F4	O1:F5
O1:F1 Verbal	1.000	.387	.673	.616	.337
O1:F2 Spatial	.387	1.000	.412	.334	.065
O1:F3 Verbal Fluency	.673	.412	1.000	.642	.498
O1:F4 Reasoning	.616	.334	.642	1.000	.310
O1:F5 General Speed	.337	.065	.498	.310	1.000

parallels elsewhere in the literature (e.g., Sternberg, 1977). High performers on visualization and reasoning tasks tend to be more careful, and thus take more time. The finding also suggests that there are wide individual differences in how people handle the tradeoff between speed and accuracy in performing difficult tasks (Lohman, 1989).

On the whole, however, considerable evidence found in the table suggests that at least for adult populations, speed and level factors are generally orthogonal or only minimally correlated. Datasets in which speed and level factors are orthogonal are CARR42, DUBO01, FREN11, KYLL01, LORD01, and MANG01A. This conclusion refers particularly to speed factors defined by rate-of-test-taking measures, or in some cases (e.g., KYLL01) to speed factors defined by latencies of correct responses in computerized tests of traditional psychometric dimensions (verbal ability, reasoning ability, numerical ability, etc.). It is generally consistent with research reviewed earlier in this chapter when the distinctness of speed and level dimensions was considered.

At the same time, it is probably unwise to accept this conclusion finally or unconditionally. Most of the available research studies were unable to take advantage of recent technologies in the construction and administration of psychometric tests. It is entirely possible that relations between speed and level dimensions are much more complex than would appear from the data in Table 11.8. Certainly this field of research is ripe for further investigation. Matters of concern in such research should be:

1.   For what types of cognitive ability dimensions do speed and level measures consistently show correlations significantly different from zero?
2.   What variations in subjects' attitudes and strategies of performance affect correlations between speed and level?
3.   What variations in subject populations (age, sex, etc.) make for differences in speed/level relations?

Evidence from Studies of Reaction Time

The story of how reaction time measures were investigated, in the early days of psychological testing, as possible indicants of intelligence, and then abandoned because of disappointing results has often been recounted (see Chapter 2). Due to the efforts of Eysenck (1979, 1987), Jensen (1979, 1987), Hunt (Hunt, Frost, & Lunneborg, 1973), and others, there has been a resurgence of interest in the possibility that reaction time measures could throw light on the nature of intelligence. P. A. Vernon, who has been one of the more recent contributors to research in this field (Vernon, 1981a, b), has edited a volume (Vernon, 1987a) that presents views and data from a number of authors who have concerned themselves with this possibility. It is beyond our scope to review and critique the many studies of the issue that have appeared over the last decade or so. We can, however, possibly adduce some conclusions from the substantial number of our datasets in which measures of reaction time or latency have been included in batteries for factor analysis. Table 11.9 lists 27 such datasets, with brief summaries of relevant results from these studies.

Factor analysis has the advantage that it focuses attention on detailed relationships between different kinds of reaction time tasks (or ECTs) and different dimensions of cognitive ability, whether at a first-order (primary) factor level or at some higher-order level. Many studies of relations between reaction time measures and cognitive ability measures have relied on one or a small number of measures of cognitive ability – e.g., a standardized test of intelligence or IQ, such as the Wechsler Intelligence Scale, or a test in the Raven Progressive Matrices series, all of which have been regarded by some as "highly g-loaded" (Jensen, 1987, p. 102). The opinion that the Wechsler Intelligence Scale is a good measure of g is based on the fact that its subtests tap a diverse set of abilities that are linked at a higher-order of analysis. The asserted g-loadedness of Raven Progressive Matrix tests needs to be examined in the context of factorial studies employing these tests. Hunt, Frost, and Lunneborg's (1973) claim that reaction time measures are related to general intelligence (with a correlation of approximately $-.3$) was based on a finding that related various reaction time parameters to scores on a college admissions test (the University of Washington Pre-College battery) similar to the College Board Scholastic Aptitude Test (SAT). What needs to be explored further is what aspects of such a test are responsible for such relations. For example, it is known that the SAT is to some extent speeded, because time-limits are used in its administration. Presumably this would also be true of the Washington Pre-College Battery used by Hunt et al. Are the relations between reaction time parameters and the Washington Pre-College Battery, then, due to the speededness of the test, as suggested by Schwartz, Griffin, and Brown (1983), or would the relations continue to hold with an unspeeded level test? Even if a Raven test is administered without a time-limit, as is often the case, does its relation with reaction time parameters depend on a linkage with some particular feature of the Raven test – and thus at the first-order of analysis, or is the linkage rather at a more general, higher order of analysis?

The information contained in Table 11.9 is shown in two columns, one labeled "evidence from first-order factors," and the other "evidence from higher-order factors." It is thus possible to consider linkages of the first type separately from the second type. A linkage of the first type could occur even in a factor solution that is completely at the first order, and not obliquely rotated, but it could also occur for hierarchical factor solutions that have factors at the second or third orders. It would occur if a reaction-time variable has a significant loading *on the same factor* as a psychometric variable. (For present purposes, I use "reaction-time variable" to refer to any variable that employs reaction time, including simple or choice reaction times, or a variable derived from reaction times, such as the NI–PI variable, that is, the difference obtained by subtracting physical-identity (PI) RT from name-identity (NI) RT in the Posner paradigm. I use "psychometric variable" to refer to scores from psychological tests of the more conventional kind, in which speed or reaction time would be reflected, if at all, only in the number of items attempted, or the number of items correct, within a time-limit.) There are circumstances, however, when we would not expect a linkage at the first-order. Suppose, for example, one first-order factor is a reaction-time factor and another is a psychometric factor, and the two factors are substantially correlated upon oblique simple-structure rotation. The hierarchical analysis would produce a second-order factor representing the correlation between the factors, and in its orthogonalized version this second-order factor would show loadings for both the reaction-time and the psychometric variables, and thus a linkage at the second order. The orthogonalized version of the *first* first-order factor would have high or at least salient loadings for the reaction-time variables and vanishing loadings for the psychometric variables, while the orthogonalized version of the *second* first-order factor would have high or at least salient loadings for the psychometric variables and vanish-

Table 11.9. *Evidence on relations of RT variables to psychometric variables and factors (see text for explanations)*

Dataset	Evidence from first-order factors	Evidence from higher-order factors
AFTA01	RT vars. have small, non-salient loadings on a Perceptual Speed factor	None (2nd-order factors are difficult to interpret)
CARL41	Neither DT nor MT load on F3 (CTBS, Raven)	Small linkage between Raven & RT represented in a 2nd-order factor biased toward speed
CHIA01	Intercept (but not slope) variables from Visual & Memory Search tasks show loadings (.264 & −.318) on a factor defined by SAT-M and SAT-V. $N = 30$	(Orthogonal factors)
CLAU01	No RT variables loaded on F3 (Raven, PMA-IQ)	Substantial loadings of F2 (RT) and F3 (Cog. Devt.) vars. on 2nd-order g
CLAU02	No RT vars. loaded on F2 (Raven, Porteus MA)	Substantial loadings of F2 (Cog. Devt.) and F3 (RT) vars. on 2nd-order g
CLAU03	No RT vars. loaded on F2 (Cog. Devt.) but Visual RT loads .459 on F6 (Mirror-Drawing Errors)	Substantial loadings of F2 (Cog. Devt.) and F3 (RT) vars. on 2nd-order g
CLAU04	No RT vars. loaded on F3 (Cog. Devt.)	(3 orders of factors) Slight linkage of RT and psychometric variables on F1 (3rd-order), none on F2 (2nd-order Cog.Devt.)
DETT00	No RT variables load on F2 (Info.Proc'g Accuracy)	F3 (DT) vars. load somewhat on F1 (2nd-order spanning accuracy & speed)
EGAN01	No RT variables load on F3 (Spatial Accuracy)	F3 (Spatial Accuracy) correlates .313 with F2 (latencies). Linkage shown on F1 (general ability?)
FAIR01	No RT variables load on F2:2H	(3 orders of factors) F2:2H correlates .40 with F8 (Speed). Linkage between RT and psychometric vars. shown in F1(g)
FAIR02	No RT vars. (in F5 & F8) load on F2 (Verbal)	2nd-order F1(2H) orthogonal to 2nd-order F6 (speed). Little linkage shown.
FLEI12	RT vars. have no sig. loadings on other factors	Intercorrelations among F2, F3, F4, but on 2nd-order F1, RT loads only .125. Discrim. RT loads .549 (see text for remark)
HUGH01	Posner vars. not loaded on other factors	2nd-order F1 and F4 orthogonal. Linkage between Posner RTs and certain psychometric variables shown in F1.
HUNT71	No sig. loadings of RT vars. on F1 (Reasoning & Verbal); sporadic loadings of psychometric vars. on RT factors	Orthogonal factors
JACK12	—	Linkage between F2 (Language Knowledge, Reading Comp. &

Table 11.9 (*cont.*)

Dataset	Evidence from first-order factors	Evidence from higher-order factors
		Speed) & F3 (Speed of Mental Comparison) shown in 2nd-order F1(2H)
JENS41	Only linkage is loading of .522 for Raven on F1 (Choice DT Slope) but not for Terman Concept Mastery test	(Orthogonal factors)
KRAN01A	No RT variables loaded on F4 (MAB performance sub-tests) or F5 (MAB verbal subtests)	On F1 (*g*?), substantial loadings of all decision variables and factors, as well as F4 (MAB performance subtests) and F5 (MAB verbal subtests).
		On F7 (2nd-order movement time factor orthog. to F1), loadings of MAB subtests ranging from .007 to .330.
		[Author reports multiple $R = .542$ for ECT battery predicting hierarchical *g* of MAB (Multiple Apt. Battery)]
LANS21	No RT vars. loaded on F2 (Digit Span & WPC – Washington Pre-College Composite)	No linkage found
LANS22	WPC highly correlated with RTs but not accuracy in a sentence verification task	Little linkage in F1 (*g*)
LANS31	See text	Little linkage in 2nd-order
PARK01	No loadings of RT vars. on other factors	No linkages
ROBE11	—	Some linkage between speed and accuracy RT vars. in 2nd-order F1 (*g* this battery)
SCHA11	RT vars.: no loadings on other 1st-order factors	No linkages at higher order
THUR41	RT vars.: no loadings on other 1st-order factors	RT variables have moderate loadings on 2nd-order general factor
VERN01	Vars. in F3 (DT – Semantic Tasks): no loadings on other 1st-order factors	Vars. in F3 have moderate loadings on F1 (*g*);
	Vars. in F5 (DT & RT): no loadings on other 1st-order factors, except .283 for DT on F3	Vars. in F5 have moderate loadings on F1 (*g*)
VERN11	Neither F2 nor F3 RT vars. have sig. loadings on F4 (Raven, Figure Copying)	Linkage on F1 (biased toward RT); most F2 & F3 RT vars. have substantial loadings on F1; Raven: .329
VERN21	No sig. loadings of F5 (Inform. Processing Speed) vars. on other 1st-order factors	Substantial linkage of RT of RT & psychometric vars. shown in F1 (*g*)

ing loadings for the reaction time variables. The evidence for linkage between reaction-time variables and psychometric variables would be at the second order, in that both types of variables would have significant loadings on the second-order factor. It is this kind of linkage that is shown in the second column of Table 11.9.

In a number of datasets, linkage is shown (if at all) only at a higher order, that is, in the second column of the table. It is still logically and theoretically possible, however, for linkage to occur both at the first order and at a higher order. This can happen if either a reaction time variable or a psychometric variable is factorially complex, with substantial loadings on both a reaction-time factor and a psychometric factor. (An example occurs in dataset CLAU03, where Visual Reaction time has first-order loadings of .558 on factor 3 (reaction time) and .459 on factor 6 (a difficult-to-interpret factor having salient loadings on a mirror-drawing task and lower-arm speed of movement); it also has a loading of .566 on a second-order general factor.)

I now give further details on the datasets for which information is shown in Table 11.9.

AFTA01: The RT variables are simple and choice reaction time, and they have salient loadings of .716 and .516, respectively, on a factor 7, Reaction Time. They also have small, nonsalient loadings of .301 and .365 on factor 4, interpreted as Perceptual Motor Speed because of salient loadings of scores on the Purdue Pegboard. On a second-order general factor, they have loadings of .092 and .211, respectively, too small to allow inference of linkage, although it is interesting that choice RT has the higher loading.

CARL41: A psychometric factor 3 is defined by scores on the California Test of Basic Skills (CTBS), the Raven, and a Reading test. Because no RT measure (DT, DTSD, DT Slope, MT, MTSD) has any significant loading on this, there is no linkage at the first order. At the second order, DT and the Raven test have loadings of .458 and .348, respectively, on factor 1, interpreted as general motor speed. This could be regarded as representing a weak linkage between a reaction-time measure and a psychometric variable. There is also a possible linkage between the Reading test (but not the CTBS and the Raven) and DT and MT variables on Factor 4, which is another second-order factor, interpreted as general cognitive speed.

CHIA01: As stated in the table, there is a possible, though weak, first-order linkage between intercept variables from Visual and Memory Search tasks and a factor defined by SAT-M and SAT-V. These data are for combined male and female subjects ($N = 30$). When male and female groups ($N = 15$ each) were studied separately, Chiang and Atkinson (1976) reported high multiple R's for predicting SAT-V and SAT-M from task variables (average slopes and intercepts, and memory span), but with quite different patterns of weights for the two groups. In view of the small N's, these results are suspect and hard to interpret; to my knowledge they have not been confirmed. If there is any validity in them, it would imply that factor analysis of batteries using ECT variables should use separate data for males and females (Lohman, 1986; see also discussion of these results by Snow, 1978).

CLAU01, CLAU02, and CLAU03: These datasets were for samples of mentally retarded persons, average age 9, 13, and 22, respectively. The chief psychometric variables were Mental Age derived from an appropriate form of the Thurstone Primary Mental Abilities battery, Mental Age from the Porteus Maze test, and total score on Raven's Matrices, all loading saliently on a factor interpreted as General Cognitive Development. There were no significant linkages at the first order, but linkage was indicated at the second order, in that both the psychometric variables and several RT variables had substantial loadings on a second-order factor 1, interpreted as a general factor.

CLAU04: This dataset had the same variables as the preceding, but was for a sample of "normal" children aged 8–10 in public schools. Except for what has already been described, there was no linkage at the first order. There was a slight linkage of psychometric and RT variables on a third-order factor (g?), but none on a second-order factor of Cognitive Development.

DETT00: This was a battery of numerous ECTs administered by computer to Air Force basic trainees. The only strictly psychometric variable was that labeled FAC, representing principal component scores from the ASVAB battery. It had a modest loading on first-order factor 2, interpreted as Information-Processing Accuracy. No RT variables (loaded on factor 3) loaded on this factor. However, the correlation between oblique factors 2 and 3 was .380, and this was reflected in some linkage of factor 2 and 3 variables on a second-order general factor.

EGAN01: Various computerized two-choice spatial tasks and various psychometric variables were administered to 48 male Navy personnel who had been screened by a battery that included spatial tests. Latencies on Block Rotation, the Guilford–Zimmerman Visualization test, and Spatial Apperception defined a factor 2 interpreted as Spatial Speed. Accuracy scores on these tasks helped define a factor 3 interpreted as Accuracy (especially Spatial). The correlation between oblique factors 2 and 3 was .313 (possibly attenuated due to range restriction), and this was reflected in some linkage on a general ability factor at the second order.

FAIR01: Three orders of factors were found for this battery. At the first order, variables from the Posner task, a Word Categorization task, and simple and choice reaction times defined three speed factors, linked by a second-order factor. Psychometric variables were subtests of the ASVAB (Armed Services Vocational Aptitude Battery), defining first-order Reasoning, Verbal, Numerical, and Technical Knowledge factors. Linkage between RT and psychometric variables occurred chiefly at the third order, all reaction time variables and most psychometric variables having moderate loadings on third-order factor 1, interpreted as a general ability factor.

FAIR02: The RT variables in this battery were not the same as those of dataset FAIR01, but the psychometric variables were the same. Two RT factors were defined, respectively, by slope and intercept variables from the Sternberg memory search task (it may have been unwise to include both slope and intercept variables in the analyzed battery, because of experimental dependence), and were linked at the second order (along with a numerical facility factor) in a factor interpreted as Speed in Laboratory Tasks. This factor, however, was uncorrelated with a second-order factor derived from most of the psychometric variables, and there was little linkage between psychometric and reaction time variables shown on either of the second-order factors.

FLEI12: At the first-order, a factor 4 (Reaction Time) was defined by simple reaction time, rate of back-and-forth arm movement, rotary pursuit, and a Discrimination Reaction Time task (among others). Psychometric variables defined two factors: Perceptual Speed (P) and Mechanical Knowledge (MK). Correlations among these three factors defined a second-order factor 1 (general ability?). Little linkage is shown for simple reaction time since it had a loading of only .125 on factor 1. The Discrimination Reaction Time task, however, had a loading of .549 on this factor, actually greater than its loading on factor 4 (.321). This test presents a fairly difficult discrimination task – responding in one of four directions depending on the relative positions of green and red lights in a visual display. It was developed by the U.S. Air Force and is described by Guilford and Lacey (1947, p. 804). Many Air Force subjects were found to have difficulty understanding the task, and in fact Air Force investigators during World War II developed a special test of subjects' understanding of the task. Eysenck (1987, p. 48) has pointed out that the test had high g-loadings in certain unpublished analyses conducted by R. L. Thorndike, and it also shows a high g-loading (.527) in our own analysis of dataset GUIL46. Contrary to Eysenck's implication that it is the pure speed element in this test that is correlated with g, it is highly likely that the linkage is due to the difficulty in making the decision that is required on each trial.

HUGH01: At the first order, certain RT variables from the Posner task define a first-order factor 2, and an intelligence test and the Raven Progressive Matrices define factor 6. These factors are respectively loaded on second-order factors 1 and 4, which are orthogonal. Some linkage between the Posner variables and the psychometric variables is shown on factor 1, interpreted as general intelligence.

HUNT71: This dataset has certain drawbacks because of the unavailability of the original correlation matrix, and possible undue experimental dependence among some variables. The five orthogonal factors in its authors' Varimax matrix were accepted and not further rotated. Factors 3 and 5 could be interpreted as factors defined by ECTs. No ECT variable shows significant loadings on Factor 1 defined by psychometric variables. At the same time, a few psychometric variables show small, sporadic loadings on ECT factors 3 and 5. I find little if any evidence of linkage between ECT variables and psychometric variables in this dataset.

JACK12: This dataset was developed in a study of processing determinants of reading speed. Factor 2 is a psychometric factor defined by a listening comprehension test, a (probably speeded) verbal aptitude test, and two measures of reading speed. It is correlated .376 with a factor 3 defined by several variables from Posner tasks, and the linkage shows up in loadings of both psychometric variables and Posner task variables on second-order factor 1, interpreted as a general intelligence factor.

JENS41: This dataset was originally analyzed by Jensen (1979), inappropriately, with a single principal component that was claimed to show linkage between RT variables from the Hick paradigm and several psychometric variables. In the reanalysis, I find three orthogonal factors; the only linkage found is for a loading (.565) of the Raven test on a factor defined by several ECT variables from the Hick task. It is not found for the Terman Concept Mastery test or a Digit Span test.

KRAN01A: As indicated above, subtests of the Multidimensional Aptitude Battery (MAB) (Jackson, 1984) formed two first-order factors, factors 4 and 5, classified as GV and GC respectively. These factors and their variables have substantial loadings on a second-order factor that also comprises *decision time* factors and their variables (but not movement time factors and variables). This result may be interpreted to indicate that there is a correlation between average decision time on various tasks and whatever is measured by the psychometric tasks in common – perhaps a *g* factor. Kranzler (1990), using five principal components of the battery of 37 ECT variables, reported a multiple correlation of .542 in predicting a hierarchical *g* factor derived from the MAB, and claimed that this reflected the presence of four undefined components in *g*. Unfortunately, details of this regression that would enable one to understand what aspects of ECT variables are correlated with *g* are not given; it was only asserted that four components contributed to *g*, with the implication that *g* is a complex variable. A more parsimonious interpretation is suggested by the hierarchical analysis: there is a single second-order variable (possibly interpretable as *g*) that to varying extents influences or is involved in performances in both psychometric and ECT tasks (for further discussion of this dataset, see Kranzler & Jensen, 1991a,b; Carroll, 1991a,b).

LANS21: Of three probe RTs obtained – two in a dual task involving memory and one in a control condition – only one (easy recall) showed some small linkage (.213) with other variables, including the Washington Pre-College Composite.

LANS22: At the first order, the Washington Pre-College Composite was highly loaded (.578) on a Speed of Semantic Processing factor 4 defined by RTs on sentence verification tasks, but very little (.160) on an Accuracy of Semantic Processing factor 3 defined by error scores on sentence verification tasks. Little linkage was shown at the second order, however.

LANS31: Despite the use of an impressive number of RT and psychometric variables, there was in general little linkage between speed and accuracy at either the first or the second order, except in the case of spatial ability tasks, where latencies obtained both in laboratory and paper-and-pencil settings had high loadings on a Visualization Speed factor that also had loadings (though somewhat lower) for several standard spatial ability tests, possibly because of the time-limit administration of these tests.

PARK01: At the first order, factor 6 was loaded with several speed or reaction time tests. Psychometric tests were not well represented in the battery, but in any case no linkages between them and reaction time variables could be observed.

ROBE11: This battery did not include psychometric measures, but it yields some information on correlations between speed and accuracy of choice reaction times. Choice RT's were defined by factor 2, and accuracies were defined by factor 5. These factors, in their oblique versions, were correlated .137, and this correlation was reflected in some small linkages on a second-order factor of general ability that was biased toward speed.

SCHA11: At the first order, factor 7 was defined saliently only by a single simple reaction-time variable that had no loadings on other factors, and there were no linkages at a second order.

THUR41: At the first order, factor 3 was defined chiefly by two reaction-time variables (RT to light, sound). In its oblique version, this factor correlated highest (.201) with a spatial ability factor, and some small linkages were observable at the second order.

VERN01: This dataset was developed by P. A. Vernon (1981a) to study relations between RT variables and the subtests of the Wechsler Adult Intelligence Scale. The sample consisted of 100 university students. At the first order of the reanalysis, there were two RT factors. One (factor 5) had substantial loadings (respectively, .678 and .676) for Mean Movement Time and Mean Decision Time from the Hick Paradigm. (This result contrasts, incidentally, with the results in dataset KRAN01, where decision time and movement time variables appeared on different factors.) The other (factor 3) had salient loadings for the following variables:

Mean RT: Posner Syn–Ant (with Memory Search)	.817
Mean RT: Memory Search (with Posner Syn–Ant)	.793
Mean RT: Posner Physical (with Memory Search)	.770
Mean RT: Memory Search (with Posner Physical)	.753
Mean RT: Memory Search (only)	.742
Mean RT: Posner Physical (only)	.710
Mean RT: Posner Syn–Ant (only)	.689
Hick task: Slope of DT re bits	.400

The first four variables here were from dual tasks in which two paradigms were administered nearly simultaneously; for example, a target set of digits was presented for memorization, then a pair of words for the Posner task (to which a response was given), then the probe digit for a delayed memory search task (to which a response was given). The next three variables were for tasks given in isolation, and the last variable was a slope variable from the Hick paradigm.

In their oblique versions, these two factors correlated only .139. There were two psychometric factors, one (factor 2) defined by most of the WAIS subtests, and the other (factor 4) defined by WAIS Information and Vocabulary. With factor 2, the two RT factors (factors 5 and 3) correlated .307 and .380, respectively. With factor 4, they correlated .061 and .196, respectively. It is noteworthy that the RT factors correlated with the majority of the WAIS subtests more highly than they did with WAIS Information and Vocabulary. Note also that factor 3 (Posner and memory search tasks) correlated more highly with WAIS factors than did factor 5 (DT and MT from the Hick paradigm). The factor intercorrelations were reflected in linkages shown on a second-order general intelligence factor (factor 1).

VERN11: This dataset was obtained with a sample of 46 mildly mentally retarded young adults. At the first order of analysis, there were two factors measuring DTs in the Hick task: (1) factor 2, essentially simple reaction time and average movement time; (2) factor 3, choice reaction time (DT's from 4-button and 8-button tasks, DTSD, and slope of DT re bits). The psychometric factor was loaded with a Figure Copying test and the Raven Progressive Matrices test. These factors were all clearly defined, with essentially no overlap. Factors 2 and 3 (both from the Hick paradigm) correlated .636. They correlated with factor 4 .377 and .263, respectively. Note that the correlation was higher for simple RT than for choice RT. These correlations resulted in linkages between RT variables and psychometric variables on a second-order general factor, particularly for the 2-button DT (loading = .885) and for the Raven test (loading .329). However, linkages were zero or minimal for DT Slope and the Figure Copying test.

VERN21: With respect to design and variables used, this dataset is similar to VERN01; the sample, however, was 106 students at a vocational college, intended to include a wider variation in general ability levels. At the first order of analysis, four factors were extracted, only one (factor 5 in the hierarchical matrix) being loaded with speed-of-information-processing variables. This is probably due to the circumstance that there was only one variable from the Hick paradigm, and thus a Simple & Choice Reaction Time factor for the Hick paradigm could not be isolated and distinguished from a factor for speed of information processing variables from Posner and memory search paradigms. None of the Hick or speed-of-information variables had a significant loading on any of the three factors identified for ASVAB subtests. In oblique versions, factor 5 correlated with the three ASVAB factors as follows:

with factor 2 (ASVAB Quantitative Reasoning)   .194
with factor 3 (ASVAB Verbal and Information)   .188
with factor 4 (ASVAB Number and Coding Speed)   .196

A second-order general factor showed clear linkages between speed of information processing variables and the ASVAB subtests. The information processing variables had loadings on the second-order factor that ranged between .257 and .373, except that the Hick simple and choice DT loaded only .103.

A Cautionary Note

Although we find considerable evidence to suggest that certain variables from ECTs (elementary cognitive tasks) are correlated with psychometrically defined cognitive abilities, most of this evidence is at least problematic. It is known (Bittner, Carter, Kennedy, Harbeson & Krause, 1986) that many ECTs require considerable practice before they "stabilize" in the sense of producing unchanging intertrial correlations and homogeneous variances, apart from measurement errors. Many of the ECTs employed in the above-reviewed studies are listed by Bittner et al. as requiring stabilization times of many minutes. Yet few if any of the studies permitted enough trials for the ECT variables to stabilize. It is entirely conceivable that in a study like that of Kranzler (1990), for example, the loadings of ECT decision time variables on a second-order general factor could be attributable to individual differences in the rate and degree to which subjects were able to adapt to the requirements of any given ECT. If this is the case, one might expect the second-order factor loadings to decrease markedly with increasing practice and repeated trials. The interpretation would be that *adapting* to the task, rather than performance on it, is what is related to general intelligence.

On the other hand, it has been argued (Schwartz, 1981) that performance on practiced skills (such as those involved in ECTs) is more likely to be correlated with scores on psychometric tests than are performance measures obtained on new skills, on the ground that overlearned, automatized skills are more likely to reflect the limits of an individual's abilities. Appropriate research is needed to resolve this problem.

SUMMARY

1. *Speed*, or time or rate of performance, and *level* or accuracy of response are two logically distinguishable aspects of task performance. A speed ability has to do with the rate at which tasks of a specified kind and difficulty are performed, while a level ability has to do with the level of task difficulty at which an individual can perform with a specified amount of accuracy (for example, at a liminal or threshold accuracy of 50 percent), given an adequate amount of time to exhibit level of performance.

2. Any model of task or test performance must take into account both speed

and level aspects, as well as matters of motivation, persistence, and tendency to guess, to omit items, or to abandon attempts at solution. A number of models of task performance are available, but have seldom been employed to create variables for factor-analytic studies of the speed–level problem.

3. When tests are administered with a time-limit on performance, test scores (number correct) can reflect varying amounts of variance due to speed and to level, depending on the amount of time permitted. Speed can thus be an influential and disturbingly misleading confound in the factor analysis of relationships among test scores. Ideally, test performance should be evaluated with reference to (1) the time taken to perform each item or task and (2) the quality or accuracy of the response. The availability of computers for test administration should make this ideal more readily attainable for many psychological traits (Howell, 1978; Hunt & Pellegrino, 1985).

4. Terms such as *speed* and *power* are often incorrectly used in referring to the nature of tests and test scores, in that they do not communicate the actual conditions under which tests are administered or the meaning of test scores. For example, it has often been assumed that because speeded tests (tests given with a time-limit) often have substantial or even high correlations with power tests of the same trait given in unlimited time, they measure the same trait to the same degree. In actuality, a speeded test measures a composite of speed and level abilities, while a test given in unlimited time is more likely to be a pure measure of a level ability. The correlation between a speeded test and a test given in unlimited time is therefore artifactually high because of the overlap of the level variance in both.

5. Empirically, pure (or nearly pure) measures of speed and level abilities tend to have very low or even zero intercorrelations. This is not always the case, however. Research has yet to determine for what traits and under what conditions the correlations between speed and level are significantly different from zero. One possibility is that for traits that involve the solving of problems whose solutions can be easily evaluated by the problem solver, the correlation between speed and level can be other than zero.

6. In the whole spectrum of cognitive abilities, some can be classified as characteristically *level* abilities, while others can be classified as characteristically *speed* abilities. The present chapter presents tentative classifications, in this respect, of the major factors that have been identified in factorial studies of cognitive performances.

7. Number ability or numerical facility is, at least in most adult populations, characteristically a speed ability, in that most persons adequately exposed to education and training in basic numerical operations (addition, subtraction, etc.) can perform simple numerical operations correctly if given unlimited time to do so, but differ widely in the time they require for correct performance. In this case, speed is likely at least in part to be a function of degree and recency of practice.

8. The speed factors associated with the major dimensions of level abilities may be thought of as factors of "rate of test taking," but apparently, rates of test taking for different types of ability tend to have low intercorrelations. Nevertheless, their intercorrelations may be high enough to allow the inference that they are linked in a "general speed of test taking" or "broad speediness" factor at a second order of analysis. As yet, research findings on this matter are not sufficient to permit drawing clear generalizations. It is abundantly evident, however, that cognitive tests of level abilities given with time-limits that do not permit most individuals to attempt all items are seriously biased against individuals with low rates of test performance.

9. It appears that reaction times obtained in various kinds of elementary cognitive tasks (ECTs) define a number of speed abilities associated with the stages of information processing in these tasks. Research has not yet been sufficient to clearly define the structure of these abilities, nor the ways in which they operate in the performance of elementary cognitive tasks, although available studies provide useful suggestions on these matters. These reaction time or speed abilities appear to have small but significant correlations with certain level abilities. The size of the correlations appears to be related to the complexity of information processing. For example, ECTs involving processes of stimulus comparison and use of complex decision rules may have higher correlations with level abilities than those involving simple reaction time or very simple decisions. The linkage between reaction times and level abilities is more likely to occur at a higher level of analysis, that is, with reference to broad abilities such as fluid intelligence, or general intelligence, rather than with reference to highly specific, "primary" abilities (Smith & Stanley, 1983, 1987). In any case, the size of these relations is relatively low, with correlations seldom exceeding about .4 in magnitude (accounting for 16% of the variance in each measure).

10. In light of the evidence, my view on the role of speed in intelligence (to the extent that it can be regarded as a single entity) is as follows: Intelligence is chiefly a *level* ability, in that it indicates the level of task difficulty and complexity that is attained or attainable by an individual at a particular point of time or stage of development, when the individual is given adequate time to exhibit that level of mastery. Individuals differ in the time that they require to perform intellectual tasks; these times generally have a low or even zero correlation with levels of intelligence. However, rates of performing certain elementary cognitive tasks appear to have small but significant correlations with intelligence levels. More intelligent individuals tend to perform such tasks somewhat faster, *on the average*, than less intelligent individuals, but there are wide variations in performance times at all levels of intelligence. The correlations are not sufficiently high to justify any hope that rates of performance on elementary cognitive tasks could be used as indicants of intelligence level. As quoted at the head of this chapter, Edward L. Thorndike's "principle" that "other things being

equal, the more quickly a person produces the correct response, the greater is his intelligence" essentially reflects a societal judgment concerning the value of high intelligence combined with quickness of response or problem solving. It merely suggests that persons who combine a high level of intelligence with quickness of performance are likely to be more efficient in achieving cognitive goals than persons who cannot exhibit quickness of response. The "principle" is not to be regarded as a statement of any scientific fact or result.

12 Abilities in the Domain of Knowledge and Achievement

*V:ed subdivides into v and n, which branch
into the various linguistic and
mathematical–scientific subjects. Each such
subject, it may be assumed, would yield its
own small group factor if appropriately
investigated.*

Philip E. Vernon (1961)

The datasets for the present survey were selected with an eye to their relevance for the study of basic cognitive abilities and aptitudes. There was less interest in recovering information about tests of special achievements, such as achievements in various subjects studied in school. Indeed, in many instances variables that obviously measured such achievements were dropped from the correlation matrices before factor analysis, in order to focus attention on data for cognitive ability tests. But this was not done in all cases, and consequently some of the factors identified in my analyses can be interpreted as measures of general or special achievements. Partly as a matter of record and for reference purposes, but also for their intrinsic interest, they are considered in the present chapter.

It is hard to draw the line between factors of cognitive abilities and factors of cognitive achievements. Some will argue that *all* cognitive abilities are in reality learned achievements of one kind or another. Such an argument is difficult to counter, because it is obvious that the performances required on even the most general tests of intelligence depend on at least some learnings – learnings of language and its uses, of commonly used symbols such as numbers and digits, or of procedures for solving various kinds of problems. Currently, cognitive psychologists (e.g., Anderson, 1983) frequently appeal to a distinction between *declarative* and *procedural* knowledge. Essentially, declarative knowledge has to do with knowledge of facts and propositions: knowledge *that* such and such is the case. Procedural knowledge has to do with knowledge about *how* things are done, or about *how* tasks are properly and successfully performed. Any analysis of the tasks set in cognitive ability tests would inevitably deal with both declarative and procedural knowledge aspects of those tasks. Individual differences shown in any cognitive ability task refer, at least in part, to differences in the extent to which persons have acquired and can demonstrate the declarative and procedural knowledges required in such a task.

Rather than trying to draw a hard and fast line between cognitive abilities and achievements, it seems best to conceptualize a continuum that extends from the most general abilities to the most specialized types of knowledges. In the domain

510

of reasoning, for example, the factor here designated I (Induction) appears to tap a very generalized ability to notice similarities and differences between stimuli and to make inferences about the rules and regularities that govern a given series of instances. This factor stands near one end of the continuum between ability and achievement. Near the other end would stand, for example, ability in mathematics. The field of mathematics – particularly in its more advanced manifestations – concerns highly specialized regularities involving the properties of numbers and certain other symbolic systems. A test of achievement in mathematics exhibits the extent to which individuals have learned these regularities (including both declarative and procedural knowledges) and can use them in solving mathematical problems. Similarly, the factor that has been designated RG (Reasoning) has to do with elementary processes of reasoning from premises, and would stand near the ability end of the continuum, while a test of competence in formal symbolic logic would be a measure of highly specialized knowledge.

Such contrasts might be drawn in any one of the domains of ability that have been considered in this volume. In the domain of language abilities, for example, the generalized ability refers to one's knowledge of, and competence in, the use of the native language. But it seems to be correlated with the acquisition of general information about the world, its history, current events, and many topics of general interest. Each area of information, however, has its specialized aspects, embraced in specialized disciplines such as history, political science, physics, etc., or topical areas such as entertainment, sports, geography, current events, etc., and one could expect that individuals differ enormously in the particular disciplines or topical areas in which they could show knowledge.

Some years ago, Skager (1961) demonstrated that individual difference factors (as would be found by factor analysis of relevant data) could be "created" by exposing individuals differentially to different learning experiences. Consider the following thought experiment: Suppose we took a sample of individuals and divided it randomly into four groups. Each group would then receive instruction in a different subject-matter unknown to them and to all the other groups. At the end of the instructional period, all groups would be tested with at least two or three tests of each of the subject-matters. Undoubtedly, a factor analysis of the battery of tests would disclose four factors, one for each of the subject-matters. Possibly the factors would be somewhat correlated because a general learning ability might affect achievement in all four groups, but the four factors would be distinct or – in the language of factor analysis – linearly independent.

Any culture or society, in effect, conducts this kind of experiment – a "natural experiment" that is not as systematic as what our thought experiment might be, but an experiment nevertheless – in the sense that individuals in any culture or society have differential experiences, both because of the different circumstances in which they find themselves and because of the different choices they make about schooling, work, hobbies, travel, etc. To a considerable extent, the "factors" that arise from the analysis of psychological and educational test data, as considered in the present volume, can be interpreted as indicating the different kinds of learnings, achievements, and experiences that individuals in our culture have. As noted in Chapter 4, Table 4.1, the datasets examined in this survey come from at least nineteen different countries; although these countries diverge considerably in their cultures, it would appear that those cultures have many common aspects, to the extent that the same kinds of basic cognitive abilities can be discerned in all of them. For discussion of the possibility that different cultures develop different abilities, see Irvine and Berry (1983, 1988). For further discussion of the idea that factors can be created by the differential experiences of people, see Carroll (1962c).

The fact that the differentiation of factors comes about in part because of the operation of differential experiences of individuals does not exclude the possibility that genetic factors also play a part in this differentiation. Reviewing the evidence for genetic sources of special cognitive abilities, Plomin, DeFries, and McClearn (1990, pp. 362ff.) conclude that there are genetic influences on (at least) verbal, spatial, and perceptual speed abilities that go beyond those on general intelligence or IQ. To the extent that such genetic influences exist, this may also explain the fact that such influences can be detected in measures of academic performance. It is often observed that individuals who are gifted in verbal performances, for example, are not necessarily talented in mathematics and science, and vice versa. Verbal performances apparently depend upon a somewhat different set of basic aptitudes from those affecting mathematical performances. Behavioral genetics research is as yet not far enough advanced to yield clear statements on the genetics of special abilities, in part because studies have not yet taken sufficient account of knowledge about dimensions of ability (as set forth in this volume, for example), but one can conceive mechanisms whereby individuals who show early promise in a special field, because of genetic endowments, are more likely to pursue that field and develop their talents in it.

In recent years there has been much interest in studying what are the characteristics of "expertise" in a particular subject-matter. What differentiates, for example, the performances of "novices" or early learners of physics from those of "experts" in physics? (See, e.g., Larkin, McDermott, Simon, & Simon, 1980; Chi, Glaser, & Farr, 1988.) One technique that has yielded promising results for this question is that of protocol analysis (Ericsson & Simon, 1984), where there is an attempt to elicit the thought processes of individuals solving problems. As far as I am aware, there have been no factor-analytic studies using such techniques. The variables employed in the factorial studies considered here are generally quite conventional tests of school achievement; the presumption would be, at least, that experts would make far higher scores on such tests than novices. At the same time, it seems that novices and experts can differ markedly in the cognitive abilities and strategies they use in solving problems; this would not necessarily be revealed in factor-analytic studies.

FACTORS OF KNOWLEDGE AND ACHIEVEMENT

In considering the factor-analytic evidence on the differentiation of achievements, we must take into account, as always, the composition of factorial batteries – whether the battery is adequately designed to show such differentiation. Some batteries, for example, have only enough variables to show that school achievements constitute a factor separate from one or more basic cognitive abilities. Other batteries, however, have enough variables to define each of several factors of knowledge or school achievement.

Table 12.1 lists 127 factors of knowledge and achievement identified in 87 datasets included in the present survey. For convenience, they are classified into five groups:

1. General school achievement. Factors are classified here if they cover a range of school subjects, or indicate the overall level of accomplishment in school.
2. Verbal information and knowledge. Factors are classified here if they indicate level and range of knowledge in one or more aspects of verbal and humanistic disciplines such as English, history, social studies, etc., or very general information as might be acquired in any of many ways.
3. Information and knowledge, mathematics and science. Factors are classified here if they indicate level and range of knowledge in mathematics and/or science, or related topics.
4. Technical and mechanical knowledge. Factors are classified here if they indicate level of knowledge and competence in such specialized areas as automotive mechanics, shopwork, or electronics, or more generally, in comprehension of simple mechanics and mechanical principles.
5. Knowledge of behavioral content. The term *behavioral content* is to be understood in the sense in which it was used by Guilford, as referring to "information, essentially nonverbal, involved in human interactions, where awareness of attention, perceptions, thoughts, desires, feelings, moods, emotions, intentions, and actions of other persons and of ourselves is important" (Guilford, 1967, p. 77). In Guilford's Structure-of-Intellect model, behavioral content was one of the four types of content that were presumed to interact with products and operations (figural, symbolic, and semantic being the other three). I regard behavioral content as constituting a specialized type of acquired knowledge. (The term *behavioral content* is not very satisfactory, but I can think of no other more satisfactory one; I therefore rely on usage established by Guilford. Some readers may prefer to use the term *personal–social*, corresponding to Gardner's (1983) discussion of what he calls "personal intelligences.")

I discuss each of these groups in turn. There is some evidence in the table for differentiation of factors within and between groups, but in general the design of datasets in this domain has failed to focus on such differentations.

Factors of General School Achievement (A0, A1, A2, AS, L6)

Symbols for factors of general school achievement are as follows:
A0: General school achievement (as indicated by average grades, class ranks, and the like).

Table 12.1. *127 factors of achievement and knowledge in 87 datasets*

Dataset	Codes[a] D C	A	T	M/F	Factor group[b] 1 Schl	2 Verb	3 Math	4 Tech	5 Beh.	Symbol, description
ALLI02	'60U	19	2	1				4		MK: Tech. Judgment
ALLI03	'60U	19	2	1				8		MK: Mech. Knowledge
BOLT11	'73U	19	E	3		5				KF: Signing & Fingerspelling
BUND11	'67U	19	6	1		2				K0: Verbal Knowledge
CANI01	'62U	16	6	2			6			KM: Math. Knowledge
"	"	"	"	"			7			KM: Math. Knowledge
"	"	"	"	"			8			KM: Math. Knowledge
CHRI01	'58U	19	2	1				8		MK: Tech. Knowledge
"	"	"	"	"		12				K0: Verb. Information
CORN01	'83U	71	1	3					5	BC: Beh. Cognition
CORY01	'77U	21	2	1				10		MK: Tech. Knowledge
CRAW01	'76C	14	1	3	3					A0: School Achvt.
CURE11	'68U	16	6	1				8		MK: Tech. Knowledge
CURE12	'68U	16	6	2			9			KM: Math. Knowledge
DEVR02	'74U	5	9	3	3					A1: Tested Achvt.
FAIR01A	'84U	19	2	3				9		MK: Tech. Knowledge
FAIR02	'84U	19	2	3				4		MK: Tech. Knowledge
FAVE01	'79U	9	6	3					2	BC: Beh. Cognition
"	"	"	"	"					3	BD: Diverg. Beh. Production
FEDE02	'80U	21	2	3				7		MK: Tech. Knowledge
FLAN01	'64U	17	1	1			3			KM: Math. Knowledge
"	"	"	"	"		4				EU: English Usage
FLEI12	'54U	19	2	1				3		MK: Tech. Judgment
FREN11	'57U	18	3	3				10		MK: Tech. Knowledge
FRUC21	'52U	21	2	1				7		MK: Tech. Knowledge
GUIL17	'52U	21	3	1				6		MK: Mech. Knowledge

Study	Yr	N	(1)	(2)	(3)	(4)	(5)	(6)	(7)	Measure
GUIL32	'47U	17	1	1			3			MK: Mech. Judgment
GUIL32A	'47U	21	3	1			2			MK: Mech. Judgment
GUIL33	'47U	21	3	1			3			MK: Mech. Knowledge
GUIL34	'47U	21	3	1			4			MK: Mech. Judgment
GUIL35	'47U	21	3	1			9			MK: Mech. Knowledge
GUIL38	'47U	21	3	1			2			MK: Mech. Judgment
"	"	"	"	"			5			MK: Tech. Knowledge
GUIL39	'47U	21	3	1		6	7			KM: Math. Knowledge
"	"	"	"	"			5			MK: Mech. Knowledge
GUIL41	'47U	21	3	1			4			MK: Mech. Knowledge
GUIL42	'47U	21	3	1			2			MK: Mech. Judgment
GUIL43	'47U	21	3	1						MK: Mech. Judgment
"	"	"	"	"	5					KA: Info., Aviation
GUIL44	'47U	21	3	1	3					K2: Verbal Info.
"	"	"	"	"		4				KM: Math. Background
"	"	"	"	"	6					KA: Info., Aviation
GUIL45	'47U	21	3	1	4					KA: Info., Aviation
"	"	"	"	"			5			MK: Mech. Judgment
GUIL46	'47U	21	3	1			9			KA: Info., Aviation
GUST11A	'84S	11	1	3	10					MK: Mech. Knowledge
"	"	"	"	"						A6: Verbal Achvt.
HAKS01	'74C	24	1	1		12				A3: Math Achvt.
HEND01	'69U	16	6	3			25			MK: Mech. Knowledge
"	"	"	"	"					2	BD: Diverg. Behav. Production
"	"	"	"	"					4	BD: Diverg. Behav. Production
"	"	"	"	"					6	BC: Behav. Cognition
"	"	"	"	"					8	BD: Diverg. Behav. Production
"	"	"	"	"					9	BC: Behav. Cognition
HOLM11	'66U	16	K	3			6			MK: Mech. Knowledge
HOLT11	'71U	21	2	1			6			MK: Tech. Knowledge
JEFF11	'57U	16	$	3			3			MK: Tech. Judgment
KELL01	'64U	22	3	1			10			MK: Mech. Judgment
LUCA01	'53U	21	3	1		11				KM: Math. Knowledge
MCGU01	'61U	12	1	1				3		A1: Tested Achvt.
MCGU02	'61U	12	1	2				2		A1: Tested Achvt.

Table 12.1 (*cont.*)

Dataset	Codes[a]				Factor group[b]					Symbol, description
	D C	A	T	M/F	1 Schl	2 Verb	3 Math	4 Tech	5 Beh.	
MEEK01	'71U	14	1	1	7					A1: Tested Achvt.
NIHI01	'64U	16	8	3	13					A1: Tested Achvt.
NIHI02	'64U	16	8	3	6					A1: Tested Achvt.
OLSO51	'66U	14	E	3		2				KF: Fingerspelling
"	"	"	"	"		6				LP: Lipreading
OSUL01	'65U	16	6	3					4	BC: Beh. Knowledge
PARA03	'69U	5	1	3		3				KO: Know. Objects
PARA08	'69U	10	1	3		4				KO: Know. Objects
PARK01	'60U	19	T	1		7				K2: Cultural Info.
PEDU01	'80I	10	1	3	3					A2: Rated Achvt.
"	"	"	"	"	4					A1: Tested Achvt.
PROG01	'71U	7	1	3		2				KO: Know. Objects
"	"	"	"	"		6				KO: Know. Objects
PROG11	'71U	7	1	3	3					A1: Tested Achvt.
"	"	"	"	"	4					A2: Rated Achievement
"	"	"	"	"			5			A3: Math. Achievement
PROG12	'71U	9	1	3			3			A3: Math. Achievement
"	"	"	"	"			4			A4: Rated Math. Achvt.
ROFF11	'52U	21	3	1				6		MK: Mech. Knowledge
SATT11	'79E	11	6	3			2			A3: Math. Achievement
"	"	"	"	"		3				A5: Geography Achvt.
"	"	"	"	"		4				A6: English Achvt.
SAUN21	'60U	18	6	1		2				K0: Gen. Information
"	"	"	"	"		3				K0: Gen. Information
"	"	"	"	"		5				K0: Gen. Information
"	"	"	"	"		6				K2: Cultural Info.
"	"	"	"	"		7				K0: Gen. Information

Code	Year									Description
SCHU00	'62U	40	4	3		6				KO: Know. Objects
SHAY01	'67U	14	1	1			3	(3)		K1: Science Info.
"	"	"	"	"		4	5			A6: English Achvt.
"	"	"	"	"						A3: Math. Achievement
SHAY02	'67U	14	1	2		6				A6: English Achvt.
"	"	"	"	"		7				K2: Cultural Info.
"	"	"	"	"		8				EU: English Usage
"	"	"	"	"			10	(10)		K1: Science Info.
"	"	"	"	"			11			A3: Math. Achvt.
SISK01	'39U	18	A	1			2			A7: Science Achvt.
"	"	"	"	"			4			A8: Hygiene/Drawing
"	"	"	"	"			5			A9: Woodwork/Geometry
SLAT01	'40E	18	A	1				2		MK: Mech. Knowledge
SPEA02	'62A	11	6	2		5				A6: Eng. Sch'l Marks
SPEA31	'77A	11	6	1		4				EU: Eng. Punctuation
SPEA32	'77A	11	6	2		2				EU: Eng. Punctuation
SPEA33	'77A	11	O	1		7				EU: Eng. Punctuation
SPEA34	'77A	11	O	2		4				EU: Punctuation/Perc. Speed.
STAK01	'61U	12	1	3	10					A0: School Grades
STEP01B	'72U	12	%	3	3					A1: Tested Achvt. & Wechsler Verbal IQ
TAYL31	'75C	6	1	3		4				KO: Know. Objects
TENO01	'69U	15	1	3						BC: Beh. Cognition
THUR71	'49U	16	$	1				8	5	MK: Mech. Judgment
TILT11	'53U	9	6	3	1					L6: Learning Gains
VAND61	'78U	17	1	3				4		MK: Tech. Knowledge
VERY01	'67U	19	6	1			2			A3: Math. Achvt.
WEDE01	'47E	14	1	2		2			2	BC: Beh. Judgments
"	"	"	"	"					5	BC: Beh. Judgments
WEIS11	'55U	15	M	3			3			A3: Geometry Achvt.
"	"	"	"	"			5			A3: Geometry Info.
"	"	"	"	"			14			A3: Alg. Computing Speed
WERD01	'58S	14	6	1			6			KM: Math. Knowledge

Table 12.1 (*cont.*)

Dataset	Codes[a]				Factor group[b]					Symbol, description
	D C	A	T	M/F	1 Schl	2 Verb	3 Math	4 Tech	5 Beh.	
WILL11	'75C	10	*	1		3				K0: Wechsler Info. & Arithmetic
WOLF11	'85U	17	1	3	6					AS: Curriculum Level
"	"	"	"	"	7					A0: School Achvt.
WOLI01	'65U	17	1	1	5					A0: School Achvt.
WOOD13	'77U	6	1	3		2				K0: Verbal Knowledge
WOOD18	'77U	30	1	3		2				K0: Verbal Knowledge
WOTH01	'90U	21	1	3				14		MK: Tech. Knowledge
WRIG21	'58U	15	8	1			2			KM: Math. Knowledge

[a]Codes: D(date), C(country), A(age), T(sample type), M/F(1 = male, 2 = female; 3 = both); see Appendix A for further information on codes.

[b]Factor Groups:

1: School achievement, general and specific subjects
2: Verbal information & knowledge
3: Information & knowledge, mathematics & science
4: Technical and mechanical knowledge
5: Knowledge of "behavioral content"

Entries in these columns are factor numbers in hierarchical matrices in Appendix B.

A1: School achievement as reflected in standardized achievement tests.
A2: School achievement as rated by teachers.
AS: Curriculum level (academic, general, vocational, etc.).
L6: Learning Gains (in dataset TILT11).

The seventeen token factors classified here occur for datasets in which the variables measuring school achievement are not sufficiently diverse or clustered to define separate areas of such achievement. For example, factor 3 (coded A0) of dataset CRAW01, for a group of ninth-grade students in a high school in British Columbia, is saliently loaded with school marks (teachers' grades) in science (.620), social studies (.600), English (.553), and mathematics (.545). A vocabulary test has a nonsalient loading on it of .236.

Some of the datasets (CRAW01, STAK01, WOLF11, WOLI01) employ school grades as the achievement variables; others (DEVR02, MCGU01, MCGU02, MEEK01, NIHI01, STEP01B) employ scores on standardized educational achievement tests at appropriate grade levels. Interestingly, two studies (PEDU01 and PROG11) employ as variables both grades or teachers' ratings *and* scores on achievement tests. In both instances, the grades and achievement test scores define linearly independent factors, but of course the factors are highly correlated, as would be expected. In dataset PEDU01, for example, the correlation is .752 and the two factors (coded A1 and A2 respectively) define a second-order factor of school achievement. This is evidence that assessments of school achievement are somewhat different depending on whether achievement is evaluated by teachers or by standardized paper-and-pencil achievement tests. Obviously each kind of assessment has errors peculiar to it; possibly a weighted combination of the two (as indicated by the second-order factor loadings in dataset PEDU01) would be a more construct-valid measure of achievement. See Pedulla, Airasian, and Madaus (1980) for further discussion.

Dataset TILT11 (Tilton, 1953) consists of a set of measures of gains in achievement for various school subjects over grades four to five. The analysis indicates that at least on a statistical basis these reflect the operation of a single factor (coded L6). In other words, gains tend to be similar or proportional in all subjects.

In a number of instances (especially in datasets DEVR02, MCGU01, MCGU02, MEEK01, PEDU01, PROG11, and STEP01B), school achievement variables are accompanied on the same achievement factors with measurements of intelligence, IQ, or various cognitive ability tests. There are a number of possible explanations for this: (1) the battery is not sufficiently diverse to define achievement factors separate from cognitive ability measures at the first-order level; (2) some cognitive ability tests reflect learned achievements in school-taught subject matters; or (3) school achievement is correlated with cognitive ability to the maximum possible given the reliabilities of the measurements. The weight of evidence is that the third explanation is less probable than the other two.

Dataset WOLF11 comes from a study (Wolfle, 1985) of determinants of postsecondary educational attainment among whites and blacks, based on data from the National Longitudinal Study of the high school class of 1972. Data were available, for 6825 whites and 433 blacks, on fathers' occupations, fathers' and mothers' educations, two tests of ability (mathematics and reading), and student grades and curriculum levels, for statistical prediction of a measure of post-secondary educational attainment. Wolfle tested path models for this prediction and concluded that "the process of educational attainment is *not* different for blacks and whites" (p. 516). I was curious whether a conventional factor analysis of the data (presented by Wolfle in the form of a variance-covariance matrix in his Table A, for whites, and Table B, for blacks) would present a structure consistent with Wolfle's path model. My analysis was conducted, however, only for whites. Exploratory factor analysis was performed on the correlation matrix reduced from the variance-covariance matrix; it yielded four correlated first-order factors: fathers' occupational and educational level, mothers' occupational and educational level, student curriculum level (i.e., academic vs. other), and student grades. At the second-order level, the first two of these factors defined a parental background factor and a general student achievement level factor. These in turn were correlated in such a way as to define a single third-order factor of combined background and achievement level on which all variables had substantial loadings. This structure appeared to be consistent with Wolfle's model, although it may not have been as revealing as Wolfle's path analysis. Postsecondary educational attainment was loaded chiefly (.500) on the third-order background/achievement factor, and secondarily (.353) on the second-order student achievement factor, in addition to small but probably significant loadings on two of the first-order factors (.133, fathers' occupation/education; .292, curriculum level).

Of interest in the study of the dimensionality of school achievement is the fact that student achievement was shown to be composed of two factors: curriculum level (academic vs. other) and student grades. In a large-scale study such as this, it is important to note that grades may not mean the same thing in different curricula.

Factors of Information and School Achievement in the Verbal Domain (A5, A6, EU, K0, K2, KA, KE, KF, KO, LP)

Thirty-seven token factors were classified here. They can be subclassified into further areas:

Knowledge of English and its conventions, particularly in writing and composition (A6: English achievement; EU: Knowledge of English usage, punctuation, etc.; KE: Knowledge of English as a second language). Factors of differences in English achievement, whether shown by tests or by school grades, were found in datasets SATT11 and SPEA02. In the latter case, the factor appeared only for girls; in dataset SPEA01, for boys, English grades appeared on a speed of reading factor. This is only one example of several in this domain where achievement appears to be more factorially differentiated for girls than for boys.

Accomplishment in English as a second language appeared on factor 7 (coded KE) of dataset GUST11A, distinct from achievement in Swedish as a native language, which appeared on a more conventional verbal factor (factor 9).

In a number of datasets (FLAN01, SHAY01, SHAY02, SPEA31, SPEA32, SPEA33, SPEA34) knowledge of conventions of English writing with respect to capitalization, punctuation, usage, and spelling appeared on factors (coded EU) distinct from general verbal knowledge factors (V). In SHAY02, for girls in the PROJECT TALENT sample, two separate factors appeared. Factor 6 (coded A6) was saliently loaded with English spelling, a test of sensitivity to grammatical functions, and a test of punctuation. Factor 8 (EU) was saliently loaded with tests of knowledge of capitalization, English usage, and effective expression.

Factor 2 (coded A0) in dataset BUND11 was loaded with a Word Coding test in which subjects had to suggest English words that could be made of letters and digit names, e.g., K9 = "canine," NE = "any", and also with a Decoding test whose problems required knowledge of such symbols as "'" = minute, ♂ = "male," etc. These tests tap a special kind of knowledge about conventions of printed language.

Other verbal subject-matters and general information (A5: Geography achievement; K0: General (verbal) information; K2: Cultural information (art, music, etc.); KA: Knowledge of aviation; KF: Knowledge of signing and fingerspelling as used in deaf communities; KO: Knowledge about objects (in young children); LP: Skill in lipreading). Factor 3 (coded K2) in dataset GUIL44 is saliently loaded with tests of history, geography, vocabulary, and reading comprehension. Factor 3 (A5) in dataset SATT11 is loaded with two tests of geography knowledge, distinct from factor 4 (A6) concerned with tests of achievement in English. Factor 2 in WOOD13 and factor 2 in WOOD18 (both coded A0) are loaded with various tests of subject-matter achievement (science, social studies, humanities) and a test of picture vocabulary that has many items drawing on general cultural knowledge. Factor 12 in CHRI01 and factor 7 in PARK01 are loaded with tests of knowledge of current affairs.

The PROJECT TALENT study (Flanagan, Dailey, Shaycoft, Gorham, Orr, & Goldberg, 1962) had a wealth of tests of specialized information included in those administered to large samples of American high school students. For example, there were tests of information on such topics as the Bible, sports, hunting, and farming. Datasets CURE11 and SHAY01 are for boys, and CURE12 and SHAY02 are for girls, for samples given a large number of PROJECT TALENT tests. (Dataset FLAN01 is only for boys, and for a limited sample of tests.) In all cases, tests of general information tend to load with tests of vocabulary and reading comprehension on factors identified as V (verbal knowledge), and nearly all the different information tests tend to load together, to different degrees. However, there is some suggestion that for girls, these factors tend to be loaded with tests of specialized cultural information at higher levels than tests of general vocabulary and reading comprehension. For example, factor 2 (coded as V and listed in Table 5.2) in dataset CURE12 has its highest loadings on tests of social studies and literature. Factor 7 (coded K2) for dataset SHAY02 has its highest loadings on information tests in theatre and ballet, art, and music. Other tests loaded highly are for information on literature, social studies, accounting and business, sports, and health. I have not tested whether the factor structures are significantly different for boys and girls, but if they are, it could mean that girls' knowledges and interests are on the average more differentiated than boys', and that these interests have a greater tendency to include such topics as theatre, art, and literature. It would be possible to pursue this matter in more detail using PROJECT TALENT or other data.

Dataset SAUN21 comes from an interesting attempt to factor-analyze the *items* of the Information and Arithmetic subtests of the (original) Wechsler Adult Intelligence Scale. Factor 4 was loaded with most of the Arithmetic Items, and factor 2 was loaded with most of the Information items, although there was some overlap, and the oblique factors were correlated .306, giving rise to a second-order factor of general ability or knowledge on these tests. (Essentially, this is the same dimension as factor 3 of dataset WILL11, which was loaded simply with the Information and Arithmetic subtests of the Wechsler test.) There were, however, several more specialized factors. Factor 6, for example, was loaded with items asking specialized cultural information such as "What is the Apocrypha?," "Who wrote Faust?," and "What's the Vatican?"; except for the last, these had near-zero loadings on the second-order factor. Factor 7 showed, for some reason, a significant *negative* correlation between knowing the height of the average woman and knowing the name of the capital of Italy. It is hard to claim any generality for such findings; they could be functions of sampling fluctuations. In any case, it appears that what can be called "general cultural information" is a function of how such information happens to get disseminated in the populace.

During World War II, the U. S. Air Force psychology program (Guilford & Lacey, 1947) found that tests of specialized information about aviation and aeronautics, as well as specially scored biographical information questionnaires, contributed to the prediction of success in pilot and navigator training programs. These tests are loaded on pertinent factors (coded KA) in datasets GUIL43, GUIL44, and GUIL45.

Dataset OLSO51 comes from a study of the language abilities of deaf adolescents (Olson, 1966), especially in relation to abilities in visual perception. Factor 2 (coded KF) is loaded with a number of measures of speed in perceiving finger-spelled words, presumably depending on knowledge and skill with the conventional fingerspellings of letters. Factor 6 (coded LP) concerns skill in speechreading (or lipreading), presumably depending on learning, experience, and practice. Measures of speechreading correlate rather highly with measures of reading speed and comprehension, indicating, possibly, that there is some interaction between learning to read and learning to speechread.

Another dataset concerned with language abilities of deaf adolescents was BOLT11. Factor 5 (coded KF) was loaded with measures of abilities to use manual signs and fingerspelling in communication, and thus represents a dimension of special knowledges and skills.

Datasets PARA03 and PARA08 come from the standardization data for the Illinois Test of Psycholinguistic Abilities (ITPA) (Paraskevopoulos & Kirk, 1969), for ages five and ten respectively. Factor 3 in PARA03 and factor 4 in PARA08 are interpreted here as Knowledge of Objects (KO) because a close inspection of the tests with highest loadings, Manual Expression and Verbal Expression, shows that they depend at least in part on the child's having knowledge about objects referred to, e.g., a telephone. Similar interpretations can be given to factors 2 and 6 in dataset PROG01 and to factor 4 in dataset TAYL31, which also derive from scores on the ITPA.

Dataset SCHU00 comes from a study of the language abilities of aphasic patients (Schuell, Jenkins, & Carroll, 1962). Factor 6 (coded KO) seems to be differentiated from other factors in the study by the fact that it requires "recognition of stimulus equivalence" – as when the patient is required to point to items named or to match printed letters, or to explain a proverb (requiring, as the authors note, "recognition of the equivalence between common situations and experiences"). Whether the factor belongs in the general information category is debatable, because it also seems to require a particular kind of integrative mental process. Nevertheless, it is mentioned here because it seemed to fit well in no other domain.

Factors of Achievement and Knowledge in Mathematics and Science (A3, A4, A7, A8, A9, K1, KM)

The 25 token factors classified here can be further divided into two groups, as follows:

Factors of achievement in mathematics (A3: Tested math achievement; A4: Teacher-rated math achievement; KM: Tested knowledge of mathematics). In terms of approximate average age of samples, the token factors found here range from age seven (dataset PROG11) to age twenty-one (LUCA01). At age seven, mathematics competence can be distinguished from achievement in verbal subject-matters, at least when tested with the appropriate subtest of the Stanford Achievement Test. Both datasets PROG11 and PROG12 show that mathematics achievement is slightly different when rated by teachers, but the correlation is high (.693 between factors 3 and 4 in PROG12). At age eleven, dataset SATT11 shows a mathematics achievement factor (factor 2, coded A3) distinct from factors of English and geography achievement. Scores on an IQ test and an Embedded Figures test have modest salient loadings on the mathematics factor.

A clear factor of mathematics achievement appears in dataset SHAY01 for fourteen-year-old boys in the PROJECT TALENT sample, but in dataset SHAY02 for girls, it is much less clear. On the other hand, in two datsets for different samples from PROJECT TALENT, a mathematical knowledge factor appears *only* for girls (factor 9, dataset CURE12). In dataset CURE11, for boys, tests of mathematics achievement tend to load on a factor of general information and verbal ability (factor 3), possibly because of underfactoring of this battery. (As did the author, I accepted only eight factors of the published factor matrix.)

Mathematics achievement factors occur in two Swedish studies by Werdelin (1958; datasets WERD01 and WERD02, both for fourteen-year-old boys). The measures are a variety of tests of arithmetic, solving equations, and plane and solid geometry.

For Weiss's (1955) sample of fifteen-year-old high school students (dataset WEIS01), three factors of mathematics achievement were found: factor 3, Geometry Achievement: factor 5, Geometry Knowledge; and factor 14, Facility in Algebraic Computation. Likewise, for Canisia's (1962) sample of Grade 11 high-school girls (dataset CANI01), three factors of tested mathematics achievement were identified: factor 6 was loaded with a test Formulas and Figures in which subjects were to match algebraic expressions with graphs, also with a score (Figure Matrix) from the Raven Progressive Matrices; factor 7 was loaded with Fluency with Mathematical Expressions (write different ways of expressing certain quantities) and Statement Translation (choose mathematical expression that correctly translates a verbal problem statement); and factor 8 had further measures of comprehension of algebraic inequalities and functional relationships. Because all these factors involve algebraic relations, it appears that they measure rather specific aspects of algebraic knowledge.

At somewhat older ages, single factors of mathematics achievement were found in datasets FLAN01, WRIG21, VERY01, GUIL44, and LUCA01. In factor 11 in dataset LUCA01, the two salient loadings were for a test of mathematical knowledge and a test of ability to solve problems in relative movement – a subject concerned with plotting and predicting the relative movements of ships navigating at sea.

Factors of achievement in scientific subjects (A7: Tested science achievement; K1: General science information; A8: Hygiene/drawing – in dataset SISK01; A9: Woodworking/Geometry – in dataset SISK01). For the fourteen-year-olds in the PROJECT TALENT sample, Shaycoft (1967) found a factor of scientific and technical information both for the boys (dataset SHAY01, factor 3) and girls (dataset SHAY02, factor 10). The measures were tests of information in such subjects as electricity and electronics, physical science, mechanics, biological science, engineering, and aeronautics and space. These factors were linearly distinct from corresponding factors of mathematics knowledge and achievement, but the interfactor correlations were .474 for the boys and .320 for the girls.

Sisk (1939) performed a factor analysis of subtests of the American Council of

Education Psychological Examination together with grades in the nine courses of an engineering curriculum at Cornell University. In the reanalysis, five of these courses defined a factor of science achievement: Engineering Laboratory, Chemistry, Physics, Analytic Geometry and Calculus, and Surveying. Grades in Hygiene and Drawing defined another factor, and in Woodwork and Descriptive Geometry still another factor.

Factors of Mechanical and Technical Knowledge (MK)

The datasets yielded 35 factors interpreted as measuring mechanical and technical knowledge, primarily about the machines and equipment that support our modern society – not necessarily computers or the more recent innovations such as copying and fax machines, but ordinary tools and their functions, automotive parts, aircraft engines, simple electronic devices, and the like. Many of the tests were originally developed in military organizations during or prior to World War II, but modern versions of them still appear to be useful. For example, the Armed Services Vocational Aptitude Battery (ASVAB), currently one of the most widely administered tests in the U.S.A., contains two subtests – Auto and Shop Knowledge, and Electronics Information – that deal with this kind of technical knowledge and information (Foley & Rucker, 1989). In several factor analyses, e.g., dataset FEDE02, the Auto and Shop Knowledge test appears as two variables – Automotive Information and Shop Information – and together with Electronics Information the three tests load on a single separate factor of Mechanical Knowledge, but each test appears to have useful specific variance for use in military classification procedures.

Striking facts about the 35 factors classified here are that (1) all are derived from samples of average age 16 or above, or modally 21; and (2) none is from a sample composed only of females, and only a few are from samples composed of both sexes. Because most samples are from the military, only a few of the more recent factor analyses have had samples with both sexes – reflecting changes in the composition of the U. S. armed forces. It is noteworthy that in Cureton's (1968) samples of boys and girls given PROJECT TALENT tests, only the boys' data yield a mechanical knowledge factor. For the girls' data, variables appearing on the boys' mechanical knowledge factor have low communalities.

In only one dataset – GUIL38 (a dataset from a World War II study in the U. S. Air Force) – is there a suggestion of a possible separation between two kinds of factors, one concerned mainly with *knowledge* of mechanical and technical terminology, tool functions, and the like, and the other concerned with *judgments* or *processing of information* about mechanical operations. Specifically, factor 5 in dataset GUIL38 is loaded with variables designated Tool Function, Mechanical Information, and Mechanical Function. Factor 2 is loaded with variables designated as Mechanical Movements, Mechanical Comprehension, and Mechanical Principles. The two oblique factors are correlated .358.

In examining the remaining factors classified here, one has the impression that some emphasize sheer knowledge and information, and some emphasize judgment and information processing about mechanical operations, but that most are combinations of the two types of factors. Even single variables can be two-dimensional, but I am unaware of any studies of the dimensionality of tests of mechanical information and judgment. It is sometimes the case (e.g., in dataset ALLI02) that tests of mechanical comprehension and judgment are aligned factorially with tests of spatial abilities; that is, spatial tests occasionally appear on the same factor as a mechanical comprehension test. This may be partly because mechanical comprehension tasks frequently employ pictorial representations of mechanical objects, and the examinee must visualize mechanical movements or operations. Nevertheless, there are numerous datasets in which mechanical knowledge factors are factorially distinguished from spatial ability factors. This is true of datasets CURE11, FEDE02, FREN11, FRUC21, GUIL17, GUIL35, GUIL46, HAKS01, JEFF11, ROFF11, and THUR71, and in some of these (e.g., GUIL35, ROFF11), even if tests of mechanical comprehension appear on the mechanical knowledge factor, they also have substantial loadings on a VZ (Visualization) factor.

There is little more to say about the factors classified here, except to point out that in the last column of Table 12.1, there is an indication of whether each factor in this group appears to emphasize knowledge or information or to emphasize "judgment," that is, information processing about mechanical devices. These indications come purely from my subjective judgments, and in many cases the indication given is actually a compromise. The subdomain is in need of further research to clarify the relative roles of knowledge, as such, and ability to process information about mechanical and electronic operations.

Factors of Knowledge of "Behavioral Content" (BC, BD)

As noted earlier, the term "behavioral content" was introduced by Guilford (1967; Guilford & Hoepfner, 1971) to refer to information involved in human interactions. At least some of this information pertains to those aspects of human communication systems that go beyond the words and sounds of a particular language – vocal inflections of pitch and loudness, facial expressions, gestures, and the like that are to a considerable extent culturally patterned and that communicate feelings, emotions, and intentions (Birdwhistell, 1970; Hall, 1959). Other types of information are of a more general character, dealing with the general nature of human activities and the likelihoods that particular types of individuals will have given objectives, intentions, and behaviors under given conditions or circumstances.

It is at least possible that people have "social intelligence" to the extent that they possess knowledges about these types of behavioral content, or are sensitive to behaviors on the part of others that communicate feelings and intentions.

Guilford and his colleagues developed a series of pencil-and-paper tests that sought to measure such knowledges, in the belief that they would measure social intelligence. Sternberg (1985, chapter 9) reviews the work of Guilford and others on social intelligence, but expresses some skepticism that measures of behavioral content knowledge will prove to be externally valid. Indeed, he points out that it is difficult to find satisfactory criteria of social intelligence, however it might be defined.

For present purposes, I can only report and comment on what dimensions of individual differences of knowledge of behavioral content seem to have been established. The available evidence is very meager, because the database includes only five or six studies that have used a factor-analytic approach to social intelligence.

Wedeck (1947) conducted a study, in Spearman's laboratory at the University of London, of what he called "the psychological ability" – "an ability to judge correctly the feelings, moods, motivations of individual" (p. 133). He devised a series of tests intended to test such an ability. One, for example, presented "40 little pictures" portraying a wide range of facial expression – of laughter, doubt, curiosity, vexation, and the like. Each picture was accompanied by four alternative verbal phrases and the subjects (secondary-school girls about 14 years of age) were asked to indicate which phrase best suited the picture. The items were graded for difficulty. Various other tests involved rating pictures or verbal descriptions of people for their probable personality traits. Correlations were obtained between these tests and several verbal and nonverbal tests of intellectual skills. Wedeck concluded that although there was some correlational overlap between the "psychological ability" tests and the verbal and nonverbal tests, the former exhibited some distinctness, and he was at considerable pains to try to explain this psychologically. In my reanalysis of this dataset (WEDE01) the "psychological ability" tests showed two factors. Tentative interpretations are: (factor 2) a factor concerned with ability to choose appropriate verbal character-izations of personalities from verbal descriptions, and (factor 5) a factor concerned with ability to recognize feelings and emotions portrayed by pictures of facial expressions, poses, and the like. All tests – both those of "psychological ability" and the verbal and nonverbal intelligence tests – had substantial loadings on a second-order general factor. This result could be interpreted in various ways. Possibly the "psychological ability" tests had too much of a verbal component, in that they required knowledge of words referring to emotions. Or it could be simply that general intelligence is a component in the acquisition of knowledge of behavioral content.

Dataset OSUL01 comes from the first large study of behavioral content conducted under Guilford's supervision (O'Sullivan, Guilford, & de Mille, 1965). Although the authors claimed to identify six factors of "behavioral cognition" (one for each of the six types of "products" postulated in Guilford's Structure-of-Intellect model), reanalysis shows only a single factor. In order of their orthogonalized loadings, the tests are as follows (listing only those tests with loadings ⩾ .3):

> Expression Grouping (.484): Given three pictures of facial expressions, gestures, and the like, all showing the same theme or feeling, choose the one of four others that shows the same theme.
>
> Expressions (.398): Given one picture of a facial expression or gesture, choose one of four others that shows that same feeling or theme.
>
> Missing Cartoons (.373): Given a four-frame comic strip with one frame missing, choose the one of four possible frames that properly completes the strip, making sense of the thoughts and feelings of the characters.
>
> Cartoon Implications (.322): Given one picture of a social situation, choose the one of four others that sensibly shows what happened before.
>
> Inflections (.315): Given four pictured facial expressions accompanied by a tape-recorded spoken word or phrase, choose the one picture that properly goes with the auditory stimulus. The reported reliability of this measure, incidentally, was only .26; higher reliability could probably be obtained by further test construction efforts.
>
> Facial Situations (.312): Given two pictures of facial expressions, choose the one of three statements that describes a situation that goes with *both* of the pictures. (Reported Kuder-Richardson reliability, .33.)
>
> Odd Strip Out (.311): Choose one of three cartoon strips in which the main character behaves differently.

At least in the case of the behavioral content facet, it appears that the six "product" facets of Guilford's Structure-of-Intellect model pertain mainly to the format of the items. Format differences were apparently not sufficiently prominent to yield factorial differentiation among the tests, all of which appear to depend simply on knowledge of, or ability to handle, behavioral content as defined above.

Some of the tests of behavioral cognition used by O'Sullivan et al. were included in a study of symbolic memory abilities by Tenopyr, Guilford, and Hoepfner (1966). Although the authors claimed to find five of the six behavioral cognition factors identified by O'Sullivan et al., reanalysis of this dataset (TENO01) disclosed only a single factor (factor 5) in the behavioral cognition domain, similar to the factor from dataset OSUL01.

The last study of behavioral content conducted in Guilford's project was that by Hendricks, Guilford, and Hoepfner (1969). In addition to tests already used by O'Sullivan et al., tests were designed to measure divergent production for each one of Guilford's product facets. The authors reported twelve factors, for the convergent and divergent operations facets crossed with the six product facets (in addition to factors in other domains from reference tests for those domains). With more conservative factoring of this dataset (HEND01), I found only two convergent factors and three divergent factors in the behavioral content domain. The convergent factors are clearly distinguished from the divergent factors, but chiefly by the formats of the tests in each category. The convergent tests are typically multiple-choice tests scored for matching keyed answers; the divergent tests almost always require writing of free-response answers that must be evaluated by trained scorers. The behavioral content, however, is the same; examinees have to exhibit their knowledge of that content in different ways.

The two convergent factors appear to be distinguished by the type of content tested. Factor 6 is loaded chiefly with the tests Missing Pictures and Missing Cartoons, both using comic-strip materials to test examinees' ability to interpret the social situations that are presented, usually involving multiple characters exhibiting different intentions and feelings. Factor 9, in contrast, is loaded with tests that require the interpretation of facial expressions, poses, and gestures.

Of the three divergent production factors, factor 2 is the most prominent, having salient loadings on thirteen tests. All tests require examinees to write "many different things" to describe or otherwise respond to the stimuli presented. Scores depend heavily on the number of responses given, although in many cases trained scorers evaluated responses for adequacy or appropriateness. For example, each item of test 6, Alternate Picture Meanings, presents a photograph of a person showing a certain facial expression, or making a certain gesture. The subject is asked to "write many different things that a person might say if he felt as the person in the picture does." Test 12, Creating Social Relations, shows a drawing of two people performing a certain social interaction with accompanying gestures or facial expressions. The examinee is asked to "write many different things the second person might be saying to the first one." The tests require writing ability, a special kind of ideational fluency, and perhaps persistence, in addition to familiarity with the meanings of facial expressions, gestures, and the like. Like all divergent-production factors, it can be regarded as a rate-of-production factor. Yet, factor 2 appears to be distinct from a more conventionally measured ideational fluency factor (factor 3), presumably because of the special behavioral content knowledge it involves.

The other two divergent-production factors are more difficult to interpret. They generally deal with the same kind of behavioral contents as the other factors. I have the impression that they represent different kinds of response biases in responding to the material. Thus, factor 4 is saliently loaded with a series of tasks in which examinees are asked to indicate different pairs or groups of responses that are supposed to satisfy certain criteria. For example, in test 4, Alternate Facial Relations, from a set of photographs of faces the examinee is to choose pairs that fit interpersonal relationships indicated by a remark that one person is saying to the other. Almost any pair might be defended as appropriate; the high scoring subject is one who realizes this fact, and gives many pairs. (This is not inconsistent with the fact that the reported reliability of the test is high, .96.)

Factor 8 is weakly loaded with only two tests, Multiple Behavioral Grouping and Alternate Expressional Groups. In each item, the first of these presents six verbal comments; the subject is to group comments into different sets according to psychological states they express. It could be that the high scoring subjects are those who indicate more such sets, regardless of their appropriateness. (The reliability of this test is reported as .64, not a very satisfactory figure.) Similarly, Alternate Expressional Groups presents five pictured expressions or actions; the task is "to make many different groups of at least three so that each group expresses a different thought, feeling, or emotion." The test's reliability is reported as only .48. In any case, it would appear that the factor exists mainly by virtue of the similar formats of the tests loaded on it.

Except for a weakly defined behavioral cognition factor in dataset CORN01, the only other available factorial evidence about the behavioral content domain is from a study, obviously inspired by Guilford's work, by Favero, Dombrower, Michael, and Dombrower (1979; dataset FAVE01). These authors administered seventeen variables from Guilford's behavioral content domains (one test from each claimed behavioral cognition factor and the score from a test of memory for behavioral units, but a Fluency Score and a Quality score for each of five divergent-production factors), together with the Comprehensive Tests of Basic Skills (CTBS), to 152 children in grades two through six. My analysis of this dataset omitted the fluency scores because they were very highly correlated with the quality scores, and exhibited experimental dependence. It disclosed only two factors, one for the behavioral cognition tests and one for the divergent-production tests. The total score from the CTBS was saliently loaded on the behavioral cognition factor, suggesting that the behavioral cognition factor had a component closely related to scholastic achievement. All tests – both those from the behavioral cognition factor and the divergent-production factor, together with the total score on the CTBS – had substantial loadings on a second-order factor. This second-order factor was, of course, specific to this rather limited battery; it would probably be best interpreted as simply a composite of a behavioral content knowledge factor and whatever scholastic achievement factor underlies the total score on the CTBS.

Indeed, all the datasets discussed in this section disclosed second-order factors in reanalyses, and all behavioral knowledge factors tended to have substantial loadings on the second-order factor. It is tempting to attribute such a result to the operation of a general intellectual factor, but the evidence provided by these datasets is too meager to make a firm assertion to that effect.

Research on the behavioral content domain needs to pay close attention to the kinds of behavioral knowledges being measured, for example separating tests of sensitivity to expressive cues (facial expressions, gestures, and the like) from tests of the understanding of social situations in which expressive cues have been eliminated or held constant. Test construction and analysis should seek to develop appropriate scales of difficulty; in the literature covered here, the only example of operations to scale items for difficulty was in the study by Wedeck (1947).

In my opinion, attempts to obtain or develop measures of divergent production of behavioral knowledge have only introduced confounds (writing ability, a speed factor, and others). People can create divergent productions only when they possess the knowledges on which such productions would be based. More useful would be the development of a reasonable taxonomy of behavioral content knowledges, and the construction of measures of different subclassifications of such a taxonomy.

A study that was unfortunately not included in the datasets examined here is one by Ford and Tisak (1983; see also Ford, 1986) that reported the finding of a distinct factor of social intelligence, for adolescents, in several measures selected as being congruent with a "behavioral effectiveness criterion" (p. 198). One came from a personality test, Hogan's Empathy Scale (Hogan, 1969). Others were ratings of social competence obtained from the subjects themselves, peers, and teachers on a Social Competence Nomination Form, and a rating of social competence obtained in an interview setting. It is noteworthy that these measures are strikingly different from those employed by Guilford and his colleagues. Considering the manner in which some of them were obtained, one might expect them to correlate with measures of certain language skills factors such as OP (Oral Production) and CM (Communication Ability) as discussed in Chapter 5.

SUMMARY

Various factors of general school achievement, achievement in special school subjects or disciplines, knowledge of general and technical information, and knowledge of information pertaining to social interactions have appeared in the datasets examined in this survey. Most can be interpreted as indicating not only general population differences in tendencies to acquire this knowledge and information but also the ways in which knowledge acquisition tends to specialize as a function of individual experiences and choices.

13   *Psychomotor Abilities*

My survey of cognitive abilities was not intended to cover the domain of physical and psychomotor abilities, but many of the datasets included measures of psychomotor abilities, with the result that a number of interpretable factors in this domain appeared. The first section of this brief chapter presents, without extensive comment or discussion, a classified list of those factors in this group that appear to match factors that have been covered in previous literature surveys. In the second section, there is presentation and discussion of certain psychomotor factors that appear not to have been well recognized in previous surveys, or that seem particularly relevant in considering the measurement of cognitive abilities.

PHYSICAL AND PSYCHOMOTOR ABILITIES COVERED IN PREVIOUS SURVEYS

Fleishman (1964, 1972; see also Fleishman & Quaintance, 1984) has summarized the results of research by himself and others on dimensions of physical and psychomotor abilities. A further summarization of these results is to be found in a chapter by Peterson and Bownas (1982), who list and describe, in their Figure 3.1, eighteen psychomotor and physical proficiency abilities identified by Theologus, Romashko, and Fleishman (1973); brief information on measures of these abilities is given in a section of their Figure 3.3. Using this information, I have attempted to classify, in Table 13.1, relevant factors yielded by my datasets. The table repeats the descriptions presented by Peterson and Bownas and lists token factors from the datasets under each ability described. Only abilities for which my datasets yield factors are included. In some cases, the classifications are tentative because there are various ambiguities in the descriptions; I find several seemingly different factors classifiable under one or the other of the abilities listed by Peterson and Bownas.

532

Table 13.1. *Factors of physical and psychomotor abilities cross-identified with similar factors listed by Peterson and Bownas (1982) (all factor descriptions are taken from Peterson and Bownas, 1982, pp. 70–72)*[a]

Dataset	Codes[b] D C	A	T	M/F	Factor no.	Detail

1. *Static Strength* (P3). "This ability involves the *degree* of muscular force exerted against a fairly immovable or heavy *external object* in order to lift, push, or pull that object. Force is exerted *continuously* up to the amount needed to move the object. This ability is general to different muscle groups (e.g., hand, arm, back, shoulder, leg). This ability does not extend to prolonged exertion of physical force over time and is not concerned with the number of times the act is repeated."

Dataset	D C	A	T	M/F	no.	Detail
CLAU03	'66U	22	R	3	5	Hand Strength
CLAU04	'66U	9	1	3	5	Hand Strength
SUNG01	'81U	16	Z	3	9	Hand Strength
SUNG02	'81U	16	#	3	8	Hand Strength
SUNG03	'81U	16	W	3	10	Hand Strength
SUNG04	'81U	16	1	1	10	Hand Strength
SUNG05	'81U	16	1	2	11	Hand Strength
THOR51	'39U	19	6	3	4	Sex, Grip, Height, Weight, Breath

7. *Gross Body Equilibrium* (P4). "This is the ability to maintain the body in an upright position or to regain body balance especially in situations where equilibrium is threatened or temporarily lost. This ability involves only *body balance*; it does *not* extend to the balancing of objects."

Dataset	D C	A	T	M/F	no.	Detail
CLAU01	'66U	9	R	3	6	Ataxiometry
CLAU04	'66U	9	1	3	11	Railwalking; Tapping

8. *Choice Reaction Time* (R2). "This is the ability to select and initiate the appropriate response relative to a given stimulus in the situation where *two or more stimuli* are possible, and where the appropriate response is selected from *two or more* alternatives. The ability is concerned with the *speed* with which the appropriate response can be *initiated* and does not extend to the speed with which the response is carried out. This ability is independent of mode of stimulus presentation (auditory or visual), and also of type of response required."

Factors in our datasets falling in this category are considered in Chapter 11 (See Table 11.5).

9. *Reaction Time* (R1). "This ability involves the *speed* with which a *single motor response* can be initiated after the onset of a *single stimulus*. It does *not* include the speed with which the response or movement is carried out. This ability is independent of the mode of stimulus presentation (auditory or visual), and also of the type of motor response required."

Factors in our datasets falling in this category are considered in Chapter 11 (See Table 11.5).

10. *Speed of Limb Movement* (R3). "This ability involves the *speed* with which discrete movements of the arms or legs can be made. The ability deals with the speed with which the movement can be carried out after it has been initiated; it is not concerned with the speed of initiation of the movement. In addition, the precision, accuracy, and coordination of the movement is not considered under this ability."

An example of a factor falling in this category is the following:

Dataset	D C	A	T	M/F	no.	Detail
JENS41	'79U	19	6	3	3	Hand Movement Speed

Table 13.1 (*cont.*)

Dataset	Codes[b]				Factor no.	Detail
	D C	A	T	M/F		

In addition, all "movement time" factors mentioned in Chapter 11 would fall under this category. Note that the definitions of Choice Reaction Time, [Simple] Reaction Time, and Speed of Limb Movement given here support the distinction between decision time and movement time.

11. *Wrist-finger Speed* (P5). "This ability is concerned with the speed with which discrete movements of the fingers, hands, and wrists can be made. The ability is not concerned with the speed of the initiation of the movement. It is only concerned with the speed with which the movement is carried out. This ability does not consider the question of the accuracy of the movement, nor does it depend on precise eye–hand coordination."

Dataset	D C	A	T	M/F	Factor no.	Detail
DUNC01	'69U	10	9	3	3	Tapping; Walking
MANG01A	'59R	14	6	2	9	Dotting (speed)
PATE01	'30U	13	6	1	4	Tapping A
"	"	"	"	"	7	Tapping B & C
ROSE01	'74U	19	6	3	2	Fine Motor Hand Control
ROSE02	'74U	19	6	3	6	Fine Motor Hand Control
ROSE03	'74U	19	6	3	6	Fine Motor Hand Control
ROYC11	'76C	40	4	3	6	Finger Tapping
VERS01	'81K	30	U	1	5	Psychomotor Speed (Tapping)
VERS02	'81K	30	U	2	5	Psychomotor Speed (Tapping)
VERS03	'41K	30	Z	1	4	Psychomotor Speed (Tapping)
YELA21	'68P	19	3	1	6	Manual Speed

13. *Multilimb Coordination* (P6). "This is the ability to coordinate the movements of two or more limbs (e.g., two legs, two hands, one leg and one hand). The ability does *not* apply to tasks in which trunk movements must be integrated with limb movements. It is most common to tasks where the body is at rest (e.g., seated or standing) while two or more limbs are in motion."

Dataset	D C	A	T	M/F	Factor no.	Detail
GUIL17	'52U	21	3	1	9	Psychomotor Coordination
GUIL35	'47U	21	3	1	7	Psychomotor Coordination
GUIL41	'47U	21	3	1	4	Psychomotor Coordination
GUIL42	'47U	21	3	1	5	Psychomotor Coordination
GUIL43	'47U	21	3	1	3	Psychomotor Coordination
GUIL44	'47U	21	3	1	5	Psychomotor Coordination
GUIL45	'47U	21	3	1	2	Psychomotor Coordination
GUIL46	'47U	21	3	1	5	Psychomotor Coordination
PARK01	'60U	19	T	1	4	Psychomotor Control
PATE01	'30U	13	6	1	3	Psychomotor: Card Sorting
YELA21	'68P	19	3	1	5	Cybernetic Coordination

14. *Finger Dexterity* (P2). "This is the ability to make skillful, coordinated movements of the fingers where manipulations of objects may or may not be involved. This ability does *not* extend to manipulation of machine or equipment control mechanisms. Speed of movement is *not* involved in this ability."

Dataset	D C	A	T	M/F	Factor no.	Detail
AFTA01	'69C	43	1	3	4	Purdue Pegboard scores
ANDR01	'37U	30	C	2	5	Finger & Tweezer Dexterity
BOLT11	'73U	19	E	3	6	Purdue Pegboard scores
CURE11	'68U	16	6	1	4	Pegboard scores
CURE12	'68U	16	6	2	10	Pegboard scores

Table 13.1 (*cont.*)

Dataset	Codes[b] D C	A	T	M/F	Factor no.	Detail
HARR01	'40U	30	5	1	3	Peg Sort; Peg Sticking; Tracing
"	"	"	"	"	4	Placing Bolts; Taking Nuts Off
"	"	"	"	"	9	Pinboard scores
JEFF11	'57U	16	$	3	6	Crissey test; Purdue Assembly
MORR11	'41U	18	P	1	7	Minnesota Assembly Box; O'Connor Finger Dexterity
PARK01	'60U	19	T	1	5	Finger Dexterity scores
ROYC11	'76C	40	4	3	11	Purdue Pegboard scores
SUNG01	'81U	16	Z	3	3	Finger Dexterity
SUNG02	'81U	16	#	3	7	Finger Dexterity
SUNG03	'81U	16	W	3	4	Finger Dexterity
SUNG04	'81U	16	1	1	5	Finger Dexterity
SUNG05	'81U	16	1	2	10	Finger Dexterity

15. *Manual Dexterity* (P1). "This is the ability to make skillful, coordinated movements of a hand, or a hand together with its arm. This ability is concerned with coordination of movement within the limb. It may involve manipulation of objects (e.g., blocks, pencils) but does not extend to machine or equipment controls (e.g., levers, dials)."

HARR01	'40U	30	5	1	5	Assembly tasks

16. *Arm–hand Steadiness* (P7). "This is the ability to make precise, steady arm–hand positioning movements, where both strength and speed are minimized. It includes steadiness during movement as well as minimization of tremor and drift while maintaining a static arm position. This ability does *not* extend to the adjustment of equipment controls (e.g., levers, dials)."

PATE01	'30U	13	5	1	5	Tracing Board, Tracing Paper, Steadiness

18. *Control Precision* (P8). "This is the ability to make controlled muscular movements necessary to adjust or position a machine or equipment control mechanisms. The adjustments can be anticipatory motor movements in response to changes in the speed and/or direction of a moving object whose speed *and* direction are perfectly predictable."

ALLI01	'60U	19	2	1	8	Rotary Pursuit task
ROFF11	'52U	21	3	1	8	Rotary Pursuit; Complex Coordination; Two-Hand Pursuit
WICK01	'80U	20	6	1	4	Critical Tracking Task (the assignment of the factor to this classification is only speculative)
YELA21	'68P	19	3	1	7	Manual Precision tasks

[a] Factor descriptions are taken, with permission, from Theologus, Romashko, and Fleishman (1973), and Peterson and Bownas (1982, pp. 70–72). With some slight changes, these descriptions are also to be found in a work by Fleishman and Quaintance (1984, pp. 324–326). In the latter, the name of the factor Choice Reaction Time was changed to Response Orientation, but the description remained the same. Note also that the tables in these references list a number of further physical strength and psychomotor factors that were not found in our datasets.
[b] Codes: D (date), C (country), A (age), T (sample type), M/F (1 = male, 2 = female; 3 = both); see Appendix A for further information on codes.

SOME FURTHER PSYCHOMOTOR ABILITIES

Table 13.2 lists a number of token factors, in three groups, that could not readily be classified in Table 13.1, or that appeared to have special relevance for the analysis of cognitive tests and factors.

Aiming (AI). The first group consists of several token factors that probably should be classified under the factor *Aiming* that was recognized by French (1951) as "the ability to carry out quickly and precisely a series of movements requiring eye–hand coordination" or "the accurate positioning of a pencil mark on paper" (p. 202). This factor was also mentioned by Fleishman (1972, p. 87) but for some reason was omitted in Peterson and Bownas's listing. The factor is illustrated by factor 4 of dataset FREN11, which employed tracing and dotting tasks. Tracing tasks require quickly and accurately making marks between lines such that the marks do not touch the lines. Dotting tasks require rapid marking (e.g., by pencil) of dots clearly within small circles. The factor is also represented in dataset HAKS01, but Hakstian and Cattell (1974) did not specify exactly what kind of aiming task they used. Insofar as cognitive tests may require rapid marking of marks in designated spaces, as on many types of answer sheets (see Hartigan & Wigdor, 1989, p. 102, discussing the answer sheet format of the General Aptitude Test Battery), it is possible that individual differences in this so-called Aiming factor may have some influence on performance in cognitive tests. I have found no evidence, however, that this is the case, unless one considers dataset PATE01, which showed a factor (factor 2) whose highest loading was for total score on the Army Alpha intelligence test – a speeded test, followed by loadings for an aiming test, a digit–symbol test, a Packing Blocks test, a body balancing test, a Rhythm test (similar to tests discussed in Chapter 9 under factor U8), and a Slow Movement test (carefully tracing a line slowly with a pencil). The correlations among these rather diverse variables, if they are not somehow artifactual, could conceivably be explained by assuming that the underlying trait is one concerned with precision and speed in handling pencils and other objects – as might be required even in responding to the Army Alpha intelligence test.

Speed of Articulation (PT). The second group of token factors may be presumed to measure a factor called Speed of Articulation, recognized by French (1951, p. 203). The factor appears in two datasets, CARR01 and MARG01, chiefly in measures of the speed of performing fast articulations with the speech musculature, as when a subject is asked to utter "p–p–p–....." as fast as possible. In speech and hearing research, such movements are termed *diadochokinetic* (from Greek words meaning "successive movements"). In dataset CARR01, measures of subjects' maximum and normal speeds of oral reading also appeared in this factor. The fact that a measure of *normal* oral reading speed was loaded on the factor suggests that even normal oral reading speed is to some extent governed by a psychomotor component.

A factor that appeared in dataset SCHU00, for aphasic patients, is classified

Table 13.2. *Some further psychomotor abilities*

Dataset	Codes[a]				Factor no.	Detail
	D C	A	T	M/F		
Aiming (AI)						
FREN11	'57U	18	3	1	4	Tracing and Dotting tasks
HAKS01	'74C	24	1	3	11	Aiming tasks
HORN25	'67U	30	Q	1	3	Follow the Line; Aiming; Cancel Numbers
HORN26	'67U	30	Q	1	3	Cancel Numbers; Follow the Line; Dot in Circle (all wrong scores)
MCGU01	'61U	12	1	1	6	Clerical Speed; Discrimination Reaction Time; Dotting
MCGU02	'61U	12	1	2	5	(Same as for MCGU01)
PATE01	'30U	13	6	1	2	Army Alpha; Aiming; Digit–Symbol; Packing Blocks; Rhythm; Slow Movement
Speed of articulation (PT)						
CARR01	'41U	20	6	3	4	Maximum Speed of Oral Reading; Diadochokinetic Lip Movements
MARG01	'64U	11	6	3	6	Diadochokinetic Lip Movements
SCHU00	'62U	50	4	3	5	Speech Musculature Movements (Aphasic Patients)
Speed of writing (WS)						
ALLI02	'60U	19	2	1	5	Writing X's; Tapping; Turning; Writing Digits
ALLI03	'60U	19	2	1	5	(same as for ALLI02)
ANDR01	'37U	30	C	2	3	Number & Letter Cancellation
BAIR01	'51U	16	D	3	2	Copying Numbers; Arithmetic
BECH01	'47U	19	6	3	3	Writing X's; Writing Words (Speed)
FREN11	'57U	18	3	1	5	Writing Digits; Writing Words; Writing X's
HARG12	'27E	13	1	3	4	Writing Figures; Copying Prose
MANG01A	'59E	14	6	3	3	Copying H's; Copying Paragraphs
PEMB01	'52U	22	6	3	5	Writing Phrases; Writing X's; Sentences
SCHE11	'52C	19	6	3	4	[Opposites]; Writing Backward tasks
"	"	"	"	"	5	Writing Forward tasks
SUMI01	'58N	14	1	1	3	Speed of Writing
SUMI02	'58N	12	1	1	3	Speed of Writing
SUMI03	'58N	10	1	1	3	Speed of Writing
SUMI04	'58N	8	1	1	4	Checking Shapes/Numbers; Writing Speed
SUNG02	'81U	16	Z	3	5	[Rhythm; Word Association], Writing Speed
SUNG04	'81U	16	1	1	6	[Rhythm], Writing Speed

[a]Codes: D (date), C (country), A (age), T (sample type), M/F (1 = male, 2 = female; 3 = both); see Appendix A for further information on codes.

here because of its general similarity to the factors obtained for normal subjects in datasets CARR01 and MARG01. It has to do with gross movements of the speech musculature, including difficulty in swallowing, imitating the examiner's tongue and jaw movements, and repeating syllables rapidly. The authors (Schuell, Jenkins, & Carroll, 1962) considered that this factor reflected the kind of gross motor impairment that occurs with certain types of brain damage.

Speed of Writing (WS). The token factors in the third group in Table 13.2 are classified as measuring *Speed of Writing.* Represented here is considerable variation in procedures of measuring writing speed. Some procedures employ very simple writing tasks, such as writing the letter X, the letter H, or a series of digits like 234567, over and over again as rapidly as possible. Others require examinees to copy sentences or paragraphs; the rate at which these tasks are performed is measured. Investigators sometimes fail to state what instructions are given to subjects – whether subjects are instructed to write as fast as possible, or to write at their normal or usual speed.

Clear evidence is lacking as to whether writing speeds measured in these various ways tend to intercorrelate highly or load on the same underlying factor of writing speed. Evidence is also ambiguous as to whether different kinds of writing speed measurements correlate significantly with other psychomotor factors, such as Finger Dexterity, Manual Dexterity, or Aiming. Finally, evidence is not clear concerning whether writing speed affects measurement of such cognitive ability factors as Ideational Fluency (FI) when the required free responses are to be made in writing, as they usually are.

In dataset ALLI02, simple writing tasks such as Writing X's and Writing Digits correlate highly with psychomotor tests Tapping (hitting two metal plates alternately with a stylus), Turning (reversing small objects in holes, in the Minnesota Rate of Manipulation Test), Placing (rapidly placing pegs in holes, again on the Minnesota Rate of Manipulation Test), and Dotting (making pencil dots in a series of circles 1/16″ in diameter). Thus, the simple writing speed measures are loaded on the same factor as tests of Aiming, Manual Dexterity, and Finger Dexterity. The dataset has no tests of copying extended prose. Nor does this dataset have tests of Ideational Fluency or other free-response cognitive ability tests.

Dataset ANDR01 shows a Cancellation factor on which is loaded tests of Number Cancellation and Letter Cancellation. Subjects are asked to cancel (mark through) given letters or digits in long series of such symbols, as rapidly as possible. This factor is, however, distinct from a Perceptual Speed factor (factor 2) and a Finger Dexterity factor (factor 5). It is a writing speed factor only in the sense that it involves manipulating a pencil in a writing position.

Dataset BAIR01 shows a weak Writing Speed factor (factor 2) with loadings on Copying Numbers ("from one side of the page to another"), Copying ("names, initials, and numbers ... from one column to another"), and Speed of Writing (copying the Gettysburg Address from a printed copy). The factor is distinguished from a possible Perceptual Speed factor, and all these measures are loaded on a second-order factor whose interpretation is not clear because nearly all measures are of a clerical nature.

Dataset BECH01 has a clear Writing Speed factor (factor 3) loaded with Speed of Writing X's and Speed of Writing Words (repeatedly writing, as fast as possible, the phrase "Now is the time for all good men"). The latter test had a significant loading (.318) on the Ideational Fluency factor in this study.

Dataset FREN11 has a Writing Speed factor (factor 5) loaded with Writing Digits, Writing "Lack" (over and over), and Writing X's. The factor is distinct from an Aiming factor (factor 4) and from a Fluency of Expression factor (factor 3) in which free written responses are required. French (1957) interpreted this factor as Finger Dexterity, but the tasks are not those ordinarily loaded on that factor (as listed in section 14 of Table 13.1).

Speed of Writing Digits (234567 to be written repeatedly) and Copying Prose are both loaded on a Writing Speed factor (factor 4) in dataset HARG12. Copying Prose also loaded .279 on Ideational Fluency. There were rather similar findings in dataset MANG01A, where the Writing Speed factor (factor 3) was loaded with both simple letter copying tasks and paragraph copying tasks. One of the copying variables had a significant loading (.306) on an Ideational Fluency factor (factor 2).

The Writing Speed factor (factor 5) in dataset PEMB01 was loaded with both simple letter copying tasks and phrase and sentence copying tests, and was distinct from a Word Fluency factor that required free responses in writing.

I found *two* writing speed factors in dataset SCHE11, in contrast to the authors' finding only one (due to underfactoring). However, all measures were very simple letter- or digit-copying tasks; there was no measure requiring copying of extended prose. The more conventional writing speed factor was factor 5. Factor 4 used essentially the same tasks as those loaded on factor 5, but subjects were asked to write *backward*; the authors' notion was that a factor of "motor rigidity" could be measured in this way. Factor 4 could indeed be called a factor of motor rigidity, or actually, lack of rigidity, i.e., the ability not to decrease speed in undertaking the unusual backward writing tasks. The two factors were distinct, but intercorrelated .305.

Factors saliently loaded with speed of writing tests occurred in four datasets from Japan: SUMI01, SUMI02, SUMI03, and SUMI04. They were loaded with simple writing tasks, repeatedly writing short series of digits, Japanese letters, or special symbols, as rapidly as possible. Other measures on these factors included reaction time and various simple speeded tasks.

Speed of Writing tests (copying sentences as rapidly as possible) were included in a series of datasets using the Ball Aptitude Battery (Sung & Dawis, 1981). Because of the small size of this battery, not well designed for factor analysis, the status of writing speed was not well defined. In datasets SUNG02 and SUNG04, separate Speed of Writing factors were identified but they had accompanying loadings on variables such as Rhythm and Word Association. In datasets SUNG01, SUNG03, and SUNG05, on the other hand, the speed of writing tests tended to have salient loadings on an Ideational Fluency factor, a result suggesting that writing speed can be implicated in performance on ideational fluency tests.

Results from all the datasets considered here leave little doubt that speed of writing is a distinct dimension of individual differences, as might be expected. Just how it should be measured, however, is uncertain. The weight of evidence suggests that it can be measured *both* by simple tasks such as having people copy words or sentences repeatedly *and* by more complex tasks such as copying an extended paragraph. In all cases, rate of performance rather than any kind of accuracy or neatness is of most concern. But asking people to write "as rapidly as possible" probably confounds the measurement of writing speed by encouraging them to write more carelessly and illegibly than they might otherwise do. What is wanted, it seems, is a measure of "normal" writing speed so that it can be used, possibly, as a control or covariate in any measures that require free written responses, such as tests of ideational fluency, for there is evidence that measured performance on these tests is to some extent affected by variations in writing speed.

The interpretation of a writing speed factor is still unclear. On the one hand, measurements may simply indicate the degree to which writing has been practiced, or the stage of development in writing skill that the individual has reached. On the other hand, measurements may reflect neurophysiological conditions affecting writing as a psychomotor activity. The factor-analytic evidence, at least, is silent on these matters. It is beyond my scope to consider information from other sources that may have addressed these questions.

SUMMARY AND DISCUSSION

Tests of various psychomotor factors appear in some factor-analytic studies of cognitive abilities, but in general these factors are clearly distinct from factors defined by tests of more strictly cognitive abilities.

Reaction time measurements, however, may present a special case, insofar as they may be considered to reflect psychomotor abilities. As discussed in Chapter 11, some measures of reaction time, particularly those derived from tasks involving the more complex forms of encoding and decision processes, tend to be correlated with various tests of cognitive ability, though weakly, and the connection is probably chiefly at a second- or higher-order of analysis.

Further special cases concern measures of speed of speech articulation and of speed of writing, which can and do sometimes generate separate factors of psychomotor ability. As far as is known, speed of speech articulation is uncorrelated with speed of writing in typical populations, but each of these factors can interact with performance on certain kinds of cognitive ability tests that require speech or writing responses. Efforts should be made to obtain good measures of these factors so that they can be used to make appropriate adjustments in measures of cognitive abilities that require open-ended speech or writing.

14 *Miscellaneous Domains of Ability and Personal Characteristics*

Chapters 5 to 13 present discussions of factors in our datasets as classified into a number of fairly broad domains of ability – generally, domains that embrace abilities commonly thought of as belonging under the general concept of intelligence. Many hundreds of token factors identified in the datasets are listed in those chapters. But in any enterprise that attempts to classify a large number of entities there will inevitably remain a residue not easily classified. This chapter deals with those token factors that do not easily fit into the domains previously discussed, or that for some reason defy meaningful classification and interpretation.

Factors discussed in this chapter are not necessarily less important than those dealt with in previous chapters. Some of them concern dimensions of personal characteristics that may not strictly belong under the concept of intelligence or cognitive ability. Others may have to do with cognitive ability, but they have not been widely investigated.

As far as possible, factors presented here are classified into a number of somewhat arbitrary, unrelated domains. But there are other factors that appear only rarely in the datasets, or that appear only in the form of "*n*-lets" (doublets, triplets) because they relate to highly specific kinds of variance. These are presented mainly in the form of lists, with appropriate discussion. The chapter ends with a list of factors in the datasets that remain uninterpreted; in general, these are regarded as resulting from statistical artifacts.

SENSORY ABILITY FACTORS

Table 14.1 lists 20 token factors, in 13 datasets, that refer to individual differences in sensitivity to stimuli in visual, olfactory, and tactile/kinesthetic modalities. (Factors of auditory sensitivity are dealt with in Chapter 9.)

Visual sensitivity (VC) factors. Datasets CLAU01, CLAU02, and CLAU03 are for groups of retarded persons at three age levels; dataset CLAU04 is for a group of normal children at age 9. A measure of uncorrected visual acuity, obtained with the Bausch and Lomb Orthorater, appears with high salient

542

Table 14.1. *20 factors of sensory ability in 13 datasets*

Dataset	Codes[a]				Factor no.	Details (saliently loaded variables)
	D C	A	T	M/F		
Visual sensitivity factors (VC)						
CLAU01	'66U	9	R	3	4	Visual Identification Threshold, Color Vision, Visual Acuity, Railwalking, RT to Pictures
CLAU02	'66U	13	R	3	6	Visual Acuity, Visual Identification Threshold, Two-Point Tactile Threshold
CLAU03	'66U	22	R	3	4	Visual Acuity, Visual Identification Threshold, Color Vision
CLAU04	'66U	9	1	3	4	Visual Acuity, Visual Identification Threshold
JACK12	'79U	18	6	3	4	Single Letter Threshold, Peripheral Letter Span
SMIT51	'66U	8	1	3	3	Binocular Acuity; Visual Acuity for Right Eye
SMIT52	'66U	18	1	3	10	Visual Acuity for Right Eye, Binocular Acuity
Color vision factors (V1, V2, V3, respectively)						
JONE21	'48U	30	1	3	2	Stimuli in Red region of spectrum
"	"	"	"	"	3	Stimuli in Green region of spectrum
"	"	"	"	"	4	Stimuli in Blue region of spectrum
Olfactory sensitivity factors (O1, O2, O3, O4, respectively)						
JONE22	'57U	21	6	3	3	isomeric butanols
"	"	"	"	"	4	pyridine; *n*-butyric acid
"	"	"	"	"	6	ethylene chloride; ethyl acetate
"	"	"	"	"	7	*n*-caprylic acid; *n*-propanol
Tactile-kinesthetic sensitivity factors (TP)						
ADEV01	'68U	18	1	1	2	Tactile localization; Laterality orientation
"	"	"	"	"	4	Two-point discrimination; Traced letter identification (negative)
HALS01	'47U	30	H	1	2	Tactual performance speed; Tactual performance localization
MOUR01	'52E	10	6	1	6	Touch discrimination; Weight discrimination
ROYC11	'76C	40	4	3	5	3 tactual localization variables: spatial body orientation
"	"	"	"	"	7	5 tactual performance variables: speed and accuracy

[a]Codes: D (date), C (country), A (age), T (sample type), M/F (1 = male, 2 = female; 3 = both); see Appendix A for further information on codes.

loadings on the respective factors in all four datasets, suggesting that the basic trait involved is visual acuity – a purely physiological characteristic. Some of the other measures appear to be affected by visual acuity, for example, Visual Identification Threshold, which was a tachistoscopic picture-naming task in which visual thresholds were obtained by the method of ascending limits. For the retarded groups, salient loadings also sometimes appeared for measures such as Color Vision, Railwalking, and Two-Point Tactile Threshold. One can only speculate about the interpretation of these findings; one possibility is that mental retardation can involve a very general depression of sensory functions. It is noteworthy that in all four datasets, the Visual Acuity measures had substantial loadings (.224 for the normal group, and ranging from .376 to .460 for the retarded groups) on a general factor for the battery – a battery that contained a considerable number of cognitive ability tests.

Factor 4 in dataset JACK12 was from a study of processing determinants of reading speed. Its positive salient loadings (.47 and .34, respectively) were for two variables: Single Letter Threshold and Peripheral Letter Span. These measures were taken in tachistoscopic stimulus presentations in which single letters were to be reported either when presented foveally or at various distances from the fovea, and either with or without surrounding masking material. Subjects were allowed to use visual corrections. Although this factor may not represent visual acuity as such, it has do with sensory processing. The authors concluded that it was not related to reading speed. At the same time, our analysis of the dataset showed that both of these variables showed substantial *negative* loadings ($-.47$ and $-.24$, respectively) on a second-order factor for the battery. Unfortunately, the sample consisted of only 24 subjects; the negative loadings may, therefore, be chance phenomena.

Datasets SMIT51 and SMIT52, for subjects with mean ages of 8 and 18, respectively, were from a study (Smith & Smith, 1966) of developmental changes in spatial judgments. Although the authors stated that "measures of acuity logically could be expected to constitute a factor with loadings on spatial tasks" (p. 6), both datasets produced visual acuity factors that were generally unrelated to other measures in the batteries; the factors had negligible loadings on second-order factors.

Color vision (V1, V2, V3) factors. Much of our knowledge about color vision comes from observations of individual differences in sensitivity to different wavelengths of the visible light spectrum. Partly to test the effectiveness of factor analysis in confirming theories of color perception, Jones (1948) analyzed data that had been obtained by flicker spectrophotometry by Coblentz and Emerson (1918) on sensitivities of 92 subjects to twenty wavelengths from 493 to 678 nm (nanometers). Jones concluded that three first-order factors were sufficient to account for the data. This was confirmed by my reanalysis, except that I obtained a second-order factor of chromatic flicker sensitivity, with the first-order factors more purely defined. This was true despite Jones's observation that "the raw data

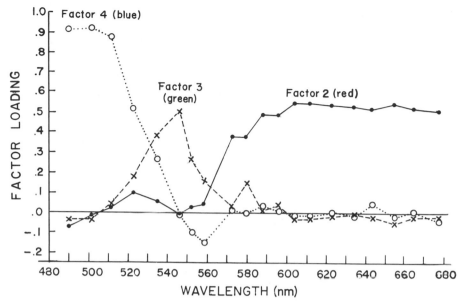

Figure 14.1. Plot of orthogonalized factor loadings on factors 2 (red), 3 (green), and 4 (blue) against stimulus wavelength; reanalysis of dataset JONE 21 (Jones, 1948).

were adjusted separately for every *S* to indicate sensitivity relative to his own maximum" (p. 362), thus presumably eliminating the possibility of a general factor of overall sensitivity. Figure 14.1 is a plot of the factor loadings I obtained against wavelength. Interestingly, this is substantially different from a similar plot presented by Jones (his Figure 1), and shows a peak for factor 3 (green) at 546 nm, near where, as Jones noted, it ought to be according to the Young–Helmholtz color theory (see, for example, Figure 4.6 in Hochberg, 1988).

My reanalyzed results vindicate the use of factor analysis in psychophysics, somewhat contrary to the opinion of Luce and Krumhansl (1988, p. 31) who state that "the few attempts to employ factor analysis in psychophysics have for the most part been deemed failures." They cite Ekman's (1954) finding of *five* factors in color similarity data – two more than the number known to be correct. Two possibilities suggest themselves: either Ekman used incorrect procedures in determining the number of factors, or the use of similarity data introduced complications that were not present in the color sensitivity data used by Jones. Actually, Luce and Krumhansl overlooked Weckroth's (1961) reanalysis of Ekman's data, which confirmed a proper three-factor solution.

Olfactory sensitivity (O1, O2, O3, O4) factors. Encouraged by his successful use of factor analysis in investigating color vision, Jones (1957) turned his attention to identifying dimensions of olfactory sensitivity, feeling that in view of the lack of well-accepted theories of dimensions in this domain, factor analysis would be more appropriate as an exploratory technique than in the color domain. Data were collected on olfactory sensitivities of 84 subjects to the odors of twenty chemical substances. Factor analysis yielded four first-order factors and a general factor of olfactory sensitivity. My reanalysis likewise yielded four first-order factors (similar to those identified by Jones), but analysis of factor intercorrelations showed two second-order factors and one third-order factor measuring general sensitivity to odors. One second-order factor linked factors 2 and 3, and the other linked factors 6 and 7. I present this analysis for its possible interest to those competent to evaluate it substantively. Jones could not find correspondences between the factors and any "chemical dimensions or homogeneous odor-qualities," and I am unable to make further comment, except to point out that the results indicate that there are wide individual differences in olfactory sensitivity, both in general and in response to particular categories of odors.

These results do not seem inconsistent with present views on the dimensional analysis of odor sensitivities. Jones's study must be regarded as only a limited exploratory study (see Cain, 1988, p. 435).

Tactile-kinesthetic sensitivity (TP) factors. Information on tactile and kinesthetic sensitivity factors is meager.

A study by Adevai, Silverman, and McGough (1968) appears to indicate that tactile localization – i.e., identifying where on the skin one has been touched – is uncorrelated with the classic two-point discrimination task. Factor 2 of dataset ADEV01 is saliently loaded with two variables: (8) Tactile localization, and (4) Laterality orientation. Tactile localization was measured by distance errors on 20 trials, in each of which S was lightly touched at some point on the ventral surface of the hand (out of sight), and then asked to mark an outline drawing where he thought he had been touched. Laterality orientation was measured by having S mark drawings of right or left body parts as either right or left. (The test has some similarity, therefore, to the Hands test that appears to load on a spatial ability factor; see Chapter 8.) Tentatively, it may be speculated that the common element in these tests is a general orientation to bodily locations. Factor 4 is loaded positively with a two-point discrimination task and *negatively* with a Traced Letter Identification task in which S had to sense (blindfolded) which of four letters was traced on the back of his hand. The authors regard this result as inconclusive.

A tactual performance factor appears in dataset HALS01, based mainly on scores from a test in which the (blindfolded) subject is asked to fit ten blocks into a formboard, and later to remember the formboard and the positions at which the blocks fit. There is obviously an element of tactile perception as well as, possibly, spatial visualization. The Tactual Performance test is part of the Halstead–Reitan battery for neuropsychological assessment (see Jarvis & Barth, 1984). I am unaware of any information that would indicate whether tactual sensitivity as measured by this battery is related to either of the factors suggested by the analysis of dataset ADEV01.

In Moursy's (1952) study, my analysis shows a Sensory-Motor Process factor saliently loaded with four variables: Touch Discrimination, Weight Discrimination, Writing Speed, and Reaction Time. The Touch Discrimination test is described as measure of a cutaneous threshold obtained "in the usual way by an aesthesiometer." The Weight Discrimination test involved having subjects arrange shot-filled cans in order of weight. The Writing Speed task required subjects to write the digits 1 through 9 over and over again as rapidly as possible. The Reaction Time test required response to an auditory stimulus, latency being measured with a chronoscope. While some rationale could be given for the appearance of touch and weight discrimination measures on this factor, interpreting the presence of the last two variables is problematical. Separate writing speed and reaction time factors, as found in other datasets (see Chapters 11 and 13), did not appear here because of the incomplete design of the battery. All variables had small but possibly significant loadings on a second-order "practical" factor, and larger loadings (about .31) on a third-order general intelligence factor.

Finally, in dataset ROYC11 there appear two tactile sensitivity factors. Factor 5 is loaded with several variables measuring the ability to localize objects touched to the face or hands; it seems to be similar to factor 2 in dataset ADEV01. Factor 7 is a Tactual Performance factor similar to that found in dataset HALS01, being based on several scores from Halstead's (1947) tactual performance test.

FACTORS IN ABILITY TO ATTEND (AC)

Attention is a very broad category in psychological theory. As Shiffrin (1988, p. 739) remarks, "*Attention* has been used to refer to all those aspects of human cognition that the subject can control (like those aspects that Atkinson and Shiffrin, 1968, termed *control processes*), and to all aspects of cognition having to do with limited resources or capacity, and methods of dealing with such constraints." This being the case, it can be argued that attention is involved, in varying degrees, in *all* cognitive performances and thus in all performances that are regarded as indicating cognitive abilities. One can expect it to be very difficult to separate the attentional components of such performances from those components that represent latent traits of abilities other than the ability to attend. An individual differences factor could often be equally well interpreted either as a factor of some particular cognitive ability or as a factor of attentional ability. For example, a popular interpretation of one of the factors measured by tests in the Wechsler intelligence scales is that it represents "freedom from distractibility" (Kaufman, 1975) – that is, the ability to attend to tasks without being distracted, but this same factor can also be interpreted as measuring an ability to perform simple coding and arithmetical tasks (see factor 2 in dataset VANH01).

Conventionally, it is assumed that individuals taking tests devote an adequate amount of attention to the tasks, but actually common experience suggests that there can be considerable variation in degree of attention, even when subjects are well motivated and under pressure to perform well. I am unaware of any observational studies of test-taking behavior that would provide information on this matter.

Information on whether there are different kinds of attentional abilities is relatively sparse. Much of what is available has been summarized by Davies, Jones, and Taylor (1984), who point out that in experimental psychology there has been little concern with individual differences in attention. They review the field under two broad rubrics: *selective* attention and *sustained* attention (or *vigilance*). Selective attention tasks, they state, can be broadly divided into those that involve *focused* attention and those that involve *divided* attention (simultaneous attending to more than one task). They consider five types of selective attention tasks: selective and dichotic listening, central–incidental learning, speeded classification and visual search, the Stroop task, and time-sharing. Individual differences occur in all these tasks, but inasmuch as investigators generally study only one type of task at a time, there is little information on intercorrelations among tasks. Davies et al. reported their impression that there is no strong evidence for a general time-sharing factor. In the domain of sustained attention, they state their belief that individual differences are mainly "task-type specific" – that is, that they depend mainly on the type of discrimination involved in signal detection tasks.

I find very few factor-analytic studies addressed to attentional abilities. An early study by Wittenborn (1943; dataset WITT01) appears to have yielded only one or possibly two factors of attention (both to be discussed below). In a study by Sack and Rice (1974, not included in our datasets), three factors were reported: degree of selectivity (ability to attend selectively to relevant cues), resistance to distraction, and shifting (ability to make a voluntary change in the focus of attention). The authors had hypothesized these abilities and prepared tests for them. However, the degree of selectivity factor was loaded principally with measures of factor CS (speed of closure) or CF (closure flexibility). The other two factors possibly correspond to factors found by Wittenborn. Neither of these studies begins to cover the range of tasks considered by Davies et al. (1984), and even that range was admittedly only a sample of the attention tasks that have been considered by experimentalists. The domain is much in need of further study from a multidimensional, individual-differences point of view.

Table 14.2 lists 21 factors, in 20 datasets, that possibly measure aspects of attentional ability. They are listed in alphabetical order by dataset and factor number. There is no claim or guarantee that any of them can be cross-identified with others. The list is presented only as a possible resource for researchers.

Factor 4 in dataset ANGL11 (a study of "behavioral rigidity") was positively loaded with three variables: (17) the nonrigidity or speed score from a "capitals" test designed by Schaie (1955) to measure an aspect of rigidity; (19) the nonrigidity

Table 14.2. *21 factors of attentional ability (AC) in 20 datasets*

Dataset	D C	A	T	M/F	Factor no.	Details (saliently loaded variables)
ANGL11	'75G	22	6	3	4	Concentration tests
BAIR01	'51U	16	D	3	4	Carefulness tests: Number checking, filing, checking copy
FOGA00	'87U	19	P	3	8	Timesharing letter tasks
FREN11	'57U	18	3	1	7	Reflected wrongs scores on tests of P and N: carefulness
GUIL41	'47U	21	3	1	3	Reflected wrongs scores on plotting and complex scale reading tests
HORN01	'66U	28	Q	3	6	Reflected wrongs scores from various tests
HORN02	'82U	28	Q	3	11	Carefulness; Experimenting
LANS22	'78U	19	6	3	3	Reflected error scores on sentence verification tasks
LUMS01	'65A	19	P	3	10	Oral and written directions on the Army Alpha test
MOON01	'54C	21	3	1	2	Reversed Reading; New Words; Arithmetic Test; Alphabet Test
SU"L01	'54G	21	6	3	5	Tasks requiring parallel information processing
THUR11	'38U	17	1	3	8	Reflected proportions wrong on visual search tasks
THUR41	'44U	19	6	3	10	Two-Hand Coordination; Color-Form Memory; Hidden Pictures
VALT01	'70G	9	V	3	2	Complex visual cancellation tasks
VALT02	'70G	9	1	3	4	" " " "
VALT03	'70G	9	%	3	3	" " " "
VANH01	'75U	12	R	3	2	Freedom from distractibility (WISC subtests)
WICK01	'80U	20	6	1	2	Auditory running memory tasks
WITT11	'43U	21	2	1	6	Tonal memory; Philip's alphabet test
"	"	"	"	"	7	Complex auditory stimulus manipulation tasks
YELA21	'68P	19	3	1	4	Tracing precision tasks

[a]Codes: D (date), C (country), A (age), T (sample type), M/F (1 = male, 2 = female; 3 = both); see Appendix A for further information on codes.

score from an opposites test, also from Schaie's rigidity battery; and (13) a perceptual speed and accuracy test from W. Horn's German adaptation of Thurstone's Primary Mental Abilities test. Apparently these were all very simple tasks requiring close attention if errors were to be avoided. The authors of this study (Angleitner & Rudinger, 1975) interpreted the factor as "set to concentrate" (*Konzentrativer Anpassung*). It was distinct from factors interpreted as CS (speed of closure) and CF (flexibility of closure).

Factor 4 in dataset BAIR01 had loadings on several simple clerical tasks that might otherwise be regarded as measures of P (perceptual speed). However, it was distinct from factor 3, which being loaded with such tests as Number Comparison and Name Checking could be interpreted as a more usual perceptual speed factor. Factor 4 is therefore tentatively interpreted as a Carefulness or Closeness of Attention factor. It is similar to factors identified in datasets FREN11 and HORN01, which also involve simple clerical tasks.

Factor 8 in dataset FOGA00 (Fogarty, 1987) appears to be one of the few examples of a "time-sharing" factor, i.e., a factor measuring the extent to which the subject can attend to two tasks at once. Fogarty claimed that the corresponding factor in his study could not be isolated except by confirmatory factor anlysis techniques, but I had no difficulty in identifying it by exploratory procedures. The factor was saliently loaded mainly with scores from tests that were performed as dual tasks; for example, variable 31 was the score on a Hidden Words task presented to the right ear while a Chord Decomposition task was presented to the left ear, both tasks being scored. Hidden Words consisted of series of spoken letters from which the subject had to detect a sequence spelling a four-letter word, while Chord Decomposition required stating whether three-note sequences were same or different. (The score for the Chord Decomposition task appeared on a general auditory ability factor.) Some of the tasks involved combined visual and auditory presentations, but all scores loaded on this factor were from tasks involving alphabet letters and spelling. The battery contained numerous other time-sharing tasks; not all of them appeared on this factor. If factor 8 is truly a time-sharing factor, it appears to be limited to tasks that involve detecting word-spellings from spoken letters during the performance of other tasks that did not involve letters.

Fogarty's time-sharing factor may be compared to time-sharing factors identified by Jennings and Chiles (1977) and Brookings (1990). These authors concluded, however, that their time-sharing factors were specific to tasks involving visual monitoring. Brookings stated his belief that Fogarty's study did not provide sufficient practice to allow the tasks to become automatized, suggesting that Fogarty's evidence for a time-sharing factor was not conclusive. It is not clear, however, that Fogarty's tasks did not involve automatized processes; it is also not clear why a time-sharing factor would necessarily have to involve automatized processes, although normally they could be expected to do so. In any event, these studies suggest ways in which true time-sharing factors may finally be established if such exist (see also Ackerman, Schneider, & Wickens, 1982).

A clear Carefulness factor was identified in dataset FREN11 (French, 1957) in four measures of degree of error in performing simple numerical and perceptual speed tasks. These variables were reflected in my analysis to produce positive manifold, and the factor is distinct from Perceptual Speed and Numerical Facility factors.

The carefulness factor (factor 3) identified in dataset GUIL41 involved wrongs scores on complex plotting and scale-reading tasks. (The number-right speed scores appeared on other factors, suggesting that wrongs scores can indeed measure something different from speed scores.) Because the dataset did not include measures of perceptual speed, the possible distinctness of carefulness measured with plotting and scale-reading tasks cannot be evaluated.

Factor 3 of dataset LANS22 has been classified here partly because the study's author was specifically interested in measuring attention. The factor is loaded with error scores on Sentence Verification tasks – in which the correctness of sentences as descriptions of visual displays is to be evaluated. These error scores were linearly independent of latency scores on the same tasks. The sentence verification task is often found to be related to verbal ability inasmuch as performance is controlled partly by the grammatical complexity of the sentences. In this dataset, however, the error scores on the sentence verification tasks were linearly independent of a verbal score (variable 12).

Lumsden's (1965, dataset LUMS01) factor 10 can be interpreted as a Carefulness factor because it is loaded with very simple oral and written directions tests of the Army Alpha battery; it is distinct from other factors (such as factor 9, Verbal Comprehension) on which these tests are also (nonsaliently) loaded.

The variables loaded on factor 2 of dataset MOON01 have the feature that they present simple tasks with novel manipulations. Reversed Reading requires subjects to respond True or False to sentences in which the words are in proper order but with the letters of each word in reverse order. New Words requires subjects to recognize, for example, *SKRINK* as an "abbreviation" for *skating rink*. The test Arithmetic presents problems where " + " means *subtract*, " − " means *add*, " × " means *divide*, and " ÷ " means *multiply*. Presumably attention is required to break highly practiced habits.

Factor 5 in dataset SU"L01 (from a study of attention conducted in Germany, Süllwold, 1954) is loaded with two tests that seem to involve a kind of time-sharing or attention to simultaneous tasks. In one of them (variable 7), subjects are visually presented alternately with words from two eleven-word sentences, the first word from sentence A, the first word from sentence B, the second word from sentence A, the second word from sentence B, and so forth; they then have to reproduce the two sentences. Probably there is a memory span component in this task, but the dataset did not include any conventional tests of memory span or even verbal comprehension. The second test loaded here (variable 6) involved presentation of a series of cards, each containing varying numbers of circles, triangles, and stars in random order. As the cards were presented, the subject was to accumulate counts of each type of figure. It would be interesting to use these or similar tasks in future studies of attention.

Factor 8 in dataset THUR11 corresponds to one that Thurstone (1938a) interpreted as a possible "carefulness" factor. It is loaded with reflected proportions of omitted or wrong responses in two perceptual speed tests: in Highest

Number, S is to find the highest number in each of 80 columns of 40 three-digit numbers; in Scattered X's, the task is to find X's in rows of pied type. Number-correct scores on these tests, which are essentially rate-of-work scores, load on perceptual speed factors.

Factor 10 in dataset THUR41 is saliently loaded with three variables: (20) Two-Hand Coordination: two plates were to be tapped with a stylus, one with the left hand and one with the right hand. In the first part of the test, S had to tap with the right hand successively in four numbered sections of the right-hand plate, and in a second part, with the left hand successively in the four numbered sections of the left-hand plate, each for 30 seconds. The patterning of the numbered sections differed between the two plates. In a third part (also 30 seconds), S had to tap the two plates simultaneously but according to the numbered patterns on each. The final score was a ratio measuring how well S could tap with both hands as well as with the hands separately. (57) Color–Form Memory: In each of ten items, S was exposed, for about 40 ms, to a display showing four forms each with a different color. The score was the number of forms and colors correctly reported. (44) Hidden Pictures: S was to find and point to human or animal figures hidden in a large drawing. Thurstone (1944a, p. 111) interpreted the factor underlying these measures as "the ability to shake off one set in order to take a new one." Further, "Freedom from *Gestaltbindung* might be an appropriate description in that it implies flexibility in manipulating several more or less irrelevant or conflicting gestalts." We might, therefore, interpret the factor as one involving the ability to switch attention – for example, between the two plates of the Two-Hand Coordination test or between the forms and colors presented in the Color–Form Memory test.

In each of datasets VALT01, VALT02, and VALT03 is found a "concentra-tion" factor loaded principally with scores on the Bourdon–Viersma concentra-tion test that requires subjects to work through rows of dot-groups, ignoring groups with three dots, striking horizontally through groups with four dots, and striking vertically through groups with five dots. The duration of this very tedious task is 10 minutes. Also loaded on this factor is a digit–symbol task of the kind found in many other studies.

Factor 2 in dataset WICK01 is loaded with auditory tasks (one alone and the other accompanied with another task) in which an alphabetic letter is heard every three seconds. The task is to judge whether each letter is in alphabetical order with the previous one.

Wittenborn's (1943) study is one of the few factorial studies addressed specifically to measuring attention. The battery consisted of a number of specially prepared attention tests along with marker tests for Number, Perceptual Speed, Associative Memory, and Space. Factor 6 in my reanalysis is saliently loaded with only two variables: a score from Seashore's Tonal Memory test (requiring subjects to detect whether two sequences of tones are same or different), and a score from Philip's alphabet test, that Woodrow (1914) had found to be predictive of an experimental criterion of attention, namely, according to Wittenborn (p.19), "the inverse of the difference between reaction time with widely varying preparatory intervals and reaction time with a uniform preparatory interval of 2 seconds." In the test, each item read aloud by the examiner consists of a letter and two digits. For example, if the examiner reads D-2-3 the subject would write F I, the digits indicating the number of letters to be read forward in the alphabet. It is thus a type of auditory vigilance task. It can be argued that Seashore's Tonal Memory test also requires auditory vigilance.

Factor 7 in my reanalysis of dataset WITT11 is also loaded with a number of auditory vigilance tests. What seems to distinguish these tests from those loading on factor 6 (discussed above) is that the subject must hold in mind fairly complex rules for dealing with the sequences of auditory stimuli. For example, in test 17, with the highest loading on this factor, the subject hears a random series of alphabet letters. In a series of corresponding spaces on the answer sheet, he is to mark " + " for a vowel following a consonant, " − " for a consonant following a vowel, and for two successive vowels or consonants, " + " for the *next* letter no matter what it is. Thus, what may be involved is not so much close attention to the stimuli but the ability to hold in mind and follow the rules for the markings.

Factor 4 in dataset YELA21 is highly loaded with two scores from MacQuarrie's tracing test – possibly introducing experimental dependence. The test requires the subject to trace a line through gaps or openings in a series of vertical lines without touching those lines. One score is simply the number of gaps successfully traversed. The other score is a special scoring for the manner or orientation in which the subject's traced line approaches each gap. Also weakly loaded on this factor is the score from a questionnaire in which *S* is asked about the extent to which he tends to pay attention to details.

The attentional factors reviewed here appear to fall into two main classes: (1) those measuring the subject's ability to pay close attention, or to be careful in monitoring behavior to perform a task according to instructions or stated rules, and (2) those measuring the subject's ability to attend to two tasks simultaneously, or at least to switch attention readily from one task to the other. It would be necessary to develop appropriate tests and designs for factorial studies that might provide better information on the structure of attentional abilities. Careful thought would have to be given to the problem of distinguishing attentional components from straightforward ability components such as Perceptual Speed.

Although it did not use factor analysis, a study by Aks and Coren (1990) has suggested procedures for measuring attention. These authors found that highly distractible subjects (university undergraduates) obtained lower scores on cognitive tests than low-distractible subjects. Distractibility was measured by comparing performance on a speeded visual search task with and without extraneous auditory and visual stimuli.

In this connection, readers may be reminded of Berger's (1977) finding (see Chapter 7) of a relation between a certain memory span factor, Resistance to

Interference, and scores on a questionnaire in which subjects report the degree to which they are able to maintain attention during demanding tasks like listening to lectures (Singer & Antrobus, 1963).

FACTORS OF COGNITIVE STYLE (CY)

Cognitive styles, according to Messick (1970), are "dimensions of individual differences in the performance of cognitive tasks that appear to reflect consistencies in the manner or form of cognition, as distinct from the content of cognition or the level of skill displayed in the cognitive performance.... [They] represent a person's typical modes of perceiving, remembering, thinking, and problem solving" (p. 188). Messick gives the following examples of such dimensions (references given in the source are omitted here):

1. *Field independence versus field dependence* – "an analytical, in contrast to a global, way of perceiving [which] entails a tendency to experience items as discrete from their backgrounds and reflects ability to overcome the influence of an embedding context."

2. *Scanning* – a dimension of individual differences in the extensiveness and intensity of attention deployment, leading to individual variations in vividness of experience and the span of awareness.

3. *Breadth of categorizing* – consistent preferences for broad inclusiveness, as opposed to narrow exclusiveness, in establishing the acceptable range for specified categories.

4. *Conceptualizing styles* – individual differences in the tendency to categorize perceived similarities and differences among stimuli in terms of many differentiated concepts, which is a dimension called *conceptual differentiation*, as well as consistencies in the utilization of particular conceptualizing approaches as bases for forming concepts – such as the routine use in concept formation of thematic or functional relations among stimuli as opposed to the analysis of descriptive attributes or the inference of class membership.

5. *Cognitive complexity versus simplicity* – individual differences in the tendency to construe the world, and particularly the world of social behavior, in a multi-dimensional and discriminating way.

6. *Reflectiveness versus impulsivity* – individual consistencies in the speed with which hypotheses are selected and information processed, with impulsive subjects tending to offer the first answer that occurs to them, even though it is frequently incorrect, and reflective subjects tending to ponder various possibilities before deciding.

7. *Leveling versus sharpening* – reliable individual variations in assimilation in memory. Subjects at the leveling extreme tend to blur similar memories and to merge perceived objects or events with similar but not identical events recalled from previous experience. Sharpeners, at the other extreme, are less prone to confuse similar objects and, by contrast, may even judge the present to be less similar to the past than is actually the case.

8. *Constricted versus flexible control* – individual differences in susceptibility to distraction and cognitive interference.

9. *Tolerance for incongruous or unrealistic experiences* – a dimension of differential willingness to accept perceptions at variance with conventional experience (Messick, 1970, pp. 188-189).

As Messick points out, these cognitive styles, if they can be accepted as valid dimensions of individual differences, can apply over a broad range of cognitive performances. If we conceive a cognitive ability in terms of the paradigm presented in Chapter 1 – as a dimension in which ability interacts with task difficulty – a cognitive style may modulate the operation of such an ability in the actual performance of a task. For example, the cognitive style *leveling versus sharpening* could modulate the manner in which any one of the memory factors discussed in Chapter 7 might affect performance on learning and memory tasks. Messick also suggests that some of the commonly accepted ability factors, such as factors of speed or fluency, may be thought of as cognitive styles rather than abilities. This suggestion would have to be investigated by considering whether these factors conform to paradigms of level or of speed abilities, or to some special paradigm that might be devised for cognitive styles. I am unaware that any such special paradigm has been developed or tested, although further suggestions of Messick (1984, 1987) might lead to an appropriate paradigm. Specifically, Messick pointed out that cognitive style dimensions are nearly always of a bipolar nature.

With due respect to the diligent efforts of researchers who have investigated cognitive styles, it must be said that differential dimensions of cognitive style have not as yet been well established. An often-cited factor-analytic study of cognitive styles was that of Gardner, Holzman, Klein, Linton, and Spence (1959). This study contained two datasets, GARD01 ($N = 30$ males) and GARD02 ($N = 30$ females), which I attempted, without success, to reanalyze. Apparently the published correlation matrices contained errors, or were based on too much missing data to permit their reanalysis. In any case, factor analysis of these matrices would be highly questionable in view of the fact that the number of variables in them was greater than the number of cases. Wardell (1974) also tried reanalyzing these datasets, using only 20 variables, and concluded that the results were "disappointing." Only "leveling versus sharpening and perhaps extensiveness of scanning and field articulation could be identified" (p. 774), and the factor patterns were quite different for the two sexes.

A further study (Gardner, Jackson, & Messick, 1960) attempted to determine relations between a series of cognitive tests and "cognitive controls" of field-articulation, leveling-sharpening, equivalence range [another term, apparently, for Messick's *breadth of categorizing*], and constricted versus flexible control. An interbattery factor analysis based on data from 63 female undergraduates demonstrated considerable covariance between cognitive control measures and ability tests, chiefly centered, according to the authors, in dimensions of field-articulation and leveling-sharpening. In my reanalysis of the data from this study (dataset GARD05A), it appeared that most of the measures of cognitive controls (variables designated CC3 through CC7) did not pass muster under Kaiser's (1981) measure of sampling adequacy and had to be dropped from the analysis. The most prominent result was that a time score from the Embedded

Table 14.3. *8 factors of cognitive style (CY) in 5 datasets*

Dataset	Codes[a] D C	A	T	M/F	Factor no.	Details (saliently loaded variables)
ADEV01	'68U	18	1	1	3	Mirror-Tracing tests; Rod & Frame
FEDE02	'80U	21	2	3	9	Category Width; Nonimpulsivity
SATT01	'76E	11	6	1	4	Embedded Figures; Haptic Perception; Analytic Style Preference
SATT11	'79E	11	6	3	5	Leveling/Sharpening; Extraversion
WIDI01	'80U	19	P	3	2	Form Memory; Form Preference
″	″	″	″	″	3	Element Memory; Contextual Score
″	″	″	″	″	5	Gestalt Completion; Background Memory; Analytic Ability; Background Preference Score
″	″	″	″	″	7	Global Tendency (negative); Analytic Tendency; Element Preference

[a]Codes: D (date), C (country), A (age), T (sample type), M/F (1 = male, 2 = female; 3 = both); see Appendix A for further information on codes.

Figures test and a (reflected) error score from the Rod and Frame test were strongly and saliently loaded on a Flexibility of Closure factor. This factor is listed in Table 8.6, not in Table 14.3, because it appears more like a factor following the paradigm of an ability rather than of a cognitive style – that is, it does not represent a dimension along which individuals can choose to operate at any point, as might be true of a cognitive style.

In the years that have elapsed since these studies were done in the 1950s and 1960s, it seems that no adequate factor-analytic study of cognitive styles has been conducted – certainly not one that included all nine of the dimensions listed above, and there is little reliable information about relations between cognitive styles and cognitive abilities. There is possibly a methodological difficulty in investigating such relations, in that linear correlational and factor analysis may not be appropriate for such studies. It is conceivable, for example, that individuals with different profiles of cognitive styles could make identical scores on ability tests; such differences, therefore, might not show up in conventional correlational analyses.

The present survey was not designed to focus on factors of cognitive style. Nevertheless, Table 14.3 lists eight token factors that appeared in five of our datasets and that merit discussion as possibly measuring dimensions of cognitive style.

Factor 3 from dataset ADEV01 (Adevai, Silverman, & McGough, 1968) was from a study of perceptual correlates of the Rod-and-Frame test, a standard test for field independence vs. field dependence (also used in dataset GARD05A mentioned above). In this test, the subject is seated in a dark room and shown a luminous rod within a luminous tilted frame. *S*'s task is to adjust the rod so that it appears to be truly vertical. In a series of trials, the tilting of the frame is varied; the subject's score is a function of how close to vertical he is able to adjust the rod. (The tilted frame can produce the illusion that the rod is vertical when it is actually not exactly vertical.) In this dataset, there were two measures of performance on this task – one in which the experimenter made the adjustments as directed by the subject, and one in which the subject himself adjusted the rod by a remote control device. Both measures had high salient loadings on the factor (.645 and .571, respectively). Even higher, however, were loadings for measures of speed (.758) and accuracy (.752) on a mirror-tracing task, in which *S* traced a path around a double-ruled six-pointed star guided only by a mirror reflection of the star. Relatively low salient loadings (.391 and .270, respectively), were found for the Gottschaldt Embedded Figures test and a Draw-a-Person test. The Embedded Figures test has been described in Chapter 8 since it is usually found to be a measure of Flexibility of Closure; however, like the Rod-and-Frame test, it is also considered to be a measure of field independence.

These findings illustrate the problem of distinguishing a cognitive style from a cognitive ability. Were it not for the extensive research of Witkin, Dyk, Faterson, Goodenough, & Karp (1962) investigating personality correlates of field independence as measured by the Embedded Figures test and the Rod-and-Frame test, one would be inclined to label this factor simply as Flexibility of Closure, and it might well have been listed in Table 8.6 devoted to that factor.

Further illustrations of confusions between styles and abilities come from a study by Federico and Landis (1980) investigating relationships among cognitive styles and selected abilities and aptitudes. In my reanalysis of their correlation matrix, I found two factors that might represent cognitive styles. Factor 10 was saliently loaded principally with Hidden Figures and a Figure Classification test. It could be interpreted as a field independence factor, but I classified it under Flexibility of Closure because the tests are clearly measures of ability, and it is listed in Table 8.6. Factor 9 was saliently loaded with three cognitive style measures: Category Width Scale, Role Construct Repertory, and Impulsivity Scale – all in a positive direction (in view of the *negative* loading of the *reflected* score on the Impulsivity Scale). The Category Width Scale (Pettigrew, 1958) purports to measure the "consistency of cognitive range." The Role Construct Repertory (Bieri, Atkins, Briar, Leaman, Miller, & Tripodi, 1966) purports to measure "cognitive complexity" or the multidimensionality of perceptions of the environment. The Impulsivity Scale (from Jackson's, 1974, Personality Research Form) is intended to measure reflectiveness versus impulsivity. Note that these are three different claimed cognitive styles; no one of these styles was represented by more than one measure. The fact that they were grouped into one factor here would indicate that they have something in common, but it is not clear what this is. In any event, they showed little if any relation to any cognitive ability test.

Factors 9 and 10 were loaded rather weakly on a second-order factor, factor 8, that could be interpreted as a general cognitive style factor.

In two studies, Satterly (1976, 1979) has investigated relations between cognitive styles, intelligence (particularly spatial ability), and school achievement, compiling datasets SATT01 and SATT11 respectively. In the first of these, I find factor 4 saliently loaded with Embedded Figures, Haptic Shape Perception, and Analytic Style Preference. It was also nonsaliently loaded, though weakly, with the Gottschaldt Simple Figures test, a mathematics understanding test, and a verbal reasoning intelligence test; it was distinct from a spatial visualization factor (factor 2). It might well be classified as Flexibility of Closure, but the presence of the Analytic Style Preference score on this factor suggests that it may be substantially influenced by the cognitive style of field independence. The Analytic Style Preference score came from a special test devised by Satterly and Brimer (1971) in which, according to Satterly, "high scores indicate a withholding of closure and the suppression of the 'common' response in a picture-grouping test" (p. 38). Embedded Figures and Haptic Shape Perception had substantial loadings (.369 and .404, respectively) on a second-order factor for the battery.

The second of Satterly's datasets (SATT11) included measures of field independence, analytic-synthetic, and level-sharpening styles, along with measures of IQ and school achievement. In reanalysis, however, I was able only to identify a factor (factor 5) for the leveling-sharpening style, and even this was suspect because of the experimental dependence involved in the measures. The measure of analytic-synthetic style had negligible correlations with all other variables, and the single measure of field-independence loaded only on a second-order factor.

A study by Widiger, Knudson, and Rorer (1980) deserves attention because it attempted to separate stylistic and ability components. Their review of the literature was in effect a scathing critique that suggested that most previous studies had failed to show that cognitive styles were independent of abilities, and that most tests purporting to measure cognitive styles are actually measures of ability. Their study attempted to establish the independence of four constructs: analytic style, global style, analytic ability, and global ability. The style constructs were measured with tests in which the manner in which a subject grouped visual patterns would supposedly show whether the subject adopted an analytic or a global approach. The ability constructs were measured with tests in which subjects were required to adopt either an analytic or a global approach. (The reader is referred to the original article for details.) In their factor analysis of the data, they found that the ability measures (which included the Group Embedded Figures test) formed an ability factor, but that the stylistic measures "failed to converge and formed four factors." This approximately describes the outcome of my reanalysis of this dataset (WIDI01). Factor 6 was a Spatial ability factor loaded with a Global Ability score, the Group Embedded Figures test, and the Advanced Progressive Matrices. The remaining four factors did not align themselves with the stylistic constructs hypothesized by the authors. Factor 7, loaded with Analytic Tendency and (negatively) Global Tendency, seems to indicate a bipolar analytic/global style factor that is independent of ability. The other three factors are specifics that draw on both ability and style tests. One can agree with the authors' conclusion that "present field dependence-independence measures are best interpreted as ability tests rather than measures of a cognitive style" (p. 116). At the same time, the bipolar analytic/global style factor identified here deserves further investigation.

The overall impression presented by these limited results – admittedly perhaps only a small sample of what may be available – is that cognitive styles have not yet been well established and differentiated, and that most putative measures of cognitive style depend too much on speed and accuracy ability parameters. The domain of cognitive styles is in need of much more careful and thorough investigation than it has received thus far. It may be too much to expect that cognitive style measures will be uncorrelated with ability measures, for it is possible or even probable that abilities are associated with particular cognitive styles, but cognitive style measures must be based on a psychometric paradigm that is different from the paradigms on which speed and accuracy ability measures are based.

A possible dimension of cognitive style is that which has long been a matter of speculation and research – the distinction between "verbal" and "visual" modes of cognition and thinking. Paivio (1971, Chapter 14) presents a review of work on this distinction, particularly with reference to his proposed "dual-coding" approach to semantic memory, according to which language and world knowledge are represented in interconnected but distinct representational systems – verbal and imaginal. He reports factor-analytic work, derived partly from objective measures of verbal and spatial abilities and partly from subjective reports of the use of verbal and imaginal processes, that gives support to the dual-process theory. However, one gets the impression from this work, also from a factor-analytic study of questionnaire responses on verbal and imaginal modes of thought (Paivio & Harshman, 1983), that any distinction between verbal and imaginal processes is mainly a *reflection* of different profiles of individual differences in verbal and spatial abilities. That is, Paivio's results can be parsimoniously interpreted as showing that people differ in the balance of their verbal and spatial abilities – as we could expect from the fact that verbal abilities and spatial abilities are virtually uncorrelated dimensions – and that individuals' subjective reports of the extent to which they use verbal and imaginal processes are, so to speak, merely epiphenomenal.

Perhaps this remark can be generalized to all instances of postulated "cognitive styles." If we assume that people use whatever abilities they possess to make decisions and solve problems, it can be expected that the manner in which decisions are made or problems are solved will vary depending on what profile of abilities is present in an individual. Referring to different modes of behavior as resulting from different "cognitive styles" is merely a manner of speaking; there is no necessary implication that cognitive styles exist independently of profiles of ability. For further discussion of cognitive styles vs. abilities, see Guilford (1980b), McKenna (1984), and Tiedeman (1989).

FACTORS OF MOTIVATION (MO), INTEREST (I#), AND PERSONALITY (PR)

This survey was not designed to cover the domains of motivation, interest, and personality, and it would be too selective and overparticular to discuss the factors in these domains that emerged from my reanalyses of the relatively few datasets that disclosed such factors. For purposes of record, Table 14.4 lists 27 factors in 14 datasets that were classified in these domains.

Dimensions of motivation have been reviewed and discussed by Boyle (1988). There has been extensive use of factor-analytic techniques in the construction of occupational interest inventories such as the Kuder Preference Record – Vocational (Kuder, 1934–76) and the Jackson Vocational Interest Survey (Jackson, 1977). For a summary of the enormous literature that exists on the factor analysis of personality, see B. D. Smith (1988).

FACTORS OF ADMINISTRATIVE BEHAVIOR (AM)

Because of its possible relevance to the analysis of cognitive abilities, a dataset from a study of administrative behavior of elementary school principals by Hemphill, Griffiths, Frederiksen, Stice, Iannaccone, Coffield, and Carlton (1961) was included in our database and subjected to reanalysis. The variables were scores assigned to 232 elementary school principals who responded to an "in-basket test" in which they were presented with simulated problems arising in an imaginary school of which they were to suppose themselves to be a principal. My reanalysis produced eight factors highly similar to those presented by the authors, except that it produced only one second-order factor, in contrast to the authors' two second-order factors. Also, my factors tend to be "purer" than those presented by the authors, with fewer high loadings, probably due to better simple-structure rotational procedures than those available to the authors in 1961. The interpretations of the first-order factors are listed in Table 14.5, in order of their loadings on the one second-order factor (which are also given), and these too are similar to the authors' interpretations. In effect, the first-order factors represent estimates of the likelihoods that any particular subject would take actions of the types specified, in confronting the kinds of problems he or she might encounter in administering an elementary school, on the assumption that the in-basket test is a valid simulation of real-life behavior. That is, subjects would vary in the profiles of responses they would take. The loadings on the second-order factor indicate the degree to which any particular subject, adopting a particular course of action, conforms to the overall pattern of response. (It is

Table 14.4. *27 factors of motivation, interests, and personality in 14 datasets*

Dataset	Codes[a]				Factor no.	Details (saliently loaded variables)
	D C	A	T	M/F		
Motivation (MO)						
CRAW01	'76C	14	1	3	4	Fear; Vocabulary
"	"	"	"	"	7	Superego; Self; Protectiveness; School Sentiment
"	"	"	"	"	8	Mating; Pugnacity-Sadism; Home-Parental; Assertiveness; Narcism-Comfort
MANG01A	'59E	14	6	3	7	Tests of persistence
PEDU01	'80I	10	1	3	7	Measures of school motivation
THOR51	'39U	19	6	3	2	Measures of persistence
"	"	"	"	"	6	Measures of ability to withstand discomfort
Interests						
GRIM01	'71U	18	6	3	2	Interests in art and music (I1)
"	"	"	"	"	3	Interests in biology & health (I2)
"	"	"	"	"	4	Interests in science (I3)
"	"	"	"	"	5	Interests in business, etc. (I4)
PIMS02	'62U	19	F	3	3	Interest in for. lang. study (I6)
TAYL13A	'67U	19	6	1	5	Interest in speaking (I5)
Personality (PR)						
DENT01	'55U	17	1	3	4	Social Introversion (negative); Rhathymia ("Happy-go-lucky")
"	"	"	"	"	5	Thinking Introversion
"	"	"	"	"	6	Cycloid Tendency; Depression
HORN01	'66U	28	Q	3	5	Early Risk-Taking
"	"	"	"	"	10	Positive Self-Image
"	"	"	"	"	11	Premsic Sensitivity
HORN02	'82U	28	Q	3	5	Early Risk-Taking
"	"	"	"	"	6	Positive Self-Image
"	"	"	"	"	7	Self-Sentiment
"	"	"	"	"	10	Sensitivity; Assertive Ego
REMO01	'62Y	15	6	1	4	Behavior in group conversation
TAYL12A	'67U	21	2	1	9	Anxiety items
TAYL13A	'67U	19	6	1	12	Anxiety measures
THOR51	'39U	19	6	3	3	Feelings of adequacy

[a]Codes: D (date), C (country), A (age), T (sample type), M/F (1 = male, 2 = female; 3 = both); see Appendix A for further information on codes.

Table 14.5. *8 factors of administrative behavior (AM) in dataset HEMP21*

Dataset	Codes[a] D C	A	T	M/F	Factor no.	Loading on 2nd-order factor	Factor interpretation
HEMP21	'61U	30	G	3	2	.82	Discuss before acting
"	"	"	"	"	3	.72	Maintain organizational relations
"	"	"	"	"	4	.65	Direct work of others
"	"	"	"	"	5	.60	Exchange information
"	"	"	"	"	6	.29	Analyze situation
"	"	"	"	"	7	.27	Organize work
"	"	"	"	"	8	.13	Comply with suggestions
"	"	"	"	"	9	−.35	Respond to outsiders

[a]Codes: D (date), C (country), A (age), T (sample type), M/F (1 = male, 2 = female; 3 = both); see Appendix A for further information on codes.

a little ironic that this study, if anything, revealed dimensions of cognitive style, rather than abilities. Surely the authors did not intend their measures of in-basket behavior to be measures of cognitive styles.)

The subjects in this study were also given extensive batteries of psychological tests, including tests of ability, knowledge, personality, and interest. Many of the administrative style factors showed significant relations with ability and knowledge test scores. These relationships are too numerous and detailed to present here. The interested reader is referred to the original report, or to a discussion of this and other studies of administrative behavior by Frederiksen (1986).

MISCELLANEOUS FACTORS OF INFANT AND CHILD BEHAVIOR

Partly as a matter of historical interest, three datasets from an early study of infant abilities (Richards & Nelson, 1939) were reanalyzed. It was considered useful to reanalyze them because the methods employed by the authors (or by Holzinger, who also analyzed the data), were somewhat primitive, and gave incorrect or at least inadequate results according to contemporary standards. The authors gave 80 children appropriate tests from Gesell's (1925) series at each of the ages 6, 12, and 18 months; these are datasets RICH31, RICH32, and RICH33 respectively, some details of which are listed in Table 14.6. My analyses agreed with Holzinger's more than with those of the authors. In each case, I obtained a general factor and three first-order factors. At age 6 months, these latter could be interpreted as (factor 2) motor development, (factor 3) a cognitive development factor loaded with two tests – *splashes in tub* and *regards pellet*, and (factor 4) an alertness and attention factor. The two tests loading on factor 3 have

Table 14.6. *10 factors of infant and child behavior (XC) in 6 datasets*

Dataset	Codes[a]					Factor no.	Details (saliently loaded variables)
	D C	A	T	M/F			
RICH31	'39U	.5	N	3	2	Inhibits 1 hand & head; Pats table; Dangling ring/persist; etc.
,,	,,	,,	,,	,,	3	Splashes in tub; Regards pellet
,,	,,	,,	,,	,,	4	Music/laughs; Music/stops crying; Looks for fallen object
RICH32	'39U	1	N	3	2	Tries shoes; Walks alone; Imitates scribble; Climbs
,,	,,	,,	,,	,,	4	Tower of Two; Third Cube
RICH33	'39U	1.5	N	3	2	Asks for Toilet; Bladder Control; Repeats things said; Listens to stories
WACH03	'81U	2	N	3	2	Means; Space; Causality
WIEB11	'80U	4	O	1	4	Imitative action; Leg coordination; Block building
WIEB12	'80U	4	O	2	2	Arm Coordination; Draw-a-design; Draw-a-child; Verbal memory II
,,	,,	,,	,,	,,	4	Verbal Memory I; Leg coordination; Imitative action; Numerical Memory I; Verbal fluency

[a]Codes: D (date), C (country), A (age), T (sample type), M/F (1 = male, 2 = female; 3 = both); see Appendix A for further information on codes.

the special characteristic, as the authors note, that they "rank above all other tests in correlating rather highly with later mental status" (p. 310). At age 12 months, the three factors are (2) gross motor development, (3) language development, and (4) fine motor development. At age 18 months, the three factors could be interpreted as (2) alertness (?), (3) visualization ability (VZ), and (4) language development. The language development factors are listed in Table 5.1 and the spatial ability factor is listed in Table 8.3.

Also listed in Table 14.6 are two factors obtained in reanalyses of correlation matrices (supplied by the authors) for two datasets obtained by Wiebe and Watkins (1980) for males' and females' scores on the McCarthy Scales of Children's Abilities given to a sample of 200 children aged $2\frac{1}{2}$ to 5 years. In reanalyses, I obtained six factors for each matrix (in contrast to the authors' three and five factors, respectively). Most of these factors have been listed in appropriate tables earlier in this volume. The two factors listed in Table 14.6 are those that could not be interpreted in terms of familiar categories. They appear to be largely dependent on motor development. The presence of a second-order factor obtained for each matrix can probably be attributed to the wide age range of the sample.

Brief mention may be made of a factor-analytic study of infant behavior conducted by Wachs and Hubert (1981), yielding datasets WACH01, WACH02, and WACH03 for subscales of the Infant Psychological Development Scale (Uzgiris & Hunt, 1975) given to samples of 25 infants at each age 14, 18, and 22 months, respectively. My reanalyses of these datasets were somewhat more conservative than those of the authors; I accepted one less factor at each age (i.e., two at ages 14 and 18 months. and three at age 22 months). They tended, however, to confirm the main factors described by Wachs and Hubert, who were interested in changes in the structure of cognitive-intellectual performance during the second year of life. Striking changes in correlational and factorial patterns over the three ages were noted; whether these changes are real or statistical artifacts of some sort is a problem.

FACTORS OF EARLY SCHOOL BEHAVIOR

Table 14.7 lists five factors of early school behavior in two datasets. These factors pertain to largely noncognitive aspects of children's behavior in the early school years. Factors 3, 5, 6, and 7 of dataset JOHA01 come from reanalysis of Johansson's (1965) study of school readiness as measured by ratings and tests given to 235 children in grade two of Swedish schools, and show that several noncognitive aspects of school behavior are factorially distinguishable among themselves and from measures of cognitive development (indicated in factors 2 and 4). All first-order factors in this study, however, are loaded on a second-order factor (factor 1) that is interpreted as "general school readiness." Factor 6 for dataset PEDU01 derives from several rated measures of "school deportment": manners/politeness, behavior in school, getting along with others, personal appearance, and attendance, that are thus shown to be independent of various cognitive measures and measures of school motivation.

FACTORS OF SOCIAL AND EDUCATIONAL BACKGROUND

Table 14.8 lists several factors of social and educational background that appeared in our datasets, despite the fact that for most datasets, variables indicating age, sex, or educational and social background were dropped from correlation matrices prior to their analysis because they were deemed not immediately relevant to identifying factors of cognitive ability.

MISCELLANEOUS SPECIAL (s0) FACTORS

In Table 14.9 are listed 19 token factors – most of a cognitive nature – that do not fit readily into any previously considered category but that merit special comment. They are all "unique," in the sense that similar factors do not appear

Table 14.7. *5 factors of early school behavior in 2 datasets*

| Dataset | Codes[a] | | | | Factor no. | Details (saliently loaded variables) |
	D C	A	T	M/F		
JOHA01	'65S	7	1	3	3	Rated Motor Readiness; Paired Comparison Assessments of Fine Motor Readiness (DM)
”	”	”	”	”	5	Self-Confidence; Positive Attitude Toward Classmates (DA)
”	”	”	”	”	6	Ratings of Social and Emotional Aspects of Readiness (DS)
”	”	”	”	”	7	Rated Attitude toward Teacher (AT)
PEDU01	'80I	10	1	3	6	Rated School Deportment (DT)

[a]Codes: D (date), C (country), A (age), T (sample type), M/F (1 = male, 2 = female; 3 = both); see Appendix A for further information on codes.

Table 14.8. *5 background factors in 3 datasets*

| Dataset | Codes[a] | | | | Factor no. | Details (saliently loaded variables) |
	D C	A	T	M/F		
FRUC21	'52U	21	2	1	5	SES Status; Biographical Inventory; Education (Yrs. Schooling) (E0)
HOLM01	'67U	15	E	3	2	Grade Level; Chronol. Age (AG)
”	”	”	”	”	3	Age Onset Deafness; Etiological Classification; Degree of Deafness (AD)
WOLF11	'85U	17	1	3	3	Father's Education; Occupation (AA)
”	”	”	”	”	4	Mother's Education (AB)

[a]Codes: D (date), C (country), A (age), T (sample type), M/F (1 = male, 2 = female; 3 = both); see Appendix A for further information on codes.

to occur anywhere else in our database. In most cases, however, they seem to be of psychological interest and worthy of further investigation. They are discussed in a series of separate paragraphs below, by dataset.

Dataset BLAC21. This study by Blackwood (1980) was an investigation of visual imagery and its correlates. In contrast to the eight-factor solution favored by Blackwood, my reanalysis identified five orthogonal factors, including factor 1 (Visual Imagery, IM; see Table 8.10), factor 3 (Visualization, VZ; see Table 8.3), and factor 4 (Verbal Ability, V; see Table 5.2). Factor 2 apparently represents individual differences in the extent to which subjects exhibit marked physiological responses to situations in which they were asked to imagine looking at scenes of several sorts, such as eye movements while imagining watching a tennis game,

Table 14.9. *19 miscellaneous special factors (S0) in 15 datasets*

| Dataset | Codes[a] | | | | Factor no. | Details (saliently loaded variables) |
	D C	A	T	M/F		
BLAC21	'80U	19	P	2	2	Physiological responses to scenes
"	"	"	"	"	5	Responses to emotional scenes
CARR41	'76U	19	6	3	6	Variables from Crowder syllable task: Consonant errors minus vowel errors
HAKS01	'74C	24	1	3	10	Design preference tests (esthetic judgment)
"	"	"	"	"	22	Representational drawing tests
HEND11A	'82E	16	6	3	4	EEG string response
"	"	"	"	"	7	EEG variance measure
HORN21	'78U	30	Q	1	6	Category free sort measures
KARL11	'42U	16	6	3	7	Incidental closure measures?
RANK01	'66U	19	P	3	2	Errors in Porteus maze tracing I
"	"	"	"	"	3	Errors in Porteus maze tracing II
REYN01	'79U	5	1	3	2	Symbol manipulation tasks
SEIB02	'67U	19	6	3	10	Viewing conditions in a perceptual task
SUNG01	'81U	16	Z	3	4	Word association & clerical tasks
SUNG03	'81U	16	W	3	6	Word association & clerical tasks
SUNG04	'81U	16	1	1	11	Word association & clerical tasks
SUNG05	'81U	16	1	2	8	Word association & clerical tasks
THUR81	'41U	13	6	3	11	Dot-counting (subitizing?) tasks
VOSS01	'77G	8	1	3	1	Visual exploration tasks

[a]Codes: D (date), C (country), A (age), T (sample type), M/F (1 = male, 2 = female; 3 = both); see Appendix A for further information on codes.

or breath rate while imagining a "fearful" scene such as being ready to make a first parachute jump or hurrying to get out of a building which is on fire. Unfortunately, some of the variables measuring this factor were experimentally dependent on each other, but there was sufficient correlation among nondependent variables to justify the construct validity of the factor. Factor 5 seems to represent individual differences in the extent to which subjects report anxiety and vivid imagery in imagining being in emotional and fearful scenes – not related, however, to actual physiological responses recorded during the imagining of such scenes.

Dataset CARR41. Factor 6 is loaded with measures derived from several versions of a memory span test for which Crowder (1971) studied what he called a "suffix effect." In some versions, the signal to the subject to begin reproducing the series of stimuli was a tone; in other versions, the signal was a distinct syllable "go!" Crowder had found that memory performance was affected by which type of signal was employed. This was not, however, the critical element in factor 6. What was critical was whether the stimuli in the series (of lengths ranging from

7 to 9) were distinguished by vowel phonemes or consonant phonemes. For example, consonant stimuli were composed of the syllables /ba/, /da/, and /ga/, while vowel stimuli were composed of the syllables /gah/, /giy/, and /guw/. It was found that a reliable variable for each version of the task (whether the responses were made orally or in writing, and whether the series had a syllable or a tone "suffix") was the difference between the number of errors for the consonant version and the number of errors for the vowel version. Factor 6 was loaded with this measure for the oral task and for the written task. Unexpectedly, it was also loaded saliently with the Mathematics score from the Scholastic Aptitude Test. These results are interesting but puzzling; they need to be replicated, because they are based on N = only 33.

Dataset HAKS01. Factor 10 in this dataset is based on scores on three forms of a Design Preference or Esthetic Judgment test. Similarly, factor 22 is derived from three subtests of a Representational Drawing test. The report (Hakstian & Cattell, 1974) fails to specify the exact nature of these tests.

Dataset HEND11A. Factors 4 and 7 are derived from my analysis of selected variables from a correlation matrix presented by D. E. Hendrickson (1982) from research involving relations between subtests of the Wechsler Adult Intelligence Scale (Wechsler, 1955, or actually as modified for Great Britain by Saville, 1971) and EEG (electroencephalographic) responses. The sample consisted of 219 older schoolchildren (average age 15.6 years). EEG measures were taken for responses to a 1000-Hz tone over 100 trials (but only the last 90 trials were used in the analysis). Two "epochs" were employed: 256 ms, as being close to the "average human pulse train," and 512 ms, for comparative purposes. For each epoch, there was a "string measure" (essentially a mean) and a variance measure. Factor 4 represents the string measure taken at the two epochs (r = .67) and factor 5 represents the *reflected* variance measure for the two epochs (r = .60). The interesting result of the reanalysis was that at the second-order, the string measure tended to be associated with the performance subtests of the WAIS (Object Assembly, Blocks, Digit-symbol, and Picture Arrangement), while the reflected variance measure was associated with the verbal subtests (Vocabulary, Information, Digit Span, Similarities, Arithmetic, and Comprehension). All measures (WAIS subtests and EEG measures) loaded on a third-order factor – presumably general intelligence; true to the author's hypothesis that the 256-epoch measures more closely represented the average human pulse train length, the 256-epoch measures had higher loadings on the third-order factor (.658 and .631) than the 512-epoch measures (.370 and .278, respectively, for the string and variance measures). These findings deserve serious consideration as evidence of important physiological correlates of intelligence, and also, to the extent that performance subtests of the WAIS represent fluid intelligence and verbal subtests represent crystallized intelligence, support for a Horn–Cattell theory of intelligence amplified to include reference to physiological correlates.

Dataset HORN21. Factor 6 is based on several variables in which subjects were asked to categorize lists of words, with either high or low interassociational values; scores were the number of categories used by the subjects. The author (Horn, 1978b) labeled this factor CDE but there is no indication in his report as to what this mnemonic is supposed to mean; also, there is no explicit interpretation of the factor. Possibly it could be interpreted as a measure (reflected) of the breadth-of-categorizing cognitive style mentioned above.

Dataset KARL11. As did Karlin (1942) I obtained a factor (factor 7) loaded saliently with the IQ from the Henmon–Nelson Intelligence test, a Sensory Masking test in which *S* had to write words heard against an increasingly loud buzzing background noise, a Memory for Limericks test in which *S* was shown a series of limericks on a screen and subsequently had to write their last lines, and a Memory for Drawings test in which *S* had to recognize drawings (geometric designs) that had previously been shown on a screen. It is difficult to classify or interpret this factor. Karlin called it an Incidental Closure factor, "a closure effect transcending sense modality, dependent on partial cues from the source of stimulation" (p. 271).

Dataset RANK01. Rankin and Thompson (1966a) obtained correlations among eight "qualitative" (Q) scores that Porteus had developed for performance on the Porteus Maze Test (Porteus, 1914–65, 1950). These authors obtained five factors for these correlations – obviously too many for eight variables. Reanalysis showed two weakly correlated factors at the first order. Factor 2 appears to indicate impulsivity in performing Porteus maze tasks, as indicated by such errors as cutting corners and crossing lines. Factor 3 is loaded with more general types of error scores. There were no impressive correlations with a vocabulary test.

Dataset REYN01. Reynolds (1979) factor-analyzed the responses of 322 beginning first graders to the six subtests of the Metropolitan Readiness Test. Initially, he obtained two- and three-factor solutions, but using the criterion attributed to Kaiser (1960a) – number of eigenvalues greater than one – he concluded that the test "has a single factor (General Readiness) accounting for the vast majority of reliable variance available" (p. 317). Reanalysis indicated that a better description would be obtained by considering two first-order factors: factor 2, loaded with various symbol manipulation tasks (copying, letter matching, numbers, and matching), and factor 3, loaded with word meaning and listening tasks. These factors, however, are highly correlated in their oblique form. Factor 1 is the second-order factor, with loadings on all six tests.

Dataset SEIB02. Factor 10 in this dataset arises from the (negative) correlation between two control variables, viewing distance and viewing angle, assigned to each subject in a testing situation in which the *S*s viewed a screen at the front of a room. These variables showed certain significant correlations with scores on tests that depended on viewing stimuli on the screen. It would have been appropriate to partial out these variables from the test scores, rather than allowing them to remain in the matrix to be factored.

Datasets SUNG01, SUNG03, SUNG04, and SUNG05. These datasets are for correlations, for different subject groups, among subtests of a so-called Ball Aptitude Battery (Sung & Dawis, 1981). The factors listed in Table 14.9 are consistent in being loaded with the subtests called Word Association and Clerical. In Word Association, the task is to give a word associated with the given stimulus word; scoring is on the basis of similarity of response to normative responses. The Clerical test presents the task of identifying as quickly as possible all pairs of identical members from two columns of numbers. Why these two tests should be correlated is not clear. The result is of possible interest for future investigation; these datasets appear to be the only ones available in which a normatively scored word-association task is presented. (Note, however, that Word Association and Clerical scores did not show special correlational association in dataset SUNG02, for a Hispanic group in which it might be expected that the usual word association norms would not apply.)

Dataset THUR81. Thurstone and Thurstone (1941) had little to suggest about the nature of a factor (factor 11 in our reanalysis) that was saliently loaded chiefly with dot-counting tasks. To quote from these authors,

> ... In one of them [Dot Counting I], the dots were arranged in a row with frequent blank spaces that were intended to encourage grouping of the spots in counting them. The question was raised whether this performance would show a saturation on the number factor *N*, but such was not the case. In the second of the dot-counting tests [Dot Counting II], the spots were arranged irregularly in a square, and the subject was asked to count them quickly by any suitable grouping, or singly, if he so preferred. In the third test of this set [Dot Counting III], the spots were arranged in groups of two, three, four, or five, and their spatial arrangement was varied. It was thought that the perception of the geometrical pattern might be perceived as symbolic of numerical quantity by the children without explicit counting of each spot (Thurstone & Thurstone, 1941, p. 23).

The process that Thurstone and Thurstone had in mind is probably what has more recently been called *subitizing* (Kaufman, Lord, Reese, & Volkman, 1949; Chi & Klahr, 1975; Chase, 1978, pp. 64–71), that is, the immediate apprehension of the quantity of objects when the quantity is in the range one to somewhere between three and seven. Factor 11 in dataset THUR81 may be taken, perhaps, as a subitizing ability factor. Future investigation should attempt to measure this factor more directly, possibly by obtaining latencies for naming groups of dots – either randomly arranged or arranged in symmetric designs like those employed by Thurstone and Thurstone. Presumably the use of symmetric designs would yield lower latencies.

Dataset VOSS01. Voss and Keller (1977) investigated whether a so-called Obscure Figures Test (Acker & McReynolds, 1965) could be taken as an instrument to measure "cognitive innovation," using a series of measures of curiosity and creativity given to children aged seven to ten years. Reanalysis of their correlation matrix confirmed the two orthogonal factors they obtained, factor 1 being loaded with various measures of curiosity or "visual exploration," and factor 2 being loaded with the Obscure Figures Test as well as other creativity measures. Factor 2 was interpreted as measuring factor FO, Originality (see Table 10.8), but factor 1 has no parallel elsewhere in our database. It is loaded chiefly with various scores, derived from a task devised by Berlyne (1960), reflecting the degree to which subjects spend more time looking at "irregular" visual patterns than "regular" patterns. This factor is possibly a measure of a cognitive style dimension rather than an ability.

SOME DOUBLET OR SPECIFIC (S&) FACTORS

The reader may here be reminded that the basic factor model for the composition of a variable posits three types of variance: common factor variance, specific variance, and error variance. In theory, the communality of a variable measures the common factor variance; the difference between the reliability of a variable and the communality is a measure of specific variance, and what is left over from these is error variance. But specific variance refers to an ability that occurs in only a single test *of a particular battery*. In theory, it is always possible to convert what is specific variance in one battery to common factor variance in another battery, simply by insuring that the second battery has *two* (or more) variables measuring the specific variance in the first battery. This feature of factor theory has in some cases made it possible to expand the number of verified and confirmed factors by providing additional variables in successive factor studies. On the other hand, providing additional variables has often had the effect of artifactually, as it were, elevating what is properly regarded as highly specific variance to the level of common factor variance. Common factors produced in this way have often been called *doublets*, or *triplets* when the high loadings are restricted to two or three variables.

Actually, and unfortunately, it is a matter of subjective judgment to decide whether a factor found in the common factor space is truly a common factor or merely an artifactual representation of what would normally be specific variance. That is, there is no statistical or other procedure, as far as I am aware, to guide such a decision. Judgments on this matter have to rely on psychological considerations concerning how "basic" a factor is in terms of psychological processes, domains of knowledge, or methods of measurement, or in terms of the conceivable generality and construct validity of what is measured.

Table 14.10 lists a number of factors, found in the common factor spaces of our datasets (at least as I have analyzed them – for sometimes a "doublet" factor can be made to vanish by reducing the number of factors accepted for analysis), that are candidates for being either artifactual doublet factors or nonartifactual real common factors. If they are the latter, one could contemplate investigating their nature in further studies.

Table 14.10. *11 doublet or specific factors (S&) in 9 datasets*

Dataset	Codes[a]				Factor no.	Details (saliently loaded variables)
	D C	A	T	M/F		
ADKI03	'52U	19	2	1	9	Verbal Classification tests
CHRI01	'58U	19	2	1	5	Content triplet: Position recall
COOM01	'41U	17	1	3	2	Alphabet and ABC tasks
"	"	"	"	"	7	Substitution tasks
GUIL18	'53U	23	3	1	4	Word checking tasks
GUIL66	'52U	21	3	1	11	Social institutions doublet
PENF01	'67E	17	8	3	5	Scores on "Interpretations" task
TAYL12A	'67U	21	2	1	7	Telegram Writing: Number of words used; Number of ideas
THUR11	'38U	17	1	3	10	Scores on Designs test
THUR41	'44U	19	6	3	9	Rorschach scores
"	"	"	"	"	11	Schmidt task scores

[a]Codes: D (date), C (country), A (age), T (sample type), M/F (1 = male, 2 = female; 3 = both); see Appendix A for further information on codes.

Dataset ADKI03. There are no variables with salient loadings on factor 9, but two forms of a Verbal Classification test have small but possibly significant loadings on it. These tests have their salient loadings on factor 4 (Verbal Reasoning). It is likely, therefore, that factor 9 is a doublet factor capturing the specific variance of these tests associated with their particular format and content.

Dataset CHRI01. Christal's (1958) factor VII is the same as our factor 5, loaded with three tests that were designed to measure memory for position in space. According to him, however, "This factor is due entirely to use of the same subject matter for all three tests. The factor has no psychological significance and will be called simply the position recall content triplet" (p. 19). It should be pointed out, however, that variables 18 and 19 (loaded on this factor) have small but possibly significant loadings on factor 3, which appears to be a valid factor measuring memory for position in space.

Dataset COOM01. Two factors are to be considered here. Factor 2 is saliently loaded with 6 variables, all special tests designed by Coombs (1941) to test several hypotheses about the nature of the number factor, N (see Chapter 11). The three Alphabet tests required Ss to solve problems such as $B\ C\ C\ A\ C = ?$, where successive pairs of letters were to be combined according to the rules $AB = C$, $AC = B$, $BC = A$, $AA = A$, $BB = B$, $CC = C$. The AB and ABC tests were simpler forms of the Alphabet tests involving finding the proper solution for only two or three letters. The Forms test was like the ABC test except that three nonmeaningful geometrical designs replaced the letters A, B, and C. Coombs regarded his factor A, corresponding to our factor 2, as a triplet that could not be interpreted with any certainty because of the high similarity of the tests. Possibly this was too hasty a conclusion. Although factor 9 was linearly independent of factor 3, the Number (N) factor, it was highly correlated with it, and in fact the tests loaded on factor 9 had among the highest loadings of all variables on the second-order factor in this battery – higher than those of Number factor tests. These tests deserve to be further investigated as measures of a distinct and possibly interpretable factor of facility in learning and following simple rules. The only other dataset in which some of these variables have been employed is WERD02, where they loaded on a numerical facility factor, possibly because there were not enough of them to define a distinct factor.

Factor 7 in the reanalysis corresponds to Coombs's factor B, which he regarded as an uninterpretable triplet. It is loaded with three Substitution tests, "designed to see if an increasing familiarity with the translation of an arbitrary symbolism would have any significance in relation to number ability" (Coombs, 1941, pp. 173–174). Each test used 90 words in code which are to be translated; since the same code is used throughout the tests, there was opportunity to learn it. It might be of interest to investigate this type of task further; I do not find it employed in any other dataset. The three variables had substantial loadings on a second-order factor.

Dataset GUIL18. Factor 4 was saliently loaded chiefly with two Word Checking tests, and both of these had substantial loadings on a second-order factor. These were multiple-choice tests in which S had to choose which word fits given criteria (e.g., "man-made object," "object must not be growing and smaller than a football"). It is difficult to judge whether it represents a distinct factor; most likely it reflects some special feature of the tests.

Dataset GUIL66. The only salient loading on Factor 11 was a *negative* one, $-.583$, for scoring of a Social Institutions task for the number of "indirect" or "remote" improvements suggested by S on a series of social institutions. The factor was (nonsaliently) loaded with a scoring for the number of "direct" or "obvious" improvements. This factor therefore is an artifact resulting from the two scorings of a single test. It illustrates a type of experimental dependence that should not be allowed to occur in the design of a test battery for factor analysis.

Dataset PENF01. Factor 5 is saliently loaded with three scores from an "Interpretations" test. The source (Penfold & Abou-Hatab, 1967) is not clear as to the nature of this test. Either the factor is an artifact resulting from experimental dependence, or it reflects an important process in critical thinking that should be further investigated.

Dataset THUR11. Factor 10 is saliently loaded with two scores from a Designs test. It is undoubtedly to be regarded as a doublet resulting from experimental dependence. (In later studies by Thurstone, the Designs test is generally interpreted as measuring factor CF, Flexibility of Closure.)

Dataset THUR41. Factor 9 is saliently loaded with two scores from the

Table 14.11. *87 uninterpreted factors (IO) in 65 datasets*

Dataset	Codes[a] D C	A	T	M/F	Factor no.	Details (saliently loaded variables)
AFTA01	'69C	43	1	3	3	Kahn test recall; Critical flicker fusion deviation
,,	,,	,,	,,	,,	6	Minnesota Percepto-Diagnostic test
,,	,,	,,	,,	,,	8	Proverbs; Kahn test symbolization; Halstead rhythm (tapping) test
,,	,,	,,	,,	,,	11	Grassi time credits; Halstead speech sounds; Grassi accuracy
ALLE11	'78U	30	U	3	4	Letter Rotations Intercept; Sentence Recognition Mean Error; Sentence Recall Clustering
ALLE12	'78U	30	U	3	4	Sentence Recall Clustering; Sentence Recognition Task
ANGL11	'75G	22	6	3	5	Schaie & Breskin rigidity tests
,,	,,	,,	,,	,,	6	Tempo factor for Cattell S-Z rigidity test
ARNO01	'67A	16	1	3	6	Sentence completion; limericks
BRAD01	'69U	16	1	3	10	Object Class Memory
BROW11	'66U	16	6	3	6	Picture arrangement; memory for test order
CARR41	'76U	19	6	3	4	Craik memory test; Words in Sentences (Modern Language Aptitude Test)
,,	,,	,,	,,	,,	7	Craik Rehearsal-Recog. Position 1
CARR43	'77U	19	6	3	13	Continuous memory task; Disguised Spelling
CLAU01	'66U	9	R	3	7	Word association
CLAU02	'66U	13	R	3	5	Kinesthetic response
CLAU03	'66U	22	R	3	6	Mirror drawing errors; Lower-arm movement
CLAU04	'66U	9	1	3	9	Lower-arm movement; Scrambled reaction time
,,	,,	,,	,,	,,	10	Reaction time to pictures; Ataxiometry measure
,,	,,	,,	,,	,,	12	Mirror drawing errors; Azimuth arithmetic
DETT00	'85U	21	2	2	2	Various ECT's scored for accuracy
DUNC11	'64U	11	6	3	9	Verbal Paired Associates Component 2
GARR11	'35U	9	6	1	2	Geometric Forms; Making Gates (test descriptions unavailable)
GERS01	'63U	19	3	1	2	Alternate additions & 11 other diverse tests
,,	,,	,,	,,	,,	7	Dot systems; Alternate letter groups
GERS02	'63U	14	1	3	8	Varied Symbols
GUIL11	'55U	21	3	1	6	Picture arrangement; Mechanical principles
GUIL12	'56U	21	3	1	6	Alternate headlines
,,	,,	,,	,,	,,	11	Alternate headlines--rearrangement
GUIL14	'57U	21	3	1	5	Riddles (clever)
,,	,,	,,	,,	,,	8	Riddles (obvious)

Table 14.11 (cont.)

Dataset	Codes[a]				Factor no.	Details (saliently loaded variables)
	D C	A	T	M/F		
GUIL17	'52U	21	3	1	10	Practical judgment
GUIL19	'55U	21	3	1	5	Problem Solving
GUIL37	'47U	21	3	1	5	Memory for plane silhouettes; SAM Complex Coordination
GUIL39	'47U	21	3	1	4	Table Reading; SAM Complex Coordination
GUIL40	'47U	21	3	1	4	Table Reading
GUIL51	'61U	14	1	3	7	Letter analogies
GUIL57	'61U	14	I	2	8	Multiple Grouping; Marking speed
GUIL58	'61U	14	8	3	6	Make a Code; Planning air maneuvers
HALS01	'47U	30	H	1	4	Halstead Dynamic Visual Field Test: Control Color; Control Form; Finger-Oscillation; Flicker Fusion
HANL01	'52U	19	6	3	7	(No salients)
HARR51	'73U	10	1	1	7	Number Exclusion; Seeing Trends; Circle Reasoning
HARR52	'73U	10	1	2	8	Word Linkage (other variables loaded negatively)
HOEP31	'64U	17	6	3	5	Form reasoning (Blakey); SCAT Verbal
HOLZ01	'39U	12	6	3	6	Straight/curved capitals
JONE31	'49U	7	1	3	4	Counting taps (Stanford–Binet)
"	"	"	"	"	5	Give number of fingers; Memory for stories (Stanford–Binet)
JONE33	'49U	11	1	3	6	Repeat 6 digits; Finding reasons; Word naming (animals)
KAMM01	'53U	19	F	3	2	Auditory test in Spanish; Word Fluency (PMA)
MANG01A	'59E	14	6	2	5	Birds (fluency); Identical Pictures
MERR41	'60U	21	3	1	9	Predicaments
MERR51	'63U	11	1	3	6	Marking Speed; Problems (negative)
NIHI01	'64U	16	8	3	5	Double Descriptions, Picture Gestalt; Product Choice (Evaluation of Semantic Units?)
"	"	"	"	"	7	Word Systems
"	"	"	"	"	11	Best Word Class; Word Linkage; Commonsense Judgment
"	"	"	"	"	12	Verbal Classification; Useful Changes
OSUL01	'65U	16	6	3	5	Picture Arrangement; Picture Exclusion (negative)
"	"	"	"	"	9	Plot Titles (low quality)
ROBE11	'76U	50	U	1	3	Dichotic Digit Pairs; Delayed Recognition
ROGE11	'53E	14	6	3	5	Indirect Fluency
ROSE03	'74U	19	6	3	4	Rotate Letters; Continuous PA Memory
ROYC11	'76C	40	4	3	8	Halstead Category tests (errors) Color Cognition Sorting; Color Cognition Memory

Table 14.11 (*cont.*)

	Codes[a]				Factor	
Dataset	D C	A	T	M/F	no.	Details (saliently loaded variables)
ROYC11	'76C	40	4	3	9	Halstead Category tests; Minute Estimation
"	"	"	"	"	12	Critical Flicker Fusion; Wepman–Jones Aphasia (Errors)
SCHA11	'40U	19	6	1	6	Figure Recognition; Backward Writing
SING21	'65U	9	1	3	6	Holmes Language Perception: Figure & Ground; Cue Symbol Closure
SNOW21	'76U	19	6	3	7	Raven; Short-Term Visual Memory
SPEA32	'77A	11	6	2	5	Ambiguous sentences
SPEA33	'77A	11	6	2	6	(no salients)
STAK01	'61U	12	1	3	5	Learning Tasks 7 and 10
"	"	"	"	"	14	Learning Tasks 2 and 5
STOR01A	'72U	67	1	3	3	Volume Conservation (reflected); Test of Behavioral Rigidity: Personality-Perceptual
SUMI02	'58N	12	1	1	7	Memory of Numbers; Weight Discrimination
SUMI03	'58N	10	1	1	2	Length Discrimination; Four-Letter Words; Reaction Time
"	"	"	"	"	5	Memory of Rhythms; Space-Cards; Correlated Eduction
SUMI04	'58N	8	1	1	3	Memory of Rhythms; Correlated Eduction; Space-Cards
TAYL11	'67U	21	3	1	5	Words used in telegram writing
TAYL13A	'67U	19	6	1	6	Leader Situation 6; Revision II
"	"	"	"	"	8	Sound Identification Situation 12; Oral Reading Situation 2
"	"	"	"	"	10	Written Interpretation Situation 17; First and Last Letters
"	"	"	"	"	11	Verbal Classification; Topics
TAYL32	'75C	6	1	3	4	Block Design
TAYL51	'76K	19	1	1	8	Mental Alertness; Hidden Patterns
TENO01	'69U	15	1	3	7	Circle Reasoning; Memory for Number Classes
WALL52	'67S	8	6	2	4	Cancellation Quality; Dissected Words; Raven Matrices; Sound Discrimination
WEIS11	'55U	15	M	3	7	Choice of Method; Letter Series
WISL01	'69U	5	8	3	3	ITPA: Auditory-Vocal-Automatic; Visual-Motor Sequencing

[a]Codes: D (date), C (country), A (age), T (sample type), M/F (1 = male, 2 = female; 3 = both); see Appendix A for further information on codes.

Rorschach test, in addition to, inexplicably, a time score from a Size–Weight Illusion task and (negatively) a score from Brightness Constancy. The factor has its artifactual aspects due to experimental dependence, but further investigation might lead to an explanation of the structure of correlations with the Rorschach test. Factor 11 is also a doublet arising at least in part from experimental dependence of two scores from the Schmidt test, an elaborate experimental procedure designed to measure color vs. form dominance in visual perception. Thurstone (1944a) himself recognized the problem of experimental dependence, but discussed various possibilities for investigating problems of form vs. color dominance:

> It seems likely that the particular tests that we have used are not adapted for bringing out the differentiation between color and form dominance if such a classification is in any sense fundamentally valid. If the subject is investigated again, it might be well to inquire also whether the fundamental difference here is in the relative sensitivity of the subject to texture of the surface as contrasted with the sensitivity to the outlines or shapes of those surfaces. If this distinction has fundamental psychological validity, then we should not be dealing with color versus form but rather with surface texture versus outline. We did not set up the tests in this battery to investigate these possibilities (p. 116).

Unfortunately, to my knowledge these possibilities have never been explored.

UNINTERPRETED (IO) FACTORS

Table 14.11 lists 87 factors, in 65 datasets, that I have not been able to interpret because it has not been possible to detect meaningful common elements in the variable – usually only one or two – which have loadings on them. For the most part they are residual factors that appear as one or more of the last factors extracted from a matrix, and thus are factors likely resulting from chance deviations in particular correlation values. They are listed here mainly to make the record of our reanalyses complete. (It should be noted, however, that further "first-order" factors are listed in Chapter 15 as actually representing broader "second stratum" abilities.) It is possible that some readers, more knowledgeable than I about the variables involved, will be able to interpret some of these factors.

15 *Higher-Order Factors of Cognitive Ability*

... all the ground that has been, or ever can be, covered by mental tests may forthwith be mapped out in at least general outlines.

Charles Spearman (1923, p. 354)

The previous chapters, from Chapter 5 on, have presented a survey of first-order cognitive ability factors found in the database for this project. They are "first-order" factors in the sense that they emerged from direct analysis of the correlation matrices of the datasets. The factorial procedures chosen for use in the project, however, dictated that when first-order factors rotated to simple structure were found to have substantial intercorrelations, their correlation matrices were to be subjected to further analysis to find one or more "second-order" factors. This process could continue for a further step when second-order factors had substantial intercorrelations, to produce "third-order" factors – in principle, possibly more than one for a given dataset, but it was never the case, for my datasets, that more than one meaningful third-order factor emerged in the analysis. (This was true even for reanalysis of one dataset, HAKS01, whose authors, Hakstian and Cattell, 1978, believed it necessary and desirable to extract three oblique factors at the third order.)

The present chapter reports the results of the higher-order analyses conducted, wherever applicable, on the 467 datasets selected for study in this survey. The chapter thus constitutes a study of the higher-order *structure* of cognitive abilities. The complete orthogonalized hierarchical factor matrices for the datasets are shown in Appendix B.

It is necessary to introduce a distinction, explicitly discussed by Cattell (1971, pp. 83ff), between the *order* of a factor and the *stratum* at which it belongs or to which it can be assigned.[1] The *order* of a factor refers to the purely operational level of analysis at which it is found. The *stratum* of a factor would refer to an absolute measure of its degree of generality over the domain of cognitive abilities. Highly specific factors, as might be obtained, say, in the factor analysis of the items of a particular test (see, for example, Saunders', 1960a, study of the picture completion items of the WAIS, dataset SAUN11), would be at a low-level stratum, whereas the g factor postulated by Spearman (1927) would be at a high-level stratum, possibly at the highest stratum, because of its generality. Any factor that one might identify could belong at a particular stratum,

577

regardless of the order at which it is operationally isolated in a particular factor-analytic study. Normally, the first-order factors identified in typical analyses of batteries of diverse tests, such as the battery analyzed by Thurstone (1938b, dataset THUR21A), may be regarded as belonging to what we may call *stratum I*, while second-order factors derived from the correlations of these first-order factors could be classified as belonging to *stratum II*. Third-order factors derived from the correlations of these second-order factors would be classified as belonging to *stratum III*. However, for reasons that are mentioned below, some investigators have analyzed batteries of tests or variables chosen to represent stratum I factors in such a way that the first-order factors derived in these studies correspond to stratum II factors. For example, Horn and Stankov (1982; dataset HORN31) analyzed a battery comprised of groups of tests selected so that second-stratum factors would emerge at the first order. Thus, one group of tests consisted of several tests, each of which was known or postulated to measure a different first-stratum factor dominated by a "broad visualization" factor at stratum II; as a consequence, one of their first-*order* factors was indeed a broad visualization factor. Strictly speaking, the present chapter should perhaps be entitled "Higher *Stratum* Factors of Cognitive Ability," but because in most datasets the orders of factors and the strata to which they belong are the same, I have not renamed the chapter. The first-order factors identified in studies like Horn and Stankov's will, however, be considered as factors at stratum II.

In performing the hierarchical analyses whose results are discussed in this chapter, it was my hope that the evidence would have a bearing on the acceptability of the hierarchical theories of intelligence and cognitive ability offered by such writers as Vernon (1961), Cattell (1971), and Horn (1988). These theories are briefly outlined in Chapter 2.

DIFFICULTIES AND LIMITATIONS IN HIERARCHICAL FACTOR ANALYSIS

The procedures of analysis and interpretation at any higher order of analysis should ideally follow the same principles as are operative at the first order of analysis. That is, the same criteria for condensation of data, number of factors, rotation of axes, and interpretation of factors should apply at the second- and any higher order of analysis as at the first order. Unfortunately, with ascending orders it becomes increasingly difficult to follow these principles strictly.

The major problem is the inevitable consequence of the fact that the number of variables (factors) automatically decreases with the order of analysis. If one starts with what has often been thought of as a large number of original variables (e.g., the 57 variables studied by Thurstone, 1938b, dataset THUR21A), there might be somewhere around, say, seven to fifteen first-order factors identified, if the study is well designed. But at the second order of analysis, even fifteen factors (as *variables*) are barely enough to support a highly determined solution. One is fortunate to obtain as many as three second-order factors, and this is the minimum number required to support an analysis for a single factor at the third order. If only two correlated second-order factors are obtained, their loadings on a third-order factor are indeterminate. (In practice, these loadings are both estimated to equal the square root of the factor intercorrelation.) In effect, study of higher-order structures by exploratory factor analysis requires very large batteries of tests, designed to include variables representing a wide variety of first- and second-order factors. In our datasets, only one or two (HAKS01, WOTH01) can be found that minimally meet this requirement. Most of our evidence, therefore, on higher-order structures comes from studies that sample the cognitive ability domain in a piecemeal fashion, largely because of the logistical problems in conducting large factor-analytic studies.

In the hope of circumventing this difficulty, some investigators have designed their batteries of variables in such a way that at least some of the first-order factors are expected to constitute second-stratum factors. Examples are datasets FOGA00, HORN01 and HORN02 (actually two analyses of the same dataset), HORN31, and UNDH21. In some such studies, the variables are sums or averages of scores obtained on two or more tests of a given first-stratum factor. The procedure, which may be called *higher-stratum design*, requires great caution in selecting tests to represent a factor adequately.

Even if datasets are not designed to yield second-order factors at the first order, determination of second-order factors depends on the adequacy with which first-order factors are represented in the variables selected to represent them. For example, there are apparently many different types of variables that can be selected to represent a Visualization (VZ) factor, as pointed out in Chapter 8. Some of these variables evidently depend more than others on Reasoning (RG) and Induction (I) factors. The variables taken to represent VZ in one study may be essentially different from those representing this factor in another study, with the result that the VZ factor in the first study has a different composition in a second-order factor from that it has in the second study. The differential representation of speed components in the VZ factors of different datasets is a particularly vexing problem – as where the VZ variables of one study are all speeded tests, whereas they may be chiefly untimed level of mastery tests in another study. Under these conditions, at the second order the VZ factor of the first study may tend to load on a general speed factor whereas the VZ factor of the second study may load on a second-order factor that has loadings on several first-order factors emphasizing level of mastery. All these remarks apply with equal force to factors other than VZ, which is cited here merely as an example.

Another difficulty stems from the assumptions underlying the factorization of first-order factor correlation matrices, that is, the assumptions underlying the simple structure principle. The possible effect of these assumptions in

Table 15.1. *Analysis of a plasmode to illustrate a problem in higher-order factor analysis*

A Plasmode (hypothesized factor pattern)			B Varimax solution		
factor			factor		
Var.	I	II	h^2	A	B	h^2
1	.85	.00	.7225	.785	.325	.7225
2	.85	.00	.7225	.785	.325	.7225
3	.85	.00	.7225	.785	.325	.7225
4	.85	.00	.7225	.785	.325	.7225
5	.60	.60	.7200	.325	.784	.7200
6	.60	.60	.7200	.325	.784	.7200
7	.60	.60	.7200	.325	.784	.7200
8	.60	.60	.7200	.325	.784	.7200
SMSQ	4.33	1.44	5.7700	2.889	2.881	5.7700

C Oblique reference-vector solution			D Hierarchical solution			
factor			factor			
Var.	A′	B′	g	a	b	h^2
1	.602	.001	.714	.461	.000	.723
2	.602	.001	.714	.461	.000	.723
3	.602	.001	.714	.461	.000	.723
4	.602	.001	.714	.461	.000	.723
5	.001	.600	.713	.000	.460	.720
6	.001	.600	.713	.000	.460	.720
7	.001	.600	.713	.000	.460	.720
8	.001	.600	.713	.000	.460	.720
	$r = .706$		SMSQ 4.076	.849	.845	5.770

analyzing data at a higher order can be seen by consideration of a simple case. In Table 15.1, a hypothetical factor pattern ("plasmode," to use a term introduced by Cattell and Jaspars, 1967) is shown (at A) in which all variables have substantial loadings on factor I, but only some of the variables have substantial loadings on factor II. (The factor pattern is constructed so that all variables have approximately equal communalities.) Applying standard factorization procedures to the correlation matrix generated by this pattern, we find the Varimax solution, shown at B, and a simple-structure oblique reference vector matrix, shown at C; the correlation between the factors of matrix C is .706. The orthogonalized hierarchical factor matrix, shown at D, has a second-order general factor (g) on which all variables have approximately equal loadings, but two first-order factors appear, one (a) with salient loadings on variables 1–4 and the other (b) with salient loadings on variables 5–8. The hierarchical factor matrix fails to correspond to the original hypothetical factor pattern (at A), although that factor pattern could be obtained by a certain rotation of the Varimax solution. That rotation, however, would violate the simple structure principle. The point is that the "standard" factorization procedures employed throughout our survey may in some cases have failed to provide a proper solution for datasets in which the "true" factor pattern contains a general (second-order) factor with some variables having no significant loadings on any of the first-order factors; one or more of the hierarchical first-order factors may be artifacts representing variables with insignificant loadings (in the "true" factor pattern) on first-order factors. This fact should be borne in mind in assessing the hierarchical factor solutions that are presented for each of the datasets reanalyzed in this survey.

The hierarchical factorization procedures work best when each second-order factor "dominates" two or more second-order factors, as is the case for the factor solution at D in Table 15.1. Note that if that factor solution had been the hypothesized factor pattern (plasmode) generating the correlation matrix, our "standard" factorization procedures would be able to reproduce it exactly. The problem arises partly because of a conflict between the simple structure principle and the principle of parsimony. The factor pattern at A in Table 15.1 emphasizes parsimony, whereas that at D violates parsimony in order to capture simple structure.

Note that when oblique first-order factors are highly correlated, their hierarchical loadings on a second-order factor tend to be high. Orthogonalization of these factors with the Schmid and Leiman (1957) procedure can drastically decrease the magnitudes of their first-order salient loadings. For example, in dataset CLAU04, the hierarchical first-order factor 3 has a loading of .72 on the third-order factor 1 and a loading of .68 on the second-order factor 2; the variables defining factor 3, however, have unusually low salient loadings on it, ranging from .10 down to .06.

HIGHER-ORDER ANALYSIS OF THE DATABASE: OVERVIEW

As may be seen from Table 15.2, about 91 percent of the 467 datasets analyzed yielded – in consideration of criteria for the obliqueness of lower-order factors and the number of factors at a higher order – one or more higher-order factors: 423 second-order factors and 37 third-order factors; 313 datasets yielded only one second-order factor; 110 datasets yielded two or more second-order factors. As noted previously, no dataset yielded more than one third-order factor. Most of the third-order factors came from datasets having only two second-order factors, in which case the loadings of second-order factors on them were indeterminate.

Table 15.2. *Yields of higher-order factors, 467 datasets*

No. of 1st-order factors	No. of 2nd-order factors							No. of 3rd-order factors
	0	1	2	3	4	5	Total	
1	6	—	—	—	—	—	6	—
2	19	32	—	—	—	—	51	—
3	7	96	1	—	—	—	104	—
4	4	46	21	—	—	—	71	10
5	5	50	13	—	—	—	68	3
6	—	35	18	—	—	—	53	4
7	1	25	13	7	—	—	46	7
8	1	12	13	2	—	—	28	2
9	—	9	5	2	—	—	16	3
10	1	5	8	3	—	—	17	5
11	—	3	—	1	1	—	5	2
12	—	—	—	—	—	—	—	—
13	—	—	—	1	—	—	1	—
...								
19	—	—	—	—	—	1	1	1
Total	44	313	92	16	1	1	467	37

No. of 2nd-order factors	No. of 3rd-order factors		
	0	1	Total
2	68	24	92
3	5	11	16
4	—	1	1
5	—	1	1
Total	73	37	110

The number of higher-order factors yielded by a dataset is undoubtedly partly a function of its design – the number of variables employed and the manner in which they were selected to cover one or more domains or subdomains of cognitive ability. The number of higher-order factors identified in a study could also be a function of the ability range of the sample of subjects underlying a dataset. Higher-order factors may be more likely to emerge for samples with wide ranges of general ability.

In interpreting each higher-order factor, consideration was given mainly to the names and interpretations of the first-order factors that had salient loadings on it, just as in interpreting a first-order factor, one pays attention to the characteristics of the variables with salient loadings on it in contrast to variables having low or vanishing loadings. Some attention, however, was paid to the magnitudes of loadings of the original variables on a higher-order factor as they are shown in the orthogonalized factor matrix for the dataset (presented in Appendix B).

Many of the higher-order factors that were found could be readily classified into one of the categories of second-order factors described by Hakstian and Cattell (1974), Horn (1988), and others. It was believed that classification and interpretation of the factors could best be done by considering cases in which two or more second-order factors were yielded by a dataset, such that classification could be guided by the possible distinctions between and among factors. (This procedure was frequently employed, it will be recalled, in arriving at characterizations of first-order factors in Chapters 5–14.) Table 15.3 shows classifications of the higher-order factors found in 110 datasets that yielded two or more such factors, or that were designed so that second-stratum factors would emerge at the first order of analysis (as in the case of dataset UNDH21, for example). The entries in the table are the numbers designating factors in the relevant hierarchical factor matrix. The categories used were a slight expansion of those suggested by previous investigators. Also, a number of factors did not fit into those categories and are listed in a column headed "Other." The categories may be briefly described as follows:

G: "General Intelligence." The table shows whether this factor emerged at the second- or the third-order. Generally this category was used when two or more second-order factors were dominated by a third-order factor, or when (as in the case of such datasets as FOGA00, HAKS21, HORN01, HORN02, HORN31, KRAN01A, and UNDH21), one or more first-order factors could be interpreted as second-stratum abilities dominated by a second-order factor interpretable as a stratum III ability. Further remarks are made below on the nature of general intelligence.

2F: Fluid intelligence. In this and other symbols, the first character, 2, indicates that the factor is at the second stratum; the second character indicates the classification of the factor. Category 2F was used whenever the higher salient loadings of first-stratum factors were for factors such as RG (Reasoning) or I (Induction), involving basic intellectual processes of manipulating abstractions, rules, generalizations, and logical relationships. (See below for further details.)

2C: Crystallized intelligence. This category was used for second-stratum factors with salient loadings on first-stratum factors such as LD (Language development) and V (Verbal ability) that appear to reflect the role of learning and acculturation.

2H: This category was established to include factors that appeared to be indeterminate combinations of factors 2F and 2C. In some cases (e.g., in dataset ALLI02), a factor classified here might be simply an instance of a *g* (general intelligence) factor appearing at the second order, with no third-order factor dominating it. In other cases (e.g., in dataset ALLI03) a factor that might otherwise be classified as G or 2G (at the second order) was classified here because it was dominated by a third-order G factor.[2]

2V: Broad visual perception. This category was used when the factor tended to have its highest salient loadings for factors such as VZ (Visualization), SR (Spatial Relations), CS (Speed of Closure), and CF (Flexibility of Closure), or others in the visual perception domain covered in Chapter 8.

2U: Broad auditory perception. A factor was classified here when it dominated first-stratum factors in the domain of auditory perception, as covered in Chapter 9. (Note that my symbol or code for this factor is GU or 2U, as opposed to the symbol Ga used by previous writers. Mnemonically, *U* is the second letter of *auditory*.)

2S: Broad cognitive speediness. A factor was classified here when it dominated first-stratum factors measuring speed of mental activity or response, such as P (Perceptual Speed) or R1 (Reaction Time). It seems, however, that there are several different second-stratum speed factors, as discussed below.

2R: Broad retrieval ability. Factors were classified here when they dominated first-stratum factors such as FI (Ideational Fluency), FW (Word Fluency), and FO (Originality) – generally, factors involving the ready production (retrieval) of a variety of responses from long-term memory storage. In some instances more than one such factor appeared; these instances are discussed below.[3]

2Y: Broad memory ability. These factors dominated several first-stratum factors in the domain of memory and learning as discussed in Chapter 7. Multiple instances of such factors are discussed below.[4]

For most pairs of factors, Table 15.3 contains instances of datasets that show distinctions between such pairs of factors. The exceptions are two: (1) There is no instance of a distinction between factor 2H and either factor 2F or factor 2C. This is simply because factor 2H was defined to be an indeterminate combination of 2F and 2C, and thus a dataset could not contain both factor 2H and one or the other of factors 2F and 2C. (2) There are few instances of distinctions between factor 2U and other factors, mainly because factor 2U occurs infrequently in the datasets.

Study of factors listed in Table 15.3 was the basis for subsequent efforts to classify a large proportion of higher-order factors yielded by the datasets, that is, all higher-order factors coming from datasets with at least three first-order factors, in addition to a few others that appeared to be of special interest. The interpretation of higher-order factors coming from datasets with only two or three first-order factors was thought to be more problematical because it would be more difficult to characterize distinctions between factors.

First, however, special attention was given to the possible distinction between factors 2F and 2C in datasets that contained both of these factors. It must be recognized that there can be a certain element of self-fulfilling prophecy or bias in the classification of factors. In the present case, a factor was generally assigned to group 2F if the higher salient loadings were for such first-stratum factors as I (Induction) or RG (Serial Reasoning), but was assigned to group 2C if the higher salient loadings were for such first-stratum factors as LD (Language Development) or V (Verbal Ability). To the extent that factors actually have loadings on the first-order factors named, this procedure automatically insures distinctions between factors. It is justified only to the extent that the loadings are in contrast, that is, that higher-order factors with high loadings for I and RG have low loadings for LD and V, and vice versa. Unfortunately, it is difficult

Table 15.3. *Higher-order factors in 110 datasets yielding two or more such factors (entries are factor numbers in hierarchical factor matrices)*

Dataset	Higher-order factor[a]									
	G*	2F	2C	2H	2V	2U	2S	2R	2Y	Other
ADKI03	—	1	7	—	—	—	—	—	—	1,9:Uninterpreted
AFTA01	—	—	—	—	—	—	—	—	—	4:Motor learning
ALLI01	—	1	—	—	—	—	—	—	—	
ALLI02	—	—	—	1	—	—	—	—	6	
ALLI03	3:1	—	—	6	—	—	—	—	2	
BRAD01	—	—	—	—	6	—	—	—	1	
CARL41	—	—	—	—	—	—	1,4	—	—	
CARR01	—	—	1	—	—	—	—	7	—	
CARR43	3:1	—	2	—	—	—	5	—	—	10:Linguistic element sensitivity
CATT01A	3:1	6	2	—	—	—	—	—	—	
CHRI01	3:1	—	10	—	7	—	—	—	2	
CLAU04	3:1	—	—	2	—	—	8	—	—	
CORY01	—	—	—	6	—	—	—	—	1	
CURE12	—	—	1	—	6	—	—	—	—	
DETT00	—	—	—	—	—	—	—	—	—	1:Info. Processing Accuracy 6:Rapid Learning
EKST11	3:1	—	—	—	2	—	7	—	—	
FAIR01A	—	—	—	5	—	—	1	—	—	
FAIR02	—	—	—	1	—	—	6	—	—	
FEDE02	—	1	5	—	—	—	—	—	—	8:Cognitive Style
FOGA00	2:1	3#	2#	—	4#	5#	—	—	—	7:Timesharing
FRED12	—	—	1	8	—	—	—	—	—	6:Word Recognition
FREN11	—	—	—	—	—	—	1	—	—	12:Uninterpreted
FRUC21	2:1	—	—	—	—	—	—	—	—	
FULG31	3:1	—	—	—	—	—	—	2,5	—	8:Uninterp. Residual

Table 15.3 (cont.)

Dataset	Higher-order factor[a]									
	G*	2F	2C	2H	2V	2U	2S	2R	2Y	Other
GAME01	—	—	—	—	—	—	—	—	1,4	
GERS01	—	—	—	—	—	—	—	1,5	—	
GERS02	—	—	—	—	—	—	6	1	—	
GRIM12	2:6	—	—	—	—	—	—	—	—	1:Interests
GUIL12	—	—	8	—	—	—	—	1	—	
GUIL14	—	—	—	1	—	—	—	6	—	
GUIL16	3:1	—	—	2	—	—	7	—	—	
GUIL56	3:1	—	—	7	—	—	—	2	—	
GUIL57	—	—	—	6	—	—	—	1	—	
GUST11A	3:1	6	9	—	2	—	—	—	—	
HAKS01	3:1	—	13	—	5	—	—	21	2	24:Gen. Information
HAKS21	2:1	2#	5,6#	—	8#	—	3#	7#	4#	
HARR01	3:1	—	—	6	—	—	—	—	—	2:Manual speed
HECK01	3:1	—	5	10	2	—	—	—	2,5	
HEND11A	3:1	—	—	—	—	—	—	—	—	
HOEP11	—	—	—	—	—	—	—	1,5	—	1:Uninterpreted
HOEP21	—	—	6	1	—	—	—	—	—	
HOEP31	—	—	—	—	1	—	7	—	—	5:Uninterpreted
HOFF01	—	—	—	4	—	—	—	1	—	
HOLT11	—	—	—	—	—	—	—	1	—	
HORN01	2:1	4#	7,9#	—	2#	—	3#	8#	—	5#,10#,11#:PR;6#:CA
HORN02	2:1	4#	3#	—	2#	—	8,9#	—	—	5#,6#,7#:PR;11#:CA;10#:IO
HORN21	—	9,10#	1	—	—	—	—	—	—	
HORN31	2:1	3#	2#	—	4#	6	1	—	5#	
HUGH01	—	4,6#	—	—	—	—	1	—	—	
HUNT61	—	—	—	—	—	—	5	—	—	
JACK12	—	—	—	1	—	—	—	—	1,4	
JAY01	—	—	1	—	—	—	—	—	—	7:Reading Decoding

Case													
	1:3O (Olfactory Sens.)	2:2O (Olfaction I)	5:2O (Olfaction II)	7:Movt. time, RT task	6:Persistence/Reasoning	2:Gen.School Achvt. 5:School Deportment/Motivation	(5:Gen.Memory Span)	1:Mother's Speech Complexity	5:Mother's Pref. for Declarative Sents.	2:Info: sci, math	5:Reading Skills	8:Uninterpreted	(7,1 dominate auditory variables)
JONE22	—	—	—	—	—	—	—	—	—	—	—	—	—
KEIT21	3:1	2	—	—	—	6	—	—	—	2	—	—	—
KELL01	—	—	—	—	—	6	—	—	—	—	—	—	1
KRAN01A	2:1	5#	—	—	1	4#	—	—	8	—	—	—	—
LORD01	—	—	1	—	7	5	—	—	—	—	—	—	—
LUCA01	—	1	—	—	—	—	—	—	—	—	—	—	—
LUMS01	—	1	8	—	—	—	—	—	—	—	—	—	—
MANG01A	—	—	—	—	1	—	—	—	—	—	—	—	—
MEEK01	3:1	—	—	6	—	8#	—	—	—	2	—	—	2
MOUR01	3:1	2	—	—	—	5	—	—	—	—	—	—	3#
NIHI01	3:1	—	—	2	—	—	8	—	—	—	—	—	—
PEDU01	3:1	—	—	—	—	—	—	—	—	—	—	—	—
PENF01	3:1	2	—	—	—	—	7	—	—	—	—	—	—
PIMS01	—	1	6	—	—	—	—	—	—	—	—	—	—
RIMO11	3:1	2	—	—	—	—	—	—	—	—	—	—	5
ROND02	—	—	—	—	—	—	—	—	—	—	—	—	—
SCHA11	3:1	—	—	2	8	—	—	—	—	—	—	—	—
SCHU11	3:1	5	2	—	—	—	—	—	—	2	—	—	—
SEGE01	3:1	—	—	2	6	—	—	—	—	—	—	—	—
SEGE02	3:1	—	—	2	6	—	—	—	—	—	—	—	—
SHAY02	3:1	—	—	5	—	—	—	—	—	5	—	—	—
SIMR01	—	—	—	4	1	2	—	—	—	—	—	—	—
SLAT01	—	—	—	1	—	5	—	—	—	—	—	—	—
SNOW21	—	—	—	1	5	1	—	—	—	—	—	—	—
SPEA34	—	1	—	—	—	—	—	—	—	1	—	—	—
STAK01	—	—	—	1	—	12	—	—	—	—	—	—	—
STAN31	—	7	1	—	—	1	—	—	—	1	—	—	8
STOR12	3:1	—	—	2	—	—	—	—	—	2	—	—	—

Table 15.3 (*cont.*)

Dataset	Higher-order factor[a]									
	G*	2F	2C	2H	2V	2U	2S	2R	2Y	Other
SUMI02	—	—	—	1	—	—	5	—	—	
SUNG01	—	—	—	1	5	—	—	—	—	8:Strength
SUNG02	3:1	—	—	2	—	—	—	10	—	6:Strength
SUNG03	3:1	—	—	5	8	—	—	2	—	
SUNG04	3:1	—	—	2	—	—	—	7	—	9:Uninterpreted
SUNG05	3:1	—	—	5	—	—	—	2	—	9:Psychomotor
TAYL01	—	—	—	1	—	—	—	6	—	
TAYL31	—	—	1	—	—	6	—	—	—	
THUR11	—	—	—	9	—	—	1,4	—	—	
THUR21A	—	1	7	—	—	—	—	—	—	
THUR81	3:1	—	—	2	12	—	8	—	—	
THUR82	3:1	—	—	2	—	—	8	—	—	
UNDE12	—	—	—	—	—	—	—	—	1,6	
UNDH01	—	—	—	1	10	—	—	—	—	
UNDH21	2:1	2#	6#	—	3#	—	4#	5#	—	
VALT01	—	—	—	4	—	—	—	—	—	1:Carefulness?
VERN51	—	—	—	1	5	—	—	—	—	
VERS01	—	—	—	—	—	—	1	—	—	4:Motor Speed
VERS02	—	—	—	—	—	—	1	—	—	4:Motor Speed
VERS03	—	—	—	—	—	—	5	—	—	1:Motor Speed

											Interpretation
VERY03	—	1	5	—	—	—	—	—	—	—	2:Uninterpreted
WEIS11	3:1	8	4	—	—	—	—	—	—	—	1:Cognitive Style
WIDI01	—	—	—	4	—	—	—	—	—	—	3:1 Gen.Level Background and Achvt.
WOLF11	—	—	—	—	—	—	—	—	—	—	2 Parental Backgrnd. / 5 Student Achvt.
WOOD13	—	4	1	—	—	—	—	—	—	—	
WOOD15	—	5	1	—	—	—	—	—	—	—	
WOOD17	—	5	1	—	—	—	—	—	—	—	
WOOD18	—	5	1	—	—	—	—	—	—	—	
WOTH01	3:1	2	—	1	12	—	15	—	—	—	8:Uninterpreted / 5:Math. Achievement
WRIG21	—	—	—	1	—	—	—	—	—	—	

*Entries are 3:1 or 2:1 showing whether factor emerged at third or second order.

#Second-stratum factor emerging at first order.

"Interpretations of higher-order factors (some of which exhibit several variations):

G: General intelligence factor (at second order)
2F: fluid intelligence (at second order)
2C: crystallized intelligence (at second order)
2H: indeterminate combination of 2F and 2C
2V: general visual perception ability
2U: general auditory perception ability
2S: broad cognitive speediness
2R: general retrieval/production ability
2Y: general memory ability

to validate the classifications in this way because due to their designs, not all datasets have instances of all the factors involved in the classification. Furthermore, loadings tend to show wide variations, possibly because of the different compositions of sets of variables defining them. For example, in nine datasets containing factor V at the first-order, its loadings on factors classified (for any reason) as factor 2F ranged from $-.09$ to $.69$, while its loadings on factors classified as 2C ranged from $.36$ to $.80$.

It seems inappropriate to report the average loadings of various first-stratum factors on factors 2F and 2C in view of wide variation of these loadings and wide variation in what factors have loadings at all (and thus, wide variations in how many values are averaged). To give an impression, however, of how factors 2F and 2C differ, I can report that the first-stratum factors that have the most generally consistent salient loadings on 2F are I (Induction), VZ (Visualization), SR (Spatial Relations), RQ (Quantitative Reasoning), and MA (Associative Memory), while the factors with the most consistent salient loadings on factor 2C are K0 (General Information), SG (Spelling and English Usage), RC (Reading Comprehension), FW (Word Fluency), V (Verbal Ability), FI (Ideational Fluency), and VL (Lexical Knowledge). Although the loadings of factor RG (Reasoning) tended to guide the assignment of a factor as 2F, the loadings of RG on factors 2F and 2C were not very consistent, sometimes being higher on factor 2C than on factor 2F (e.g., in dataset CATT01A). This is possibly due to different compositions of factor RG in different datasets – sometimes being dependent on highly verbal tests and sometimes being dependent on nonverbal tests.

Following are a series of sections devoted to each of the higher-stratum factors identified in our database. Each section is accompanied by a table listing datasets containing the relevant factor. For each dataset and factor, there is an indication of the number of that factor in the pertinent hierarchical factor matrix (shown in Appendix B), the order at which it appears, and the loadings (in order of algebraic magnitude) for lower-order factors or variables that define the factor. When the factor is defined by lower-order factors, the latter are specified in terms of their symbols (as listed in Appendix A), and the loadings are given (to two decimals) for all such lower-order factors – even low, vanishing, or negative loadings, in order to give a maximum amount of data for interpretation of the factor. (On occasion, two or more factors with the same symbol are listed; sometimes these factors are actually quite different but are given the same symbol because their differences are not of interest. For example, in some datasets there are personality factors, symbolized PR, but this volume is not concerned with personality factors. In other cases the factors are alternates of the same cognitive factor, as discussed elsewhere in this volume. In all such instances the symbols are suffixed with *a*, *b*, etc. to distinguish them.) When the order of the factor is *one*, only the names and loadings of variables with salient loadings on the factor are given.

Occasionally the list of loadings for a given factor includes not only those for lower-order factors that it directly dominates, but also any loadings for other factors. Such other loadings are preceded by the word *also*, as in the case of dataset HAKS21 in Table 15.4.

This makes for what may appear as an excessively large amount of tabular material. It must be noted, however, that these tables summarize data from almost the complete range of the database. To keep the tabular material as limited as possible, the tables are restricted, in most cases, to higher-order factors found in datasets that yielded at least four first-order factors. Readers interested in higher-order factors found in smaller datasets can still refer to the relevant hierarchical factor matrices found in Appendix B.

FACTORS CLASSIFIED AS G (GENERAL INTELLIGENCE)

Table 15.4 lists 153 factors, in 146 datasets, classified as measuring "general intelligence" or possibly Spearman's factor *g*. They include not only the factors listed as G in Table 15.3 but also numerous factors found in datasets not listed in that table, that is, in numerous datasets that yielded only a single higher-stratum factor. Note that these factors could occur at any order of analysis. Thirty-three of them occurred at order 3, in which case they were symbolized as 3G; sixteen occurred at order 1, in which case they were symbolized as 1G; and the remainder (the majority) at order 2, symbolized as 2G. Those occurring at order 3 dominated at least two second-order factors, and those occurring at order 2 normally dominated at least three or four first-order factors, sometimes many more than four. Those occurring at order 1 had loadings on a series of variables on which the first-order correlation matrix was based.

In classifying a factor as G, the most important criterion, regardless of the order of a factor, was the variety of its lower-order factors or variables. On the supposition that a general factor should show great generality of application over the total domain of cognitive abilities, it should have substantial loadings for lower-order factors or variables in several different domains; the more domains covered, the greater the generality. Most factors occurring at order three dominated only two second-order factors; as was seen in Table 15.2, only thirteen third-order factors in our whole database dominated three or more second-order factors. The degree to which generality could be demonstrated for third-order factors was thus limited. Greater generality could be exhibited in the case of second-order factors, because they could dominate a fair number of first-order factors.

Classification of a factor as G was strengthened when it was a third-order factor, or a second-order factor derived from a dataset designed (with higher-stratum design) to yield a third-stratum factor at the second order. Nevertheless, not all such factors were classified as G. If the lower-order factors having salient loadings on a factor were restricted to a single domain, the higher-order factor

Table 15.4. *153 factors classified as G in 147 datasets*

Dataset	Factor no.	Order	Loadings for lower-order factors or variables[a]
ALLI03	1	3	2:2Y(.61);6:2H(.61)
ARNO01	1	2	2:I(.87);3:VL(.76);4:SR(.51);5:MS(.48);6:I0(.43)
BACH21	1	2	2:CS(.72);3:GH(.67);4:CF(.67);5:MS(.33)
BLAK01	1	2	2:I(.75);3:VZ(.68);4:P(.50)
BOLT11	1	2	2:VZ(.72);3:P(.71);4:CM(.70);5:KF(.68);6:P2(.51); 7:UU(.08);8:S&(−.09)
BOTZ01	1	2	2:I(.97);3:VZ(.68);4:N(.50);5:I0(.23);6:V(.23);7:FW(.19); 8:CS(.17);9:CF(−.03)
BROW11	1	2	2:MM(.83);3:V(.82);4:FI(.57);5:M6(.40);6:I0(.29);7:RG(−.11)
BROW21	1	2	2:I(.82);3:VZ(.66);4:P(.62);5:V(.48)
BUND11	1	2	2:K0(.67);3:RG(.44);4:FX(.36);5:P(.35);6:MSa(.28);7:MSb(.14)
CARR43	1	3	2:2C(.59);5:2S(.57);10:2∗(.09)
CATT01A	1	3	2:2C(.66);6:2F(.66)
CHRI01	1	3	2:2Y(.81);7:2V(.55);10:2C(.44)
CLAU01	1	2	2:R1(.94);3:DC(.63);4:VC(.33)
”	3	1	DC:Cognitive Development vars.(.63 to .39)
CLAU02	1	2	2:DC(.88);3:R1(.66);4:UA(.49)
”	2	1	DC:Cognitive Development vars.(.44 to .18)
CLAU03	1	2	2:DC(.92);3:R1(.70);4:VC(.40);5:P3(.38)
”	2	1	DC:Cognitive Development vars.(.29 to .14)
CLAU04	1	3	2:2H(.68);8:2P(.68)
COOM01	1	2	2:S&(.77);3:N(.66);4:I(.65);5:V(.55);6:SR(.54);7:S&(.45); 8:P(.38);9:MA(.32)
CORN01	1	2	2:I(.94);3:V(.81);4:MS(.57);5:BC(.51);6:P(.20)
CRAW01	1	2	2:FI(.71);3:A0(.61);4:MO(.49);5:I(.45);6:FF(.38);7:MOa(.37); 8:MOb(−.18)
CURE11	1	2	2:VZ(.80);3:V(.59);4:P2(.31);5:N(.21);6:I0(.12);7:MA(.11); 8:MK(−.10);9:P(−.15)
DEMI01A	1	2	2:RG(.80);3:V(.80);4:FO(.66);5:N(52)
DEMI02A	1	2	2:FO(.86);3:N(.78);4:V(.73);5:RG(−.13)
DENT01	1	2	2:1G(.67);3:GR(.66);4:PR(.15);5:PRa(−.03);6:PRb(−.04)
”	2	1	Reasoning(.43);Number(.42);Word Fluency(.30); Memory(.29);Perceptual Speed(.28)
DEVR02	1	2	2:DC(.77);3:A1(.66);4:RP(.58)
”	2	2	DC:Cognitive Development variables
DUBO01	2	1	1G:‘Level’ variables
DUNC01	1	2	2:GC(.75);3:P5(.75)
DUNH11	1	2	2:RG(.85);3:V(.74);4:I(.62);5:FW(.55);6:I0(.50);7:FO(.46); 8:I0(.01)
DUPO01	1	2	2:RP(.90);3:N(.80);4:V(.66);5:VZ(.41)
EKST11	1	3	2:2V(.63);3:2S(.63)
FLEI51	1	2	2:V(.89);3:RQ(.51);4:VZ(.43);5:P(−.07);6:FW(−.29)
FOGA00	1	2∗	2:GC(.89);3:GF(.62);4:CF(.60);5:U5(.58);6:UK(−.30)
FRUC21	1	2	2:V(.88);3:N(.86);4:VZ(.85);5:E0(.63);6:P(.35);7:MK(.32)
GARR11	1	2	2:I0(.84);3:GC(.78);4:VZ(.13)
GARR14	1	2	2:GC(.75);3:MA(.52);4:MS(.23)

Table 15.4 *(cont.)*

Dataset	Factor no.	Order	Loadings for lower-order factors or variables[a]
GARR16	1	2	2:RG(.92);3:GH(.66);4:MA(.32)
GOOD01	1	2	2:I(.64);3:N(.57);4:P(.53);5:V(.47);6:MA(.18);7:VZ(−.24); 8:Ia(−.30)
GOOD11	1	2	2:GS(.60);3:GF(.60)
GRIM01	6	2	7:RQ(.62);8:(.58)
GUIL11	1	2	2:RG(.90);3:V(.55);4:SP(.43);5:FX(.39);6:I0(.35);7:FO(.30); 8:N(.28)
GUIL16	1	3	2:2H(.58);7:2S(.58)
GUIL17	1	2	2:V(.78);3:P(.57);4:RQ(.51);5:VZ(.41);6:MK(.37);7:I(.33); 8:N(.33);9:P6(.11);10:I0(.03)
GUIL18	1	2	2:I(.94);3:RG(.76);4:S&(.48);5:FA(.45);6:VZ(.34);7:Ia(.24); 8:FI(.16)
GUIL19	1	2	2:RG(.83);3:RQ(.56);4:V(.35);5:I0(.34)
GUIL21	1	2	2:RG(.99);3:RGa(.70);4:FI(.61);5:I(.58);6:RQ(.23)
GUIL31	1	2	2:VZ(.91);3:V(.63);4:SR(.46);5:P(.42);6:N(.12)
GUIL32	1	2	2:RG(.89);3:MK(.75);4:V(.64),5.I(.57)
GUIL32A	1	2	2:MK(.95);3:RG(.69);4:V(.68);5:I(.54)
GUIL33	1	2	2:RQ(.80);3:MK(.62);4:P(.49)
GUIL34	1	2	2:RG(.91);3:N(.56);4:MK(.56);5:P(.29)
GUIL35	1	2	2:RG(.94);3:RGa(.69);4:P(.53);5:V(.46);6:N(.45);7:P6(.18); 8:VZ(.05);9:MK(−.20)
GUIL36	1	2	2:GH(.54);3:VZ(.54)
GUIL38	1	2	2:MK(.70);3:VZ(.55);4:V(.42);5:MKa(.38);6:LE(.35)
GUIL40	1	2	2:RQ(.98);3:P(.78);4:I0(.47);5:SR(.36);6:LE(.29);7:LEa(.13)
GUIL41	1	2	2:RQ(.88);3:AC(.46);4:P6(.28);5:MK(.14)
GUIL46	1	2	2:RG(.95);3:VZ(.68);4:MA(.66);5:P6(.41);6:V(.37)7:P(.20); 8:IL(.16);9:MK(−.01)
GUIL51	1	2	2:RG(.96);3:FW(.81);4:V(.59);5:N(.32);6:I(.26);7:I0(.25); 8:I0(−.05)
GUIL56	1	3	2:2R(.65);7:2H(.65)
GUST11A	1	3	2:2V(.96);6:2F(.71);9:2C(.62)
HAKS01	1	3	2:2Y(.76);5:2F(.62);13:2C(.52);21:2R(.22); 24:Gen. information(.21)
HAKS21	1	2*	2:GF(.79);3:GS(.77);4:GY(.58); Also (salient on Factor 5): 7:GR(.50);8:GV(.34)
HARG01	1	2	2:GC(.77);3:FO(.73);4:FOa(−.10)
HARR01	1	3	2:2P(.71);6:2H(.71)
HARR51	1	2	2:V(.96);3:MM(.79);4:SR(.58);5:I(.37);6:FW(.27);7:I0(.17); 8:P(.17)
HARR52	1	2	2:V(1.00);3:I(.75);4:MM(.67);5:FW(.55);6:P(.33);7:VZ(.08); 8:I0(.08);9:NA(−.16)
HARR53	1	2	2:MM(.62);3:P(.61);4:I(.55);5:CS(.55);6:SG(.47)
HARR54	1	2	2:RQ(.60);3:CS(.59);4:I(.56);5:P(.56);6:MM(.50);7:V(.45)
HEND11A	1	3	2:2V(.83);5:2C(.83)
HISK03	1	2	2:VZ(.88);3:MS(.88)

Table 15.4 *(cont.)*

Dataset	Factor no.	Order	Loadings for lower-order factors or variables[a]
HISK04	1	1	7 cognitive variables, loadings .72 to .56
HOLT11	5	1	8 cognitive variables, loadings .60 to .22
HORN01	1	2*	2:VZ(.77);3:R9(.64);4:GF(.58);5:PR(.38);6:CA(−.07)
HORN02	1	2*	2:GV(.85);3:GC(.52);4:GF(.51);5:PR(.43);6:PRa(.29); 7:PRb(.19);8:PRc(−.42)
HORN25	1	2*	2:M0(.83);3:AI(.74);4:GH
HORN26	1	2*	2:GH(.67);3:AI(.64);4:GR(−.14)
HORN31	1	2*	2:GC(.86);3:GF(.69);4:GV(.57);5:GY(.45);8:2U(.42)
HUEF01	1	1	DC:8 cognitive variables, 7 from WISC
JENS41	2	1	Terman Concept Mastery Test (.94);Digit-Span (.49)
JOHA01	1	2	2:DC(.95);3:DM(.80);4:V&(.70);5:DA(.59);6:DS(.57); 7:AT(−.04)
"	2	1	DC:7 cognitive variables
KEIT21	1	3	2:2C(.78);5:2F(.78)
KRAN01A	1	2	2:R4(.70);3:R7(.57);4:2V(.52);5:2C(.43);6:R1(.37)
MASN01	2	1	5 cognitive variables
MCGU01	1	2	2:RG(.78);3:A1(.58);4:FI(.69);5:CS(.59);6:P(.47)
MCGU02	1	2	2:A1(.92);3:RG(.78);4:FI(.67);5:P(.38)
MEEK01	1	3	2:2Y(Mem.Span)(.60);6:2H(.60)
MICH62	1	2	2:VZ(.81);3:V(.65);4:N(.42);5:P(.27)
MOON01	1	2	2:AC(.90);3:RG(.58);4:CS(.46);5:CSa(.23)
MORR11	1	2	2:P(.70);3:U3(.52);4:V(.45);5:I(.44);6:VZ(.19);7:P2(−.07)
MOUR01	1	3	2:2F(.91);5:2V(.91)
NIHI01	1	3	2:2H(.62);8:2R(.62)
NIHI02	1	2	2:I(.87);3:RG(.85);4:SP(.69);5:RGa(.53);6:A1(.51);7:SPa(.36); 8:FI(.22);9:V(.01)
OSUL01	1	2	2:RQ(.87);3:V(.73);4:BC(.69);5:I0(.27);6:FO(.19);7:SP(.04); 8:CS(−.01);9:I0(−.28)
PARK01	1	2	2:RG(.95);3:VZ(.61);4:P6(.57);5:P2(.29);6:R1(.22);7:K2(.05)
PEDU01	1	3	2:School Achvt.(.85);5:23(.85)
PENF01	1	3	2:2F(.49);7:2R(.49)
PETE11	1	2	2:I(.83);3:V(.71);4:RQ(.67);5:N(.61);6:RG(.24)
PETE12	1	2	2:I(.92);3:V(.67);4:RG(.66);5:RGa(.65);6:N(.43)
PRIC01	4	1	4 cognitive variables
PROG12	1	2	2:V(.88);3:A3(.88);4:A4(.76);5:2F(.70)
RAND01	1	2	2:M0(.77);3:CZ(.58);4:VZ(.49);5:MS(.37)
RAND02	1	2	2:CZ(.68);3:M0(.59);4:VZ(.44);5:MS(−.17)
REMO01	1	2	2:2F(.95);3:VZ(.65);4:PR(.20)
REMO02	1	2	2:N(.65);3:2F(.49);4:V(.45)
REYN11	1	2	2:LD(.82);3:VZ(.82)
REYN11	2	1	DC:5 cognitive development variables
RIMO11	1	3	2:2F(.74);5:2Y(memory span)(.74)
RIMO21	1	2	2:RG(.70);3:I(.50);4:Ia(.48);5:RQ(.35)
SAUN03	1	2	2:VZ(.68);3:V&(.58);4:LD(.53);5:LDa(.42);6:MS(.06)
SCHA11	1	3	2:2H(.51);8:2S(.51)
SCHU11	1	3	2:2C(.80);5:2F(.80)
SEGE01	1	3	2:2H(.45);6:2S(.45)

Table 15.4 (*cont.*)

Dataset	Factor no.	Order	Loadings for lower-order factors or variables[a]
SEGE02	1	3	2:2H(.75);6:2S(.75)
SHAY02	1	3	2:2V(.79);5:2H(.51);9:tech.infor.(.30)
SING21	1	2	2:RD(.71);3:VZ(.63);4:LS(.49);5:U3(.37);6:IO(.18)
SNOW11	1	2	2:CS(.69);3:VZ(.51);4:MS(.51);5:RG(.47);6:P(.44)
SNOW12	1	2	2:MS(.67);3:RQ(.64);4:LD(.61);5:P(.56);6:VZ(.32);7:IO(− .10); 8:MM(− .15)
SNOW21	8	1	SAT-Verbal(.71);Visual Memory Slope(.70); SAT-Quantitative(.44)
STEP01B	1	2	2:RP(.93);3:A1(.90);4:RPa(.81);5:RPb(.18)
STOR11	1	2	2:2H(.81);3:FX(.71);4:LD(.58);5:I(.57);6:OP(.30);7:FO(.30); 8:RQ(.25);9:VL(.22);10:RG(.00);11:VZ(− .01)
STOR12	1	3	2:2H(.52);8:2R(.52)
STOR13	1	2	2:RG(.93);3:RQ(.67);4:VZ(.50);5:FX(.34);6:MS(.33);7:FO(.24); 8:LD(.22);9:CZ(.18);10:RGa(.08);11:RGb(.01)
SUMI03	1	2	2:IO(.84);3:WS(.81);4:V(.74);5:IO(.61);6:LE(.17)
SUNG02	1	3	2:2H(.99);6:2P(.44);10:?R(− .19)
SUNG03	1	3	2:2R(.56);5:2H(.10);8:2V(− .42)
SUNG04	1	3	2:2H(.80);7:2R(.77);9:2O(− .11)
SUNG05	1	3	2:2R(.71);5:2H(.55);9:2P(.16)
TENO01	1	2	2:I(.85);3:MA(.80);4:P(.58);5:BC(.29);6:SG(.14);7:IO(.03)
THUR31	1	2	2:I(.94);3:SR(.52);4:P(.46);5:V(.41);6:Pa(.40);7:MA(.37); 8:N(.35);9:RG(.31);10:FW(− .12)
THUR41	6	1	4 PMA tests, loadings .70-.53
THUR81	1	3	2:2H(.72);8:2S(.58);12:2V(.28)
THUR82	1	3	2:2H(.75);8:2S(.75)
UNDH11	1	2	2:FW(.90);3:V(.79);4:I(.74);5:R9(.45);6:VZ(.44)
UNDH21	1	2*	2:GF(.90);3:GV(.67);4:GS(.64);5:GR(.56);6:GC(.04)
VERN01	1	2	2:2V(.87);3:R7(.47);4:VL(.37);5:R2(.29);6:MS(.08);7:IO(− .37)
VERN21	1	2	2:RQ(.67);3:V(.58);4:N(.36);5:R4(.34)
VERY01	1	2	2:A3(.87);3:VZ(.60);4:RG(.46);5:V(.39);6:N(.21)
VERY02	1	2	2:RG(.62);3:N(.48);4:VZ(.39);5:V(.14);6:RQ(.07)
VIDL01	1	2	2:FI(.83);3:GC(.83)
WEIN11	1	2	2:I(.91);3:FW(.88);4:V(.68);5:WA(.55);6:FI(.48)
WEIS11	1	3	2:2O(.72);4:2C(.53);8:2F(.51)
WERD01	1	2	2:RG(.76);3:RQ(.72);4:VZ(.72);5:V(.64);6:KM(.47);7:N(.25); 8:I(− .01)
WERD02	1	2	2:RQ(.81);3:V(.61);4:RG(.58);5:VZ(.53);6:N(.38);7:RGa(.32)
WERD51	1	2	2:N(.75);3:P(.75);4:RG(.61);5:VZ(.58)
WEXL01	1	1	8 measures of mental development, including 4 subtests of WPPSI; loadings .80 to .49
WIEB11	1	2	2:VZ(.73);3:LD(.70);4:XC(.70);5:MS(.09);6:MM(.00)
WIEB12	1	2	2:XC(.63);3:MS(.58);4:XCa(.58);5:I(.27);6:LD(.12)
WOTH01	1	3	2:2F(.82);8:IO(.50);12:2V(.00);15:2R(− .32)
WRIG01	1	2	2:N/MS(.98);3:LD(.65);4:VZ(.37);5:RG(.20)

*Study designed for second-stratum analysis at first order.

[a]See Appendix A for factor codes. See text for explanation of entries.

would be regarded as representing an ability at stratum II, while the lower-order factors would represent abilities in some sort of limbo between stratum I and II. For example, hierarchical factor 1 at the third-order in dataset HECK01 dominates two second-order memory factors, with loadings of .75 and .64 respectively, while another second-order factor has a vanishing loading ($-.13$) on it. Factor 1 was classified, therefore, not as G but as a stratum II memory ability.

Occasionally, as may be seen in Table 15.4, two factors from a given dataset were classified as G, each at a different order of analysis. This could be the result of the analytic problem noted earlier, whereby a factor could appear artifactually if it is of such a general character that it should have no loadings on a lower-order factor. For example, datasets CLAU01, CLAU02, and CLAU03 were each found to contain a first-order factor labeled as "Cognitive Development" and covering mental growth in a number of domains. Such a factor could be regarded as a first-order factor measuring G, but its variance overlaps with the variance found at the second-order. A similar phenomenon occurs in dataset JOHA01.

Classification of factors as G in Table 15.4 should not be taken as indicating that all these factors are exactly identical. Presumably, if it were possible to obtain factor scores for each of these factors in some appropriate population, these factor scores might be highly correlated, especially after correction for attenuation. But it is unlikely that they would be perfectly correlated, because the G factor for a given dataset is dependent on what lower-order factors or variables are loaded on it. One could say that a higher-order factor is "colored" or "flavored" by its ingredients.

For each factor listed in Table 15.4, there are listed, in order of magnitude, the loadings of the lower-order factors or variables that it dominates. The reader is encouraged to scan these entries in order to get an impression of what kinds of lower-order factors or variables are likely to have high loadings on the G factors listed, and the degree of variation in loadings that occurs for a given lower-order factor. This variation will sometimes appear extreme. For example, for dataset BACH21, the highest loading on factor 1 is .72, for factor CS, while for dataset BOTZ01, factor CS has a loading of only .17. Such variation could probably be traced to numerous sources – the types of variables subsumed under the factors, the interpretation of the factors, vagaries in rotational procedures, and sheer sampling fluctuation. Over the whole table, however, a considerable degree of consistency can be observed. For example, the G factor usually has high loadings for factor I (Induction), and low loadings for psychomotor factors.

Note that for factors at the third order, the loadings are for second-order factors; for factors at the second order, the loadings are for first-order factors. For factors at the first order, the loadings are for the raw variables. It is useful

Table 15.5. *Central tendencies of loadings of first-order factors on the third-order G factors in selected datasets*

Factor	Median	Mean	Range	No. of loadings
I (Induction)	.57	.57	.49 to .65	6
VZ (Visualization)	.57	.55	.22 to .79	12
RQ (Quantitative Reasoning)	.51	.51	.26 to .73	7
V (Verbal Ability)	.49	.49	.19 to .66	13
CF (Flexibility of Closure)	.45	.57	.39 to .88	3
N (Numerical Facility)	.45	.39	.01 to .61	9
MA (Associative Memory)	.43	.46	.10 to .89	9
FW (Word Fluency)	.43	.40	.26 to .50	5
CS (Speed of Closure)	.42	.37	.11 to .57	3
RG (Sequential Reasoning)	.41	.39	−.08 to .83	13
SR (Spatial Relations)	.40	.40	.20 to .67	12
FI (Ideational Fluency)	.38	.40	.38 to .46	4
FO (Originality)	.37	.40	.34 to .50	3
VL (Lexical Knowledge)	.37	.37	.30 to .44	2
P (Perceptual Speed)	.37	.34	.11 to .45	10
MS (Memory Span)	.36	.38	.28 to .54	10
SP (Sensitivity to Problems)	.34	.34	.31 to .38	3
MK (Mechanical Knowledge)	.26	.23	.02 to .38	4
R1 (Reaction Time)	−.08	−.06	−.02 to −.11	2

also to consider, for third-order factors, the loadings of first-order factors on them. These can be found in the second-order hierarchical factor matrices contained in Appendix B. However, Table 15.5 presents a summarization of these loadings for most of the datasets shown in Table 15.4 as containing a G factor. Data are presented only for factors that occurred in these datasets at least twice. (Some datasets, namely CARR43, GUIL56, PEDU01, SUNG02–05, and WEIS11 were excluded from this analysis because there were various reasons to doubt that the third-order factor was a good representation of G. For example, in the case of dataset GUIL56 most of the first-order factors represented the general retrieval factor 2R; the dataset was designed to investigate factors in "creative thinking.") As may be seen from the table, factors I, VZ, RQ, V, and CF had fairly consistent high loadings on G, while factors such as MS, SP, MK, and R1 tended to have low loadings. This suggests that factor G involves complex higher-order cognitive processes. The eventual interpretation of factor G must resort to analysis of what processes are common to the tasks used in the measurement of such factors as I, VZ, RQ, and V, and to the analysis of what attributes of such tasks are associated with their difficulties.

FACTORS CLASSIFIED AS Gf OR 2F (FLUID INTELLIGENCE)

The possible distinction between factor Gf (2F) and Gc (2C) has been discussed above. Table 15.6 lists 46 factors, at either order 2 or 1, that were classified as measuring factor Gf (fluid intelligence). The factor is regarded as essentially indicating a second-stratum ability. In some instances (e.g., datasets FOGA00, HAKS21, HORN01), the factor appeared at order 1 in the analysis because the dataset had what we call higher-stratum design. In other instances (e.g., datasets GOOD11, HALS01, PROG12) the factor appeared at order 1 because a group of relatively diverse variables (as listed in the table with their loadings) defined it at this level.

To gain an impression of what kinds of stratum I factors tended to define this stratum II factor, a tabulation was made of the first-order factors that had either one of the two highest loadings, in the case of all factors listed as appearing at order 2 in the table. Factors appearing at least twice in this tabulation were as follows:

> Factor I (Induction): 19 times, average loading .64
> Factor VZ (Visualization): 10 times, average loading .62
> Factor RG (Sequential Reasoning): 7 times, average loading .55
> Factor RQ (Quantitative Reasoning): 6 times, average loading .65
> Factor FI (Ideational Fluency): 3 times, average loading .60
> Factor GF (Fluid Intelligence): 2 times, average loading .54
> Factor SR (Spatial Relations): 2 times, average loading .46

Miscellaneous other factors appeared in this tabulation once. In order of their loadings, these are: L0 (Learning Ability, .68); U3 (General Sound Discrimination, .59); P (Perceptual Speed, .58); M0 (Unidentified Memory Ability, .57); LA (Foreign Language Aptitude, .57); N (Numerical Facility, .54); MS (Memory Span, .54); MA (Associative Memory, .54); CF (Flexibility of Closure, .51); UR (Resistance to Auditory Distortion, .45); GY (General Memory Ability, .43); and VL (Lexical Knowledge, .41). In the case of factors U3 and UR, the classification was based on the recommendation of the authors of the dataset, STAN31 (Stankov & Horn, 1980), who sought to show that auditory tasks could measure fluid intelligence. My own preference would be to classify the second-order factor as 2U (General Auditory Function), on the supposition that the general intellective function would appear, with appropriate battery design, in a stratum III factor.

The possible criticism could be advanced that these results are partly an artifact of the fact that the presence of high loadings on I or RG (or both) was used as one of the bases for classifying a factor as GF or 2F. In response, I may point out that in a number of datasets, the factor was clearly distinct from other second-stratum factors that dominated rather different sets of first-order factors. The factors classified here deserved interpretation, regardless of whether they dominated factors I or RG. The presence of a high loading on such factors as RQ and VZ was not used as a sole basis for classification, yet factors I and RG were frequently associated with them.

The types of variables that had high salient loadings on first-order factors classified as Gf tend to confirm the characterization of this factor as one involving difficult tasks of induction, reasoning, problem solving, and visual perception.

FACTORS CLASSIFIED AS GC OR 2C (CRYSTALLIZED INTELLIGENCE)

Table 15.7 lists 84 factors, in 81 datasets, that were classified as measuring what Cattell (1971) and others have called "crystallized intelligence," that is, a type of broad mental ability that develops through the "investment" of general intelligence into learning through education and experience. As in the case of other factors, there are some instances (in datasets HAKS21, HEND11A, and HORN01) where a dataset yielded a Gc factor at both the second and the first order, mainly because of its design but also possibly because of anomalies in the factorization process.

A tabulation of the first-order factors that appeared most often with one of the two highest loadings on the Gc factor showed the following:

Factor V (Verbal Ability), 23 times, average loading .71
Factor LD (Language Development), 11 times, average loading .78
Factor RC (Reading Comprehension), 7 times, average loading .75
Factor RG (Sequential Reasoning), 7 times, average loading .69
Factor K0 (General Information), 5 times, average loading .73
Factor FI (Ideational Fluency), 5 times, average loading .68
Factor SG (Spelling), 5 times, average loading .67
Factor N (Numerical Facility), 5 times, average loading .55

Most of these factors involve language either directly or indirectly. Although factors RG, FI, and N may not directly involve language, many tests of these factors are verbal. Numerical facility is often acquired through schooling, or at least through practical experience.

Other factors that often had high loadings were: LS (Listening Comprehension); FW (Word Fluency); RQ (Quantitative Reasoning); R& (a special reading comprehension factor); and MA (Associative Memory). Note that some of these factors were also found to have loadings on factor Gf. It is reasonable to think that factors could have multiple loadings – i.e., that their variance could depend on both Gc and Gf.

In dataset STAN31, factors UK (Temporal Tracking) and US (Speech Sound Discrimination) had loadings of .96 and .57, respectively, on a second-order factor that was classified as Gc, in accord with Stankov and Horn's (1980) assignment. The second-order factor could, however, have been equally well classified as factor 2U (see below).

Table 15.6. *46 factors classified as Gf or 2F (fluid intelligence) in 43 datasets*

Dataset	Factor no.	Order	Loadings for lower-order factors or variables[a]
ADKI03	1	2	2:I(.96);3:VZ(.80);4:RG(.69);5:N(.38);6:CS(.34)
ALLI01	1	2	2:L0(.68);3:I(.68)
BURN11	1	2	2:I(.68);3:RQ(.55);4:VZ(.51);5:V(.21)
CANI01	1	2	2:RG(.93);3:RQ(.93);4:I(.62);5:N(.38);6:KM(.34); 7:KMa(.09);8:KMb(−.02)
CARL40	1	2	2:I(.85);3:Ia(.47);4:Ib(.30);5:Ic(.27)
CATT01A	6	2	7:SR(.49);8:I(.42)
ELKO01	1	2	2:I(.68);3:Ia(.63);4:Ib(.55);5:U8(.53);6:VZ(.47);7:P(.42)
FEDE02	1	2	2:FI(.75);3:N(.54);4:VZ(.44). Also 10:CF(.48)
FOGA00	3	1*	Number Series(.52);Sets STV-Visual(.44); Number Series(.43);Hidden Words(.39); Tonal Counting(.31);Sets STV/Visual(.29); Matrices(.20)
GOOD11	3	1	Induction(.54); Reasoning (.54)
GUST11A	6	2	7:VZ(.25);8:I(.23)
HAKS21	2	1*	Spatial(.52);Numerical(.37);Induction(.37); Perceptual Speed(.34);Closure Flexibility(.20)
HALS01	3	1	Halstead Category(.69);Carl Hollow-Square(.45); Henmon−Nelson(.44);Halstead Time-Sense(.26)
HORN01	4	1*	Induction(.54);Intellectual Level(.53); Figural Relations(.49);Semantic Relations(.46); Formal Reasoning(.40);General Reasoning(.39); Associative Memory(.33)
HORN02	4	1*	Intellectual Level(.64);Induction(.58);Formal Reasoning(.54);Number Facility(.53);Semantic Relations(.49);General Reasoning(.43);Perceptual Speed(.41);Intellectual Speed(.39);Associative Memory(.33);Figural Relations(.30)
HORN21	9	2*	10:GF(.66);11:GV(−.27). Also 4:VL(.41).
"	10	1*	Matrices,Time(.54);Paper Folding,Time(.51); Matrices(.50);Letter Series,Time(.48);Common Analogies,Time(.45);Letter Series(.44); Analogies(.36)
HORN31	3	1*	Auditory Immed. Memory(.57);Figural Relations(.54); Visualization(.40);Speed of Closure(.20)
HUGH01	4	2	5:MA(.54);6:GF(.43). Also 3:MS(.43)
"	6	1	ACER Intelligence(.73);Raven Matrices(.58); Piaget Rod Flexibility(.38);Flapboard(.24)
LANS31	7	1	Letter Series(.53);Common Analogies(.48);Matrices(.32)
LUCA01	1	2	2:RG(.79);3:VZ(.76);4:RGa(.61);5:I(.57);6:V(.13) Also 9:Ia(.48)
LUMS01	1	2	2:FI(.71);3:VZ(.66);4:MS(.49);5:MA(.39);6:N(.36);7:CS(.32) Also 9:RC(.44)

Table 15.6 (*cont.*)

Dataset	Factor no.	Order	Loadings for lower-order factors or variables[a]
MOUR01	2	2	3:GY(.43);4:RG(.26)
PENF01	2	2	3:RQ(.76);4:RG(.40);5:S&(.38);6:RGa(.28)
PIMS01	1	2	2:I(.84);3:LA(.57);4:RS(.31);5:KL(−.32). Also 7:V(.39)
"	6	1	H.S.Math-Sci Grades(.54);Ship Destinations(.47); Linguistic Analysis I(.36)
PROG12	5	1	Lorge-Thorndike Nonverbal(.44);Otis–Lennon Total(.34);Metropolitan Readiness(.23)
REMO01	2	1	Numerical Operations(.24);Disordered Sentences(.23);Weekday Test(.22);Reasoning(.20); Factor V(.19);Factor R(.19);Factor V(.18); Numerical Operations(.15)
REMO02	3	1	Test of Factor R(.50);Factor S(.44);Factor V(.41); Test of Factor S(.37)
RIMO11	2	2	3:I(.53);4:VZ(.40)
ROYC11	1	2	2:P(.58);3:I(.52);4:Ia(.51);5:TP(.48);6:P5(.45);7:TPa(.45); 8:I0(.38),9.I0a(.37);10:LD(.33);11:P2(.32);12:I0(−.14)
SCHU11	5	2	6:SR(.42);7:RG(.34)
STAN31	7	2	8:U3(.59);9:UR(.45). Also 4:U1(.48);3:US(.38); See text for comment.
THUR21A	1	2	2:VZ(.84);3:RG(.60);4:P(.59);5:N(.48);6:MA(.45). Also 9:FW(.45)
UNDH21	2	1*	Necessary Facts(.32);Circle Reasoning(.32); Verbal Analogies(.31);Sentence Selection(.30); Letter Series(.27);Matrices(.18)
VALT02	2	1	Perceptual Speed(.53);IQ(.34);Rey-Test(.20); Footprints Test(.20);Embedded Figures(.16)
VALT03	2	1	IQ(.44);Perceptual Speed(.40);Rey-Test(.32); Embedded Figures(.25);Footprints Test(.24)
VERY03	1	2	2:VZ(.81);3:RG(.36);4:N(.26). Also 6:RQ(.54)
WEIS11	8	2	9:I(.75);10:Ia(.65);11:RQ(.55);12:N(.52);13:VZ(.52); 14:A3a(.35). Also 5:A3(.33)
WHEA01	1	2	2:I(.71);3:CF(.51);4:CS(.29);5:MA(.25);6:U3(.03); 7:U(−.39).
WOOD13	4	2	5:I(.79);6:VZ(.42). Also 3:RC(.31)
WOOD15	5	2	6:VZ(.63);7:I(.60). Also 4:RQ(.34)
WOOD17	5	2	6:MS(.54);7:VZ(.49). Also 4:SG(.58)
WOOD18	5	2	6:RQ(.77);7:VZ(.34). Also 3:SG(.50)
WOTH01	2	2	3:FI(.34);4:RQ(.33);5:MS(.33);6:P(.24);7:VL(.19)

*Study designed for second-stratum analysis at first order.
[a]See Appendix A for factor codes. See text for explanation of entries.

Table 15.7. *84 factors classified as Gc or 2C (crystallized intelligence) in 81 datasets*

Dataset	Factor no.	Order	Loadings for lower-order factors or variables[a]
ADKI03	7	2	8:FI(.61);9:S&(.31);10:P(.16). Also 4:RG(.46);5:N(.36)
CARR01	1	2	2:MA(.67);3:V(.64);4:PT(.53);5:MAa(.43);6:NA(.43)
CARR11	1	2	2:RG(.92);3:V(.64);4:MA(.27);5:VL(−.54)
CARR43	2	2	3:VL(.28);4:M0(−.16). Also 6:R9(−.31);7:MOa(−.31); 11:PC(.48);12:RG(−.39)
CATT01A	2	2	3:RG(.55);4:N(.47);5:V(.36)
CHRI01	10	2	11:N(.58);12:K0(.54)
CUMM01	1	2	2:O&(.71);3:LD(.65);4:MS(.45);5:RP(.43);6:I(.28)
CURE12	1	2	2:V(.88);3:SG(.69);4:P(.38);5:MA(.03)
DAVI01	1	2	2:Verbal Speed(.95);3:RG(.57);4:Reasoning Speed(.45);5:N(.02)
DUNC01	2	1	Stanford Achvt Battery(.65);Reading(.59);IQ(.53); Reading(.53);Arith.(.52);Calculate(.46);Answering(.25)
DUNC11	1	2	2:N(.89);3:V(.64);4:MA(.44);5:MAa(.25);6:L0(.12);7:I(.09); 8:RQ(.05);9:I0(−.08);10:Ia(−.11)
FEDE02	5	2	6:V(.80);7:MK(.65). Also 10:CF(.33)
FOGA00	2	1*	12 GC variables (per author) (.28 to .14)
FRED12	1	2	2:R&(.83);3:R&a(.53);4:RD(.19);5:R&b(−.34)
GARD05A	1	2	2:V(.67);3:MA(.53);4:CF(.51);5:RG(.32)
GARR11	3	1	Arithmetic(.53);Objects(.50);Vocabulary(.46); Word Retention(.37);Logical Prose(.36); Digit Span(.15)
GARR14	2	1	Vocabulary(.55);Logical Prose(.44);Form Board(.39); Arithmetic(.35);Making Gates(.31)
GUIL12	8	2	9:FW(.89);10:V(.50);11:I0(−.13);12(−.16)
GUIL20	1	2	2:V(.91);3:FA(.35);4:RQ(.28);5:FO(.16);6:FI(.13)
GUIL22	1	2	2:FI(.78);3:I(.74);4:Ia(.60);5:FA(.48);6:RG(.43)
GUIL66	1	2	2:RG(.80);3:FW(.69);4:FO(.52);5:N(.49);6:CS(.38); 7:VZ(.36);8:SP(.28);9:FX(.06);10:FI(.03);11:S&(−.12); 12:SPa(−.12)
GUST11A	9	2	10:A6(.69);11:VL(.62);12:A3(.40);13:MS(.22)
HAKS01	13	2	14:SG(.66);15:FW(.61);16:V(.47);17:FI(.45);18:N(.43); 19:CS(.41);20:FO(.35)
HAKS21	5	2*	6:GC(.63);7:FI or GR(.58);8:GV(.42)
"	6	1*	Mechanical Ability(.43);Verbal Ability(.35)
HARG01	2	1	Images(.54);Verbal IQ(.51);Remote Associates(.48); Perceptual IQ(.47); Word Meanings(.35); Picture Completion(.20)
HEND11A	5	2	6:GC(.41);7:EEG Variance(.33)
"	6	1	WAIS Subtests:Vocab.(.40);Info.(.33);Digit Span(.32); Similarities(.31);Arith.(.26);Comprehension(.25)
HOEP21	6	2	7:SP(.82);8:V(.42);9:RQ(.22);10:FO(−.23). Also 2:FW(.34);4:CS(−.39)

Table 15.7 (*cont.*)

Dataset	Factor no.	Order	Loadings for lower-order factors or variables[a]
HOLM11	1	2	2:V(.79);3:CS(.77);4:PC(.71);5:U3(.56);6:MK(.09)
HORN01	7	2*	8:FI(.64);9:GC(.55);10:PR(.20);11:PRa(−.23)
"	9	1*	Verbal Comprehension(.39);Experience Evaluate(.39); Self-Sentiment(.38);Experimenting(.36); Mech.Knowledge(.34)
HORN02	3	1*	Associative Fluency(.52);Verbal Comprehension(.35)
HORN21	9	2*	2:M0(.68);3:P(.66);4:VL(.51);5:MOa(.49);6:S0(.49); 7:MOb(.39);8:MOc(.29)
HORN31	2	1*	Semantic Systems(.44);Verbal Comprehension(.42); Semantic Relations(.40);Listening Comprehension(.30);Induction(.22)
JACK11	1	2	2:RC(.91);3:LS(.75);4:RS(.46)
JAY01	1	2	2:V(.81);3:SG(.70);4:RS(.69);5:MM(.59);6:RG(.30)
JONE31	1	2	2:LD(.88);3:I(.72);4:I0(.32);5:I0(.18);6:MS(.10)
JONE32	1	2	2:LD(.88);3:MM(.72);4:I(.64);5:MS(.47);6:FI(.21);7:VZ(.18)
JONE33	1	2	2:MS(.87);3.LD(.78);4:I(.51);5:VZ(.44);6:I0(.00)
JONE34	1	2	2:LD(.99);3:V&(.62);4:VZ(.59);5:I(.55);6:MS(.20);7:FO(.11)
KAMM01	1	2	2:I0(.66);3:RG(.63);4:US(.62);5:KL(.54);6:N(.36);7:LS(.24)
KEIT21	2	2	3:LD(.52);4:RC(.49);5:MS(.22)
KRAN01A	5	1	Subtests of Mental Abilities Battery: Vocabulary(.76); Information(.66);Comprehension(.65);Similarities(.64); Picture Completion(.34)
LANG31	1	2	2:P(.65);3:RS(.64);4:RQ(.53);5:VL(.40)
LANS31	6	1	Esoteric Analogies(.77);Vocabulary(.72); General Information(.61);Remote Associations(.32)
LUMS01	8	2	9:RC(.53);10:AC(.33);11:CS(.26);12:VL(.23)
LUNZ11	1	2	2:LD(.84);3:RP(.73);4:MS(.72);5:MM(.69);6:MV(.57); 7:RPa(.20);8:MSa(−.07)
MASN01	1	2	2:GC(.80);3:KL(.80)
MESS01	1	2	2:V(.60);3:VU(.59);4:CF(.57);5:P(.42);6:FW(.42);7:FI(.35); 8:CS(.21);9:RQ(−.04)
OLSO51	1	2	2:KF(.87);3:RS(.56);4:WA(.56);5:VZ(.47);6:LP(.41); 7:PI(.38);8:CS(.33)
PIMS01	6	2	7:V(.68);8:FE(.60)
PROG11	1	2	2:V(.96);3:A1(.80);4:A2(.74);5:A3(.55)
ROSE01	6	1	A–B Task(.53);SAT(.53)
ROSE02	3	1	Continuous PA Memory(.44);SAT(.43); Rotated Letters(.40)
ROSE03	2	1	A–B Task(.50);RT Slope(.34);SAT(.30)
SAUN21	1	2	2:K0(.85);3:K0a(.54);4:N(.38);5:K0b(.21);6:K2(.07); 7:K0c(.03)
SCHE11	1	2	2:I0(.61);3:N(.53);4:WS(.49);5:WSa(.33);6:I(.30)
SCHO31	1	2	ESL Factors:2:Reading & Grammar(.88);3:Listening(.65); 4:Oral Interview(.61);5:Writing(.61); 6:Auditory Memory(.45)

Table 15.7 (*cont.*)

Dataset	Factor no.	Order	Loadings for lower-order factors or variables[a]
SCHU00	1	2	2:RC(.99);3:LD(.74);4:VZ(.57);5:PT(.32);6:KO(−.02)
SCHU11	2	2	3:V(.48);4:N(.26)
SHAY01	1	2	2:V(.91);3:K1(.82);4:A6(.75);5:A3(.53);6:N(.28);7:VZ(.15); 8:P(.13)
SPEA01	1	2	2:RG(.90);3:LS(.82);4:MS(.54);5:RS(.43);6:MA(.07)
SPEA02	1	2	2:LS(.87);3:MS(.64);4:I(.61);5:A6(.41);6:MA(.14)
SPEA31	1	2	2:V(.87);3:R&(.86);4:EU(.57);5:P(.55);6:R&(.49);7:I(−.04)
SPEA32	1	2	2:EU(.72);3:I(.64);4:V(.60);5:I0(.43);6:R&(.26);7:Va(.12); 8:P(−.08);9:PC(−.20)
SPEA33	1	2	2:I(.71);3:V(.57);4:P(.30);5:R&(.12);6:I0(.10);7:EU(.07); 8:I0(.04)
SPEA34	1	2	2:V(.89);3:I(.56);4:EU(.42). Also 6:R&(.53)
STAN31	1	2	2:UK(.96);3:US(.57);4:U1(.57);5:U8(.27);6:MS(.24). See text for comment.
STOR01A	4	1	Stanford–Binet Vocabulary(.83);Schaie Test of Behavioral Rigidity:Psychomotor(.56), Motor-Cognitive(.52)
TAYL11	1	2	2:V(.94);3:FI(.72);4:FE(.39);5:I0(.02);6:WA(.01); 7:FO(−.02);8:FW(−.17)
TAYL31	1	2	2:LD(.71);3:FI(.64);4:KO(.55);5:MS(.26)
THUR21A	7	2	8:V(.56);9:FW(.56);10:PC(.38). Also 4:P(.38);3:RG(.30)
TRAU01	1	2	2:V(.71);3:MA(.55);4:L0(.51);5:N(.51);6:RQ(.45);7:MS(.22); 8:I0(.21)
UNDE12	10	1	SAT-Math(.71);Verbal Discrimination(.31); Simul.Acq./Free Recall/Pairs(−.38)
UNDH21	6	1*	Arith.Reasoning(.53);Information(.46); Card Rotation(.26)
VERY03	5	2	6:RQ(.68);7:V(.56)
VIDL01	3	1	Word-Group Naming(.35);Ordering I(.32); Associations III(.31);Sequential Associations(.30);Test Anxiety(.28); Word Grouping(.25);New Uses(.21)
WEIS11	4	2	5:A3(.60);6:VL(.43);7:I0(−.42);8:I(−.50)
WOLI01	1	2	2:RC(.75);3:RQ(.51);4:I(.39);5:A0(.18);6:V(.14);7:VZ(.01)
WOOD13	1	2	2:K0(.78);3:RC(.72)
WOOD15	1	2	2:LD(.85);3:SG(.68);4:RQ(.59)
WOOD17	1	2	2:LD(.75);3:RQ(.73);4:SG(.72). Also 7:VZ(−.32)
WOOD18	1	2	2:K0(.95);3:SG(.64);4:MS(.29)

*Study designed for second-stratum analysis at first order.
[a]See Appendix A for factor codes. See text for explanation of entries.

FACTORS CLASSIFIED AS Gh OR 2H (COMBINATION
OF GF AND GC)

Table 15.8 lists 54 factors in the database that had to be classified as belonging to what may be called a hybrid factor Gh or 2H, usually appearing at the second-order, coordinate with one or more other second-order factors, and often dominated by a third-order factor that was classified as G (as listed in Table 15.4). The lower-order factors or variables having salient loadings on such factors covered the territory for *both* factors Gf and Gc. Essentially this classification was established in order to have one that was distinct from that of a factor G that also appeared in a dataset at the third-order. In future research, it would be desirable to attempt to design batteries so that a clear distinction between Gf and Gc would be obtained, thus preventing the appearance of a hybrid factor Gh. Nevertheless, whenever such a hybrid factor appeared in our datasets, Gh was highly similar to G. Indeed, a tabulation of the lower-order factors that had one of the two highest loadings on this factor (in a given dataset) showed a distribution very similar to that of G as presented in Table 15.5:

> Factor V (Verbal Ability), 18 times, average loading .62
> Factor VZ (Visualization), 10 times, average loading .59
> Factor RG (Sequential Reasoning), 8 times, average loading .70
> Factor RQ (Quantitative Reasoning), 7 times, average loading .69

Other first-order factors appearing at least twice in this tabulation were: U3 (General Sound Discrimination, .55); MK (Mechanical Knowledge, .55); FW (Word Fluency, .54); GF (Fluid Intelligence – at first order, .78); SG (Spelling, .73); KM (Mathematics Knowledge, .72); P (Perceptual Speed, .66); RD (Reading Decoding, .56); GH (this factor at the first order, .56); and I (Induction, .41).

FACTORS CLASSIFIED AS Gy OR 2Y
(GENERAL MEMORY)

Table 15.9 lists 25 factors classified as Gy or 2Y, General Memory, in 20 datasets. There is considerable basis for believing that there are actually *several* second-order factors of memory, but our database does not include enough information to clarify the true structure of memory and learning abilities at higher strata. (For that matter, as was noted in Chapter 7, information on the structure of stratum I abilities in this domain was far from clear and sufficient.) If we tabulate the first-order factors that most frequently have one of the two highest salient loadings on a second-order memory factor, we find the following:

> Factor MA (Associative Memory), 13 times, average loading .66
> Factor MS (Memory Span), 8 times, average loading .36
> Factor L0 (one of several "Learning Ability" factors), 5 times, average loading
> .56

Table 15.8. *54 factors classified as Gh or 2H (combination of Gf and Gc) in 53 datasets*

Dataset	Factor no.	Order	Factor loadings for lower-order factors or variables
ALLI02	1	2	2:V(.86);3:P(.71);4:MK(.55);5:WS(.49)
ALLI03	6	2	7:V(.53);8:MK(.52);9:N/P(.08)
BACH21	3	1	Lorge-Thorndike Verbal(.58),Non-Verbal(.44); Backward Digit-Span(.30)
CARL41	3	1	Calif.Test of Basic Skills(.81); Raven(.64);Reading(.43)
CHIA01	4	1	SAT-Math(.75);SAT-Verbal(.46)
CLAU04	2	2	3:GH(.68);4:VC(.26);5:P3(.20);6:UT(.06);7:R1(−.31)
"	3	1	Raven(.10);Porteus(.10);Stereognosis(.09);Pegboard(.08); PMA MA(.08);Recognition Memory(.08); Apprehension Span(.06)
CORY01	6	2	7:RG(.85);8:CS(.50);9:CSa(.30);10:MK(.24)
FAIR01A	5	2	6:RQ(.75);7:V(.64);8:N(.37);9:MK(−.22)
FAIR02	1	2	2:V(.79);3:RQ(.64);4:MK(.64);5:R5(.17)
FLAN01	1	2	2:V(.71);3:KM(.66);4:EU(.60);5:VZ(.43);6:P(.24)
FREN11	8	2	9:VZ(.95);10:MK(.42);11:V(.35)
GARR16	3	1	Arithmetic(.62);Vocabulary(.52);Form Board(.35); Digit Span(.23)
GUIL14	1	2	2:FX(.76);3:RG(.60);4:V(.45);5:I0(.29). Also 7:FI(.32)
GUIL16	2	2	3:RG(.69);4:RQ(.69);5:VZ(.46);6:RGa(.29)
GUIL36	2	1	Reading Comp.(.70);Arith.Reasoning(.49);Map Memory(.47);Memory for Tactical Plans(.42); Map Memory(.40);Mech.Compreh.(.29);Memory for Landmarks(.26)
GUIL56	7	2	8:FO(.59);9:V(.44);10:FF(.30);11:FX(.14)
GUIL57	6	2	7:FW(.73);8:I0(.55);9:V(.51);10:FF(.41). Also 4:FO(.31)
HARR01	6	2	7:V(.57);8:VZ(.47);9:P2(−.09)
HECK01	10	2	11:V(.65);12:RG(.65);13:M6(.52). Also 4:MM(.35)
HOEP31	1	2	2:RQ(.70);3:RG(.63);4:V(.49);5:I0(.21);6:P(.19)
HOLT11	4	2	5:1G(.71);6:MK(.70)
HORN25	4	1*	Dominoes(.70);Remote Assns.(.60);Letter Series(.50); Analogies(.45);Gen.Info.(.42);Copy the Pattern (.29)
HORN26	2	1*	Analogies(.60);Dominoes(.57);Gen.Info.(.49); Copy the Pattern((.40);Memory Span(.28)
JACK12	1	2	2:LS(.77);3:R7(.37);4:VC(−.76)
MEEK01	6	2	7:A1(.72);8:GH(.45)
NIHI01	2	2	3:RG(.76);4:V(.67);5:I0(.29);6:FI(.25);7:IO(.00)
SCHA11	2	2	3:VL(.76);4:SR(.41);5:FW(.35);6:I0(.24);7:R1(−.36)
SEGE01	2	2	3:RQ(.89);4:VZ(.68);5:V(.66)
SEGE02	2	2	3:VZ(.59);4:RQ(.56);5:V(.43)
SHAY02	5	2	6:A6(.82);7:K2(.55);8:EU(.55). Also 10:K1(.45)
SLAT01	4	2	5:LE(.61);6:V(.37). Also 3:VZ(.66).
STAK01	1	2	2:V(.81);3:P(.62);4:L0(.59);5:I0(.39);6:N(.37);7:MA(.31). Also 11:L0a(.41)

Table 15.8 (*cont.*)

Dataset	Factor no.	Order	Factor loadings for lower-order factors or variables
STOR11	2	1	18 cognitive variables, loadings .52 to .23.
STOR12	2	2	3:RG(.79);4:RQ(.61);5:VZ(.44);6:RGa(.42);7:V(.26)
SUMI02	1	2	2:V(.85);3:WS(.69);4:U3(.32)
SUNG01	1	2	2:U3(.73);3:P2(.63);4:S0(.53). Also 10:I(.42).
SUNG02	2	2	3:I(.15);4:VZ(.14);5:WS(.09)
SUNG03	5	2	6:S0(.65);7:U3(.49). Also 10:P3(−.35)
SUNG04	2	2	3:U3(.51);4:VZ(.42);5:P2(.14);6:WS(−.36)
SUNG05	5	2	6:U3(.58);7:V(.47);8:S0(.46). Also 4:VZ(.32).
TAYL01	1	2	2:I(.67);3:V(.46);4;FI(.41);5:N(.35)
THUR11	9	2	10:Designs Doublet(.48);11:V(.41)
THUR81	2	2	3:V(.59);4:FW(.40);5:I(.35);6:MA(.32);7:N(.27)
THUR82	2	2	3:V(.55);4:FW(.49);5:MA(.40);6:I(.39);7:N(.32)
UNDH01	1	2	2:MS(.73);3:VZ(.72);4:VZa(.69);5:I(.65);6:P(.56);7:CS(.45);8:LD(.44);9:N(.23)
VALT01	4	2	5:RG(.65). Also 3:RD(.52)
VALT02	1	2	2:GF(.78);3:RD(.59),4.AC(.49)
VALT03	1	2	2:GF(.78);3:AC(.70);4:RD(.17)
VALT11	1	2	2:VZ(.60);3:V(.57);4:US(.41);5:N(−.24)
VALT12	1	2	2:V(.55);3:SG(.54);4:SGa(.51);5:VZ(.47);6:US(.40);7:N(−.12)
VERN51	1	2	2:SG(.92);3:N(.85);4:I(.81)
WIDI01	4	2	5:CY(.56);6:CF(.43);7:CYa(.23)
WRIG21	1	2	2:KM(.78);3:VZ(.67);4:V(.54)

*Study designed for second-stratum analysis at first order.
[a]See Appendix A for factor codes. See text for explanation of entries.

Factor M0 (one of several "miscellaneous" memory factors), 5 times, average loading .52
Factor MM (Meaningful Memory), 5 times, average loading .46
Factor M6 (Free Recall Memory), 3 times, average loading .79

However, there are *two* second-order memory factors in each of three datasets: HECK01, HUNT61, and UNDE12. It is not clear how they can be cross-identified, if at all. Furthermore, some of the second-order factors listed in the table appear to be specialized to the subdomain of memory span. This is true of second-order factor 1 in dataset MEEK01 and second-order factor 5 in dataset RIMO11. On the other hand, factor MS is associated with several "typical" memory abilities in several datasets, though it tends to have lower loadings on a second-order memory ability than the other memory factors.

The two second-order factors in dataset GAME01 are interpretable as two somewhat different learning ability factors, and they seem not to be associated

Table 15.9. *25 factors classified as Gy or 2Y (general memory) in 20 datasets*

Dataset	Factor no.	Order	Loadings for lower-order factors or variables[a]
ALLI02	6	2	7:MA(.52);8:N(.47)
ALLI03	2	2	3:MA(.64);4:M0(.46);5:WS(.24)
BRAD01	1	2	2:MA(.86);3:MV(.75);4:CS(.37);5:FF(.26)
CARL31	1	2	2:MA(.95);3:MAa(.83);4:MAb(.57);5:MAc(.13)
CHRI01	2	2	3:M0(.49);4:MA(.40);5:S&(.30);6:MAa(.30)
CORY01	1	2	2:MA(.90);3:RQ(.59);4:M6(.51);5:P(.37). Also 8:CS(−.37)
GAME01	1	2	2:L0(.73);3:M&(.57). Also 6:L0a(.60).
”	4	2	5:L0b(.64);6:MS(.51);7:MA(−.05)
HAKS01	2	2	3:MM(.58);4:MA(.32)
HECK01	1	3	2:2Ya(.75);5:2Yb(.64);10:2H(−.13)
”	2	2	3:M0(.35);4:MM(−.30). Also 6:MMa(−.38)
”	5	2	6:MMa(.66);7:MA(.40);8:MS(.30);9:PI. Also 11:V(.37)
HORN31	5	1*	Maintain & Judge Rhythm(.54);Visual Memory(.34)
HUNT61	1	2	2:M6(.75);3:MS(−.72)
”	4	2	5:R6(.60);6:MS(.55);7:M0(.39)
INGH01	1	2	2:L0(.54);3:L0a(.30);4:L0b(.29);5:L0c(.20);6:L0d(.16); 7:L0e(.15);8:L0f(.05)
KELL01	1	2	2:MM(.77);3:MA(.43);4:MS(.39);5:V(.38). Also 8:RQ(.33)
MALM01	1	2	2:M6(.96);3:MA(.92);4:MM(.38)
MEEK01	2	2	3:MS(.57);4:MSa(.50);5:MSb(.47)
MOUR01	3	1	Memory for Shapes(.18);Imagery(.16);Memory for Numbers(.14);Association(.11)
PETR01	1	2	2:MS(.74);3:MA(.68);4:MAa(.37);5:MSa(.36)
RIMO11	5	2	6:MS(.38);7:MSa(.37)
SEIB02	1	2	2:PI(.80);3:M0(.52);4:MM(.50);5:M0a(.44);6:MA(.28); 7:VL(.17);8:MS(.11);9:M0b(.09);10:S0(−.07)
UNDE12	1	2	2:MA(.74);3:M6(.67);4:MS(.40);5:VL(.40). Also 8:MM(.52)
”	6	2	7:M0(.78);8:MM(.58);9:M0a(.14);10:GC(−.29). Also 2:MA(.38)

*Study designed for second-stratum analysis at first order.
[a]See Appendix A for factor codes. See text for explanation of entries.

with memory abilities, except possibly memory span. The second-order factor in dataset INGH01 is entirely associated with first-order learning abilities, and the evidence for their association with the more typical type of memory ability is unclear or absent.

It must be concluded that our database does not furnish clear information as to the higher-order structure of memory abilities, except to the extent that Table 15.5 suggests that certain memory abilities have moderate loadings on a general intelligence factor. Factor MA (Associative Memory) is reported to have loadings ranging from .10 to .89 (median, .43), and factor MS (Memory Span) has loadings ranging from .28 to .54 (median, .36), at least in certain datasets.

From Table 15.10, which lists 40 factors (mostly at the second order) classified as measuring Gv or 2V (Broad Visual Perception) found in 30 datasets, one finds that the first-order factors which most frequently had one of the two highest loadings on factor 2V were the following:

> Factor VZ (Visualization), 22 times, average loading .67
> Factor SR (Spatial Relations), 16 times, average loading .60
> Factor MK (Mechanical Knowledge), 4 times, average loading .70
> Factor P (Perceptual Speed), 3 times, average loading .47

Factors that occurred in this tabulation twice, with their average loadings, were I (.54), CF (.47), and N (.40).

The appearance of factors VZ and SR in this list is readily understandable from the fact that they involve perceptions and manipulations of visual shapes and forms. Tests of factor MK often involve perception and comprehension of visual presentations of mechanical objects and mechanisms. Factors P, I, and CF are often measured with tasks involving visual forms; for example, a frequently found test of I is the Progressive Matrices test due to Raven (1938–65). Factor Gv or 2V is therefore readily interpretable as measuring a general ability to deal with visual forms, particularly those that would be generally characterized as figural or geometric, and particularly those whose perception or mental manipulation is complex and difficult. Presumably, high status on this factor would signal an ability to perceive and deal with such forms accurately. It is not clear to what extent the factor involves *speed* of perception, although the presence of factors SR and P as often having high loadings on it suggests that speed is at least sometimes a component.

Evidence on the higher-order structure of auditory abilities is very meager because of the little attention that has been given to this domain, at least from the standpoint of individual differences and factor analysis. Table 15.11 lists 7 factors, in 5 datasets, that were classified as measuring one or more second-order factors in the domain.

The single second-order factors found in each of datasets HANL01, KARL11, and STAN21 are reasonably good evidence for a single general auditory perception factor that dominates a variety of first-order factors in the auditory domain, both those involving speech perception and those involving perception of musical sounds. On the other hand, dataset HORN31, designed for second-stratum analysis at the first order, yielded a second-order factor that dominates two first-order factors in the auditory domain. The second-order factor (factor

Table 15.10. *40 factors classified as Gv or 2V (broad visual perception) in 40 datasets*

Dataset	Factor no.	Order	Loadings for lower-order factors or variables[a]
BRAD01	6	2	7:VZ(.70);8:M6(.33);9:V(.07);10:I0(−.45). Also 3:MV(.64);4:CS(.32)
CHRI01	7	2	8:MK(.56);9:SR(.46). Also 12:K0(.48)
CURE12	6	2	7:VZ(.79);8:N(.38);9:KM(.33);10:P2(.22). Also 3:SG(.35)
EGAN01	1	2	2:SR(.58);3:VZ(.55);4:N(−.11)
EKST11	2	2	3:SR(.66);4:SRa(.48);5:VZ(.48);6:CS(.26)
GUIL39	1	2	2:SR(.62);3:VZ(.60);4:I0(.56);5:P(.35);6:KM(.32);7:MK(.30)
GUST11A	2	2	3:CF(.23);4:SR(.17);5:CS(.08)
HAKS01	5	2	6:SR(.63);7:I(.56);8:CF(.53);9:P(.51);10:S0(.28);11:AI(.27); 12:MS(.26). Also 22:S0(.42);19:CS(.33);18:N(.30)
HEND11A	2	2	3:VZ(.38);4:EEG String Measure(.33)
HOFF01	1	2	2:VZ(.91);3:VZa(.72);4:RQ(−.52). Also 7:V(.37)
HORN02	2	1*	Visualization(.37);Spatial Orientation(.34); Closure Flexibility(.31);Speed of Closure(.25); Adaptive Flexibility(.23)
HORN31	4	1*	Spatial Orientation(.51);Closure Flexibility(.40); Figural Classes(.29)
JEFF11	1	2	2:VZ(.90);3:MK(.81);4:I(.69);5:SR(.54);6:P2(.17); 7:CS(−.12)
KEIT21	6	2	7:VZ(.46);8:N(.42)
KELL01	6	2	7:MV(.56);8:P(.56);9:RQ(.33);10:MK(.33)
KRAN01A	4	1*	Subtests of Mental Abilities Battery: Spatial(.65),Object Assembly(.55),Picture Arrangement(.44),Digit-Symbol(.32); Raven Adv. Progressive Matrices(.41)
LORD01	5	2	6:VZ(.76);7:RQ(.40);8:VL(.09);9:R9(−.65). Also 4:R9a(.37);3:P(−.36)
MEEK01	8	1	Subtests of Differential Aptitudes Battery: Mechanical(.53),Abstract(.50),Spatial Orientation(.47)
MICH51	1	2	2:VZ(.78);3:P(.65);4:V(.12);5:N(−.04)
MICH61	1	2	2:VZ(.95);3:SR(.80);4:V(.46);5:P(.41);6:N(.35)
MOUR01	5	2	6:TP(.33);7:VZ(.22)
PEMB01	1	2	2:SR(.66);3:FW(.55);4:CS(.52);5:WS(.37);6:CF(.32)
PRIC01	1	2	2:VZ(.71);3:VZa(.64);4:1G(.38)
ROFF11	1	2	2:V&(.86);3:CS(.61);4:V&a(.48);5:VZ(.45);6:MK(.39); 7:V&b(.25);8:P8(.19);9:LE(.19);10:V(.08)
SHAY02	2	2	3:VZ(.53);4:P(.20)
SIMR01	5	2	6:SR(.73);7:SRa(.58). Also 4:P(.37)
SLAT01	1	2	2:MK(.78);3:VZ(.68)
SNOW21	1	2	2:PI(.82);3:MS(.77);4:PIa(.42). Also 7:I0(.34)
STAK01	12	2	13:SR(.61);14:I0(.44);15:L0(.21);16:I(−.40)
SUNG01	5	2	6:VZ(.75);7:FI(.50). Also 2:U3(.36)
SUNG03	8	2	9:VZ(.71);10:P3(.35);11:I0(−.75)

Table 15.10 (*cont.*)

Dataset	Factor no.	Order	Loadings for lower-order factors or variables[a]
THUR41	1	2	2:VZ(.69);3:R1(.34);4:IL(.27);5:CS(.24);6:1G(.20); 7:CSa(.15);8:PN(.13);9:S&(.07);10:AC(.06);11:S&(.02)
THUR71	1	2	2:CF(.66);3:SR(.62);4:I(.60);5:MV(.49);6:MVa(.49); 7:CS(.47);8:MK(.45);9:VZ(.36);10:IM(.30)
THUR81	12	2	13:SR(.63);14:SS(.62). Also 5:I(.43)
UNDH01	10	2	11:SR(.53);12:IO($-.60$). Also 4:VZ(.61);5:I(.32)
UNDH21	3	1*	Surface Development(.48);Street Gestalt(.47); Hidden Figures(.36)
VERN01	2	1	Raven Adv. Prog. Matrices(.44); Subtests of WAIS: Object Assembly(.36), Block Design(.35), Picture Arrangement(.33), Comprehension(.24), Picture Completion(.22), Arith. Reasoning(.21), Similarities(.21)
VERN11	4	1	Figure Copy(.75);Raven Prog. Matrices(.63)
VERN51	5	2	6:VZ(.65). Also 4:I(.51)
WOTH01	12	2	13:SR(.73);14:MK(.64). Also 4:RQ(.42);6:P($-.36$)

*Study designed for second-stratum analysis at first order.
[a]See Appendix A for factor codes. See text for explanation of entries.

Table 15.11. *7 factors classified as Gu or 2U (broad auditory perception) in 5 datasets*

Dataset	Factor no.	Order	Loadings for lower-order factors or variables[a]
HANL01	1	2	2:UR(.64);3:U3(.61);4:UU(.61);5:URa(.58);6:VL(.48); 7:IO(.27);8:UA(.23);9:UT(.22);10:URb(.18);11:UM(.06)
HORN31	6	2*	7:UR(.71);8:GU(.51). Also 4:GV(.46)
”	7	1*	SPUD:Perceive Distorted Speech(.69); Auditory Acuity(.25)
”	8	1*	DASP:Discriminate Sound Patterns(.55); ACOR:Auditory Cognitive Relations(.27) TC:Temporal Tracking(.24)
KARL11	1	2	2:UR(.60);3:U6(.54);4:U5(.52);5:UM(.48);6:MS(.28); 7:S0(.26);8:UMa($-.38$)
STAN21	1	2	2:U5(.93);3:UK(.57);4:LD(.34);5:U8(.03)
TAYL31	6	2	7:PC(.78);8:MS(.56). Also 4:KO(.37)

*Study designed for second-stratum analysis at first order.
[a]See Appendix A for factor codes. See text for explanation of entries.

6) seems to present a mixture of analysis strata and might well have been classified as an instance of G to be listed in Table 15.4, but it is distinct from factor 1 as already listed there. The two first-order (but stratum II) factors may be interpreted as representing a possible division of auditory factors into two types, one (factor 7) having to do with perception of speech and the other (factor 8) having to do with the perception of musical sounds.

The assignment of factor 6 in dataset TAYL31 in this table is dubious; it relies on weak definitions of a possible Phonetic Coding factor and an Auditory Memory Span factor.

It can be stated again that the auditory domain is in need of much further research. It may be noted that the only first-order factor that occurred more than once in a tabulation of such factors having loadings among the two highest for a second-order factor was factor UR (Resistance to Auditory Stimulus Distortion). Research should investigate the hypothesis that an important component of the general auditory perception factor is the degree to which the individual can cognitively control the perception of auditory stimulus inputs.

FACTORS CLASSIFIED AS Gr OR 2R (BROAD RETRIEVAL ABILITY)

For these second-stratum factors, I use the term "broad retrieval ability," following the suggestions of such writers as Cattell (1971, p. 40), Hakstian and Cattell (1978), and Horn (1988), to denote a capacity to readily call up concepts, ideas, and names from long-term memory. Such a capacity seems to be involved in the entire domain of abilities discussed in Chapter 10 of the present volume, and also in certain abilities (OP, Oral Production, and WA, Writing Ability) in the domain of language as discussed in Chapter 5. Retrieval is not, of course, the only process involved in these factors; many of them also imply constructive or other processes. Table 15.12 lists 44 higher-order factors, found in 40 datasets of this survey, that have been classified in this category. Most of these factors are found at the second order of analysis, and in most cases a given dataset yielded only one such factor. A tabulation of the first-order factors that most frequently occurred as having one of the two highest loadings on the factor yielded the following:

> Factor FI (Ideational Fluency), 31 times, average loading .68
> Factor FO (Originality/Creativity), 7 times, average loading .58
> Factor FE (Fluency of Expression), 4 times, average loading .76
> Factor FF (Figural Fluency), 4 times, average loading .67
> Factor SP (Sensitivity to Problems), 4 times, average loading .55
> Factor FA (Associational Fluency), 4 times, average loading .52
> Factor WA (Writing Ability), 3 times, average loading .81
> Factor FX (Figural Flexibility), 3 times, average loading .63
> Factor OP (Oral Production), 3 times, average loading .53

Factors occurring twice in this tabulation, with their average loadings, included 2R (because of a mixture of levels of analysis, .82), V (Verbal Ability, .78), RG (Sequential Reasoning, .75), NA (Naming Facility), and FW (Word Fluency, .64).

The only datasets that yielded more than one factor in this category were FULG31, GERS01, and HOEP11. It is not clear that these second-order factors could be cross-identified. Dataset FULG31 yielded one second-order factor dominating factors FI and NA – factors characterized as involving production of ideas without any particular restrictions on their originality, and another second-order factor dominating factors FA and FO – factors for which ideas produced possibly had a higher degree of originality. These two factors were in turn dominated by a third-order factor that is still restricted to idea production. This dataset was of rather limited scope in terms of the types of variables, even though there were 24 of them. In dataset GERS01, many of the first-order factors were difficult to interpret, having loadings on collections of rather diverse speeded variables in the domain of what its authors (Gershon, Guilford, & Merrifield, 1963) called "divergent symbolic production abilities." Second-order factors 1 and 5 were distinguished mainly by high loadings for factor FI on factor 1 and high loadings for factor FX on factor 5. Dataset HOEP31 (another in the series from Guilford's group) yielded no third-order factor; its two second-order factors were distinguished by the appearance of two versions of factor FX in factor 1 and the appearance of factors FA, FF (in two versions), and FI in factor 5. But FA and FF also had loadings on factor 1. The results can only be characterized as puzzling. Like many other domains, the domain of general retrieval ability is in need of further research to clarify its structure, using variables that would be better defined than previously in terms of types of tasks and the extent to which they are given under pressure for speed.

FACTORS CLASSIFIED AS GS OR 2S (BROAD SPEEDINESS)

Various symbols have been employed in the factorial literature to denote one or more broad factors of speediness in performing cognitive tasks. For example, the symbol Gps (General Perceptual Speed) has been used by Hakstian and Cattell (1978). I use the symbol Gs or 2S to refer to any factor at stratum II that essentially measures speed of cognitive performance, without intending to imply that all such factors are necessarily the same. Horn has discussed the general problem of identifying higher-order factors of speed in dealing with intellectual problems, pointing out (as I have in this volume, Chapter 11) that many studies have used artifactual correlations that have "contributed to the belief that speed and power are equivalent" (Horn, 1988, p. 666). He states that two broad factors of speed have been identified, one that he calls Attentive Speediness, Gs: "This is a quickness in identifying elements, or distinguishing between elements, of a (visual) stimulus pattern, particularly when measured

Table 15.12. *44 factors classified as Gr or 2R (broad retrieval ability) in 40 datasets*

Dataset	Factor no.	Order	Loadings for lower-order factors or variables[a]
BENN01	1	2	2:WA(.81);3:RG(.79);4:FI(.42)
BENN02	1	2	2:WA(.93);3:RG(.71);4:FI(.65)
BERE01	1	2	2:FF(.85);3:FE(.76);4:FI(.71);5:FA(.66);6:FFa(.35); 7:FW(.25)
BERE02	1	2	2:FE(.89);3:FI(.74);4:FIa(.70);5:FF(.62);6:FFa(−.03); 7:FW(−.64)
CARR01	7	2	8:FE(.61);9:OP(.59). Also 4:PT(.33)
FRED13	1	2	2:FI(.82);3:CS(.66);4:P(.45);5:CF(.21);6:FW(.16)
FULG31	1	3	2:2R(.82);5:2Ra(.82)
"	2	2	3:FI(.39);4:NA(.38)
"	5	2	6:FA(.37);7:FO(.26)
GERS01	1	2	2:I0(.82);3:FI(.61);4:V(.25). Also 7:I0(.42);6:FF(.32)
"	5	2	6:FX(.58);7:I0(.52);8:FF(−.32)
GERS02	1	2	2:FX(.52);3:FI(.52);4:FF(.44);5:I(.38)
GUIL12	1	2	2:FI(.90);3:FE(.80);4:FA(.48);5:FO(.27);6:I0(.17); 7:WA(.12). Also 10:V(.48)
GUIL14	6	2	7:FI(.63);8:I0(.45)
GUIL23	1	2	2:NA(.89);3:FA(.61);4:FI(.45)
GUIL55	1	2	2:FI(.93);3:FW(.78);4:FX(.29);5:FIa(.27);6:FF(.26); 7:FXa(.24);8:N(.22)
GUIL56	2	2	3:FI(.63);4:FIa(.54);5:FW(.39);6:FF(.22)
GUIL57	1	2	2:FF(.66);3:FI(.59);4:FO(.47);5:FX(.26). Also7:FW(.47); 10:FFa(.31)
GUIL58	1	2	2:FO(.66);3:FI(.66);4:FIa(.57);5:FF(.55);6:I0(.32); 7:FW(.32);8:FA(.31);9:V(.17);10:FX(.06)
HAKS01	21	2	22:S0(.46);23:FO(.44). Also 17:FI(.41);20:FOa(.33)
HEND01	1	2	2:BD(.92);3:FI(.82);4:BDa(.55);5:FO(.51);6:BC(.42); 7:V(.35);8:BDb(.10);9:BCa(−.07)
HOEP11	1	2	2:FX(.80);3:N(.64);4:FXa(.33). Also 6:FA(.57);8:FF(.40)
"	5	2	6:FA(.67);7:FFa(.63);8:FFb(.48);9:FI(.44)
HOLT11	1	2	2:FO(.78);3:FI(.77)
INNE01A	1	2	2:FO(.50);3:FI(.50)
KNOE11	1	2	2:FI(.60);3:FA(.44);4:FW(.37);5:FAa(.35);6:FE(.33); 7:FEa(.26)
MARK01	1	2	2:FI(.93);3:FIa(.76);4:FO(.63);5:RG(.40)
MAY01	1	2	2:FI(.76);3:FIa(.61);4:FO(.59);5:FOa(.58)
MERR41	1	2	2:FI(.72);3:SP(.63);4:FIa(.59);5:V(.58);6:FO(.46);7:FA(.38); 8:I(.37);9:I0(.35);10:RG(.26)
MERR51	1	2	2:FO(.95);3:V(.77);4:SP(.41);5:FI(.28);6:I0(.22);7:GF(−.08)
NIHI01	8	2	9:FI(.49);10:SP(.42);11:I0(.12);12:I0(.11);13:A1(−.02)
OLIV01	1	2	2:FI(.81);3:FIa(.81)
PENF01	7	2	8:SP(.75);9:SPa(.39);10:V(.24)
ROGE11	1	2	2:FI(.91);3:WA(.70);4:OP(.41);5:I0(.11)

Table 15.12 (*cont.*)

Dataset	Factor no.	Order	Loadings for lower-order factors or variables[a]
STOR12	8	2	9:FO(.47);10:MS(.45);11:RG(.27);12:RGa(−.17); 13:I(−.18)
SUNG02	10	2	11:FI(.66). Also 8:P3(−.43)
SUNG03	2	2	3:FI(.56);4:P2(.41). Also 9:VZ(.49);7:U3(.38)
SUNG04	7	2	8:FI(.48). Also 11:S0(.37)
SUNG05	2	2	3:FI(.57);4:VZ(.39)
TAYL01	6	2	7:FW(.49);8:P(.41);9:MA(.27). Also 3:V(.38);4:FI(.37)
TAYL12A	1	2	2:FI(.83);3:OP(.57);4:V(.49);5:WA(.26);6:OPa(.12); 7:S&(.05);8:RG(−.07);9:PR(−.24)
TAYL13A	1	2	2:V(.79);3:OP(.44);4:FO(.37);5:I5(.35);6:I0(.28);7:FI(.27); 8:I0(.16);9:FE(.12);10:I0(−.10);11:I0(−.18); 12:PR(−.29)
UNDH21	5	1*	Ideational Fluency(.64);Synonym Fluency-FA(.47); Word Fluency(.47);Vocabulary(.38);Uses(.37)
WOTH01	15	2	16:FF(.53). Also 3:FI(.41)

*Study designed for second-stratum analysis at first order.
[a]See Appendix A for factor codes. See text for explanation of entries.

under press to maintain focused attention" (p. 666). The other speed factor he calls "quickness in deciding on answers" – a measure of "just how quickly one produces answers, both correct and incorrect, to problems of moderate difficulty" (p. 666).

Table 15.13 lists 57 token higher-order factors, from 52 datasets, that are classified as Gs or 2S (Broad Speediness). It is necessary to examine whether they can be further subclassified. First, a tabulation of the first-order factors that most frequently occur as having one of the two highest loadings on each token second-order factor yields the following:

> Factor P (Perceptual Speed), 27 times, average loading .65
> Factor N (Numerical Facility), 8 times, average loading .66
> Factor R2 (Choice Reaction Time), 7 times, average loading .81
> Factor R9 (Speed of Test Performance), 6 times, average loading .70
> Factor WS (Writing Speed), 5 times, average loading .63
> Factor R7 (Speed of Mental Comparison), 4 times, average loading .76
> Factor VZ (Visualization), 4 times, average loading .73
> Factor R3 (Movement Time in RT paradigms), 4 times, average loading .53
> Factor P6 (Multilimb Coordination), 3 times, average loading .60. (This factor is probably identical to factor R3.)

First-order factors occurring twice in this tabulation, with their average loadings, included P5 (Wrist–Finger Speed, .84), R5 (Slope of Visual/Memory

Table 15.13. *57 factors classified as Gs or 2S (Broad speediness) in 52 datasets*

Dataset	Factor no.	Order	Loadings for lower-order factors or variables[a]
ANDR01	1	2	2:P(.83);3:WS(.68);4:VZ(.67);5:P2(.37)
BAIR01	1	2	2:WS(.91);3:P(.81);4:AC(.66);5:V(.53)
BECH01	1	2	2:P(.92);3:WS(.57);4:Pa(.53);5:N(.49);6:Pb(.35);7:SR(.30); 8:FI(.28);9:Pc(.18);10:CS(.01);11:CF(−.26)
CARL41	1	2	2:R2(.90);3:GH(.30). Also 6:R3(.30)
”	4	”	5:R2a(.85);6:R3(.48)
CARR43	5	2	6:R9(.46);7:M0(.44);8:M0a(.42);9:M0b(.30). Also 13:I0(−.35)
CLAU04	8	2	9:I0(.55);10:I0(.39);11:P4(.29);12:I0(.16)
EKST11	7	2	8:P(.49);9:CF(.49)
FAIR01A	1	2	2:R7(.93);3:R4(.73);4:R1(.45)
FAIR02	6	2	7:N(.97);8:R6(.30). Also 3:RQ(.30)
FREN11	1	2	2:R9(.64);3:FE(.49);4:AI(.47);5:WS(.44);6:P(.39); 7:CA(−.41)
GERS02	6	2	7:P(.58);8:I0(.28). Also 3:FI(.45)
GOOD11	2	1*	PMA tests: Perceptual Speed(.51);Number(.37); Space(.36);Verbal(.36);Memory(.14)
GUIL16	7	2	8:P(.55);9:RG(.49)
GUIL42	1	2	2:P(.69);3:V(.56);4:MK(.45);5:P6(.42);6:N(.28)
GUIL43	1	2	2:P(.76);3:P6(.53);4:MK(.36);5:KA(.35);6:N(.34)
GUIL44	1	2	2:P(.88);3:K2(.53);4:KM(.35);5:P6(.29);6:KA(.06)
GUIL45	1	2	2:P6(.85);3:P(.50);4:KA(.41);5:MK(.39);6:N(.21)
HAKS21	3	1*	Spelling(.42);Speed of Closure(.39);Word Fluency(.26); Auditory Ability(.15)
HARR01	2	2	3:P2(.47);4:P2a(.45);5:P1(.42)
HOEP31	7	2	8:N(.66);9:CS(.48). Also 2:RQ(.51)
HOLM01	1	1	Finding A's(.75);Subtraction & Multiplication(.74); Number Comparisons(.70);Letter Sets(.53); Object-Number(.46);Omelet Test(.44); Word Changes(.30);Hidden Figures(.24); Gestalt Completion(.18)
HORN02	8	2*	9:R9(.61);10:PR(.49);11:CA(−.45)
HUGH01	1	2	2:R7(.57);3:MS(.55). Also 6:GF(.42)
JACK12	5	2	6:R5(.67). Also 2:LS(.36)
KRAN01A	7	2	8:R3(.88);9:R3a(.47). Also 4:GV(.42)
LANS31	1	2	2:P(.81);3:Pa(.69);4:R4(.66);5:VZ(.16);6:GC(−.09); 7:GF(−.32)
LORD01	1	2	2:N(.82);3:P(.78);4:R9(.69)
LUCA01	7	2	8:N(.59);9:I(.58);10:P(.45);11:KM(.33). Also 5:Ia(.42)
MANG01A	1	2	2:FI(.75);3:WS(.43);4:N(.35);5:I0(.28). Also 8:I(.36)
PATE01	1	2	2:AI(.48);3:P6(.42);4:P5(.41);5:P7(.36);6:P(.26);7:P5a(.24); 8:VZ(.21)
ROBE11	1	2	2:R2(.87);3:I0(.53);4:M6(.49);5:R8(.10)
ROSE11	1	2	2:R5(.94);3:R4(.75);4:S0(.34);5:S0a(.30);6:S0b(.04); 7:S0c(−.08);8:S0d(−.36)

Table 15.13 (*cont.*)

Dataset	Factor no.	Order	Loadings for lower-order factors or variables[a]
ROSE12	1	2	2:R7(.79);3:R6(.63);4:R5(.63);5:R4(.61);6:S0(.56);7:S0a(.17); 8:S0b(.14)
SCHA11	8	2	9:P(.69);10:N(.40);11:SR(.34);12:Pa(.21);13:MA(.15). Also 7:R1(.33)
SEGE01	6	2	7:P(.29)
SEGE02	6	2	7:P(.27)
SIMR01	1	2	2:MA(.76);3:P(.71);4:Pa(.51)
SNOW21	5	2	6:R7(.73);7:I0(.71);8:1G(.34)
SU″L01	1	2	2:SS(.64);3:SSa(.56);4:P(.39);5:AC(.09)
SUMI01	1	2	2:P(.74);3:WS(.55);4:MA(.13);5:V(.13);6:LE(−.47)
SUMI02	5	2	6:P(.74);7:I0(.60)
THUR11	1	2	2:FW(.69);3:P(.63). Also 7:MA(.35)
″	4	2	5:P(.57);6:N(.51);7:MA(.40);8:CA(.32)
THUR81	8	2	9:P(.52);10:NA(.46);11:S0(.45). Also 3:V(−.30)
THUR82	8	2	9:P(.46);10:SR(.37)
UNDH21	4	1*	Number Additions(.60);Symbol Identities(.60); Coding(.60);Identical Forms(.35)
VERN11	1	2	2:R1(.95);3:R2(.67);4:GV(.40)
VERS01	1	2	2:R9(.89);3:P(.78). Also 6:R2(.39)
″	4	2	5:P5(.83);6:R2(.73). Also 3:P(.53)
VERS02	1	2	2:VZ(.92);3:R9(.80). Also 6:R2(.56)
″	4	2	5:P5(.85);6:R2(.75)
VERS03	1	2	2:R2(.91);3:VZ(.84);4:P5(.73)
″	5	2	6:R9(.81). Also 3:VZ(.54)
WERD41	1	2	2:N(.54);3:P(.52);4:RG(−.02)
WITT11	1	2	2:N(.77);3:P(.53);4:MA(.37);5:SR(.25);6:AC(.11); 7:ACa(−.16)
YELA21	1	2	2:P(.69);3:VZ(.62);4:AC(.58);5:P5(.47);6:P5a(.40); 7:P8(−.01)

*Study designed for second-stratum analysis at first order.
[a]See Appendix A for factor codes. See text for explanation of entries.

Search, .80), R4 (Speed of Semantic Processing, .74), SS (Spatial Scanning, .69), R6 (RT/Intercept of Visual/Memory Search, .46), and P2 (Finger Dexterity, .46). A large variety of first-order factors occurred once: R1 (Simple Reaction Time, .95), MA (Associative Memory, .76), FI (Ideational Fluency, .75), FW (Word Fluency, .69), I (Induction, .58), V (Verbal Ability, .56), MS (Memory Span, .55), K2 (Cultural Information), RQ (Quantitative Reasoning, .51), RG (Sequential Reasoning, .49), PR (a personality factor, .49), FE (Fluency of Expression, .49), CF (Flexibility of Closure, .49), AI (Aiming, .48), NA (Naming Facility, .46), M0 (an unspecified memory factor, .44), SR (Spatial Relations, .37), and LS (Listening

Ability, .36), probably reflecting the fact that tests of these factors often involve speeding or time constraints.

There are good reasons for making further classifications of the factors listed in the table, even though there are only five instances of datasets yielding more than one factor. In making such classifications, the primary consideration is what kinds of first-order factors are subsumed by a second-stratum factor, and the similarity of these factors. It is reasonably clear that most of the factors in the table can be interpreted as instances of Horn's (1988) Attentive Speediness, that is, factors that tend to dominate such first-order factors as P (Perceptual Speed), N (Numerical Facility), R9 (Speed of Test Taking), or other factors that arise because of the presence of speeded, relatively easy tests among those that have salient loadings on them. Because of their number, they will not be separately listed.

A fairly clear second classification comprises second-order factors that tend to dominate various kinds of reaction time tasks such as the Hick paradigm. For this reason it is henceforth symbolized as Gt or 2T. Its measures are chiefly *decision time* measures. (Factors covering movement time measures are regarded as psychomotor factors and are placed in a third category, below.) Instances (coded by dataset and hierarchical factor number) of factor 2T are as follows:

> CARL41:1 has a loading of .90 on factor 2, measuring S. D. and slope (with respect to bits) of reaction time measurements in the Hick paradigm, but lesser loadings of .30 each on a movement time factor and at least two tests of general cognitive ability (the California Test of Basic Skills and the Raven Progressive Matrices Test). (CARL41:4, orthogonal to CARL41:1, is classified below as a psychomotor factor.)
>
> FAIR01A:1 dominates several factors arising from reaction time tests. (Note that it contrasts with an Attentive Speediness factor in dataset FAIR02.)
>
> JACK12:5 rests on several measures of reaction time in responding to "multiple-letter displays."
>
> ROBE11:1 rests on measures of simple and choice reaction time.
>
> ROSE11:1 and ROSE12:1 dominate factors measuring various reaction time tasks.
>
> SNOW21:5 is difficult to interpret, but seems to depend largely on speed in several reaction time and visual search tasks.
>
> VERN11:1 has loadings chiefly on scores from Hick paradigm tasks.

Factor 2T is very probably the general processing speed factor involved in the studies examined by Kail (1991) as showing that throughout childhood and adolescence, there are consistent age differences in speed of processing as measured by reaction-time tasks. Kail stated that his results were "consistent with the view that age differences in processing speed reflect some general (i.e., nontask specific) component that changes rapidly during childhood and more slowly during adolescence" (p. 490).

A third category of second-order speed factors is what will henceforth be symbolized as Gp or 2P, interpreted as General Psychomotor Speed, in that it is primarily concerned with the speed of finger, hand, and arm movements, relatively independent of cognitive control. Instances are as follows:

> CARL41:4 possibly falls in this category since its largest loadings are for measures of (arm) movement time in the Hick paradigm.
>
> CLAU04:8 has loadings on various psychomotor tasks and performances.
>
> HARR01:2 has loadings chiefly on measures of hand speed in manipulating or assembling small objects.
>
> KRAN01A:7 is chiefly dependent on measures of (arm) movement time in the Hick paradigm.
>
> PATE01:1 has its higher loadings on a variety of psychomotor tasks, such as "aiming," packing blocks, tapping, and card sorting. Lower loadings occur for what appear to be Perceptual Speed and Spatial Relations factors.
>
> VERS01:4, VERS02:4, and VERS03:1 are factors found in three datasets using the same variables on different samples (in South Africa, adult white males and females, and black males); in these samples, they contrast with factors classified as 2S and not separately listed here. They have loadings chiefly for measures of sensory discrimination and of psychomotor speed in simple tasks such as tapping.

This leaves the second order factors in several datasets unclassified. HUGH01:1 embraces several kinds of measures: speed of mental comparison in the Posner task, and memory span. At the first order of analysis, it also has loadings on an intelligence test and the Raven Progressive Matrices task. It is a speed factor only by virtue of its loadings on variables from the Posner task. Possibly it should be classified as a general intelligence factor, but it contrasts with factors 4 and 6, classified as 2F and already listed in Table 15.6. MANG01A:1 has its chief loadings on FI (Ideational Fluency) and WS (Writing Speed), but also smaller loadings on a factor combining numerical facility and perceptual speed, and an uninterpretable factor probably measuring further aspects of cognitive speed. Factor THUR11:1 contrasts with factor THUR11:4 (already classified in the first large group of factors); its loadings are for FW (Word Fluency) and P (Perceptual Speed). It is not clear how it should be classified.

MISCELLANEOUS HIGHER-ORDER FACTORS

Table 15.14 lists a number of other higher-order factors that do not appear to be readily classifiable in any of the categories previously presented. For the most part, however, they represent special broad abilities in certain domains. In each case, the table gives the complete list of lower-order factors, and their loadings on the factor (in order of size). From this information, as well as information about the lower-order factors (to be found elsewhere in this volume), the reader should be able to derive some impression of the nature of the factor. Brief interpretations are given in the table, and the factors are listed by the broad domain into which they appear to fall. It is not believed necessary to enter into any extended discussion of these factors, even though many of them

Table 15.14. *44 special higher-order factors, by domain*

Dataset	Factor no.	Order	Loadings for lower-order factors or variables; possible interpretation[a]
Domain: Language:			
CARR21	1	2	2:MY(.58);3:PC(.54);4:VL(.49);5:FW(.45);6:L0(.35); 7:NA(.19).
			Linguistic Element Sensitivity?
CARR43	10	2	11:PC(.65);12:RG(.61);13:I0(.53);14:M0(.51);15:MY(.45).
			Linguistic Element Sensitivity?
FRED11	1	2	2:RD(.98);3:RDa(.59);4:RDb(.52);5:RDc(.41);6:RS(.32).
			Reading Ability
FRED12	6	2	7:R&(.64);8:RD(.50);9:RDa(.43);10:RDb(.37)
			Word Recognition Ability
JAY01	7	2	8:RD(.46). Also 2:V(.53);3:SG(.54);4:RS(.55).
			Reading Decoding – Accuracy & Speed
MARG01	1	2	2:OP(.65);3:OPa(.64);4:OPb(.60);5:OPc(.55);6:PT(.32); 7:OPd(.16);8:OPe(.01).
			General Oral Communication Skill
ROND01	1	2	2:O&(.84);3:O&a(.56);4:O&b(.27)
			Mother's Speech Complexity
"	5	2	6:O&c(.64);7:O&d(.36)
			Mother's Preference for Declarative Sentences
SPEA34	5	2	6:R&(.67);7:CZ(.57);8:RG(−.17)
			Special Reading Skills
Domain: Memory and learning:			
ALLE11	1	2	2:N(.80);3:MS(.49);4:I0(.14);5:R∗(.06);6:R5(.04);7:R4(−.20)
			Numerical/Memory Span?
ALLE12	1	2	2:MS(.71);3:N(.68);4:I0(.52);5:R4(−.01);6:R5(−.18); 7:R∗(−.19)
			Numerical/Memory Span?
ALLI01	4	2	5:L0(.55);6:L0a(.42);7:L0b(−.18);8:P8(−.29). Also 2:I(.41).
			Rote Learning?
DETT00	6	2	7:L0(.65);8:L0a(.54);9:R∗(.23);10:R∗a(−.21). Also 2:I0(.39).
			Learning Rate?
Domain: Visual perception:			
ANGL11	1	2	2:CF(.88);3:CS(.74);4:AC(.32);5:I0(.13);6:I0(−.04).
			General Closure?
OHNM11	1	2	2:CZ or VU(.76);3:CS(.76).
			General Closure?
SMIT52	1	2	2:LE(.64);3:LEa(.55);4:LEb(.51);5:LEc(.44);6:LEd(.36); 7:LEe(.35);8:LEf(.08);9:LEg(.02);10:VC(.02);LEh(−.05).
			General Spatial Judgment Ability?
TAYL51	1	2	2:IL(.73);3:ILa(.59);4:ILb(.55);5:P(.27);6:ILc(.14); 7:CS(.13);8:I0(.09).
			General Resistance to Illusions

Table 15.14 (*cont.*)

Dataset	Factor no.	Order	Loadings for lower-order factors or variables; possible interpretation[a]
Domain: Speed; information processing:			
DETT00	1	2	2:I0(.77);3:R2(.56);4:R*(.40);5:R3(−.18) Information Processing Accuracy
FOGA00	7	2	8:AC(.86);9:SG(.49). Also 2:GC(.37). Timesharing.
MANG01A	6	2	7:MO(.68);8:I(.38);9:P5(−.39). Rate of Work: Difficult Tasks
Domain: Knowledge:			
FAVE01	1	2	2:BC(.52);3:BD(.52). Knowledge of "Behavioral Content"
HAKS01	24	2	25:MK(.84). Also 16:V(.49);23:FO(.39). General Information
PEDU01	2	2	3:A2(.51);4:A1(.38). School Ability
SATT11	1	2	2:A3(.92);3:A5(.79);4:A6(.65);5:CY(.34) General School Achievement
SHAY02	9	2	10:K1(.67);11:A3(.45). Also 7:K2(.34). General Information (Math. & Science)
SISK01	1	2	2:A7(.56);3:RG(.55);4:A8(.41);5:A9(.10). General School Achievement
WRIG21	5	2	6:N(.74). Also 2:KM(.53) Mathematical Ability
Domain: Psychomotor			
SUNG01	8	2	9:P3(.65);10:I(−.43). Also 2:U3(.35). Psychomotor (Strength)
SUNG02	6	2	7:P2(.50);8:P3(.46);9:U3(−.50). Also 3:I(−.55). Psychomotor
SUNG05	9	2	10:P2(.42);11:P3(.34). Also 8:S0(.36). Psychomotor
Domain: Miscellaneous			
FEDE02	8	2	9:CY(.65);10:CF(.58). Also 2:FI(.39). Cognitive Style
GRIM01	1	2	2:I1(.65);3:I2(.63);4:I3(.27);5:I4(.10) Interests
HEMP21	1	2	2:AM(.82);3:AMa(.72);4:AMb(.65);5:AMc(.60); 6:AMd(.29);7:AMe(.27);8:AMf(.13);9:AMg(−.35). School Administration Ability
JONE21	1	2	2:V1(.84);3:V2(.80);4:V3(.33) Sensitivity to Chromatic Flicker
JONE22	1	3	2:2O(.84);5:2Oa(.84) General Olfactory Sensitivity
"	2	2	3:O1(.49);4:O2(.30) Group Factor for O1 and O2

Table 15.14 (*cont.*)

Dataset	Factor no.	Order	Loadings for lower-order factors or variables; possible interpretation[a]
JONES	5	2	6:O3(.27);7:O4(.19)
			Group Factor for O3 and O4
PEDU01	5	2	6:DT(.51);7:MO(.42)
			School Deportment and Motivation
THOR51	1	2	2:MO(.73);3:PR(.55);4:P3(.49);5:V(.23);6:MOa(.04).
			General Persistence/Motivation
VALT01	1	2	2:AC(.72);3:RD(.66).
			Carefulness?
WIDI01	1	2	3:CY(.73);4:CYa(−.72).
			Cognitive Style
WOLF11	1	3	2:Parental Backgrnd(.72);5:Student Achvt.(.72)
			General Level of Background & Achievement.
"	2	2	3:AA(.63);4:AB(.43).
			Parental Background
"	5	2	6:AS(.51);7:AO(.50).
			Student Achievement

[a]See Appendix A for factor codes. See text for explanation of entries.

are or should be of considerable interest. For example, the Timesharing factor identified in dataset FOGA00 possibly serves to answer a long-standing question in the individual-differences literature as to whether such a factor exists.

THE MEANING OF HIGHER-ORDER FACTORS

When a higher-order factor is found, dominating (usually) *several* lower factors which have salient loadings on it, it can be taken to represent a dimension of individual differences that is more general – covering a broader range of tasks and performances – than the lower-order factors. It is defined not only by the lower-order factors that have salient loadings on it but also by the range of still lower-order factors (if any) and test variables that have substantial loadings on it. The interpretation of a higher-order factor must take into account whatever aspects of ability and performance seem to function in common over all these lower-order factors and variables. Such an interpretation, in effect, provides a "theory" of the factor, with potential to be tested in further research by examining whether this interpretive theory predicts the loadings of new variables or factors on it.

The lower-order factors, in turn, represent specializations of abilities in certain directions, possibly in different content or process areas, or in terms of different strategies of performance that apply to them.

The fundamental ideas about the nature of an ability that have been introduced in Chapter 1 can be applied to abilities at all levels of analysis. That is, an ability can be thought of as specifying a series of tasks or performances that differ in their difficulty or complexity level, and that are differentially responded to by individuals at different levels of ability in accordance with the model of task performance specified in the person characteristic function. However, insofar as a given series of tasks may be loaded on, or influenced by, factors at different levels of analysis, analysis of task performance must take into account these different levels. In effect, performance on a series of tasks that are loaded on abilities at three levels of analysis must be explained, first, in terms of individual differences on the factor at the highest level of analyis. These differences must be controlled for or partialled out in studying variation at the second level of analysis – variation that will depend upon the particular aspects of ability represented in tasks at the second level of analysis. A similar process of control or partialling occurs in the transition to the explanation of differences at the first level of analysis. To my knowledge these ideas have never been formally developed in the theory of test analysis. Conventional item response theory usually assumes unidimensionality or homogeneity of items or tasks, and thus implies that only one level of analysis applies (in the terms considered here).

To make these ideas a little more concrete, suppose that we are considering a task, such as an ideational fluency task like Thing Categories: "In 3 minutes, list all the things you can think of that are red or are red more often than any other color." Suppose further that this task has, in an orthogonalized hierarchical factor matrix, a loading of .5 on a third-order general factor, a loading of .5 on the second-order factor 2R (General Retrieval Ability), and a loading of .5 on factor FI (Ideational Fluency), and that its loadings on all other factors in a large matrix are zero. This means that the variation in scores on the Thing Categories task is controlled or predicted partly by the individual's score or status on a general factor, partly by status on the second-order factor, and partly by status on factor FI. In applying the person characteristic function to the second-order ability 2R, we would have to make analyses for different levels of status on the third-order factor, e.g., for individuals grouped by quintiles on this factor. For each such group, individuals would be further subdivided by status on factor 2R, and the relative levels of difficulties of all tasks subsumed under this factor noted (including all tasks subsumed under factor FI and a series of other factors dominated by factor 2R). Person characteristic functions would be drawn as a function of these difficulties, and the nature of factor 2R would presumably become clear as related to how the attributes of these tasks change as their difficulties increase.

Presumably, the same process could be carried out to investigate the nature of the first-order factor FI; it might be done by studying person characteristic functions for individuals selected in each cell of a 5×5 matrix representing levels of status on the general factor crossed with levels of status on the second-order factor 2R, or as many cells of that matrix as might be adequately filled.

Whether these kinds of analysis would actually be practical, I do not know, for they have never been tried. They would obviously require large samples of individuals and tasks. The purpose of this thought-experiment, however, is to establish that (1) there is a conceptual basis for the existence of factors at different levels of analysis, and that (2) in principle it is possible to establish the nature of ability factors at different levels of analysis by use of the person characteristic function.

For example, it would in principle be possible to establish the nature of the general factor of intelligence, G, by analyzing the attributes of all tasks (however diverse their nature otherwise) that yield probabilities of successful performance that are systematically related to status on such a factor. Similarly, it would be possible in principle to establish the nature of a second-order or second-stratum factor, such as 2R, by studying variation in task performance as a function of type of task and status on this factor when status on the third-order factor is controlled for.

SUMMARY AND COMMENT

From the database studied in this survey, it has been possible to confirm and amplify the hierarchical theory of higher-order abilities put forth by such writers as Cattell (1971) and Horn (1988). Specifically:

(1) There is abundant evidence for a factor of general intelligence, G (or 3G), found at the highest order (usually 2 or 3) of analysis for a given dataset and thus at stratum III, that dominates factors or variables that emphasize the level of difficulty that can be mastered in performing induction, reasoning, visualization, and language comprehension tasks. There is also some evidence that the G factor is likely to be correlated (though at a low level) with measures of speed of information processing and capacity of working memory.

(2) At a lower order of analysis, or at stratum II, a number of broad ability factors can be distinguished. These are:

> 2F: Fluid Intelligence, concerned with basic processes of reasoning and other mental activities that depend only minimally on learning and acculturation.
>
> 2C: Crystallized Intelligence, concerned with mental processes that reflect not only the operation of fluid intelligence but also the effects of experience, learning, and acculturation.
>
> 2H: A factor that apparently combines the roles of fluid and crystallized intelligence, but that can be analytically distinct from the factor of general intelligence, G.
>
> 2Y: General Memory Ability, probably involved in any task that calls for learning and memory of new content or responses. However, there may be several varieties of this factor; one subvariety is a higher-order memory span

factor 2X. Present evidence is not sufficient to permit a clear specification of the structure of learning and memory abilities.

2V: Broad Visual Perception, involved in any task that requires the perception of visual forms *as such*. (That is, it is involved only minimally, if at all, in the perception of printed language forms.)

2U: Broad Auditory Perception, involved in any task or performance that requires the perception or discrimination of auditory patterns of sound or speech, particularly when such patterns present difficulties because of fine discriminations, auditory distortion, or complex musical structure.

2R: Broad Retrieval Ability, involved in any task or performance that requires the ready retrieval of concepts or items from long-term memory. It is possible that there are several varieties of this factor, depending on the degree of "originality" required in the responses.

2S: Broad Cognitive Speediness, involved in any task or performance that requires rapid cognitive processing of information. There appear to be several subvarieties of this ability, including factor 2T, governing speed of decision in various types of reaction-time tasks, and factor 2P, speed of psychomotor response performance in reaction-time tasks. Factor 2P, however, has minimal cognitive content and should not taken to be strictly a cognitive ability.

(3) In addition, various other second-order factors can be identified in language, memory and learning, visual perception, information-processing, knowledge, and other domains, indicating certain generalizations of abilities in these domains.

(4) The analysis of abilities at several orders and strata offers insight into the structure of abilities and can be the basis for a theory of cognitive abilities.

Figure 15.1 is a diagram showing the general outline of the three-stratum structure of the major cognitive abilities that have been identified in this survey. At stratum III, factor G (3G) dominates a series of broad abilities at stratum II. Because of inadequacies of available data, it is deemed not advisable to attempt to assign numbers or coefficients that would indicate how strong this domination is in the case of each second-stratum factor. Roughly, however, the strength of domination is indicated in the figure by the closeness of each box representing a second-stratum factor to the box representing G. The stratum I factors listed under each second-stratum factor are those regarded as being most likely to be dominated by the respective factor. In actuality, as suggested in the text of the present chapter, it is frequently the case that first-stratum factors have loadings on more than one second-order factor, indicating that first-stratum factors and the variables measuring them are frequently factorially complex.

Some readers may ask why our analysis has not disclosed higher-order factors corresponding to everyday concepts of ability like "mathematical ability," "musical ability," and "problem-solving ability." Several reasons for this can be offered. Consider, as an example, "mathematical ability."

Already in Chapter 1 it was pointed out that any ability refers to variations in performance on some defined class of tasks. If there is such a thing as

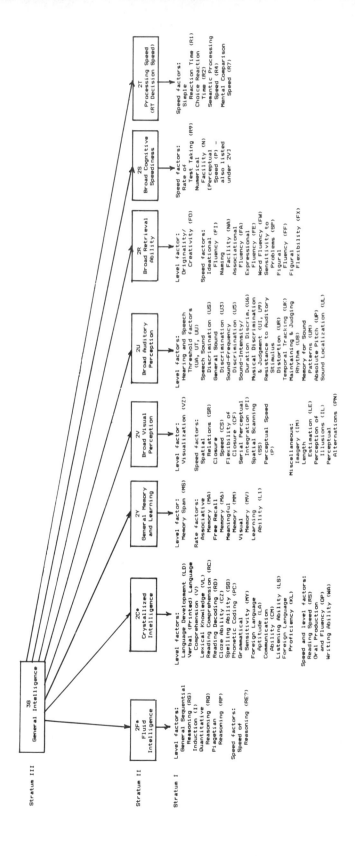

Figure 15.1. The structure of cognitive abilities.

Stratum III

3G
General Intelligence

Stratum II

2F*
Fluid Intelligence

2C*
Crystallized Intelligence

2Y
General Memory and Learning

2V
Broad Visual Perception

2U
Broad Auditory Perception

2R
Broad Retrieval Ability

2S
Broad Cognitive Speediness

2T
Processing Speed (RT Decision Speed)

Stratum I

2F* Fluid Intelligence

Level factors:
General Sequential
Reasoning (RG)
Induction (I)
Quantitative
Reasoning (RQ)
Piagetian
Reasoning (RP)

Speed factors:
Speed of
Reasoning (RE?)

2C* Crystallized Intelligence

Level factors:
Language Development (LD)
Verbal (Printed) Language
Comprehension (V)
Lexical Knowledge (VL)
Reading Comprehension (RC)
Reading Decoding (RD)
Cloze Ability (CZ)
Spelling Ability (SG)
Phonetic Coding (PC)
Grammatical
Sensitivity (MY)
Foreign Language
Aptitude (LA)
Communication
Ability (CM)
Listening Ability (LS)
Foreign Language
Proficiency (KL)

Speed and level factors:
Reading Speed (RS)
Oral Production
and Fluency (OP)
Writing Ability (WA)

2Y General Memory and Learning

Level factor:
Memory Span (MS)

Rate factors:
Associative
Memory (MA)
Free Recall
Memory (M6)
Meaningful
Memory (MM)
Visual
Memory (MV)
Learning
Ability (L1)

2V Broad Visual Perception

Level factor:
Visualization (VZ)

Speed factors:
Spatial
Relations (SR)
Closure
Speed (CS)
Flexibility of
Closure (CF)
Serial Perceptual
Integration (PI)
Spatial Scanning
(SS)
Perceptual Speed
(P)

Miscellaneous:
Imagery (IM)
Length
Estimation (LE)
Perception of
Illusions (IL)
Perceptual
Alternations (PN)

2U Broad Auditory Perception

Level factors:
Hearing and Speech
Threshold factors
(UA, UT, UU)
Speech Sound
Discrimination (US)
General Sound
Discrimination (U3)
Sound-Frequency
Discrimination (U5)
Sound-Intensity/
Duration Discrim. (U6)
Musical Discrimination
& Judgment (U1, U9)
Resistance to Auditory
Stimulus
Distortion (UR)
Temporal Tracking (UK)
Maintaining & Judging
Rhythm (UB)
Memory for Sound
Patterns (UM)
Absolute Pitch (UP)
Sound Localization (UL)

2R Broad Retrieval Ability

Level factor:
Originality/
Creativity (FO)

Speed factors:
Ideational
Fluency (FI)
Naming
Facility (NA)
Associational
Fluency (FA)
Expressional
Fluency (FE)
Word Fluency (FW)
Sensitivity to
Problems (SP)
Figural
Fluency (FF)
Figural
Flexibility (FX)

2S Broad Cognitive Speediness

Speed factors:
Rate of
Test Taking (R9)
Numerical
Facility (N)
(Perceptual
Speed (P) -
also listed
under 2V]

2T Processing Speed (RT Decision Speed)

Speed factors:
Simple
Reaction Time (R1)
Choice Reaction
Time (R2)
Semantic Processing
Speed (R4)
Mental Comparison
Speed (R7)

* In many analyses, factors 2F and 2C cannot be distinguished;
they are represented, however, by a factor designated 2H,
a combination of 2F and 2C.

mathematical ability, it would refer to individual differences in performing a large class of mathematical tasks – e.g., those tasks normally taught and assigned in mathematics courses in school, at different grade levels from elementary to graduate school. One would have to specify the grade level that is of interest in speaking of mathematical ability, but whatever the answer it is evident that the mathematical tasks taught or assigned at any particular grade level exhibit much diversity, especially at the more advanced levels. Such tasks might differ markedly in their characteristics and requirements; it is not a foregone conclusion that there is only *one* mathematical ability.

Secondly, recall the statement, also in Chapter 1, that "the investigations dealt with in this book can be regarded as attempts to identify abilities by systematically classifying different tasks with respect to the abilities they require." The results that have been reviewed and discussed in Chapters 5 through the present Chapter 15 indicate that mathematical tasks involve a variety of abilities, not only higher-order abilities such as G, Gf, and Gc, but also lower-order abilities such as I (Induction), RG (Sequential Reasoning), RQ (Quantitative Reasoning), and sometimes VZ (Visualization). In addition they have loadings on a number of specialized mathematical knowledge and achievement factors coded KM (Knowledge of Mathematics). These are the findings, for example, in datasets that were designed specifically to study mathematical abilities at the secondary school level, datasets CANI01, WEIS01, WERD01, and WERD02. (See the hierarchical factor matrices for these datasets in Appendix B.)

"Mathematical ability," therefore, must be regarded as an inexact, unanalyzed popular concept that has no scientific meaning unless it is referred to the structure of abilities that compose it. It cannot be expected to constitute a higher-level ability.

Similar statements could be made about other everyday concepts like "musical ability," "artistic ability," "creative ability," "problem-solving ability," and the like.

For that matter, a similar conclusion can be reached regarding the concept of "intelligence," which is also an inexact, unanalyzed popular concept that has no scientific status unless it is restated to refer to the abilities that compose it, as described in the present volume. Early in this century, Spearman (1923) recognized this in placing the term *intelligence* in quotation marks in the title of his work *The Nature of 'Intelligence' and the Principles of Cognition*, for in this way he hoped to distinguish *g* from intelligence as ordinarily conceived. In our present state of knowledge, "intelligence" can be referred not only to *g* but also to a great variety of other constructs, approximately as suggested in Figure 15.1. The long-discussed problem of defining intelligence is transformed into one of defining the various factorial constructs that underlie it and specifying their structure.

NOTES

1. The problem of levels of analysis has been discussed by Humphreys (1962) and Coan (1964), among others. What I refer to as *stratum* is treated by Coan as a matter of *referent generality*.

2. It was necessary to assign a special symbol or code "2H" for this category in order to distinguish it from factor G in cases where it was one of the second-order factors that was dominated by G. In many of these cases, a 2H factor was accompanied by other second-order factors such as 2V and 2R, all dominated by a third-order factor 3G. The impossibility of recognizing or distinguishing factors 2F and 2C in such a dataset may be attributed to weakness in battery design such that there were not enough first-order factors to produce this distinction. The category 2H is not to be taken to represent a factor that is actually distinct from 2F or 2C.

3. R in the code "2R" may be taken to be a merely arbitrary symbol, although it is mnemonically related to *retrieval*, a term used by several previous writers (Cattell, Horn, Hakstian). It should not be taken seriously as an indicant of a psychological process. Although all the first-order factors normally dominated by factor 2R appear to reflect a process of retrieval from long-term memory, some of them, e.g., factor FO (Originality/Creativity) may involve other, more constructive processes. In assigning symbols to factors, I have been captive to my decision to limit factor codes to two characters. In the case of higher-order factors, the first character is an indication of the order or stratum, so that only one character is left to specify the nature of the factor.

4. In the present context, "learning ability factor" is to be taken to refer only to a certain class of factors, discussed in Chapter 7, that were identified in factor studies of variables derived from learning tasks. The term may be misleading in that it does not embrace a number of other factors that can be taken to measure learning ability in the sense of controlling or predicting learning rates. Elsewhere in this volume, in discussing the distinction between *aptitude* and *achievement*, I have claimed that many cognitive abilities are aptitudes in the sense that they control or predict rates of learning. The third-stratum factor G and 3G can be thought of as a learning ability factor, like several other higher-order factors such as Gf and Gc.

PART III

Issues

The presentation of the voluminous results in Chapters 5–15 calls for discussion of their meaning and implications. Above all, there is need for the formulation of a theory to account for and explain them. In Chapter 16, a three-stratum theory of cognitive abilities is offered, with discussion of how the theory relates to current views of the nature of cognitive processes and performances. Moreover, the results themselves have implications for further research and for the resolution of many problems concerning cognitive abilities – their measurement and their applications in various domains of practical life. Chapter 17 touches on some of these issues. Chapter 18 is directed toward implications for further research on cognitive abilities, test construction, test use, and public policy on testing.

One could address a very long list of issues that pertain to cognitive abilities, their measurement, and their implications. Many of these issues are related, in a general way, to what is often called the "nature–nurture problem," that is, the problem of whether there are genetic determinants of abilities, and of whether the environment, experience, learning, education, and training can contribute to the development and enhancement of abilities. There has been interest in how abilities mature or otherwise change with age – through childhood and adolescence to adulthood, and in the later stages of life. There is also the issue of whether abilities are malleable through specific interventions designed to improve them or alter their operation. There has also been interest in the so-called differentiation hypothesis whereby it is maintained that the number of differentiable abilities increases with age, at least through pre-adult life.

It is not my intention to give anything like a full treatment of these issues, because in view of the enormous literature that has accumulated about them it would be practically impossible to do so, short of devoting a further volume to such a treatment. Most of these issues are discussed extensively in the respective chapters of handbooks such as those of Sternberg (1982) and Wolman (1985). What I hope to do, however, is to comment on how the results of this survey of differentiable abilities might be taken account of in future thinking and research about these issues.

629

16 *A Theory of Cognitive Abilities: The Three-Stratum Theory*

A theory, according to most accounts, is a set of hypotheses or verifiable statements that seek to explain a set of observed data. In the present case, the data for which a theory is to be constructed are voluminous, albeit not as complete or satisfactory as one might like. The data consist, essentially, of information on the correlations of variables that come primarily from psychological tests, but occasionally also from observations of behavior from sources other than tests, such as school marks, ratings of competence and various personal attributes, and the like. They consist also of the results of factor analyses of such data according to a scheme that displays the loadings of variables or factors on latent traits at several levels of a hierarchy of abilities from fairly specific (at the first stratum) to highly general (at a third stratum). An adequate theory of cognitive abilities should provide statements concerning the nature and placement of abilities at each level of this hierarchy. Desirably, it should also provide statements or hypotheses about the sources of individual differences in these abilities, at whatever level in the hierarchy.

Certain methodological assumptions must underlie any theory developed to account for factor-analytic results:

1. A properly designed psychological test (or any type of observation that is the basis for a variable used in a factor analysis) provides an indication of the degree of ability that the individual can demonstrate in performing some class of tasks. In any representative sample of individuals, persons differ in their degrees of ability, and this assumption is confirmed when tests show high reliability and test score distributions show wide variance. For many types of tests, when the items (or tasks) of a test are arranged in order of difficulty, an individual's probability of success decreases as difficulty increases. The test score is an indicator of the level of difficulty that an individual can attain. Other types of tests are designed to indicate the speed with which the individual can perform certain types of tasks or test items.
2. The individual differences represented by a variable in a factor analysis are relatively stable over time, even though they are measured at a particular point of time.

631

3.   These individual differences are accounted for, at least on a statistical basis, by a linear model in which performance on a test is assumed to be a function of the individual's standing on one or more factors or latent traits. The degree to which each factor is associated with performance on a given test is indicated by the weight of that factor in the factorial equation for the test; these weights can range from -1 to $+1$, but in practice the weights are generally either near zero or strikingly positive. The factorial equation for the test is initially assumed to be the same for all individuals in a sample, and in principle generalizable over different samples.

These assumptions are made in the common factor model that underlies most factor-analytic work. The model is regarded as a close approximation to the way in which abilities actually operate in the "real world"; in some cases, it is possible to modify the model in order to account for discrepancies with data. If data could be better fit by assuming that factorial equations actually should differ over individuals (or even over occasions for the same individual) this would have to be taken care of by refinements made in special studies that depart from the usual factor-analytic methodology.

Note that the use of linear equations implies an assumption about the way in which abilities act in combination to determine test performance. Specifically, it implies that abilities can compensate for each other. That is, for example, if an individual is low on one ability that is important in determining performance on a test, it would be assumed that high ability on another ability that is involved in the test can compensate for this, producing an average score on the test for the individual. In reality, abilities may not act in combination in this way. For example, successful performance on a task may require at least a certain minimum level on each of two abilities. The possibility of discovering such a way in which abilities combine is normally excluded by the linear methodology of factor analysis. This methodology can be modified in special studies, however, or replaced by an entirely different methodology. These special studies and methodologies would in no way conflict with the basic three-stratum theory of abilities; they would only address different ways in which the abilities defined in this theory operate or show their effects.

The interpretation of a factor can be thought of as a kind of theory construction. As applied to a factor identified in a particular study, it is an effort to develop a statement or a series of statements to explain why variables have high salient loadings on the factor, in contrast to variables that have low or vanishing loadings. If factors found in different studies are considered to be identical, the statements developed to interpret them must be shown to be properly descriptive of all such factors and applicable to explaining the high and low loadings of variables on them. The interpretive statements must also serve to explain why factors that are shown to be distinct from a given factor are theoretically expected to be distinct. It is also desirable that interpretive statements about factors be productive of hypotheses to be tested in further factor-analytic studies. In this way factor-analytic research can be a cumulative enterprise leading to more exact and more comprehensive theories of data.

These comments about factor interpretation apply equally to factors at each of the different orders or strata of ability. At the second order, for example, the goal in interpreting a factor is to develop a statement that explains the variation in factor loadings of first-order factors on that factor. Similarly, a third-order factor is to be interpreted by a theoretical statement explaining variation in factor loadings of second-order factors on that factor. Such statements are intended to be applicable to the interpretation of similar factors found in different studies; in this way, a generalization of theory is to be achieved. Unfortunately, at the higher orders of analysis, it is common to find that the number of factors at a lower order is small, thus limiting the information available for factor interpretation. However, in this case it is often helpful to refer to the loadings of individual variables on a higher-order factor, noting variation in these loadings in terms of the interpretation proposed for the higher-order factor.

Interpretation of a factor is often enhanced by considering information about what characteristics of items or tasks that are loaded on the factor make them differentially difficult. A description of these characteristics often can be directly incorporated in the description of the factor. See, for example, Carroll, Meade, and Johnson's (1991) analyses of characteristics of spatial ability tasks that make for variation in difficulty. One such characteristic, seen in a range of items in a Block Counting test, is the degree to which the individual has to visualize the presence of blocks that are not directly visible in a pictured pile of blocks. The most difficult items in the test are, generally, those in which there is the greatest problem of inferring the presence of blocks that are not directly visible. This leads to the interpretation of the factor on which this test loads as one requiring imaginal visualization, taking into account the structure of a pile of blocks (or similar materials) in terms of which blocks must support others.

Chapters 5 through 15 have presented interpretations of numerous first-stratum and second-stratum factors, as well as of a single third-stratum factor, that were developed according to the above principles. In many cases the interpretations were qualified as speculations that would need to be tested and confirmed in further studies. Taken together, however, the interpretations offered in the previous chapters can be regarded as constituting a *three-stratum theory of cognitive abilities*. The abilities found at each of the strata may be called *narrow* (stratum I), *broad* (stratum II), and *general* (stratum III).

At this point it is useful to examine these interpretations from a somewhat wider perspective. We ask whether there is anything that seems to be characteristic of narrow, first-stratum factors as contrasted with what characterizes broad, second-stratum factors, or with what characterizes the single general, third-stratum factor. First consider the second-stratum factors. It appears that they are very general abilities that lie in broad domains of behavior. Insofar as they are distinct from the general ability represented by the third-stratum factor, they represent moderate specializations of ability into such spheres as ratiocinative processes (fluid intelligence); prior acquisition of knowledge, particularly in language (crystallized intelligence); learning and memorial processes; visual perception; auditory perception; facile production of ideas; and speed. There appear to be at least two second-stratum abilities in the domain of cognitive speed, one concerned with the speed of response and one concerned with speed in processing information accurately. A third second-stratum speed factor concerns psychomotor movements, and probably contains very little in the way of a cognitive component. All these second-stratum abilities, including some additional ones that research has not yet clearly defined, appear to represent basic constitutional and long-lasting characteristics of individuals that can govern or influence a great variety of behaviors in a given domain. The domains appear to differ in the relative emphases they give to process, content, and manner of response. Thus, *process* is emphasized in factors 2F (fluid intelligence), 2Y (memory and learning), and 2R (general retrieval); *content* is emphasized in factors 2C (crystallized intelligence), 2V (general visual perception), and 2U (general auditory perception); *response* is emphasized in factor 2S (broad speediness).

In contrast, narrow, first-stratum abilities represent greater specializations of abilities, often in quite specific ways that reflect the effects of experience and learning, or the adoption of particular strategies of performance. For example, in the domain covered by factor 2F (fluid intelligence), factor I (Induction) possibly represents the prior acquisition of specialized strategies for examining situations in order to induce rules and generalizations, factor VZ (Visualization) represents the prior acquisition of perceptual processes and strategies for dealing with visual shapes and forms, and factor RG (Sequential Reasoning) represents the prior acquisition of strategies for attending to and dealing with sequential reasoning problems. Similarly, in the domain covered by factor 2C, factor LD (Language Development) represents differential amounts of opportunity to be exposed to the learning of the native language in its oral form, factors V (Verbal Ability) and RC (Reading Comprehension) represent degrees of experience and learning of the native language in its printed form, and factor K0 reflects variations in ability and opportunity to acquire general information beyond language.

Roughly, the above characterizations of factors at different strata correspond to those made by Cattell (1971, Chapter 11) in what he calls a *triadic* theory of abilities that deals with (1) *capacities*, (2) *provincial powers*, and (3) *agencies*. I cannot attempt to rehearse the details of Cattell's quite elaborate theory, except to point out, first, that Cattell tends to discount the existence of a third-stratum general factor. He believes that most second-stratum abilities are *powers* that express "limiting properties of the brain"; of these, some are *capacities* (such as what I designate as 2F, 2Y, and 2R) that permit or limit action over the whole cognitive field, and others (such as 2V and 2U) are *provincial powers* that represent neural organizations in the brain for visual or auditory perception. He regards most first-order or first-stratum abilities as *agencies*: "They take their shape largely from cultural and general learning, and are the agencies through which fluid intelligence and the powers express themselves" (p. 297). Cattell might well have reservations about my attempt to characterize factors strictly in terms of the strata at which they are found; he cautions that "because a set of patterns crop up as factors at the same order (stratum) it does not follow that they are the same kind of *psychological entity*" (p. 296).

In a more recent exposition of his triadic theory, Cattell (1982, Chapter 8) has addressed its possible implications for studying the inheritance of abilities. I find myself in general agreement with him in emphasizing that behavioral genetic research must be based on appropriate definition and measurement of the traits studied; specifically, research must take care to differentiate between strata of ability. The various factors of ability at the second and third strata may differ in their heritabilities; Cattell believes that data already available show, for example, that Gf (2F) is more highly heritable than Gc (2C) – which may indeed not be heritable at all if properly measured independently of Gf (2F). Primary factors – which Cattell regards as usually being "agencies," would generally have low or vanishing heritabilities, except possibly for certain special traits like spelling ability or sense of absolute pitch. Cattell recommends that genetic research should use as its variables the scores obtained in his SUD (stratified unrelated determiners) model – essentially the same model that we determine by the Schmid and Leiman (1957) orthogonalized hierarchical procedure. Thus, in studying the inheritance of a primary factor, one would use what Cattell calls a "stub factor" – the specific part left in a primary factor when the variance due to a second or higher order factor is removed. Both Cattell and I would emphasize that much behavior-genetic research can be faulted for not having properly assessed factorially independent sources of variance.

Some Further Details of the Three-Stratum Theory

Before comparing the three-stratum theory with other theories of cognitive abilities, it is necessary to specify certain qualifications on the theory.

First, it is not intended that the three strata be rigidly defined. The stratum to which an ability belongs is conceived to be an indication of its degree of generality in covering the possible domain of cognitive abilities and performances. Generality is a matter of degree rather than of strict categories. It is therefore only a matter of convenience – to some extent borrowed from the notion of *order of analysis* in factor analysis, that we tend to think of three distinct strata. Actually, there may be intermediate strata between these three distinct levels. We have seen, in studying the higher-order structure of abilities in Chapter 15, that it is sometimes difficult to assign factors to strata, particularly when a factor appearing, say, at the third order of analysis is clearly not identifiable with a perfectly general factor of ability, or when a factor appearing at the second order is better regarded as a first-stratum ability. This can be simply a result of the way in which variables in a factor analysis are defined – variables, for example, that differ in incidental matters of format or administration such that they define first-order factors that are in reality lower than what would be usually first-stratum factors. (For example, in dataset LANS31 factor 2 was a Perceptual Speed factor defined by paper-and-pencil tests, while factor 3 was a Perceptual Speed factor defined by responses in a laboratory setting; at the second order, it was dominated by a broad speediness factor (factor 1) that could be regarded as a mixture of first-stratum and second-stratum abilities.) Presumably, these problems could be resolved by appropriate design of factor-analytic batteries, or possibly by special techniques of analysis that could be devised.

Second, the three-stratum theory of cognitive abilities is not intended to imply a strict tree-structure whereby higher-stratum abilities dominate only certain lower-stratum abilities. That is, the structure of abilities is not to be thought of as represented by a tree structure in which factors branch only from single higher-stratum nodes into distinct groups of lower-stratum abilities. In actuality, the dependence of lower-stratum abilities on higher-stratum abilities is indicated by their loadings on them, or perhaps even better by the loadings of the original variables on them. Certainly at the first-stratum level, a test can have substantial loadings on more than one first-stratum factor, and/or more than one second-stratum factor. A first-stratum *factor* can have loadings on more than one second-order factor, depending on the variables of which it is composed. For example, a test of some kind of spatial ability could have a loading on factor 2F because of the way in which the test demands cognitive information processing, but also a loading on 2V because of the complexity of spatial representation that is presented by the test stimuli.

COMPARISON WITH OTHER THEORIES OF COGNITIVE ABILITIES

The full import of the three-stratum theory can be explicated by comparing it with certain other theories of cognitive abilities, most of them having been mentioned in Chapter 2.

Spearman's Two-Factor Theory; The Holzinger–Spearman Bi-Factor Model

In *The Abilities of Man*, Spearman (1927) developed what was probably the first formal theory of cognitive abilities, the so-called two-factor theory whereby any cognitive test was conceived to be "saturated" with a general factor g and a specific factor, s, unique to that test. Both in this book and in his earlier work *The Nature of Intelligence and the Principles of Cognition* (1923), the postulated nature of the *g* factor was thoroughly expounded. A careful reading of Spearman's work reveals, however, that he was also interested in the nature of the specific factor *s*. The specific factor was not simply a place-holder for whatever was measured by a test other than *g*; it could be an ability deserving of attention in its own right. The symbol *s* stood for any ability of this nature, and there could be a host of such abilities. (Although Spearman seldom mentioned the matter, he realized that *s* could include an error component; indeed, he frequently corrected correlations for attenuation in order to estimate the correlation freed of the effects of an error term.) Around 1925, together with Karl Holzinger and others, Spearman began investigating such "specific" factors, or what came to be called *group factors*. Techniques for computing factorial models and results were, of course, relatively primitive in those days. The model that Spearman and Holzinger eventually settled on (the bi-factor model, as it was termed by Holzinger) is essentially a two-stratum model, *g* occupying the higher stratum and assorted group factors occupying the lower stratum.

The three-stratum model or theory offered here is highly similar to the Spearman–Holzinger model. Stratum III is essentially the same as what Spearman called *g*; stratum I is essentially the same as the level occupied by the Spearman/Holzinger group factors. The major difference is that the three-stratum theory recognizes an intermediate stratum II containing *broad* group factors. The existence of such a stratum is supported by (a) computational procedures that are much more advanced than those available in Spearman and Holzinger's time, and (b) a large array of datasets, surveyed in the present volume, that disclose factors in stratum II.

In the main, I accept Spearman's concept of *g*, at least to the extent of accepting for serious consideration his notions about the basic processes measured by *g* – the apprehension of experience (what might now be called *metacognition*) and the eduction of relations and correlates. These notions, however, require much more confirmation and refinement than Spearman was able to provide. Objective procedures must be developed, if possible, for appraising or measuring the extent to which a task involves metacognitive and eductive processes. Spearman's characterizations of tests as eductive or noneductive ("reproductive") were based largely on his own subjective judgments. The loadings of variables on factor 2G or 3G reported in this volume could serve as criteria for assessing the success of any objective task-analysis procedures that might be devised to measure eductive metacomponents.

Thurstone's Theory of Cognitive Abilities

The three-stratum theory is a direct outgrowth of Thurstone's model in the sense that it relies on successive factorizations of correlation matrices at higher orders. The notion of successive factorizations was contained in Thurstone's latest work on factor analysis (1947), and Thurstone and Thurstone (1941) extracted a second-order general factor for their battery of tests given to eighth-grade children. The model of intelligence presented in Thurstone's well-known early work, *Primary Mental Abilities* (1938b), with seven or more orthogonal primary abilities and no general factor, was a one-stratum model, but it should not be taken as the model that Thurstone espoused in his later years.

Guilford's Structure-of-Intellect Theory

The three-stratum model is very different from Guilford's Structure-of-Intellect model, which as originally proposed (Guilford, 1967) contained facets rather than strata, and recognized no higher-order factors. Instead, it was a model in which the abilities manifested by particular variables depended on the manner in which they were assumed to sample various operation, content, and product facets. Abilities were classified into the cells of a $5 \times 4 \times 6$ cube according to the particular values of facets they were held to measure. Although it might be possible to classify the stratum I abilities disclosed by our survey into cells defined by Guilford's system, it does not seem worthwhile to do so in view of the questionable nature of Guilford's facets. There are certain rough correspondences between our stratum II factors and the facets of Guilford's system; for example, factor 2R (General Retrieval) is chiefly (but not entirely) concerned with Guilford's divergent production operation, and factor 2Y (General Memory) tends to correspond to Guilford's memory operation. There was no place in Guilford's system for a third-stratum g factor; this was a consequence of Guilford's somewhat idiosyncratic methodology (see Horn, 1970; Horn & Knapp, 1973, 1974).

P. E. Vernon's Hierarchical Model of Intelligence

The three-stratum theory is in many ways similar to Vernon's (1950, 1961) hierarchical theory of intelligence, except that it is much more explicit about the factors that belong at different strata. As discussed in Chapter 2, Vernon's theory was never worked out in detail; even Vernon granted that it was probably an oversimplification to assume two factors, *v:ed* (verbal/educational) and *k:m* (spatial/mechanical), as occupying a stratum just below g. The three-stratum theory recognizes, just as Vernon did, that strata are not necessarily distinct; its stratum II, in effect, contains perhaps as many as a dozen broad factors with varying degrees of generality over the cognitive domain, and with varying loadings on a third-stratum factor. It does not recognize Vernon's *v:ed* and *k:m* factors; these are probably different mixtures of broad factors at stratum II. The theory agrees with Vernon's model, however, in recognizing a very broad factor, g, at stratum III.

The Cattell–Horn–Hakstian Gf/Gc Theory

Like some other models discussed here, the model of intelligence and cognitive abilities presented in various writings by Horn, Cattell, and Hakstian (e.g., Cattell, 1971, 1982; Cattell & Horn, 1978; Hakstian & Cattell, 1974, 1978; Horn, 1988) depends on successive factorizations of correlation matrices at different orders. Sometimes, as in the work of Hakstian and Cattell (1978), the factorization is taken up to a fourth stratum. Nevertheless, in most presentations of what has usually been called Gf–Gc theory (Horn, 1988), only two strata are seriously recognized – a first-order stratum consisting of a large number of narrow abilities, and a second stratum consisting of a limited number of broad abilities such as Gf, Gc, Gv, Gr, etc. Gf–Gc theory thus appears to be essentially a two-stratum theory. Our three-stratum theory is similar to Gf–Gc theory except that it postulates, and provides much support for, a third-stratum factor *g* which derives from the common factor variance of the second-stratum factors. It is true, as Horn (1988) points out, that the third-stratum factor computed (by the Schmid–Leiman technique) in a given study can be somewhat different from one computed in another study, for its nature depends in part on the types of variables and factors present or emphasized in the battery as a whole. Nevertheless, if a battery contains an adequate diversity of variables the third-stratum factor that is computed can be regarded as an estimator of a true latent-trait *g*; the accuracy of estimation depends in part on whether the battery contains variables selected to represent second-stratum factors known to have high loadings on *g*. In principle, it should be possible to derive scores on a third-stratum factor that weight the scores on the original variables to provide optimal estimation of *g*.

Other Theories

The work of Richard Meili has been updated and presented in a 1981 publication (Meili, 1981) that is available only in German. In its present form, Meili's theory appears to have a taxonomic character somewhat similar to that of Guilford's Structure-of-Intellect, in that it postulates four main broad factors – Complexity, Globalization, Plasticity, and Fluency – interacting with verbal, symbolic, and figural content facets. Meili also postulates "components" or processes underlying factors and insists that a theory of intelligence can be formulated only by taking these components into account. It is possible to find general correspondences between Meili's theory and the three-stratum theory presented here; results of his researches could undoubtedly be incorporated into a three-stratum theory. Unfortunately they were largely overlooked in conducting the present survey.

The same could be said of recent work of Jäger (1984) in developing a "Berlin model of intelligence structure" – a model that is in some respects similar to Meili's (see Chapter 2).

The theory of cognitive abilities presented by Royce and Powell (1983) is a three-stratum theory essentially similar to that presented here. At stratum I it claims 23 cognitive factors, at stratum II six cognitive factors (*verbal, reasoning, spatiovisual, memorization, fluency,* and *imaginativeness* – roughly parallel to those of the present theory), and at stratum III three cognitive factors (*perceiving, conceptualizing,* and *symbolizing*). No general factor at a fourth stratum is admitted because, according to them, "positive manifold can be attributed to cooperative functioning among all the cognitive abilities rather than general intelligence" (p. 108). Alignment of the present three-stratum theory with Royce and Powell's would be possible, presumably, by detailed comparisons of the respective datasets and analyses. The database underlying the present three-stratum theory is undoubtedly broader than Royce and Powell's; yet, I do not find any clear evidence of their three factors at stratum III.

Although I have not undertaken such a task, the results of the present survey could probably be accommodated in the "radex" or "facet" theory of intelligence advocated by Guttman (1957, 1965; see also Guttman, Epstein, Amir, & Guttman, 1990), which offers a possible refinement that I have been unable to take advantage of, namely the analysis of certain variables in terms of a simplex or circumplex whereby variables can often be ranged along a line or a circle such that the distances between them correspond to their correlations. I would hypothesize, however, that simplex arrangements reflect mainly differences in task prerequisites and difficulties that interfere with the handling of data through conventional correlational techniques (Carroll, 1945, 1983c).

Somewhat similar to Guttman's interpretation of cognitive abilities is that underlying the nonmetric multidimensional analyses conducted by Snow, Kyllonen, and Marshalek (1984), as mentioned in Chapter 2. These authors claim that "the radex ... emerges as the most general theoretical model to date on both substantive and methodological grounds" (p. 88). Despite this claim, I continue to believe that a three-stratum factorial model provides a more elegant, comprehensive, and accurate depiction of the structure of cognitive abilities, in that it specifies latent dimensions on which variables and factors have specified, quantified weights. Nonmetric scaling does not possess this feature. Consider the two-dimensional circular plots of assorted abilities created by Snow et al. (pp. 66, 68) in a reanalysis of data from Thurstone (1938b; dataset THUR21A). While it is true that the positioning of test points with respect to the approximate center of the plot corresponds to loadings on g (as determined in a more conventional factor analysis), with the highest g-loaded tests close to the center, any further detail on structure comes only by examining the clustering of the test points and their positioning with respect to what they call "content wedges" – verbal, figural, and numerical. I am not so sure that the nonmetric scaling brings out patterns in the data "that are hidden or obscured in the results of factor analyses" (p. 70). I would hope that all the patterns they observe would also be observable in a three-stratum hierarchical analysis that would give loadings of each test on factors at each of the three strata, with indications of factorial complexity that would not be readily observable in a nonmetric analysis.

Unfortunately, my reanalysis of the Thurstone data was not successful in depicting a three-stratum analysis, possibly because of defects in the design of the dataset, Thurstone's use of tetrachoric correlations (less reliable than Pearsonians), difficulties in simple-structure factor rotations, the linearity of the factoring process, and the confounding of many of the factors with speededness. If I had been able to develop a three-stratum structure, stratum III (the g factor) would correspond to the degree to which a test point was close to the center of a two-dimensional plot, stratum II would correspond to broad clusters of points in different areas of the plot, and stratum I would correspond, presumably, to narrower clusters of points generally within the broad clusters. The three-stratum theory is thus essentially similar to the theory assumed in Snow et al.'s nonmetric analysis.

A "theory of multiple intelligences" presented by Gardner (1983) has received much attention in the popular press. It is based not on factor-analytic evidence but rather, for the most part, on Gardner's analysis of information on domains in which extraordinary degrees of talent and giftedness, or deficits in brain-damaged individuals, are found to occur. It is interesting, nevertheless, that the kinds of "intelligences" described by Gardner show a fairly close correspondence with the broad domains of ability represented by factors found at stratum II in the present theory. Gardner's "linguistic intelligence" corresponds best to factor 2C (crystallized intelligence); "musical intelligence" to factor 2U (auditory perception ability), or at least some special subfactors of it; "logical-mathematical intelligence" to factor 2F (fluid intelligence); and "spatial intelligence" to factor 2V (visual perception). However, Gardner's "bodily-kinesthetic intelligence" has no direct counterpart in the theory, partly because tests of kinesthetic abilities have not appeared in factorial studies and partly because the theory does not recognize psychomotor ability as a central component of cognitive ability. One of Gardner's "personal intelligences" – "ability to notice and make distinctions among other individuals" (p. 239) – would possibly be represented in the present theory in one of our knowledge factors, BC (knowledge of behavioral content), but his other personal intelligence factor – "access to one's own feeling life" – has no counterpart in our theory, principally because adequate measurements of such an ability have never, to my knowledge, appeared in factor-analytic studies. Although Gardner is aware of the tradition that posits a general factor of intelligence, he discounts this (mistakenly, in my opinion) as arising from the largely paper-and-pencil character of most intelligence tests and the fact that they emphasize what he calls "linguistic" and "logical-mathematical" abilities. He also discounts multifactorial theories of intelligence such as Thurstone's because, he claims, they fail to account for the full diversity of abilities that can be observed. Generally, Gardner has neglected the evidence on the basis of which the present three-stratum theory has been constructed. Nevertheless, Gardner's research provides a useful source that suggests further explorations of cognitive abilities that could be conducted within the framework of the present theory.

THE ASSUMED STATUS OF FACTORS IN THE THREE-STRATUM THEORY

In the factorial literature there has been much discussion (e.g., Coan, 1964) of the status of the factors that emerge from factor analysis: are they merely mathematical artifacts, or do they correspond to something real in the constitution of individuals?

Certainly at certain stages in the computation of factors, they can be considered mathematical artifacts, in the sense that they arise in part from the mathematical operations performed in such computations. A principal component, or an unrotated principal factor would often exemplify such an artifact.

However, when factors have been rotated to simple structure, or (particularly in the case of a single factor accounting for all the common factor variance in a matrix of correlations) have been accepted as revealing the extent to which variables or lower-order factors measure a characteristic of individuals, a factor must be regarded as meaningfully reflecting something that exists in the individual. A factor can, for example, summarize the degree to which an individual masters a particular domain of knowledge, such as the vocabulary of his or her native language. In many instances a factor reflects the status of an individual with respect to a dimension of ability in which the tasks subsumed under that dimension can be ordered in difficulty or complexity; this would be the case for what I have termed *level* factors (see Chapter 11). In other instances, a factor can reflect the characteristic speed with which individuals can perform tasks in a certain class of tasks; this would be case for what I have termed *speed* factors. In all these instances, factors can be regarded as real rather than artifactual. In my view, it makes no sense to be concerned with whether factors represent *reifications*, as some have claimed (e.g., Gould, 1981). Dictionaries define reification as the treatment of an abstraction or idea as if it had material existence. Consider, for example, the factor of Static Strength that has been identified in numerous studies of physical abilities (see Table 13.1, where it is coded P3). It would seem absurd to claim that this factor is simply a reification of an abstract idea; rather, the factor reflects differences in the ability of individuals to perform certain tasks requiring physical strength. These differences undoubtedly have an underlying physiological source in characteristics of groups of muscles and their innervation. Analogously, it is absurd to claim that factors of cognitive abilities are reifications, because they reflect observable differences in individuals' performances of certain classes of tasks. The fact that it is difficult to specify the precise physiological sources of such differences does not make the corresponding factors any less real.

These remarks apply equally to factors at all levels of the hierarchy assumed in the three-stratum theory. The general factor found at stratum III can be said to reflect differences in the performances of individuals in broad classes of tasks.

It is possible to speculate about the physiological basis of differences represented in this general factor, as Spearman (1927) did, or to conduct research on the psychoneurological bases of such differences, as has been attempted in recent years (Eysenck, 1982; Hartlage & Telzrow, 1985). It should be noted, however, that lower-order factors as presented here in hierarchical matrices represent factors from which the influence of higher-order factors has been partialled out, to the extent permitted by the design of a particular factor-analytic study. To this extent, but only to this extent, lower-order hierarchical factors are in a sense artifactual. They still represent the extent to which individuals are specialized in their patterns of abilities, apart from their differences in higher-order abilities.

In my view, the object of factor-analytic research is to discover what abilities exist, irrespective of the strata at which they exist. Taxonomies such as Guilford's (1967) Structure-of-Intellect or Guttman's (1982) facet theory may have had a useful heuristic function in exploring the domain of cognitive abilities, but it seems unreasonable to expect that distinct factors should exist in every cell or facet combination ("structuple") of such a taxonomy. In fact, such taxonomies seem to be antithetical to the notion of a hierarchy such as is supported in the present survey.

The hierarchical structure favored here does propose, however, that there exist a finite number of distinct factors, at different strata, that can account for a large part of the covariance of all possible measures of cognitive abilities. It proposes that these factors are generalizable over different samples and populations of subjects to the extent that the factors are relevant to such samples or populations. (We would not expect a factor of English vocabulary knowledge to apply to a population whose native language is not English, for example, except possibly to the extent that such a population had had an opportunity to learn English. But vocabulary factors appear to exist in populations of native speakers of any language.) Nevertheless, it is conceivable and even probable that particular tasks would be approached or solved differently depending on the ability patterns of the persons attempting such tasks. A by now classic result in the study of cognitive tasks was the finding of MacLeod, Hunt, and Mathews (1978) that subjects' performance on the Clark and Chase (1972) sentence verification task was dependent on their pattern of verbal and spatial abilities. In effect, the factorial equations for certain measurements from this task were different depending on the subjects' abilities. Nevertheless, the basic verbal and spatial abilities that affected performance could still be accorded independent and permanent status, and the factorial equations governing the measurement of verbal and spatial abilities, as such, would not have differed over subjects.

THE THREE-STRATUM THEORY OF COGNITIVE ABILITIES AND GENERAL PSYCHOLOGICAL THEORY

Although the three-stratum theory offered here is concerned with what are called cognitive abilities, the theory does not subscribe to, or rely on, any particular psychological theory – neither, for example, a cognitive theory nor a behavioristic theory. The abilities with which it deals are called cognitive only because they are concerned with various ways of applying skills and knowledge to the processing or production of information. Its data, however, derive from observations (in the main, quite objective) of individuals' responses to tasks with defined characteristics in terms of stimuli and situational conditions. Insofar as these data are based on performance, the theory qualifies as what Sternberg and Powell (1982, p. 975) would classify as an *explicit* theory of intelligence.

The totality of the theory includes not only specifications of dimensions (factors at several strata) but also descriptions of these dimensions in terms of statements or testable hypotheses about what characteristics of tasks, and what measurements of responses to such tasks, are to be regarded as predictive of the loadings of such tasks on the dimensions. Descriptions of factorial dimensions may also include statements or hypotheses concerning the characteristics of individuals or samples to which these dimensions apply. By virtue of the testability of factorial hypotheses, they should form a part of a body of scientific knowledge in psychology, and thus a part of general psychological theory.

In Chapter 11, lists and descriptions of the cognitive ability factors identified in the present survey provide a convenient summary of the statements and hypotheses that have been made about these factors. For what are there called *level* factors, the statements summarize what characteristics of tasks or performances make for differentiation with respect to factorial assignment and difficulty of tasks for a given factor. For what are there called *speed* factors, statements indicate what kinds of responses are to be timed to produce measurements of given factors. (If any broad taxonomic classification of cognitive ability factors were to be formulated, in fact, it might be one based on the distinction between level and speed – a classification that is not included, or even mentioned, in Guilford's 1967 taxonomic Structure-of-Intellect model.)

Thus, the theory offered here has largely to do with the classification of abilities according to types of tasks or performances and types of measurements (in most cases, accuracy vs. speed), as well as according to the generality of factors over the domain of cognitive performances. Most or perhaps all of these classifications can be handled within a purely behavioristic framework. Nevertheless, as I have pointed out elsewhere (Carroll, 1988a), names and interpretations of factors often imply hypotheses as to the *processes* that underlie performances in tests of ability. Names of processes like "closure," "induction," and "visualization" often appear in descriptions of factors, and concepts from cognitive psychology like "working memory" and "long-term memory" are sometimes mentioned in interpreting factors. The naming of a factor in terms of a process, or the assertion that a given process or component of mental architecture is involved in a factor, can be based only on inferences and makes little if any contribution to explaining or accounting for that process unless clear criteria exist for defining and identifying processes.

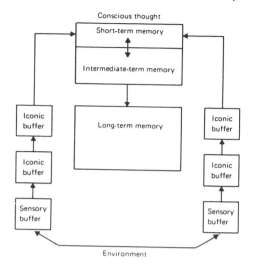

Figure 16.1 A schematic model of human cognitive processing. (From Hunt, 1971.) Copyright © 1971, Academic Press. Reproduced by permission.

On the other hand, to the extent that it is valid to infer processes involved in different factors, factor analysis can help in differentiating processes, and even in differentiating *components* of processes. With suitable experimental arrangements, it is possible to investigate individual differences in the stages of a complex mental task like solving an analogy (Sternberg, 1977) or performing a stimulus comparison task (Kyllonen, 1985; see Chapter 11). Elsewhere (Carroll, 1980c) I have pointed out that some of Sternberg's data on analogies tasks could be factor-analyzed to show the generality of components over different tasks. There are many promising opportunities for factor-analytic research to suggest what kinds of components operate in mental tasks, and possibly to suggest *how* they operate.[1]

Also important in interpreting factors would be statements concerning what kinds of procedural and declarative knowledge are involved. Many of the factors in the language domain (Chapter 5), such as V (Verbal Ability) or VL (Lexical Knowledge), represent differences in the extent of people's declarative knowledge about their native language – the meanings of words and grammatical constructions. Factors in the reasoning domain (Chapter 6) can be interpreted as in part measures of procedural knowledge – implicit knowledge of the algorithms that are to be employed in solving verbal or quantitative reasoning problems.

Cognitive psychologists have found it useful to develop schematic models of human information processing. One such model was proposed by Hunt (1971), as shown in Figure 16.1, and it was on the basis of this model that I (Carroll, 1976a) attempted to interpret the factors identified in the 1963 ETS *Kit of*

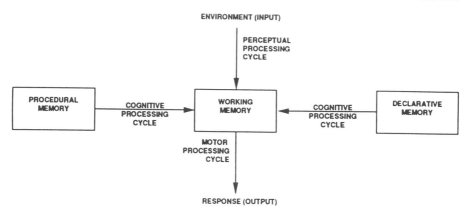

Figure 16.2. Information-processing model depicting memories and processing cycles. (From Kyllonen & Christal, 1990, p. 391.) Copyright © 1990, Ablex Publishing Corporation. Reproduced by permission.

Reference Tests for Cognitive Factors (French, Ekstrom, & Price, 1963). A more recent model – the "four-source framework" – was proposed by Kyllonen and Christal (1990) as a basis for a major research program (the Learning Abilities Measurement Program, LAMP) on learning abilities and aptitudes; this is shown in Figure 16.2. The concept of a central processor, as studied extensively by Baddeley (1986), was embodied in the box labeled "Working Memory." Kyllonen and Christal speculate, with reference to their model, that individual differences may occur in either the capacity and contents of the memories (procedural, declarative, or working) or the speed of the processing cycles (perceptual, cognitive, or motor). They state, for example, that "individual differences in reasoning proficiency may be due entirely to differences in working memory capacity" (Kyllonen & Christal, 1989, p. 158); they have reported (Kyllonen & Christal, 1990) a factor-analytic study claiming that reasoning ability is "little more than" working-memory capacity. Although there are some technical problems with this report, it is apparent that at least certain kinds of reasoning performances are affected by working-memory capacity as measured by certain simple tasks which, according to Baddeley (1986, p. 34), require "the temporary storage of information that is being processed in any of a range of cognitive tasks." Obviously, the research strategy that must be followed is to investigate ways of measuring working memory and to study its role in various cognitive tasks.

The concept of working memory is strongly appealed to in Carpenter, Just, and Shell's (1990) analysis of what is measured by the Raven Progressive Matrices test, often held to be a highly effective measure of general intelligence. According to their analysis, "[t]he processes that distinguish among individuals are primarily the ability to induce abstract relations and the ability to dynamically manage a large set of problem-solving goals in working memory" (p. 404). One is allowed to speculate, therefore, whether the general factor presumably measured by the Raven Progressive Matrices test is principally a measure of the capacity of working memory. Although some evidence supports such a speculation, one must be cautious in accepting it because as yet there has not been sufficient work on measuring working memory, and the validity and generality of the concept have not yet been well established in individual difference research. Carpenter et al.'s analysis may be compared with an analysis by Tullos (1987), who found that the primary source of individual differences on the Raven test seemed to be ability to apply rules of inference, along with lack of knowledge of certain types of rules frequently involved in Raven test items.

THE THREE-STRATUM THEORY AND THE COGNITIVE CORRELATES APPROACH

Pellegrino and Glaser (1979) noted that many research activities in the study of individual differences from the point of view of cognitive psychology could be classified under two headings: the "cognitive correlates" approach and the "cognitive components" approach. Work by Earl Hunt and his colleagues (e.g., Hunt, 1978; Hunt, Lunneborg, & Lewis, 1975) could be classified under the former, since it sought to find significant and meaningful correlations between psychometric indicators and performances on various elementary cognitive tasks. (For example, it found correlations of about −.3 between scholastic aptitude measures and mean reaction times on certain simple information processing tasks, such as the Posner physical/name letter-matching task). Work by Sternberg (1977) was regarded as belonging in the latter category, because it sought to break down complex cognitive tasks into their components. Here I want to draw attention to problems with the cognitive correlates approach, which has continued to be pursued in recent years. I argue that the cognitive correlates approach is likely to be unsuccessful and misleading unless it is viewed from the perspective of the three-stratum theory being put forth here. It is likely to be unsuccessful because the "correlates" that it claims to find are difficult to interpret if they are not referred to a broader theory. It is likely to be misleading because it may not correctly identify the locus or source of a correlate.

A study exemplifying the cognitive correlates approach is one by Palmer, MacLeod, Hunt, and Davidson (1985) that attempted to find information-processing correlates of reading ability. A variety of tests were given to college students selected to represent a wide range of reading comprehension ability; complete data were available for $N = 67$. Information-processing tasks included visual search, visual matching, span of apprehension, memory span, lexical decision, picture-sentence verification, and semantic decision. Some of the information-processing tasks involved alphabetic letters; others involved single words. Reading tests included measures of reading comprehension and reading speed; there was also a single test of listening comprehension (with scores from two alternate forms). Other measures included the Raven Progressive Matrices test and several tests from a multiple aptitude battery; actually most of these latter tests did not enter into the authors' analysis at all. Why these data were not actually used is something of a mystery; possibly the number of cases available was not large enough to allow sufficient degrees of freedom in their procedures of analysis.

The authors' approach was to investigate a series of hypothesized models concerning relations between information-processing tasks and reading ability measures, using the Analysis of Covariance Structure method developed by Jöreskog and Sörbom (1978). A preliminary model tested whether reading comprehension was different from listening comprehension; because these factors were found to be correlated .96, it was concluded that in this sample listening comprehension was virtually the same as reading comprehension. (Clearly, reading comprehension would not be the same as listening comprehension in a sample of, say, third-graders.) It was also found that reading comprehension was different from reading speed, because the correlation between these factors was only .63.

Next, the authors tested models concerned with the relations between reading (comprehension and speed) and performance (speed or correctness) in what were called "elementary" information-processing tasks – search, matching, and span of apprehension. In the search tasks, subjects were visually presented with a target item for 250 ms, after which they had to detect whether this item was present in a search set of from two to five further items. Target items were either single alphabetic letters or single words. The matching task was the familiar Posner task (see Chapter 11) in which subjects had to detect whether two items had the same "name" or not. Paired items were either uppercase and/or lowercase letters, or single words with one letter that might be changed (e.g., *SINK, SINK*; *SINK, WINK*). In the search and matching tasks, scores were reaction times. The span of apprehension test determined, by a method of limits, the number of items (letters or words) that the subject could correctly report when the items were visually presented simultaneously for 100 ms. (It was like a memory-span task except that the items were presented simultaneously.) From their data and the statistical tests they conducted, the authors concluded that the letter and word tasks "involve distinct abilities that have different relationships to reading ability. The letter tasks are not related to reading while the same tasks with words are related to reading." Further, "the word tasks were more related to reading speed than [to?] reading comprehension" (p. 77).

The authors similarly tested models concerning relationships between reading and "higher-order" information processing tasks. These tasks were: lexical decision (speed in deciding whether a stimulus was a word, e.g., *king*, or a non-word, e.g., *dake*), picture-sentence verification (speed in determining whether a sentence accurately described a "picture" consisting of an asterisk and a plus sign aligned vertically; see Chapter 11), and semantic decision (speed in determining whether a sentence was true or not, e.g. A VIPER IS A VOLCANO). At one point the authors considered whether the lexical decision task correctly belonged with the "higher-order" tasks rather than with the "elementary" tasks; a statistical test led them to conclude that it did. Further tests led them to conclude that "[t]he higher-order tasks involve skills not tapped by either choice reaction time or elementary-word tasks" and "are related to both reading comprehension and reading speed, while word tasks appear to be related to speed but not to comprehension" (p. 78).

The correlation matrices presented by the authors in their Tables 11, 12, and 13 made it possible to perform a reanalysis of their data by the exploratory factor analysis techniques employed throughout the present survey, with a resulting hierarchical factor matrix (Table 16.1) that presents a message about relationships between reading and information-processing tasks that is rather different from the one presented by Palmer et al.

A number of things are to be noted in Table 16.1. Above all, there is a fairly strong second-order factor (factor 1) spanning the first-order factors, but more about this later. For now, consider the first-order factors, which are arranged according to their loadings on the second-order factor. With respect to factor 2, which has a loading of .74 on factor 1, the single listening comprehension measure has the highest loading (.63) on that factor, which I interpret as a Language Comprehension factor because of the heavy loadings of several reading comprehension tests, the listening comprehension test, and a vocabulary test. Whether listening comprehension could be distinguished from reading comprehension could not be determined in this analysis because there was only one measure of the former included in the published correlation matrix. Evidence cited in Chapter 5 shows that listening comprehension can be factorially distinguished from reading comprehension if there are adequate measures of each of these skills, certainly if the sample contains a substantial proportion of individuals whose reading comprehension is relatively poorer than their listening comprehension, as would be true in samples at educational levels lower than college.

Factor 3 contained a melange of measures of quantitative reasoning and spatial skills – measures that for some reason did not enter any of the model test analyses of Palmer et al. It approximates a factor of fluid intelligence.

Factor 4 corresponds to the reading speed factor of Palmer et al. except that in my analysis variable 13, an "experimental" reading speed measure, has a relatively lower loading, in contrast to the high loadings that Palmer et al. obtained for subvariables (Form 1, Form 2) of this variable. The correlation matrices that they presented did not show separate correlations for Form 1 and Form 2 of this variable, and thus I was unable to study these. It appears that the reading speed factor they obtained contained artifactually high amounts of whatever specific variance was present in the two forms of their experimental test, described as consisting of 300- to 500-word passages that subjects were to

Table 16.1. First- and second-order hierarchical factor matrices. Palmer J./Macleod C. M./Hunt E./Davidson J. E. Information processing correlates of reading. Journal of Memory and Language 1985 24 59–88

N = 67

*** Hierarchical factor matrix, order 1 ***

V#		1	2	3	4	5	6	7	8	h^2
Factor 1: O2:F1 general this battery: order 2										
Factor 2: O1:F2 language comprehension: order 1										
1 + 18	Listening Comp'n – Davis	**.68**	**.63**	.08	-.02	-.10	-.00	.00	-.03	.87
2 + 17	Reading Comp'n – Davis	**.65**	**.56**	-.04	.05	.00	.15	-.13	-.09	.79
3 + 20	Vocabulary – WPC	**.64**	**.55**	-.02	-.00	.12	-.18	.18	.01	.78
4 + 16	Reading Comp'n – Nelson–Denny	**.67**	**.48**	-.03	.23	-.02	.02	.07	.02	.74
5 + 19	Reading Comp'n – WPC	**.61**	**.45**	.02	.06	.17	-.10	.00	.09	.62
6 + 21	Grammar – WPC	**.61**	**.33**	.13	-.07	**.34**	.11	-.08	.12	.65
Factor 3: O1:F3 quant. reasoning/spatial: order 1										
7 + 23	Quantitative Skill – WPC	**.47**	.05	**.73**	-.04	.06	-.00	-.15	.01	.79
8 + 24	Quantitative Achvt – WPC	**.49**	-.05	**.65**	.02	.23	.07	.00	-.01	.72
9 + 28	Raven Matrices	**.38**	.05	**.56**	.00	-.06	.03	-.02	.23	.52
10 + 27	Spatial – WPC	**.25**	-.08	**.52**	-.01	.00	-.07	.15	**.30**	.45
11 + 25	Applied Quantitative – WPC	**.54**	.10	**.51**	.07	.14	.05	.00	-.11	.61
12 + 26	Mechanical – WPC	**.43**	.23	**.43**	-.00	-.20	-.08	.13	**.39**	.63
Factor 4: O1:F4 reading speed: order 1										
13 + 14	Reading Speed – Nelson–Denny	**.44**	-.00	-.01	**.88**	-.10	-.03	.01	.09	.99
14 + 15	Reading Speed – Minnesota	**.38**	.03	.02	**.56**	.07	.01	-.12	.04	.48
15 + 13	Reading Speed – Experimental	**.58**	.21	.04	**.43**	.05	.12	.05	-.12	.60
Factor 5: O1:F7 spelling: order 1										
16 + 22	Spelling – WPC	**.40**	.03	.01	-.06	**.73**	-.04	.06	.05	.71

Factor 6: O1:F1 processing speed: order 1

										h^2
17 + 8	Matching – Letters	.17	−.08	.00	−.08	−.04	**.79**	.01	.14	.69
18 + 6	Search – Letters	.23	−.03	.08	−.09	−.06	**.79**	−.07	.14	.72
19 + 1	Two-Choice Reaction Time	.31	.12	−.08	−.03	−.11	**.78**	−.01	−.01	.74
20 + 10	Lexical Decision	.42	.04	−.11	.04	.29	**.74**	−.11	.01	.84
21 + 9	Matching – Words	.46	−.03	.03	.09	.18	**.73**	.18	−.16	.84
22 + 7	Search – Words	.34	−.07	.06	.04	.09	**.72**	.16	−.12	.69
23 + 12	Semantic Decision	.61	.08	.03	.11	**.34**	**.58**	.09	−.01	.85
24 + 11	Picture–Sentence Verification	.48	.14	.06	.02	.15	**.45**	.04	.14	.50

Factor 7: O1:F6 span of apprehension: order 1

										h^2
25 + 5	Span of Apprehension – Words	.35	.03	.05	.09	.05	.06	**.78**	−.01	.74
26 + 4	Span of Apprehension – Letters	.14	.05	−.03	−.13	−.06	.12	**.65**	.09	.49

Factor 8: O1:F5 memory span: order 1

										h^2
27 + 2	Memory Span–Letters	.20	.04	−.01	.08	.14	.05	−.08	**.76**	.65
28 + 3	Memory Span – Words	.34	.21	−.05	−.01	.10	.12	.03	**.60**	.54
SMSQ		6.05	1.78	2.06	1.42	1.15	4.14	1.26	1.40	19.27

*** Hierarchical factor matrix, order 2 ***

HF # 1st-order factor	1	h^2
Factor 1: O2:F1 general this battery: order 2		
HF 2 O1:F2 Language Comprehension	**.74**	.55
HF 3 O1:F3 Quant. Reasoning/Spatial	**.51**	.26
HF 4 O1:F4 Reading Speed	**.50**	.25
HF 5 O1:F7 Spelling	**.48**	.23
HF 6 O1:F1 Processing Speed	**.37**	.13
HF 7 O1:F6 Span of Apprehension	**.24**	.06
HF 8 O1:F5 Memory span	.07	.00
SMSQ	1.49	1.49

read in order to answer multiple-choice questions. The scores used for measuring speed were the line numbers that the subjects reported reaching within 45 seconds of starting each passage. (Apparently, correctness scores from the multiple-choice questions did not enter the authors' analyses.)

Factor 5 was defined chiefly by the Spelling subtest of the multiple aptitude battery, and did not enter the authors' analyses. It also has possibly significant loadings for the Grammar test and for speeds in the lexical decision and semantic decision tasks. Evidently, good spellers tend to make faster decisions about whether letter strings are words or non-words, or about whether the simple sentences in the semantic decision tasks are true or false.

Factor 6 may be interpreted as a Processing Speed factor, containing salient loadings for speeds on most (but not all) of the information processing tasks. Simple matching and search tasks involving letters, and a two-choice reaction time measure, have the highest loadings on this factor, although some tasks involving words also have loadings of .72 or greater. There is no evidence of separate factors for "elementary" and "higher-order" tasks, as the authors assumed in their analyses. Instead, this analysis suggests that the variables differed with respect to their loadings on the second-order factor 1: "elementary" tasks had lower loadings on this factor than "higher-order" tasks did. Among the information-processing tasks, the highest loading on the second-order factor was for the semantic decision task.

Factor 7 had loadings for the two span of apprehension tasks, and factor 8 had loadings for the two memory-span tasks. The presence of a separate Span of Apprehension factor suggests that Palmer et al. were in error in classifying span of apprehension tasks with processing speed tasks in their Tables 7 and 8, and in fact span of apprehension had lower loadings on their factors 1 (choice reaction time) and 4 (letter processing) factors in both of those tables. In view of the separateness of the memory-span tasks, it is perhaps fortunate that the authors did not use these tasks in their analyses.

The second-order hierarchical matrix in Table 16.1 shows the loadings of the first-order factors on the single second-order factor, ranging from .74 for Language Comprehension down to .07 for Memory Span. This second-order factor may be interpreted as close to, but probably not identical with, the theoretical g or general intelligence factor postulated by Spearman (1927). Because of the large number of measures of language ability in the battery, the factor is probably somewhat biased toward the Gc or 2C (crystallized intelligence) factor described by Cattell (1971) and others, but it also has a component of the Gf or 2F (fluid intelligence) factor because of the substantial loading of a combined Quantitative Reasoning and Spatial factor on it. What is of most interest in the present context is the fact that nearly every conclusion that Palmer et al. reached about relations between reading measures and information processing tasks can be accounted for, or in some cases denied, by the structure shown in Table 16.1.

When Palmer et al. state that "the letter and word tasks involve distinct abilities that have different relationships to reading ability" (p. 77), a more appropriate observation would be, not that the letter and word tasks involve distinct abilities (for they do not), but that the letter tasks have lower loadings on the general factor than the word tasks; further, the reading speed measures tend to have lower loadings on the general factor than the reading comprehension measures do. Actually my results contradict the conclusion of Palmer et al. that word tasks are related more to reading speed than to reading comprehension. According to the pattern shown in Table 16.1, by virtue of loadings on the second-order factor word tasks should be found more highly related to reading comprehension than to reading speed. Examination of the zero-order correlations shows, in fact, that the word search and word matching tasks show higher correlations with reading speed measures *only* when the experimental reading speed measure is used, and this is due to the fact that the experimental reading speed measure has almost as high a loading (.58) on the second-order factor as the language comprehension measures have. Also, the experimental reading speed measure has a small but possibly significant loading (.21) on the Language Comprehension factor, suggesting that it tends to be influenced by comprehension ability. It is thus not a pure measure of reading speed; it measures general ability and language comprehension as well. The correlations of word matching and word search speeds with the other measures of reading speed (the Nelson–Denny and the Minnesota tests) are generally no higher than their correlations with comprehension measures.

It can be stated, therefore, that the conclusions of Palmer et al. about correlates of reading and information-processing measures were incorrect due partly to misclassification of their information-processing measures and partly to failure to take account of relations of all measures to a higher-order factor of ability. This higher-order factor of ability is likely to be the locus of the correlations between reading measures and information processing measures.

The reader may be reminded that a similar conclusion was reached in Chapter 11 with respect to correlations between intelligence and speed of mental processing. That is, any linkage between intelligence and speed exists at a higher level of analysis – in higher-order factors of ability, such that persons whose scores on such factors are high tend to exhibit faster speeds of information processing. Whether the linkage exists at the highest level – that is, with respect to the postulated g factor at stratum III – or at a lower level – that is, with respect to a second-stratum factor of processing speed – is not yet clear from the available research.

SUMMARY

1. The data assembled in the present survey and the methodological assumptions and procedures that were adopted led to the construction or confirmation of a

three-stratum theory of cognitive abilities that recognizes abilities classified at three strata – narrow, broad, and general, with respect to the generality of factors over the total domain. The interpretation of individual factors, at each stratum, is a process of theory construction that specifies testable hypotheses regarding the characteristics of variables that measure (load significantly on) each factor at a higher stratum. The totality of the theory embodies specifications for numerous narrow, first-stratum factors, for a smaller number of broad, second-stratum factors, and for a single, general factor at stratum three.

2. The three strata that are assumed in the theory are not intended to be rigidly defined; generality is a matter of degree rather than of strict categories. Further, it is not assumed that the three strata exhibit strict subsumption relations; that is, although first-stratum factors may characteristically be classified under particular second-stratum factors, they may also show relations to other second-stratum factors.

3. The three-stratum theory assumes a hierarchical rather than a taxonomic model. It may be regarded as an expansion and elaboration of factor models proposed by Spearman, Holzinger, Thurstone, P. E. Vernon, R. B. Cattell, Horn, and others. It is fundamentally different from taxonomic theories such as those proposed by Guilford and Guttman, but can be accommodated within, or show correspondences with, radex theories that assume hierarchical structures.

4. Factors, at whatever stratum, may be assumed to correspond to real phenomena, in individuals, that govern cognitive performances. Factors are not to be regarded as reifications.

5. The three-stratum theory is an *explicit* theory of cognitive abilities in the sense that it seeks to account for observed covariation in the total range of cognitive performances. It is neutral with respect to particular types of psychological theory, e.g., behavioristic or cognitive. Interpretations of factors, however, often appeal to models of cognitive performances that assume the operation of cognitive processes in different aspects of a cognitive architecture such as sensory buffers, perceptual processors, short-term working memory, and long-term memories containing procedural and declarative knowledge.

6. The three-stratum theory provides a framework within which correlations between psychometric variables and information-processing variables are to be interpreted. The cognitive correlates approach that has sometimes been adopted in studying such correlations is likely to be unsuccessful or at least misleading if its results are not properly referred to the three-stratum framework.

NOTE

1. In the realm of memory, Richardson–Klavehn and Bjork (1988) and Hintzman (1990) discuss the role of "dissociations" as a basis for concluding that different processes are involved. A dissociation is a finding of different results from different testing methods. Dunn and Kirsner (1988), however, argue that dissociation does not guarantee that different processes are involved; they introduce a new technique, *reversed association*,

that is claimed to overcome the limitations of dissociation. Reversed association is defined as any nonmonotonic relation between two tasks. Both Dunn and Kirsner and Hintzman cite factor analysis as possibly enjoying the properties of reversed association, in that it shows that subjects are ordered differently by different tasks (and consequently, by different factors). This line of argument gives support to the hope that factor analysis can contribute to the identification of cognitive processes. Dunn and Kirsner state, however, that "factor analysis ... is primarily a technique to inform about the number rather than the nature of things. ... The observation of reversed association, or functional dissociation for that matter, does not relieve the experimenter of the burden of theoretical development. All it is able to do is establish the need for more than one process and perhaps suggest their likely characteristics" (p. 100). I regard this as an unduly pessimistic evaluation of factor analysis.

17 Issues About Abilities: Nature and Nurture, and Others

This chapter considers a variety of issues that stem from the classic "nature vs. nurture problem" – centrally, how heritable are the cognitive abilities described in this survey, and to what extent are they products of the individual's environment and learning experiences? But also, how do they develop and change over the individual's life span? How malleable or improvable are they? Do abilities multiply and become differentiated as individuals mature and become exposed to different environments and learning experiences? Do factor structures differ across groups differing in sex, race, or ethnicity?

In the scope of this volume, no one of these issues can be given anything like the treatment it would deserve in a volume exclusively devoted to them. The approach taken here is briefly to summarize present knowledge and opinion, to draw attention to relevant information assembled in the present survey, and to suggest possible implications that the three-stratum theory may have for further research on these issues, none of which is close to resolution in contemporary scientific work.

Some of these issues have usually been studied with reference to global measures of intelligence such as IQs from standardized intelligence tests. In view of the known factorial complexity of global measures of intelligence, one can raise the question of whether the answers that have been thus far obtained on the various issues mentioned above are sufficiently precise and adequate. It is conceivable, at least, that the answers would vary for different factors of cognitive ability. In this chapter, particular attention is paid to studies, insofar as they are available, that address questions with respect to different factors of ability.

GENETIC DETERMINANTS OF ABILITIES

It hardly needs to be pointed out that the question of genetic influences on abilities is one of the most controversial issues in the life sciences. It has been studied over many years, but particularly in recent years in the emerging science of behavioral genetics. Plomin, DeFries, and McClearn (1990) present the basic

656

theories and methods of behavioral genetics, with special reference to methods used for studying the heritability of human traits, including family, twin, and adoption methods. Most studies of the heritability of cognitive abilities have relied on measures of IQ. For example, Bouchard and McGue (1981) compiled intraclass IQ correlations for a large number of family, twin, and adoption studies. Using model-fitting procedures, Plomin et al. (p. 365) report the estimated heritability of IQ from these data as .58. (Heritability, h^2, is the ratio of the genetic variance of a measured trait to the total variance in a given population; the ratio can range from .0 to 1.0. In all instances, I refer to heritability in the broad sense, i.e., the heritability from both additive and nonadditive variance. See Plomin et al. for further explanation of these terms.)

Scarr and Carter–Saltzman (1982, p. 792) note that while some experts believe that evidence to date is insufficient to permit concluding that intelligence has any heritability at all, most investigators have concluded that "about half ($\pm$.1) of the current differences among individuals in U. S. and European white populations in measured intelligence result from genetic differences among them." Vandenberg and Vogler (1985, p. 50) state that "[w]hile methodological advances have resulted in a refinement of estimates of the genetic contribution to phenotypic variability from around 80% to a more moderate 30% to 40%, studies have consistently demonstrated familial resemblance for measures of intelligence for more than a century." A recent report on heritability, based on a study of more than 100 twins raised apart, is by Bouchard, Lykken, McGue, Segal, and Tellegen (1990), who state in their abstract:

...about 70% of the variance in IQ was found to be associated with genetic variation. ...These findings extend and support those from numerous other twin, family, and adoption studies. It is a plausible hypothesis that genetic differences affect psychological differences largely indirectly, by influencing the effective environment of the developing child. This evidence for the strong heritability of most psychological traits, sensibly construed, does not detract from the value or importance of parenting, education, and other propaedeutic interventions (p. 223).

Given that IQ measures are likely to be diverse and factorially complex (see dataset WRIG01, Wright, 1939; datasets JONE31–34, Jones, 1949; datasets STOR11–13, Stormer, 1966), one can ask which aspects of IQ are more subject to genetic influences. It is conceivable that estimates of the heritability of IQ, as a measure that is flawed in many ways, are actually underestimates of the heritability of some component or components of IQ. It would seem desirable, if possible, to study the heritability of separate components of IQ measures, or in the context of factor-analytic work, of any separate factors that can be isolated among measures of cognitive abilities.

Note that heritability is defined as a characteristic of a *population*, not of a trait or indicator. Heritabilities may therefore vary as a function of the population. For example, when Tambs, Sundet, and Magnus (1984) obtained unusually high heritabilities for Norwegians' scores on the WAIS subtests, they attributed this to a presumed greater than average egalitarian character of Norwegian society that allowed genetic factors to express themselves to a greater extent than usual. When I speak of different heritabilities for different factors or traits, it should be understood that they are to be taken relative to a given population.

As a hypothesis, assume that the factors postulated in the three-stratum theory presented here differ in their heritabilities. It is reasonable to think of the general factor g or G, at stratum III, as having higher heritability than factors at lower strata. At stratum II, the postulated factors may differ in their degrees of heritability, with factor Gf (2F) probably having the highest degree. Factor Gc (2C) reflects the degree to which the individual has been able to profit from environmental influences such as exposure to language, culture, and schooling; the role of heredity in such a factor would arise only to the extent that genetic characteristics predispose the individual to profit, or fail to profit, from this environmental exposure. The heritability of other factors at stratum II might be lower, but still significant. At stratum I, factors would have still lower heritabilities because they reflect mainly specializations of ability that occur through practice, training and exceptional exposures or adaptations (or lack thereof) to certain learning opportunities, independent of the genetic constitution of the individual.

Testing these hypotheses would require that the variables whose heritabilities are investigated be measures of abilities, at the various strata, that have been cleansed as much as possible of the effects of other abilities at the same or different strata. I have already mentioned (Chapter 16) Cattell's (1982) recommendation that the abilities to be investigated be what he calls "stub" factors, or essentially what would be obtained as factor scores based on hierarchical orthogonalized matrices. It appears that such a technique has thus far only seldom been employed in studying heritabilities of separate factors.

Discussions of the heritabilities of special abilities are available in writings of Plomin, DeFries, and McClearn (1990, pp. 368–371), Scarr & Carter–Saltzman (1982, pp. 865–879), Storfer (1990, passim), and Vandenberg and Vogler (1985, pp. 36–48). It is generally agreed that the inheritance of intelligence is polygenic, and thus it is reasonable to suppose that different sets of genes control different abilities. Although there is considerable evidence for differential genetic influences on special abilities, the evidence is as yet not clearcut and convincing. Scarr and Carter–Saltzman remark that "[m]any behavior geneticists continue to doubt that different kinds of intellectual functioning are differentially heritable (Loehlin & Nichols, 1976; R. Nichols, 1978)" (p. 865). Vandenberg and Vogler cite a study by DeFries, Kuse, and Vandenberg (1979) in which the parent–offspring correlations for fifteen different cognitive tests were partitioned into genetic and environmental covariances and separately factor-analyzed. Four factors – spatial, verbal, perceptual speed and accuracy, and memory – were found in each matrix, and the factorial structures in the two matrices were highly similar. They comment that

This perhaps somewhat surprising result has been interpreted as evidence that environment – for example, educational influences – can develop only abilities that are potentially there. Note that the environment need not consist only of formal, academic instruction (p. 45).

A further comment would be that these data show that the four factors identified are all heritable, but somewhat separately. In further tables from this source, it appears that spatial and verbal abilities tend to have higher heritabilities than perceptual speed and accuracy and visual memory. (We have seen, in Chapter 15, that the latter two factors tend to have lower loadings on 3G than the former factors do.) Vandenberg and Vogler further cite a study of the heritability of information-processing tasks (Cole, Johnson, Ahern, Kuse, McClearn, Vandenberg, & Wilson, 1979), remarking that the study "suggests that information-processing tasks may be under genetic control to about the same degree as standard measures of intelligence, but more work is clearly needed before we can be certain of this" (p. 47).

In reviewing the literature, McGue and Bouchard (1989) discuss issues of heritability of special abilities in terms of two questions: (a) Are cognitive abilities equally or differentially heritable, and (b) are genetic influences the result of a single and general factor, or are there genes that specifically influence some abilities but not others? In response to the first question, they confirm the conclusion cited above that some abilities are more heritable than others. With respect to the second question, they feel that the data are unequivocally in support of the proposition that "a single general genetic factor does not account for all genetic influences upon cognitive abilities" (p. 10). They cite Martin and Eaves (1977) and Martin, Jardine, and Eaves (1984) as finding evidence for genetic contributions not only to a general factor, but also to different abilities. For Primary Mental Abilities subtests, Martin and Eaves found genetic influences for Verbal Comprehension, Spatial Ability, and Word Fluency, but not for Numerical and Reasoning.

In their own study of twins raised apart, McGue and Bouchard found specific genetic influences on several abilities, not only those measured by psychometric tests but also some derived from information-processing measures: "On average, the proportion of the variance associated with genetic factors appears to be largest for the Spatial Ability tests, next for the Verbal Reasoning and Perceptual Speed and Accuracy measures, and least for Visual Memory.... Among the other measures, significant genetic effects were found for NI + PI, the two Sternberg intercepts, and the spatial processing measures" (p. 31). It is noteworthy, in this study, that the four psychometric factors that were found were largely uncorrelated, as indicated by the fact that the authors presented a Varimax-rotated factor matrix for them such that there would be little temptation to further rotate it obliquely to produce a second-order general factor. (Possibly this was because the correlations were corrected for age and sex effects before factoring.) Because of this, it appears that there was little evidence of a genetic effect on a general factor, contrary to results from other studies. On the other hand, it is evident that there was covariance between psychometric measures and information-processing measures, so that, for example, the genetic effect found for Verbal Reasoning was also an effect for certain information-processing measures.

In a study of monozygotic (MZ) and dizygotic (DZ) twins, Vernon (1987b) has found heritable components in several information-processing speed variables. According to him,

Only one of three specific speed of information-processing variables – STM storage-processing trade-off, was found to be heritable. Measures of speed of STM scanning of information, and of LTM retrieval of information, showed low MZ and DZ intraclass correlations, replicating the results of the only other study to have investigated this issue (McGue et al., 1984) (Vernon, 1987b, p. 18).

The findings of the present survey suggest many dimensions of ability whose possible genetic aspects require exploration.

PSYCHONEUROLOGICAL BASES FOR COGNITIVE ABILITIES

To the extent that cognitive abilities may be regarded as reflecting differences in the physiological constitution of individuals, they may be assumed to have psychoneurological bases – regardless of whether those differences are genetically influenced or not. Even if there are strong genetic factors in one or more abilities, many abilities also reflect the cumulated effects of experiences that result in learning and memories, and these also must be assumed to have some psycho-neurological basis. Study of such matters is at the forefront of current research in neuropsychology. Haier (1990), however, points out that although the 1990s have been declared the "decade of the brain" this has had little impact on intelligence research; he calls for funding support that would enable neuro-psychologists more readily to use the high-technology instrumentation that is now available to study brain function.

Hynd and Willis (1985), in writing a chapter on the neurological foundations of intelligence, felt that their chapter might have three possible outcomes: It might adequately reflect our current state of knowledge, which is relatively slight and tentative. Viewed from several decades hence, however, it might well seem naive and erroneous. But on the positive side, it might encourage further research into "the intriguing relationship between intelligence and its neurological correlates" (p. 122). They present an excellent review of past work on such correlates, extending over the past century or more. Work has focused on cerebral organization and its possible meaning not only for the fact of individual differences in general intelligence, but also for the specialization of abilities. Lateralization of function in the left and right hemispheres is possibly correlated with certain special abilities.

Hynd and Willis favor Luria's (1980) theories of successive and simultaneous processing, as applied particularly by Das, Kirby, and Jarman (1979) to the study of individual differences. Successive processing implies that information is considered in terms of serial order, while simultaneous processing "involves the synthesis of separate elements into a group, thus permitting integration and the construction of gestalt perception" (p. 145). Successive processing occurs primarily in processing of language and auditory inputs, while simultaneous processing occurs in perception and manipulation of visual gestalts. Hynd and Willis cite a number of investigations that "have suggested that successive (or analytic) processing is primarily a function of the left cerebral hemisphere and simultaneous (or holistic) processing is primarily a function of the right cerebral hemisphere" (p. 146). Nevertheless, they point out (p. 147) a possible confound of processing style and response modality in this research, in that "successively processed tasks are more often presented and responded to verbally, and simultaneously processed tasks are more often presented and responded to nonverbally" (p. 147). They also warn against accepting the assumption made by many educators that teaching to preferred modalities (left brain vs. right brain) is worthwhile, since research has not supported such an assumption.

Eysenck (1982, 1988; Eysenck & Barrett, 1985) has emphasized the possible neurological correlates of g or general intelligence, particularly when it is regarded as a biological phenomenon, with control of the effects of learning and acculturation. He cites evidence that g is to a considerable extent correlated with electroencephalograph (EEG) measurements, average evoked potentials (AEP), and other physiological indicators. He refers in particular to the work of A. E. Hendrickson (1982) and D. E. Hendrickson (1982) on correlations of EEG measures with Wechsler Adult Intelligence Scale (WAIS) subtests. It is interesting, incidentally, that in my reanalysis of D. E. Hendrickson's data (dataset HEND11A), the measure of the *complexity* of the EEG waveform (the string measure) had its primary loading on a second-order 2V (general visual perception) factor, while a measure (taken negatively) of the *variance* of the waveform across time-slices had its primary loading on a second-order 2C (crystallized intelligence) factor. The second-order factors had an intercorrelation of .69 and had loadings on a third-order 3G factor, as did all the WAIS subtests. This finding, which may seem surprising, obviously needs replication.

The topic of neurobiological correlates of cognitive abilities is rife with speculation. Fodor (1983), for example, offers rationale and evidence for a theory that the brain is organized into independent "modular" systems. Possibly some of these systems would correspond to broad factors of cognitive ability (Carroll, 1985). Waterhouse (1988) makes the interesting suggestion that "special cognitive talents or abilities are different in source from human intelligence in general." She hypothesizes that "special cognitive abilities are based on a set of skills that involve the acutely accurate and extremely extensive representation of visual images and sounds, and the rapid recognition and facile manipulation of patterns involving those visual and auditory representations" (p. 495). In terms of brain morphology, these talents would be found in specialized visual and auditory processing systems.

Perhaps some of these speculations can be tested with recently developed methodology for the noninvasive investigation of brain function during intellectual work, namely, positron emission tomography. Illustrating use of this methodology is a study by Haier, Siegel, Nuechterlein, Hazlett, Wu, Paek, Browning, and Buchsbaum (1988) of cortical glucose metabolic rate correlates of abstract reasoning and attention performances. Even with very small numbers of subjects, highly significant *negative* correlations between cortical metabolic rates and scores on the Raven Advanced Progressive Matrices (RAPM) test were obtained, tending to suggest that intelligence is related to the efficiency of neural circuits, in the sense that low scorers have to "work harder" to perform a test such as the RAPM. There was some evidence in this study for activation of specific cortical areas.

I would suggest that neurobiological work be guided by factor-analytic results, as set forth in the present volume, that indicate what kinds of abilities are measured by various tests. The Raven Advanced Progressive Matrices test, for example, measures only one kind of abstract reasoning, and tends to measure spatial abilities as well. To the extent possible, neuropsychological research should attempt to find correlates between physiological phenonomena and measures of particular abilities freed of the influence of other abilities.

THE STABILITY OF COGNITIVE ABILITIES OVER TIME

As mentioned earlier at various points (e.g., Chapter 16), a widely held assumption is that cognitive abilities are relatively stable over time, in the sense that while these abilities may tend to increase with maturation, education, and other effects, individuals tend to hold approximately the same position relative to an age cohort, and thus the correlations of abilities from one age to another tend to be high. This matter has been much studied with respect to measures of IQ or global intelligence taken during childhood and adolescence. Cronbach and Snow (1977, pp. 111f., 142–150) discuss the so-called overlap hypothesis that was proposed by John E. Anderson (1939) whereby it was thought that mental growth from one year to the next was characterized by random increments that were not predictable from current status. Or as Roff (1941) put it, "... the so-called 'constancy of the I.Q.' [was thought to be] due primarily to the retention by each child of the skills and knowledge which determined his scores in earlier years, and is not due at all to correlation between earlier scores and later gains or increments" (p. 385). By several lines of reasoning and statistical analysis, Cronbach and Snow were able to reject the overlap hypothesis. They showed, essentially, that the bases of the overlap hypothesis are statistical artifacts due to measurement and scaling errors. This being the case, the overlap hypothesis would presumably also be rejected for specific abilities, but longitudinal data on special abilities are harder to come by than data for global IQ measures. I am not aware of any analysis of growth in special abilities similar to the one that Cronbach and Snow performed on data used by Anderson and Roff.

For the adult years, Conley (1984) has assembled and analyzed the available data on the longitudinal consistency of global measures of intelligence in terms of a procedure devised by Converse and Markus (1979) whereby the observed retest correlation over a given number of years, n, is estimated as the product of R, the internal consistency or period-free reliability of the measuring instrument, and a stability coefficient, s, raised to the nth power. He found that the intelligence data correspond to a curve having an annual stability coefficient $s = 0.99$ and a period-free reliability $R = .95$. This stability coefficient is higher than that, 0.98, for personality variables.

Several sets of longitudinal data may be used to assess the stability of special abilities over periods of years. (Here, stability refers to consistency of rank-order in a cohort.) From the Seattle Longitudinal Study, Schaie and Strother (1968) reported seven-year test–retest reliabilities for PMA subtests as follows: Verbal Meaning, .88; Space, .75; Reasoning, .93; Number, .91; and Word Fluency, .86. Working with data from this study collected over the years 1956, 1963, and 1970, Hertzog is reported to have found that "factor covariances remained high over the three occasions . . . , indicating consistency of individual differences over time" (Schaie, 1983, p. 110). Hertzog is also reported to have found that factor covariances were greatest in the older group (mean ages 58, 65, and 72), indicating that the factor space became more oblique as the sample aged. Somewhat similar results were obtained by Horn and McArdle (1980) for (partially simulated) longitudinal data on subtests of the WAIS. For example, they report:

The numbers suggest that P [performance] ability at age 30 is significantly and notably predictive of P at age 40 (.54) and that the same is true for the V [verbal] abilities at the two ages (.37). However, early-age V is not very predictive of later-age P, and similarly, early-age P is not very predictive of later-age V (p. 520).

In general, the data suggest considerable stability of specific abilities over time periods measured in years. But this conclusion must be qualified to the extent that the phenotypic measures of special abilities probably include variance from higher-stratum abilities. A more satisfactory answer to the question of the stability (test–retest reliabilities) of special abilities would come from analyses that would partial out the effect of higher-stratum abilities. That is, we want to know: How stable is the g factor (stratum III)? Eliminating the effect of the stratum III g, how stable are the broad factors of ability at stratum II? And eliminating the effects of strata III and II, how stable are abilities at stratum I? To some extent, these questions have been addressed in a longitudinal factor analysis of the Seattle Longitudinal Study data by Schaie and Hertzog (1986), who show that there is high stability for a general factor, and also "an impressive degree of stability of interindividual differences in PMA performance across the adult life span" (p. 103). These conclusions are limited, of course, by the fact that they deal only with five PMA abilities and the second-order general factor defined by them, which may reflect in part the speededness of the PMA tests.

DEVELOPMENT AND CHANGE OF ABILITIES OVER AGE

Plentiful information and discussion about development and changes in global intelligence through childhood and young adulthood as measured, for example, by the Stanford–Binet and instruments in the Wechsler series are available (Anastasi, 1988; Sattler, 1982). The mental age and derived score scales used for these instruments are developed in such a way that mean values can be plotted over ages. Much less information is available for special abilities such as those isolated in factor-analytic studies. At one time in the planning of the present work I had the intention of trying to glean from factor-analytic studies information from which I could derive growth curves for special abilities. Several problems arose in any attempt to do this. One is the fact that factor-analytic studies have used such diverse samples in terms of age, type of sample, etc. that it is not clear that meaningful growth curves could be constructed. Another is the fact that the tests and scores used in factor-analytic studies have been highly diverse in terms of test content, length, timing, and other aspects, so that scales are not generally comparable over different studies. Finally, the effort that would be required to estimate growth curves from factor-analytic studies, in view of the unsatisfactory nature of the data, appeared to be much greater than I could afford to expend in view of the many other tasks that demanded attention. I therefore decided to abandon the attempt.

The age norms given for various multifactorial standardized tests of mental abilities give some partially satisfactory information for constructing growth curves, but because the units of the scales are not necessarily equal, there is no assurance that a change of a certain number of units at the low end of the scale is in any way equal to growth of the same number of units at the high end of the scale. Possibly this problem is somewhat diminished by the use of certain test theory models, such as the Rasch model, that have been employed by those who have constructed multifactorial tests such as the British Ability Scales (Elliott, 1983) or the Woodcock–Johnson Psycho-Educational Battery (Woodcock & Johnson, 1989). It would be difficult to interpret growth curves constructed from these norms, however, because the influence of abilities at different strata of the ability hierarchy would be uncontrolled. That is, for example, growth curves for stratum I abilities would undoubtedly reflect the effect of growth in stratum II and III abilities. Furthermore, there would be difficulties in interpreting the actual levels of ability attained at different ages because most abilities have no absolute metric for making such interpretations. A possible exception is memory-span ability; see Figure 7.1, which plots average forward and backward digit span performance on memory-span tests in the Wechsler series over ages 6 to adult.

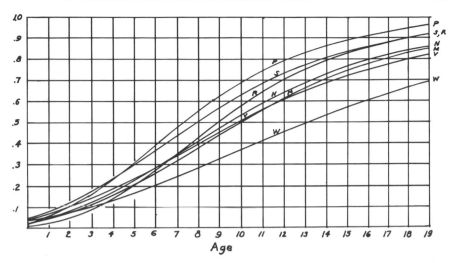

Figure 17.1. Growth curves for Primary Mental Ability tests. (From Thurstone, 1955.) P: Perceptual Speed; S: Space; R: Reasoning; N: Number, M: Memory; V: Verbal; W: Word Fluency. The ordinate shows proportion of estimated asymptotic adult level. Reproduced by permission of the L. L. Thurstone Psychometric Laboratory, University of North Carolina at Chapel Hill.

When test scores do not constitute an absolute metric, as is true of most such scores, it is still possible to employ techniques of behavioral scaling (Carroll, 1992) to develop scales for plotting growth over chronological age.

Partly for its historical interest and partly because it is not widely available, I reproduce in Figure 17.1 Thurstone's (1955) plot of mental growth curves for subtests of the Primary Mental Abilities battery. Thurstone derived these curves from standardization data and fitted them to Gompertz curves such that an asymptotic "adult" value was estimated for each ability. Each curve shows the rate at which this asymptotic value was approached. On this basis, Thurstone wrote:

From this figure we can make a rough comparison of the rate of maturation of these abilities. For this purpose we note the age at which the average mental growth curve reaches four-fifths of the adult performance. With this criterion the Perceptual Speed factor P reaches 80% of the adult performance at the age of 12. The Space and Reasoning factors attain the same relative performance at the age of 14. The Number and Memory factors reach this level at about 16. The Verbal Comprehension factor develops more slowly and it reaches the same relative level at the age of 18. The Word Fluency factor W matures later than 20 (p. 4).

An excellent review of the development and change of cognitive abilities from a life-span developmental perspective has been written by Dixon, Kramer, and

Baltes (1985), with consideration not only of the history of the field but also of current research. They mention a few stable findings:

First, until early adulthood, intellectual development is characterized primarily in terms of growth or progression in cognitive operations and knowledge. Second, the structure of mental abilities and associated interindividual differences reach [*sic*] a fairly high level of stabilization by early adolescence. The level of stabilization is not perfect – there is room for further change – but present genetic and social conditions appear to be prevalent. Third, by early adulthood, most individuals can exercise sufficient cognitive skills to engage in further knowledge acquisition, providing that social and ecological conditions (for example, occupation) permit, since the capacity for continued learning and for maintaining and expanding on both general knowledge systems and specific knowledge domains is a prototypical feature of adulthood. Fourth, deviations from this general pattern of intellectual development are often the result of environmental insult, serious disease, or substantial social deprivation. ...

With regard to adulthood and old age, this general pattern of universal growth and stabilization of interindividual differences in structure and function is not (or is not yet) the dominant position in research and theory. If applied to the adult portion of the life span, most such summary statements regarding childhood intelligence would represent issues of controversy. ... The widespread aging of the population is a fairly recent phenomenon. Thus it may be understandable that the course of intellectual development during adulthood and old age is less structured, less stable, and less predictable than it is during childhood (p. 302).

The authors describe two important longitudinal studies of change in mental abilities over adulthood. One of these is that of Schaie (1979, 1983), who collected scores on five of Thurstone's tests of primary mental abilities for stratified samples of adults ranging in age from 20 to 70, starting in 1956 and continuing in successive waves of testing in 1963, 1970, and 1977. These data provide much evidence concerning age changes in the five abilities tested – Verbal Meaning, Space, Reasoning, Number, and Word Fluency. Unfortunately, all these tests tend to emphasize speed at least as much as power (or *level*, as defined in Chapter 11), so that the observed declines of mean test scores that begin to appear around age 60 may imply declines of speed more than level. Dixon et al. remark that "[a]ppropriate data to address the question of the validity of the Schaie results (for example, a comparable design using a low speed and high power test) are simply not available" (p. 326). On the other hand, Schaie (1983) reported data on a small sample ($N = 31$) that suggested that even when the Thurstone PMA tests were administered without a time limit, "differential performance levels were greater and in the same order as under the standard conditions of instruction" (p. 83).

The other important longitudinal study alluded to by Dixon et al. is that of Horn and Cattell (1967; see also Horn, 1982, 1985). Horn and Cattell reported distinct differences in age curves for different second-stratum abilities. Actually, Horn has been responsible for collecting and analyzing a number of different datasets on maintenance or decline of abilities with age (Horn, Donaldson, & Engstrom (1981); Horn & McArdle, 1980). The net results have persuaded Horn that there are real declines, but declines are different for different abilities. To quote Horn: "From young adulthood to old age there is regular year-to-year decline in the averages for some of the abilities of intelligence – namely, the *Gf*, *Gv*, and *Gs* abilities; in the same samples of subjects there is also regular year-to-year increase in the averages for other abilities that are said to indicate intelligence – namely, the *Gc* and *TSR* abilities" (Horn, 1985, p. 280).

Research on the change of mental abilities in adulthood and old age has been dogged by many methodological problems, including not only the cross-sectional vs. longitudinal controversy, but also the problem of how to deal with differences between cohorts and the problem of exactly what is to be measured, and how (speed versus level). Data to resolve all the controversies are not now available. If one could now initiate a study that would properly take account of all these problems, the final results, of course, would not be known for years, perhaps not until the middle of the twenty-first century.

TO WHAT EXTENT ARE COGNITIVE ABILITIES MALLEABLE?

The question of whether, and to what extent, cognitive abilities are changeable through treatments or interventions specially designed or intended to change them is exceedingly complex. The answer, or answers, depend on what abilities, or aspects of abilities, are involved, and what kinds of operations or interventions are meant to produce changes in levels of abilities. Certainly some kinds of ability – those representing the results of learning, or school achievements, are improvable through further education, training, or practice, but there is inadequate systematic information in the literature as to whether there are any limits on the improvability of these abilities that are set by levels of more "basic" abilities.

Most discussions of the improvability of abilities have concerned the improvability of general intelligence or IQ as measured by various standard tests of intelligence, with little concern for the separate abilities that might be thought of as constituting intelligence, that is, the stratum I and stratum II abilities that have been described in the present survey. In a comprehensive review of the large literature on environmental effects on intelligence, Bouchard and Segal (1985) conclude that "no single environmental factor appears to have a large influence on IQ" (p. 452). They feel that environmental effects are multifactorial. One possibility that needs to be considered in further research is that the effects are different for different abilities.

It is evident that environmental effects must have accounted for a large part of the striking increases in overall mean IQ noted by Flynn (1987) in many countries, including the U.S. – from 5 to 25 points in a single generation. Some of the largest gains have occurred for "culturally reduced" tests of fluid intelligence like the Raven Progressive Matrices Test; the gains are somewhat smaller for tests of crystallized intelligence, such as the verbal scores for the

Wechsler Adult Intelligence Scale. Flynn argues that these results suggest that IQ tests do not measure intelligence; rather, they measure a "correlate with a weak causal link to intelligence" (p. 187) that may be called abstract problem-solving ability (APSA), that is, an ability that is only remotely related to intelligence as it operates in the real world to create all sorts of innovations in culture, social life, science, art, etc. Perhaps it is too strong to say that IQ has only a "weak causal link" to real-world intelligence; I would argue that the causal link is actually quite strong, and not well reflected in Flynn's data on IQ gains because these concern only central tendencies. In any event, Flynn finds it impossible to identify the precise environmental changes that are responsible for IQ gains.

EFFECTS OF SCHOOLING ON COGNITIVE ABILITIES

One type of experience to which almost every individual is subject is *schooling*. The study of the effects of schooling is the major objective of research in educational psychology, and it can be said that thousands of research studies have been conducted on the effects of schooling on knowledge and performance. Strangely, it cannot be said that there exists systematic information on the effects of schooling on cognitive abilities, neither global intelligence nor specific mental abilities. This is partly due to the fact that producing changes in mental abilities is not usually thought to be an objective of education. This point is arguable, however, as may be seen by considering that the success of schooling is sometimes (probably mistakenly) judged by success in producing higher scores on the College Board Scholastic Aptitude Test and similar measures of scholastic aptitude. Rather, cognitive abilities are often thought to be determinants of success in schooling, or at least predictors of it. It would in any case be difficult, ordinarily, to specify how cognitive abilities are affected by schooling, because of the complex interrelations of cognitive abilites and educational success.

There have, however, been attempts to study causal relations between aptitudes and school achievements. Crano, Kenny, and Campbell (1972) developed the technique of cross-lagged panel analysis for this purpose. Briefly, Crano (1974) found that at least in high SES (socioeconomic status) groups, general intelligence tests (and particularly those measuring fluid intelligence) given at grade 4 predicted school achievement at grade 6 better than achievement tests given at grade 4 predicted intelligence tests given at grade 6. The findings were not as clear-cut in a low SES group, prompting Crano to suggest that "fundamentally different patterns of cognitive development might well operate in groups differentiated on the basis of SES and initial intellectual endowment" (p. 250). These conclusions must be taken with caution, however, because Rogosa (1980) has shown that the technique of cross-lagged correlation can be seriously flawed. Humphreys (1991) has suggested possible ways of circumventing flaws in the procedure.

School programs and curricula differ widely; it should not be too difficult to assess the effect of different programs or curricula on results of different cognitive tests. In one interesting experiment, Härnqvist (1968) studied the effect of tracking in the Swedish secondary school. His results suggest that students selecting more rigorous curricula may gain as much as two-thirds of a standard deviation in cognitive ability as compared to students who select a vocational education curriculum. (This is reminiscent of the finding of Wolfle (1985; dataset WOLF11) that curriculum level is a strong predictor of educational achievement.) It is interesting that Härnqvist found a canonical correlation of .78 between general intelligence measured at age 13 and at age 18. However, the correlation was only .38 for a second unrotated component measuring a contrast between spatial and verbal abilities. The lowered correlation was probably due to differential experiences in school and occupational experiences between ages 13 and 18. Balke-Aurell (1982) replicated and extended Härnqvist's analyses on the 1948 cohort that he studied, and also studied data on a further, 1953, cohort. She found that the higher the educational level reached, the more positive was the increase in the intelligence (g) factor. Changes in the contrast between spatial and verbal abilities were strikingly related to the type of education and occupational experiences of the subjects. Those educated in verbally dominated curricula showed a greater verbal orientation in ability, while those educated in curricula dominated by technical subjects changed more in a spatial/technical direction. These changes were interpreted as caused by educational experiences and not merely the result of self-selective influences.

EFFECTS OF TRAINING AND OTHER INTERVENTIONS

The question of whether intelligence can be raised has usually been framed in terms of whether it is possible in some way to improve the intelligence of persons who are "retarded" or "mentally weak," whose IQs, when they are tested, fall far below the norm. Spitz (1986), a psychologist associated with one of the best known centers for training and research on mental retardation in America, has written a fascinating and moving account of the long history of the many diverse attempts to improve intelligence. He has amassed extensive and plentiful evidence to support his skepticism about the possibility of doing this. As he remarks, "the unsubstantiated claims that there are ways to raise intelligence and thereby cure retarded people come from earnest and dedicated workers on the one hand, as well as from scoundrels and psychopaths on the other, with all gradations in between" (p. 218). But, he cautions:

surely the accumulation of evidence that intelligence cannot be substantially and permanently raised by special training is unrelated to the humanistic concern to educate and assist mentally retarded persons to the best of our ability. *All retarded persons must be given the best education and the best environment possible to allow them to grow to their fullest potential, and training for academic, social and vocational adjustment must be vigorously pursued* (p. 219).

Earlier, a group of experts invited to write chapters in a book edited by Detterman and Sternberg (1982) had presented, on the whole, a slightly more optimistic view about the possibilities of improving intelligence. In the first chapter, Snow (1982) considered the question of "training intellectual aptitude," not necessarily only for the mentally retarded, but also for persons of normal or above average intelligence. In fact, Snow points out that "education is primarily an aptitude development program" (p. 29). Further,

> General intellectual aptitudes have long been regarded as impervious to change through direct training interventions, even while being susceptible to long-term development through education. Present evidence supports the hypothesis that superficial interventions based on practice, coaching, expectancy changes, and the like, have little or no effect on ability development, but that substantial educational interventions based on direct training of component skills and metacognitive strategies can sometimes have important positive effects. To the extent that further research can expose the cognitive components and metacomponents that are susceptible to training, and can suggest how effective training can be designed, adaptive instruction that develops aptitude directly may be envisioned (pp. 31f.).

Snow's chapter is followed by a group of chapters devoted to the topic of modifying general intelligence, introduced by Detterman (1982b). Detterman expresses the view that

> research to date would conservatively suggest that increases in IQ of 10 to 20 points are the maximum to be anticipated. If this upper limit merely represents our ignorance of environmental effects, or actually represents biological limitations of the organism, is a question that can only be answered by additional research (p. 43).

In a following chapter, Caruso, Taylor, and Detterman (1982) review several early intervention efforts designed to increase intelligence and promote school achievement in needy children, with major focus on project Headstart as conducted in the U. S. According to these authors, none of these programs has been shown to produce any lasting effects on intellectual functioning. They attribute the lack of success partly to a failure to link research to the conduct of social policy. In further chapters, results from other programs of early intervention are reviewed. One of these is the so-called Milwaukee Project, touted as "the first modern attempt to conduct a methodologically sound study of the effects of early intervention" (Detterman, 1982b, p. 42). Interestingly, this is the program that Page (1985) called "scandalous" in its unverified claims and misappropriation of research funds. Garber's (1988) final report of the Milwaukee project, that contended that it was able to raise IQ an average of 30 points at age 6, was assessed by Jensen as giving results that are "most plausibly interpreted as a specific training effect of the intervention on the item content of the IQ tests without producing a corresponding change in g" (Jensen, 1989, p. 234).

Underlying all these reports of possible effects of intervention on intellectual status is the basic question of what is actually being changed or improved, if anything. Further in the Detterman and Sternberg volume, Brown and Campione

(1982) put the question as follows, in the title of their chapter: "Modifying intelligence or modifying cognitive skills: more than a semantic quibble?" They think it *is* more than a semantic quibble. If it is a matter of modifying intelligence, they would insist on seeing evidence of transfer of skills, or of improving learning-to-learn skills:

> ... we would argue that in order to say anything about whether successful training tells us anything about modifying intelligence, we would need to know if anything else improved (i.e., what transfer of training accrued). We believe that transfer criteria are not just nice but necessary, not only because transfer is an integral part of our theory about what intelligence is, but also because considering transfer, one is forced to ask: transfer of what? mastery of what? ... hence one is forced to make explicit what one is trying to train, what one is attempting to modify – and hence, by extension, just what one thinks intelligence is (p. 228, with text corrected for typographical errors).

But Brown and Campione are apparently more comfortable with the notion of training cognitive skills, where the issue of intelligence and its modifiability does not enter:

> ... if the child writes better, reads more fluently, progresses to word problems in arithmetic, etc., most people would be satisfied with the cognitive skills program that accomplished these results (p. 229).

The issue can be framed in terms of the three-stratum theory offered here. Improving intelligence, or certain components of intelligence, would refer chiefly to enhancing levels of stratum III or stratum II abilities; improving cognitive skills would refer to enhancing levels of stratum I abilities like V (verbal ability), VL (lexical knowledge), RG (sequential reasoning), etc., apart from the effects of stratum II and III abilities that dominate those stratum I abilities. It would be interesting to conduct a transfer-of-training experiment in which it might be shown that training a particular verbal skill, like vocabulary knowledge, would transfer to another verbal skill, like reading comprehension. Or to give another example, it might be shown that training on a particular inductive skill, like solving number series problems (Holzman, Glaser, & Pellegrino, 1976), would transfer to another inductive skill, like solving problems in the Raven Progressive Matrices test. The basic question would be whether transfer occurred only across different tests of a stratum I ability or across different factors dominated by a particular stratum II ability. Few transfer-of-training experiments have been explicitly guided by a factorial model of this sort, although such a model appears to be implicit in the "general analytic scheme" underlying Glaser and Pellegrino's (1982) program of research on improving learning skills, and Pellegrino (1984) has obtained some results suggesting that training transfers across certain measures of spatial visualization (VZ) ability. Transfer to training across different tasks measuring a particular ability is also the basis of the perspective adopted by Hogan (1978) in reviewing the general problem of the trainability of abilities. She refers to experiments discussed by Postman (1971) as concerned with "nonspecific transfer" in the general area of verbal learning. She states her belief that if abilities can be trained, such training "may provide a more efficient approach for training individuals to perform a variety of different tasks than training for each specific task" (p. 2).

The literature contains a number of examples of programs designed to enhance special abilities; on examination, most of these abilities can be classified as stratum I abilities. Programs for coaching performance on scholastic aptitude tests may fall into this category, but their objectives and methods tend to be diverse. Cole (1982) points out that many such programs emphasize the teaching of "test-wiseness" – knowing how to pace one's performance, or knowing strategies for guessing when one is unsure of answers, and so forth. Other programs emphasize motivation and the reduction of "test anxiety." It seems that relatively few programs stress teaching of knowledge (e.g., vocabulary, mathematical problem-solving procedures) that is likely to be covered by the tests. Messick and Jungeblut (1981) found that the major variable associated with score increases is the amount of student contact time. They conclude that

... improvement of the comprehension and reasoning skills measured by the SAT, when it occurs, is a function of the time and effort expended and that each additional score increase may require increasing amounts of time and effort, probably geometrically increasing amounts. If this is the case, the time required to achieve average score increases much greater than 20 to 30 points (on a 200- to 800-point scale) rapidly approaches that of full-time schooling, especially in Verbal; hence it quickly becomes unfeasible to augment the already full-time requirements of secondary school with sufficient additional contact time devoted to coaching to obtain large improvements in comprehension and reasoning skills over those afforded by a high school education (p. 215).

In reviewing the literature on training particular facets of intelligence, Sternberg, Ketron, and Powell (1982) cite studies focused on verbal ability, reasoning ability, problem-solving ability, spatial ability, or memory ability. Their own approach emphasizes "componential analysis," the goal of which is "to isolate information-processing components of intelligent task performance, and to relate these components to each other and to performance on standard psychometric tests and factors of intelligence" (p. 156). Some success, though surprisingly limited, is reported in training components of performance in linear syllogisms, "people–piece analogies", and verbal comprehension tasks in high school or college subjects. Apparently, some strategies for solving problems can be taught, but often people fail to use these strategies even when trained to do so. From these studies, the evidence for true improvement in the underlying abilities is meager at best. It is possible that these abilities can be enhanced only by very long periods of training and practice.

It has long been believed that spatial abilities are very resistant to improvement through any form of training or practice. Studies conducted by Fleishman and his associates (Levine, Brahlek, Eisner, & Fleishman, 1979; Levine, Schulman, Brahlek, & Fleishman, 1980) would seem to confirm this belief. Little or no effect of practice or training was noted, in control group designs, on visualization, flexibility of closure, and spatial scanning abilities. Even when small but significant effects for spatial scanning ability were observed, they did not transfer to a task (electronic trouble-shooting) that had been demonstrated to require this ability.

Pellegrino (1984), however, claimed substantial success in the training of spatial ability by means of extended practice. This was confirmed in a later report (Pellegrino, 1988, p. 64), with evidence of both item-specific and general transfer effects. Posttest means on several spatial ability tests were in most cases significantly greater than pretest means. However, initial status on the spatial aptitude tests was generally not predictive of amount or rate of change with practice, except possibly for the more complex tasks. Pellegrino concluded that the issue of whether aptitude tests can predict practice or training effects needed much further investigation.

There is good evidence that aptitude patterns and training methods interact in training spatial visualization abilities. Salomon (1974) found that low-verbal-ability subjects profited from a filmed demonstration of procedures for visualizing surface development tasks, while high-verbal-ability subjects' performance on such tasks was actually harmed by this treatment, in comparison to being allowed to use their own strategies. Kyllonen, Lohman, and Snow (1984) worked with paper-folding tasks and showed that spatial and verbal ability patterns interacted not only with type of training but also with characteristics of items that made them easier for some subjects and more difficult for other subjects. This study is a good illustration of the fact that research in ability training can become very complex. Snow and Lohman (1984) have offered theory and prescriptions for improving this area of research.

From several studies (Politzer & Weiss, 1969; Yeni-Komshian, 1965), it appears that components of foreign language aptitude are very little susceptible to training, and even if they are, they do not transfer to increased efficiency or success in learning foreign languages.

With regard to all such training studies, however, questions can be asked: If training was generally unsuccessful, was this because the training was not the best for the purpose? Could greater effects be obtained if the training were improved or changed entirely? Obviously, such questions can be answered only by conducting further research, with as much insight and creativity in devising improved training procedures as one might muster. Perhaps because of the recognized difficulties in conducting successful training experiments, educational research workers have not devoted sufficient effort to this task. From the perspective of the survey of cognitive abilities that has been undertaken here, there are large areas of the cognitive domain that have been practically untouched by efforts in ability training. For example, except for a program of research by Maltzman (1960) there seems to have been very little attention devoted to improving performance in the domain of idea production, as described in Chapter 10, despite the great interest in enhancing "creativity" (see Sternberg, 1988; Sternberg & Lubart, 1991). But even in domains in which considerable work has been accomplished, such as verbal ability, reasoning ability, and spatial ability, there is much more to be done.

COGNITIVE ABILITIES AND LEARNING:
AN ASPECT OF VALIDITY

The question addressed here is somewhat different from, though related to, the question taken up above (whether cognitive abilities are improvable). It is the question of whether any cognitive abilities, at any stratum in the hierarchy of abilities, are predictive of learning, either in general or in specific areas. This question is also closely related to the question of test validity, because tests of cognitive ability are often validated with respect to the degree that they predict success in learning – either in the school curriculum or in particular curriculum areas, or in highly specialized courses of training.

I must confess to feeling considerable dismay when I find statements, as I sometimes do in the popular press or even in professional literature, to the effect that cognitive ability (or intelligence) is not related to learning. Such statements appear to have reflected frequent textbook assertions on the matter based on early experiments and findings of Woodrow (1938, 1946; see extensive discussion in Cronbach & Snow, 1977) that gains with practice on certain simple cognitive tasks could not be predicted from intelligence tests. But it is difficult to generalize from Woodrow's findings because the learning tasks he studied in the laboratory are not highly similar to learning tasks in normal schooling or training courses. The context of learning in such courses – where time and opportunity to learn is much greater – is not at all similar to the context of Woodrow's experiments. In any case, Zeaman and House (1967) were able to conclude that intelligence tests do indeed correlate moderately with a variety of laboratory learning tasks. They pointed out that Woodrow's findings have been questioned by a number of investigators for unreliability of the learning measures, restriction of range, and poor control of individual differences in starting level.

Brody (1985, pp. 359–363) provides a good summary of the evidence on the relation of intelligence and learning. "There is no doubt," he says, "that intelligence scores are correlated with academic success. ... Usually the correlations are somewhat higher for the elementary grades and decrease at the college level due to restrictions in range of talent." (People who criticize college admissions tests because of their alleged low predictive validity tend to overlook the restriction of range of talent entailed in validity studies, to say nothing of the problem of the truncation of the distribution curve that takes place as a result of selection.) Brody also mentions that intelligence tests given early in school are good predictors of the number of years of education that a person will obtain; at least, this was the case in a report by Benson (1942). (Even given the fact that the average number of years of schooling attained is higher in recent years than it was in 1942, this relation would probably still hold true, although there are probably complicating factors such as the possible effect of intelligence score records on school dropout.) In commenting on Cronbach and Snow's (1977) comprehensive review of the literature on aptitude-treatment interactions (ATIs), Brody is struck by the fact that most of the few significant interactions that were found are with respect to general abilities rather than with respect to specialized abilities. "Thus," Brody points out, "with occasional exceptions a more differentiated view of intellectual abilities has not been found to be the most useful basis for individuating the curriculum" (p. 360). The bulk of evidence suggests, therefore, that the stratum III ability represented by g is more relevant to ability-are specific to certain classes of learning tasks.

Factor-analytic research on learning abilities discussed in Chapter 7 generally supports the proposition that learning ability is closely related to the third-stratum g factor, but that there also exist stratum II or I learning abilities that are specific to certain classes of learning tasks.

Based on my studies of foreign language aptitudes as predictors of second-language learning, I proposed (Carroll, 1963) a "model of school learning" that asserted, among other things, that aptitudes are predictors of learning success mainly to the extent that they predict *rate of learning*. This was certainly true in the case of second-language learning, as I showed in several studies (Carroll, 1966, 1974) and it seemed likely to be true in other domains. Nevertheless, my model also asserted the relevance of aptitude for *understanding* instruction, particularly instruction that is poorly organized or difficult for the student to comprehend; such an aptitude would probably center in either g – a stratum III ability, or the second-stratum abilities 2C and 2F. In any case, my model of school learning was the basis for Bloom's (1968, 1974) concept of "mastery learning," whereby each student would be given adequate time to master concepts. The notion was that schooling does not ordinarily provide enough time to allow all children to reach mastery, with the consequent artifactually high correlation between cognitive ability tests and school achievement. Use of mastery learning techniques would presumably reduce the correlation between aptitudes and eventual school achievement, mainly by reducing variation in school achievement.

Commenting on mastery learning theory, Brody (1985) remarks:

It may be the case that educational changes in instructional formats my help students with lower ability to develop greater mastery of the educational program of the schools. However, no known instructional formats will eliminate individual differences in general ability as an index of the ability to acquire more complex intellectual skills (p. 361).

Brody goes on to cite Cronbach and Snow's (1977) general conclusions on the relationship between general ability and treatment interactions for instruction:

We once hoped that instructional methods might be found whose outcomes correlate very little with general ability. This does not appear to be a viable hope. Outcomes from extended instruction almost always correlate with pretested ability unless a ceiling is artificially imposed.

The pervasive correlations of general ability with learning rate or outcomes in education limits the power of ATI findings to reduce individual differences (*sic*, Cronbach & Snow, 1977, p. 500).

Nevertheless, there is no reason to cease efforts to search for special abilities that may be relevant for predicting learning. One promising possibility is to be found in the work of Gettinger (1984), who has studied individual differences in the time needed for learning, in general or in specific domains. She points out that this variable has not been adequately researched, measured, or effectively used in educational diagnosis. Gettinger and White (1980) found that work-sample tests of time needed to learn were more effective in predicting eventual achievement than standard measures of intelligence.

Ackerman (1986, 1987, 1988a, 1989a; Ackerman & Schneider, 1985) has embarked on an extensive program of research on relations between psychometric variables and the learning of skills that require a considerable amount of practice and training before satisfactory competence is achieved. Appeal is made to theories of automatic and controlled processing (Schneider & Shiffrin, 1977) and performance-resource functions (Norman & Bobrow, 1975). In general, Ackerman's studies have shown that general and content abilities are predictive of learning effects when the tasks require "controlled processing," i.e., slow, conscious efforts to apply rules to novel situations; in contrast, a different set of abilities predicts performance when the tasks have been practiced to the point of attaining "automatization," i.e., fast, effortless performance.

A program of research on learning abilities – the Learning Abilities Measurement Program (LAMP) – is under way in U.S. Air Force psychological laboratories (Kyllonen & Christal, 1989). (Some results of these studies have already been cited in Chapter 11.) In this program, it is theorized that learning involves four underlying sources: As *mediators* it involves (1) effective cognitive processing speed and (2) effective processing capacity, while as *enablers* it involves (3) conceptual or declarative knowledge and (4) procedural knowledge and strategic skill. Much effort has been expended on developing measures of working memory, which appears to be at least an important component of performance on reasoning tests (Kyllonen & Christal, 1990). An example of a study issuing from this program is Kyllonen and Stephens's (1990) experiment on cognitive abilities as determinants of success in acquiring skill in tracing signals through logic gates – a skill that is involved in studying and trouble-shooting computer circuits. Kyllonen and Stephens argue, on the basis of their findings, that ability in acquiring this kind of logic skill is little more than working memory capacity and a highly task-specific component. It is not yet clear, however, how working memory capacity is to be interpreted in terms of the three-stratum theory outlined in Chapter 16. Is working memory capacity a component of a stratum III g factor, or is it to be associated with some ability at a lower level in the hierarchy, for example Memory Span? The latter seems unlikely in view of the generally low correlations obtained between reasoning tasks and memory span.

THE DIFFERENTIATION OF FACTORS WITH AGE

Throughout the history of studies of individual differences in cognitive abilities, there has been interest in whether abilities tend to become more differentiated as age increases. As Anastasi (1970) points out, Cyril Burt had proposed a differentiation hypothesis as early as 1919. On the basis of results available to him, Garrett (1938, 1946; see also Garrett, Bryan, & Perl, 1935) believed that the evidence supported such a hypothesis. Methodological problems, however, have caused the available research to give conflicting answers. Results have been found to depend on the samples of subjects, on the variety and kinds of variables used, and on whether the data are cross-sectional or longitudinal.

From both a common sense and a theoretical perspective, there is every reason to expect that there should be at least some differentiation of abilities, insofar as abilities are formed through the accumulation of experiences and learnings, and through transfer of learning (Ferguson, 1954, 1956). It has been demonstrated a number of times (Skager, 1961; Whimbey & Denenberg, 1966) that differentiated abilities – "factors" – can be formed by the manipulation of learning experiences. In Chapter 5, Figure 5.1, I graphically depicted the possible age-differentiation of language abilities, based on the notion that many such abilities, for example abilities depending on reading, cannot be formed until individuals have become exposed to relevant instructional experiences. I also stressed the possibility of this type of differentiation in a paper on language abilities published in 1962 (Carroll, 1962).

On the other hand, considering the data amassed in the present survey, I am struck by the fact that nearly all the major types of abilities can be detected and isolated over a wide range of ages – often at a quite early age – and as a rule they appear to be the same factors regardless of age level. Tests measuring a given factor may indeed vary from age to age in difficulty and other characteristics, but they are all associated with the same basic type of content and process. Either or both of two possible circumstances can be mentioned to account for this. One is that differences in very early experiences – before age 5, say, before tests of differentiated abilities are normally administered – give rise to differentiation of factors. For example, children undoubtedly differ in the extent to which they are exposed to toys that might enhance spatial abilities. The other is that some abilities may be under a considerable degree of specific genetic control, so that they may appear as differentiated even at early ages.

A number of datasets were based on samples taken at different ages, usually employing the same or highly similar test variables. Table 17.1 gives a list of these, showing the ages or grade levels involved, the number of variables, the

Table 17.1. *Datasets that could show contrasts over ages or grades*

Dataset	Age (A) or grade (G)	No. of variables	No. of factors[a] m	m'
ANDE01	G 1–3	11	3	4
ANDE02	G 4–6	12	3	4
ANDE03	G 7–9	12	3	4
GARR11	A 9 (Males)	10	3	4
GARR12	A 9 (Females)	10	3	4
GARR13	A 12 (Males)	10	3	4
GARR14	A 12 (Females)	10	3	4
GARR15	A 15 (Males)	10	3	4
GARR16	A 15 (Females)	10	3	4
JONE31	A 7	24	5	6
JONE32	A 9	35	6	7
JONE33	A 11	30	5	6
JONE34	A 13	30	6	7
PARA01	A 3	12	3	4
PARA02	A 4	12	3	4
PARA03	A 5	12	3	4
PARA04	A 6	12	3	4
PARA05	A 7	12	3	4
PARA06	A 8	12	3	4
PARA07	A 9	12	3	4
PARA08	A 10	12	3	4
REIN01	A 10:6;IQ 106	18	3	4
REIN02	A 12:6;IQ 94	18	3	4
REIN03	A 10:1;IQ 99	18	3	4
REIN04	A 13:1;IQ 100	18	3	4
RICH31	A 6 mos.	17	3	4
RICH32	A 12 mos.	14	3	4
RICH33	A 18 mos.	16	3	4
RIEB01	A 6	7	2	3
RIEB02	A 8	7	2	3
SCHU01	A 20	8	2	2
SCHU02	A 64	8	2	2
SMIT51	A 5–11	40	10	10
SMIT52	A 12–30+	40	10	11
SULL01	G 6	8	2	3
SULL02	G 8	8	2	3
SUMI04	G 3	17	3	4
SUMI03	G 5	17	5	6
SUMI02	G 7	17	5	7
SUMI01	G 9	17	5	6
TOUS01	G 1	9	1	1
TOUS02	G 2	9	1	1
WACH01	A 14 mos.	8	2	2

Table 17.1 (*cont.*)

Dataset	Age (A) or grade (G)	No. of variables	No. of factors[a]	
			m	*m'*
WACH02	A 18 mos.	8	2	2
WACH03	A 22 mos.	8	3	3
WOOD13	G 1	22	4	6
WOOD15	G 5	22	5	7
WOOD17	G 12	22	5	7
WOOD18	A 30	22	5	7

[a]*m* = number of first-order factors extracted; *m'* = number of hierarchical factors.

number of first-order factors extracted from the relevant matrix, and the total number of hierarchical factors. (The reader is reminded that all datasets were analyzed blindly and independently by the same criteria for number of factors, so that the analysis was not biased in favor of any particular hypothesis concerning age-differentiation of factors. In the case of some datasets, the number of factors was determined by the original investigators, but even for these, there is no evidence of bias with respect to an age-differentiation hypothesis.) In nearly all instances, the same number of factors was extracted at each age. In datasets JONE31–34, either five or six factors were extracted, but without any systematic relation to age; also, the samples varied somewhat in the number and identity of test variables included. The only instances in which a slight age- or grade-related trend appeared were the following:

For dataset SUMI04, at grade 3, there were three factors, while five factors appeared for the rest, for grades 5, 7, and 9. A similar phenomenon occurred for datasets WOOD13–18, where there were four factors for the grade 1 data (WOOD13) and five factors for the rest (grades 5 and 12, and an adult sample). For datasets WACH01–03, there were two factors for the two younger samples (14 and 18 months), and three factors for the oldest sample (22 months). Thus, our data yield very little evidence for age-differentiation of factors. This is true despite the fact that several datasets (datasets GARR11–16 and REIN01–04) were from studies designed to test the hypothesis of age-differentiation.

Actually, datasets REIN01–04 represent a special case, from a study by Reinert, Baltes, and Schmidt (1965) designed to investigate what they called a "performance differentiation hypothesis" according to which ability differentiation occurs as a function of the overall level of ability manifested by a sample, even when age is constant. Reinert et al. tested this hypothesis by creating from their data two groups (datasets REIN01 and REIN02) that were equal in "level of performance" (i.e., average test scores) though different in age and IQ; for such groups, they predicted no differences in the factor structure, whereas for two other groups that were created (datasets REIN03 and REIN04), levels of performance were high and low, respectively, but the intelligence levels (IQs) were equal. For the latter two groups they predicted greater factor differentiation in the high performance group. They claimed to find some support for this prediction, although according to both their and our analyses, the numbers of factors were the same; there were differences in mean correlations and communalities, according to them. I computed congruence coefficients between corresponding factors in the two sets of data and found no striking differences, however. My conclusion is that there was no significant evidence of factor differentiation even in the datasets for which such differentiation was predicted.

Distinct evidence for age-differentiation of factors was claimed also by Atkin, Bray, Davison, Herzberger, Humphreys, and Selzer (1977b). Methodologically, their study was superior in that cases were selected from a large national longitudinal sample such that the same individuals were tested at each grade with the same variables, and the number of meaningful factors in each matrix was estimated by the Montanelli and Humphreys (1976) criterion that has also been used frequently in the present survey. For white males, ability differentiation was clearest; only two factors were retained at grade 5, four at grades 7 and 9, and five at grade 11. Approximately similar results were obtained for white females. For black males and females, there was less differentiation. Unfortunately, the applicability of these results to the differentiation of cognitive abilities is at least problematical, because most of the variables in the matrices were either school achievement measures or measures of information in various domains (industrial arts, home arts, physical science, music, art, etc.). Only two of the sixteen variables could be regarded as measures of cognitive abilities in the usual sense – the Verbal and the Quantitative scores from the School and College Ability Tests. The "abilities" that became differentiated at grade 11 were chiefly small factors of information about cultural matters (music, entertainment, home arts), science, and history. The authors acknowledged the limitations in their data, but contended that qualitative differences between intelligence, aptitude, and achievement measures are not as great as they are alleged to be. I find it difficult to accept this contention in the context of drawing a conclusion about the ability differentiation hypothesis.

Unfortunately, adequate data on the age-differentiation of the chief cognitive abilities are not available, to my knowledge, if one requires them to be on a long-range longitudinal basis. As a weak substitute for such data, I decided to examine the intercorrelations of the eleven subtests that occur at all levels of the British Ability Scales (Elliott, 1983). These intercorrelations are available in the test manual for three age groups on a cross-sectional basis: ages 5–7, ages 8–13, and ages 14–16. For each age group, I analyzed the correlation matrix for the number of meaningful factors by the criteria I have used throughout this study and found no evidence of increased factor differentiation over these ages; four factors were evident throughout, although the fourth factor tended to change in its composition.

My general conclusion on age-differentiation of cognitive ability factors is that it is a phenomenon whose existence is hard to demonstrate. Results depend on the types of factors whose differentiation is to be investigated; basic cognitive abilities are apparently less subject to differentiation than factors measuring specialized learnings. The question of age differentiation is probably of little scientific interest except possibly at very young ages. It is, if anything, of more scientific interest that the same factors are found throughout the life span – evidence for invariances in important aspects of human behavior.

ARE THERE DIFFERENCES IN FACTOR STRUCTURES ACROSS MALE AND FEMALE SAMPLES?

There has been much interest in possible differences across the sexes in means and variances of different cognitive abilities. In a recent review of available research, Sadker, Sadker, and Klein (1991) note that differences in mathematical, verbal, and spatial abilities have been declining over recent years. Because the interest of the present survey has been almost exclusively in correlational data, I do not feel it appropriate to try to analyze my data for information regarding such sex differences. Table 17.2 lists datasets representing separate samples for males and females, with information on the number of variables and the numbers of factors identified in my analyses. In all instances, the variables used for males and females were identical across the relevant pair of datasets. Some of the published investigations failed to report, separately for males and females, means and standard deviations for the cognitive variables used. Furthermore, the data come from many different epochs over the past half century. I feel, therefore, that the only issue in this area that I can legitimately address is that of whether factor structures differ across male and female groups. Because of the diversity of historical periods, and for other reasons, the data are of limited value even for addressing this issue.

As may be seen from the table, most pairs of datasets yielded the same number of factors for males and females, and where there were differences, they were small, possibly resulting from chance statistical fluctuations that influenced decisions on the number of factors to be analyzed. The differences are somewhat more frequent with respect to the total number of hierarchical factors yielded by the analyses; whether these differences are actually meaningful and supportable by the data could probably be determined only by structural equation testing methods. An approximate method of analysis that was much easier to apply, and that seemed to yield useful information, was the use of congruence coefficients among all the orthogonal hierarchical factors in a given pair of datasets. (Essentially, a congruence coefficient is similar to a correlation coefficient, but without adjustment for means and variances, intended to measure similarity of factorial structure across two groups. See Gorsuch, 1983, p. 285.) This procedure made it possible to evaluate the cross-identification of factors across gender

Table 17.2. *Datasets that could show contrasts over gender groups*

Dataset	Male (M) or female (F)	No. of variables	No. of factors[a]	
			m	m'
BENN01	M	9	3	4
BENN02	F	9	3	4
BERE02	M	18	6*	7
BERE01	F	18	6*	7
CURE11	M	91	8*	9
CURE12	F	91	8*	10
GARR11	M	10	3	4
GARR12	F	10	3	4
GARR13	M	10	3	4
GARR14	F	10	3	4
GARR15	M	10	3	4
GARR16	F	10	3	4
GUIL56	M	31	8	11
GUIL57	F	31	8	10
HARR51	M	56	7	8
HARR52	F	56	8	9
HARR53	M	31	5	6
HARR54	F	31	6	7
INNE01A	M	8	2	3
INNE02A	F	8	2	2
MCGU01	M	18	5	6
MCGU02	F	18	4	5
MICH61	M	15	5	6
MICH62	F	15	4	5
RAND01	M	11	4	5
RAND02	F	11	4	5
SCHI11	M	12	3	4
SCHI12	F	12	3	4
SEGE01	M	9	4	7
SEGE02	F	9	4	7
SHAY01	M	47	7*	8
SHAY02	F	47	7*	11
SPEA01	M	37	5	6
SPEA02	F	37	5	6
SPEA31	M	42	6*	7
SPEA32	F	42	8*	9
SPEA33	M	42	7*	8
SPEA34	F	42	6*	8
SUNG04	M	17	7	11
SUNG05	F	17	7	11

Table 17.2 (*cont.*)

Dataset	Male (M) or female (F)	No. of variables	No. of factors[a]	
			m	*m'*
THOM11	M	11	2	3
THOM12	F	11	2	3
VERS01	M	12	4*	6
VERS02	F	12	4*	6
VERY01	M	30	5	6
VERY02	F	30	5	6

*Number of first-order factors determined by original author(s) of study.

[a]m = number of first-order factors extracted; m' = number of hierarchical factors.

groups. Even if the same numbers of factors were yielded by the datasets in a pair, the factors could be quite different.

In general, there was excellent cross-identification of factors across male and female datasets, suggesting no appreciable differences in factor structure. Of considerable interest was the fact that higher-order factors, when present, almost always had congruence coefficients across sex groups ranging in the high .80s or .90s. Corresponding first-order factors generally had congruence coefficients in the .70s and up. I comment only on the datasets for which cross-identification of factors was in some cases poor. Except where noted, the first dataset in a pair was for males.

> Datasets BERE01 (females), BERE02 (males): Congruence was .986 for the two second-order factors, but was poor for most first-order factors, being only .589 for corresponding FI factors, .669 for FE, .607 for FF, .641 for another FF factor, .568 for FW, and .458 for two factors originally interpreted as FA and FF, respectively. Identification and interpretation of factors in these datasets had been difficult in any case, but it appears that boys and girls had somewhat different factor structures for variables in the domain of idea production. Note, however, that my analysis was based on factor matrices and numbers of factors specified by the original investigator, correlation matrices not being available. If it had been possible to analyze correlation matrices, congruence coefficients might have been more acceptable.
> Datasets CURE11 and CURE12: My analyses were limited by the fact that they were based on 8-factor solutions specified by the original investigator. Dataset CURE11 (males) yielded only one higher-order factor, with a congruence coefficient of .927 with a corresponding factor in dataset CURE12, which had an additional higher-order factor. Congruence coefficients were regarded as acceptable for the following factors: .875 (Verbal Information), .883 (Visualization), .663 (Numerical Facility), .935 (Perceptual Speed), .703 (Clerical or Spelling factors), and .745 (Finger Dexterity). Congruence was, inexplicably,

only .206 for corresponding factors in the memory domain. A Mechanical Knowledge factor for males had no clear counterpart in the female matrix, possibly because of inadequate variance for this factor among females. It is difficult to explain why a Mathematical Knowledge factor for the females had no clear counterpart in the male matrix, except possibly the fact that mathematical knowledge variables were generally loaded on the Verbal Information factor for males but not for females. Mathematical Knowledge is thus possibly a more specialized ability for females.

Datasets GARR11–16: Odd-numbered datasets are for males, even-numbered for females, over ages 9, 12, and 15. Congruence was generally good for the single second-order factor (except, inexplicably, for males at age 15). Congruence was only moderate across sex and age groups for the first-order factors; no pattern of interest emerged.

Datasets GUIL56, GUIL57: In my analyses of correlation matrices, two second-order factors emerged for both males and females, with congruence coefficients of .886 for factor 2R and .872 for factor 2H. For males but not for females, these factors were correlated sufficiently to yield a third-order general factor, having congruence coefficients of .971 and .924 respectively for factors 2R and 2H for females. For readily interpretable first-order factors, the male–female congruence coefficients were: .820 (FW), .821 (V), .803 (FI), .910 (FX), and .760 (FF). Coefficients were lower for other factors, but this is possibly because they were not well defined in the original study.

Datasets HARR51, HARR52: Factors 2G, V, I, MM, SR, FW, and P had acceptable congruence coefficients ranging from .646 to .991. A Reasoning factor identified for the females was not readily identifiable with a male factor, and the structure of spatial ability factors was somewhat different across sex groups.

Datasets HARR53, HARR54: All five first-order factors for males were cross-identifable with female factors (congruence coefficients ranging from .761 to .879), but an additional factor (factor 4, Classification) for females was difficult to cross-identify with male factors.

Datasets MCGU01, MCGU02: Congruence was excellent for factors 2G, V, RG, and FI. However, factors CS and P for males seemed to correspond to a single P factor for females.

Datasets MICH61, MICH62: In this study of spatial ability factors, congruence was excellent for factors 2G, V, and N. Congruence was only .670 for factor P. The VZ factor found for females seemed to split into factors VZ and SR for males. Whether this result is of any great significance would have to be explored in further investigation, probably with more precise control of speed and level aspects of spatial ability tests.

Datasets SEGE01, SEGE02: In both male and female samples, a single third-order factor, two second-order factors, and four first-order factors were obtained. All congruence coefficients were at least .959 except for the second-order speed factor, where congruence was −.234. For males, the only possibly significant loadings on this factor were for two spatial relations tests; for females, they were chiefly for verbal, clerical, and computation tasks. I cannot offer any interpretation for this finding, if indeed it is significant.

Datasets SHAY01, SHAY02: The major difference between the male and female analyses, both based on factor rather than correlation matrices such that I could not determine the true number of first-order factors, was that the analysis for females showed three second-order factors and a third-order factor, while the analysis for males showed only a single second-order factor. Congruence was generally excellent for all first-order factors. One can only say that for females, the first-order factors tended to group themselves (be specifically intercorrelated) more than was the case for males.

Datasets SPEA01, SPEA02: Congruence coefficients were at least .813 for factors 1–4 (2G, LS, I, and MS), but were only .459 for factors interpreted as Reading Comprehension and .541 for factors interpreted as Associative Memory.

Datasets SPEA31, SPEA32: A low congruence coefficient was again found for factors interpreted as Reading Compehension, suggesting different patterns of reading abilities for boys and girls. Mismatches of factors were even more drastic for datasets SPEA33 and SPEA34, which were for students in Australian urban lower-class areas.

Datasets VERY01, VERY02: Factors showed close correspondences except that a factor interpreted as Mathematical Knowledge (KM) in the male matrix did not appear for females; for females, separate RG and RQ factors appeared. The male KM factor showed a congruence coefficient of −.184 with the female RQ factor.

In summary, there were few cases in which factor structures were appreciably different for males and females. Differences occurred, if at all, chiefly with respect to reading, mathematical, reasoning, and spatial skills – domains in which male–female mean and variance differences have historically been found. It should be remembered that many of our datasets were assembled many decades ago. Whether similar differences in factor structures would be found for datasets assembled contemporarily is a question that could be answered only with new empirical studies.

DO FACTOR STRUCTURES DIFFER ACROSS CULTURAL, ETHNIC, OR RACIAL GROUPS?

The datasets were gathered in a number of different countries. There were only two instances in which similar test batteries were administered to samples in different countries – datasets VERN61 (in the U.S.) and VERN62 (in Britain), and datasets GUIL15 (in the U.S.) and FULG31 (in Yugoslavia). In both instances the same factors manifested themselves. Apart from these cases, I have not attempted to make an analysis of whether there are systematic differences across countries in factor identifications or structures. Because of the diversity of the samples and test batteries, it would be difficult to make such an analysis. I have the impression, however, that nothing would be gained in this way. The same factors of cognitive ability can be observed or at least sampled in all countries for which we have data.

The datasets are not sufficiently diverse with respect to ethnic or racial differences to support any definitive statement about differences in factor structures across these groups. In the few instances in which the same or similar test batteries were administered to different racial or ethnic groups (datasets NAGL01, for blacks, and NAGL02, for whites; datasets VERS01 and VERS02 for white males and females and VERS03 for black males, all in South Africa; datasets SUNG01 for blacks, SUNG02 for Hispanics, and SUNG03 for whites) the same or highly similar factor structures were observed. As in the case of differences across countries, it is my impression that no significant differences would be found for other datasets that might seek to contrast racial or ethnic groups. This is, in fact, essentially the conclusion that has been reached by investigators concerned with cross-cultural studies of abilities (e.g., Irvine, 1969, 1979, 1981).

SUMMARY

1. From the literature, it is evident that there are substantial genetic influences not only on a general intellectual factor but also on a number of the major types of cognitive factors, possibly as distinguished in the stratum II factors postulated in the three-stratum theory. Further behavioral genetic research needs to take into account the delineation of the structure of cognitive abilities offered in the present survey, as well as the three-stratum theory, in developing further knowledge about genetic influences on cognitive abilities.

2. The literature of neuropsychology suggests that the factorial organization of cognitive abilities can be shown to have at least some important and meaningful correspondences with the organization of the brain and the central nervous system. Increasingly, significant correlations between psychometric variables and certain neuropsychological indicators are being found. In further neuropsychological research, it will undoubtedly be profitable to give systematic consideration to the types of cognitive ability dimensions that have been identified here.

3. Thus far there is only limited information about the long-term stability of particular cognitive abilities, apart from global intelligence. Presently available evidence suggests that most of the major types of cognitive ability are stable to a substantial extent, in the sense that individuals generally maintain their status relative to their age cohort with only minor deviations over long periods of time, from childhood to old age. There is some evidence, however, that abilities differ in their courses of maturational development and later decline in terms of absolute levels. Much more information on these matters is needed in order to attain better understanding of life-span developmental patterns. Furthermore, there is need for continued monitoring of average levels of different cognitive abilities for the population as a whole, in view of the fact that at least some abilities have shown striking secular increases in various populations.

4. No simple answer can be given to the question of whether cognitive abilities are malleable or improvable through specific types of experiences and interventions. Undoubtedly some abilities are more malleable than others. The evidence suggests that general intelligence and the major types of stratum II abilities may be relatively less malleable than more specific abilities at stratum I, but there is

as yet inadequate information as to the limits, if any, to which these abilities may be improved, or as to the effects of different types of environments, training, and intervention. The question of the improvability of abilities must be looked at from the standpoint of the generality of transfer effects.

5. Cognitive abilities, measured at particular points of time, are at least moderately predictive of subsequent school success and rates of learning of particular skills. Evidence suggests that the locus of this relation is primarily in the stratum III general intelligence factor, but abilities in lower strata can also be implicated. Further research, based on the three-stratum theory and analysis of abilities required in particular learning tasks, is needed to make our information on ability-learning relations more definitive and systematic.

6. Except possibly for the very early developmental period, there is little evidence to support the hypothesis that cognitive abilities become more and more differentiated with age, up to the period of adulthood and beyond. As far as presently available knowledge indicates, all the major types of cognitive ability are observable, differentiable, and measurable from early in the life-span, i.e., from the earliest school years, up to old age. To the extent that differentiation actually occurs, it centers in abilities having to do with different areas of learning and skill formation.

7. With reference to the major types of cognitive ability, there is little evidence that factorial structure differs in any systematic way across male and female groups, different cultures, racial groups, and the like. What differentiation occurs may be attributed to differences in schooling and other environmental experiences encountered by different sexes, or different cultural and racial groups.

18 *Implications and Recommendations*

*The key to understanding the IQ controversy lies in
the historical conflict between two strands in American
thought: the desire for increasingly efficient and
objective assessment, and the belief in human
equipotentiality.*
Mark Snyderman and Stanley Rothman (1986, p. 11)

Human beings, we have come to appreciate, are immensely diverse, not only in their physical characteristics, but even more in their behaviors, personalities, and capabilities. It is with a sense of wonderment that the scientist or even the ordinary person on the street contemplates this enormous diversity and hopes to make sense of it by reducing it to some set of cardinal ideas or principles.

In this book, I have focused on just one domain of human diversity – the domain of what may be called cognitive abilities. This domain alone, it appears, is far-flung and finely divided. For more than a century, since the days of those who first broached the possibility of studying individual differences in cognitive abilities – Francis Galton, James McKeen Cattell, Alfred Binet, William Stern, Charles Spearman, and others – psychologists have attempted to find ways of understanding the diversity of these abilities, first by developing procedures for objectively measuring them and then by formulating ways of classifying them and investigating their structure. Two principal instruments for doing these things have been (1) the mental test and (2) the statistical technique known as factor analysis. I have surveyed and reanalyzed the results of a significant sample of the many studies that have been conducted to investigate the structure of the abilities revealed by mental tests and other indicators. Despite many apparent contradictions and difficulties of interpretation, I believe that the portrait of cognitive abilities that has emerged, along with the three-stratum theory that I have outlined and supported, presents a reasonable, well-articulated, and clearly understandable account of diversity in human capabilities.

The picture is far from complete, however. Many factors remain inadequately specified, and many aspects of the three-stratum theory need to be tested and refined. My first concern in the present chapter is to state what implications my results and conclusions have for further research in the study of human cognitive abilities. A further concern is to indicate what significance my results have for present and future practices in the use of tests and other indicators of cognitive abilities. I also want to spell out in what ways my results and conclusions contain suggestions for increased public knowledge and understanding, and improved public policies, concerning the roles of cognitive abilities in a highly technological, culturally diverse society.

My remarks, therefore, are addressed to at least three audiences. First, they are addressed to research workers in many disciplines and specialties concerned with the development and validation of tests, and with the use of tests in a variety of studies of cognitive abilities, including, for example, factor analysis, educational and developmental psychology, experimental psychology, and general psychological theory. Secondly, they are addressed to practitioners employing cognitive ability tests in any one or more of a variety of contexts, including, for example, clinical psychology, and testing for selection, admission, and placement in education, government, the military, and private enterprise. Third, they are addressed to members of the general public who are concerned with policies on uses of cognitive ability tests in any of these contexts.

The chapter has three major sections. The first has to do with implications for research in cognitive abilities. The second addresses the issue of what abilities are measured by cognitive ability tests that are standardized and commercially available. The third addresses issues of broad public policy on uses of tests.

IMPLICATIONS FOR FURTHER RESEARCH IN COGNITIVE ABILITIES

I must emphasize at the start that the initial goal of further research in cognitive abilities should be, in the spirit of pure science, to determine what cognitive abilities exist and can be measured, irrespective of their "importance" or prospect of ultimate utility of validity in practical affairs (Carroll & Horn, 1981). In this regard, abilities are analogous to the elements in the periodic table: Some, like fluid intelligence, are obviously as important as carbon or oxygen; others are more like the rare earth elements whose importance has not always been appreciated or become apparent – their possible importance is unpredictable.

It must have been obvious to the reader of the previous chapters that there are numerous gaps in the literature of factor-analytic research available for constructing a systematic account of what cognitive abilities exist. In every domain of ability that I have considered, many questions remain concerning what factors of ability can be identified and distinguished, and how they can be interpreted. Even in the case of widely recognized factors such as V (Verbal Ability), I (Induction), RG (Sequential Reasoning), MA (Associative Memory), VZ (Visualization), and FI (Ideational Fluency), there are problems about exactly what ranges of behaviors are covered by the factor, and thus how the factor can be related to theories of cognitive behavior. An almost universal problem has to do with whether there are separate speed and level aspects of a factor, and if so, what relationships exist between speed and level (see Chapter 11). Another frequent problem concerns the status of factors in the three-stratum hierarchy, particularly at the second stratum, and the relationships among factors at different levels of the hierarchy (see Chapter 15). It would be unnecessarily redundant to list all these questions here; they are mentioned and usually extensively discussed in the relevant chapters. The important point is that despite its sixty- or seventy-year history, factor-analytic research still has much to do, partly to clarify and expand results already attained, but also to explore new domains of inquiry.

Elsewhere (Carroll, 1989) I have argued that factor-analytic research is a poor exemplar of a cumulative research enterprise. Except perhaps in the "golden age" of the 1940s and early 1950s, there has been continued failure to build upon the results of previous research, and to answer questions and test hypotheses generated by studies as they are completed. Early Thurstonian results were accepted uncritically and used as the basis for repetitive, largely uninformative studies year after year, up to the present. The same rather inadequately designed tests were used in study after study, investigators often failing to take the opportunity to redesign tests to permit checking of interesting hypotheses concerning the nature of the factors that were measured. It is my hope that the publication of the present volume will serve the purpose of informing researchers as to what results have been firmly established, and at the same time alerting them to the many problems that still remain to be resolved.

Problems of test construction. A major implication of my survey is that many of the tests frequently used in factor-analytic research are in need of revision – sometimes, radical revision. They need to be redesigned with two major purposes in mind: (1) to improve the construct validity of the testing materials and the procedures of administration, by considering exactly what aspects of cognitive performance are tapped by the tests, and (2) to better appraise and differentiate the speed and level aspects of ability. Presently available methods of test construction and analysis, derived chiefly from item response theory (Hambleton, 1983; Lord, 1980), could make a substantial contribution to this effort, but also logical analysis of test tasks is needed from the standpoint of cognitive psychology. Tasks should be designed so that difficulty is systematically related to observable features of the tasks (Carroll, Meade, & Johnson, 1991; Embretson, 1985). Tests should be constructed so that item responses in typical samples conform as closely as possible to the person characteristic functions expected on the basis of the theory of ability outlined in Chapter 1 (see also Carroll, 1990). This would help to insure that the tests are as internally unidimensional as possible. At the same time, psychometric research may be necessary to permit taking account of the fact that from a factor-analytic standpoint, many tests are inevitably multidimensional, in the sense that their scores simultaneously measure factors at different levels of the three-stratum hierarchy. Whether this represents a fundamental contradiction between factor-analytic and item-response theory approaches is not clear at the present time. If there is indeed a contradiction, it could possibly be resolved by research into the properties of factor scores derived from hierarchical factor matrices – research that could determine how best to produce "factorially pure" (unidimensional) scores from measures that are found fundamentally multidimensional. Specifically, it would be a goal of research to show how best to produce scores for first-, second-, and third-stratum factors freed of the effects from the other strata.

To facilitate developmental studies – that is, studies of the development of abilities over age, groups of vertically, equated tests need to be constructed in order to provide a common scale of ability, for given factors, over a wide range of ages. Such tests could be used in factor-analytic studies investigating the question of the differentiation of abilities. They would also provide comparable scales whereby the growth of abilities could be investigated and more accurately calibrated.

The ideal in test construction would be approached if it were possible to develop a standardized series of tests, with alternate forms, for each of the known factors of cognitive ability, that would be maximally construct-valid and appropriate for a wide range of ages, ability levels, and samples such that the scores would have comparable meanings over these ages, ability levels, and samples. At the same time the scores would have high reliabilities and low standard errors of measurement. In the course of research towards this ideal, one would seek to find out whether the constructs measured by tests could in fact be made comparable over different ages, ability levels, and samples, or whether it would be necessary to formulate and test different constructs over different ages, ability levels, and types of samples.

Problems of battery design. There is need for improved design of batteries of measures for factor-analytic studies. At many points in the present survey, it has been noted that unresolved questions have arisen because of deficiencies in battery design. Studies have often failed to include sufficient numbers of univocal measures of given factors. Ideally, at least three or four measures of a given factor should be included, but not so many as to produce unnecessary redundancy or require excessive testing time. Results of the present survey should be helpful in guiding the selection of measures to meet this requirement. In the past, it has been difficult to meet this requirement because there has been inadequate knowledge concerning what factors exist and what factors a given test or variable is likely to measure.

The need for cross-sectional and longitudinal factor-analytic studies. As has been pointed out in Chapter 17, there are few factor-analytic datasets that permit examination of the growth and differentiation of abilities across chronological or mental ages. This circumstance is partly attributable to the difficult and expensive logistics of conducting such studies; it is also due in part to the lack of tests that are scaled in such a way to provide comparable measures of factors across a range of ages – particularly those of childhood and adolescence. A more complete understanding of the growth and development of cognitive abilities would, however, be very desirable and would justify concerted effort and expense in conducting studies that are properly designed to yield such understanding.

The organization of factor-analytic research. Because of its difficulty, cost, and complexity, factor-analytic research is inevitably an enterprise that must be conducted in piecemeal fashion, usually by focusing on one or two domains or subdomains at a time, but with appropriate "marker" or reference tests to insure that the interpretation of the results in a given domain of ability can be done with reference to selected abilities in other domains. The problem arises chiefly because it is difficult to secure adequate testing time from examinee samples of adequate size (e.g., with N's of 100 or more). Even marker tests take up valuable testing time, and there must be sufficient marker tests (preferably, three or more) for each factor that is included in a battery just for the purpose of differentiating factors in a target domain from those of other domains. The marker tests provided in the ETS Kit of Factor Reference Tests (Ekstrom et al., 1976) must be used with caution, partly because they do not adequately permit differentiation between speed and level aspects of abilities, but also because they are not, in some cases, univocal tests of the factors they are intended to represent. It is possible, however, to use the ETS Kit tests with adequate control of speed and level aspects by appropriate procedures of test administration. Computerized versions of at least some of the ETS Kit tests could be constructed, and in fact have been constructed in some research laboratories.

In contrast to studies that focus on a particular domain or subdomain of abilities, there is need for studies to clarify the identification of higher-stratum abilities and their relations with first-stratum abilities. It should now be more readily possible to construct batteries in which the variables are selected to directly define second-stratum abilities by representing different first-stratum abilities. The tests of first-stratum abilities would be selected in such a way as to minimize the possibility that first-stratum factors would contribute to the rank of the matrix. This kind of design – which may be called *higher-stratum design* – is illustrated in datasets HORN01 and HORN31, but those datasets were constructed at a time when the structure of the relevant abilities was not as well known as it is now.

Confirmatory factor-analytic studies. This survey has used almost exclusively exploratory factor-analytic techniques, for various reasons stated in Chapter 3. I would expect in general, however, that our findings could be confirmed by applying confirmatory techniques (e.g., LISREL or EQS analyses[1]) to the datasets, to the extent that it is feasible to use such techniques with datasets having large numbers of variables. The hierarchical matrices computed in our survey would provide guides to the structures to be initially tested in structural equation models. Indeed, in my view the models derived from exploratory results should be more reliable guides than hypotheses derived on other bases. (See my discussion,

Chapter 16, of a dataset analyzed with both exploratory and confirmatory techniques.)

Validity Studies

This survey of cognitive abilities has paid very little attention to the importance, validity, or ultimate usefulness of the ability factors that have been identified, for several reasons: (1) as stated above, my purpose was mainly to identify, catalog, and interpret the known abilities, without regard for their importance or validity; (2) attention to validity studies would have taken us into a vast and uncertain literature, thus constituting a distraction from our main purpose; and (3) like tests, factors do not intrinsically and for themselves have validity; they could be said to have validity only with respect to given purposes or uses. A factor that might be "valid" with respect to a given use or criterion might have no validity whatsoever for another use or criterion.

Note, however, that it is assumed that if a *factor* has validity for a given purpose, all tests or measurements of that factor can be assumed to have validity for that purpose, to the extent that they have high or significant loadings on the factor. It would usually be profitable to test this assumption in validity studies, for example, by noting whether multiple tests of a factor have approximately equal validity coefficients against the criterion, and also whether only one of these tests would carry the main burden of prediction when the criterion is regressed on sets of measurements loaded with a given factor. Alternatively, is a structural model in which a path from a latent variable to the criterion is evaluated, the latent variable underlying the set of measurements would carry the burden of prediction.

Validity of a test against a criterion is assumed to be dependent on whether the same elements of ability are present or required in both the test and the criterion. Judgment of whether this condition may be true depends on careful task analysis of both the test and the criterion. For example, the potential validity of a spatial ability test against criterion performance in, say, flying an airplane would depend upon whether it could be shown that the visualization behavior required by the test would also be required, at least under certain circumstances, in flying an airplane.

Although it has been impossible here to survey information on the validities of cognitive ability tests in predicting or assessing various aspects of real-life behavior such as school success and occupational success, the reader may be assured that cognitive abilities and their tests do indeed have very substantial relevance for these real-life behaviors, contrary to the widespread impression that was apparently created by an essay published by David McClelland (1973). As summarized by Barrett and Depinet (1991), McClelland's claims were that grades in school do not predict occupational success or other important life outcomes, that intelligence and aptitude tests do not predict occupational success, that tests and academic performance predict job performance (if at all) only because of an underlying relationship with social status, that tests are unfair to minorities, and that "competencies" would be better able to predict important behaviors than would more traditional tests. Barrett and Depinet found only very limited support in the research literature for these claims; indeed, most of the research findings surveyed tended to support quite their opposite.

Developmental Studies

On the assumption of the availability of factor measures that are adequately comparable across ages, there is need for cross-sectional, or even better, longitudinal studies to investigate the "normal" development of factors over age, that is, development that takes place in the course of normal maturation without any special intervention that is designed to improve abilities. As I noted in Chapter 17, I deemed it difficult or perhaps impossible to construct adequate developmental information from the published results of available factor-analytic studies. As an example of the kind of developmental information that might be developed, I reproduced (Figure 17.1) Thurstone's (1955) fitted growth curves for seven "primary mental abilities," but these growth curves are based on questionable assumptions and data. (For one thing, Thurstone's primary mental ability scores are substantially influenced by speed factors.) Better information is needed, for more factors and for better-measured factors, partly to provide baselines for evaluating the results of studies of special interventions designed to improve abilities, as discussed below.

Cognitive-Process Studies

Here I call attention to the need for studies concerning the cognitive processes underlying at least a substantial number of the cognitive ability factors that have been identified. Such studies would presumably lead to the better understanding of what is measured by each of these factors. One example of research of this type is that of Ippel (1986) using what he calls *component-testing*; Ippel's work focused on three types of tasks – embedded figures tasks (as measuring factor CF, Flexibility of Closure), the block design task (as measuring factor VZ, Visualization), and the mental rotation task (as measuring factor SR, Spatial Relations). Many other examples could be given from recent literature.

Modifiability Studies

As discussed in Chapter 17, there is a surprising paucity of information on the extent to which abilities associated with specific cognitive factors can be improved or enhanced by specially designed training programs. It would, of course, require a major effort to remedy this lack, especially if the effort is to be cast over the numerous domains of cognitive ability that have been covered here. Basically, the question to be answered for each ability (at any given stratum) can be framed somewhat as follows: For an individual whose ability is currently measured at level X, at what rate Y over time can this ability be increased by treatment T, and is there an asymptotic level Z beyond which the ability cannot be increased? In this statement, the rate Y may be complex, as where the learning might be found to be initially fast but ultimately much slower, or to follow an S-shaped curve. The treatment T might be one of only a number of possible treatments, the problem being one of selecting the optimally effective treatment. The statement allows for different learning rates as a function of initial ability level, but these could possibly also be a function of status on other abilities. For example, it might be that learning rate could depend not only on level X of the ability in question, but also on status on the third-statum g factor. It becomes apparent that studies of the trainability or malleability of ability factors could become very difficult and complex – probably one reason that so few of them have been attempted. Nevertheless, it would be highly valuable, from the standpoint of framing realistic educational policies, to have more information on what possibilities there are in the training of abilities. Sternberg (1983) and Halford (1989) have outlined principles for conducting studies to yield this kind of information; present knowledge and technology should make such studies much more feasible than they have previously been.

Miscellaneous Methodological Matters

One can agree with several points made by Detterman (1989) in discussing the future of intelligence research. He trusts or hopes that this research will employ larger and more adequate samples of subjects, that greater attention will be paid to achieving high reliability of tests, and that research will be more theoretically based than previously.

AVAILABLE MEASURES OF COGNITIVE ABILITY FACTORS

During its long history, factor-analytic research has been the basis for the construction and development of a number of cognitive ability tests and test batteries that are available either commercially or from special sources. The results of the present survey of cognitive ability factors make it possible to comment on the adequacy of these tests and batteries for measuring the factors that have been identified in the survey.

Following is a list of some of these tests and batteries, arranged in chronological order of their first publication, with information about their subtests, their likely factor composition, and datasets in our survey in which they appear as variables in factor-analytic batteries. Most of these tests are listed in a publication of the

Buros Institute of Mental Measurements, *Tests in Print III: An Index to Tests, Test Reviews, and the Literature on Specific Tests* (*TIP III*) (Mitchell, 1983), a publication that gives extensive information on publishers, subtest scores, reviews in previous publications of the Buros Institute or its predecessor (Buros' own Gryphon Press), and bibliographical references. (*TIP III* is the latest of this series available at this writing, but I am informed that a fourth edition is planned for publication in 1992.) As a matter of convenience and interest I give the index number of each test in *TIP III* and the total number of bibliographical references given. (The references themselves appear either in *TIP III* or in previous publications of the Buros Institute or its predecessor.)

> *Progressive Matrices* (Raven, 1938–1965). (*TIP III*: 1914; 899 references. See also Court, 1977, for a "researcher's bibliography.") The construction of this test, in Great Britain, was inspired by Spearman's (1927) work; it was intended as a measure of Spearman's g. Three forms differing somewhat in difficulty are available: *Standard Progressive Matrices* (for ages 6 and over); *Coloured Progressive Matrices* (for ages 5–11 and mental patients and senescents); and *Advanced Progressive Matrices* (ages 11 and over, of above-average intellectual ability). One or more variables from these (or closely similar) tests appear in the following datasets: ADKI03, AFTA01, ARNO01, BACH21, BARR00, BOLT11, CARL40, CARL41, CLAU01–04, CORN01, CRAW01, CUMM01, CURE11, CURE12, GUST11, HUGH01, JARM31, JENS41, LUNZ11, MASN01, RIMO11, ROYC11, SCHU01, SNOW11, SNOW12, SNOW20, SNOW21, SPEA01–02, SPEA31–34, STAN61, STOR01A, VERN01, VERN11, and WALL51–52. Information on the factorial composition of the variables is somewhat varied, depending on the design of the relevant battery. For example, in datasets SCHU01, STAN61, and WALL51–52 the communality for the Progressive Matrix variable was low, suggesting that there were not enough variables in the battery to define the factor or factors it measured. Dataset CARL40 was a factor analysis of the *items* of the Coloured Progressive Matrix test, suggesting that four separate factors, plus a general factor, are measured by this test. In most other cases, the one or more Progressive Matrix variables had substantial loadings on a higher-order general factor, plus a first-order factor generally interpreted as I (Induction). In some datasets, e.g., CURE11, CURE12, JARM31, SNOW11, and VERN01, the first-order factor on which it was loaded tended also to have spatial ability variables, suggesting that the Progressive Matrix test may have a spatial ability component. In dataset GUST11A, however, the matrix test variables (odd and even scores on the test) had loadings only on a first-order factor of their own, interpreted as "cognition of figural relations," with no significant loadings either on I (Induction) or VZ (Visualization). Our evidence suggests that the Progressive Matrix test is a good measure of g and of the second-stratum factor 2F, but the degree to which this test measures first-order factors I and VZ is not clear. On the basis of an extensive theoretical and empirical analysis of this test, Carpenter, Just, and Shell (1990) conclude that "the processes that distinguish among individuals are primarily the ability to *induce* [emphasis added] abstract relations and the ability to dynamically manage a large set of problem-solving goals in working memory" (p. 404). In use of the test for factorial studies, I would recommend that there

be control of the speed and level aspects of performance, i.e., by obtaining separate scores for level and rate of performance.

Culture Fair Intelligence Test (Cattell & Cattell, 1933–1973). (*TIP III*: 643; 177 references.) This test represents an attempt by its authors to measure fluid intelligence as free as possible of cultural effects. It has four subtests: Series, Classifications, Matrices, and Conditions, all of which appear in dataset CATT01A, where it appears that they measure an induction (I) factor at the first order and a general intelligence factor (2G) at the second order.

SRA Primary Mental Abilities (Thurstone and Thurstone, 1938–65). (*TIP III*: 2269; 483 references.) Early editions, no longer in print, were *Tests for Primary Mental Abilities, Experimental Edition, 1938* and *Chicago Tests of Primary Mental Abilities*, with tests for several age levels. The 1962 edition has tests for five levels: Grades K–1: verbal meaning, perceptual speed, number facility, spatial relations; Grades 2–4: subtests as for grades K–1; Grades 4–6: subtests as for grades K–1 plus reasoning; Grades 6–9: subtests: verbal meaning, number facility, reasoning, spatial relations; Grades 9–12: subtests: as for grades 6–9. One or more variables from these tests appear in our datasets ARNO01, BARR00, BECH01, CATT01A, GOOD01, GOOD11, SING21, and STAK01, in addition to Thurstone's studies from which the tests were developed. Because the tests are all given with time-limits, they tend to be correlated beyond what can be expected from the loadings of level scores on a higher-order factor. Factorially, they provide only gross and not completely adequate measures of their intended factors: V, P, N, VZ, and RG. That is, the measures of V tend to measure VL (lexical knowledge) more than comprehension of printed language, the measures of reasoning are a combination of measures of I, RG, and RQ, and the measures of spatial abilities do not provide differentiation between factors VZ and SR.

USES General Aptitude Test Battery (GATB) (United States Employment Service, 1946–82). (*TIP III*: 2537; 566 references.) Form B-1002 of the GATB has twelve separately-timed tests and yields nine scores: Intelligence, Verbal, Numerical, Spatial, Form Perception, Clerical Perception, Motor Coordination, Finger Dexterity, and Manual Dexterity. Scores from this or other forms of the GATB appear in datasets CURE11, CURE12, and SEGE01–02, and cover factors I (Induction), RG (Serial Reasoning), RQ (Quantitative Reasoning), VZ (Visualization), SR (Spatial Relations), and P (Perceptual Speed), in addition to factors in the psychomotor domain. The total score on the cognitive tests would tend to measure a general factor. Hartigan and Wigdor (1989) give a detailed description of the battery and comment on its major shortcomings as the central element in an employment referral system, namely, the highly speeded nature of the test and the paucity of available test forms.

Guilford–Zimmerman Aptitude Survey (Guilford & Zimmerman, 1947–56). (*TIP III*: 1044; 64 references.) This battery, designed for grades 9–16 and adults, has seven subtests: Verbal Comprehension, General Reasoning, Numerical Operations, Perceptual Speed, Spatial Orientation, Spatial Visualization, and Mechanical Knowledge. One or more variables from these subtests appear in our datasets ALLI02, EGAN01, and GUIL11. The scores fail to differentiate speed and level aspects of the factors they are intended to cover.

Differential Aptitude Tests (Forms V and W) (Bennett, Seashore, & Wesman, 1947–82). (*TIP III*: 732; 414 references.) Designed for grades 8–12 and adults, this has eight subtests: Verbal Reasoning, Numerical Ability, Abstract

Reasoning, Clerical Speed and Accuracy, Mechanical Reasoning, Space Relations, Spelling, and Language Usage. All these subtests have time-limits. One or more variables from these subtests appear in our datasets CURE11, CURE12, FRUC21, MEEK01, OSUL01, PETE11, and PETE12.

Flanagan Aptitude Classification Tests (Flanagan, 1951–60). (*TIP III*: 899; 20 references.) The "16-test edition," designed for grades 10–12 and adults, has the following subtests: Inspection, Coding, Memory, Precision, Assembly, Scales, Coordination, Judgment and Comprehension, Arithmetic, Patterns, Components, Tables, Mechanics, Expression, Reasoning, and Ingenuity. A "19-test edition" for grades 9–12 has these same subtests plus Vocabulary, Planning, and Alertness. Variables from these subtests appear in our datasets CURE11 and CURE12.

ETS Kit of Factor Referenced Cognitive Tests. (*TIP III*: 1257; 181 references.) Note that *TIP III* lists only the 1963 edition of this kit (French, Ekstrom, & Price, 1963) but mentions the 1954 edition (French, 1954). It fails to list the 1976 edition (Ekstrom, French, & Harman, 1976), which has been frequently cited in previous chapters of the present volume. These kits have been issued for research purposes only, generally for samples at grades 9 and up, including adults. Their factor content has varied somewhat over the various editions; see Table 3.1 for a concordance of these kits. Variables from these ETS kits occur frequently in our datasets – so frequently that it is not practical to list the relevant datasets here. A large number of variables from the 1976 edition were analyzed by Wothke, Bock, Curran, Fairbank, Augustin, Gillet, and Guerrero (1991) in dataset WOTH01; for various technical reasons, my reanalysis disclosed only 11 first-order factors in the Kit, as opposed to the 23 factors that the tests in the 1976 version were intended to measure. (Wothke et al. recovered only six factors in the dataset.) According to the analyses made in the current survey, however, nearly all the factors that the Kit purports to measure are identifiable and distinguishable if they are adequately defined in the variables of a factor-analytic battery. One factor that I have not been able to identify is factor IP, Integrative Processes; its tests are probably measures in the reasoning domain. Also, the status of the Verbal Closure factor is questionable. Major problems with the use of tests from the ETS Kits arise because (1) they are relatively short and thus less reliable than longer tests would be, (2) they are normally administered with time-limits, so that scores are unknown combinations of speed and level dimensions, and (3) the subtests assigned to each of the factors are not necessarily all tests of the same first-order factor. Note that the Kit purports to measure only first-order factors. Presumably, higher-order factors would arise from the correlations of first-order factors measured by the Kit; my reanalysis of dataset WOTH01 disclosed one third-order factor and four second-order factors.

Armed Services Vocational Aptitude Battery (ASVAB) (United States Department of Defense, 1967–82). (*TIP III*: 202; 13 references.) This group-administered battery (at least in a form available in 1982) has 12 subtests: General Information, Numerical Operations, Attention to Detail, Word Knowledge, Arithmetic Reasoning, Space Perception, Mathematics Knowledge, Electronics Information, Mechanical Comprehension, General Science, Shop Information, and Automotive Information. For more recent information, see Foley and Rucker (1989), who indicate that certain of the above subtests (Attention to Detail and Space Perception) have been dropped, while others have been added or combined. Sets of variables from the ASVAB appear in several of our datasets: FAIR01–02, FEDE02, VERN21, VAND61, and WOTH01. My reanalyses indicate that one or more subtests of the ASVAB measure the following factors: V (Verbal Ability), RQ (Quantitative Reasoning), N (Numerical Facility), MK (Mechanical Knowledge, plus special varieties of technical information), KM (Knowledge of Mathematics), P (Perceptual Speed), and K0 (General Information, including scientific information). Most of the tests are designated as power tests (measuring level of ability); only Numerical Operations and a Coding Speed test are speeded. Cronbach (1979) has commented critically on various characteristics of the battery from the standpoint of its use in career guidance.

Comprehensive Ability Battery (CAB) (Hakstian & Cattell, 1975–77). (*TIP III*: 547; 8 references.) These group tests are designed for ages 15 and over, and yield 20 scores, each for a presumably separate factor: Verbal Ability, Numerical Ability, Spatial Ability, Speed of Closure, Perceptual Speed and Accuracy, Inductive Reasoning, Flexibility of Closure, Rote Memory, Mechanical Ability, Memory Span, Meaningful Memory, Spelling, Auditory Ability, Esthetic Judgment, Spontaneous Flexibility, Ideational Fluency, Word Fluency, Originality, Aiming, and Representational Drawing. Scores from tests of these factors appear in dataset HAKS01; a higher-stratum analysis of twenty factor scores appears in dataset HAKS21.

Structure of Intellect Learning Abilities Test (Meeker & Meeker, 1975–81). (*TIP III*: 2320; 2 references.) There are eight forms of this test, for different age levels and/or special testing purposes. The basic form, for grades 2–12, yields 26 scores in five test areas: Comprehension, Memory, Evaluation, Convergent Production, and Divergent Production, i.e., the operation facets of Guilford's (1967) Structure-of-Intellect (SOI) model. Generally, the scores in each area represent different combinations of the "content" and "product" factors of the SOI model. These particular tests or subtests do not appear in any of my datasets, but representative subtests from the Structure-of-Intellect model appear in numerous datasets analyzed in this survey. In general, my analyses make it doubtful that the tests of this battery measure as many as 26 distinguishable factors.

British Ability Scales (Elliott, Murray, & Pearson, 1977–79). (*TIP III*: 322; no references.) The tests referred to in *TIP III* were first published in 1979, but were revised for publication in 1983 (Elliott, 1983). The 1983 battery contains 23 individually administered tests yielding 24 scores (the Block Design test yielding both a level and a power score). Some of the tests are meant to be administered only at certain age levels. The 23 tests are as follows: Speed of Information Processing, Matrices, Formal Operational Thinking, Similarities, Social Reasoning, Block Design, Rotation of Letter-Like Forms, Visualization of Cubes, Copying, Matching Letter-Like Forms, Verbal–Tactile Matching, Recall of Designs, Immediate Visual Recall, Delayed Visual Recall, Recall of Digits, Visual Recognition, Naming Vocabulary, Word Reading, Verbal Comprehension, Word Definitions, Verbal Fluency, Basic Arithmetic, and Early Number Skills. It is notable that nearly all of these tests were constructed on the basis of the Rasch (1960) model of item response; also, factor-analytic research had a strong influence on the selection of scales. Because the tests are individually administered, with rules of discontinuation, most tests are measures of level of ability rather than speed; several scales, however, are expressly constructed to yield measures of speed. Factor analyses of test intercorrelations show that the British Ability Scales measure chiefly three factors: Verbal Ability, Visual Perception, and Memory (Recall), in addition to a Speed of Mental Processing factor.

Woodcock–Johnson Psycho-Educational Battery (Woodcock and Johnson, 1977–78). (*TIP III*: 2639; 3 references.) This individually administered battery, with scales that can be applied over ages 3 to 80, has 27 subtests divided into 3 parts: Part I (cognitive ability), 12 scores: Picture Vocabulary, Spatial Relationships, Memory for Sentences, Visual–Auditory Learning, Blending, Quantitative Concepts, Visual Matching, Antonyms–Synonyms, Analysis–Synthesis, Numbers Reversed, Concept Formation, Analogies; Part II (achievement), 10 scores: Letter–Word Identification, Word Attack, Passage Comprehension, Calculation, Applied Problems, Dictation, Proofing, Science, Social Studies, Humanities; Part III (interest level): 5 scores: Reading Interest, Mathematics Interest, Language Interest, Physical Interest, and Social Interest. Scores from Parts I and II appear as variables in our datasets WOOD13, WOOD15, WOOD17, and WOOD18; the hierarchical factor matrices in Appendix B may be consulted for information on factorial content. The battery has now been revised (Woodcock & Johnson, 1989), with an expanded set of scales; Woodcock (1990) discusses an eight-factor model derived from Gf-Gc theory as the theoretical basis for the battery, and compares its factorial content with that of several other cognitive batteries. The eight factors correspond to second-stratum abilities; as designated by Woodcock, they are as follows: Gf (Fluid Reasoning), Gc (Comprehension–Knowledge), Gv (Visual Processing), Ga (Auditory Processing), Gs (Processing Speed), Gsm (Short-Term Memory), Glr (Long-Term Retrieval), and Gq (Quantitative Ability). Note, however, that Woodcock's Glr ability is not the same as what I have designated Gr or 2R (General retrieval or idea-production ability); rather, it is essentially intermediate-term learning and memory ability. The WJ-R battery does not contain any tests of Gr or idea-production ability.

Ball Aptitude Battery (Sung, Dawis, & Dohm, 1981). This battery is described in a brochure issued by the Ball Foundation, the publisher, as "a multiple-ability test battery designed to measure aptitudes related to successful work behavior in both apprentice training positions and job positions." It contains fourteen tests, some of which are paper-and-pencil tests; others are individually administered performance tests. The separately scored tests are: Clerical, Idea Fluency, Tonal Memory, Pitch Discrimination, Inductive Reasoning, Word Association, Writing Speed, Paper Folding, Vocabulary, Ideaphoria, Finger Dexterity, Grip, Shape Assembly, and Analytical Reasoning. These variables appear in our datasets SUNG01–05.

Multidimensional Aptitude Battery (MAB) (Jackson, 1984). This group-administered battery, appropriate for high school and college students and adults, has the following subtests: (1) Information, (2) Arithmetic, (3) Comprehension, (4) Vocabulary, (5) Similarities, (6) Digit Symbol, (7) Picture Completion, (8) Spatial, (9) Picture Arrangement, and (10) Object Assembly. These subtests closely parallel those present in the Wechsler Adult Intelligence Scale-Revised (*TIP III*: 2598), and thus may be expected to measure verbal and performance aspects of intelligence, or roughly the second-stratum factors 2C and 2V. The MAB variables appear in dataset KRAN01A, where it is found that variables 1, 3, 4, 5, and 7 measure principally factor 2C and variables 2, 6, 8, 9, and 10 measure factor 2V; all variables have moderate loadings on a higher-order factor interpreted as approximately the same as *g*. (Probably because of restriction of range in the sample of college students, the loadings on the higher-order factor are only moderate.) Although this battery is advertised as multidimensional it covers only a small range of the domain of cognitive abilities.

The tests or batteries described above cover various ranges of ability factors, from the *g* factor presumably measured by the Progressive Matrices test to the fairly diverse sets of factors measured by the ETS Kits of Factor Referenced Cognitive Tests, the Woodcock–Johnson Psycho-Educational Battery, and the Ball Aptitude Test. All have been strongly influenced by factor-analytic research. Less influenced by such research have been various tests or batteries of tests developed primarily to measure general intelligence, or aspects thereof, often for clinical diagnosis of persons' strengths and weaknesses in cognitive functioning. Interpretation of scores of these tests and test batteries must nevertheless take factor-analytic research into account. The single scores or indices derived from such tests, such as MA (Mental Age) and IQ (Intelligence Quotient), are too readily interpreted without consideration of the differential patterns of scores from individual parts of the test. A listing of the major individually administered intelligence tests in common use follows, with comments on their factorial structure.

Stanford–Binet Intelligence Scale, Third Revision (Terman & Merrill, 1960). (*TIP III*: 2289; 1793 references). This is a series of individually administered scales for ages 2 and over that is designed to yield a mental age and an IQ. Variables from these scales (or earlier editions thereof) appear in our datasets JONE31–34, STOR11–13, and WRIG01. The chief factors measured are LD (Language Development), I (Induction), RG (Reasoning), and MS (Memory Span); in addition, certain small subsets of scales measure RQ (Quantitative Reasoning), VZ (Visualization), MM (Meaningful Memory), and even FO (Originality). Because of the great emphasis on measures of language development, the total MA or IQ is strongly biased toward the second-stratum factor Gc, but this is partly counterbalanced by an emphasis on reasoning tests that contributes to an influence of the second-stratum factor Gf. A fourth edition of the Stanford–Binet Intelligence Scale was published in 1985 by Thorndike, Hagen, and Sattler (1985). P. E. Vernon (1987) lamented that the structure of the test had changed considerably. Its 15 subtests are grouped under four areas – Verbal, Nonverbal, Numerical, and Short-Term Memory, apparently in response to opinions, based on factor-analytic research, that separate scales would be desirable. Vernon felt that there was inadequate evidence that differences between area scores would be diagnostically significant.

Wechsler Adult Intelligence Scale – Revised (WAIS-R) (Wechsler, 1971). (*TIP III*: 2598; 1867 references.) This is an individually administered test intended primarily for clinical use. Subtests include six yielding a Verbal score (information, comprehension, arithmetic, similarities, digit span, vocabulary) and six yielding a Performance score (digit symbol, picture completion, block design, picture arrangement, and object assembly). One or more of these variables (from the WAIS-R or earlier editions) appear in our datasets

HEND11A, ROYC11, SAUN03, SNOW11–12, SPRA11, VERN01, and WILL11. Datasets SAUN11 and SAUN21 address the factorial composition of the individual items in the Picture Completion, Information, and Arithmetic subtests. Factorial studies almost invariably show three factors, a verbal or language development factor found principally in some of the verbal subtests, a spatial or visualization factor found principally in some of the Performance subtests, and a further factor in the memory span and digit symbol subtests that is probably a combination of factor MS (Memory Span) and P (Perceptual Speed). Actually, the scales are not designed for factor-analytic investigation; the factors derived in studies that employ only the subscales of this battery are not well defined. Other factors measured by individual subtests are N (Numerical Facility), K0 (General Information), and RG (Reasoning). The Verbal scale can be taken as an approximate measure of the second-stratum factor Gc, while the Performance scale can be taken as an approximate measure of factor Gv, or somewhat less validly, of factor Gf. The Total scale can be taken as an approximate measure of factor g.

Wechsler Intelligence Scale for Children – Revised (WISC-R) (Wechsler, 1974). (*TIP III*: 2602; 2230 references.) This is an individually administered test that is a downward extension of the WAIS-R, with essentially the same scales, for ages 6–16. One or more variables from the WISC (the original edition) or WISC-R appear in our datasets HUEF01, KEIT21, NAGL01-03, PROG01, STEP01, UNDH01, VANH01, and WALL01. The factorial composition is highly similar to that of the WAIS. Kaufman (1975) reported factor analyses of WISC-R intercorrelations as published in the test manual for eleven age levels between $6\frac{1}{2}$ and $16\frac{1}{2}$ years; he interpreted the three factors that emerged at each level as Verbal Comprehension, Perceptual Organization, and Freedom from Distractibility, but these interpretations must be regarded with caution because the WISC-R battery is too restricted to permit identification of all the factors it measures. (A revision, WISC-III, was published in 1991.)

Wechsler Preschool and Primary Scale of Intelligence (WPPSI) (Wechsler, 1967). (*TIP III*: 2608; 250 references.) This is a further downward extension of the WAIS-R and WISC-R; in fact, it overlaps considerably with the WISC-R. One or more variables from this test appear in our datasets TAYL31 and WEXL01. The factorial composition of the test is essentially like that of the WISC-R.

Frank (1983) has critically examined all of Wechsler's tests of intelligence from the standpoint of their adequacy for clinical work, considering their psychometric characteristics, the factorial content of the scales, and their appropriateness for clinical judgments. He finds many inadequacies, concluding:

The Wechsler tests are like the dinosaur, too large, cumbersome and ill-fitted and awkward in the age in which they developed, unable to remain viable in a psychometric age which has passed it by in conceptualization. As with the dinosaur it is time for the Wechsler test to become extinct (p. 126).

Although Frank's views may be somewhat extreme, I would regard them as essentially correct. Presently available knowledge and technology would permit the development of tests and scales that would be much more adequate for their purpose than the Wechsler scales.

Apparently intended to replace at least some parts of the WPPSI and the WISC-R, the *Kaufman Assessment Battery for Children (K–ABC)* (Kaufman & Kaufman, 1983) offers scales that purport to profit from recent research on cognitive abilities. The 16 scales are grouped into a "mental processing" set and an "achievement" set. The "mental processing" scales yield two global scores, one reflecting "sequential processing of information" and the other reflecting "simultaneous processing," these categories being based on the work of Das, Kirby, and Jarman (1975) and indirectly on the work of Luria (1966). The achievement scales have been shown to be more highly *g*-loaded than the mental processing scales (Jensen, 1984). Variables from the K–ABC test appear in our datasets KEIT21 and NAGL01–03, all of which also include variables from the WISC-R. In all cases, it appears that the essential factor structure of the K–ABC is similar if not identical to that of the WISC-R. In datasets NAGL01 and NAGL02, for matched groups of black and white children, respectively, the factors are Verbal (V or LD), Visualization (VZ), and Memory Span (MS). The simultaneous processing tests can be interpreted in more traditional terms as tests of VZ (Visualization); the successive processing tests are tests of language processing (factor LD) and short-term memory (factor MS). In dataset KEIT21 these same factors (LD, VZ, and MS) are present, but a factor of Reading Ability also appears. Further, three orders of factors appear: Gf and Gc factors at the second order and a *g* factor at the third order. With respect to factorial content, there is little if anything that is new in the K–ABC test.

Particularly in its early history, factor-analytic research was an attempt to isolate separate factors of ability by constructing and studying tests each of which focused on particular types of items that were found in group intelligence tests, e.g., vocabulary items, verbal analogy items, number-series items, quantitative reasoning items, etc. The factors isolated by Thurstone (1938b) and many other factor analysts reflected, therefore, specific abilities sampled by group intelligence tests. With the presently available evidence from factor-analytic studies, it is now possible to understand what these group intelligence tests measured.

There exist literally dozens or even hundreds of paper-and-pencil intelligence tests designed to be administered to groups of individuals (for example, see Mitchell's 1983 compilation of tests in print). Typically these tests are composed of collections of items or tasks selected to measure a variety of intellectual functions without necessarily distinguishing among such functions in terms of producing separate scales or scores, except in some cases to produce "verbal" and "nonverbal" scores. In terms of factorial content at the *item* level, they tend to measure certain factors in the language, reasoning, and (occasionally) the spatial domains, to the extent that these factors are found valid for predicting scholastic success or success in occupations. The total scores thus tend to represent composites of general intelligence (*g* or 3G), crystallized intelligence (Gc or 2C), and fluid intelligence (Gf or 2F), but they are normally biased toward measuring developed abilities that depend on reading ability, vocabulary knowledge, and verbal comprehension, in view of the fact that they present *printed* verbal stimuli; thus, they are usually strongly biased towards measuring the second-stratum factor Gc or 2C, in addition to specific abilities involved in decoding print.

We may illustrate these conclusions by considering two widely used tests of general ability: the Cognitive Abilities Test and the College Board Scholastic Aptitude Test.

> *Cognitive Abilities Test (CAT)* (Thorndike, Hagen, & Lorge, 1954–74). (*TIP III*: 483; 44 references.) This paper-and-pencil group intelligence test is a revision of the Lorge–Thorndike Intelligence Tests (Lorge, Thorndike, & Hagen, 1954–66; *TIP III*: 1341) and exists in several formats for different grade levels. The Multi-Level edition is a single booklet that covers grades 3 through 12, but the examinee takes only items appropriate for his or her age or grade level. There are 10 subtests at each level, but they are graded in difficulty over the 8 levels. They are grouped into three batteries, each yielding a single score, as follows:
>
> > *Verbal Battery*: Vocabulary, Sentence Completion, Verbal Classification, Verbal Analogies.
> >
> > *Quantitative Battery*: Quantitative Relations, Number Series, Equation Building.
> >
> > *Nonverbal Battery*: Figure Classification, Figure Analogies, Figure Synthesis.
>
> Each subtest contains a series of highly similar items; considering each subtest individually, one can see that it might be analogous to a variable used in a factorial study. For example, in the Verbal Battery the vocabulary test is a multiple-choice test in which the examinee has to find a word that means the same as a given word. The sentence completion test requires choosing one of five words that best fits the empty space in a sentence; the verbal classification test requires choosing one of five words that "goes together" with three given words (e.g., *gull* would "go together with" *dove, hawk,* and *sparrow*); and the verbal analogies test requires choosing a word that best completes a verbal analogy of the form $A:B::C:$____. On the basis of the evidence compiled in this survey of cognitive abilities, these items would be expected to measure factor VL (Lexical Knowledge), I (Induction), and perhaps RC (Reading Comprehension) and RG (Serial Reasoning). Similarly, items in the Quantitative Battery would be expected to measure I (Induction), N (Numerical Facility), and RQ (Quantitative Reasoning), and items in the Nonverbal Battery would be expected to measure VZ (Visualization) and I (Induction). Consequently, it could be expected that the subtests would intercorrelate rather highly, partly because of the overlaps in their factorial compositions, and partly because the subtests tend to measure higher-order factors. Indeed, factor analyses presented by the test's authors indicate three primary factors (verbal, "figural-nonverbal," and quantitative), plus a large general factor (which they interpret as "relational thinking"). The authors recommend reporting separate scores for the three batteries rather than combining them into a total score. Reviewers of the test in *The Eighth Mental Measurements Yearbook* (Buros, 1978) questioned the need for giving all three batteries, believing that the Verbal battery alone is sufficient for most purposes.
>
> *College Board Scholastic Aptitude Test (SAT)* (Educational Testing Service, issued periodically). *TIP III*: 501; 936 references.) This three-hour pencil-and-paper test for college admissions testing is usually referred to as the SAT, with two scores, SAT-V (verbal) and SAT-M (mathematics), and a total score. The test's authors prefer to avoid calling it an intelligence test because so

doing would tend to imply that it measures a fixed intellectual capacity; rather, they feel, it should be regarded as a test of developed abilities. The verbal sections normally contain three types of items: antonyms (essentially, a multiple-choice vocabulary test), verbal analogies (in which the examinee must choose one of five sets of $C{:}D$ terms that properly completes an analogy that starts with a lead stimulus of the form $A{:}B{::}$____) and sentence completions (in which the examinee must choose one of five pairs of words or phrases that properly fill corresponding blanks in a sentence). Successful responses to such items require adequate vocabulary knowledge (factor VL), reading comprehension (factor RC), and probably inductive ability (factor I). The quantitative or mathematical portion contains varied items chiefly requiring quantitative reasoning (factor RQ) and inductive ability. For the population taking the test, SAT-V and SAT-M scores typically have a correlation of about .67 (Donlon, 1984) and are widely thought of as having separate meanings; factorially, they may regarded as measuring factor V (verbal ability) and factor RQ (quantitative reasoning), respectively. The combined total score is probably best regarded as a measure of the second-stratum ability 2C (crystallized intelligence), but it would also correlate fairly highly with a third-stratum general factor. Scores on the SAT are, however, subject to the influences of growth and special training (or coaching) (Messick, 1980), a fact that justifies calling the SAT a test of developed abilities; however, the test probably reflects native ability to the extent that there appear to be limits to the extent that scores can improve with education and/or special training. Using the person characteristic function to describe test scores as a function of difficulty levels reached by groups of different levels of ability, I (Carroll, 1980b) have published an account of the SAT's construct validity.

Like most group tests of mental ability, both of these tests are *timed*; consequently, scores for individuals who are unable to consider or answer all items on a given subtest will reflect a component of lack of speed. However, the time limits in each case are fairly generous, so that the scores usually reflect power or level of ability much more than rate of test-taking.

These tests have evolved in response to particular requirements in their use – in the case of the Cognitive Abilities Battery, the mass testing of school children in order to obtain measures of developed mental abilities, and in the case of the SAT, efficient testing of candidates for college admission in order to obtain assessments of probability of success in higher education. As we have seen, both of the tests have separate scores for presumably differentiable aspects of ability. There is always a question of how many scores on such tests there should be. For certain purposes, a single overall score may be adequate, as when one wants to obtain a single ranking of a group of students. When multiple scores are available, however, there is the possibility of making differential diagnoses of probable success in different courses of education and training, or in different educational institutions. Whether multiple scores are useful is an empirical question whose answer depends on whether the use of multiple scores makes for greater efficiency and more satisfactory decisions overall. For example, does a multiple regression based on two or more scores produce significantly more accurate predictions than a regression based on only one predictor variable? Are clinical judgments based on a profile of scores more sensitive and accurate than those based on a single score?

These questions are the echo of a more general and fundamental controversy that pertains to the whole realm of cognitive abilities. On the one hand, there is the extreme view that all cognitive abilities can most usefully be summed up in a single index, such as the IQ or a score on factor g. At the other extreme is the view that there exist a very large number of separate abilities, all of which must be taken into account, perhaps with almost equal weight, in assessing human capabilities. Those who argue for a single index point out that in many situations, a single index of ability contributes most of the variance in predicting a criterion of success, and that any further measures of ability make only small or even negligible contributions. Those who call for measures of multiple abilities can, however, cite circumstances or settings in which a single index does not suffice – where measures of further abilities do indeed make significant individual contributions.

In my view, there is no universally valid resolution of this controversy. The issue has to be settled on a case-by-case basis, taking account, of course, of the practical exigencies of the situation (e.g., costs, available testing time, etc.). We can now be certain that many separate, partially independent abilities exist, and there is always the possibility that a multiplicity of abilities, at different strata of the ability hierarchy, will be operative in any given situation. This possibility can be investigated only by assessing the role of multiple abilities, or of multiple scales from a test battery. If it is found that a single index is sufficient, that conclusion must be accepted for the case that is investigated, but the conclusion cannot be generalized to other cases. It can be expected that cases in which it is more profitable to employ measures of multiple abilities will present themselves.

On this basis, it is reasonable to tolerate or even encourage the availability of measures of multiple abilities.

IMPLICATIONS FOR PUBLIC POLICY ON TESTING

Already in Chapter 1 it was pointed out that the study of cognitive abilities can have important implications for social policy. In an essay on policy issues arising from the study of intelligence, Zigler and Seitz (1982, p. 586) remarked that researchers often find themselves "entangled" in such issues. In recent years there has been what has been called a "sea change" in American ideologies on civil rights, equality of educational opportunity and outcomes, and the equipotentiality of human beings of whatever gender, race, ethnic group, or social class. The so-called IQ controversy, which has been of long standing, has been especially exacerbated by this change in the focus of social thought.

There has been a veritable deluge of books, articles, and media presentations protesting, in one way or another, the alleged myth of the IQ and its measurability and possible genetic basis, or the lack of validity of scholastic aptitude tests (see, for example, Kamin, 1974; Block & Dworkin, 1976; Houts, 1977; CBS, 1975; Nairn, 1980; Gould, 1981; Crouse & Trusheim (1988); Mensh & Mensh, 1991). It cannot be said that these presentations are all bad or totally misinformed. They have raised important issues and in some cases have led to useful improvements in tests and their uses. Nevertheless, to the extent that they are misinformed or draw incorrect conclusions, it is necessary to issue corrective information. For example, a frequent statement found in these presentations is to the effect that "we do not know what intelligence is" or that "there is no theory of intelligence." The thesis of the present volume is that we know a great deal about intelligence and its component abilities, and that it is possible to state an acceptable theory of intelligence (such as the three-stratum theory offered here).

Partly in response to criticisms of psychological tests and their uses, there have been numerous conferences or commissions convened to examine ability testing and research, the effects of testing on education and the society, and possible modifications in policies concerning tests. For example, in 1968 the Black Psychological Association presented to the American Psychological Association (APA) a manifesto that called for a moratorium on the testing of students with "disadvantaged" backgrounds. As a result, the APA appointed a task force to study educational uses of tests with disadvantaged students; the task force's report was eventually published (Cleary, Humphreys, Kendrick, & Wesman, 1975). The report contained, among other things, a discussion of the theory of human abilities, including a definition of intelligence as "the entire repertoire of acquired skills, knowledge, learning sets, and generalization tendencies considered intellectual in nature that are available at any one period of time" (p. 19). In the meantime another APA task force was at work on employment testing of minority groups in industry; for its report, see Baxter (1969).

In 1974, a research conference on the nature of intelligence was held at the Learning Research and Development Center, University of Pittsburgh, resulting in a book on this subject (Resnick, 1976). Even at that time there was already much discussion of the role of cognitive psychology in contributing to the understanding of intellectual behavior and performance. Some stress was laid on the implications of theories of intelligence for education.

In 1977, the National Research Council (an arm of the National Academy of Sciences) appointed a Committee on Ability Testing, composed of nearly a score of distinguished specialists from various disciplines (about half of them from psychology), to "conduct a broad examination of the role of testing in American life" (Wigdor & Garner, 1982, Part I, p. vii). Its report, released in 1982, has two parts: part I, a seven-chapter summary of its findings and conclusions, including general information on concepts, methods, and results of testing, its historical and legal contexts, and uses of tests in employment and in schools; and part II, a series of eleven prepared papers on these subjects that were used as background for the committee's deliberations. In part I, chapter 2 provided for the lay reader a summary of basic concepts of ability and ability testing, pointing out that tests can measure ability only at the moment of testing and that tests do not portray a fixed or inherent characteristic of an individual. It urged that "intelligence" can be a misleading concept insofar as it encourages misunderstandings about the kind of measurement involved or the false notion that intelligence is a tangible and well-defined entity or even that it is a unitary ability. In general the committee concluded that despite many limitations, tests are useful in education and in employment. With respect to employment tests it stated, "the committee has seen no evidence of alternatives to testing that are equally informative, equally adequate technically, and also economical and politically viable" (Wigdor & Garner, 1982, Part I, p. 144). It recognized, above all, that "the quest for a more equitable society has placed ability testing at the center of the controversy and has given it an exaggerated reputation for good and for harm" (p. 239). My comment would be that while this was in general an excellent and balanced report, it was perhaps a little too cautious in laying forth the scientific evidence about the nature and structure of abilities. The notion, for example, that intelligence is a tangible and well-defined entity is not entirely false, in light of the perspective taken in the present volume.

In 1978, the National Institute of Education within the U. S. Department of Health, Education and Welfare sponsored two conferences on uses of tests (chiefly, achievement tests) in education. One was entitled the National Conference on Achievement Testing and Basic Skills, the other was the Conference on Research in Testing. The proceedings of the latter, with a brief account of the former, were published in a report by Tyler and White (1979). Although these conferences were not explicitly concerned with ability testing, they raised many issues applicable to ability tests as well as to achievement tests. For example, one recommendation made by a subgroup at the conference on research was that the National Institute of Education should

Make explicit to everyone (pupils, parents, public and professionals of all kinds) that a person's abilities, activities, and attitudes can not be measured. The public, especially, misperceives that hard data exist, and that test scores constitute these data. The public does not realize how quickly the point is reached where we do not know how to discriminate validly among people, but where the data mislead us to think we do. This is what is meant by the myth of measurability (Tyler & White, 1979, p. 376).

It is most unfortunate that a statement like this was allowed to appear in the report without comment.

The most recent broad commission on testing was the National Commission on Testing and Public Policy, formed in 1987 under the chairmanship of Bernard R. Gifford of the University of California at Berkeley, with the support of the Ford Foundation. The commission had seventeen members from a variety of public and private organizations. Its overall report (National Commission on Testing and Public Policy, 1990), *From Gatekeeper to Gateway: Transforming Testing in America*, called for a fundamental restructuring of testing such that tests would be used to "open gates of opportunity rather than close them off"

(p. x), and gave a number of specific recommendations on how this could be accomplished:

1. Testing policies and practices must be reoriented to promote the development of all human talent.
2. Testing programs should be redirected from overreliance on multiple-choice tests toward alternative forms of assessment.
3. Test scores should be used only when they differentiate on the basis of characteristics relevant to the opportunities being allocated.
4. The more test scores disproportionately deny opportunities to minorities, the greater the need to show that the tests measure characteristics relevant to the opportunities being allocated.
5. Test scores are imperfect measures and should not be used alone to make important decisions about individuals, groups, or institutions; in the allocation of opportunities, individuals' past performance and relevant experience must be considered.
6. More efficient and effective assessment strategies are needed to hold institutions accountable.
7. The enterprise of testing must be subjected to greater public accountability.
8. Research and development programs must be expanded to create assessments that promote the development of the talents of all our peoples (National Commission on Testing and Public Policy, 1990, pp. x–xi).

As background for its work and to promote public understanding of testing problems, the commission has sponsored the publication of several volumes containing prepared papers. As of this writing, two such volumes have appeared (Gifford, 1989a, b), one concerned primarily with political and legal factors in test development and interpretation, and the other concerned chiefly with uses of tests in education, particularly as testing affects minority groups.

A highly useful work on the history of the IQ controversy and the ways in which it is understood by members of the testing profession and presented to the public through newspaper and broadcast media is a book entitled *The IQ Controversy, the Media and Publc Policy* (Snyderman & Rothman, 1988). Its first author is a Ph.D. in psychology trained at Harvard University under Richard Herrnstein, who is known for his views on the role of intelligence in economic and social mobility in the U.S. (Herrnstein, 1973). The second author is a professor of political science and government, interested in the impact of the media on the formation of political and social attitudes. Along with its well-documented discussion of the IQ controversy, the book reports two interesting surveys. One was a survey of the opinions of experts (in psychology and education) on such matters as the nature of intelligence, its heritability, and the proper uses of intelligence tests. The other was a content analysis of the information and views on intelligence testing put forth in major news and broadcast media over the period 1969 to 1983. (The starting date was selected because it was the date when the IQ controversy was brought into public prominence with the publication of Arthur Jensen's (1969) article, "How Much Can We Boost IQ and Scholastic Achievement?" in the *Harvard Educational Review*.) The major finding of these surveys was the striking contrast between the views of the experts and the information and views purveyed by the news media. In the words of the authors:

By stressing the indeterminacy of a definition of intelligence, the limitations of tested ability, the ubiquitousness of test misuse, the inordinate control exerted by test makers, and cultural bias in tests, the news media have presented to the reading and viewing public a distorted image of testing, one more consistent with the opinion of a disappointed test taker than that of those who know most about tests. The views of the expert community are lost when Herrnstein, Jensen, and Shockley, in addition to being frequently misrepresented, are cast as intellectual loners in their defense of substantial heritability and the validity of tests. Moreover, whether as a result of disinclination to clarify issues that would put testing and its supporters in a better light, or because of inadequate technical training, journalists have done a great disservice to their audience by portraying IQ heritability as an all-or-none phenomenon, and by confusing within- and between-group heritability, cultural deprivation and cultural bias, and aptitude and achievement. Such inaccuracies add fuel to the fires of the IQ controversy just as surely as does portraying Leon Kamin as a spokesman for a substantial portion of the psychological community .... (p. 247).

During the 1950's, scientists and the informed public accepted as a matter of course the assumption that genetic factors were importantly involved in individual differences in measured intelligence, as well as the argument (against the position taken by many as late as the 1920s) that differences in IQ among various ethnic or racial groups were wholly the result of environmental factors.

In the past twenty-five years this conventional wisdom has changed dramatically. Intelligence and aptitude tests have fallen into disfavor among the literate public, as have attempts to define intelligence. However intelligence is defined, the suggestion that individual differences in intelligence, like individual capacities for painting or composing, may have a genetic component has become anathema.

More significantly, the literate and informed public today is persuaded that the majority of experts in the field believe it is impossible to adequately define intelligence, that intelligence tests do not measure anything that is relevant to life performance, and that they are biased against minorities, primarily blacks and Hispanics, as well as against the poor. It appears from book reviews in popular journals and from newspaper and television coverage of IQ issues that such are the views of the vast majority of experts who study questions of intelligence and intelligence testing (Snyderman & Rothman, 1988, pp. 249–250).

The actual views of experts, as reported both in the book and (somewhat more succinctly) in a separate article (Snyderman & Rothman, 1987), are on the whole quite different from what they are portrayed to be by the media, even though experts' opinions are far from unanimous on some issues. A majority of experts agreed that there is a consensus among psychologists and educators as to the kinds of behaviors that are labeled "intelligent." Further, there is near unanimity on the important elements of intelligence being "abstract thinking or reasoning," "the capacity to acquire knowledge," and "problem-solving ability." When asked, "Is intelligence, as measured by intelligence tests, better described in terms of a primary general intelligence factor and subsidiary group and special ability factors, or entirely in terms of separate faculties?," 58% favored some form of a general intelligence solution, whereas 13% felt intelligence consisted mainly of separate faculties. With respect to the heritability of intelligence, there was a consensus that there is a significant genetic component; on the average, experts believed that 60% of the variation in IQ in the American white population is associated with genetic variation, but few believed there was sufficient evidence to estimate the heritability of IQ in the American black population.

Experts were inclined to believe that there is some racial bias in intelligence tests. However, responses were mixed on the question of the source of the black–white difference in IQ. Forty-five percent believe the difference to be a product of both genetic and environmental variation, whereas only 15% felt the difference is entirely due to environment effects; 24% felt there was insufficient evidence for any conclusion, and 14% did not respond to the question.

The respondents indicated that while various types of test misuse sometimes occurred, this did not seem to present a serious problem. They were generally satisfied with current uses of tests in schools and in employment.

Implications of the Three-Stratum Theory of Cognitive Abilities for Social Policy Issues

The theory of cognitive abilities offered in the present volume does not, and cannot be expected to, provide answers to all the problems of social policy that have been raised by critics of testing and the various commissions that have examined the relevance of testing to such problems. Many of these problems depend more on social values than upon scientific theories or knowledge. For example, the question of whether scores on employment tests should be adjusted to equalize mean reported scores of different racial/ethnic groups, as was recommended by a commission appointed to study this issue with reference to the General Aptitude Test Battery (Hartigan & Wigdor, 1989), depends not so much on the psychometric characteristics of the tests (their reliability, validity, etc.) as upon the judged social value of making the adjustments. The theory does, however, give the lie to allegations that science has not yet offered a satisfactory definition of intelligence, a theory of intelligence, or a body of sound knowledge about cognitive abilities. To the extent that it may be possible to inform the general public about the scientific bases for judgments about the role of abilities and their measurements in social policy decisions, a number of points may be made. For the sake of brevity and clarity, these points are stated below without all the qualifications and refinements that could be added to them.

1. It is important that the public understand what an ability is, and how variations in ability express themselves. We have in mind here any one of many abilities – from the most general to the most specific. An ability expresses itself in variations – even within a single individual – in success or lack of success in performing particular tasks over a range of tasks of a certain kind and of different difficulties. Typically, an individual will be able to perform tasks (of a certain kind) that are very easy, but will be unable to perform tasks (of that same kind) that are very difficult. But there are variations over individuals in the levels of

task difficulty that these individuals can perform with a satisfactory degree of success. Individuals who can perform difficult tasks are said to be more able or capable than individuals who cannot perform those difficult tasks. An individual's degree of ability corresponds to the highest level of difficulty of the tasks that the individual is able to perform successfully about half the time. The individual's score on a test of the ability corresponds to an estimate of that level of task difficulty. In any population of individuals, scores on tests of the ability tend to range from low to high; their distribution often approximates the so-called bell-shaped normal distribution, and it may be assumed that the levels of task difficulty that individuals can perform are distributed in this same way. Usually, when the distributions of scores are compared for different groups, there are large overlaps in these distributions, even though the means and standard deviations may be somewhat different.

2. In the above discussion, we have been speaking of the psychological abilities that are intrinsically characteristic of human populations, as *inferred* from tests and other observations of performance. Although the score on a particular psychological test given to a particular individual at a given point of time may not be a completely accurate estimate of that individual's ability, the masses of data that can be collected from large groups of individuals are adequate for inferring the levels and characteristics of the abilities that are tapped by the tests. Psychological tests of cognitive abilities contain samples of the tasks that define those abilities. Although there are many technical problems in designing adequate tests and testing procedures, most of these problems are solvable, and in fact have been solved in the construction of many psychological tests that are available. With due caution and attention to their characteristics and limitations, psychological tests are useful devices for producing estimates of abilities. Tests employing the multiple-choice format are in many cases the most reliable, valid, and efficient estimates of relevant abilities in many domains. Abilities in some domains, however, such as the domains of idea production and memory, cannot be effectively measured with multiple-choice formats; free response formats are generally more appropriate in these domains.

3. A basic claim of the three-stratum theory of cognitive abilities, supported by much scientific evidence, is that there exists a substantial number of different intellectual abilities, all showing characteristics such as what has just been described. They are differentiated not only by the fact that their intercorrelations are often far from perfect, but also by the fact that they pertain to different classes of tasks. For example, one class of tasks, corresponding to what may be called verbal ability, is comprised of tasks involving the understanding of language; another class of tasks, corresponding to what may be called reasoning ability, are tasks involving correct reasoning from given assumptions and premises. Describing and defining any given ability involves describing the kinds of tasks, of different difficulties, that give rise to the ability, or that allow the ability to express itself when individuals or groups of individuals are asked to perform

those tasks. A further claim of the theory is that abilities differ in generality or specificity. Abilities are classified at three levels of generality – general, broad, and narrow. The evidence suggests that there is only one general ability, an ability that applies in varying degrees to all cognitive, intellectual tasks. There are about ten broad abilities that apply to different domains of cognitive tasks. Finally, there are numerous narrow abilities that apply to fairly specific kinds of cognitive tasks or performances, usually reflecting the effects of specialized learning or training.

4. The scientific evidence for the existence of these three classes of ability comes from analysis of the variations in test performance observed in typical groups of individuals of different ages found in different developed countries. In effect, it is a "fact of nature" that individuals in these samples show variations in different kinds of ability. Further investigations have tried to determine the reasons for, or the sources of, these differences. To a large extent, the differences can be accounted for by differences in the maturity and learning experiences of individuals. There is also evidence that some abilities, particularly the general and broad abilities, are also somewhat affected by genetic factors. Under the prevailing conditions of social structure and educational opportunities, typically about half of the observed variation in abilities can be traced to heredity and about half to environmental factors. The fact that part of the variation is traceable to genetic factors implies that there may be limits to which abilities subject to genetic influences can be enhanced or improved through education, specific training, or other interventions. As yet, however, there is not adequate information as to what these limits, if any, may be. The evidence available suggests that the limits in most cases lie within a relatively narrow range of tested ability levels. For example, for an individual with a tested IQ of 100, although it might be relatively easy for the individual, with appropriate education, training, and effort to attain an IQ 10 points higher, the attainment of an IQ much beyond this range would become increasingly difficult or improbable.

5. From the standpoint of educational and social policy, these findings bring both good news, and news that is less favorable, to the notion that "all human beings are created equal" at least with respect to potential cognitive ability and mental development. The good news is that because there are many kinds of ability, it can be expected that a large proportion of the population can be, or can through effort become, at least close to or above average in *some* ability, or perhaps in many abilities. The multiplicity of abilities means that there is a psychological basis for specialization in education and the world of work. Furthermore, only average ability is sufficient to meet many of the requirements of life in the real world. For example, it may not take a large amount of cognitive ability to learn to read at a basic level, to run a small store, or to manage a small farm. Many people who are below average in general mental ability are able to adapt to the requirements of everyday life. The bad news is that variations in general ability (the *g* factor), which are apparently associated to a considerable extent

with genetic variation, may control variations in both broad and narrow abilities, and thus somewhat limit potentialities for development in many people. Coupled with the fact that job requirements in technically oriented economies are becoming increasingly more demanding, this means that a substantial portion of the population at any given time may not have, or be able to develop, the abilities to meet these requirements. Just how society can confront and deal with these circumstances will undoubtedly be an enduring problem that is only in very small measure attributable to tests and testing. Tests are only messengers about differences in abilities that are relevant to social issues and policies. (For further discussion, see articles in a special issue of the *Journal of Vocational Behavior*, Volume 29, December 1986; in particular, articles by Gottfredson, 1986b, Jensen, 1986, and Hunter, 1986.)

6. Finally, it should be recognized and remembered that tests of ability reveal real differences in people's abilities. Well-designed ability tests, administered to groups for which they are designed, are normally not biased against particular groups; any group differences in scores that appear reflect real mean group differences in present abilities, at least with respect to the samples of individuals tested. But as noted previously, there are almost always large overlaps in score distributions; there should be less interest in group differences than in the performances of particular individuals.

NOTE

1. LISREL (Linear Structural Relationships) is a computer program for structural equation analysis developed by Jöreskog and Sörbom (1978, 1984). EQS is a program for structural equation analysis, developed by Bentler (1985), that dispenses with some of the constraints of the LISREL program.

References and List of Datasets

Note: This list contains all references to citations in the text as well as to the datasets and their reanalyses in the literature. Embedded in it is also a list of datasets, which are designated by standard 5- to 7-character codes as explained in Chapter 3. These codes, preceded by "DS-" (for "dataset"), are found in the alphabetical list under the relevant author citations. For each dataset, the symbols # in $H1.\#\#.\#.\#$ indicate, respectively, the number of 1st-, 2nd , and 3rd-order factors in the hierarchical analysis as shown in Appendix B. For example, $H1.10.2$ would signify that there are ten first-order factors and two second-order factors (and no third-order factors) in the dataset.

Abelson, A. R. (1911). The measurement of mental ability of 'backward' children. *British Journal of Psychology*, *4*, 268–314.

Aby, S. H. (Compiler) (1990). *The IQ debate: A selective guide to the literature*. New York: Greenwood.

Acker, M., & McReynolds, P. (1965). The Obscure Figures Test: An instrument for measuring "cognitive innovation." *Perceptual and Motor Skills*, *21*, 815–821.

Ackerman, P. L. (1986). Individual differences in information processing: An investigation of intellectual abilities and task performance during practice. *Intelligence*, *10*, 101–139.

Ackerman, P. L. (1987). Individual differences in skill learning: An integration of psychometric and information processing perspectives. *Psychological Bulletin, 102*, 3–27.

Ackerman, P. L. (1988a). Determinants of individual differences during skill acquisition: Cognitive abilities and information processing. *Journal of Experimental Psychology: General, 117*, 288–318.

Ackerman, P. L. (1988b). A review of Linda S. Gottfredson (Ed.), The *g* factor in employment (*Journal of Vocational Behavior*, Special Issue, 1986, 29:3). *Educational & Psychological Measurement, 48*, 553–558.

Ackerman, P. L. (1989a). Individual differences and skill acquisition. In P. L. Ackerman, R. J. Sternberg, & R. Glaser (Eds.), *Learning and individual differences: Advances in theory and research* (pp. 165–217). New York: Freeman.

Ackerman, P. L. (1989b). Abilities, elementary information processes, and other sights to see at the zoo. In R. Kanfer, P. L. Ackerman, & R. Cudeck (Eds.), *Abilities, motivation, and methodology* (pp. 281–293). Hillsdale, NJ: Erlbaum.

Ackerman, P. L. (1989c). Individual differences in learning and cognitive abilities. Report

No. 89–01 Contract N00014-86-k-0478. Minneapolis, MN: Department of Psychology, University of Minnesota.

Ackerman, P. L. (1989d). Within-task intercorrelations of skilled performance: Implications for predicting individual differences? (A comment on Henry & Hulin, 1987.) *Journal of Applied Psychology, 74,* 360–364.

Ackerman, P. L., & Schneider, W. (1985). Individual differences in automatic and controlled information processing. In R. F. Dillon (Ed.), *Individual differences in cognition,* Vol. 2 (pp. 35–66). Orlando, FL: Academic.

Ackerman, P. L., Schneider, W., & Wickens, C. D. (1982). Individual differences and time-sharing ability: A critical review and analysis. Champaign: University of Illinois Psychology Department, Human Attention Research Laboratory, Report HARL-ONR-8102.
   Reanalysis of DS-WICK01.

Adams, J. A., & Montague, W. E. (1967). Retroactive inhibition and natural language mediation. *Journal of Verbal Learning and Verbal Behavior, 6,* 528–535.

Adevai, G., Silverman, A. J., & McGough, W. E. (1968). Perceptual correlates of the rod-and-frame test. *Perceptual & Motor Skills, 26,* 1055–1064.
   DS-ADEV01 *HI.3.1*

Adkins, D. C., & Lyerly, S. B. (1952). *Factor analysis of reasoning tests.* Chapel Hill, NC: Univ. of North Carolina Press.
   DS-ADKI03 *HI.8.2*
   Reanalyzed: Ahmavaara (1957), Humphreys, Tucker, & Dachler (1970), Matin & Adkins (1954)

Advisory Panel on the Scholastic Aptitude Test Score Decline (1977). *On further examination.* 2 vols. New York: College Entrance Examination Board.

Aftanas, M. S., & Royce, J. R. (1969). A factor analysis of brain damage tests administered to normal subjects with factor score comparisons across ages. *Multivariate Behavioral Research, 4,* 459–481.
   DS-AFTA01 *HI.10.2*

Ahmavaara, V. (1957). *On the unified factor theory of mind.* Helsinki, Finland: Suomalaisen Tiedeakatemian Toimituksia. (Annales Akademiae Scientiarum Fennicae, Series B, Vol. 106.)
   Reanalyses of ADKI03, BOTZ01, CARR01, GUIL17, GUIL18, GUIL31, GUIL46, GUIL66, HARR01, KARL11, KNOE11, MORR11, PEMB01, RIMO21, TAYL01, THUR21, THUR41.

Aks, D. J., & Coren, S. (1990). Is susceptibility to distraction related to mental ability? *Journal of Educational Psychology, 82,* 388–390.

Allen, T. W., Rose, A. M., & Kramer, L. J. (1978). An information processing approach to performance assessment: III. An elaboration and refinement of an information processing performance battery. Washington, DC: American Institutes for Research. (Technical Report No. 3, AIR 58500-11/78-TR)
   DS-ALLE11 *HI.6.1* (Day 1)
   DS-ALLE12 *HI.6.1* (Day 2)

Allison, R. B., Jr. (1960). Learning parameters and human abilities. Princeton, NJ: Educational Testing Service and Princeton University Technical Report.
   DS-ALLI01 *HI.6.2* (learning measures)
   DS-ALLI02 *HI.6.2* (reference variables)
   DS-ALLI03 *HI.6.2.1* (combined variables)
   Reanalyzed: Snow, Kyllonen, & Marshalek (1984)

Anastasi, A. (1932). Further studies on the memory factor. *Archives of Psychology (N.Y.), 22,* No. 142.

DS-ANAS11 *HI.3.1*
Reanalyzed: Garrett (1938)
Anastasi, A. (1970). On the formation of psychological traits. *American Psychologist, 25,* 899–910.
Anastasi, A. (1983). Traits, states, and situations: A comprehensive view. In H. Wainer & S. Messick (Eds.), *Principals of modern psychological measurement: A Festschrift for Frederic M. Lord* (pp. 345–356). Hillsdale, NJ: Erlbaum.
Anastasi, A. (1988). *Psychological testing* (6th edition). New York: Macmillan.
Anderson, H. E., Jr., & Leton, D. A. (1964). Factor analysis of the California Test of Mental Maturity. *Educational & Psychological Measurement, 24,* 513–523.
DS-ANDE01 *HI.3.1* (Gr. 1–3)
DS-ANDE02 *HI.3.1* (Gr. 4–6)
DS-ANDE03 *HI.3.1* (Gr. 7–9)
Anderson, J. E. (1939). The limitations of infant and preschool tests in the measurement of intelligence. *Journal of Psychology, 8,* 351–379.
Anderson, J. R. (1983). *The architecture of cognition.* Cambridge, MA: Harvard University Press.
Anderson, J. R. (1990). *Cognitive psychology and its implications* (3rd edition). New York: Freeman.
Andrew, D. M. (1937). An analysis of the Minnesota Vocational Test for Clerical Workers. *Journal of Applied Psychology, 21,* 18 47, 139–172.
DS-ANDR01 *HI.4.1*
Andrew, D. M., & Paterson, D. G. (1934). *Measured characteristics of clerical workers.* Minneapolis: University of Minnesota Press. (Bulletins of the University of Minnesota Employment Stabilization Research Institute, 3(1).)
Angermaier, M. (1973) Drei Faktorenanalysen zum Thema 'Legasthenie.' [Three factor analyses on reading disability.] *Zeitschrift für experimentelle und angewandte Psychologie, 20,* 1–19.
Reanalysis of VALT01-03
Angleitner, A., & Rudinger, G. (1975). Eine Untersuchung zur faktoriellen Beschreibung von Intelligenz und Rigidität. [An investigation of the factorial description of intelligence and rigidity.] *Archiv für Psychologie, 127,* 35–50.
DS-ANGL11 *HI.5.1*
Applebee, A. N., Langer, J. A., & Mullis, I. V. S. (1986). *The writing report card: Writing achievement in American schools.* Princeton, NJ: Educational Testing Service. (NAEP Report No. 15-W-02)
Arnold, E. M. (1967). Is temporal integration a distinct mental ability? *Australian Journal of Psychology, 19,* 41–47.
DS-ARNO01 *HI.5.1*
Atkin, R., Bray, R., Davison, M., Herzberger, S., Humphreys, L., & Selzer, U. (1977a). Cross-lagged panel analysis of sixteen cognitive measures at four grade levels. *Child Development, 48,* 944–952.
Atkin, R., Bray, R., Davison, M., Herzberger, S., Humphreys, L., & Selzer, U. (1977b). Ability factor differentiation grades 5 through 11. *Applied Psychological Measurement, 1,* 65–76.
Atkinson, R. C., Bower, G. H., & Crothers, E. J. (1965). *An introduction to mathematical learning theory.* New York: Wiley.
Atkinson, R. C., & Shiffrin, R. M. (1968). Human memory: A proposed system and its control processes. In K. W. Spence & J. T. Spence (Eds.), *The psychology of learning and motivation: Advances in research and theory,* Vol. 2 (pp. 89–195). New York: Academic.

Bachelder, B. L., & Denny, M. R. (1977a). A theory of intelligence: I. Span and the complexity of stimulus control. *Intelligence, 1,* 127–150.

Bachelder, B. L., & Denny, M. R. (1977b). A theory of intelligence: II. The role of span in a variety of intellectual tasks. *Intelligence, 1,* 237–256.

Bachem, A. (1954). Time factors in relative and absolute pitch discrimination. *Journal of the Acoustical Society of America, 26,* 751–753.

Bachman, L. F. (1982). The trait structure of cloze test scores. *TESOL Quarterly, 16,* 61–70.
    DS-BACH01 *HI.3.1*

Bachman, L. F., & Palmer, A. S. (1982). The construct validation of some components of communicative proficiency. *TESOL Quarterly, 16,* 449–465.
    DS-BACH11 *HI.3.1*

Bachor, D. G. (1977). Information processing capacity and teachability of low achieving students. *Dissertation Abstracts, 38*(6A), 3373 (Canadian Microfiche 30331).
    DS-BACH21 *HI.4.1*

Baddeley, A. (1986). *Working memory.* Oxford, England: Clarendon Press.

Bair, J. T. (1951). Factor analysis of clerical aptitude tests. *Journal of Applied Psychology, 35,* 245–249. [ADI Doc. 3180]
    DS-BAIR01 *HI.4.1*

Balke-Aurell, G. (1982). *Changes in ability as related to educational and occupational experience.* Göteborg: Göteborg Studies in Educational Sciences 40.

Ball, J. M. (1952). An experimental study of the relationship between the ability to impart information orally and the primary mental abilities, verbal comprehension, and general reasoning. *Speech Monographs, 19,* 112.

Bannatyne, A. D., & Wichiarajote, P. (1969). Relationships between written spelling, motor functioning, and sequencing skills. *Journal of Learning Disabilities, 2,* 4–16.
    DS-BANN11 matrix not analyzable

Barratt, P. E. H. (1953). Imagery and thinking. *Australian Journal of Psychology, 5,* 154–164.
    DS-BARR00 *HI.2.1*

Barrett, G. V., Alexander, R. A., Doverspike, D., & Cellar, D. (1982). The development and application of a computerized information-processing test battery. *Applied Psychological Measurement, 6,* 13–29.
    DS-BARR01 *HI.4*
    DS-BARR02 *HI.4* (retest)

Barrett, G. V., & Depinet, R. L. (1991). A reconsideration of testing for competence rather than for intelligence. *American Psychologist, 46,* 1012–1024.

Barrett, P., Eysenck, H. J., & Lucking, S. (1986). Reaction time and intelligence: A replicated study. *Intelligence, 10,* 9–40.

Bartlett, F. C. (1932). *Remembering: A study in experimental and social psychology.* Cambridge, England: Cambridge University Press.

Bates, E., Bretherton, I., & Snyder, L. (1987). *From first words to grammar: Individual differences and dissociable mechanisms.* New York: Cambridge University Press.

Baxter, B. N. (1941). An experimental analysis of the contributions of speed and level in an intelligence test. *Journal of Educational Psychology, 32,* 285–296.

Baxter, B. N. (1942). On the equivalence of time-limit and work-limit methods. *American Journal of Psychology, 55,* 407–411.

Baxter, B. N. (Ed.) (1969). American Psychological Association, Task Force on Employment Testing of Minority Groups. Job testing and the disadvantaged. *American Psychologist, 24,* 637–650.

Beaton, A. E., et al. (1987). *Implementing the new design: The NAEP 1983–84 technical report.* Princeton, NJ: National Assessment of Educational Progress, Educational Testing Service. (Report No. 15-TR-20)

Bechtoldt, H. P. (1947). Factorial study of perceptual speed. Unpublished Ph.D. thesis, University of Chicago.
DS-BECH01 *HI.10.1*

Bechtoldt, H. P. (1953). Factor analysis of the Airman Classification Battery with civilian reference tests. *USAF Human Resources Research Center Research Bulletin*, 53–59.

Bejar, I. I., Chaffin, R., & Embretson, S. E. (1991). *Cognitive and psychometric analysis of analogical problem solving*. New York: Springer-Verlag.

Bellak, L. (1950). *Children's Apperception Test*. Melbourne: Australian Council for Educational Research.

Bennett, G. K., Seashore, H. G., & Wesman, A. G. (1947–82). *Differential Aptitude Tests*. New York: The Psychological Corporation.

Bennett, S. N. (1973). Divergent thinking abilities – a validation study. *British Journal of Educational Psychology*, 43, 1–7.
DS-BENN01 *HI.3.1* (males)
DS-BENN02 *HI.3.1* (females)

Benson, V. E. (1942). The intelligence and later scholastic success of sixth grade pupils. *School & Society*, 55, 163–167.

Bentler, P. M. (1977). Factor simplicity index and transformations. *Psychometrika*, 12, 277–295.
Reanalysis of HOLZ01

Bentler, P. M. (1985). *Theory and implementation of EQS, a structural equations program*. Los Angeles, CA: BMDP Statistical Software.

Bentler, P. M., & Wingard, J. A. (1977). Function invariant and parameter scale-free transformation methods. *Psychometrika*, 42, 221–240.
Reanalysis of HOLZ01

Bereiter, C. (1960). Verbal and ideational fluency in superior tenth grade students. *Journal of Educational Psychology*, 51, 337–345.
DS-BERE01 *HI.6.1* (females)
DS-BERE02 *HI.6.1* (males)

Berger, E. (1977). Field dependence and short-term memory. *Dissertation Abstracts International*, 38(4-B), 1870. (University Microfilm 77–21266)
DS-BERG21 *HI.3.1*

Berger, M. (1982). The "scientific approach" to intelligence: An overview of its history with special reference to mental speed. In H. J. Eysenck (Ed.), *A model for intelligence* (pp. 13–43). Berlin: Springer-Verlag.

Berger, R. M., Guilford, J. P., & Christensen, P. R. (1957). A factor-analytic study of planning. *Psychological Monographs*, 71 (6, Whole No. 435).
Further report of DS-GUIL11

Berlyne, D. E. (1960). *Conflict, arousal, and curiosity*. New York: McGraw–Hill.

Bernstein, E. (1924). Quickness and intelligence: An enquiry concerning the existence of a general speed factor. *British Journal of Psychology, Monograph Supplements*, 3, 1–55.

Bethell-Fox, C. E., Lohman, D. F., & Snow, R. E. (1984). Adaptive reasoning: Componential and eye movement analysis of geometric analogy performance. *Intelligence*, 8, 205–238.

Bieri, J., Atkins, A. L., Briar, S., Leaman, R. L., Miller, H., & Tripodi, T. (1966). *Clinical and social judgment: The discrimination of behavioral information*. New York: Wiley.

Binet, A. (1890). Perceptions d'enfants. [Children's perceptions.] *Revue Philosophique*, 30, 582–611.

Binet, A. (1903). *L'étude expérimentale de l'intelligence.* [The experimental study of intelligence.] Paris: Schleicher.

Binet, A., & Henri, V. (1896). La psychologie individuelle. [Individual psychology.] *Année Psychologique, 2,* 411–465.

Binet, A., & Simon, T. (1905). Méthodes nouvelles pour le diagnostic du niveau intellectuel des anormaux. [New methods for diagnosing the intellectual level of abnormals.] *Année Psychologique, 11,* 191–336.

Binet, A., & Simon, T. (1908). Le développment de l'intelligence chez les enfants. [The development of intelligence in children.] *Année Psychologique, 14,* 1–94.

Bingham, W. V. (1937). *Aptitudes and aptitude testing.* New York: Harper. [Reprinted, 1942]

Birdwhistell, R. L. (1970). *Kinesics and context: Essays on body motion communication.* Philadelphia: University of Pennsylvania Press.

Birke, W. (1981). Item response time as a basis for ability and difficulty measures. Paper for the 23rd Annual Conference of the Military Testing Association.

Birnbaum, A. (1968). Some latent trait models and their use in inferring an examinee's ability. In F. M. Lord & M. R. Novick, *Statistical theories of mental test scores* (pp. 395–479). Reading, MA: Addison–Wesley.

Birren, J. E., & Botwinick, J. (1951). Rate of addition as a function of difficulty and age. *Psychometrika, 16,* 219–232.

Bittner, A. C. Jr., Carter, R. C., Kennedy, R. S., Harbeson, M. M., & Krause, M. (1986). Performance evaluation tests for environmental research (PETER): Evaluation of 114 measures. *Perceptual & Motor Skills, 63,* 683–708.

Blackwood, L. C., Jr. (1980). Visual imagery: An analysis of structure. Unpublished Ph.D. dissertation, University of North Carolina at Chapel Hill.
DS-BLAC21 *HI.5*

Blakey, R. I. (1940). A re-analysis of a test of the theory of two factors. *Psychometrika, 5,* 121–136.
Reanalysis of DS-BROW21

Blakey, R. I. (1941). A factor analysis of a non-verbal reasoning test. *Educational & Psychological Measurement, 1,* 187–198.
DS-BLAK01 *HI.3.1*

Block, N. J., & Dworkin, G. (1974). IQ heritability and inequality. *Philosophy & Public Affairs, 3,* 331–407.

Block, N. J., & Dworkin, G. (Eds.) (1976). *The IQ controversy–Critical readings.* New York: Pantheon.

Bloom, B. S. (1968). Learning for mastery. *Evaluation Comment, 1(2).*

Bloom, B. S. (1974). Time and learning. *American Psychologist, 29,* 682–688.

Bloxom, B. (1972). Alternative approaches to factorial invariance. *Psychometrika, 37,* 425–440.
Reanalysis of HOLZ01

Bock, R. D., & Aitken, M. (1981). Marginal maximum likelihood estimation of item parameters: Application of an EM algorithm. *Psychometrika, 46,* 443–459.

Bolton, B. (1973). An alternative solution for the factor analysis of communication skills and nonverbal abilities of deaf clients. *Educational & Psychological Measurement, 33,* 459–463.
DS-BOLT11 *HI.7.1*

Bolton, B. (1978). Differential ability structure in deaf and hearing children. *Applied Psychological Measurement, 2,* 147–149.
Analyses of HISK01–04

Bolton, B., Hinman, S., & Tuft, S. (1973). *Annotated bibliography: Factor analytic studies*

1941–1970. 4 vols. Fayetteville, AR: Arkansas Rehabilitation Research & Training Center.

Botzum, W. A. (1951). A factorial study of the reasoning and closure factors. *Psychometrika, 16*, 361–386.

DS-BOTZ01 *HI.8.1*

Reanalyzed: Ahmavaara (1957)

Bouchard, T. J., Jr. (1984). Twins reared together and apart: What they tell us about human diversity. In S. W. Fox (Ed.), *Individuality and determinism* (pp. 147–184). New York: Plenum.

Bouchard, T. J., Jr., Lykken, D. T., McGue, M., Segal, N. L., & Tellegen, A. (1990). Sources of human psychological differences: The Minnesota study of twins reared apart. *Science, 250*, 223–228.

Bouchard, T. J., Jr., & McGue, M. (1981). Familial studies of intelligence: A review. *Science, 212*, 1055–1058.

Bouchard, T. J., Jr., & Segal, N. L. (1985). Environment and IQ. In B. B. Wolman (Ed.), *Handbook of intelligence: Theories, measurements, and applications* (pp. 391–464). New York: Wiley.

Boyle, G. J. (1988). Elucidation of motivation structure by dynamic calculus. In J. R. Nesselroade & R. B. Cattell (Eds.), *Handbook of multivariate experimental psychology* (pp. 737–787). New York: Plenum.

Bradley, P. A., Hoepfner, R., & Guilford, J. P. (1969). A factor analysis of figural memory abilities. Los Angeles: Reports from the Psychological Laboratory, University of Southern California, No. 43.

DS-BRAD01 *HI.8.2*

Reanalyzed: Kelderman, Mellenbergh, & Elshout (1981); Merrifield (1974)

Brener, R. (1940). An experimental investigation of memory span. *Journal of Experimental Psychology, 26*, 467–482.

DS-BREN01A *HI.3.1*

Brody, N. (1985). The validity of tests of intelligence. In B. B. Wolman (Ed.), *Handbook of intelligence: Theories, measurements, and applications* (pp. 353–389). New York: Wiley.

Brookings, J. B. (1990). A confirmatory factor analytic study of time-sharing performance and cognitive abilities. *Intelligence, 14*, 43–59.

Brown, A. L., & Campione, J. C. (1982). Modifying intelligence or modifying cognitive skills: More than a semantic quibble? In D. K. Detterman & R. J. Sternberg (Eds.), *How and how much can intelligence be increased.* (pp. 215–231). Norwood, NJ: Ablex.

Brown, R. W. (1957). Linguistic determinism and the part of speech. *Journal of Abnormal & Social Psychology, 55*, 1–5.

Brown, R. W. (1973). *A first language: The early stages.* Cambridge, MA: Harvard University Press.

Brown, R. W. & McNeill, D. (1966). The "tip of the tongue" phenomenon. *Journal of Verbal Learning and Verbal Behavior, 5*, 325–337.

Brown, S. W., Guilford, J. P., & Hoepfner, R. (1966). A factor analysis of semantic memory abilities. Los Angeles: Reports from the Psychological Laboratory, University of Southern California, No. 37.

DS-BROW11 *HI.6.1*

Further publication: Brown, Guilford, & Hoepfner (1968)

Reanalyzed: Horn & Knapp (1973)

Brown, S. W., Guilford, J. P., & Hoepfner, R. (1968). Six semantic-memory abilities. *Educational and Psychological Measurement, 28*, 691–717.

Brown, W. (1910). Some experimental results in the correlation of mental abilities. *British Journal of Psychology, 3,* 296–322.

Brown, W., & Stephenson, W. (1933). A test of the theory of two factors. *British Journal of Psychology, 23,* 352–370.
  DS-BROW21 *HI.4.1*
  Reanalyzed: Blakey (1940)

Bruner, J. S., & Potter, M. C. (1964). Interference in visual recognition. *Science, 144,* 424–425.

Bunderson, C. V. (1967). Transfer of mental abilities at different stages of practice in the solution of concept problems. Princeton, NJ: Educational Testing Service Research Bulletin RB-67-20.
  DS-BUND11 *HI.6.1*

Burns, R. B. (1980). Relation of aptitudes to learning at different points in time during instruction. *Journal of Educational Psychology, 72,* 785–795.
  DS-BURN11 *HI.4.1*

Buros, O. K. (Ed.) (1953). *The fourth mental measurements yearbook.* Highland Park, NJ: Gryphon.

Buros, O. K. (Ed.) (1959). *The fifth mental measurements yearbook.* Highland Park, NJ: Gryphon.

Buros, O. K. (Ed.) (1978). *The eighth mental measurements yearbook.* Highland Park, NJ: Gryphon.

Burt, C. (1909). Experimental tests of general intelligence. *British Journal of Psychology, 3,* 94–177.

Burt, C. (1911). Experimental tests of higher mental processes and their relation to general intelligence. *Journal of Experimental Pedagogy, 1,* 93–112.

Burt, C. (1917). *The distribution and relations of educational abilities.* London: King & Son.

Burt, C. (1921). *Mental and scholastic tests.* London: P. S. King.

Burt, C. (1939). The factorial analysis of ability. III. Lines of possible reconcilement. *British Journal of Psychology, 30,* 84–93.

Burt, C. (1940). *The factors of the mind: An introduction to factor-analysis in psychology.* London: University London Press. [New York: Macmillan, 1941]

Burt, C. (1949). Alternative methods of factor analysis and their relations to Pearson's method of 'principal axes.' *British Journal of Psychology, Statistical Section, 2,* 98–121.

Cain, W. S. (1988). Olfaction. In R. C. Atkinson, R. J. Herrnstein, G. Lindzey, & R. D. Luce (Eds.), *Stevens' Handbook of experimental psychology,* 2nd edition. Vol. 1: *Perception and motivation* (pp. 409–459). New York: Wiley.

Calhoun, D. (1973). *The intelligence of a people.* Princeton, NJ: Princeton University Press.

Canisia, M. (1962). Mathematical ability as related to reasoning and use of symbols. *Educational & Psychological Measurement, 22,* 105–127.
  DS-CANI01 *HI.7.1*
  Reanalyzed: DeGuire (1982)

Canter, D. (Ed.) (1985). *Facet theory: Approaches to social research.* New York: Springer.

Carey, N. (1915). Factors in the mental processes of school children. II. On the nature of the specific mental factors. *British Journal of Psychology, 8,* 71–92.

Carlson, H. B. (1937). Factor analysis of memory ability. *Journal of Experimental Psychology, 21,* 477–492.
  DS-CARL31 *HI.4.1*

Carlson, J. S., & Jensen, C. M. (1980). The factorial structure of the Raven Coloured Progressive Matrices Test: A reanalysis. *Educational & Psychological Measurement, 40,* 1111–1116.
  DS-CARL40 *HI.4.1*

Carlson, J. S., Jensen, C. M., & Widaman, K. F. (1983). Reaction time, intelligence, and attention. *Intelligence, 7*, 329–344.
DS-CARL41 *HI.4.2*

Carpenter, P. A., Just, M. A., & Shell, P. (1990). What one intelligence test measures: A theoretical account of the processing in the Raven Progressive Matrices Test. *Psychological Review, 97*, 404–431.

Carroll, J. B. (1941). A factor analysis of verbal abilities. *Psychometrika, 6*, 279–307.
DS-CARR01 *HI.7.2*
Reanalyzed: Ahmavaara (1957), Wendeler (1970)

Carroll, J. B. (1943). The factorial representation of mental ability and academic achievement. *Educational & Psychological Measurement, 3*, 307–332.
DS-CARR11 *HI.4.1*

Carroll, J. B. (1945). The effect of difficulty and chance success on correlations between items or between tests. *Psychometrika, 10*, 1–19.

Carroll, J. B. (1953). An analytical solution for approximating simple structure in factor analysis. *Psychometrika, 18*, 23–38.

Carroll, J. B. (1957). Biquartimin criterion for rotation to oblique structure in factor analysis. *Science, 126*, 1114–1115.

Carroll, J. B. (1958). A factor analysis of two foreign language aptitude batteries. *Journal of General Psychology, 59*, 3–19.
DS-CARR21 *HI.6.1*
DS-CARR22 *HI.3.1*

Carroll, J. B. (1960). Vectors of prose style. In T. A. Sebeok (Ed.), *Style in language.* Cambridge, MA: Technology Press, 1960.

Carroll, J. B. (1961). The nature of the data, or how to choose a correlation coefficient. *Psychometrika, 26*, 347–372.

Carroll, J. B. (1962a). Computer applications in the investigation of models in educational research. In A. G. Oettinger (Ed.), Proceedings of a Harvard symposium on digital computers and their applications. *Annals of the Computation Laboratory of Harvard University, 31*, 48–58.

Carroll, J. B. (1962b). The prediction of success in intensive foreign language training. In R. Glaser (Ed.), *Training research and education* (pp. 87–136). Pittsburgh, PA: University of Pittsburgh Press. [ERIC Doc. ED 038 051]

Carroll, J. B. (1962c). Factors of verbal achievement. In P. L. Dressel (Ed.), *Proceedings of the Invitational Conference on Testing Problems, 1961* (pp. 11–18). Princeton, NJ: Educational Testing Service. [Reprinted in A. Anastasi (Ed.), (1966). *Testing problems in perspective* (pp. 406–413). Washington D. C.: American Council on Education.]

Carroll, J. B. (1963). A model of school learning. *Teachers College Record, 64*, 723–733.

Carroll, J. B. (1966). *A parametric study of language training in the Peace Corps.* Cambridge, MA: Harvard Graduate School of Education. [ERIC Document ED 010 877]

Carroll, J. B. (1968a). The psychology of language testing. In A. Davies (Ed.), *Language testing symposium: A psycholinguistic approach* (pp. 46–69). London: Oxford University Press.

Carroll, J. B. (1968b). Review of J. P. Guilford's *The nature of human intelligence* (New York: McGraw–Hill, 1967). *American Educational Research Journal, 5*, 249–256.

Carroll, J. B. (1971). Development of native language skills beyond the early years. In C. Reed (Ed.), *The learning of language* (pp. 97–156). New York: Appleton-Century-Crofts.

Carroll, J. B. (1972). Stalking the wayward factors; Review of J. P. Guilford & R. Hoepfner's *The analysis of intelligence* (New York: McGraw-Hill, 1971). *Contemporary Psychology, 17*, 321–324.

Carroll, J. B. (1974). The aptitude–achievement distinction: The case of foreign language aptitude and proficiency. In D. R. Green (Ed.), *The aptitude–achievement distinction* (pp. 286–303). Monterey, CA: CTB/McGraw-Hill.

Carroll, J. B. (1975). Speed and accuracy of absolute pitch judgments: Some latter-day results. Princeton, NJ: Educational Testing Service Research Bulletin RB-75-35. [ERIC Document ED 150 153].

Carroll, J. B. (1976a). Psychometric tests as cognitive tasks: A new "Structure of Intellect." In L. Resnick (Ed.), *The nature of intelligence* (pp. 27–56). Hillsdale, NJ: Erlbaum.

Carroll, J. B. (1976b). Word retrieval latencies as a function of frequency and age-of-acquisition priming, repeated trials, and individual differences. Princeton, NJ: Educational Testing Service Research Bulletin RB-76-7. [ERIC Document ED 150 154]

　　DS-CARR31 *HI.2.1*

Carroll, J. B. (1977). The nature of certain linguistic abilities. Unpublished Ms.

　　DS-CARR41 *HI.6.1*
　　DS-CARR42 *HI.7*
　　DS-CARR43 *HI.11.3.1*

Carroll, J. B. (1978). How shall we study individual differences in cognitive abilities? – Methodological and theoretical perspectives. *Intelligence, 2*, 87–115.

　　Reanalysis of JARM31

Carroll, J. B. (1980a). Individual difference relations in psychometric and experimental cognitive tasks. Chapel Hill, NC: The L. L. Thurstone Psychometric Laboratory, University of North Carolina, Report No. 163. [NTIS Doc. AD-A086 057; ERIC Doc. ED 191 891]

Carroll, J. B. (1980b). Measurement of abilities constructs. In *Construct validity in psychological assessment; Proceedings from a colloquium on theory and application in education and employment* (pp. 23–41). Princeton, NJ: Educational Testing Service. [ETS Microfiche 1939]

Carroll, J. B. (1980c). Remarks on Sternberg's "Factor theories of intelligence are all right almost." *Educational Researcher, 9*(8), 14–18.

Carroll, J. B. (1980d). Discussion. In D. J. Weiss (Ed.), *Proceedings of the 1979 Computerized Adaptive Testing Conference* (pp. 278–283, 449–452). Minneapolis: University of Minnesota, Department of Psychology, Psychometric Methods Program.

Carroll, J. B. (1981a). Ability and task difficulty in cognitive psychology. *Educational Researcher, 10*(1), 11–21.

　　Reanalysis of JENS41

Carroll, J. B. (1981b). Twenty-five years of research on foreign language aptitude. In K. C. Diller (Ed.), *Individual differences and universals in language learning aptitude* (pp. 83–118). Rowley, MA: Newbury House.

Carroll, J. B. (1982). The measurement of intelligence. In R. J. Sternberg (Ed.), *Handbook of human intelligence* (pp. 29–120). New York: Cambridge University Press.

Carroll, J. B. (1983a). Psychometric theory and language testing. In J. W. Oller, Jr. (Ed.), *Issues in language testing research* (pp. 80–107). Rowley, MA: Newbury House.

　　Reanalysis of SCHO31

Carroll, J. B. (1983b). Studying individual differences in cognitive abilities: Through and beyond factor analysis. In R. F. Dillon & R. R. Schmeck (Eds.), *Individual differences in cognition*, Vol. 1 (pp. 1–33). New York: Academic.

Carroll, J. B. (1983c). The difficulty of a test and its factor composition revisited. In H. Wainer & S. Messick (Eds.), *Principals of modern psychological measurement: A Festschrift in honor of Frederic M. Lord* (pp. 257–283). Hillsdale, NJ: Erlbaum.

Carroll, J. B. (1984). Raymond B. Cattell's contributions to the theory of cognitive abilities. *Multivariate Behavioral Research, 19*, 300–306. [References, in pp. 344–380]

Carroll, J. B. (1985). Exploratory factor analysis: A tutorial. In D. K. Detterman (Ed.), *Current topics in human intelligence*, Vol. 1 (pp. 25–58). Norwood, NJ: Ablex.

Carroll, J. B. (1987a). Measurement and educational psychology: Beginnings and repercussions. In J. A. Glover & R. R. Ronning (Eds.), *Historical foundations of educational psychology* (pp. 89–106). New York: Plenum.

Carroll, J. B. (1987b). The national assessments in reading: Are we misreading the findings? *Phi Delta Kappan, 68*, 424–430.

Carroll, J. B. (1988a). Editorial: Cognitive abilities, factors, and processes. *Intelligence, 12*, 101–109.

Carroll, J. B. (1988b). The NAEP Reading Proficiency Scale is not a fiction; A reply to McLean and Goldstein. *Phi Delta Kappan, 69*, 761–764.

Carroll, J. B. (1989). Factor analysis since Spearman: Where do we stand? What do we know? In R. Kanfer, P. L. Ackerman, & R. Cudeck (Eds.), *Abilities, motivation, and methodology: The Minnesota Symposium on Learning and Individual Differences* (pp. 43–67). Hillsdale, NJ: Erlbaum.

Carroll, J. B. (1990). Estimating item and ability parameters in homogeneous tests with the person characteristic function. *Applied Psychological Measurement, 12*, 109–125.

Carroll, J. B. (1991a). No demonstration that *g* is not unitary, but there's more to the story: Comment on Kranzler and Jensen. *Intelligence, 15*, 423–436.

Carroll, J. B. (1991b). Still no demonstration that *g* is not unitary: Further comment on Kranzler and Jensen. *Intelligence, 15*, 449–453.

Carroll, J. B. (1992). Test theory and the behavioral scaling of test performance. In N. Frederiksen, R. J. Mislevy, & I. Bejar (Eds.), *Test theory for a new generation of tests* (pp. 297–322). Hillsdale, NJ: Erlbaum.

Carroll, J. B., & Burke, M. L. (1965). Parameters of paired-associate verbal learning: Length of list, meaningfulness, rate of presentation, and ability. *Journal of Experimental Psychology, 69*, 543–553.

Carroll, J. B., Davies, P., & Richman, B. (1971). *The American Heritage word frequency book*. Boston: Houghton Mifflin.

Carroll, J. B., & Horn, J. L. (1981). On the scientific basis of ability testing. *American Psychologist, 36*, 1012–1020.

Carroll, J. B., Kohlberg, L. & DeVries, R. (1984). Psychometric and Piagetian intelligences: Toward resolution of controversy. *Intelligence, 8*, 67–91.
  Reanalysis of DEVR02, STEP01B

Carroll, J. B., Meade, A., & Johnson, E. S. (1991). Test analysis with the person characteristic function: Implications for defining abilities. In R. E. Snow & D. E. Wiley (Eds.), *Improving inquiry in social science: A volume in honor of Lee J. Cronbach* (pp. 109–143). Hillsdale, NJ: Erlbaum.
  DS-CARR85 HI.2.1

Carroll, J. B., & Sapon, S. M. (1959). *Modern Language Aptitude Test, Form A*. New York: The Psychological Corporation.

Carroll, J. B., & Sapon, S. M. (1967). *Modern Language Aptitude Test – Elementary*. New York: The Psychological Corporation.

Carroll, J. B., & White, M. N. (1973a). Word frequency and age of acquisition as determiners of picture-naming latency. *Quarterly Journal of Experimental Psychology, 25*, 85–95.

Carroll, J. B., & White, M. N. (1973b). Age-of-acquisition norms for 220 picturable nouns. *Journal of Verbal Learning and Verbal Behavior, 12*, 563–576.

Caruso, D. R., Taylor, J. J., & Detterman, D. K. (1982). Intelligence research and intelligent policy. In D. K. Detterman & R. J. Sternberg (Eds.), *How and how much can intelligence be increased* (pp. 45–65). Norwood, NJ: Ablex.

Carver, R. P. (1990). *Reading rate: A review of research and theory*. San Diego: Academic.

Carver, R. P., Johnson, R. L., & Friedman, H. L. (1971–72). Factor analysis of the ability to comprehend time-compressed speech. *Journal of Reading Behavior, 4*, 40–49.

Cattell, J. M. (1885). Ueber die Zeit der Erkennung und Benennung von Schriftzeichen, Bildern und Farben. *Philosophische Studien, 2*, 635–650. [Translated: On the time required for recognizing and naming letters and words, pictures and colors. In A. T. Poffenberger (Ed.), *James McKeen Cattell: Man of Science; Vol. 1: Psychological research* (pp. 13–25), Lancaster, PA: Science Press, 1947]

Cattell, J. M. (1890). Mental tests and measurements. *Mind, 15*, 373–381.

Cattell, J. M., & Farrand, L. (1896). Physical and mental measurements of the students of Columbia University. *Psychological Review, 3*, 618–648.

Cattell, R. B. (1943). The measurement of adult intelligence. *Psychological Bulletin, 40*, 153–193.

Cattell, R. B. (1952). *Factor analysis: An introduction and manual for the psychologist and social scientist.* New York: Harper.

Cattell, R. B. (1957). A universal index for psychological factors. *Psychologia, 1*, 74–85.

Cattell, R. B. (1963). Theory of fluid and crystallized intelligence: A critical experiment. *Journal of Educational Psychology, 54*, 1–22.
  DS-CATT01A *HI.5.2* (13 variables)
  Reanalyzed: Humphreys (1967), Humphreys, Tucker, & Dachler (1970)

Cattell, R. B. (1966). The scree test for the number of factors. *Multivariate Behavioral Research, 1*, 245–276.

Cattell, R. B. (1967a). La théorie de l'intelligence fluide et cristallisée, sa relation avec les tests "culture fair" et sa vérification chez les enfants de 9 à 12 ans. [The theory of fluid and crystallized intelligence, its relation with "culture fair" tests and its verification with children of 9 to 12 years.] *Revue de Psychologie Appliquée, 17*, 134–154.

Cattell, R. B. (1967b). The theory of fluid and crystallized general intelligence checked at the 5–6 year-old level. *British Journal of Educational Psychology, 37*, 209–224.

Cattell, R. B. (1971). *Abilities: Their structure, growth, and action.* Boston: Houghton Mifflin. [Revised edition: Amsterdam: North-Holland, 1987.]

Cattell, R. B. (1978). *The scientific use of factor analysis in behavioral and life sciences.* New York: Plenum.

Cattell, R. B. (1982). *The inheritance of personality and ability: Research methods and findings.* New York: Academic Press.

Cattell, R. B., & Cattell, A. K. S. (1957). *The IPAT Culture Fair Intelligence Scales.* Champaign, IL: Institute for Personality and Ability Testing.

Cattell, R. B., & Horn, J. L. (1978). A check on the theory of fluid and crystallized intelligence with description of new subtest designs. *Journal of Educational Measurement, 15*, 139–164.

Cattell, R. B., & Jaspars, J. (1967). A general plasmode (No. 30-10-5-2) for factor analytic exercises and researchers. *Multivariate Behavior Research Monograph, 67–3.*

CBS (1975). News special *The IQ Myth*, broadcast April 22.

Chase, W. G. (1978). Elementary information processes. In W. K. Estes (Ed.), *Handbook of learning and cognitive processes*, Vol. 5: *Human information processing* (pp. 19–90). Hillsdale, NJ: Erlbaum.

Chein, I. (1939). An empirical study of verbal, numerical, and spatial factors in mental organization. *Psychological Record, 3*, 71–94.
  Reanalysis of DS-SMIT01

Chi, M. T. H., Glaser, R., & Farr, M. J. (Eds.) (1988). *The nature of expertise.* Hillsdale, NJ: Erlbaum.

Chi, M. T. H., & Klahr, D. (1975). Span and rate of apprehension in children and adults. *Journal of Experimental Child Psychology, 19*, 434–439.

Chiang, A., & Atkinson, R. C. (1976). Individual differences and interrelationships among a select set of cognitive skills. *Memory & Cognition, 4*, 661–672.
    DS-CHIA01 *HI.4*

Christal, R. E. (1958). Factor analytic study of visual memory. *Psychological Monographs, 72* (13; Whole No. 466).
    DS-CHRI01 *HI.8.3.1*

Christal, R. E. (1986). Learning abilities measurement program (LAMP); Description, plans, and preliminary findings. San Antonio, TX: AFHHRL Newsletter, Department of the Air Force.

Christensen, P. R., & Guilford, J. P. (1963). An experimental study of verbal fluency factors. *British Journal of Statistical Psychology, 26*, 1–26.
    Further publication of GUIL12.

Clark, H. H., & Chase, W. G. (1972). On the process of comparing sentences against pictures. *Cognitive Psychology, 3*, 472–517.

Clausen, J. (1966). *Ability structure and subgroups in mental retardation.* Washington, DC: Spartan Books.
    DS-CLAU01 *HI.6.1* (Age 8–10 retarded)
    DS-CLAU02 *III.6.1* (Age 12–15 retarded)
    DS-CLAU03 *HI.6.1* (Age 20–24 retarded)
    DS-CLAU04 *III.9.2.1* (Age 8–10 normals)

Cleary, T. A., Humphreys, L. G., Kendrick, S. A., & Wesman, A. (1975). Educational uses of tests with disadvantaged students. *American Psychologist, 30*, 15–41.

Cliff, N. (1966). Orthogonal rotation to congruence. *Psychometrika, 31*, 33–42.

Coan, R. W. (1964). Facts, factors and artifacts: The quest for psychological meaning. *Psychological Review, 71*, 123–140.

Coblentz, W. W., & Emerson, W. H. (1918). Relative sensitivity of the average eye to light of different colors and some practical application to radiation problems. *Bulletin of the Bureau of Standards, 4*(2), 167–236.

Cofer, C. N. (Ed.) (1961). *Verbal learning and verbal behavior.* New York: McGraw-Hill.

Cohen, J. D., Dunbar, K., & McClelland, J. L. (1990). On the control of automatic processes: A parallel distributed processing account of the Stroop effect. *Psychological Review, 97*, 332–361.

Cohen, P. C. (1983). *A calculating people: The spread of numeracy in early America.* Chicago: University of Chicago Press.

Colberg, M. (1985). Logic-based measurement of verbal reasoning: A key to increased validity and reliability. *Personnel Psychology, 38*, 347–359.

Colberg, M., & Nester, M. A. (1987). The use of illogical biases in psychometrics. Paper presented at the VIIIth International Congress of Logic, Methodology, and Philosophy of Science, Moscow, USSR.

Colberg, M., Nester, M. A., & Cormier, S. M. (1982). Inductive reasoning in psychometrics: A philosophical corrective. *Intelligence, 6*, 139–164.

Colberg, M., Nester, M. A., & Trattner, M. H. (1985). Convergence of the inductive and deductive models in the measurement of reasoning abilities. *Journal of Applied Psychology, 70*, 681–694.

Cole, D. A., & Maxwell, S. E. (1985). Multitrait–multimethod comparisons across populations: A confirmatory factor analytic approach. *Multivariate Behavioral Research, 20*, 389–417.

Cole, N. (1982). The implications of coaching for ability testing. In A. K. Wigdor &

W. R. Garner (Eds.), *Ability testing: Uses, consequences, and controversies* (Part II, pp. 389–414). Washington, DC: National Academy Press.

Cole, R. E., Johnson, R. C., Ahern, F. M., Kuse, A. R., McClearn, G. E., Vandenberg, S. G., & Wilson, J. R. (1979). A family study of memory processes and their relations to cognitive test scores. *Intelligence, 3*, 127–138.

Comrey, A. L. (1973). *A first course in factor analysis.* New York: Academic.

Comrey, A. L., & Lee, H. B. (1992). *A first course in factor analysis.* Second edition. Hillsdale, NJ: Erlbaum.

Conley, J. J. (1984). The hierarchy of consistency: A review and model of longitudinal findings on adult individual differences in intelligence, personality, and self opinion. *Personality and Individual Differences, 5*, 11–25.

Converse, R. P., & Markus, G. B. (1979). Plus ca change ...: The new CPS Election Study panel. *American Political Science Review, 73*, 32–49.

Cooley, C. H. (1897). Genius, fame, and the comparison of races. *Annals of the American Academy of Political & Social Science, 9*(3, May), 1–42.

Coombs, C. H. (1941). A factorial study of number ability. *Psychometrika, 6*, 161–189. DS-COOM01 *HI.9.1*

Cooper, L. A. (1976). Individual differences in visual comparison processes. *Perception & Psychophysics, 19*, 433–444.

Cooper, L. A., & Regan, D. T. (1982). Attention, perception, and intelligence. In R. J. Sternberg (Ed.), *Handbook of human intelligence* (pp. 123–169). Cambridge, England: Cambridge University Press.

Coren, S., & Girgus, J. S. (1978). *Seeing is deceiving: The psychology of visual illusions.* Hillsdale, NJ: Erlbaum.

Coren, S., Girgus, J. S., Ehrlichman, H., & Hakstian, A. R. (1976). An empirical taxonomy of visual illusions. *Perception & Psychophysics, 20*, 129–137.

Cornelius, S. W., Willis, S. L., Nesselroade, J. R., & Baltes, P. B. (1983). Convergence between attention variables and factors of psychometric intelligence in older adults. *Intelligence, 7*, 253–269. DS-CORN01 *HI.5.1*

Corso, J. F. (1973). Hearing. In B. B. Wolman (Ed.), *Handbook of general psychology* (pp. 348–381). Englewood Cliffs, NJ: Prentice–Hall.

Cory, C. H., Rimland, B., & Bryson, R. A. (1977). Using computerized tests to measure new dimensions of abilities: An exploratory study. *Applied Psychological Measurement, 1*, 101–110. DS-CORY01 *HI.8.2*

Court, J. H. (Compiler) (1977). *Researcher's bibliography for Raven's Progressive Matrices and Mill Hill Vocabulary Scales* (4th edition). Adelaide: School of Social Sciences, Flinders University of South Australia.

Cox, G. M. (1939). The multiple factor theory in terms of common elements. *Psychometrika, 4*, 59–68.

Cox, J. W. (1928). *Mechanical aptitude: Its existence, nature and measurement.* London: Methuen.

Craik, F. I. M. (1971). Age differences in recognition memory. *Quarterly Journal of Experimental Psychology, 23*, 316–323.

Crano, W. D. (1974). Causal analyses of the effects of socioeconomic status and initial intellectual endowment on patterns of cognitive development and academic achievement. In D. R. Green (Ed.), *The aptitude–achievement distinction* (pp. 223–261). Monterey, CA: CTB/McGraw–Hill.

Crano, W. D., Kenny, D. A., & Campbell, D. T. (1972). Does intelligence cause achievement? A cross-lagged panel analysis. *Journal of Educational Psychology, 63*, 258–275.

Cravens, H. (1978). *The triumph of evolution: American scientists and the heredity–environment controversy, 1900–1941.* Philadelphia: University of Pennsylvania Press.

Crawford, C. B., & Ferguson, G. A. (1970). A general rotation criterion and its use in orthogonal rotation. *Psychometrika, 35,* 321–332.
 Reanalysis of HOLZ01

Crawford, C. B., & Nirmal, B. (1976). A multivariate study of measures of creativity, achievement, motivation, and intelligence in secondary school students. *Canadian Journal of Behavioral Science, 8,* 189–201.
 DS-CRAW01 *HI.7.1*

Crockenberg, S. B. (1972). Creativity tests: A boon or boondoggle for education? *Review of Educational Research, 42,* 27–45.

Cronbach, L. J. (1968). Intelligence? Creativity? A parsimonious reinterpretation of the Wallach–Kogan data. Stanford, CA: School of Education, Stanford University.
 Reanalysis of WALL01

Cronbach, L. J. (1975). Five decades of public controversy over mental testing. *American Psychologist, 30,* 1–14.

Cronbach, L. J. (1979). The Armed Services Vocational Aptitude Battery – A test battery in transition. *Personnel & Guidance Journal, 57,* 232–237.

Cronbach, L. J. (1990). *Essentials of psychological testing* (5th ed.). New York: Harper and Row.

Cronbach, L. J., & Snow, R. E. (1977). *Aptitudes and instructional methods: A handbook for research on interactions.* New York: Irvington.

Cronbach, L. J., & Warrington, W. G. (1951). Time-limit tests: Estimating their reliability and degree of speeding. *Psychometrika, 16,* 167–188.

Crouse, J., & Trusheim, D. (1988). *The case against the SAT.* Chicago: University of Chicago Press.

Crowder, R. G. (1971). The sound of vowels and consonants in immediate memory. *Journal of Verbal Learning and Verbal Behavior, 10,* 587–596.

Cudeck, R. (1982). Methods for estimating between-battery factors. *Multivariate Behavioral Research, 17,* 47–68.
 Reanalysis of MALM01

Cummins, J. P. (1979). Language functions and cognitive processing. In J. P. Das, J. R. Kirby, & R. F. Jarman (Eds.), *Simultaneous and successive cognitive processes* (pp. 175–185). New York: Academic.
 DS-CUMM01 *HI.5.1*

Cureton, E. E., et al. (1944). Verbal abilities experiment: Analysis of new word meaning and verbal analogies tests (Personnel Research Section, Adjutant General's Office, PRS Report No. 548). Arlington, VA: War Department.
 DS-CURE01 *HI.2.1*

Cureton, E. E. (1968). A factor analysis of Project TALENT tests and four other test batteries. Palo Alto, CA: Project TALENT Office. [ERIC Doc. ED 025 819]
 DS-CURE11 *HI.8.1* (males)
 DS-CURE12 *HI.8.2* (females)

Cureton, E. E., & D'Agostino, R. B. (1983). *Factor analysis: An applied approach.* Hillsdale, NJ: Erlbaum.
 Reanalysis of THUR82

Das, J. P., Kirby, J. R., & Jarman, R. F. (1975). Simultaneous and successive syntheses: An alternative model for cognitive abilities. *Psychological Bulletin, 82,* 87–103.

Das, J. P., Kirby, J. R., & Jarman, R. F. (1979). *Simultaneous and successive cognitive processes.* New York: Academic.

Davidson, W. M., & Carroll, J. B. (1945). Speed and level components in time-limit scores: A factor analysis. *Educational & Psychological Measurement, 5,* 411–427.

DS-DAVI01 *HI.4.1*
Reanalyzed: Lohman (1979a)
Davies, D. R., Jones, D. M., & Taylor, A. (1984). Selective- and sustained attention tasks: Individual and group differences. In R. Parasuram & D. R. Davies (Eds.), *Varieties of attention* (pp. 395–447). Orlando, FL: Academic.
Davis, F. B. (1944). Fundamental factors of comprehension in reading. *Psychometrika, 9,* 185–197.
DS-DAVI11 *HI.1*
Reanalyzed: Thurstone (1946)
Rejoinder: Davis (1946)
Reanalyzed: Jennrich & Robinson (1969), Jöreskog (1967), Martin & McDonald (1975).
Davis, F. B. (1946). A brief comment on Thurstone's note on a reanalysis of Davis' reading tests. *Psychometrika, 11,* 249–255.
Rejoinder to Thurstone (1946) on DAVI11
Davis, P. C. (1956). A factor analysis of the Wechsler–Bellevue scale. *Educational & Psychological Measurement, 16,* 127–146.
DS-DAVI41 not analyzable
Deary, I. J., Head, B., & Egan, V. (1989). Auditory inspection time, intelligence and pitch discrimination. *Intelligence, 13,* 135–147.
Deese, J. (1965). *The structure of associations in language and thought.* Baltimore: The Johns Hopkins Press.
DeFries, J. C., Kuse, A. R., & Vandenberg, S. G. (1979). Genetic correlations, environmental correlations and behavior. In J. R. Royce & L. P. Mos (Eds.), *Theoretical advances in behavior genetics* (pp. 389–421). Alphen aan den Rijn, Netherlands: Sijthoff Noordhoff International.
DeFries, J. C., Vandenberg, S. G., & McClearn, G. E. (1976). Genetics of specific cognitive abilities. *Annual Review of Genetics, 10,* 179–207.
Degan, J. W. (1950). Mechanical aptitude VI: A re-analysis of the Army Air Force battery of mechanical tests. Chicago: Psychometric Laboratory Report No. 58, University of Chicago.
Reanalysis of GUIL38
DeGuire, L. J. (1983). Reanalyses of factor-analytic studies of mathematical abilities. Unpublished Ed. D. dissertation, University of Georgia. [University Microfilms No. 83-14713]
Reanalyses of CANI01, VERY01–02, WEIS01, WERD01, and several other datasets not included here
de Mille, R. (1962). Intellect after lobotomy in schizophrenia: A factor-analytic study. *Psychological Monographs, 76*(16, Whole No. 535). [ADI Document 7260]
DS-DEMI01A *HI.4.1* (lobotomized schizophrenics)
DS-DEMI02A *HI.4.1* (normals, control)
Denton, J. C., & Taylor, C. W. (1955). A factor analysis of mental abilities and personality traits. *Psychometrika, 20,* 75–81.
DS-DENT01 *HI.5.1*
Detterman, D. K. (1982a). Does "g" exist? *Intelligence, 6,* 99–108.
Detterman, D. K. (1982b). Questions I would like answered. In D. K. Detterman & R. J. Sternberg (Eds.), *How and how much can intelligence be increased.* (pp. 41–44). Norwood, NJ: Ablex.
Detterman, D. K. (1989). Editorial: The future of intelligence research. *Intelligence, 13,* 199–203.
Detterman, D. K. (unpublished). [A study of learning rates]

DS-DETT00 *HI.8.2*

Detterman, D. K., & Sternberg, R. J. (Eds.) (1982). *How and how much can intelligence be increased.* Norwood, NJ: Ablex.

DeVries, R. (1974). Relationships among Piagetian, IQ, and achievement assessments. *Child Development, 45,* 746–756.

DS-DEVR02 *HI.3.1*

Reanalyzed: Carroll, Kohlberg, DeVries (1984)

Dixon, R. A., Kramer, D. A., & Baltes, P. B. (1985). Intelligence: A life-span developmental perspective. In B. B. Wolman (Ed.), *Handbook of intelligence: Theories, measurements, and applications* (pp. 301–350). New York: Wiley.

Donlon, T. F. (Ed.) (1984). *The College Board technical handbook for the Scholastic Aptitude Test and Achievement Tests.* New York: College Entrance Examination Board.

Doughtie, E. B., Wakefield, J. A., Jr., Sampson, R. N., & Alston, H. L. (1974). A statistical test of the theoretical model for the representational level of the Illinois Test of Psycholinguistic Ability. *Journal of Educational Psychology, 66,* 410–415.

Reanalysis of PARA01–08

Drake, R. M. (1954–57). *Drake Musical Aptitude Tests.* Chicago, IL: Science Research Associates.

DuBois, P. H. (1932). A speed factor in mental tests. *Archives of Psychology, 22* (Whole No. 141).

DS-DUBO01 *HI.2*

DuBois, P. H. (1970). *A history of psychological testing.* Boston: Allyn & Bacon.

Dudek, F. J. (1948). The dependence of factorial composition of aptitude tests upon population differences among pilot trainees. I. The isolation of factors. *Educational & Psychological Measurement, 8,* 613–633.

Replication of GUIL44 with a different sample.

Duncan, A. D. W. (1969). Behavior rates of gifted and regular elementary school children. *Monograph of the National Association for Creative Children and Adults.* [Reprinted in L. Willerman & R. G. Turner (Eds.), *Readings about individual and group differences* (pp. 217–223). San Francisco, CA: Freeman.]

DS-DUNC01 *HI.2.1*

Duncanson, J. P. (1964). Intelligence and the ability to learn. Princeton, NJ: Educational Testing Service Research Bulletin RB-64-29.

Further report, Duncanson (1966)

Duncanson, J. P. (1966). Learning and measured abilities. *Journal of Educational Psychology, 57,* 220–229.

DS-DUNC11 *HI.9.1*

Dunham, J. L., Guilford, J. P., & Hoepfner, R. (1966). Abilities pertaining to classes and the learning of concepts. Los Angeles: Reports from the Psychological Laboratory, University of Southern California, No. 39.

DS-DUNH11 *HI.7.1*

Further reported: Dunham, Guilford, & Hoepfner (1968; 1969)

Reanalyzed: Kelderman, Mellenbergh, & Elshout (1981)

Dunham, J. L., Guilford, J. P., & Hoepfner, R. (1968). Multivariate approaches to discovering the intellectual components of concept learning. *Psychological Review, 75,* 206–221.

Further report of DUNH11

Dunham, J. L., Guilford, J. P., & Hoepfner, R. (1969). The cognition, production, and memory of class concepts. *Educational & Psychological Measurement, 29,* 615–638.

Further report of DUNH11

Dunlap, W. P., Kennedy, R. S., Harbeson, M. M., & Fowlkes, J. E. (1989). Problems with individual difference measures based on some componential cognitive paradigms. *Applied Psychological Measurement, 13*, 9–17.

Dunn, J. C., & Kirsner, K. (1988). Discovering functionally independent mental processes: The principle of reversed association. *Psychological Review, 95*, 91–101.

Dupont, J–B., Gendre, F., & Pauli, L. (1975). Èpreuves opératoires et tests factoriels classiques; Contribution à l'étude de la structure des aptitudes mentales durant l'adolescence. [Tests of operations and classic factorial tests; Contribution to the study of the structure of mental aptitudes during adolescence.] *Revue Européenne des Sciences Sociales et Cahiers Vilfredo Pareto, 13* (No. 35), 137–198.
DS-DUPO01 *HI.4.1*

Dwyer, P. S. (1937). The determination of the factor loadings of a given test from the known factor loadings of other tests. *Psychometrika, 2*, 173–178.

Ebbinghaus, H. (1896–97). Ueber eine neue Methode zur Prüfung geistiger Fähigkeiten und ihre Anwendung bei Schulkindern. [On a new method for testing mental abilities and its use with school children.] *Zeitschrift für Psychologie und Physiologie der Sinnesorgane, 13*, 401–459.

Educational Testing Service (issued periodically). *College Board Scholastic Aptitude Test.* Princeton, NJ: Author.

Egan, D. E. (1978). Characterizing spatial ability: Different mental processes reflected in accuracy and latency scores. Murray Hill, NJ: Bell Laboratories. (USN AMRL Technical Report No. 1250.)
DS-EGAN01 *HI.3.1*

Ekman, G. (1954). Dimensions of color vision. *Journal of Psychology, 38*, 467–474.

Ekstrom, R. B. (1967). A comparison of two groups of reference tests measuring selected perception and closure factors. Unpublished doctoral dissertation, Rutgers University. (University Microfilms No. 67–14421)
DS-EKST11 *HI.6.2.1*

Ekstrom, R. B. (1979). Review of cognitive factors. *Multivariate Behavioral Research Monographs,* No. 79-2, 7–56.

Ekstrom, R. B., French, J. W., & Harman, H. H., with D. Dirmen (1976). *Manual for kit of factor-referenced cognitive tests, 1976.* Princeton, NJ: Educational Testing Service.

Eliot, J., & Smith, I. M. (1983). *An international directory of spatial tests.* Windsor, England: NFER/Nelson; and Atlantic Highlands, NJ: Humanities Press.

El Koussy, A. A. H. (1935). The visual perception of space. *British Journal of Psychology Monograph Supplement, 7,* No. 20.
DS-ELKO01 *HI.6.1*

Elliott, C. D. (1983). *British ability scales. Manual 1: Introductory handbook. Manual 2: Technical handbook.* Windsor, England: NFER/Nelson.

Elliott, C. D., Murray, D. J., & Pearson, L. S. (1979–82). *British ability scales: Manuals.* Windsor, England: National Foundation for Educational Research.

Embretson, S. E. (Ed.) (1985). *Test design: Developments in psychology and psychometrics.* Orlando, FL: Academic.

English, H. B., & English, A. C. (1958). *A comprehensive dictionary of psychological and psychoanalytical terms: A guide to usage.* New York: McKay.

Ericsson, K. A. (1985). Memory skill. *Canadian Journal of Psychology, 39*, 188–231.

Ericsson, K. A., & Simon, H. A. (1984). *Protocol analysis.* Cambridge, MA: MIT Press.

Eysenck, H. J. (1939). Review of Thurstone's *Primary Mental Abilities,* 1938. *British Journal of Educational Psychology, 9,* 270–275.
Reanalysis of DS-THUR21

Eysenck, H. J. (1967). Intellectual assessment: A theoretical and experimental approach. *British Journal of Educational Psychology, 37*, 81–98.

Eysenck, H. J. (Ed.) (1973). *The measurement of intelligence.* Baltimore: Williams & Wilkins.

Eysenck, H. J. (1979). *The structure and measurement of intelligence.* With contributions by David W. Fulker. New York: Springer-Verlag.

Eysenck, H. J. (Ed.) (1982). *A model for intelligence.* Berlin: Springer-Verlag.

Eysenck, H. J. (1987). Speed of information processing, reaction time, and the theory of intelligence. In P. A. Vernon (Ed.), *Speed of information-processing and intelligence* (pp. 21–67). Norwood, NJ: Ablex.

Eysenck, H. J. (1988). Editorial: The concept of "intelligence": Useful or useless? *Intelligence, 12*, 1–16.

Eysenck, H. J., & Barrett, P. (1985). Psychophysiology and the measurement of intelligence. In C. R. Reynolds & V. L. Willson (Eds.), *Methodological and statistical advances in the study of individual differences* (pp. 1–49). New York: Plenum.

Eysenck, H. J., & Kamin, L. (1981). *The intelligence controversy.* New York: Wiley-Interscience.

Fairbank, B. A., Jr. (1988). Mathematical analysis of reaction time distribution. Paper presented at the annual meeting of the Human Factor Society, Anaheim, CA.

Fairbank, B. A., Jr., Tirre, W., & Anderson, N. S. (1991). Measures of thirty cognitive tasks: Intercorrelations and correlations with aptitude battery scores. In P. L. Dann, S. M. Irvine, & J. Collis (Eds.), *Advances in computer-based human assessment* (pp. 51–101). Dordrecht & Boston: Kluwer Academic.
  DS-FAIR01A *HI.7.3*
  DS-FAIR02 *HI.6.2*

Fancher, R. B. (1985). Spearman's computation of *g*: A model for Burt? *British Journal of Psychology, 76*, 341–352.

Faulds, B. (1959). The perception of pitch in music. Princeton, NJ: Educational Testing Service Technical Report.
  DS-FAUL11 *HI.2*

Favero, J., Dombrower, J., Michael, W. B., & Dombrower, E. (1979). The concurrent validity and factor structure of seventeen Structure-of-Intellect measures reflecting behavioral content. *Educational & Psychological Measurement, 39*, 1019–1034.
  DS-FAVE01 *HI.2.1*

Federico, P-A., & Landis, D. B. (1980). *Relationships among selected measures of cognitive styles, abilities, and aptitudes.* San Diego, CA: Navy Personnel Research and Development Center Report No. 80-23.
  DS-FEDE02 *HI.7.3*

Fee, F. (1968). An alternative to Ward's factor analysis of Wallach and Kogan's "creativity" correlations. *British Journal of Educational Psychology, 38*, 319-321.
  Reanalysis of DS-WALL01

Ferguson, G. A. (1954). On learning and human ability. *Canadian Journal of Psychology, 8*, 95–112.

Ferguson, G. A. (1956). On transfer and the abilities of man. *Canadian Journal of Psychology, 10*, 121–131.

Fernandes, K., & Rose, A. M. (1978). An information processing approach to performance assessment: II. An investigation of encoding and retrieval processes in memory. Washington, DC: American Institutes for Research Technical Report AIR 58500-11/78-TR.
  DS-FERN01 *HI.2* (day 1)
  DS-FERN02 *HI.2* (day 2)

Fitts, P. M. (1964). Perceptual-motor skill learning. In A. W. Melton (Ed.), *Categories of human learning* (pp. 243–285). New York: Academic.

Flanagan, J. C. (1951–60). *Flanagan Aptitude Classification Tests.* Chicago: Science Research Associates.

Flanagan, J. C., Dailey, J. T., Shaycoft, M. F., Gorham, W. F., Orr, D. B., & Goldberg, I. (1962). *Design for a study of American youth.* Boston: Houghton Mifflin.

Flanagan, J. C., Davis, F. B., Dailey, J. T., Shaycoft, M. F., Orr, D. B., Goldberg, I., & Neyman, C. A., Jr. (1964). *The American high school student* (Cooperative Research Project No. 635). Pittsburgh: University of Pittsburgh.
DS-FLAN01 *HI.5.1*

Flavell, J. H. (1977). *Cognitive development.* Englewood Cliffs, NJ: Prentice-Hall.

Fleishman, E. A. (1963). Factor analyses of physical fitness tests. *Educational & Psychological Measurement, 23,* 647–661.

Fleishman, E. A. (1964). *The structure and measurement of physical fitness.* Englewood Cliffs, NJ: Prentice–Hall.

Fleishman, E. A. (1972). Structure and measurement of psychomotor abilities. In R. N. Singer (Ed.), *The psychomotor domain: Movement behaviors* (pp. 78–106). Philadelphia: Lea & Febiger.

Fleishman, E. A., & Hempel, W. E., Jr. (1954). Changes in factor structure of a complex psychomotor test as a function of practice. *Psychometrika, 19,* 239–252.
DS-FLEI12 *HI.3.1*
Critique: Bechtoldt (1962); Humphreys (1960)

Fleishman, E. A., & Quaintance, M. K. (1984). *Taxonomies of human performance: The description of human tasks.* Orlando, FL: Academic.

Fleishman, J. J., & Dusek, E. R. (1971). Reliability and learning factors associated with cognitive tests. *Psychological Reports, 29,* 523–530.
DS-FLEI51 *HI.5.1*

Flynn, J. R. (1987). Massive IQ gains in 14 nations: What IQ tests really measure. *Psychological Bulletin, 101,* 171–191.

Fodor, J. A. (1983). *The modularity of mind: An essay on faculty psychology.* Cambridge, MA: MIT Press.

Fogarty, G. (1987). Time sharing in relation to broad ability domains. *Intelligence, 11,* 207–231.
DS-FOGA00 *HI.7.2*

Foley, P., & Rucker, L. S. (1989). An overview of the Armed Services Vocational Aptitude Battery (ASVAB). In R. F. Dillon & J. W. Pellegrino (Eds.), *Testing: Theoretical and applied perspectives* (pp. 16–35). New York: Praeger.

Ford, M. E. (1986). A living systems conceptualization of social intelligence: Outcomes, processes, and developmental change. In R. J. Sternberg (Ed.), *Advances in the psychology of human intelligence,* Vol. 3 (pp. 119–171). Hillsdale, NJ: Erlbaum.

Ford, M. E., & Tisak, M. S. (1983). A further search for social intelligence. *Journal of Educational Psychology, 75,* 196–206.

Forrest, D. W. (1974). *Francis Galton: The life and work of a Victorian genius.* New York: Taplinger.

Frank, G. (1983). *The Wechsler enterprise: An assessment of the development, structure, and use of the Wechsler tests of intelligence.* New York: Pergamon.

Franklin, E. (1956). *Tonality as a basis for the study of musical talent.* Gothenburg: Gumperts Forlag.

Franzbach, M. (1965). *Lessings Huarte-Uebersetzung (1752): Die Rezeption und Wirkungsgeschichte des "Examen de Ingenios para las Ciencias" (1575) in Deutschland. [Lessing's translation (1752) of Huarte: History of the reception and impact of*

"Examen de Ingenios para las Ciencias" (1575) in Germany.] Hamburg: Cram, De Gruyter.

Frederiksen, J. R. (1967). Cognitive factors in the recognition of ambiguous auditory and visual stimuli. *Journal of Personality and Social Psychology, 7*, 1–17.
   DS-FRED01 *HI.2*

Frederiksen, J. R. (1978). A chronometric study of component skills in reading. Cambridge, MA: Bolt Beranek & Newman Report No. 3757.
   DS-FRED11 *HI.5.1*

Frederiksen, J. R. (1982). A componential theory of reading skills and their interactions. In R. J. Sternberg (Ed.), *Advances in the psychology of intelligence*, Vol. 1 (pp. 125–180). Hillsdale, NJ: Erlbaum.
   DS-FRED12 *HI.8.2*
   DS-FRED13 *HI.5.1*

Frederiksen, N. (1986). Toward a broader conception of human intelligence. In R. J. Sternberg & R. K. Wagner (Eds.), *Practical intelligence: Origins of competence in the everyday world* (pp. 84–116). Cambridge, England: Cambridge University Press.

French, J. W. (1951). The description of aptitude and achievement tests in terms of rotated factors. *Psychometric Monographs*, No. 5.

French, J. W. (Ed.) (1954). Manual for Kit of Selected Tests for Reference Aptitude and Achievement Factors. Princeton, NJ: Educational Testing Service.

French, J. W. (1957). The factorial invariance of pure-factor tests. *Journal of Educational Psychology, 48*, 93–109.
   DS-FREN11 *HI.10.4*

French, J. W. (1965). The relationship of problem-solving styles to the factor composition of tests. *Educational & Psychological Measurement, 25*, 9–28.

French, J. W., Ekstrom, R. B., & Price, L. A. (1963). *Manual and kit of reference tests for cognitive factors*. Princeton, NJ: Educational Testing Service.

Frick, J. W., Guilford, J. P., Christensen, P. R., & Merrifield, P. R. (1959). A factor-analytic study of flexibility in thinking. *Educational & Psychological Measurement, 19*, 469–496.
   Further report of DS-GUIL14

Friedman, H. L., & Johnson, R. L. (1968). Compressed speech: Correlates of listening ability. *Journal of Communication, 18*, 207–218.

Fruchter, B. (1948). The nature of verbal fluency. *Educational & Psychological Measurement, 8*, 33–47.
   Reanalysis of 20 variables in DS-THUR21; see also Thorndike (1970)

Fruchter, B. (1952). Orthogonal and oblique solutions of a battery of aptitude, achievement and background variables. *Educational & Psychological Measurement, 12*, 20–38.
   DS-FRUC21 *HI.8.2*
   Further analysis: Fruchter & Novak (1958)

Fruchter, B. (1954). *Introduction to factor analysis*. New York: Van Nostrand.

Fruchter, B., & Novak, E. (1958). A comparative study of three methods of rotation. *Psychometrika, 23*, 211–221.
   Reanalyses of DS-FRUC21

Fryer, D. (1922). Occupational intelligence standards. *School & Society, 16*, 273–277.

Fürntratt, E. (1969). Hauptachsenanalyse und Varimax-Rotation von Thurstone's Primary Mental Abilities-Testbatterie. [Principal-axis analysis and Varimax-rotation of Thurstone's Primary Mental Abilities test battery.] *Diagnostica, 15*, 161–177.
   Reanalysis of THUR21

Fulgosi, A., & Guilford, J. P. (1966). Fluctuation of ambiguous figures and intellectual flexibility. *American Journal of Psychology, 79*, 602–607.
DS-FULG21 *HI.2*

Fulgosi, A., & Guilford, J. P. (1972). Factor structures with divergent- and convergent-production abilities in groups of American and Yugoslavian adolescents. *Journal of General Psychology, 87*, 169–180.
DS-FULG31 *HI.4.2.1*

Furneaux, W. D. (1948). Some factors affecting the design of 'g' with particular reference to the relation of 'speed' and 'power'. *Proceedings of the Twelfth International Congress of Psychology* (p. 65). Edinburgh.

Furneaux, W. D. (1960). Intellectual abilities and problem-solving behavior. In H. J. Eysenck (Ed.), *Handbook of abnormal psychology* (pp. 167–192). London: Pitman Medical.

Galton, F. (1869). *Hereditary genius: An enquiry into its laws and consequences.* London: Collins.

Galton, F. (1883). *Inquiries into human faculty and its development.* London: Macmillan.

Games, P. A. (1962). A factorial analysis of verbal learning tasks. *Journal of Experimental Psychology, 63*, 1–11.
DS-GAME01 *HI.5.2*

Garber, H. L. (1988). *The Milwaukee Project: Preventing mental retardation in children at risk.* Washington, D. C.: American Association on Mental Retardation.

Gardner, H. (1983). *Frames of mind: The theory of multiple intelligences.* New York: Basic Books.

Gardner, R. W., Holzman, P., Klein, G., Linton, H., & Spence, D. (1959). Cognitive control: A study of individual consistencies in cognitive behavior. In G. S. Klein (Ed.), *Psychological Issues*, I, Monograph 4. New York: International Universities Press.
DS-GARD01 Considered not analyzable
DS-GARD02 Considered not analyzable
Reanalyzed: Wardell (1974)

Gardner, R. W., Jackson, D. N., & Messick, S. (1960). Personality organization in cognitive controls and intellectual abilities. *Psychological Issues, 2* (Monograph 8), 1–149.
DS-GARD05A *HI.4.1*

Garnett, J. C. M. (1919). General ability, cleverness and purpose. *British Journal of Psychology, 9*, 345–366.

Garrett, H. E. (1938). Differentiable mental traits. *Psychological Record, 2*, 259–298.
Reanalyses of ANAS11, SCHN01

Garrett, H. E. (1946). A developmental theory of intelligence. *American Psychologist, 1*, 372–378.

Garrett, H. E., Bryan, A. I., & Perl, R. E. (1935). The age factor in mental organization. *Archives of Psychology* (N.Y.), No. 176.
DS-GARR11 *HI.3.1* (Gr. 9 boys)
DS-GARR12 *HI.3.1* (Gr. 9 girls)
DS-GARR13 *HI.3.1* (Gr. 12 boys)
DS-GARR14 *HI.3.1* (Gr. 12 girls)
DS-GARR15 *HI.3.1* (Gr. 15 boys)
DS-GARR16 *HI.3.1* (Gr. 15 girls)
Reanalyzed: Richards (1941)

Geiselman, E. E., Woodward, J. A., & Beatty, J. (1982). Individual differences in verbal memory performance: A test of alternative information-processing models. *Journal of Experimental Psychology: General, 111*, 109–134.
DS-GEIS01 *HI.2*

DS-GEIS02 *HI.2*
(Note: Analyses based on corrected correlation matrices supplied by authors.)
Gershon, A., Guilford, J. P., & Merrifield, P. R. (1963). Figural and symbolic divergent-production abilities in adolescent and adult populations. Los Angeles: Reports from the Psychological Laboratory, University of Southern California, No. 29.
DS-GERS01 *HI.6.2* (adults)
DS-GERS02 *HI.6.2* (adolescents)
Reanalyzed: Merrifield (1974)
Gesell, A. (1925). *The mental growth of the preschool child: A psychological outline of normal development from the fifth to the sixth year, including a system of developmental diagnosis.* New York: Macmillan.
Gettinger, M. (1984). Individual differences in time needed for learning: A review of the literature. *Educational Psychologist, 19*, 15–29.
Gettinger, M., & White, M. A. (1980). Evaluating curriculum fit with class ability. *Journal of Educational Psychology, 72*, 338–344.
Getzels, J. W., & Jackson, P. W. (1962). *Creativity and intelligence: Explorations with gifted students.* New York: Wiley.
Gewirtz, J. L. (1948). Studies in word fluency: Its relation to vocabulary and mental age in young children. *Journal of Genetic Psychology, 72*, 165–176.
Ghiselli, E. E. (1966). *The validity of occupational aptitude tests.* New York: Wiley
Gibson, J. J. (Ed.) (1947). *Army Air Forces Aviation Psychology Program, Report No. 7: Motion picture testing and research.* Washington, DC: U. S. Government Printing Office.
Gifford, B. R. (Ed.) (1989a). *Test policy and the politics of opportunity allocation: The workplace and the law.* Boston: Kluwer.
Gifford, B. R. (Ed.) (1989b). *Test policy and test performance: Education, language, and culture.* Boston: Kluwer.
Glaser, R., & Pellegrino, J. (1982). Improving the skills of learning. In D. K. Detterman & R. J. Sternberg (Eds.), *How and how much can intelligence be increased.* Norwood, NJ: Ablex.
Glass, G. V. (1966). Alpha factor analysis of infallible variables. *Psychometrika, 31*, 545–561.
Reanalysis of GUIL51
Goddard, H. H. (1910). A measuring scale for intelligence. *Training School, 6*, 146–154.
Goldman, S. R., & Pellegrino, J. W. (1984). Deductions about deduction: Analyses of developmental and individual differences. In R. J. Sternberg (Ed.), *Advances in the psychology of human intelligence*, Vol. 2 (pp. 147–197). Hillsdale, NJ: Erlbaum.
Goodman, C. H. (1943a). A factorial analysis of Thurstone's sixteen Primary Mental Ability tests. *Psychometrika, 8*, 141–151.
DS-GOOD01 *HI.7.1*
Reanalyzed: Guttman (1957)
Goodman, C. H. (1943b). Factorial analysis of Thurstone's seven primary abilities. *Psychometrika, 8*, 121–129.
DS-GOOD11 *HI.2.1*
Gordon, E. (1969). Intercorrelations among Musical Aptitude Profile and Seashore Measures of Musical Talent subtests. *Journal of Research in Music Education, 17*, 263–271.
DS-GORD01 *HI.3.1*
Gordon, N. G., & O'Dell, J. W. (1980). Reassessment of factor solution of Halstead's matrix. *Perceptual & Motor Skills, 51*, 123–128.
Reanalysis of DS-HALS01

Gordon, R. A. (1986). IQ commensurability of black–white differences in crime and delinquency. Paper presented at the convention of the American Psychological Association, Washington, DC.

Gorsuch, R. L. (1974, 1983). *Factor analysis*. Philadelphia: W. B. Saunders. (2nd edition: Hillsdale, NJ: Erlbaum, 1983.)
Reanalysis of DS-HOLZ01

Goss, A. E., & Nodine, C. F. (1965). *Paired-associates learning*. New York: Academic.

Gottfredson, L. S. (1984). The role of intelligence and education in the division of labor. Baltimore, MD: Center for Social Organization of Schools, Johns Hopkins University, Report No. 355.

Gottfredson, L. S. (1986a). IQ versus training: Job performance and black–white occupational inequality. Paper presented at the convention of the American Psychological Association, Washington, DC.

Gottfredson, L. S. (1986b). Societal consequences of the *g* factor in employment. *Journal of Vocational Behavior, 29*, 379–410.

Gottschaldt, K. (1926). Ueber den Einfluß der Erfahrung auf die Wahrnehmung von Figuren. I. Ueber den Einfluß gehäufter Einprägung von Figuren auf ihre Sichtbarkeit in umfassenden Konfigurationen. [On the influence of experience on the perception of figures. I. On the influence of cumulated impression of figures on their visibility in surrounding configurations.] *Psychologische Forschung, 8*, 261–317.

Gould, S. J. (1981). *The mismeasure of man*. New York: Norton.

Green, D. R. (Ed.) (1974). *The aptitude–achievement distinction: Proceedings of the Second CTB/McGraw-Hill Conference on Issues in Educational Measurement*. Monterey, CA: CTB/McGraw-Hill.

Green, R. F., Guilford, J. P., Christensen, P. R., & Comrey, A. L. (1953). A factor-analytic study of reasoning abilities. *Psychometrika, 18*, 135–160.
Further report of GUIL16

Greene, E. B. (1937–49). *Michigan Vocabulary Profile Test*. New York: Harcourt, Brace & World.

Greeno, J. G., & Simon, H. A. (1988). Problem solving and reasoning. In R. C. Atkinson, R. J. Herrnstein, G. Lindzey, & R. D. Luce (Eds.), *Stevens' Handbook of experimental psychology*, 2nd edition, Volume 2: *Learning and cognition* (pp. 589–672). New York: Wiley.

Grimaldi, J., Loveless, E., Hennessy, J.. & Prior, J. (1971). Factor analysis of 1970–71 version of the Comparative Guidance and Placement Battery. *Educational & Psychological Measurement, 31*, 959–963.
DS-GRIM01 *HI.6.2*

Groen, G. J., & Parkman, J. M. (1972). A chronometric analysis of simple addition. *Psychological Review, 79*, 329–343.

Guertin, A. S., Guertin, W. H., & Ware, W. B. (1981). Distortion as a function of the number of factors rotated under varying levels of common variance and error. *Educational & Psychological Measurement, 41*, 1–9.
Rotation reanalysis of HOLZ01

Guertin, W. H., & Bailey, J. P., Jr. (1970). *Introduction to modern factor analysis*. Ann Arbor, MI: Edwards.

Guilford, J. P. (1950). Creativity. *American Psychologist, 5*, 444–454.

Guilford, J. P. (1956). The structure of intellect. *Psychological Bulletin, 53*, 267–293.

Guilford, J. P. (1967). *The nature of human intelligence*. New York: McGraw-Hill.

Guilford, J. P. (1974). Rotation problems in factor analysis. *Psychological Bulletin, 81*, 498–501.
Reply to Horn & Knapp (1973), but see Horn & Knapp (1974)

Guilford, J. P. (1980a). Fluid and crystallized intelligences: Two fanciful concepts. *Psychological Bulletin, 88*, 406–412.
Critique of HORN01; see also Horn & Cattell (1982)

Guilford, J. P. (1980b). Cognitive styles: What are they? *Educational & Psychological Measurement, 40*, 715–735.

Guilford, J. P. (1981). Higher-order structure-of-intellect abilities. *Multivariate Behavioral Research, 16*, 411–435.

Guilford, J. P. (1982). Cognitive psychology's ambiguities: Some suggested remedies. *Psychological Review, 89*, 48–59.

Guilford, J. P. (1985). The structure-of-intellect model. In B. B. Wolman (Ed.), *Handbook of intelligence: Theories, measurements, and applications* (pp. 225–266). New York: Wiley.

Guilford, J. P., Berger, R. M., & Christensen, P. R. (1955). A factor-analytic study of planning: II. Administration of tests and analysis of results. Los Angeles: Reports from the Psychological Laboratory, University of Southern California, No. 12.
DS-GUIL11 *HI.7.1*
Further report: Berger, Guilford, & Christensen (1957)
Reanalysis: Harris (1967), Harris & Harris (1971), Harris & Liba (1965)

Guilford, J. P., & Christensen, P. R. (1956). A factor-analytic study of verbal fluency. Los Angeles: Reports from the Psychological Laboratory, University of Southern California, No. 17.
DS-GUIL12 *HI.10.2*
Further report: Christensen & Guilford (1963)
Reanalyzed: Wendeler (1970)

Guilford, J. P., Christensen, P. R., Kettner, N. W., Green, R. F., & Hertzka, A. F. (1954). A factor-analytic study of Navy reasoning tests with the Air Force Aircrew Classification Battery. *Educational & Psychological Measurement, 14*, 301–325.
Further report of GUIL17

Guilford, J. P., Frick, J. W., Christensen, P. R., & Merrifield, P. R. (1957). A factor-analytic study of flexibility in thinking. Los Angeles: Reports from the Psychological Laboratory, University of Southern California, No. 18.
DS-GUIL14 *HI.6.2*
Further report: Frick, Guilford, Christensen, & Merrifield (1959)

Guilford, J. P., Fruchter, B., & Zimmerman, W. S. (1952). Factor analysis of the Army Air Force's Sheppard Field battery of experimental aptitude tests. *Psychometrika, 17*, 45–68.
Reanalysis of GUIL46

Guilford, J. P., Fulgosi, A., & Hoepfner, R. (1970). A multivariate analysis of some controlled-association tasks. *Journal of General Psychology, 83*, 119–134.
DS-GUIL15 *HI.3.1*
See also DS-FULG31

Guilford, J. P., Green, R. F., & Christensen, P. R. (1951). A factor-analytic study of reasoning abilities: II. Administration of tests and analysis of results. Los Angeles: Reports from the Psychological Laboratory, University of Southern California, No. 3.
DS-GUIL16 *HI.6.2.1*
Further report: Green, Guilford, Christensen, & Comrey (1953)

Guilford, J. P., Green, R. F., Christensen, P. R., Hertzka, A. F., & Kettner, N. W. (1952). A factor-analytic study of Navy reasoning tests with the Air Force Aircrew Classification Battery. Los Angeles: Reports from the Psychological Laboratory, University of Southern California, No. 6.

DS-GUIL17 *HI.9.1*
Further report: Guilford, Christensen, Kettner, Green, & Hertzka (1954)
Reanalyzed: Ahmavaara (1957)
Guilford, J. P., Hertzka, A. F., & Christensen, P. R. (1953). A factor-analytic study of evaluative abilities: II. Administration of tests and analysis of results. Los Angeles: Reports from the Psychological Laboratory, University of Southern California, No. 9.
DS-GUIL18 *HI.7.1*
Further report: Hertzka, Guilford, Christensen, & Berger (1954)
Reanalyzed: Ahmavaara (1957), Harris (1967), Harris & Harris (1971), Harris & Liba (1965)
Guilford, J. P., & Hoepfner, R. (1966a). Sixteen divergent-production abilities at the ninth-grade level. *Multivariate Behavioral Research, 1,* 43–66.
Further report of HOEP11
Guilford, J. P., & Hoepfner, R. (1966b). Structure-of-intellect factors and their tests, 1966. Los Angeles: Reports from the Psychological Laboratory, University of Southern California, No. 36.
Guilford, J. P., & Hoepfner, R. (1971). *The analysis of intelligence.* New York: McGraw-Hill.
Reanalyses of numerous studies by Guilford and associates.
Guilford, J. P., Hoepfner, R., & Petersen, H. (1965). Predicting achievement in ninth-grade mathematics from measures of intellectual-aptitude factors. *Educational & Psychological Measurement, 25,* 659–682.
Further report of PETE11–12.
Guilford, J. P., Kettner, N. W., & Christensen, P. R. (1955a). A factor-analytic investigation of the factor called general reasoning. Los Angeles: Reports from the Psychological Laboratory, University of Southern California, No. 14.
DS-GUIL19 *HI.4.1*
Further report: Guilford, Kettner, & Christensen (1956)
Reanalyzed: Harris (1967), Harris & Harris (1971), Harris & Liba (1965), Thorndike (1970)
Guilford, J. P., Kettner, N. W., & Christensen, P. R. (1955b). The relation of certain thinking factors to training criteria in the U.S. Coast Guard Academy. Los Angeles: Reports from the Psychological Laboratory, University of Southern California, No. 13.
DS-GUIL20 *HI.5.1*
Further report: Kettner, Guilford, & Christensen (1959b)
Guilford, J. P., Kettner, N. W., & Christensen, P. R. (1956a). A factor-analytic study across the domain of reasoning, creativity, and evaluation: II. Administration of tests and analysis of results. Los Angeles: Reports from the Psychological Laboratory, University of Southern California, No. 16.
DS-GUIL21 *HI.5.1* (Table 4, p. 11)
DS-GUIL22 *HI.5.1* (Table 5, p. 12)
DS-GUIL23 *HI.3.1* (Table 6, p. 13)
Further report: Kettner, Guilford, & Christensen (1959a)
Reanalysis: Harris (1967), Harris & Harris (1971), Harris & Liba (1065)
Guilford, J. P., Kettner, N. W., & Christensen, P. R. (1956b). A factor analytic study of the factor called general reasoning. *Educational & Psychological Measurement, 16,* 438–453.
Further report of GUIL19
Guilford, J. P., & Lacey, J. I. (Eds.) (1947). *Printed classification tests.* Army Air Force

Aviation Psychology Program Research Reports, No. 5. Washington, DC: U.S. Government Printing Office.

Note: Many of these datasets are discussed or reanalyzed by Lohman (1979a)

DS-GUIL31 *HI.5.1* (p. 114, Nonverbal reasoning)

Reanalyzed: Ahmavaara (1957)

DS-GUIL32 *HI.4.1* (p. 148, Table 8.9, judgment & reasoning)

DS-GUIL32A *HI.4.1* (p. 148, Table 8.10, judgment & reasoning)

DS-GUIL33 *HI.3.1* (p. 181, foresight & planning)

DS-GUIL34 *HI.4.1* (p. 183, foresight & planning)

DS-GUIL35 *HI.8.1* (p. 216, integration tests)

DS-GUIL36 *HI.2.1* (p. 262, Memory I)

Reanalyzed: Humphreys & Fruchter (1945)

DS-GUIL37 *HI.4.1* (p. 262, Memory II)

Reanalyzed: Humphreys & Fruchter (1945)

DS-GUIL38 *HI.5.1* (p. 334, mechanical tests)

Reanalyzed: Degan (1950)

DS-GUIL39 *HI.6.1* (p. 409, Perceptual I)

DS-GUIL40 *HI.6.1* (p. 410, Perceptual II)

Reanalyzed: Lohman (1979a)

DS-GUIL41 *HI.4.1* (p. 687, carefulness battery)

DS-GUIL42 *III.5.1* (p. 799, Dec. '42 classification battery)

DS-GUIL43 *HI.5.1* (p. 801, Jul. '43 classification battery)

DS-GUIL44 *HI.5.1* (p. 802, Nov. '43 classification battery)

See Dudek (1948), replication with different sample

DS-GUIL45 *HI.5.1* (p. 803, Sep. '44 classification battery)

Reanalyzed: Humphreys (1964), Linn (1968)

DS-GUIL46 *HI.8.1* (Appendix C, Sheppard Field battery)

Reanalyzed: Adkins & Lyerly (1952), Ahmavaara (1957), Guilford, Fruchter, & Zimmerman (1952), Lohman (1979a), Roff (1951). [Note: The analysis presented here is based on Roff's corrected data matrix.]

Guilford, J. P., & Merrifield, P. R. (1960). The structure of intellect model: Its uses and implications. Los Angeles: Reports from the Psychological Laboratory, University of Southern California, No. 24.

Guilford, J. P., Merrifield, P. R., Christensen, P. R., & Frick, J. W. (1960). An investigation of symbolic factors of cognition and convergent production. Los Angeles: Reports from the Psychological Laboratory, University of Southern California, No. 23.

DS-GUIL51 *HI.7.1*

Further report: Guilford, Merrifield, Christensen, & Frick (1961)

Reanalyzed: Glass (1966), Harris (1967), Harris & Harris (1971), Harris & Liba (1965), Horn & Knapp (1973)

Guilford, J. P., Merrifield, P. R., Christensen, P. R., & Frick, J. W. (1961). Some new symbolic factors of cognition and convergent production. *Educational & Psychological Measurement*, 21, 515–541.

Further report of GUIL51

Guilford, J. P., Merrifield, P. R., & Cox, A. B. (1961). Creative thinking in children at the junior high school levels. Los Angeles: Reports from the Psychological Laboratory, University of Southern California, No. 26. (Cooperative Research Project No. 737.)

DS-GUIL55 *HI.7.1* (boys & girls, full range IQ)

DS-GUIL56 *HI.8.2.1* (boys, IQ 95–119)

DS-GUIL57 *HI.8.2* (girls, IQ 95–119)

DS-GUIL58 *HI.9.1* (boys & girls, IQ 120+)

Guilford, J. P., & Pandey, R. E. (1974). Abilities for divergent production of symbolic and semantic systems. *Journal of General Psychology, 91*, 209–220.
DS-GUIL61 *HI.3*
Guilford, J. P., Wilson, R. C., & Christensen, P. R. (1952). A factor-analytic study of creative thinking: II. Administration of tests and analysis of results. Los Angeles: Reports from the Psychological Laboratory, University of Southern California, No. 8.
DS-GUIL66 *HI.11.1*
Further report: Wilson, Guilford, Christensen, & Lewis (1954)
Reanalyzed: Ahmavaara (1957), Harris (1967), Harris & Harris (1971), Harris & Liba (1965)
Guilford, J. P., & Zimmerman, W. S. (1947–56). *Guilford-Zimmerman Aptitude Survey*. Orange, CA: Sheridan Psychological Services.
Guilford, J. P., & Zimmerman, W. S. (1948). The Guilford-Zimmerman Aptitude Survey. *Journal of Applied Psychology, 32*, 24–34.
Gulliksen, H. (1934). A rational equation of the learning curve based on Thorndike's Law of Effect. *Journal of General Psychology, 2*, 395–434.
Gulliksen, H. (1950). *Theory of mental tests*. New York: Wiley.
Gullion, C. M. (1985). The usefulness of number-of-factors criteria under empirically relevant conditions: A Monte Carlo study. Unpublished Ph.D. dissertation, University of North Carolina at Chapel Hill.
Gusfield, J. (1986). Review of J. Q. Wilson & R. J. Herrnstein, *Crime and human nature* (New York: Simon & Schuster, 1985). *Science, 231*, 413–414.
Gustafsson, J–E. (1984). A unifying model for the structure of intellectual abilities. *Intelligence, 8*, 179–203.
DS-GUST11A *HI.9.3.1*
Gustafsson, J–E. (1988). Hierarchical models of individual differences in cognitive abilities. In R. J. Sternberg (Ed.), *Advances in the psychology of human intelligence*, Vol. 4 (pp. 35–71). Hillsdale, NJ: Erlbaum.
Gustafsson, J–E. (1989). Broad and narrow abilities in research on learning and instruction. In R. Kanfer, P. L. Ackerman, & R. Cudeck (Eds.), *Abilities, motivation, and methodology: The Minnesota Symposium on Learning and Individual Differences* (pp. 203–237). Hillsdale, NJ: Erlbaum.
Gustafsson, J–E., Lindström, B., & Björck–Akesson, E. (1981). A general model for the organization of cognitive abilities. Mölndal, Sweden: Department of Education, University of Göteborg, Report 1981:06.
Reanalyses of BOTZ01, UNDH11, & first presentation of GUST11.
Guttman, L. (1941). The quantification of a class of attributes: A theory and method for scale construction. In P. Horst (Ed.), *The prediction of personal adjustment* (pp. 3l9–348). New York: Social Science Research Council.
Guttman, L. (1953). Image theory for the structure of quantitative variates. *Psychometrika, 18*, 277–296.
Guttman, L. (1954). A new approach to factor analysis: The radex. In P. F. Lazarsfeld (Ed.), *Mathematical thinking in the social sciences* (pp. 258–348). Glencoe, IL: Free Press.
Guttman, L. (1955). A generalized simplex for factor analysis. *Psychometrika, 20*, 173–192.
Guttman, L. (1957). Empirical verification of the radex structure of mental abilities and personality traits. *Educational & Psychological Measurement, 17*, 391–407.
Reanalyses of selected variables from GOOD01, PATE01, THUR21, THUR32, THUR41, THUR81.
Guttman, L. (1965). A faceted definition of intelligence. *Studies in Psychology, Scripta Hierosolymitana* (Jerusalem: Hebrew University), *14*, 166–181.

Guttman, L. (1966). Order analysis of correlation matrices. In R. B. Cattell (Ed.), *Handbook of multivariate experimental psychology* (pp. 438–458). New York: Rand McNally.

Guttman, L. (1982). Facet theory, smallest space analysis, and factor analysis. *Perceptual & Motor Skills, 54,* 491–493.

Guttman, R., Epstein, E. E., Amir, M., & Guttman, L. (1990). A structural theory of spatial abilities. *Applied Psychological Measurement, 14,* 217–236.

Härnqvist, K. (1968). Relative changes in intelligence from 13 to 18. *Scandinavian Journal of Psychology, 9,* 50–82.

Haier, R. J. (1990). Editorial: The end of intelligence research. *Intelligence, 14,* 371–374.

Haier, R. J., Siegel, B. V. Jr., Nuechterlein, K. H., Hazlett, E., Wu, J. C., Paek, J., Browning, H. L., & Buchsbaum, M. S. (1988). Cortical glucose metabolic rate correlates of abstract reasoning and attention studied with positron emission tomography. *Intelligence, 12,* 199–217.

Hakstian, A. R. (1971). A comparative evaluation of several prominent methods of oblique factor transformation. *Psychometrika, 36,* 175–193.
    Reanalysis (rotation) of HOLZ01, RIMO11

Hakstian, A. R. (1972). Optimizing the resolution between salient and non-salient factor pattern coefficients. *British Journal of Mathematical and Statistical Psychology, 25,* 229–245.

Hakstian, A. R., & Abell, R. A. (1974). A further comparison of oblique factor transformation methods. *Psychometrika, 39,* 429–444.
    Reanalysis (rotation) of HOLZ01, PEMB01

Hakstian, A. R., & Cattell, R. B. (1974). The checking of primary ability structure on a broader basis of performances. *British Journal of Educational Psychology, 44,* 140–154.
    DS-HAKS01 *HI.19.5.1*

Hakstian, A. R., & Cattell, R. B. (1975–77). *Comprehensive Ability Battery.* Champaign, IL: Institute for Personality and Ability Testing.

Hakstian, A. R., & Cattell, R. B. (1978). Higher-stratum ability structures on a basis of twenty primary abilities. *Journal of Educational Psychology, 70,* 657–669.
    DS-HAKS21 *HI.6.2*

Halford, G. S. (1989). Cognitive processing capacity and learning ability: An integration of two areas. *Learning and Individual Differences, 1,* 125–153.

Hall, E. T. (1959). *The silent language.* Garden City, NY: Doubleday.

Hall, W. E., & Robinson, F. P. (1945). An analytical approach to the study of reading skills. *Journal of Educational Psychology, 36,* 429–442.
    DS-HALL11 not analyzable

Halstead, W. C. (1947). *Brain and intelligence: A quantitative study of the frontal lobes.* Chicago: University of Chicago Press.
    DS-HALS01 *HI.3.1*
    Reanalyzed: Gordon & O'Dell (1980), Russell (1973)

Hambleton, R. K. (Ed.) (1983). *Applications of item response theory.* Vancouver, BC: Educational Research Institute of British Columbia.

Hanley, C. M. (1956). Factorial analysis of speech perception. *Journal of Speech and Hearing Disorders, 21,* 76–87.
    DS-HANL01 *HI.10.1*

Hargreaves, D. J., & Bolton, H. (1972). Selecting creativity tests for use in research. *British Journal of Psychology, 63,* 451–462.
    DS-HARG01 *HI.3.1*

Hargreaves, H. L. (1927). The 'faculty' of imagination: An enquiry concerning the existence of a general 'faculty,' or group factor, of imagination. *British Journal of Psychology Monograph Supplement, 3,* No. 10.

DS-HARG11A *HI.2.1* (p. 18)
DS-HARG12 *HI.3.1* (p.32)
Harman, H. H. (1960, 1967). *Modern factor analysis.* Chicago: University of Chicago Press. (Second edition, 1967)
Harman, H. H. (1976). *Modern factor analysis,* Third edition revised. Chicago: University of Chicago Press.
Reanalysis of HOLZ01
Harré, R., & Lamb, R. (Eds.) (1983). *The encyclopedic dictionary of psychology.* Cambridge, MA: MIT Press.
Harrell, W. (1940). A factor analysis of mechanical ability tests. *Psychometrika, 5,* 17–33.
DS-HARR01 *HI.6.2.1*
Reanalysis: Ahmavaara (1957)
Harris, C. W. (1967). On factors and factor scores. *Psychometrika, 32,* 363–379.
Reanalyses: see Harris & Liba (1965)
Harris, C. W., & Liba, M. R. (1965). Component, image, and factor analysis of tests of intellect and of motor performance. Cooperative Research Project No. S-094, University of Wisconsin. (ERIC Doc. ED 003 683)
Reanalyses: GUIL11, GUIL18, GUIL19, GUIL21-23, GUIL51, GUIL66, MERR41
Harris, M. L., & Harris, C. W. (1971). A factor analytic interpretation strategy. *Educational & Psychological Measurement, 31,* 589–606.
Reanalyses: See Harris & Liba (1965)
Harris, M. L., & Harris, C. W. (1973). *A structure of concept attainment abilities.* Madison, WI: Wisconsin Research and Development Center for Cognitive Learning.
DS-HARR51 *HI.7.1* (boys tested 1970)
DS-HARR52 *HI.8.1* (girls tested 1970)
DS-HARR53 *HI.5.1* (boys tested 1971)
DS-HARR54 *HI.6.1* (girls tested 1971)
Harrison, R. (1941). Personal tempo and the interrelationships of voluntary and maximal rates of movements. *Journal of General Psychology, 24,* 343–379.
Hart, B., & Spearman, C. (1912). General ability, its existence and nature. *British Journal of Psychology, 5,* 51–84.
Hartigan, J. A., & Wigdor, A. K. (Eds.) (1989). *Fairness in employment testing: Validity generalization, minority issues, and the General Aptitude Battery.* Washington, DC: National Academy Press.
Hartlage, L. C., & Telzrow, C. F. (Eds.) (1985). *The neuropsychology of individual differences: A developmental perspective.* New York, NY: Plenum.
Hass, W. A., & Wepman, J. M. (1974). Dimensions of individual difference in the spoken syntax of school children. *Journal of Speech and Hearing Research, 17,* 455–469.
DS-HASS01 *HI.5*
Haynes, J. R. (1970). Hierarchical analysis of factors in cognition. *American Educational Research Journal, 7,* 55–68.
DS-HAYN01 Matrix not analyzable
Hearnshaw, L. S. (1979). *Cyril Burt: Psychologist.* Ithaca, NY: Cornell University Press.
Hebb, D. O. (1942). The effects of early and late brain injury upon test scores and the nature of normal adult intelligence. *Proceedings of the American Philosophical Society, 85,* 275–292.
Heckman, R. W. (1967). Aptitude-treatment interactions in learning from printed-instruction: A correlational study. Unpublished Ph.D. thesis, Purdue University. (University Microfilm 67–10202)
DS-HECK01 *HI.9.3.1*
Heider, F., & Simmel, M. (1944). An experimental study of apparent behavior. *American Journal of Psychology, 57,* 243–259.

Helmstadter, G. C., & Ortmeyer, D. H. (1953). Some techniques for determining the relative magnitude of speed and power components of a test. *Educational & Psychological Measurement, 13*, 280–287.

Hemphill, J. K., Griffiths, D., Frederiksen, N., Stice, G., Iannaccone, L., Coffield, W., & Carlton, S. (1961). *Dimensions of administrative performance.* New York & Princeton: Teachers College, Columbia University, & Educational Testing Service.
DS-HEMP21 *HI.8.1*

Hendricks, M., Guilford, J. P., & Hoepfner, R. (1969). Measuring creative social abilities. Los Angeles: Reports from the Psychological Laboratory, University of Southern California, No. 42.
DS-HEND01 *HI.8.1*

Hendrickson, A. E. (1982). The biological basis of intelligence. Part I: Theory. In H. J. Eysenck (Ed.), *A model for intelligence* (pp. 151–196). Berlin: Springer

Hendrickson, A. E., & White, P. O. (1964). PROMAX: A quick method for rotation to oblique simple structure. *British Journal of Statistical Psychology, 17*, 65–70.
Promax analysis of HOLZ01

Hendrickson, D. E. (1982). The biological basis of intelligence. Part II: Measurement. In H. J. Eysenck (Ed.), *A model for intelligence* (pp. 197–228). Berlin: Springer.
DS-HEND11A *HI.4.2.1* (15 selected variables)

Herbart, J. F. (1816). *Lehrbuch zur Psychologie. [Textbook on psychology.]* (Translated, M. K. Smith, Appleton, 1891.)

Herrnstein, R. J. (1973). *IQ in the meritocracy.* Boston: Little, Brown.

Herrnstein, R. J. (1982). IQ testing and the media. *Atlantic Monthly, 250* (2, August), 68–74.

Hertzka, A. F., Guilford, J. P., Christensen, P. R., & Berger, R. M. (1954). A factor-analytic study of evaluative abilities. *Educational & Psychological Measurement, 14*, 581–597.
Further report of GUIL18

Hick, W. E. (1952). On the rate of gain of information. *Quarterly Journal of Experimental Psychology, 4*, 11–26.

Higgins, L. C. (1978). A factor analytic study of children's picture interpretation behavior. *Educational Communication & Technology, 26*, 215–232.
DS-HIGG01 *HI.3.1*

Hinman, S., & Bolton, B. (1979). *Factor analytic studies 1971–1975.* Troy, NY: Whitston.

Hintzman, D. L. (1990). Human learning and memory: Connections and dissociations. *Annual Review of Psychology, 41*, 109–139.

Hintzman, D. L., Carre, F. A., Eskridge, V. L., Owens, A. M., Shaff, S. S., & Sparks, M. E. (1972). "Stroop" effect: Input or output phenomenon? *Journal of Experimental Psychology, 95*, 458–459.

Hiskey, M. (1966). *Manual for the Hiskey–Nebraska Test of Learning Aptitude.* Lincoln, NE: Union College Press.
DS-HISK03 *HI.2.1*
DS-HISK04 *HI.1*
Analyzed: Bolton (1978)

Ho, W-C. (1957). Higher order factors in factor analysis. Unpublished Ed.D. dissertation, Harvard Graduate School of Education.
Reanalysis of MOUR01

Hochberg, J. (1988). Visual perception. In R. C. Atkinson, R. J. Herrnstein, G. Lindzey, & R. D. Luce (Eds.), *Stevens' Handbook of experimental psychology*, 2nd edition. Vol. 1: *Perception and motivation* (pp. 195–276). New York: Wiley.

Hoepfner, R. (1967). A "construct item analysis" of some aptitude tests. *Educational & Psychological Measurement, 27*, 287–299.
DS-HOEP01 *HI.3.1*

Hoepfner, R., & Guilford, J. P. (1965). Figural, symbolic, and semantic factors of creative

potential in ninth-grade students. Los Angeles: Reports from the Psychological
Laboratory, University of Southern California, No. 35.
DS-HOEP11 *HI.7.2*
Further report: Guilford & Hoepfner (1966)
Reanalyzed: Horn & Knapp (1973)

Hoepfner, R., Guilford, J. P., & Bradley, P. A. (1968). Identification of transformation
abilities in the structure-of-intellect model. Los Angeles: Reports from the Psy-
chological Laboratory, University of Southern California, No. 41.
DS-HOEP21 *HI.8.2*
Further report: Hoepfner, Guilford & Bradley (1970)
Reanalyzed: Khattab, Michael, & Hocevar (1982)

Hoepfner, R., Guilford, J. P., & Bradley, P. A. (1970). Information-transformation abilities.
Educational & Psychological Measurement, 30, 785–802.
Further report of HOEP21

Hoepfner, R., Guilford, J. P., & Merrifield, P. R. (1964). A factor analysis of the symbolic-
evaluation abilities. Los Angeles: Reports from the Psychological Laboratory,
University of Southern California, No. 33.
DS-HOEP31 *HI.7.2*
Further report: Hoepfner, Nihira, & Guilford (1966)

Hoepfner, R., Nihira, K., & Guilford, J. P. (1966). Intellectual abilities of symbolic and
semantic judgment. *Psychological Monographs, General & Applied, 80* (16, Whole
No. 624).
Further report of HOEP31 and NIHI01

Hoffman, K., Guilford, J. P., Hoepfner, R., & Doherty, W. (1968). A factor analysis of the
figural-cognition and figural-evaluation abilities. Los Angeles: Reports from the
Psychological Laboratory, University of Southern California, No. 40.
DS-HOFF01 *HI.7.2*
Reanalyzed: Kelderman, Mellenbergh, & Elshout (1981), Lohman (1979a)

Hogan, J. C. (1978). *Trainability of abilities: A review of nonspecific transfer issues relevant
to ability testing.* Technical Report. Washington, DC: Advanced Research Resources
Organization.

Hogan, R. (1969). Development of an empathy scale. *Journal of Consulting and Clinical
Psychology, 33*, 307–316.

Holmberg, G. R. (1966). A factor analytic study of the intellective abilities of deaf children,
as measured by the "structure of intellect" model. Unpublished doctoral dissertation,
University of Nebraska. (University Microfilms 66–11740)
DS-HOLM01 *HI.3*

Holmes, J. A. (1954). Increased reliabilities, new keys, and norms for a modified
Kwalwasser–Dykema Test of Musical Aptitudes. *Journal of Genetic Psychology, 85*,
65–73.

Holmes, J. A., & Singer, H. (1966). *Speed and power of reading in high school.* U.S. Office
of Education Cooperative Research Program Monograph No. 14. Washington, DC:
Government Printing Office.
DS-HOLM11 *HI.5.1*

Holtz, R. R. (1971). A study of selected creative thinking tests in conjunction with measures
of intelligence and personality. Unpublished doctoral dissertation, University of
California, Berkeley. (University Microfilms 72–3754.)
DS-HOLT11 *HI.4.2*

Holyoak, K. J. (1984). Analogical thinking and human intelligence. In R. J. Sternberg (Ed.),
Advances in the psychology of human intelligence, Vol. 2 (pp. 199–230). Hillsdale, NJ:
Erlbaum.

Holzinger, K. J. (1934a). Preliminary report on Spearman–Holzinger unitary trait study, No. 1. Chicago: Statistical Laboratory, Department of Education, University of Chicago.

Holzinger, K. J. (1934b). Preliminary report on Spearman–Holzinger unitary trait study, No. 2. Chicago: Statistical Laboratory, Department of Education, University of Chicago.

Holzinger, K. J. (1935a). Preliminary report on Spearman–Holzinger unitary trait study, No. 3. Chicago: Statistical Laboratory, Department of Education, University of Chicago.

Holzinger, K. J. (1935b). Preliminary report on Spearman–Holzinger unitary trait study, No. 4. Chicago: Statistical Laboratory, Department of Education, University of Chicago.

Holzinger, K. J. (1935c). Preliminary report on Spearman–Holzinger unitary trait study, No. 5. Chicago: Statistical Laboratory, Department of Education, University of Chicago.

Holzinger, K. J. (1935d). Preliminary report on Spearman–Holzinger unitary trait study, No. 6. Chicago: Statistical Laboratory, Department of Education, University of Chicago.

Holzinger, K. J. (1936). Recent research on unitary mental traits. *Character & Personality*, 4, 335–343.

Holzinger, K. J., & Crowder, N. A. (1952–55). *Holzinger-Crowder Uni-Factor Tests*. Yonkers-on-Hudson: World Book.
Analyzed: Schutz (1958)

Holzinger, K. J., & Harman, H. H. (1937). Relationships between factors obtained from certain analyses. *Journal of Educational Psychology*, 28, 321–345.

Holzinger, K. J., & Harman, H. H. (1938). Comparison of two factorial analyses. *Psychometrika*, 3, 45–60.
Reanalysis of THUR21

Holzinger, K. J., & Harman, H. H. (1941). *Factor analysis: A synthesis of factorial methods*. Chicago: University of Chicago Press.

Holzinger, K. J., & Swineford, F. (1936a). Preliminary report on Spearman-Holzinger unitary trait study, No. 7. Chicago: Statistical Laboratory, Department of Education, University of Chicago.

Holzinger, K. J., & Swineford, F. (1936b). Preliminary report on Spearman–Holzinger unitary trait study, No. 8. Chicago: Statistical Laboratory, Department of Education, University of Chicago.

Holzinger, K. J., & Swineford, F. (1936c). Preliminary report on Spearman–Holzinger unitary trait study, No. 9. Chicago: Statistical Laboratory, Department of Education, University of Chicago.

Holzinger, K. J., & Swineford, F. (1939). A study in factor analysis: The stability of a bi-factor solution. *Supplementary Education Monographs*, No. 48. Chicago: Department of Education, University of Chicago.
DS-HOLZ01 *HI.5.1*
Reanalyzed: Bentler (1977), Bentler & Wingard (1977), Bloxom (1972), Crawford & Ferguson (1970), Gorsuch (1974), Guertin, Guertin, & Ware (1981), Hakstian (1971), Hakstian & Abell (1974), Harman (1976), Hendrickson & White (1964), Jennrich & Sampson (1966), Jöreskog (1978), Katz & Rohlf (1974), Kashiwagi (1965), Koopman (1973), Lee & Comrey (1979), Lee & Jennrich (1979), Linn (1968), Lohman (1979a), Meredith (1964b), Tryon & Bailey (1970), Tucker & Lewis (1973)

Holzman, T. C., Glaser, R., & Pellegrino, J. W. (1976). Process training derived from a computer simulation theory. *Memory and Cognition*, 4, 349–356.

Horn, J. L. (1965a). Fluid and crystallized intelligence: A factor analytic study of the structure among primary mental abilities. Unpublished doctoral dissertation, University of Illinois. (University Microfilms 65–7113)
  DS-HORN01 *HI.9.2*
  Reanalyzed: Lohman (1979a)
  DS-HORN02 See Horn & Cattell (1982)
  Further report: Horn & Cattell (1967)
Horn, J. L. (1965b). A rationale and test for the number of factors in factor analysis. *Psychometrika, 30,* 179–185.
  Preliminary analysis of HORN01
Horn, J. L. (1970). Organization of data on life-span development of human abilities. In L. R. Goulet & P. B. Baltes (Eds.), *Life-span developmental psychology* (pp. 423–466). New York: Academic.
Horn, J. L. (1976). Human abilities: A review of research and theory in the early 1970s. *Annual Review of Psychology, 27,* 437–485.
Horn, J. L. (1978a). Human ability systems. In P. B. Baltes (Ed.), *Life-span development and behavior,* Vol. 1 (pp. 211-256). New York: Academic.
Horn, J. L. (1978b). A study of speed, power, carefulness, and short-term learning components of intelligence and changes in these components in adulthood. Denver, CO: Final report, Department of Psychology, University of Denver.
  DS-HORN21 *HI.9.2* (Varimax matrix, p. 89)
Horn, J. L. (1982). The aging of human abilities. In B. B. Wolman (Ed.), *Handbook of developmental psychology* (pp. 847–870). Englewood Cliffs, NJ: Prentice-Hall.
Horn, J. L. (1985). Remodeling old models of intelligence. In B. B. Wolman (Ed.), *Handbook of intelligence: Theories, measurements, and applications* (pp. 267–300). New York: Wiley.
Horn, J. L. (1988). Thinking about human abilities. In J. R. Nesselroade & R. B. Cattell (Eds.), *Handbook of multivariate experimental psychology,* Second edition (pp. 645–685). New York, NY: Plenum.
Horn, J. L., & Bramble, W. J. (1967). Second-order ability structure revealed in rights and wrongs scores. *Journal of Educational Psychology, 58,* 115–122.
  DS-HORN25 *HI.4.1* (rights scores)
  DS-HORN26 *HI.3.1* (wrongs scores)
Horn, J. L., & Cattell, R. B. (1966). Refinement of the theory of fluid and crystallized general intelligences. *Journal of Educational Psychology, 57,* 253–270.
  Further report of HORN01; see Guilford (1980) for critique.
Horn, J. L., & Cattell, R. B. (1967). Age differences in fluid and crystallized intelligence. *Acta Psychologica, 26,* 107–129.
  Further report of HORN01
Horn, J. L., & Cattell, R. B. (1982). Whimsy and misunderstandings of Gf-Gc theory: A comment on Guilford. *Psychological Bulletin, 91,* 623–633.
  Further analysis of HORN01 as DS-HORN02 in reply to Guilford (1980)
Horn, J. L., Donaldson, G., & Engstrom, R. (1981). Apprehension, memory, and fluid intelligence decline in adulthood. *Research on Aging, 3,* 33–84.
Horn, J. L., & Knapp, J. R. (1973). On the subjective character of the empirical base of Guilford's Structure-of-Intellect model. *Psychological Bulletin, 80,* 33–43.
  Reanalysis of BROW21, GUIL51, HOEP11; see Guilford (1974)
Horn, J. L., & Knapp, J. R. (1974). Thirty wrongs do not make a right: Reply to Guilford. *Psychological Bulletin, 81,* 502–504.
  Reply to Guilford (1974)
Horn, J. L., & McArdle, J. J. (1980). Perspectives on mathematical/statistical model building (MASMOB) in research on aging. In L. W. Poon (Ed.), *Aging in the 1980's:*

Psychological issues (pp. 503–541). Washington DC: American Psychological Association.

Horn, J. L., & Stankov, L. (1982). Auditory and visual factors of intelligence. *Intelligence*, 6, 165–185.
DS-HORN31 *HI.6.2*

Horst, P. (1941). A non-graphical method for transforming an arbitrary factor matrix into a simple structure matrix. *Psychometrika*, 6, 79–99.
Reanalysis of THUR11

Horst, P. (1965). *Factor analysis of data matrices*. New York: Holt, Rinehart & Winston.

Hotelling, H. (1933). Analysis of a complex of statistical variables into principal components. *Journal of Educational Psychology*, 24, 417–441, 498–520.

Hotelling, H. (1936). Simplified calculation of principal components. *Psychometrika*, 1(1), 27–35.

Householder, A. S. (1964). *The theory of matrices in numerical analysis*. New York: Dover.

Houts, P. L. (Ed.) (1977). *The myth of measurability*. New York: Hart.

Howell, G. C., Jr. (1978). An investigation of response time in computerized psychological tests. *Dissertation Abstracts International*, 1978(Jan.), Vol. 38(7-B), 3448.

Howie, D. (1956). Speed and accuracy. *Australian Journal of Psychology*, 8, 111–118.

Huarte de San Juan, J. (1575). *Examen de ingenios para las ciencias. [Examination of talents for the sciences.]* Madrid: Baeza.

Hueftle, M. K. (1967). A factor analytic study of the Frostig Developmental Test of Visual Perception, the Illinois Test of Psycholinguistic Abilities, and the Wechsler Intelligence Scale for Children. Unpublished doctoral dissertation, Colorado State College. (University Microfilm 67–13679)
DS-HUEF01 *HI.5*

Huey, E. B. (1908). *The psychology and pedagogy of reading*. New York: Macmillan. [Reprinted: Cambridge, MA: MIT Press, 1968]

Hughes, O. (1983). Learning, intelligence and human problem solving. Unpublished Ph.D. thesis, University of Newcastle.
DS-HUGH01 *HI.4.2*

Hull, C. L. (1928). *Aptitude testing*. Yonkers-on-Hudson: World Book.

Humphreys, L. G. (1960). Investigations of the simplex. *Psychometrika*, 25, 313–323.
Reanalysis of FLEI12

Humphreys, L. G. (1962). The organization of human abilities. *American Psychologist*, 17, 475–483.

Humphreys, L. G. (1964). Number of cases and number of factors: An example where *N* is very large. *Educational & Psychological Measurement*, 24, 457–466.
Reanalysis of GUIL45

Humphreys, L. G. (1967). Critique of Cattell's "Theory of fluid and crystallized intelligence: A critical experiment." *Journal of Educational Psychology*, 58, 129–136.
Reanalysis of CATT01, HORN01

Humphreys, L. G. (1982). The hierarchial factor model and general intelligence. In N. Hirschberg & L. G. Humphreys (Eds.), *Multivariate applications in the social sciences* (pp. 223–239). Hillsdale, NJ: Erlbaum.

Humphreys, L. G. (1991). Causal inferences from observational data: Use a redesigned cross-lagged methodology. *Intelligence*, 15, 151–156.

Humphreys, L. G., & Fruchter, B. (1945). Re-analysis of Memory Batteries I and II. San Antonio Psychological Research Unit, Research Bulletin T 45–15.
Reanalysis of GUIL36, GUIL37

Humphreys, L. G., & Ilgen, D. R. (1969). Note on a criterion for the number of common factors. *Educational & Psychological Measurement*, 29, 571–578.
Reanalysis of THUR11, THUR31, THUR81

Humphreys, L. G., & Park, R. K. (1981). Analysis of variances and covariances is misleading as a guide to a common factor model. *Intelligence, 5,* 157–163.
Reanalysis of SCHU01

Humphreys, L. G., & Parsons, C. K. (1977). Partialing out intelligence: A methodological and substantive contribution. *Journal of Educational Psychology, 69,* 212–216.
Reanalysis of SATT01

Humphreys, L. G., & Parsons, C. K. (1979). Piagetian tasks measure intelligence and intelligence tests assess cognitive development: A reanalysis. *Intelligence, 3,* 369–382.
Reanalysis of STEP01

Humphreys, L. G., & Taber, T. (1973). A comparison of squared multiples and iterated diagonals as communality estimates. *Educational & Psychological Measurement, 33,* 225–229.

Humphreys, L. G., Tucker, L. R, & Dachler, P. (1970). Evaluating the importance of factors in any given order of factoring. *Multivariate Behavioral Research, 5,* 209–215.
Reanalysis of ADKI03, CATT01

Hundal, P. S., & Horn, J. L. (1977). On the relationships between short-term learning and fluid and crystallized intelligence. *Applied Psychological Measurement, 1,* 11–21.

Hunsicker, L. M. (1925). A study of the relationship between rate and ability. *Teachers College Contributions to Education,* No. 185.

Hunt, E. (1971). What kind of computer is man? *Cognitive Psychology, 2,* 57–98.

Hunt, E. (1978). Mechanics of verbal ability. *Psychological Review, 85,* 109–130.

Hunt, E. B., Davidson, J., & Lansman, M. (1981). Individual differences in long-term memory access. *Memory & Cognition, 9,* 599–608.
DS-HUNT51 *HI.3.1*

Hunt, E. B., Frost, N., & Lunneborg, C. (1973). Individual differences in cognition: A new approach to intelligence. In G. Bower (Ed.), *The psychology of learning and motivation: Advances in research and theory,* Vol. 7 (pp. 87–122). New York: Academic.
DS-HUNT61 *HI.5.2*

Hunt, E. B., Lunneborg, C., & Lewis, J. (1975). What does it mean to be high verbal? *Cognitive Psychology, 7,* 194–227.
DS-HUNT71 *HI.5*

Hunt, E., & Pellegrino, J. (1985). Using interactive computing to expand intelligence testing: A critique and prospectus. *Intelligence, 9,* 207–236.

Hunt, K. W. (1965). *Grammatical structures written at three grade levels.* Champaign, IL: National Council of Teachers of English. (NCTE Research Report No. 3.)

Hunter, J. E. (1986). Cognitive ability, cognitive aptitudes, job knowledge, and job performance. *Journal of Vocational Behavior, 29,* 340-362.

Hurley, I. R., & Cattell, R. B. (1962). The procrustes program: Producing direct rotation to test a hypothesized factor structure. *Behavioral Sciences, 7,* 258–262.

Hynd, G. W., & Willis, W. G. (1985). Neurological foundations of intelligence. In B. B. Wolman (Ed.), *Handbook of intelligence: Theories, measurements, and applications* (pp. 119–157). New York: Wiley.

Ingham, J. G. (1952). Memory and intelligence. *British Journal of Psychology, 43,* 20–32.
DS-INGH01 *HI.7.1*

Inman, W. (personal communication). [Unpublished paper]
Reanalysis of THUR21

Innes, J. M. (1972). The relationship of word-association commonality response set to cognitive and personality variables. *British Journal of Psychology, 63,* 421–428.
DS-INNE01A *HI.2.1* (males)
DS-INNE02A *HI.2* (females)

Ippel, M. J. (1986). *Component-testing: A theory of cognitive aptitude measurement.* Amsterdam: Free University Press.

Irvine, S. H. (1969). Factor analysis of African abilities and attainments: Constructs across cultures. *Psychological Bulletin, 71,* 20–32.

Irvine, S. H. (1979). The place of factor analysis in cross-cultural methodology and its contribution to cognitive theory. In L. H. Eckensberger, W. J. Lonner, & Y. H. Poortinga (Eds.), *Cross-cultural contributions to psychology* (pp. 300–341). Lisse: Swets & Zeitlinger.
Survey of 91 factor-analytic studies

Irvine, S. H. (1981). Culture, cognitive tests and cognitive models: Pursuing cognitive universals by testing across cultures. In M. P. Friedman, J. P. Das, & N. O'Connor (Eds.), *Intelligence and learning* (pp. 407–426). New York: Plenum.

Irvine, S. H., & Berry, J. W. (Eds.) (1983). *Human assessment and cultural factors.* New York: Plenum.

Irvine, S. H., & Berry, J. W. (Eds.) (1988). *Human abilities in cultural contexts.* New York: Cambridge University Press.

Irwin, R. J. (1984). Inspection time and its relation to intelligence. *Intelligence, 8,* 47–65.

Jackson, D. N. (1974). *Personality Research Form, Manual.* Goshen, NY: Research Psychologists Press.

Jackson, D. N. (1977). *Jackson Vocational Interest Survey: Manual* Port Huron, MI: Research Psychologists Press.

Jackson, D. N. (1984). *Multidimensional Aptitude Battery, Manual.* Port Huron, MI: Research Psychologists Press.

Jackson, M. D., & McClelland, J. L. (1979). Processing determinants of reading speed. *Journal of Experimental Psychology: General, 108,* 151–181.
DS-JACK11 *HI.3.1*
DS-JACK12 *HI.4.2*

Jacobs, S. S., & Shin, S. H. (1975). Interrelationships among intelligence, product dimension of Guilford's model and multilevel measure of cognitive functioning. *Psychological Reports, 37,* 903–910.
DS-JACO01 *HI.3.1*

Jäger, A. O. (1967). *Dimensionen der Intelligenz.* [*Dimensions of intelligence.*] Göttingen: Hogrefe.

Jäger, A. O. (1984). Intelligenzstrukturforschung: Konkurrierende Modelle, neue Entwicklungen, Perspectiven. [Research on intelligence structure: Competing models, new developments, perspectives.] *Psychologische Rundschau, 35,* 21–35.

Jarman, R. F., & Das, J. P. (1977). Simultaneous and successive syntheses and intelligence. *Intelligence, 1,* 151–169.
DS-JARM31 *HI.2.1*
Reanalyzed: Carroll (1978)

Jarvis, P. E., & Barth, J. T. (1984). *Halstead–Reitan Test Battery: An interpretive guide.* Odessa, FL: Psychological Assessment Resources.

Jay, E. S. (1950). A factor study of reading tasks. Unpublished Ph.D. dissertation, University of Chicago.
DS-JAY01 *HI.6.2*

Jeffress, L. A. (1948). The nature of 'primary abilities.' *American Journal of Psychology, 61,* 107-111.

Jeffrey, T. E. (1957). A factorial study of three space factors. Unpublished Ph.D. thesis, University of Chicago.
DS-JEFF11 *HI.6.1*

Jenkins, J. J., & Palermo, D. S. (1964). *Word association norms.* Minneapolis, MN: University of Minnesota Press.

Jennings, A. E., & Chiles, W. D. (1977). An investigation of time-sharing ability as a factor in complex performance. *Human Factors, 19*, 535–547.

Jennrich, R. I., & Robinson, S. M. (1969). A Newton-Raphson algorithm for maximum likelihood factor analysis. *Psychometrika, 34*, 111–123.
Reanalysis of DAVI11 (See Rao, 1955)

Jennrich, R. I., & Sampson, P. F. (1966). Rotation for simple loadings. *Psychometrika, 31*, 313-323.
Reanalysis of HOLZ01.

Jensen, A. R. (1964). Individual differences in learning: Interference factor. Berkeley, CA: Cooperative Research Report No. 1867, University of California.
DS-JENS01 not analyzable due to negative roots

Jensen, A. R. (1965). Scoring the Stroop test. *Acta Psychologica, 24*, 398–408.
DS-JENS02 *HI.3*

Jensen, A. R. (1968). Patterns of mental ability and socioeconomic status. *Proceedings of the National Academy of Science, 60*, 1330–1337.

Jensen, A. R. (1969). How much can we boost IQ and scholastic achievement? *Harvard Educational Review, 39*, 1–123.

Jensen, A. R. (1970). Hierarchical theories of mental ability. In W. B. Dockrell (Ed.), *On intelligence: The Toronto symposium on intelligence, 1969* (pp. 119–190). London: Methuen.

Jensen, A. R. (1973). Level I and Level II abilities in three ethnic groups. *American Educational Research Journal, 10*, 263–276.

Jensen, A. R. (1979). *g*: Outmoded theory or unconquered frontier? *Creative Science & Technology, 2*(3), 16–29.
DS-JENS41 *HI.3*
Reanalyzed: Carroll (1981)

Jensen, A. R. (1980). *Bias in mental testing.* New York: Free Press.

Jensen, A. R. (1984). The black-white difference on the K-ABC: Implications for future tests. *Journal of Special Education, 18*, 377–408.

Jensen, A. R. (1986). *g*: Artifact or reality? *Journal of Vocational Behavior, 29*, 301–331.

Jensen, A. R. (1987). Individual differences in mental ability. In J. A. Glover & R. R. Ronning (Eds.), *Historical foundations of educational psychology* (pp. 61–88). New York: Plenum.

Jensen, A. R. (1989). Raising IQ without increasing *g*? Review of [H. L. Garber,] *The Milwaukee Project: Preventing mental retardation in children at risk. Developmental Review, 9*, 234–258.

Jensen, A. R., & Figueroa, R. A. (1975). Forward and backward digit span interaction with race and IQ: Predictions from Jensen's theory. *Journal of Educational Psychology, 67*, 882–893.

Jöreskog, K. G. (1963). *Statistical estimation in factor analysis.* Uppsala, Sweden: Almqvist & Wiksells.

Jöreskog, K. G. (1967). Some contributions to maximum likelihood factor analysis. *Psychometrika, 32*, 443–482.
Reanalysis of DAVI11, LORD01

Jöreskog, K. G. (1978). Structural analysis of covariance and correlation matrices. *Psychometrika, 43*, 443–477.
Reanalysis of HOLZ01, LORD01

Jöreskog, K. G., & Sörbom, D. (1978). LISREL: Analysis of linear structural relationships by the method of maximum likelihood. User's Guide. Chicago: International Educational Services.

Jöreskog, K. G., & Sörbom, D. (1979). *Advances in factor analysis and structural equation models.* With an introduction by W. W. Cooley. Cambridge, MA: Abt.

Jöreskog, K. G., & Sörbom, D. (1983). *LISREL: Analysis of linear structural relationships by the method of maximum likelihood: User's guide*. Chicago: International Educational Services.

Jöreskog, K. G., & Sörbom, D. (1984). *LISREL VI: Analysis of linear structural relationships by the method of maximum likelihood: User's guide*. Mooresville, IN: Scientific Software.

Johansson, B. A. (1965). *Criteria of school readiness: Factor structure, predictive value and environmental influences*. Stockholm: Almqvist & Wiksell. (Stockholm Studies in Educational Psychology 9.)
  DS-JOHA01 *HI.6.1*

Johnson, R. C., McClearn, G. E., Yuen, S., Nagoshi, C. T., Ahern, F. M., & Cole, R. E. (1985). Galton's data a century later. *American Psychologist, 40*, 875–892.

Johnson-Laird, P. N. (1985). Deductive reasoning ability. In R. J. Sternberg (Ed.), *Human abilities: An information-processing approach* (pp. 173–194). New York: Freeman.

Jones, F. N. (1948). A factor analysis of visibility data. *American Journal of Psychology, 61*, 361–369.
  DS-JONE21 *HI.3.1*

Jones, F. N. (1957). An analysis of individual differences in olfactory thresholds. *American Journal of Psychology, 70*, 227–232.
  DS-JONE22 *HI.4.2.1*

Jones, L. V. (1949). A factor analysis of the Stanford-Binet at four age levels. *Psychometrika, 14*, 299–331.
  DS-JONE31 *HI.5.1* (age 7)
  DS-JONE32 *HI.6.1* (age 9)
  DS-JONE33 *HI.5.1* (age 11)
  DS-JONE34 *HI.6.1* (age 13)
  Reanalyzed: Jones (1954)

Jones, L. V. (1954). Primary abilities in the Stanford-Binet, age 13. *Journal of Genetic Psychology, 84*, 125–147.
  Reanalysis of JONE34

Jones, L. V., & Wepman, J. M. (1967). Grammatical indications of speaking style in normal and aphasic speakers. In K. Salzinger & S. Salzinger (Eds.), *Research in verbal behavior and some neurophysiological implications* (pp. 169–180). New York: Academic.

Joynson, R. B. (1989). *The Burt affair*. New York: Routledge, Chapman & Hall.

Judd, C. H. (1936). *Education as cultivation of the higher mental processes*. New York: Macmillan.

Kail, R. (1991). Developmental change in speed of processing during childhood and adolescence. *Psychological Bulletin, 109*, 490–501.

Kaiser, H. F. (1958). The varimax criterion for analytic rotation in factor analysis. *Psychometrika, 23*, 187–200.

Kaiser, H. F. (1960a). The application of electronic computers to factor analysis. *Educational & Psychological Measurement, 20*, 141–151.

Kaiser, H. F. (1960b). Varimax solution for primary mental abilities. *Psychometrika, 25*, 153–158.
  Reanalysis of THUR21

Kaiser, H. F. (1970). A second generation Little Jiffy. *Psychometrika, 35*, 401–416.

Kaiser, H. F. (1974). An index of factorial simplicity. *Psychometrika, 39*, 31–36.

Kaiser, H. F. (1981). A revised measure of sampling adequacy for factor-analytic data matrices. *Educational & Psychological Measurement, 41*, 379–381.

Kaiser, H. F., & Rice, J. (1974). Little Jiffy, Mark IV. *Educational & Psychological Measurement, 34*, 111–117.

Kamin, L. J. (1974). *The science and politics of IQ*. New York: Wiley.

Kamman, J. F. (1953). A comparison of factor patterns in a native language and an auxiliary language. Unpublished Ph.D. thesis, University of Illinois.
DS-KAMM01 *HI.6.1*

Kaplan, R. M. (1985). The controversy related to the use of psychological tests. In B. B. Wolman (Ed.), *Handbook of intelligence: Theories, measurements, and applications* (pp. 465–504). New York: Wiley.

Karlin, J. E. (1941). Music ability. *Psychometrika, 6,* 61–65.
DS-KARL01 *HI.3* (Analysis 1)

Karlin, J. E. (1942). A factorial study of auditory function. *Psychometrika, 7,* 251–279.
DS-KARL11 *HI.7.1*
Reanalyzed: Ahmavaara (1957)

Karlin, J. E., & Abrams, M. H. (1946). Auditory tests of the ability to hear speech in noise. (OSRD Publication Board, No. 22847). Washington, D.C.: U.S. Department of Commerce.

Kashiwagi, S. (1965). Geometric vector orthogonal rotation method in multiple-factor analysis. *Psychometrika, 30,* 515–530.
Reanalysis of HOLZ01, THUR21, THUR41

Katz, J. O., & Rohlf, F. J. (1974). Functionplane – A new approach to simple structure rotation. *Psychometrika, 39,* 37–51.
Reanalysis of HOLZ01

Kaufman, A. S. (1975). Factor analysis of the WISC-R at 11 age levels between 6 1/2 and 16 1/2 years. *Journal of Consulting and Clinical Psychology, 43,* 135–147.

Kaufman, A. S. (1978). WISC-R research: Implications for interpretation. *School Psychology Digest, 8,* 5–27.

Kaufman, A. S., & Kaufman, N. (1982). *The Kaufman Assessment Battery for Children.* Circle Pines, MN: American Guidance Service.

Kaufman, E. L., Lord, M. W., Reese, T. W., & Volkman, J. (1949). The discrimination of visual numbers. *American Journal of Psychology, 62,* 498–528.

Keating, D. P., & Bobbitt, B. L. (1978). Individual and developmental differences in cognitive-processing components of mental ability. *Child Development, 49,* 155–167.

Keith, T. Z., & Novak, C. G. (1987). What is the *g* that the K-ABC measures? Paper presented at the meeting of the National Association of School Psychologists, New Orleans, LA.
DS-KEIT21 *HI.5.2.1*

Kelderman, H., Mellenbergh, G. J., & Elshout, J. J. (1981). Guilford's facet theory of intelligence: An empirical comparison of models. *Multivariate Behavioral Research, 16,* 37–61.
Reanalysis of BRAD01, DUNH11, HEND01, HOFF01, OSUL01, TENO01

Kelley, H. P. (1964). Memory abilities: A factor analysis. *Psychometric Monographs,* No. 11.
DS-KELL01 *HI.8.2*
Reanalyzed: Ross (1961)

Kelley, T. L. (1927). *The interpretation of educational measurements.* Yonkers-on-Hudson, NY: World Book.

Kelley, T. L. (1928). *Crossroads in the mind of man: A study of differentiable mental abilities.* Stanford, CA: Stanford University Press.

Kelley, T. L. (1935). *Essential traits of mental life.* Cambridge, MA: Harvard University Press. (Harvard Studies in Education, No. 26.)

Kessel, F. S., & Bevan, W. (1985). Notes toward a history of cognitive psychology. In C. E. Buxton (Ed.), *Points of view in the modern history of psychology* (pp. 259–294). New York: Academic.

Kettner, N. W., Guilford, J. P., & Christensen, P. R. (1956). A factor analytic investigation of the factor called general reasoning. *Educational & Psychological Measurement, 16*, 438–453.
Further report of GUIL19

Kettner, N. W., Guilford, J. P., & Christensen, P. R. (1959a). A factor-analytic study across domains of reasoning, creativity, and evaluation. *Psychological Monographs: General & Applied, 73*, 1–31.
Further report of GUIL21–23

Kettner, N. W., Guilford, J. P., & Christensen, P. R. (1959b). The relation of certain thinking factors to training in the U. S. Coast Guard Academy. *Educational & Psychological Measurement, 19*, 381–394.
Further report of GUIL20

Khattab, A–M., Michael, W. B., & Hocevar, D. (1982). The construct validity of higher order structure-of-intellect abilities in a battery of tests emphasizing the product of transformations: A confirmatory maximum likelihood factor analysis. *Educational & Psychological Measurement, 42*, 1089–1105.
Reanalysis of HOEP21

Kim, J–O., & Mueller, C. W. (1978a). *Introduction to factor analysis: What it is and how to do it.* Beverly Hills: Sage.

Kim, J–O., & Mueller, C. W. (1978b). *Factor analysis: Statistical methods and practical issues.* Beverly Hills: Sage.

Kirsch, I. S., & Jungeblut, A. (1986). *Literacy: Profiles of American's young adults.* Princeton, NJ: Educational Testing Service.

Knoell, D. M., & Harris, C. W. (1952). A factor analysis of word fluency. *Journal of Educational Psychology, 43*, 131–148.
DS-KNOE11 *HI.6.1*
Reanalyzed: Ahmavaara (1957)

Knower, F. H. (1938). A study of speech attitudes and adjustments. *Speech Monographs, 5*, 130–203.

König, E. (1957). Effect of time on pitch discrimination thresholds under several psychophysical procedures: Comparison with intensity discrimination thresholds. *Journal of the Acoustical Society of America, 29*, 606–612.

Koestler, A. (1964). *The act of creation* (with a foreword by Sir Cyril Burt). New York: Macmillan.

Koop, T. (1985). Replication of Guttman's structure of intelligence. In D. Canter (Ed.), *Facet theory: Approaches to social research* (pp. 237–244). New York: Springer.

Koopman, R. F. (1973). Determining parameter values in the generalized image system. *Psychometrika, 38*, 495–511.
Reanalysis of HOLZ01

Kranzler, J. H. (1990). The nature of intelligence: A unitary process or a number of independent processes? Unpublished doctoral dissertation, University of California at Berkeley.
DS-KRAN01A *HI.7.2*

Kranzler, J. H., & Jensen, A. R. (1991a). The nature of psychometric *g*: Unitary process or a number of independent processes? *Intelligence, 15*, 297–422.

Kranzler, J. H., & Jensen, A. R. (1991b). Unitary *g*: Unquestioned postulate or empirical fact? *Intelligence, 15*, 437–448.

Kuder, F. (1934–76). *Kuder Preference Record – Vocational.* Chicago: Science Research Associates.

Kwalwasser, J., & Dykema, P. W. (1930). *Kwalwasser-Dykema Music Tests.* New York: Carl Fischer.

Kyllonen, P. C. (1985). *Dimensions of information processsing speed*. Brooks Air Force Base, TX: Air Force Systems Command, AFHRL-TP-84-56.

Kyllonen, P. C., & Christal, R. E. (1989). Cognitive modeling of learning abilities: A status report of LAMP. In R. F. Dillon & J. W. Pellegrino (Eds.), *Testing: Theoretical and applied perspectives* (pp. 146–173). New York: Praeger.

Kyllonen, P. C., & Christal, R. E. (1990). Reasoning ability is (little more than) working memory capacity?! *Intelligence, 14,* 389–433.

Kyllonen, P. C., Lohman, D. F., & Snow, R. E. (1984). Effects of aptitudes, strategy training, and task facets on spatial task performance. *Journal of Educational Psychology, 76,* 130–145.

Kyllonen, P. C., Lohman, D. F., & Woltz, D. J. (1984). Componential modeling of alternative strategies for performing spatial tasks. *Journal of Educational Psychology, 76,* 1325–1345.

Kyllonen, P. C., & Stephens, D. L. (1990). Cognitive abilities as determinants of success in acquiring logic skill. *Learning and Individual Differences, 2,* 129–160.

Lachman, R., Shaffer, J. P., & Hennrikus, D. (1974). Language and cognition: Effects of stimulus codability, name-word frequency, and age of acquisition on lexical reaction. *Journal of Verbal Learning and Verbal Behavior, 13,* 613–625.

Lado, R. (1965). Memory span as a factor in second language learning. *International Review of Applied Linguistics, 3,* 123–129.

Lang, R. J., & Ryba, K. A. (1976). The identification of some creative thinking parameters common to the artistic and musical personality. *British Journal of Educational Psychology, 46,* 267–279.
   DS-LANG01 *HI.3.1*

Langsam, R. S. (1941). A factorial analysis of reading ability. *Journal of Experimental Education, 10,* 57–63.
   DS-LANG31 *HI.4.1*

Lanier, L. H. (1934). The interrelations of speed of reaction measurements. *Journal of Experimental Psychology, 17,* 371–399.

Lansman, M. (1978). An attentional approach to individual differences in immediate memory. Unpublished Ph.D. dissertation, University of Washington. [*Dissertation Abstracts International, 39*(5-B), 2542–2543]
   DS-LANS21 *HI.3.1*
   DS-LANS22 *HI.3.1*

Lansman, M., Donaldson, G., Hunt, E., & Yantis, S. (1982). Ability factors and cognitive processes. *Intelligence, 6,* 347–386.
   DS-LANS31 *HI.6.1*

Larkin, J., McDermott, J., Simon, D., & Simon, H. A. (1980). Expert and novice performance in solving physics problems. *Science, 208,* 1335–1342.

Lawley, D. N. (1940). The estimation of factor loadings by the method of maximum likelihood. *Proceedings of the Royal Society of Edinburgh, 60,* 64–82.

Lawley, D. N., & Maxwell, A. E. (1963). *Factor analysis as a statistical method.* London: Butterworths.

Lee, H. B., & Comrey, A. L. (1979). Distortions in a commonly used factor analytic procedure. *Multivariate Behavioral Research, 14,* 301–321.
   Reanalysis of HOLZ01

Lee, S-Y., & Jennrich, R. I. (1979). A study of algorithms for covariance structure analysis with specific comparisons using factor analysis. *Psychometrika, 44,* 99–113.
   Reanalyses of HOLZ01, THUR81

Leibovitz, M. P., London, P., Cooper, L. M., & Hart, J. T. (1972). Dominance in mental imagery. *Educational & Psychological Measurement, 32,* 679–703.
   DS-LEIB01 not analyzable

Leino, J. (1981). Psychometric test theory and cognitive processes: A theoretical scrutiny and empirical research. Helsinki: Institute of Education, University of Helsinki, Research Bulletin No. 57.

Lemmon, V. W. (1927). The relation of reaction time to measures of intelligence, memory, and learning. *Archives of Psychology*, No. 94.

Lenk, W. (1983). *Faktorenanalyse: Ein Mythos? Historische und konzeptionelle Untersuchungen zur Faktorenanalyse und Intelligenzforschung. [Factor analysis: A myth? Historical and conceptual investigations into factor analysis and research on intelligence.]* Weinheim & Basel: Beltz.

Levine, J. M., Brahlek, R. E., Eisner, E. J., & Fleishman, E. A. (1980). Trainability of abilities: Training and transfer of abilities related to electronic fault-finding. *Catalog of Selected Documents in Psychology, 10*, 60. MS. 2098.

Levine, J. M., Schulman, D., Brahlek, R. E., & Fleishman, E. A. (1980). Trainability of abilities: Training and transfer of spatial visualization. *Catalog of Selected Documents in Psychology, 10*, 82. MS. 2119.

Linden, K. W., & Linden, J. D. (1968). *Modern mental measurement: A historical perspective*. Boston: Houghton Mifflin.

Line, W., & Kaplan, E. (1932). The existence, measurement and significance of a speed factor in the abilities of public school children. *Journal of Experimental Education, 1*, 1–8.

Linn, R. I. (1968). A Monte Carlo approach to the number of factors problem. *Psychometrika, 33*, 37–71.
    Reanalysis of GUIL45, HOLZ01, THUR81–82

Lippmann, W. (1922). The mental age of Americans. *New Republic, 32*, 213–215.
    Subsequent articles in this series: The mystery of the 'A' men, pp. 246–248; The reliability of intelligence tests, pp. 275–277; The abuse of the tests, pp. 297–298; Tests of hereditary intelligence, pp. 328–330; A future for the tests, Vol. 33, pp. 9–10.

Lipsitz, L. (Ed.) (1977). *The test score decline: Meaning and issues*. Englewood Cliffs: Educational Technology Publications.

Loeffler, F. J. (1963). An extension and partial replication of Meyers' primary mental abilities at mental age six. Paper delivered at symposium of Society for Research in Child Development, University of California at Berkeley.

Loehlin, J. C., & Nichols, R. C. (1976). *Heredity, environment, and personality: A study of 850 sets of twins*. Austin, TX: University of Texas Press.

Lohman, D. F. (1979a). *Spatial ability: A review and reanalysis of the correlational literature*. Stanford, CA: Aptitude Research Project, School of Education, Stanford University Technical Report No. 8.
    Reanalyses of DAVI01, GUIL40, GUIL46, HOFF01, HORN01, LORD01, MICH51, MICH61–62, THUR41, THUR71

Lohman, D. F. (1979b). *Spatial ability: Individual differences in speed and level*. Stanford, CA: Aptitudes Research Project, School of Education, Stanford University Technical Report No. 9.

Lohman, D. F. (1986). The effect of speed–accuracy tradeoff on sex differences in mental rotation. *Perception & Psychophysics, 39*, 427–436.

Lohman, D. F. (1989). Human intelligence: An introduction to advances in theory and research. *Review of Educational Research, 59*, 333–373.

Lohman, D. F., Pellegrino, J. W., Alderton, D. L., & Regian, J. W. (1987). Dimensions and components of individual differences in spatial abilities. In S. H. Irvine & S. E. Newstead (Eds.), *Intelligence and cognition: Contemporary frames of reference* (pp. 253–312). Dordrecht: Martinus Nijhoff.

Long, J. S. (1983). *Confirmatory factor analysis: A preface to LISREL*. Beverly Hills: Sage.

Longstaff, H. P., & Porter, J. P. (1928). Speed and accuracy as factors in objective tests in general psychology. *Journal of Applied Psychology, 12*, 636–642.

Lord, F. M. (1952). A theory of test scores. *Psychometric Monographs*, No. 7.

Lord, F. M. (1956). A study of speed factors in tests and academic grades. *Psychometrika, 21*, 31–50.
DS-LORD01 *HI.7.2*
Reanalyzed: Jöreskog (1967,1978), Lohman (1979a), Tucker & Lewis (1973)

Lord, F. M. (1980). *Applications of item response theory to practical testing problems.* Hillsdale, NJ: Erlbaum.

Lord, F. M., & Novick, M. R. (1968). *Statistical theories of mental test scores.* With contributions by A. Birnbaum. Reading, MA: Addison–Wesley.

Lorenz, C. A., & Neisser, U. (1986). Ecological and psychometric dimensions of spatial ability. Atlanta, Ga: Department of Psychology, Emory University, Report #10.

Lorge, I., Thorndike, R. L., & Hagen, E. (1954–66). *Lorge-Thorndike Intelligence Tests.* Chicago, IL: Riverside Publishing Co.

Lucas, C. M., & French, J. W. (1953). A factorial study of experimental tests of integration, judgment, and planning. Princeton, NJ: Educational Testing Service Research Bulletin RB-53-16.
DS-LUCA01 *HI.9.2*

Luce, R. D., & Krumhansl, C. L. (1988). Measurement, scaling, and psychophysics. In R. C. Atkinson, R. J. Herrnstein, G. Lindzey, & R. D. Luce (Eds.), *Stevens' Handbook of experimental psychology*, Second edition, Vol. 1: *Perception and motivation* (pp. 3–74). New York: Wiley.

Lumsden, J. (1965). The structure of immediate memory. Unpublished doctoral dissertation, University of Western Australia.
DS-LUMS01 *HI.10.2*

Lundin, R. W. (1949). The development and validation of a set of musical ability tests. *Psychological Monographs: General and Applied, 63*(10), Whole No. 305, 1–20.

Lunneborg, C. E. (1977). Choice reaction time: What role in ability measurement? *Applied Psychological Measurement, 1*, 309–330.
DS-LUNN21 *HI.2*

Lunzer, E. A., Wilkinson, J. E., & Dolan, T. (1976). The distinctiveness of operativity as a measure of cognitive functioning in five-year-old children. *British Journal of Educational Psychology, 46*, 280–294.
DS-LUNZ11 *HI.7.1*

Luria, A. R. (1966, 1980). *Higher cortical functions in man.* New York: Basic Books.

Luria, A. R. (1968). *The mind of a mnemonist.* New York: Basic Books.

Luria, A. R. (1973). *The working brain.* Harmondsworth: Penguin.

MacCallum, R. (1983). A comparison of factor analysis programs in SPSS, BMDP, and SAS. *Psychometrika, 48*, 223–231.

MacCorquodale, K., & Meehl, P. (1948). On a distinction between hypothetical constructs and intervening variables. *Psychological Review, 55*, 95–107.

MacLeod, C. M. (1991). Half a century of research on the Stroop effect: An integrative review. *Psychological Bulletin, 109*, 163–203.

MacLeod, C. M., Hunt, E. B., & Mathews, N. N. (1978). Individual differences in the verification of sentence-picture relationships. *Journal of Verbal Learning and Verbal Behavior, 17*, 493–507.

Malmi, R. A., Underwood, B. J., & Carroll, J. B. (1979). The interrelationships among some associative learning tasks. *Bulletin of the Psychonomic Society, 13*, 121–123.
DS-MALM01 *HI.3.1*
Reanalyzed: Cudeck (1982)

Maltzman, I. (1960). On the training of originality. *Psychological Review, 67*, 229–242.

Mangan, G. L. (1959). A factorial study of speed, power and related temperament variables. *British Journal of Educational Psychology, 29*, 144–154.
DS-MANG01A *HI.7.2*

Marge, M. (1964). A factor analysis of oral communication skills in older children. *Journal of Speech and Hearing Research, 7*, 31–46.
DS-MARG01 *HI.7.1*

Marks, A., Guilford, J. P., & Merrifield, P. R. (1959). A study of military leadership in relation to selected intellectual factors. Los Angeles: Reports from the Psychological Laboratory, University of Southern California, No. 21.
DS-MARK01 *HI.4.1*

Marr, D. B., & Sternberg, R. J. (1987). The role of mental speed in intelligence: A triarchic perspective. In P. A. Vernon (Ed.), *Speed of information-processing and intelligence* (pp. 271–294). Norwood, NJ: Ablex.

Marsh, H. W., & Hocevar, D. (1983). Confirmatory factor analysis of multitrait multimethod matrices. *Journal of Educational Measurement, 20*, 231–248.

Marshalek, B. (1981). *Trait and process aspects of vocabulary knowledge and verbal ability.* Stanford, CA: Aptitude Research Project, School of Education, Stanford University (Technical Report No. 15).

Marshalek, B., Lohman, D. F., & Snow, R. E. (1983). The complexity continuum in the radex and hierarchical models of intelligence. *Intelligence, 7*, 107–127.
Reanalysis of SNOW11–12

Martin, J. K., & McDonald, R. P. (1975). Bayesian estimation in unrestricted factor analysis: A treatment for Heywood cases. *Psychometrika, 40*, 505–517.
Reanalysis of DAVI11

Martin, M. (1978). Memory span as a measure of individual differences in memory capacity. *Memory & Cognition, 6*, 194–198.

Martin, N. G., & Eaves, L. J. (1977). The genetical analysis of covariance structure. *Heredity, 38*, 79–95.

Martin, N. G., Jardine, R., & Eaves, L. J. (1984). Is there only one set of genes for different abilities? A reanalysis of the National Merit Scholarship Qualifying Test (NMSQT) data. *Behavior Genetics, 14*, 355–370.

Masny, D. (1983). Cognitive and linguistic correlates of second language grammaticality judgements. Unpublished doctoral dissertation, University of Montreal.
DS-MASN01 *HI.2.1*

Matin, L., & Adkins, D. C. (1954). A second-order factor analysis of reasoning abilities. *Psychometrika, 19*, 71–78.
Reanalysis of ADKI03

Matthews, G., & Dorn, L. (1989). IQ and choice reaction time: An information processing analysis. *Intelligence, 13*, 299–317.

Maxwell, S. E. (1977). Ideational fluency and retrieval from semantic memory. Unpublished Ph.D. dissertation, University of North Carolina at Chapel Hill.

May, F., & Metcalf, A. (1965). A factor-analytic study of spontaneous flexibility measures. *Educational & Psychological Measurement, 25*, 1039–1050.
DS-MAY01 *HI.4.1*

May, M. A. (1921). Psychological examining in the U. S. Army. *Memoirs of the National Academy of Sciences, 15*, 416.

Mayer, R. E. (1986). Mathematics. In R. F. Dillon & R. J. Sternberg (Eds.), *Cognition and instruction* (pp. 127–154). Orlando, FL: Academic.

Mayer, R. E., Larkin, J. H., & Kadane, J. B. (1984). A cognitive analysis of mathematical problem-solving ability. In R. J. Sternberg (Ed.), *Advances in the psychology of human intelligence*, Vol. 2 (pp. 231–273). Hillsdale, NJ: Erlbaum.

McCartin, R. A., & Meyers, C. E. (1966). An exploration of six semantic factors at first grade. *Multivariate Behavioral Research, 1,* 74–94.
DS-MCCA21 *HI.2.1*

McClelland, D. C. (1973). Testing for competence rather than for "intelligence." *American Psychologist, 28,* 1–14.

McDonald, R. P. (1985). *Factor analysis and related methods.* Hillsdale, NJ: Erlbaum.

McFarland, R. A. (1928). The röle of speed in mental ability. *Psychological Bulletin, 25,* 595–612.

McFarland, R. A. (1930). An experimental study of the relationship between speed and mental ability. *Journal of General Psychology, 3,* 67–97.

McFarlane, M. (1925). A study of practical ability. *British Journal of Psychology Monograph Supplements, 3,* No. 8.

McGue, M., & Bouchard, T. J., Jr. (1989). Genetic and environmental determinants of information processing and special mental abilities: A twin analysis. In R. J. Sternberg (Ed.), *Advances in the psychology of human intelligence,* Vol. 5 (pp. 7–45). Hillsdale, NJ: Erlbaum.

McGue, M., Bouchard, T. J., Jr., Lykken, D. T., & Feuer, D. (1984). Information processing abilities in twins reared apart. *Intelligence, 8,* 239–258.

McGuire, C., Hindsman, E., King, F. J., & Jennings, E. (1961). Dimensions of talented behavior. *Educational & Psychological Measurement, 21,* 3–38.
DS-MCGU01 *HI.5.1* (males, selected variables)
DS-MCGU02 *HI.4.1* (females, selected variables)

McKenna, F. P. (1984). Measures of field independence: Cognitive style or cognitive ability? *Journal of Personality and Social Psychology, 47,* 593–603.

McKenna, M. C. (1986). Cloze procedure as a memory-search process. *Journal of Educational Psychology, 78,* 433–440.

McKeown, M. G., & Curtis, M. E. (Eds.) (1987). *The nature of vocabulary acquisition.* Hillsdale, NJ: Erlbaum.

McNemar, Q. (1938). The equivalence of the general factors found for successive levels on the new Stanford Revision. *Psychological Bulletin, 35,* 657.

McNemar, Q. (1964). Lost: Our intelligence? Why? *American Psychologist, 19,* 871–882.

Mednick, S. A. (1962). The associative basis of the creative process. *Psychological Review, 69,* 220–232.

Meeker, M., & Meeker, R. (1975–81). *Structure of Intellect Learning Abilities Test.* El Segundo, CA: SOI Institute.

Meeker, M., & Meyers, C. E. (1971). Memory factors and school success of average and special groups of ninth-grade boys. *Genetic Psychology Monographs, 83,* 275–308.
DS-MEEK01 *HI.5.2.1*

Meili, R. (1946). L'analyse de l'intelligence. [The analysis of intelligence.] *Archives de Psychologie, 31,* No. 121.

Meili, R. (1979). Charakteristika der Globalisationsaufgaben. [Characteristics of globalization tasks.] *Psychologie – Schweizerische Zeitschrift für Psychologie und ihre Anwendungen, 38,* 22–42.

Meili, R. (1981). *Struktur der Intelligenz: Faktorenanalytische und denkpsychologische Untersuchungen.* [Structure of intelligence: Factor-analytic and cognitive psychology investigations.] Bern: Huber.

Mellon, J. C. (1969). *Transformational sentence combining: A method for enhancing the development of syntactic fluency in English composition.* Champaign, IL: National Council of Teachers of English. (NCTE Research Report No. 10.)

Melton, A. W. (1963). Implications of short-term memory for a general theory of memory. *Journal of Verbal Learning and Verbal Behavior, 2,* 1–21.

Mensh, E., & Mensh, H. (1991). *The IQ mythology: Class, race, gender, and inequality.* Carbondale, IL: Southern Illinois University Press.

Meredith, W. (1964). Rotation to achieve factorial invariance. *Psychometrika, 29,* 187–206. Reanalysis of HOLZ01

Merrifield, P. R. (1974). Factor analysis in educational research. *Review of Research in Education, 2,* 393–434. Reanalysis of BRAD01, GERS01-02, MERR41

Merrifield, P. R., Guilford, J. P., Christensen, P. R., & Frick, J. W. (1960). A factor-analytic study of problem-solving abilities. Los Angeles: Reports from the Psychological Laboratory, University of Southern California, No. 22. DS-MERR41 *HI.9.1* Further report: Merrifield, Guilford, Christensen, & Frick (1962) Reanalyzed: Harris & Liba (1965), Merrifield (1974)

Merrifield, P. R., Guilford, J. P., Christensen, P. R., & Frick, J. W. (1962). The role of intellectual factors in problem solving. *Psychological Monographs: General & Applied, 76*(10, Whole No. 529). Further report of MERR41

Merrifield, P. R., Guilford, J. P., & Gershon, A. (1963). The differentiation of divergent-production abilities at the sixth-grade level. Los Angeles: Reports from the Psychological Laboratory, University of Southern California, No. 27. DS-MERR51 *HI.6.1*

Messick, S. (1970). The criterion problem in the evaluation of instruction: Assessing possible, not just intended, outcomes. In M. C. Wittrock & D. E. Wiley (Eds.), *The evaluation of instruction: Issues and problems* (pp. 183–220). New York: Holt, Rinehart & Winston.

Messick, S. (1980). *The effectiveness of coaching for the SAT: Review and reanalysis of research from the fifties to the FTC.* Princeton, NJ: Educational Testing Service.

Messick, S. (1984). The nature of cognitive styles: Problems and promise in educational practice. *Educational Psychologist, 19,* 59–74.

Messick, S. (1987). Structural relationships across cognition, personality, and style. In R. E. Snow & M. J. Farr (Eds.), *Aptitude, learning, and instruction,* Vol. 3: *Cognitive and affective process analysis* (pp. 35–75). Hillsdale, NJ: Erlbaum.

Messick, S., & French, J. W. (1975). Dimensions of cognitive closure. *Multivariate Behavioral Research, 10,* 3–16. DS-MESS01 *HI.8.1*

Messick, S., & Jungeblut, A. (1981). Time and method in coaching for the SAT. *Psychological Bulletin, 89,* 191–216.

Michael, W. B., Zimmerman, W. S., & Guilford, J. P. (1950). An investigation of two hypotheses regarding the nature of the spatial-relations and visualization factors. *Educational & Psychological Measurement, 10,* 187–213. DS-MICH51 *HI.4.1* Reanalyzed: Lohman (1979a)

Michael, W. B., Zimmerman, W. S., & Guilford, J. P. (1951). An investigation of the nature of the spatial-relations and visualization factors in two high school samples. *Educational & Psychological Measurement, 11,* 561–577. DS-MICH61 *HI.5.1* (males) DS-MICH62 *HI.4.1* (females) Reanalyzed: Lohman (1979a)

Miller, G. A. (1956). The magical number seven, plus or minus two: Some limits on our capacity for processing information. *Psychological Review, 63,* 81–97.

Miller, G. A., Galanter, E., & Pribram, K. H. (1960). *Plans and the structure of behavior.* New York: Holt, Rinehart & Winston.

Miller, G. A., & Nicely, P. (1955). An analysis of perceptual confusions among some English consonants. *Journal of the Acoustical Society of America, 27,* 338–352.

Miller, T. W., & Weiss, D. J. (1976). *Effects of time-limits on test-taking behavior.* Minneapolis, MN: Psychometric Methods Program, University of Minnesota, Research Report 76–2.

Mitchell, J. V., Jr. (1983). *Tests in print III: An index to tests, test reviews, and the literature on specific tests.* Lincoln, NE: University of Nebraska Press.

Miyajima, K. (1972). The analytical study of speed components in intelligence test with time-limits: Proposition of a new approach to the speed and power problem. *Psychologia, 15,* 232–239.

Montanelli, R. G., Jr., & Humphreys, L. G. (1976). Latent roots of random data correlation matrices with squared multiple correlations on the diagonal: A Monte Carlo study. *Psychometrika, 41,* 341–348.

Mooney, C. M. (1954). A factorial study of closure. *Canadian Journal of Psychology, 8,* 51–60.
  DS-MOON01 *HI.4.1*

Moore, T. V (1933). The essential psychoses and their fundamental syndromes. *Studies in Psychology and Psychiatry, Catholic University of America, 3,* No. 3.

Morrow, R. S. (1941). An experimental analysis of the theory of independent abilities. *Journal of Educational Psychology, 32,* 495–512.
  DS-MORR11 *HI.4.1*
  Reanalyzed: Ahmavaara (1957)

Moursy, E. M. (1952). The hierarchical organization of cognitive levels. *British Journal of Statistical Psychology, 5,* 151–180.
  DS-MOUR01 *HI.4.2.1*
  Reanalyzed: Ho (1957)

Mulaik, S. A. (1972). *The foundations of factor analysis.* New York: McGraw-Hill.

Mulaik, S. A. (1986). Factor analysis and *Psychometrika*: Major developments. *Psychometrika, 51,* 23–33.

Mulla, M. A. (1979). Aptitude, attitude, motivation, anxiety, intolerance of ambiguity, and other biographical variables as predictors of achievement in English as a Foreign Language by high school science majors in Saudi Arabia. Unpublished Ph.D. dissertation, University of Michigan.
  DS-MULL01 *HI.3.1*

Muraki, E., & Engelhard, G., Jr. (1985). Full-information item factor analysis: Applications of EAP scores. *Applied Psychological Measurement, 9,* 417–430.

Murdock, B. B. (1960). The immediate retention of unrelated words. *Journal of Experimental Psychology, 60,* 222–224.

Murphy, L. W. (1936). The relation between mechanical ability tests and verbal and non-verbal intelligence tests. *Journal of Psychology, 2,* 353–366.
  DS-MURP01 *HI.3.1*

Murray, H. A. (1943). *Thematic Apperception Test.* Cambridge, MA: Harvard University Press.

Mursell, J. L. (1937). *The psychology of music.* New York: Norton.

Myers, C. T. (1952). The factorial composition and validity of differentially speeded tests. *Psychometrika, 17,* 347–352.

Naglieri, J. A., & Jensen, A. R. (1987). Comparison of black-white differences on the WISC-R and the K-ABC: Spearman's hypothesis. *Intelligence, 11,* 21–43.
  DS-NAGL01 *HI.3.1* (blacks)
  DS-NAGL02 *HI.3.1* (whites)
  DS-NAGL03 *HI.3.1* (combined)

Nairn, A., & Associates (1980). *The reign of ETS: The corporation that makes up minds.* Washington, DC: Learning Research Project.

National Assessment of Educational Progress (1985). *The reading report card: Progress toward excellence in our schools; Trends in reading over four national assessments, 1971–1984.* Princeton, NJ: Educational Testing Service. (ETS Report No. 15-R-01.)

National Commission on Testing and Public Policy (1990). *From gatekeeper to gateway: Transforming testing in America.* Chestnut Hill, MA: Author.

Neisser, U. (1967). *Cognitive psychology.* New York: Appleton–Century–Crofts.

Nettelbeck, T. (1987). Inspection time and intelligence. In P. A. Vernon (Ed.), *Speed of information-processing and intelligence* (pp. 295–346). Norwood, NJ: Ablex.

Newell, A. (1973). Production systems of control processes. In W. G. Chase (Ed.), *Visual information processing* (pp. 463–526). New York: Academic.

Newell, A., & Simon, H. A. (1972). *Human problem solving.* Englewood Cliffs, NJ: Prentice-Hall.

Nichols, R. (1978). Twin studies of ability, personality, and interests. *Homo, 29,* 158–173.

Nickerson, R. S. (1988). On improving thinking through instruction. *Review of Research in Education, 15,* 3–57.

Nihira, K., Guilford, J. P., Hoepfner, R., & Merrifield, P. R. (1964). A factor analysis of the semantic-evaluation abilities. Los Angeles: Reports from the Psychological Laboratory, University of Southern California, No. 32.
DS-NIIII01 *HI.10.2.1* (Group A)
DS-NIHI02 *HI.8.1* (Group B)
Further report: Hoepfner, Nihira, & Guilford (1966)

Norman, D., & Bobrow, D. (1975). On data limited and resource limited processes. *Cognitive Psychology, 7,* 44–64.

Oakes, W. F. (1955). An experimental study of pitch naming and pitch discrimination reactions. *Journal of Genetic Psychology, 86,* 237–259.

Odoroff, M. E. (1935). A correlational method applicable to the study of the time factor in intelligence tests. *Journal of Educational Psychology, 26,* 307–311.

Ohnmacht, F. W., Weaver, W. W., & Kohler, E. T. (1970). Cloze and closure: A factorial study. *Journal of Psychology, 74,* 205–217.
DS-OHNM11 *HI.2.1*

Oldfield, R. C., & Wingfield, A. (1964). The time it takes to name an object. *Nature, 202,* 1031–1032.

Oldfield, R. C., & Wingfield, A. (1965). Response latencies in naming objects. *Quarterly Journal of Experimental Psychology, 17,* 273–281.

Oléron, P. (1957). *Les composantes de l'intelligence d'après les recherches factorielles.* [*The components of intelligence according to factorial researches.*] Paris: Presses Universitaires de France.

Olive, H. (1972). The relationship of divergent thinking to intelligence, social class, and achievement in high-school students. *Journal of Genetic Psychology, 121,* 179–186.
DS-OLIV01 *HI.2.1*

Oller, J. W., Jr. (1976). Evidence for a general language proficiency factor: An expectancy grammar. *Die Neueren Sprachen, 75,* 165–174.

Olson, J. R. (1966). A factor analytic study of the relation between the speed of visual perception and the language abilities of deaf adolescents. Unpublished doctoral dissertation, Ohio State University. (University Microfilms 67-2507)
DS-OLSO51 *HI.7.1*

O'Sullivan, M., & Guilford, J. P. (1975). Six factors of behavioral cognition: Understanding other people. *Journal of Educational Measurement, 12,* 255–271.
Further report of OSUL01

O'Sullivan, M., Guilford, J. P., & de Mille, R. (1965). The measurement of social intelligence. Los Angeles: Reports from the Psychological Laboratory, University of Southern California, No. 34.
DS-OSUL01 *HI.8.1*
Further report: O'Sullivan & Guilford (1975)
Reanalyzed: Kelderman, Mellenbergh, & Elshout (1981)

Otis, A. S. (1918). An absolute point scale for the group measure of intelligence. *Journal of Educational Psychology, 9*, 238–261, 333–348.

Page, E. B. (1986). The disturbing case of the Milwaukee Project. In H. H. Spitz, *The raising of intelligence: A selected history of attempts to raise retarded intelligence* (pp. 115–140). Hillsdale, NJ: Erlbaum.

Paivio, A. (1971). *Imagery and verbal processes.* New York: Holt, Rinehart & Winston.

Paivio, A., & Cohen, M. (1979). Eidetic imagery and cognitive abilities. *Journal of Mental Imagery, 3*, 53–64.
DS-PAIV11 Matrix not analyzable

Paivio, A., & Harshman, R. A. (1983). Factor analysis of a questionnaire on imagery and verbal habits and skills. *Canadian Journal of Psychology, 37*, 461–483.

Palmer, J., MacLeod, C. M., Hunt, E., & Davidson, J. E. (1985). Information processing correlates of reading. *Journal of Memory and Language, 24*, 59–88.
DS-PALM01 *HI.7.1*

Paraskevopoulos, J. N., & Kirk, S. A. (1969.) *The development and psychometric characteristics of the revised Illinois Test of Psycholinguistic Abilities.* Urbana, IL: University of Illinois Press.
DS-PARA01 *HI.3.1* (age 2–7/3–1)
DS-PARA02 *HI.3.1* (age 3–7/4–1)
DS-PARA03 *HI.3.1* (age 4–7/5–1)
DS-PARA04 *HI.3.1* (age 5–7/6–1)
DS-PARA05 *HI.3.1* (age 6–7/7–1)
DS-PARA06 *HI.3.1* (age 7–7/8–1)
DS-PARA07 *HI.3.1* (age 8–7/9–1)
DS-PARA08 *HI.3.1* (age 9–7/10–1)
Reanalyzed: Doughtie, Wakefield, Sampson, & Alston (1974), Ramanaiah, O'Donnell, & Adams (1978)

Parker, J. F., Jr., & Fleishman, E. A. (1960). Ability factors and component performance measures as predictors of complex tracking behavior. *Psychological Monographs: General & Applied, 74*(16, Whole No. 503).
DS-PARK01 *HI.6.1*
Reanalyzed: Tucker (1967)

Paterson, D. G., Elliott, R. M., Anderson, L. D., Toops, H. A., & Heidbreder, E. (1930). *Minnesota Mechanical Ability Tests.* Minneapolis, MN: University of Minnesota Press.
DS-PATE01 *HI.7.1*
Reanalyzed: Guttman (1957), Wittenborn (1945)

Paterson, D. G., & Tinker, M. A. (1930). Time-limit vs. work-limit methods. *American Journal of Psychology, 42*, 101–104.

Pawlik, K. (1967). *Dimensionen des Verhaltens: Eine Einführung in Methodik und Ergebnisse faktorenanalytischer psychologischer Forschung.* [*Dimensions of behavior: Introduction to methods and results of factor-analytic psychological research.*] Bern: Hans Huber.

Peak, H., & Boring, E. G. (1926). The factor of speed in intelligence. *Journal of Experimental Psychology, 9*, 71–94.

Pearson, E. S. (1938). *Karl Pearson: An appreciation of some aspects of his life and work.* London: Cambridge University Press.

Pearson, K. (1901). On lines and planes of closest fit to systems of points in space. *Philosophical Magazine, 2,* 559–572.

Pedulla, J. J., Airasian, P. W., & Madaus, G. F. (1980). Do teacher ratings and standardized test results of students yield the same information? *American Educational Research Journal, 17,* 303–307.
DS-PEDU01 *HI.4.2.1*

Pellegrino, J. W. (1984). Information processing and intellectual ability. Paper presented at the annual meeting of the American Educational Research Association, New Orleans.

Pellegrino, J. W. (1985). Inductive reasoning ability. In R. J. Sternberg (Ed.), *Human abilities: An information-processing approach* (pp. 195–225). New York: Freeman.

Pellegrino, J. W. (1988). *Individual differences in skill acquisition: Information processing efficiency and the development of automaticity.* Brooks Air Force Base, TX: Air Force Human Resources Laboratory, Report AFHRL-TP-87-52.

Pellegrino, J. W., Alderton, D. L., & Shute, V. J. (1984). Understanding spatial ability. *Educational Psychologist, 19,* 239–253.

Pellegrino, J. W., & Glaser, R. (1979). Cognitive correlates and components in the analysis of individual differences. *Intelligence, 3,* 187–218.

Pellegrino, J. W., & Glaser, R. (1982). Analyzing aptitudes for learning: Inductive reasoning. In R. Glaser (Ed.), *Advances in instructional psychology,* Vol. 2 (pp. 269–345). Hillsdale, NJ: Erlbaum.

Pellegrino, J. W., & Hunt, E. B. (1989). Computer-controlled assessment of static and dynamic spatial reasoning. In R. F. Dillon & J. W. Pellegrino (Eds.), *Testing: Theoretical and applied perspectives* (pp. 174–198). New York: Praeger.

Pellegrino, J. W., & Kail, R., Jr. (1982). Process analyses of spatial aptitude. In R. J. Sternberg (Ed.), *Advances in the psychology of intelligence,* Vol. 1 (pp. 311–365). Hillsdale, NJ: Erlbaum.

Pemberton, C. (1952). The closure factors related to other cognitive processes. *Psychometrika, 17,* 267–288.
DS-PEMB01 *HI.5.1*
Reanalyzed: Ahmavaara (1957), Hakstian & Abell (1974)

Penfold, D. M., & Abou–Hatab, F. A. H. (1967). The factorial dimensions of verbal critical thinking. *Journal of Experimental Education, 36*(2), 1–12.
DS-PENF01 *HI.7.2.1*

Perfetti, C. A. (1985). *Reading ability.* New York: Oxford University Press.

Perkins, D. N. (1981). *The mind's best work.* Cambridge, MA: Harvard University Press.

Petersen, H., Guilford, J. P., Hoepfner, R., & Merrifield, P. R. (1963). Determination of "Structure-of-Intellect" abilities involved in ninth-grade algebra and general mathematics. Los Angeles: Reports from the Psychological Laboratory, University of Southern California, No. 31.
DS-PETE11 *HI.5.1* (general math. students)
DS-PETE12 *HI.5.1* (algebra students)
Further report: Guilford, Hoepfner, & Petersen (1965)

Peterson, J. (1925). *Early conceptions and tests of intelligence.* Yonkers-on-Hudson: World Book.

Peterson, L. R., & Peterson, M. J. (1959). Short term retention of individual verbal items. *Journal of Experimental Psychology, 58,* 193–198.

Peterson, N. G., & Bownas, D. A. (1982). Skill, task structure, and performance acquisition. In M. D. Dunnette & E. A. Fleishman (Eds.), *Human performance and productivity*, Vol. 1: *Human capability assessment* (pp. 49–105). Hillsdale, NJ: Erlbaum.

Petrov, Y.I. (1970). [Memory structure as a psychic function] (Russian). *Voprosy Psikhologii, 16*(3), 132–136.
    DS-PETR01 *HI.4.1*

Pettigrew, T. F. (1958). The measurement and correlates of category width as a cognitive variable. *Journal of Personality, 26*, 532–544.

Pickens, J. D., & Pollio, H. R. (1979). Patterns of figurative language competence in adult speakers. *Psychological Research, 40*, 299–313.
    DS-PICK01 Matrix not analyzable

Pieters, J. P. M., & van der Ven, A. H. G. S. (1982). Precision, speed, and distraction in time-limit tests. *Applied Psychological Measurement, 6*, 93–109.

Pimsleur, P., Stockwell, R. P., & Comrey, A. L. (1962). Foreign language learning ability. *Journal of Educational Psychology, 53*, 15–26.
    DS-PIMS01 *HI.6.2* (sample 1)
    DS-PIMS02 *HI.8* (a second sample one year later)

Plomin, R., DeFries, J. C., & McClearn, G. E. (1990). *Behavioral genetics: A primer* (2nd edition). New York: Freeman.

Politzer, R. L., & Weiss, L. (1969). *An experiment in improving achievement in foreign language learning through learning of selected skills associated with language aptitude.* Stanford, CA: Stanford University. (ERIC Doc. ED 046 261.)

Polson, P., & Jeffries, R. (1982). Problem solving as search and understanding. In R. J. Sternberg (Ed.), *Advances in the psychology of intelligence*, Vol. 1 (pp. 367–411). Hillsdale, NJ: Erlbaum.

Poltrock, S. E., & Agnoli, F. (1986). Are spatial visualization ability and visual imagery ability equivalent? In R. J. Sternberg (Ed.), *Advances in the psychology of human intelligence*, Vol. 3 (pp. 255–296). Hillsdale, NJ: Erlbaum.

Poltrock, S. E., & Brown, P. (1984). Individual differences in visual imagery and spatial ability. *Intelligence, 8*, 93–138.

Porebski, O. R. (1954). A psychological and statistical study of speed and power as variables of human ability. *Occupational Psychology, 28*, 218–231.

Porebski, O. R. (1960). Speed and power factors of intelligence: Further evidence. *Occupational Psychology, 34*, 184–194.

Porter, E. L. H. (1938). Factors in the fluctuation of fifteen ambiguous phenomena. *Psychological Record, 2*, 231–253.
    DS-PORT01 matrix not analyzable

Porteus, S. D. (1914–65). *The Porteus Maze Test.* New York: The Psychological Corporation.

Porteus, S. D. (1950). *The Porteus Maze Test and intelligence.* Palo Alto, CA: Pacific Books.

Posner, M. I. (1978). *Chronometric explorations of mind.* Hillsdale, NJ: Erlbaum.

Posner, M. I., & Mitchell, R. (1967). Chronometric analysis of classification. *Psychological Review, 74*, 392–409.

Postman, L. (1971). Transfer, interference, and forgetting. In J. W. Kling & L. A. Riggs (Eds.), *Woodworth and Schlosberg's experimental psychology* (pp. 1019–1132). New York: Holt, Rinehart & Winston.

Price, E. J. J. (1940). The nature of the practical factor (*f*). *British Journal of Psychology, 30*, 341–351.
    DS-PRIC01 *HI.3.1*

Proger, B. B., Mann, L., Bayuk, R. J., Jr., Burger, R. M., Cross, L. H., & Green, P. A. (1973). Factorial structure of the Illinois Test of Psycholinguistic Abilities. *Psychological Reports, 32*, 931–935.

DS-PROG01 *HI.5.1*
Proger, B. B., McGowan, J. R., Bayuk, R. J., Jr., Mann, L., Trevorrow, R. L., & Massa, E. (1971). The relative predictive and construct validities of the Otis–Lennon Mental Ability Test, the Lorge–Thorndike Intelligence Test, and the Metropolitan Readiness Test in grades two and four: A series of multivariate analyses. *Educational & Psychological Measurement, 31*, 529–538.
DS-PROG11 *HI.4.1* (grade 2)
DS-PROG12 *HI.4.1* (grade 4)
Ramanaiah, N. V., O'Donnell, J. P., & Adams, M. (1978). A test of the theoretical model of the revised Illinois Test of Psycholinguistic Abilities. *Applied Psychological Measurement, 2*, 519–525.
Reanalyses of PARA01–08
Randhawa, B. S., & Hunt, D. (1979). Some further evidence in successive and simultaneous integration and individual differences. *Canadian Journal of Behavioural Science, 11*, 340–355.
DS-RAND01 *HI.4.1* (males)
DS-RAND02 *HI.4.1* (females)
Rankin, R. J., & Thompson, K. (1966a). A factorial investigation of scores on the Porteus Maze. *Perceptual & Motor Skills, 23*, 1255–1260.
DS-RANK01 *HI.2.1*
Rankin, R. J., & Thompson, K. (1966b). A factor analytic approach to impulse as measured by Arrow Dot I, Q, and SORT. *Perceptual & Motor Skills, 23*, 1239–1245.
DS-RANK11 matrix not analyzable
Rao, C. R. (1955). Estimation and tests of significance in factor analysis. *Psychometrika, 20*, 93–111.
Reanalysis of DAVI11
Rasch, G. (1960, 1980). *Probabilistic models for some intelligence and attainment tests.* Copenhagen: Danmarks Paedagogiske Institut. (Expanded edition: Chicago: University of Chicago Press, 1980)
Raskin, E. (1937). The interrelationships of speed of response measured on levels of varying difficulty. Unpublished Ph.D. thesis, University of Minnesota.
Raven, J. C. (1938–65). *Progressive Matrices.* New York: The Psychological Corporation, & London: H. K. Lewis & Co.
Reinert, G., Baltes, P., & Schmidt, L. R. (1965). Faktorenanalytische Untersuchungen zur Differenzierungshypothese der Intelligenz: Die Leistungsdifferenzierungshypothese. [Factor-analytic investigations of the hypothesis of intelligence differentiation: The hypothesis of differentiation by performance level.] *Psychologische Forschung, 28*, 246–300.
DS-REIN01 *HI.3.1* (Table 14)
DS-REIN02 *HI.3.1* (Table 15)
DS-REIN03 *HI.3.1* (Table 24)
DS-REIN04 *HI.3.1* (Table 25)
Remondino, C. (1962). Recherche sur la signification du facteur numérique. [Research on the signification of the numerical factor.] *Revue de Psychologie Appliquée, 12*, 63-81.
DS-REMO01 *HI.3.1* (one random half)
DS-REMO02 *HI.3.1* (2nd random half)
Resnick, L. B. (Ed.) (1976). *The nature of intelligence.* Hillsdale, NJ: Erlbaum.
Reuchlin, M. (1964). *Méthodes d'analyse factorielle à l'usage des psychologues.* [*Methods of factor analysis used by psychologists.*] Paris: Presses Universitaires de France.
Revenstorf, D. (1980). *Faktorenanalyse.* [*Factor analysis.*] Stuttgart: Kohlhammer.
Reyburn, H. A., & Taylor, J. G. (1941). Some factors of intelligence. *British Journal of Psychology, 31*, 249–261.

DS-REYB01 *HI.3.1*
Reynolds, C. R. (1979). A factor analytic study of the Metropolitan Readiness Test. *Contemporary Educational Psychology, 4,* 315–317.
DS-REYN01 *HI.2.1*
Reynolds, C. R. (1980). Differential construct validity of a preschool battery for Blacks, Whites, males, and females. *Journal of School Psychology, 18,* 112–125.
DS-REYN11 *HI.2.1*
Richards, T. W. (1941). Genetic emergence of factor specificity. *Psychometrika, 6,* 37–42. Reanalysis of GARR11–16
Richards, T. W., & Nelson, V. L. (1939). Abilities of infants during the first eighteen months. *Journal of Genetic Psychology, 55,* 299–318.
DS-RICH31 *HI.3.1* (age 6 mo.)
DS-RICH32 *HI.3.1* (age 12 mo.)
DS-RICH33 *HI.3.1* (age 18 mo.)
Richardson–Klavehn, A.; & Bjork, R. A. (1988). Measures of memory. *Annual Review of Psychology, 39,* 475–543.
Rieben, L., & Mengal, P. (1977). Intelligence globale, créativité et operativité chez l'enfant: Analyse factorielle et analyse discriminante. [Global intelligence, creativity, and operativity in the child: Factorial and discriminant analysis.] *Psychologie – Schweizerische Zeitschrift für Psychologie und ihre Anwendungen, 36,* 100–108.
DS-RIEB01 *HI.2.1* (age 6)
DS-RIEB02 *HI.2.1* (age 8)
Rimoldi, H. J. A. (1948). Study of some factors related to intelligence. *Psychometrika, 13,* 27–46.
DS-RIMO11 *HI.4.2.1*
Reanalyzed (rotation): Hakstian (1971)
Rimoldi, H. J. A. (1951a). The central intellective factor. *Psychometrika, 16,* 75–101.
DS-RIMO21 *HI.4.1*
Reanalyzed: Ahmavaara (1957)
Rimoldi, H. J. A. (1951b). Personal tempo. *Journal of Abnormal and Social Psychology, 46,* 283-303.
Rindler, S. E. (1979). Pitfalls in assessing test speediness. *Journal of Educational Measurement, 16,* 261–270.
Rips, L. J. (1984). Reasoning as a central intellective activity. In R. J. Sternberg (Ed.), *Advances in the psychology of human intelligence,* Vol. 2 (pp. 105–147). Hillsdale, NJ: Erlbaum.
Robertson–Tchabo, E., & Arenberg, D. (1976). Age differences in cognition in healthy educated men: A factor analysis of experimental measures. *Experimental Aging Research, 2,* 75–89.
DS-ROBE11 *HI.4.1*
Roff, M. E. (1941). A statistical study of the development of intelligence test performance. *Journal of Psychology, 11,* 371–386.
Roff, M. E. (1951). Personnel selection and classification procedures: Spatial tests: A factorial analysis. Randolph Field, TX: USAF School of Medicine. (Project No. 21-29-002 Final Report)
Reanalysis of GUIL46
Roff, M. E. (1952). A factorial study of tests in the perceptual areas. *Psychometric Monographs,* No. 8.
DS-ROFF11 *HI.9.1*
Rogers, C. A. (1953). The structure of verbal fluency. *British Journal of Psychology, 44,* 368–380.

DS-ROGE11 *HI.4.1*
Reanalyzed: Wendeler (1970)

Rogosa, D. (1980). A critique of cross-lagged correlation. *Psychological Bulletin, 88,* 245–258.

Rondal, J. A. (1978). Patterns of correlations for various language measures in mother–child interactions for normal and Down's syndrome children. *Language & Speech, 21,* 242–252.
DS-ROND01 *HI.2* (children)
DS-ROND02 *HI.5.2* (mothers)

Rosanoff, A. J. (Ed.) (1927). *Free Association Test (Kent–Rosanoff)* (6th edition). New York: Wiley.

Rose, A. M. (1974). Human information processing: An assessment and research battery. Ann Arbor: Human Performance Center, Department of Psychology, University of Michigan. (Technical Report No. 46)
DS-ROSE01 *HI.5.1* (day 1)
DS-ROSE02 *HI.5.1* (day 2)
DS-ROSE03 *HI.5.1* (day 3)

Rose, A. M., & Fernandes, K. (1977). An information processing approach to performance assessment: I. Experimental investigation of an information processing performance battery. Washington: American Institutes for Research, Technical Report No. 1.
DS-ROSE11 *HI.7.1* (day 1)
DS-ROSE12 *HI.7.1* (day 2)

Roskam, E. E., van Breukelen, G., & Jansen, R. (1989). Concentration, speed, and precision in time-limited tasks. In D. Vickers & P. L. Smith (Eds.), *Human information processing: Measures, mechanisms, and models* (pp. 291–310). Amsterdam: Elsevier (North Holland).

Ross, J. (1961). A factor test of a memory model. Princeton, NJ: Educational Testing Service Research Bulletin RB-61-14.
Reanalysis of KELL01

Royce, J. R. (1980). Factor analysis is alive and well. *American Psychologist, 35,* 390–392.

Royce, J. R., & Powell, A. (1983). *A theory of personality and individual differences: Factors, systems, and processes.* Englewood Cliffs, NJ: Prentice–Hall.

Royce, J. R., Yeudall, L. T., & Bock, C. (1976). Factor analytic studies of human brain damage. I. First and second-order factors and their brain correlates. *Multivariate Behavioral Research, 11,* 381–418.
DS-ROYC11 *HI.11.1*

Ruch, G. W., & Koerth, W. (1923). "Power" vs. "speed" in Army Alpha. *Journal of Educational Psychology, 11,* 193–208.

Russell, E. W. (1973). Reanalysis of Halstead's biological intelligence factor matrix. *Perceptual & Motor Skills, 37,* 699–705.
Reanalysis of HALS01

Sachs, J. S. (1967). Recognition memory for syntactic and semantic aspects of connected discourse. *Perception & Psychophysics, 2,* 437–442.

Sack, S. A., & Rice, C. E. (1974). Selectivity, resistance to distraction, and shifting as three attentional factors. *Psychological Reports, 34,* 1003–1012.

Sadker, M., Sadker, D., & Klein, S. (1991). The issue of gender in elementary and secondary education. *Review of Research in Education, 17,* 269–334.

Salomon, G. (1974). Internalization of filmic schematic operations in interaction with learners' aptitudes. *Journal of Educational Psychology, 66,* 499–511.

Sapon, S. M. (1955). A work sample test for foreign language prognosis. *Journal of Psychology, 39,* 97–104.

Satterly, D. J. (1976). Cognitive styles, spatial ability, and school achievement. *Journal of Educational Psychology*, 68, 36–42.
  DS-SATT01 *HI.3.1*
  Critique: Humphreys & Parsons (1977)
Satterly, D. J. (1979). Covariation of cognitive styles, intelligence and achievement. *British Journal of Educational Psychology*, 49, 179–181.
  DS-SATT11 *HI.4.1*
Satterly, D. J., & Brimer, M. A. (1971). Cognitive style and school learning. *British Journal of Educational Psychology*, 41, 294–303.
Sattler, J. M. (1982). *Assessment of chldren's intelligence and special abilities* (2nd edition). Boston: Allyn & Bacon.
Saum, A. L. (1938). The relative significance of time as a factor in tests of ability at the college level. *Journal of Applied Psychology*, 22, 192–210.
Saunders, D. R. (1953). An analytic method for rotation to orthogonal simple structure. Princeton, NJ: Educational Testing Service Research Bulletin RB-53-10.
Saunders, D. R. (1959). On the dimensionality of the WAIS battery for two groups of normal males. *Psychological Reports*, 5, 529–541.
  DS-SAUN03 *HI.5.1* (combined samples A & B)
Saunders, D. R. (1960a). A factor analysis of the picture completion items of the WAIS. *Journal of Clinical Psychology*, 16, 146–149.
  DS-SAUN11 *HI.3.1*
Saunders, D. R. (1960b). A factor analysis of the information and arithmetic items of the WAIS. *Psychological Reports*, 6, 367–383.
  DS-SAUN21 *HI.6.1*
Saville, P. (1971). *A British supplement to the manual of the Wechsler Adult Intelligence Scale*. New York: The Psychological Corporation.
Scarr, S., & Carter–Saltzman, L. (1982). Genetics and intelligence. In R. J. Sternberg (Ed.), *Handbook of human intelligence* (pp. 792–896). Cambridge, England: Cambridge University Press.
Schaefer, W. C. (1940). Test difficulty and factorial composition. Unpublished Ph.D. dissertation, University of Chicago.
  DS-SCHA11 *HI.10.2.1*
Schaie, K. W. (1955). A test of behavioral rigidity. *Journal of Abnormal and Social Psychology*, 51, 604–610.
Schaie, K. W. (1979). The primary mental abilities in adulthood: An exploration in the development of psychometric intelligence. In P. B. Baltes & O. G. Brim, Jr. (Eds.), *Life-span development and behavior*, Vol. 2 (pp. 67–115). New York: Academic.
Schaie, K. W. (Ed.) (1983). *Longitudinal studies of adult psychological development*. New York: Guilford.
Schaie, K. W., & Hertzog, C. (1986). Toward a comprehensive model of adult intellectual development: Contributions of the Seattle Longitudinal Study. In R. J. Sternberg (Ed.), *Advances in the psychology of human intelligence*, Vol. 3 (pp. 79–118). Hillsdale, NJ: Erlbaum.
Schaie, K. W., & Strother, C. R. (1968). A cross-sequential study of age changes in cognitive behavior. *Psychological Bulletin*, 70, 671–680.
Scheffler, I. (1985). *Of human potential: An essay in the philosophy of education*. Boston: Routledge & Kegan Paul.
Scheier, I. H., & Ferguson, G. A. (1952). Further factorial studies of tests of rigidity. *Canadian Journal of Psychology*, 6, 18–30.
  DS-SCHE11 *HI.5.1*
Schiff, W., & Dytell, R. S. (1972). Deaf and hearing children's performance on a tactual perception battery. *Perceptual & Motor Skills*, 35, 683–706.

DS-SCHI01 (deaf) matrix not analyzable

DS-SCHI02 (hearing) matrix not analyzable

Schiller, B. (1934). Verbal, numerical and spatial abilities of young children. *Archives of Psychology (N.Y.)*, *24*, No. 161.

DS-SCHI11 *HI.3.1* (boys)

DS-SCHI12 *HI.3.1* (girls)

Schmid, J., & Leiman, J. M. (1957). The development of hierarchical factor solutions. *Psychometrika*, *22*, 53–61.

Schmitt, N., & Stults, D. M. (1986). Methodology review: Analysis of multitrait–multimethod matrices. *Applied Psychological Measurement*, *10*, 1–22.

Schneck, M. M. R. (1929). The measurement of verbal and numerical abilities. *Archives of Psychology (N. Y.) 17*, No. 107.

DS-SCHN01 *HI.2.1*

Analyzed: Garrett (1938)

Schneider, W., & Shiffrin, R. M. (1977). Controlled and automatic human information processing: I. Detection, search, and attention. *Psychological Review*, *84*, 1–66.

Scholz, G., Hendricks, D., Spurling, R., Johnson, M., & Vandenberg, L. (1980). Is language ability divisible or unitary? A factor analysis of 22 English language proficiency tests. In J. W. Oller, Jr., & K. Perkins (Eds.), *Research in language testing* (pp. 24–33). Rowley, MA: Newbury House.

DS-SCIIO31 *HI.5.1*

Reanalyzed: Carroll (1983a), Vollmer & Sang (1983)

Schreiner, R. L., Hieronymus, A. N., & Forsyth, R. (1969). Differential measurement of reading abilities at the elementary school level. *Reading Research Quarterly*, *5*, 84–99.

DS-SCHR11 *HI.3.1*

Schuell, H., Jenkins, J. J., & Carroll, J. B. (1962). A factor analysis of the Minnesota Test for Differential Diagnosis of Aphasia. *Journal of Speech and Hearing Research*, *5*, 349–369.

DS-SCHU00 *HI.5.1*

Schultz, N. R., Jr., Kaye, D. B., & Hoyer, W. J. (1980). Intelligence and spontaneous flexibility in adulthood and old age. *Intelligence*, *4*, 219–231.

DS-SCHU01 *HI.2* (younger adults)

DS-SCHU02 *HI.2* (older adults)

Reanalyzed: Humphreys & Park (1981)

Schutz, R. E. (1958). Factorial validity of the Holzinger–Crowder Uni-Factor Tests. *Educational & Psychological Measurement*, *18*, 873–875.

DS-SCHU11 *HI.4.2.1*

Schwartz, S. (1981). Verbal ability, attention and automaticity. In M. P. Friedman, J. P. Das, & N. O'Connor (Eds.), *Intelligence and learning* (pp. 567–574). New York: Plenum.

Schwartz, S., Griffin, T. M., & Brown, J. (1983). Power and speed components of individual differences in letter matching. *Intelligence*, *7*, 369–378.

Seashore, C. E. (1919). *Manual of instructions and interpretations for Measures of Musical Talent.* Chicago: Stoelting.

Seashore, C. E., Lewis, D., & Saetveit, J. G. (1939–60). *Seashore Measures of Musical Talents, Revised Edition.* New York: The Psychological Corporation.

Seashore, R. H., Buxton, C. E., & McCollom, I. N. (1940). Multiple factorial analysis of fine motor skills. *American Journal of Psychology*, *53*, 251–259.

DS-SEAS01 Matrix not analyzable

Segel, D. (1957). The multiple aptitude tests. *Personnel & Guidance Journal*, *35*, 424–432.

DS-SEGE01 *HI.4.2.1* (males)

DS-SEGE02 *HI.4.2.1* (females)

Seibert, W. F., Reid, J. C., & Snow, R. E. (1967). *Studies in cine-psychometry II: Continued factoring of audio and visual cognition and memory.* West Lafayette, IN: Purdue University Audio Visual Center. [ERIC Doc. 019 877]
[DS-SEIB01 see DS-HECK01]
DS-SEIB02 *HI.9.1*

Seibert, W. F., & Snow, R. E. (1965). *Studies in cine-psychometry. I: Preliminary factor analysis of visual cognition and memory.* Lafayette, IN: Purdue University Audio Visual Center. [ERIC Doc. ED 003 624]

Shankweiler, D. P. (1961). Performance of brain-damaged patients on two tests of sound localization. *Journal of Comparative and Physiological Psychology, 54,* 375–381.

Sharp, S. E. (1898–99). Individual psychology: A study in psychological method. *American Journal of Psychology, 10,* 329–391.

Shaycoft, M. F. (1967). *Project TALENT: The high school years: Growth in cognitive skills.* Pittsburgh, PA: American Institutes for Research & School of Education, University of Pittsburgh. (Interim Report 3)
DS-SHAY01 *HI.7.1* (males)
DS-SHAY02 *HI.7.3.1* (females)

Shepard, R. N. (1981). Individual differences in the perception of musical pitch. In *Documentary Report of the Ann Arbor symposium: Applications of psychology to the teaching and learning of music* (pp. 152–174). Reston, VA: Music Educators National Conference.

Shepard, R. N., & Metzler, J. (1971). Mental rotation of three-dimensional objects. *Science, 171,* 701–703.

Shepard, R. N., & Teghtsoonian, M. (1961). Retention of information under conditions approaching a steady state. *Journal of Experimental Psychology, 62,* 302–309.

Shiffrin, R. M. (1988). Attention. In R. C. Atkinson, R. J. Herrnstein, G. Lindzey, & R. D. Luce (Eds.), *Stevens' Handbook of experimental psychology,* 2nd edition, Vol. 2: *Learning and cognition* (pp. 739–811). New York: Wiley.

Shuter–Dyson, R., & Gabriel, C. (1981). *The psychology of musical ability,* 2nd edition. London: Methuen.

Siegel, J. A., & Siegel, W. (1977). Absolute identification of notes and intervals by musicians. *Perception & Psychophysics, 21,* 143–152.

Simrall, D. (1947). Intelligence and the ability to learn. *Journal of Psychology, 23,* 27–43.
DS-SIMR01 *HI.5.2*

Singer, H. (1965). Validity of the Durrell–Sullivan Reading Capacity Test. *Educational & Psychological Measurement, 25,* 479–491.
DS-SING21 *HI.5.1*

Singer, J., & Antrobus, J. (1963). A factor-analytic study of daydreaming and conceptually-related cognitive and personality variables. *Perceptual & Motor Skills, 17*(Monog. Suppl. 3), 187–209.

Sisk, H. L. (1939). A multiple factor analysis of mental abilities in the freshman engineering curriculum. *Journal of Psychology, 9,* 165–177.
DS-SISK01 *HI.4.1*

Skager, R. W. (1961). The effects of two training procedures on the differentiation of numerical ability. Unpublished doctoral dissertation, University of California at Los Angeles.

Skeels, H. M., & Dye, H. B. (1939). A study of the effects of differential stimulation on mentally retarded children. *Proceedings of the American Association for Mental Deficiency, 44,* 114–136.

Skehan, P. (1980). Memory, language aptitude and second language performance. *Polyglot, 2* (Fiche 3), D11–E14.

DS-SKEH01 *HI.2.1*

Slater, P. (1938). Speed of work in intelligence tests. *British Journal of Psychology, 29,* 55–68.

Slater, P. (1940). Some group tests of spatial judgment or practical ability. *Occupational Psychology, 14,* 40–55.
DS-SLAT01 *HI.4.2*

Smith, B. D. (1988). Personality: Multivariate systems theory and research. In J. R. Nesselroade & R. B. Cattell (Eds.), *Handbook of multivariate experimental psychology,* 2nd edition (pp. 687–736). New York: Plenum.

Smith, G. A., & Stanley, G. (1983). Clocking *g*: Relating intelligence and measures of timed performance. *Intelligence, 7,* 353–368.

Smith, G. A., & Stanley, G. (1987). Comparing subtest profiles of *g* loadings and correlations with RT measures. *Intelligence, 11,* 291–298.

Smith, G. M., Jr. (1933). Group factors in mental tests similar in material or in structure. *Archives of Psychology (N.Y.), 25,* No. 156.
DS-SMIT01 *HI.3.1*
Reanalyzed: Chein (1939)

Smith, H. W. (1977). Intelligence, reading, and spelling abilities. *Dissertation Abstracts International, 38*(5-A), 2676–2677. (University Microfilm 77-24347)
DS-SMIT11 *HI.3.1*

Smith, O. W., & Smith, P. C. (1966). Developmental studies of spatial judgments by children and adults. *Perceptual & Motor Skills, 22,* 3–73 (Monograph Supplement 1-V22).
DS-SMIT51 *HI.10* (children)
DS-SMIT52 *HI.10.1* (adults)

Snow, C. E., & Hoefnagel-Höhle, M. (1979). Individual differences in second-language ability: A factor-analytic study. *Language & Speech, 22,* 151–162.
DS-SNOW01 *HI.3.1* (time 1)
DS-SNOW02 *HI.3.1* (time 2)
DS-SNOW03 *HI.3.1* (time 3)

Snow, R. E. (1976). Research on aptitude for learning: A progress report. *Review of Research in Education, 4,* 50–105.

Snow, R. E. (1978a). Theory and method for research on aptitude processes. *Intelligence, 2,* 225–278.

Snow, R. E. (1978b). Eye fixation and strategy analyses of individual differences in cognitive aptitudes. In A. M. Lesgold, J. W. Pellegrino, S. D. Fokkema, & R. Glaser (Eds.), *Cognitive psychology and instruction* (pp. 299–308). New York: Plenum.

Snow, R. E. (1980). Aptitude processes. In R. E. Snow, P-A. Federico, & W. E. Montague (Eds.), *Aptitude, learning, and instruction,* Vol. 1: *Cognitive process analyses of aptitude* (pp. 27–63). Hillsdale, NJ: Erlbaum.

Snow, R. E. (1981). Toward a theory of aptitude for learning: I. Fluid and crystallized abilities and their correlates. In M. P. Friedman, J. P. Das, & N. O'Connor (Eds.), *Intelligence and learning* (pp. 345–362). New York: Plenum.

Snow, R. E. (1982). The training of intellectual aptitude. In D. K. Detterman & R. J. Sternberg (Eds.), *How and how much can intelligence be increased.* (pp. 1–37). Norwood, NJ: Ablex.

Snow, R. E., Kyllonen, P. C., & Marshalek, B. (1984). The topography of ability and learning correlations. In R. J. Sternberg (Ed.), *Advances in the psychology of human intelligence,* Vol. 2 (pp. 47–103). Hillsdale, NJ: Erlbaum.

Snow, R. E., & Lohman, D. F. (1984). Toward a theory of cognitive aptitude for learning from instruction. *Journal of Educational Psychology, 76,* 347–376.

Snow, R. E., & Lohman, D. F. (1989). Implications of cognitive psychology for educational measurement. In R. L. Linn (Ed.), *Educational measurement*, 3rd edition (pp. 263–331). New York: American Council on Education & Macmillan.

Snow, R. E., Lohman, D. F., Marshalek, B., Yalow, E., & Webb, N. (1977). Correlational analyses of reference aptitude constructs. Stanford, CA: Aptitude Research Project, School of Education, Stanford University, Technical Report No. 5.
    DS-SNOW11 *HI.5.1* (high school sample)
    DS-SNOW12 *HI.7.1* (college sample)
    Reanalyzed: Marshalek, Lohman, & Snow (1983)

Snow, R. E., Marshalek, B., & Lohman, D. F. (1976). Correlation of selected cognitive abilities and cognitive processing parameters: An exploratory study. Stanford, CA: Aptitude Research Project, School of Education, Stanford University, Technical Report No. 3.
    DS-SNOW20 *HI.5* (Table 3)
    DS-SNOW21 *HI.6.2* (Table 7)

Snyderman, M., & Rothman, S. (1986). Science, politics, and the IQ controversy. *The Public Interest*, No. 83, 79–97.

Snyderman, M., & Rothman, S. (1987). Survey of expert opinion on intelligence and aptitude testing. *American Psychologist, 42*, 137–144.

Snyderman, M., & Rothman, S. (1988). *The IQ controversy, the media and public policy.* New Brunswick, NJ: Transaction Books.

Sokal, M. M. (Ed.) (1987). *Psychological testing and American society, 1890–1930.* New Brunswick: Rutgers University Press.

Soltow, L., & Stevens, E. (1981). *The rise of literacy and the common school in the United States: A socioeconomic analysis to 1870.* Chicago: University of Chicago Press.

Spearman, C. (1904a). The proof and measurement of association between things. *American Journal of Psychology, 15*, 72–101. [Reprinted, 1987, *100*, 441–471]

Spearman, C. (1904b). "General intelligence," objectively determined and measured. *American Journal of Psychology, 15*, 201–293.

Spearman, C. (1910). Correlation calculated from faulty data. *British Journal of Psychology, 3*, 271–295.

Spearman, C. (1923). *The nature of 'intelligence' and the principles of cognition.* London: Macmillan. [Reprinted: New York: Arno, 1973]

Spearman, C. (1927). *The abilities of man: Their nature and measurement.* New York: Macmillan. [Reprinted: New York: AMS Publishers, 1981]

Spearman, C. (1930). Autobiography. In C. Murchison (Ed.), *A history of psychology in autobiography*, Vol. 1 (pp. 299–334). Worcester, MA: Clark University Press.

Spearman, C. (1939). Thurstone's work reworked. *Journal of Educational Psychology, 30*, 1–16.
    Reanalysis of THUR21

Spearman, C., & Holzinger, K. J. (1924). The sampling error in the theory of two factors. *British Journal of Psychology, 15*, 17–19.

Spearman, C., & Holzinger, K. J. (1925). Note on the sampling error of tetrad differences. *British Journal of Psychology, 16*, 86–88.

Spearman, C., & Wynn Jones, L. (1950). *Human ability: A continuation of "The abilities of man."* London: Macmillan.

Spearritt, D. (1962). *Listening comprehension – a factorial analysis.* Melbourne: Australian Council for Educational Research. (ACER Research Series No. 76)
    DS-SPEA01 *HI.5.1* (boys)
    DS-SPEA02 *HI.5.1* (girls)

Spearritt, D., with Spalding, D., & Johnston, M. (1977). *Measuring reading comprehension in the upper primary school*. Canberra: Australian Government Publishing Service. (Education Research and Development Committee Report No. 11)

DS-SPEA31 *HI.6.1* (middle-class boys)

DS-SPEA32 *HI.8.1* (middle-class girls)

DS-SPEA33 *HI.7.1* (lower-class boys)

DS-SPEA34 *HI.6.2* (lower-class girls)

Spitz, H. H. (1986). *The raising of intelligence: A selected history of attempts to raise retarded intelligence*. With a chapter by Ellis B. Page. Hillsdale, NJ: Erlbaum.

Sprague, R. L., & Quay, H. C. (1966). A factor analysis study of the responses of mental retardates on the WAIS. *American Journal of Mental Deficiency, 70*, 595–600.

DS-SPRA11 *HI.3.1*

Stake, R. E. (1961). Learning parameters, aptitudes, and achievements. *Psychometric Monographs*, No. 9.

DS-STAK01 *HI.13.3*

Stankov, L. (1983). Attention and intelligence. *Journal of Educational Psychology, 75*, 471–490.

DS-STAN21 *HI.4.1*

Stankov, L., & Horn, J. L. (1980). Human abilities revealed through auditory tests. *Journal of Educational Psychology, 72*, 21–44.

DS-STAN31 *HI.7.2*

Stankov, L., Horn, J. L., & Roy, T. (1980). On the relationship between Gf/Gc theory and Jensen's Level I/Level II theory. *Journal of Educational Psychology, 72*, 796–809.

DS-STAN41 Matrix as published not analyzable.

Stanovich, K. E. (1981). Relationships between word decoding speed, general name-retrieval ability, and reading progress in first-grade children. *Journal of Educational Psychology, 73*, 809–815.

DS-STAN51 *HI.2.1*

Stanovich, K. E. (Ed.) (1988). *Children's reading and the development of phonological awareness*. Detroit, MI: Wayne State University Press.

Stanovich, K. E., Cunningham, A. E., & Feeman, D. J. (1984). Intelligence, cognitive skills, and early reading progress. *Reading Research Quarterly, 29*, 278–303.

DS-STAN61 *HI.3.1*

Stanton, H. M., & Koerth, W. (1930). Musical capacity measures of adults repeated after music education. *University of Iowa Studies*, First Series No. 189.

Stenquist, J. L. (1923). Measurements of mechanical ability. *Teachers College Columbia Contributions to Education*, No. 130.

Stephens, B., McLaughlin, J. A., Miller, C. K., & Glass, G. V. (1972). Factorial structure of selected psycho-educational measures and Piagetian reasoning assessments. *Developmental Psychology, 6*, 343–348.

DS-STEP01B *HI.4.1*

Reanalyzed: Humphreys & Parsons (1979); Carroll, Kohlberg, & DeVries (1984).

Stephenson, W. (1953). *The study of behavior*. Chicago: University of Chicago Press.

Sternberg, R. J. (1977). *Intelligence, information processing, and analogical reasoning: The componential analysis of human abilities*. Hillsdale, NJ: Erlbaum.

Sternberg, R. J. (1979). The nature of mental abilities. *American Psychologist, 34*, 214–230.

Sternberg, R. J. (Ed.) (1982). *Handbook of human intelligence*. New York: Cambridge University Press.

Sternberg, R. J. (1983). Criteria for intellectual skills training. *Educational Researcher, 12*(2), 6–12.

Sternberg, R. J. (1985). *Beyond IQ: A triarchic theory of human intelligence*. New York: Cambridge University Press.

Sternberg, R. J. (Ed.) (1988). *The nature of creativity: Contemporary psychological perspectives.* New York: Cambridge University Press.

Sternberg, R. J., & Berg, C. (1986). Quantitative integration: Definitions of intelligence: A comparison of the 1921 and 1986 symposia. In R. J. Sternberg & D. K. Detterman (Eds.), *What is intelligence? Contemporary viewpoints on its nature and definition.* Norwood, NJ: Ablex.

Sternberg, R. J., & Detterman, D. K. (Eds.) (1986). *What is intelligence? Contemporary viewpoints on its nature and definition.* Norwood, NJ: Ablex.

Sternberg, R. J., Ketron, J. L., & Powell, J. S. (1982). Componential approaches to the training of intelligence performance. In D. K. Detterman & R. J. Sternberg (Eds.), *How and how much can intelligence be increased.* (pp. 155–172). Norwood, NJ: Ablex.

Sternberg, R. J., & Lubart, T. I. (1991). An investment theory of creativity and its development. *Human Development, 34,* 1–31.

Sternberg, R. J., & McNamara, T. P. (1985). The representation and processing of information in real-time verbal comprehension. In S. E. Embretson (Ed.), *Test design: Developments in psychology and psychometrics* (pp. 21–43). Orlando, FL: Academic.

Sternberg, R. J., & Powell, J. S. (1982). Theories of intelligence. In R. J. Sternberg (Ed.), *Handbook of human intelligence* (pp. 975–1005). Cambridge, England: Cambridge University Press.

Sternberg, R. J., & Powell, J. S. (1983). Comprehending verbal comprehension. *American Psychologist, 38,* 878–893.

Sternberg, R. J., & Turner, M. E. (1981). Components of syllogistic reasoning. *Acta Psychologica, 47,* 245–265.

Sternberg, S. (1966). High speed scanning in human memory. *Science, 153,* 652–654.

Sternberg, S. (1969). Memory-scanning: Mental processes revealed by reaction-time experiments. *American Scientist, 57,* 421–457.

Sternberg, S. (1975). Memory scanning: New findings and current controversies. *Quarterly Journal of Experimental Psychology, 27,* 1–32.

Stevens, S. S. (1951). Mathematics, measurement, and psychophysics. In S. S. Stevens (Ed.), *Handbook of experimental psychology* (pp. 1–49). New York: Wiley.

Stewart, N. (1947). AGCT scores of Army personnel grouped by occupations. *Occupations, 26,* 5–41.

Stoll, P. D. (1972). A study of the construct and criterion-related validity of the Stanford Diagnostic Reading Test. *Journal of Educational Research, 66,* 184–189.
DS-STOL01 *HI.2*

Storck, P. A., Looft, W. R., & Hooper, F. H. (1972). Interrelationships among Piagetian tasks and traditional measures of cognitive abilities in mature and aged adults. *Journal of Gerontology, 27,* 461–465.
DS-STOR01A *HI.3.1*

Storfer, M. D. (1990). *Intelligence and giftedness: The contributions of heredity and early environment.* San Francisco: Jossey–Bass.

Stormer, G. E. (1966). Dimensions of intellect unmeasured by the Stanford–Binet. Unpublished Ed.D. dissertation, University of Illinois. (University Microfilm 66-12432).
DS-STOR11 *HI.10.1* (upper IQ range)
DS-STOR12 *HI.10.2.1* (middle IQ range)
DS-STOR13 *HI.10.1* (lower IQ range)

Street, R. F. (1931). *A gestalt completion test.* New York: Teachers College, Columbia University.

Stroop, J. R. (1935). Studies of interference in serial verbal reactions. *Journal of Experimental Psychology, 18,* 643–662.

Stumpf, H., & Zimmer, G. (1974). *Zur Intelligenzstruktur bei emotional labilen und stabilen Personen.* [*On the structure of intelligence in emotionally labile and stable individuals.*] Bonn: Psychologisches Institut der Universität Bonn.
DS-STUM11 *HI.4.1*

Süllwold, F. (1954). Ein Beitrag zur Analyse der Aufmerksamkeit. [A contribution to the analysis of attention.] *Zeitschrift für experimentelle und angewandte Psychologie, 2,* 495–513.
DS-SU″L01 *HI.4.1*

Sullivan, J. (1973). The relationship of creative and convergent thinking to literal and critical reading ability of children in the upper grades. *Journal of Educational Research, 66,* 374–377.
DS-SULL01 *HI.2.1* (grade 6)
DS-SULL02 *HI.2.1* (grade 8)

Sumita, K., & Ichitani, T. (1958). A factor analytic study on the differentiation of intellectual abilities. *Tohoku Psychologica Folia, 16,* 51–85.
DS-SUMI01 *HI.5.1* (grade 9)
DS-SUMI02 *HI.5.2* (grade 7)
DS-SUMI03 *HI.5.1* (grade 5)
DS-SUMI04 *HI.3.1* (grade 3)

Sung, Y. H., & Dawis, R. V. (1981). Level and factor structure differences in selected abilities across race and sex groups. *Journal of Applied Psychology, 66,* 613–624.
DS-SUNG01 *HI.7.3* (blacks)
DS-SUNG02 *HI.7.3.1* (Hispanics)
DS-SUNG03 *HI.7.3.1* (whites)
DS-SUNG04 *HI.7.3.1* (males)
DS-SUNG05 *HI.7.3.1* (females)

Sung, Y. H., Dawis, R. V., & Dohm, T. E. (1981). *Ball Aptitude Battery: Administrator's Manual.* Glen Ellyn, IL: Ball Foundation.

Sutherland, J. D. (1934). The speed factor in intelligent reactions. *British Journal of Psychology, 24,* 276–294.

Swineford, F. (1941). Some comparisons of the multiple-factor and the bi-factor methods of analysis. *Psychometrika, 6,* 375–382.
Reanalysis of THUR82

Swineford, F. (1948). A study in factor analysis: The nature of the general, verbal, and spatial bi-factors. *Supplementary Educational Monographs,* No. 67. Chicago: University of Chicago Press.
DS-SWIN11 *HI.3.1*
Reanalyzed: Cureton & D'Agostino (1983, p. 163)

Tambs, K., Sundet, J. M., & Magnus, P. (1984). Heritability analysis of the WAIS subtests: A study of twins. *Intelligence, 8,* 283–293.

Tate, M. W. (1947). Speed of response in mental test materials of varying degrees of difficulty. Unpublished doctoral dissertation, Harvard Graduate School of Education.

Tate, M. W. (1948). Individual differences in speed of response in mental test materials of varying degrees of difficulty. *Educational & Psychological Measurement, 8,* 353–374.

Taylor, C. W. (1947). A factorial study of fluency in writing. *Psychometrika, 12,* 239–262.
DS-TAYL01 *HI.7.2*
Reanalyzed: Ahmavaara (1957), Wendeler (1970)

Taylor, C. W., Ghiselin, B., & Yagi, K. (1967). *Exploratory research on communication abilities and creative abilities.* Salt Lake City, UT: University of Utah.
DS-TAYL11 *HI.7.1* (Battery A)
DS-TAYL12A *HI.8.1* (Battery B)
DS-TAYL13A *HI.11.1* (Battery C)

Taylor, L. J. (1975). The Peabody Picture Vocabulary Test: What does it measure? *Perceptual & Motor Skills, 41*, 777–778.
  DS-TAYL31 *HI.6.2* (WPPSI data)
  DS-TAYL32 *HI.3.1* (ITPA data)
Taylor, T. R. (1976). The factor structure of geometric illusions: A second study. *Psychologia Africana, 16*, 177–200.
  DS-TAYL51 *HI.7.1*
Taylor, W. L. (1953). Cloze procedure: A new tool for measuring readability. *Journalism Quarterly, 30*, 415–433.
Tenopyr, M. L. (1966). A factor-analytic study of symbolic-memory abilities. Unpublished doctoral dissertation, University of Southern California. (University Microfilm 67-2128)
  DS-TENO01 *HI.6.1*
  Further report: Tenopyr, Guilford, & Hoepfner (1966)
  Reanalyzed: Kelderman, Mellenbergh, & Elshout (1981)
Tenopyr, M. L., Guilford, J. P., & Hoepfner, R. (1966). A factor analysis of symbolic memory abilities. Los Angeles: Reports from the Psychological Laboratory, University of Southern California, No. 38.
  Further report of TENO01
Terman, L. M. (1916). *The measurement of intelligence: An explanation of and a complete guide for the use of the Stanford revision and extension of the Binet–Simon intelligence scale.* Boston: Houghton Mifflin.
Terman, L. M., & Merrill, M. A. (1937). *Measuring intelligence.* Boston: Houghton Mifflin.
Terman, L. M., & Merrill, M. A. (1960). *Stanford–Binet Intelligence Scale: Manual for the Third Revision Form L-M.* Boston: Houghton Mifflin.
Theologus, G. C., Romashko, T., & Fleishman, E. A. (1973). Development of a taxonomy of human performance: A feasibility study of ability dimensions for classifying human tasks. *JSAS Catalog of Selected Documents in Psychology, 3*, 25–26 (Ms. No. 321).
Thissen, D. (1980). Latent trait scoring of timed ability tests. In D. J. Weiss (Ed.), *Proceedings of the 1979 Computerized Adaptive Testing Conference* (pp. 257–277). Minneapolis, MN: Computerized Adaptive Testing Laboratory, Psychometric Methods Program, Department of Psychology, University of Minnesota.
Thissen, D. (1983). Timed testing: An approach using item response theory. In D. J. Weiss (Ed.), *New horizons in testing: Latent trait test theory and computerized adaptive testing* (pp. 179–203). New York: Academic.
Thomson, G. H. (1916). A hierarchy without a general factor. *British Journal of Psychology, 8*, 271–281.
Thomson, G. H. (1939, 1946, 1951). *The factorial analysis of human ability.* Boston: Houghton Mifflin. [2nd edition, 1946; 5th edition, 1951]
Thomson, G. H. (1940). *An analysis of performance test scores of a representative group of Scottish children.* London: University of London Press.
  See Thomson (1941)
Thomson, G. H. (1941). The speed factor in performance tests. *British Journal of Psychology, 32*, 131–135.
  DS-THOM11 *HI.2.1*
  DS-THOM12 *HI.2.1*
  See also Thomson (1940)
Thorndike, E. L., et al. (1921). Intelligence and its measurement: A symposium. *Journal of Educational Psychology, 12*, 123–147, 195–216, 271–275.
Thorndike, E. L., Bregman, E. O., Cobb, M. V., Woodyard, E., & the Staff of the Division of Psychology of the Institute of Educational Research of Teachers College,

Columbia University. (n.d.[1926]). *The measurement of intelligence*. New York: Bureau of Publications, Teachers College, Columbia University.

Thorndike, E. L., & Lorge, I. (1944). *The teacher's word book of 30,000 words*. New York: Bureau of Publications, Teachers College, Columbia University.

Thorndike, R. L. (1936). Factor analysis of social and abstract intelligence. *Journal of Educational Psychology, 27,* 231–233.
DS-THOR21 *HI.3.1*

Thorndike, R. L., Hagen, E., & Lorge, I. (1954–74). *Cognitive Abilities Test*. Chicago, IL: Riverside Publishing.

Thorndike, R. L., Hagen, E. P., & Sattler, J. M. (1985). *Stanford–Binet Intelligence Scale,* 4th edition. Chicago, IL: Riverside Publishing.

Thorndike, R. M. (1970). Method of extraction, type of data, and adequacy of solutions in factor analysis. Unpublished Ph.D. dissertation, University of Minnesota. (University Microfilm 70-20242)
Reanalysis of GUIL19

Thorndike, R. M., & Lohman, D. F. (1990). *A century of ability testing*. Chicago, IL: Riverside Publishing.

Thornton, G. R. (1939). A factor analysis of tests designed to measure persistence. *Psychological Monographs, 51,* No. 229.
DS-THOR51 *HI.5.1*

Thurstone, L. L. (1924). *The nature of intelligence*. London: Kegan Paul, Trench, Trubner. [Reprinted: Westport, CT: Greenwood Press, 1973]

Thurstone, L. L. (1926). Scoring of individual performance. *Journal of Educational Psychology, 17,* 446–457.

Thurstone, L. L. (1928). The absolute zero in intelligence measurement. *Psychological Review, 35,* 175–197.

Thurstone, L. L. (1930). The relation between learning time and length of task. *Psychological Review, 37,* 44–58.

Thurstone, L. L. (1931). Multiple factor analysis. *Psychological Review, 38,* 406–427.

Thurstone, L. L. (1936a). The factorial isolation of primary abilities. *Psychometrika, 1,* 175–182.
Preliminary report of THUR21A

Thurstone, L. L. (1936b). A new concept of intelligence and a new method of measuring primary abilities. *Educational Record, 17*(Suppl. 10), 124–138.
A further preliminary report of THUR21A

Thurstone, L. L. (1937). Ability, motivation, and speed. *Psychometrika, 2,* 249–254.

Thurstone, L. L. (1938a). The perceptual factor. *Psychometrika, 3,* 1–17.
DS-THUR11 *HI.8.3*
Reanalyzed: Horst (1941), Humphreys & Ilgen (1969)

Thurstone, L. L. (1938b). Primary mental abilities. *Psychometric Monographs,* No. 1.
DS-THUR21A *HI.8.2* (52 vars.)
Preliminary report: Thurstone (1936a, b)
Reanalyzed: Ahmavaara (1957), Eysenck (1939), Fürntratt (1969), Fruchter (1948), Guttman (1957), Holzinger & Harman (1938), Inman (1980), Kaiser (1960b), Kashiwagi (1965), Lohman (1979a), Spearman (1938), Wrigley, Saunders, & Neuhaus (1955), Zimmerman (1953).

Thurstone, L. L. (1938c). A new rotational method in factor analysis. *Psychometrika, 3,* 199–218.

Thurstone, L. L. (1940). Experimental study of simple structure. *Psychometrika, 5,* 153–168.
DS-THUR31 *HI.9.1*
Reanalyzed: Guttman (1957), Humphreys & Ilgen (1969)

Thurstone, L. L. (1944a). A factorial study of perception. *Psychometric Monographs*, No. 4.
 DS-THUR41 *HI.10.1*
 Reanalyzed: Ahmavaara (1957), Guttman (1957), Kashiwagi (1965), Lohman (1979a).
Thurstone, L. L. (1944b). Second-order factors. *Psychometrika*, *9*, 71–100.
Thurstone, L. L. (1946). Note on a reanalysis of Davis' reading tests. *Psychometrika*, *11*,
 185–188.
 Reanalysis of DAVI11; see Davis (1946)
Thurstone, L. L. (1947). *Multiple factor analysis: A development and expansion of* The
 Vectors of Mind. Chicago, IL: University of Chicago Press.
Thurstone, L. L. (1949). Mechanical aptitude III: Analysis of group tests. Chicago:
 University of Chicago Psychometric Laboratory Report No. 55.
 DS-THUR71 *HI.9.1*
 Reanalyzed: Lohman (1979a)
Thurstone, L. L. (1952). Autobiography. In E. G. Boring (Ed.), *A history of psychology in
 autobiography*, Vol. 4 (pp. 295–321). New York: Russell and Russell.
Thurstone, L. L. (1955). The differential growth of mental abilities. Chapel Hill, NC:
 Psychometric Laboratory, University of North Carolina, Report No. 14.
Thurstone, L. L., & Thurstone, T. G. (1941). Factorial studies of intelligence. *Psychometric
 Monographs*, No. 2.
 DS-THUR81 *HI.10.3.1* (Table 1)
 DS-THUR82 *HI.7.2.1* (Table 4)
 Reanalyzed: Bechtoldt (1961), Guttman (1957), Humphreys & Ilgen (1969), Lee &
 Jennrich (1979), Linn (1968), Swineford (1941), Tucker (1958), Yates (1981)
Thurstone, L. L, & Thurstone, T. G. (1946–65). *Primary Mental Abilities.* Chicago: Science
 Research Associates.
Tiedeman, J. (1989). Measures of cognitive styles: A critical review. *Educational Psycho-
 logist*, *24*, 261–275.
Tilton, J. W. (1953). The intercorrelations between measures of school learning. *Journal
 of Psychology*, *35*, 169–179.
 DS-TILT11 *HI.1*
Torrance, E. P. (1963). *Education and the creative potential.* Minneapolis, MN: University
 of Minnesota Press.
Torrance, E. P. (1966). *Torrance Tests of Creative Thinking, Research Edition.* Princeton,
 NJ: Personnel Press.
Toussaint, N. A. (1974). An analysis of synchrony between concrete-operational tasks in
 terms of structure and performance demands. *Child Development*, *45*, 992–1001.
 DS-TOUS01 *HI.1* (grade 1)
 DS-TOUS02 *HI.1* (grade 2)
Traub, R. E. (1970). A factor analysis of programmed learning and ability measures.
 Canadian Journal of Behavioural Sciences, *2*, 44–59.
 DS-TRAU01 *HI.7.1*
Traub, R. E. (1983). A priori considerations in choosing an item response model. In R. K.
 Hambleton (Ed.), *Applications of item response theory* (pp. 57–70). Vancouver, BC:
 Educational Research Institute of British Columbia.
Travis, L. E., & Hunter, T. A. (1928). The relation between 'intelligence' and reflex
 conduction rate. *Journal of Experimental Psychology*, *11*, 342–354.
Travis, L. E., & Young, C. W. (1930). The relations of electromyographically measured
 reflex times in the patellar and Achilles reflexes to certain physical measurements and
 to intelligence. *Journal of General Psychology*, *3*, 374–400.
Tryon, C. M. (1933). On the nature of "speed" and its relation to other variables. *Journal
 of General Psychology*, *8*, 198–216.

Tryon, C. M., & Jones, H. E. (1933). The relationship between 'speed' and 'altitude.' *Journal of Experimental Psychology, 16*, 98–114.

Tryon, R. C., & Bailey, D. E. (1970). *Cluster analysis.* New York: McGraw-Hill.
Reanalysis of HOLZ01

Tucker, L. R (1940). A matrix multiplier. *Psychometrika, 5*, 289–294.

Tucker, L. R (1944). A semi-analytical method of factorial rotation to simple structure. *Psychometrika, 9*, 43–68.

Tucker, L. R (1955). The objective definition of simple structure in linear factor analysis. *Psychometrika, 20*, 209–225.

Tucker, L. R (1958). An inter-battery method of factor analysis. *Psychometrika, 23*, 111–136.
Reanalysis of THUR81 (selected variables)

Tucker, L. R (1967). Three-mode factor analysis of Parker–Fleishman complex tracking behavior data. *Multivariate Behavioral Research, 2*, 139–151.
Reanalysis of PARK01

Tucker, L. R (1980). Functional representation of Montanelli–Humphreys weights for judging number of factors by the parallel analysis technique. Unpublished manuscript.

Tucker, L. R, & Finkbeiner, C. T. (1981). Transformation of factors by artificial personal probability functions. Princeton, NJ: Educational Testing Service Research Report RR-81-58.

Tucker, L. R, & Finkbeiner, C. T. (1991). Transformation of factors by artificial personal probability functions. Unpublished manuscript.

Tucker, L. R, & Lewis, C. (1973). A reliability coefficient for maximum likelihood factor analysis. *Psychometrika, 38*, 1–10.
Reanalyses of HOLZ01, LORD01

Tuddenham, R. D. (1962). The nature and measurement of intelligence. In L. Postman (Ed.), *Psychology in the making: Histories of selected research problems* (pp. 464–525). New York: Knopf.

Tuddenham, R. D. (1970). A 'Piagetian' test of cognitive development. In W. B. Dockrell (Ed.), *On intelligence: The Toronto symposium on intelligence, 1969* (pp. 49–70). London: Methuen.

Tuddenham, R. D. (1971). Theoretical regularities and individual idiosyncrasies. In D. R. Green, M. P. Ford, & G. B. Flamer (Eds.), *Measurement and Piaget: Proceedings of the CTB/McGraw-Hill Conference on Ordinal Scales of Cognitive Development* (pp. 64–75). New York: McGraw-Hill.

Tullos, D. (1987). Individual differences in reasoning: An analysis of solution processes in figural matrix problems. Unpublished Ph. D. dissertation, Stanford University.

Turse, P. L. (1937–40). *Turse Shorthand Aptitude Test.* Yonkers-on-Hudson: World Book Co.

Tyler, R. W., & White, S. H. (Chairmen) (1979). *Testing, teaching, and learning: Report of a Conference on Research on Testing, August 17–26, 1978.* Washington, DC: National Institute of Education.

Underwood, B. J., Boruch, R. F., & Malmi, R. A. (1978). Composition of episodic memory. *Journal of Experimental Psychology: General, 107*, 393–419.
DS-UNDE12 HI.8.2

Underwood, B. J., & Schulz, R. W. (1960). *Meaningfulness and verbal learning.* New York: Lippincott.

Undheim, J. O. (1976). Ability structure in 10-11-year-old children and the theory of fluid and crystallized intelligence. *Journal of Educational Psychology, 68*, 411–423.
DS-UNDH01 HI.10.2
Reanalyzed: Undheim & Gustafsson (1985)

Undheim, J. O. (1978). Broad ability factors in 12- to 13-year-old children, the theory of fluid and crystallized intelligence, and the differentiation hypothesis. *Journal of Educational Psychology, 70*, 433–443.
DS-UNDH11 *HI.5.1*
Reanalyzed: Gustafsson, Lindström, & Björck–Akesson (1981)

Undheim, J. O. (1981). On intelligence I: Broad ability factors in 15-year-old children and Cattell's theory of fluid and crystallized intelligence. *Scandinavian Journal of Psychology, 22*, 171–179.
DS-UNDH21 *HI.5.1*
Reanalyzed: Undheim & Gustafsson (1987)

Undheim, J. O., & Gustafsson, J–E. (1987). The hierarchical organization of cognitive abilities: Restoring general intelligence through the use of linear structural relations (LISREL). *Multivariate Behavioral Research, 22*, 149–171.
Reanalyses of UNDH01, UNDH11, UNDH21

United States Department of Defense (1967–91). *Armed Services Vocational Aptitude Battery*. Washington, DC: Author.

United States Employment Service (1946–77). *USES General Aptitude Battery*. Washington, DC: Author.

United States Employment Service (1970). *Manual for the General Aptitude Test Battery, Section III: Development*. Washington, DC: U. S. Department of Labor, Manpower Administration.

Uzgiris, I. C., & Hunt, J. McV. (1975). *Assessment in infancy: Ordinal scales of psychological development*. Urbana, IL: University of Illinois Press.

Valtin, R. (1970). *Legasthenie: Theorien und Untersuchungen*. [*Reading disability: Theories and investigations.*] Weinheim: Beltz.
DS-VALT01 *HI.3.2* (reading retarded)
DS-VALT02 *HI.3.1* (normals, controls)
DS-VALT03 *HI.3.1* (above combined)
Reanalyzed: Angermaier (1973)

Valtin, R., Jung, U. O. H., & Scheerer–Neumann, G. (1981). *Legasthenie in Wissenschaft und Unterricht: Leseprozessmodell, Fremdsprachenlegasthenie und Erstlesedidaktik.* [*Reading disability in scientific perspective and in instruction: Model of the reading process, disability in foreign language learning, and beginning reading instruction.*] Darmstadt: Wissenschaftliche Buchgesellschaft.
DS-VALT11 *HI.4.1* (Table 25)
DS-VALT12 *HI.6.1* (Table 26)

Vandenberg, S. G. (1962). The hereditary abilities study: Hereditary components in a psychological test battery. *American Journal of Human Genetics, 14*, 220–237.

Vandenberg, S. G., & Vogler, G. P. (1985). Genetic determinants of intelligence. In B. B. Wolman (Ed.), *Handbook of intelligence: Theories, measurements, and applications* (pp. 3–57). New York: Wiley.

VanderPloeg, A. J., & Mueller, S. G. (1978). An examination of the Armed Services Vocational Aptitude Battery. *Measurement & Evaluation in Guidance, 11*, 70–77.
DS-VAND61 *HI.3.1*

Van der Ven, A. H. G. S. (1971). Time-limit tests: A critical review. *Nederlands Tijdschrift voor de Psychologie, 26*, 580–591.

Van der Ven, H. G. (1976). The reliability of speed and precision in time-limit tests. *Tijdschrift voor Onderwijs Research, 1*, 68–73.

Van Hagen, J., & Kaufman, A. S. (1975). Factor analysis of the WISC-R for a group of mentally retarded children and adolescents. *Journal of Consulting and Clinical Psychology, 43*, 661–667.
DS-VANH01 *HI.3.1*

Velicer, W. F., & Jackson, D. N. (1990). Component analysis versus common-factor analysis: Some issues in selecting an appropriate procedure. *Multivariate Behavioral Research, 25*, 1–28.

Vernon, P. A. (1981a). Speed of information processing and general intelligence. Unpublished Ph.D. thesis, University of California at Berkeley.

DS-VERN01 *HI.6.1*

Further report: Vernon (1983)

Vernon, P. A. (1981b). Reaction time and intelligence in the mentally retarded. *Intelligence, 5*, 345–355.

DS-VERN11 *HI.3.1*

Vernon, P. A. (1981c). Level I and Level II: A review. *Educational Psychologist, 16*, 45–64.

Vernon, P. A. (1983). Speed of information processing and general intelligence. *Intelligence, 7*, 53–70.

Further report of VERN01

Vernon, P. A. (Ed.) (1987a). *Speed of information-processing and intelligence.* Norwood, NJ: Ablex.

Vernon, P. A. (1987b). New developments in reaction time research. In P. A. Vernon (Ed.), *Speed of information-processing and intelligence* (pp. 1–20). Norwood, NJ: Ablex.

Vernon, P. A., & Jensen, A. R. (1984). Individual and group differences in intelligence and speed of information processing. *Personality & Individual Differences, 5*, 411–423.

DS-VERN21 *HI.4.1*

Vernon, P. E. (1947). Research on personnel selection in the Royal Navy and the British Army. *American Psychologist, 2*, 35–51.

DS-VERN51 *HI.4.1*

Vernon, P. E. (1950, 1961). *The structure of human abilities.* London: Methuen. [2nd edition, 1961]

Vernon, P. E. (1962). The determinants of reading comprehension. *Educational & Psychological Measurement, 22*, 269–286.

DS-VERN61 *HI.2.1* (male American college students)

DS-VERN62 *HI.2.1* (male British college students)

Vernon, P. E. (1987). The demise of the Stanford–Binet scale. *Canadian Psychology, 28*, 251–258.

Vernon, P. E., & Parry, J. B. (1949). *Personnel selection in the British forces.* London: University of London Press.

Verster, J. M. (1983). The structure, organization and correlates of cognitive speed and accuracy: A cross-cultural study using computerised tests. In S. H. Irvine & J. W. Berry (Eds.), *Human assessment and cultural factors* (pp. 275–292). New York: Plenum.

DS-VERS01 *HI.4.2* (white male adults)

DS-VERS02 *HI.4.2* (white female adults)

DS-VERS03 *HI.4.2* (black male adults)

Very, P. S. (1967). Differential factor structures in mathematical ability. *Genetic Psychology Monographs, 75*, 169–207.

DS-VERY01 *HI.5.1* (males)

DS-VERY02 *HI.5.1* (females)

DS-VERY03 *HI.5.2* (combined)

Reanalyzed: DeGuire (1983)

Vidler, D. (1974). Convergent and divergent thinking, test-anxiety, and curiosity. *Journal of Experimental Education, 43*, 79–85.

DS-VIDL01 *HI.2.1*

Vollmer, H., & Sang, F. (1983). Competing hypotheses about second language ability: A plea for caution. In J. W. Oller, Jr. (Ed.), *Issues in language testing research* (pp. 29–79). Rowley, MA: Newbury House.

Reanalysis of SCHO31

Voss, H. G., & Keller, H. (1977). Critical evaluation of the Obscure Figures Test as an instrument for measuring cognitive innovation. *Perceptual & Motor Skills, 45,* 495–502.

DS-VOSS01 *HI.2*

Wachs, T. D., & Hubert, N. C. (1981). Changes in the structure of cognitive-intellectual performance during the second year of life. *Infant Behavior & Development, 4,* 151–161.

DS-WACH01 *HI.2* (14 mo.)
DS-WACH02 *HI.2* (18 mo.)
DS-WACH03 *HI.3* (22 mo.)

Wagner, R. K., & Torgesen, J. K. (1987). The nature of phonological processing and its causal role in the acquisition of reading skills. *Psychological Bulletin, 101,* 192–212.

Walker, D. A. (1931, 1936, 1940). Answer pattern and score scatter in tests and examinations. *British Journal of Psychology, 22,* 73–86; *26,* 301–308; *30,* 248–260.

Walker, H. M. (1929). *Studies in the history of statistical method.* Baltimore: Williams & Wilkins.

Wallach, M. A., & Kogan, N. (1965). *Modes of thinking in young children: A study of the creativity–intelligence distinction.* New York: Holt, Rinehart & Winston.

DS-WALL01 *HI.4*

Reanalyzed: Cronbach (1968), Fee (1968), Ward (1967)

Wallin, E. (1967). *Spelling: Factorial and experimental studies.* Stockholm: Almqvist & Wiksell.

DS-WALL51 *HI.3.1* (boys)
DS-WALL52 *HI.3.1* (girls)

Walsh, M. D. (1978). Factor analytic study of the Embedded Figures and Rod and Frame tests. *Perceptual & Motor Skills, 47,* 531–537.

DS-WALS21 *HI.3.1*

Ward, J. (1967). An oblique factorization of Wallach and Kogan's "creativity" correlations. *British Journal of Educational Psychology, 37,* 380–382.

Reanalysis of WALL01

Ward, W. D., & Burns, E. M. (1982). Absolute pitch. In D. Deutsch (Ed.), *The psychology of music* (pp. 431–451). New York: Academic.

Wardell, D. (1974). Note on factor analysis of cognitive styles. *Perceptual & Motor Skills, 38,* 774.

Reanalysis of GARD01, GARD02

Waterhouse, L. (1988). Speculations on the neuroanatomical substrate of special talents. In L. K. Obler & D. Fein (Eds.), *The exceptional brain: Neuropsychology of talent and special abilities* (pp. 493–512). New York: Guilford.

Weaver, W. W., & Bickley, A. C. (1967). Sources of information for responses to reading test items. *Proceedings of the 75th Annual Convention of the American Psychological Association, 2,* 293–294.

Weaver, W. W., & Kingston, A. J. (1963). A factor analysis of the Cloze procedure and other measures of reading and language ability. *Journal of Communication, 13,* 252–261.

DS-WEAV01 *HI.3.1*

Weber, H. (1953). Untersuchungen zur Faktorenstruktur numerischer Aufgaben. [Investigations of the factor structure of numerical tasks.] *Zeitschrift für experimentelle und angewandte Psychologie, 1,* 336–391.

DS-WEBE01 *HI.3.1* (boys)

DS-WEBE02 *HI.3.1* (girls)

Webster, P. R. (1977). A factor of intellect approach to creative thinking in music. Unpublished Ph.D. dissertation, University of Rochester, Eastman School of Music. [*Dissertation Abstracts International*, 38(6-A), 3136–3137; Order No. 77-26,619.]

Wechsler, D. (1955). *Manual for the Wechsler Adult Intelligence Scale.* New York: The Psychological Corporation.

Wechsler, D. (1967). *Wechsler Preschool and Primary Scale of Intelligence: Manual.* New York: The Psychological Corporation.

Wechsler, D. (1971). *Manual for the Wechsler Adult Intelligence Scale – Revised.* New York: The Psychological Corporation.

Wechsler, D. (1974). *Manual for the Wechsler Intelligence Scale for Children – Revised.* New York: The Psychological Corporation.

Wechsler, D. (1981). *Manual for the Wechsler Adult Intelligence Scale – Revised.* New York: The Psychological Corporation.

Weckroth, J. (1961). Dimensions of color sensation. *Scandinavian Journal of Psychology*, 2, 65–70.

Wedeck, J. (1947). The relationship between personality and 'psychological ability'. *British Journal of Psychology*, 37, 133–151.
DS-WEDE01 *HI.4.1*

Weinfeld, F. D. (1959). A factor analytic approach to the measurement of different effects of training: An evaluation of three methods of teaching English composition. Unpublished Ed.D. thesis, Graduate School of Education, Harvard University.
DS-WEIN11 *HI.5.1*

Weiss, D. J. (Ed.) (1983). *New horizons in testing: Latent trait test theory and computerized adaptive testing.* New York: Academic.

Weiss, E. S. (1955). A factor analysis of mathematical ability. Unpublished Ed.D. dissertation, Graduate School of Education, Harvard University.
DS-WEIS11 *HI.10.3.1*
Reanalyzed: DeGuire (1983)

Wendeler, J. (1970). Vergleich einiger Faktorenanalysen muttersprachlicher Leistungen. [Comparison of some factor analyses of native-language performances.] *Diagnostica*, 16, 76–94.
Reanalyses of CARR01, GUIL12, ROGE11, TAYL01

Wepman, J. M. (1958–73). *Auditory Discrimination Test, Ages 5–8.* Palm Springs, CA: Language Research Associates. (Revised edition, 1973).

Werdelin, I. (1958). *The mathematical ability: Experimental and factorial studies.* Lund, Sweden: Gleerups.
DS-WERD01 *HI.7.1* (Table VI)
DS-WERD02 *HI.6.1* (Table VII)
Reanalyzed: DeGuire (1983)

Werdelin, I., & Stjernberg, G. (1969). On the nature of the perceptual speed factor. *Scandinavian Journal of Psychology*, 10, 185–192.
DS-WERD41 *HI.3.1*

Werdelin, I., & Stjernberg, G. (1971). The relationship between difficulty and factor loadings of some visual–perceptual tests. *Scandinavian Journal of Psychology*, 12, 21–28.
DS-WERD51 *HI.4.1*

Wesche, M., Edwards, H., & Wells, W. (1982). Foreign language aptitude and intelligence. *Applied Psycholinguistics*, 3, 127–140.

Wexley, K., Guidubaldi, J., & Kehle, T. (1974). An evaluation of Montessori and day care programs for disadvantaged children. *Journal of Educational Research*, 68, 95–99.
DS-WEXL01 *HI.1*

Wheaton, G. R., Eisner, E. J., Mirabella, A., & Fleishman, E. A. (1976). Ability requirements as a function of changes in the characteristics of an auditory signal identification task. *Journal of Applied Psychology, 61*, 663–676.
Further report of DS-WHEA01

Wheaton, G. R., Shaffer, E. J., Mirabella, A., & Fleishman, E. A. (1973). *Methods for predicting job-ability requirements: 1. Ability requirements as a function of changes in the characteristics of an auditory signal identification task.* Silver Spring, MD: American Institutes for Research.
DS-WHEA01 *HI.6.1*
Further report: Wheaton et al. (1976)

Whellams, F. S. (1971). The aural musical abilities of junior school children: A factorial investigation. Unpublished doctoral dissertation, University of London.

Whimbey, A. E., & Denenberg, V. H. (1966). Programming life histories: Creating individual differences by the experimental control of early experiences. *Multivariate Behavioral Research, 1*, 279–286.

White, B. W. (1954). Visual and auditory closure. *Journal of Experimental Psychology, 48*, 234–240.
DS-WHIT01 *HI.2*

White, P. O. (1973). Individual differences in speed, accuracy and persistence: A mathematical model for problem solving. In H. J. Eysenck (Ed.), *The measurement of intelligence* (pp. 246–260). Baltimore: Williams & Wilkins.

White, P. O. (1982). Some major components in general intelligence. In H. J. Eysenck (Ed.), *A model for intelligence* (pp. 44–90). Berlin: Springer-Verlag.

Wickens, C. D., Mountford, S. J., & Schreiner, W. (1980). Task dependent differences and individual differences in dual task performance. New Orleans, LA: Naval Biodynamics Laboratory.
DS-WICK01 *HI.3.1*
Further report: Wickens, Mountford, & Schreiner (1981)
Reanalyzed: Ackerman, Schneider, & Wickens (1982)

Wickens, C. D., Mountford, S. J., & Schreiner, W. (1981). Multiple resources, task-hemispheric integrity, and individual differences in time-sharing. *Human Factors, 23*, 211–229.
Further report of DS-WICK01

Widaman, K. F., & Carlson, J. S. (1989). Procedural effects on performance on the Hick paradigm: Bias in reaction time and movement time parameters. *Intelligence, 13*, 63–85.

Widiger, T. A., Knudson, R. M., & Rorer, L. G. (1980). Convergent and discriminant validity of measures of cognitive styles and abilities. *Journal of Personality & Social Psychology, 39*, 116–129.
DS-WIDI01 *HI.5.2*

Wiebe, M. J., & Watkins, E. O. (1980). Factor analysis of the McCarthy Scales of Children's Abilities on preschool children. *Journal of School Psychology, 18*, 154–162.
DS-WIEB11 *HI.5.1* (boys)
DS-WIEB12 *HI.5.1* (girls)

Wigdor, A. K., & Garner, W. R. (Eds.) (1982). *Ability testing: Uses, consequences, and controversies, Parts I and II.* Washington, DC: National Academy Press.

Williams, D. S. (1972). Computer program organization induced from problem examples. In H. A. Simon & L. Siklóssy (Eds.), *Representation and meaning: Experiments with information processing systems* (pp. 143–205). Englewood Cliffs, NJ: Prentice-Hall.

Williams, T. H. (1975). The Wechsler scales: Parents and (male) children. *Journal of Educational Measurement, 12*, 119–128.

DS-WILL11 *HI.3.1* (male children)

DS-WILL12 *HI.3.1* (parents)

Wilson, J. Q., & Herrnstein, R. J. (1985). *Crime and human nature.* New York: Simon & Schuster.

Wilson, R. C., Guilford, J. P., Christensen, P. R., & Lewis, D. J. (1954). A factor-analytic study of creative-thinking abilities. *Psychometrika, 19,* 297–311.

Further report of GUIL66

Windholz, G., & McIntosh, W. A. (1967). Concurrent validation of Guilford's six convergent tests. *Educational & Psychological Measurement, 27,* 393–400.

DS-WIND01 *HI.3*

Wing, H. D. (1941). A factorial study of musical tests. *British Journal of Psychology, 31,* 341–355.

DS-WING01 *HI.2*

Wishart, J. (1928). Sampling errors in the theory of two factors. *British Journal of Psychology, 19,* 180–187.

Wisland, M., & Many, W. A. (1969). A factorial study of the Illinois Test of Psycholinguistic Abilities with children having above-average intelligence. *Educational & Psychological Measurement, 29,* 367–376.

DS-WISL01 *HI.2.1*

Wissler, C. (1901). The correlation of mental and physical traits. *Psychological Monographs, 3,* 1–62.

Witkin, H. A., Dyk, R. B., Faterson, H. F., Goodenough, D. R., & Karp, S. A. (1962). *Psychological differentiation.* Potomac, MD: Erlbaum.

Witkin, H. A., & Goodenough, D. R. (1981). *Cognitive styles: Essence and origins –Field dependence and independence.* New York: International Universities Press.

Witkin, H. A., Oltman, P. K., Raskin, E., & Karp, S. A. (1971). *A manual for the Embedded Figures Tests.* Palo Alto, CA: Consulting Psychologists Press.

Wittenborn, J. R. (1943). Factorial equations for tests of attention. *Psychometrika, 8,* 19–35.

DS-WITT11 *HI.6.1*

Reanalysis: Stankov (1983)

Wittenborn, J. R. (1945). Mechanical ability, its nature and measurement. I. An analysis of the variables employed in the preliminary Minnesota experiment. *Educational & Psychological Measurement, 5,* 241 260.

Reanalysis of PATE01

Wolfle, D. (1940). Factor analysis to 1940. *Psychometric Monographs.* No. 3.

Wolfle, L. M. (1985). Postsecondary educational attainment among whites and blacks. *American Educational Research Journal, 22,* 501–525.

DS-WOLF11 *HI.4.2.1*

Wolins, L., & Perloff, R. (1965). The factorial composition of AGCT "subtests" along with college aptitude items and high school grades. *Educational & Psychological Measurement, 25,* 73–78.

DS-WOLI01 *HI.6.1*

Wolman, B. B. (Ed.) (1973). *Dictionary of behavioral science.* New York: Van Nostrand Reinhold.

Wolman, B. B. (Ed.) (1985). *Handbook of intelligence: Theories, measurements, and applications.* New York: Wiley.

Woltz, D. J. (1988). An investigation of the role of working memory in procedural skill acquisition. *Journal of Experimental Psychology: General, 117,* 319–331.

Wood, D. A. (1962). *Louis Leon Thurstone: Creative thinker, dedicated teacher, eminent psychologist.* Princeton, NJ: Educational Testing Service.

Woodcock, R. W. (1990). Theoretical foundations of the WJ-R measures of cognitive ability. *Journal of Psychoeducational Assessment, 8*, 231–258.

Woodcock, R. W., & Johnson, M. B. (1977–78). *Woodcock–Johnson Psycho-Educational Battery.* Hingham, MA: Teaching Resources.

  DS-WOOD13 *HI.4.2* (grade 1)

  DS-WOOD15 *HI.5.2* (grade 5)

  DS-WOOD17 *HI.5.2* (grade 12)

  DS-WOOD18 *HI.5.2* (adults age 20–39)

Woodcock, R. W., & Johnson, M. B. (1989). *Woodcock–Johnson Psycho-Educational Battery – Revised.* Allen, TX: DLM Teaching Resources.

Woodrow, H. (1914). The measurement of attention. *Psychological Monographs, 17*, No. 76.

Woodrow, H. (1938). The relation between abilities and improvement with practice. *Journal of Educational Psychology, 29*, 215–230.

Woodrow, H. (1946). The ability to learn. *Psychological Review, 53*, 147–158.

Woodworth, R. S. (1938). *Experimental psychology.* New York: Henry Holt.

Woodworth, R. S. (1941). *Heredity and environment.* New York: Social Science Research Council.

Woodworth, R. S., & Schlosberg, H. (1954). *Experimental psychology, Revised edition.* New York: Holt, Rinehart & Winston.

Wothke, W., Bock, R. D., Curran, L. T., Fairbank, B. A., Augustin, J. W., Gillet, A. H., & Guerrero, C., Jr. (1991). *Factor analytic examination of the Armed Services Vocational Aptitude Battery (ASVAB) and the kit of factor-referenced tests.* Brooks Air Force Base, TX: Air Force Human Resources Laboratory Report AFHRL-TR-90-67.

  DS-WOTH01 *HI.11.3*

Wright, B. D., & Stone, M. H. (1979). *Best test design.* Chicago: MESA.

Wright, R. E. (1939). A factor analysis of the original Stanford–Binet scale. *Psychometrika, 4*, 209–220.

  DS-WRIG01 *HI.4.1*

Wrigley, C., Saunders, D. R., & Neuhaus, J. O. (1958). Application of the quartimax method of rotation to Thurstone's Primary Mental Abilities study. *Psychometrika, 23*, 151–170.

  Reanalysis of THUR21

Wrigley, J. (1958). The factorial nature of ability in elementary mathematics. *British Journal of Educational Psychology, 28*, 61–78.

  DS-WRIG21 *HI.4.2*

Yates, A. (1987). *Multivariate exploratory data analysis: A perspective on exploratory factor analysis.* Albany, NY: State University of New York Press.

  Reanalysis of THUR81

Yela, M., & Pascual, M. (1968). La estructura factorial de la inteligencia tecnica. [The factorial structure of technical intelligence.] *Revista de Psicologia General y Aplicada, 23*(94), 1–66.

  DS-YELA21 *HI.6.1*

Yeni–Komshian, G. (1965). Training procedures for developing auditory perception skills in the sound system of a foreign language. Unpublished doctoral dissertation, McGill University.

Yerkes, R. M. (Ed.) (1921). Psychological examining in the United States Army. *Memoirs of the National Academy of Sciences*, No. 15.

Zeaman, D., & House, B. J. (1967). The relation of IQ and learning. In R. M. Gagné (Ed.), *Learning and individual differences* (pp. 192–212). Columbus, OH: Merrill.

Zigler, E., & Seitz, V. (1982). Social policy and intelligence. In R. J. Sternberg (Ed.), *Handbook of human intelligence* (pp. 586–641). Cambridge, England: Cambridge University Press.

Zimmerman, W. S. (1946). A simple graphical method for orthogonal rotation of axes. *Psychometrika, 11,* 51–55.

Zimmerman, W. S. (1953). A revised orthogonal rotational solution for Thurstone's original Primary Mental Abilities test battery. *Psychometrika, 18,* 77–93.
Reanalysis of THUR21

Appendix A: *Codes for Countries, Samples, and Factors*

These codes are used in tables listing factors and in many other contexts, for example in the hierarchical factor matrices shown in Appendix B.

Codes for Country in Which a Sample Was Taken

0   Unknown
A   Australia
B   Belgium
C   Canada
D   Scotland
E   England/Wales
F   France
G   Germany/Austria
H   Holland/Netherlands
I   Ireland
J   Yugoslavia
K   South Africa
L   Saudi Arabia
N   Japan
O   Norway
P   Spain
R   Russia/USSR
S   Sweden
T   Argentina
U   United States
W   Switzerland
Y   Italy
Z   New Zealand

Codes for Description of Sample

!   Music & non-music students
Hispanics
$ Technical high school or vocational college
%   Combined normals & remedials or retardates
&   Disadvantaged students, day care, etc.

790

*	Children of persons in another sample
0	Not stated, information not available
1	"Normal" sample at given age or grade
2	Enlisted military persons
3	Military (officers, NCO's, officer candidates, plebes)
4	Brain-damaged persons, aphasics
5	Employed, not otherwise specified
6	Students at given age/grade
7	Low-achieving students, "retarded" children, of low IQ
8	Above normal in IQ/achievement
9	Mixture of normal and gifted
A	Engineering students/apprentices
B	Architecture students
C	Clerical workers
D	Commercial students
E	Deaf persons
F	Learners of a second or foreign language
G	Students or professionals in education
H	Healthy, recently recovered from head injury
I	Restricted range around IQ of 100
J	Emotionally disturbed persons
K	Summer make-up students
L	Lobotomized schizophrenics
M	Students in math or science courses
N	Infants
O	Persons/students in lower-class areas
P	Students in introductory psychology courses
Q	Prison inmates
R	Retarded persons
S	Schizophrenics
T	ROTC students
U	Adult volunteers, paid or not paid
V	Remedial reading students
W	Whites (vs. blacks or others)
X	Down's syndrome children
Y	Mothers/parents of children in another sample
Z	Blacks (vs. other ethnic groups)

Codes for Factor Classifications

Note: It is emphasized that these codes are used only to indicate the classification of a factor, not to indicate the precise identity of a factor. It is frequently the case that even within a particular dataset, a given factor code is used to indicate the classification of more than one factor.

1C	– Crystallized intelligence (at first order)
1G	– General cognitive ability (at first order)
2'	– Broad communication ability (at second order)
2"	– Parental background (at second order)
2&	– Broad administrative ability (at second order)
2(	– General school achievement (at second order)

2*   – Any special second-order factor
20   – An uninterpreted second-order factor
21   – A second-order factor combining fluid intelligence and broad visual perception
22   – Accuracy of information processing (at second order)
25   – A second-order factor emphasizing mother's high relative frequency of declarative sentences
28   – Strength (at second order)
2B   – General information (at second order)
2C   – Crystallized intelligence (at second order)
2D   – General cognitive development (at second order)
2E   – Any special cognitive style factor (at second order)
2F   – Fluid intelligence (at second order)
2G   – General cognitive ability (at second order)
2H   – A second-order factor combining fluid and crystallized intelligence
2I   – General interest (at second order)
2L   – Learning ability (at second order)
2O   – A second-order olfactory sensitivity factor
2P   – General psychomotor ability (at second order)
2R   – Broad retrieval ability (at second order)
2S   – Broad speediness (at second order)
2T   – Broad reaction time (at second order)
2U   – Broad auditory ability (at second order)
2V   – Broad visual perception ability (at second order)
2X   – Broad memory-span ability (at second order)
2Y   – Broad memory ability (at second order)
3(– General favorable background and achievement level (at third order)
3G   – General cognitive ability (at third order)
3O   – General olfactory sensitivity (at third order)
3R   – Broad retrieval ability (at third order)
3Y   – Broad memory ability (at third order)

Note: All subsequent codes are for factors found at the first order.

A0 – School achievement
A1 – School achievement (as shown by achievement tests)
A2 – School achievement (teacher-rated)
A3 – Mathematics achievement (tested)
A4 – Mathematics achievement (teacher-rated)
A5 – Geography achievement
A6 – Achievement in English (school course)
A7 – Achievement in science (school course)
A8 – Achievement: Hygiene/drawing
A9 – Achievement: Geometry/woodworking
AA – Father's occupation/education
AB – Mother's education
AC – Attention/concentration
AD – Type of deafness
AG – Age relative to grade level
AI – Aiming ability
AM – An administrative behavior factor
AP – Apprehension span
AS – Curriculum level

AT – Attitude to teacher
BC – "Behavioral content" knowledge
BD – Divergent production of "behavioral content"
CF – Closure flexibility
CM – Communication ability
CS – Closure speed
CY – A cognitive style factor
CZ – "Cloze" ability
DA – Development: Self-confidence
DM – Development: Motor readiness
DS – Development: Social/emotional readiness
DT – School deportment
E0 – Socioeconomic status/education
EU – English usage knowledge
FA – Associational fluency
FE – Expressional fluency
FF – Figural fluency
FI – Ideational fluency
FO – Originality/creativity
FW – "Word fluency"
FX – Figural flexibility
G   – General cognitive ability (at first order)
GC – Crystallized intelligence (at first order)
GF – Fluid intelligence (at first order)
GH – Fluid/crystallized intelligence (at first order)
GR – Broad retrieval ability (at first order)
GS – Broad speediness (at first order)
GU – Broad auditory ability (at first order)
GV – Broad visual perception ability (at first order)
GX – Broad memory span (at first order)
GY – Broad memory ability (at first order)
I   – Inductive reasoning
I0 – An uninterpreted first-order factor
I1 – Interest in art/music
I2 – Interest in biology
I3 – Interest in science
I4 – Interest in business
I5 – Interest in speaking/communication
I6 – Interest in foreign language study
IL – Resistance to illusions
IM – Imagery
K0 – General (verbal) information
K1 – General science information
K2 – Information about "culture" (art, music, etc.)
K7 – Achievement in English as a second language (assessed by interview, free writing samples)
K8 – Achievement in English as a second language (self-rated)
K9 – Achievement in English as a second language (assessed by multiple-choice achievement tests)
KA – Knowledge of aviation
KE – Knowledge of English as a second language
KF – Knowledge of signing/fingerspelling (for deaf persons)

KL　– Proficiency in a foreign language
KM – Knowledge of mathematics
KO – Knowledge about objects (in infants and children)
L0　– An uninterpreted learning ability factor
L1　– Learning ability
L6　– Learning gains
L7　– Rate of learning in programmed instruction
LA　– Foreign language aptitude
LD　– Development in the native language
LE　– Length estimation
LP　– Skill in lipreading
LS　– Listening ability
M0　– A miscellaneous memory factor
M6　– Free recall memory
MA　– Associative memory
MD　– Movement detection (visual)
MK　– Mechanical knowledge
MM – Meaningful memory
MO　– A motivation factor
MS　– Memory span
MV　– Visual memory
MY　– Grammatical sensitivity
N　　– Numerical facility
NA　– Naming facility
O&　– An oral style factor
O1　– An olfactory sensitivity factor (See DS-JONE22)
O2　– ”　　”　　　　”　　　”　　　”　”　　　”
O3　– ”　　”　　　　”　　　”　　　”　”　　　”
O4　– ”　　”　　　　”　　　”　　　”　”　　　”
OP　– Oral production ability
P　　– Perceptual speed
P1　– Manual dexterity
P2　– Finger dexterity
P3　– Static strength
P4　– Gross body equilibrium
P5　– Wrist–finger speed
P6　– Multilimb coordination
P7　– Arm–hand steadiness
P8　– Motor control precision
PC　– Phonetic coding
PI　– Serial perceptual integration
PN　– Perceptual alternations (rate)
PQ　– Plotting ability
PR　– A personality factor
PT　– Speech articulation speed
R&　– A special reading comprehension factor
R∗　– A reaction time factor specific to a paradigm
R1　– Simple reaction time
R2　– Choice reaction time
R3　– Movement time (in a reaction time paradigm)
R4　– Semantic processing speed
R5　– Visual/memory search: Slope

R6 – Visual/memory search: RT/intercept
R7 – Mental comparison speed
R8 – Complex information processing: Accuracy
R9 – Rate-of-test-taking
RC – Reading comprehension
RD – Reading decoding
RE – Speed of reasoning
RG – Sequential reasoning
RP – Piagetian reasoning
RQ – Quantitative reasoning
RS – Reading speed
S& – A doublet or specific factor
S0 – A miscellaneous special factor
S1 – Mental comparison accuracy
SG – Spelling ability
SP – Sensitivity to problems
SR – Spatial relations
SS – Spatial scanning
TP – Tactile–kinesthetic sensitivity
TS – Time sharing
TT – Auditory cognitive relations
U3 – General sound discrimination
U5 – Pitch/timbre discrimination
U6 – Sound intensity/duration/rhythm discrimination
U8 – Maintaining and judging rhythm
U9 – Musical sensitivity
UA – Hearing threshold
UI – Tonal memory
UK – Temporal tracking
UL – Binaural sound localization
UM – Memory for sound patterns
UP – Absolute pitch ability
UR – Resistance to auditory stimulus distortion
US – Speech sound discrimination
UT – Speech sound threshold
UU – Speech synthesis in speech audiometry
V   – Verbal ability
V& – Any special visual factor
V1 – Color sensitivity – red portion of spectrum
V2 –   ”   ”   – green ”   ”   ”
V3 –   ”   ”   – blue   ”   ”   ”
VC – Visual acuity/sensitivity
VL – Lexical knowledge/vocabulary
VN – Verbal discrimination memory
VU – Verbal closure
VZ – Visualization
WA – Writing production ability
WS – Handwriting speed
XC – A factor of infant/child behavior
ZP – Stroop interference

Appendix B: *Hierarchical Factor Matrix Files*

Appendix B consists of 468 ASCII-character files recorded on three 3.5-inch high-density disks that accompany this volume, although sold separately. Each file, when printed, is a hierarchical factor matrix (on one or more pages) for one of the datasets examined in the volume. The format of such tables is described in Chapter 3, with reference to Tables 3.2G, 3.3, and 3.5.

The files are designed to be printed on wide ($14\frac{7}{8}''$) computer paper using an IBM or IBM-compatible personal computer and a dot-matrix printer that will accommodate such paper and that is capable of printing boldface and italicized characters. Values printed in boldface are those for variables that are salient for a given factor. Values that are printed both in boldface and italics are those that are not salient for a given factor but are nevertheless greater than .295 in absolute magnitude. A file can be printed using a normal DOS command such as A > print a:ADEV01.HI (assuming that the disk is in drive A and that one desires to print file ADEV01.HI, as listed in the directory of the disk). In alphabetical order, files ADEV01.HI through GUST11A.HI are on the disk labeled APPENDIX_B1; files HAKS01.HI through ROYC11.HI are on disk APPENDIX_B2; files SATT01.HI through YELA21.HI are on disk APPENDIX_B3.

If all 468 files are printed, 780 pages are produced. Users are cautioned not to attempt to print the files in compressed-type mode because the characters that control boldface and italic type are not permissible in this mode, having the effect of defeating the compressed-type mode and printing misaligned columns.

796

Name Index

Subject Index